67th ART DIRECTORS ANNUAL AND 2nd INTERNATIONAL EXHIBITION

ADC PUBLICATIONS INC.

Board of Directors
Paula Scher, President
Walter Kaprielian
Kurt Haiman
B. Martin Pedersen
Louis Silverstein
Andrew Kner, Advisory Board

ADC Executive Director
Diane Moore

Editors
Debbie Mackler
Jonathan Gregory

Hall of Fame Copy
Dan Forté

Database Consultant
Marie Gangemi

Interior Design
Robert Anthony

Interior Design Associate
Steve Madison

Divider Photos
Harold Zipkowitz

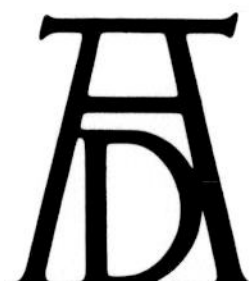

Published in 1988 by
Madison Square Press Inc.
10 E 23 Street
New York, NY 10010
for
The Art Directors Club Inc.
250 Park Avenue South
New York, NY 10003

ISSN: 0735-2026
ISBN: 0-8230-4890-X

Printed in Japan

Distributed to the trade in the
United States & Canada by
Watson-Guptill Publications
1515 Broadway
New York, NY 10036

International Distribution
RotoVision SA
Route de Suisse 9
CH-1295 MIES/VD
Switzerland

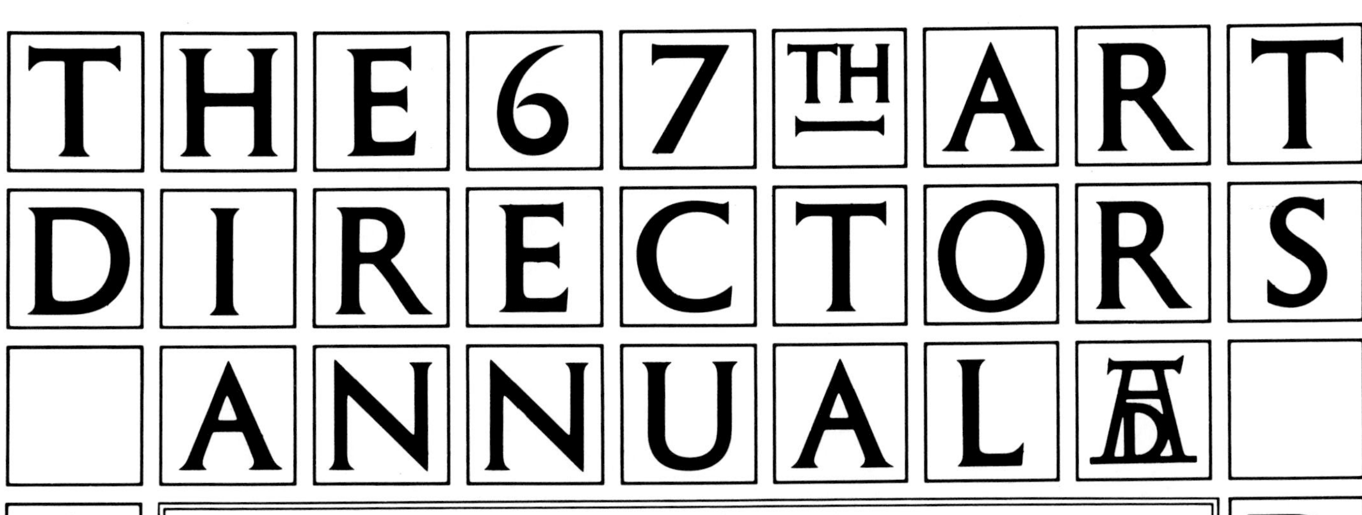

A INCLUDING THE SECOND INTERNATIONAL EXHIBITION D

COMMITMENT

6 7

CONTENTS

ROBERT ANTHONY

Robert Anthony, this year's interior book designer, heads his own graphic design firm, Robert Anthony, Inc. Founded in 1967, his firm has serviced clients as varied as financial, restaurant-hotel, publishing, and travel. Anthony is an active member of The Art Directors Club of New York, the Graphic Artists Guild, The American Institute of Graphic Arts, and the Society of Illustrators. He has received numerous design awards including AIGA Communication Graphics, AIGA Cover Shows, Creativity, Society of Illustrators, Print Case Books, Type Directors Club, and Art Directors Club.

MILTON GLASER

Milton Glaser, this year's International Call for Entries designer, is president of Milton Glaser Inc., a full-service graphic design company, active in all areas of visual communication from corporate identity to entertainment to food packaging. He has been honored with every award and tribute possible and his work has been exhibited around the world. In 1979, Glaser was inducted into the Art Directors Club Hall of Fame. In addition to his immediately recognizable poster designs, Glaser has had a hand in architectural design as well, creating the World Trade Center's observation deck and Sesame Place, the children's educational theme park. Glaser is a graduate of The Cooper Union and resides in New York City.

ALAN PECKOLICK

Alan Peckolick, this year's National Call for Entries designer, is president of Peckolick + Partners, a graphic design firm specializing in corporate identity, logos, and packaging. He has received countless awards for design excellence. Peckolick is on the advisory boards of *Design World* in Australia and The Herb Lubalin Study Center at The Cooper Union in New York City. In addition, he continues to lecture art students and professional design organizations worldwide. Peckolick is a graduate of Pratt Institute and resides in New York City.

COMMITMENT
A
D
FOR THE TRUE BELIEVERS
WHEN THE PHILISTINES
THE PRODUCT BIGGER AND THE IDEA
IT'S TIME TO ENTER THE 67TH ANNUAL
ART DIRECTORS CLUB SHOW.
6
7
THE 67TH ART DIRECTORS ANNUAL
INCLUDING THE SECOND INTERNATIONAL EXHIBITION
COMMITMENT
SECOND INTERNATIONAL EXHIBITION
The Art Directors Club, Inc.
CALL FOR ENTRIES
NEW YORK, NY 10003 U.S.A.
The Art Directors Club of New York is extending its prestigious annual awards program to the international design and advertising community. The 2nd International Exhibition, a juried competition for excell-ence in print, television and film art direction, will be judged by a distinguished panel of ADC Hall of Fame laureates and designers of international stature.

HALL OF FAME

HALL OF FAME MEMBERS

1972
M. F. Agha
Lester Beall
Alexey Brodovitch
A. M. Cassandre
René Clark
Robert Gage
William Golden
Paul Rand

1973
Charles Coiner
Paul Smith
Jack Tinker

1974
Will Burtin
Leo Lionni

1975
Gordon Aymar
Herbert Bayer
Cipe Pineles Burtin
Heyworth Campbell
Alexander Liberman
L. Moholy-Nagy

1976
E. McKnight Kauffer
Herbert Matter

1977
Saul Bass
Herb Lubalin
Bradbury Thompson

1978
Thomas M. Cleland
Lou Dorfsman
Allen Hurlburt
George Lois

1979
W. A. Dwiggins
George Giusti
Milton Glaser
Helmut Krone
Willem Sandberg
Ladislav Sutnar
Jan Tschichold

1980
Gene Federico
Otto Storch
Henry Wolf

1981
Lucian Bernhard
Ivan Chermayeff
Gyorgy Kepes
George Krikorian
William Taubin

1982
Richard Avedon
Amil Gargano
Jerome Snyder
Massimo Vignelli

1983
Aaron Burns
Seymour Chwast
Steve Frankfurt

1984
Charles Eames
Wallace Elton
Sam Scali
Louis Silverstein

1985
Art Kane
Len Sirowitz
Charles Tudor

1986
Walt Disney
Roy Grace
Alvin Lustig
Arthur Paul

1987
Willy Fleckhaus
Shigeo Fukuda
Steve Horn
Tony Palladino

1988
Ben Shahn
Bert Steinhauser
Mike Tesch

ADC SPECIAL HALL OF FAME AWARD TO SILAS RHODES

Painting by Patrick Pigott

ALLAN BEAVER, Ivan Chermayeff, Paul Davis, Phil Dusenberry, Bob Gill, Bob Giraldi, Milton Glaser, Tony Palladino – a few of the many prominent visual communicators who have either studied or taught at the School of Visual Arts since its founding by Silas Rhodes in 1947, 41 years ago.

Originally called the School for Cartoonists and Illustrators, SVA first opened its doors to only 3 faculty members and 35 students, most of whom had enrolled under the G.I. Bill of Rights. Although Rhodes had earned a Ph.D. in literature from Columbia, he did not believe that strict and formal studies prepared students for the real world. He once wrote "What good is an education that prepares you to read Schopenhauer or Goethe if it *cannot* help you find work?" This philosophy has been SVA's underlying credo and commitment to the countless students who have studied there.

What was unique about Rhodes' school was that he recruited only practicing artists and illustrators to teach there, in their "spare" time. Realizing that the field of visual communication was constantly expanding into related fields, he looked for instructors who worked in advertising, editorial design, photography, and more recently, media arts. Under Rhodes' direction, SVA has grown from a 3-year institution that did not grant degrees to a fully accredited, board-certified college offering B.A.s and M.F.A.s in art education, communication arts, film arts, media arts, photography, painting, sculpture, and illustration. In 1986, SVA became the first accredited college in the United States to offer an M.F.A. in computer art. With 690 faculty members, 2,500 fulltime, and 4,000 continuing-education students, SVA is the nation's largest, independent, degree-granting art school. Its ever-increasing course catalogue and reputation are testimonials to Rhodes' leadership.

SVA's contributions to visual communications are immeasurable. Its effect is seen even in New York City's subways, enriched by SVA posters. A strong and viable gallery committee helps promote group and individual shows at the Cooper-Hewitt Museum and elsewhere. Most recently, it presented the gala 40th Anniversary Retrospective Show at the Art Directors Club.

No matter how one quantifies SVA's impressive growth in size and influence, one thing remains constant, however–Silas Rhodes' strong-willed dedication to its continued success. For his unwavering devotion to the tradition of practical education in visual communications, the Art Directors Club proudly presents its Special Hall of Fame Award to Silas Rhodes.

BEN SHAHN

Ben Shahn; Sol Libsohn photographer

BEN SHAHN. His codified signature neatly scribbled under any of his images conjures up a peerless world of visual and emotional realism. Born in Kovno Lithuania in 1898, Ben Shahn and his family immigrated to the United States in 1906. Like many artists, he later used his childhood experiences in both Lithuania and Brooklyn to create works of fine art.

As a young boy, Shahn delighted in reading the *Old Testament*. He would spend hours visually interpreting biblical scenes and Hebrew typefaces, all in a style distinctly his own. Shahn's thirst for knowledge was partially quenched by his uncle, a bookbinder who brought him books from his shop, while his parents–his mother, a potter and his father, a woodcarver–no doubt instilled in him an early affinity for creating with his hands.

His teenage years were spent as a lithographer's apprentice by day and a high-school student by night. During the 1920s, Shahn studied at New York University, the City College of New York, and the National Academy of Design. His fascination with biology earned him two summer semesters at Woods Hole in Massachusetts. Realizing the need to explore the world he had read so much about, Shahn, in 1925, began two years of extensive traveling throughout Europe and North Africa. These trips yielded many sketches, paving the way for his first exhibition at New York's Downtown Gallery in 1930.

In 1932 Shahn produced a series of 23 highly compassionate and controversial gouaches dealing with the celebrated Sacco & Vanzetti murder trial, proving his deftness in portraying sociopolitical events as well as scenic images. The inconclusive evidence revealed in the trial and reflected in the sentence had aroused international outcry. Shahn's work mirrored this protest. He joined the ranks of artists and writers who believed that both men were executed, not because of their guilt, but because of their ethnic origin and unpopular political affiliations. Shahn's paintings are harsh and twisted linear studies, powerful visual editorials protesting the tragedy of a social injustice.

Despite his strong political views, Shahn collaborated on and was commissioned to produce several murals and frescoes for various public and federal buildings. In 1933, Mexican artist Diego Rivera, impressed by Shahn's work, asked for his assistance in creating *Man at the Crossroads*. This ill-fated fresco in New York's RCA Building was later destroyed by an act of political censorship. Shahn's other egg-tempera murals, produced in the Renaissance method of painting over original cartoons or sketches, grace post offices in New York City and the Health, Education, and Welfare Building in Washington, DC. Particularly noteworthy are the 13 murals that cover the walls of the Bronx Central Annex Post Office. For two years, beginning in 1938, Shahn and his wife, Bernarda Bryson Shahn, worked to create the large mural panels in the building's main lobby.

During this period, Shahn's work became recognized, exhibited, and praised around the world. His first contact with graphic design, however, came in 1942 when he was invited to work in the Office of War Information. There began his long and fruitful association with fellow ADC Hall of Famer, William Golden.

Their first joint venture was a war poster entitled *We French Workers Warn You*. It proved to be "round one" as Shahn referred to his initial skirmish with Golden on visual ideology and artistic convictions. The friction occurred after both discussed and evidently agreed on what the poster should convey. Shahn created a totally different version, incensing Golden. In an essay written for a retrospective volume on Bill Golden, Shahn fondly recalled the now legendary incident.

I think Bill and I solidified our graphic futures more through that impasse than through any subsequent single experience. What I learned was a hardened determination to put the integrity of an image first and above all other considerations. One must be prepared to retire from any job whatever, rather than abandon the clear vision.

This early clash of two visual titans strengthened rather than dissolved their personal and professional admiration for each other. The poster turned out to be a wonderfully expressive piece, showing a solemn group of French workers under arrest and stripped of their fervent national pride. To this day, the poster remains a much sought-after item in the Ben Shahn collection.

During the war, Shahn created other posters for the Office of War Information, with subjects ranging from Nazi brutality to post-war employment for veterans. Only two posters, however, were widely distributed. His war work contrasts sharply with the World War I patriotism of Walter Whitehead and F. Strothmann. Shahn's posters appealed to the conditions of human suffering on a more abstract visual and cerebral plane. His images, full of horrific expressions and disproportionate body language succeed without actually depicting war's carnage.

After the war, Shahn was selected as one of the "World's Ten Best Artists" by *Look* magazine. His considerable talents were also gaining favor with many innovative art directors and designers in the advertising and editorial fields. Magazines like *Charm*, *Esquire*, *Harper's*, *Scientific American*, and *Vogue* had begun to appreciate the immense graphic potential of a Ben Shahn visual. Shahn had once described this type of work as just another way to earn extra income to support his "real" artistic endeavors. He quickly realized that, contrary to his earlier beliefs, this so-called "illegitimate" method of creating images could be just as challenging and rewarding as "high art."

In 1947, Shahn renewed his working relationship with William Golden at CBS. From promotional brochures to print ads, the team of Golden and Shahn helped make CBS flourish. Their first post-war collaboration for the network was a promotional brochure publicizing an early television documentary on juvenile delinquency entitled *The Eagle's Brood*. Shahn's visual is a study in silent frustration. Like human time-bombs, two boys sit poignantly staring out, practically begging for help. One cannot help noticing the wrinkles in their clothing and their morose, almost bitter facial expressions. Ironically, one boy's pose is reminiscent of Rodin's *Thinker*. Shahn created an image that uniquely reflected the content of the documentary it advertised. Viewing this disturbing image today, over four decades later, one is still captivated by its underlying tension, which, like the problem, has not lessened.

From 1947 until Golden's untimely death in 1959, the "dynamic duo" produced many inspired graphics for CBS. One of the most memorable is *The Empty Studio*. Originally illustrated for a network radio advertising sales pamphlet in 1948, Shahn, through his visual acuity, brilliantly captured the starkness of a vacant radio studio. The cold maze of metal folding chairs and music stands, numerous microphones, and a lone cello resting gingerly between two chairs establish the mood voiced in the brochure copy.

The empty studio. . . . No voice is heard now. The music is still. The studio audience has gone home. But the work of the broadcast has just begun. . . . Between broadcasts, people everywhere are buying the things this program has asked them to buy.

Other fine examples of work Shahn did for CBS are print ads entitled *Harvest* (1955) and *The Big Push* (1957). The former looks at the incredible growth and popularity of television through the clutter of rooftop antennas. The latter sells the power of television advertising by a cacophonous array of overlapping supermarket shopping carts. These wonderfully eclectic ads elevated advertising, Bill Golden, and Ben Shahn to new heights of graphic expression.

Fred W. Friendly, broadcast journalism pioneer and champion of a free press, along with his CBS colleague, Edward R. Murrow, commissioned Shahn to do a number of pieces for their prestigious news documentary unit. One such project was *Ambassador Satchmo*, a 1956 profile of the life and music of Louis Armstrong. Shahn's sketches and paintings played a major role in the documentary. Friendly recalls Shahn as being

the graphic conscience and the promise of broadcasting. He artistically chronicled television during its golden age. Ben helped make television more than just lights and wires in a box.

Throughout the late 1950s and early 1960s, Shahn renewed his early interest in the Bible. He created a vast and beautiful array of work based on both testaments, richly adorning them with his inimitable calligraphic impressions. They remain prized examples of his immense artistic legacy.

Shahn died in March 1969 at the age of 71. He is considered to be one of the greatest masters of the twentieth century. Honors, books, and gallery retrospectives continue to rekindle interest in his work, almost 20 years after his death. Ben Shahn was an innovative and free graphic spirit. He conveyed the human condition in a style few could hope even to imitate. Shahn had only to touch his brush or pencil to paper to produce a masterpiece. His cryptic, yet graceful lines and shapes still leave all who view them in awe of his talent.

Always a champion of the less fortunate and of the need for social and spiritual leadership, Shahn once wrote

Society cannot grow upon negatives. If man has lost his Jehovah, his Buddha, his Holy Family, he must have new, perhaps more scientifically tangible beliefs to which he may attach his affections....In any case, if we are to have values, a spiritual life and a culture, these things must find the imagery and interpretations through the arts.

Amen, Ben!

"Eagles Brood," CBS, 1947

Sacco & Vanzetti, 1932

Detail from Bronx Central Annex Post Office mural, 1939

Poster for Jerome Robbins' "Jazz Ballet," 1958

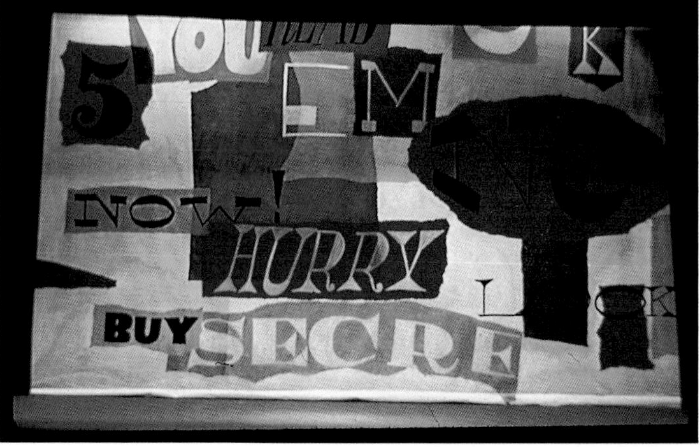

Set design for "Jazz Ballet," 1958

"Third Allegory," 1955

"Harvest," CBS, 1955

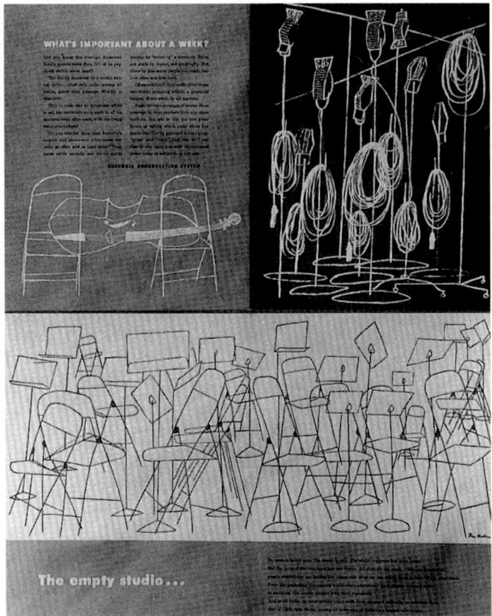

"Empty Studio," CBS, 1948

"Big Push," CBS, 1957

"We French Workers Warn You" poster, 1942

"Triple Dip," 1959

"Truman & Dewey," CBS, 1948

MIKE TESCH

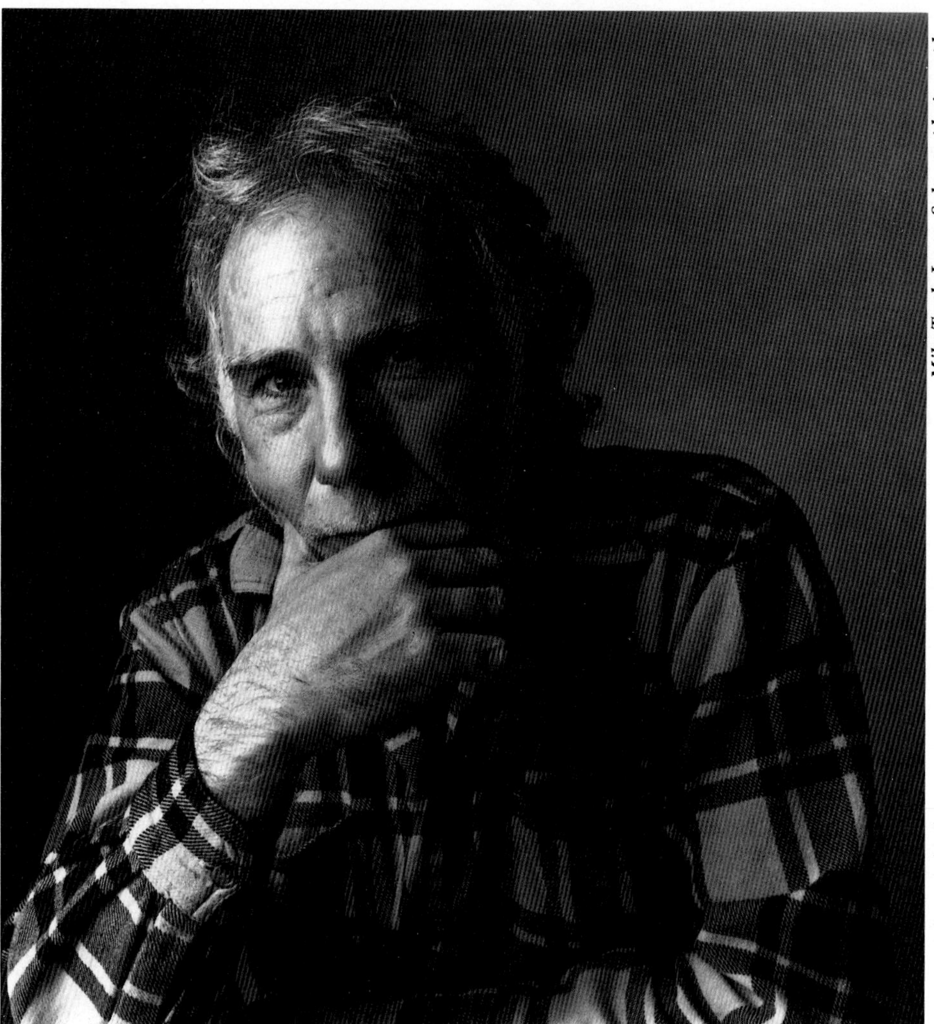

Mike Tesch; James Salzano photographer

MEETING with Mike Tesch is like communicating with a spirited, soft-spoken, gray-bearded philosopher in a disconcertingly dark corner office. Blinds drawn, the only light comes from a harsh table lamp that glares out from a desk crammed with storyboards, reels, and books ranging from Eisenstadt to Ogilvy. "I was a very insecure and protected kid. My mother sheltered me with the hope I'd become a dentist." Fortunately Tesch did not accede to his mother's wishes. He has, however, touched countless people with his unique brand of advertising.

Born in Brooklyn in 1938, Tesch and his family moved to Far Rockaway, Queens, a year later. His first encounter with art came at Far Rockaway High School where he worked on the yearbook art staff before graduating in 1954. Tesch remarks, "I got As in Art while other kids got As in Math." After graduation, he moved back to Brooklyn, once again enjoying the sights and sounds of that special melting pot. The ethnic variations there eventually helped shape his advertising.

After graduating from Pratt Institute in 1959, Tesch decided to take some design courses at the School of Visual Arts where he encountered his first inspirational figure, teacher and designer Bob Gill. Gill taught Tesch how to think conceptually.

Bob gave me a good kick in the butt. He taught me not just to decorate a page, but to have an idea and make sure you always say something, be it a letterhead or a matchbook cover. He sent me on my way and was certainly one of the most unforgettable characters I've met.

Armed with the Gospel-according-to Gill, Tesch landed his first job, in *Redbook's* promotion department. With his boss, art director Mike Pennette, the two helped make the department one of the best in the business. As a result, Tesch won his first AIGA award, the first of hundreds.

Sensing the urgency to get "artsy," Tesch left *Redbook* in 1961 for greener pastures. He showed his portfolio to future ADC Hall of Famer, Tony Palladino, who suggested he see designer Ivan Chermayeff (another future Hall of Famer). Chermayeff immediately hired Tesch as a senior designer. At Chermayeff & Geismar Associates, Tesch worked on a wide variety of assignments for Pepsi-Cola. One was a poster announcing a Pepsi-sponsored exhibition on Pop-Art. Entitled *Vernacular Ameri-*

ca, the poster was done in lime green with the announcement in a comic-book dialogue balloon–reminiscent of Roy Lichtenstein without a comic-like visual. The exhibition, as Tesch recalls, was probably one of the shortest on record.

I had a pink Cadillac parked on the sidewalk–right in front of Pepsi's headquarters on Park Avenue. The president of Pepsi arrived and was outraged because Pop-Art was "un-American." We had to strike the show the very next day.

Wanting to do ads and commercials, Tesch left graphic design and embarked on his advertising career. In 1965, he was hired by his former boss, Mike Pennette, who had just formed his own agency, Fladell, Winston & Pennette. Tesch found himself working on clients such as Lender's Bagels, The Associated Press, *Evergreen Review*, and King Features. His admittedly nonmemorable work, coupled with the company's instability, resulted in his being fired.

Advertising history was made the very next day. Tesch, unemployed, called Amil Gargano, an art director at Carl Ally Inc. Gargano arranged for Tesch to meet with Ed McCabe and Ralph Ammirati, who agreed with Gargano's assessment of Tesch's work. Tesch was hired at Carl Ally Inc. in August 1966. To this day, Tesch believes he was hired because the agency needed a good shortstop to play on their softball team!

His first assignment for Ally was Hertz Rent-a-Car. With writer Jim Parry, Tesch created trailblazing advertising. One that particularly stands out is "Death of a Traveling Salesman," which portrays the trials and tribulations of a modern day "traveler." Mike Cuesta's photograph of a man–back to camera–suit wrinkled and shoulders rounded from carrying his overstuffed suitcases–adds to the overall atmosphere of the concept. One vignette, for example, says:

You've just landed in a city that gets only seven inches of rain a year.... All on the day you arrive.

Through the late 1960s and early 1970s, Tesch also worked on clients like Chris-Craft, Travelers Insurance, Pan Am, and Tonka Toys. Chris-Craft presented this creative challenge: How do you sell a $30,000 houseboat to someone who thinks he has no time left to use it? Tesch and writer Steve Smith solved the problem by producing a chart showing that the average person actually has four months off a year. The ad sold the boats!

His work for Travelers Insurance produced one of his most intriguing commercials. Entitled "Auto," the spot sold automobile insurance through the concept of showing a brand new car, legally parked, being crushed by a truck backing into it as the mortified owner comes out of an ice cream parlor. Created with writer Tom Messner, the spot was also an engineering feat, for, by using hydraulics and electronics, the car was crushed in 20 seconds.

His Traveler's work also includes a very effective print ad. The visual shows a 55mph sign on a gravel highway shoulder. The copy states: "If saving your life isn't important, think of the gas you'll save."

Tesch's advertising for Pan Am is an example of perfect timing. The energy crises and recession of the 1970s all but killed airline travel. After eight consecutive years of losses, Pan Am needed a new concept to halt the skid. By taking advantage of the *Roots* phenomenon, Tesch and writer Tom Messner created Pan Am's "Heritage" campaign. "Every American has two heritages. Pan Am is going to help you discover the other one." Tesch, Messner, and ADC Hall of Famer, director Steve Horn created a spot called "Roots" about Americans going back to their ancestral homelands. Pan Am's revenues rose to a record $122 million.

A by-product of Tesch's work for the Tonka Toys account was his collaboration with writer Patrick Kelly and the beginning of a professional and personal relationship that still endures. To Tesch, Kelly is "unequivocally the best writer I've worked with. Without him, I wouldn't be here."

One of Tesch's favorite spots, "Elephant," was done for Tonka. To demonstrate how strongly-built Tonka's toys were, the spot featured Nelly the elephant stepping on a yellow Tonka dump truck. Tesch recalls the shoot:

It took us weeks to make Nelly feel at ease stepping on the yellow truck. It seems she was afraid of yellow. When we put yellow in her path, she spooked. Steve Horn finally captured the moment on film and Nelly became a star.

Toward the end of the 1970s, Tesch was selected as one of "America's 100 Outstanding Creative People" by *AdDay/USA*. Carl Ally Inc., now known as Ally & Gargano, rewarded him for his creative efforts by making him a vice president and creative director. And along came Federal.

The overnight delivery business was a new and exciting service to consumers in 1976. The Federal Express account was a fabulous vehicle for Tesch's random studies into the vulnerabilities of human behavior. He took the basic elements of fear and anxiety and exploited them in bizarre, comic ways that have yet to be duplicated. With Patrick Kelly and director Joe Sedelmaier, Tesch helped make Federal the country's leading overnight courier. With spots like "Paper Blob," "Fast-Paced World," "Pacing the Floor," "Promise Them Anything," and others, consumers and advertisers were propelled into a world of slapstick frenzy. Ally & Gargano and their client dominated advertising and have the awards to prove it. In a span of four years, 1978–82, Tesch won ten ADC Gold Awards for his Federal Express commercials. The spots are even included in the Smithsonian Institute's permanent collection of modern advertising.

Tesch says that the key to the incredible success of the Federal Express commercials was the client's willingness to take chances. The spontaneity associated with these classic spots could never have happened if Federal had conducted the customary research and test marketing. "You can't animatic humor," Tesch emphatically insists.

In 1981, Tesch, along with Bill Bernbach, Ed McCabe, and Hal Riney, was elected to *Adweek's* "All American Creative Team." He is now a member of Ally & Gargano's executive committee and Executive Vice President and Director of Creative Services. Despite the management titles, Tesch continues to create exceptional advertising.

If I'm going to do something, I'm going to do it right. I'm not one of those people who bury themselves in a newspaper while riding the subway. I look around at faces, expressions, and body language. I don't close myself off. I'm always learning.

Tesch has already given the advertising business a legacy of love, compassion, sensitivity, and of course, humor. His intensity and dedication to his craft are reflected in his work. Perhaps fellow ADC Hall of Famer Amil Gargano has said it best.

Mike is an enormously tenacious guy. Once you give up, nothing very good happens. Mike has never given up.

"Elephant," Tonka Toys, 1974

"Fast-Paced World," Federal Express, 1981

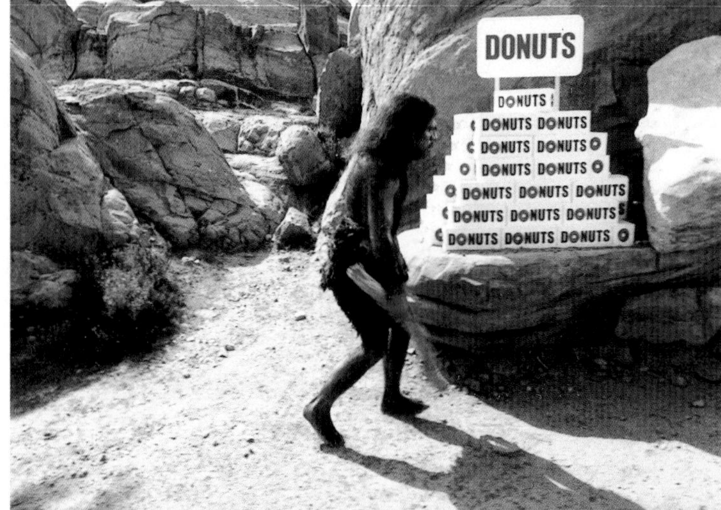

"3,000,000 BC," Dunkin' Donuts, 1988

Travelers Insurance ad, 1973

What's it like to be the mother of three kids when you're already the father?

There's no one way to describe it because it's different for every man who loses his wife.

But no matter what kind of an emotional adjustment he has to make, he still has to deal with the economic realities. Somebody's got to take care of the kids and the house. Which may mean hiring a full-time housekeeper.

If his wife had a job, as four out of ten mothers* do these days, that extra money is gone. Money that could have helped later on with the mortgage or the kids' education.

Maybe that's why the traditional idea of insuring the wife with only a token amount doesn't make as much sense anymore.

The Travelers life insurance people have developed a number of plans to meet the needs of today's family.

Since each plan is a little different, you really ought to look up your local Travelers agent in the Yellow Pages to find out which one's right for you.

But do it soon. And do it together.

THE TRAVELERS
Maybe we can help.

*U.S. Department of Labor Statistics

Travelers Insurance ad, 1973

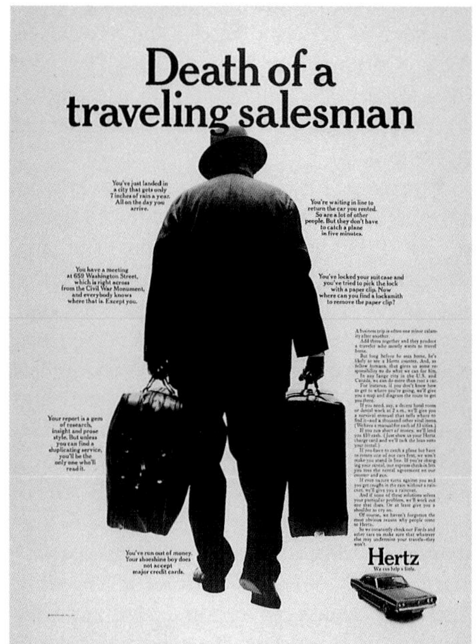

Hertz ad, 1968

"Auto," Travelers Insurance, 1982

"Roots," Pan Am Heritage campaign, 1971

Gallery announcement poster, 1961

Barney's ad, 1977

What are you going to do with the 4 months you have off this year?

	Days off
Vacation	10
Saturdays	52
Sundays	52
Holidays	8
Total	122

These days you don't have to be rich, retired or unemployed to have a lot of time off.

Even if you're forced to work for a living, you still have about 4 months a year available for leisure. Which is probably a good deal more free time than you thought you had.

And while you're taking a fresh look at all your leisure, you ought to look at a fresh way to enjoy it. You ought to look at a new Chris-Craft Aqua-Home.

It's a combination resort, vacation home and boat that will turn a day off into a vacation day and a weekend or a week into a vacation.

It's also the one vacation place that will let you tow a water skier, fish out the back door, dive off the sundeck, entertain 20 to 30 people without creating a crowd and move to a new neighborhood whenever you like.

And speaking of moving, there are over 30,000 miles of interlocking waterways throughout the U.S. and Canada. So it's quite conceivable that you could spend all your free time cruising them without seeing the same sight twice.

The home part of the Aqua-Home

Then, to make the time when you're not cruising as enjoyable as when you are, the Chris-Craft Aqua-Home offers more house than any houseboat in its class.

Whether you pick the 34-ft. or 46-ft. model you get all the conveniences of home and then some. Including wall-to-wall carpeting and wood paneling throughout. For the ship's cook, otherwise known as your wife, there's an all-electric galley with a 3-burner range with oven and rotisserie, and a refrigerator-freezer, instead of the usual archaic ice box. And since no home should be without a bathroom, there's a bathroom with a vanity and stall shower.

The difference between our two models is in the length not the luxury: our 34-footer sleeps six; our 46-footer sleeps eight.

The aqua part of the Aqua-Home

Now you might think that to get this much house in a houseboat you might have to give up something in the boat. Not in an Aqua-Home.

Below decks, our 46-footer has twin 230-hp Chris-Craft engines that'll get you and your house up over 27 mph to tow that water skier we mentioned before.

Then, since we know that a nice house on a bad foundation is not a nice house, we build the foundation (hull) out of the strongest fiberglass around. It was developed with the experience gained in over 70 years of designing and building power cruisers and yachts. (Try to find another houseboat builder with as much experience building power cruisers and yachts.)

Prices start at $14,990 for the 34-footer and at $29,990 for the 46-footer. And don't forget, there's no charge for real estate or real estate taxes.

All told, a Chris-Craft Aqua-Home gives you the advantages of a resort attached to the advantages of a house attached to the advantages of a boat. Just the thing for a man of leisure, like yourself.

The Aqua-Home
Chris-Craft

Chris-Craft ad, 1970

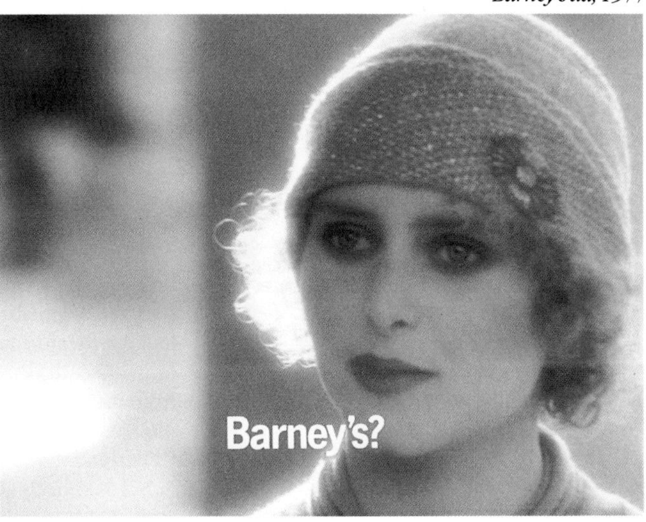

"Paris," Barney's, 1980

BERT STEINHAUSER

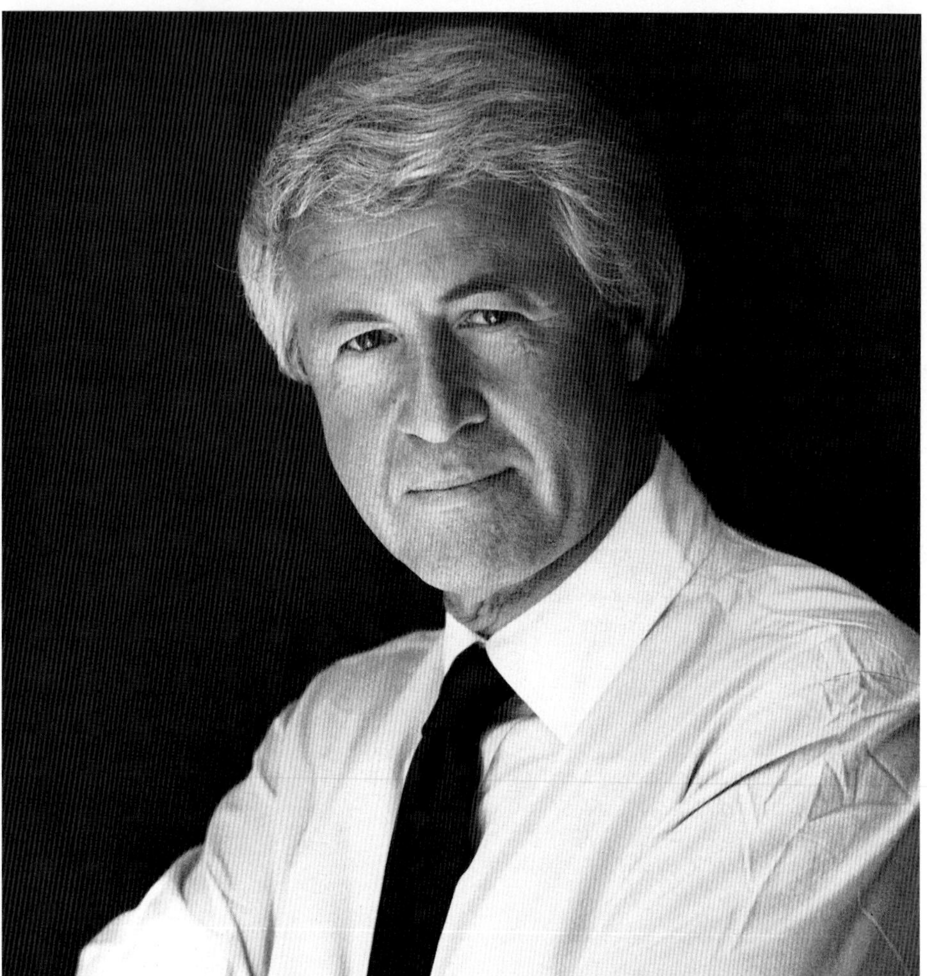

Bert Steinhauser, Michael Miller, photographer

SPENDING time with Bert Steinhauser, either in person or through his work, is an exhilarating experience. His ebullient personality, coupled with his love for his craft and for humanity make him a dynamic one-man show.

Born in Brooklyn in 1928, Steinhauser attended Samuel J. Tilden High School and received the school's art medal. From there he went on to study at Brooklyn College where he was deeply influenced by his design professors. He augmented his studies with courses in advertising at Pratt Institute. After graduating from college in 1949, he accepted an offer from the William Becker Studio but soon moved on to Altman & Stoller, Kurnit & Geller, and to C. J. Herrick.

Bill Bernbach hired Steinhauser to work at DDB in 1955. In addition to his art directing responsibilities, Bernbach recruited him to represent the agency at advertising seminars. Most importantly, Bernbach encouraged Steinhauser to be different. The late 1950s and 1960s were advertising's years of grandeur. DDB's pool of talent during those years included Bob Gage, Phyllis Robinson, Helmut Krone, Bob Levenson, Len Sirowitz, Ron Rosenfeld, Bill Taubin, and Dave Reider. Steinhauser's ever-increasing role helped solidify the agency's leading position. His work for clients like Clairol, Chivas Regal, El-Al, Hartmann, Heinz, Jamaica Tourism, Porsche, S.O.S., Volkswagen, and Wedgewood are timeless testimonials to DDB and Steinhauser alike.

Steinhauser's first major account was Clairol. He was asked to come up with a way to show Clairol's extensive hair-coloring line in one ad. Steinhauser helped create a new photographic technique using convex mirror-imaging. One woman with a neutral hair color was photographed through a succession of convex mirrors. Each section was individually retouched to match the Clairol color scheme. The ad earned Steinhauser his first ADC Gold Award.

Steinhauser next went on to pursue new creative objectives with the Chivas Regal account. For eight glorious years, his work for Chivas graced numerous magazines, making Chivas one of them most sought-after scotches in the world. During this time, Steinhauser became interested in photography. The images of Art Kane, Mel Sokolsky, and Bert Stern affected him deeply. Steinhauser's need for more photographic control and his dedication to perfection led well-known advertising photographer and friend, Wingate Paine to remark jokingly and with admiration, "Bert, shoot it yourself." More than 50,000 stills later, Steinhauser continues to photograph images for personal and professional purposes. He was, for example, one of the first photographers to tap the resources of the 35mm camera for professional advertising photo shoots.

An early Steinhauser ad for Chivas showed a crocodile belt (his) wrapped around the famous bottle. The headline said, "Give Dad and expensive belt." The visual, bathed in deep black shadows, became Steinhauser's photographic trademark. His pictorial excursions into trompe-l'oeil and silhouettes made simple, yet stunning, visual statements. Bernbach, increasingly aware of Steinhauser's talents as a photographer, supported him totally. Steinhauser remembers many weekends when he turned his office into a photo studio, giving him the added capabilities he needed as a complete visual communicator.

Other classic concepts for Chivas included a series of wonderfully eclectic magazine cartoons. Steinhauser hired artists like Charles Addams and Chuck Saxon to interpret the visuals. Although the tops of the pages said "Advertisement," *New Yorker* readers were regularly fooled into believing that these stylishly subtle ads were part of the magazine's editorial content.

Steinhauser's work for Heinz represented his commitment to supporting the underdogs of advertising. His "skinny chicken" ad for their soup line helped bolster sales in a Campbell's-dominated market. The superb, western-themed, stop-action spots Steinhauser did for Heinz Ketchup are masterpieces of comparative advertising. Shot in Holland because of superior technique and attractive production costs, "High Noon" and others like it made Heinz the slowest-pouring and fastest-selling ketchup in the "West, East, North, and South."

Again employing the editorial advertising idea that had worked so effectively for Chivas, Steinhauser and writer Ron Rosenfeld produced one of the most spectacular sales reversals in advertising history. Rival Dog Food sales were so low that grocers sold more generic kibble than Rival. Steinhauser and Rosenfeld developed an ad that looked like a feature story from *Life* magazine. Using *Life's* typeface and photo-layout design, they told the very readable and enjoyable saga of an overweight man and his overweight pet. Entitled "Funny, fat people have fat dogs!" the ad reported on the problems caused by giving dogs non-nutritious food. No product shot or tag-line was used. Rival's name appeared only three times, buried in the copy. Nevertheless, Rival's sales skyrocketed.

During the late 1960s, Steinhauser's personal quest for "advertising having to motivate, not just communicate," was realized again and again. His work for Close-Up toothpaste, Yardley, and "Big Blue" for S.O.S. were cases in point.

His favorite, however, was a 1967 public service print ad that chided Congress for not passing the Rat Extermination Bill. The visual was a photograph of a huge, menacing rat. The headline read "Cut this out and put it in bed next to your child." The copy, powerfully written by Chuck Kollewe tells how rats have "killed more humans than all the generals in history put together...that thousands of our children are bitten by rats each year – some killed or disfigured." At the bottom of the ad was a list of all who had voted for or against the bill's passage, asking all who read it to take action. One person who did was President Johnson.

In a personal letter to Steinhauser, LBJ thanked him for his "timely and imaginative ad that surely played an important part in persuading Congress to pass this vital legislation" the second time around. Steinhauser is justly proud of this citation, more so than any of the hundreds of others he has received. This initial venture into the powerful worlds of public service and politics paved the way for his work with the Anti-Defamation League and the Democratic National Committee.

During the late 1970s, Steinhauser did a number of extraordinary ads for Porsche and Jamaica Tourism. His eye for color and typefaces literally made ads explode off the pages. He approached each assignment as if it were a 24-page poster. "Before you read it, you need to see it," he once remarked. In the Porsche ads, he used bold metallic colors and a Renaissance linear perspective that cut through two Carreras with razor-sharp perfection. On the other hand, the warm, colorful waters of Jamaica were exquisite foils for Steinhauser's layouts for Jamaica Tourism. Almost three-dimensional, the picturesque pastiche of images appear as if they jumped out of a children's pop-up book, capturing the allure and beauty of the island.

Steinhauser's last body of work for DDB was for Volkswagen. The recurrent energy crises, with odd- and even-day gas rationing paved the way for the country's attraction to the economics of owning a small car. In response, VW developed the Rabbit and Steinhauser and Bob Levenson developed the "Does It Again" campaign. Steinhauser also began to try his hand at directing commercials. His extensive knowledge of still photography made the transition smooth and logical. His work for VW on both fronts earned him four ADC Gold Awards in two years. Particularly effective was the "Sheik" spot. Shot in Jerusalem, a group of disgruntled Arab oilmen complain about the new Rabbit Diesel's being the best low-mileage car in America. Other gems in the campaign include Wilt Chamberlain singing the praises of the Rabbit's headroom: "more than my Rolls Royce," and the North Carolina Highway Patrol explaining how they use Rabbits to catch speeders.

Steinhauser left DDB in 1980, after almost 25 years of inspired visual communicating, to form his own production company. As Steinhauser explains, "Once I hit 50, my first half was over. I went out on my own because I wanted to explore new avenues. The second half of my life is what really counts." Bert Steinhauser Productions flourished for eight years. Its spots for clients ranging from Miller Lite to General Electric have won many Clios and New York Film Festival awards along the way. Steinhauser is particularly proud of an Illinois Bell commercial he shot in 1987. Simply titled "Stormy Weather," it features young lovers after an obvious quarrel, waiting to see who will pick up the telephone and apologize first. Beautifully shot in soft focus with pastel colors, the title track is played by a breathy tenor saxophonist reminiscent of Coleman Hawkins.

In 1982, Silas Rhodes, founder of New York's School of Visual Arts, persuaded Steinhauser to put on a one-man retrospective. For months on end, he planned what was to be a multi-media event. His work on both slides and film graced the gallery's stark white walls in carefully-timed, overlapping intervals.

Always an advocate of education, Steinhauser helped form the country's first M.F.A. program at Syracuse University. He still serves as a visiting professor there and also continues to lecture on advertising at seminars around the world.

An intensely private man who once wanted to be a rabbi, Steinhauser is proud of his close-knit family, wishing only to be remembered as a good husband and father. His legacy, however, extends far beyond his family, to the countless people within and out of the business who have been touched by his gentle, heartfelt celebration of life.

Rival Dog Food ad, 1964

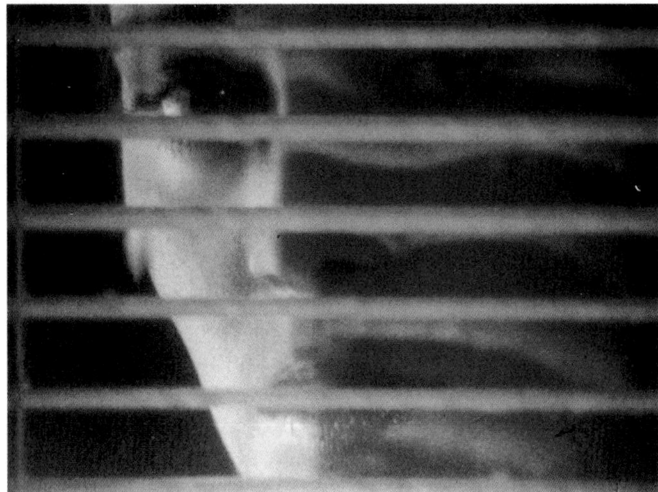

Illinois Bell, "Stormy Weather," 1987

Volkswagen "Sheik," 1980

Chivas Regal ad, 1963

Close-Up Toothpaste ad, 1967

Jamaica Tourism ad, 1978

Porsche ad, 1979

Clairol ad, 1960

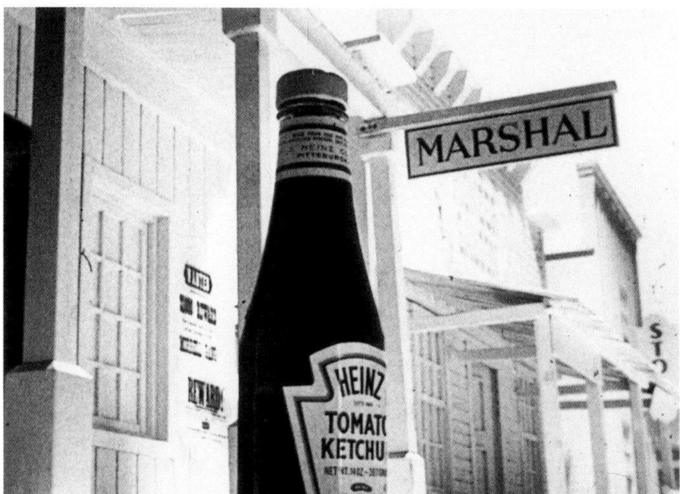

Heinz Ketchup, "High Noon," 1964

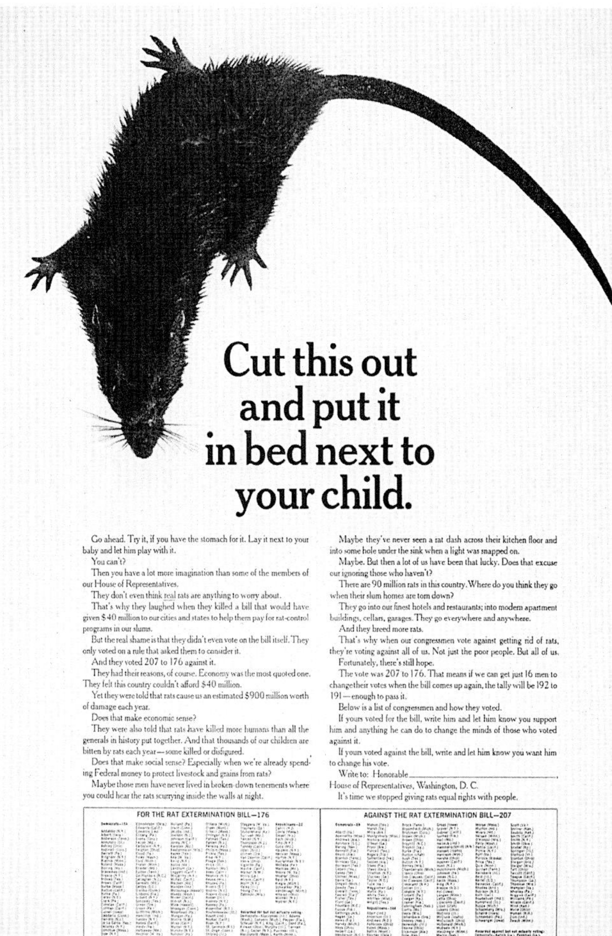

Rat Extermination public service ad, 1967

Chivas Regal ad, 1961

Heinz Soup ad, 1961

NEWSPAPER ADVERTISING

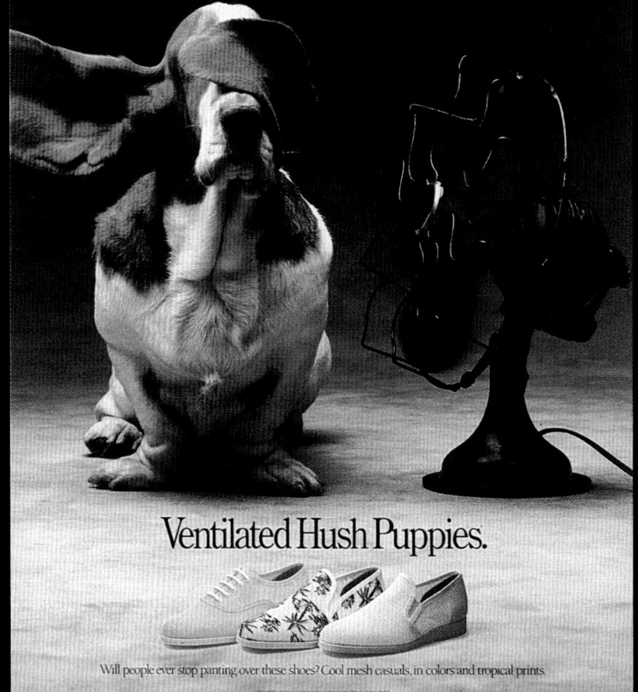
Ventilated Hush Puppies.
Will people ever stop panting over these shoes? Cool mesh casuals, in colors and tropical prints.

Corporate Hush Puppies.
Dress Lites with our super-lightweight soles. They'll make someone at the office drool.

Sophisticated Hush Puppies.
Our classic pumps. For those with a nose for the finer things.

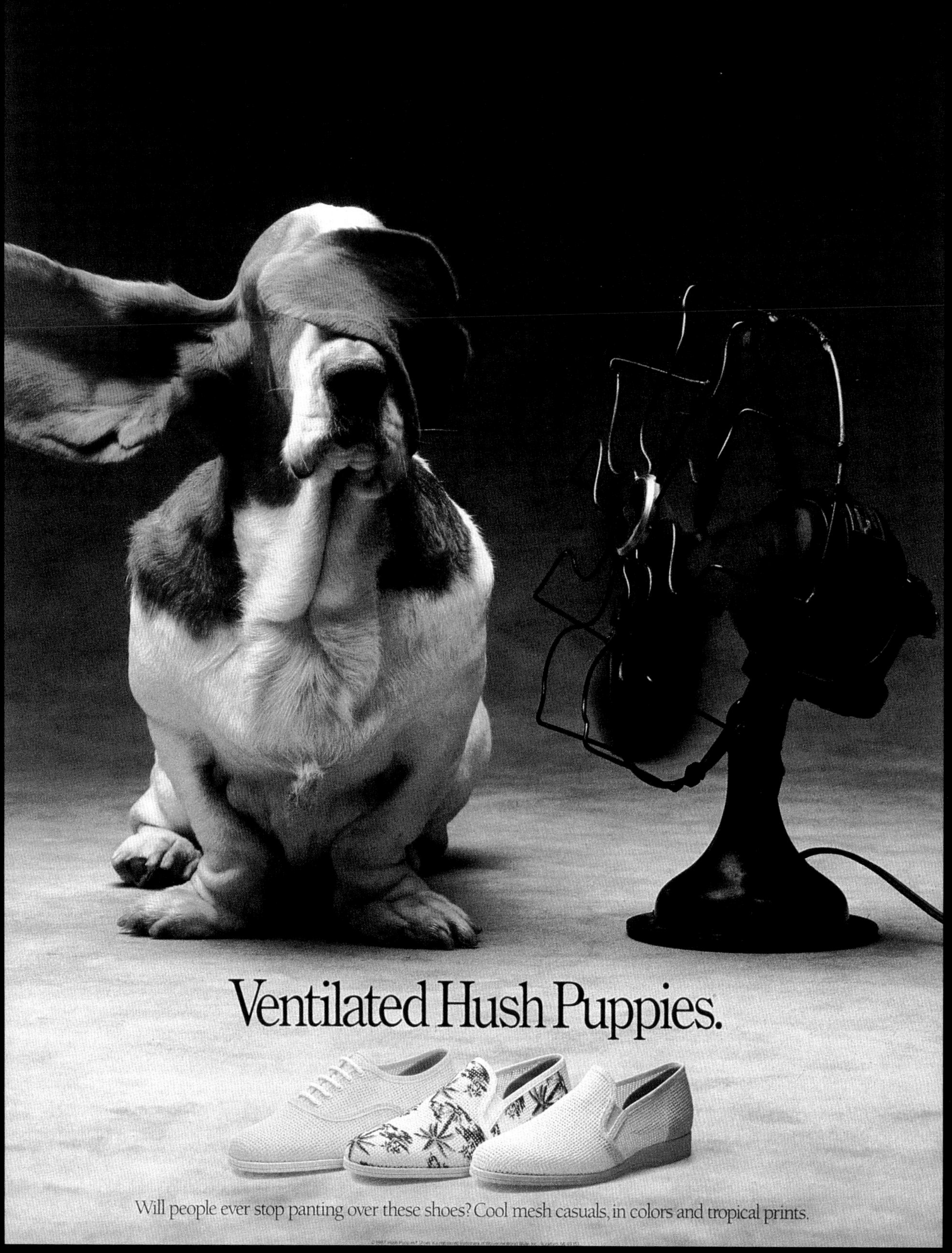

2 Silver Award

Art Director: Bob Barrie
Designer: Bob Barrie
Photographer: Rick Dublin
Writer: Jarl Olsen
Creative Director: Tom McElligott
Client: Hush Puppies
Agency: Fallon McElligott
Model: Jason

Malcolm Forbes, 1925

62 years ago when I was
on my father's knee, motorcycles
and hot air in balloons and print
weren't even gleams in this kid's eye —
Malcolm Forbes

For one hundred years, Bloomingdale's has been as rich and diverse as the people who shop there.

bloomingdale's

It wouldn't be the same without you.

3 Silver Award

Art Director: Houman Pirdavari
Designer: Houman Pirdavari
Writer: Bill Miller
Creative Director: Tom McElligott
Client: Bloomingdale's
Agency: Fallon McElligott

Malcolm Forbes, 1925

62 years ago when I was
on my father's knee, motorcycles
and hot air in balloons and print
weren't even gleams in this kid's eye—
Malcolm Forbes

For one hundred years, Bloomingdale's has been as rich and diverse as the people who shop there.

bloomingdale's

It wouldn't be the same without you.

Joseph Papp, 1935

a year after my Bar Mitzvah
and deep in the throes of memorizing
marc antony's speech from Shakespeare's
Julius Caesar (soon to be recorded on
a small metal disc in a store on 14th St,
price 10 cents — included use of background
music, Stravinsky's "Firebird Suite").
Photograph courtesy of adjacent photo-booth —
price, one nickle. year 1935.
Joseph (Yussel) Papp

For 100 years, Bloomingdale's has seen the fortunes of young men turn on how well they spend their nickels.

bloomingdale's

It wouldn't be the same without you.

Mickey Mantle, 1936

If I'd have known then
what I know now
I'd of named my horse Yogi
He's a lot smarter than he looks!
"My Heroes Have Always Been Cowboys"
Mickey Mantle

For 100 years, our heroes have always been customers.

bloomingdale's

It wouldn't be the same without you.

4 Silver Award

Art Director: Houman Pirdavari
Designer: Houman Pirdavari
Writer: Bill Miller
Creative Director: Tom McElligott
Client: Bloomingdale's
Agency: Fallon McElligott

5

Art Director: David Fox
Illustrator/Artist: Oasis Studio
Writer: Joe Alexander
Creative Director: Jac Coverdale
Client: North Memorial Hospital
Trauma Center
Agency: Clarity, Coverdale, Rueff

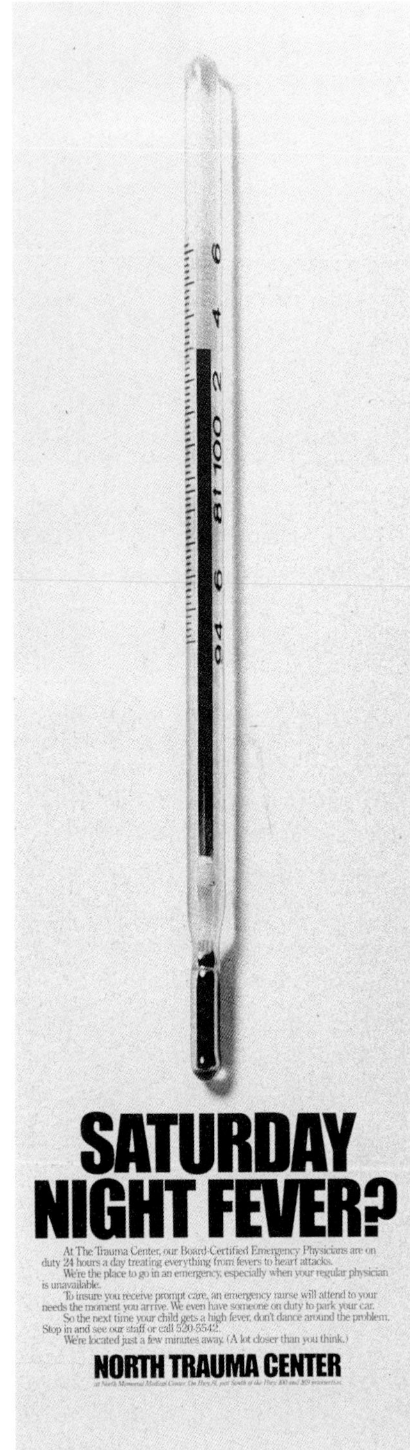

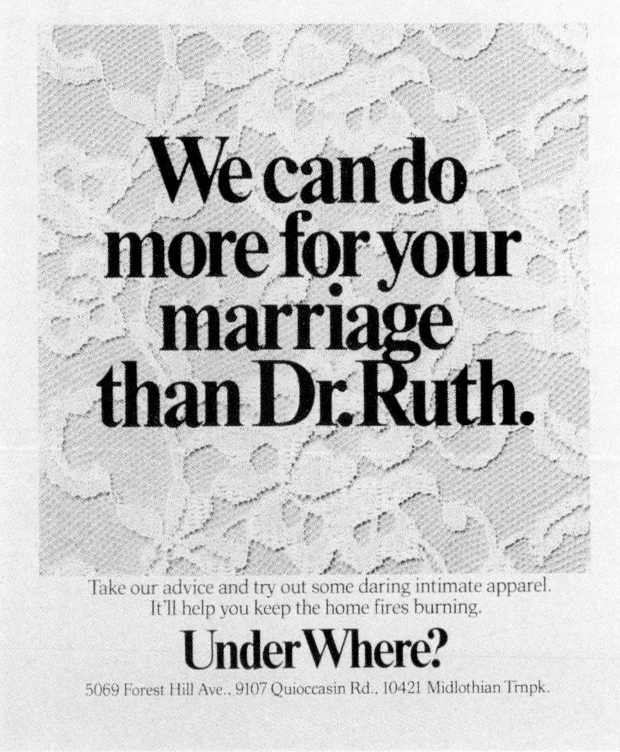

6

Art Director: Cabell Harris
Photographer: Pat Edwards
Writer: Ken Hines
Creative Director: Ken Hines
Client: Under Where
Agency: Lawler Ballard Advertising

7

Art Director: William Murphy
Photographer: Michael Pierce
Writer: Margaret Wilcox
Creative Director: Richard Pantano
Client: The Boston Globe
Agency: Hill, Holliday, Connors, Cosmopulos Inc.
Production Manager: Guy Silverio

8

Art Director: Houman Pirdavari
Designer: Houman Pirdavari
Writer: Bill Miller
Creative Director: Tom McElligott
Client: Bloomingdale's
Agency: Fallon McElligott

9

Art Director: Bob Barrie
Designer: Bob Barrie
Photographer: Rick Dublin
Writer: Jarl Olsen
Creative Director: Tom McElligott
Client: Hush Puppies
Agency: Fallon McElligott
Model: Jason

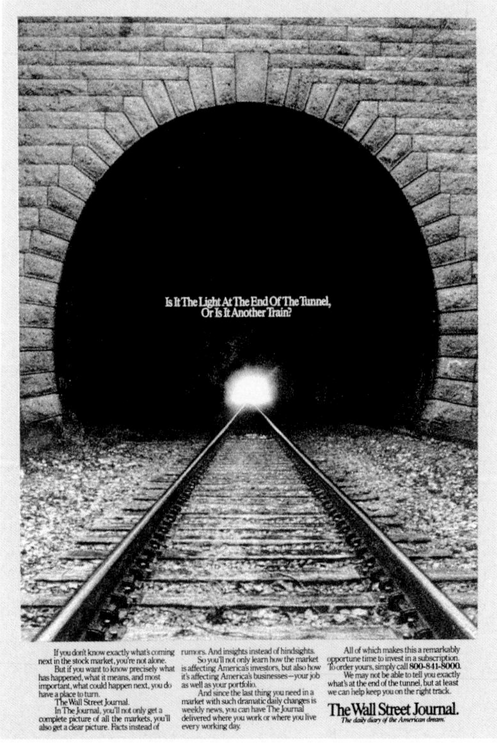

10

Art Director: Dean Hanson
Designer: Dean Hanson
Photographer: Rick Dublin
Writer: Bruce Bildsten
Creative Director: Tom McElligott
Client: The Wall Street Journal
Agency: Fallon McElligott

11
Art Director: Keith Evans
Designer: Keith Evans
Illustrator/Artist: Robert Grossman
Writer: Bryan Buckley
Creative Director: James Lawson
Client: Seagrams/Crown Royal
Agency: DDB Needham Worldwide

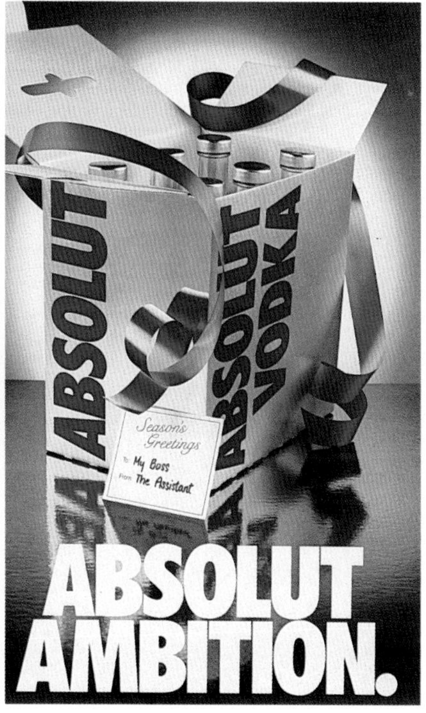

12
Art Director: Steve Feldman
Designer: Steve Feldman
Photographer: Steve Bronstein
Writer: Patrick Hanlon
Creative Director: Arnie Arlow, Peter Lubalin
Client: Carillon Importers Ltd.
Agency: TBWA Advertising Inc.

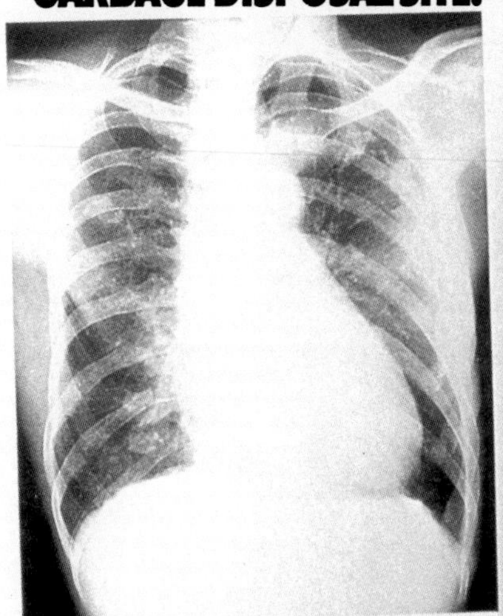

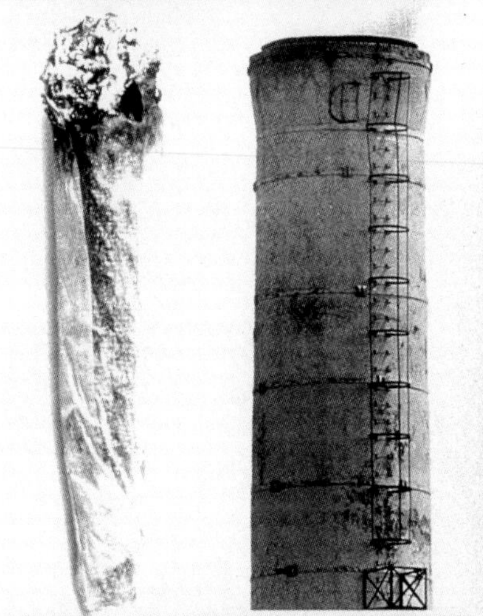

13

Art Director: Jac Coverdale
Photographer: Jim Arndt, Steve Umland
Writer: Joe Alexander
Creative Director: Jac Coverdale
Client: Earth Protector
Agency: Clarity, Coverdale, Rueff

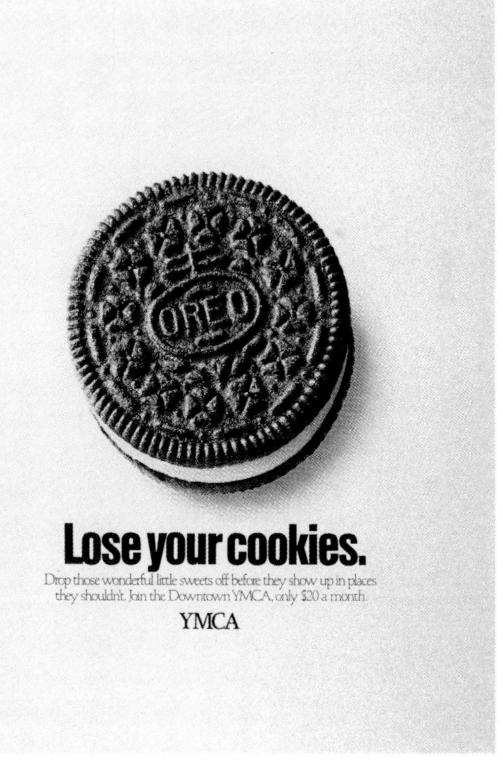

14
Art Director: David Fox
Photographer: Rick Dublin
Writer: Jerry Fury
Creative Director: Jac Coverdale
Client: YMCA
Agency: Clarity, Coverdale, Rueff

15
Art Director: Rachel Stephens
Designer: Rachel Stephens
Writer: Effie Meyer
Creative Director: Effie Meyer
Client: Northwest Fashion Square
Agency: R. L. Meyer Advertising

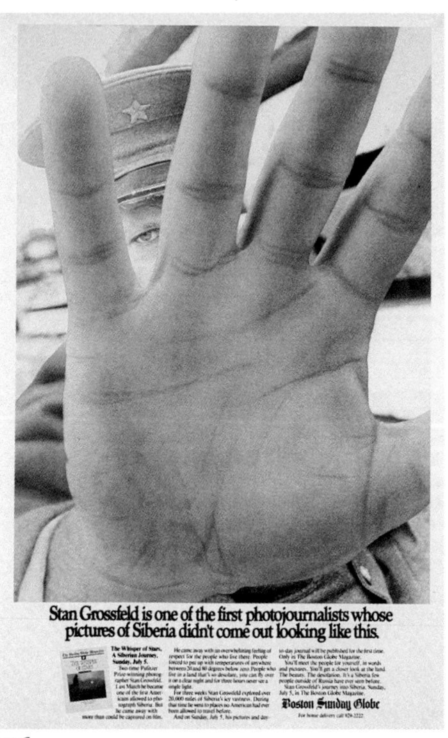

16
Art Director: William Murphy
Photographer: Michael Pierce
Writer: Margaret Wilcox
Creative Director: Richard Pantano
Client: The Boston Globe
Agency: Hill, Holliday, Connors, Cosmopulos Inc.
Production Manager: Guy Silverio

17

Art Director: Roy Grace
Designer: Roy Grace
Photographer: Bruno
Illustrator/Artist: Roy Grace
Writer: Diane Rothschild
Creative Director: Roy Grace, Diane Rothschild
Client: Whittle Communications
Agency: Grace & Rothschild

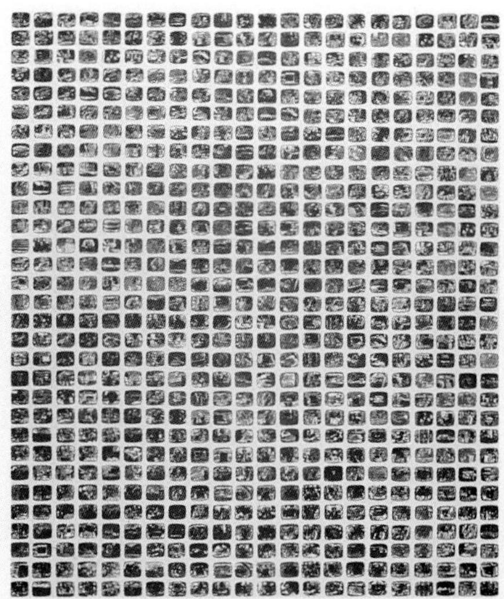

THIS AD COULD CAUSE CANCER.

The paper this ad is printed on could end up in the new Hennepin County garbage burning plant. Where it could eventually be released into the air in the form of cancer causing dioxins and other harmful pollutants. Please call or write Earth Protector for more information on how you can stop the incinerator. 1138 Plymouth Bldg., Mpls., MN 55402. (612) 375-0202. Donations are welcome. Because even though this ad is small, the problem isn't.

MINNESOTANS AGAINST THE GARBAGE BURNING PLANT

18

Art Director: David Fox
Photographer: Rick Dublin
Writer: Joe Alexander
Creative Director: Jac Coverdale
Client: Earth Protector
Agency: Clarity, Coverdale, Rueff

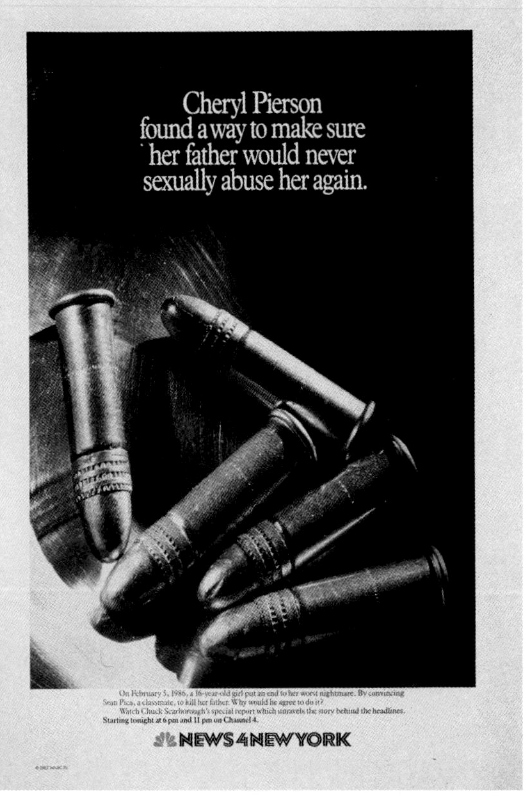

19

Art Director: Dan Krippahne, Rony Herz, Jill McClabb
Writer: Sandy Mairs, Richard Gamer, Shawne Cooper
Client: WNBC-TV
Agency: Lord, Geller, Federico, Einstein

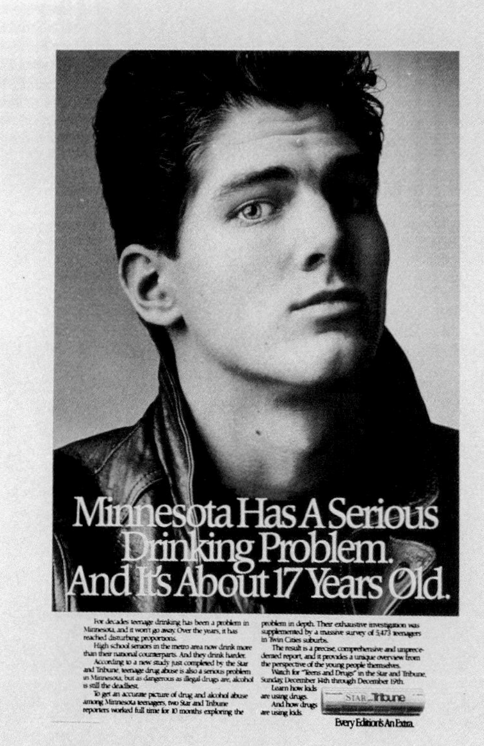

20

Art Director: Ron Anderson, Gregg Byers
Writer: Dick Thomas
Creative Director: Bert Gardner
Client: The Minneapolis Star Tribune
Agency: Bozell, Jacobs, Kenyon, & Eckhardt
Production Manager: Jim Grismer

21

Art Director: Kathy Izard
Writer: Steve Lasch, E. L. Jones, Melissa van Halsema
Creative Director: Jim Mountjoy
Client: WJZY-TV 46
Agency: Loeffler, Ketchum, Mountjoy

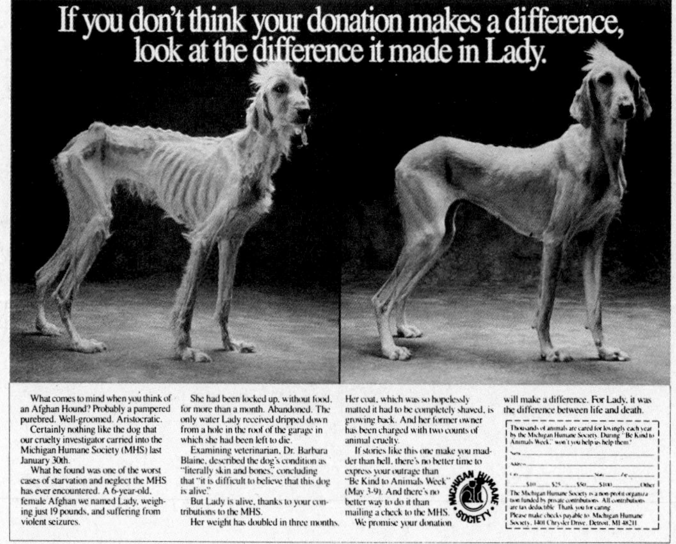

22

Art Director: Bryan McPeak, Tony Gaudin
Photographer: Jerry Farber
Writer: Craig Piechura, Dave Michalak
Creative Director: John DeCerchio
Client: Michigan Humane Society
Agency: W. B. Doner & Co.

23

Art Director: Walt Taylor
Designer: Walt Taylor
Photographer: Ronn Maratea
Writer: Rebecca Flora
Creative Director: Bruce Mansfield
Client: Virginia Dept. of Alcoholic Bev. Control
Agency: Lawler Ballard Advertising

24
Art Director: John Green
Photographer: Lee Crum
Writer: John Green
Client: New Orleans Dental Association
Agency: Bauerlein

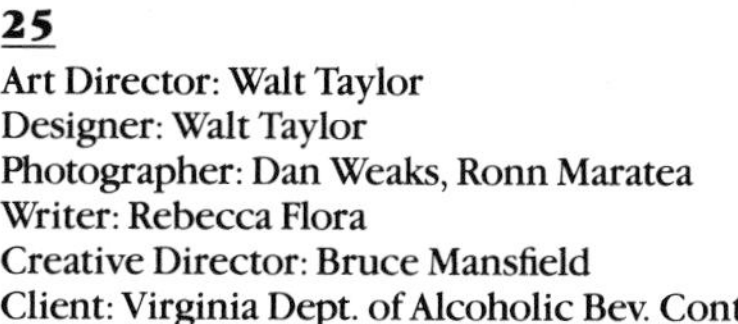

25
Art Director: Walt Taylor
Designer: Walt Taylor
Photographer: Dan Weaks, Ronn Maratea
Writer: Rebecca Flora
Creative Director: Bruce Mansfield
Client: Virginia Dept. of Alcoholic Bev. Control
Agency: Lawler Ballard Advertising

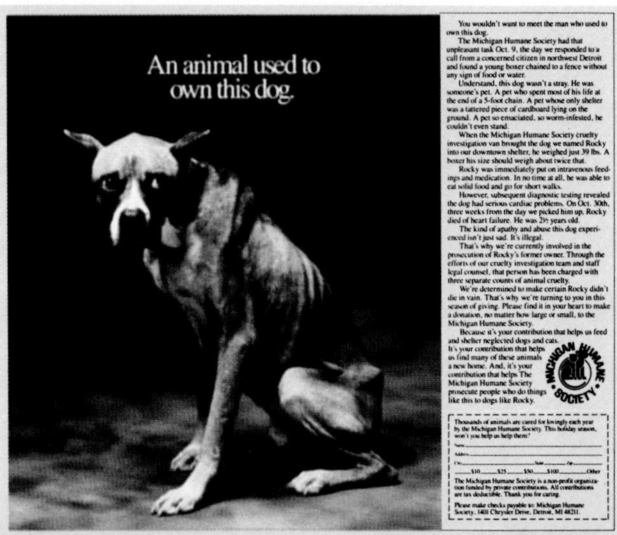

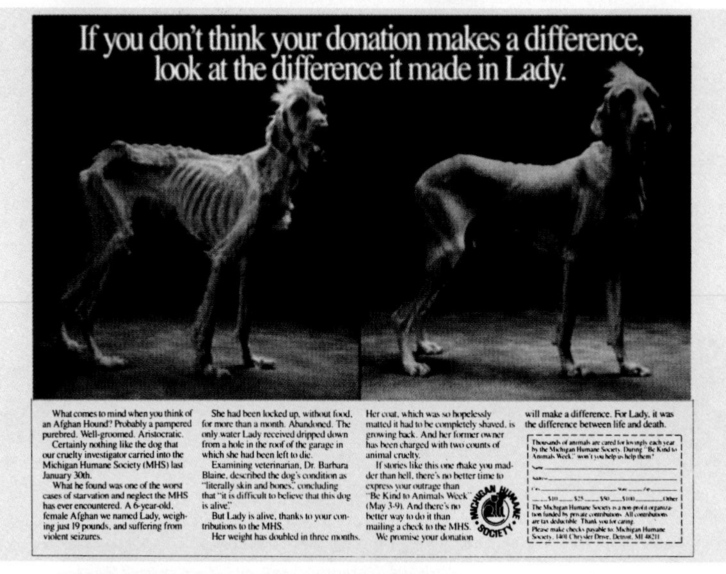

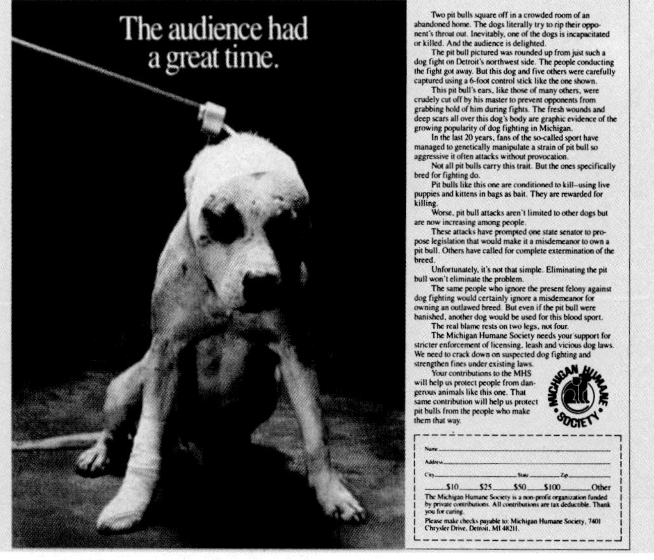

26

Art Director: Bryan McPeak, Tony Gaudin
Photographer: Jerry Farber
Writer: Craig Piechura, Dave Michalak, Joel Mitchell, Ross Lerner
Client: Michigan Humane Society
Agency: W. B. Doner & Co.

BUSINESS OPPORTUNITIES

BUSINESS OPPORTUNITIES

Tip O'Neill. Cardmember since 1973.

Wilt Chamberlain. Cardmember since 1976.
Willie Shoemaker. Cardmember since 1966.

Ray Charles. Cardmember since 1965.

27 Gold Award

Art Director: Parry Merkley, Jeff Streeper
Designer: Parry Merkley
Photographer: Annie Leibovitz
Writer: Gordon S. Bowen
Creative Director: Gordon S. Bowen
Client: American Express
Agency: Ogilvy & Mather

Itty Bitty Hush Pupp

No one looks down on our little shoes. Soft-Pu
infants and toddlers feature breathable leather
uppers. Just what this market is crying f

Hush Puppies Children's Lineup.

llowing kids home.
now come in over 50
Each has the com-
ppies are famous for.
ection for infants features
ble soles. Most uppers are leather
pairs also come with a cuddly stuffed

dog that kids (and
Our boys' styl
everywhere. An
Town shoes, w
To see the
Puppies, dial 1-800-2
Call us right away. Or we'l

Perception.

Reality.

If you think Rolling Stone readers are the great unwashed, this should send that sort of thinking right down the drain: In the last 7 days alone, Rolling Stone readers worked up a lather with soap and shampoo 40 million times. If you've got health and beauty aids to sell, you can clean up in the pages of Rolling Stone.

Rolling Stone

Perception.

Reality.

For a new generation of Rolling Stone readers, sexual freedom simply means a bigger pill to swallow. If you're looking for an informed, educated and health conscious market, get between the covers of Rolling Stone.

Rolling Stone

Perception.

Reality.

If you still think the readers of Rolling Stone are looking at the world through rose colored glasses, maybe this will open your eyes: Last year, the readers of Rolling Stone purchased a shade more than 4.5 million pairs of designer sunglasses. If you're looking for a bright spot to sell your product, the sun never sets on the pages of Rolling Stone.

Rolling Stone

There's only One Thing to LOOK for IN A Transparent Tape

We mean that little green tab, of course.

It's your assurance that the tape you sell will be recognized by 9 out of 10 of your customers.

It tells you that you're selling the kind of quality that's tried and true. And that each roll of tape you stock is backed by a reputation for service and support that's one of the best in the business.

Remember, no other tape has that little green tab, or all the positive qualities that go with it. That's the best reason we know to stock Scotch™ brand transparent tape, or any of the other fine "Scotch" tapes from 3M.

To order, call your 3M sales representative today.

3M

30 Distinctive Merit

Art Director: Sally Wagner
Photographer: Kent Severson
Writer: Emily Scott
Creative Director: Tom Weyl
Client: 3M Scotch Tape
Agency: Martin/Williams Advertising Inc

31
Art Director: Tom Lichtenheld
Designer: Tom Lichtenheld
Writer: Rod Kilpatrick
Creative Director: Tom McElligott
Client: Murray's
Agency: Fallon McElligott

Af ernoon

Afternoon isn't complete without it. **Tea Time at Murray's**
Mon.-Sat., 2-4:30 pm • 26 So. 6th St. • 339-0909

32
Art Director: Tom Lichtenheld
Designer: Tom Lichtenheld
Photographer: Mark LeFavor
Writer: Bruce Bildsten
Creative Director: Tom McElligott
Client: WFLD-TV
Agency: Fallon McElligott

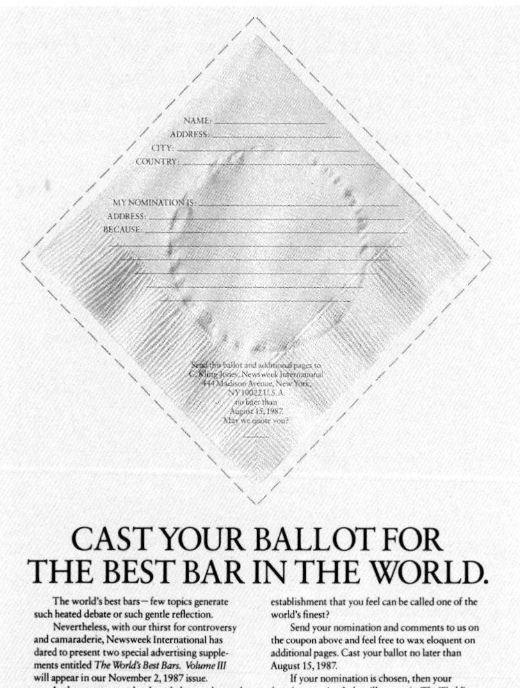

33
Art Director: Gwenne Wilcox, Tracy Wong
Designer: Gwenne Wilcox
Photographer: Susan Goldman
Writer: Laura Baudo
Client: Newsweek Inc.
Design Firm: Wilcox Design
Publisher: Newsweek Inc.
Publication: Newsweek

34

Art Director: David Jenkins
Photographer: Steve Bonini
Writer: Ken Wieden
Creative Director: Dan Wieden, Dave Kennedy
Client: Nike Inc.
Agency: Wieden & Kennedy

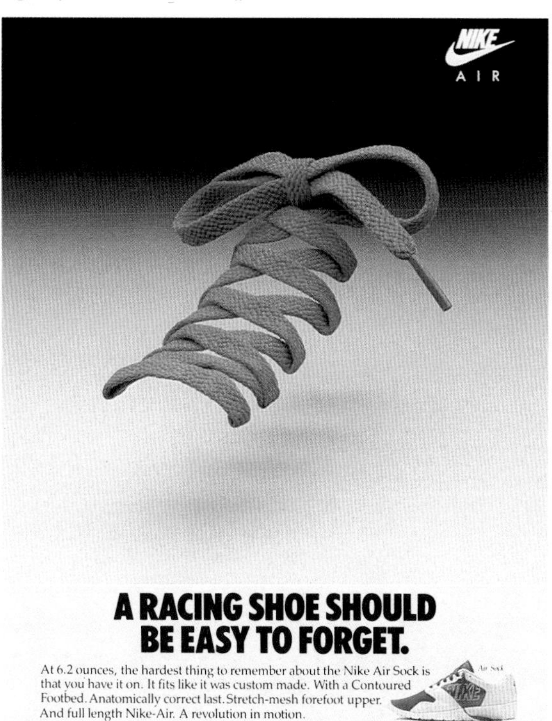

35

Art Director: Rick McQuiston
Photographer: Rick Miller
Writer: Dan Wieden
Creative Director: Dan Wieden, Dave Kennedy
Client: Speedo America
Agency: Wieden & Kennedy

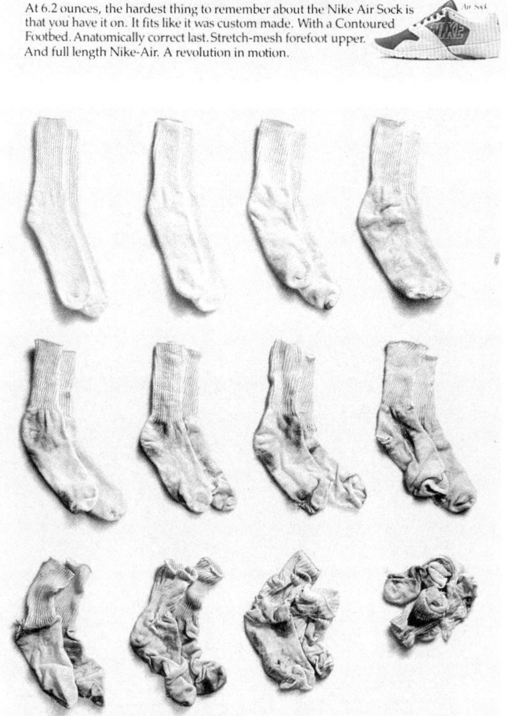

FOLLOW THE WHITE SOX ALL SEASON LONG.

WFLD is carrying seventy White Sox games this year. We suggest you tune in as often as possible. After all, you should never go too long without watching your Sox. 32 WFLD

36

Art Director: Tom Lichtenheld
Designer: Tom Lichtenheld
Photographer: Lars Hansen
Writer: Jamie Barrett
Creative Director: Tom McElligott
Client: WFLD-TV
Agency: Fallon McElligott

WOULD YOU SELL AN UNRELIABLE MOTORCYCLE TO THESE GUYS?

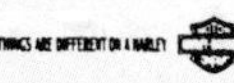

37

Art Director: Jud Smith, Chuck Anderson
Photographer: Jim Arndt
Writer: Ron Sackett, Dave Halsey
Creative Director: Ron Sackett
Client: Harley-Davidson
Agency: Carmichael Lynch
Producer: Pat Mayfield

38

Art Director: Houman Pirdavari
Designer: Houman Pirdavari
Photographer: Dave Jordano
Writer: Jarl Olsen
Creative Director: Tom McElligott
Client: Penn Tennis Balls
Agency: Fallon McElligott

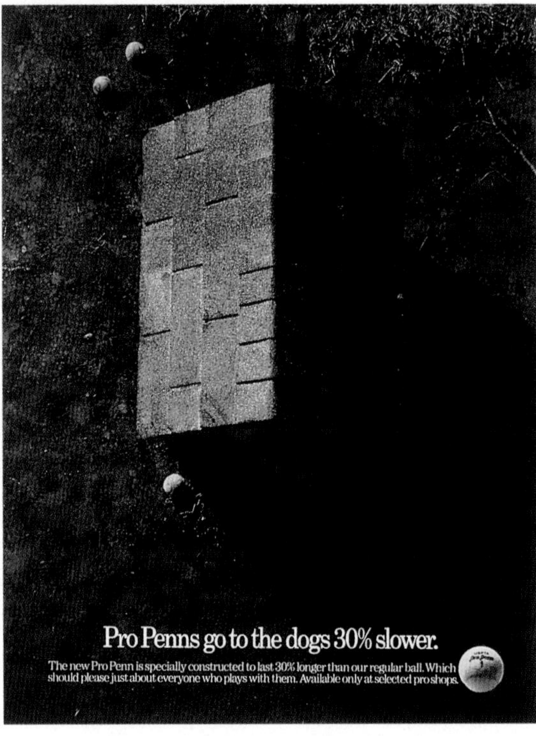

39

Art Director: Geoff Hayes
Designer: Geoff Hayes
Photographer: Steve Bronstein
Writer: Evert Cilliers
Creative Director: Arnie Arlow, Peter Lubalin
Client: Carillon Importers Ltd.
Agency: TBWA Advertising Inc.

40

Art Director: Michael Smith
Photographer: Cailor Resnick
Writer: Amelia Rosner
Creative Director: Bill Hamilton
Client: Arrow
Agency: Chiat/Day Inc., New York
Account Management: Amy Saypol, Dick O'Connell

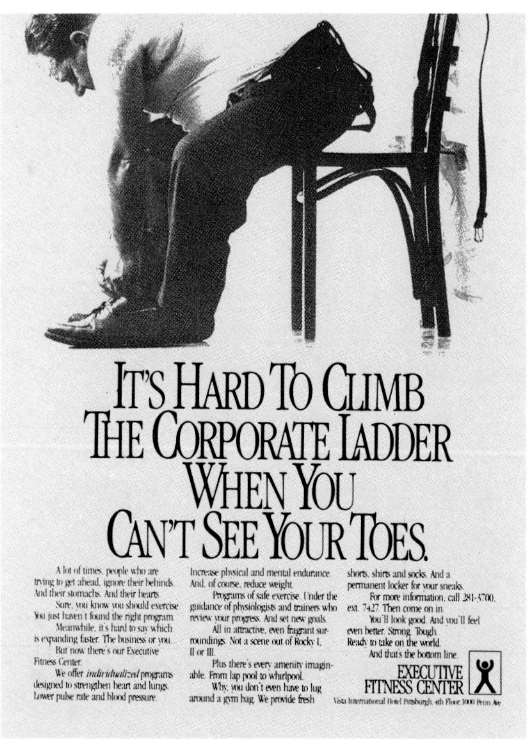

41

Art Director: John R. Chepelsky
Writer: Cathy Bowen
Creative Director: John R. Chepelsky, Ray Werner
Client: Vista International Hotel, Pittsburgh
Agency: Werner, Chepelsky & Partners Inc.

42

Art Director: Garrett Jewett
Designer: Garrett Jewett
Photographer: Billy Renshaw
Writer: Jim Walsh
Creative Director: Charlie Piccirillo
Client: Colombian Coffee
Agency: DDB Needham Worldwide

43

Art Director: Dean Hanson
Designer: Dean Hanson
Photographer: Mark LeFavor
Writer: Phil Hanft
Creative Director: Tom McElligott
Client: 3M
Agency: Fallon McElligott

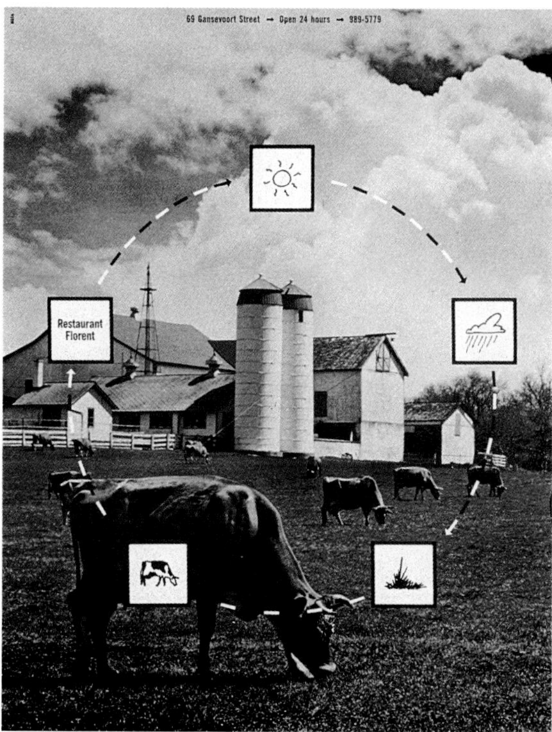

44

Art Director: Tibor Kalman
Designer: Tibor Kalman, Timothy Horn
Photographer: Fredrick Lewis
Illustrator/Artist: Timothy Horn
Client: Restaurant Florent
Agency: M & Co.

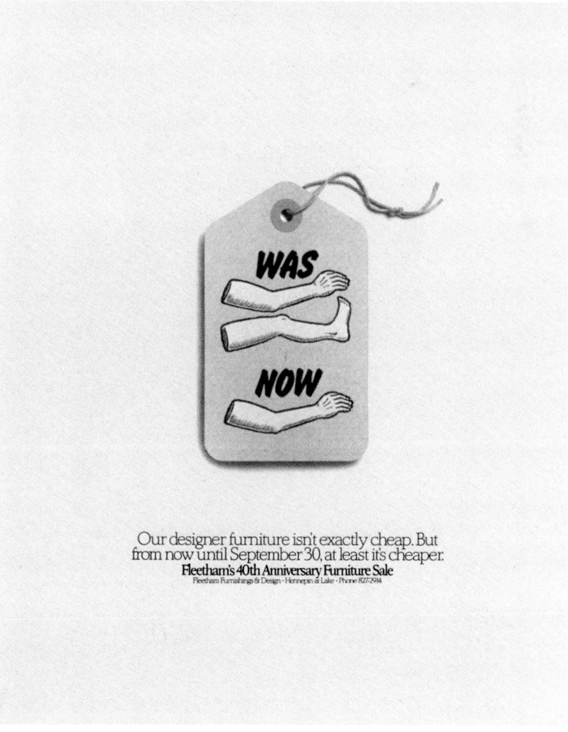

45

Art Director: Tom Lichtenheld
Designer: Tom Lichtenheld
Illustrator/Artist: Tom Lichtenheld
Writer: Rod Kilpatrick
Creative Director: Tom McElligott
Client: Fleetham's
Agency: Fallon McElligott

46

Art Director: Shelton Scott
Writer: René Mandis
Client: Hyundai Motor America

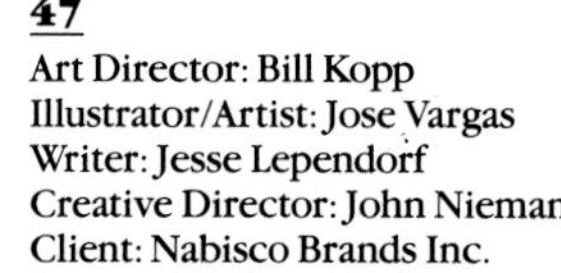

47

Art Director: Bill Kopp
Illustrator/Artist: Jose Vargas
Writer: Jesse Lependorf
Creative Director: John Nieman
Client: Nabisco Brands Inc.
Agency: McCann-Erickson

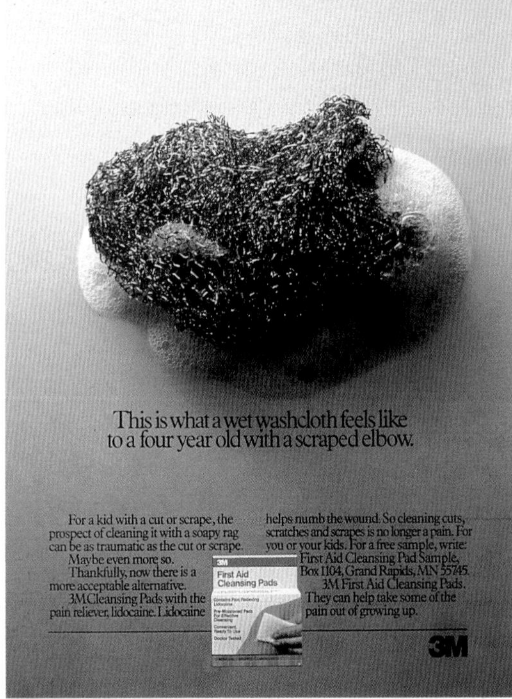

48

Art Director: Dean Hanson
Designer: Dean Hanson
Photographer: Mark LeFavor
Writer: Phil Hanft
Creative Director: Tom McElligott
Client: 3M
Agency: Fallon McElligott

49

Art Director: Bob Barrie
Designer: Bob Barrie
Writer: Jamie Barrett
Creative Director: Tom McElligott
Client: WFLD-TV
Agency: Fallon McElligott

50

Art Director: Michael Prieve
Photographer: Steve Bonini
Writer: Mark Fenske
Creative Director: Dan Wieden, Dave Kennedy
Client: Nike Inc.
Agency: Wieden & Kennedy

Nike Duellist. Extremely lightweight Phylon™ cushioning.

Nike Air Mariah. Full length Nike-Air® midsole.

THEY CAME. THEY SAW. THEY KICKED BUTT.

Most road racers will look at these shoes and wonder how anyone could run with so little on their feet. Say hello to these people at the beginning of the race. You won't see them later.

51

Art Director: Sharon Brady
Photographer: Lanpher Productions
Writer: Tom Cunniff
Creative Director: Bill Campbell
Client: Nikkal Industries
Agency: Barker, Campbell & Farley

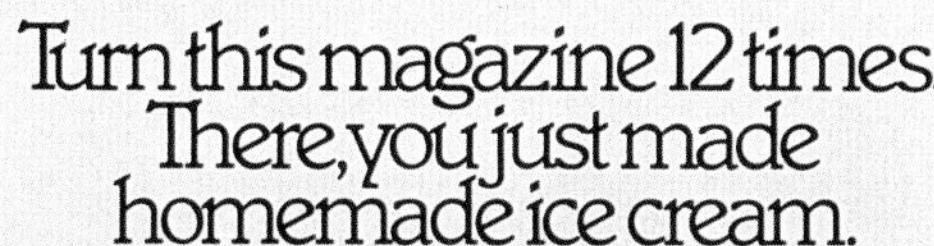

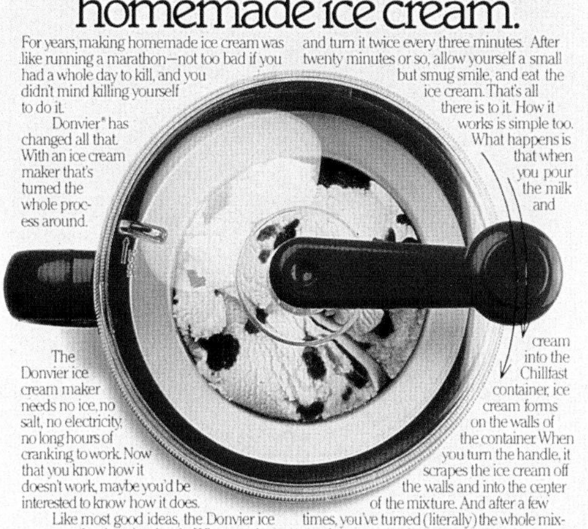

For years, making homemade ice cream was like running a marathon—not too bad if you had a whole day to kill, and you didn't mind killing yourself to do it.

Donvier® has changed all that. With an ice cream maker that's turned the whole process around.

The Donvier ice cream maker needs no ice, no salt, no electricity, no long hours of cranking to work. Now that you know how it doesn't work, maybe you'd be interested to know how it does.

Like most good ideas, the Donvier ice cream maker is quite simple. When you're ready to make ice cream, pull the frozen Chillfast™ container out of the freezer. Put it in the case, and insert the blade.

Put in some milk, some cream, a little sugar, and some other ingredients. (Other ingredients? Yes. Anything you want. Fresh peaches, strawberries, almonds, chocolate—anything you want.)

Cover the cylinder, attach the handle, and turn it twice every three minutes. After twenty minutes or so, allow yourself a small but smug smile, and eat the ice cream. That's all there is to it. How it works is simple too. What happens is that when you pour the milk and cream into the Chillfast container, ice cream forms on the walls of the container. When you turn the handle, it scrapes the ice cream off the walls and into the center of the mixture. And after a few times, you've turned (literally) the whole mixture into gourmet ice cream.

And with half-pint, pint and quart sizes all priced below $50, you might ask "What will they think of next?"

We're working on it. We're working on it.

DONVIER
ICE CREAM MAKERS

© Nikkal Industries, Ltd., P.O. Box 2636, Virginia Beach, VA 23450. For the store nearest you, call 1-800-334-4559.

IF A FLASHLIGHT WITH NEW DURACELL® BATTERIES SAT IN A DRAWER FROM JANUARY 1, 2, 3, 4, … 27, 28, 29, 30, 31, TO JANUARY 1, THREE YEARS LATER, THEY'D STILL WORK.

DURACELL

52

Art Director: Tracy Wong
Designer: Tracy Wong
Photographer: Susan Goldman
Writer: Steve Baer
Creative Director: Mike Pitts
Client: Duracell Batteries
Agency: Ogilvy & Mather

53

Art Director: Bob Brihn
Designer: Bob Brihn
Photographer: Craig Perman
Writer: Jamie Barrett
Creative Director: Tom McElligott
Client: WFLD-TV
Agency: Fallon McElligott

54
Art Director: Ron Rosen
Designer: Ron Rosen
Photographer: Jerry Cailor
Writer: Craig Demeter
Creative Director: Roy Grace, Diane Rothschild
Client: Range Rover of North America
Agency: Grace & Rothschild

55
Art Director: Bob Brihn
Designer: Bob Brihn
Photographer: Rick Dublin
Writer: Jarl Olsen
Creative Director: Tom McElligott
Client: WFLD-TV
Agency: Fallon McElligott

Created from the same plastic used by NASA, our DELRIN Snap and D Ring is virtually indestructible. Removability eliminates dangerous dangling clips.

DRYLIN lining, a new miracle fabric from the makers of Gore-Tex actively draws moisture off the skin, transferring it through the Gore-Tex membrane for quick evaporation.

A GORE-TEX membrane allows perspiration vapor to escape while preventing the passage of moisture into the glove.

Gates exclusive high density rubberized palm patch of Tuffgrip II provides a non-skid no slip surface that works like a vice grip on your ski pole.

A CORDURA Nylon blend, Ambush Cloth is the most durable yet flexible shell material available today.

With its millions of microscopic air pockets, THERMOLITE insulation provides maximum warmth with minimal thickness, and it's virtually crushproof.

NO OTHER GLOVE COMPANY HAS THE GUTS TO RUN THIS AD.

Gates

56
Art Director: David Bender
Photographer: Gil Cope
Writer: Tom Cunniff
Creative Director: David Bender
Client: Gates
Agency: Janklow Bender

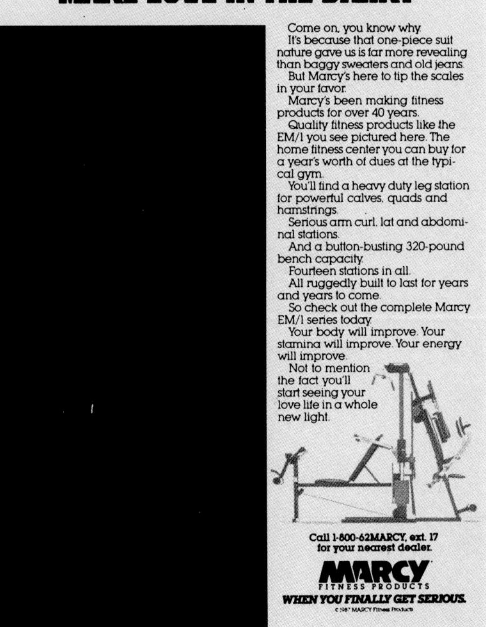

57
Art Director: Ken Sakoda
Designer: Reyes Art Works
Writer: Scott Montgomery
Creative Director: Scott Montgomery, Ken Sakoda
Client: Marcy Fitness Products
Agency: Salvati, Montgomery, Sakoda Inc.
Design Firm: Reyes Art Works

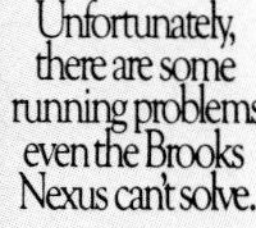
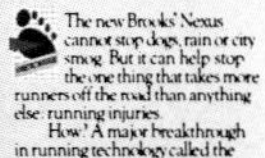

58
Art Director: Houman Pirdavari
Designer: Houman Pirdavari
Photographer: Steve Umland
Writer: Tom McElligott
Creative Director: Tom McElligott
Client: Brooks
Agency: Fallon McElligott
Model: Daisy

59
Art Director: Michael Smith
Photographer: Cailor Resnick
Writer: Jackie End
Creative Director: Bill Hamilton
Client: Arrow
Agency: Chiat/Day Inc., New York
Account Management: Amy Saypol, Dick O'Connell

60
Art Director: Michael Smith
Photographer: Steve Gross
Writer: Graham Turner
Creative Director: Bill Hamilton
Client: Arrow
Agency: Chiat/Day Inc.
Account Management: Amy Saypol, Dick O'Connell

61
Art Director: Earl Cavanah
Photographer: Henry Sandbank
Writer: Larry Cadman
Creative Director: Sam Scali
Client: Volvo of America Corp.
Agency: Scali, McCabe, Sloves Inc.

When you have over 52 parts that can break down, you need an aerobic shoe that won't.

The foot is a major engineering work of art. Protecting it from the abuse of aerobic workouts requires an equally impressive shoe.

That shoe is, without reservation, the all new Brooks Prima.

For starters, Prima's unique built-in ballet slipper reduces foot movement within the shoe for more stability and comfort.

The patented Kinetic Wedge,® a piece of soft, flexible material under the ball of the foot, reduces stress-related injuries by allowing your foot to arch more naturally.

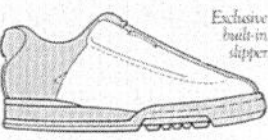

And extended sidewalls and more rounded toes help prevent foot roll, the major cause of sprains and breaks in aerobics.

But just as important as all this technical stuff is the package it comes in. An aerobic shoe that actually looks as good on the outside as it does on the inside.

The Brooks Prima. A triumph of form and function in one aerobic shoe.

Available in four colors and two widths. For a free technical bulletin and the Brooks retailer nearest you, call 1-800-233-7531 (in PA, call 1-800-722-3394).

62
Art Director: Bob Brihn
Designer: Bob Brihn
Photographer: Kerry Peterson
Writer: Phil Hanft
Creative Director: Tom McElligott
Client: Brooks
Agency: Fallon McElligott

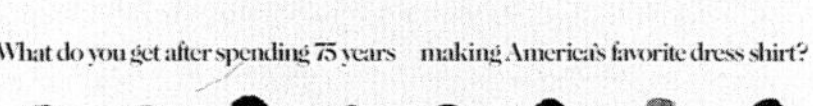

63
Art Director: Michael Smith
Photographer: Annie Leibovitz
Writer: Jackie End, Bill Hamilton
Creative Director: Bill Hamilton
Client: Arrow
Agency: Chiat/Day Inc.
Account Supervisor: Amy Saypol, Dick O'Connell

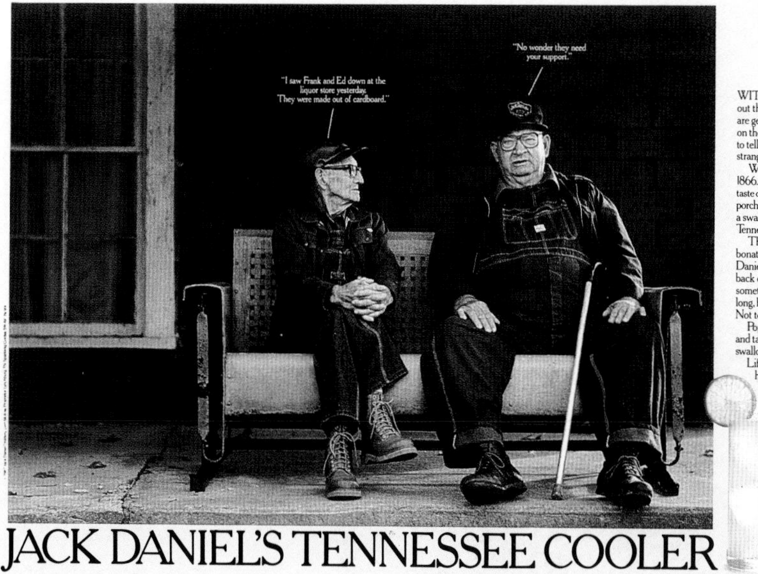

64
Art Director: Pat Burnham
Designer: Pat Burnham
Photographer: Craig Perman
Writer: Bill Miller
Creative Director: Tom McElligott
Client: Jack Daniels
Agency: Fallon McElligott

65
Art Director: Mary Morant, Charles Rosner
Photographer: Shaw & Leach
Writer: Harvey Cohen
Creative Director: Charles Rosner
Client: Chemical Bank
Agency: Lord, Geller, Federico, Einstein

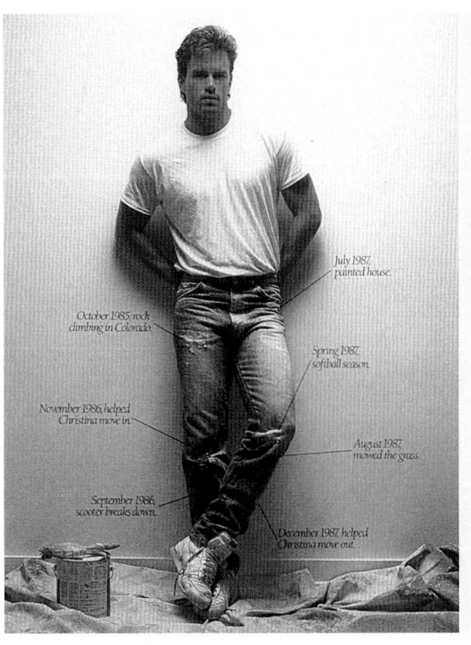

66
Art Director: Mark Johnson
Designer: Mark Johnson
Photographer: Randy Miller
Writer: Bill Miller
Creative Director: Tom McElligott
Client: Lee Jeans
Agency: Fallon McElligott

Unfortunately, some aerobic shoes are only slightly more functional.

Strangely enough, considering the dramatic growth of aerobics in recent years, the new Brooks Prima is the first aerobic shoe that's actually as functional as it is sexy.

Underneath a sleek and colorful, soft-leather upper hides a highly engineered, technically advanced shoe.

For example, the Brooks Prima's unique built-in ballet slipper contains your foot snugly and comfortably for more stability.

The Brooks patented Kinetic Wedge,™ a piece of soft, flexible material under the ball of the foot, reduces stress-related injuries by allowing your foot to arch more naturally.

A more rounded toe and extended sidewalls reduce foot roll, a leading cause of sprains and breaks in aerobics.

Patented Kinetic Wedge

The result is the first aerobic shoe that passes both the test of fashion as well as the one on the studio floor.

To borrow a phrase, Brooks Primas are a giant step forward for both aerobic shoes and the women who wear them.

Available in four colors and two widths. For a free technical bulletin and the Brooks retailer nearest you, call 1-800-233-7531 (in PA, call 1-800-722-3394).

BROOKS PRIMA

67
Art Director: Bob Brihn
Designer: Bob Brihn
Photographer: Kerry Peterson
Writer: Phil Hanft
Creative Director: Tom McElligott
Client: Brooks
Agency: Fallon McElligott

Inspiration for one of the most important advances in aerobic shoes.

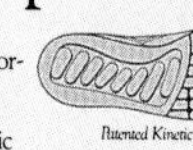

It's amazing no one thought of it before. A slipper inside the shoe.

Actually, it's more like a ballet slipper than a bedroom slipper. But the effect is the same. Extraordinary comfort.

Made of seamless, stretch material, the slipper limits foot movement within the shoe for more stability and greater support, fewer blisters and a more enjoyable workout.

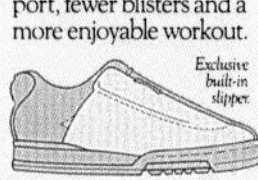

Exclusive built-in slipper.

The shoe? The new Brooks Prima, a virtual cornucopia of technological advances. Just a few:

The patented Kinetic Wedge,™ a piece of soft material under the ball of the foot, to allow your feet to arch more naturally and reduce stress-related hip, leg and foot injuries.

Patented Kinetic Wedge

Extended sidewalls and more rounded toes to minimize foot roll.

Plus, for extra cushioning, hollow lugs on the sole and a soft, removeable insert inside the shoe.

Brooks Prima. Just the inspiration your feet need to get your body out on the studio floor.

Available in four colors and two widths. For a free technical bulletin and the Brooks retailer nearest you, call 1-800-233-7531 (in PA, call 1-800-722-3394).

BROOKS PRIMA

68
Art Director: Bob Brihn
Designer: Bob Brihn
Photographer: Kerry Peterson
Writer: Phil Hanft
Creative Director: Tom McElligott
Client: Brooks
Agency: Fallon McElligott

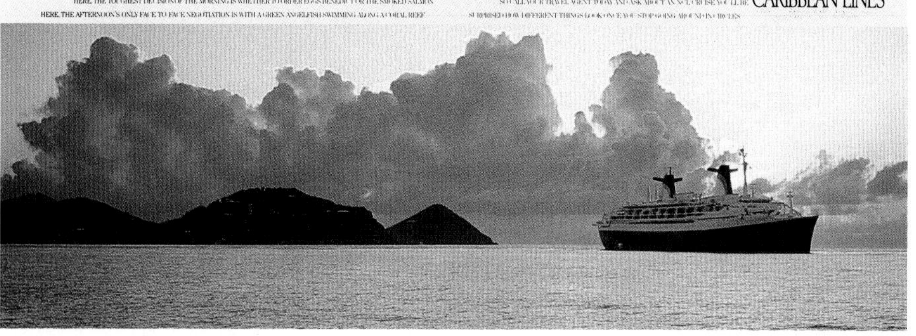

69
Art Director: Larry Bennett
Photographer: Randy Miller
Writer: Steve Bassett
Client: Norwegian Cruise Line
Agency: McKinney & Silver

70
Art Director: George D'Amato
Photographer: Irving Penn
Writer: Herbert Green
Creative Director: George D'Amato, Herbert Green
Client: Cosmair/L'Oreal
Agency: McCann-Erickson

71
Art Director: Mark Johnson
Designer: Mark Johnson
Photographer: Dan Lamb, Rick Dublin
Writer: Tom McElligott
Creative Director: Tom McElligott
Client: Hush Puppies
Agency: Fallon McElligott

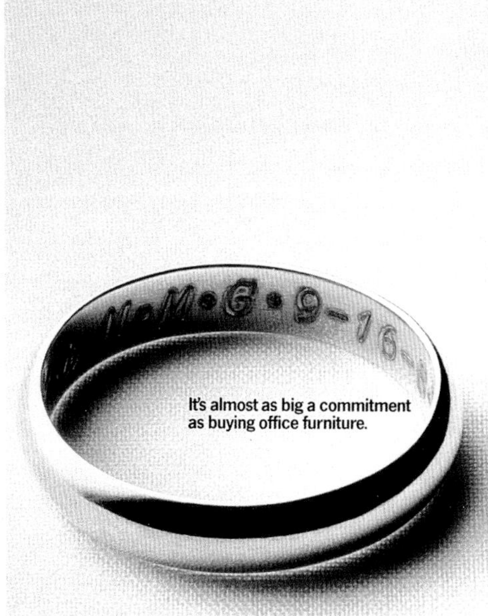

72
Art Director: Gary Goldsmith
Designer: Gary Goldsmith
Photographer: Gil Cope
Writer: Neal Gomberg
Creative Director: Gary Goldsmith
Client: Knoll International
Agency: Goldsmith/Jeffrey
Account Supervisor: Bob Jeffrey

73
Art Director: Clem McCarthy, Alain Briere
Photographer: Jeff Zwart
Writer: Rav Friedel, Paul Wolfe
Creative Director: Ralph Ammirati
Client: BMW of North America Inc.
Agency: Ammirati & Puris Inc.

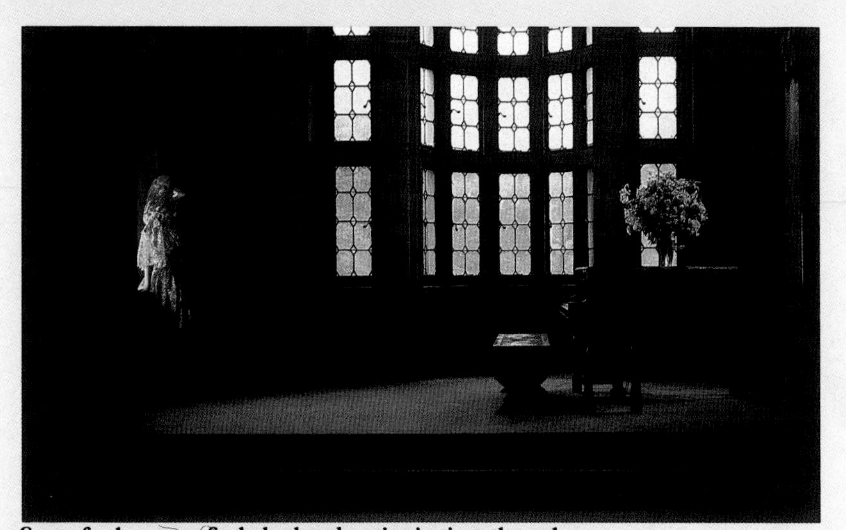

74
Art Director: Tom Wolsey

75
Art Director: Tom Kelly
Writer: Bill Borders
Creative Director: Bill Borders
Client: Blitz-Weinhard Brewing Co.
Agency: Borders, Perrin & Norrander Inc.

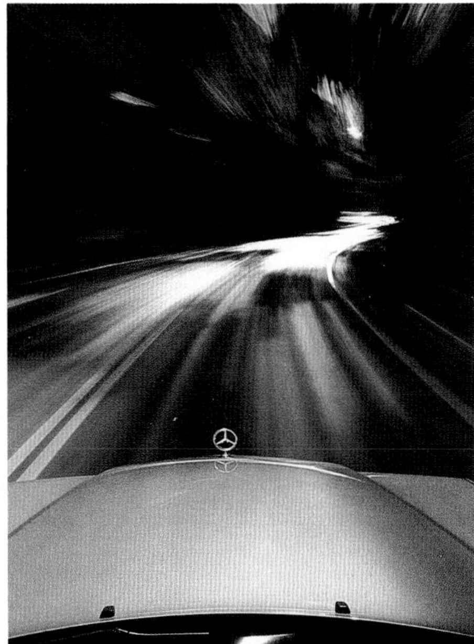

THE MERCEDES-BENZ 190 CLASS:
THE SUBTLE DIFFERENCE BETWEEN MASTERING
THE ROAD AND MERELY COPING WITH IT.

The road passes beneath you as always, but the sensations are markedly different. So is your state of mind. This is your first experience with a 190 Class sedan, but already you are driving with calm confidence. The car has earned your trust.

It feels resolutely stable, going precisely where you steer it, refusing to waver off course or wallow over potholes. Even the severest bumps seem only a minor disturbance as the suspension gently quells the violence underneath. Negotiating a run of switchback turns seems more routine business than high drama as the car shifts direction nimbly in response to your steering commands. Sports sedans might occasionally handle this adroitly, but they seldom feel this composed.

Suddenly the pavement deteriorates into washboard gravel, but the car tracks steadfastly ahead, curiously unfazed by the change in terrain. It occurs to you that you have yet to hear a squeak or rattle. The engine remains almost subliminally quiet, wind noise a faint whisper when you hear it at all. You normally feel an urge to stretch your legs after sitting for so long, but now you feel the urge to keep driving.

Even if you chose the automatic transmission, you still find it easy to shift manual-style when the mood strikes, locating each gear by feel without glancing downward. Your driving has become pleasurably instinctive, as driving at its best should be.

This ostensibly mystical exaltation of the driving experience springs from such technological advances as "the most sophisticated steel suspension ever put into volume production" (Britain's *Car* Magazine). And the simple fact that a 190 Class sedan is built like every Mercedes-Benz—not one ergonomic or safety principle sacrificed for the sake of cosmetic luxury or digital showmanship. Every detail of construction and assembly meeting universally envied standards.

The result is a sedan that does not "challenge" you in the macho sports-sedan tradition, but rather serves as a congenial and supremely capable ally—at once exciting and obedient, responsive and considerate. The road provides challenge enough.

Engineered like no other car in the world

76
Art Director: Günther Maier
Designer: Günther Maier
Photographer: Jeff Zwart
Writer: Ted Baker
Creative Director: Bruce McCall
Client: Mercedes Benz of North America
Agency: McCaffrey & McCall

Jeans Tough Enough For Construction Workers.

At Lee, we understand the kind of wear and tear a child can put jeans through. That's why we make Lee Riders with comfortable, heavyweight denim, double stitched seams, and riveted pockets. We even wear test them so you can be sure they'll last long enough to make great hand-me-downs. Lee Riders®, Storm Rider® and Built To Take It™ jeans. Because when kids get into jeans, there's no telling what they'll get into.

Lee Riders For Kids

Lee

77
Art Director: Tom Lichtenheld
Designer: Tom Lichtenheld
Photographer: Jean Moss
Writer: George Gier
Creative Director: Tom McElligott
Client: Lee Jeans
Agency: Fallon McElligott

Finally. An office furniture dealer that's as big as you are.

Or as small as you are.

Introducing Office Pavilion. The office furniture dealer that handles everything from major corporate installations to an office for one. You see, instead of the usual huge number of product lines, we concentrate on a small group of the best. Starting with Herman Miller. From the Eames lounge chair to Ethospace interiors, Herman Miller products are famous for quality and innovative design. Our other lines include Meridian, Helikon, Novikoff, Tradex and B & B Italia. At Office Pavilion, our focused approach enables us to apply our products to your best advantage. And we guarantee move-in dates in writing. Best of all, Office Pavilion is locally owned. So we'll be there when you need us. All of which is why more and more businesses are working with Office Pavilion. We're the office furniture dealer that's just your size.

PAVILION

78
Art Director: Nancy Rice, Nick Rice
Photographer: Marvy! Advertising Photography
Writer: Jim Newcombe
Creative Director: Nancy Rice
Client: Herman Miller Inc.
Agency: Rice & Rice Advertising Inc.

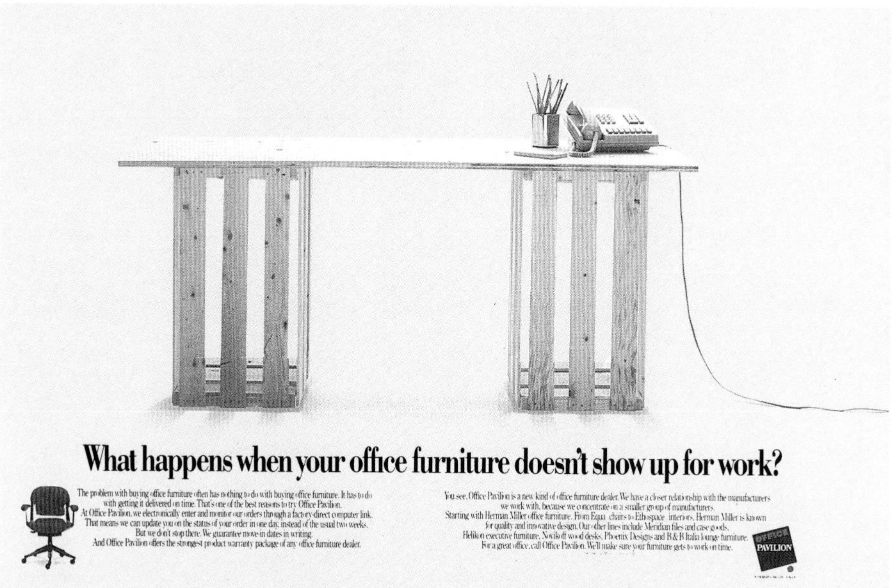

79
Art Director: Nancy Rice, Nick Rice
Photographer: Marvy! Advertising Photography
Writer: Jim Newcombe
Creative Director: Nancy Rice
Client: Herman Miller Inc.
Agency: Rice & Rice Advertising Inc.

80
Art Director: Tom Lichtenheld
Designer: Tom Lichtenheld
Photographer: Jean Moss
Writer: George Gier
Creative Director: Tom McElligott
Client: Lee Jeans
Agency: Fallon McElligott

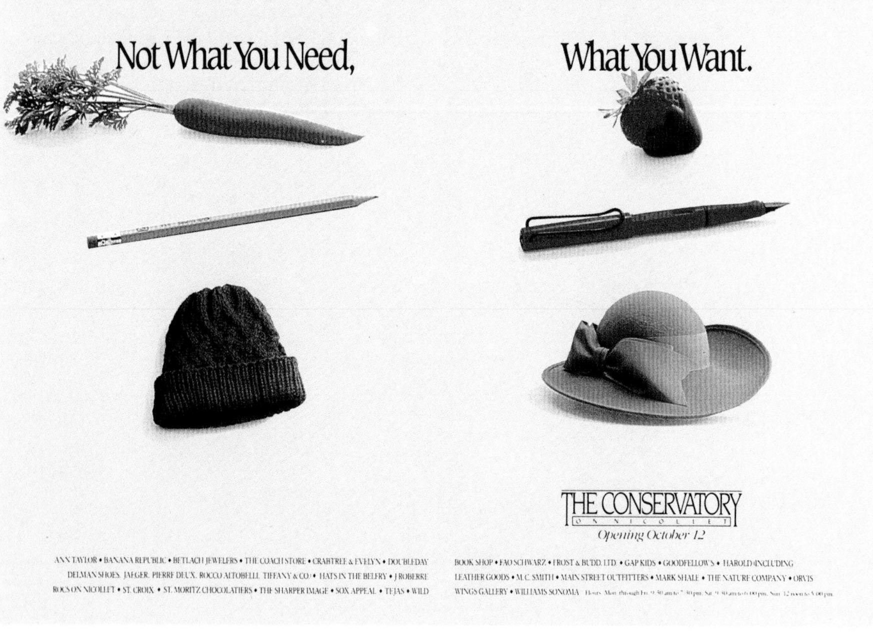

81
Art Director: Jim Henderson
Photographer: Tom Connors
Writer: Emily Scott
Creative Director: Tom Weyl
Client: The Conservatory on Nicollet
Agency: Martin/Williams Advertising Inc.

An Inc. 500 company.

A Fortune 500 company.

82

Art Director: Michael Fazende
Designer: Michael Fazende
Photographer: Jim Marvy
Writer: Phil Hanft
Creative Director: Tom McElligott
Client: Coleman
Agency: Fallon McElligott

83

Art Director: Leslie Sweet
Photographer: Reymond Meyer
Writer: Nat Whitten, Steve Salinaro
Creative Director: Bill Hamilton
Client: Reebok
Agency: Chiat/Day Inc., New York
Account Management: Steve Mitgang

84

Art Director: Houman Pirdavari
Designer: Houman Pirdavari
Photographer: Steve Umland
Writer: Tom McElligott
Creative Director: Tom McElligott
Client: Brooks
Agency: Fallon McElligott

Some of us have more finely developed nesting instincts than others.

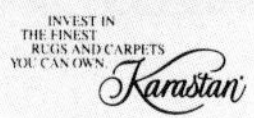

85

Art Director: Tom Wolsey

Every company has its own personality.

Maybe it's conservative.

Or flamboyant.

Or maybe it's conservative and flamboyant.

The point is your office furniture should be able to say: "This is the kind of company we are."

Something Knoll Office systems and seating happen to do very well.

They can suit almost any personality. Open plan office, private office or data processing center. From the receptionist to the CEO.

And to give all those offices their own personalities, you can choose from wood veneers like mahogany and maple. Fabrics and plastic laminates. And colors from beige to shades that can please the most flamboyant chairman of the board.

At Knoll, we offer everything from systems to seating and from desks to textiles. As well as the service that makes managing your office a lot easier.

Call 1-800-633-0034 to talk with a representative or authorized dealer nearest you.

(We promise he won't have green hair.)

86

Art Director: Gary Goldsmith
Designer: Gary Goldsmith
Photographer: Gil Cope
Writer: Neal Gomberg
Creative Director: Gary Goldsmith
Client: Knoll International
Agency: Goldsmith/Jeffrey
Account Supervisor: Bob Jeffrey

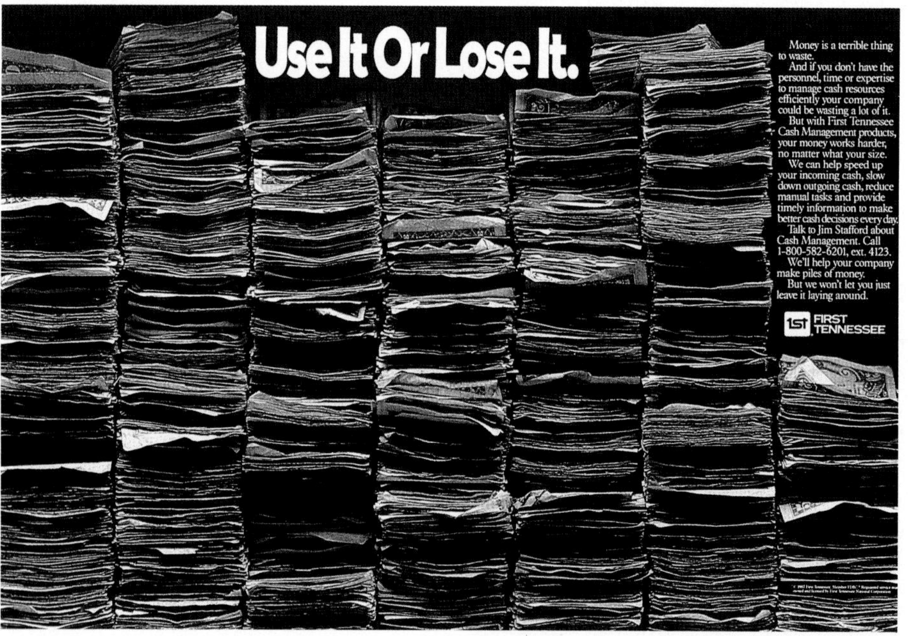

87

Art Director: Dean Hanson
Designer: Dean Hanson
Photographer: Rick Dublin
Writer: Bruce Bildsten
Creative Director: Tom McElligott
Client: First Tennessee
Agency: Fallon McElligott

88
Art Director: David Nathanson
Photographer: Bill Werts Studio
Writer: Phil Lanier
Creative Director: Bob Kuperman, Lee Clow
Client: Yamaha Motor Corp. USA
Agency: Chiat/Day
Publication: Snowmobile

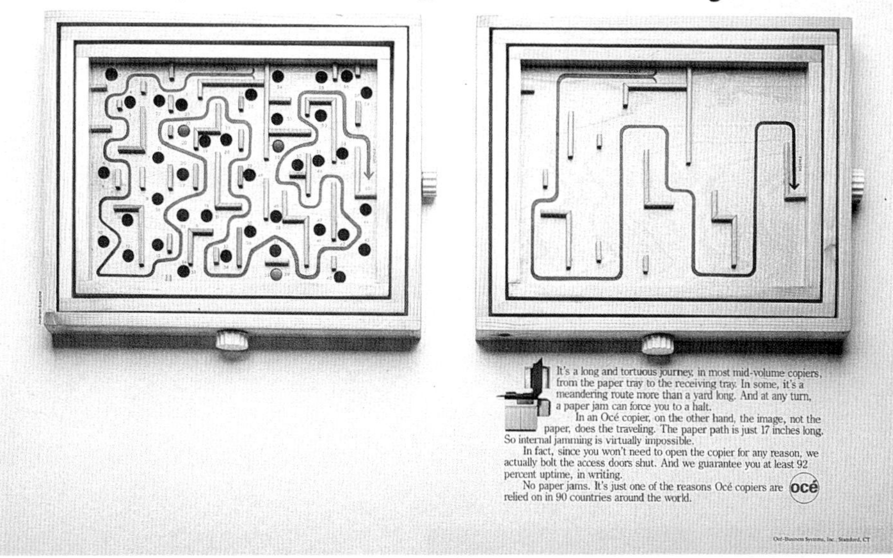

89
Art Director: Susan Casey
Designer: Nancy Manfredi
Photographer: Steve Bronstein
Writer: Dave Goldenberg
Creative Director: Steve Trygg
Client: Oce Business Systems
Agency: Anderson & Lembke

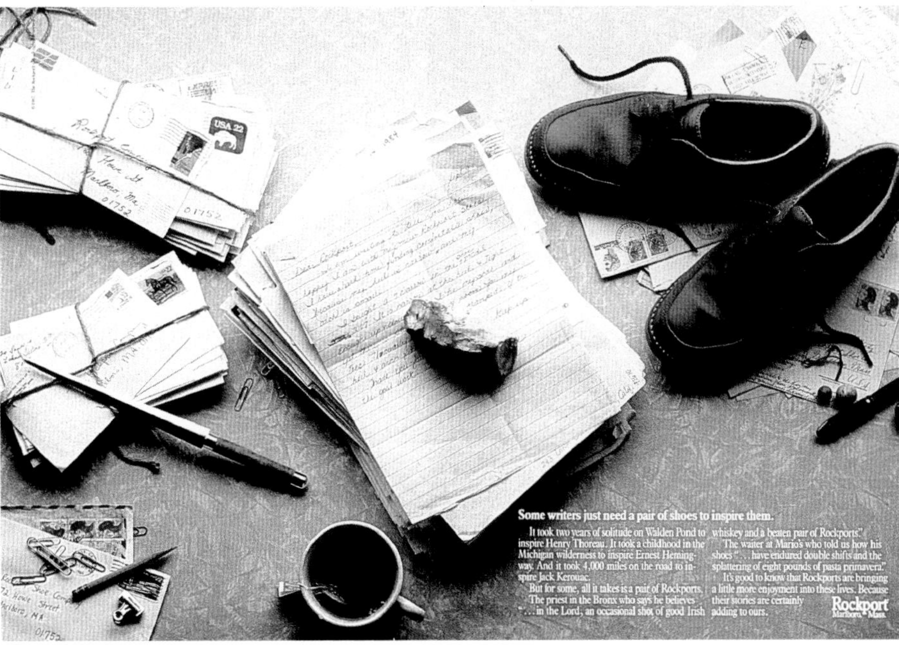

90
Art Director: Michael Smith
Photographer: Dennis Manarchy
Writer: Bryan Buckley
Creative Director: Bill Hamilton
Client: Rockport
Agency: Chiat/Day Inc., New York
Account Management: Steve Friedman

A lot of people think you can fit everything Coleman makes on one page.

91
Art Director: Michael Fazende
Designer: Michael Fazende
Photographer: Jim Marvy
Writer: Phil Hanft
Creative Director: Tom McElligott
Client: Coleman
Agency: Fallon McElligott

Now That Your Kids Can Watch Music,

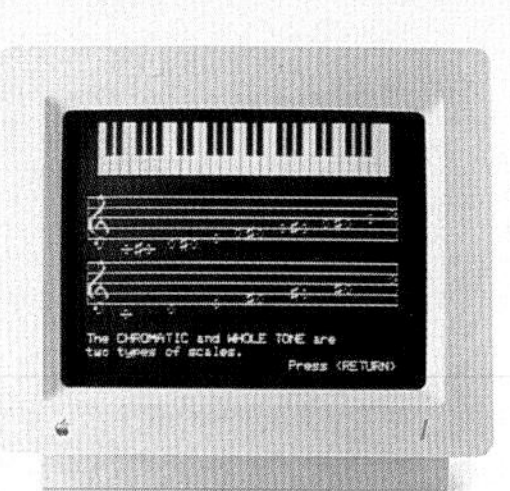

Teach Them How To Read It.

Your child is exposed to a lot of great music while watching MTV.

But now parents have an even better way to channel their child's interest in music.

It's called The Music Class: A new 5-part music software series from Wenger for kids, adults, beginners, even professionals.

With playful graphics and challenging tests, The Music Class will guide your child through the fundamentals of music.

Simple step-by-step instructions teach everything from rhythm to note reading—all at your child's own speed.

The Music Class also gives friendly advice, points out errors and applauds correct answers.

The five programs can be taught on any Apple II or IIGS computer with 64K memory:

Fundamentals: Making sense of those skinny lines with blobs and tails. All the basics from note reading to rhythm. $49.

Rhythm: What the real difference is between a waltz and a polka, ragtime and rock, and more. A comical little guy named Mr. Metro Gnome is the teacher. $49.

Ear Training: How to hear exactly what's happening in a piece of music. Your child will never listen to Madonna quite the same way again. $49.

Music Symbols: No, they aren't called squiggles, slashes, and dots. Your child will learn up to 80 musical symbols. $39.

Note Reading: Know the difference between an E-Flat eighth note and a B-Flat quarter note. This is where kids learn to read music. $39.

So order by calling toll free 1-800-843-1337. Or collect 612-854-9554. Ask about our Coda Catalog with over 600 music software products.

Who knows, with The Music Class helping them, maybe someday you'll end up watching your kids perform on MTV.

The Music Class

92
Art Director: David Fox
Photographer: Steve Umland
Writer: Joe Alexander
Creative Director: Jac Coverdale
Client: Wenger
Agency: Clarity, Coverdale, Rueff

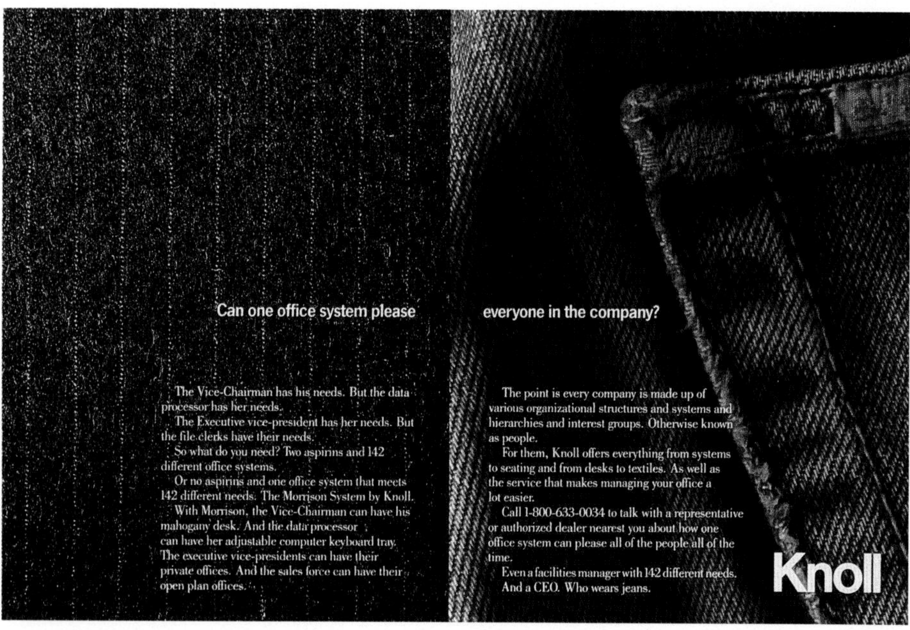

93
Art Director: Gary Goldsmith
Designer: Gary Goldsmith
Photographer: Gil Cope
Writer: Neal Gomberg
Creative Director: Gary Goldsmith
Client: Knoll International
Agency: Goldsmith/Jeffrey
Account Supervisor: Bob Jeffrey

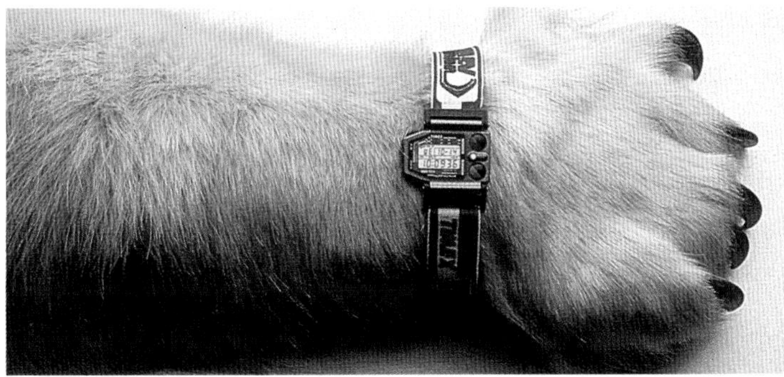

94
Art Director: Houman Pirdavari
Designer: Houman Pirdavari
Photographer: Terry Heffernan
Writer: Bruce Bildsten
Creative Director: Tom McElligott
Client: Timex
Agency: Fallon McElligott

95
Art Director: George D'Amato
Photographer: Irving Penn
Writer: Herbert Green
Creative Director: George D'Amato, Herbert Green
Client: Cosmair/L'Oreal
Agency: McCann-Erickson

96
Art Director: Susan Fitzgerald, Charles Rosner
Photographer: Kmari Kostiainen
Writer: Peter Swerdloff
Creative Director: Charles Rosner
Client: Chemical Bank
Agency: Lord, Geller, Federico, Einstein

97
Art Director: Mark Fennimore
Designer: William Wondriska
Photographer: Jay Maisel
Client: United Technologies Corp.
Agency: Ogilvy & Mather

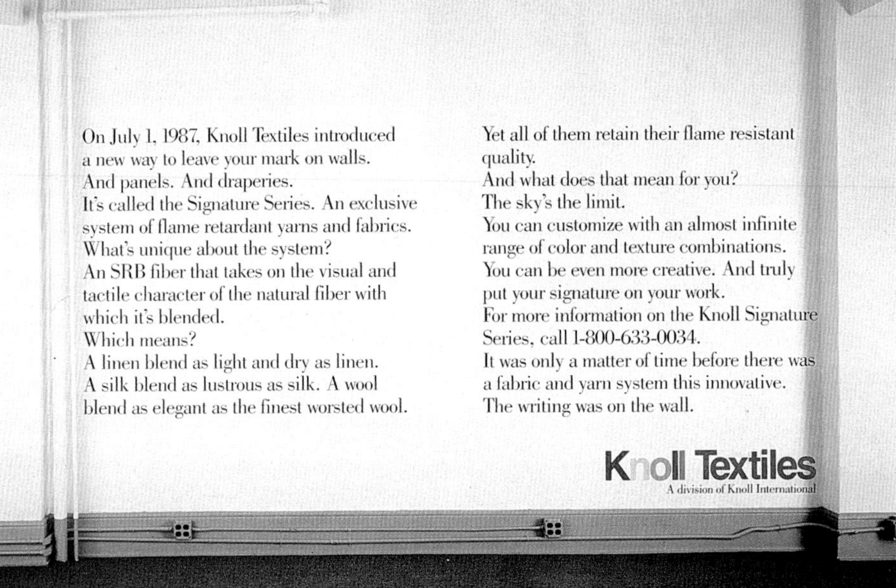

98
Art Director: Gary Goldsmith
Designer: Gary Goldsmith
Photographer: Gil Cope
Writer: Neal Gomberg
Creative Director: Gary Goldsmith
Client: Knoll International
Agency: Goldsmith/Jeffrey
Account Supervisor: Bob Jeffrey

99
Art Director: Gary Goldsmith
Designer: Gary Goldsmith
Photographer: Gil Cope
Writer: Neal Gomberg
Creative Director: Gary Goldsmith
Client: Knoll International
Agency: Goldsmith/Jeffrey
Account Supervisor: Bob Jeffrey

BOLLA. THE ITALIAN CLASSIC.

There's an Italian Classic that's been brightening lives every day for years. It's Bolla Wine. We've been producing classic premium wines for over a century.

In fact, Bolla is the only family owned and operated winery in all of Northern Italy, the richest grape producing region in the world.

It's this heritage that enables us to produce a Valpolicella, Soave, Trebbiano and Bardolino that continue to taste exactly as they should year after year.

Maybe that's one reason the most popular premium wine from Italy is Bolla. And why you may begin seeing Bolla in a slightly different light.

100
Art Director: Mark Moffett
Photographer: Christopher Broadbent
Writer: Rodney Underwood
Creative Director: Ralph Ammirati
Client: Bolla Wines
Agency: Ammirati & Puris Inc.

L O V I N G C A R E B Y C L A I R O L

Pluck.
Pluck Pluck.
Pluck Pluck Pluck.
Pluck.

Maybe it's time to change the way you deal with gray.

How many gray hairs are you going to pluck before you face up to the problem?

Are you going to let yourself go gray? Are you ready to adjust to that new image of yourself? Or will you decide to keep looking young and attractive, with hair that sends out a message of health, beauty and vigor?

It's not a decision to be taken lightly, we know. Deciding to use haircoloring is not the same as choosing a new lipstick.

But there's haircoloring and haircoloring.

Did you know there's one that's as gentle to the hair as a shampoo? It's called Loving Care,® it's made by Clairol, and it's perfect for covering gray.

Loving Care bathes each strand of hair with beautiful, natural-looking color. It washes in like a shampoo, and washes out gradually in about 6 shampoos. It stays natural-looking, too; there are no "roots".

With 23 shades to choose from, it's easy to match your own color. If you prefer, you can add warm tones or deepen your own color or even make your gray look like highlights by choosing 2 or 3 shades lighter than your own. Since there's no peroxide or ammonia, it won't hurt your hair. In fact, Loving Care will give your hair body, gloss and a healthy look.

Before you pluck another hair, wake up to the fact that nature is forcing you to make a decision: gray hair or Loving Care.

Gray hair
or Loving Care.

101
Art Director: Ron Louie
Designer: Ron Louie
Writer: Phyllis Robinson
Client: Clairol
Director of Photography: Hiro

Finding the perfect balance between power and beauty is an art form in itself. And when achieved, offers a feeling of great satisfaction. So for that reason, we fly one of the most advanced fleets in the air today.

KOREAN AIR

102
Art Director: Tom Cordner, Tom Roberts, John Wagner
Illustrator/Artist: Tom Roberts
Writer: Bill Day
Creative Director: Tom Cordner, Brent Bouchez
Client: Korean Airlines
Agency: Ogilvy & Mather L.A.

We admit there are balls which may outlast the new Pro Penn.

Pro Penns are designed to last 30% longer than our regular ball. Which puts them in a league all their own. Available only at selected pro shops.

103

Art Director: Houman Pirdavari
Designer: Houman Pirdavari
Photographer: Dave Jordano
Writer: Jarl Olsen
Creative Director: Tom McElligott
Client: Penn Tennis Balls
Agency: Fallon McElligott

Unfortunately, by the time your last pair of jeans looked this good, they were worn out.

It's such a pity. To have gone through so much together, only to part company just when your jeans finally have just the right look.

But that's the whole idea behind new Lee® Frosted Riders.®

Lee Frosted Riders give you the same worn look and character you get from jeans that are two or three years old. The difference is you don't have to wait two or three years to get it. Available in relaxed fitting jeans, jackets, skirts and bibs. Grey, black and indigo.

Frosted Riders Lee

Most jeans that look this good have ten times the mileage.

If you don't have time to wait for your jeans to look like they've been around the block a few times, new Lee® Frosted Riders® are for you.

With Lee Frosted Riders, you get the same worn look and distinctive character that normally comes with two or three years of hard living. The difference is you don't have to wait two or three years to get it.

But you better jump into a pair soon. These jeans are going faster than a bored and stroked '57 Chevy on a lonely country road.

Now available in grey, black and indigo.

Frosted Riders Lee

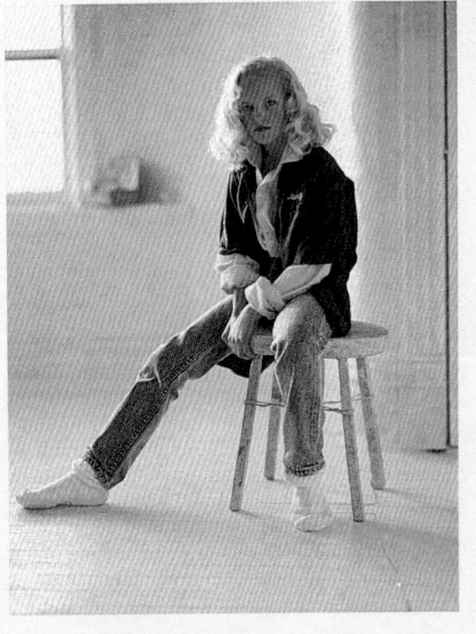

By the time most jeans look this good, you could be in college.

You don't have to be the class brain to know that if jeans started out looking this great, you'd start the year looking pretty good, too.

Which explains why new Lee® Frosted Riders® are such a hot item.

Lee Frosted Riders give you the same look and character everyone's wearing these days. So maybe, with some Lee Frosted Riders this fall, the year won't be a total waste after all. Available in relaxed fitting jeans, jackets and skirts. Grey, black and indigo.

Frosted Riders Lee

104

Art Director: Mark Johnson
Designer: Mark Johnson
Photographer: Dennis Manarchy
Writer: Phil Hanft
Creative Director: Tom McElligott
Client: Lee Jeans
Agency: Fallon McElligott

Unfortunately, some aerobic shoes are only slightly more functional.

Strangely enough, considering the dramatic growth of aerobics in recent years, the new Brooks Prima is the first aerobic shoe that's actually as functional as it is sexy.

Underneath a sleek and colorful, soft-leather upper hides a highly engineered, technically advanced shoe.

For example, the Brooks Prima's unique built-in ballet slipper contains your foot snugly and comfortably for more stability.

The Brooks patented Kinetic Wedge,* a piece of soft, flexible material under the ball of the foot, reduces stress-related injuries by allowing your foot to arch more naturally.

A more rounded toe and extended sidewalls reduce foot roll, a leading cause of sprains and breaks in aerobics.

The result is the first aerobic shoe that passes both the test of fashion as well as the one on the studio floor.

To borrow a phrase, Brooks Primas are a giant step forward for both aerobic shoes and the women who wear them.

Available in four colors and two widths. For a free technical bulletin and the Brooks retailer nearest you, call 1-800-233-7531 (in PA, call 1-800-722-3394).

BROOKS PRIMA

Inspiration for one of the most important advances in aerobic shoes.

It's amazing no one thought of it before. A slipper inside the shoe.

Actually, it's more like a ballet slipper than a bedroom slipper. But the effect is the same. Extraordinary comfort.

Made of seamless, stretch material, the slipper limits foot movement within the shoe for more stability and greater support, fewer blisters and a more enjoyable workout.

The shoe? The new Brooks Prima, a virtual cornucopia of technological advances. Just a few.

The patented Kinetic Wedge,* a piece of soft material under the ball of the foot, to allow your feet to arch more naturally and reduce stress-related hip, leg and foot injuries.

Extended sidewalls and more rounded toes to minimize foot roll.

Plus, for extra cushioning, hollow lugs on the sole and a soft, removeable insert inside the shoe.

Brooks Prima. Just the inspiration your feet need to get your body out on the studio floor.

Available in four colors and two widths. For a free technical bulletin and the Brooks retailer nearest you, call 1-800-233-7531 (in PA, call 1-800-722-3394).

BROOKS PRIMA

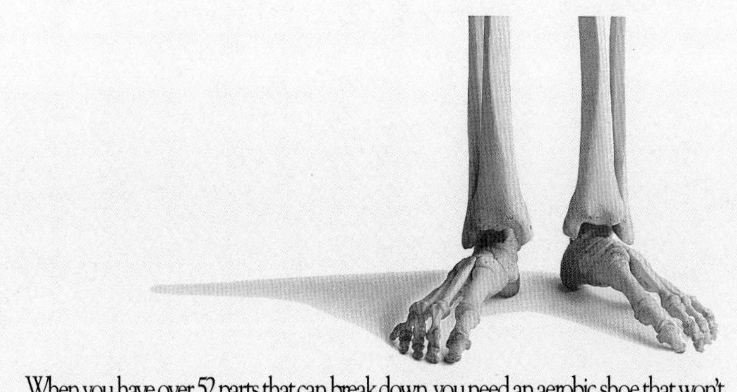

When you have over 52 parts that can break down, you need an aerobic shoe that won't.

The foot is a major engineering work of art. Protecting it from the abuse of aerobic workouts requires an equally impressive shoe.

That shoe is, without reservation, the all new Brooks Prima.

For starters, Prima's unique built-in ballet slipper reduces foot movement within the shoe for more stability and comfort.

The patented Kinetic Wedge,* a piece of soft, flexible material under the ball of the foot, reduces stress-related injuries by allowing your foot to arch more naturally.

And extended sidewalls and more rounded toes help prevent foot roll, the major cause of sprains and breaks in aerobics.

But just as important as all this technical stuff is the package it comes in. An aerobic shoe that actually looks as good on the outside as it does on the inside.

The Brooks Prima. A triumph of form and function in one aerobic shoe.

Available in four colors and two widths. For a free technical bulletin and the Brooks retailer nearest you, call 1-800-233-7531 (in PA, call 1-800-722-3394).

BROOKS PRIMA

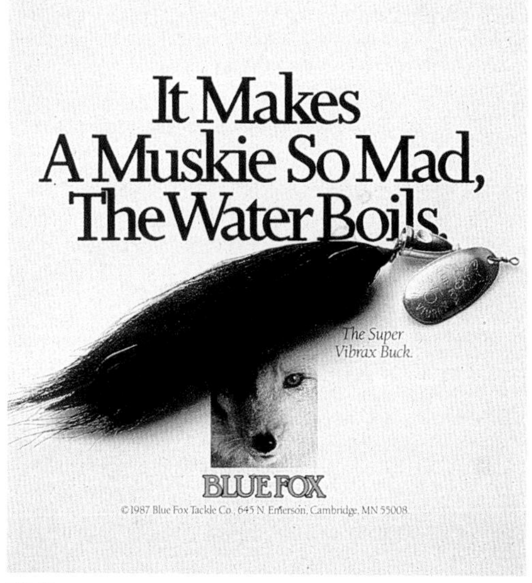

105

Art Director: Bob Brihn
Designer: Bob Brihn
Photographer: Kerry Peterson
Writer: Phil Hanft
Creative Director: Tom McElligott
Client: Brooks
Agency: Fallon McElligott

106

Art Director: Frank Haggerty
Photographer: Marvy! Advertising Photography
Writer: Kerry Casey
Creative Director: Jack Supple
Client: Blue Fox Tackle Co.
Agency: Carmichael Lynch
Producer: Linda Hines

107

Art Director: Michael Smith
Photographer: Annie Leibovitz, Cailor Resnick
Writer: Jackie End, Bill Hamilton, Amelia Rosner
Creative Director: Bill Hamilton
Client: Arrow
Agency: Chiat/Day Inc.

108
Art Director: Houman Pirdavari
Designer: Houman Pirdavari
Photographer: Steve Umland
Writer: Tom McElligott
Creative Director: Tom McElligot
Client: Brooks
Agency: Fallon McElligott

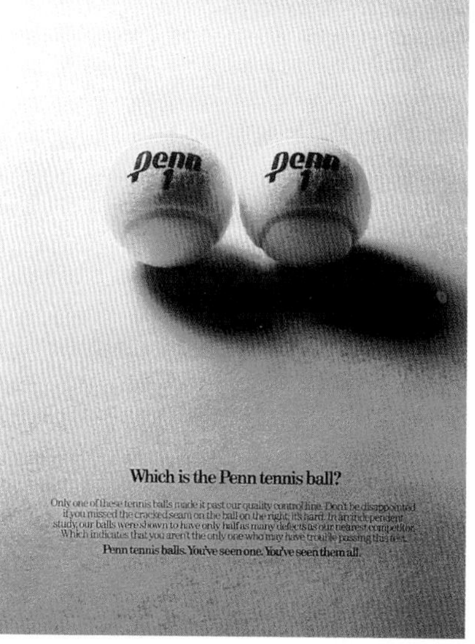

This isn't our ball. But it's our ad.

This tennis ball has just undergone half an hour of simulated court play. See how fuzzy the felt is? That's called *pilling* and it can slow down a tennis ball. At Penn, we use felt made to our unique specifications. So when you see severe pilling like this, it isn't likely that it's one of our balls. Although it could be an ad for them.

Penn tennis balls. You've seen one. You've seen them all.

109
Art Director: Houman Pirdavari
Designer: Houman Pirdavari
Photographer: Dave Jordano
Writer: Jarl Olsen
Creative Director: Tom McElligott
Client: Penn Tennis Balls
Agency: Fallon McElligott

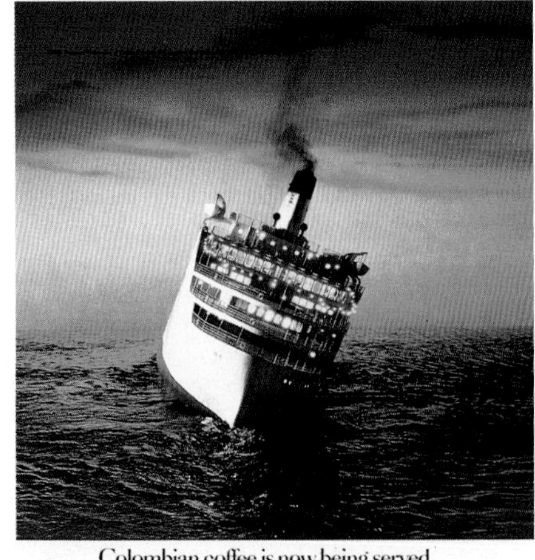

Colombian coffee is now being served in the starboard lounge.

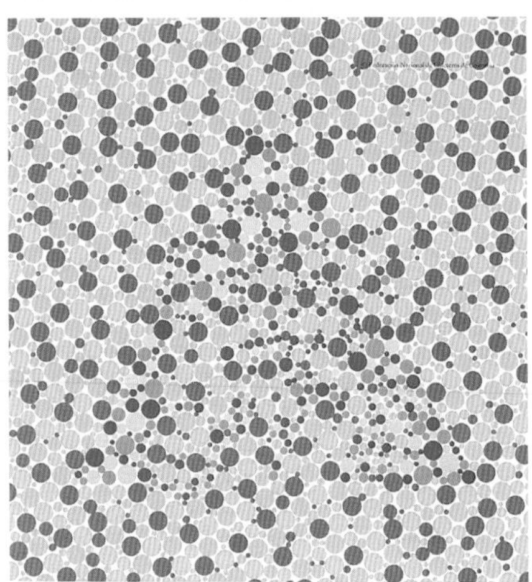

Taste test.

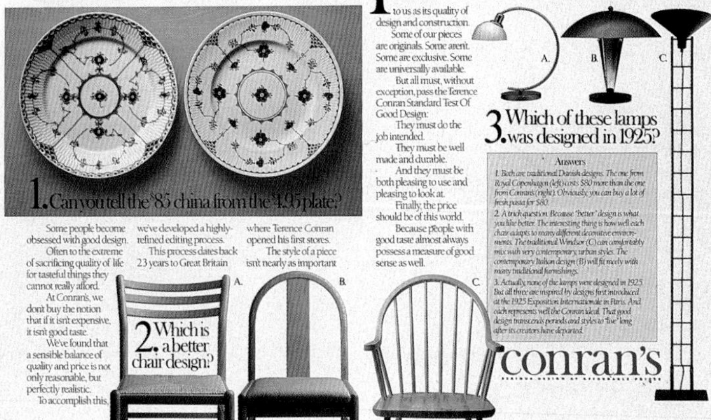

It must be a Colombian Coffee break.

110

Art Director: Dean Hanson
Designer: Dean Hanson
Photographer: Rick Dublin
Writer: Phil Hanft
Creative Director: Tom McElligott
Client: Conran's
Agency: Fallon McElligott

111

Art Director: Steve Jaeger, Garrett Jewett
Photographer: Billy Renshaw, Don Spiro
Writer: Chuck Gessner, Jim Walsh
Creative Director: Charlie Piccirillo
Client: Colombian Coffee
Agency: DDB Needham Worldwide

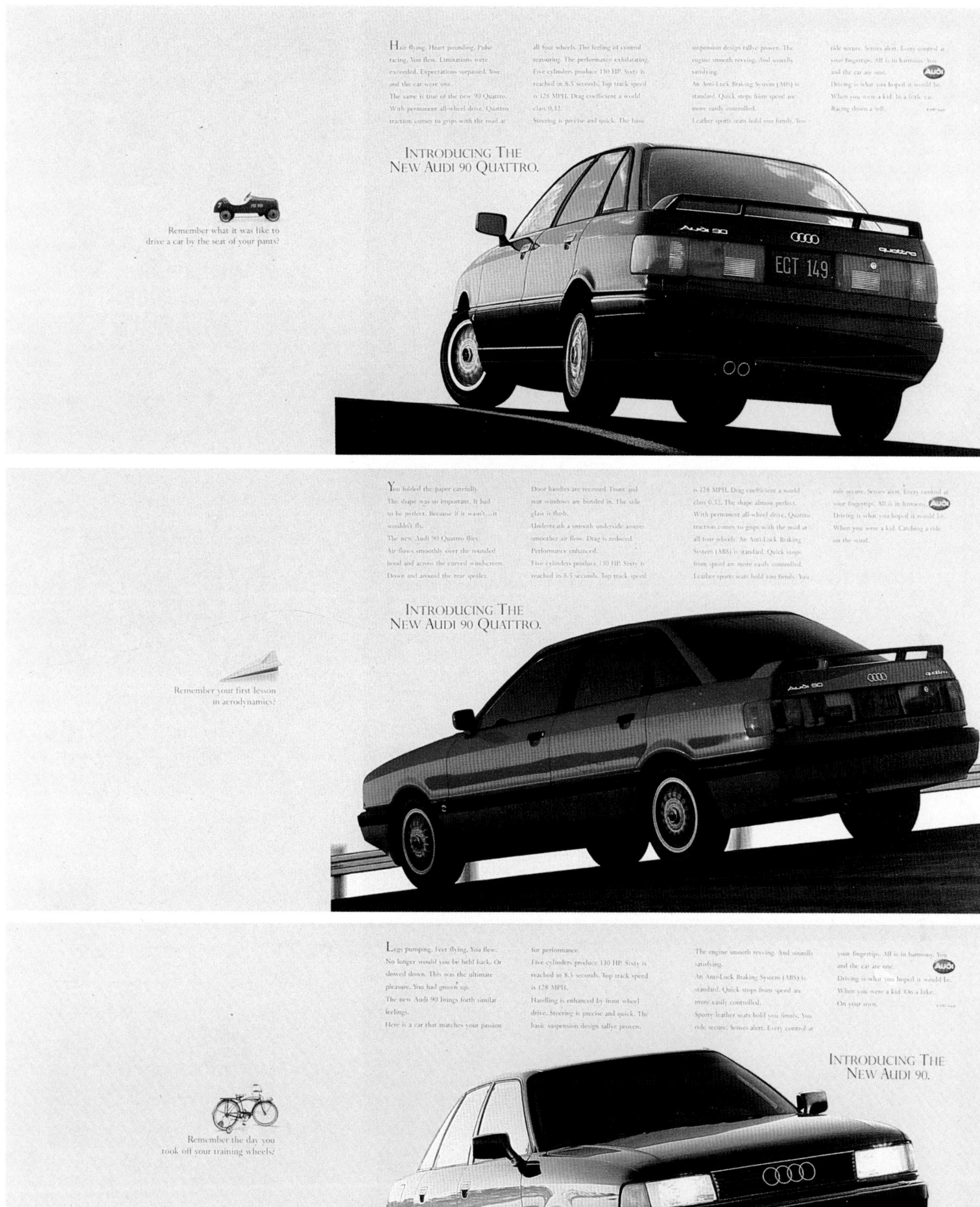

112

Art Director: Joe Gallo
Photographer: Carol Corey, Derek Gardner
Writer: Bill Klimas
Creative Director: Bill Klimas
Client: Audi of America Inc.
Agency: DDB Needham Worldwide

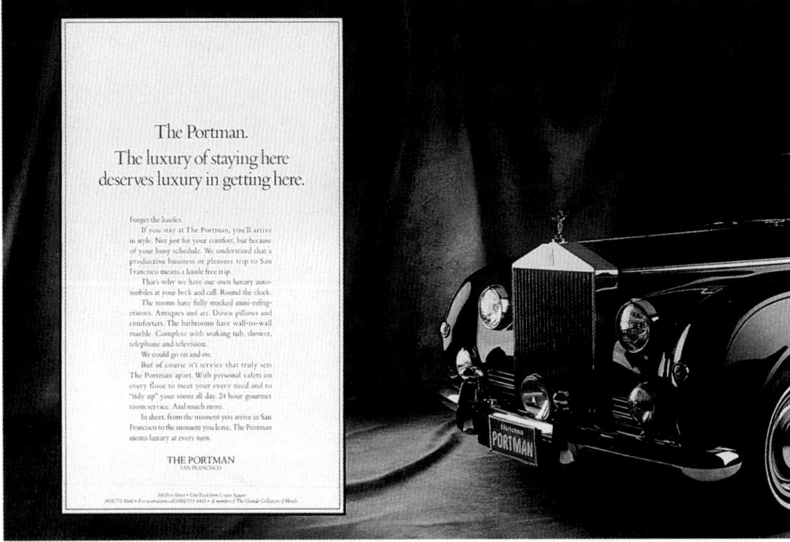

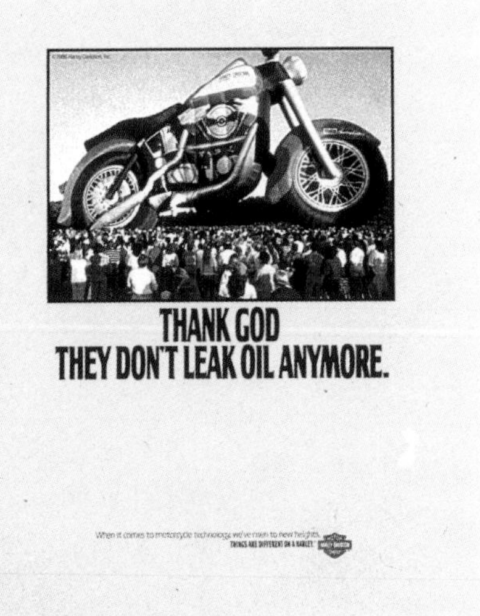

113
Art Director: Kristine Pallas
Photographer: Bob Mizono
Writer: John B. Mattingly
Creative Director: Kristine Pallas
Client: The Portman, San Francisco
Agency: Pallas Advertising Inc.

114
Art Director: Jud Smith, Chuck Anderson
Writer: Ron Sackett, Dave Halsey
Creative Director: Ron Sackett
Client: Harley-Davidson Inc.
Agency: Carmichael Lynch
Producer: Pat Mayfield

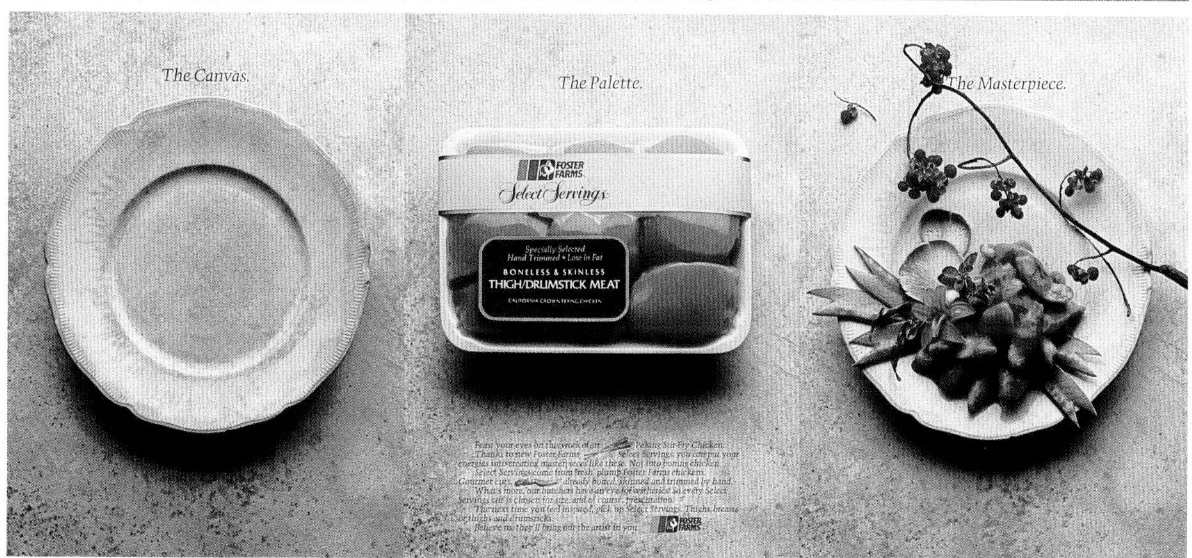

115
Art Director: Rick Boyko
Photographer: Dennis Manarchy
Illustrator/Artist: Michael Bull
Writer: Richard Kelley
Creative Director: Lee Clow
Client: Foster Farms
Agency: Chiat/Day Advertising

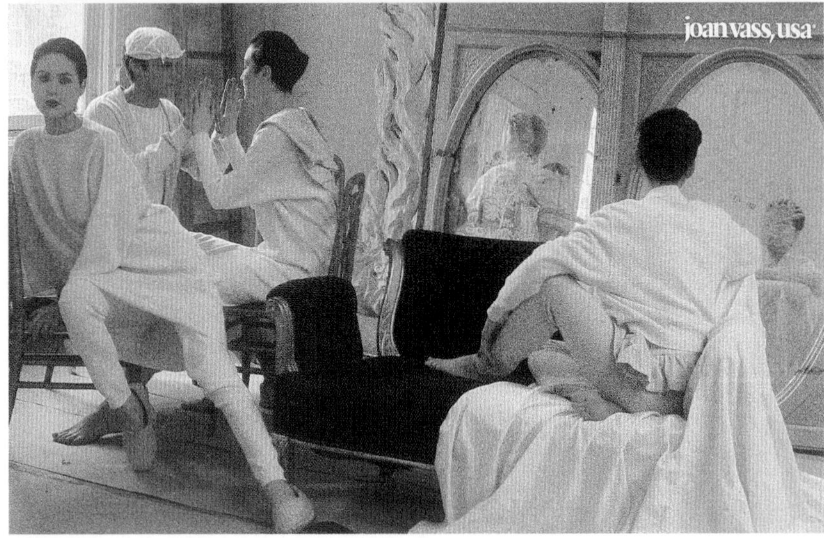

116

Art Director: Lawrence Alten
Designer: Lawrence Alten, Abby Alten
Photographer: Deborah Turbeville
Creative Director: Lawrence Alten
Client: Joan Vass, USA
Agency: Alten Advertising Inc.

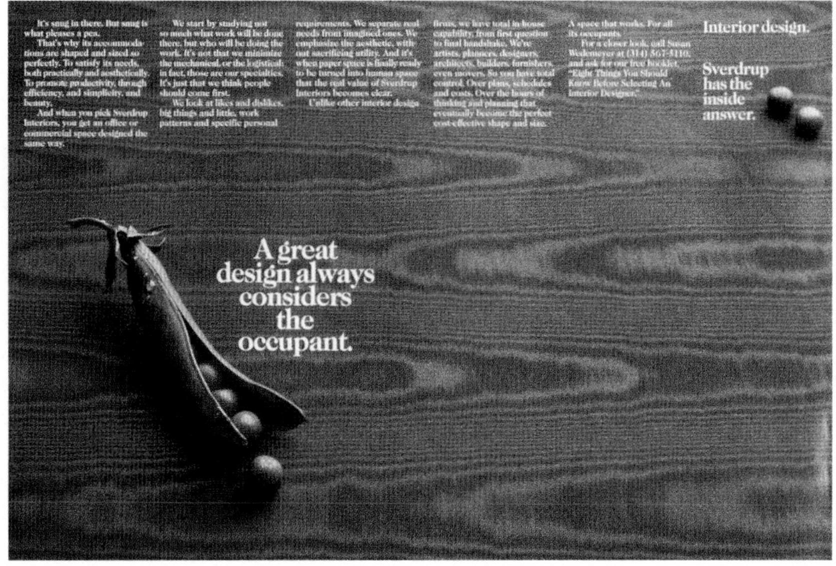

117

Art Director: Donna Hagerty-Payne
Designer: Donna Hagerty-Payne
Photographer: Jon Bruton
Writer: Donna Hagerty-Payne, Gary Apple
Creative Director: Jay Divine
Client: Sverdrup Corp.
Agency: Sverdrup Marketing, BHN

118

Art Director: Kai Mui
Writer: John Harrington, Peter Louison
Creative Director: Nicholas I. Orloff
Client: Eastman Kodak Co., Prof. Photo. Division
Agency: Rumrill-Hoyt Inc.
Account Manager: Vicki Lewis

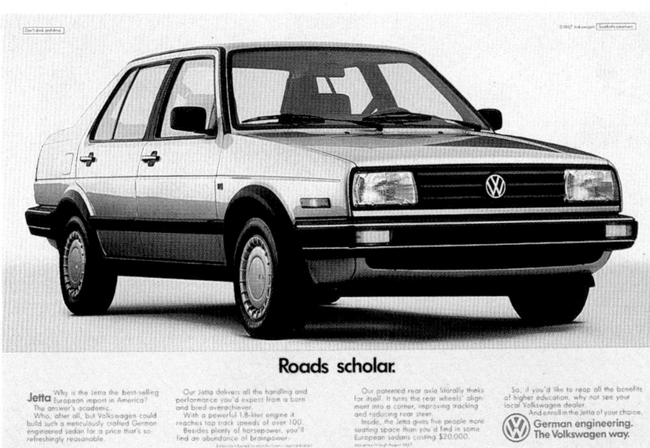

119
Art Director: Robert Tucker, John Staffen, David Martin
Photographer: Jim Hall
Writer: Ed Smith, Mike Rogers, Hal Silverman
Client: Volkswagen
Agency: DDB Needham Worldwide

120
Art Director: Roy Grace
Photographer: Henry Sandbank, Carl Furuta, Jerry Cailor
Writer: Diane Rothschild
Creative Director: Roy Grace
Diane Rothschild
Client: Range Rover of North America
Agency: Grace & Rothschild

121

Art Director: John Klimo
Photographer: Olof Wahlund
Writer: Lois Korey
Creative Director: Lois Korey, Allen Kay
Client: Halston Fragrances
Agency: Korey, Kay & Partners

122

Art Director: Bruce Arendash
Photographer: Andrew Unangst
Writer: Michael Jordan
Creative Director: Lynn Giordano
Client: Citizen Watch
Agency: Lintas USA

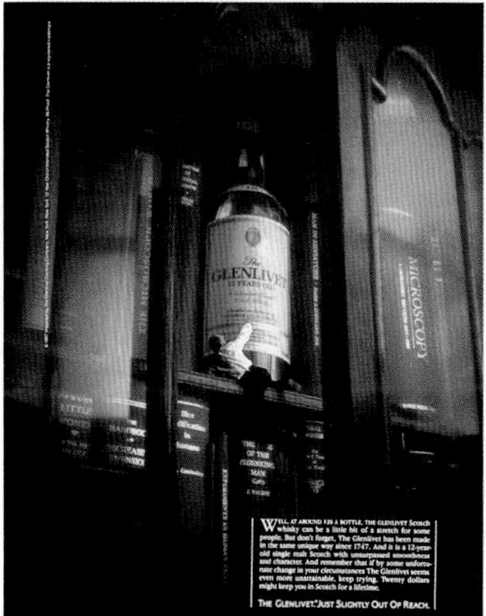

123

Art Director: Dean Stefanides
Designer: Dean Stefanides
Photographer: Dennis Manarchy
Writer: Bernie Rosner
Creative Director: Sam Scali
Client: Ralston Purina/O.N.E.
Agency: Scali, McCabe, Sloves Inc.

124

Art Director: Roy Carruthers
Photographer: Martin Thompson, Eric Michelson
Writer: Steve Jeffrey
Creative Director: Malcolm End
Client: Seagrams/The Glenlivet
Agency: Ogilvy & Mather

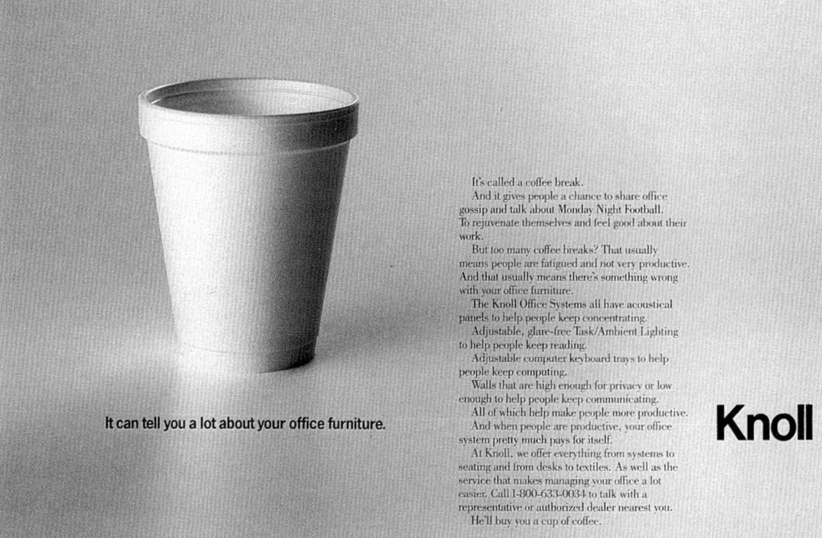

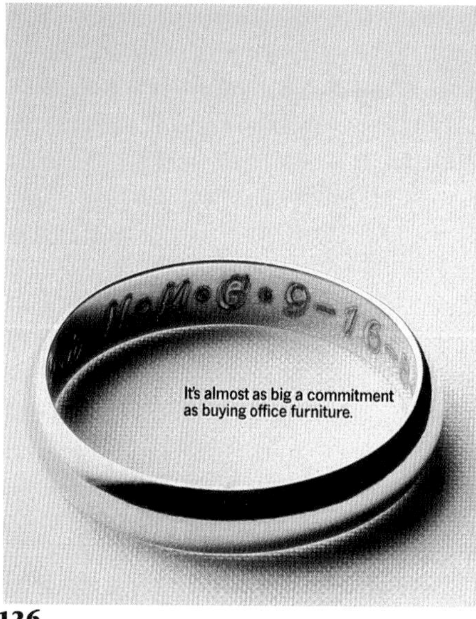

125

Art Director: Roy Grace
Designer: Roy Grace
Photographer: Bruno
Writer: Diane Rothschild
Creative Director: Roy Grace, Diane Rothschild
Client: The Paddington Corp.
Agency: Grace & Rothschild

126

Art Director: Gary Goldsmith
Designer: Gary Goldsmith
Photographer: Gil Cope
Writer: Neal Gomberg
Creative Director: Gary Goldsmith
Client: Knoll International
Agency: Goldsmith/Jeffrey
Account Supervisor: Bob Jeffrey

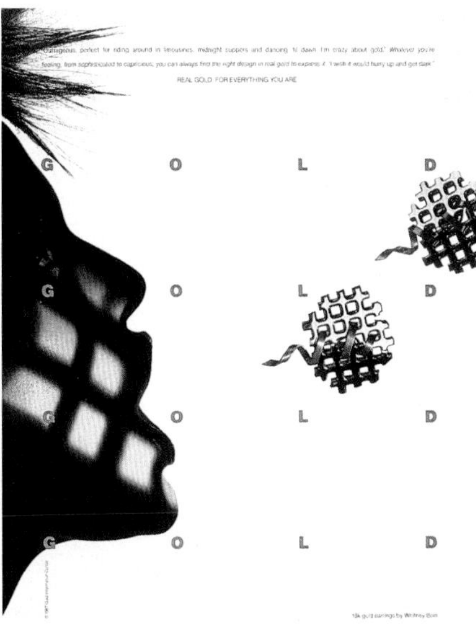

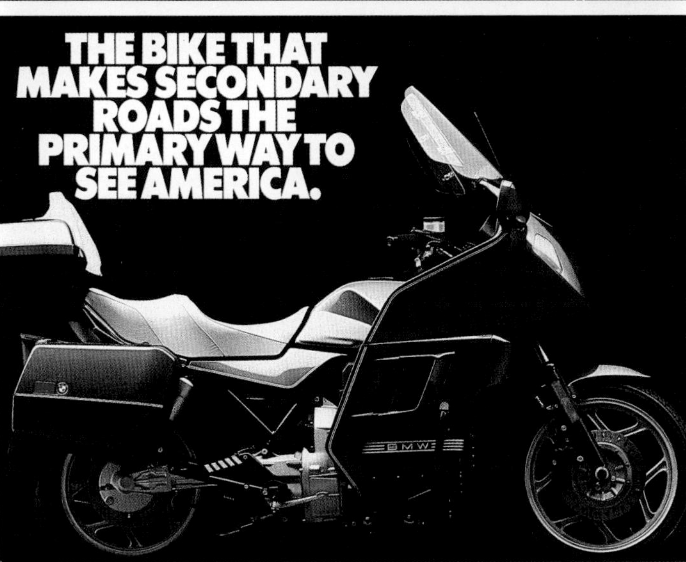

REAL GOLD. FOR EVERYTHING YOU ARE.

G O L D

G O L D

G O L D

G O L D

CREATED FOR A CONSIDERABLY HIGHER PURPOSE THAN GOING NOWHERE FAST.

To riders who possess no loftier goal than shaving tenths of seconds off the journey from point A to point B, BMW hasn't much to say.

To riders inspired by the promise of an extraordinarily agile, meticulously honed sports machine, however, we have quite a bit to say.

All of which is perfectly summed up in the BMW K100RS. A sport touring bike that multiplies the dimensions of motorcycling—from the single dimension of sheer speed, to the multidimensional, balanced performance cherished by European riders for decades.

With the K100RS, you can cut corners with surgical precision.

Tour long distances in ergonomic comfort.

Blast along straightaways courtesy of BMW's liquid-cooled, fuel-injected, in-line four-cylinder engine.

And slice through the wind with a wind tunnel sculpted fairing.

Meanwhile, you'll be enjoying a motorcycle so stunning in appearance, it has won international design awards.

Unlike many bikes, the BMW K100RS is not an instrument of self-denial.

Rather, it offers experienced motorcycle riders something far more satisfying than the opportunity to go nowhere fast.

The opportunity to go everywhere well.

THE LEGENDARY MOTORCYCLES OF GERMANY.

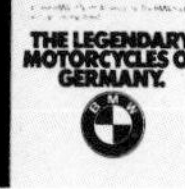

REAL GOLD. FOR EVERYTHING YOU ARE.

G O L D

G O L D

G O L D

G O L D

127

Art Director: Clem McCarthy, Marcus Kemp, William Hartwell, Alain Briere
Designer: Alain Briere
Photographer: Jeff Zwart
Writer: Paul Wolfe
Client: BMW of North America Inc. Motorcycle
Agency: Ammirati & Puris Inc.

128

Art Director: Ron Louie
Designer: Ron Louie
Photographer: Neal Barr
Writer: Dan Brooks
Creative Director: Jack Mariucci, Bob Mackall
Client: Gold Information Center Jewelry
Agency: DDB Needham Worldwide

An Inc. 500 company.

A Fortune 500 company.

Thirty years ago Coleman would have been a good bet to make the *Inc.* 500. Today, thanks to constant innovation and selective acquisition of related companies, Coleman ranks among the top corporations in America. For the numbers and facts behind our $500,000,000 enterprise and its hundreds of products in outdoor recreation, marine sports, and heating and air conditioning, call 1-800-521-8434, ext. 50. In Minnesota, 1-800-962-6996, ext. 50.

Coleman

A lot of people think you can fit everything Coleman makes on one page.

Wrong.

Coleman makes not just one, not just fifty, but hundreds of different products.

Over $500,000,000 worth last year alone. And most of them leaders in their categories, thanks to constant innovation and careful acquisition of related companies.

For a more complete look at our activities in outdoor recreation, marine sports and heating and air conditioning, call 1-800-521-8434, ext. 50. In MN, 1-800-962-6996, extension 50.

Coleman

You're wrong if you think this is everything we make.

You're wrong if you think this is everything we make.

The little-known truth about Coleman: We're a $500,000,000 company making and selling hundreds of different products all over the world. And, thanks to careful acquisition of related companies and constant product innovation, most are leaders in their categories. For a more complete story of our activities in outdoor recreation, marine sports and heating and air conditioning, call 1-800-521-8434, extension 50. In MN, 1-800-962-6996, extension 50.

Coleman

129

Art Director: Michael Fazende
Designer: Michael Fazende
Photographer: Jim Marvy
Writer: Phil Hanft
Creative Director: Tom McElligott
Client: Coleman
Agency: Fallon McElligott

WIN THE BATTLE.

WIN THE WAR.

When you make Federal part of your battle plan, you can win the war.

IT'S NOT JUST A PACKAGE.
IT'S YOUR BUSINESS.

MISSION.

FEDERAL EXPRESS
OVERNIGHT LETTER
OVERNIGHT SERVICE IS AVAILABLE WITHIN THE U.S./TO AND FROM CANADA AND PUERTO RICO.
INTERNATIONAL DELIVERY SCHEDULE VARIES BY DESTINATION.

MISSION ACCOMPLISHED.

If your mission is to manage an office, your mission is never impossible when you use Federal Express.

IT'S NOT JUST A PACKAGE.
IT'S YOUR BUSINESS.

THE CALL OF DUTY.

ABOVE AND BEYOND.

When duty calls, Federal Express answers.

IT'S NOT JUST A PACKAGE.
IT'S YOUR BUSINESS.

130

Art Director: Bob Brihn
Designer: Bob Brihn
Photographer: Mark LeFavor
Writer: Bill Miller
Creative Director: Tom McElligott
Client: Federal Express
Agency: Fallon McElligott

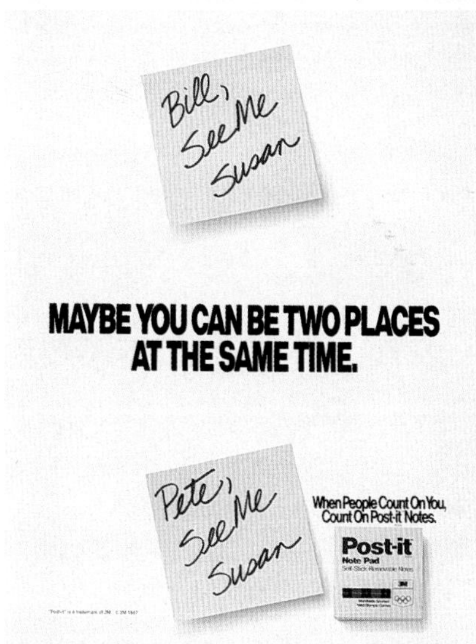

131

Art Director: Bill Zabowski
Photographer: Peter Wong
Writer: Pete Smith
Creative Director: Tom Weyl
Client: 3M Post-it Notes
Agency: Martin/Williams Advertising Inc.

132

Art Director: Michael Smith
Photographer: Dennis Manarchy
Writer: Bryan Buckley
Creative Director: Bill Hamilton
Client: Rockport
Agency: Chiat/Day Inc., New York
Account Management: Steve Friedman

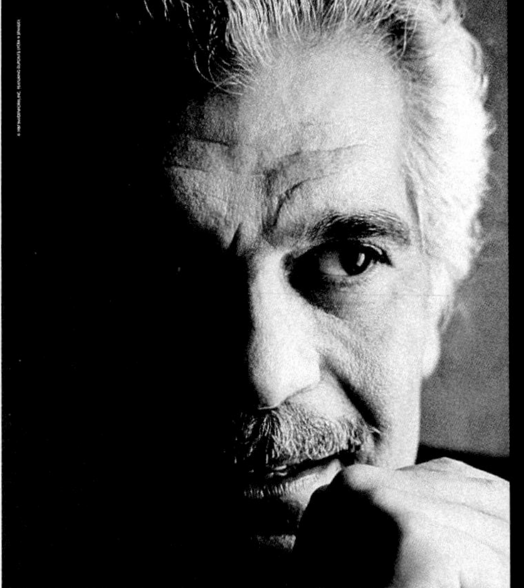

A Waterford biscuit barrel can only be made by following a recipe that's been passed down for centuries.
From the white-hot ovens of Waterford,® formed by the mouths of skilled blowers and the hands of master cutters, comes a biscuit barrel whose beauty will always remain as fresh as the day it was made.
Waterford
Steadfast in a world of wavering standards.

133

Art Director: Tod Seisser, Irv Klein
Photographer: Henry Sandbank
Writer: Jay Taub, Stephanie Arnold
Editor: Morty Ashkinos
Creative Director: Jay Taub, Tod Seisser
Client: Maidenform
Agency: Levine, Huntley, Schmidt & Beaver

134

Art Director: Sherry Pollack, Gail Bartley
Photographer: Barney Edwards
Writer: Lesley Stern, Bill McCullam, Paul Hartzell, David Tessler
Client: Waterford Crystal
Agency: Ammirati & Puris Inc.

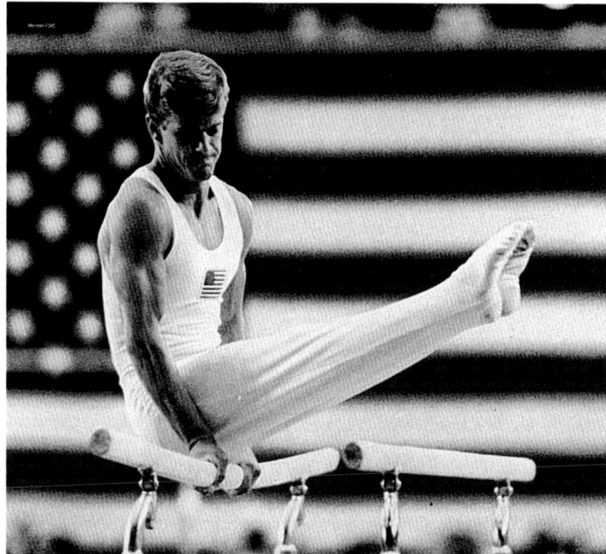

What is strength?

In banking, the single most important test of strength is capital. But it's not the only one.

At Chemical, we recently increased our capital by nearly one billion dollars, and our capital to assets ratio puts us ahead of most of our competitors.

But we set performance standards for ourselves that measure more than capital levels or ratios and emphasize the skill with which we deploy our capital for our clients.

We've invested our capital to expand into investment banking, using it to support an average securities trading volume of 40 billion dollars a day.

We've broken new ground in interstate banking—committing capital to the largest interstate merger in banking history, with Texas Commerce Bancshares, and to the largest merger between a New York and a New Jersey bank, with Horizon Bancorp.

In the end, no amount of capital will protect a bank against poor management, while there's no limit to what hard work, sound management and imagination can accomplish with the capital we have.

That's why we're proud of our bank's capital strength and even prouder of our personal strengths: financial skill and judgment.

CHEMICALBANK
The bottom line is excellence.

Is it time to teach an old law new tricks?

Just because a law is old doesn't mean it's necessarily good or bad.

But when over the years an industry changes dramatically, it seems reasonable that the laws governing it should also change. For example, America's financial services are governed by a law enacted before computer technology, globalized capital markets, and a wide variety of instruments became part of our financial system.

That law, the Glass-Steagall Act, was passed in the crisis atmosphere of the Great Depression in response to stock market abuses. This 54-year-old law keeps commercial banks from breaking into the Wall Street cartel that dominates stock and bond underwriting and has created a division of services that's outdated and harmful.

By creating a monopoly on certain lines of corporate business, Glass-Steagall has kept the cost of raising capital artificially high. And, ironically, it has prevented U.S. commercial banks from conducting business at home they can successfully pursue overseas—underwriting bonds in London but not in New York, for instance.

Chemical Bank supports appropriate regulation. But we believe that regulations must be removed if they perpetuate unfair competition, hinder our domestic banking system, or raise prices for our corporate clients. If we fail to repeal these archaic regulations, we'll continue to use yesterday's laws to govern today's markets. And that seems to us like the tail wagging the dog.

CHEMICALBANK
The bottom line is excellence.

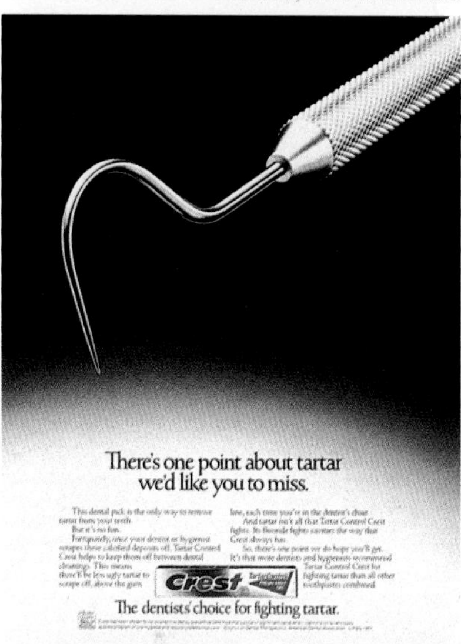

How do you stick to your credit culture when temptation's right under your nose?

Bankers are the only salesmen who must drum up business and turn down would-be buyers—simultaneously.

This process of at once soliciting and rejecting is governed by what we call our credit culture. It involves a series of tough decisions—and crucial ones—because the competition's fierce. One bank's unacceptable risk can be another's handsome profit. The bank that thinks it's only in the business of saying "no" won't be in *any* business very long—while those who say "yes" too readily can also readily get into trouble.

Our credit culture, when all is said and done, is as much an *attitude* as a set of rules. A belief that some kinds of deals, no matter how profitable they first appear, remain bad business. And a determination to look for the best ways to help our customers.

Is there anything unusual about our credit culture? We like to think there is. Perhaps it's a willingness to look a little deeper into a deal, a business or an individual before we lend. A willingness to work with customers if things get tough. An urge to solve a problem and save a promising business.

Does this apply beyond commercial banking? Absolutely. Because a sound approach to risk is vital in today's much broader, ever more competitive financial marketplace. To help our customers with foreign exchange, swaps, stand-by credits—with the dozens of new services investment banking brings—we can never forget the conscience of our bank: our credit culture.

CHEMICALBANK
The bottom line is excellence.

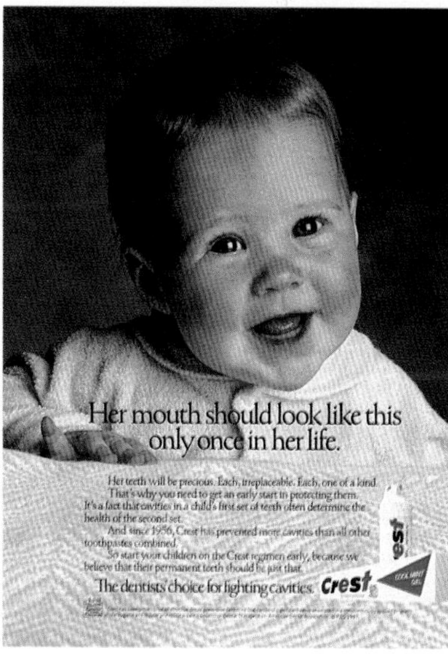

136
Art Director: John Malinowski
Photographer: Jerry Friedman, Frank Cowan
Writer: Harry Braver
Creative Director: Ken Charof
Client: Procter & Gamble
Agency: D'Arcy, Masius, Benton & Bowles

135
Art Director: Charles Rosner, Mary Morant, Susan Fitzgerald
Writer: Peter Swerdloff, Harvey Cohen
Creative Director: Charles Rosner
Client: Chemical Bank
Agency: Lord, Geller, Federico, Einstein

137
Art Director: Carlos Segura
Designer: Carlos Segura
Photographer: Chris Hawker
Writer: Carlos Segura, Bill Force
Creative Director: Carlos Segura, Jan Zwiren
Client: Aladdin
Agency: Zwiren & Partners

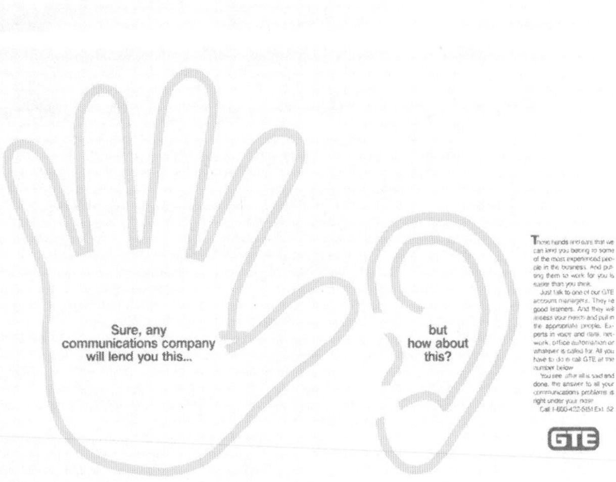

138
Art Director: Nat Harrison
Designer: Nat Harrison
Illustrator/Artist: Nat Harrison
Writer: Larry Chase
Creative Director: James Lawson
Client: GTE
Agency: DDB Needham Worldwide

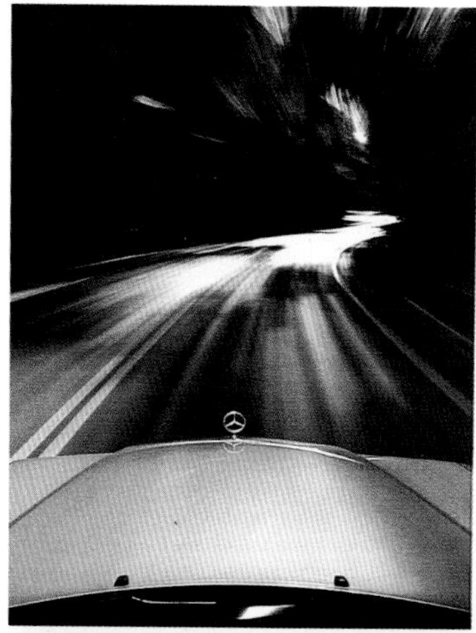

THE MERCEDES-BENZ 190 CLASS:
THE SUBTLE DIFFERENCE BETWEEN MASTERING
THE ROAD AND MERELY COPING WITH IT.

Engineered like no other car in the world

THE MERCEDES-BENZ 190 CLASS:
NO MATTER HOW HARD YOU DRIVE, YOU NEVER
LEAVE CIVILIZATION BEHIND.

Engineered like no other car in the world

THE MERCEDES-BENZ 300 CLASS:
SO TECHNOLOGICALLY ADVANCED, YOU BARELY
NOTICE THE TECHNOLOGY.

Engineered like no other car in the world

It came back as a copier.

How Océ copiers put an end to bottle feeding.

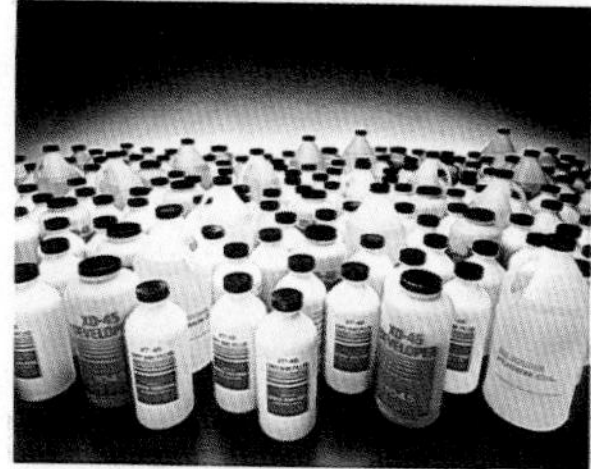

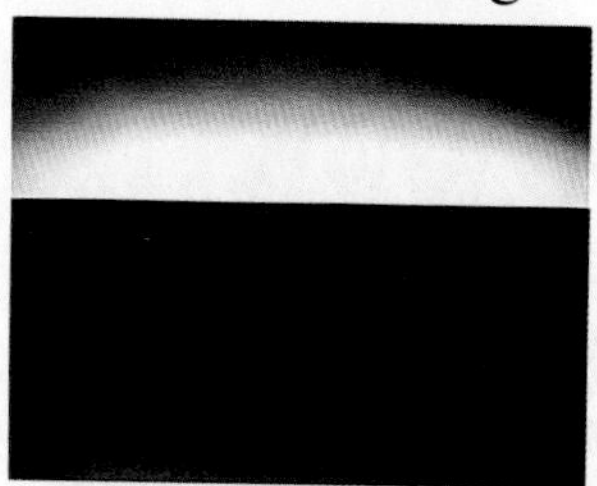

The average mid-volume copier consumes about 100 bottles of toner, 15 bottles of developer and 15 bottles of fuser oil each year.

With an Océ, you can forget all that. You never have to add toner, developer or fuser oil.

For starters, the Océ has a 90,000-copy toner reservoir which holds enough toner to last until we come by and top it off (at no additional cost to you).

Second, the patented one-component toner eliminates the need for developer in an Océ.

Finally, low heat fusing means you don't have to mess with fuser oil.

With such a meager appetite, the Océ copier saves you bottle costs and downtime. It's just one of the reasons Océ copiers are relied on in 90 countries around the world.

océ

Why an Océ copier will never jam.

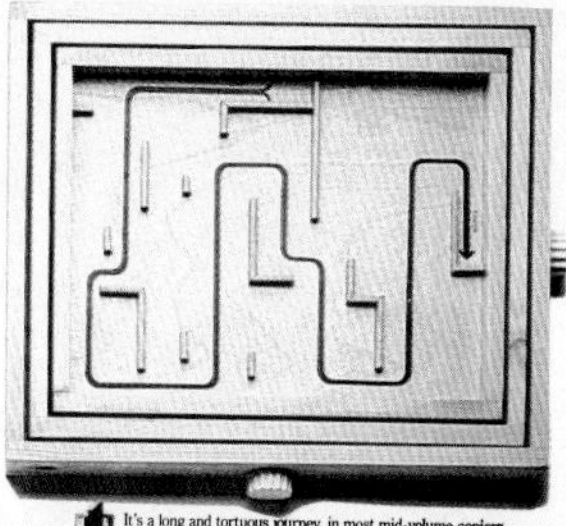

It's a long and tortuous journey, in most mid-volume copiers, from the paper tray to the receiving tray. In some, it's a meandering route more than a yard long. And at any turn, a paper jam can force you to a halt.

In an Océ copier, on the other hand, the image, not the paper, does the traveling. The paper path is just 17 inches long. So internal jamming is virtually impossible.

In fact, since you won't need to open the copier for any reason, we actually bolt the access doors shut. And we guarantee you at least 92 percent uptime, in writing.

No paper jams. It's just one of the reasons Océ copiers are relied on in 90 countries around the world.

océ

Océ Business Systems, Inc., Stamford, CT

139

Art Director: Günther Maier
Designer: Günther Maier
Photographer: Dietmar Henneka, Jeff Zwart
Writer: Ted Baker
Creative Director: Bruce McCall
Client: Mercedes Benz of North America
Agency: McCaffrey & McCall

140

Art Director: Susan Casey
Designer: Nancy Manfredi
Photographer: Steve Bronstein
Writer: Dave Goldenberg
Creative Director: Steve Trygg
Client: Oce Business Systems
Agency: Anderson & Lembke

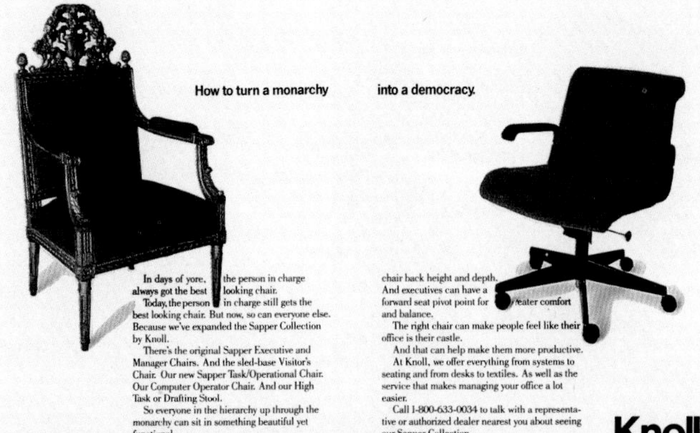

141

Art Director: Rick Paynter, Julius Weil
Photographer: Henry Wolfe
Writer: Leland Rosemond, Ray Pelletier
Creative Director: Bill Appelman, Leland Rosemond
Client: American Insurance Group
Agency: Bozell, Jacobs, Kenyon & Eckhardt Inc.

142

Art Director: Gary Goldsmith
Designer: Gary Goldsmith
Photographer: Gil Cope
Writer: Neal Gomberg
Creative Director: Gary Goldsmith
Client: Knoll International
Agency: Goldsmith/Jeffrey
Account Supervisor: Bob Jeffrey

irector: Kurt Tausche
r: Kerry Casey
ive Director: Kurt Tausche
Client: Minnesota State High School League
Agency: Bozell, Jacobs, Kenyon & Eckhardt Inc.

JUST A PINCH BETWEEN YOUR CHEEK AND WHERE YOUR GUMS USED TO BE.

Smokeless tobacco causes gum disease and mouth cancer. Chew on that before you have another chew. For more information, call the Minnesota State High School League at 427-5250.

144
Art Director: William Oberlander
Photographer: Craig Cutler
Writer: Jesse Lependorf
Creative Director: John Nieman
Client: Nabisco Brands Inc.
Agency: McCann-Erickson

145
Art Director: Michael Rosen
Designer: Michael Rosen
Writer: Michael Rosen
Creative Director: Gary Goldsmith
Client: Citizens against Cocaine Abuse
Agency: Goldsmith/Jeffrey
Account Supervisor: Bob Jeffrey

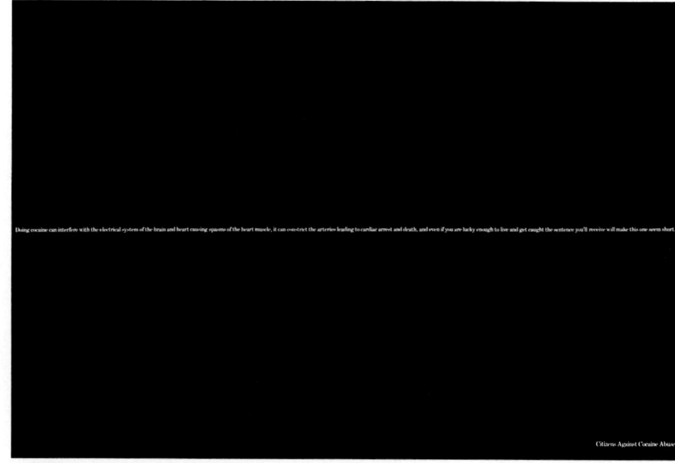

146
Art Director: Gary Goldsmith
Designer: Gary Goldsmith
Writer: Neal Gomberg
Creative Director: Gary Goldsmith
Client: Citizens against Cocaine Abuse
Agency: Goldsmith/Jeffrey
Account Supervisor: Bob Jeffrey

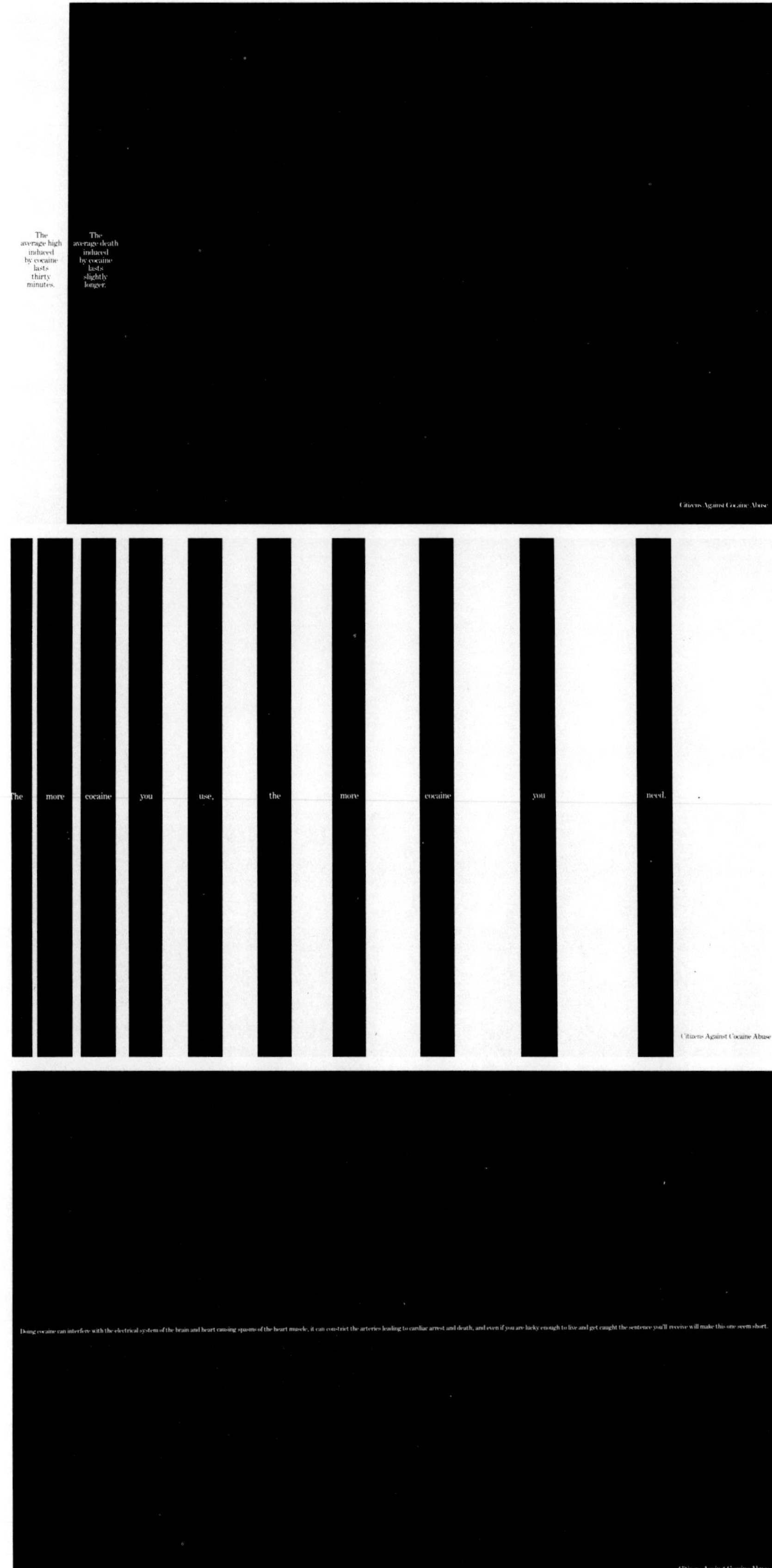

147

Art Director: Gary Goldsmith, Michael Rosen
Designer: Gary Goldsmith, Michael Rosen
Writer: Neal Gomberg, Michael Rosen
Creative Director: Gary Goldsmith
Client: Citizens against Cocaine Abuse
Agency: Goldsmith/Jeffrey
Account Supervisor: Bob Jeffrey

148
Art Director: Bob Barrie
Designer: Bob Barrie
Photographer: Rick Dublin
Writer: Jarl Olsen
Creative Director: Tom McElligott
Client: Hush Puppies
Agency: Fallon McElligott
Model: Jason

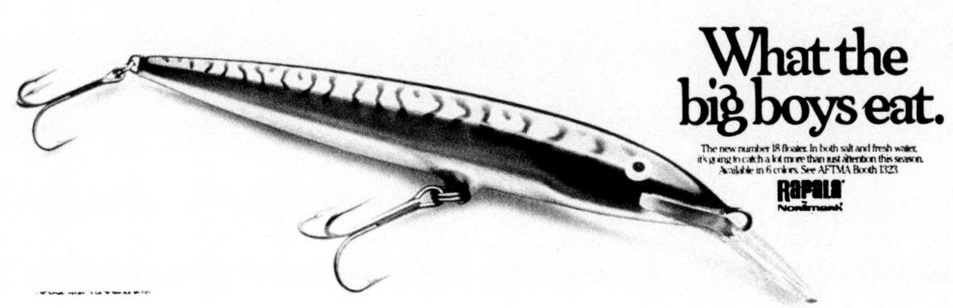

JanklowBender is looking for someone who can write well.

Submit portfolios to Peter Bregman.

257 Park Avenue So. N.Y.C. 10010.

149
Art Director: Paul Asao
Photographer: Marvy! Advertising Photography
Writer: Kerry Casey
Creative Director: Jack Supple
Client: Normark/Rapala
Agency: Carmichael Lynch
Producer: Sheila FitzPatrick

150
Art Director: David Bender
Writer: Peter Bregman
Creative Director: David Bender
Client: Janklow Bender
Agency: Janklow Bender

151
Art Director: Houman Pirdavari
Designer: Houman Pirdavari
Photographer: Rick Dublin
Writer: Bill Miller
Creative Director: Tom McElligott
Client: Rolling Stone
Agency: Fallon McElligott

152
Art Director: Houman Pirdavari
Designer: Houman Pirdavari
Photographer: Rick Dublin
Writer: Bill Miller
Creative Director: Tom McElligott
Client: Rolling Stone
Agency: Fallon McElligott

Perception.

Reality.

For a new generation of Rolling Stone readers, sexual freedom simply means a bigger pill to swallow. If you're looking for an informed, educated and health conscious market, get between the covers of Rolling Stone.

Rolling Stone

Perception.

Reality.

If you still think the readers of Rolling Stone are looking at the world through rose colored glasses, maybe this will open your eyes: Last year, the readers of Rolling Stone purchased a shade more than 4.5 million pairs of designer sunglasses. If you're looking for a bright spot to sell your product, the sun never sets on the pages of Rolling Stone.

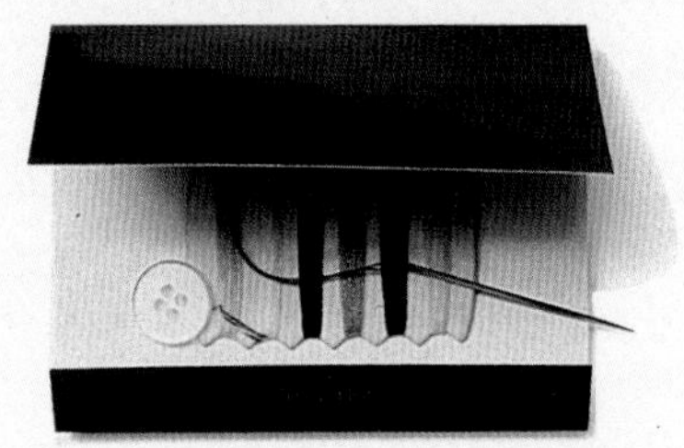

This will keep your guests from losing their buttons.

Big business is often complicated by small emergencies. That's why so many business travelers are constantly on pins and needles. But the fact is, they have to be prepared. And nothing prepares them better than The Wall Street Journal. After all, only The Journal offers the kind of detailed, daily analysis of national and international news that businesspeople need.

And only The Journal can call itself the number one newspaper among frequent hotel guests.

This will keep them from losing their shirts.

For further information on how to join our recently expanded amenities program, write to Allen Simeone, Director of Circulation Sales, Dow Jones & Co., Inc., P.O. Box 300, Princeton, New Jersey 08540.

Or call him collect at (609) 520-4275. Before you know it, your business will be bursting at the seams.

The Wall Street Journal Amenities Program.

153
Art Director: Angela Dunkle
Designer: Angela Dunkle
Photographer: Rick Dublin
Writer: Jamie Barrett
Creative Director: Tom McElligott
Client: The Wall Street Journal
Agency: Fallon McElligott

154
Art Director: Yvonne Smith
Illustrator/Artist: Chris Davey
Writer: Robert Chandler
Creative Director: Steve Hayden
Client: Northrop Corp.
Agency: BBDO/LA
Production: Gina Norton
Producer: Karen Garnett

155
Art Director: Pam Conboy
Photographer: Dennis Manarchy
Writer: Lee Schmidt
Creative Director: Tom Weyl
Client: 3M Health Care Specialties Division
Agency: Martin/Williams Advertising Inc.

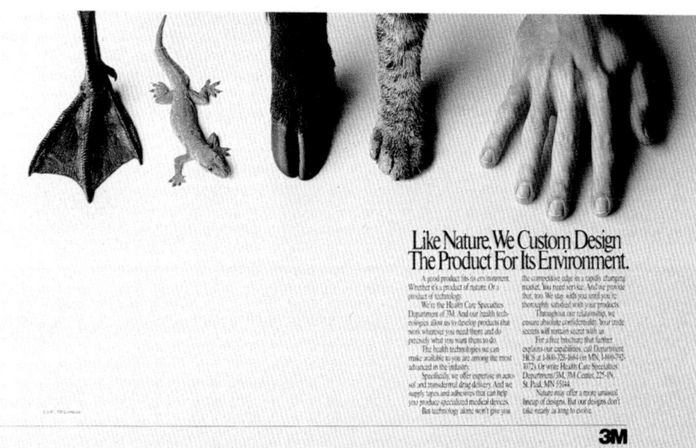

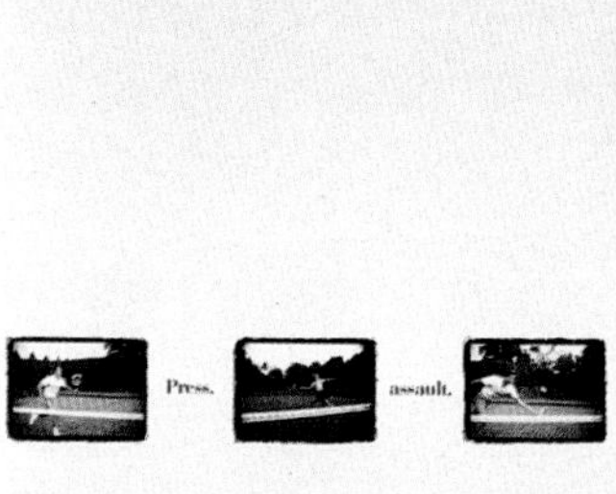

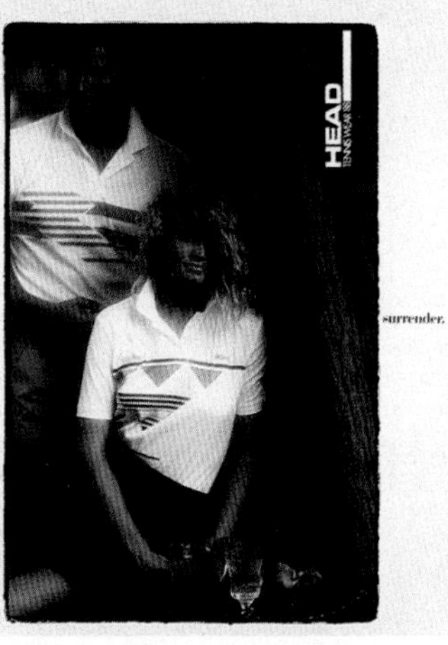

156
Art Director: Richard Smith
Designer: Richard Smith
Photographer: Helen Norman
Writer: Elise Kolaja
Creative Director: Jeff Millman
Client: Head Sports Wear
Agency: Smith, Burke & Azzam Advertising Inc.
Publication: Sports Style

157
Art Director: Dick Henderson
Photographer: Eric Henderson
Writer: Jim Cole
Creative Director: Dick Henderson, Jim Cole
Client: Masland Carpets
Agency: Cole, Henderson, Drake Inc.

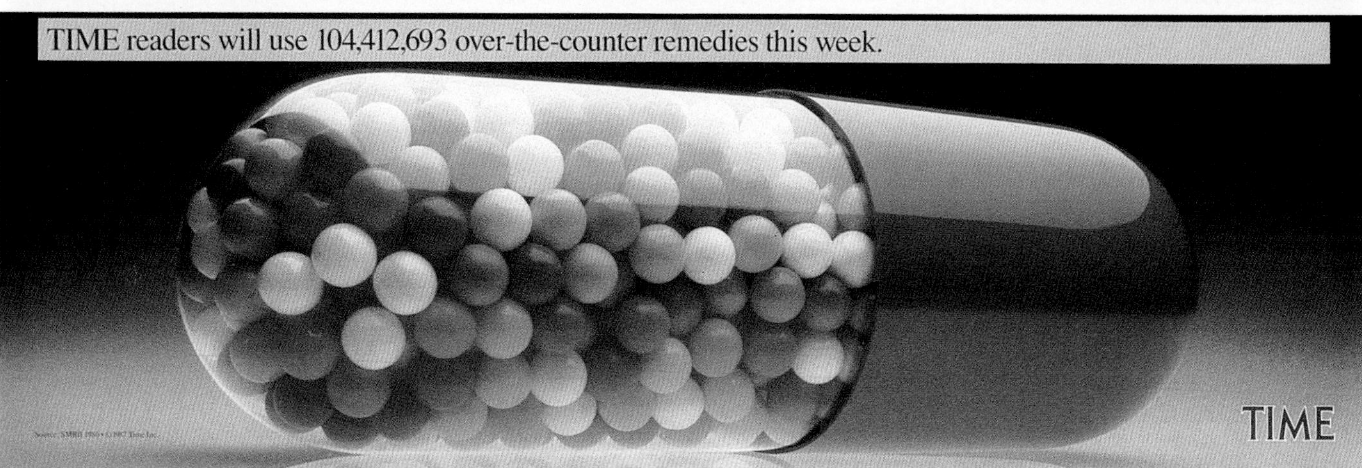

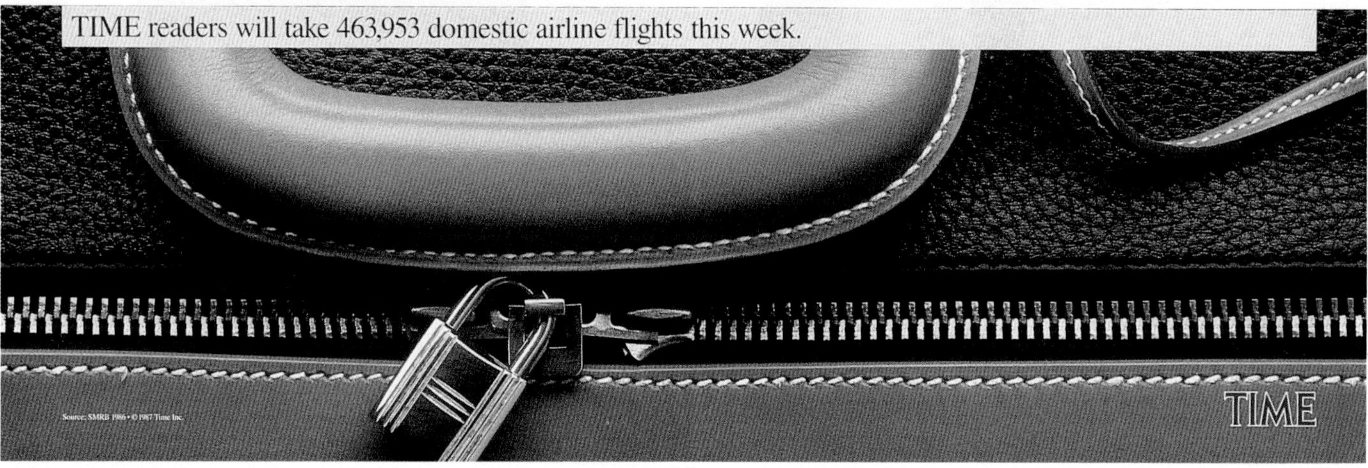

158
Art Director: Greg Elkin
Writer: Richard Hayes
Creative Director: Bob Cox
Client: Time Inc.
Agency: Young & Rubicam Inc.

Imitation may be the sincerest form of flattery, but it's no indication of quality.

In this dog-eat-dog marketplace, me-too products are beginning to proliferate. And they can be very inviting. At first glance, they may seem to meet your customer's needs perfectly. But in reality, they're designed for one purpose. To carve off a piece of your already-existing business. To cut up the sales and profit pie into smaller and smaller pieces.

Now that may be one reason to invent a product, but it's not the 3M reason. When we invent a product, we invent new business for you. We bake another totally new pie.

For example, there was no such thing as a sticky backed note until we invented Post-it brand notes. Your customers bought them by the millions and a new business was born.

Today, through constant attention to innovation, 3M expands your profits into six different arenas: tape, notes, diskettes, binding, visual products and mailroom systems.

That's one way to tell the difference between companies that talk quality, and companies that *are* quality.

Questions or comments? Write Commercial Office Supply Division/3M, 223-3S, 3M Center, St. Paul, MN 55144-1000.

3M

If something doesn't work right, it's no bargain at any price.

In today's tight economy, you may have customers requesting the so-called bargain products. Cheaper versions of quality products you and they have been quite happy with. But suppose, in your efforts to service these budget-conscious customers, you sell them products of questionable quality. Who pays the price then?

You do.

You lose money on returns. You lose time and money on extra service. And, even worse, you risk losing the loyalty of the very same customers you were working so hard to please.

At 3M, we work hard to prevent that eventuality. Unlike other manufacturers, we don't use you and your customers as a test market.

Instead, we spend time and money up-front, building consistent quality into our products before we sell them.

Ask yourself. When was the last time you had a Post-it™ brand note returned, or a roll of Scotch® brand Tape? We believe that kind of product integrity is something your customers won't mind paying for, in the long run.

Questions or comments? Write Commercial Office Supply Division/3M, 223-3S, 3M Center, St. Paul, MN 55144-1000.

3M

A marketplace based solely on price is built on a very shaky foundation.

Right now, in the office products marketplace, a dangerous game is being played. It's called the discount price game and (as we've seen time and time again) it's a game that has no winners.

Consider this. You're operating at 25% gross margin, and you're tempted to cut your selling price by only 10% to take on a copycat product. You'll find you need to sell 50% more units to maintain the same cash margin you earn now. Sure, your budget-conscious customer pays less for the same amount of product, but what happens to your profits over the long run?

You lose.

That's why, at 3M, we work to keep our value (and your profits) up. And we can do that because it's always been our policy to provide your customers with new products, innovative products. Products that really are worth the price. In short, 3M sells quality, and sells it hard. If you do the same, we can avoid costly price cutting.

And both come out winners.

Questions or comments? Write Commercial Office Supply Division/3M, 223-3S, 3M Center, St. Paul, MN 55144-1000.

3M

159

Art Director: Sally Wagner
Photographer: Kent Severson
Writer: Emily Scott
Creative Director: Tom Weyl
Client: 3M Commercial Office Supplies Division
Agency: Martin/Williams Advertising Inc.

160

Art Director: Pam Conboy
Photographer: Dennis Manarchy
Writer: Lee Schmidt
Creative Director: Tom Weyl
Client: 3M Health Care Specialties Division
Agency: Martin/Williams Advertising Inc.

Every company has its own personality.

Maybe it's conservative.

Or flamboyant.

Or maybe it's conservative and flamboyant.

The point is your office furniture should be able to say: "This is the kind of company we are."

Something Knoll Office systems and seating happen to do very well.

They can suit almost any personality. Open plan office, private office or data processing center. From the receptionist to the CEO.

And to give all those offices their own personalities, you can choose from wood veneers like mahogany and maple. Fabrics and plastic laminates. And colors from beige to shades that can please the most flamboyant chairman of the board.

At Knoll, we offer everything from systems to seating and from desks to textiles. As well as the service that makes managing your office a lot easier.

Call 1-800-633-0034 to talk with a representative or authorized dealer nearest you.

(We promise he won't have green hair.)

Knoll

Once you tie the knot, that's it. It's your office furniture.

For better or for worse, in growth periods and in slow periods, in open plans and in closed offices, 'til obsolescence do you part.

In other words, it had better last.

Something Knoll Office Systems are engineered to do very well. All of them are built with the most durable steel, wood veneers, laminates and fabrics. And all of them can change as your company changes.

Morrison can quickly create virtually any kind of work space. From open to data processing to private offices with movable full height walls.

Hannah can hide unwieldy wires and cables better than any other office system.

Zapf can give everyone in the company an open, elegant, office.

And speaking of commitment, there are our service people. Team Knoll. They'll be there for you before installation to do everything from writing specifications to developing typical workstations. During installation, to supervise assembly. And after installation for care and maintenance training with your facilities people.

At Knoll, we offer everything from systems to seating and from desks to textiles. As well as the service that makes managing your office a lot easier. Call 1-800-633-0034 to talk with a representative or authorized dealer nearest you.

We'll start the courtship.

It'll make it a lot easier for you to say, "I do."

Knoll

161

Art Director: Gary Goldsmith
Designer: Gary Goldsmith
Photographer: Gil Cope
Writer: Neal Gomberg
Creative Director: Gary Goldsmith
Client: Knoll International
Agency: Goldsmith/Jeffrey
Account Supervisor: Bob Jeffrey

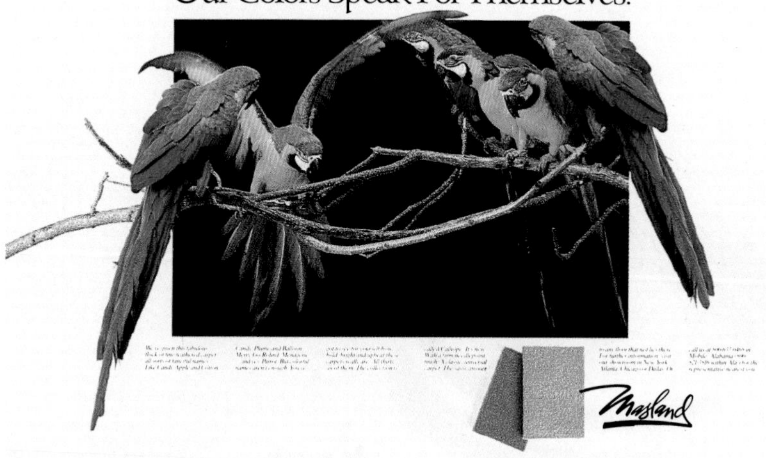

162
Art Director: Dick Henderson
Photographer: Eric Henderson, Yann Arthus-Bertrand
Writer: Jim Cole, Ken Lewis
Creative Director: Dick Henderson, Jim Cole
Client: Masland Carpets
Agency: Cole, Henderson, Drake Inc.

SOME PEOPLE WOULD BET THEIR LIFE ON METAL FRAMES.

THAT'S WHY SIXTEEN MILLION PEOPLE WEAR THESE.

UNIVERSAL

FOR SOME PEOPLE, METAL FRAME STYLES AREN'T A BIG DEAL.

BUT TO SIXTEEN MILLION OTHERS IT IS.

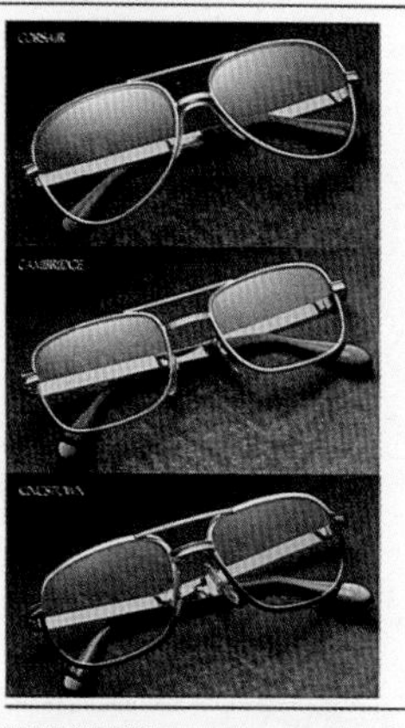

UNIVERSAL

SOME PEOPLE THINK METAL FRAME STYLES ARE A BUNCH OF BULLY.

SIXTEEN MILLION OTHERS WOULD STRONGLY DISAGREE.

UNIVERSAL

163

Art Director: John Housley
Photographer: Myron
Illustrator/Artist: Rob Bolster
Writer: Todd Diamond
Creative Director: John Housley
Client: Universal Optical
Agency: Wooding & Housley

"I'm the studio hacker. I've got just about anything you need right on disc — models, elephants, raspberries in January, bearded ladies... But if you want something really wild I hit the streets. A couple of weeks ago Mitch and I rounded up a turquoise bowling ball, a tattooed arm, punk spikes (that was easy), a 1953 Boy Scouts Manual, and oh yeah, the bear's head. So sometimes it takes more than an IBM to get what you're after. Which brings me to how I ended up here in the first place. I used to ride for Bicycle Express, the delivery service. I got to like Berthiaume's. They were pretty cool. So when they asked me to program I said sure. And I traded in my wheels for some discs."

BERTHIAUME

"It wasn't deep sea photography, but it was as close as I want to get. We're on the beach in Santa Barbara, shooting Levi's, and everything looks great—we got L.A. talent and Weby's cinnamon rolls. The sun's drifting into the Pacific leaving this hazy kind of twilight; terrific light. But there's one catch—Berthiaume's Angle. All these perspectives to choose from, and he wants to shoot from the shoreline. Nevermind that the tide's coming in. Nevermind that we're all going to be snorkeling in an hour. So here comes the water, cold water. Berthiaume's shooting like a maniac, going rung by rung up a ladder. Me, I'm loading film, trying not to get strangled by kelp or sacked by the next wave. In the end Berthiaume got wet, too, which is only right. But the film was fine, thanks to my U.S. Navy Approved Water Tight Containers. And the shot? Terrific. Stunning, in fact. And I have to say, the angle made it."

Kevin Peterson
Production Assistant
Tom Berthiaume Studio

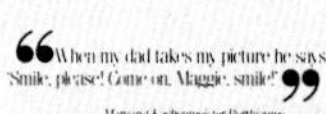

BERTHIAUME

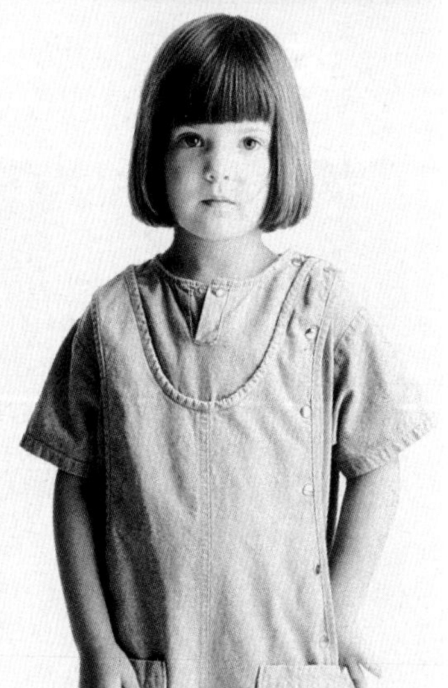

"When my dad takes my picture he says, 'Smile, please! Come on, Maggie, smile!'"

BERTHIAUME

164

Art Director: Susan Kruskopf
Designer: Susan Kruskopf
Photographer: Tom Berthiaume
Writer: John Olson, Tom Berthiaume
Client: Tom Berthiaume Studio
Agency: Kruskopf Olson Advertising

PROMOTION

The Art Directors Club, Inc.
250 Park Avenue South
New York, NY 10003
CONTROL TAG
ENTRY FEES
The Art Directors Club
67th Annual Exhibition
250 Park Avenue South
New York, NY 10003
Fill in the appropriate information below. Enclose check or money order payable to The Art Directors Club, Inc. and place in package with entries. Entries received without checks will be discarded. The Art Directors Club is not responsible for the loss of original art. Entries are not returnable.
U.S. Postage
New York, NY

monster off Duxbury Beach.

A real grand-daddy of a fish.

By Russ T. Scupper

The African fisherman had never seen a fish like it. Neither had the people at the market where they tried to sell it. Makes sense. The fish was a monster and it had been thought to have been extinct for millions of years.

WEATHER: Chance of rain, chance of sun, chance of monsoon, chance of melon size hail

Atlantis revisited.

By Tommy Cod

The famed city of Atlantis. What ever happened to this mythical town? Well, that's a topic that's been debated all week at the annual Atlantis Symposium in Newport, Rhode Island. Among the different theories offered are that Atlantis was a victim of an epidemic; that it went condo; or that the citizens moved to a different town with a better public school system.

By B.

The episo series Harry will be ism a origin that s terror revers to take specie George Mark design can wit

Printed in U.S.A. on Scott Vellum Offset Cream 70 lb.

Fish Stories

S.D. Warren Company,

a Subsidiary of Scott Paper Company 225 Franklin Street, Boston, MA 02110

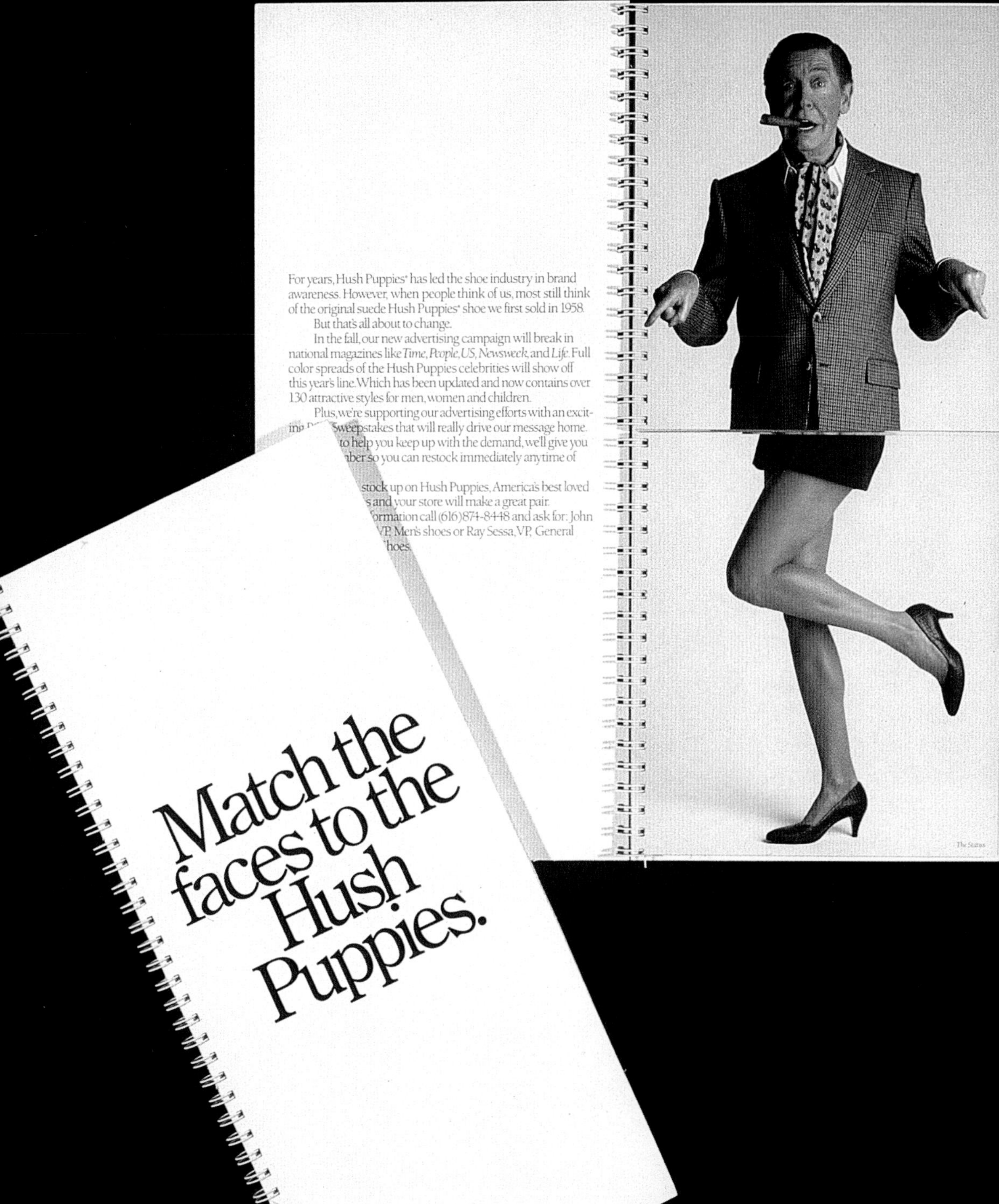

166 Distinctive Merit

Art Director: Mark Johnson
Designer: Mark Johnson
Photographer: Dan Lamb, Rick Dublin
Writer: Tom McElligott
Creative Director: Tom McElligott
Client: Hush Puppies
Agency: Fallon McElligott

167
Art Director: Bob Barrie
Designer: Bob Barrie
Writer: Mike Lescarbeau
Creative Director: Tom McElligott
Client: Continental Illinois
Agency: Fallon McElligott

168
Art Director: Jill Hawkins
Designer: Jill Hawkins, Steve Mach
Photographer: Michael Johnson
Creative Director: Jill Hawkins
Client: Ellis Inc.
Design Firm: Jill Hawkins Design
Printer: Brodnax Printing

169
Art Director: Rob Dalton
Designer: Rob Dalton
Writer: Sam Avery
Creative Director: Tom McElligott
Client: Coleman
Agency: Fallon McElligott

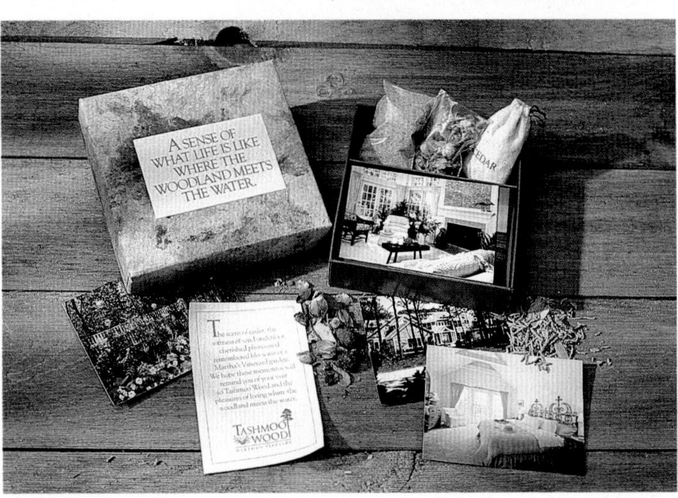

170
Art Director: Laurel Emery
Designer: Laurel Emery
Photographer: Jan Staller, Claude Furones
Writer: Lesley Teitelbaum
Client: High Street Development
Agency: Great Scott Advertising Co., Inc.
Account Supervisor: Lorraine Borden
Account Executive: Bob Baldwin

171
Art Director: Kimberly Baer
Designer: Barbara Cooper
Photographer: Jeff Corwin
Writer: Candace Pearson
Client: Jeff Corwin
Design Firm: Kimberly Baer Design Associates
Printer: Atomic Press

172
Art Director: Charlotte White
Designer: Charlotte White
Writer: Ann Waterfall
Creative Director: Peter Taflan
Client: Edward Weck & Co., Inc.
Agency: Peter Taflan Marketing Communications Inc.

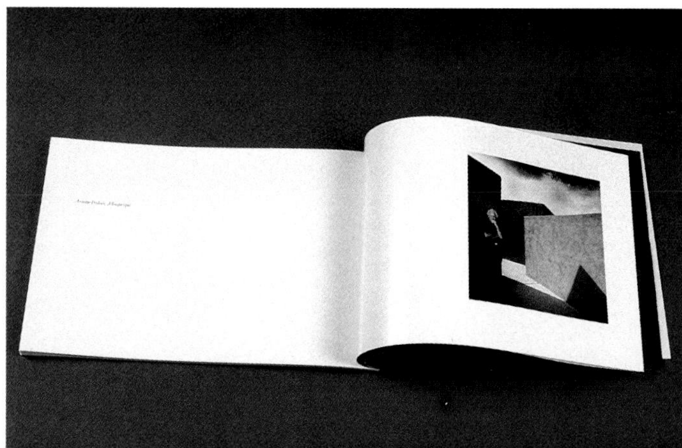

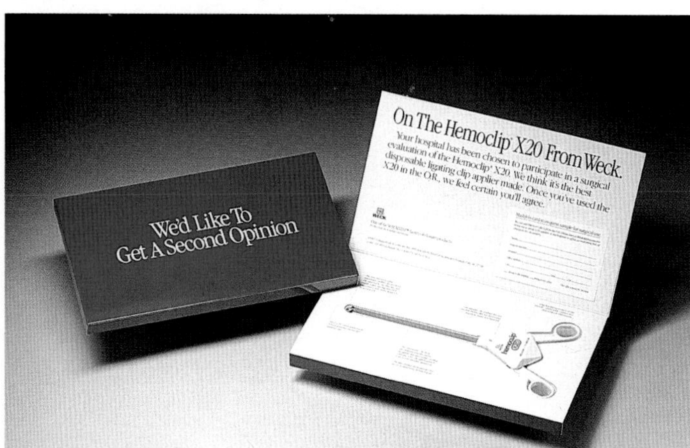

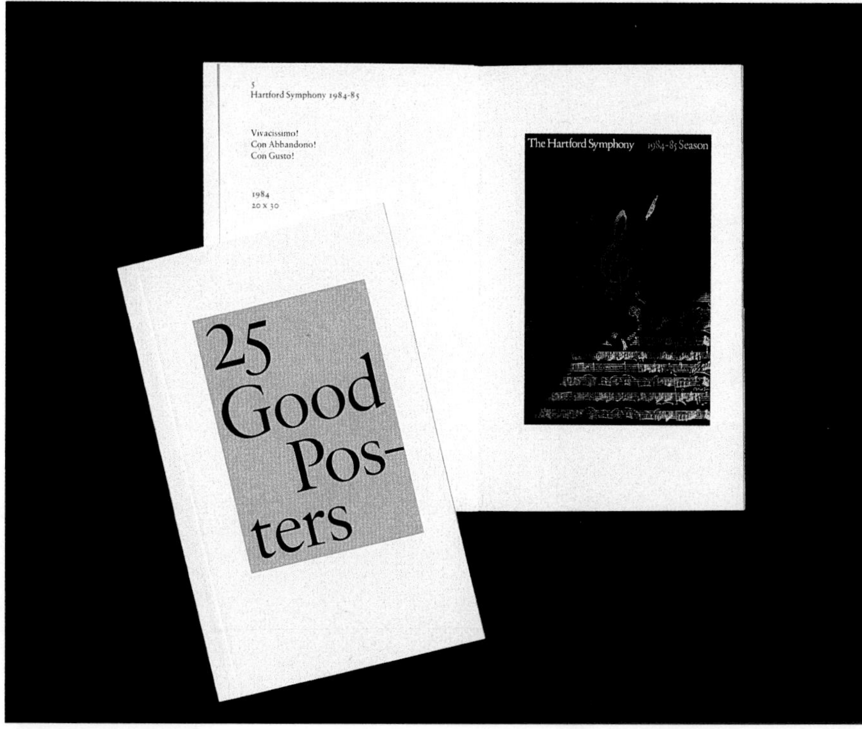

173
Art Director: Peter Good
Designer: Peter Good
Writer: Peter Good, Gordon Bowman
Creative Director: Peter Good
Client: Peter Good
Design Firm: Peter Good Graphic Design
Paper: Westvaco Paper
Printer: Hennegan Printing

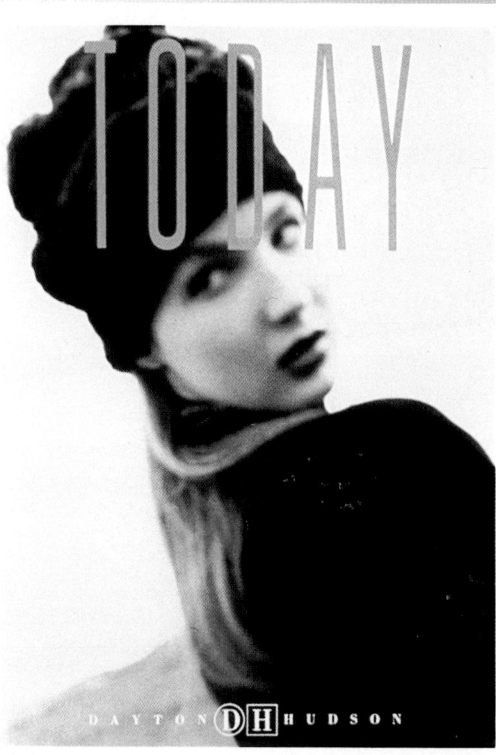

174
Art Director: Robert Valentine
Designer: Robert Valentine
Photographer: William Garrett, James Wojcik
Writer: Vicky Rossi
Cathy Berg Ostlie
Client: Dayton Hudson Department Store Co.
Agency: Dayton Hudson
Fashion Stylist: Mary Bergtold

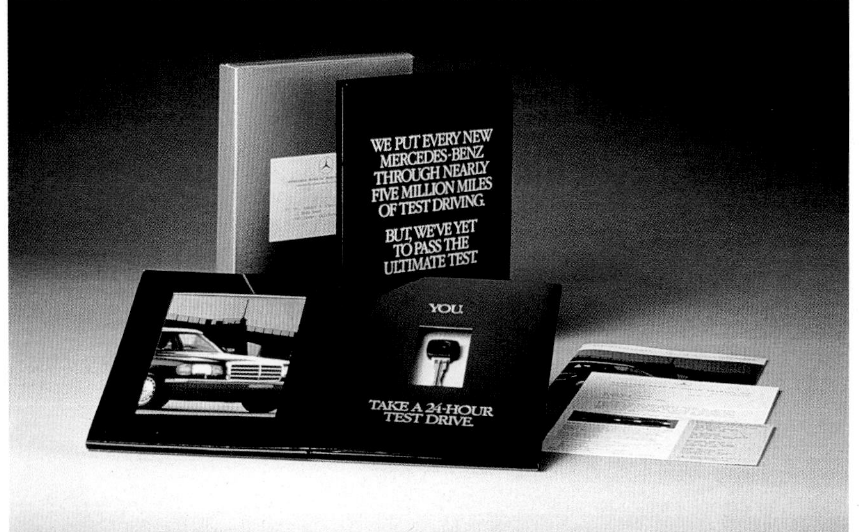

175
Art Director: Lynda Decker, Marvin Fried
Writer: Carolyn Crimmins, Judy Hultquist
Creative Director: Tim Fenton
Client: Mercedes-Benz
Agency: McCaffrey & McCall Direct Marketing
Account Supervisor: Winifred Barnes
Advertiser's Supervisor: Gerd Klauss

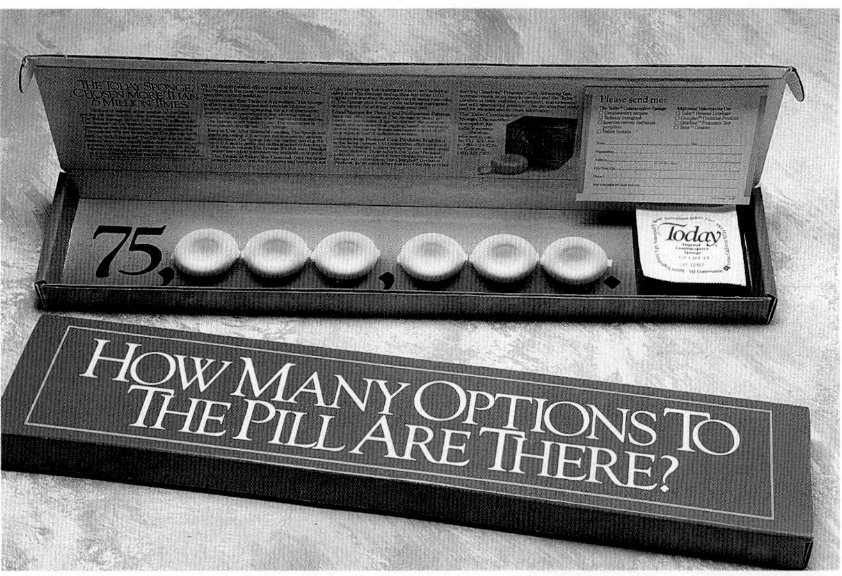

176
Art Director: William Johnson
Designer: William Johnson
Photographer: John Svoboda
Writer: Bob Pettit
Creative Director: William Johnson
Client: Today Sponge, VLI Corp.
Agency: Forsythe, Marcelli, Johnson
Printer: Greens Printing

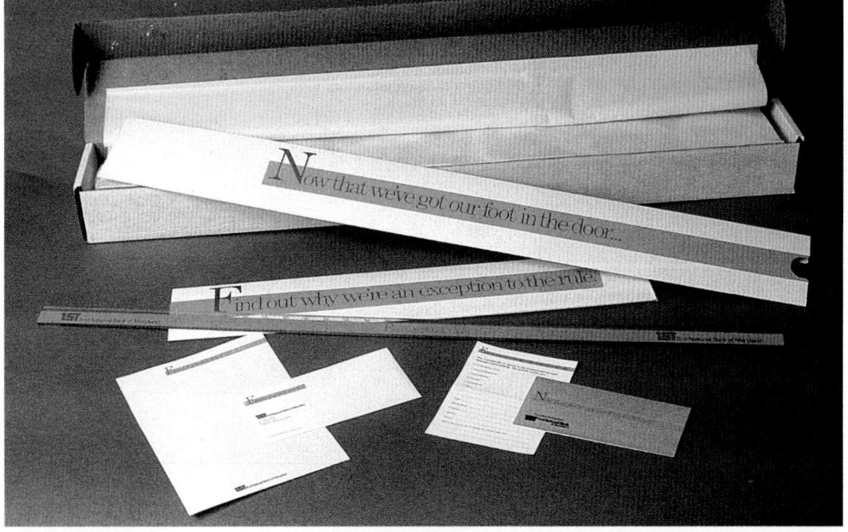

177
Art Director: David Crowder
Designer: Karen Klinedinst
Writer: Chris Nufer
Client: First National Bank of Maryland
Design Firm: Crowder Communications

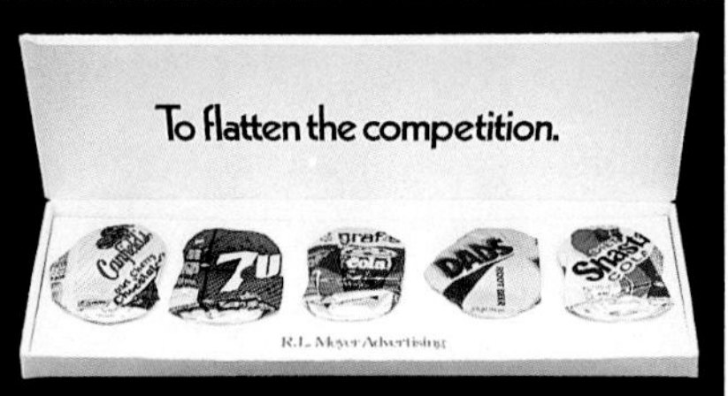

178
Art Director: Rachel Stephens
Designer: Rachel Stephens
Writer: Mike Roozen
Creative Director: Effie Meyer
Client: Jolly Good Soda
Agency: R. L. Meyer Advertising

179
Art Director: Seymour Chwast, Don Povie
Designer: Seymour Chwast
Editor: Steve Heller
Client: Mohawk Paper Mills
Design Firm: The Push Pin Group

180
Art Director: Thom Marchionna
Designer: Rich Nelson
Photographer: Bruce Ashley
Writer: Rob Price
Creative Director: Thom Marchionna
Design Firm: Apple Creative Services
Production Manager: Barbara Crow

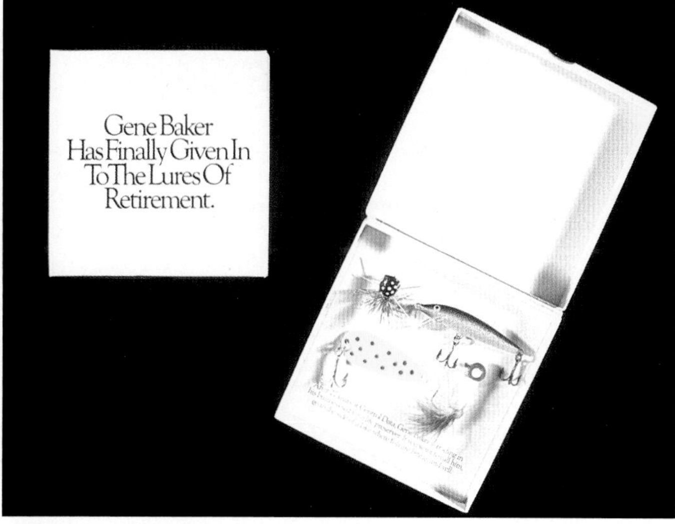

181
Art Director: Woody Kay
Designer: Doreen Velmer
Writer: Ernie Schenck
Creative Director: Ernie Schenck, Woody Ray
Client: Carl Nelson
Agency: Pagano, Schenck & Kay

182
Art Director: Rob Dalton
Designer: Rob Dalton
Writer: Mike Lescarbeau
Creative Director: Tom McElligott
Client: Gene Baker
Agency: Fallon McElligott

183
Art Director: Angela Dunkle
Designer: Angela Dunkle
Writer: Jamie Barrett
Creative Director: Tom McElligott
Client: The Wall Street Journal
Agency: Fallon McElligott

184
Art Director: Rex Peteet
Designer: Rex Peteet
Illustrator/Artist: Jack Unruh, Rex Peteet, John Evans
Writer: Mary Langridge, Rex Peteet
Client: International Paper Co.
Design Firm: Sibley/Peteet Design

185
Art Director: Jim Newbury
Designer: Jim Newbury
Illustrator/Artist: Theo Rudnak
Writer: Roger Richards
Creative Director: Ken Haas, Jerry Sullivan
Client: The Griffin Co.
Agency: Sullivan, Haas, Coyle

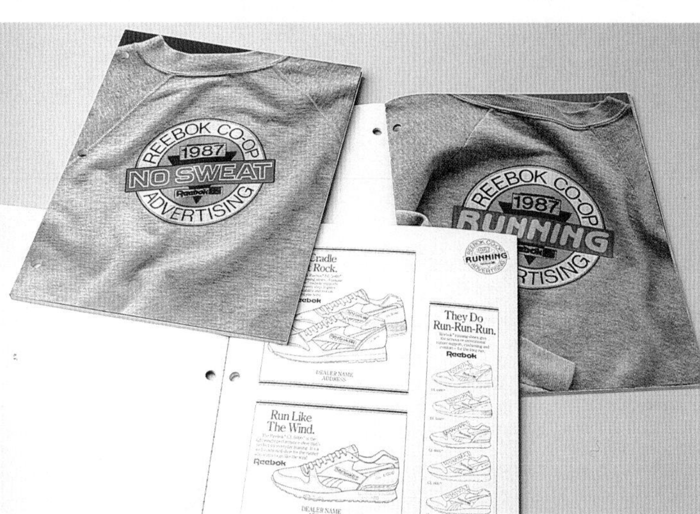

186
Art Director: Steve Snider
Designer: Steve Snider
Photographer: Marty Paul
Illustrator/Artist: Judith Dufour Love
Writer: Brian Flood
Editor: Geri Noonan
Creative Director: Steve Snider
Client: Reebok International Ltd.
Design Firm: Snider Design

187

Art Director: Lee Arters
Designer: Lee Arters
Photographer: Jade Albert, Nick Basilion
Writer: Adam Hanft
Creative Director: Don Slater
Client: SONY
Agency: Slater, Hanft, Martin Inc.
Account Supervisor: Allan Cohen

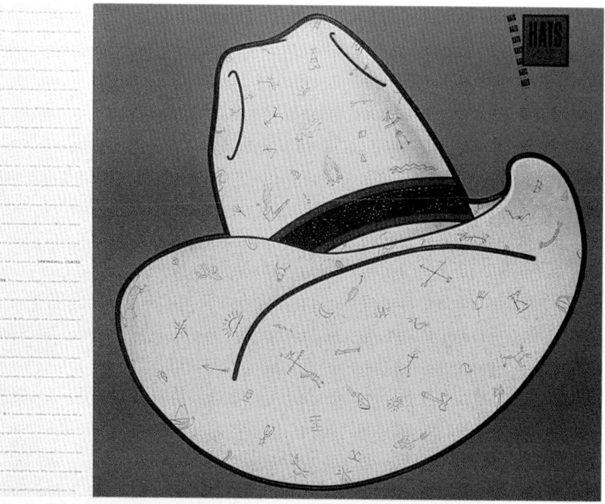

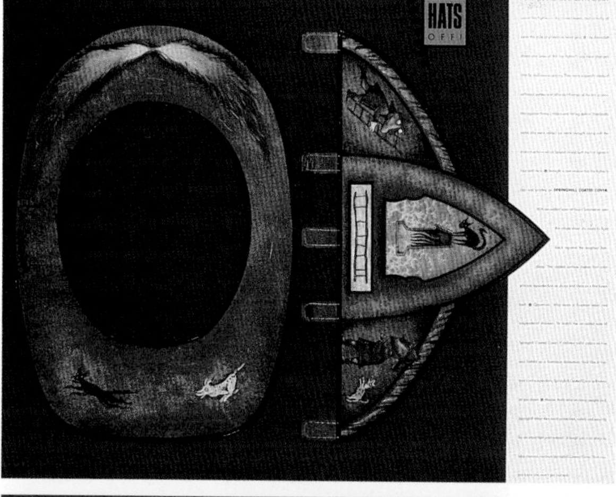

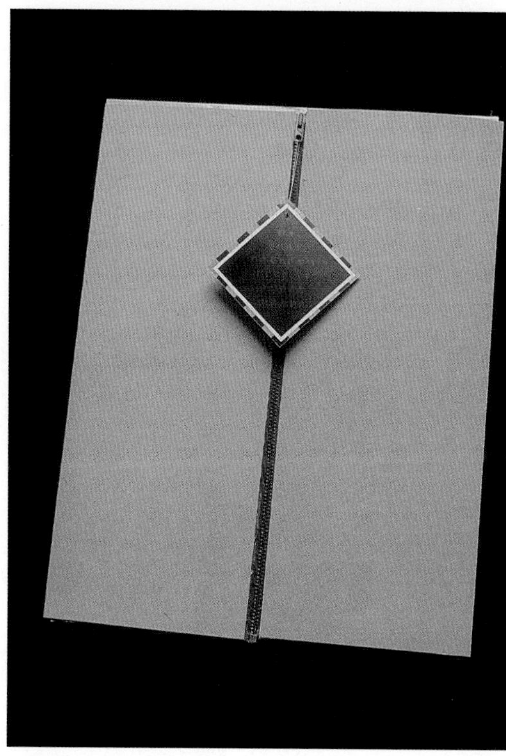

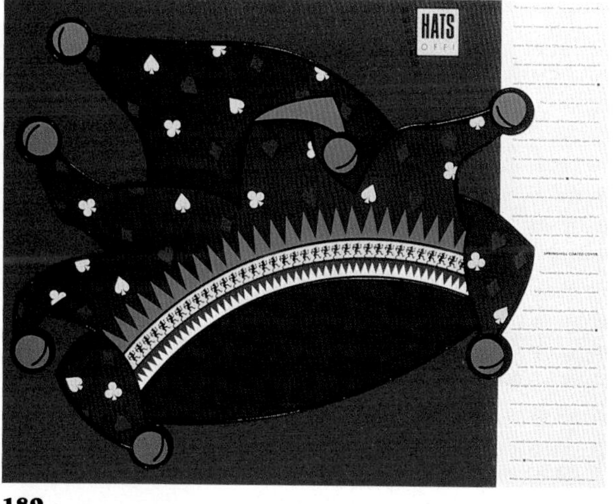

188

Art Director: Cheryl Heller
Designer: Cheryl Heller, Rose Disanto
Photographer: Herb Ritts
Writer: Jerry Cronin
Creative Director: Cheryl Heller
Client: Reebok
Agency: Heller Breene

189

Art Director: Kathy Sobb
Designer: Kathy Sobb
Illustrator/Artist: Molly Leach, Lane Smith, Kathy Sobb
Writer: James Smith
Client: International Paper Co.
Design Firm: Sobb & Associates
Print Production: Laurence Communications

190
Art Director: Cabell Harris
Illustrator/Artist: Kelly Alder
Writer: Ken Hines
Creative Director: Ken Hines
Client: Clydes Restaurant Group
Agency: Lawler Ballard Advertising

191
Art Director: Deb Miner
Designer: Deb Miner
Client: Donaldson's Department Store
Design Firm: McCool & Co.

192
Art Director: Glenn Dayton
Designer: Trish Stratton
Writer: Arthur Bradshaw
Creative Director: Bradshaw/Dayton
Client: The Beverly Heritage Hotels/Calmark
Agency: Dayton Associates

193
Art Director: Charles S. Anderson
Designer: Charles S. Anderson
Illustrator/Artist: Charles S. Anderson, Lynn Schulte
Client: Chaps/Ralph Lauren
Design Firm: The Duffy Design Group

194
Art Director: Ark Stein
Designer: Dennie Moore
Illustrator/Artist: Max Gisko
Creative Director: David Oke, J. B. Moore, Rob Caughlan
Client: California Highway Patrol
Agency: Roanoke Co., Inc.
Design Firm: Studio Silicon

195
Art Director: Joe Duffy
Designer: Joe Duffy
Illustrator/Artist: Joe Duffy, Lynn Schulte
Writer: Chuck Carlson
Client: Chaps/Ralph Lauren
Design Firm: The Duffy Design Group

NEWSPAPER EDITORIAL

Book life!

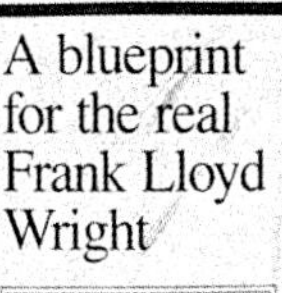

A blueprint for the real Frank Lloyd Wright

MANY MASKS: A LIFE OF FRANK LLOYD WRIGHT
By Brendan Gill
Putnam's, $22.95, illus., 576 pages
REVIEWED BY ROGER STARR

Some years ago, it seemed entertaining to play an informal parlor game in which each player was invited to name one of the 10 most overrated people of the 20th century. Some names were certain to be heard whenever the game was played, if only because the players who named them were unsure of the reason for their notoriety. Such a name was Bernard Baruch. Inevitably he was assumed to be overrated because no one present could claim to know exactly what he had done to deserve attention other than sit on a bench in Lafayette Park, feed pigeons and box as a young amateur.

Other names were controversial, even though everyone knew what they were supposed to have done. Albert Schweitzer's name was one such. Everyone knew that he opened a hospital for native Africans at Lambarane. Was it a good hospital he had established, or only a bit of goodwill? Had he actually cured patients? Since we couldn't answer, he went on the list with no protest.

The name that inevitably provoked the most heated controversy was that of Frank Lloyd Wright. Was he, as John Dos Passos told readers of "The Big Money," "a patriarch of the new building not without honor except in his own country"?

Or was he a charlatan, a mountebank, a womanizer, professionally overrated but with a positive genius for attracting attention to himself? Was he truly the greatest American architect of the 20th century? Or did critics and collectors overrate his artistic achievements in an effort to ignore more pertinent defects in his character, papering over their shame in having succumbed to his tendentious charm?

Brendan Gill, novelist, drama critic for The New Yorker magazine and a citizen with a distinguished and active public career devoted to the preservation of that city's older significant buildings, takes on, in this fascinating book, the difficult task of bringing into simultaneous focus the two contrasting views of Wright, otherwise identified as "masks."

Mr. Gill acknowledges a bond of friendship and affection between himself and Wright, whom he first met in the postwar years when Wright, after a few signal triumphs and a long train of tragedies, mistakes, failures and disgraces, was truly coming into belated prominence. Wright died in 1959 at the peak of his comeback.

What gives "Many Masks: A Life of Frank Lloyd Wright" a special interest, beyond the skill, patience and sensitivity of Mr. Gill's pursuit of a just balance and the immaculate prose in which he conveys it, is the suggestion that the writer and his subject share a deeper affinity. Brendan Gill himself demonstrated at a very early age immense talent as a novelist, just as Wright demonstrated his genius in architecture and drawing. Wright's up-and-down-and-up career was the inevitable result of his inability to put aside his stunning verbal skills of personal persuasion and salesmanship, and the fascinating challenge of relations with other real people, to concentrate entirely on the technical craft of architecture.

It requires no great stretch of the imagination to believe that Mr. Gill recognizes in himself a similarly distracting pull toward public life, human companionship and public involvement and away from the lonelier literary fields for which he early showed so marked a gift. The tension between the love of communicating in person and the loneliness of most writing may have inspired Mr. Gill's

see WRIGHT, *page E10*

Best Sellers

■ Publisher's Weekly Hardcover Best Sellers are compiled from data from large-city bookstores, bookstore chains and local best-seller lists across the United States.

FICTION

1. **PRESUMED INNOCENT**, by Scott Turow. Farrar, Straus & Giroux, $18.95
2. **PATRIOT GAMES**, by Tom Clancy. Putnam, $19.95
3. **HEAVEN AND HELL**, by John Jakes. Harcourt Brace Jovanovich, $19.95
4. **LEAVING HOME: A COLLECTION OF LAKE WOBEGON STORIES**, by Garrison Keillor. Viking, $18.95
5. **BELOVED**, by Toni Morrison. Knopf, $18.95
6. **KALEIDOSCOPE**, by Danielle Steel. Delacorte Press, $19.95
7. **MISERY**, by Stephen King. Viking, $18.95
8. **SARUM**, by Edward Rutherfurd. Crown, $19.95
9. **HOT FLASHES**, by Barbara Raskin. St. Martin's, $18.95
10. **THE NEW BREED**, by W.E.B. Griffin. Putnam, $16.95
11. **LEGACY**, by James Michener. Random House, $18.95
12. **VILLAINY VICTORIOUS**, by L. Ron Hubbard. Bridge Publications, $18.95
13. **TEAM YANKEE: A NOVEL OF WORLD WAR III**, by Harold Coyle. Presidio Press, $17.95
14. **FREEDOM**, by William Safire. Doubleday, $24.95
15. **THE PRINCE OF TIDES**, by Pat Conroy. Houghton Mifflin, $19.95

NON-FICTION

1. **VEIL: THE SECRET WARS OF THE CIA, 1981-1987**, by Bob Woodward. Simon & Schuster, $21.95
2. **SPYCATCHER: THE CANDID AUTOBIOGRAPHY OF A SENIOR INTELLIGENCE OFFICER**, by Peter Wright with Paul Greengrass. Viking, $19.95
3. **TIME FLIES**, by Bill Cosby. Dolphin Doubleday, $16.95
4. **THE GREAT DEPRESSION OF 1990**, by Ravi Batra. Simon & Schuster, $17.95
5. **MAN OF THE HOUSE: THE LIFE AND POLITICAL MEMOIRS OF SPEAKER TIP O'NEILL**, with William Novak. Random House, $19.95
6. **THE CLOSING OF THE AMERICAN MIND**, by Allan Bloom. Simon & Schuster, $18.95
7. **FAMILY: THE TIES THAT BIND . . . AND GAG!**, by Erma Bombeck. McGraw-Hill, $15.95
8. **IT'S ALL IN THE PLAYING**, by Shirley MacLaine. Bantam, $15.95
9. **THE MAKING OF "THE AFRICAN QUEEN,"** by Katharine Hepburn. Knopf, $15.95
10. **LOVE MEDICINE & MIRACLES**, by Bernie S. Siegel. Harper & Row, $17.95
11. **STRAIGHT ON TILL MORNING: THE BIOGRAPHY OF BERYL MARKHAM**, by Mary S. Lovell. St. Martin's, $16.95
12. **THE 8-WEEK CHOLESTEROL CURE**, by Robert W. Kowalski. Harper & Row, $15.95
13. **CULTURAL LITERACY**, by E.D. Hirsch Jr. Houghton Mifflin, $16.95
14. **HOW TO MARRY THE MAN OF YOUR CHOICE**, by Margaret Kent. Warner, $14.95
15. **OUT OF CONTROL: CONFESSIONS OF AN NFL CASUALTY**, by Thomas "Hollywood" Henderson and Peter Knobler. Putnam, $17.95

Walesa and the struggle of Poland

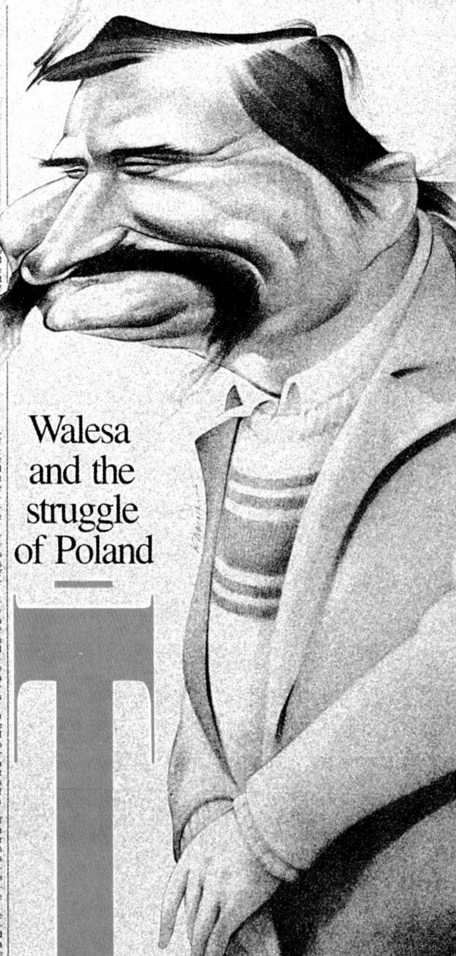

Illustration by John Kascht, The Washington Times

A WAY OF HOPE: AN AUTOBIOGRAPHY
By Lech Walesa
Henry Holt, $19.95, illus., 325 pages

LECH WALESA AND HIS POLAND
By Mary Craig
Continuum, $18.95, illus., 326 pages

REVIEWED BY JANUSZ BUGAJSKI

The long-awaited autobiography of Polish Solidarity leader Lech Walesa has finally appeared in English. Based on a recent French translation and the Polish original, Mr. Walesa's "A Way of Hope: An Autobiography" provides an important testimony by the electrician who, as a free-trade union leader, rocked the communist world and raised the hopes of millions of downtrodden working people in the Soviet bloc.

In 1980 Lech Walesa captured the imagination of the world when he became a visible symbol of a heroic struggle waged by an imprisoned society against a self-perpetuating dictatorship. Mr. Walesa's inspiring leadership qualities and his insistence on peaceful protest and negotiated compromise, despite government provocations and violence, were recognized internationally in 1983 when, much to the chagrin of the Warsaw regime, he was awarded the Nobel Peace Prize.

In Poland, Mr. Walesa continues to be admired and respected as the ordinary worker who stood up to the Communist Party monolith and refused to be corrupted, manipulated or silenced. Contrary to communist claims, he represented and still represents genuine national aspirations.

The government of Gen. Wojciech Jaruzelski has tried every trick in the book to discredit and eliminate "private citizen" Walesa as a political force. Even before martial law, the government endeavored to bribe him with offers of a plush villa in exchange for his chairmanship of the official labor unions. After a state of war was declared in December 1981, the party-military junta pressured him to collaborate. When he refused, the authorities concocted a Walesa look-alike on TV broadcasts to fool the public into believing he was involved in serious negotiations with the regime and supported Gen. Jaruzelski. When these underhanded maneuvers failed, they tried to entice him into exile; he declined to abandon his country in the middle of crisis.

Upon Mr. Walesa's release from an 11-month internment in 1982, the authorities launched a campaign of character assassination typical of the Leninist media, accusing Mr. Walesa of sexual infidelity and financial misconduct. Few were deceived, and the attacks dissipated. Despite constant harassment, around-the-clock surveillance and the barrage of accusations and disinformation, Mr. Walesa was untainted in the eyes of the public. Charges of unsavory links with "the reds," one of the milder derogatory terms for the party among Polish workers, did not stick to him.

Mr. Walesa is a doer, not a writer; but despite performing his job in the Gdansk shipyards, devoting much of his time to a continuous stream of visitors and coordinating the dispersed Solidarity movement, he was determined to record the maelstrom of events into which fate had thrust him. "A Way of Hope" furnishes details on his family background interspersed with descriptions of major events in recent Polish history, and relates his frequent confrontations with the communist authorities — at school, at work, with local officials and government dignitaries.

He gives a vivid firsthand account of the tragic demonstrations of workers in December 1970 and contrasts them with the triumphant "solidarity strikes" of August 1980. Mr. Walesa was on the frontline of both episodes as an organizer, participant, victim and eventual victor.

He was a prominent leader of the 1970 shipyard protests when scores of workers were massacred in the streets by the party police force. It was this trauma more than any other that opened his eyes to the regime's brutality, treachery and mendacity, and solidified his determination to honor his slain workmates by actively pursuing the Poland of their dreams.

Since the start of his employment at the shipyards, Mr. Walesa has campaigned on behalf of his workmates to remedy their grievances against management and their demeaning treatment by party bosses. What shines through his narrative, as well as the recollections of fellow workers and union officials included in this volume, is Mr. Walesa's stubborn individualism, his refusal to play by anyone else's rules, or to bow to any worldly authorities undeserving of his trust and loyalty.

The book charts the growth of the free-trade-union movement from a mere six members in 1976, to 600 in 1978, to several thousand in 1979, to 10 million in 1980, when the dam burst and workers' discontent spilled over. Solidarity's 500 "legal" days are detailed, from the vantage point of one of the key participants torn between often conflicting priorities — union cohesion, avoidance of violent clashes — and negotiations with a procrastinating regime plotting its counterrevolution.

During this period, and for the first time in communist Poland, workers were, in his words, "able to take charge of their own problems instead of being helpless dupes, mere

see WALESA, *page E10*

The good & the 'bad': A look at Soviet life

A DAY IN THE LIFE OF THE SOVIET UNION
By Rick Smolan and David Cohen
Introduction by Harrison Salisbury
Collins, $39.95, illus., 240 pages
REVIEWED BY PHILIP GOLD

"A Day in the Life of the Soviet Union" is a beautiful book. But then, nobody ever claimed that Russia wasn't "radiantly photogenic," as the narrative puts it. These are attractive people. But then, few have claimed that the U.S.S.R. is populated entirely by pathologically dour Marxist-Leninist fanatics.

Some will find in "A Day in the Life of the Soviet Union" a necessary reminder of our common humanity. Others doubtless will excoriate the book as an attempt to sugar over fundamental and perhaps irreconcilable differences between two systems, two powers, two philosophies. I found it both more complex and somewhat sadder. But then, I'm Russian by ancestry, or so I've been told; and it is indeed possible to be at least moderately homesick for places you've never been.

The book is one of a series of coffee-table photologs that attempt to capture the soul of a country by sending dozens of photographers to shoot it on the same day. Previous volumes in the series have covered the United States, Japan, Australia and Canada.

This project was conceived several years ago, but in a country as "morbidly camera-shy" as the Soviet Union, it took Mr. Gorbachev's glasnost to make it happen. On May 15, 1987, 100 photographers (50 Western, 50 Soviet bloc) spread out over the U.S.S.R. to use up 50 rolls of Kodachrome each. The result, as retired New York Times columnist Harrison Salisbury informs us in the introduction, is "the bad along with the good." According to Mr. Salisbury, "almost all of Russia is here."

The good is cheerily humane. Lots of babies. Lots of children, either studiously in class or exercising with a combination of energy and diffidence. Young men, military and naval cadets, either studiously in class or exercising with a combination of energy and diffidence or marching with a somehow non-threatening, wholly admirable martial devotion. The ethnics appear in typical travel-brochure style — dancing, fishing, playing games. The obligatory ballet shots also are there, and, of course, so is Russia's high-tech version of the Bolshoi, the space program. One also finds a yuppie (Soviet-style) wedding in Siberia.

Perhaps most striking are the elders. Who can look at these old men and women without an involuntary shudder at what they witnessed and experienced? Thanks to Messrs. Stalin and Hitler, there are not enough Soviet senior citizens around to place an insupportable burden on the state pension system. Two old couples, one on the day of their 50th wedding anniversary (he wears a medal), speak eloquently of bonds forged during a time of troubles whose severity few Westerners can even imagine.

The "bad" presented in this book seems absolutely inane. A peek inside a Soviet prison looks, as Mr. Salisbury admits, more like a U.S. military camp than part of the Gulag Archipelago. We see a few of the "by-products of glasnost" — body-building juvenile delinquents, some quasi-spacy teens at a rock concert, a motorcyclist restrained by the local constabulary.

And along with the inane, the inept. In the control room of a nuclear power plant, a photographer notes three emergency shutdown switches "secured with string and sealing wax." Another photographer, delighted to discover an office that still uses the abacus for its ac-

see SOVIET, *Page E9*

197

Art Director: Greg Ryan
Designer: Greg Ryan
Illustrator/Artist: Nancy Doniger
Editor: Nora Kerr
Creative Director: Tom Bodkin
Client: The New York Times
Publisher: The New York Times
Publication: The New York Times, "Travel"

The New York Times
Travel
Sunday, April 12, 1987
10

SPECIAL ISSUE
Around the World In Springtime

Ireland
Pottery of the west reflects its setting. By Christine S. Cozzens.
19

Denmark
Pedaling from inn to inn on Fyn and beyond. By Rita D. Jacobs.
9

The Caribbean
Off-season guide: Savoring spicy Guadeloupe. By Andrew Sinclair/ Island amenities. By Frank J. Prial/ Reduced rates from Anguilla to St. Thomas. By Stanley Carr/ Weather report. By Carol Plum.
14-16

France
Royal retreats of beech and pine outside Paris. By Gordon Mott.
12

Italy
In Florence, a season of dove-shaped cakes and halls filled with music. By Anne Marshall Zwack.
10

6 Homage to Herring
Fare of the Country. To the Dutch, a new season of the salted fish calls for a festival. By Theodore James Jr
23 The Other Vegas
A little town in New Mexico has a glossy name and a jackpot of historic buildings. By Kathleen Teltsch.
47 Instant Celebrity
To a black, travel abroad is a route lined with whispers, stares and questions. By Stephanie Griffith.

198

Art Director: Linda Brewer, Tom Bodkin
Designer: Linda Brewer
Photographer: Leslie E. Spatt
Editor: Michael Leahy
Creative Director: Tom Bodkin
Client: The New York Times
Publisher: The New York Times
Publication: The New York Times, "Arts & Leisure"

The New York Times
Arts & Leisure
Section 2

THEATER
A youthful American approaches 'Richard II' with fresh eyes.
By Jan Benzel
5

MUSIC
How technology and ethnicity are shaping the art of singing.
By John Rockwell
19

DANCE
The enduring legacy of Fred Astaire's elegant magic.
Anna Kisselgoff
20

ART
A major Delacroix retrospective touches all aspects of the artist's career.
By Michael Brenson
27

ABOUT THE ARTS
The two faces of Brian De Palma's 'Untouchables.'
By John Gross
31

The Bolshoi's Balancing Act

On the eve of its visit to New York this week, debate continues about the company's emphasis on classical tradition.

When the Playgoer's The Thing

Seen the Film? Read The Book!

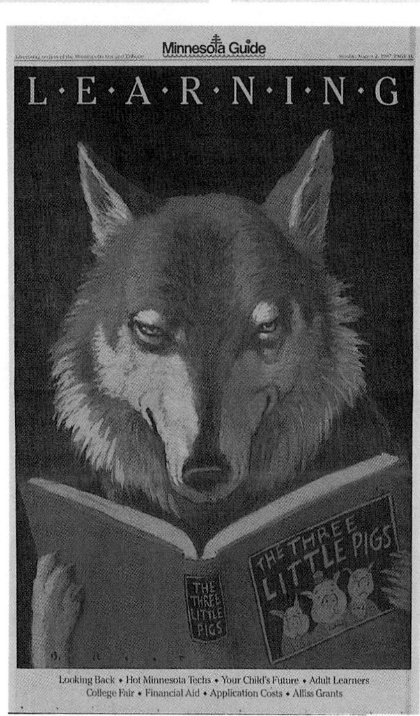

199

Art Director: Lynn Phelps
Designer: Lynn Phelps
Illustrator/Artist: Barrett Root
Editor: Jean Peterson
Client: The Minneapolis Star Tribune
Publisher: The Minneapolis Star Tribune
Publication: Minnesota Guide

200
Art Director: Joseph Scopin, John Kascht
Designer: John Kascht
Illustrator/Artist: John Kascht
Editor: Colin Walters
Publication: The Washington Times

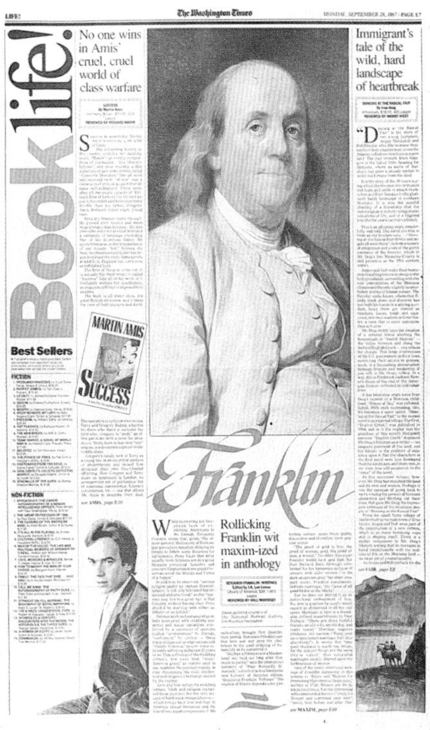
The Washington Times

Book life!

No one wins in Amis' cruel, cruel world of class warfare

Immigrant's tale of the wild, hard landscape of heartbreak

Best Sellers

FICTION

NON-FICTION

MARTIN AMIS

SUCCESS

Franklin

Rollicking Franklin wit maxim-ized in anthology

201
Art Director: Lynn Phelps
Designer: Lynn Phelps
Illustrator/Artist: Tom Lochray
Editor: Jean Peterson
Client: The Minneapolis Star Tribune
Publisher: The Minneapolis Star Tribune
Publication: Minnesota Guide

Minnesota Guide

& home HOUSE

The Mortgage Quest • Building Your Home • Money Matters • Kitchen Planning Tips • The Low Maintenance Home

FINANCING

Minnesota Guide

WHEELS

Mid Year Models • Communication • Check it Yourself
Motor Homes • Auto Styling • Dream Machines • Mini to Maxi • Summer Driving

202
Art Director: Lynn Phelps
Designer: Lynn Phelps
Illustrator/Artist: Leland Klanderman
Editor: Jean Peterson
Client: The Minneapolis Star Tribune
Publisher: The Minneapolis Star Tribune
Publication: Minnesota Guide

203

Art Director: Mare Earley
Designer: Margaret Carsello
Photographer: Anthony Berardi, Jr.
Editor: Brenda Butler
Publisher: The Chicago Tribune
Publication: The Chicago Tribune, "Style"
Project Editor: Janet Franz

Dot, Dot, Dash!

Summer fashion's sweet confections? Polka-dot party dresses.

The New York Times

Book Review

August 16, 1987

Of Moles and Men

Cloak & Gown
Yale University has always been a great nursery for spooks, according to Robin Winks, who takes a scholarly machete to the jungle of myth about the Ivy League heroes of the O.S.S. and the C.I.A. A portrait of dining-club idealists, champions of a sentimental imperialism, missionaries bent on improving the world. **7**

Conspiracy of Silence
The eminent art historian Sir Anthony Blunt was in truth part of the infamous ring of spies laced through upper levels of British society and government. A traitor's life story, told by Barrie Penrose and Simon Freeman. **11**

Spycatcher
Britain's hottest banned book. Peter Wright's memoirs recount his career bugging phones, cracking codes and feverishly pursuing supposed moles in Her Majesty's secret service. **13**

The Heirs of Calvino and the Eco Effect

By Sergio Perosa

'You Must Remember This' by Joyce Carol Oates/**3**

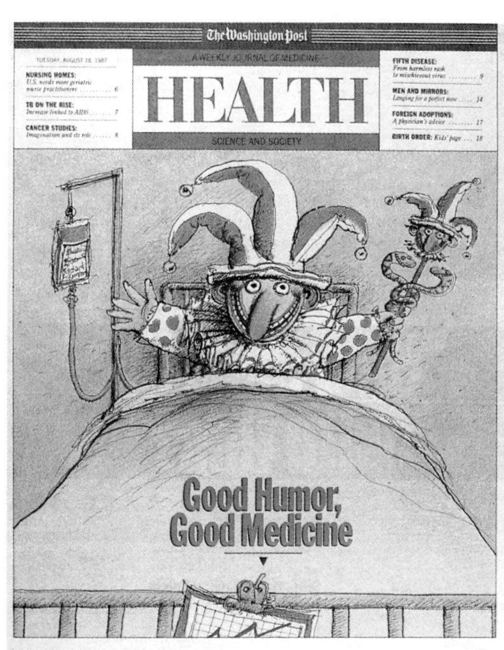

The Washington Post

TUESDAY, AUGUST 18, 1987

A WEEKLY JOURNAL OF MEDICINE

HEALTH

SCIENCE AND SOCIETY

NURSING HOMES: U.S. needs more geriatric nurse practitioners ... 6
TB ON THE RISE: Increase linked to AIDS ... 7
CANCER STUDIES: Imagination and its role ... 8
FIFTH DISEASE: From harmless rash to mischievous virus ... 9
MEN AND MIRRORS: Longing for a perfect nose ... 14
FOREIGN ADOPTIONS: A physician's advice ... 17
BIRTH ORDER: Kids' page ... 18

Good Humor, Good Medicine

204

Art Director: Steven Heller
Designer: Steven Heller
Illustrator/Artist: Mirko Ilic
Editor: Mike Levitas
Creative Director: Tom Bodkin
Client: The New York Times
Publisher: The New York Times
Publication: The New York Times, "Book Review"

205

Art Director: Alice Kresse
Designer: Alice Kresse
Illustrator/Artist: Richard Thompson
Writer: Victor Cohn
Editor: Abigail Trafford
Client: The Washington Post
Publication: The Washington Post, "Health Magazine"

206
Art Director: Lynn Phelps
Designer: Lynn Phelps
Illustrator/Artist: Daniel Craig
Editor: Jean Peterson
Client: The Minneapolis Star Tribune
Publisher: The Minneapolis Star Tribune
Publication: Minnesota Guide

207
Art Director: Lynn Phelps
Designer: Lynn Phelps
Illustrator/Artist: Jim Buckels
Editor: Jean Peterson
Client: The Minneapolis Star Tribune
Publisher: The Minneapolis Star Tribune
Publication: Minnesota Guide

208
Art Director: Joseph Scopin, John Kascht
Designer: John Kascht
Illustrator/Artist: John Kascht
Editor: Colin Walters
Publication: The Washington Times

209
Art Director: Terry Redknapp
Designer: Terry Redknapp
Photographer: Randy Leffingwell
Writer: Betsy Balsley
Editor: Betsy Balsley
Publisher: The Los Angeles Times
Publication: The Los Angeles Times, "Food"

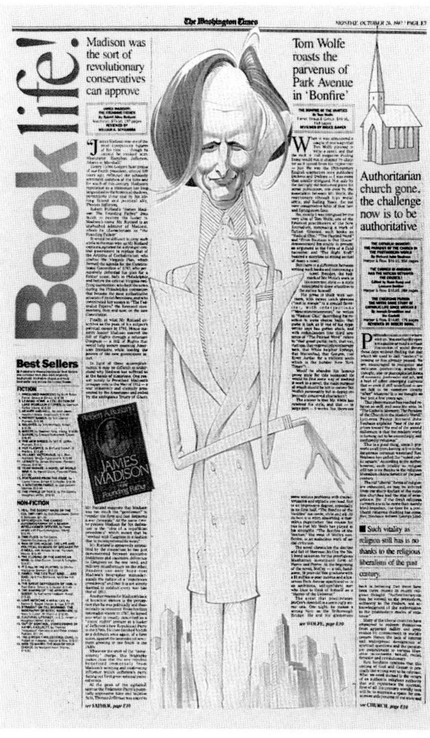
The Washington Times

Booklife!

Madison was the sort of revolutionary conservatives can approve

Tom Wolfe roasts the parvenus of Park Avenue in 'Bonfire'

Authoritarian church gone, the challenge now is to be authoritative

Best Sellers

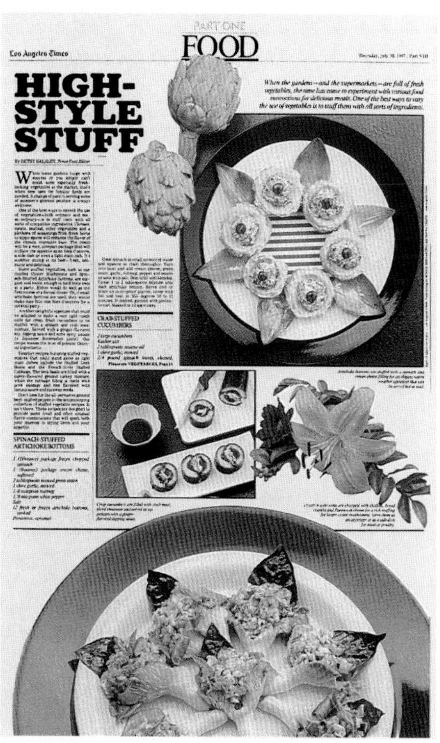
Los Angeles Times

PART ONE

FOOD

HIGH-STYLE STUFF

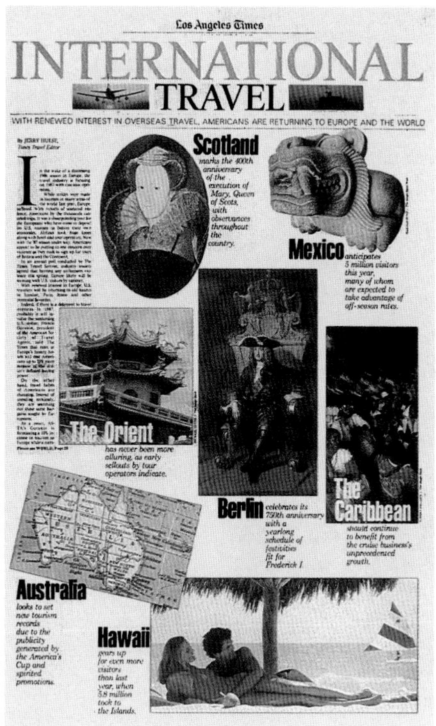
Los Angeles Times

INTERNATIONAL TRAVEL

WITH RENEWED INTEREST IN OVERSEAS TRAVEL, AMERICANS ARE RETURNING TO EUROPE AND THE WORLD

Scotland marks the 400th anniversary of the execution of Mary, Queen of Scots, with observances throughout the country.

Mexico anticipates 5 million visitors this year, many of whom are expected to take advantage of off-season rates.

The Orient has never been more alluring, as early sellouts by tour operators indicate.

Berlin celebrates its 750th anniversary with a yearlong schedule of festivities fit for Frederick I

The Caribbean should continue to benefit from the cruise business's unprecedented growth.

Australia looks to set new tourism records due to the publicity generated by the America's Cup and spirited promotions.

Hawaii gears up for even more visitors than last year, when 5.8 million took to the Islands.

210
Art Director: Terry Redknapp
Designer: Donald Burgess
Writer: Jerry Hulse
Editor: Jerry Hulse
Publisher: The Los Angeles Times
Publication: The Los Angeles Times, "Travel"

211
Art Director: Therese Shechter
Designer: Therese Shechter
Writer: Rob Salem
Editor: Patrick McCormick
Client: The Toronto Star
Publication: The Toronto Star, "What's On"

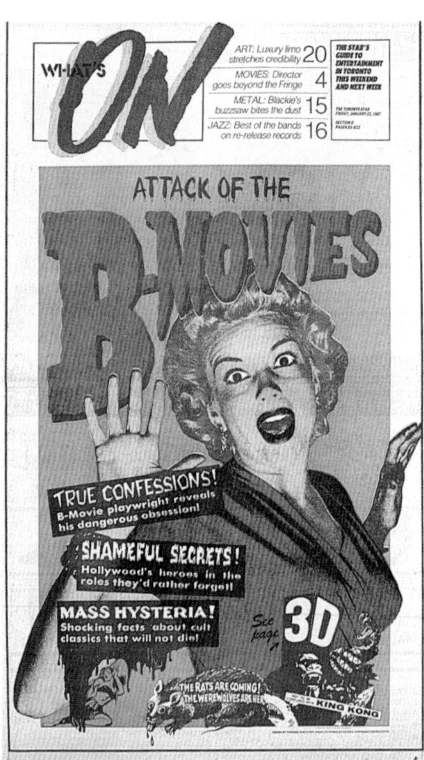

WHAT'S ON

ART: Luxury limo stretches credibility 20
MOVIES: Director goes beyond the Fringe 4
METAL: Blackie's buzzsaw bites the dust 15
JAZZ: Best of the bands on re-release records 16

THE STAR'S GUIDE TO ENTERTAINMENT IN TORONTO THIS WEEKEND AND NEXT WEEK

ATTACK OF THE B-MOVIES

TRUE CONFESSIONS! B-Movie playwright reveals his dangerous obsession!

SHAMEFUL SECRETS! Hollywood's heroes in the roles they'd rather forget!

MASS HYSTERIA! Shocking facts about cult classics that will not die!

See page 3D

THE RATS ARE COMING! THE WEREWOLVES ARE HERE!

KING KONG

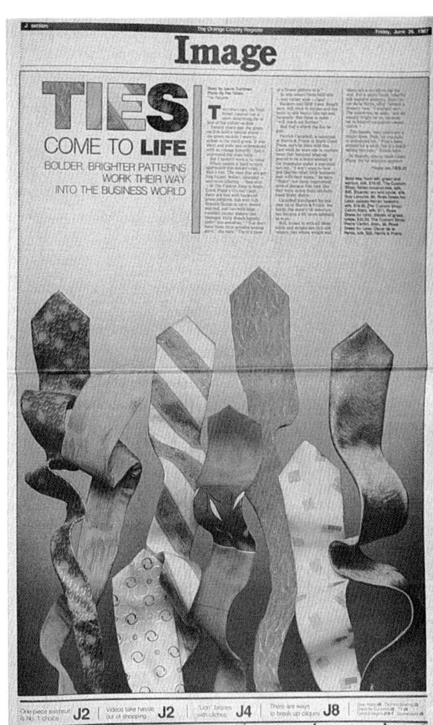

The Orange County Register

Image

TIES COME TO LIFE

BOLDER, BRIGHTER PATTERNS WORK THEIR WAY INTO THE BUSINESS WORLD

J2 J2 J4 J8

212
Art Director: Gwendolyn Wong
Designer: Gwendolyn Wong
Photographer: Pat Tehan
Writer: Laura Tuchman
Editor: Blair Charnley
Publication: Orange County Register
Color Production: Register Color Lab

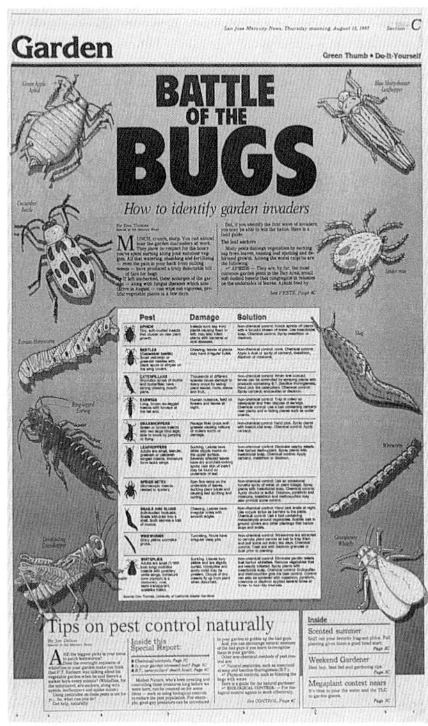

Garden

Green Thumb • Do-It-Yourself

BATTLE OF THE BUGS

How to identify garden invaders

Pest	Damage	Solution

Tips on pest control naturally

Inside
Scented summer
Weekend Gardener
Megaplant contest nears

213
Art Director: Brad Zucroff
Designer: Bob Reynolds
Illustrator/Artist: Bob Reynolds
Client: The San Jose Mercury News

214
Art Director: Aldona Charlton
Designer: Aldona Charlton
Photographer: Jan Houseworth
Illustrator/Artist: Robert Pizzo
Writer: Diane Nottle
Editor: Ralph Hubley
Client: The Boston Globe
Publisher: The Boston Globe
Publication: The Boston Globe

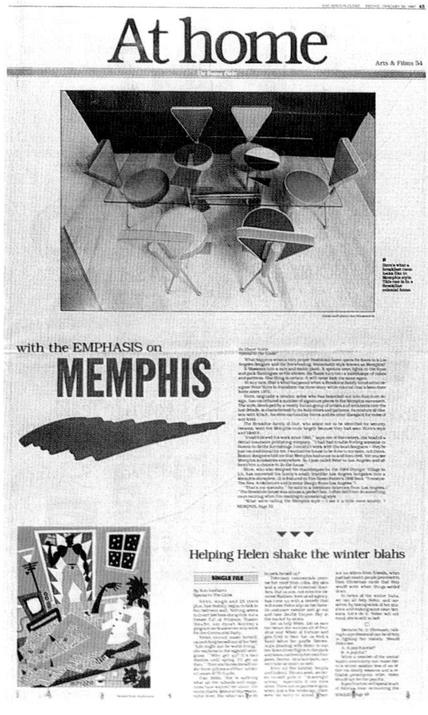
At home

with the EMPHASIS on
MEMPHIS

Helping Helen shake the winter blahs

215
Art Director: Lynn Phelps
Designer: Lynn Phelps
Illustrator/Artist: Roger Boehm
Writer: Sheryl Silver
Editor: Jean Peterson
Client: The Minneapolis Star Tribune
Publisher: The Minneapolis Star Tribune
Publication: Minnesota Guide

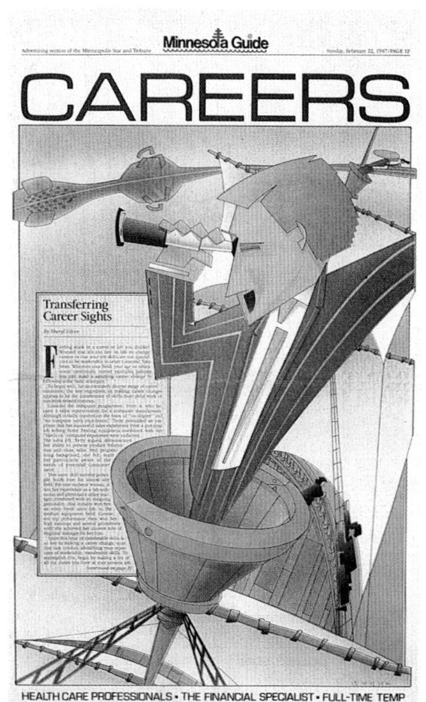
Minnesota Guide
CAREERS

Transferring Career Sights

HEALTH CARE PROFESSIONALS • THE FINANCIAL SPECIALIST • FULL-TIME TEMP

THE TORONTO STAR
FASHION
SECTION B

COTTON COOL

216
Art Director: Catherine Pike
Designer: Catherine Pike
Photographer: Bernard Weil
Writer: Catherine Patch
Editor: Ellie Tesher
Client: The Toronto Star
Publication: The Toronto Star, “Fashion”

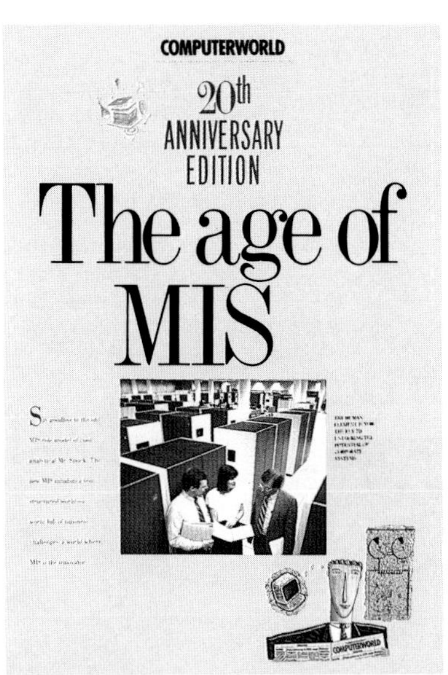

COMPUTERWORLD

20th ANNIVERSARY EDITION

The age of MIS

BY ASHLEY GRAYSON AND JOHN VORNHOLT

The new MIS

As management learns more about DP, and vice versa, the traditional lines will blur, and MIS will be poised to play a larger role in corporate decision making

If you give users the right tools, chances are they will do an outstanding job with them. The danger is that they can create islands of information, doing so in a vacuum.

TIMELINE: *Software*

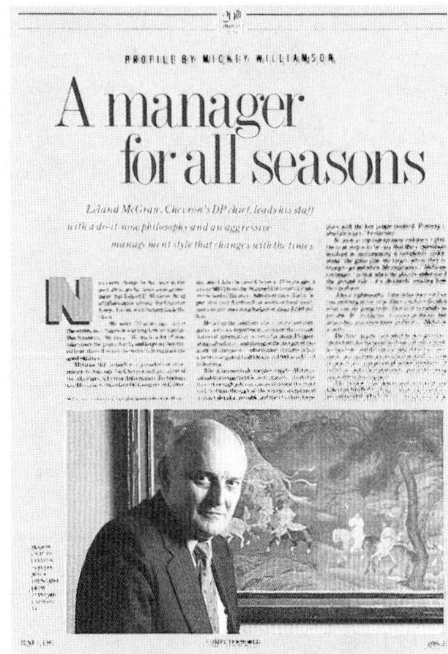

PROFILE BY MICKEY WILLIAMSON

A manager for all seasons

Leland McGrane, Chevron's DP chief, leads his staff with a do-it-now philosophy and an aggressive management style that changes with the times

217

Art Director: Marjorie Magowan
Designer: Ronn Campisi
Editor: Jan Fiderio
Publisher: CW Publishing Inc.
Publication: Computerworld
Graphics Director: Mitchell J. Hayes

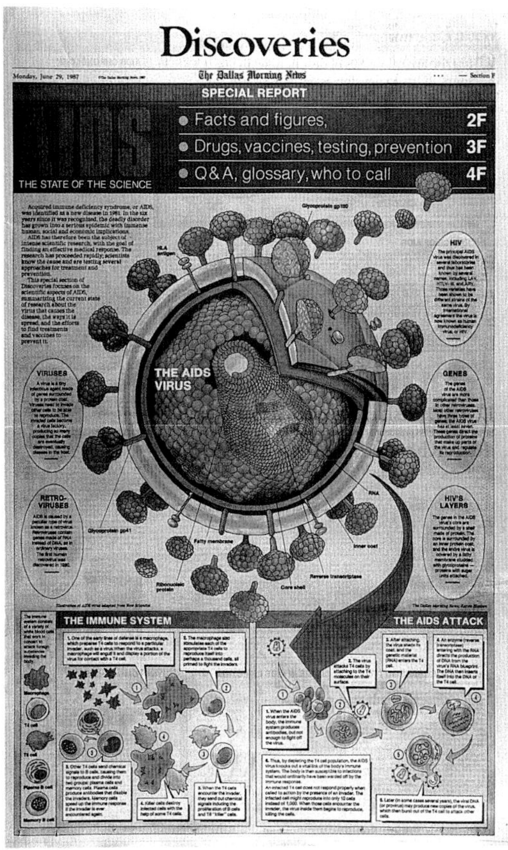

Discoveries

Monday, June 29, 1987 — The Dallas Morning News — Section F

SPECIAL REPORT

AIDS

THE STATE OF THE SCIENCE

- Facts and figures, 2F
- Drugs, vaccines, testing, prevention 3F
- Q&A, glossary, who to call 4F

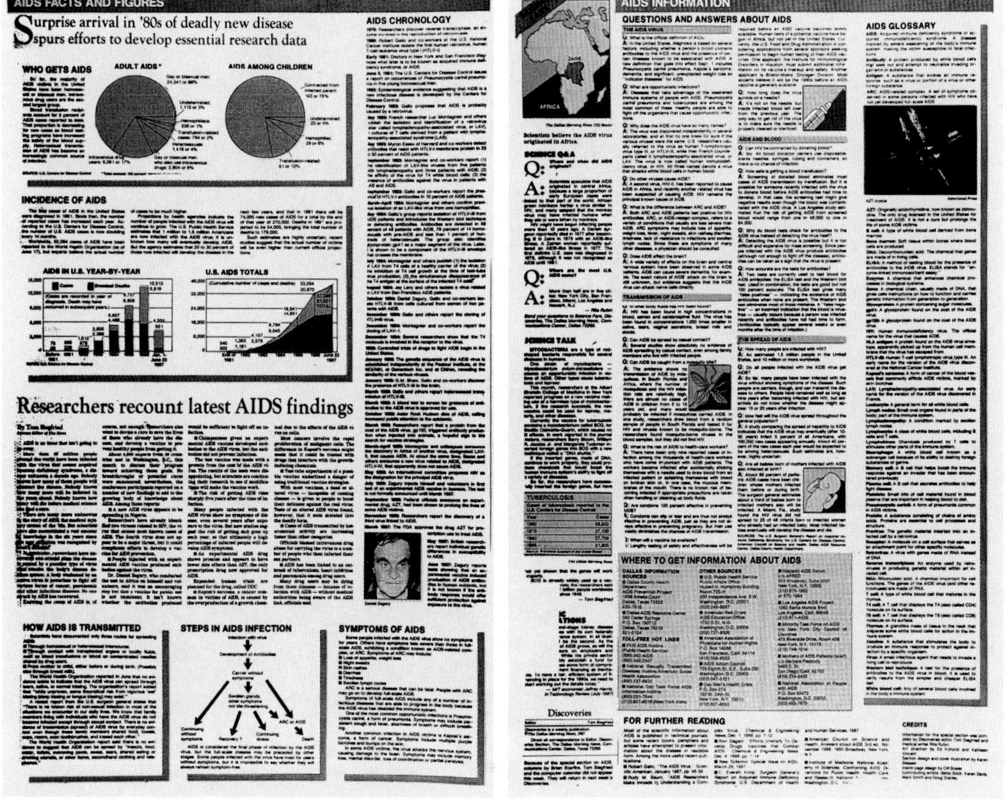

AIDS FACTS AND FIGURES

Surprise arrival in '80s of deadly new disease spurs efforts to develop essential research data

WHO GETS AIDS

ADULT AIDS

AIDS AMONG CHILDREN

AIDS CHRONOLOGY

INCIDENCE OF AIDS

AIDS IN U.S. YEAR-BY-YEAR

U.S. AIDS TOTALS

Researchers recount latest AIDS findings

HOW AIDS IS TRANSMITTED

STEPS IN AIDS INFECTION

SYMPTOMS OF AIDS

AIDS INFORMATION

QUESTIONS AND ANSWERS ABOUT AIDS

AIDS GLOSSARY

AFRICA

WHERE TO GET INFORMATION ABOUT AIDS

FOR FURTHER READING

218

Art Director: Ed Kohorst, Kathleen Vincent
Designer: Karen Blessen, Clif Bosler

THE

SIX HUNDRED AND THIRTY

The Stories of Philadelphia's Vietnam War Dead

PHILADELPHIA DAILY NEWS

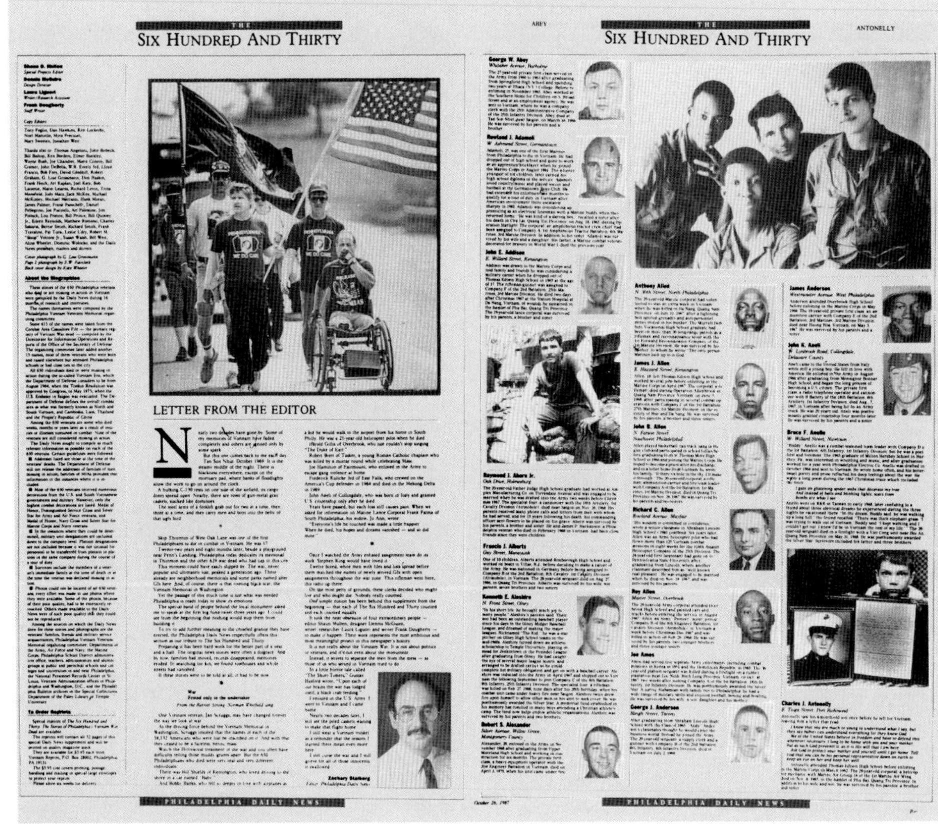
THE

SIX HUNDRED AND THIRTY

LETTER FROM THE EDITOR

ABEY

THE

SIX HUNDRED AND THIRTY

ANTONELLY

PHILADELPHIA DAILY NEWS

PHILADELPHIA DAILY NEWS

219

Art Director: Dennis McGuire
Designer: Dennis McGuire
Photographer: G. Loie Grossmann
Editor: Shaun Mullen
Publisher: The Philadelphia Daily News
Publication: The Six Hundred and Thirty

MAGAZINE EDITORIAL

IAL REPORT

COLLECTORS PHOTOGRAPHY

THROUGH THE LOOKING GLASS
WITH DEBORAH TURBEVILLE

Deborah Turbeville's work beckons us as though from the past, across time barriers. When seeing her work, we feel an acute sense of "deja-vu," the presence of Marcel Proust and Eugene Atget, of distant days filled with mysteries and intrigue, of old friends and old dreams. She searches out the "secret gardens" of the remote past, the unanswered questions, the poignant moments in time that escaped without a trace, the vague memories of one's youth, the stages upon which long-forgotten events took place.

Her pictures impart a sad sense of "these moments are gone, never to be lived again." Lyrical and unsettling, her work dictates her acceptance into the rare circle of photographers who have made images we can't forget, images that reappear in our minds, closely identified with the unresolved moments of our pasts.

28

29

220 Gold Award

Art Director: Larry Vigon
Photographer: Deborah Turbeville
Writer: Jeff Dunas
Editor: Jeff Dunas
Client: Melrose Publishing Group
Publisher: Jeff Dunas
Publication: Collector's Photography

221 Gold Award

Art Director: Kit Hinrichs
Designer: Kit Hinrichs, Lenore Bartz
Photographer: Henrik Kam, Steven A. Heller
Illustrator/Artist: John Mattos, Walid Saba
Client: Art Center College of Design
Design Firm: Pentagram Design

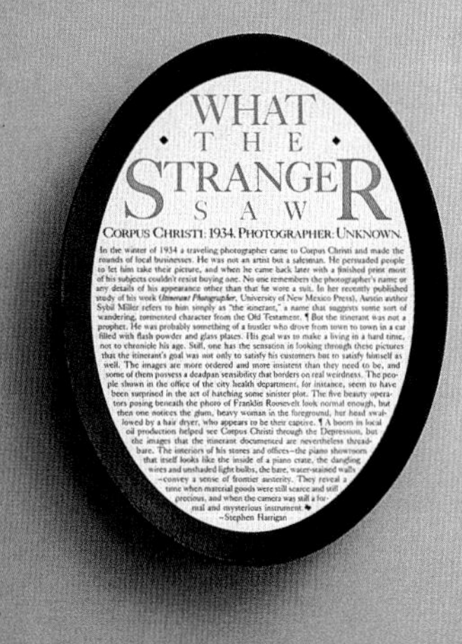

WHAT THE STRANGER SAW

CORPUS CHRISTI: 1934. PHOTOGRAPHER: UNKNOWN.

In the winter of 1934 a traveling photographer came to Corpus Christi and made the rounds of local businesses. He was not an artist but a salesman. He persuaded people to let him take their picture, and when he came back later with a finished print most of his subjects couldn't resist buying one. No one remembers the photographer's name or any details of his appearance other than that he wore a suit. In her recently published study of his work (*Itinerant Photographer*, University of New Mexico Press), Austin author Sybil Miller refers to him simply as "the itinerant," a name that suggests some sort of wandering, tormented character from the Old Testament. ¶ But the itinerant was not a prophet. He was probably something of a hustler who drove from town to town in a car filled with flash powder and glass plates. His goal was to make a living in a hard time, not to chronicle his age. Still, one has the sensation in looking through these pictures that the itinerant's goal was not only to satisfy his customers but to satisfy himself as well. The images are more ordered and more insistent than they need to be, and some of them possess a deadpan sensibility that borders on real weirdness. The people shown in the office of the city health department, for instance, seem to have been surprised in the act of hatching some sinister plot. The five beauty operators posing beneath the photo of Franklin Roosevelt look normal enough, but then one notices the glum, heavy woman in the foreground, her head swallowed by a hair dryer, who appears to be their captive. ¶ A boom in local oil production helped see Corpus Christi through the Depression, but the images that the itinerant documented are nevertheless threadbare. The interiors of his stores and offices—the piano showroom that itself looks like the inside of a piano crate, the dangling wires and unshaded light bulbs, the bare, water-stained walls—convey a sense of frontier austerity. They reveal a time when material goods were still scarce and still precious, and when the camera was still a formal and mysterious instrument.

—Stephen Harrigan

Cafe With Slot Machine

222 Silver Award

Art Director: D. J. Stout
Designer: D. J. Stout
Photographer: Tom Ryan
Writer: Stephen Harrigan
Editor: Gregory Curtis
Creative Director: D. J. Stout
Publisher: Michael R. Levy
Publication: Texas Monthly

223 Silver Award

Art Director: Kit Hinrichs
Designer: Kit Hinrichs, Lenore Bartz
Photographer: Henrik Kam
Illustrator/Artist: John Hersey, John Mattos
Writer: Susan Hoffman
Client: Art Center College of Design
Design Firm: Pentagram Design

THE NEW *C*LASSICS

This is the time to opt for classics, but with a twist. Simple, elegant and ever so important. Whether you are a new romantic or stuck on tough chic. Try a classic green suede pump instead of basic black. And feel great in an elegant soft brown cap. You'll wear these every day. Left: shoe by Charles Jourdan. Right: felt hat by Patricia Underwood. See our shopping guide, page 101. Styled by Walter S. Coordinated by Melissa Breitrose. Photographed by Andrew Macpherson.

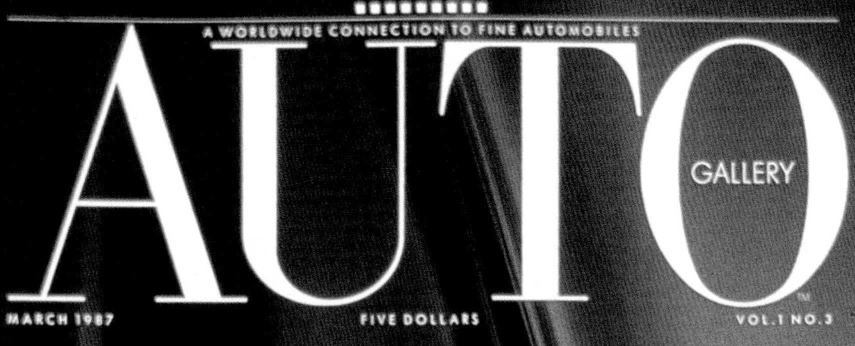

225 Distinctive Merit

Art Director: Michael Brock
Designer: Michael Brock
Photographer: Tim Hargrove
Editor: Al Esquerra
Creative Director: Michael Brock
Client: Auto Gallery
Design Firm: Michael Brock Design
Publisher: Al Esquerra
Publication: Auto Gallery

IMPERIAL EASTER Eggs

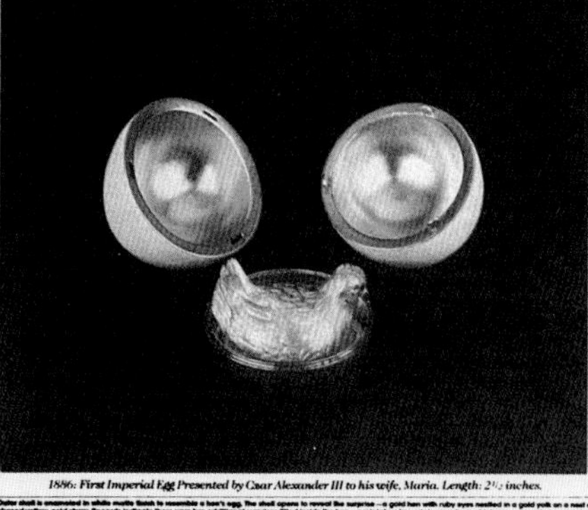

1886: First Imperial Egg Presented by Czar Alexander III to his wife, Maria. Length: 2½ inches.

Outer shell is enameled in white matte finish to resemble a hen's egg. The shell opens to reveal the surprise—a gold hen with ruby eyes nestled in a gold yolk on a nest of chased yellow-gold straw. Records indicate there were two additional surprises fitted inside the hen—a miniature imperial crown from which was suspended a miniature ruby egg. Both of these elements, however, have been lost.

Romanov

On July 16, 1918, in the final days of the Russian Revolution, Czar Nicholas II, his wife Alexandra and their five children were herded into the basement of an old house and murdered by a firing squad. The family could have been imprisoned or exiled like other deposed rulers, but the massacre was a potent demonstration that Russia had had its fill of Czars and Czarinas for all time. Nicholas II was thus the last of a dynasty named Romanov that had ruled Russia for 300 years.

For the record, the despised, autocratic Romanovs left a bequest that was not to be at all despised. In their 300-year reign they had extended the country's borders beyond Asia into Europe, brought sophisticated Western culture into their realm, engulfed a multitude of ethnic populations and their resources, established dominion over the Russian Orthodox Church and amassed a fortune in material goods that could readily be turned into hard cash.

Aside from their palaces, paintings and public artifacts, the last Romanovs had acquired a wealth of personal jewels and art objects commissioned from the legendary jeweler, Peter Carl Fabergé. Probably the most famous (and infamous) pieces were the opulent Imperial Easter Eggs.

In old Russia, Easter was the most revered and festive holiday, and it was traditional to present a colored, decorated egg to a loved one on Easter Sunday. Wealthy families, of course, indulged in more expensive manifestations of their affection. Czar Alexander III, for instance, intrigued by the fanciful creations of the jeweler, Peter Carl Fabergé, commissioned him to concoct a splendid gift for his wife, Czarina Maria. On Easter Sunday, 1886, she received the first Fabergé Imperial Easter Egg, and she continued to receive one every year for the next 30 years. When her husband died in 1894, their son Czar Nicholas II, expanded the tradition, ordering two eggs each year—one for his mother and one for his wife, Alexandra.

In all, from 1886 to 1916, the House of Fabergé created 54 Imperial Easter Eggs. Each one was a unique fantasy executed in precious metals, hard stones, diamonds, pearls, rubies, jewel-like enameling, and with embellishments of exquisite delicacy. Beyond their overt beauty, each egg opened to reveal a surprise. Every year, Fabergé invented surprises of increasing complexity and delight.

When the Bolsheviks came to power and the eggs were unveiled to the world at large, like Imelda Marcos' 3,000 pairs of shoes they became symbols of the imperial family's shocking extravagances and a moral justification for the revolution. But historians and the cognoscenti of the arts are above moralizing. They believe the eggs should not be detested for the prodigality of their patrons, but appreciated for the magnificent achievement of their creators—the craftsmen of Fabergé.

Faberge

Peter Carl Fabergé was born in 1846 in the imperial city of St. Petersburg, where the Romanovs held court and where his father, a jeweler, plied his trade in a modest shop on Bolshaya Morskaya Street. The Fabergés descended from a family of French Huguenots that had been forced out of France for their religious affiliation and had made their way to Russia via Germany. Peter Carl attended lower school in Russia, but when he determined to follow in his father's footsteps as a jeweler, he went off to Germany and apprenticed himself to a master goldsmith in Frankfurt. Aside from his training in the shop, he visited museums and master jewelers in Dresden, Venice, Rome, Florence, London and Paris. His experiences abroad filled him with visions of art objects that diverged from the jeweler's usual stock of necklaces, brooches, bracelets and rings.

When he returned to St. Petersburg in 1870, Peter Carl took over the management of his father's shops. A brother, Agathon, who had also served his apprenticeship as a jeweler, joined him in 1882. The two young men, full of enthusiasm and energy, reorganized the shop and instigated bold new merchandising plans for the firm. Instead of concentrating on the usual assortment of personal jewelry, they started to produce small utilitarian objects using precious metals, gems and artful jewelers' techniques. They created decorative snuff boxes, desk sets, buckles, clocks, picture frames, carved animals, fans, buttons and even knitting needles. When these spectacular fantasies were exhibited at the Pan-Russian Exhibition of 1882, they caused a stir. Among the numerous admirers was Czar Alexander III, who, not long after, commissioned the firm to produce a special Easter gift for his wife, the Czarina Maria.

In truth, the idea of fashioning Easter eggs out of precious metals and jewels was not original with Peter Carl Faberge. Many of the eggs designed for the imperial family and for other wealthy patrons were totally derivative of historic pieces he had seen on his excursions through museums. Contrary to popular notion, Peter Carl Faberge had no direct "hands on" experience with any of the work produced in his name. Instead, he employed a nucleus of workmasters, goldsmiths Perchin and Wigstrom, jewelers Holmstrom and Thielemann, and a master silversmith named Rappoport. All the masters who worked under his roof were autonomous; they hired, trained and paid their own crews of assistants. But they all worked under Faberge's relentless eye. He was constantly consulted about design, methods and techniques, and every piece produced had to pass his fastidious inspection. Distinguishing features of Faberge creations were the lavish details and flawless craftsmanship. No one made a more precise fitting for a stone or devised a more complex, exquisite enameling technique. Workmanship was everything to Faberge. According to legend, any piece with the tiniest imperfection was smashed with a hammer, rather than have it leave the shop bearing the Faberge name.

With the Czar as a client, the eminence of the House of Faberge was guaranteed. The business expanded, and branches were opened in Odessa, Kiev and Moscow. Throughout Europe and Russia there was no firm that matched Faberge's reputation for excellence, and the business poured in. But World War I marked the beginning of the end of the enterprise in Russia. The shop's activities were diverted to wartime priorities—manufacturing small arms and munitions. Jewelry was not in great demand, though a limited quantity was produced. Finally, when the Bolsheviks seized power, Faberge was forced to leave the country, the skilled workers abandoned the shops, and the unfinished merchandise was confiscated, as were all the royal family's Faberge holdings. Most of the Imperial Eggs, as well as countless other Faberge treasures, were sold by the financially strapped new government for hard cash. The pieces were dispersed to dealers, private collectors and museums.

1898

LILIES OF THE VALLEY EGG

Presented by Czar Nicholas II to his mother, Maria. Height: 5⁹⁄₁₆ inches closed, 7⁷⁄₈ inches open.

The pale pink enamel shell is supported on cabriole-style legs of matte green-gold leaves dripping with rose diamond dewdrops. The egg nestles in a bouquet of lilies of the valley fashioned out of pearls, diamonds and translucent green enamel leaves. A small pearl knob triggers the surprise—a trefoil of miniature portraits of Czar Nicholas and his eldest daughters. A geared mechanism raises the miniatures out of the egg and spreads them out in fan form. The portraits are framed in rose diamonds and topped with a miniature crown.

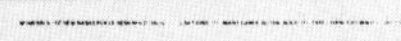

1903

CHANTICLEER EGG

Presented by Czar Nicholas II to his mother, Maria. Height: 10⁷⁄₈ inches closed, 12⁷⁄₈ inches open.

The egg and base are enameled a brilliant sapphire blue on a moire patterned gold ground. Swags and ribbons of gold encircle the grille at the top. A band of seed pearls with gold foliage ring the egg at mid point. The white enameled clock face has a gold bezel which is also trimmed with seed pearls. The surprise is a little golden chanticleer enameled in yellow, blue and green that is synchronized with the clock movement. On the hour, the bird emerges from beneath the gold grille to crow the hour with its head bobbing, wings flapping and tiny beak opening and closing.

Czar Nicholas II

1916

CROSS OF ST. GEORGE EGG: PRESENTED BY CZAR NICHOLAS II TO HIS MOTHER, MARIA. HEIGHT: 3³⁄₁₆ INCHES; WITH STAND 4⁵⁄₈ INCHES.

Forbes

It seems that destiny brought the names Forbes and Romanov and Faberge together. At least Malcolm Forbes, publisher of Forbes Magazine, was aware of the others at a very early age. He recalls, "When I was very young, I read with horrified fascination an abundantly illustrated volume on World War I. Its chapter about the Russian Revolution and the massacre of the Romanov family included a picture of a Faberge Imperial Easter Egg to illustrate the prewar extravagance of Russia's rulers."

The memory must have been firmly imprinted in his mind, for years later in London, he was irresistibly drawn to a Faberge cigarette lighter, and he purchased it as a gift for his wife. Since she, too, was captivated by the fantasy, artistry and history of Faberge, the Forbeses found themselves on the road to becoming collectors. Year after year, piece by piece, they acquired Faberge treasures, until they amassed over 250 pieces. It is the largest private collection of Faberge works in the world.

But of all the Faberge fantasies, the Imperial Easter Eggs are considered the most significant. They are the epitome of excellence in style, in technique and in integrity for the materials used. Of the 54 Imperial Easter Eggs produced, 43 are known to have survived, and of that number 12 are in the Forbes collection. It is the largest concentration of Imperial Eggs and exceeds the Kremlin's holdings by two. Christopher Forbes, Malcolm's son, calls it one of the "ironies of history" that the two institutions with the richest holdings of Imperial Easter Eggs are the Communist USSR and Forbes Magazine, "The Capitalist Tool." The word "richest" is to be taken quite literally here, as the most recent price mentioned for an Imperial Easter Egg was $1,750,000.

All of the eggs reproduced here are from the Forbes collection, but as faithful as photography is, the pictures are no match for the articles "in the flesh." Fortunately, all 12 Imperial Easter Eggs, along with over 200 other Faberge treasures, are installed in the Forbes Magazine Galleries, 62 Fifth Avenue, at the corner of 12th Street in New York City. The galleries are open Tuesday through Saturday from 10 a.m. to 4 p.m. The public is welcome; admission is free. Prepare to be astounded.
Marion Muller

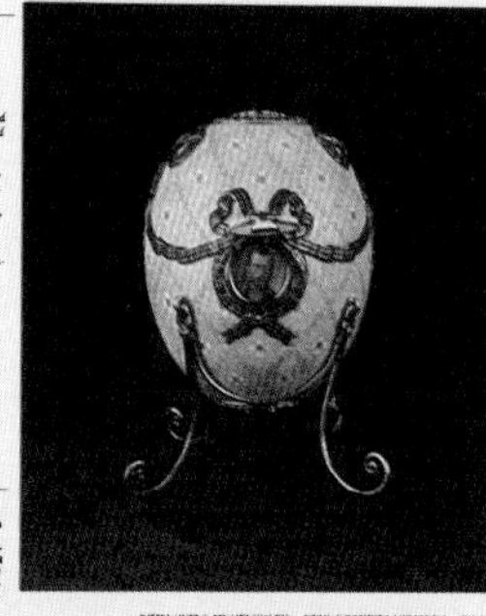

As a gesture to wartime austerity, the egg was made of silver instead of gold, and was far less lavish than earlier designs. The shell is enameled in matte opalescent white with trellised laurel garlands framing the crosses of St. George. A gold ribbon enameled in orange and black encircles the egg. Buttons concealed in the ribbons triggered the appearance of the surprises, which were miniature portraits of Czar Nicholas II and his son, Alexis. This was the only egg the Dowager Empress Maria was able to take with her when she made her escape from Russia.

226 Distinctive Merit

Art Director: B. Martin Pedersen
Photographer: H. Peter Curran, Robert Forbes, Larry Stein, Marvin Lyons
Writer: Marion Muller
Editor: Edward Gottschall
Publisher: International Typeface Corp.

227
Art Director: Lucy Bartholomay
Designer: Lucy Bartholomay
Editor: Ande Zellman
Publisher: The Boston Globe
Publication: The Boston Globe, "Magazine"

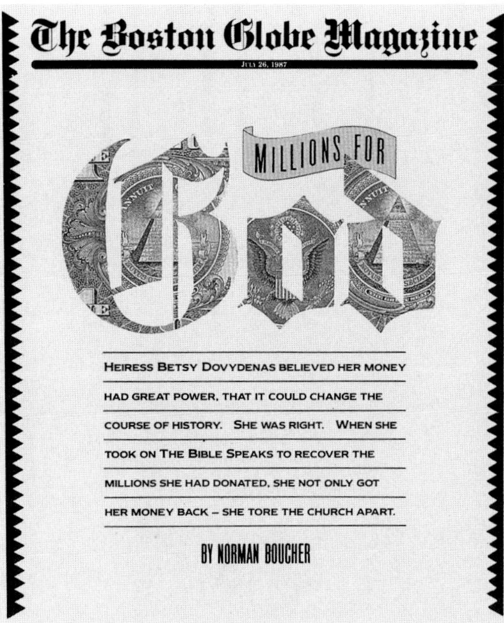

228
Art Director: Lucy Bartholomay
Designer: Lucy Bartholomay
Illustrator/Artist: Paula Munck
Editor: Alison Arnett
Publisher: The Boston Globe
Publication: The Boston Globe, "Travel"

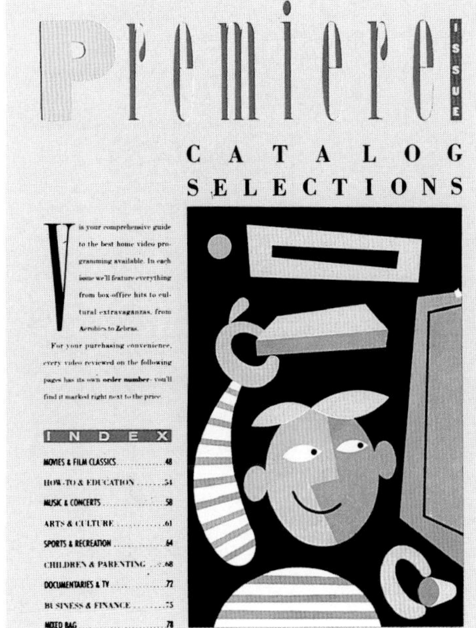

229
Art Director: Terry R. Koppel
Designer: Terry R. Koppel
Illustrator/Artist: Anders Wengren
Writer: Peter Hauck
Editor: Peter Hauck
Client: Fairfield Publishing
Design Firm: Koppel & Scher
Publisher: Fairfield Publishing
Publication: V Magazine

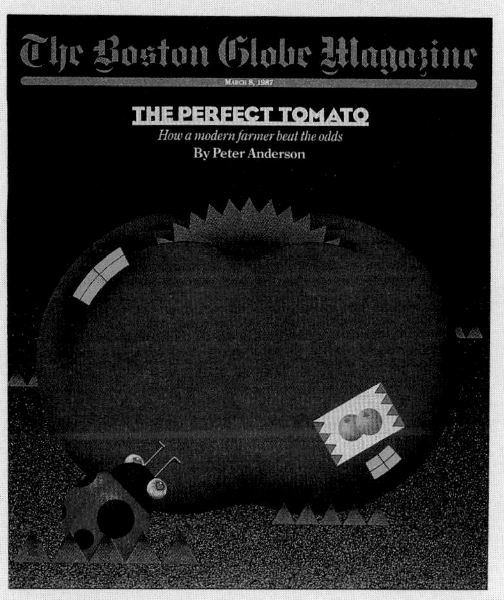

230
Art Director: Lynn Staley
Designer: Gail Anderson
Illustrator/Artist: Jose Cruz
Editor: Ande Zellman
Publisher: The Boston Globe
Publication: The Boston Globe, "Magazine"

231
Art Director: Fabien Baron
Designer: Ann Kwong
Photographer: Josef Aster
Editor: Susan B. Adams

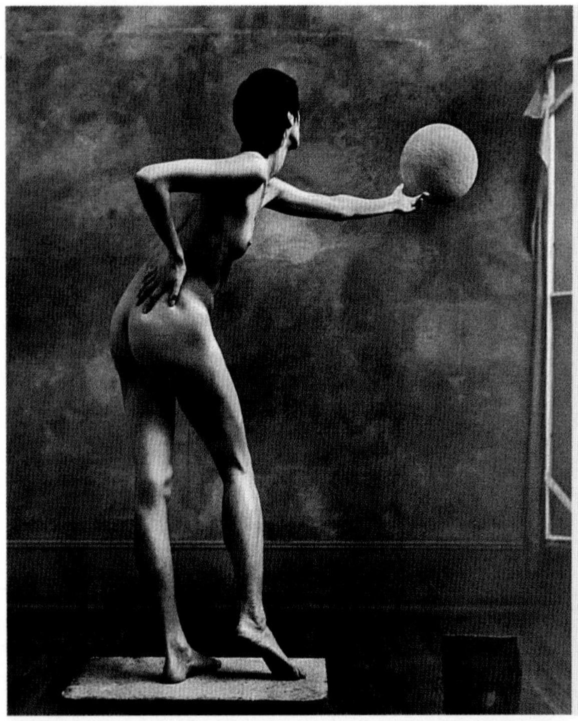

Day JOB

HER ACTOR'S TRAINING PREPARED HER FOR ALMOST EVERYTHING, BUT NOT FOR THIS.

In the fall of 1985 it had been a long time between commercials, so I was tending bar on the Upper West Side, hoping it wouldn't be long before my fortunes improved. One night I was carrying an armload of glassware down the stairs near the kitchen when I slipped on some spilled pasta and fell. The glasses flew out of my hands, and I tumbled over backward. I cut the palm of my hand when I landed, and the cement steps caught me just at the coccyx, causing a strange, worrisome numbness in my legs. I walked home that night with a pain in my ass and a determination to find a better day job.

An actor's life is full of ups and downs. One day the phone is ringing and the residuals are coming in, and then one day they're not. You think, *What did I do wrong?* And you look to everyone for advice.

Agents, when you are lucky enough to get in to see them, are terrific make-over specialists. At various times I've been told to lose weight, change my hair, get my teeth capped, use more makeup, use less makeup, be more upscale, be more down-home.

Acting teachers are make-over artists, too. One told me that I was great when I suffered, another told me all that suffering was a bore and I was more interesting when I was being sexy. Still another said, "Be zany, offbeat; that's where you shine." All this critical advice can make a person crazy. Trying to be what other people think is best makes you feel like an orphan that nobody wants.

Most actors, whether successful or struggling, suffer from image problems at some point in their careers. They need to be approved of or they don't work and they don't eat. Rejection is denial of the means of survival. Rejection is also denial of you as a person, and it's hard not to take that personally, but you try. You look for ways to keep your spirits up and your rent paid, and you keep doing that forever. No one told you it would be like this—it's just something you learn.

You learn a lot of things as an actor: how to find your inner truth, how to sing and dance or duel convincingly with a sword. Dialects

BY CLAUDIA DIXON

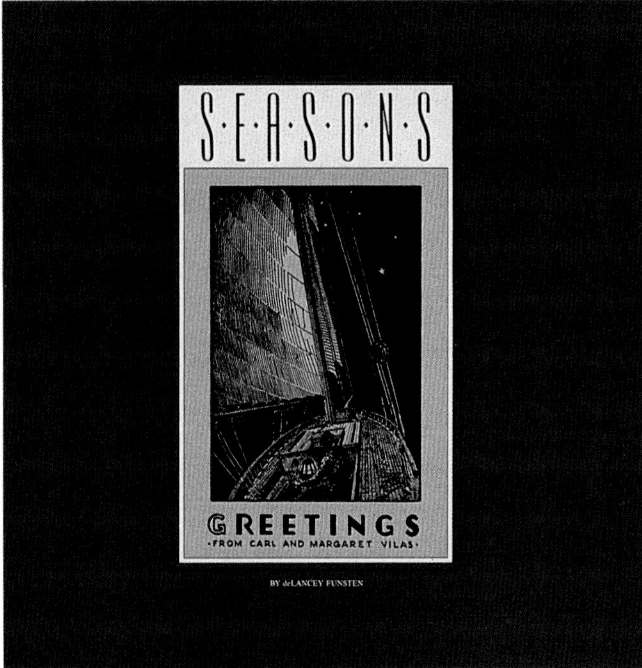

In an era of fast-paced, high-tech living, some people still prefer slow, traditional methods. For 52 years Carl and Margaret Vilas have delighted their friends and relatives at Christmastime by sending cards they designed and produced themselves. In addition to being lovely, the cards are thoroughly nautical. The Vilases have chosen their chief preoccupation — sailing — as their theme. The painstakingly made cards reflect more than half a century of Carl and Margaret's sailing adventures; they also reflect more effort given to holiday greetings than dashing out to the Hallmark shop for a mass-produced cliché. ☐ The Vilases sent their first cards in 1934, two years after their marriage and twelve years before they bought the historic yacht *Direction*. The decision to create Christmas cards nicely combined their interests and abilities. Charles Harrison Vilas II worked in the printing industry as a pressman, printing-ink technician and salesman. He became the associate editor of the Cruising Club of America's Cruising Club News in 1962 and eventually its editor, a position he still holds at age 80. Margaret Van Pelt Vilas graduated Phi Beta Kappa from Vassar, then earned a bachelors degree in Architecture from Columbia, a masters in Architecture from MIT and the honor of being a life member of the American Water Color Society.

232
Art Director: Clare Cunningham
Illustrator/Artist: Carl Vilas, Margaret Vilas
Writer: deLancey Funsten
Editor: Joseph Gribbins
Creative Director: Clare Cunningham
Client: Nautical Quarterly
Publisher: C. S. Lovelace
Publication: Nautical Quarterly

233

Art Director: Phyllis Schefer
Photographer: Greg Watermann
Publication: Elle
Publication Director: Régis Pagniez

faces

ALREADY A SUPER-STAR IN HOLLAND, DEREK DE LINT IS HOT TO TROT ON NEW TURF

THE FLYING DUTCHMAN

BY RUTH GARDNER

Derek de Lint's flight bonus plan is looking real hefty these days. With all the commuting he's doing between L.A. and Amsterdam, he literally is a flying Dutchman. He's also a happy Dutchman. After 14 years of acting—theater as well as in 15 films—he's coming into his own internationally. His name doesn't make L.A. producers jump for joy, yet, or hearts throb on this side of the Atlantic, yet, but his clean-cut good looks, his strong stage and film presence, his green-into-brown eyes, and his irresistibly charming smile make a face that's not easily forgotten. And by year's end, American audiences will have seen him in at least three movies. Last spring *The Assault*, a Dutch film in which he starred, captured the Oscar and Golden Globe awards for best foreign film. In June his first feature film, *Soldier of Orange*, was aired on prime-time TV, and this November, the much-talked-about Philip Kaufman (*The Right Stuff* director) film, *The Unbearable Lightness of Being*, will open with de Lint in the lead. And his recently completed film with Charlotte Rampling, *Mascara*, and another film, *Diary of a Mad Old Man*, will be released here. Not bad for a fella who just decided a year ago that it was time to make a name for himself in American films.

De Lint is part of a growing number of young, bona-fide European stars who, tempted by *l'Amerique*, dare to leave the comforts of stardom at home in order to capture the elusive golden apple in Hollywood. Gérard Depardieu, Christophe Lambert, Rutger Hauer, and Klaus-Maria Brandauer represent an Eighties version of the handsome, debonair foreigner of the David Niven or Marcello Mastroianni sort who was able to penetrate the closed American audience which, in general, has had a history of rejecting anything "foreign" in movies. This new crop is older than our own Eighties brat pack—Rob Lowe, Tom Cruise, and Matt Dillon—and just different enough from our older stars—Robert De Niro, Dustin Hoffman, and Robert Redford—to fascinate and intrigue. De Lint, who was 37 last July, is confident enough in his talent to risk starting all over in the U.S.

"ACTING IS GREAT, BUT I WILL NEVER TAKE MYSELF TOO SERIOUSLY"

DE LIVELY Spirited fashion for a multi-faceted talent. Pocketed cotton pants, $74, green-and-navy wool jacket, $332, and turtle-neck sweater, $117; all from Marithé and François Girbaud. Gloves, Luna D'Oro, $7. Camouflage high tops, Converse, $25. For more details, see Shopping Guide.

DESIGN

Chair Flair

Reinventing the wheel may be simpler than creating a new chair. Like a cook's perfect omelet, the chair presents a true test of the designer's skill. Here, some current creations and re-creations.

Photographs by Cy Gross
Produced by Andrew Bill
Text by Hope Batey

234

Art Director: Melissa Tardiff, Maria Bavosa
Photographer: Cy Gross
Editor: Frank Zachary
Publisher: Fred Jackson
Publication: Town & Country

The joint custody solution is changing parents' ideas about divorce—and family.

DAD'S HOUSE

MOM'S HOUSE

BY MEREDITH MARAN

"I'm glad at least Mommy and Daddy are friends now," says 11-year-old Demetria Haberfeld. "When they lived together they were always yelling at each other. This way is better than having them argue all the time. But we still think it would be funner if they lived together."

"It would be," asserts Selena, Demetria's seven-year-old sister.

Demetria and Selena's parents split up six years ago, and since then the girls have been (in their words) "switching houses" on a weekly basis. "In some ways," says Demetria, "it's better than living with one parent all the time. You get double of everything—a whole set of toys and clothes for each place, more Hanukkah and birthday presents."

"I like Mommy's boyfriend!" says Selena. "He has a mansion and two cars. And Daddy's girlfriend makes great food. Plus she has nice kids. But I still want Mommy and Daddy to get back together so I won't miss them anymore."

Once upon a time, parents breaking up called to mind the specter of children like Demetria and Selena, yearning for Mommy and Daddy to get back together. And though it may be true that children keep more couples together than does true love, many parents are developing a new working model for successful separation—one that provides the kids with two homes and a mom and dad who both play an active parental role.

The latest statistics say that in the United

(Continued from previous page)

States, one out of eight marriages ends in divorce, and 10 percent of all children have divorced parents. For divided families, joint custody is an advancing trend. Thirty-three states now have joint custody laws (which declare the state's intent to give children of divorce meaningful and frequent access to both parents), compared to eight states in 1980 and none in 1978.

The jury is still out on joint custody, however. Feminist critics contend that in giving up sole custody, divorced mothers are also surrendering adequate financial compensation. And some family therapists contend that partial care of the child often means partial commitment to him. But at its best, joint custody is an arrangement that places the well-being of the child over the problems of the parents. As Isolina Ricci, a San Francisco-based family therapist and a veteran court mediator, says, "When parents divorce they divorce each other, not their children."

Joint custody arrangements that work are much like the marriages that produced them—filled with conflict and compromise, disappointment and discovery. Yet increasing numbers of these families are surviving the struggle with familial ties intact. Demetria and Selena's family—the Rhines and Haberfelds of Oakland, California—is one. The Asches and Henkelses of Chicago and St. Louis are another.

Both families split up some years ago; both still grapple with the emotional and logistical aftershocks. But both sets of ex-

235

Art Director: Veronique Vienne
Photographer: Elma Garcia
Publication: Parenting
Picture Editor: Cathy Raymond

236

Art Director: Fabien Baron
Designer: Fabien Baron
Writer: Marcelle Clements
Editor: Betsy Carter

The Jewish American Prince

Sure, he's special. Just ask his mother.

74

Flo and Gene Simmons

I just hope no anti-Semites are reading this. Because the subject here is Jewish men, and I intend to be merciless. And in case you're wondering, yes, believe me, I feel plenty guilty about it. But let's face it, the writer's job is to betray, and guilt is therefore an occupational hazard. In any event, my sense of justice prevails over my guilt: have you noticed that no one seems to have any compunction taking potshots at Jewish women? No one worries about precipitating the next Holocaust every time they make a JAP joke. And, I ask you, why are there so many Jewish American Princess jokes and no Prince jokes?

For those of you who have been living in Kuala Lumpur and don't know what I'm talking about, here is an unexceptional example of the genre:

BY MARCELLE CLEMENTS

Kim, a pretty honors student, and Rick, her track-star boyfriend, are hanging out with their friends. As they chat, Kim chops up some lines of cocaine on a mirror. She offers it to Rick, who refuses it. "You always say you don't want any, and then you end up having some anyway," she groans. "Why do we have to go through all this?" Embarrassed, he shrugs his shoulders and picks up the mirror. A SCENE FROM THE VIDEO *SHATTERED: IF YOUR KID IS ON DRUGS.*

A New Weapon for Parents

FIGHTING Drugs WITH Video

By Nissa Simon

These two teenagers aren't dropouts or misfits; they are our children. The peer pressure they face, combined with the widespread availability of drugs, means they must fight the odds to stay clean. Some win; some don't. According to the National Institute on Drug Abuse, by their senior year 17 percent of all high school students have tried cocaine. Over 50 percent have tried marijuana; even more—56 percent—are active drinkers. There is a drug epidemic facing America's youth, and the overwhelming concern of many parents is how to keep their children from falling prey to it. Unfortunately, there is no simple solution. But there are ways to help kids avoid becoming involved with drugs in the first place. One of those ways is home video.

NISSA SIMON, *a freelance writer specializing in health, is the author of* Don't Worry, You're Normal: A Teenager's Guide to Self-Health *(Harper & Row).*

32 ▼ PREMIERE ISSUE 1987

ALEXA GRACE

It's not enough for parents to simply watch anti-drug videos with their children... they need to discuss them as well.

237

Art Director: Terry R. Koppel
Designer: Terry R. Koppel
Illustrator/Artist: Alexa Grace
Writer: Nissa Simon
Editor: Peter Hauck
Client: V Magazine
Publisher: Fairfield Publishing
Publication: V Magazine

238
Art Director: Larry Vigon
Designer: Judi Gold
Photographer: Jacques Schumacher
Writer: Jeff Dunas
Editor: Jeff Dunas
Client: Melrose Publishing Group
Publisher: Jeff Dunas
Publication: Collector's Photography

239
Art Director: Al Braverman
Designer: K. C. Witherell
Photographer: Langdon Clay
Illustrator/Artist: Sandy Ceppos
Writer: Claire Whitcomb
Editor: Joann R. Barwick
Client: The Hearst Corp.
Publisher: Marcia E. Miller
Publication: House Beautiful

240

Art Director: Fabien Baron
Designer: Margot Frankel
Illustrator/Artist: Gene Greif
Editor: Helen Rogan

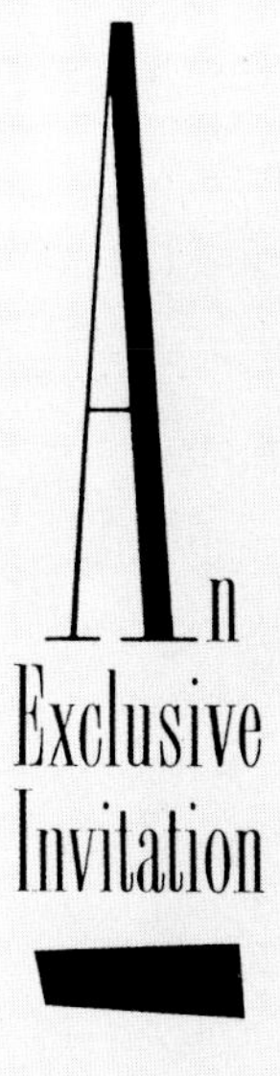

You (and a guest) are invited to visit the world of public relations. Meet the women who smile, schmooze, cajole, and hype. And find out for yourself if they get what they deserve

by David Finkle

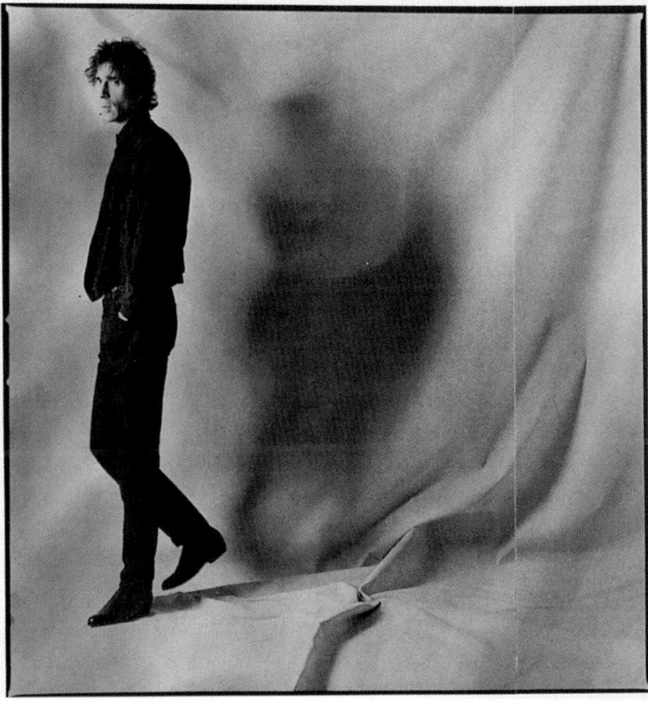

Peter Wolf Blasts Out The Past

By Steve Perry

LONE WOLF

EDDIE WATSON LIVES. So it is etched in graffiti outside Watson's practice space in an aging Boston office building. Peter Wolf is waiting his turn out in the hall while another singer wraps up his vocal workout. "Eddie's really an incredible guy," says Wolf. "What a great arranger and accompanist. During the Tin Pan Alley era he was one of the guys you'd call if you were a singer coming to town for a week at a club and needed some players." Nowadays Watson, a congenial man in his mid-seventies, supports himself with lounge gigs and music lessons. And Peter Wolf is his most illustrious— if unlikely—student.

While he waits, Wolf shuffles through photocopies of sheet music in preparation for the songs he'll be singing today: "Moon River," "Fly Me To The Moon," "This Is All I Ask." Surprise selections for his upcoming tour? Uh, no. "Eddie helps me work on phrasing, breath points, some of the finer points of singing. He also helps me understand composition better—just from the standpoint of song construction."

Self-refinement would probably be the last thing on the mind of most artists in Wolf's position. On this sunny Saturday in May, he's caught in a maelstrom of activity. Yesterday he was in New York to confirm the opening dates for his first concert tour since splitting with the J. Geils Band in 1983. Prior to that, he was in California for the editing of his video for "Can't Get Started," the second single from his new *Come As You Are* LP. And tomorrow he'll be flying back to New York to handle more tour arrangements. Tuesday the band will start daily rehearsals in Boston. And so on.

The pressures of promoting his second solo LP and getting the tour rolling are aggravated by the fact that Wolf is acting as his own business manager. "Not by choice," he emphasizes. "I just haven't found anybody to say to me, 'Hey, I deserve a percentage of your career, because I'm going to contribute *this* to it.' I could get one of these big-time managers, but they're just gonna turn me over to some young lieutenants who are on salary. They'd have no real interest in helping me.

"I have more control this way, but you can get smacked around like a ping-pong ball, too. Fortunately it's gone well so far, but it's very draining. And what's in front of me now is

Photograph by John Curtis

241

Art Director: Gary Koepke
Designer: Lisa Laarman
Photographer: John Curtis
Design Firm: Koepke Design Group

242
Art Director: David Carson
Designer: David Carson
Photographer: Grant Brittain
Client: Skateboard
Design Firm: Carson Design

243
Art Director: Edward Leida
Designer: Edward Leida
Photographer: Andrew Martin
Editor: Richard Buckley
Creative Director: Owen Hartley
Client: Fairchild Publications
Publisher: John B. Fairchild
Publication: Scene

244
Art Director: Fabien Baron
Designer: Fabien Baron
Writer: Stacy Title
Editor: Betsy Carter

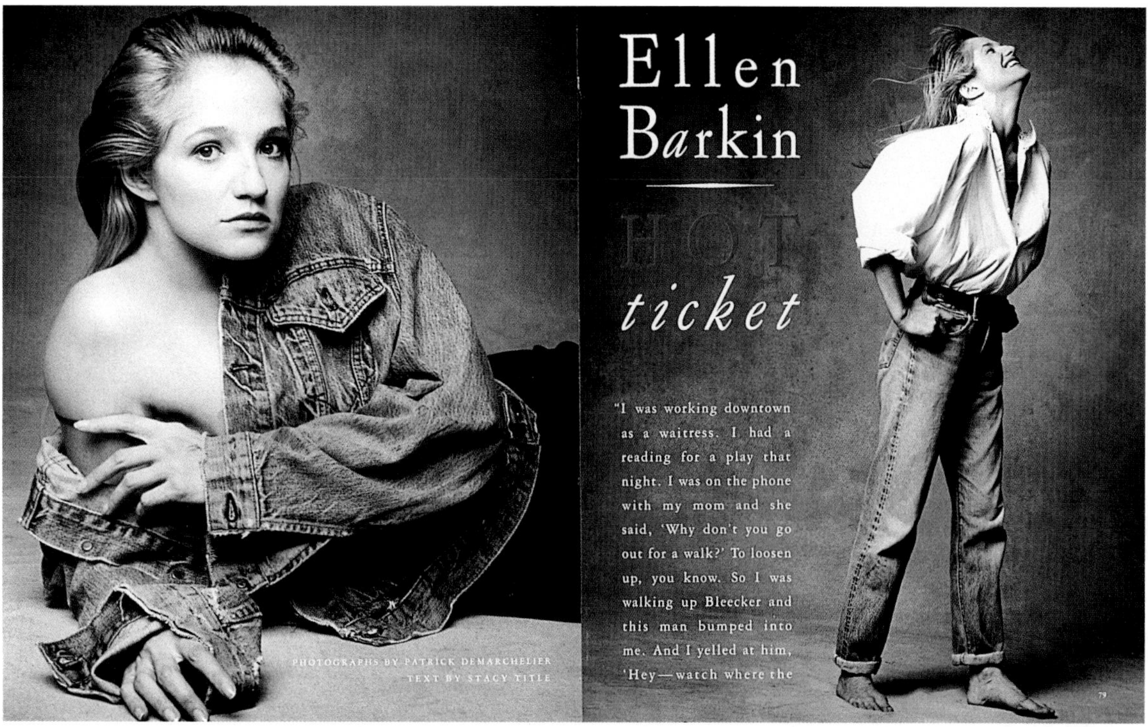

Ellen Barkin

HOT *ticket*

"I was working downtown as a waitress. I had a reading for a play that night. I was on the phone with my mom and she said, 'Why don't you go out for a walk?' To loosen up, you know. So I was walking up Bleecker and this man bumped into me. And I yelled at him, 'Hey—watch where the

PHOTOGRAPHS BY PATRICK DEMARCHELIER
TEXT BY STACY TITLE

79

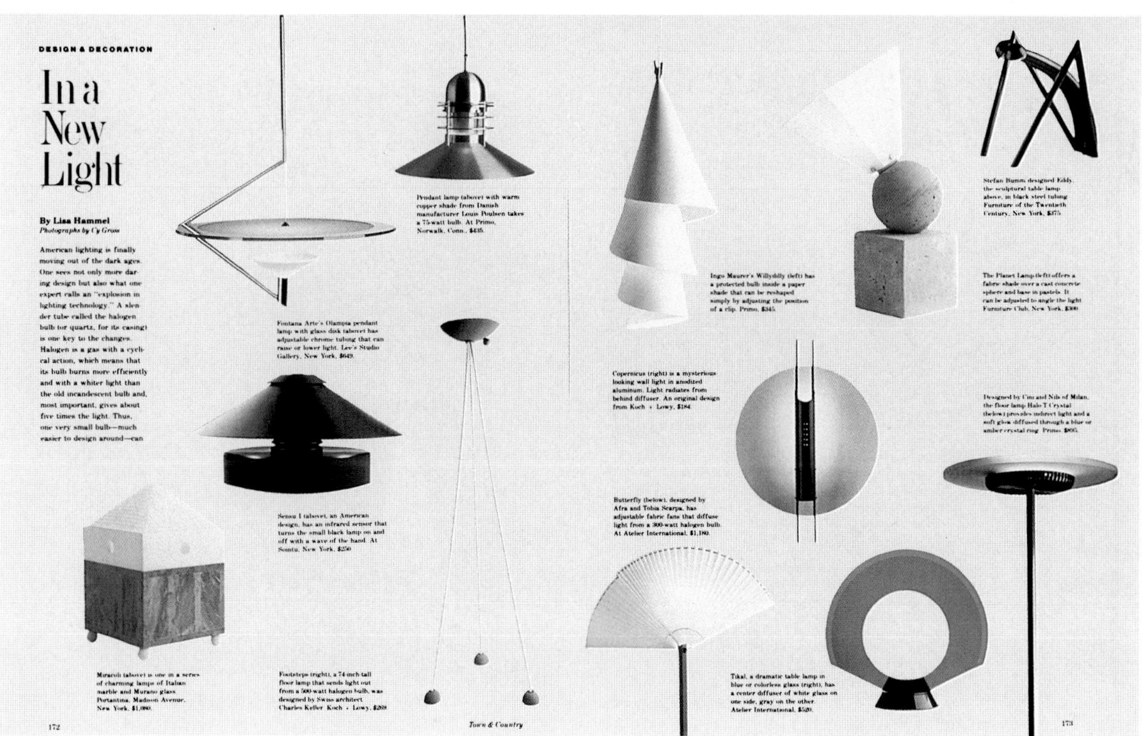

DESIGN & DECORATION

In a New Light

By Lisa Hammel
Photographs by Cy Gross

American lighting is finally moving out of the dark ages. One sees not only more daring design but also what one expert calls an "explosion in lighting technology." A slender tube called the halogen bulb (or quartz, for its casing) is one key to the changes. Halogen is a gas with a cyclical action, which means that its bulb burns more efficiently and with a whiter light than the old incandescent bulb and, most important, gives about five times the light. Thus, one very small bulb—much easier to design around—can

Fontana Arte's Olampia pendant lamp with glass disk (above) has adjustable chrome tubing that can raise or lower light. Lee's Studio Gallery, New York, $649.

Pendant lamp (above) with warm copper shade from Danish manufacturer Louis Poulsen takes a 75-watt bulb. At Primo, Norwalk, Conn., $435.

Sensu I (above), an American design, has an infrared sensor that turns the small black lamp on and off with a wave of the hand. At Sointu, New York, $250.

Miracoli (above) is one in a series of charming lamps of Italian marble and Murano glass. Portantina, Madison Avenue, New York, $1,080.

Footsteps (right), a 74-inch-tall floor lamp that sends light out from a 500-watt halogen bulb, was designed by Swiss architect Charles Keller. Koch + Lowy, $269.

Ingo Maurer's Willydilly (left) has a protected bulb inside a paper shade that can be reshaped simply by adjusting the position of a clip. Primo, $345.

Stefan Bumm designed Eddy, the sculptural table lamp above, in black steel tubing. Furniture of the Twentieth Century, New York, $375.

The Planet Lamp (left) offers a fabric shade over a cast concrete sphere and base in pastels. It can be adjusted to angle the light. Furniture Club, New York, $300.

Copernicus (right) is a mysterious-looking wall light in anodized aluminum. Light radiates from behind diffuser. An original design from Koch + Lowy, $184.

Designed by Cini and Nils of Milan, the floor lamp Halo T Crystal (below) provides indirect light and a soft glow diffused through a blue or amber crystal ring. Primo, $695.

Butterfly (below), designed by Afra and Tobia Scarpa, has adjustable fabric fans that diffuse light from a 300-watt halogen bulb. At Atelier International, $1,180.

Tikal, a dramatic table lamp in blue or colorless glass (right), has a center diffuser of white glass on one side, gray on the other. Atelier International, $520.

172 *Town & Country* 173

245
Art Director: Melissa Tardiff, Maria Bavosa
Photographer: Cy Gross
Editor: Frank Zachary
Publisher: Fred Jackson
Publication: Town & Country

246
Art Director: Tom Bentkowski
Designer: Robin Brown
Photographer: Arnold Newman
Writer: Brad Darrach
Editor: Pat Ryan
Client: Life Magazine, Time Inc.
Publisher: Lisa Valk
Publication: Life

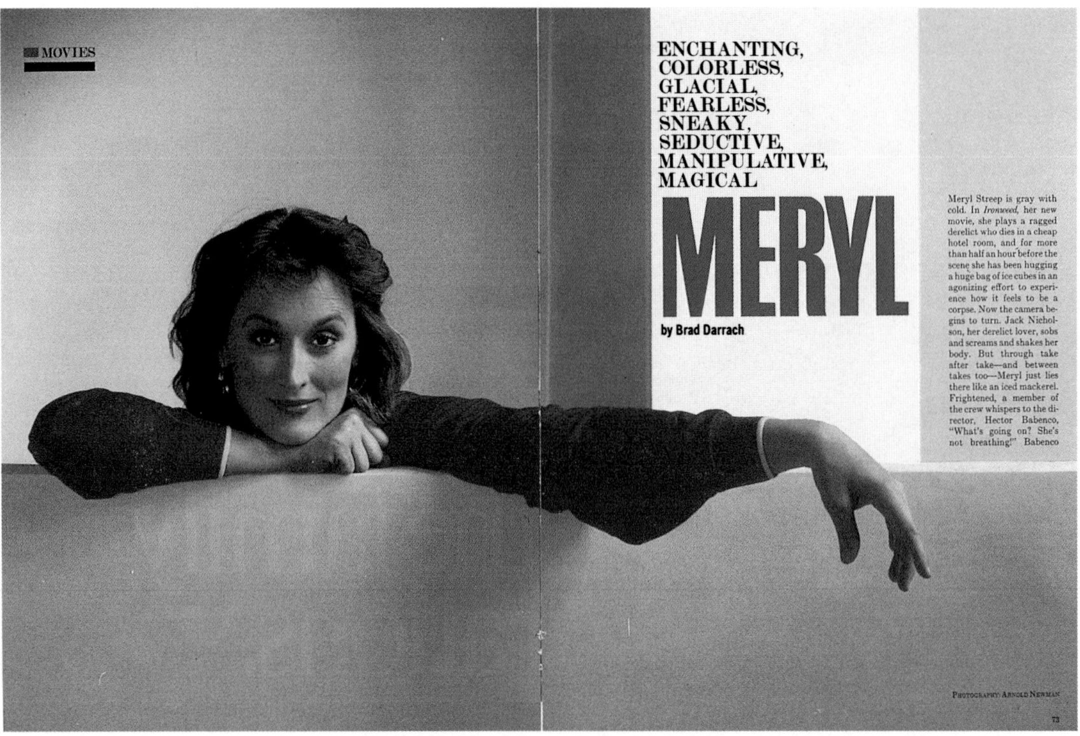

MOVIES

ENCHANTING, COLORLESS, GLACIAL, FEARLESS, SNEAKY, SEDUCTIVE, MANIPULATIVE, MAGICAL

MERYL

by Brad Darrach

Meryl Streep is gray with cold. In *Ironweed,* her new movie, she plays a ragged derelict who dies in a cheap hotel room, and for more than half an hour before the scene she has been hugging a huge bag of ice cubes in an agonizing effort to experience how it feels to be a corpse. Now the camera begins to turn. Jack Nicholson, her derelict lover, sobs and screams and shakes her body. But through take after take—and between takes too—Meryl just lies there like an iced mackerel. Frightened, a member of the crew whispers to the director, Hector Babenco, "What's going on? She's not breathing!" Babenco

Photography: Arnold Newman

73

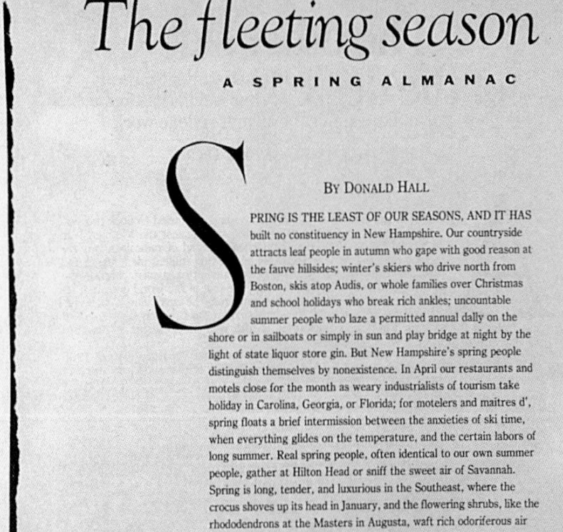

The fleeting season

A SPRING ALMANAC

By Donald Hall

SPRING IS THE LEAST OF OUR SEASONS, AND IT HAS built no constituency in New Hampshire. Our countryside attracts leaf people in autumn who gape with good reason at the fauve hillsides; winter's skiers who drive north from Boston, skis atop Audis, or whole families over Christmas and school holidays who break rich ankles; uncountable summer people who laze a permitted annual dally on the shore or in sailboats or simply in sun and play bridge at night by the light of state liquor store gin. But New Hampshire's spring people distinguish themselves by nonexistence. In April our restaurants and motels close for the month as weary industrialists of tourism take holiday in Carolina, Georgia, or Florida; for motelers and maitres d', spring floats a brief intermission between the anxieties of ski time, when everything glides on the temperature, and the certain labors of long summer. Real spring people, often identical to our own summer people, gather at Hilton Head or sniff the sweet air of Savannah. Spring is long, tender, and luxurious in the Southeast, where the crocus shoves up its head in January, and the flowering shrubs, like the rhododendrons at the Masters in Augusta, waft rich odoriferous air through the warm nights.

Of the world's seasons spring has the best press. Where are the songs of spring? Everyplace. It is when the voice of the turtle is heard in the land. A later poet told how a young man's fancy lightly turned; another called April the cruelest month; another claimed always to mourn with ever-returning spring; still another, resident of Italy, protested, "Oh, to be in England now that April's there."

Now I have never spent a whole spring *Continued on page 70*

Donald Hall lives on his family's Eagle Pond Farm in Wilmot, New Hampshire, writing poetry and prose. This essay is from *Seasons at Eagle Pond* which will be published in November by Ticknor & Fields.

22

Illustration by Merle Nacht

23

247
Art Director: Lucy Bartholomay
Designer: Gail Anderson
Illustrator/Artist: Merle Nacht
Writer: Donald Hall
Editor: Ande Zellman
Publisher: The Boston Globe
Publication: The Boston Globe, "Magazine"

248
Art Director: Larry Vigon
Designer: Linda Homler Karr
Photographer: Christian Vogt
Writer: Jeff Dunas
Editor: Jeff Dunas
Client: Melrose Publishing Group
Publisher: Jeff Dunas
Publication: Collector's Photography

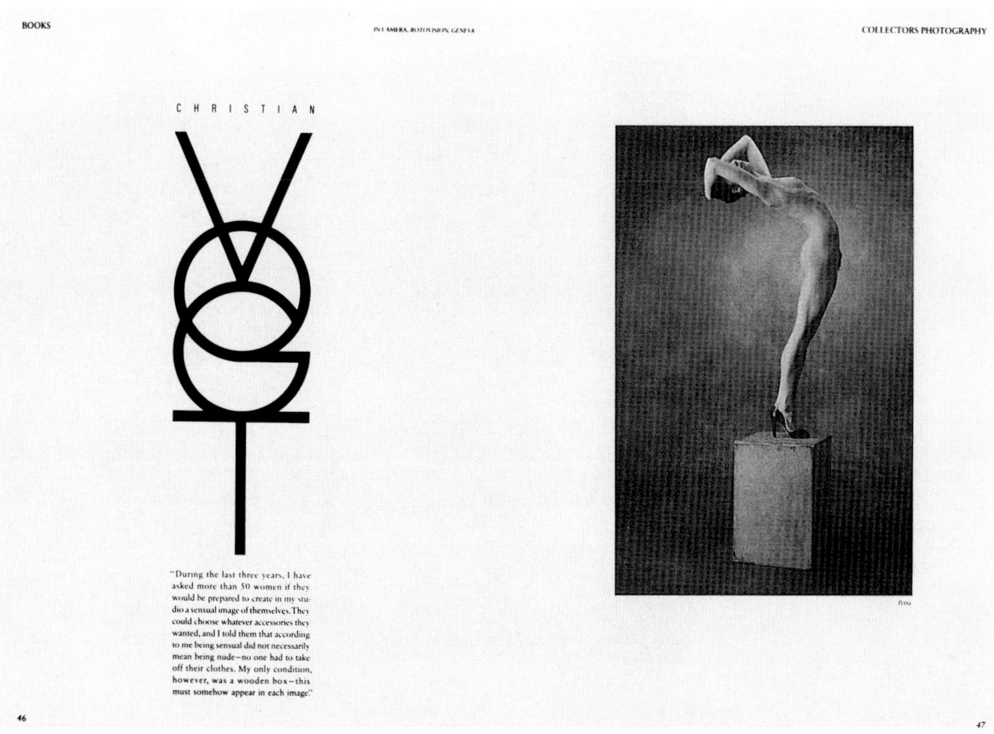

249
Art Director: Suez Kehl
Designer: Cindy Scudder
Photographer: John Dominis
Writer: Carol McCabe
Editor: Joan Tapper
Client: National Geographic Society
Publisher: National Geographic Society
Publication: National Geographic Traveler
Picture Editor: Winthrop Scudder

250

Art Director: Matthew Drace
Designer: Mark Ulriksen
Illustrator/Artist: Jamie Hogan
Writer: Laura Baker
Editor: Mark Powelson
Publisher: Earl Adkins
Publication: San Francisco Focus

FICTION

the Beachcomber

BY LAURA BAKER

The storm thundered up from the Caribbean, a sudden bitter squall that sent the pleasure boats scurrying for safety under a yellow sky. It hung offshore, boiling black before the seaview windows of the great white hotels that line the route from Miami to Palm Beach. The wind rose, sweeping the cries of birds and men alike beneath it and tumbling the striped cabañas end over end like beach balls. In the late afternoon the lights flickered once and went out, and the breakers foaming up under the palm trees pounded the beaches down into darkness. Emma turned once in her sleep: to the right into old age, and turned again, to the other side. Into what? She lay for some moments with old age to her right and something to her left. On the beach, it said.

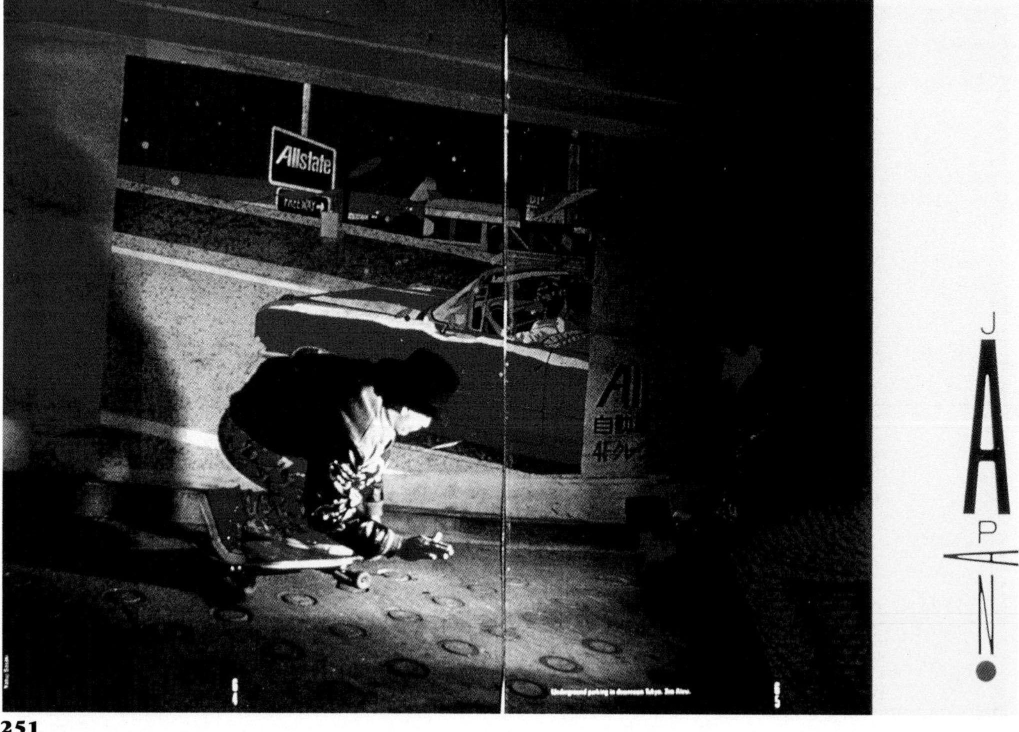

251

Art Director: David Carson
Designer: David Carson
Photographer: Grant Brittain
Client: Skateboard
Design Firm: Carson Design

252

Art Director: Eric Keller
Designer: Eric Keller
Photographer: Maria Kracjirovic
Writer: Susan Hipsley
Editor: Jane Rayburn
Client: Metropolitan Detroit
Design Firm: The Publications Co.
Publisher: Adams Communications
Publication: Metropolitan Detroit

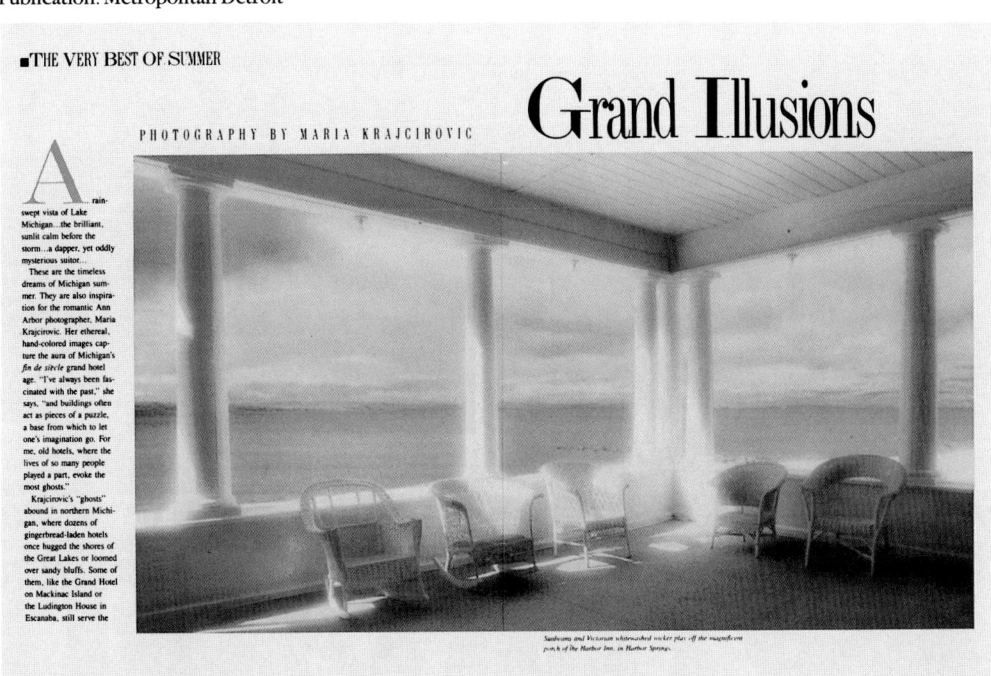

■THE VERY BEST OF SUMMER

Grand Illusions

PHOTOGRAPHY BY MARIA KRAJCIROVIC

A rain-swept vista of Lake Michigan...the brilliant, sunlit calm before the storm...a dapper, yet oddly mysterious suitor...

These are the timeless dreams of Michigan summer. They are also inspiration for the romantic Ann Arbor photographer, Maria Krajcirovic. Her ethereal, hand-colored images capture the aura of Michigan's *fin de siècle* grand hotel age. "I've always been fascinated with the past," she says, "and buildings often act as pieces of a puzzle, a base from which to let one's imagination go. For me, old hotels, where the lives of so many people played a part, evoke the most ghosts."

Krajcirovic's "ghosts" abound in northern Michigan, where dozens of gingerbread-laden hotels once hugged the shores of the Great Lakes or loomed over sandy bluffs. Some of them, like the Grand Hotel on Mackinac Island or the Ludington House in Escanaba, still serve the

Sunbeams and Victorian whitewashed wicker play off the magnificent porch of the Harbor Inn, in Harbor Springs.

68 METROPOLITAN DETROIT JUNE 1987 69

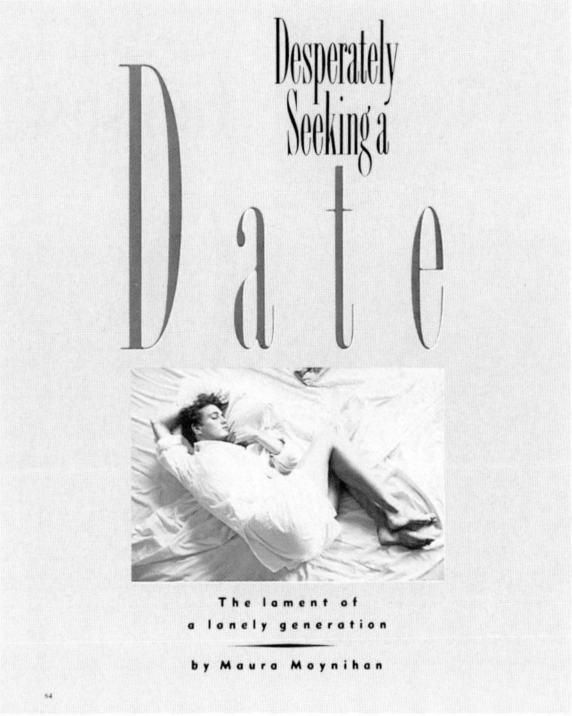

Desperately Seeking a Date

The lament of
a lonely generation

by Maura Moynihan

54

253

Art Director: Fabien Baron
Designer: Margot Frankel
Photographer: Bico Stupakoff
Editor: Betsy Carter

254

Art Director: Clare Cunningham
Designer: Clare Cunningham
Photographer: Benjamin Mendlowitz, Clare Cunningham
Writer: James P. Brown
Editor: Joseph Gribbins
Client: Nautical Quarterly
Publisher: C. S. Lovelace
Publication: Nautical Quarterly

NAUTICAL QUARTERLY

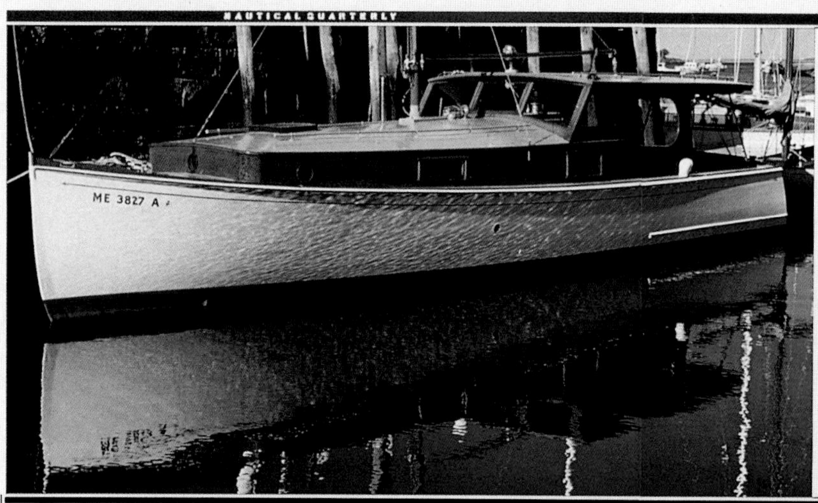

When Hugh Sharp, a former commodore of the Cruising Club of America, decided a few years ago that he and his friends were getting a little old for battling a thrashing jenny on a plunging foredeck, the retired duPont executive did not swallow the anchor. Instead he switched to a powerboat—but one with much of the aesthetic appeal and seakindliness of a well-designed sailboat. His choice was a Down-East lobsterboat, fitted out yacht-style by the John M. Williams Company of Hall's Quarry, Maine. "I've always been a sailor," says Sharp. "I didn't trust powerboats. This one I do." ☐ Sentiment was a factor in leading Dan Fales, executive editor of Motor Boating and Sailing Magazine, and his wife, Jerry, to the same choice. Their *Barnabas II* is a fiberglass Newman 36 hull from Jarvis Newman, Inc. of Manset, Maine, off a mold taken from an old wooden workboat, and given a yacht's innards by Roger Morse in Thomaston, home of her namesake, Captain Barnabas Fales, Dan's seagoing great-great-grandfather. Fales is particularly pleased with the eye-catching Maine-coast look of *Barnabas II*. "She gets an enormous amount of attention wherever we go," he reports. "The design strikes a responsive chord, especially among sailors who seem to have a deep appreciation for the lines of a boat and for seakeeping ability. Down East boats are famous for that."

LOBSTERYACHTS

BY JAMES P. BROWN

36 37

RHAPSODY IN
Gershwin

BY MARTIN F. NOLAN

On the evening of October 14, 1930, as he lifted his baton to conduct the overture to *Girl Crazy*, George Gershwin was at midpoint in his career. He had already written 20 Broadway shows and dozens of other songs, and played three of his own symphonic works in concert halls — *Rhapsody in Blue* at New York's Aeolian Hall in 1924, *Concerto in F* at Carnegie Hall in 1925, and *An American in Paris*, also at Carnegie Hall in 1928. The audience that night was to hear, for the first time, musical strains that are now as familiar as any in American music — "Bidin' My Time," "But Not for Me," and "Embraceable You." Other achievements lay ahead: the first musical awarded a Pulitzer Prize, *Of Thee I Sing*; his *Second Rhapsody*, which premiered at Symphony Hall in 1932, with Serge Koussevitsky conducting the Boston Symphony Orchestra; a full opera, *Porgy and Bess*; and scores for several movies.

Born Jacob, son of Morris and Rose Gershovitz (the family name later became Gershvin, and then Gershwin), in Brooklyn on September 26, 1898, the composer was 32 as the 1930s began, and decades of fruitful music seemed to lie ahead. Yet, 50 years ago yesterday, the world was shocked, saddened, and forced into a premature assessment of his work. George Gershwin died of a brain tumor at Cedars of Lebanon Hospital, in Los Angeles, at 10:35 a.m., July 11, 1937.

Like the armor of Patroclus, fought for by the Greeks and Trojans in the *Iliad*, the Gershwin legacy has been in dispute. Was he a genius, a jazz artist, a self-taught plugger who represented American brashness, a tunesmith with symphonic pretensions? The answer may be all of the above.

When Woody Allen needed a romantic sound track for *Manhattan* in 1979, he chose *Continued on page 32*

MARTIN F. NOLAN IS THE EDITOR OF THE GLOBE'S EDITORIAL PAGE.

ABOVE: "GEORGE BY GEORGE," A GERSHWIN SELF-PORTRAIT. FACING PAGE (INSET): THE COMPOSER AT THE PIANO IN 1926 WITH HIS LYRICIST BROTHER, IRA (RIGHT), AND DUBOSE HEYWARD, AUTHOR OF THE NOVEL *PORGY*, ON WHICH THE OPERA *PORGY AND BESS* IS BASED.

16 17

255

Art Director: Lucy Bartholomay
Designer: Lucy Bartholomay
Photographer: Nicholas Haz, Vandamn Studio
Illustrator/Artist: George Gershwin
Writer: Martin F. Nolan
Editor: Ande Zellman
Publisher: The Boston Globe
Publication: The Boston Globe, "Magazine"

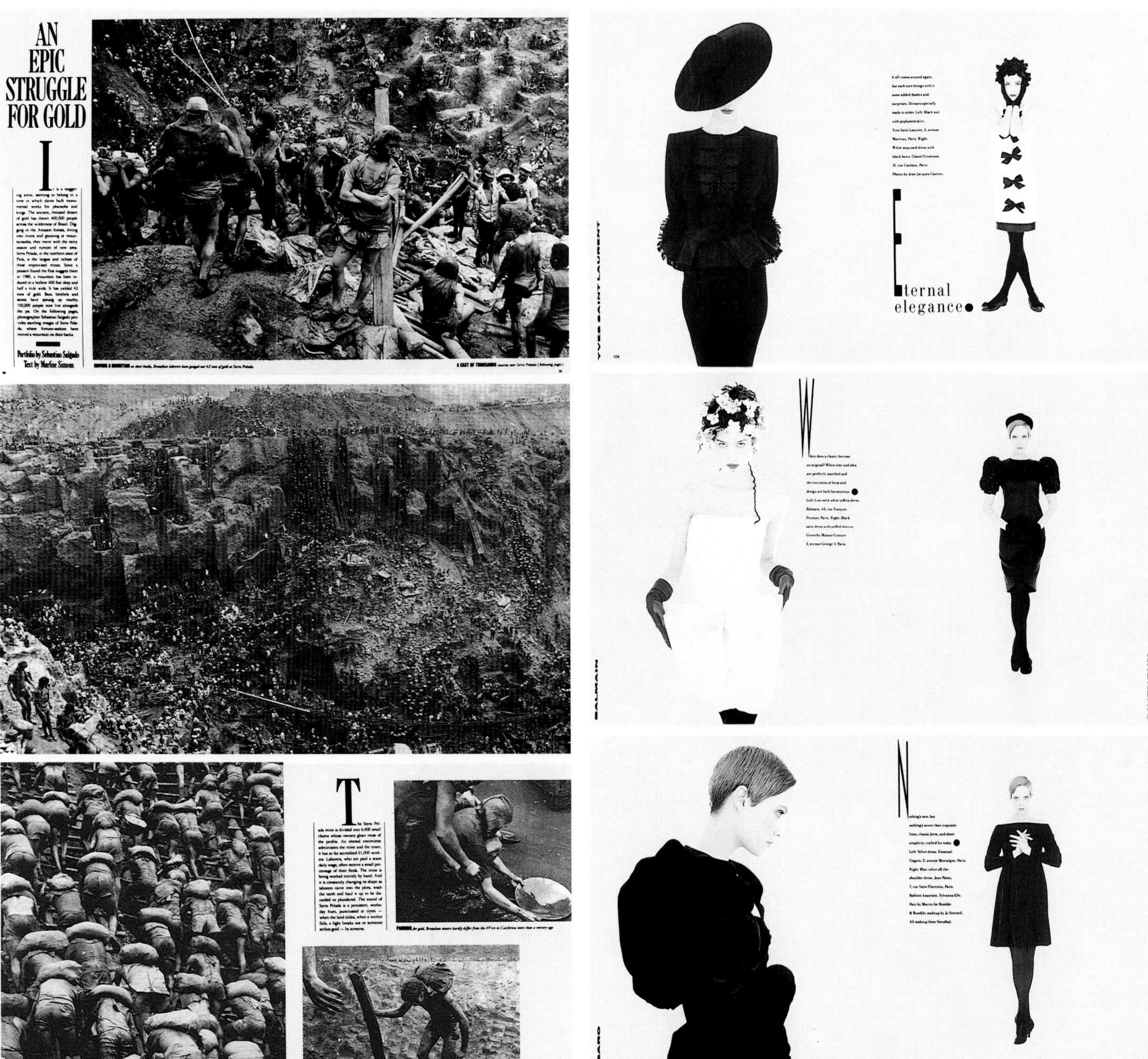

256
Art Director: Diana LaGuardia
Designer: Janet Froelich
Photographer: Sebastiao Salgado
Editor: Edward Klein
Creative Director: Tom Bodkin
Client: The New York Times
Publisher: The New York Times
Publication: The New York Times, "Magazine"

257
Art Director: Fabien Baron
Designer: Fabien Baron
Photographer: Jean-Jacques Castres
Editor: Betsy Carter

NATURAL Plants, clay and mud, marine life, trace minerals, essential oils—alone

EARTHLY DELIGHTS

or mixed together, all are potent friends to your good looks.

From the muds and fruits of the earth, to the minerals and plant life of the sea, nature holds a bounty of skin-loving treasures. The benefits of natural products have been known for centuries, the lessons handed down in rites and folklore. Ancient Egyptians used essential oils in cosmetics, medicine, and religious ceremonies, and the purveyors of these herbal preparations were held in high esteem. Natural-based substances were also found among the ancient Greeks, Romans, and Arabs. And Marco Polo, while on his famed voyage, took along an aloe plant for its seemingly miraculous healing powers when rubbed on burns, cuts, and insect bites. More recently, interest in natural products was revived by hippies during the Sixties, while "health freaks" carried the back-to-nature banner during the Seventies.

Nineteen-eighty-seven finds us on the brink of rediscovering the healing and beauty benefits of nature. Now wedded with modern technology and science, and enjoying an increasingly stronger alliance with medicine, natural products are gaining a much wider audience. Many of these advances stem from the new attention that medicine is giving to natural products, as doctors, chemists, and other researchers plumb the lessons of folklore as a starting point for developing new remedies. "The Japanese recently isolated two of the active ingredients in aloe vera that have anti-inflammatory properties," says Dr. Gary Dugan, Avon's director of skin care. "This helps explain the plant's benefits, so we are better able to understand how and why aloe vera works the way it does."

Better living through chemistry. The Europeans have a tradition, which dates back centuries, of looking to nature for cures. "When a doctor in France finds a new extract that works medicinally, beauty researchers try to discover if it has benefits for the skin as well," explains Yveline Duchesne, international training director at Clarins.

Many cosmetic companies around the world currently are learning from such diverse philosophies as ancient Chinese herbal medicine or the remedies of the American Indians. Estée Lauder, for instance, is sending its researchers to France and Italy, to work at herb farms and with plant therapists, before returning to this country to develop new products.

Although natural products have always been thought of as being ready to use—witness Polo's aloe plant—it takes a chemist to make them as effective as they presently are. And that's more effective than ever before. By studying the makeup and special properties of each natural ingredient, researchers are determining which combinations can improve the innately synergistic effect. Often this research leads, ironically, into the area of synthetics. Sometimes man-made substances can best improve nature's efficacy, helping to prolong shelf life, create formulations to better suit the needs of different body parts, or—most important—improve product penetration. "That's why mixing something yourself from a health-food store is less likely to work," says Merill Linde-

BY CATHERINE OLDS

NATURAL PLUS **When is a botanical better than just a natural? When science and modern technology unite to help make botanicals work more efficiently and more efficaciously than even nature intended. Right: Hair, Ayo for Bumble & Bumble, NYC; makeup, Craig Gadson/Moreau Inc.**

FANGO MUD **Deep conditioning via mud, botanicals, and mineral water, courtesy of Princess Marcella Borghese's Terme di Montecatini Fango Active Mud for Hair and Scalp.**

EUCALYPTUS **Oil-absorbing clay and eucalyptus oil, plus white nettle, chamomile, and witch hazel, tone the hair and scalp in Bain de Terre Eucalyptus Clay Pack.**

PALM OIL **Food for dry hair: Georgette Klinger's YH Conditioner, a blend of palm oil, egg oil, henna, panthenol, horsetail extract, and mineral oil, is mixed with two egg yolks for superrich conditioning.**

JUNIPER TAR **Normalize oily hair and scalp with Rene Furterer RF Green Cream Shampoo, a blend of essential oils—orange, cyprus, red thyme, and rosemary—juniper tar, and sulfur.**

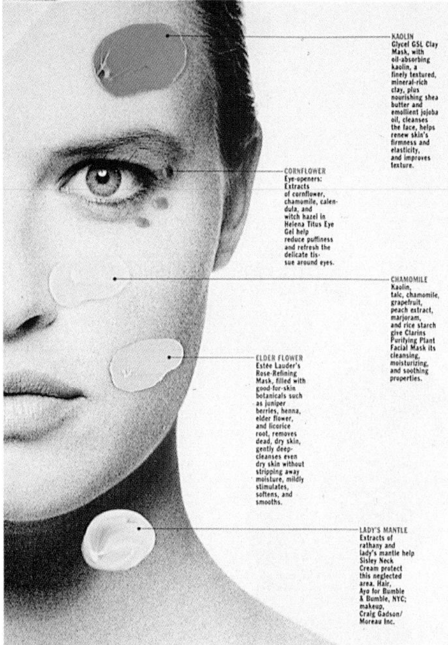

KAOLIN **Glycel GSL Clay Mask, with oil-absorbing kaolin, a finely textured, mineral-rich clay, plus nourishing shea butter and emollient jojoba oil, cleanses the face, helps renew skin's firmness and elasticity, and improves texture.**

CORNFLOWER **Eye-openers: Extracts of cornflower, chamomile, calendula, and witch hazel in Helena Titus Eye Gel help reduce puffiness and refresh the delicate tissue around eyes.**

CHAMOMILE **Kaolin, talc, chamomile, grapefruit, peach extract, marjoram, and rice starch give Clarins Purifying Plant Facial Mask its cleansing, moisturizing, and soothing properties.**

ELDER FLOWER **Estée Lauder's Rose-Refining Mask, filled with good-for-skin botanicals such as juniper berries, henna, elder flower, and licorice root, removes dead, dry skin, gently deep-cleanses even dry skin without stripping away moisture, mildly stimulates, softens, and smooths.**

LADY'S MANTLE **Extracts of rathany and lady's mantle help Sisley Neck Cream protect this neglected area. Hair, Ayo for Bumble & Bumble, NYC; makeup, Craig Gadson/Moreau Inc.**

buck, uses essential oils in environmental fragrances and in massage and bath oils. Her Oil Calmant, for example, draws on the properties of ylang ylang, chamomile, and frankincense, among other oils, to ease tension and encourage relaxation.

It came from beneath the sea. The French have long recognized the benefits of thalassotherapy—a term coined in their country in 1869 for the use of seawater and seaweed for therapeutic purposes. Seawater and seaweed are rich sources of proteins, vitamins, and minerals that are identical to and compatible with our blood. Once studies proved that they can penetrate through the skin—provided the water has been heated to 93 degrees Fahrenheit—the push was on to capture the sea's powers.

Plankton is just one of the many useful marine proteins found in today's skin-care treatments. "It works synergistically to benefit the skin, smoothing and firming it," says A. John Penicnak, Ph.D., senior vice president/corporate scientific department for Cosmair, Inc. Plankton is an essential element in all Biotherm products. Its Gel Exfoliant Smoothing Body Scrub, for instance, combines the nourishment of this marine protein with the exfoliating properties of ultra-fine granules to refine rough, uneven skin.

Algae, more sea life rich in vitamins and minerals, are thought to have a stimulating effect on skin. Flora-Spa's Body Care Kit tones and firms via their Algae Bath. And Zia Cosmetics Rejuvenating Aloe Lift Mask combines aloe, algae, and seaweed for a skin-tightening treatment. Sea peptides, a marine source with an important effect on helping skin rejuvenate its appearance, provide nourishing and antiaging properties to Estée Lauder's Skin Perfecting Creme.

The entire body, in fact, can profit from the sea. Bain de Terre's Conditioning Kelp Masque rejuvenates the hair shaft with its combination of emollient sea kelp and springwater. Repêchage's Seaweed Manicure includes a Seaweed Mask that gives hands, those often-neglected parts of the body, a deep hydrating treatment.

Trace for the face. Trace elements, essential for healthy skin, play important roles in stimulating the skin's metabolism, according to Dr. Penicnak. Copper assists elastin and collagen development and helps strengthen skin, while iron promotes cell renewal. Silicon is essential for the maintenance and growth of connective tissue, zinc aids in the repair and renewal of healthy skin, and magnesium promotes an energetic metabolism. All are present in Lancôme's Oligo Major Activating Serum with Trace Elements, which increases cell respiration while helping improve skin's tone, elasticity, firmness, and texture. Skin-care expert Ilona of Hungary claims that magnesium is the "magic mineral." And that explains why all her products—from cleansers to night creams—contain magnesium-rich water brought from her native Budapest.

More and more companies, in fact, are basing products on mineral water. Water is vital to skin cells. And the best way to make a cell membrane work is with a combination of water and minerals. Minerals control the membrane's permeability, and help transport fluid more efficiently across the membrane. And they also help the cell to hold on to water for a longer period of time. Princess Marcella Borghese's Terme di Montecatini Clinical Spa Eye Care System employs Aqua di Vita Botanico, the mineral-rich waters of the famed Italian spa, as an enriched base for its creams and compresses.

The feats of clay. Since ancient times, spa treatments have used clays and muds to absorb oils and draw impurities away from the skin. Today they're contained in more modern products in combination with other botanicals or with one another. Glycel GSL Clay Mask, for example, includes kaolin, a finely textured clay rich in minerals. Christian Dior's Hydra-Dior Refreshing Clay Masque also uses kaolin, along with chamomile, cucumber, and allantoin extracts, for deep but gentle cleansing.

L'Herbier de Provènce has found that green clay, the key ingredient in their Green Clay Masque, has special purifying and cleansing properties. Combining it with extracts of willow, leek, rosemary, and hazelnut oil gives a nourishing yet mildly astringent effect, making the mask especially beneficial for oily skin.

The good and precious earth. Nowhere is the wealth of the earth and nature more apparent than in the Crown Jewels by Vera Brown Skincare, a group of lotions and creams developed by Dr. Stephen Chang from a 400-year-old family formula. Privy to the secrets of ancient Chinese medicine—one of his ancestors was physician to the imperial court—Chang mixes pulverized jade (the Chinese used to bury their royal leaders in jade because of its skin-preserving qualities) with frankincense and myrrh. The result: Jade Cream, to moisturize and revitalize.

It stands to reason that as interest in natural products and ingredients continues to grow, more up-until-now-untapped beauty treasures will be discovered. Equipped with new knowledge and modern technology, beauty promises to work hand in hand with science to find, refine, and profit from botanicals as never before. And that can usher in a whole new era of beauty and skin care, naturally. □

FACE-OFF Natural blends exfoliate skin where it's rough, moisturize where it's dry, firm where it's slack, proving that Mother Nature knows best.

258
Art Director: Phyllis Schefer
Photographer: Guzman
Publication: Elle
Publication Director: Régis Pagniez

259
Art Director: Phyllis Schefer
Photographer: Gilles Bensimon
Publication: Elle
Publication Director: Régis Pagniez

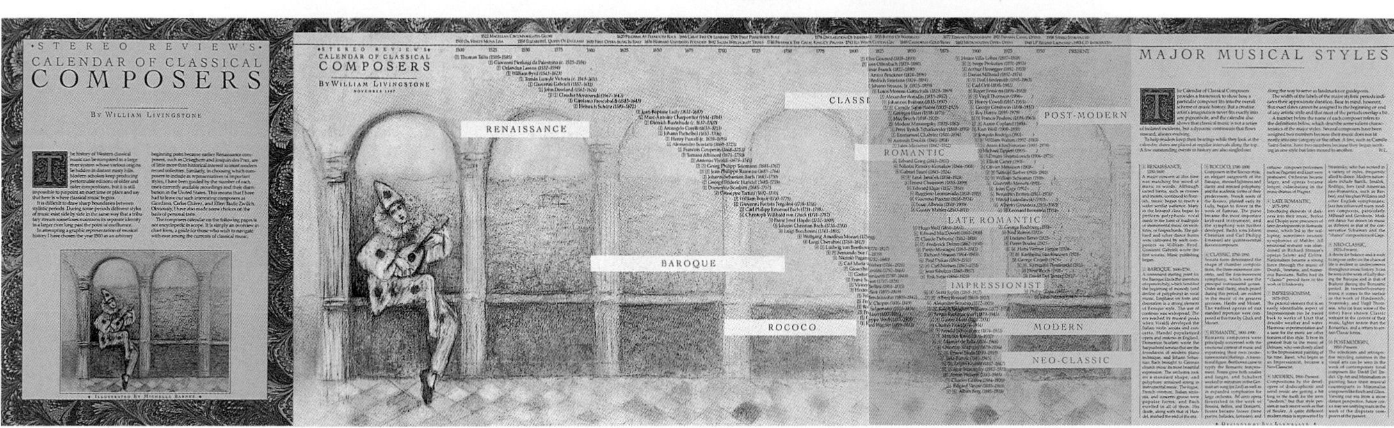

260
Art Director: Sue Llewellyn
Designer: Sue Llewellyn
Illustrator/Artist: Michelle Barnes
Writer: William Livingstone
Editor: William Livingstone
Publication: Stereo Review

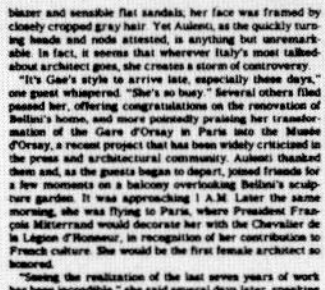

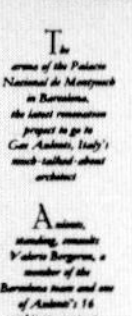

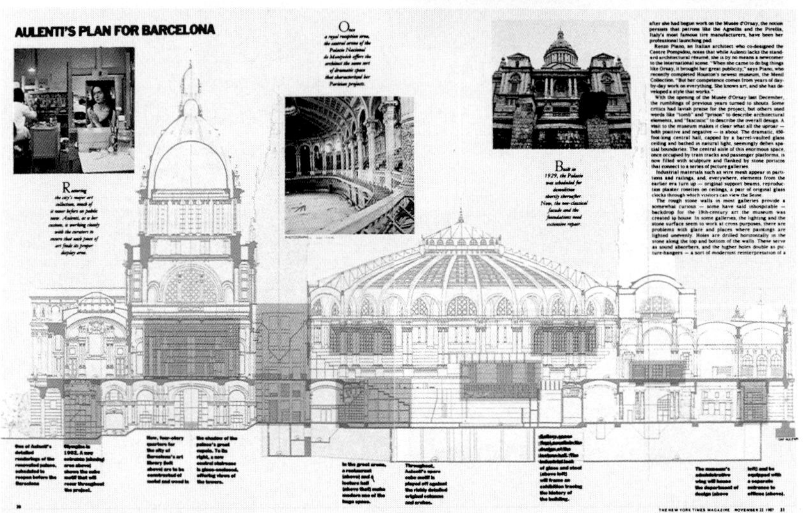

261

Art Director: Diana LaGuardia
Designer: Janet Froelich
Photographer: Lizzie Himmel
Editor: Edward Klein
Creative Director: Tom Bodkin
Client: The New York Times
Publisher: The New York Times
Publication: The New York Times, "Magazine"

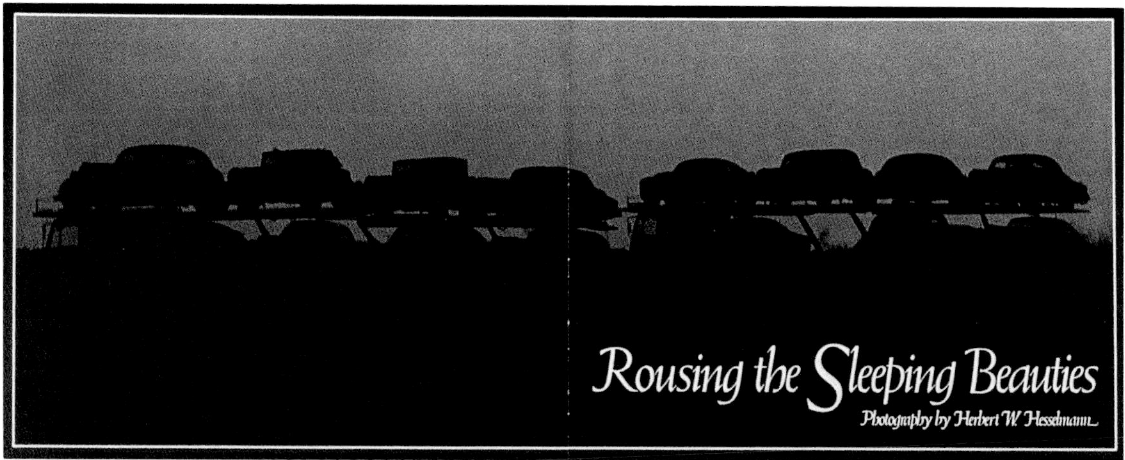

Rousing the Sleeping Beauties

Photography by Herbert W. Hesselmann

IN DEATH EXISTS a certain dignity. The sanctity of our souls demands that our earthly remains should be permitted to repose undisturbed and merge slowly with the soil surrounding them. The grave-robber's damnation shall be his to bear for life.

In Volume XXII, Number 2, we presented Herbert W. Hesselmann's disturbing portraits from this private European crypt. Included among them were examples of the world's most celebrated marques.

For reasons yet unclear, the anonymous owner of this mechanical morgue has since sought to move his collection, disrupting the peaceful slumber of his cadavers while relocating them to distant quarters.

WHAT HAS RESULTED, as Hesselmann's exclusive photographs bear witness, appears even more disquieting than his originals. Rusted, rotted and long past salvation, these plundered carcasses seem almost to mock the vaunted status of their polished, pampered and restored relations.

On the preceding page, for example, an Alfa 2300 SS lies wrecked and ruined. Below, a Lancia Flaminia has sat so long unmoved that a tree has sprouted between its bumper and body.

One by one, the Bugattis and the Astons, two Cords, a Lincoln, two Lotuses, three Lancias, a Ferrari and a host of other relics are dragged on to their rolling bier, to travel miles before they sleep again.

262

Art Director: Michael Pardo
Designer: Michael Pardo
Photographer: Herbert W. Hesselmann
Writer: Lowell C. Paddock
Editor: Lowell C. Paddock
Publication: Automobile Quarterly

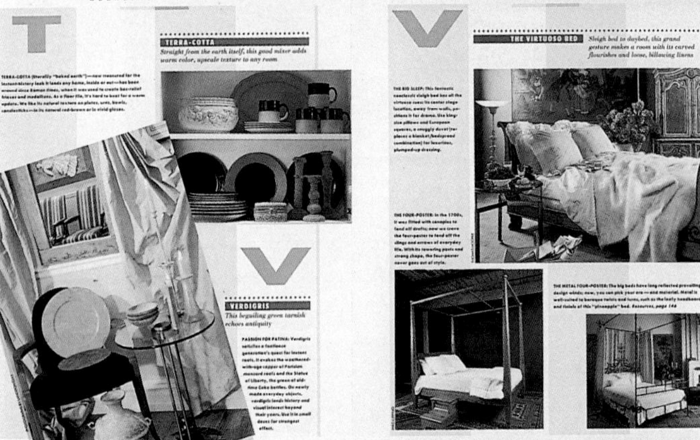

263
Art Director: Don Morris
Designer: Richard Ferretti, Don Morris
Publisher: Meredith Corp.
Publication: Metropolitan Home
Design Assistant: Kayo Dersarkissian

264
Art Director: Don Morris
Designer: Richard Ferretti, Don Morris
Photographer: John Vaughan
Publisher: Meredith Corp.
Publication: Metropolitan Home
Design Assistant: Kayo Dersarkissian
Design Assistant: Janet Stein-Folan

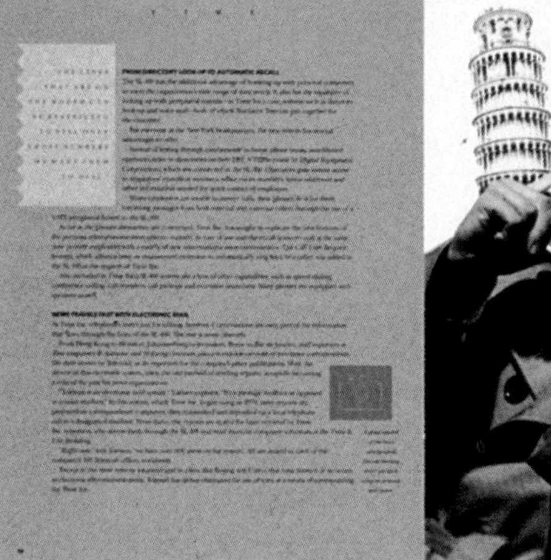

265

Art Director: D. J. Stout
Designer: D. J. Stout
Photographer: William Coupon
Editor: Gregory Curtis
Publisher: Michael Levy
Publication: Texas Monthly
Typography: Steve Gibbs

266

Art Director: Bryan L. Peterson
Designer: Bryan L. Peterson
Photographer: Geof Kern
Writer: Marsha Coburn
Editor: Sharon Larkin, Barbara Wooley
Client: Northern Telecom
Design Firm: Peterson & Co.
Publication: Access

DIETS BE DAMNED! BRING ON DESSERT!

Chocolate Pâté, Banana-Nut Pie and More from America's Top Restaurants
By Alan Richman
Photography by Constance Hansen

267
Art Director: Elizabeth Woodson
Designer: Betty Alfenito
Photographer: Constance Hansen
Publisher: American Express Publishing Corp.
Publication: Food & Wine

At the head of their class, these seven Texas fashion students have big designs on American couture.

by Helen Thompson

MOST LIKELY TO SUCCEED

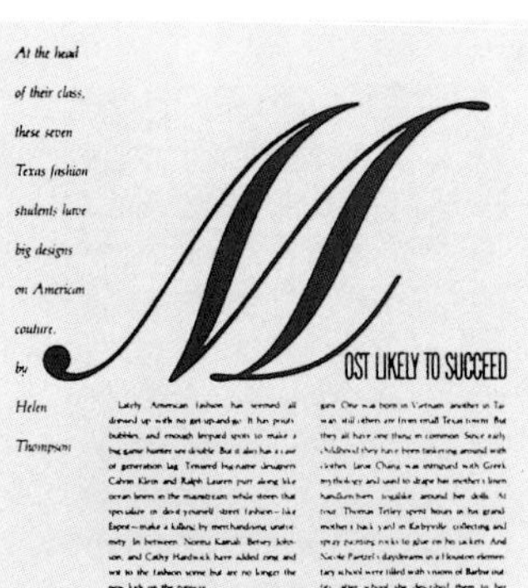

RIC GUTIERREZ

RANDY CARRELL

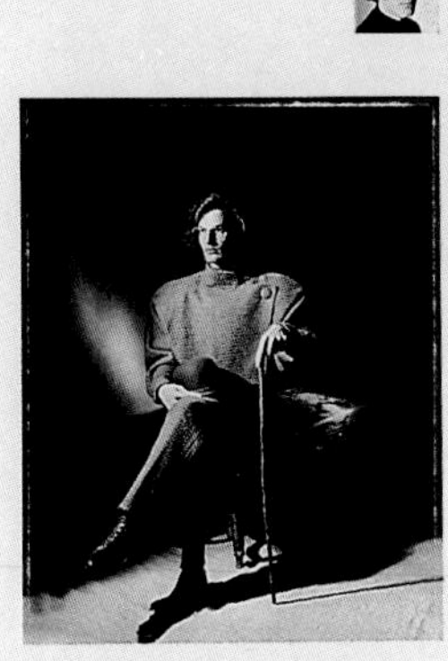

DELISA DOLAN

THOMAS TETLEY
JANIE CHANG
LAN LE

NICOLE PAETZEL

268
Art Director: D. J. Stout
Designer: D. J. Stout
Photographer: Geof Kern
Writer: Helen Thompson
Editor: Gregory Curtis
Publisher: Michael Levy
Publication: Texas Monthly

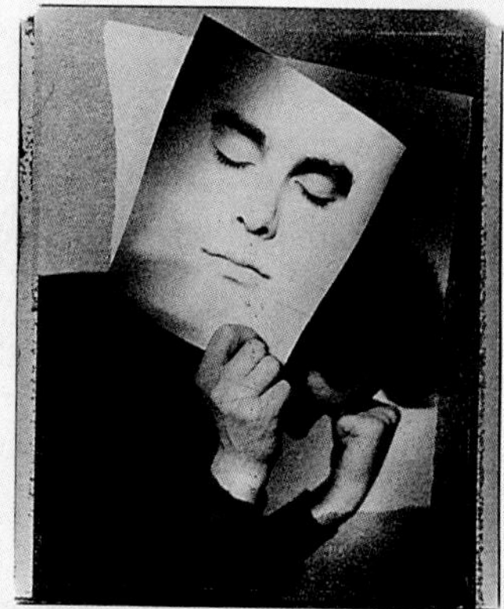

First it was no salt and no caffeine. Then no smoking, please. Then it was time to say no to drugs. Then there was herpes, and now there's AIDS, so it's no to sex. Add it all up and you've got . . .

by David Seeley

The NO *Decade*

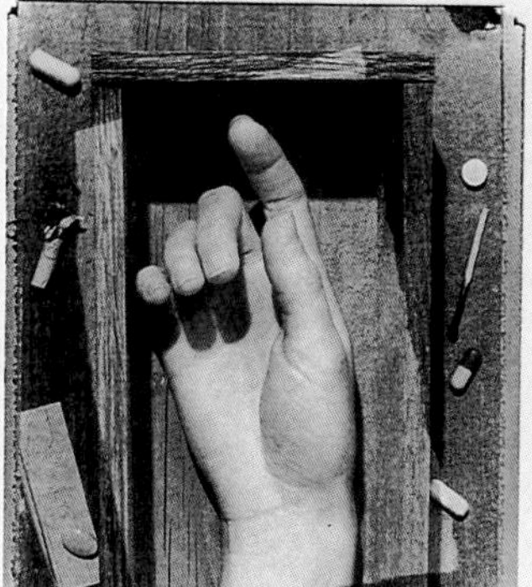

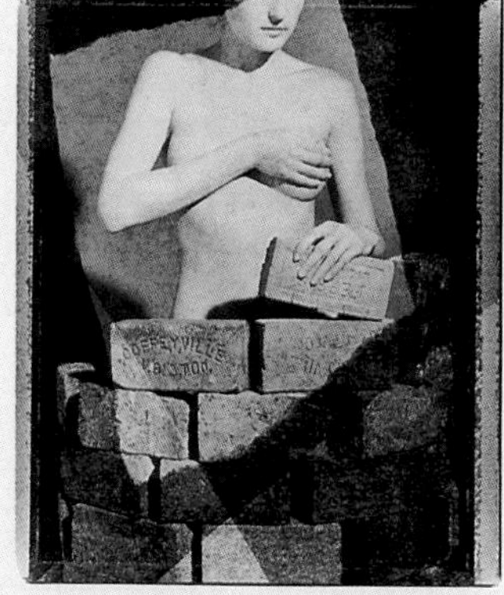

269

Art Director: D. J. Stout
Designer: D. J. Stout
Photographer: Geof Kern
Writer: David Seeley
Editor: Gregory Curtis
Publisher: Michael R. Levy
Publication: Texas Monthly

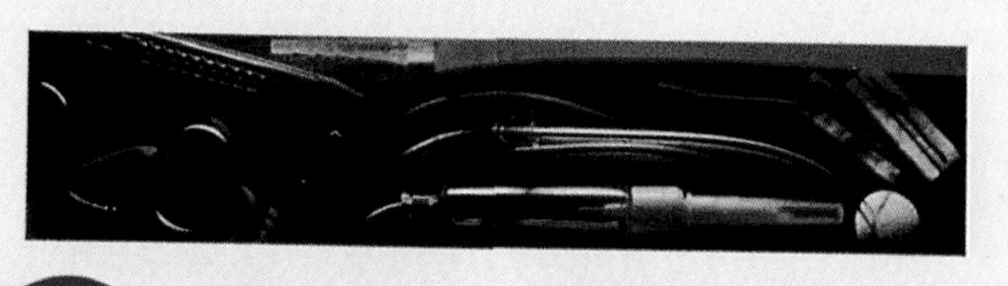

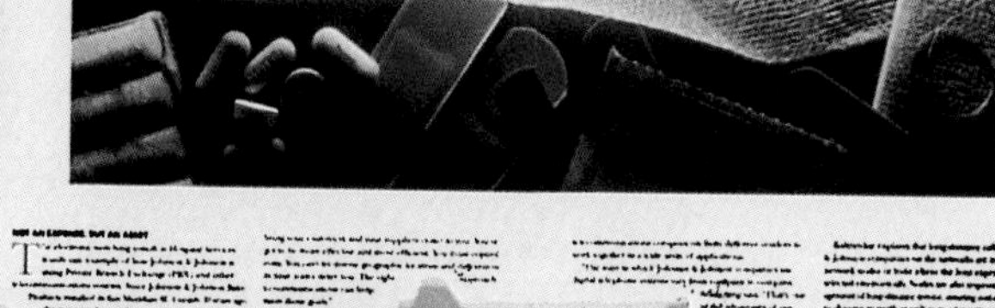

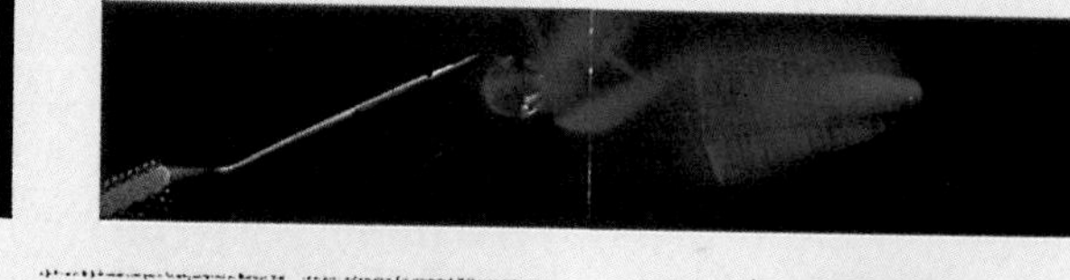

PROFILE:

270

Art Director: Bryan L. Peterson
Designer: Bryan L. Peterson
Photographer: Robb Debenport
Editor: Sharon Larkin, Barbara Wooley
Client: Northern Telecom
Design Firm: Peterson & Co.
Publication: Access

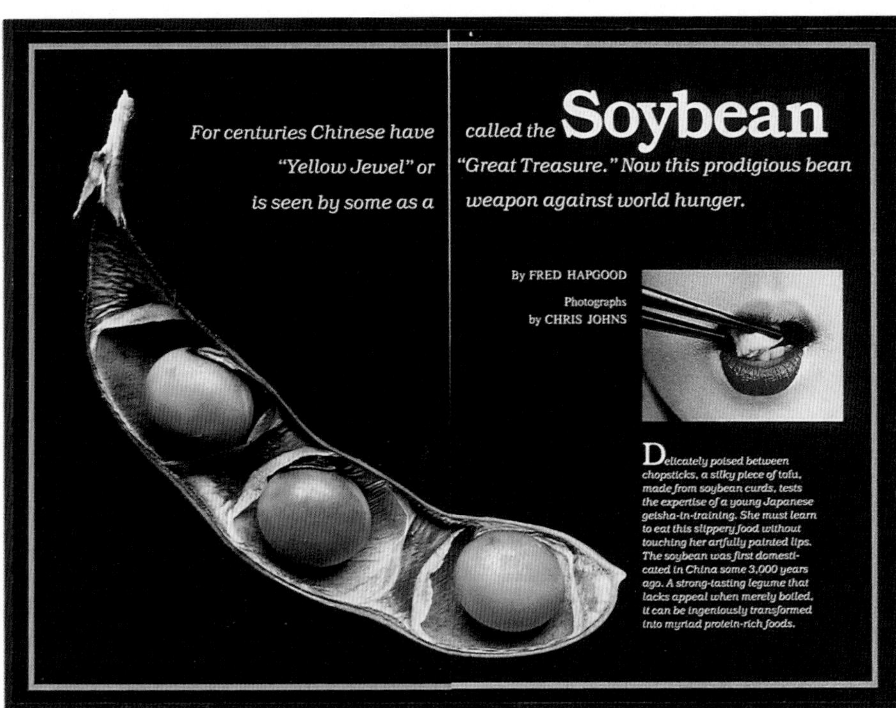

For centuries Chinese have called the Soybean "Yellow Jewel" or "Great Treasure." Now this prodigious bean is seen by some as a weapon against world hunger.

By FRED HAPGOOD

Photographs by CHRIS JOHNS

Delicately poised between chopsticks, a silky piece of tofu, made from soybean curds, tests the expertise of a young Japanese geisha-in-training. She must learn to eat this slippery food without touching her artfully painted lips. The soybean was first domesticated in China some 3,000 years ago. A strong-tasting legume that lacks appeal when merely boiled, it can be ingeniously transformed into myriad protein-rich foods.

A feast for the eyes

Japanese dishes show the soybean in its most artful incarnations.

Elegantly simple, "simmering tofu," or yudofu (left), is cooked in a wooden casket and served with a teapot of soy sauce. Decorated with tiny leaves, dengaku (above) is made by broiling skewered tofu coated in miso (fermented soybean paste).

The first and tastiest skimming of soy milk produced these mouth-watering strips of yuba (center). A trio of miso-flavored dumplings is served on a smooth rock (right).

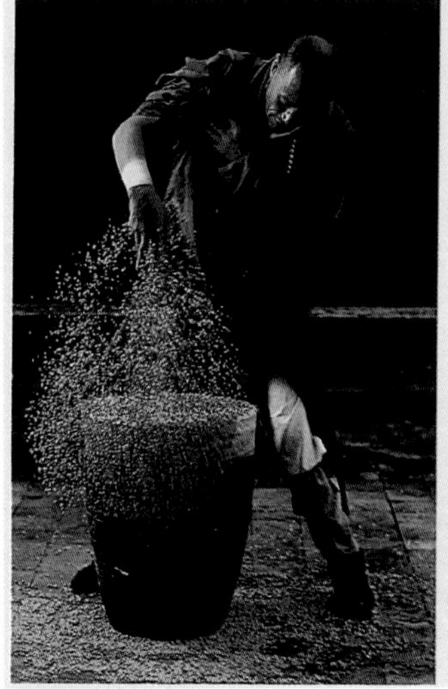

milled in the country with 5 percent soy flour. This was one of our biggest plans." Unfortunately, Sri Lanka's largest mill refused to participate in the program.

The staff of the island nation's Soyabean Foods Research Centre regrouped and developed another plan—to persuade citizens to substitute soya for an existing food. In this case they hoped to substitute it for coconut milk, which is widely used as a cooking medium. "Coconuts are a land-intensive and unpredictable crop," said S. Pathiravitana, editor of *Soyanews*. "The government hoped to wean the people from dependence on them while also improving their diets."

A factory was built to produce a soy-milk powder, to be marketed as Rajasoya. A promotion campaign was planned—and then, as if the gods themselves were rooting for the cause, at the very moment of the product rollout, the coconut crop collapsed.

"The price of a coconut went up from one rupee to five," Cecil Dharmasena, director of the research center, recalled. "Rajasoya was very successful. Everybody started using it. The factory hired a second shift and began planning a third. Then coconut prices began to slip, they went down to two and a half rupees, and back up to three—still a lot more expensive than they had been, but suddenly people just started paying the higher prices. Sales of Rajasoya plummeted. We went to one shift, two days a week."

There are Sri Lankans, I was told, who prefer soy-milk powder to coconut milk, finding the latter too heavy and greasy, but obviously they are a minority. The research center subsequently developed coconut-soy blends that native Sri Lankans (taste tests seem to show) find more acceptable, but so far no entrepreneurs have been willing to back them in the marketplace.

The campaign to win the hearts and minds of Sri Lankans for the soybean continues. The Rajasoya factory is again working near full capacity, and the government is planning to supply schoolchildren with a fresh soy beverage every day. One Muslim trader I spoke to waved away the idea that the soybean had failed in Sri Lanka. There were still lots of possibilities, he said. "This is a Buddhist country," he reminded me. "We eat meat, but we feel guilty about it."

ANOTHER REASON why soya might yet succeed in Sri Lanka, at least over the long term, is that the local farmers continue to grow the bean, and in increasing volume. "Who buys your beans? The government?" I asked the farmers. No, I was told, private traders. "And who do they sell them to?" Nobody seemed to know, so, together with Pathiravitana, I visited the Pettah on Old Moor Street in Colombo, headquarters to the traders of Sri Lanka.

There, away from the noisy, colorful circus that is the traffic of downtown Colombo, we went from stall to stall, and soon the source of this mysterious increase in demand became clear: Poultry growers were buying the bean. The livestock industry had arrived in Sri Lanka, and it was thriving. "The old ways are certainly breaking down," sighed Pathiravitana, referring to the Buddhist strictures against eating flesh. For myself, I was struck at finding a case in which livestock feed was apparently playing a positive role in the development of soy foods by stabilizing the market for the farmer while the soy-foods industry experimented with different approaches for human comestibles.

Spurred to greater efforts by initial setbacks in Sri Lanka's soybean campaign, researchers have come up with a variety of soy products, including a coffee "extender," breakfast cereal-like soybean flakes, and increasingly popular vegetarian "Soyameat," devoid of the characteristic legume taste that marked—and doomed—earlier substitutes. The experts now cite Sri Lanka's program as a model for other developing nations, noting that consumption of the nutritious, all-purpose bean has significantly increased in the past five years.

And that's not just chicken feed. □

The mighty soybean challenges a martial-arts master: Shi Yong-zhou, 56, a former Shaolin temple monk in China's Henan Province, tests his strength by plunging an arm elbow-deep into the bean-packed barrel.

The Prodigious Soybean

271

Art Director: Robert W. Madden
Photographer: Christopher Johns
Illustrator/Artist: James Gurney
Writer: Fred Hapgood
Picture Editor: Susan Welchman
Cartography: Hal Aber

SPECIAL REPORT

COLLECTORS PHOTOGRAPHY

H A N D - C O L O R I N G

Since the inception of *COLLECTORS PHOTOGRAPHY*, we have tried to publish portfolios that reflect the graphic strengths of the photographer's style and continuity of his or her vision. Often, mixed into a selection of black and white images, for example, we find several hand-tinted images. These images are often quite beautiful, but to present a consistent view of an artist's work, we select the entire portfolio from either the black-and-white work, or the color images. Some photographers prefer working in color, the majority in black and white.

Hand tinting black and white images has been a part of many a photographer's arsenal of techniques since the turn of the century. Very popular in the twenties and thirties, it seemed to have lost favor thereafter until the 1970s, when the technique was applied to all manner of photography: fashion, beauty, advertising and fine art.

Early in this decade, many photographers began experimenting with older processes; toning black and white images with sepia, selenium, and gold; carbon processes, gum bichromates, platinum printing and others. Photographers realized that these techniques only broadened their ability to create. Having mastered them, they enhanced their abilities to interpret a client's wishes, expanded the scope of their personal styles, and the necessary ability to stay with the current trends of their industry and art.

Now, in the late 1980s, hand tinting or hand coloring, depending on which you prefer, is again very popular. Photographers are discovering that collectors are often taken with the subtle possibilities hand tinting avails, galleries are showing more hand tinted work than ever, and photographers the world over are impassioned with its unique qualities. Many artists have discovered that they can blend the techniques they've mastered in painting and drawing with photography, and conversely, photographers interested in painting and drawing have found that hand tinting is an ideal means of merging these two talents into a single art statement.

COLLECTORS PHOTOGRAPHY would be remiss if we didn't assemble an entire portfolio dedicated to this phenomena, and recognize it as a vital part of today's photographic expression.

SPECIAL REPORT

COLLECTORS PHOTOGRAPHY

272

Art Director: Diana LaGuardia
Designer: Audrone Razgaitis
Editor: Edward Klein
Creative Director: Tom Bodkin
Client: The New York Times
Publisher: The New York Times
Publication: The New York Times, "Magazine"

Martine Sitbon "the new york woman is an eccentric dream."

WITH A NEW YORK ACCENT

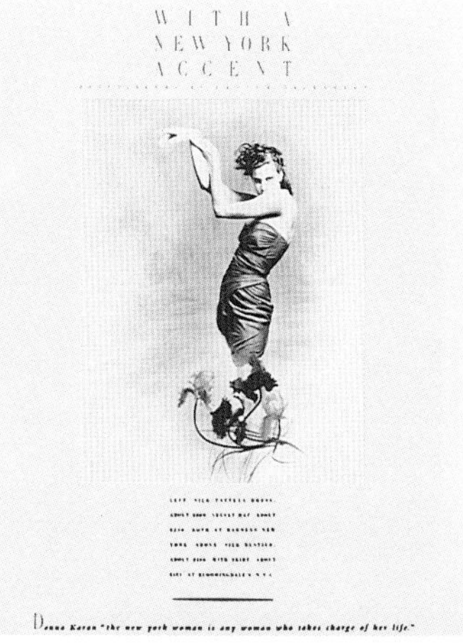

Donna Karan "the new york woman is any woman who takes charge of her life."

Rei Kawakubo "clothes reflect an attitude. the new york woman's is independent and free."

Romeo Gigli "I design for the urban woman who never loses her femininity."

Yves Saint-Laurent "fashion passes but style is eternal."

David Cameron "the new york woman is as diverse as the city itself."

273

Art Director: Fabien Baron
Designer: Fabien Baron
Photographer: Javier Valhonrat
Editor: Betsy Carter

274

Art Director: Larry Vigon
Writer: Jeff Dunas
Editor: Jeff Dunas
Client: Melrose Publishing Group
Publisher: Jeff Dunas
Publication: Collector's Photography

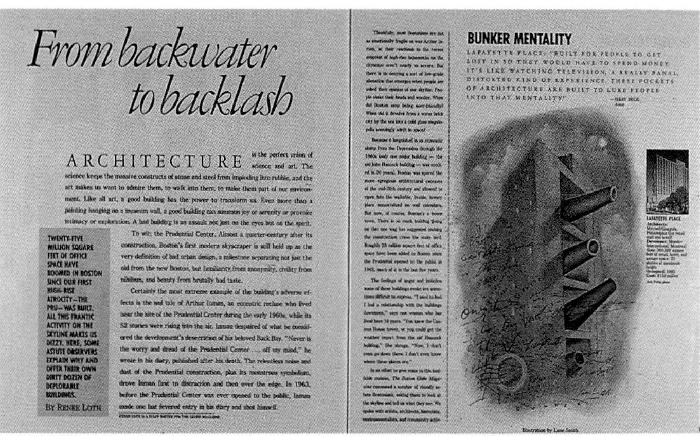

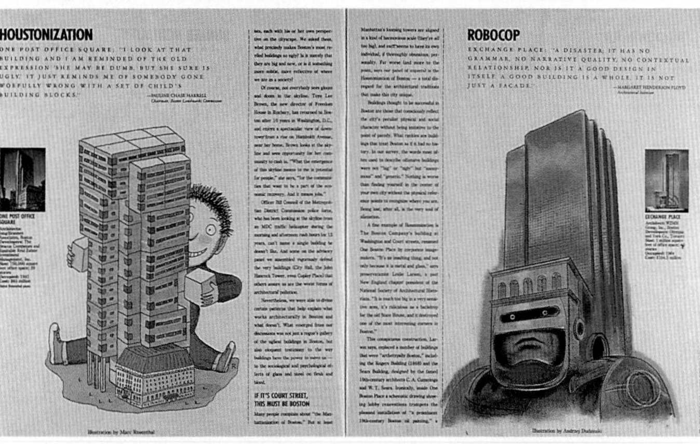

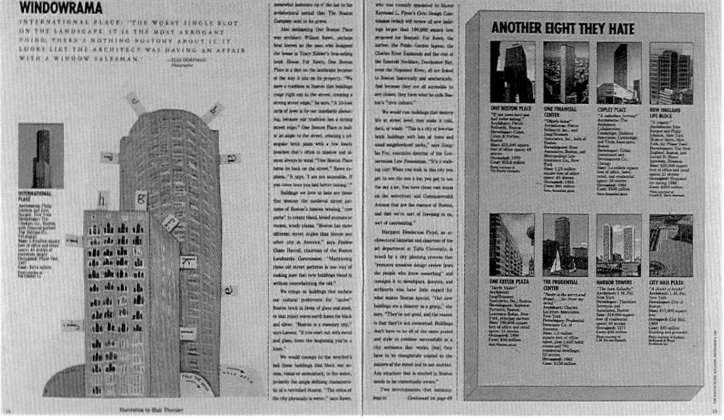

275

Art Director: Lucy Bartholomay
Designer: Lucy Bartholomay, Gail Anderson
Illustrator/Artist: Lane Smith, Marc Rosenthal, Andrzej Dudzinski, Blair Thornley
Writer: Renee Loth
Editor: Ande Zellman
Publisher: The Boston Globe
Publication: The Boston Globe, "Magazine"

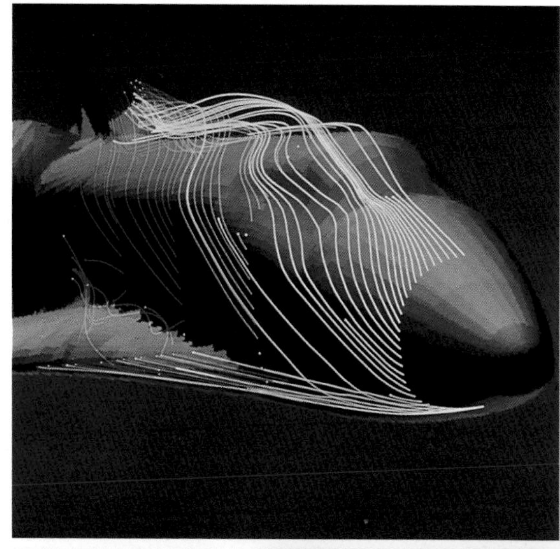

MACHINE DREAMS TAKE FLIGHT

SILICOSMS

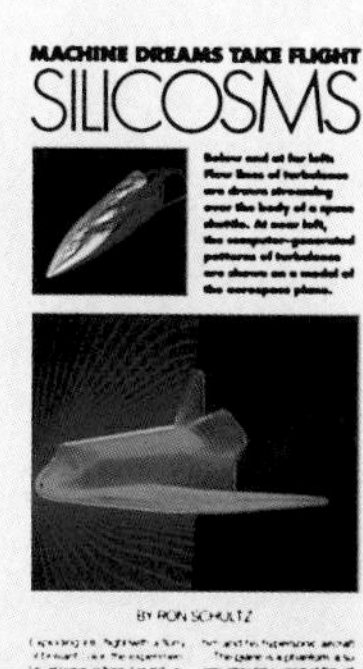

Below and at far left: Flow lines of turbulence are drawn streaming over the body of a space shuttle. At near left, the computer-generated patterns of turbulence are shown on a model of the aerospace plane.

BY RON SCHULTZ

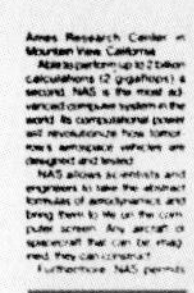
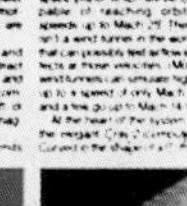
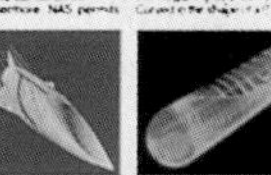
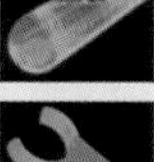

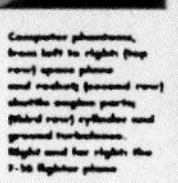

Computer phantoms, from left to right: (top row) space plane and rocket; (second row) shuttle engine parts; (third row) cylinder and ground turbulence. Right and far right: the F-16 fighter plane

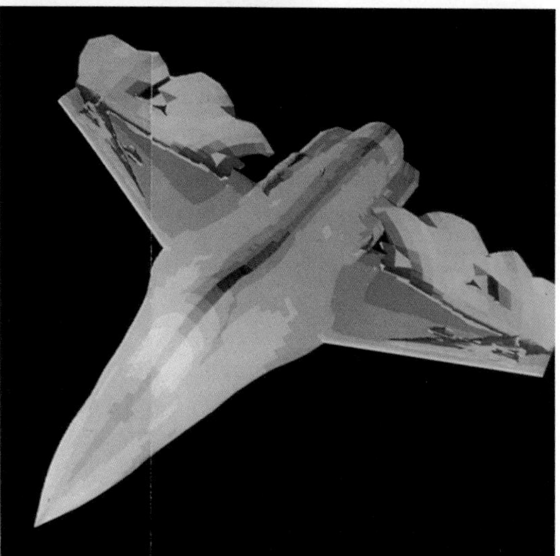

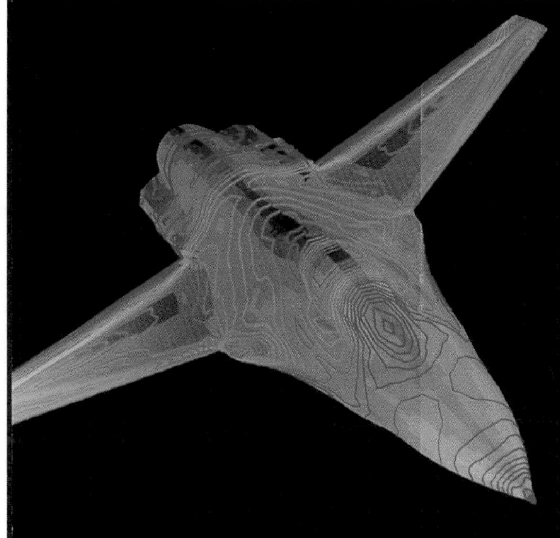

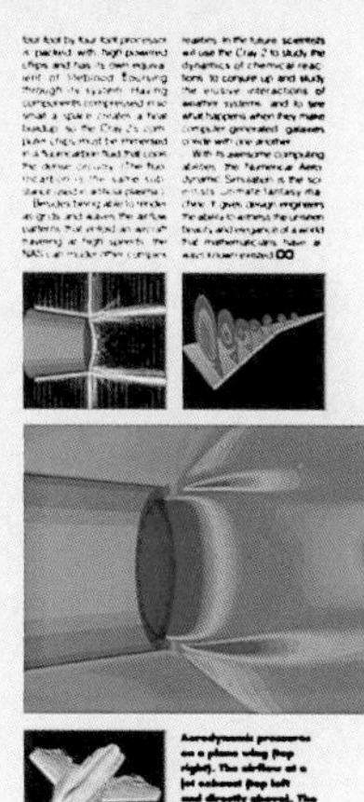

Aerodynamic pressures on a plane wing (top right). The airflow at a jet exhaust (top left and directly above). The imprint of Mach speed stress upon the fuselage and wings of a jet (left and far left)

276

Art Director: Dwayne Flinchum
Photographer: Ames Research Center, NASA
Graphics Director: Frank DeVino
Photo/Art Editor: Hilde Kron

277
Art Director: Phyllis Schefer
Photographer: Anne Pagniez
Publication: Elle
Publication Director: Régis Pagniez

278
Art Director: Phyllis Schefer
Photographer: Toscani
Publication: Elle
Publication Director: Régis Pagniez

279

Art Director: Phyllis Schefer
Photographer: Toscani
Publication: Elle
Publication Director: Régis Pagniez

280

Art Director: Wendall Harrington, John Bark
Designer: Aura Rosenberg
Photographer: Matthew Rolston

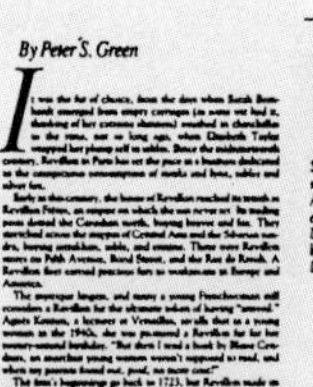
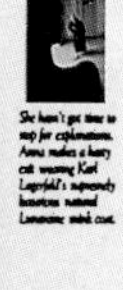
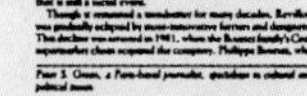

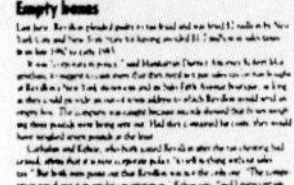
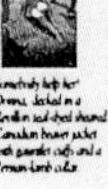

281

Art Director: Phyllis Schefer
Photographer: Gilles Bensimon
Publication: Elle
Publication Director: Régis Pagniez

282

Art Director: Sandra DiPasqua
Designer: Sandra DiPasqua
Photographer: David LaChapelle
Publisher: Hearst Magazines
Publication: Connoisseur

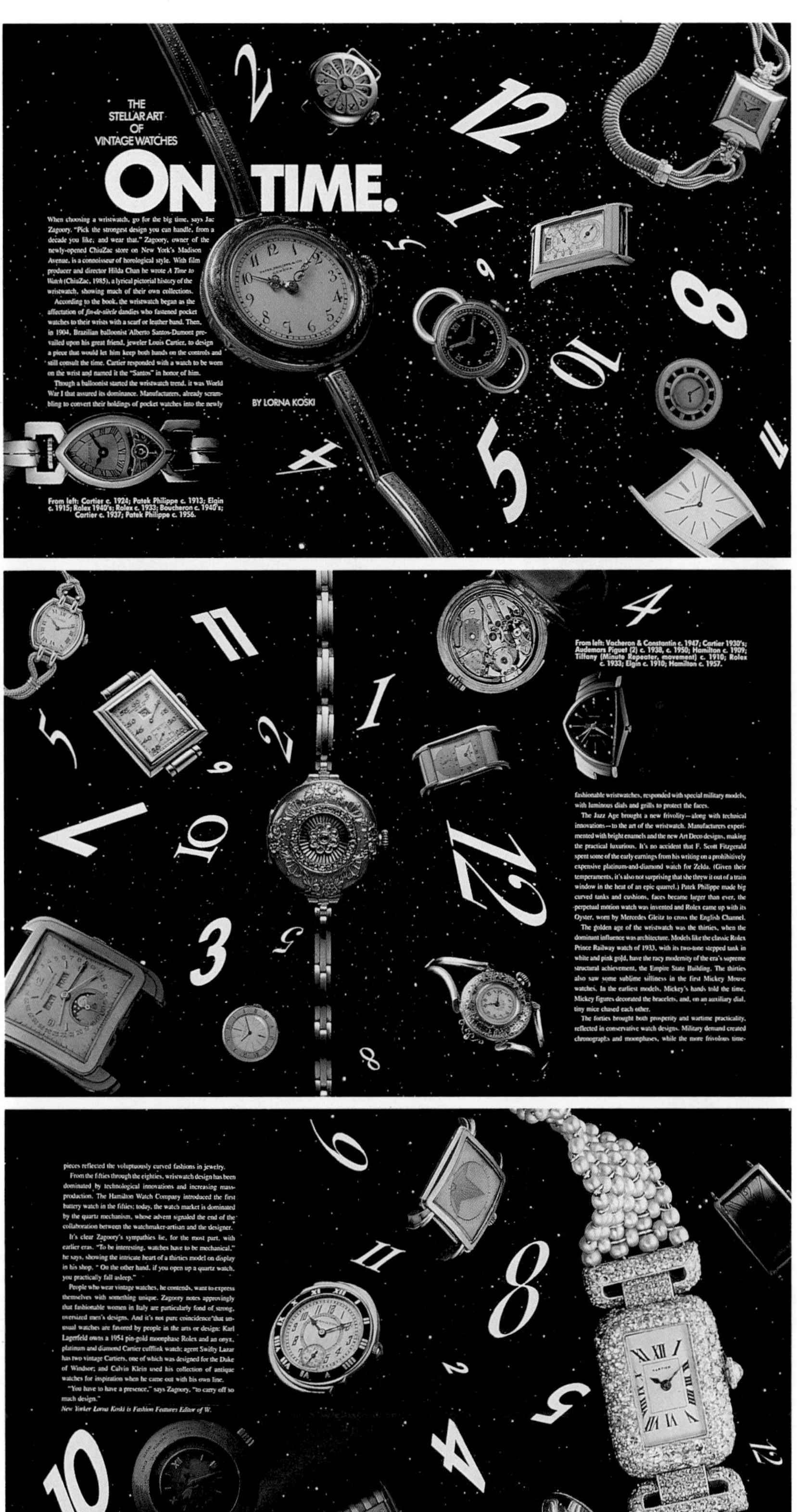

THE STELLAR ART OF VINTAGE WATCHES

ON TIME.

BY LORNA KOSKI

When choosing a wristwatch, go for the big time, says Jac Zagoory. "Pick the strongest design you can handle, from a decade you like; and wear that." Zagoory, owner of the newly-opened ChiuZac store on New York's Madison Avenue, is a connoisseur of horological style. With film producer and director Hilda Chan he wrote *A Time to Watch* (ChiuZac, 1985), a lyrical pictorial history of the wristwatch, showing much of their own collections.

According to the book, the wristwatch began as the affectation of *fin-de-siècle* dandies who fastened pocket watches to their wrists with a scarf or leather band. Then, in 1904, Brazilian balloonist Alberto Santos-Dumont prevailed upon his great friend, jeweler Louis Cartier, to design a piece that would let him keep both hands on the controls and still consult the time. Cartier responded with a watch to be worn on the wrist and named it the "Santos" in honor of him.

Though a balloonist started the wristwatch trend, it was World War I that assured its dominance. Manufacturers, already scrambling to convert their holdings of pocket watches into the newly fashionable wristwatches, responded with special military models, with luminous dials and grills to protect the faces.

From left: Cartier c. 1924; Patek Philippe c. 1913; Elgin c. 1915; Rolex 1940's; Rolex c. 1933; Boucheron c. 1940's; Cartier c. 1937; Patek Philippe c. 1956.

The Jazz Age brought a new frivolity—along with technical innovations—to the art of the wristwatch. Manufacturers experimented with bright enamels and the new Art Deco designs, making the practical luxurious. It's no accident that F. Scott Fitzgerald spent some of the early earnings from his writing on a prohibitively expensive platinum-and-diamond watch for Zelda. (Given their temperaments, it's also not surprising that she threw it out of a train window in the heat of an epic quarrel.) Patek Philippe made big curved tanks and cushions, faces became larger than ever, the perpetual motion watch was invented and Rolex came up with its Oyster, worn by Mercedes Gleitz to cross the English Channel.

The golden age of the wristwatch was the thirties, when the dominant influence was architecture. Models like the classic Rolex Prince Railway watch of 1933, with its two-tone stepped tank in white and pink gold, have the racy modernity of the era's supreme structural achievement, the Empire State Building. The thirties also saw some sublime silliness in the first Mickey Mouse watches. In the earliest models, Mickey's hands told the time, Mickey figures decorated the bracelets, and, on an auxiliary dial, tiny mice chased each other.

The forties brought both prosperity and wartime practicality, reflected in conservative watch designs. Military demand created chronographs and moonphases, while the more frivolous timepieces reflected the voluptuously curved fashions in jewelry.

From left: Vacheron & Constantin c. 1947; Cartier 1930's; Audemars Piguet (2) c. 1938, c. 1950; Hamilton c. 1909; Tiffany (Minute Repeater, movement) c. 1910; Rolex c. 1933; Elgin c. 1910; Hamilton c. 1957.

From the fifties through the eighties, wristwatch design has been dominated by technological innovations and increasing mass-production. The Hamilton Watch Company introduced the first battery watch in the fifties; today, the watch market is dominated by the quartz mechanism, whose advent signaled the end of the collaboration between the watchmaker-artisan and the designer.

It's clear Zagoory's sympathies lie, for the most part, with earlier eras. "To be interesting, watches have to be mechanical," he says, showing the intricate heart of a thirties model on display in his shop. "On the other hand, if you open up a quartz watch, you practically fall asleep."

People who wear vintage watches, he contends, want to express themselves with something unique. Zagoory notes approvingly that fashionable women in Italy are particularly fond of strong, oversized men's designs. And it's not pure coincidence that unusual watches are favored by people in the arts or design: Karl Lagerfeld owns a 1954 pin-gold moonphase Rolex and an onyx, platinum and diamond Cartier cufflink watch; agent Swifty Lazar has two vintage Cartiers, one of which was designed for the Duke of Windsor; and Calvin Klein used his collection of antique watches for inspiration when he came out with his own line.

"You have to have a presence," says Zagoory, "to carry off so much design."

New Yorker Lorna Koski is Fashion Features Editor of W.

From left: Patek Philippe c. 1948; Hamilton c. 1929; Rolex c. 1933; Gubelin c. 1930; Rolex c. 1916; Cartier c. 1920; Patek Philippe for Tiffany & Co. c. 1925.

WATCH PHOTOGRAPHS COURTESY CHIUZAC LIMITED.
BACKGROUND PHOTOS BY LIONEL BROWN/THE IMAGE BANK.

283

Art Director: Bridget DeSocio
Designer: Audemars Piguet
Photograpner: Philippe Patek
Editor: Samuel Howell Young
Client: Almanac Magazine
Publisher: Barbara Cady

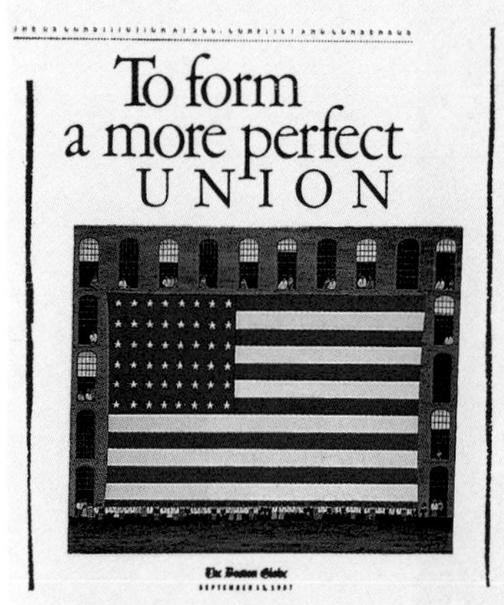

To form
a more perfect
UNION

The Boston Globe

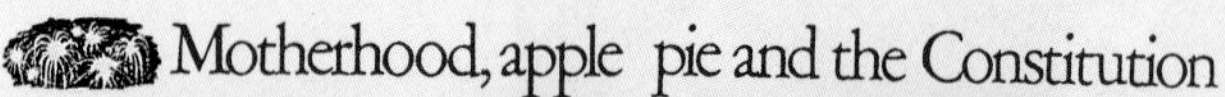

Motherhood, apple pie and the Constitution

BY RICHARD HIGGINS

"The Constitution, and the Laws of the United States which shall be made in Pursuance thereof... shall be the supreme Law of the Land."
ARTICLE VI

IN 1850, DANIEL Webster wrote that the US Constitution is "all that gives us a national character." Webster overstated the case, but the Constitution's influence on American culture as symbol and source has always been larger than the system of laws it created.

As a symbol, the Constitution has played an almost mythic role in shaping the nation's image of itself as a law-abiding, freely-constituted people baptized in the waters of liberty and justice.

To a scripturally-based people, it has been a sacred text. John Marshall, the great Supreme Court chief justice, spoke for many Americans when he described the Constitution as having sprung from a historically unique moment, guided by a force larger than its authors.

American culture is word-oriented. Since Puritan times, Americans have turned to texts, orations and sermons as easily as

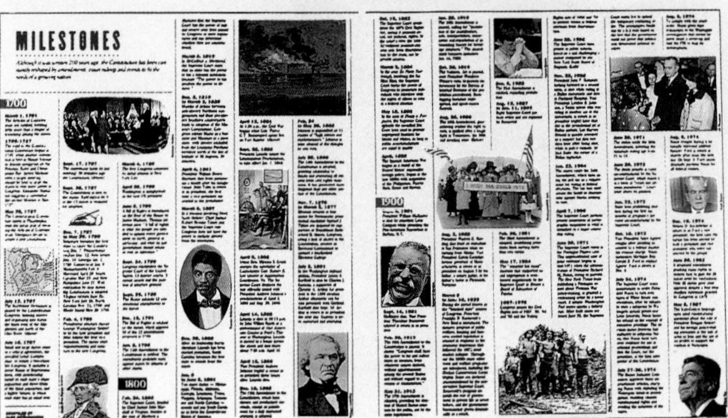

MILESTONES

RITUALS

THE BRISKER OUR PACE, THE MORE WE NEED THE RESPITE THEY OFFER FROM MILE-A-MINUTE DAYS

Give yourself, or a friend, the gift of time: These treats let you stop the treadmill—and slowly savor the process

THE MORE CONVENIENT LIFE GETS, THE FASTER WE live it. These days, time doesn't merely pass, it jogs. We send messages round the world in the blink of an eye; cross continents for lunch. At such a pace, it's not surprising that now we take comfort in things that let us linger, places that give pause. Rituals are such restful junctions, where design and manners meet. Based on step-by-step sequence, and time-after-time tradition, rituals allow us to slow down with style. Honed by generations, they offer instant roots. And though the pleasures of afternoon tea, for example, have been known for ages, the way we stage it today doesn't have to be rule-bound or stuffy. Thanks to its detail, each ritual offers plenty of scope for personal variations. What better grounds for imagination? In the words and images that follow, we focus on how to make the most of our favorite rites—how better to savor them. Whether you're pampering yourself, or giving to others, time is always at a premium, so we've found for each leisurely ritual, such as the bath, a fast-fix likeness—the shower—that's just as satisfying. If you're looking for gift ideas, the photographs in the following pages will inspire you. In these pictures you'll see many of life's small pleasures, no longer taken for granted.

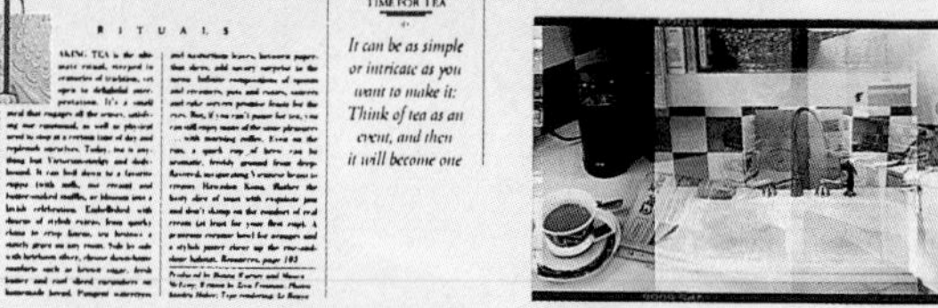

RITUALS

TIME FOR TEA

It can be as simple or intricate as you want to make it: Think of tea as an event, and then it will become one

COFFEE BREAK

Wake up workday java—a variety of aromatic beans and a few quick tricks make the daily grind much more than a chore

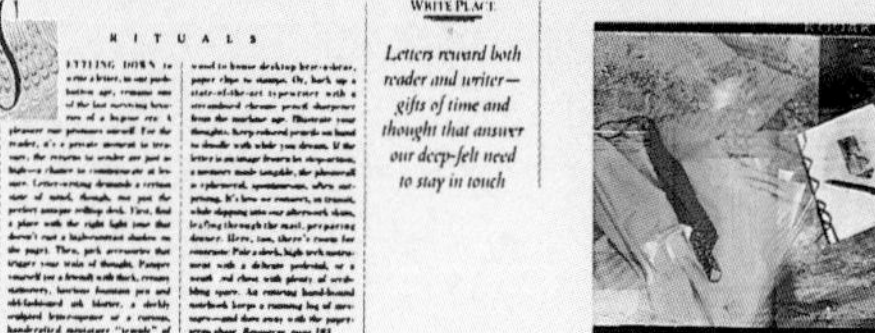

RITUALS

WRITE PLACE

Letters reward both reader and writer—gifts of time and thought that answer our deep-felt need to stay in touch

PHONE HOME

Put a little party into your line: New-age connectors help set impromptu get-togethers, join voices from the past

284
Art Director: Lynn Staley
Designer: Lynn Staley, Holly Nixholm
Illustrator/Artist: Paul Degen, Gary Hallgren
Editor: Nick King
Publisher: The Boston Globe
Publication: The Boston Globe

285
Art Director: Don Morris
Designer: Richard Ferretti, Don Morris
Photographer: Sandra Haber
Publisher: Meredith Corp.
Publication: Metropolitan Home
Typographer: Es Rouya

286

Art Director: Tom Bentkowski
Designer: Nora Sheehan
Photographer: Jan Staller
Writer: Vance Muse
Editor: Pat Ryan
Client: Time, Inc.
Publisher: Lisa Valk
Publication: Life

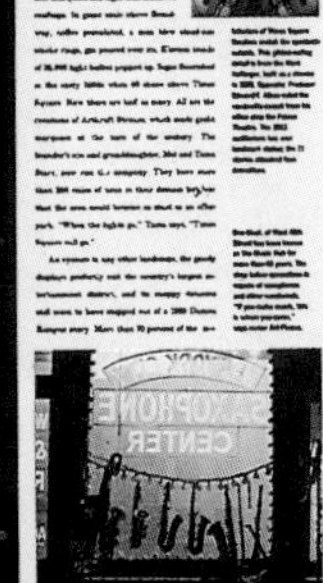

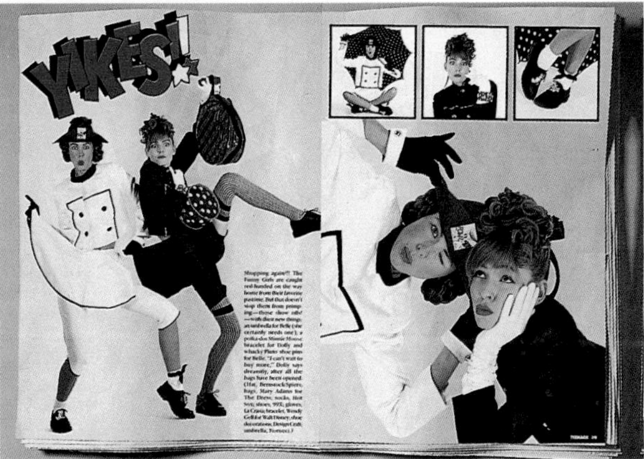

287

Art Director: Robin Poosikian
Designer: Robin Poosikian
Photographer: Beth Baptiste
Editor: Jeannie Ralston
Publication: Teenage
Hand Lettering: James Montalbano

288
Art Director: Andrew Kner
Designer: Philippe Weisbecker
Illustrator/Artist: Philippe Weisbecker
Editor: Martin Fox
Client: Print
Publisher: R C Publications
Publication: Print

289
Art Director: Andrew Kner
Designer: Joel Peter Johnson
Illustrator/Artist: Joel Peter Johnson
Editor: Martin Fox
Client: Print
Publisher: R C Publications
Publication: Print

290
Art Director: Francesca R. Messina
Illustrator/Artist: Helmut Mittendorf
Editor: William Joyce McTighe
Client: Ricochet, Atlantic Transfer Publications
Design Firm: Anthony McCall & Associates
Publisher: Suzanne L. Charity

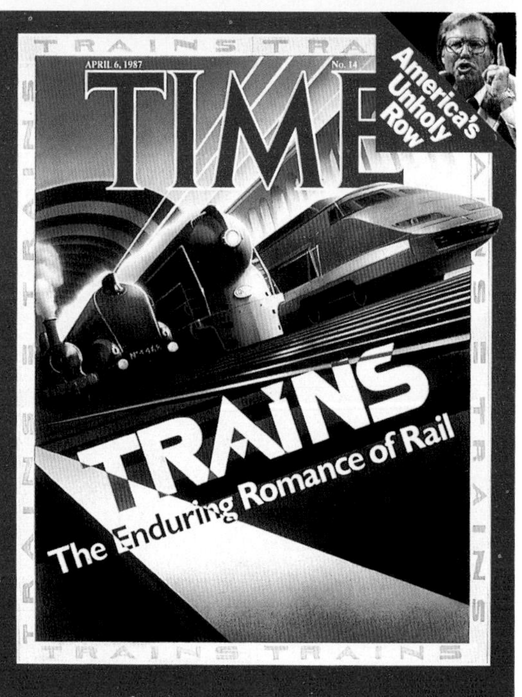

291
Art Director: Nigel Holmes
Illustrator/Artist: Philip Castle
Client: Time Inc.
Publication: Time

292
Art Director: Phyllis Schefer
Photographer: Steven Silverstein
Publication: Elle
Publication Director: Régis Pagniez

293
Art Director: Tibor Kalman
Designer: Emily Oberman
Editor: Ingrid Sischy
Client: Artforum
Design Firm: M & Co.
Publication: Artforum

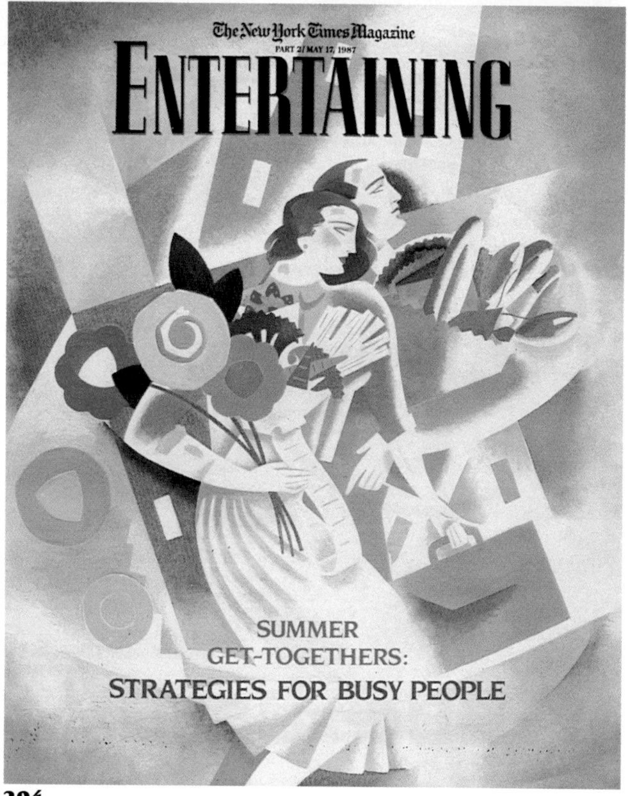

294
Art Director: Nancy Kent
Designer: Nancy Kent
Illustrator/Artist: Jeanne Fisher
Editor: Dona Guimaraes
Creative Director: Tom Bodkin
Client: The New York Times
Publisher: The New York Times
Publication: The New York Times, "Entertaining"

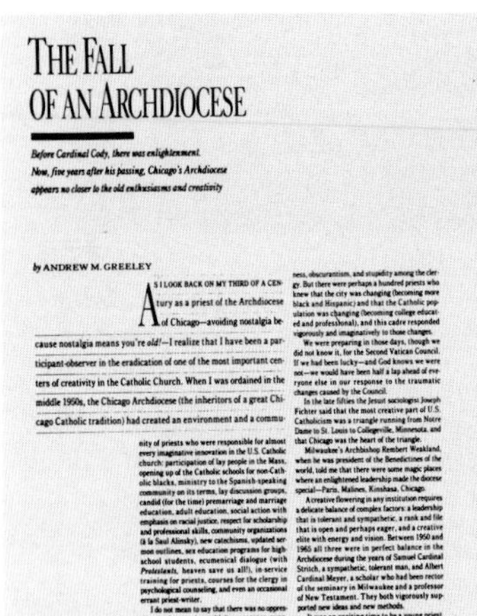

THE FALL OF AN ARCHDIOCESE

Before Cardinal Cody, there was enlightenment. Now, five years after his passing, Chicago's Archdiocese appears no closer to the old enthusiasms and creativity

by ANDREW M. GREELEY

AS I LOOK BACK ON MY THIRD OF A CENtury as a priest of the Archdiocese of Chicago—avoiding nostalgia because nostalgia means you're *old!*—I realize that I have been a participant-observer in the eradication of one of the most important centers of creativity in the Catholic Church. When I was ordained in the middle 1950s, the Chicago Archdiocese (the inheritors of a great Chicago Catholic tradition) had created an environment and a community of priests who were responsible for almost every imaginative innovation in the U.S. Catholic church: participation of lay people in the Mass, opening up of the Catholic schools for non-Catholic blacks, ministry to the Spanish-speaking community on its terms, lay discussion groups, candid (for the time) premarriage and marriage education, adult education, social action with emphasis on racial justice, respect for scholarship and professional skills, community organizations (à la Saul Alinsky), new catechisms, updated sermon outlines, sex education programs for high-school students, ecumenical dialogue (with *Protestants*, heaven save us all!), in-service training for priests, courses for the clergy in psychological counseling, and even an occasional errant priest-writer.

I do not mean to say that there was no oppression, intolerance, insensitivity, arrogance, meanness, obscurantism, and stupidity among the clergy. But there were perhaps a hundred priests who knew that the city was changing (becoming more black and Hispanic) and that the Catholic population was changing (becoming college educated and professional), and this cadre responded vigorously and imaginatively to those changes.

We were preparing in those days, though we did not know it, for the Second Vatican Council. If we had been lucky—and God knows we were not—we would have been half a lap ahead of everyone else in our response to the traumatic changes caused by the Council.

In the late fifties the Jesuit sociologist Joseph Fichter said that the most creative part of U.S. Catholicism was a triangle running from Notre Dame to St. Louis to Collegeville, Minnesota, and that Chicago was the heart of the triangle.

Milwaukee's Archbishop Rembert Weakland, when he was president of the Benedictines of the world, told me that there were some magic places where an enlightened leadership made the diocese special—Paris, Malines, Kinshasa, Chicago.

A creative flowering in any institution requires a delicate balance of complex factors: a leadership that is tolerant and sympathetic, a rank and file that is open and perhaps eager, and a creative elite with energy and vision. Between 1950 and 1965 all three were in perfect balance in the Archdiocese during the years of Samuel Cardinal Stritch, a sympathetic, tolerant man, and Albert Cardinal Meyer, a scholar who had been rector of the seminary in Milwaukee and a professor of New Testament. They both vigorously supported new ideas and new methods.

It was an exciting time to be a young priest,

illustration JAY BELMORE

138 CHICAGO SEPTEMBER 1987

photography by MICHAEL WEINSTEIN

Not far from the din of the urban jungle, we found a haven of exurban splendor, where real men find real alternatives to traditional suit dressing.

STRONG SUITS

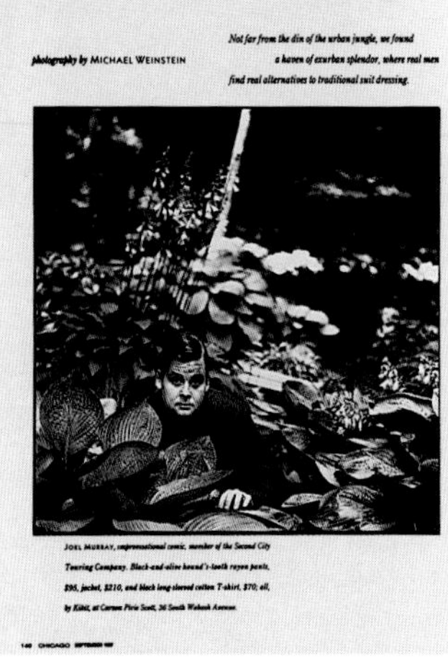

JOEL MURRAY, *improvisational comic, member of the Second City Touring Company. Black-and-olive hound's-tooth rayon pants, $95, jacket, $210, and black long-sleeved cotton T-shirt, $70; all, by Kikit, at Carson Pirie Scott, 36 South Wabash Avenue.*

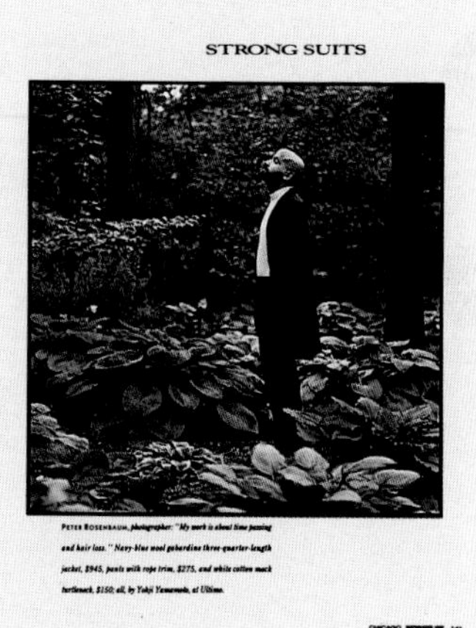

PETER ROSENBAUM, *photographer: "My work is about time passing and hair loss." Navy-blue wool gabardine three-quarter-length jacket, $945, pants with rope trim, $275, and white cotton mock turtleneck, $150; all, by Yohji Yamamoto, at Ultimo.*

140 CHICAGO SEPTEMBER 1987 · CHICAGO SEPTEMBER 1987 141

295

Art Director: Cynthia Hoffman
Designer: Barbara Solowan, Cynthia Hoffman, Kerig Pope, Susan Prosinski
Design Firm: Metropolitan Communications
Publication: Chicago
Design Director: Barbara Solowan

history

The San Franciscan Who Stole Nicaragua

By Michael Covino

"a piercing eye, a princely air, presence like a chevalier"
—Joaquin Miller on William Walker, whom he fought under in Nicaragua

ANOTHER HARD DAY IN REVOLUTIONARY MANAGUA. Tomás Martinez Borge, Nicaraguan minister of the interior, has been on the phone trying to get a shipment of Ivory soap slipped in from Texas all afternoon, ever since learning the Bulgarians failed to come through with that sandpapery stuff of theirs. Vice President Sergio Ramírez Mercado, who moonlights as a novelist—or is it the other way around?—has been busy checking up on the progress of the literacy campaign in the rural districts around Jinotega. Humberto Ortega of the defense ministry has been on the phone with Wilfredo Barreto, a Sandinista party official, coordinating the movement of troops against the contras in the southern war zone. And Humberto's brother, Daniel, president of the country—well, Daniel has been speaking to members of the press and the United States Congress all day long trying to get someone—anyone!—interested in those numbers found on a little scrap of paper inside the pocket of a downed pilot, numbers that look like they might unlock a secret Swiss account.

Now, though, it is time to relax. So they slip Alex Cox's *Repo Man* (1984) into the Zenith VCR and fill up their glasses with some Flor De Caña light rum. It's a funny movie and they laugh a lot. They enjoy Harry Dean Stanton's grizzled portrayal of a fast-talking, chain-smoking car repossessor whose motto is "ordinary f——— people, I hate 'em." They laugh at Emilio Estevez's portrayal of a tough, nihilistic punker who discovers there are still a few lessons to be learned from the Dean as the two travel around Los Angeles County searching for a '64 Chevy Malibu driven by a mad scientist and containing in its trunk some radioactive waste, or maybe some dead aliens. And when a punk teenager opens the trunk, a green light floods out, instantly vaporizing him—just his boots are left standing there. Hilarious! It's too friggin' much. The tears of laughter roll down Daniel's face. Mercado is hammering his knees with his fists. And then when the Chevy flies off into outer space at the end of the movie—

"Who do you think is really flying that Chevy?" Humberto asks, laughing.

"Hasenfus," his brother answers. "Eugene Hasenfus delivering weapons from another planet." And they all crack up.

Walker's the nightmare monster Nicaraguan mothers threaten their children with when they're bad, the epitome of the ugly, bullying American.

54 · SAN FRANCISCO FOCUS

Holiday

ENTERTAINING

by James McNair

Most of the time you can't get enough of rushing around: sampling the sand dabs at new restaurants, signing up for classes in calligraphy, battling crosstown traffic to the symphony.

On the holidays, though, something changes. The rain on the roof has a comforting sound, and you want nothing more than to stay at home, build a fire and invite friends over.

But what do you do when they get there? That's where we come in. We've got the table settings, the moods and the menus. We suggest the bubbly for you, pass on tips on everything from scenting the air to renting a fog machine, even supply the recipes. All you have to do is decide what to wear.

Photography by Patricia Brabant

296

Art Director: Matthew Drace
Photographer: Patricia Brabant
Illustrator/Artist: Seymour Chwast, Philip Burke
Writer: James McNair, Michael Covino
Editor: Mark Powelson
Publisher: Earl Adkins
Publication: San Francisco Focus

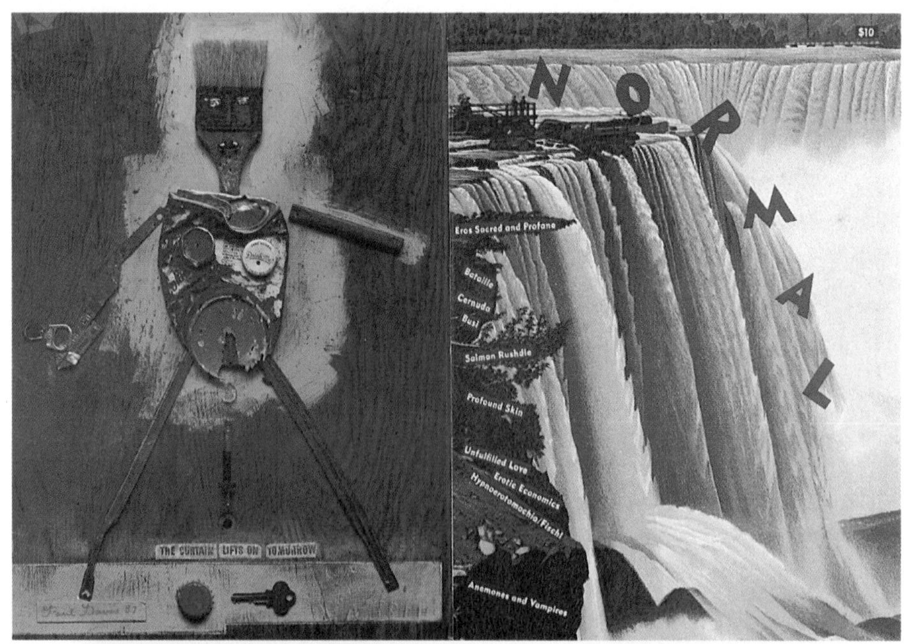

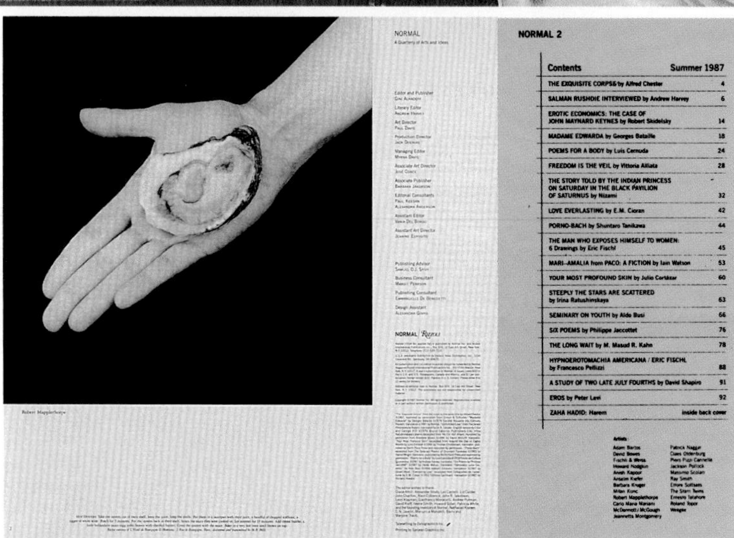

NORMAL 2

Contents Summer 1987

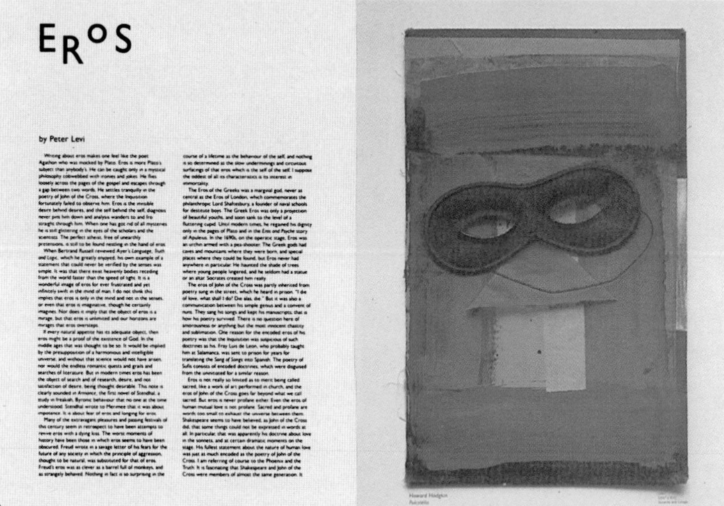

EROS

by Peter Levi

297
Art Director: Paul Davis
Designer: Paul Davis, Jose Conde, Jeanine Esposito
Editor: Gini Alhadeff
Client: Normal Inc., Rizolli
Publisher: Gini Alhadeff
Publication: Normal

A Day in The Life ...

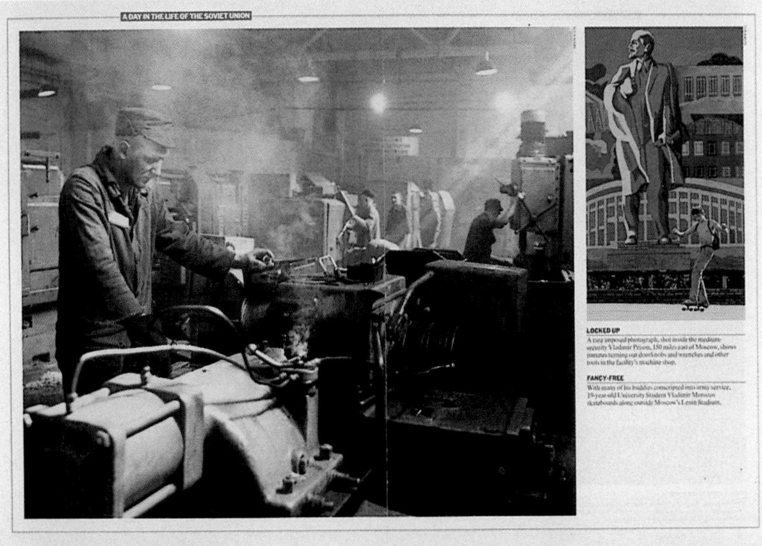

A DAY IN THE LIFE OF THE SOVIET UNION

LOCKED UP

A rare unposed photograph, shot inside the medium-security Vladimir Prison, 150 miles east of Moscow, shows inmates turning out doorknobs and wrenches and other tools in the facility's machine shop.

FANCY-FREE

With many of his buddies conscripted into army service, 19-year-old University Student Vladimir Morozov skateboards along outside Moscow's Lenin Stadium.

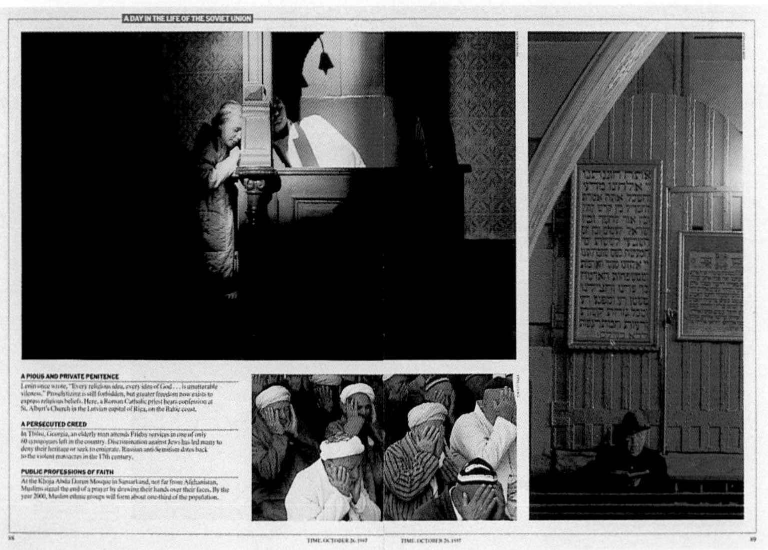

A DAY IN THE LIFE OF THE SOVIET UNION

A PIOUS AND PRIVATE PENITENCE

Lenin once wrote, "Every religious idea, every idea of God . . . is unutterable vileness." Proselytizing is still forbidden, but greater freedom now exists to express religious beliefs. Here, a Roman Catholic priest hears confession at St. Albert's Church in the Latvian capital of Riga, on the Baltic coast.

A PERSECUTED CREED

In Tbilisi, Georgia, an elderly man attends Friday services in one of only 60 synagogues left in the country. Discrimination against Jews has led many to deny their heritage or seek to emigrate. Russian anti-Semitism dates back to the violent massacres in the 17th century.

PUBLIC PROFESSIONS OF FAITH

At the Khoja Abdu Darun Mosque in Samarkand, not far from Afghanistan, Muslims signal the end of a prayer by drawing their hands over their faces. By the year 2000, Muslim ethnic groups will form about one-third of the population.

298

Art Director: Rudy Hoglund, Arthur Hochstein
Designer: Arthur Hochstein
Client: Time Inc.

TexasMonthly

The NO *Decade*

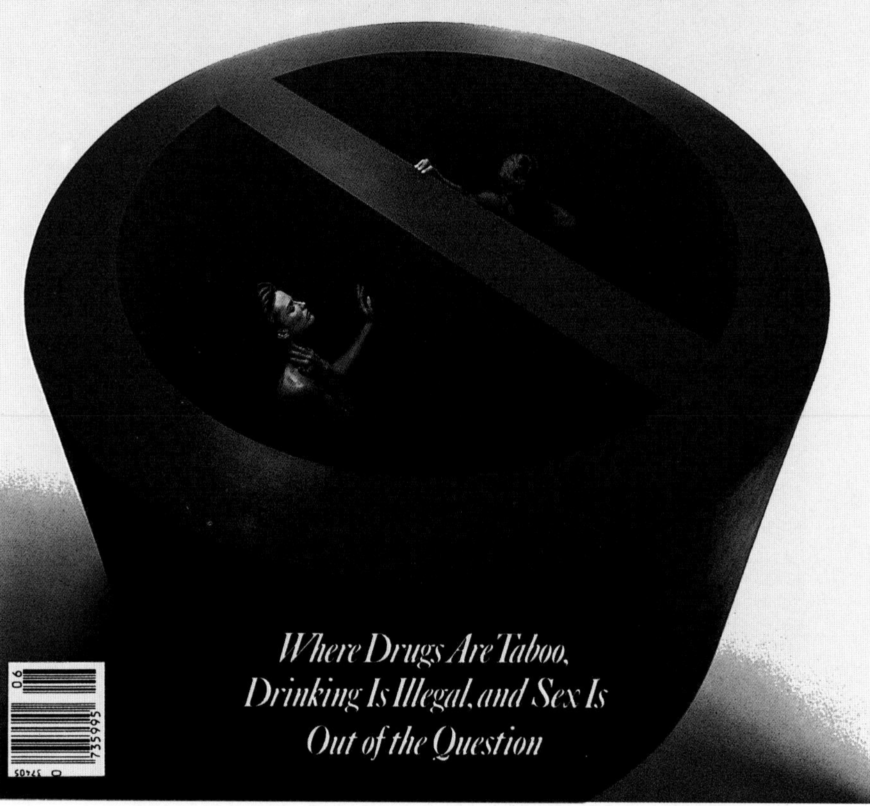

299

Art Director: D. J. Stout, Nancy E. McMillen
Designer: D. J. Stout
Photographer: Geof Kern
Editor: Gregory Curtis
Publisher: Michael R. Levy
Publication: Texas Monthly

300

Art Director: Bryan L. Peterson
Designer: Bryan L. Peterson, Scott Ray, Paul Marince
Editor: Patsy Swank
Client: Arts Illustrated
Design Firm: Peterson & Co.
Publisher: Al Schmidt, Schmidt & Associates Inc.
Publication: Arts Illustrated

SEARCHES AND SEIZURES

Amendment IV.

'...To be secure... against unreasonable searches and seizures...'

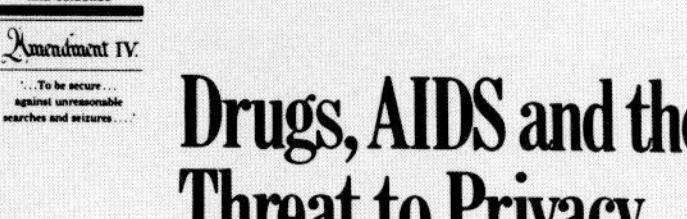

By Yale Kamisar

The 'epidemics' of the 80's have put enormous pressures on the Fourth Amendment.

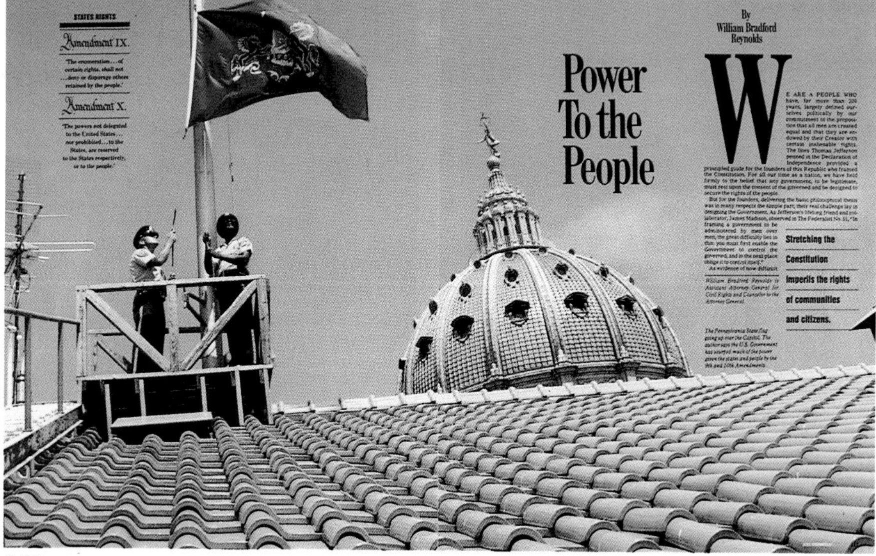

301

Art Director: Diana LaGuardia
Designer: Janet Froelich, Kevin McPhee, Audrone Razgaitis, Richard Samperi
Illustrator/Artist: Eugene Mihaesco
Creative Director: Tom Bodkin
Client: The New York Times
Publication: The New York Times, "Magazine"

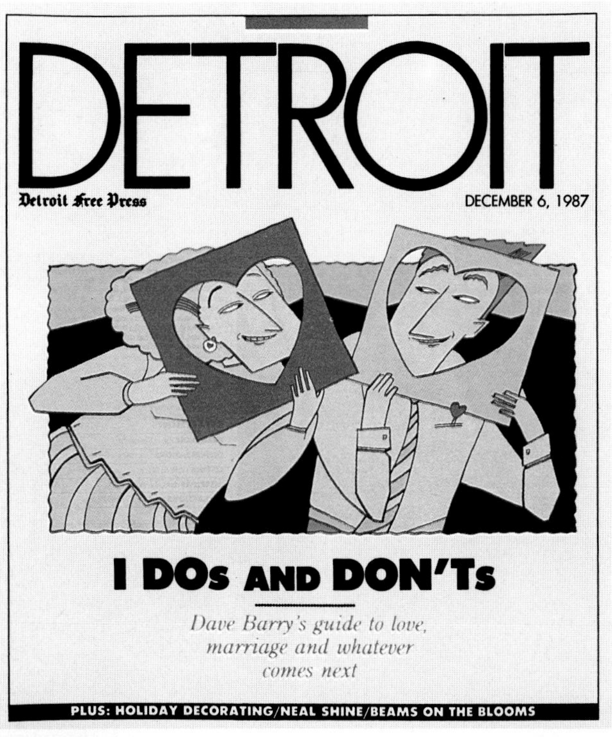

DETROIT

Detroit Free Press

DECEMBER 6, 1987

I DOs AND DON'Ts

Dave Barry's guide to love, marriage and whatever comes next

PLUS: HOLIDAY DECORATING/NEAL SHINE/BEAMS ON THE BLOOMS

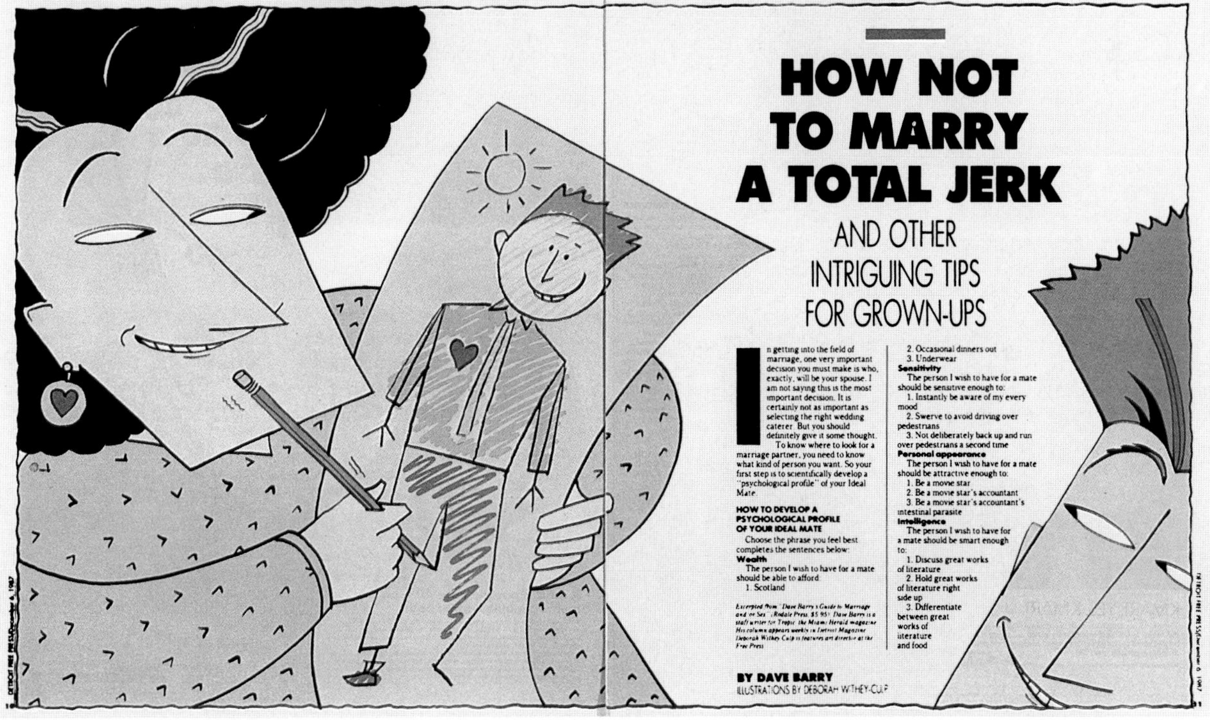

HOW NOT TO MARRY A TOTAL JERK

AND OTHER INTRIGUING TIPS FOR GROWN-UPS

In getting into the field of marriage, one very important decision you must make is who, exactly, will be your spouse. I am not saying this is the most important decision. It is certainly not as important as selecting the right wedding caterer. But you should definitely give it some thought.

To know where to look for a marriage partner, you need to know what kind of person you want. So your first step is to scientifically develop a "psychological profile" of your Ideal Mate.

HOW TO DEVELOP A PSYCHOLOGICAL PROFILE OF YOUR IDEAL MATE

Choose the phrase you feel best completes the sentences below:

Wealth

The person I wish to have for a mate should be able to afford:

1. Scotland
2. Occasional dinners out
3. Underwear

Sensitivity

The person I wish to have for a mate should be sensitive enough to:

1. Instantly be aware of my every mood
2. Swerve to avoid driving over pedestrians
3. Not deliberately back up and run over pedestrians a second time

Personal appearance

The person I wish to have for a mate should be attractive enough to:

1. Be a movie star
2. Be a movie star's accountant
3. Be a movie star's accountant's intestinal parasite

Intelligence

The person I wish to have for a mate should be smart enough to:

1. Discuss great works of literature
2. Hold great works of literature right side up
3. Differentiate between great works of literature and food

Excerpted from "Dave Barry's Guide to Marriage and/or Sex" (Rodale Press, $5.95). Dave Barry is a staff writer for Tropic, the Miami Herald magazine. His column appears weekly in Detroit Magazine. Deborah Withey Culp is features art director at the Free Press.

BY DAVE BARRY

ILLUSTRATIONS BY DEBORAH WITHEY-CULP

302

Art Director: Deborah Withey
Designer: Deborah Withey
Illustrator/Artist: Deborah Withey
Writer: Dave Barry
Editor: Charles Fancher
Client: Detroit Magazine
Publisher: Detroit Free Press

303

Art Director: Scott Menchin
Illustrator/Artist: Steve Bennett, Sibley/Peteet
Publisher: Howard Cadel

GRAPHIC DESIGN

MAGIC Show

Using printing techniques ranging from embossing to die-cuts, Dallas designer Rex Peteet creates a showcase booklet for a new line of paper.

By Joseph Kennedy

One of the Southwest's most innovative design studios, Sibley/Peteet Design of Dallas recently pulled out all the stops for a sales booklet produced for International Paper.

"Paper companies are special clients because their target audience is the graphic arts community," notes designer Rex Peteet. "That gives us an opportunity to do creative work that we don't always get to do."

The New York-based paper company wanted to showcase the possibilities of its new paper, Springhill Coated Cover—with an eye on the annual report and brochure market.

"The paper had an improved coated surface and was also available for the first time in 8-point weight," Peteet states.

Portrait of designers Rex Peteet (left) and Don Sibley.

"Our assignment was to highlight the paper and the new weight."

Sibley/Peteet put together about nine different creative concepts, sketching the ideas in pencil on 19" x 24" tissue.

"One concept played off the number eight—to emphasize that this is an 8-point paper—featuring objects like an 8 ball and a V-8 engine," he explains.

Magic, however, has an inherent, universal appeal, a color and excitement that fasci

Opposite page, this envelope was printed to look like a three-dimensional box of cards. It contains an oversized ace of spades (actually a sales representative's card). It's just one part of an elaborate promotional project.

44 HOW

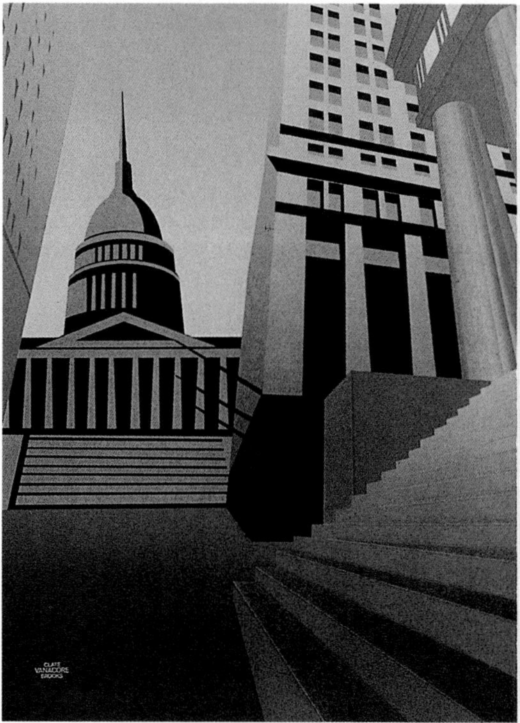

TAKING STOCK

by
SHEILA KAPLAN

Congressmembers' investments often coincide with their congressional responsibilities. Congressional ethics rules, however, do little to guard against conflicts of interest.

When the stock market sank 508 points on Black Monday, investors across the nation went into a frenzy. Among the worried shareholders were members of Congress, who suddenly found themselves contemplating two painful prospects — the potential collapse of the international economy and the instant collapse of their personal portfolios.

Members of Congress, like many Americans, invest on Wall Street, giving them a personal stake in the market. While it can be argued that owning stock gives them an opportunity to express confidence in American business, these investments also can pose conflicts of interest because members of Congress are in the unusual position of being able to influence the financial ups and downs of businesses that rely on federal programs and policies.

Consider the case of Sen. Frank Murkowski (R-Alaska). A member of the Senate Energy and Natural Resources Committee, Murkowski is also a major partner in a venture that owns part of an Alaskan oil refinery. The refinery relies on oil from Alaska's North Slope, and earlier this year the senator introduced a bill, now before the committee, that would open a federal wildlife refuge on the North Slope to oil exploration and drilling.

Few instances involving conflicts of interest are as troubling as Murkowski's, but many members of Congress do experience similar, if subtler, ethical binds in their dual roles as investors and policy makers. Currently, the loose rules that govern congressional ethics, coupled with a general laissez-faire atmosphere on Capitol Hill, reveal Congress's failure to face up to the very real problems created by members' private investments.

In sharp contrast with executive branch officials, who have more restrictive investment guidelines, members of Congress are free to invest as much as they like wherever they like; the one requirement is that they disclose these investments on annual financial reports. Under ethics rules adopted in the mid-1970s, members make public financial disclosures of their outside holdings and income. Holdings are listed by broad ranges — $50,000 to $100,000, $100,000 to $250,000, etc. — with their largest investments listed as more than $250,000.

The nature of some of these investments, particularly those corresponding to a member's committee assignments, may at the very least give the appearance of a conflict of interest. Further questions are raised by members who own or trade stocks while an industry or particular business is undergoing congressional scrutiny, receiving government funds or negotiating contracts.

For example, Sen. John Glenn (D-Ohio), the former astronaut and one-time presidential contender, is not only one of Congress's largest investors in government defense contractors but also a member of the Armed Services Committee, which considers all proposed legislation related to weapons research, development and acquisition. Last year Glenn also served on the Defense Acquisition Policy Subcommittee.

Based on his 1986 financial disclosure statement, Glenn last year held between

Sheila Kaplan is a staff writer. Anna Mangum also contributed to this story. Research assistance was provided by magazine interns Dom Brown, Anne Nichols and Scott Thomsen, and former interns Elizabeth Cornwell and Andrew James.

November/December 1987 Common Cause Magazine 29

304

Art Director: Jeffrey L. Dever
Designer: Jeffrey L. Dever
Illustrator/Artist: Clara Vanacore Brooks
Editor: Deborah Baldwin
Client: Common Cause
Design Firm: Dever Designs
Publisher: Common Cause
Publication: Common Cause

305

Art Director: Tom Monahan
Designer: Ronn Campisi
Illustrator/Artist: Tim Lewis
Client: CW Publishing

SECURITY
MANAGEMENT STRATEGIES

A new vigilance

Security has piqued the interest of MIS and management at all levels

BY STAN KOLODZIEJ

As if MIS managers don't have enough work dealing with applications backlogs, fielding user complaints and grooming themselves to become chief information officers, they must also shoulder the growing chore of computer security.

Safeguarding systems is no mean task. Computer security runs the gamut from individual passwords and data access controls to multimillion-dollar

JUNE 3, 1987 COMPUTERWORLD FOCUS 21

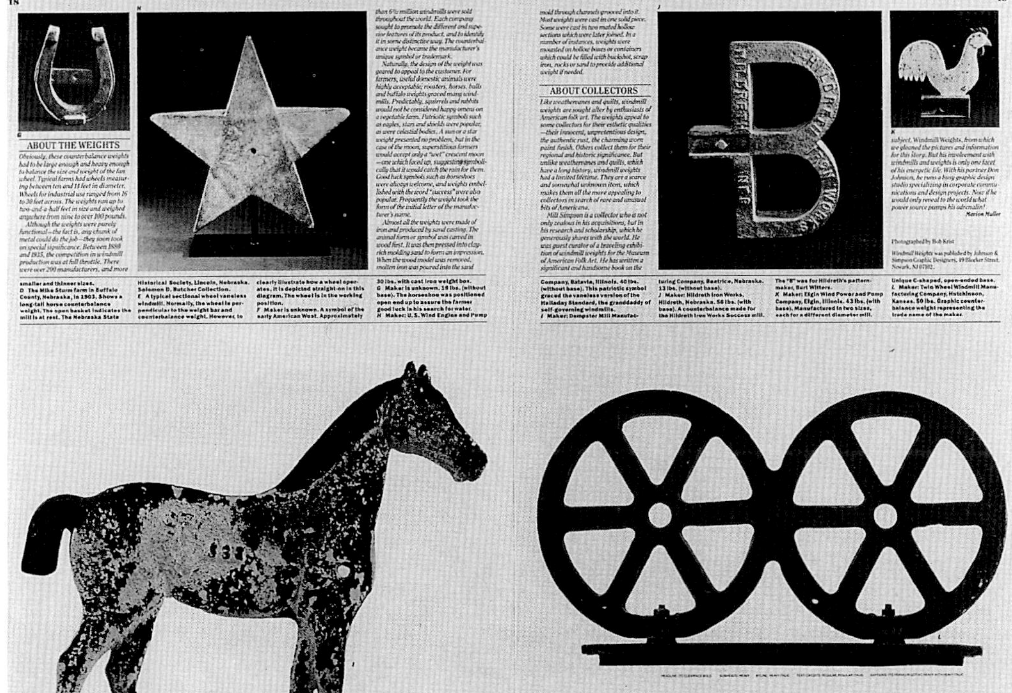

ABOUT THE WEIGHTS

ABOUT COLLECTORS

306

Art Director: B. Martin Pedersen
Photographer: Bob Krist
Writer: Marion Muller
Editor: Edward Gottschall
Creative Director: B. Martin Pedersen
Client: International Typeface Corp.
Design Firm: Jonson, Pedersen, Hinricks & Shakery Inc.
Publisher: International Typeface Corp.
Publication: U&LC

They won't kill you, but they can sure make your life miserable. Here's how to keep them from getting the best of you and recognize trouble when it's on the way.

DIGESTIVE UPSETS

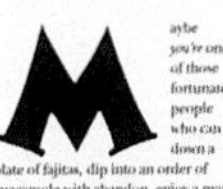

Maybe you're one of those fortunate people who can down a plate of fajitas, dip into an order of guacamole with abandon, enjoy a margarita, and spice up an already fiery meal with a side dish of jalapenos—all without the slightest digestive discomfort. Most of us can't, but we do anyway—and suffer the consequences.

No one is immune to occasional upsets caused by overeating, seasonal viruses, or foods that just don't meet our stomachs' standards. Learning to read the symptoms of these upsets and associate them with troublesome foods are the first steps toward maintaining a healthy digestive tract.

"Most of us eat too much, too fast, too often," advises V. Hugh Gilmore, M.D., a family practice physician on staff at the Memorial Health Center in Sugar Land. "We're gluttons for punishment, unwilling to sacrifice something that's pleasurable for an instant, but ends up causing us misery for hours, or even days, afterwards." In the article that follows, Gilmore and other Memorial physicians work their way through the digestive system, offering their advice for keeping misery to a minimum.

HEARTBURN

That familiar burning sensation can occur as soon as you start eating, immediately after a meal, or hours later, when you're just about to doze off. Almost everyone has occasional heartburn, usually from too much food, combined with smoking and bad posture. But some people have daily symptoms, including intense pain that can be confused with ulcers or angina.

The medical name for heartburn is reflux esophagitis, so named because the burning sensation occurs when stomach acid refluxes up through the lower esophageal sphincter muscle into the esophagus. "The lower esophageal sphincter acts like a door," explains Frank Lanza, M.D., a gastroenterologist on staff at Memorial Southwest Hospital. "It opens to allow food to move from the esophagus to the stomach and then closes immediately to prevent the stomach's contents from escaping upward into the esophagus. We've found that some individuals who suffer frequent attacks of reflux esophagitis have a weakness in this muscle, which lets hydrochloric acid from the stomach move up and burn the esophageal walls."

When you feel heartburn coming on, stand up and walk around, and take a liquid antacid, which works faster than tablets. Some sufferers find relief with Gaviscon, an over-the-counter medication that thickens stomach contents, making them less likely to move upward into the esophagus. If you find the taste of liquid antacids disagreeable, try storing the bottle in your refrigerator. Some people find chilled antacids more palatable.

Avoid milk. It may act as a buffer initially, but its fat content may actually relax the esophageal sphincter muscle and cause further reflux. Its high calcium content can also stimulate increased acid production.

Avoid carbonated beverages and over-the-counter effervescent products, like Alka-Seltzer, which actually aggravate the problem. Both tend to make you belch, which may force up more stomach acid along with the air.

To prevent heartburn, try eating smaller, more frequent meals, and don't eat for at least three hours before bed. When you do go to bed, use blocks to raise the head of your bed at least eight inches. Avoid foods that may be causing your heartburn, like fatty foods, chocolate, alcohol, peppermint, onions, cabbage, citrus fruits, chili, coffee, and tomatoes.

ACID INDIGESTION

Doctors call it dyspepsia. To some sufferers, it means mild discomfort after a meal, marked by a bloated feeling or a burning sensation. To others, it's nausea, stomach spasm, a bitter taste in the mouth, or belching. Whatever the complaint, dyspepsia results when foods are not digested properly.

Robert Davis, M.D., a gastroenterologist on staff at Memorial Southwest Hospital, advises sufferers to refrain from overeating, especially fatty foods, and avoid stomach irritants like coffee, tea, smoking, alcohol, and aspirin. Certain foods, including lobster, crab, sardines, peanuts, and pickles, are difficult to digest and should be avoided by those who suffer regular attacks.

Vegetables and fruits that form gas, among them raw apples, garlic, onions, beans, peppers, celery, artichokes, and pineapples, may also cause discomfort because of their high cellulose content. Overcooking can change foods, making them difficult to digest, and people who bolt down food or live on coffee and pastries leave themselves vulnerable to indigestion.

If you give in to that irrational craving for foods that make you miserable—and wind up with indigestion—try loosening any tight-fitting clothing you're wearing and experimenting to see whether lying on your side, lying prone, standing, or walking helps.

If your indigestion is mild but recurs persistently, you'll be wise to schedule an appointment with your doctor. If it's severe and accompanied by difficulty in breathing, sudden nausea or vomiting, fainting, heavy sweating, or a cold, clammy feeling, call a doctor immediately. Many conditions can cause dyspepsia, including disease of the liver or pancreas. Your doctor can help you find and eliminate its cause.

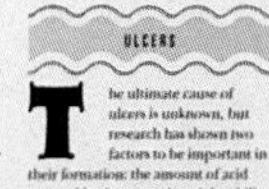

ULCERS

The ultimate cause of ulcers is unknown, but research has shown two factors to be important in their formation: the amount of acid secreted by the stomach and the ability of the stomach and intestinal walls to resist erosion by the acid. If enough acid is secreted, it can overpower the walls' protective mucus.

GAS

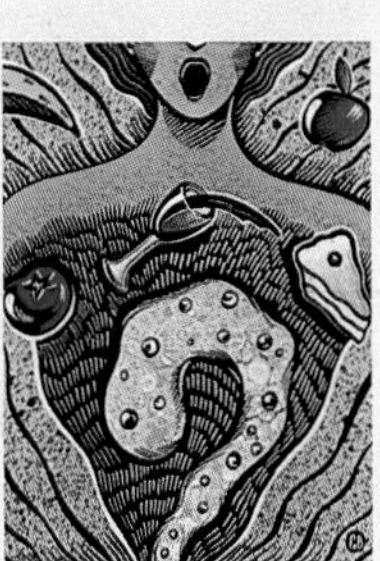

Eating foods with a high air content, smoking, chewing gum, gasping, and sipping through straws all add to a gas sufferer's misery.

CROHN'S DISEASE

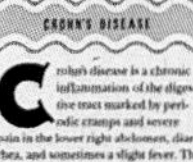

IRRITABLE BOWEL SYNDROME

DIVERTICULAR DISEASE

Anger, anxiety, and other negative emotions can slow down digestion and bring on that familiar burning sensation.

CONSTIPATION

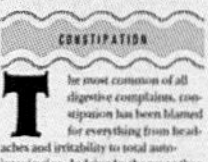

HEMORRHOIDS

307

Art Director: Mark Geer, Richard Kilmer
Designer: Mark Geer
Illustrator/Artist: Cathie Bleck
Writer: Karen Kephart
Client: Memorial Care Systems
Design Firm: Kilmer/Geer Design
Publication: Caring

300 CE

Elegance. Movement. Sensuality. Power. Classic coupes hold a breathless excitement in their essence. The 1988 300CE, pictured here and on the following pages, is a coupe for the 300 Class with a truly breathtaking shape.

The 300CE Coupe bears a close family resemblance to the Mercedes-Benz 300 Class sedans—from its aerodynamically angled grille to its superb, powerful, smooth-running, 177-hp, in-line six-cylinder engine. But its new body, 3.3 inches shorter in wheelbase and 1.4 inches lower than the sedans, marks it exclusively as a powerful grand touring car. The more compact dimensions of a coupe challenged Mercedes-Benz engineers to carefully alter the 300 Class body design and reinforce the chassis—a challenge from which elegant solutions emerged. B-pillars have been cleverly eliminated, making the rolled up windows appear to be one solid panel that virtually blends into the exterior skin. The C-pillars are gently raked at 25 degrees from

6

7

8

the vertical and dip to the rear deck lid, which is 1.4 inches lower than on the sedans, in a smooth, sensuous sweep. The rear window panel smoothly overlaps into the roof and C-pillars, forming an integrated, harmonious line. Streamlined protective lower body panels extend from the coupe's front wheels to the rear. The new coupe's system of air management tells in not only its remarkably low 0.30 coefficient of aerodynamic drag, but also in the quiet of the cabin, at high speed, with even one window down.

9

What is it like to drive this remarkable coupe? *Automobile* magazine thrilled to the coupe's "wonderful feeling of airiness," and found that it equaled in every way the 300E Sedan's "nearly perfect blend of handling, roadholding and comfort." *Auto, Motor und Sport* said simply that the 300CE is "perhaps the best six cylinder the world has to offer."

Reinforcements for safety ingeniously bolster the 300CE's monocoque chassis, from a stronger roof frame that acts as a roll bar to a forked longitudinal member design in the front to dissipate forces in the event of a severe frontal impact.

You would expect a Mercedes-Benz coupe to have an exceptional, *exclusive* appeal. But the 300CE is something more. A coupe both superbly made *and* superbly functional—even at top speed—and yet so rare as to be among automobiles evocative of an age. An automobile built solidly in the tradition of such grand touring classics as the great Mercedes-Benz 1930s coupes. Yet original enough to found a tradition of its own.

10

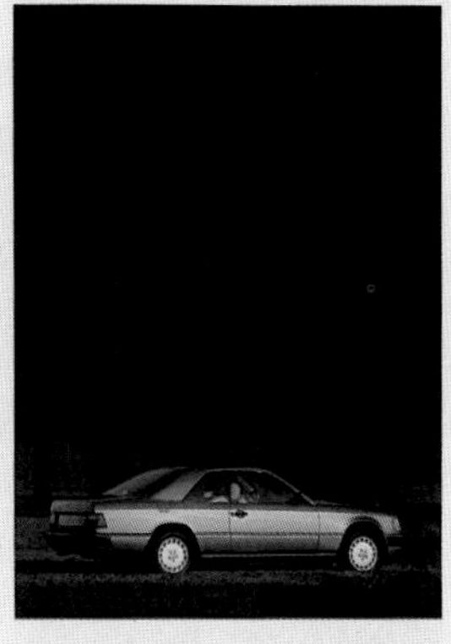

11

308

Art Director: John Tom Cohoe
Designer: John Tom Cohoe
Photographer: Clint Clemens
Writer: Tom Leander
Editor: Tom Leander
Creative Director: Tom Parrett
Client: Mercedes-Benz of North America
Agency: McCaffrey & McCall
Publication: Mercedes

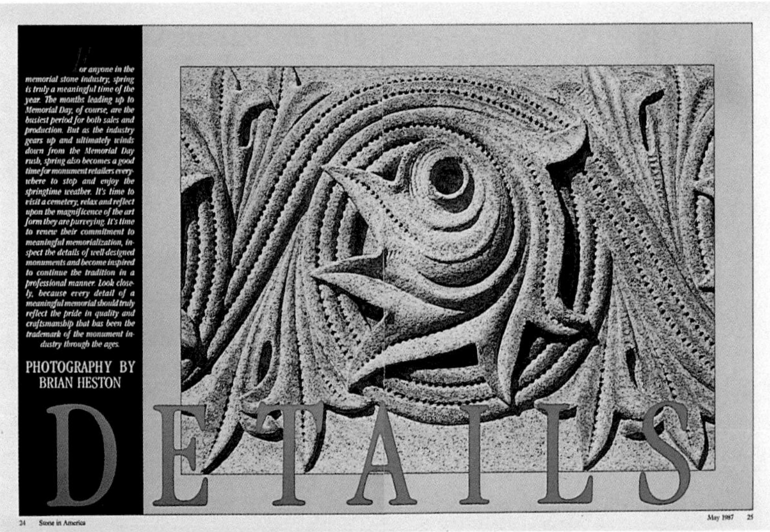

For anyone in the memorial stone industry, spring is truly a meaningful time of the year. The months leading up to Memorial Day, of course, are the busiest period for both sales and production. But as the industry gears up and ultimately winds down from the Memorial Day rush, spring also becomes a good time for monument retailers everywhere to stop and enjoy the springtime weather. It's time to visit a cemetery, relax and reflect upon the magnificence of the art form they are purveying. It's time to renew their commitment to meaningful memorialization, inspect the details of well-designed monuments and become inspired to continue the tradition in a professional manner. Look closely, because every detail of a meaningful memorial should truly reflect the pride in quality and craftsmanship that has been the trademark of the monument industry through the ages.

PHOTOGRAPHY BY BRIAN HESTON

DETAILS

24 Stone in America

May 1987 25

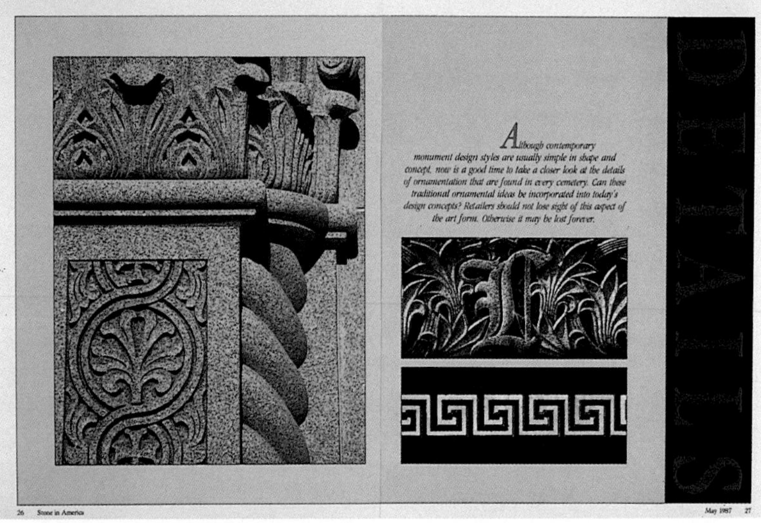

Although contemporary monument design styles are usually simple in shape and concept, now is a good time to take a closer look at the details of ornamentation that are found in every cemetery. Can these traditional ornamental ideas be incorporated into today's design concepts? Retailers should not lose sight of this aspect of the art form. Otherwise it may be lost forever.

DETAILS

26 Stone in America

May 1987 27

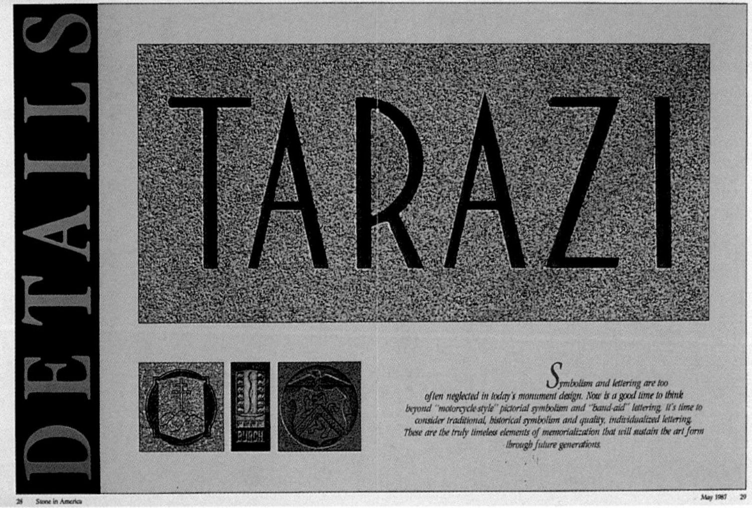

DETAILS

Symbolism and lettering are too often neglected in today's monument design. Now is a good time to think beyond "motorcycle-style" pictorial symbolism and "band-aid" lettering. It's time to consider traditional, historical symbolism and quality, individualized lettering. These are the truly timeless elements of memorialization that will sustain the art form through future generations.

28 Stone in America

May 1987 29

309

Art Director: Bob Moon
Designer: Bob Moon
Photographer: Brian Heston
Editor: Bob Moon
Publisher: American Monument Association
Publication: Stone in America

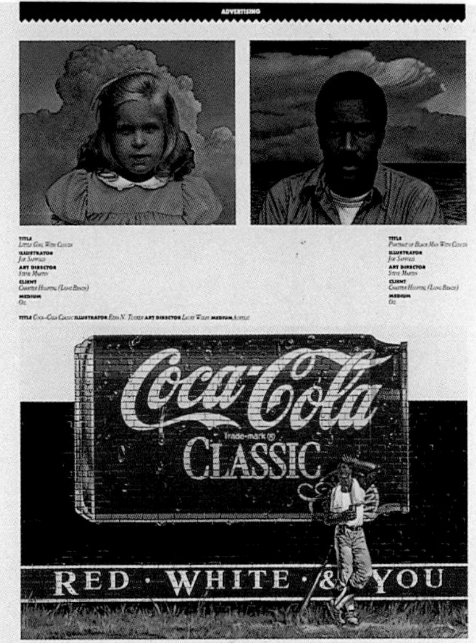

310

Art Director: B. Martin Pedersen
Designer: B. Martin Pedersen
Editor: B. Martin Pedersen
Creative Director: B. Martin Pedersen
Design Firm: Graphis US Inc.
Publisher: Graphis US Inc./Graphis Press Corp.
Publication: Graphis 250

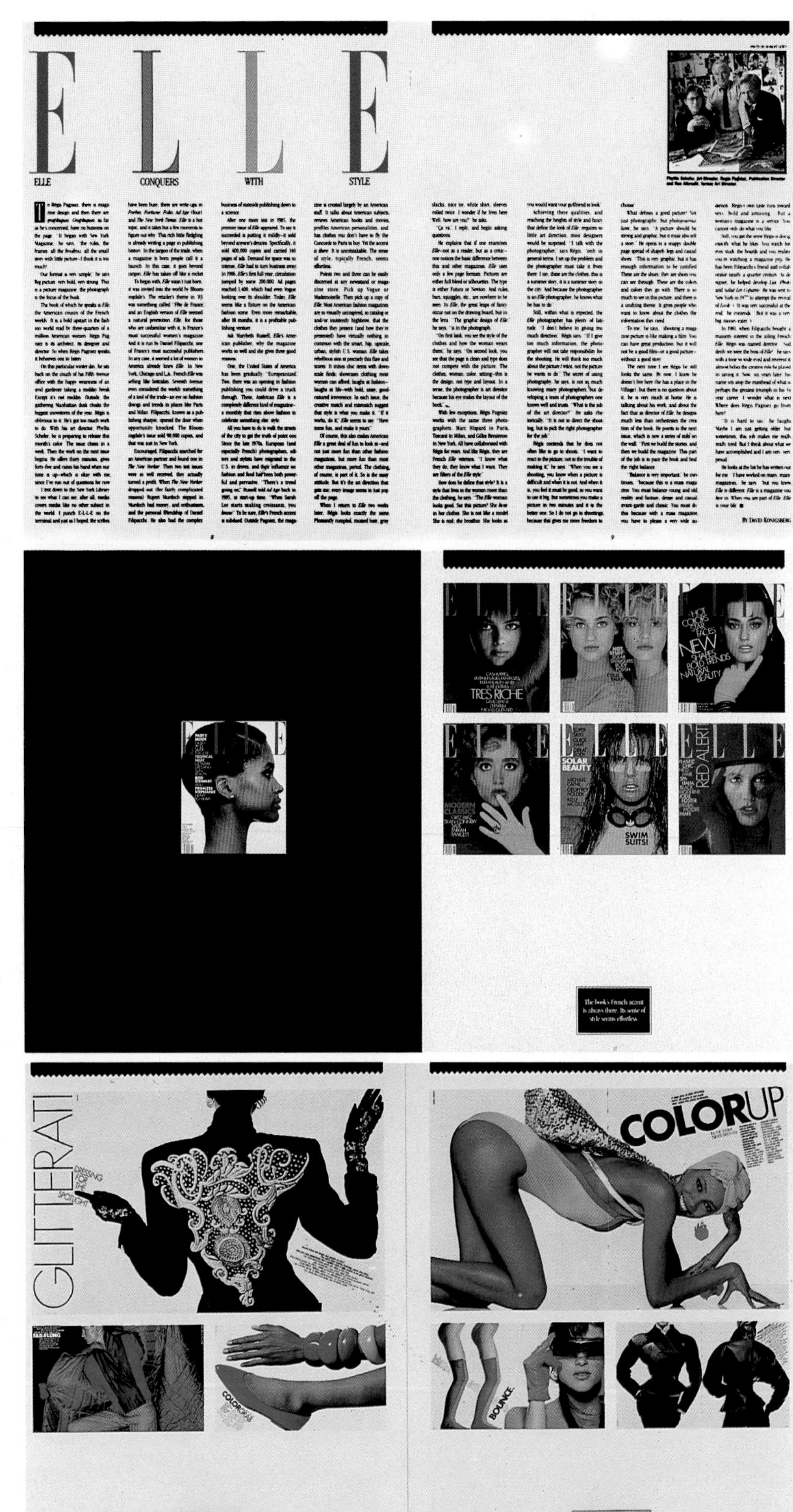

311

Art Director: B. Martin Pedersen
Photographer: Toscani, Gilles Bensimon
Writer: David Konigsberg
Editor: B. Martin Pedersen
Creative Director: B. Martin Pedersen
Design Firm: Graphis U.S. Inc.
Publisher: Graphis US Inc./Graphis Press Corp.
Publication: Graphis 250

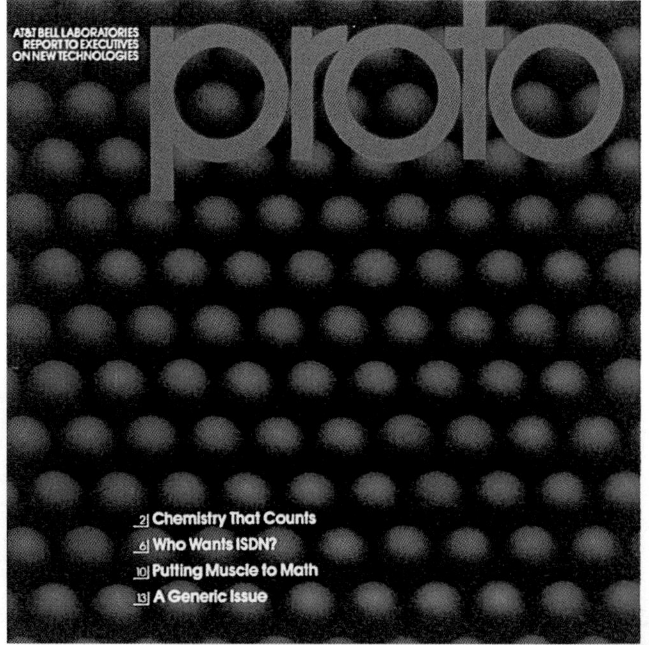

BY JOYCE DRAPER

A MATERIAL HASN'T A CHANCE OF GETTING INTO AN AT&T PRODUCT UNTIL IT REVEALS ITS CHEMISTRY, RIGHT DOWN TO THE LAST IMPURITY.

Somewhere among the billion people who inhabit North America, Europe, and Russia, an extraterrestrial humanoid—or two, or three, or dozens—may be living unnoticed. The assignment: identify any and all of them. Will the assignment be successfully completed? In a sci-fi thriller, it may be; in the analytical chemistry labs at AT&T Bell Laboratories, it must be. There, dealing with fact, not fiction, Jim Mitchell and other analytical chemists know that even a one-in-a-billion impurity can make a material difference in a telecommunication device—the difference between useful and useless.

A trace of cobalt, unnoticed in the glass from which optical fiber is drawn, can cause the fiber to lose unacceptable amounts of information-laden light. But traces of boron and phosphorus, properly distributed in silicon, turn semiconductor material into the stuff transistors are made of. In information-age products, little things mean a lot—for better or worse.

The need for analytical chemistry spans research, development, and manufacture; filling the need takes the combined efforts of groups dispersed throughout AT&T. The Analytical Chemistry Research Department, which Mitchell heads, has a varied role: advancing analytical chemistry through fundamental research, serving as a central source of analytical expertise, and collaborating with other analytical groups in the close, continuing support of specific development or manufacturing organizations.

There's plenty of work for all. A researcher, who has fabricated a new material with a highly complex, multilayered structure, wants a "characterization" of that material—a complete profile of its composition and structure. A developer needs characterizations too, to determine which material will best contribute needed properties to a future product.

Before manufacture, raw materials must be scrutinized for impurities that could cause trouble. During manufacture, product quality must be monitored to ensure that what started out right doesn't go chemically awry. And after manufacture, products that fail while being tested or used must return to the analytical chemist for diagnosis. Until a product's chemistry holds no surprises, the analysts won't let it alone.

Analytical chemistry has an overwhelming variety of substances to deal with, thanks to nature's basic set of 106 chemical elements. If 106 doesn't sound like much, think of the 450,000 words English-speaking people have created from an alphabet of 26 elements. There's a lot of raw material, chemically speaking.

What happens to that raw material is that atoms from each of those 106 elements bond chemically with other atoms, like or unlike themselves, to form molecules, the basic unit of chemical compounds. To date, chemists have identified some four million chemical compounds (which, in turn, can form an endless number of complex mixtures).

Given the unique anatomies of their atoms and molecules, elements and compounds react uniquely when prodded with light or heat or electricity or magnetic fields or mechanical stress or the chemistry of other substances. The

312

Art Director: Nancy Koch
Designer: Steve Phillips Design
Photographer: David Arky
Writer: Joyce Draper
Editor: Michael Miller
Client: AT&T Bell Laboratories
Publisher: AT&T Bell Laboratories
Publication: Proto
Model Maker: Bruce Morozko

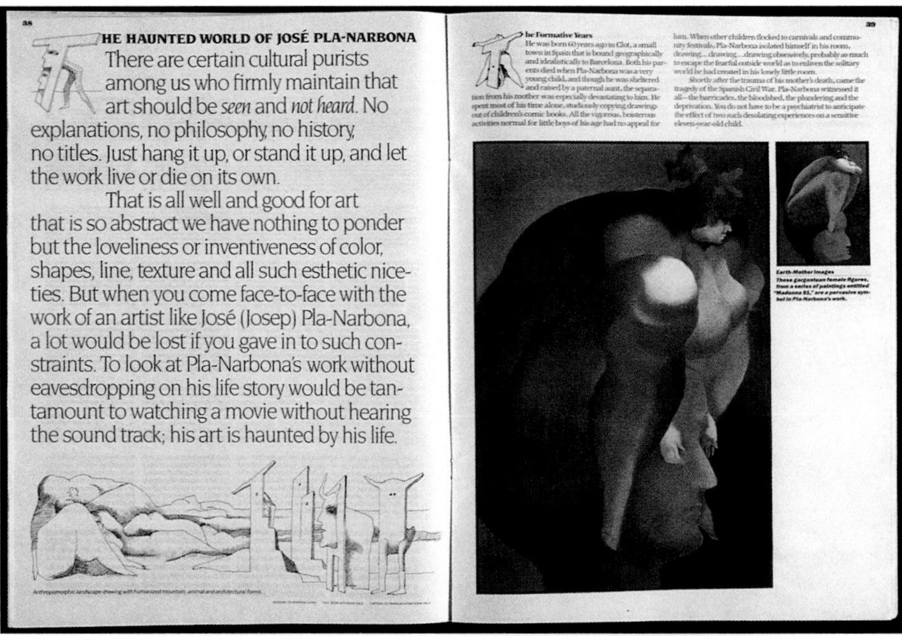

38

THE HAUNTED WORLD OF JOSÉ PLA-NARBONA

There are certain cultural purists among us who firmly maintain that art should be *seen* and *not heard*. No explanations, no philosophy, no history, no titles. Just hang it up, or stand it up, and let the work live or die on its own.

That is all well and good for art that is so abstract we have nothing to ponder but the loveliness or inventiveness of color, shapes, line, texture and all such esthetic niceties. But when you come face-to-face with the work of an artist like José (Josep) Pla-Narbona, a lot would be lost if you gave in to such constraints. To look at Pla-Narbona's work without eavesdropping on his life story would be tantamount to watching a movie without hearing the sound track; his art is haunted by his life.

39

The Formative Years

He was born 60 years ago in Clot, a small town in Spain that is bound geographically and idealistically to Barcelona. Both his parents died when Pla-Narbona was a very young child, and though he was sheltered and raised by a paternal aunt, the separation from his mother was especially devastating to him. He spent most of his time alone, studiously copying drawings out of children's comic books. All the vigorous, boisterous activities normal for little boys of his age had no appeal for him. When other children flocked to carnivals and community festivals, Pla-Narbona isolated himself in his room, drawing…drawing…drawing obsessively, probably as much to escape the fearful outside world as to enliven the solitary world he had created in his lonely little room.

Shortly after the trauma of his mother's death, came the tragedy of the Spanish Civil War. Pla-Narbona witnessed it all—the barricades, the bloodshed, the plundering and the deprivation. You do not have to be a psychiatrist to anticipate the effect of two such desolating experiences on a sensitive eleven-year-old child.

Earth-Mother Images
These gargantuan female figures, from a series of paintings entitled "Madonna 81," are a pervasive symbol in Pla-Narbona's work.

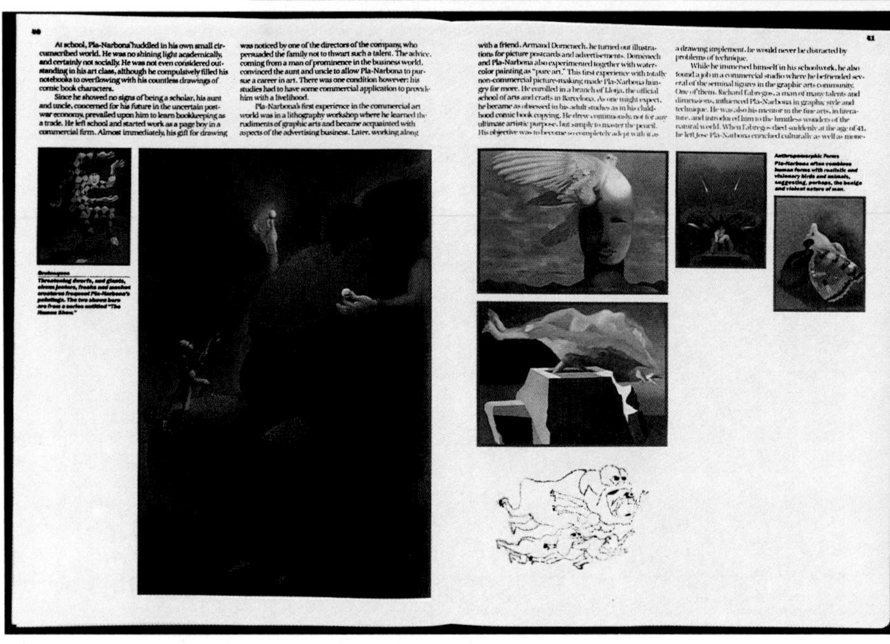

40

At school, Pla-Narbona huddled in his own small circumscribed world. He was no shining light academically, and certainly not socially. He was not even considered outstanding in his art class, although he compulsively filled his notebooks to overflowing with his countless drawings of comic book characters.

Since he showed no signs of being a scholar, his aunt and uncle, concerned for his future in the uncertain post-war economy, prevailed upon him to learn bookkeeping as a trade. He left school and started work as a page boy in a commercial firm. Almost immediately, his gift for drawing was noticed by one of the directors of the company, who persuaded the family not to thwart such a talent. The advice, coming from a man of prominence in the business world, convinced the aunt and uncle to allow Pla-Narbona to pursue a career in art. There was one condition however: his studies had to have some commercial application to provide him with a livelihood.

Pla-Narbona's first experience in the commercial art world was in a lithography workshop where he learned the rudiments of graphic arts and became acquainted with aspects of the advertising business. Later, working along with a friend, Armand Domenech, he turned out illustrations for picture postcards and advertisements. Domenech and Pla-Narbona also experimented together with watercolor painting as "pure art." This first experience with totally non-commercial picture-making made Pla-Narbona hungry for more. He enrolled in a branch of Llotja, the official school of arts and crafts in Barcelona. As one might expect, he became as obsessed in his adult studies as in his childhood comic book copying. He drew continuously, not for any ultimate artistic purpose, but simply to master the pencil. His objective was to become so completely adept with it as a drawing implement, he would never be distracted by problems of technique.

While he immersed himself in his schoolwork, he also found a job in a commercial studio where he befriended several of the seminal figures in the graphic arts community. One of them, Richard Fabregas, a man of many talents and dimensions, influenced Pla-Narbona in graphic style and technique. He was also his mentor in the fine arts, in literature, and introduced him to the limitless wonders of the natural world. When Fabregas died suddenly at the age of 41, he left Jose Pla-Narbona enriched culturally as well as mone-

Grotesques
Threatening dwarfs, and giants, clowns, jesters, freaks and macabre creatures frequent Pla-Narbona's paintings. The two shown here are from a series entitled "The Human Show."

41

Anthropomorphic Forms
Pla-Narbona often combines human forms with realistic and visionary birds and animals, suggesting, perhaps, the benign and violent nature of man.

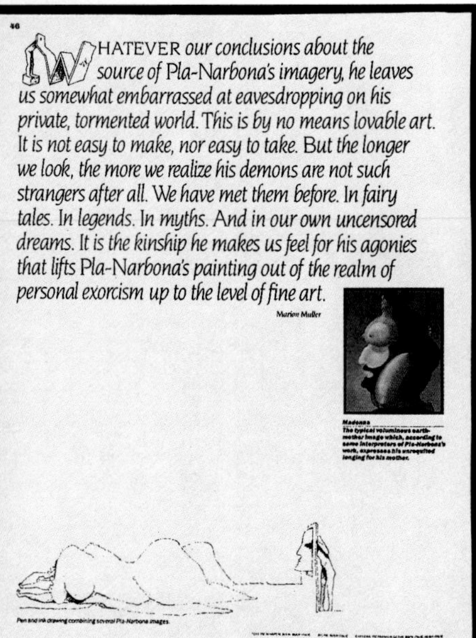

46

WHATEVER *our conclusions about the source of Pla-Narbona's imagery, he leaves us somewhat embarrassed at eavesdropping on his private, tormented world. This is by no means lovable art. It is not easy to make, nor easy to take. But the longer we look, the more we realize his demons are not such strangers after all. We have met them before. In fairy tales. In legends. In myths. And in our own uncensored dreams. It is the kinship he makes us feel for his agonies that lifts Pla-Narbona's painting out of the realm of personal exorcism up to the level of fine art.*

Marion Muller

Madonna
The typical voluminous earth-mother image which, according to some interpreters of Pla-Narbona's work, expresses his unrequited longing for his mother.

313

Art Director: Mo Lebowitz
Designer: Mo Lebowitz
Illustrator/Artist: José Pla-Narbona
Writer: Marion Muller
Editor: Edward Gottschall
Client: International Typeface Corp.
Design Firm: International Typeface Corp.
Publisher: International Typeface Corp.
Publication: U&LC

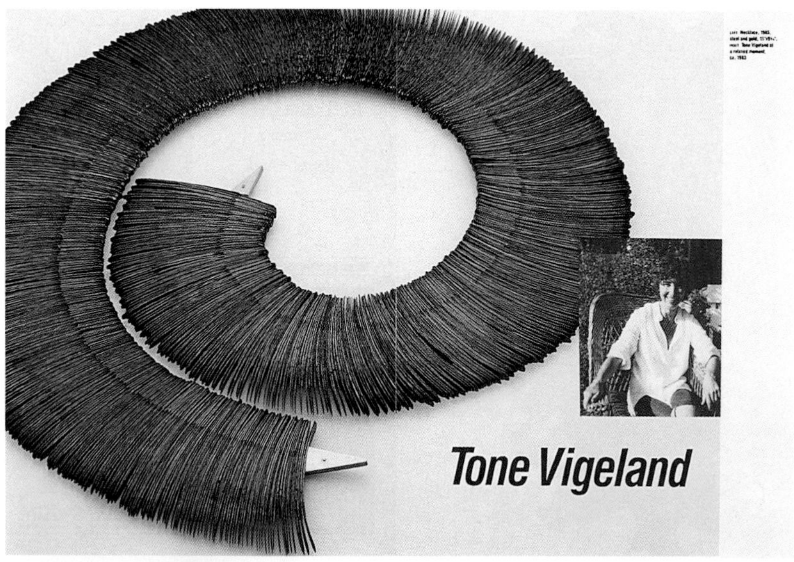

BY JAMES EVANS PHOTOGRAPHS BY ABEL

"Jewelry should enhance the wearer. It must feel nice, even sensual, and it must work with that body."

314

Art Director: Kiyoshi Kanai
Designer: Andrea Wollensak
Photographer: Abel
Writer: James Evans
Editor: Lois Moran
Client: American Craft Council
Agency: Kiyoshi Kanai Inc.
Publisher: American Craft Council
Publication: American Craft

Strolling into spring

Spring returns. Not with timid, small steps but in big, bold strides: color, fabric and silhouette point to a fashion-right market.

All new colors, prints, fabrications, silhouettes and themes have popped up in the girls' sportswear market for spring, giving this season of new beginnings an unjaded feeling of freshness.

Short and boxy is the mainstream of fashion for spring '88 with crop length and swing tops over short pouf skirts and shorts; minis, bubbles, tiered, ruffled, flippy skirts and skorts (split-skirt) shorts. Rib yoke treatments are important as are low torso, pocket, leg and ankle treatments. Baseball stitching is another detail for this season as well.

The major statement in fabrications for spring includes 100 percent cotton in various interpretations such as knits, wovens and garment washed canvas. While ecru, natural, or oatmeal denim is making inroads into the market, crinkle, seersucker and pucker fabrics also prove to be winners. Eyelet is another hot number, especially used for detailed accents and trims. French terry follows through for spring as well.

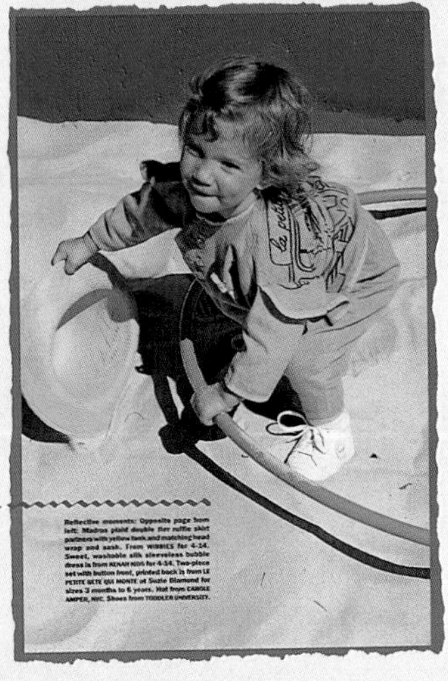

315

Art Director: Catherine Connors, Dana Dolan
Photographer: James Levin
Publication: Earnshaw's

316
Art Director: Jack Lefkowitz
Designer: Jack Lefkowitz
Illustrator/Artist: Jack Lefkowitz
Writer: David Ritchey
Editor: David Ritchey
Client: Industrial Launderer
Agency: Jack Lefkowitz Inc.
Publisher: Institute of Industrial Launderers
Publication: Industrial Launderer

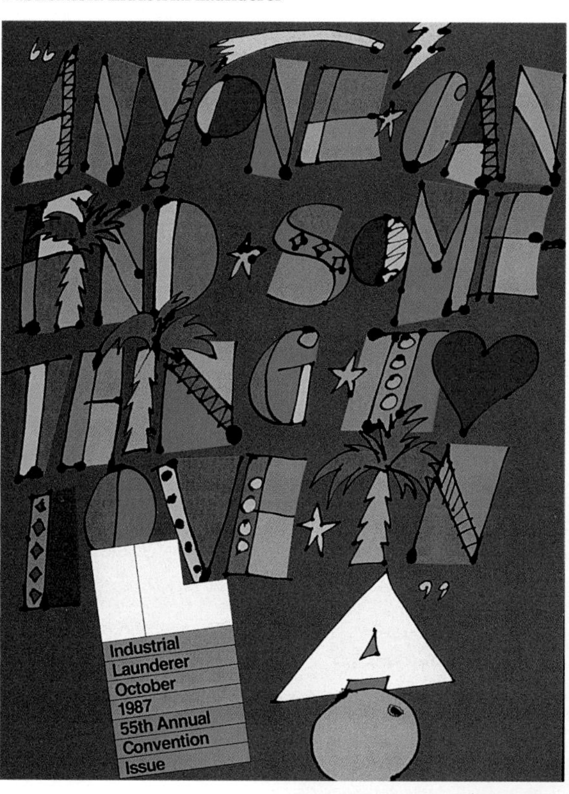

317
Art Director: John Hair
Designer: Bob Cato
Photographer: Ian Bradshaw
Editor: Dick Kagan
Creative Director: Bob Cato
Client: Pan American World Airways
Publisher: David Bannister, East/West Network
Publication: Pan Am Clipper

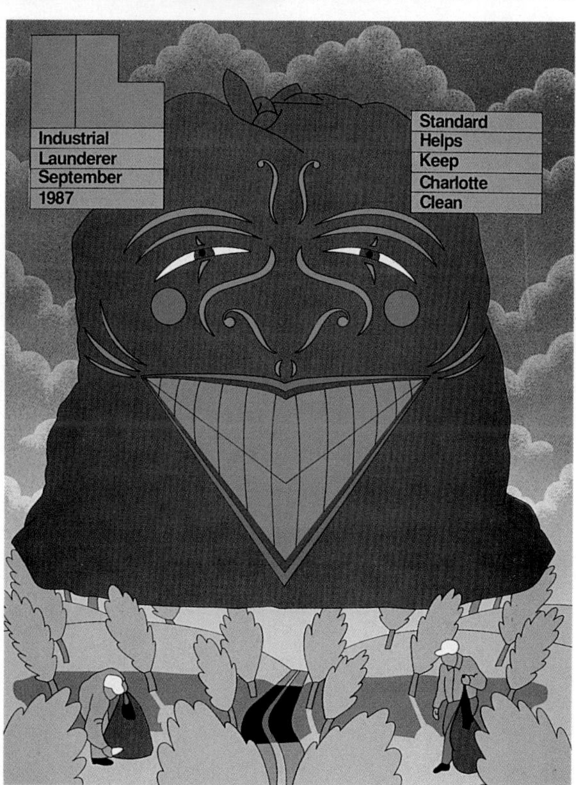

318
Art Director: Jack Lefkowitz
Designer: Jack Lefkowitz
Illustrator/Artist: Patricia Winters
Writer: David Ritchey
Editor: David Ritchey
Client: Industrial Launderer
Agency: Jack Lefkowitz Inc.
Publisher: Institute of Industrial Launderers
Publication: Industrial Launderer

319
Art Director: Lyle Metzdorf
Designer: Lyle Metzdorf
Illustrator/Artist: John Alcorn
Editor: Lyle Metzdorf
Creative Director: Lyle Metzdorf
Client: Chemical Bank
Design Firm: Jonson, Pirtle, Pedersen, Alcorn, Metzdorf & Hess
Publisher: Jutta Matijasic
Publication: Chemical Bank Review

320
Art Director: Tom Monahan
Designer: Ronn Campisi
Illustrator/Artist: Simon Ng
Client: CW Publishing

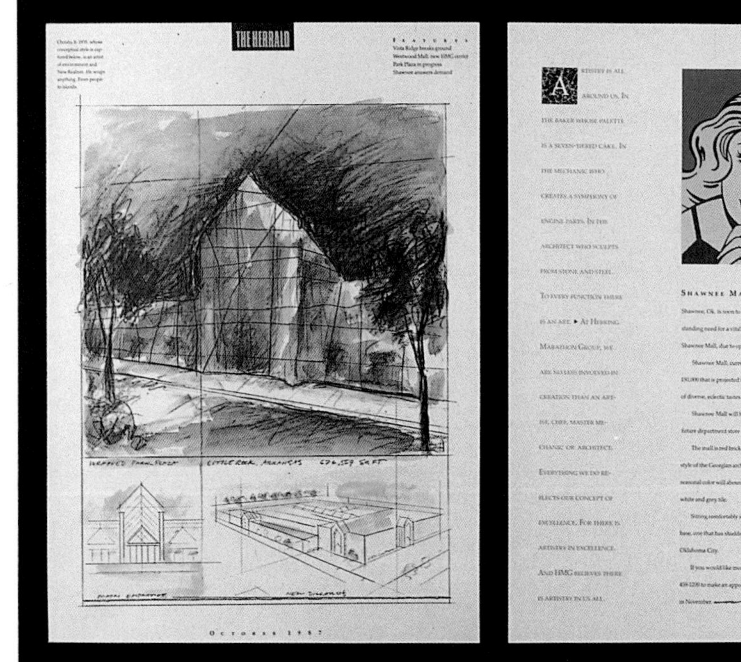

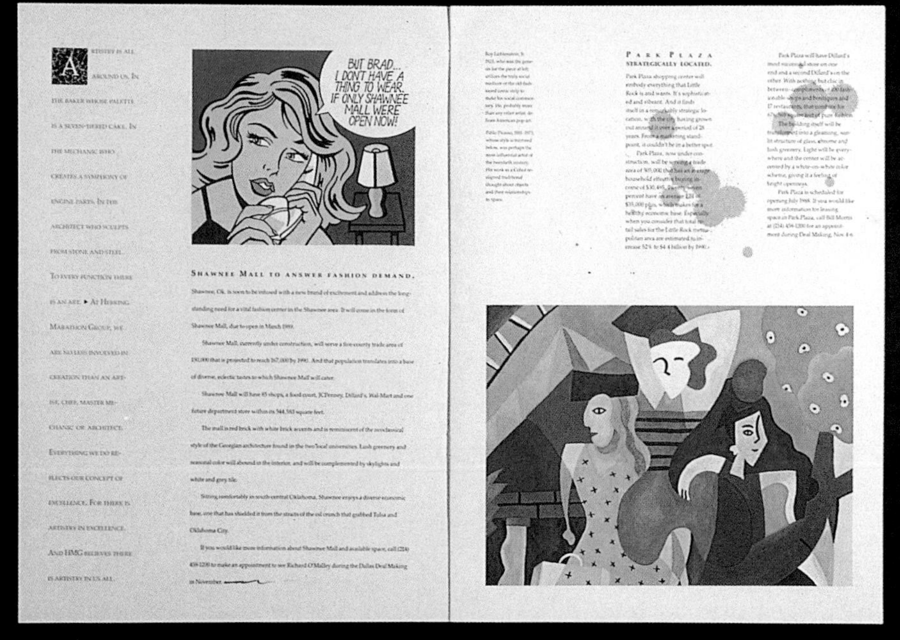

321
Art Director: Chuck Johnson, Bob Dennard, Jan Wilson
Illustrator/Artist: Chuck Johnson, Brad Wines, Jan Wilson
Writer: Susan Nelson
Client: Herring Marathon Group
Design Firm: Dennard Creative Inc.

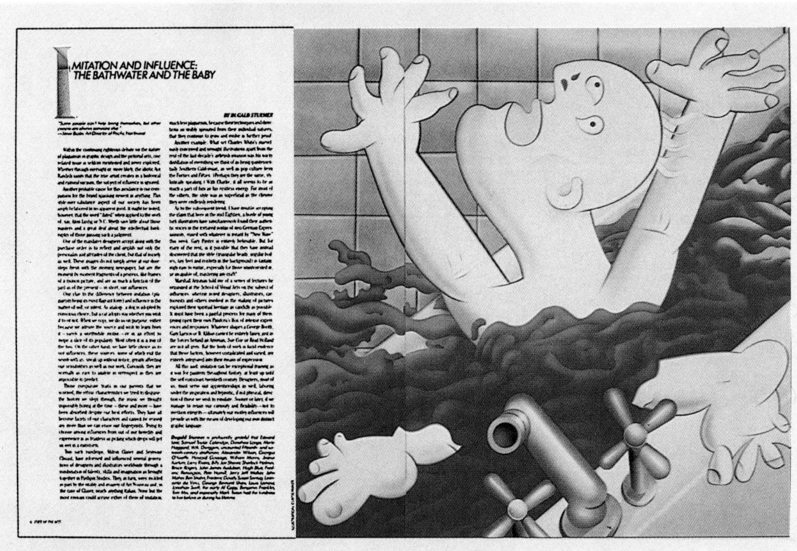

IMITATION AND INFLUENCE: THE BATHWATER AND THE BABY

CAVEAT VENDOR

322
Art Director: Curtis Parker, Art Lofgreen, Julie Sand
Editor: Leslie Johnson, Susan McCrillis
Client: Phoenix Society of Communicating Arts
Design Firm: Parker, Johnson, Lofgreen Design Assoc.
Publisher: Phoenix Society of Communicating Arts
Publication: State of the Arts

QUEENS

INDUSTRY UPDATE

TRENDS ISSUES NEWS DEVELOPMENTS

1987

INDUSTRY TREND TOWARD BOARD VS. PLASTIC

MUSIC PACKAGING

GRAPHICS

Critical Factor in CD and Cassette Packaging

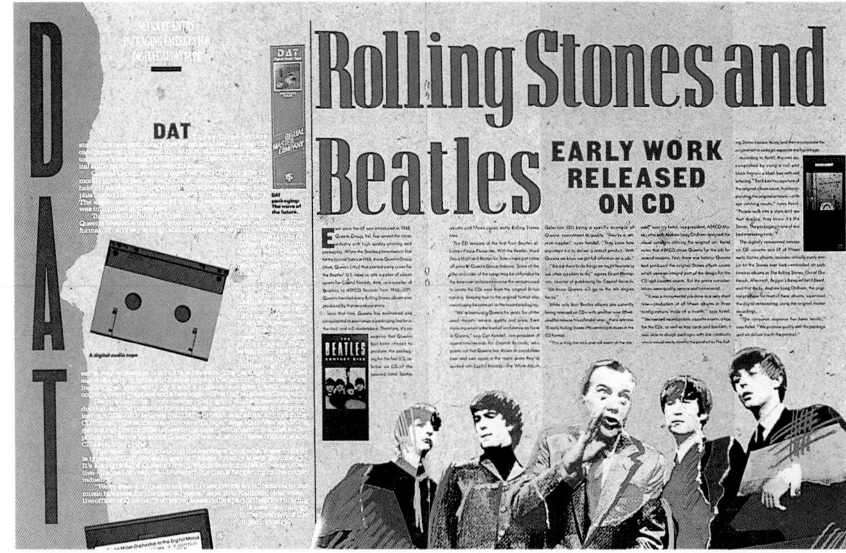
DAT

Rolling Stones and Beatles

EARLY WORK RELEASED ON CD

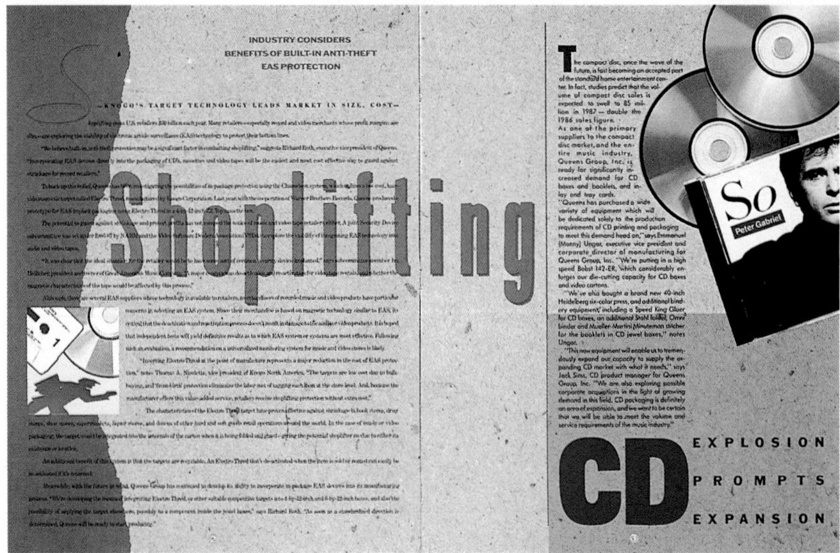
INDUSTRY CONSIDERS BENEFITS OF BUILT-IN ANTI-THEFT EAS PROTECTION

Shoplifting

CD EXPLOSION PROMPTS EXPANSION

323

Art Director: Terry R. Koppel
Designer: Terry R. Koppel
Writer: Melissa Mojo
Editor: Richard Roth, Melissa Mojo
Client: Queens Group
Design Firm: Koppel & Scher
Publisher: Queens Group

I went to work on this project before I ever saw the photographs we were to use. The guidelines had been laid out so I knew the most basic but most important considerations. The audience would be made up primarily of photographers. I knew the size, the context, and that I would be writer, editor, art director and designer. Out of respect for the contributors, I decided to use the photos the way they were given to me, without manipulation. Ideally I wanted to tell a story while giving each photo a space of its own.

"because I couldn't see what they found so interesting I had to let my imagination take over."

As soon as I took the photographs out of the envelope I saw what I was looking for. Although the photos were very different from each other there was one that I knew I could build my story on. The people, mostly men, were all looking in the same general direction but they each seemed to be looking at something different. Because I couldn't see what they found so interesting I had to let my imagination take over. The men with the binoculars reminded me of photographers, using their lenses to bring their subject closer and to crop and select what they individually wanted to see.

Next came the design and editorial decisions. To help direct the reader into my story I started by making the main image noticeably larger and centering it on the spread. I pulled out and enlarged the woman with the hat and strong facial expression and butted it up against an image in a very obvious way to show what I thought might be behind her expression. I gave the impression of a close-up of the plants on the far right, and put the baseball player in action by repeating the same photo in various sizes and positions. Beyond this I would like your imagination to take over.

The rest of the design has to do with balance and mood. I chose to use a layout with some tension, some dissonance, and to resolve this tension with the pretty woman as my close. I felt that photographers and designers would be attracted to this and it would make for a more intriguing story.

324

Art Director: Henry Brimmer
Designer: Michael Mabry, Vincent Romaniello
Photographer: Charly Franklin
Design Firm: Henry Brimmer Design
Publication: Photo Metro
Printer: Singer Printing

CHICAIGAO

AIGA in Chicago

A quarterly publication of the Chicago Chapter, the American Institute of Graphic Arts

Autumn 1987

Defining the Profession of Graphic Design
Our first issue of AIGA in Chicago explores the ongoing evolution of the graphic design profession based on the insights and perceptions of designers themselves.

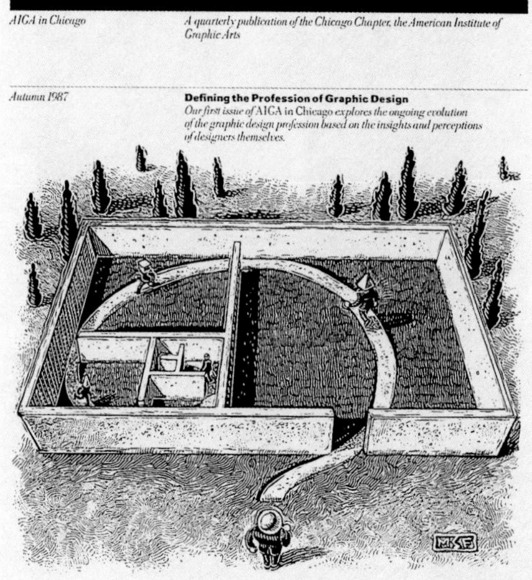

Identifying the Issues: A Roundtable Discussion

"A key to being perceived as professional is when everybody in our industry adheres to the same guidelines, the same language, and the same ethics."

325

Art Director: Bart Crosby
Designer: Carl Wohlt
Illustrator/Artist: Mary Flock
Editor: John Ortbal, Michael Lange
Creative Director: Bart Crosby
Client: AIGA, Chicago Chapter
Design Firm: Crosby Associates Inc.

GRAPHIC DESIGN

ESPRIT'S GRAPHIC WORK 1984-1986

SPECKLETONE
COLOURS
NEW HUES FROM AFAR
Clarion
RADIO

MARTEX

MANON
GIVENCHY
ATELIER MARTEX
1-2080

CERTIFIABLY NUTS

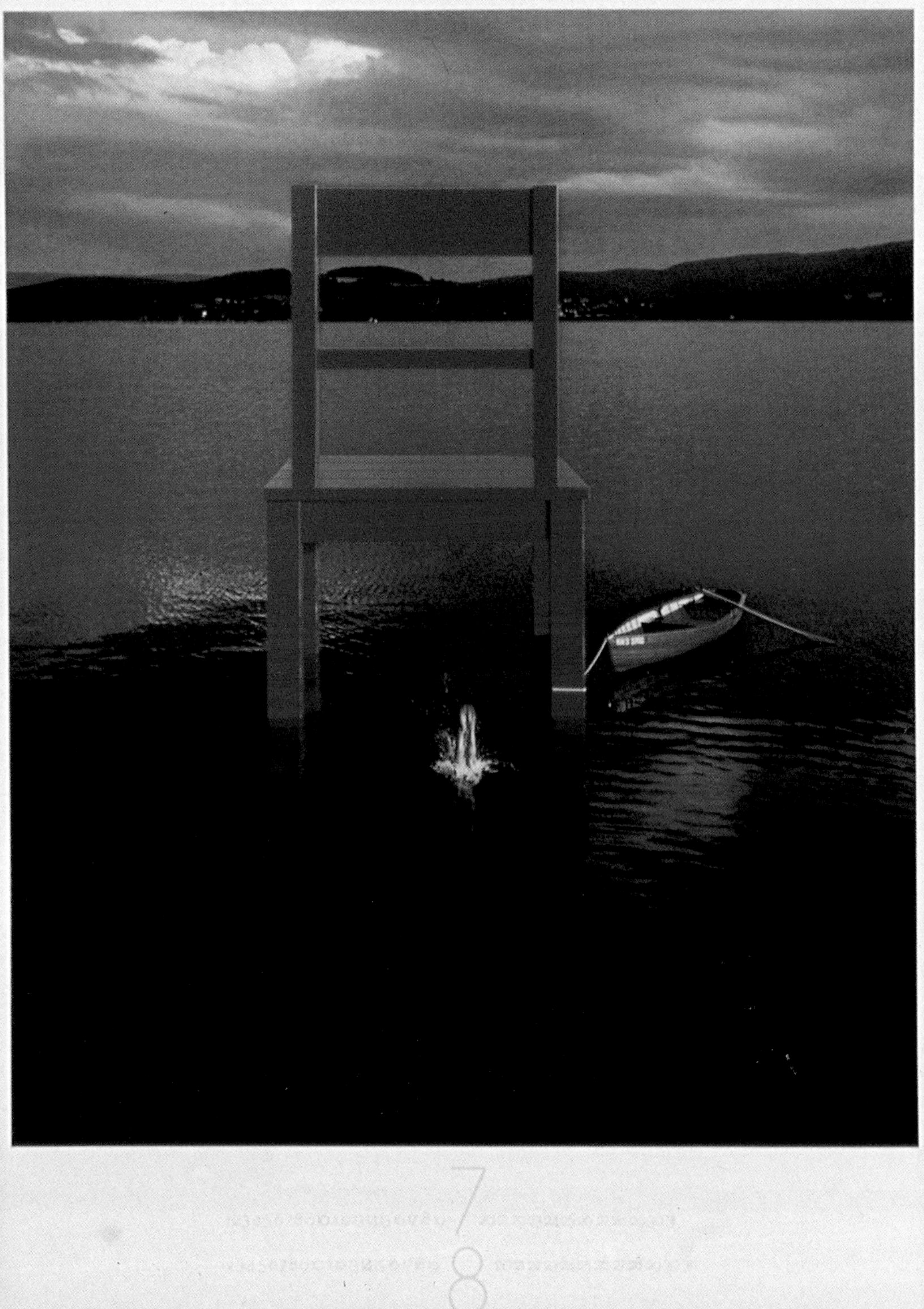

333 Distinctive Merit

Art Director: Joseph Polzelbauer
Photographer: Otto Kasper
Client: Sinar AG

334
Art Director: Peter Harrison, Suzanne Morin
Designer: Suzanne Morin, Peter Harrison
Photographer: Bruce Wolf
Writer: Robert C. Hubbell
Client: Hasbro Inc.
Design Firm: Pentagram Design

335
Art Director: Colin Forbes
Designer: Michael Gericke
Client: Drexel, Burnham, Lambert
Design Firm: Pentagram Design

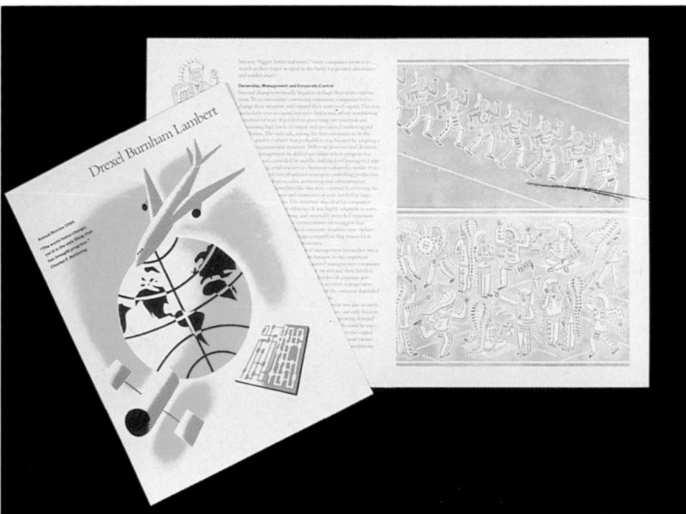

336
Art Director: Brian Boyd
Designer: Brian Boyd
Photographer: Robert Latorre
Illustrator/Artist: Brian Boyd
Writer: Rich Flora
Client: Chili's Inc.
Agency: The Richards Group
Design Firm: Richards, Brock, Miller, Mitchell & Assoc.

337
Art Director: Ivan Chermayeff
Designer: Bill Anton
Photographer: Alan Shortall
Illustrator/Artist: Ivan Chermayeff
Client: Hechinger
Design Firm: Chermayeff & Geismar Associates

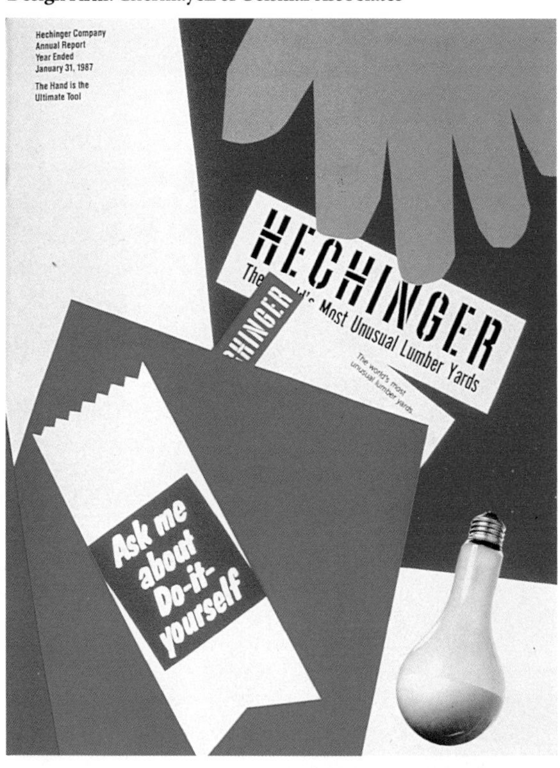

338
Art Director: Lauren Smith
Designer: Lauren Smith, Cliff Rusch
Photographer: David Powers
Writer: Del Tycer
Creative Director: Lauren Smith
Client: Western Micro Technologies
Agency: Tycer Associates
Design Firm: Lauren Smith Design

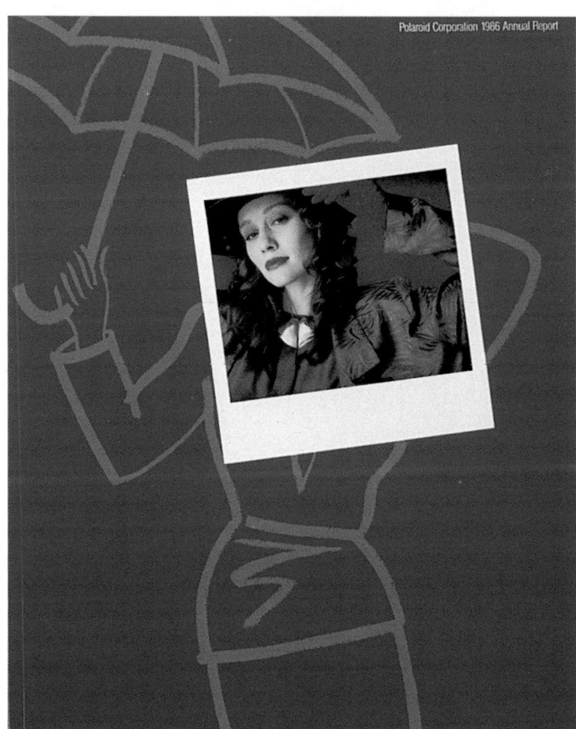

339
Art Director: Mike Benes, Marie McGinley
Designer: Mike Benes, Marie McGinley, Vartus Artinian
Illustrator/Artist: Lark Carrier, Jamie Hogan, Marie McGinley
Writer: Sam Yanes

340
Art Director: Pat Samata
Designer: Pat Samata, Greg Samata
Photographer: Mark Joseph
Illustrator/Artist: Paul Thompson
Writer: Jennette LoCurto
Editor: Kate Walsh
Client: Carson, Pirie, Scott & Co.
Agency: Samata Associates

341
Art Director: Craig Frazier
Designer: Craig Frazier
Photographer: Jock McDonald
Illustrator/Artist: John Hersey
Writer: Barbara Shapiro
Client: 3Com Corp.
Design Firm: Frazier Design

342
Art Director: Peter Harrison
Designer: Susan Hochbaum
Photographer: Scott Morgan
Writer: David Bither
Client: Warner Communications Inc.
Design Firm: Pentagram Design

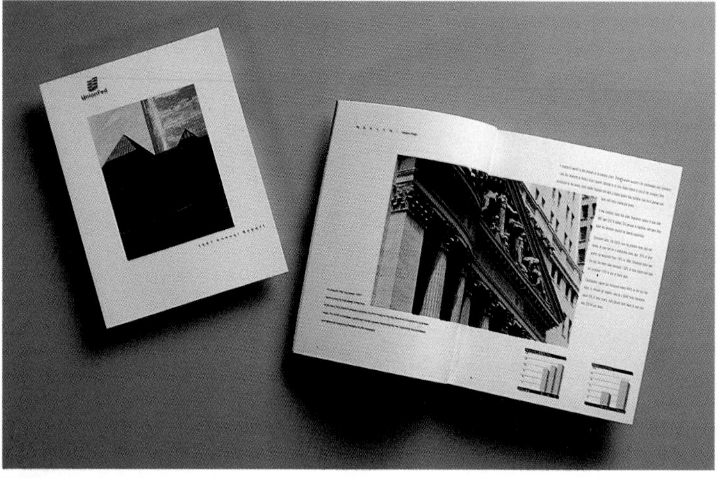

343
Art Director: James Cross
Designer: Joseph Jacquez
Photographer: Pete Saloudos
Editor: Jennifer Barrett
Client: Unionfed Financial Corp.
Design Firm: Cross Associates

344
Art Director: Kit Hinrichs
Designer: Kit Hinrichs, Lenore Bartz
Photographer: Tom Tracy, Paul Fusco, Gerald Bybee
Writer: Holly Hutchins
Client: Potlatch Corp.
Design Firm: Pentagram Design

345
Art Director: Pat Samata
Designer: Pat Samata
Photographer: Terry Heffernan, Mark Joseph
Illustrator/Artist: Paul Thompson
Writer: Dave Prichard
Editor: Elizabeth Higashi
Client: International Mineral & Chemical Corp.
Design Firm: Samata Associates

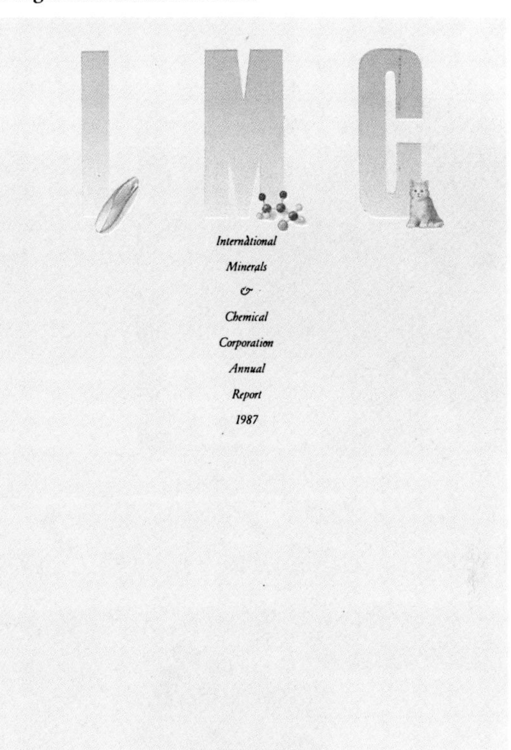

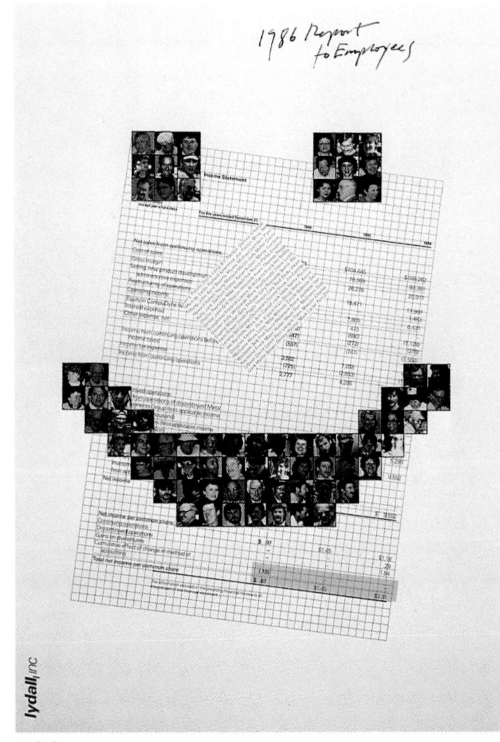

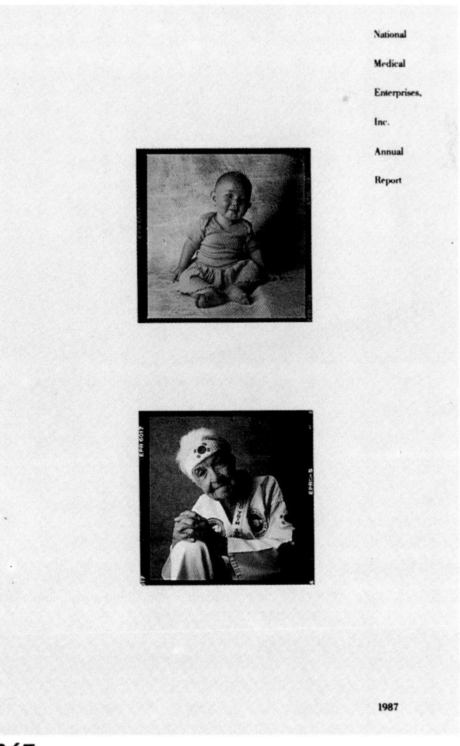

346
Art Director: Robert Appleton
Designer: Robert Appleton
Writer: Carole F. Butenas
Client: Lydall Inc.
Printer: Allied Printing Services
Typographer: Typographic House

347
Art Director: James Berte
Designer: James Berte
Photographer: William Coupon
Illustrator/Artist: Martin Ledyard
Client: National Medical
Design Firm: Robert, Miles, Runyan & Associates

348

Art Director: Ron Jefferies
Designer: Susan Garland
Photographer: Russ Widstrand
Writer: Peter Churm, Ron Bissell
Creative Director: Ron Jefferies
Client: The Flourocarbon Company
Agency: The Jefferies Association
Design Firm: The Jefferies Association

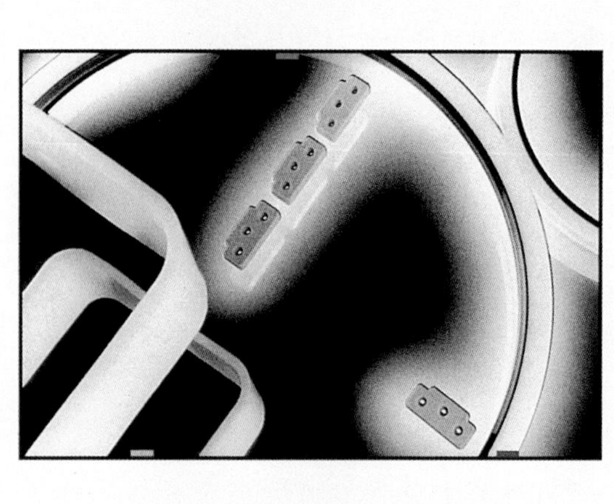

349

Art Director: Michael Gunselman
Designer: Michael Gunselman, Ralph Billings, Jr.
Photographer: Ed Eckstein
Writer: Marla Mathias
Client: U.S. Healthcare Inc.
Design Firm: Michael Gunselman Inc.
Project Coordinator: Picture That Inc.

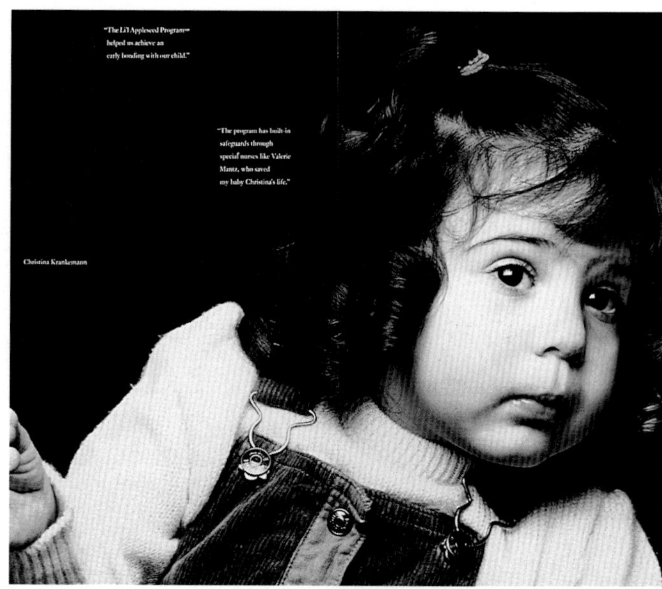

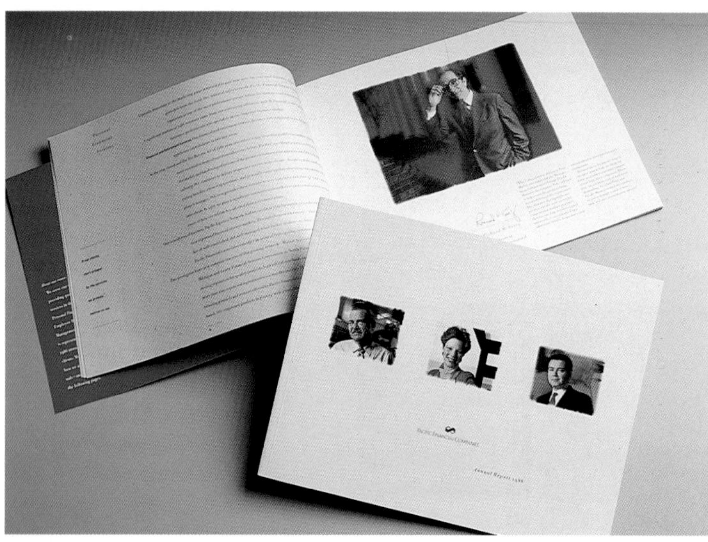

350

Art Director: Lisa Levin, Ken White
Designer: Lisa Levin
Photographer: Eric Myer
Writer: Alison Edwards
Creative Director: Ken White
Client: Pacific Financial Companies
Design Firm: White & Associates
Publisher: Pacific Financial Companies

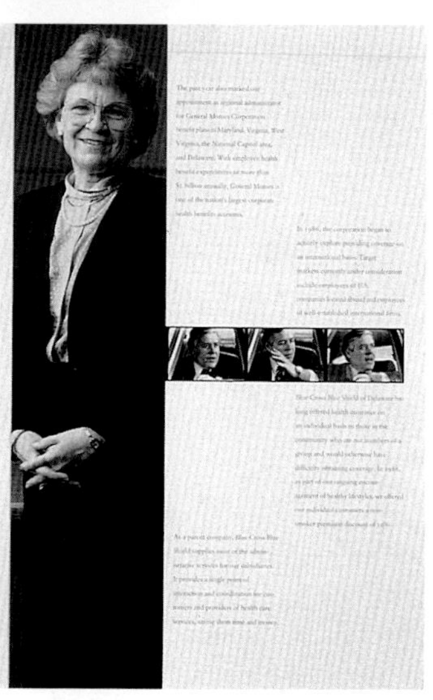

351

Art Director: Michael Gunselman
Designer: Michael Gunselman
Photographer: Ed Eckstein
Writer: Kerin Hearn
Client: Blue Cross/Blue Shield of Delaware
Design Firm: Michael Gunselman Inc.
Printer: Lebanon Valley Offset

352
Art Director: Pat Samata
Designer: Pat Samata, Greg Samata
Photographer: Mark Joseph
Writer: Mary Jo Bohr
Editor: Ed Joyce
Client: Peoples Energy Corp.
Agency: Samata Associates
Design Firm: Samata Associates

353
Art Director: Bennett Robinson
Designer: Bennett Robinson, Erika Siegel
Photographer: Various
Illustrator/Artist: Various
Writer: Various
Creative Director: Bennett Robinson
Client: Simpson Paper Co.
Design Firm: Corporate Graphics Inc.
Printer: Anderson Lithograph

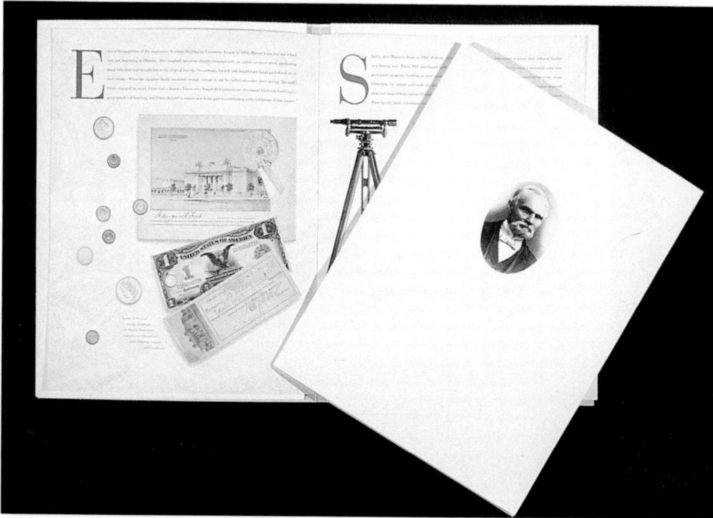

354
Art Director: McRay Magleby
Designer: McRay Magleby, Linda Sullivan
Photographer: John Snyder
Illustrator/Artist: McRay Magleby
Writer: Norman A. Darais
Client: Brigham Young University
Design Firm: BYU Graphics
Typographer: Jonathan Skousen

355
Art Director: John Vosbikian
Photographer: Giandomenico & Fiore
Client: Quickie Manufacturing Corp.
Design Firm: Hovaness Design Inc.

356
Art Director: James Cross
Designer: Anne Burdick, John Clark
Writer: Arnold & Underwood
Client: Simpson Paper Co.
Design Firm: Cross Associates

357
Art Director: Steven Sessions
Designer: Steven Sessions
Photographer: Steve Brady
Illustrator/Artist: LeeLee Brazeal, Jeffery Masara
Writer: Clarisse Burns
Creative Director: Steven Sessions
Client: Charter Hospital
Agency: Steven Sessions Inc.

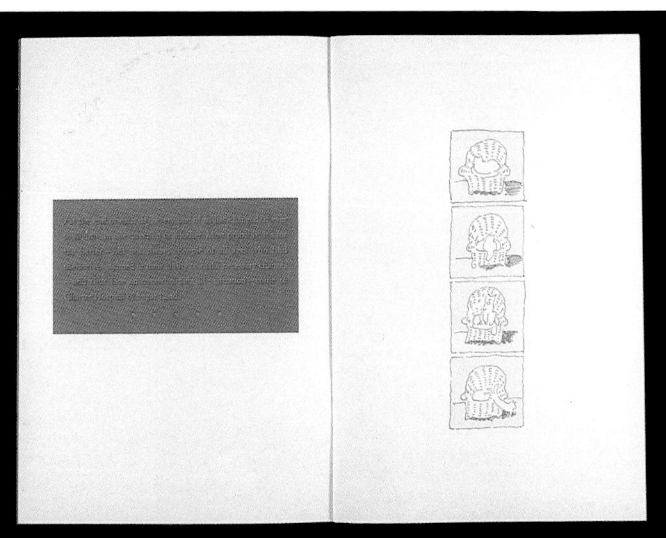

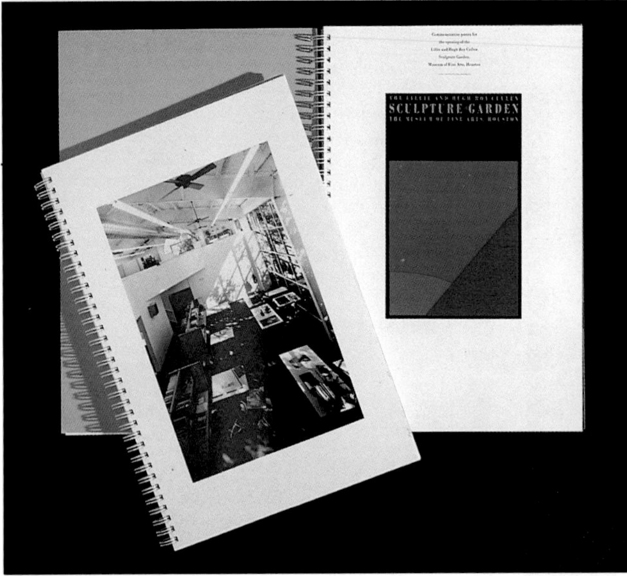

358
Art Director: Lowell Williams
Designer: Lowell Williams, Bill Carson
Photographer: Ron Scott
Writer: Lowell Williams
Client: Lowell Williams Design Inc.
Design Firm: Lowell Williams Design Inc.

359
Art Director: James Cross, Jay Novak
Designer: Joseph Jacquez
Photographer: Warren Faubel, Charles Imstepf
Illustrator/Artist: Disney Art Dept.
Client: Euro Disneyland
Design Firm: Cross Associates

360
Art Director: Mitchell Mauk
Designer: Mitchell Mauk
Writer: Mitchell Mauk, Demian Martin, Raymond Burnham
Client: Entertainment Technologies
Design Firm: Mauk Design
Printer: AR Lithographers
Typographer: Z Typography

361
Art Director: Peter Richards
Photographer: Langley Penoyar Photography
Writer: Tom McCarthy
Creative Director: Bob Wheatley, Peter Richards
Client: GNA
Agency: Ogilvy & Mather Public Relations/West
Account Group Supervisor: Bob Wheatley
Hand Tinting: Daniel Langley

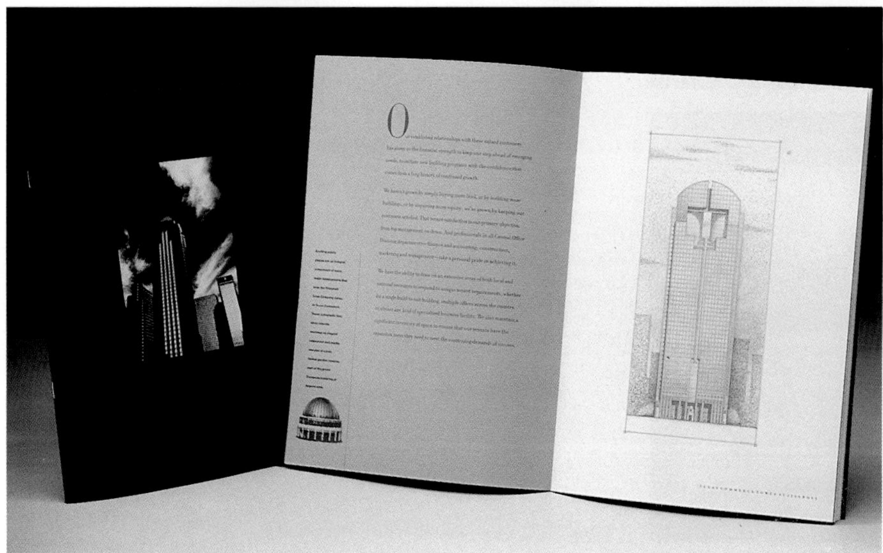

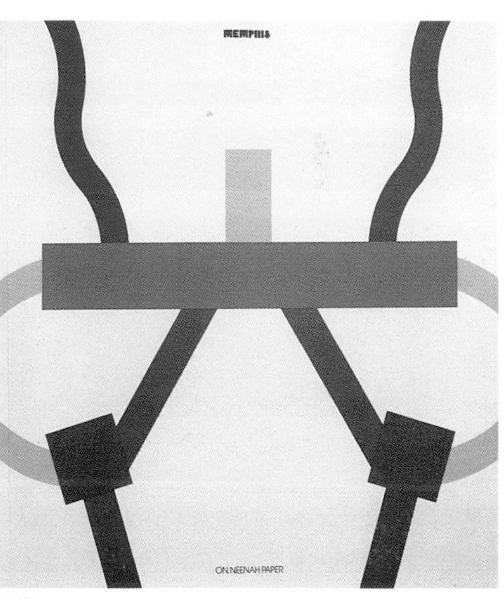

362
Art Director: Don Sibley
Designer: Don Sibley
Photographer: Joe Aker
Illustrator/Artist: Mark Domiteaux
Writer: Lee Herrick
Client: Trammell Crow Co.
Design Firm: Sibley/Peteet Design

363
Art Director: Glen Smith
Photographer: Ettore Sottass, Michele de Lucchi, Joe Giannetti
Writer: Steve Holt, Michael McDonough
Creative Director: Tom Wright
Client: Neenah Paper
Printer: Litho Specialties

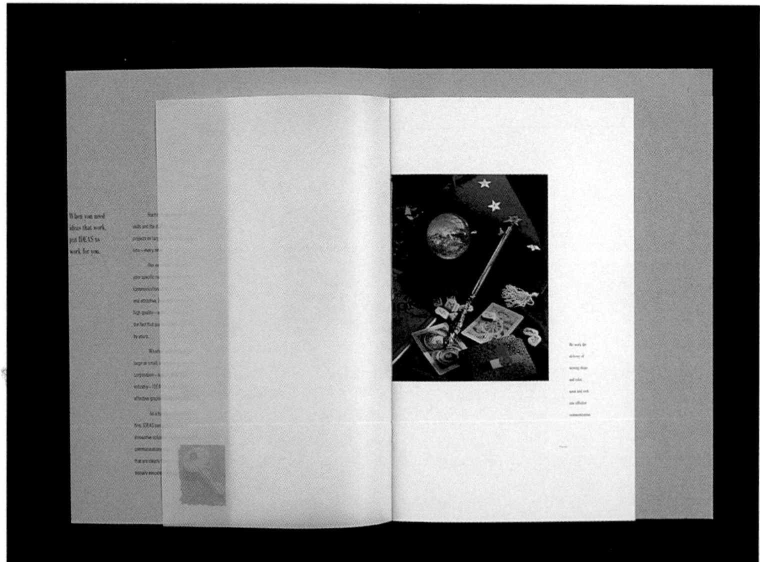

364
Art Director: Cynde Starck, Robin Brandes
Designer: Cynde Starck, Lisa Pettibone
Photographer: John Lund
Illustrator/Artist: Michèle Manning
Design Firm: Ideas
Printer: Reliable Graphics

365
Art Director: Paul Huber
Designer: Paul Huber
Photographer: Steve Marsel
Illustrator/Artist: Marc Rosenthal
Writer: Dan Altman
Creative Director: Bob Manley
Client: Tristar Sports
Agency: Altman & Manley Advertising
Design Firm: Altman & Manley Design

366
Art Director: Dick Mitchell, Greg Booth
Designer: Dick Mitchell
Photographer: Greg Booth
Writer: Mark Perkins
Client: Lomas & Nettleton Financial Corp.
Agency: The Richards Group
Design Firm: Richards, Brock, Miller, Mitchell & Associates

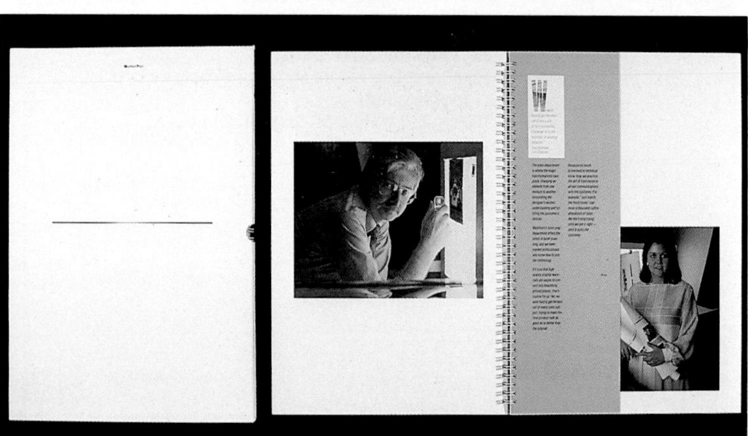

367
Art Director: James A. Stygar
Designer: James A. Stygar
Photographer: Richard Ustinich
Writer: Penelope Stygar, Betse Feuchtenberger
Client: Washburn Press
Design Firm: Stygar Group Inc.

368
Art Director: Alan Peckolick
Illustrator/Artist: Lynn Boyer-Pennington
Design Firm: Peckolick & Partners
Lettering: Tony Dispigna

369
Art Director: Young Kim
Designer: Young Kim
Photographer: Dan Salzman
Writer: Jeff Seglin
Client: The Banque Indosuez, Todreas/Hanley
Design Firm: The Brownstone Group

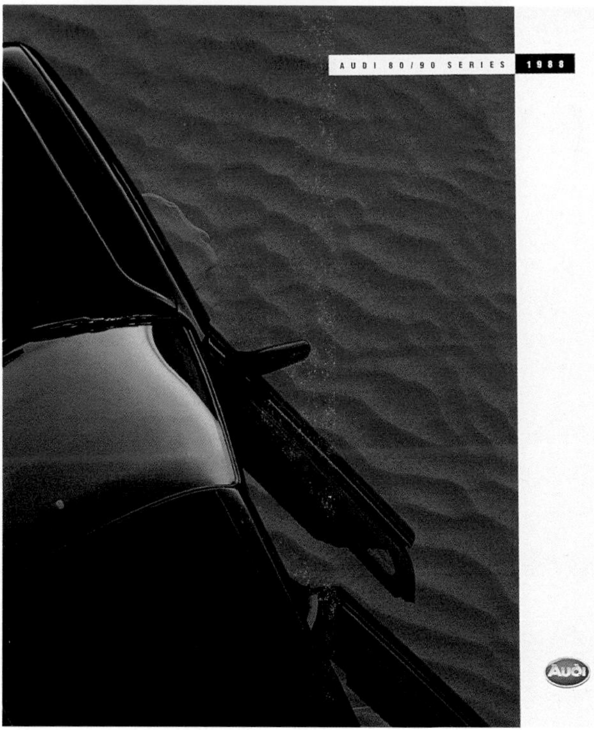

370
Art Director: Tyler Smith
Designer: Tyler Smith
Photographer: Myron
Writer: Craig Walker
Creative Director: Tyler Smith
Client: Louis, Boston
Agency: Tyler Smith
Design Firm: Tyler Smith

371
Art Director: Barry Shepard
Designer: Steve Ditko, Karin Burklein Arnold, Douglas Reeder
Photographer: Rick Rusing, Rick Gayle
Client: Audi of America Inc.
Design Firm: SHR Communications Planning & Design
Production Manager: Roger Barger

372
Art Director: John Harris
Writer: Barbara Kaplan
Publisher: Sarah Lawrence Publications Office

373
Art Director: John Luke
Designer: John Luke
Client: John Luke Publishing
Cover Design: Paul Rand

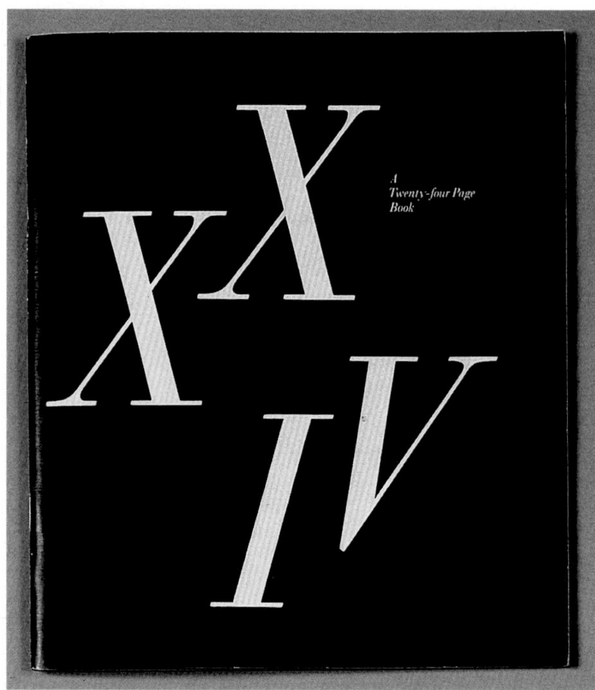

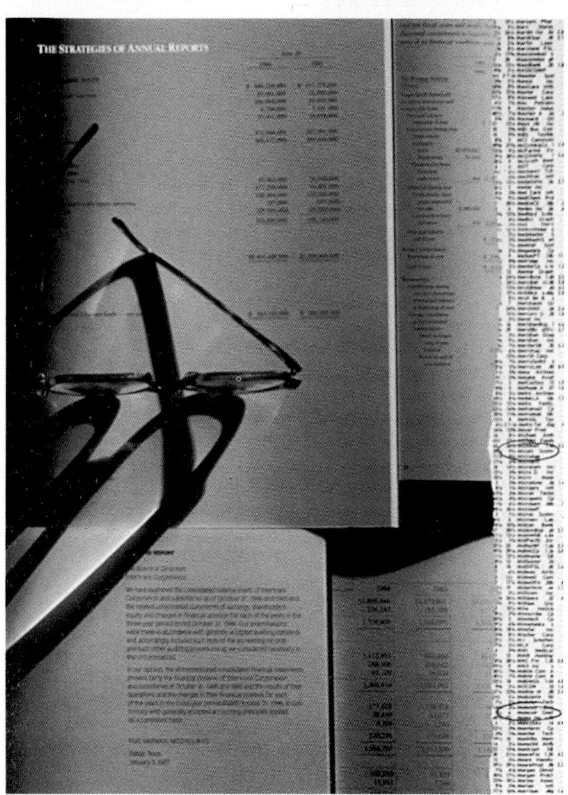

374
Art Director: Kevin B. Kuester
Designer: Kevin B. Kuester, Tim Sauer
Photographer: Terry Heffernan
Writer: Dick Cinquina
Client: Potlatch Corp.
Design Firm: Madsen & Kuester Inc.
Project Coordinator: Marjorie Oknick

375
Art Director: Bill Cahan
Designer: Cathy Locke
Photographer: Burton Pritzker
Illustrator/Artist: David Gambale
Writer: David Crane
Client: Babcock & Brown Inc.
Agency: Cahan & Associates
Design Firm: Cahan & Associates

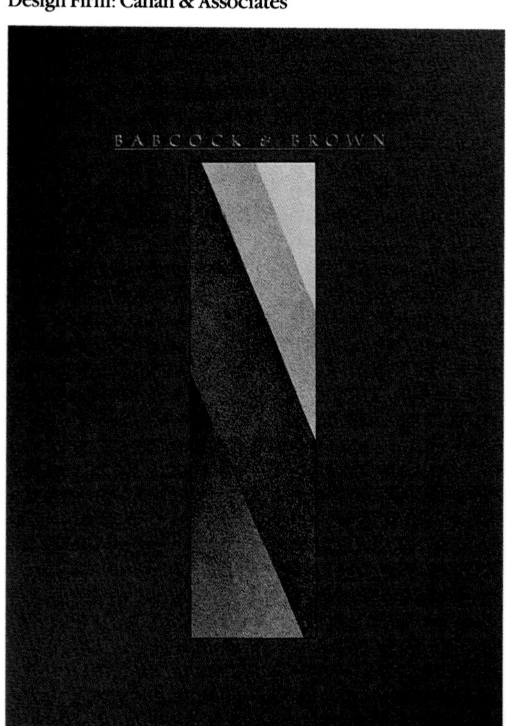

376
Art Director: Susan Casey
Designer: Nancy Manfredi
Illustrator/Artist: Mark Hess
Writer: Dave Goldenburg
Creative Director: Steve Trygg
Client: Oce Business Systems
Agency: Anderson & Lembke

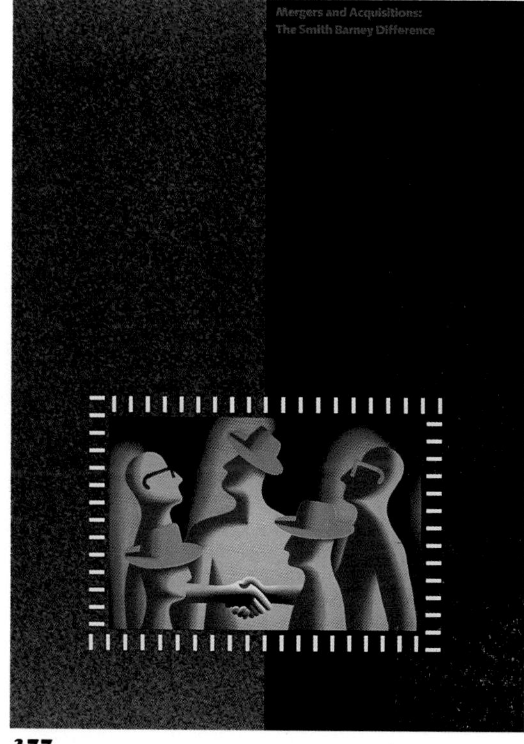

377
Art Director: Leslie Smolan
Designer: Alyssa A. Adkins
Illustrator/Artist: Jean-Charles Blais, Jack Goldstein, Mark Kostabi, Andrew Stevovich
Editor: Rita Jacobs
Client: Smith Barney
Design Firm: Carbone Smolan Associates

378
Art Director: Carole Bouchard
Designer: Carole Bouchard
Photographer: Christopher Harting
Writer: David Abend
Creative Director: Cheryl Heller
Client: Reebok
Agency: Heller Breene

379
Art Director: James A. Stygar
Designer: James A. Stygar
Photographer: Brent Cavedo
Writer: Betse Feuchtenberger
Client: Thetford Associates Inc.
Design Firm: Stygar Group Inc.

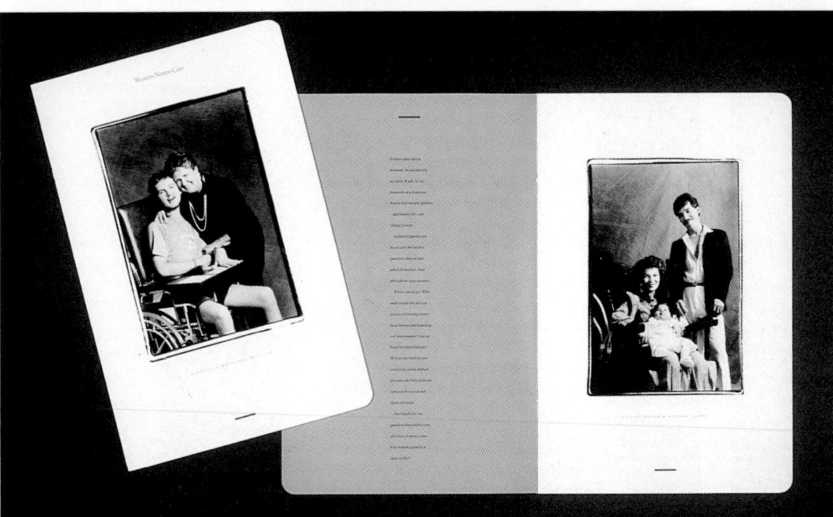

380
Art Director: Paul Huber, Brent Croxton
Designer: Brent Croxton, Paul Huber
Photographer: Steve Brady
Writer: Neil Ray
Creative Director: Paul Huber
Client: Western Neuro Care
Design Firm: Altman & Manley

381
Art Director: John T. Cleveland
Designer: John T. Cleveland
Writer: Rose DeNeve
Client: S. D. Warren Co.
Design Firm: John Cleveland Inc.

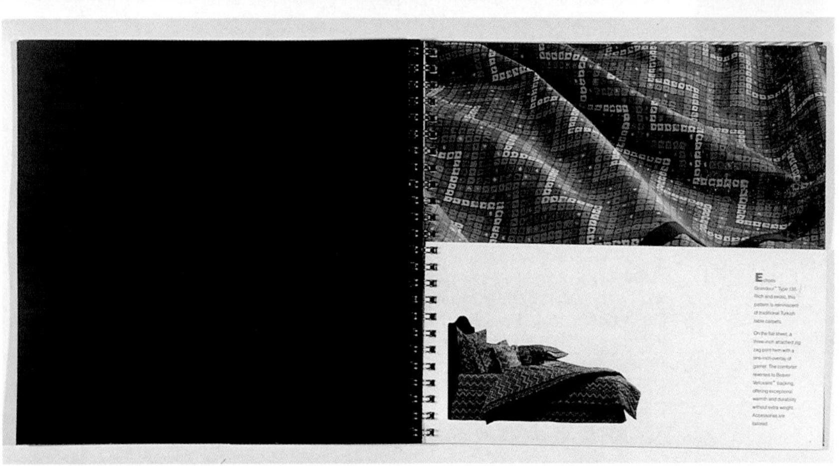

382
Art Director: Jean McCartney
Designer: Jean McCartney
Photographer: George Kleiman
Creative Director: Bryan Dixon
Client: Lady Pepperell
Agency: West Point Pepperell
Design Firm: West Point Pepperell
Stylist: Susan Dalglish

384

Art Director: Deborah Van Rooyen
Designer: Deborah Van Rooyen
Illustrator/Artist: Jean Michel Folon
Writer: Sharyn Rogers
Creative Director: Sharyn Rogers,
Deborah Van Rooyen
Client: Fidelity Investments, Systems Division
Agency: Bernard Hodes Advertising
Design Firm: BHA Design Group
Printer: Dynagraf

383

Art Director: Jennifer Morla
Designer: Jennifer Morla
Photographer: Jeffrey Newbury
Writer: Jennifer Morla
Client: Levi Strauss & Co.
Design Firm: Morla Design Inc.

385

Art Director: James Cross
Designer: Yee-Ping Cho
Writer: Arnold & Underwood
Client: Simpson Paper Co.
Design Firm: Cross Associates

386
Art Director: Jennifer Morla
Designer: Jennifer Morla
Photographer: Elaine Keenan
Writer: Jennifer Morla
Client: Levi Strauss & Co.
Design Firm: Morla Design Inc.

387
Art Director: Cheryl Heller
Designer: Cheryl Heller, Joanne Biron, Julie Edwards
Photographer: Christopher Harting
Illustrator/Artist: Heller Breene Designers
Writer: Denis Jakuc
Creative Director: Cheryl Heller
Agency: Heller Breene

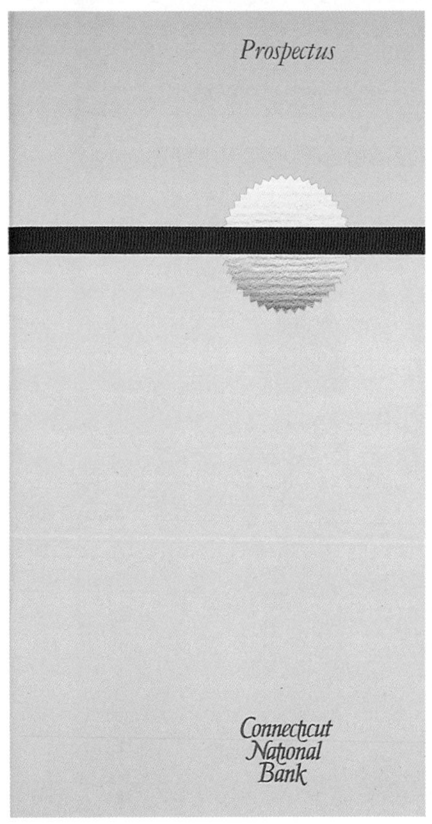

388
Art Director: Ted Bertz
Designer: Wendy Weeks
Photographer: Jack McConnell
Writer: Robert Ford
Client: Connecticut National Bank
Design Firm: Ted Bertz Design Inc.

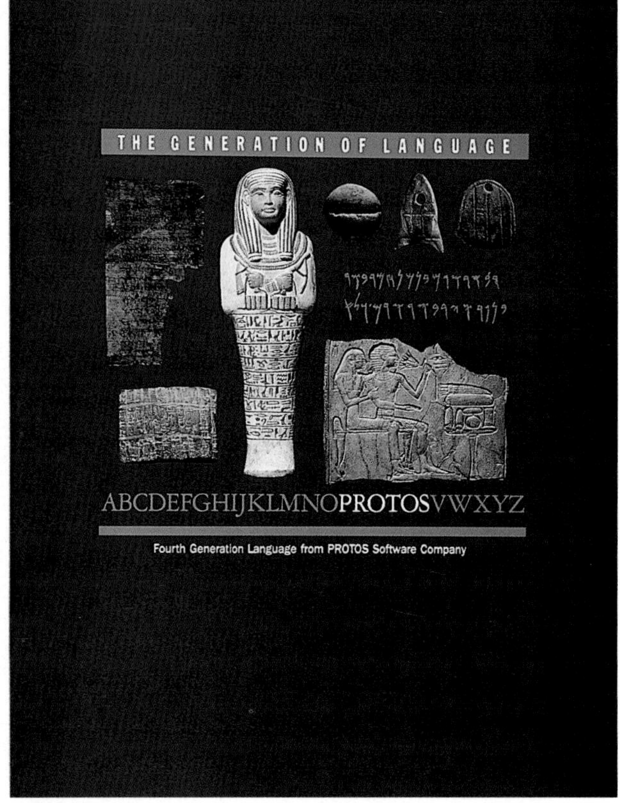

389
Art Director: Jane Wu
Designer: Jane Wu
Writer: Anita Harvey
Client: Protos Software Co.
Design Firm: Wu Graphic Design

390
Art Director: Gordon Hochhalter
Designer: Dan La Rocca
Photographer: Rod Cooke, Jack O'Grady
Illustrator/Artist: Bob Conge, Dan La Rocca
Writer: Sheila Fagan, Gordon Hochhalter
Client: R. R. Donnelley Financial

391
Art Director: Cheryl Heller
Designer: Cheryl Heller, David Lopes
Photographer: Clint Clemens
Writer: Peter Caroline
Creative Director: Cheryl Heller
Client: S. D. Warren
Agency: Heller Breene

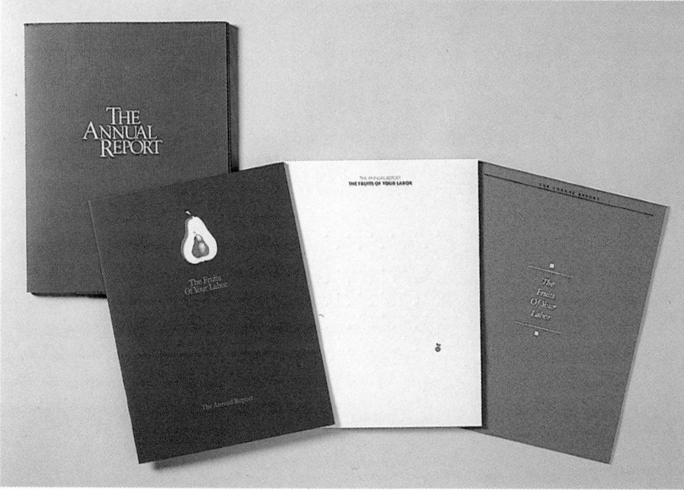

392
Art Director: L. Cameron Hyers
Designer: Tom Fowler, Elizabeth P. Ball, Karl S. Maruyama
Writer: Brad Elliott
Client: James River Corp.

393
Art Director: Lowell Williams
Designer: Lana Rigsby
Photographer: Ron Scott, Bob Harr
Illustrator/Artist: Lana Rigsby, Cindy White
Writer: Lee Herrick
Client: Gerald D. Hines Interests
Design Firm: Lowell Williams Design Inc.

394

Art Director: Peter W. Johnson
Designer: Peter W. Johnson
Photographer: Thomas A. Brown, Richard Wahlstrom
Writer: David H. Crippen
Client: Perkin-Elmer Corp.
Technical Editor/Writer: Mark S. Feder
Printer: Allied Printing Services
Project Manager: Frank H. Fitzsimmons

395

Art Director: Craig Frazier
Designer: Craig Frazier, Grant Peterson, Deborah Hagemann
Writer: Michael Wright
Creative Director: Michael Wright
Client: American Inroads
Design Firm: Frazier Design

396

Art Director: Charles Davidson
Designer: Joe Feigenbaum
Photographer: John Manno
Writer: Deanne Torbert Dunning
Creative Director: Charles Davidson
Client: Movado Watch Corp.
Agency: Harry Viola Advertising

397

Art Director: Arnold Goodwin
Designer: Chris Cacci, Arnold Goodwin
Writer: Michael F. Knab
Client: Consolidated Papers
Agency: Wardrop, Murtaugh & Temple
Design Firm: Goodwin, Knab & Co.

398
Art Director: Paula Scher
Designer: Paula Scher
Photographer: Lynn Sugarman
Writer: Paula Scher
Client: Lynn Sugarman
Design Firm: Koppel & Scher

399
Art Director: Nicolas Sidjakov, Jerry Berman
Designer: Barbara Vick
Photographer: Hank Benson, Alan Krosnick, Nikolay Zurek, Henrik Kam
Writer: Dennis Foley
Creative Director: Nicolas Sidjakov, Jerry Berman
Design Firm: Sidjakov, Berman, Gomez & Partners

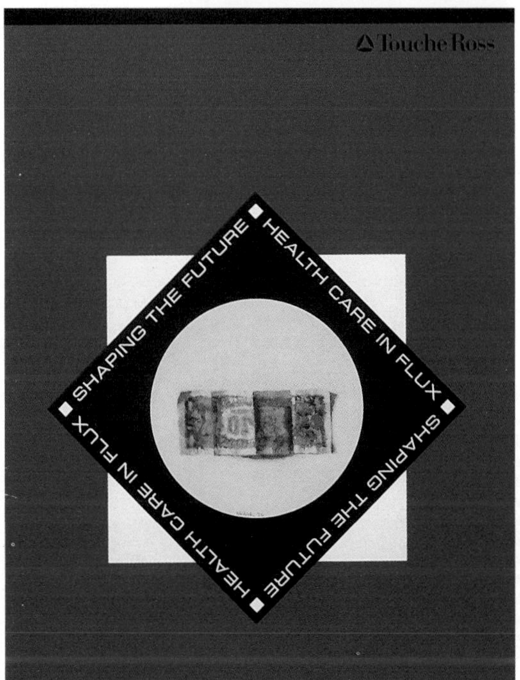

400
Art Director: Leslie Smolan
Designer: Alyssa A. Adkins
Illustrator/Artist: Robert M. Kulicke, Tony King, Hai Knafo, Barton Licice Benes
Writer: Wilma Ross
Client: Touche Ross & Co.
Design Firm: Carbone Smolan Associates

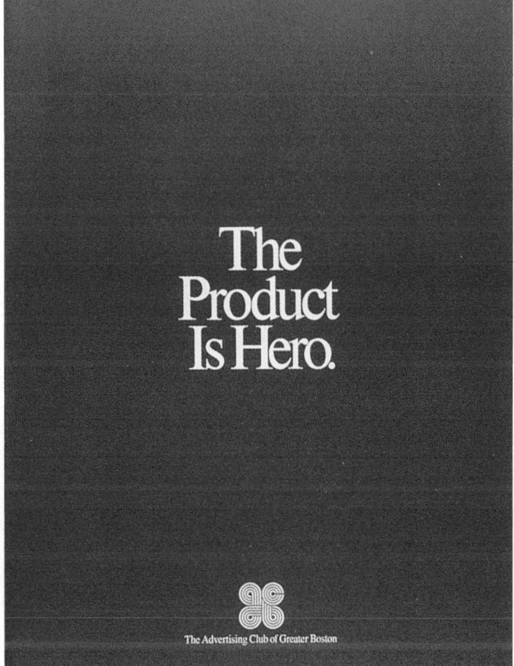

401
Art Director: Nick deSherbinin
Writer: Marc Simon
Creative Director: Rick Cohn
Client: Advertising Club of Greater Boston
Agency: Rizzo, Simons, Cohn Inc.
Production Manager: Marian K. Edom

402
Art Director: Kevin B. Kuester
Designer: Kevin B. Kuester, Bob Goebel
Photographer: Jim Sims
Writer: Dick Cinquina
Client: BCE Development Properties Inc.
Design Firm: Madsen & Kuester Inc.

403
Art Director: Kevin B. Kuester
Designer: Kevin B. Kuester, Tim Sauer
Photographer: Jim Sims
Writer: Dick Cinquina
Client: Potlatch Corp.
Design Firm: Madsen & Kuester Inc.

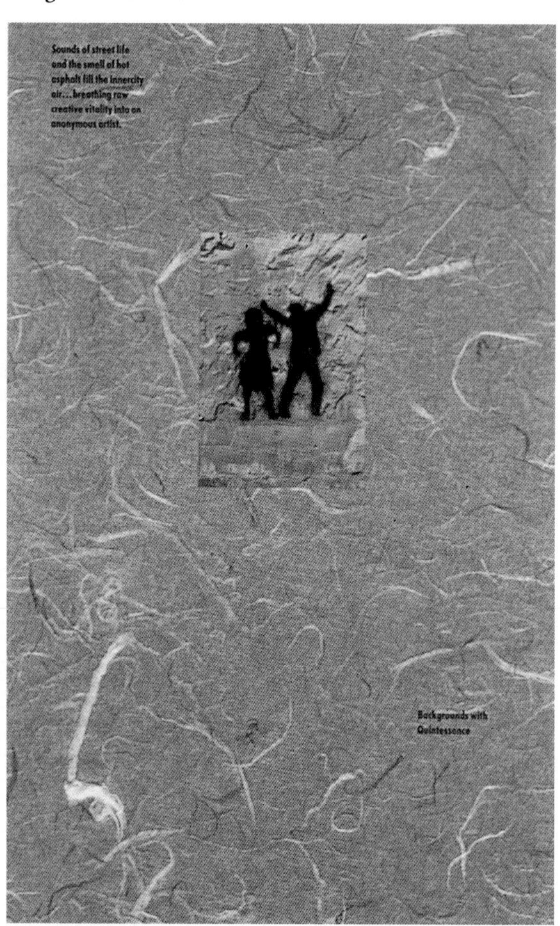

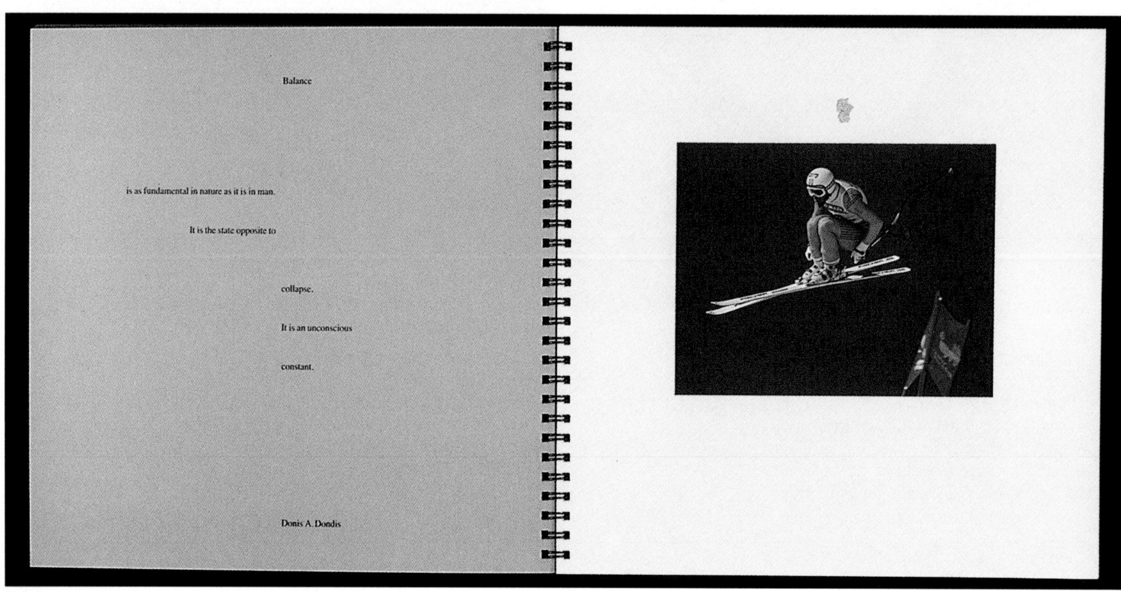

404
Art Director: Diana Graham
Designer: Debra Thompson, Wing Chan
Photographer: John McDermott
Client: John McDermott
Design Firm: Diagram Design & Marketing Communications Inc.
Publisher: Overseas Printing Corp.

405
Art Director: Lauren Smith
Designer: Lauren Smith
Illustrator/Artist: Lauren Smith
Writer: Lauren Smith
Client: Douglas Larson D.D.S.
Agency: Lauren Smith Design
Design Firm: Lauren Smith Design

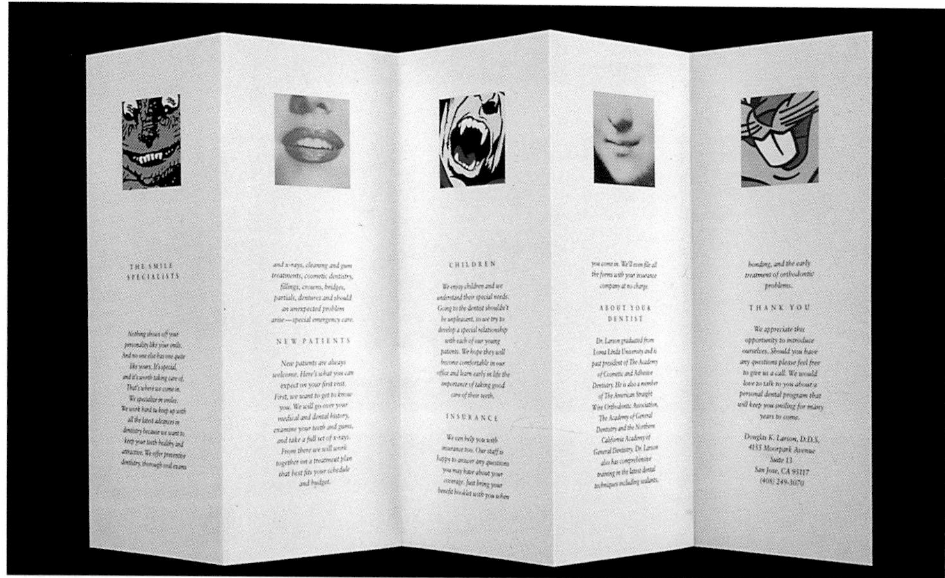

406
Art Director: Young Kim, Brent Marmo
Designer: Young Kim
Photographer: Susie Cushner, Betsy Cullen
Illustrator/Artist: Steve Oles
Writer: Jeri Quinzio
Client: The Codman Company
Design Firm: The Brownstone Group

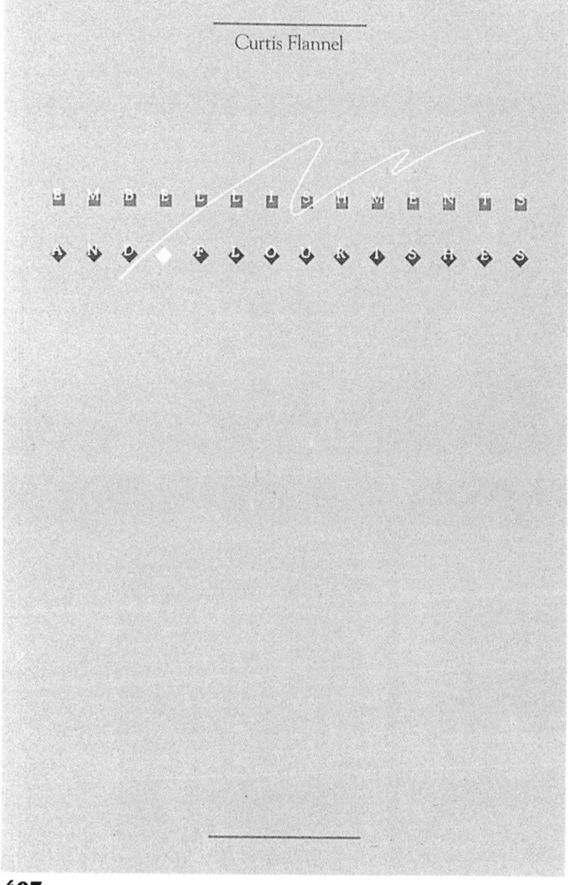

407
Art Director: Tom Fowler
Designer: Elizabeth Ball, Karl Maruyama
Writer: Brad Elliott
Client: James River Corp.
Agency: Hyers/Smith Inc.

408
Art Director: James Sebastian
Designer: Margaret Wollenhaupt, Michael McGinn, Gretchen Grace
Photographer: Peter Bosch
Writer: David Konigsberg
Client: Hopper Paper, Georgia Pacific
Design Firm: Designframe Inc.

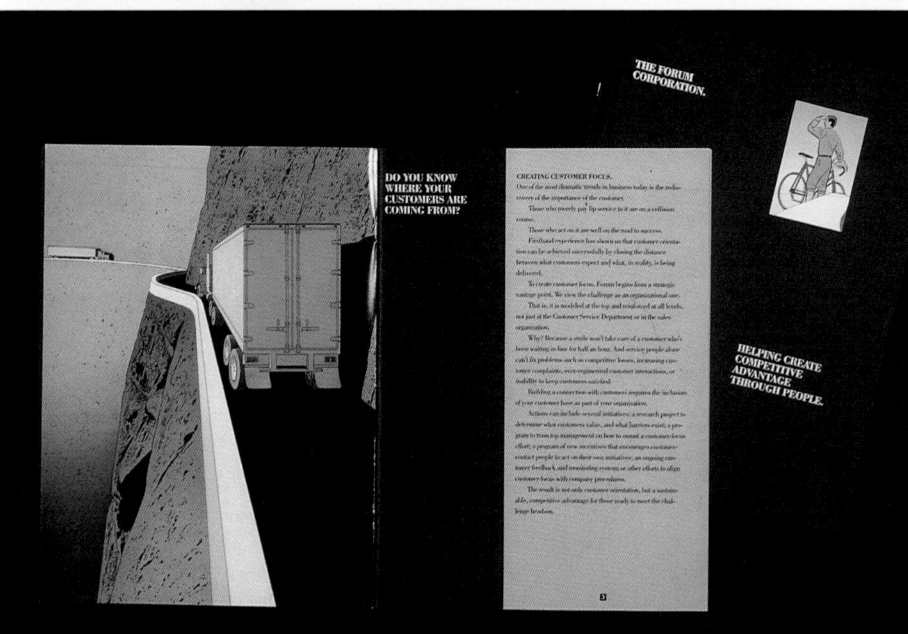

409
Art Director: Paul Huber
Designer: Paul Huber
Illustrator/Artist: Guy Billout
Writer: Craig Walker
Client: The Forum Corp.
Design Firm: Altman & Manley Design

410
Art Director: James A. Stygar
Designer: James A. Stygar
Photographer: Richard Ustinich, James A. Stygar
Writer: Jay Jenkins
Client: Lawyers Title Insurance Corp.
Design Firm: Stygar Group Inc.

411
Art Director: Domenica Genovese
Designer: Elizabeth G. Clark
Photographer: Jeremy Green
Illustrator/Artist: Kelly Walsh
Writer: Bernice Thieblot
Editor: Linda Thorne
Creative Director: Bernice Thieblot
Client: Agnes Scott College
Design Firm: The North Charles Street Design Organization

412
Art Director: Pat Samata
Designer: Greg Samata
Photographer: Terry Heffernan, Dennis Dooley
Illustrator/Artist: Kate Pagni
Writer: Dan Fredricks
Editor: Robert Walker
Client: The Parker Pen Co.
Design Firm: Samata Associates

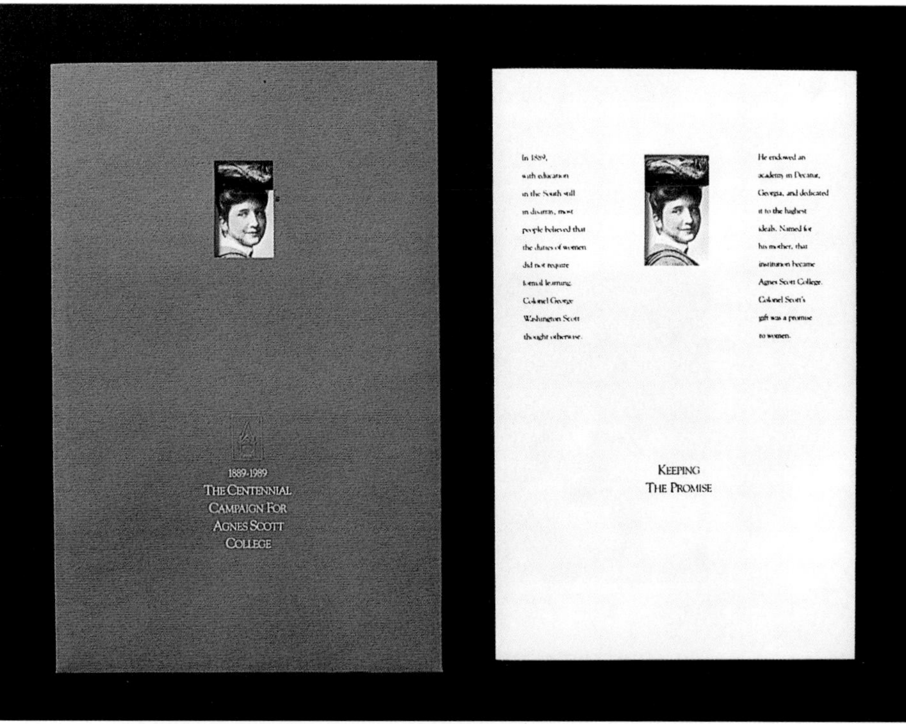

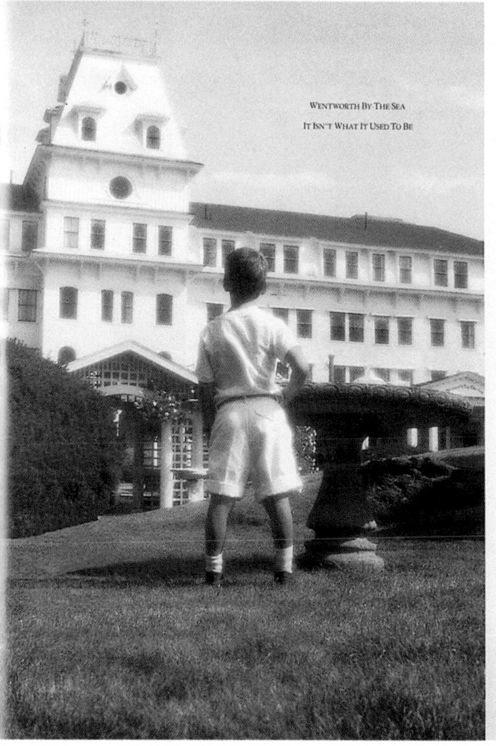

413
Art Director: Tyler Smith
Designer: Tyler Smith
Photographer: Aldo Fallai
Illustrator/Artist: Fritz Dumville
Writer: Lee Nash
Creative Director: Tyler Smith
Client: Louis, Boston
Agency: Tyler Smith
Design Firm: Tyler Smith

414
Art Director: Tom Kaminsky
Photographer: John Goodman
Writer: Craig Walker
Agency: Clarke, Goward, Fitts Design Group

415
Art Director: Robin Ayres
Designer: Robin Ayres
Photographer: Greg Booth, John Wong
Writer: Lee Herrick
Client: MCorp
Agency: The Richards Group
Design Firm: Richards, Brock, Miller, Mitchell & Assoc.

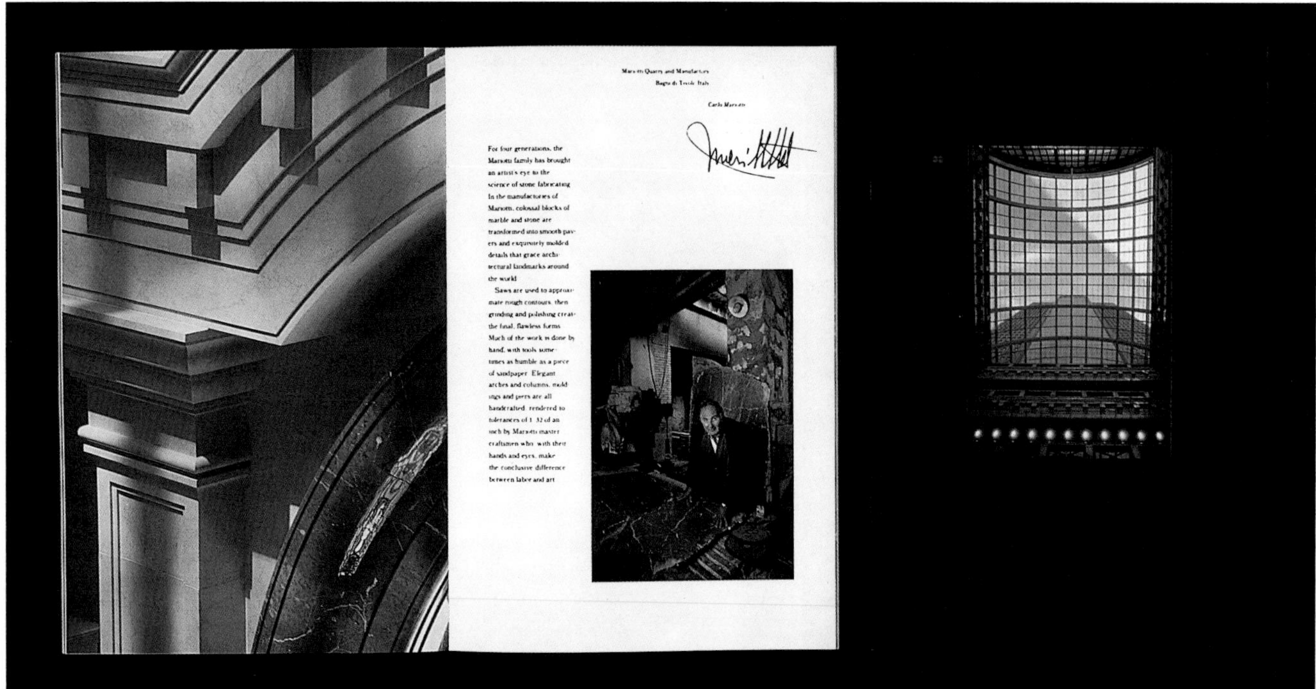

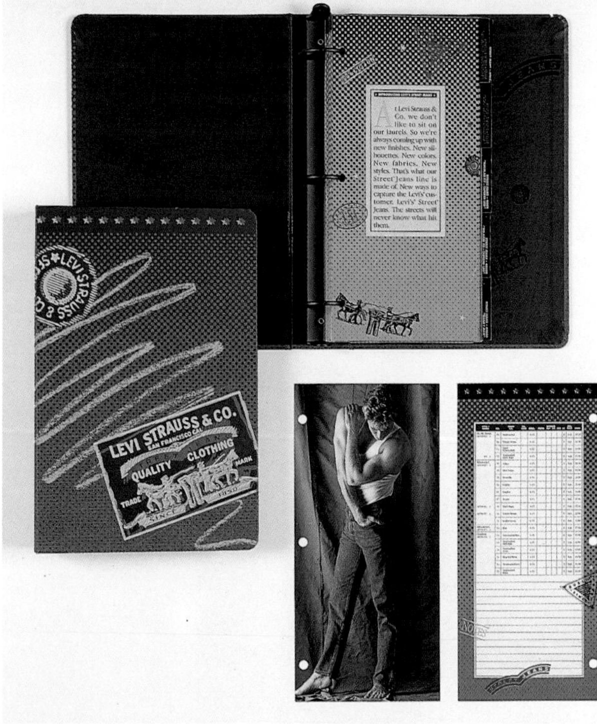

416
Art Director: Jennifer Morla
Designer: Jennifer Morla
Photographer: Jeffrey Newbury
Illustrator/Artist: Jim Fulp
Writer: Stacey Bovero
Client: Levi Strauss & Co.
Design Firm: Morla Design Inc.

417
Art Director: Richard Kilmer, Mark Geer
Writer: Pat Byers
Creative Director: Don Boswell, Pat Byers
Client: Bruce Belin & Associates
Agency: Boswell Byers Advertising
Design Firm: Kilmer/Geer Design Inc.

418
Art Director: Marty Neumeier
Designer: Kathleen Joynes, Marty Neumeier
Photographer: Barrie Schwortz
Illustrator/Artist: Gary Kelley
Writer: Kathleen Joynes, Marty Neumeier
Client: Creative Education
Design Firm: Neumeier Design Team

419
Art Director: Robin Soltis Brach
Designer: Robin Soltis Brach
Photographer: John Cororan
Illustrator/Artist: Bob Conge
Writer: David Pickall
Client: AMP Inc.
Design Firm: F. E. Worthington Inc.

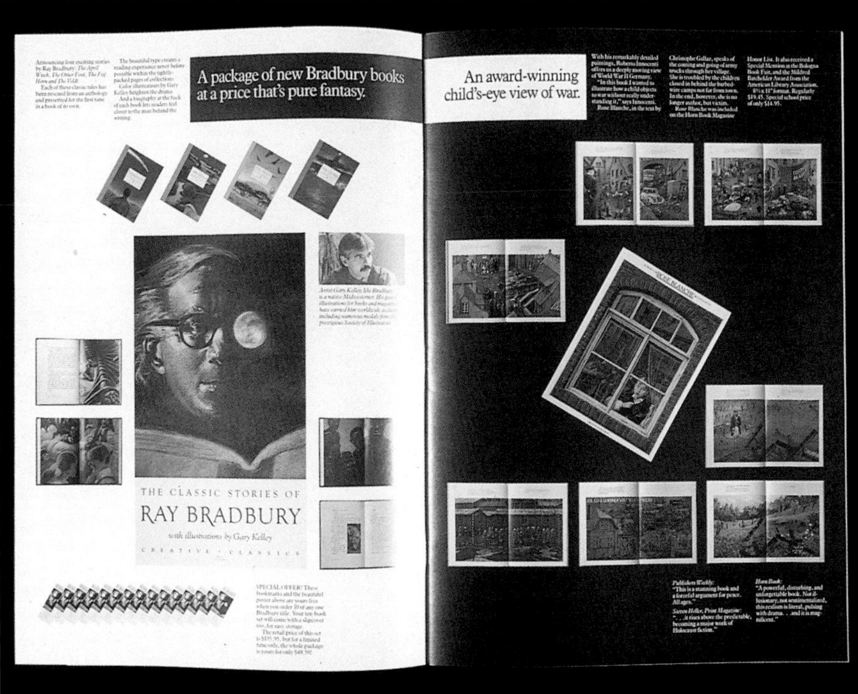

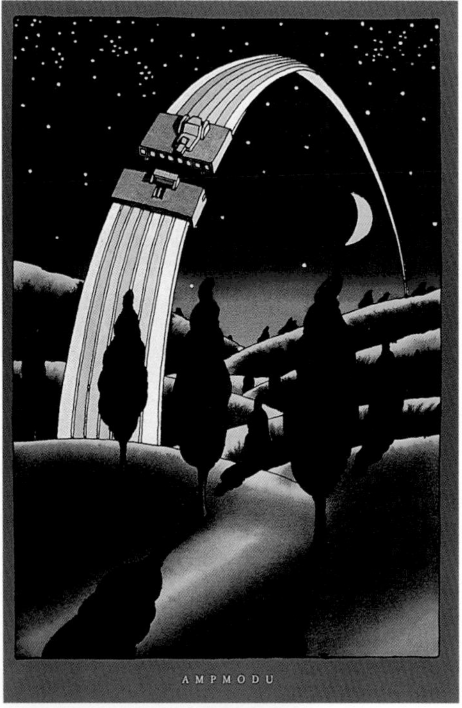

420
Art Director: Joyce Nesnadny
Photographer: Stephen Tannock
Illustrator/Artist: Jo Novosel
Writer: Sue Piatt
Editor: Suzanne Dickson
Client: The Progressive Corporation
Agency: Nesnadny & Schwartz
Printer: Custom Graphics

421
Art Director: Linda Powell
Designer: Linda Powell
Photographer: Peter Kiar
Writer: Deb Wierenga
Client: Herman Miller Inc.
Printer: Hennegan Company

422
Art Director: Tom Geismar
Designer: Tom Geismar
Photographer: Len Gittleman
Illustrator/Artist: Cathy Rediehs
Writer: Paul Rosenthal
Client: Champion Papers
Design Firm: Chermayeff & Geismar Associates

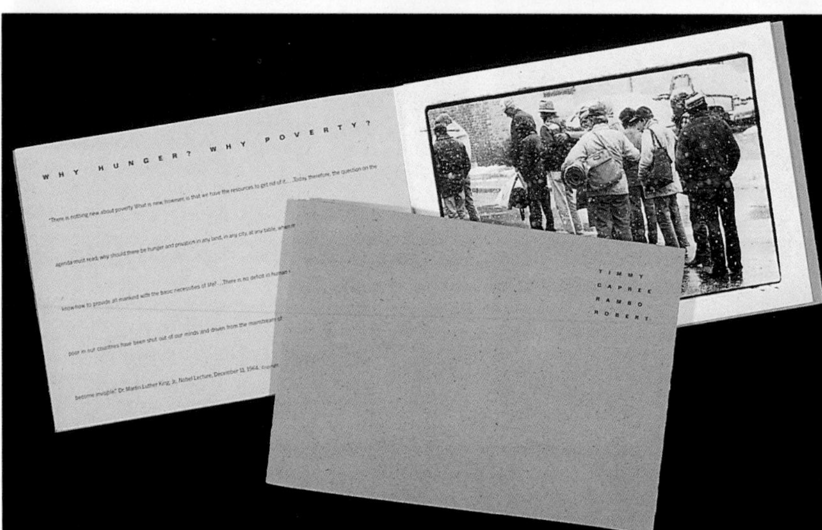

423
Art Director: Joleen Roos
Designer: Joleen Roos
Photographer: John Snyder
Writer: Joleen Roos
Editor: Joleen Roos, David Mack
Client: The St. Vincent de Paul Center
Design Firm: BYU Graphics
Typographer: Jonathan Skousen

424
Art Director: John Swieter
Designer: John Swieter
Illustrator/Artist: John Swieter
Writer: Craig Melcher
Creative Director: John Swieter
Client: The Dallas Sidekicks
Agency: Swieter Design
Publisher: Jarvis Press
Client Contact: Kent Russell

425
Art Director: Woody Pirtle, Joe Rattan
Designer: Joe Rattan, Woody Pirtle
Photographer: Image Bank
Writer: Mary Langridge
Client: Champion International Corp.
Design Firm: Pirtle Design

426
Art Director: Douglas Wolfe
Designer: Buck Smith
Photographer: Bishop Photography Inc.,
Comstock Inc.
Writer: Laurie Vincent
Client: Southwestern Bell Telephone Co.
Design Firm: Hawthorne/Wolfe

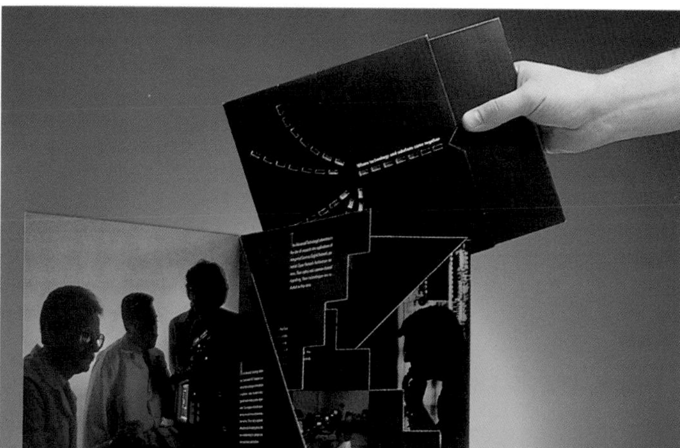

427
Art Director: Craig Frazier
Designer: Craig Frazier, Conrad Jorgensen
Writer: Craig Frazier, Conrad Jorgensen
Client: AIGA, San Francisco
Design Firm: Frazier Design,
Jorgensen Design Associates

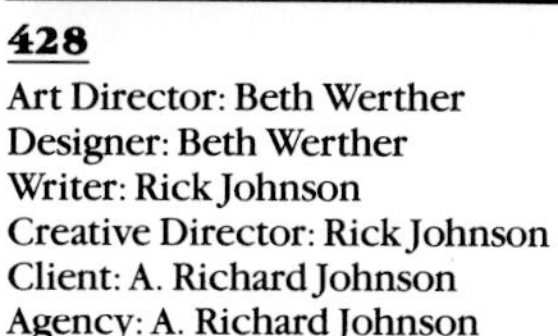

428
Art Director: Beth Werther
Designer: Beth Werther
Writer: Rick Johnson
Creative Director: Rick Johnson
Client: A. Richard Johnson
Agency: A. Richard Johnson

429
Art Director: Paul Huber, Holly Russell
Designer: Holly Russell, Paul Huber
Photographer: Mike Malyszko
Illustrator/Artist: Jude Johnson
Writer: Linda Bradford
Client: NeuroCare Inc.
Agency: Altman & Manley Advertising

430
Art Director: David Fox
Writer: Joe Alexander
Creative Director: Jac Coverdale
Client: Office Solutions Inc.
Agency: Clarity, Coverdale, Rueff

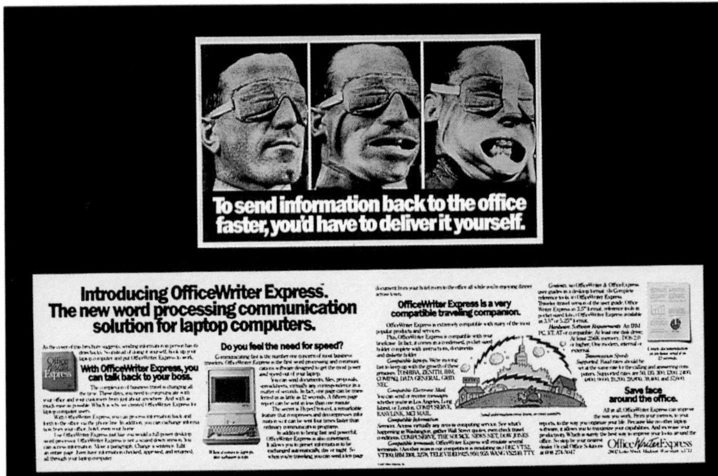

431
Art Director: Steven Sessions
Designer: Steven Sessions
Photographer: Jack Mitchell
Illustrator/Artist: David Walker
Writer: Robert Larkin
Editor: Linda Sease
Creative Director: Steven Sessions
Client: Houston Ballet
Agency: Steven Sessions Inc.

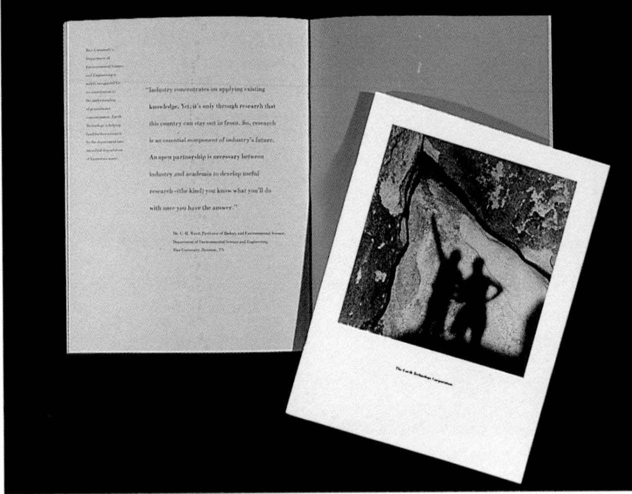

432
Art Director: Lowell Williams
Designer: Lowell Williams, Bill Carson
Photographer: Jeff Corwin
Writer: JoAnn Stone
Client: The Earth Technology Corp.
Design Firm: Lowell Williams Design Inc.

433
Art Director: Jann Church
Designer: Shelly Beck
Photographer: Mike Morgan
Writer: Marion Manchester
Creative Director: Jann Church
Client: Kimoto
Agency: Jann Church Partners
Design Firm: Jann Church Partners

434
Art Director: Angela Dunkle
Designer: Angela Dunkle
Photographer: Rick Dublin
Writer: Jamie Barrett
Creative Director: Tom McElligott
Client: Marecek & Cairns
Agency: Fallon & McElligott

435
Art Director: Jennifer Morla
Designer: Jennifer Morla
Photographer: David Robin
Writer: Jennifer Morla
Client: Bradmill U.S.A. Ltd.
Design Firm: Morla Design Inc.

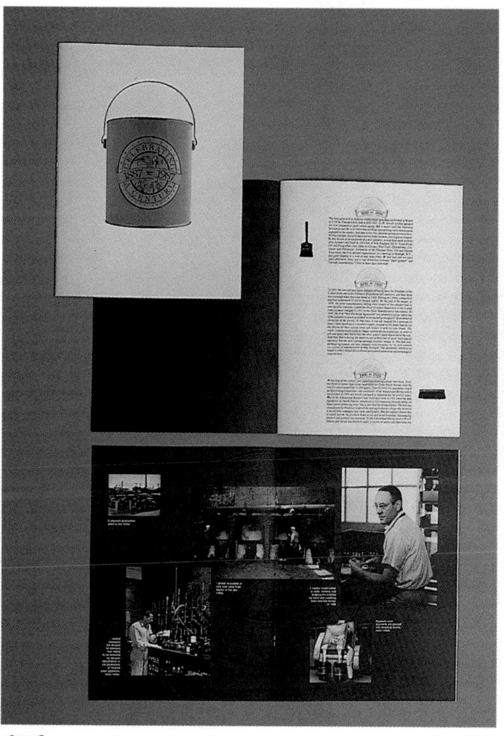

436
Art Director: Susan J. Hasten
Designer: Jeffrey S. Dale
Illustrator/Artist: Jeffrey S. Dale
Writer: Muriel F. Campaglia
Editor: Kristina C. Cook
Client: National Paint & Coatings Association
Design Firm: Hasten & Hunt Graphic Design Inc.

437
Art Director: Leslie Smolan
Designer: Eric A. Pike
Photographer: Barbara Bordnick, Dana Gluckstein, Steve Krongard, John Marmaras
Client: Merrill Lynch, Pierce, Fenner & Smith
Design Firm: Carbone Smolan Associates

438
Art Director: Peter Comitini
Designer: Peter Comitini
Illustrator/Artist: Max Guiterrez
Writer: Steve Jaffe
Creative Director: Elaine Zeitsoff
Client: NBC, Sales Marketing
Agency: NBC
Design Firm: NBC

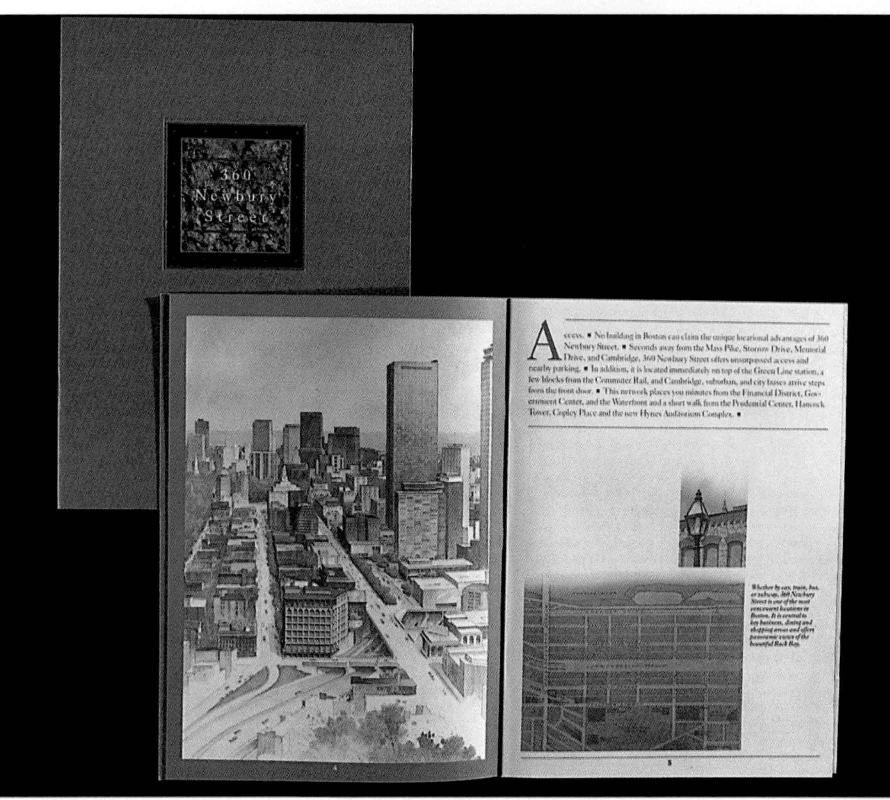

439
Art Director: Ken Harris, Diana Parziale
Designer: Diana Parziale
Illustrator/Artist: Jack Crompton
Creative Director: Ken Harris
Client: The Cohen Companies
Design Firm: Grand Design

THE RIGHT TOOL FOR THE JOB

The paper requirements of the forms converter are more demanding today than ever before. Champion has responded by tailoring its forms papers to the specific needs of the converter, paying special attention to different converting equipment and rapidly changing technology. Our line of communications papers is larger than ever, and includes new products and basis weights. This line of communications papers includes:

Champion Register Bond. This product is designed to run problem-free on high-speed converting equipment. Made for use in continuous forms and unit sets, Champion Register Bond features a lint-free, smooth, sized surface that enhances printability. It is available in seven basis weights: 12, 13.5, 15, 16, 18, 20, and 24 lb.

440
Art Director: Robert Meyer
Designer: Robert Meyer
Illustrator/Artist: Steve Björkman
Writer: Bruce Rogowski
Client: Champion International
Design Firm: Robert Meyer Design Inc.

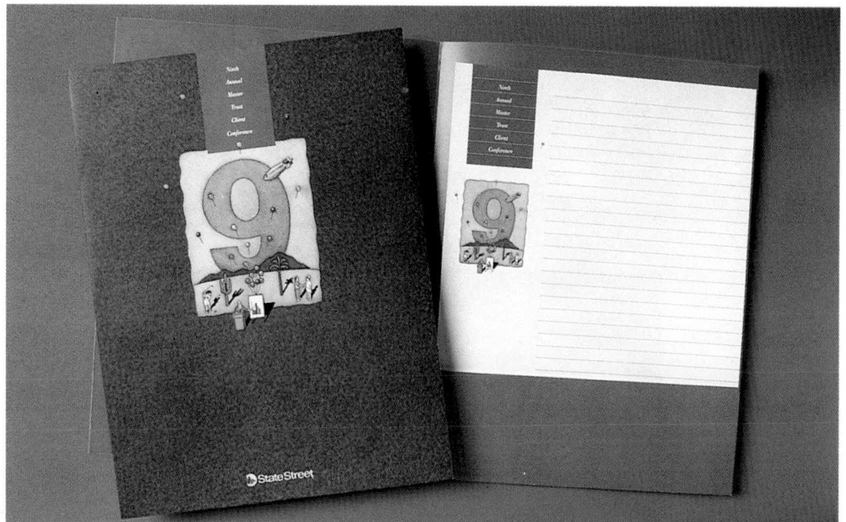

441
Art Director: Carol Doherty
Designer: Carol Doherty
Illustrator/Artist: Rob Saunders
Client: State Street Bank
Agency: State Street Bank
Printer: W. E. Andrews Co., Inc.

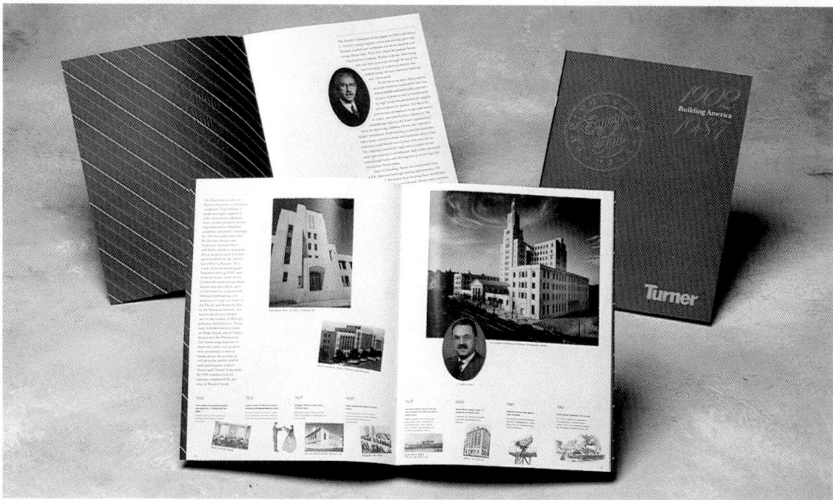

442
Art Director: Andrew Jackson
Designer: Andrew Jackson
Illustrator/Artist: Chris Duke
Writer: Sandra L. Salisbury
Client: The Turner Corporation
Design Firm: Steve Burnett Inc.
Printer: Garner Publishing

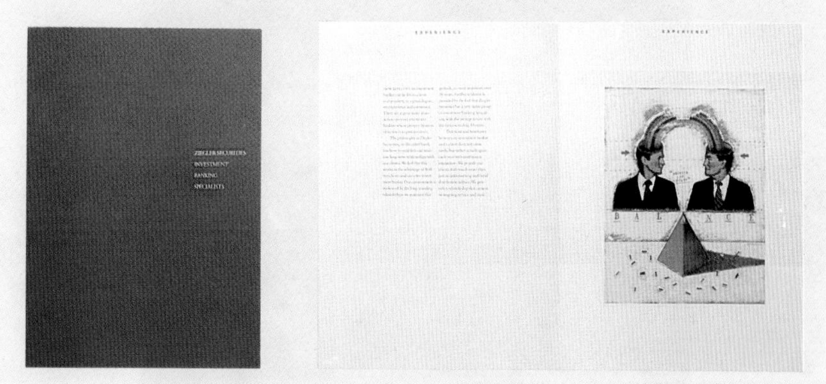

443
Art Director: Andrew Brown
Designer: Lisa Romanowski
Illustrator/Artist: David Lesh
Writer: Ziegler Securities
Editor: Paul Johnson
Client: Ziegler Securities
Design Firm: Hill & Knowlton Inc.

444
Art Director: Bradford Ghormley
Designer: Bradford Ghormley
Photographer: Steve Heiner
Writer: Sara Harrell
Client: Geneva Pipe Company
Design Firm: Smit, Ghormley, Sanft
Printer: Woods Lithographics
Typography: Andresen Typographics

445
Art Director: Julie Ray
Designer: Steven Sessions
Photographer: Jack Mitchell, Jim Sims
Writer: Julie Ray
Creative Director: Julie Ray
Client: Houston Ballet
Design Firm: Steven Sessions Inc.

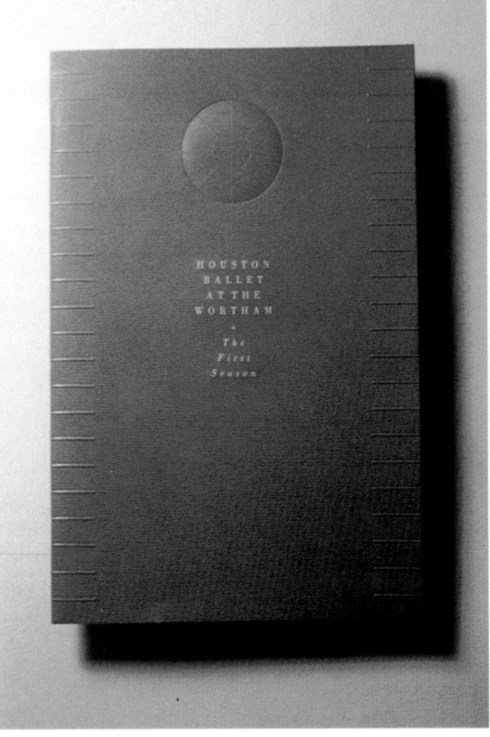

446
Art Director: Eugene Grossman
Designer: Tom Devine, Robert Wolf
Photographer: Irvin Blitz
Writer: Bill Hartley
Creative Director: Eugene Grossman
Client: Anspach Grossman Portugal Inc.
Typographer: Typogram
Printer: Lithographix Inc.

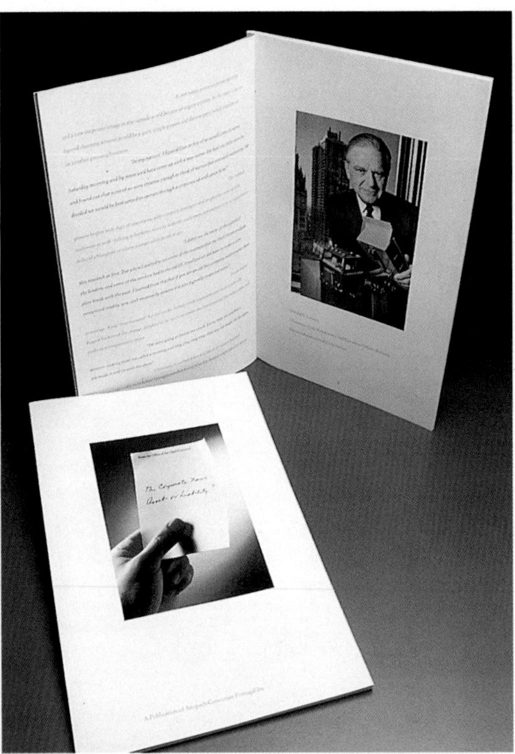

447
Art Director: Susan Turner
Designer: Susan Turner
Photographer: Susie Cushner
Creative Director: Susan Turner
Client: The Markuse Corp.
Design Firm: Clifford Selbert Design Inc.

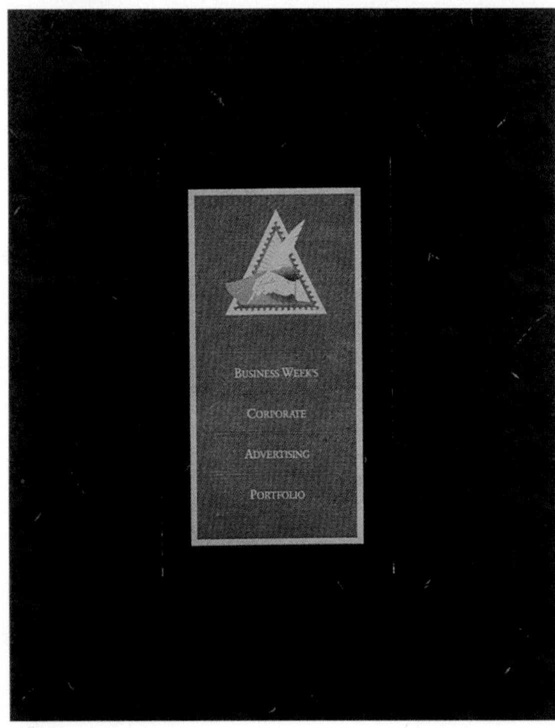

448
Art Director: John C. Reger
Designer: Dan Olson
Client: Business Week
Agency: Design Center Inc.
Design Firm: Design Center Inc.
Publisher: Business Week
Publication: Business Week Corp. Ad. Portfolio

449
Art Director: Stan Elder
Designer: Stan Elder
Photographer: Jim Erickson, Greg Plachta
Writer: Ann Waterfall
Creative Director: Peter Taflan
Client: Garden View Realty Inc.
Agency: Peter Taflan Marketing Communications Inc.

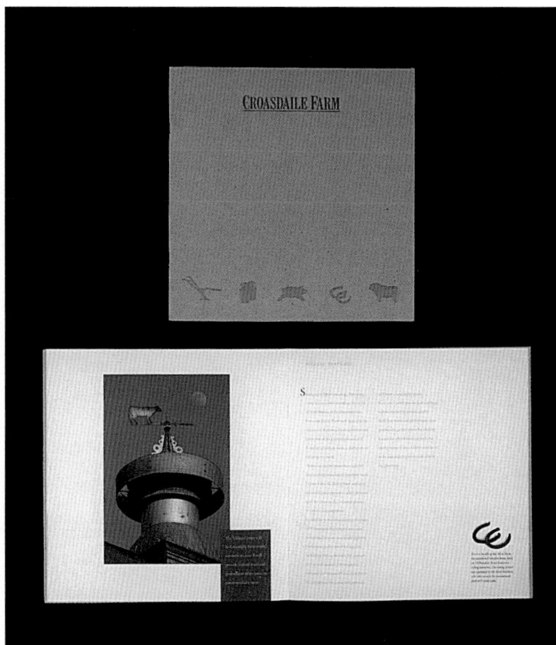

450
Art Director: Gordon Fisher
Designer: Seymour Chwast
Illustrator/Artist: Seymour Chwast
Writer: Stephen Heller
Creative Director: Tom Wright
Client: Neenah Paper
Design Firm: Gordon Fisher
Publisher: Neenah Paper
Printer: Neenah Printing

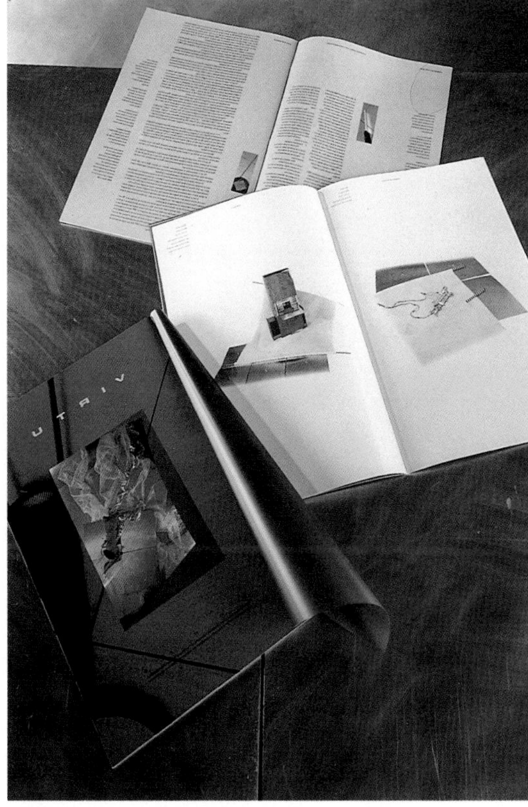

451
Art Director: Del Terrelonge
Designer: Del Terrelonge
Photographer: Ron Baxter Smith
Writer: Allan Klusacek, Esther Shipman
Client: Virtu–Forum & Function
Design Firm: Terrelonge Design Inc.
Painted Backdrop: Kurtz Mann

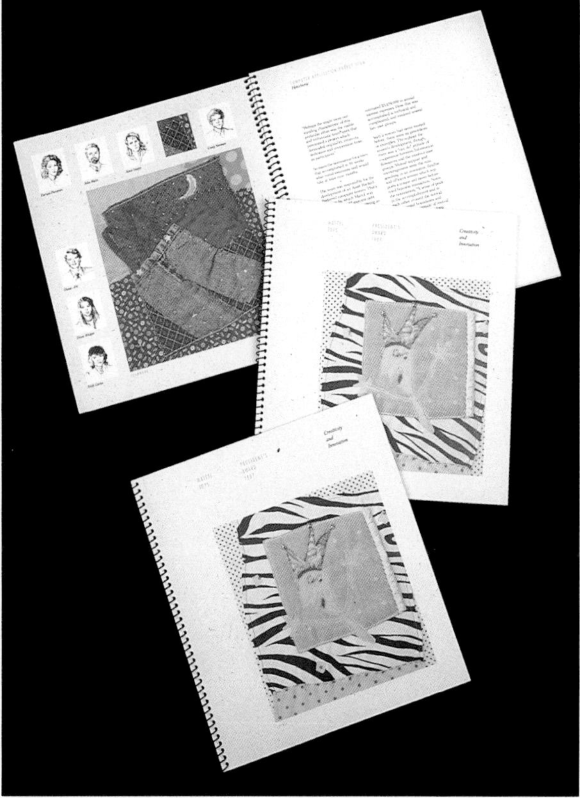

452
Art Director: Linda Warren
Designer: Linda Warren, Tracy duCharme
Illustrator/Artist: Tracy duCharme, Linda Warren
Editor: Shel Holtz
Client: Mattel Toys
Design Firm: The Warren Group

453
Art Director: Bob Defrin
Designer: Bob Defrin
Photographer: Charles Stewart
Client: Atlantic Records

454
Art Director: Thomas Starr
Designer: Jennifer Schumacher
Illustrator/Artist: Mauricio Varela
Writer: John Elias Michalakis
Editor: Richard Hirsh
Client: Periclean Motion Picture Co.
Agency: Thomas Starr & Associates
Design Firm: Thomas Starr & Associates
Publisher: Enigma Records

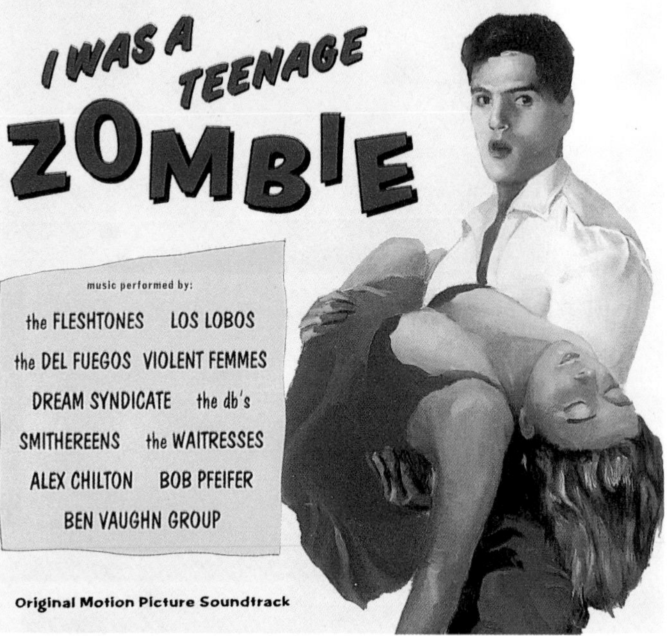

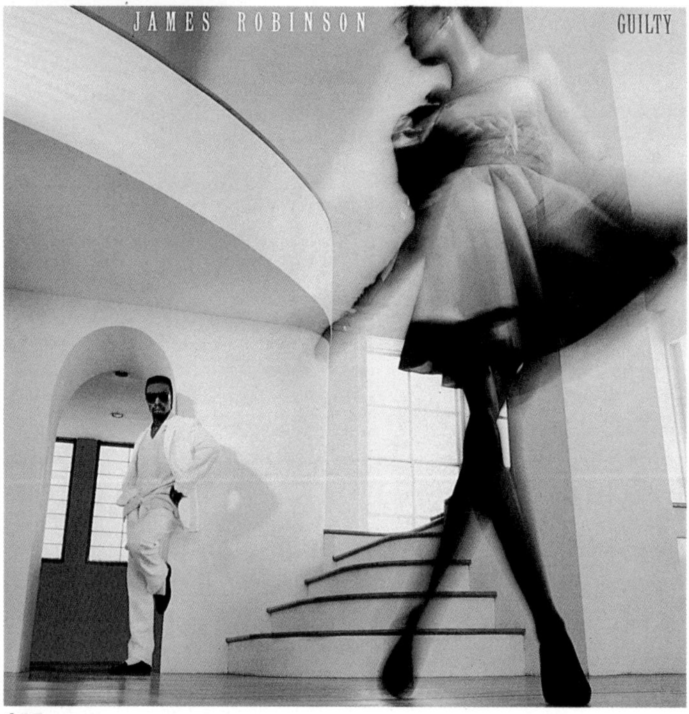

455
Art Director: Stacy Drummond
Designer: Stacy Drummond
Photographer: Hans Neleman
Client: Epic Records
Agency: CBS Records

456
Art Director: Christopher Austopchuk
Illustrator/Artist: Francesco Clemente
Client: Tony King

457
Art Director: Stacy Drummond
Designer: Stacy Drummond
Client: Epic Records
Agency: CBS Records

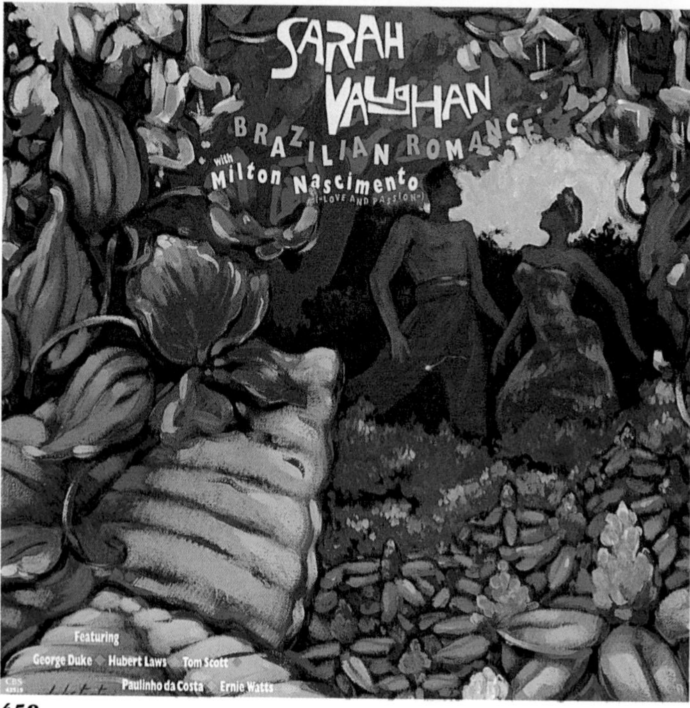

458
Art Director: Stacy Drummond
Designer: Stacy Drummond
Illustrator/Artist: Lori Lohstoeter
Client: CBS Records
Agency: CBS Records

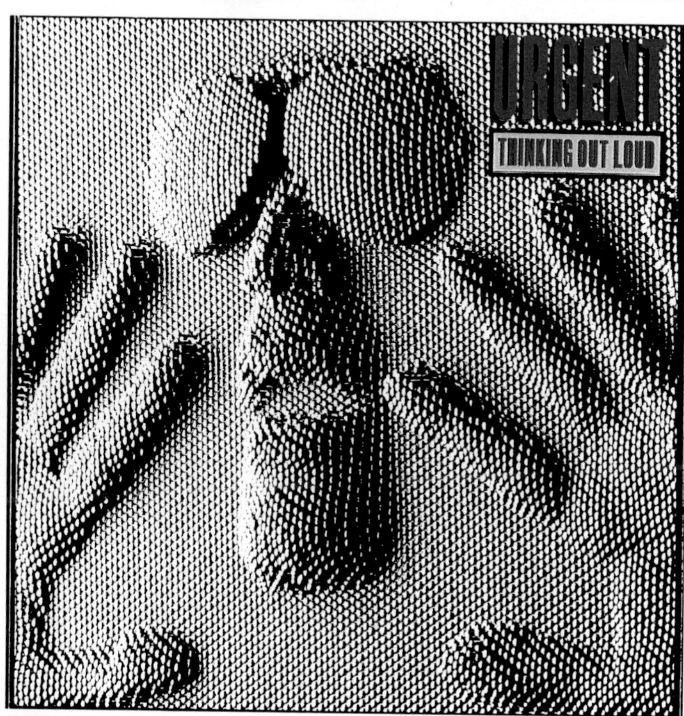

459
Art Director: Paula Scher
Designer: Paula Scher
Photographer: John Paul Endress
Client: EMI-Manhattan Records
Design Firm: Koppel & Scher

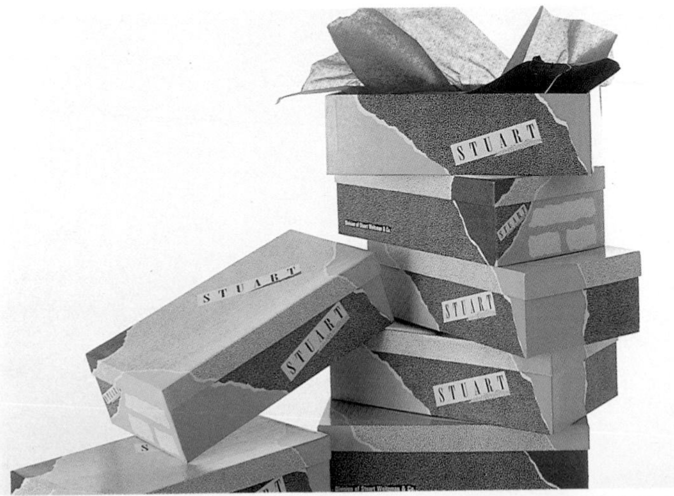

460
Art Director: Gwenne Wilcox
Designer: Gwenne Wilcox, Zia Khan
Illustrator/Artist: Gwenne Wilcox
Client: Stuart Weitzman & Co.
Design Firm: Wilcox Design

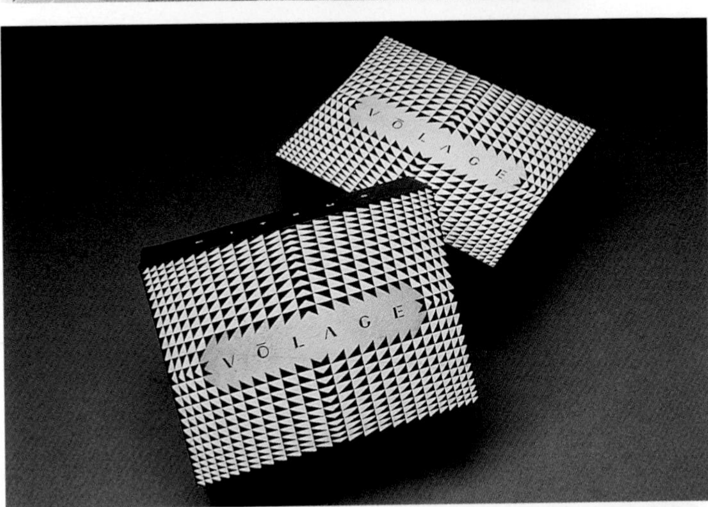

461
Art Director: Woody Pirtle
Designer: Woody Pirtle, Jeff Weithman
Illustrator/Artist: Jeff Weithman
Creative Director: Woody Pirtle
Client: Neiman-Marcus
Design Firm: Pirtle Design

462
Art Director: Bruce Dean, Scott Johnson
Illustrator/Artist: Bruce Dean, Scott Johnson
Client: Tenth Pan American Games
Design Firm: Dean Johnson Design

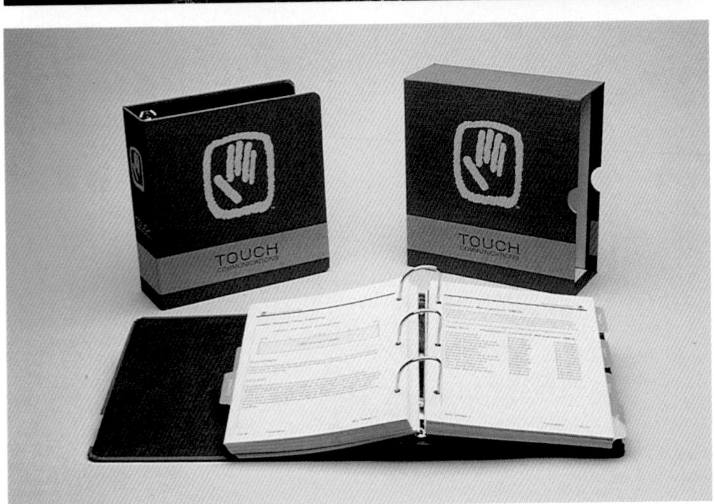

463
Art Director: Gary Cook
Creative Director: Clay Pamphilon
Agency: Rigoli, Pamphilon, Demeter
Account Manager: Sue Harden

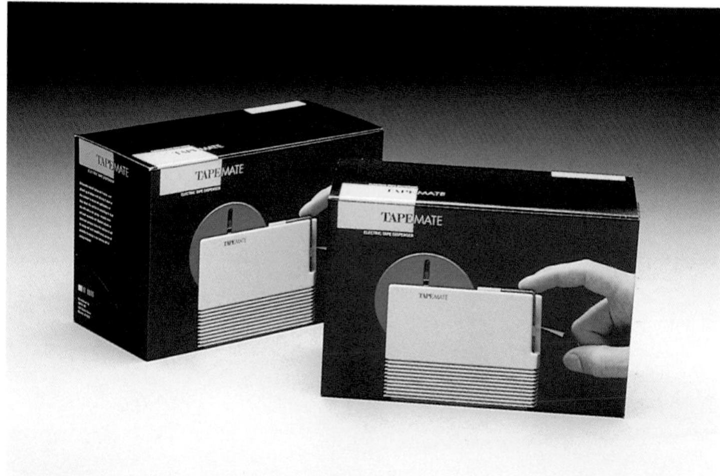

464
Art Director: Ken White
Designer: Vernon Hahn, Tracy Mitchell
Photographer: Henry Blackham
Writer: Aileen Farnan Antonier
Creative Director: Ken White
Client: Simtek Inc.
Design Firm: White & Associates
Publisher: Simtek Inc.

465
Art Director: Lannie Hart
Designer: Shinzo Saiki, Kuniaki Nomura
Illustrator/Artist: Laurie Horwitz
Creative Director: Mark Rosen
Client: Elizabeth Arden Inc.
Design Firm: Saiki & Associates Inc.

466
Art Director: Peter Windett
Designer: Peter Windett
Illustrator/Artist: Glynn Boyd Harte
Client: Crabtree & Evelyn Ltd.
Design Firm: Peter Windett & Associates

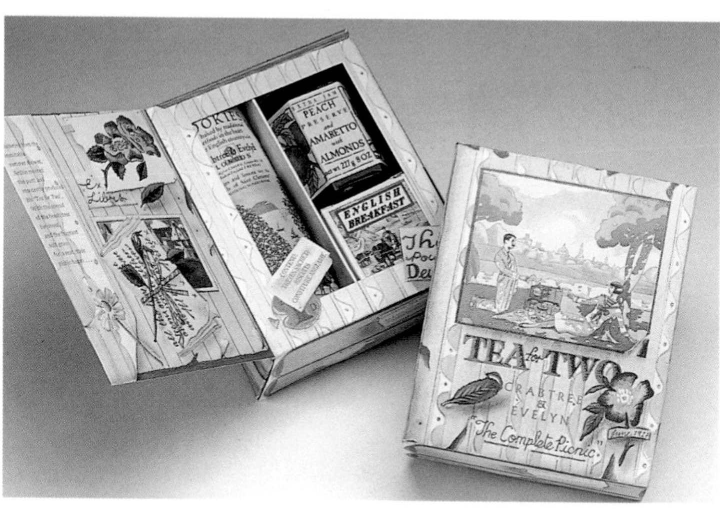

467
Art Director: Peter Windett
Designer: Peter Windett
Illustrator/Artist: Ian Beck
Client: Crabtree & Evelyn Ltd.
Design Firm: Peter Windett & Associates

468
Art Director: Nicolas Sidjakov, Jerry Berman
Designer: Barbara Vick
Illustrator/Artist: Carolyn Vibbert, Rebecca Archey, Karen Montgomery
Creative Director: Nicolas Sidjakov, Jerry Berman
Client: Heritage Kitchen Specialty Foods
Design Firm: Sidjakov, Berman, Gomez & Partners

469
Art Director: Ron Sullivan
Designer: Linda Helton, Darrel Kolosta
Writer: Max Wright
Creative Director: Ron Sullivan, Mark Perkins
Client: The Rouse Co., North Star
Design Firm: Sullivan Perkins

470
Art Director: Charles Hively
Designer: Charles Hively
Illustrator/Artist: Dave Maloney
Writer: Charles Hively
Creative Director: Charles Hively
Client: Del Sol Food Co.
Agency: The Hively Agency
Design Firm: The Hively Agency

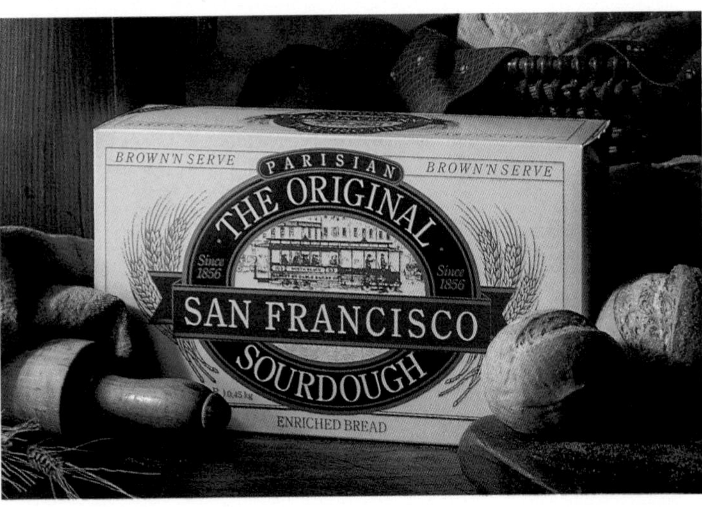

471
Art Director: Nicolas Sidjakov, Jerry Berman
Designer: Mark Bergman
Illustrator/Artist: Dave Stevenson
Creative Director: Nicolas Sidjakov, Jerry Berman
Client: Kraft Foods
Design Firm: Sidjakov, Berman, Gomez & Partners

472
Art Director: Dominic Pangborn
Designer: Norri del Rosario
Client: Wolverine Technologies Inc.
Design Firm: Pangborn Design Ltd.
Client Contact: Kathy Kirsch
Printer: ColorTech Graphics Inc.
Manufacturer: M & M Manufacturing

473
Art Director: Dominic Pangborn
Designer: Norri del Rosario
Client: Wolverine Technologies Inc.
Design Firm: Pangborn Design Ltd.
Client Contact: Kathy Kirsch
Printer: ColorTech Graphics Inc.
Manufacturer: M & M Manufacturing

474
Art Director: Rik Besser, Douglas Joseph
Designer: Rik Besser
Client: Vuarnet-France

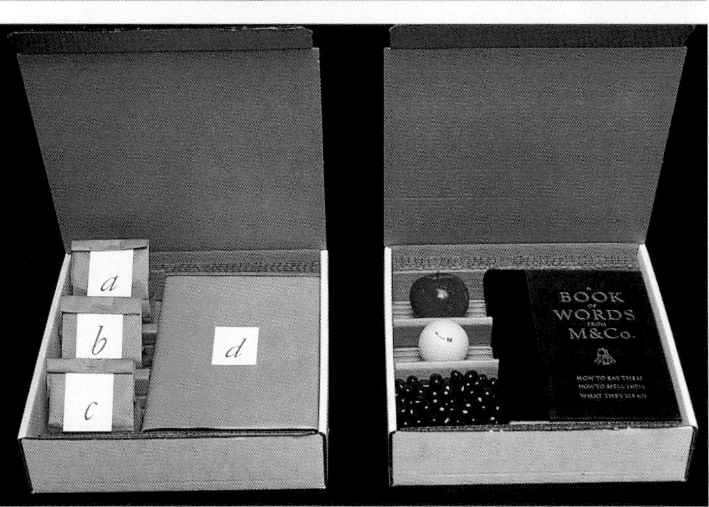

475
Art Director: Tibor Kalman
Designer: Alexander Isley
Illustrator/Artist: Tibor Kalman, Alexander Isley, Sean Kelly
Client: M & Co.

476
Art Director: Bob Newman
Designer: Bob Newman
Illustrator/Artist: Gunnar Skillins
Client: Marco Inc.
Design Firm: Newman Design Associates Inc.

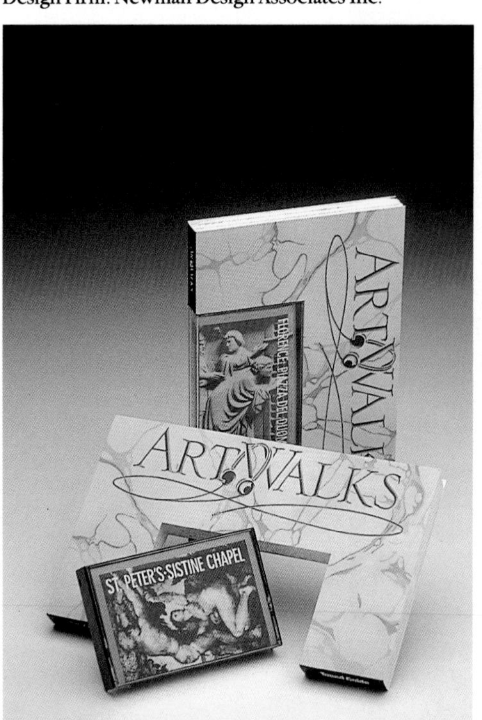

477
Art Director: Don Weller
Designer: Don Weller
Illustrator/Artist: Don Weller
Creative Director: Don Weller
Client: Schirf Brewing Co.
Agency: The Weller Institute for
the Cure of Design Inc.
Design Firm: The Weller Institute for
the Cure of Design Inc.

478
Art Director: Craig Frazier
Designer: Craig Frazier
Illustrator/Artist: Craig Frazier
Client: Merlion Winery
Design Firm: Frazier Design

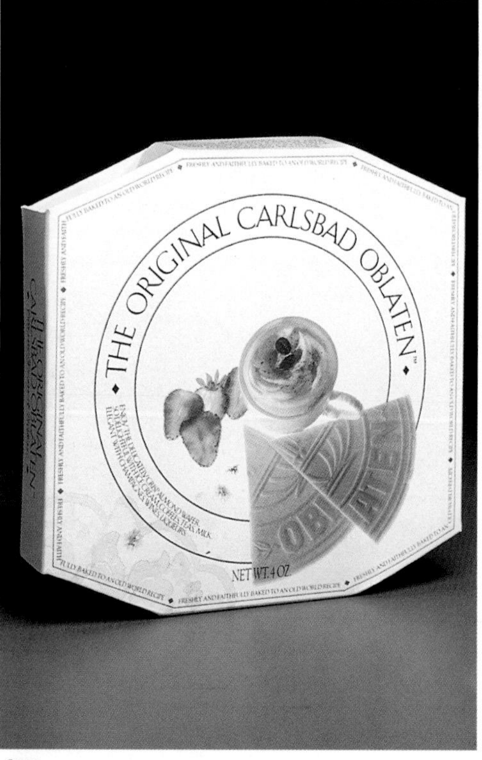

479
Art Director: Siegfried Gesk
Designer: Kris Morgan
Photographer: Hans Rott, Shigeta & Assoc.
Creative Director: Siegfried Gesk
Client: The Austrian Oblaten Co.
Design Firm: Pedersen & Gesk Inc.

480

Art Director: Charles S. Anderson
Designer: Charles S. Anderson
Illustrator/Artist: Charles S. Anderson, Lynn Schulte
Writer: Chuck Carlson
Client: Brooks Shoes
Design Firm: The Duffy Design Group

481

Art Director: Charles S. Anderson
Designer: Charles S. Anderson, Haley Johnson
Illustrator/Artist: Charles S. Anderson, Lynn Schulte
Writer: Chuck Carlson
Client: Chaps/Ralph Lauren
Design Firm: The Duffy Design Group

482

Art Director: Joe Duffy
Designer: Joe Duffy, Sharon Werner
Illustrator/Artist: Joe Duffy, Lynn Schulte
Writer: Chuck Carlson
Client: Lee Jeans
Design Firm: The Duffy Design Group

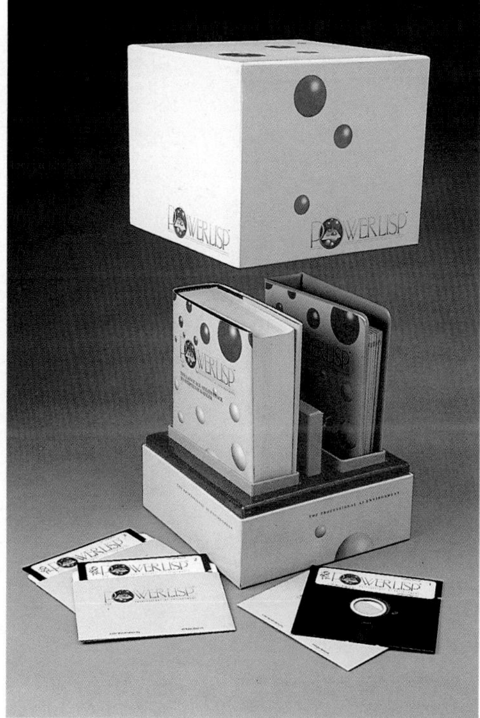

483

Art Director: Lars Hall
Designer: Jessica von Horn
Creative Director: Lars Hall
Client: Cederroth's
Agency: Hall & Cederquist
Design Firm: Hall & Cederquist

484
Art Director: Haley Johnson
Designer: Haley Johnson
Photographer: Dave Bausman
Illustrator/Artist: Haley Johnson
Writer: Chuck Carlson
Client: The Duffy Design Group
Design Firm: The Duffy Design Group

485
Art Director: Madeleine Corson
Designer: Madeleine Corson
Photographer: Thomas Heinser
Creative Director: Madeleine Corson, Randall Grahm
Client: Bonny Doon Vineyard
Design Firm: Madeleine Corson Design

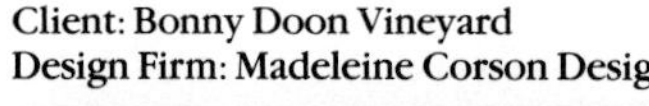

486
Art Director: Woody Pirtle
Designer: Woody Pirtle, Jeff Weithman, Alan Colvin
Illustrator/Artist: Jeff Weithman, Alan Colvin
Creative Director: Woody Pirtle
Client: Alberini Vineyards
Design Firm: Pirtle Design

487
Art Director: Allan Woolwine
Designer: Michael Leary
Illustrator/Artist: John Burgoyne
Writer: Doug Goransson
Creative Director: Doug Goransson
Client: Boston Beer Co.
Agency: Gearon, Hoffman, Goransson
Printer: Allegheny Label

488
Art Director: Charles S. Anderson
Designer: Charles S. Anderson
Illustrator/Artist: Charles S. Anderson, Lynn Schulte
Client: Timex Corp.
Design Firm: The Duffy Design Group

489
Art Director: Tim Girvin
Designer: Stephen Pannone
Photographer: Phil Banko, Mark Burnside
Creative Director: Laura Perry
Client: Aldus Corp.
Design Firm: Tim Girvin Design

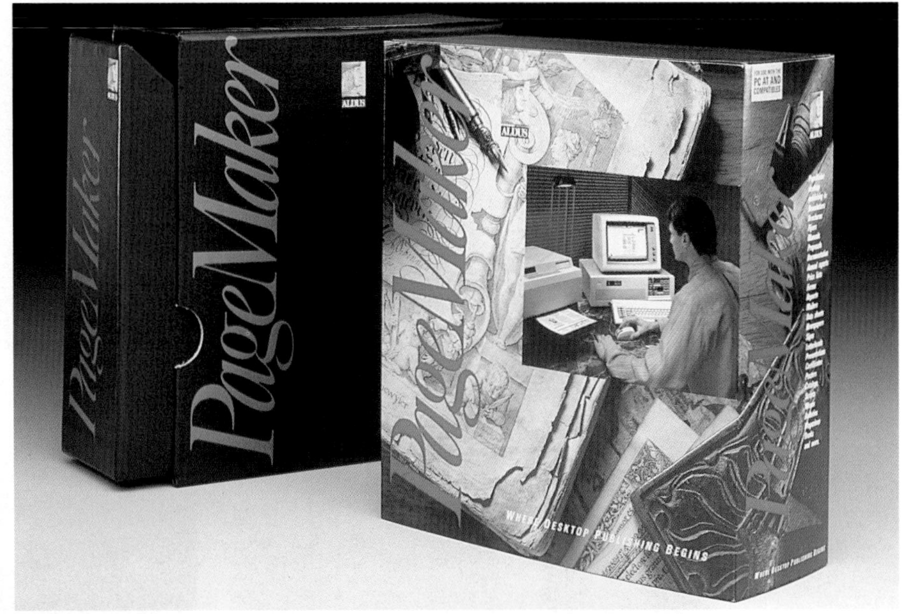

490
Art Director: Joe Duffy
Designer: Joe Duffy, Sara Ledgard
Illustrator/Artist: Joe Duffy, Lynn Schulte
Client: Chaps/Ralph Lauren
Design Firm: The Duffy Design Group

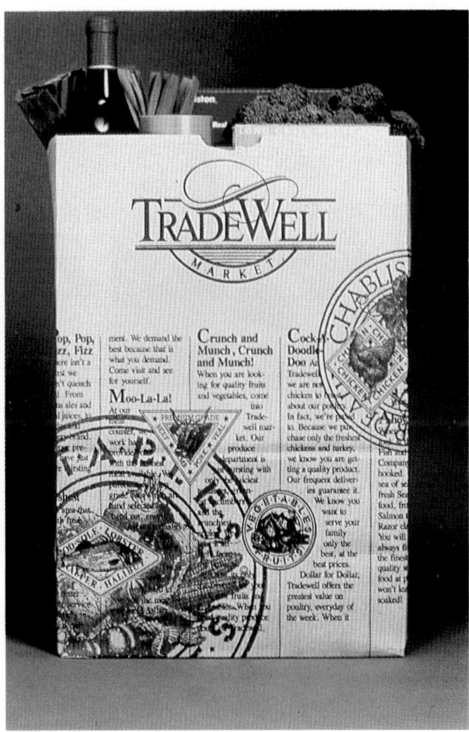

491
Art Director: Jack Anderson
Designer: Jack Anderson, Mary Hermes,
Cheri Huber, Julie Tanagi
Illustrator/Artist: Jani Drewfs
Writer: Hal Hilts
Client: Tradewell
Design Firm: Hornall Anderson Design Works

492
Art Director: Robert Cummings
Designer: Robert Cummings
Illustrator/Artist: Dawne Holmes
Creative Director: Robert Cummings
Client: MicroProducts Inc.
Design Firm: Cummings Communications Design Inc.

493
Art Director: Eric Read
Designer: Eric Read
Illustrator/Artist: Eric Read
Creative Director: Robert P. DeVito
Client: Plantronics
Design Firm: Axion Design Inc.
Product Manager: John Campanella
Industrial Designer: Alan Stephenson

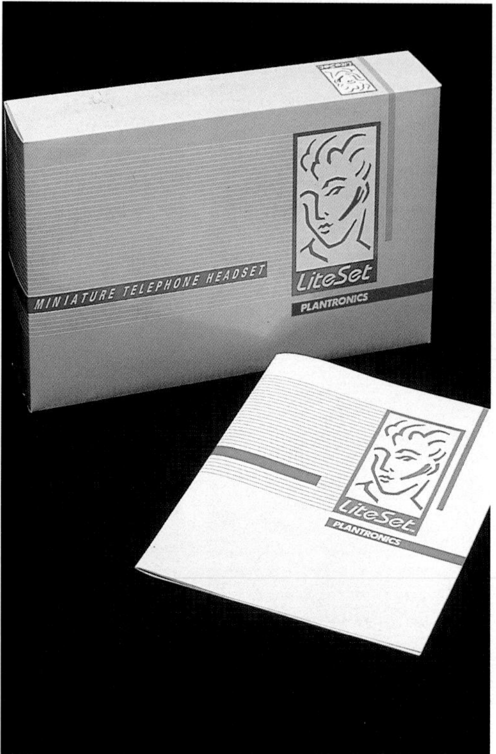

494
Art Director: Mitchell Mauk
Designer: Mitchell Mauk
Client: Amdek Inc.
Agency: Metaphor Inc.
Design Firm: Mauk Design
Printer: Curry Signs
Typographer: Z Typography

495
Art Director: Marty Neumeier
Designer: Marty Neumeier, Kathleen Joynes
Photographer: George Fry III
Writer: Paul Cuneo
Client: Activision
Design Firm: Neumeier Design Team

496
Art Director: Steve Lageson
Designer: Steve Lageson
Illustrator/Artist: Steve Lageson
Client: M. L. McJak Corp.
Agency: Falcon Advertising Art
Design Firm: Falcon Advertising Art

497
Art Director: Scott A. Mednick
Designer: Scott A. Mednick, Cheryl Rehman,
Jamie Graupner, Tak-Kean Kwan
Writer: Dana Precious
Creative Director: Scott A. Mednick
Client: Echo Design Group
Design Firm: Scott Mednick & Associates

498
Art Director: Paul Zwiefelhofer
Designer: Paul Zwiefelhofer
Illustrator/Artist: Art Factory
Writer: Linda Peterson
Creative Director: Paul Zwiefelhofer
Client: Columbia Food Co., Inc.
Agency: Jacobson Rost
Design Firm: Jacobson Rost
Color Separator: Colorcraft

499
Art Director: Jeffrey Pacione
Designer: Jeffrey Pacione, Diana Pasquarello
Photographer: Dennis Helmar
Illustrator/Artist: Leslie Worth
Client: Big Ben Games Inc.
Design Firm: RichardsonSmith Inc.

500
Art Director: Ronald Peterson
Designer: Jacquie Fauter-MacConnell
Client: R. G. Barry Corp.
Design Firm: Peterson & Blyth Associates Inc.

501
Art Director: Kit Hinrichs
Designer: Kit Hinrichs
Illustrator/Artist: Mark Summers
Client: The Nature Company
Design Firm: Pentagram Design

502

Art Director: Robert Consoli
Illustrator/Artist: Robert Consoli
Writer: Robert Consoli
Client: Whitmore Printing
Agency: Fuller Consoli Inc.
Airbrush: Jason Levinson

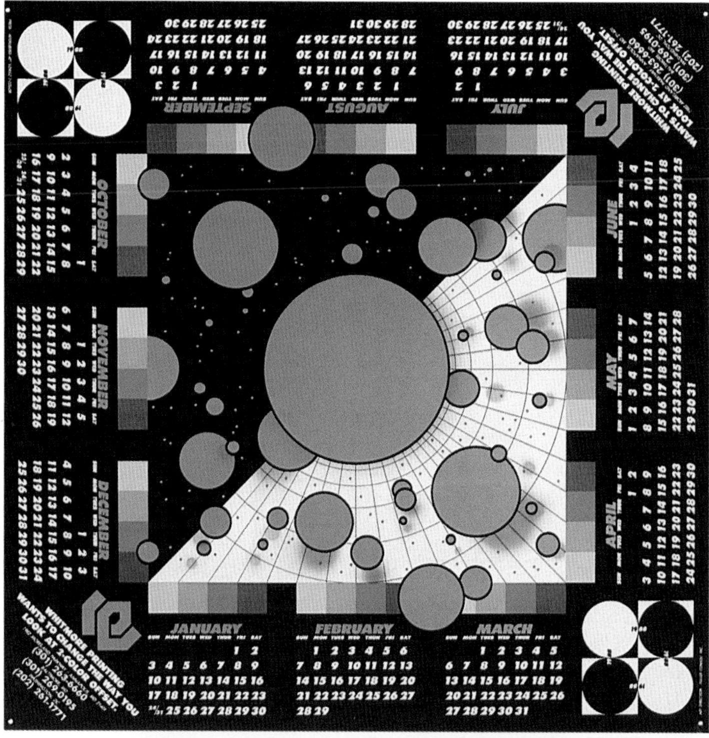

504

Art Director: Woody Pirtle
Designer: Woody Pirtle, Jeff Weithman
Photographer: Phil Branner
Writer: Woody Pirtle
Creative Director: Woody Pirtle
Client: Pirtle Design
Design Firm: Pirtle Design

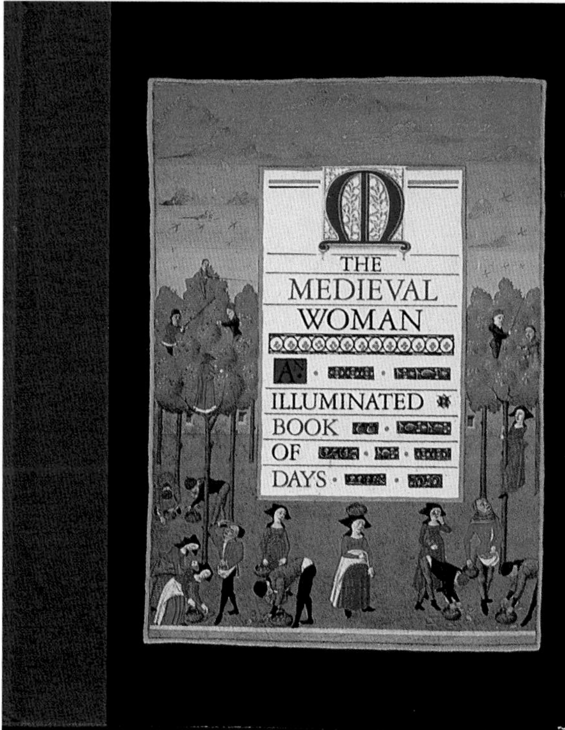

503

Art Director: Clifford Selbert
Designer: Clifford Selbert, Ellen Magurn
Creative Director: Clifford Selbert
Client: New York Graphic Society
Design Firm: Clifford Selbert Design Inc.

505
Art Director: Peter Morance
Designer: Peter Morance
Editor: Leo Levine
Client: Mercedes-Benz of North America, National Multiple Sclerosis Society
Design Firm: Peter Morance Inc.

506
Art Director: Malcolm Waddell
Designer: Malcolm Waddell
Photographer: John Blaustein
Client: Eskind Waddell
Design Firm: Eskind Waddell
Specifications Manager, Mead Paper: Janet Blank
Printer: MacKinnon-Moncur Ltd.

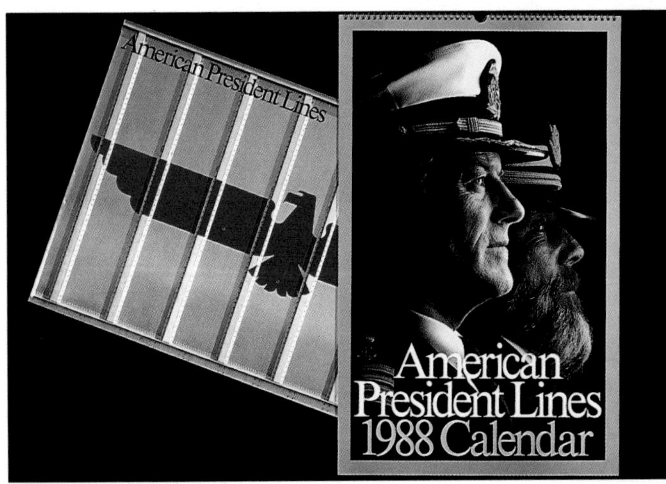

507
Art Director: Kit Hinrichs
Designer: Kit Hinrichs, Gwyn Smith, Karen Berndt
Photographer: Terry Heffernan
Illustrator/Artist: Sara Anderson
Writer: Peterson & Dodge
Client: American President Co.
Design Firm: Pentagram Design

508
Art Director: Kai Mui, Ron Sullivan
Photographer: Co Rentmeester
Creative Director: Nicholas I. Orloff
Client: Eastman Kodak, Consumer Products Div.
Agency: Rumrill-Hoyt Inc.
Account Manager: Vicki Lewis

509

Art Director: Jim Bohan
Illustrator/Artist: Dennis Johnson, Erik Belgvad
Writer: Chuck Rednick
Creative Director: Jim Black
Client: Dow Chemical
Agency: HDM Dawson, Johns & Black

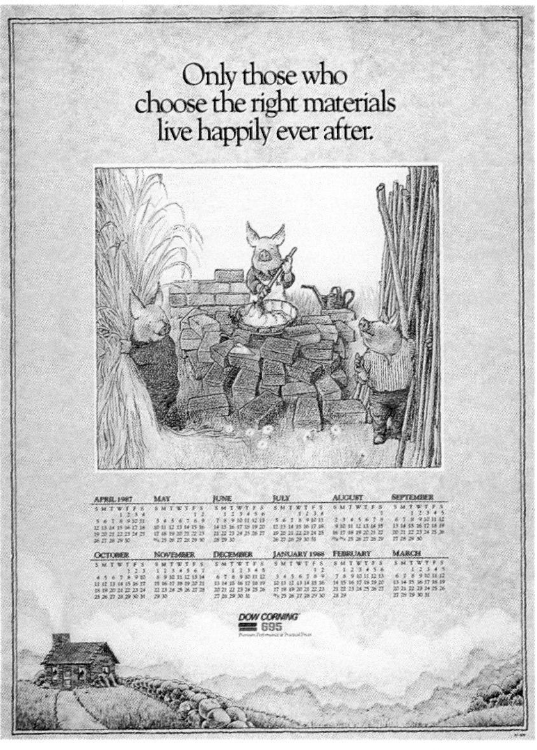

510

Art Director: Milton Glaser
Designer: Milton Glaser, Suzanne Zumpano
Illustrator/Artist: Juan Suarez Botas
Creative Director: Milton Glaser
Client: Queens College, CUNY
Design Firm: Milton Glaser Inc.
President, Queens College: Shirley Strum Kenny

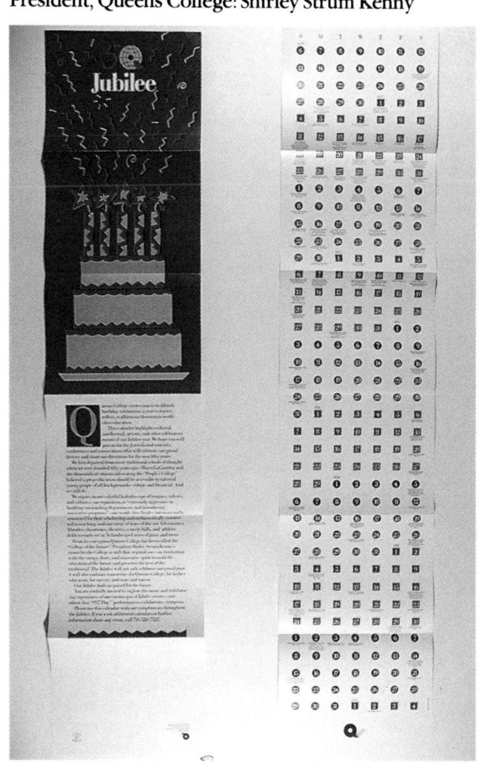

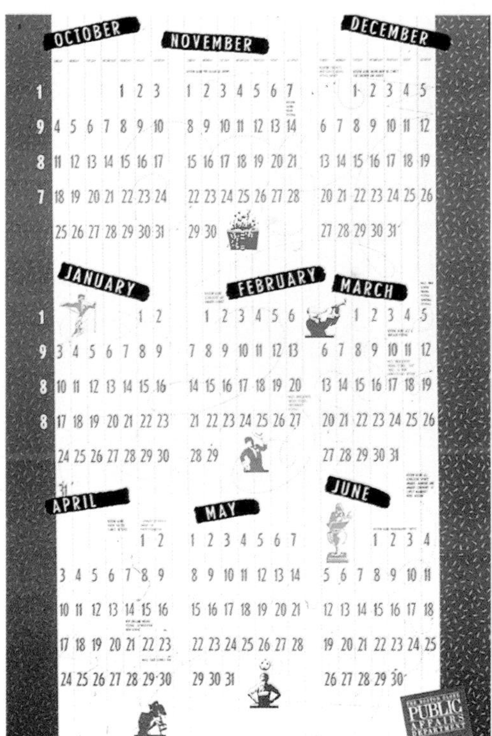

511

Art Director: John Avery
Designer: John Avery
Illustrator/Artist: Jim McKiernan, Bob Boucher
Client: The Boston Globe
Agency: Hill, Holliday, Connors, Cosmopulos, Inc
Design Firm: Hill Holliday Design

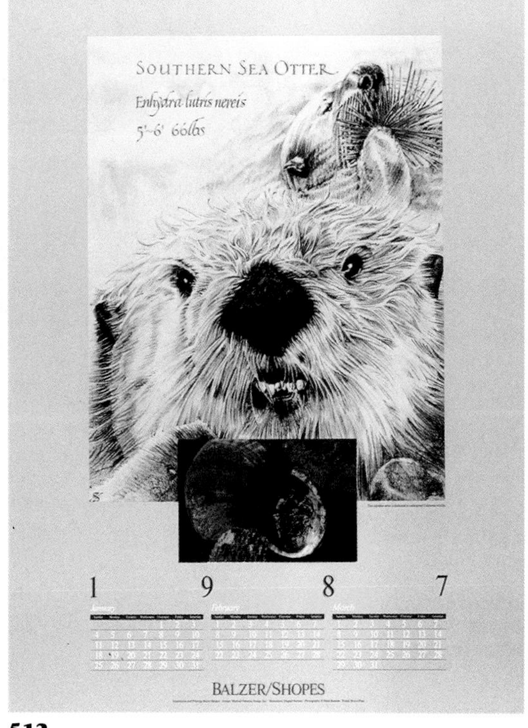

512

Art Director: Michael Osborne
Designer: Michael Osborne
Photographer: Hank Benson
Illustrator/Artist: Dugald Stermer
Client: Balzer/Shopes
Design Firm: Michael Osborne Design

513
Art Director: Ronald Emmerling
Illustrator/Artist: Whitman Studio Inc.
Client: Gemini Industries Inc.
Design Firm: Ronald Emmerling Design Inc.
Printer: Sterling/Roman Press

Accessorize.

GEMINI

514
Art Director: Rex Peteet, Judy Dolim
Designer: Judy Dolim
Illustrator/Artist: Judy Dolim
Writer: Rex Peteet
Client: LaSalle Partners/Renaissance Tower
Design Firm: Sibley/Peteet Design

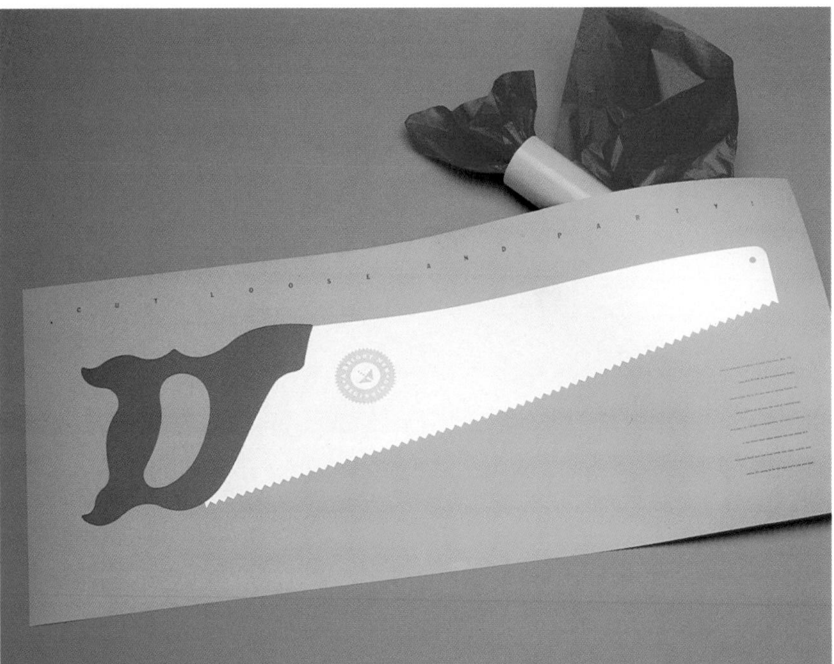

515
Art Director: Jill Hawkins, Leon Banowetz
Designer: Jill Hawkins, Leon Banowetz
Illustrator/Artist: Maciek Pinno
Writer: Mark Seal
Creative Director: Jill Hawkins
Client: Hotel del Coronada
Design Firm: Jill Hawkins Design

516
Art Director: Ron Sullivan
Designer: Darrel Kolosta
Illustrator/Artist: Darrel Kolosta
Writer: Max Wright
Creative Director: Ron Sullivan, Mark Perkins
Client: The Friends of Bonnie Legro
Design Firm: Sullivan Perkins

517
Art Director: Vin Scheihagen
Designer: Vin Scheihagen
Illustrator/Artist: Larry Adams
Writer: Vin Scheihagen
Creative Director: Pat Carrithers
Client: Bright Banc
Agency: Evans/Dallas Inc.

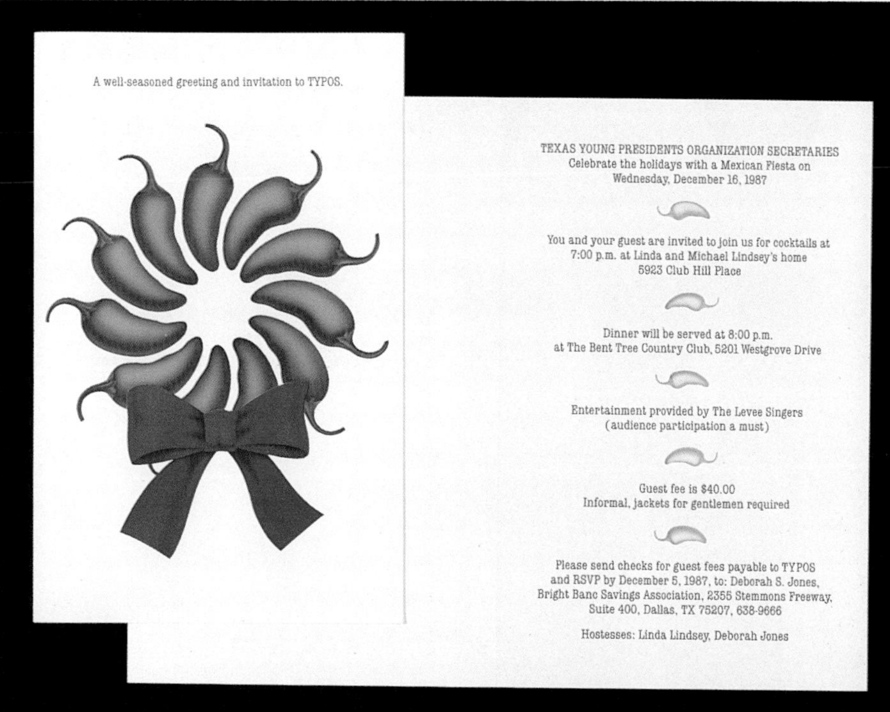

518
Art Director: Jerry Sullivan
Designer: Jerry Sullivan
Illustrator/Artist: R. O. Blechman
Writer: Ken Haas
Creative Director: Ken Haas, Jerry Sullivan
Client: Art Directors Club of Atlanta
Agency: Sullivan Haas Coyle

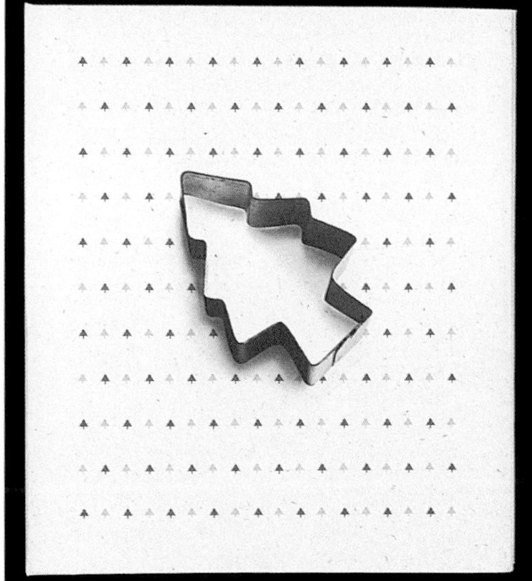

519
Art Director: Pat Samata, Greg Samata
Photographer: Mark Joseph
Illustrator/Artist: Paul Thompson
Writer: Nancy Bishop
Editor: Pat Samata, Greg Samata,
Client: Samata Associates
Publication: Samata Associates Holiday Cookbook

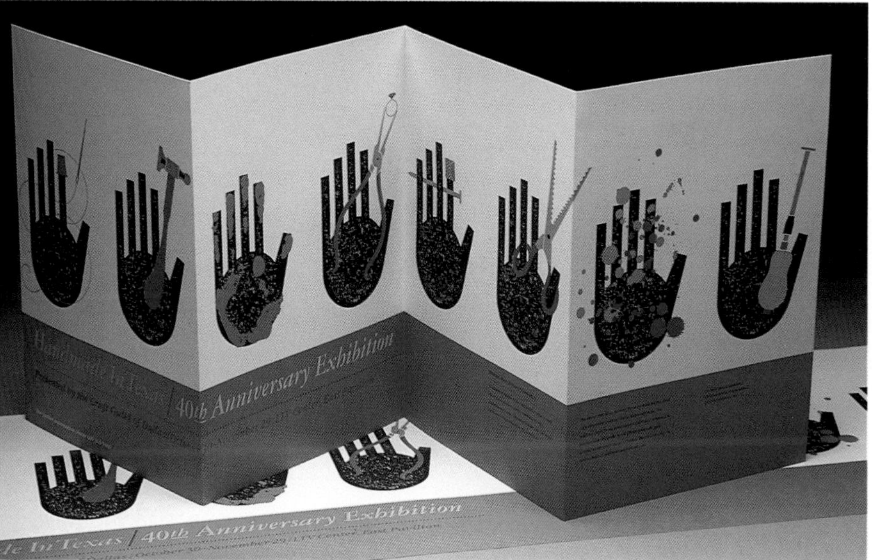

520
Art Director: Rex Peteet
Designer: Rex Peteet
Illustrator/Artist: David Beck, Julia Albanesi
Writer: Rex Peteet
Client: Craft Guild of Dallas
Design Firm: Sibley/Peteet Design

521
Art Director: Lesley Rucker
Designer: Lesley Rucker
Photographer: Andy Vracin
Writer: Doug Rucker
Creative Director: Doug Rucker
Client: Pat Sweeney, Mike Sweeney
Printer: Brodnax Printing

522
Art Director: Scott Paramski
Designer: Scott Paramski
Writer: Melinda Marcus
Client: Kayren Schwandt, Mark Schwandt
Design Firm: Peterson & Co.

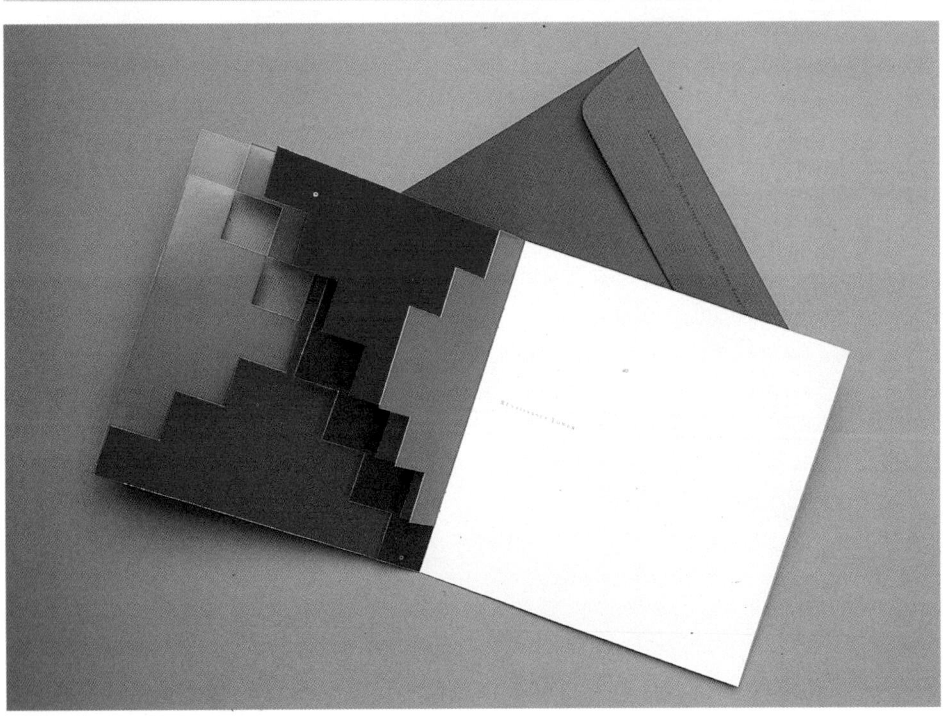

523
Art Director: Don Sibley
Designer: Don Sibley
Illustrator/Artist: Don Sibley
Writer: Don Sibley
Client: LaSalle Partners/Renaissance Tower
Design Firm: Sibley/Peteet Design

524
Art Director: Rex Peteet
Designer: Rex Peteet
Illustrator/Artist: Rex Peteet
Writer: Bob Downs
Client: Heritage Press
Design Firm: Sibley/Peteet Design

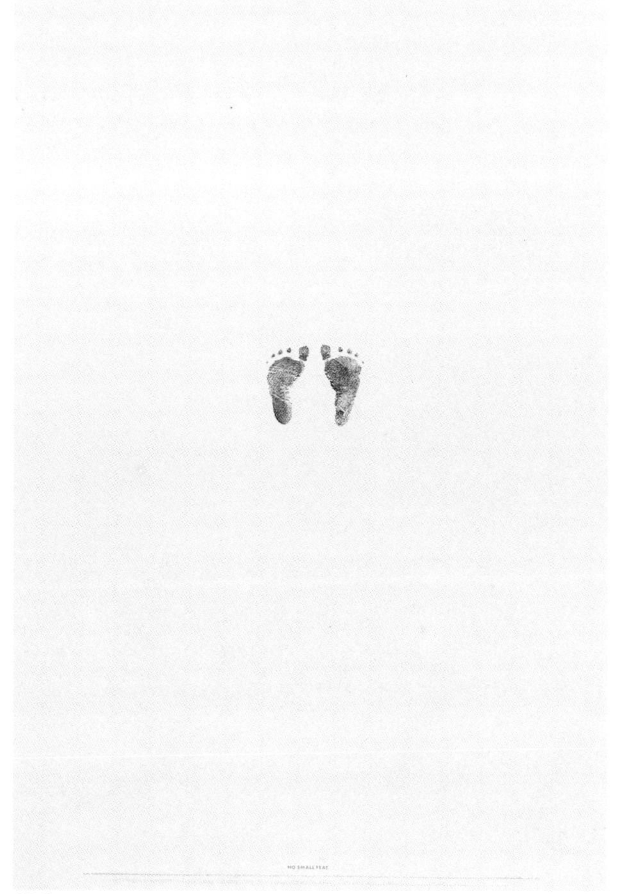

525
Art Director: Gary Templin
Designer: Gary Templin
Writer: Gary Templin, Dick Mitchell
Client: Ann McKinley, Michael McKinley
Agency: The Richards Group
Design Firm: Richards, Brock, Miller, Mitchell & Assoc.
Printer: Brodnax Printing

526
Art Director: Judy Dolim
Designer: Judy Dolim
Illustrator/Artist: Judy Dolim
Writer: Carol St. George
Client: Dallas Society of Visual Communications
Design Firm: Sibley/Peteet Design

527
Art Director: Warren Johnson
Illustrator/Artist: Joan Hall
Writer: Phil Calvit
Creative Director: Harry Beckwith
Client: Hotel Sofitel, Chicago
Agency: Carmichael Lynch
Agency Producer: Linda Hines

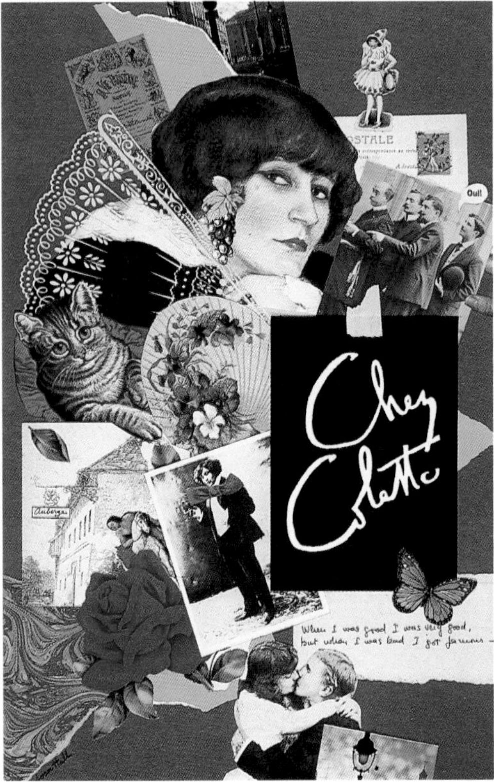

528
Art Director: Ron Sullivan
Designer: Diana McKnight
Illustrator/Artist: Linda Helton
Writer: Max Wright
Creative Director: Ron Sullivan, Mark Perkins
Client: The Friends of Cathy Case
Design Firm: Sullivan Perkins

529
Art Director: Clifford Selbert
Designer: Melanie Lowe
Illustrator/Artist: Mark Fisher
Client: Schneider & Associates
Design Firm: Clifford Selbert Design

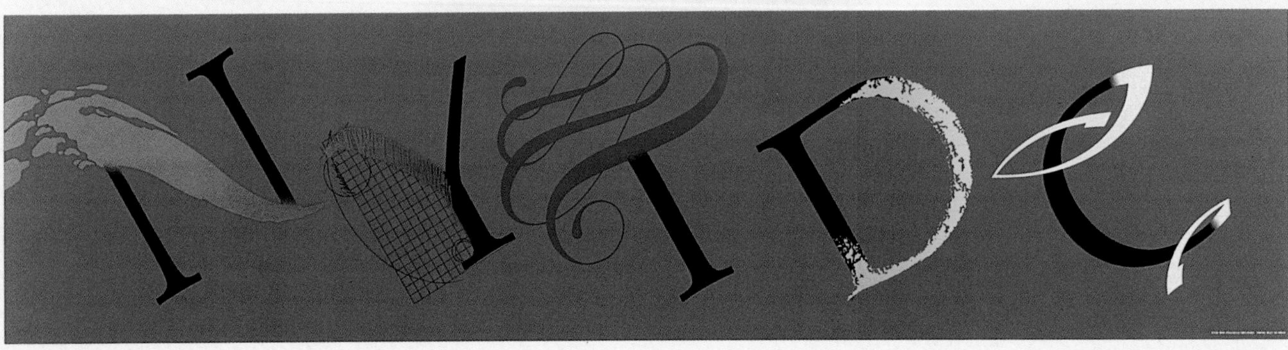

530
Art Director: Mark Steele
Designer: Mark Steele
Writer: Eric Johansen; Don Crum & Co.
Client: AIGA, Texas Chapter
Agency: Don Crum & Co.
Design Firm: The Dallas Times Herald Promotion Art
Calligrapher: Mark Steele

531
Art Director: Michael Blair
Illustrator/Artist: Michael Bacus
Client: U.S. Suzuki
Agency: HDM, Los Angeles

532
Art Director: Sharon Brady, Tammy Deane
Photographer: Mark Atkinson
Writer: Tom Cunniff, Greg Jordan
Creative Director: Bill Campbell
Client: Greg Jordan, Laurie Jordan
Agency: Barker, Campbell & Farley

533
Art Director: Ron Sullivan
Designer: Diana McKnight
Illustrator/Artist: Linda Helton, Diana McKnight
Creative Director: Ron Sullivan, Mark Perkins
Client: Turtle Creek Center for the Arts
Agency: Howe Associates
Design Firm: Sullivan Perkins

534
Art Director: Anthony Rutka
Designer: Anthony Rutka
Writer: Joan Weadock, Anthony Rutka
Client: Bacon Academy, Class of 1967
Agency: Rutka Weadock Design
Printer: Britannia Ltd.

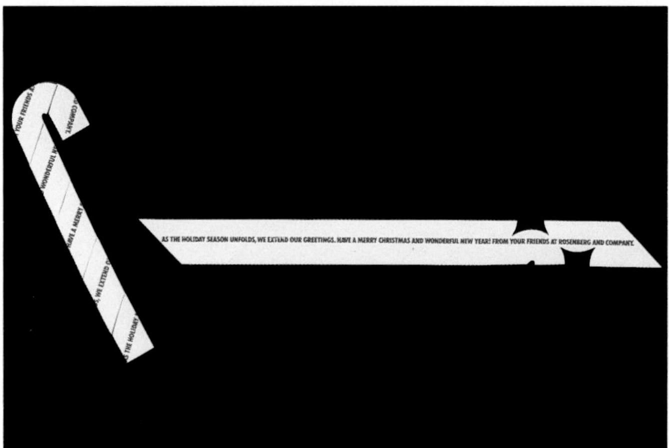

535
Art Director: David Martin
Designer: Bryan Collins
Writer: David Martin
Creative Director: Alan Lidji
Client: Rosenberg & Co.
Agency: Rosenberg & Co.

536
Art Director: Howard R. Swaim
Designer: Howard R. Swaim
Illustrator/Artist: Andrzej Dudzinski
Writer: Joellen Kitchen
Creative Director: Robert Robinson, Cylvia Santillan
Client: The Los Angeles Times
Agency: The Los Angeles Times, Promotion Dept.
Production Manager: Patty Kellman

537
Art Director: Montena Fink
Writer: James Schlankey
Creative Director: Sandy Steele
Client: EDS Corp.
Agency: EDS Corp. Communications

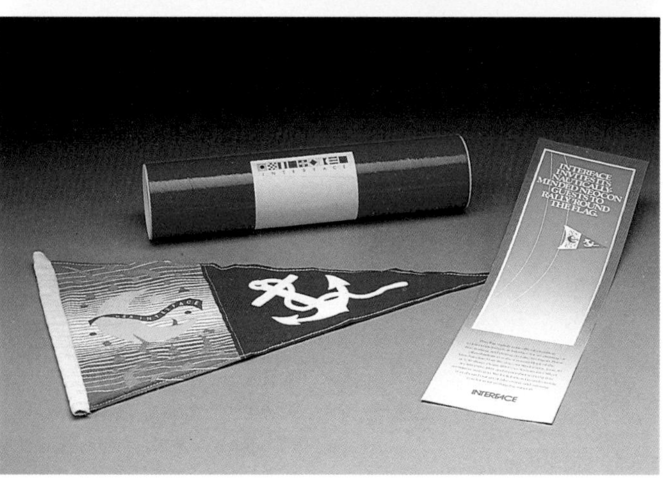

538
Art Director: Don Trousdell
Designer: Tina Trousdell
Illustrator/Artist: Tina Trousdell
Writer: Rich Maender
Client: Interface
Design Firm: Don Trousdell Design

539
Art Director: Gina Federico
Designer: Gina Federico
Client: David Cundy Inc.
Design Firm: David Cundy Inc.

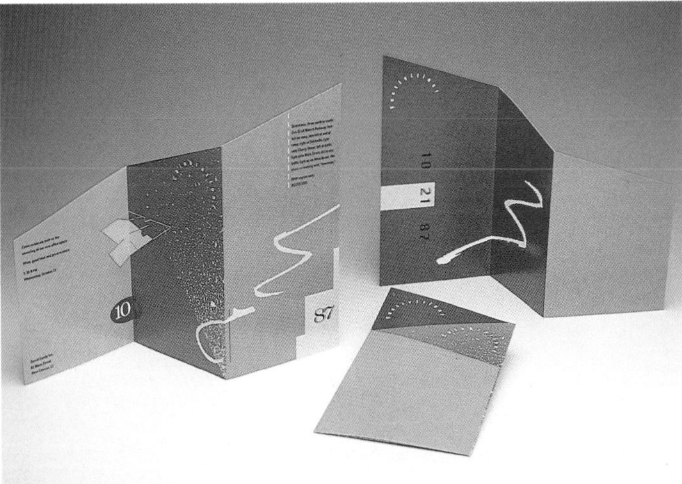

540
Art Director: Michael Osborne
Designer: Michael Osborne, Bill Reuter
Client: Friends of Classics, San Diego State U.
Design Firm: Michael Osborne

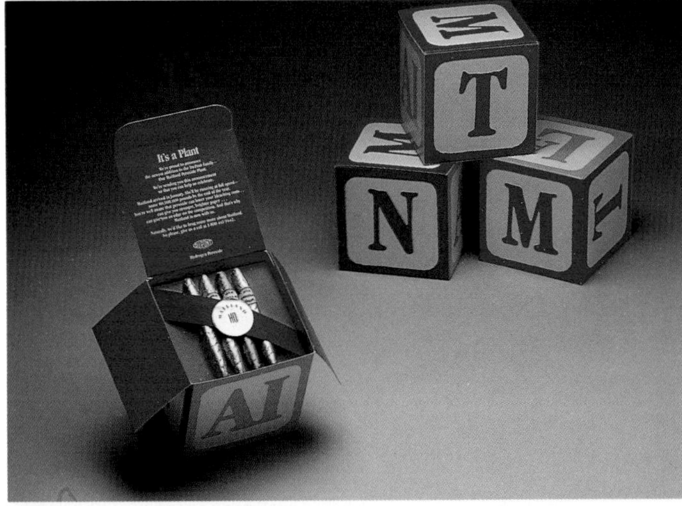

541
Art Director: Elizabeth Krewson
Designer: Elizabeth Krewson
Writer: Sara Bender
Creative Director: Donna Perzel
Client: Du Pont Co.
Agency: Janet Hughes & Associates

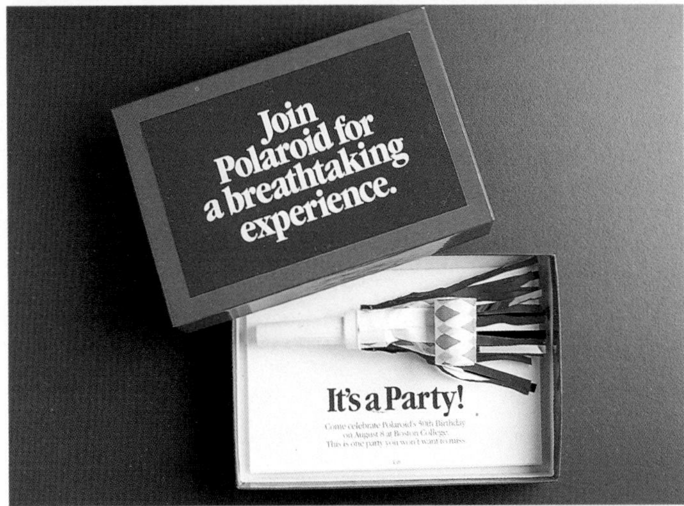

542
Art Director: Sue Merfeld
Designer: Sue Merfeld
Writer: Brian Flood
Creative Director: Mike Benes
Client: Polaroid Corp.
Design Firm: Polaroid Corporate Graphics
Printer: United Lithograph

543
Art Director: Hoi L. Chu
Designer: Hoi L. Chu, Martine Channon
Illustrator/Artist: Martine Channon
Client: H. L. Chu & Company Ltd.
Design Firm: H. L. Chu & Company Ltd.

545
Art Director: Glenn A. Staada
Designer: Ben Geist
Design Firm: Staada & Koorey Inc.
Printer: Gordonian

544
Art Director: Peter Harrison
Designer: Michael Gericke
Client: Domore Corp.
Design Firm: Pentagram Design

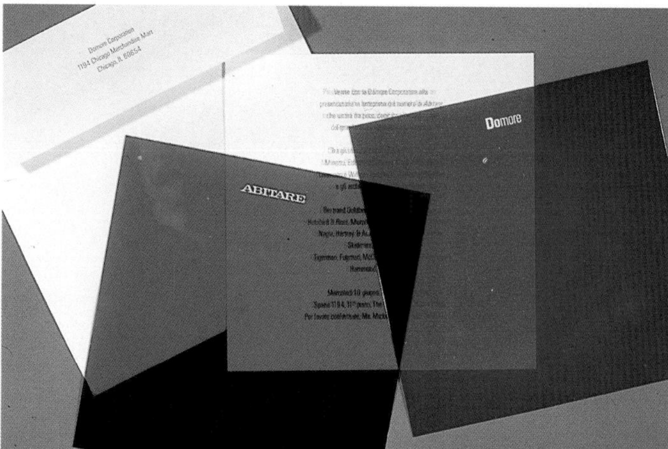

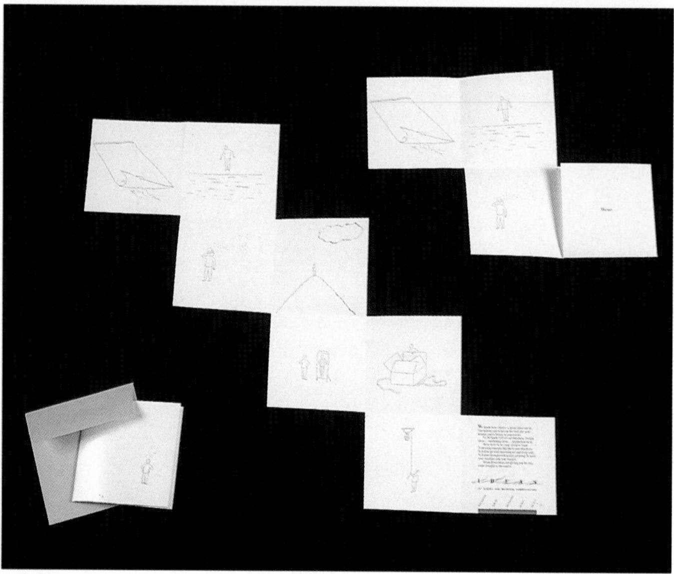

546
Art Director: Cynde Starck, Robin Brandes
Designer: Cynde Starck
Illustrator/Artist: Lonni Sue Johnson
Writer: Joan Siboni
Creative Director: Cynde Starck
Client: Ideas
Design Firm: Ideas
Printer: Reliable Graphics

547
Art Director: John Baxter
Designer: John Baxter
Photographer: Raymond Lavoie
Writer: John Baxter
Editor: T. George Harris
Client: American Health
Design Firm: John Baxter Design
Publisher: Owen Lipstein
Promotion Director: Elizabeth Schick

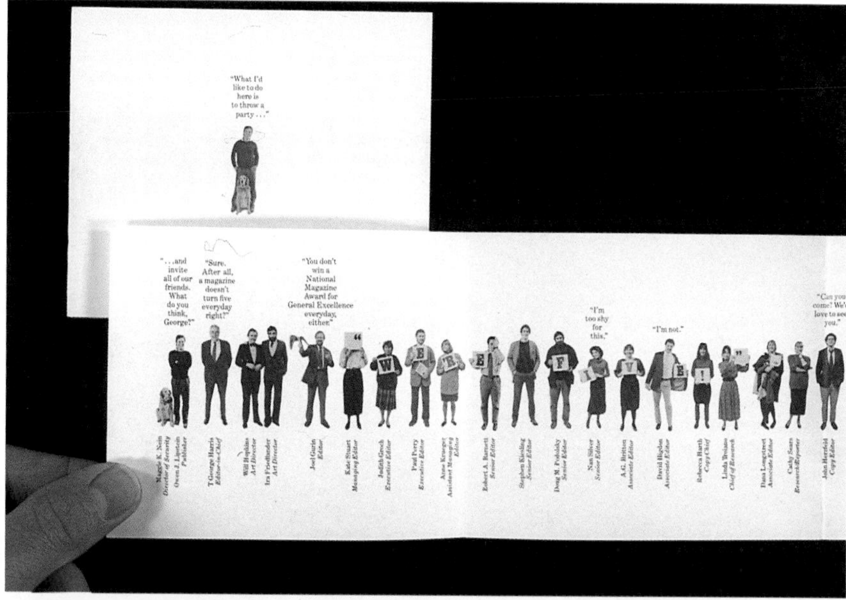

548
Art Director: Steve Gibbs
Designer: Bill Pierce
Writer: Carol St. George
Client: Corry Hiebert
Design Firm: Gibbs Design Inc.

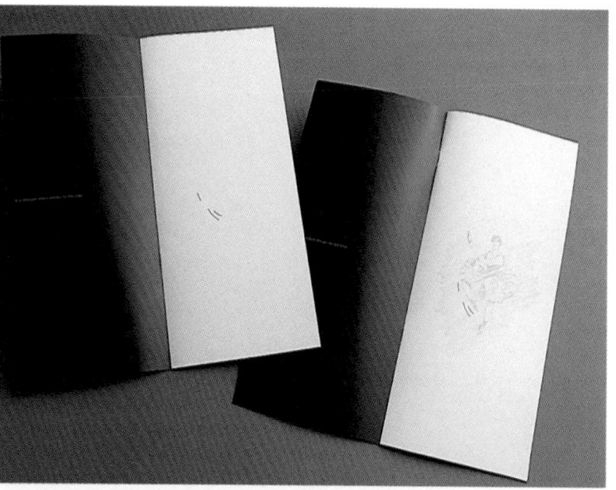

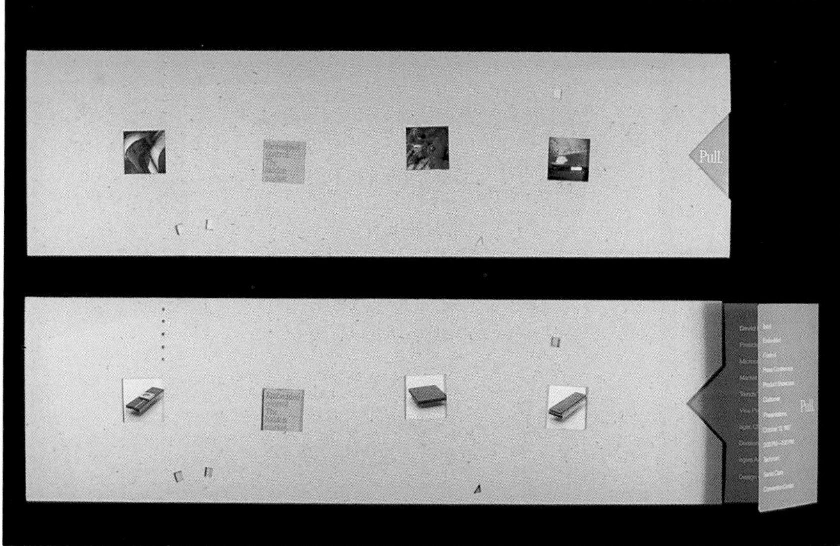

549
Art Director: Robert Holmes
Designer: Robert Holmes
Photographer: Dave Siegel
Writer: Larry Thelen
Creative Director: Larry Thelen
Client: Intel
Agency: Thelen Plus

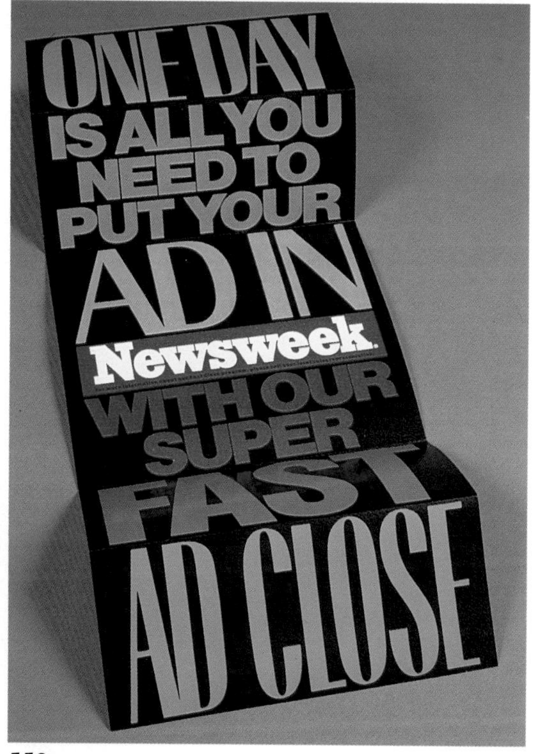

550
Art Director: Deborah Dalton
Designer: Deborah Dalton
Writer: Deborah D. Dalton, Tom Pletcher
Creative Director: Carmile S. Zaino
Client: Newsweek Inc.

551
Art Director: Danny Sadler
Designer: Danny Sadler
Writer: Marilyn Giasson, Danny Sadler
Client: Brown Bloyed & Associates
Agency: Brown Bloyed & Associates
Printer: Rodgers Litho

552
Art Director: Roslyn Eskind, Malcolm Waddell
Designer: Roslyn Eskind, Malcolm Waddell, Christopher Campbell
Client: Eskind Waddell
Design Firm: Eskind Waddell
Printer: Tom Steele, MacKinnon-Moncur
Typesetter: Ken Mokedanz, Cooper & Beatty

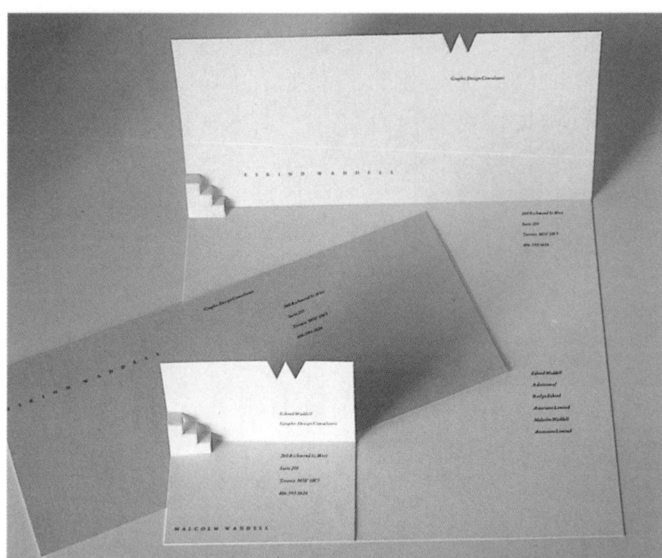

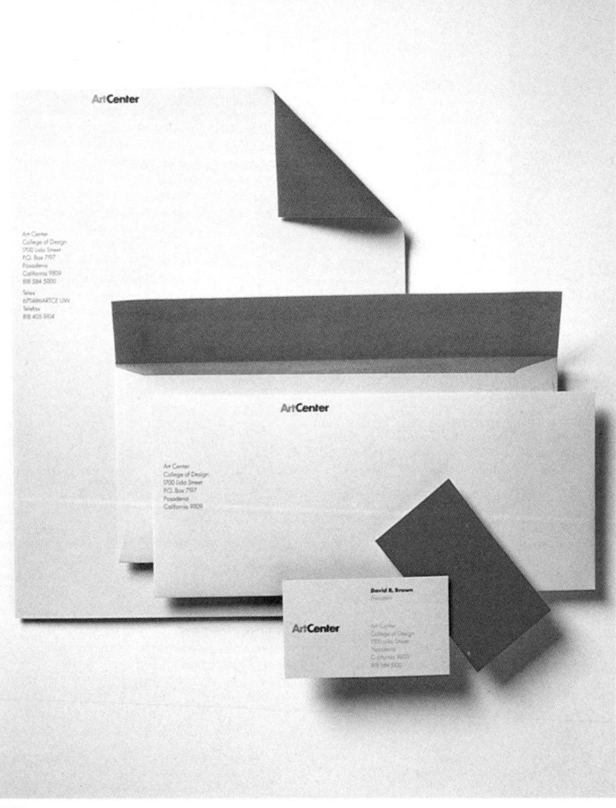

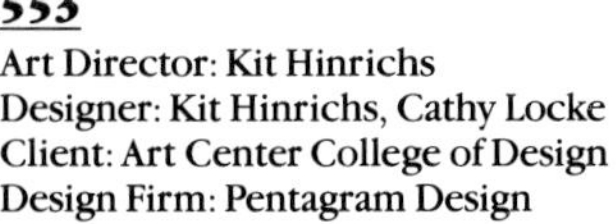

553
Art Director: Kit Hinrichs
Designer: Kit Hinrichs, Cathy Locke
Client: Art Center College of Design
Design Firm: Pentagram Design

554
Art Director: Lauren Smith
Designer: Lauren Smith
Illustrator/Artist: Donna Lang
Client: Weaver Photography
Design Firm: Lauren Smith Design

555
Art Director: Robert E. Wages
Designer: Robert E. Wages
Illustrator/Artist: Walt Floyd
Design Firm: Wages Design

556
Art Director: Will Brown
Client: Tawn Chi & Associates Inc.

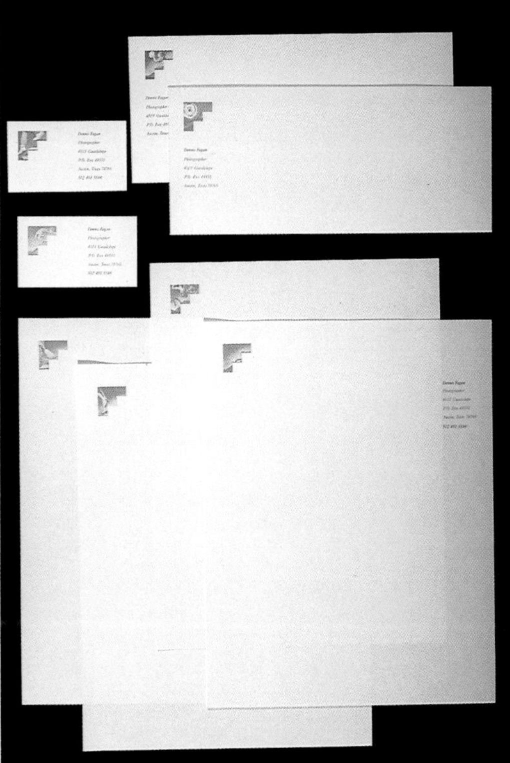

557
Art Director: Jane Wu
Designer: Jane Wu
Photographer: Dennis Fagan
Client: Dennis Fagan Photographer
Design Firm: Wu Graphic Design
Marketing Consultant: Elaine Sorel
Photo Assistant: Ron Sawasky

558
Art Director: Ursula Bendixen, Suzanne Redding
Designer: Ursula Bendixen, Suzanne Redding
Client: Bendixen Redding
Design Firm: Bendixen Redding

559
Art Director: Woody Pirtle
Designer: Woody Pirtle
Illustrator/Artist: Woody Pirtle
Creative Director: Woody Pirtle
Client: Robin Bugbee
Design Firm: Pirtle Design

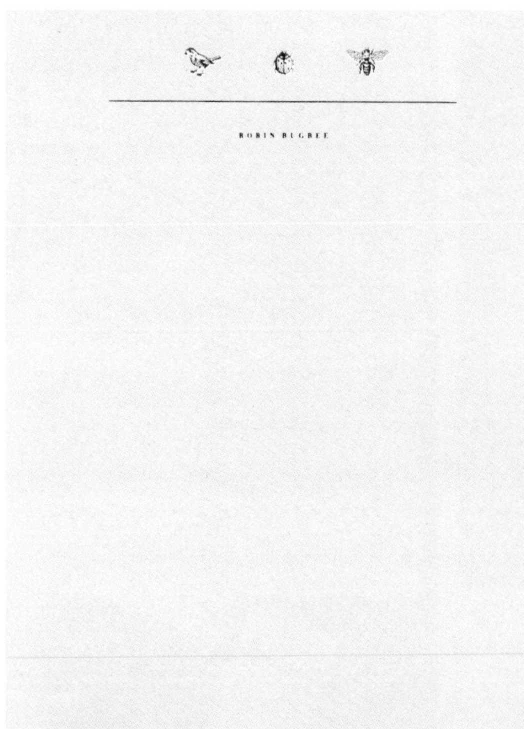

560
Art Director: James A. Stygar
Designer: James A. Stygar
Writer: Jay Jenkins, Betse Feuchtenberger
Design Firm: Stygar Group Inc.

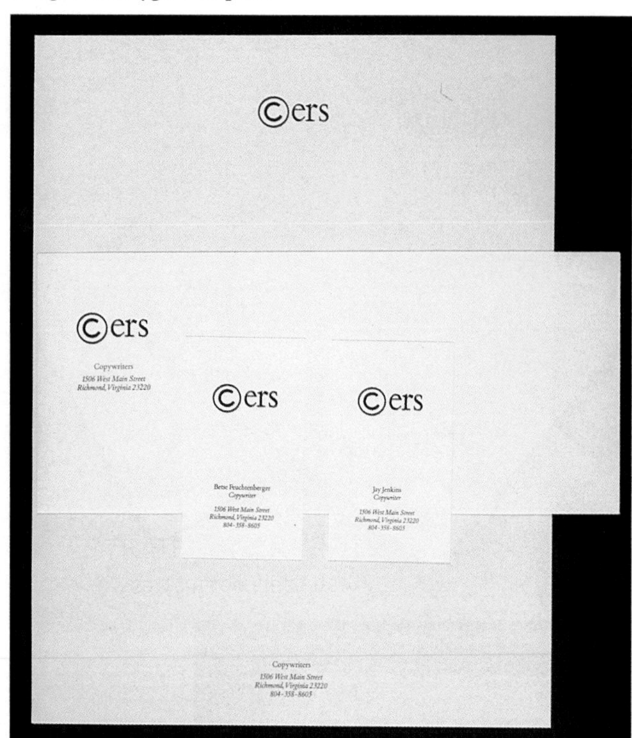

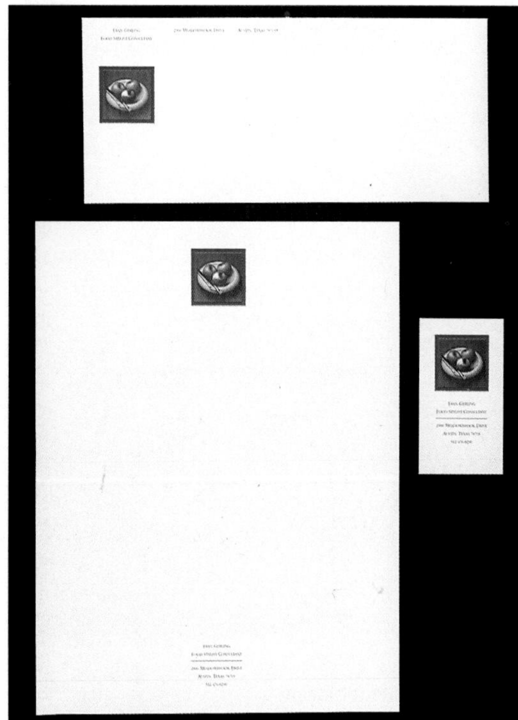

561
Art Director: Jane Wu
Designer: Jane Wu
Photographer: Michael Flahive
Client: Fran Gerling, Food Stylist
Design Firm: Wu Graphic Design

562
Art Director: Cap Pannell
Designer: Cap Pannell
Client: Pannell/St. George
Design Firm: Pannell/St. George

563
Art Director: Terry O'Connor
Designer: Helena O'Connor, May Fong
Calligrapher: Bill Fong

564
Art Director: Kevin B. Kuester
Designer: Bob Goebel
Illustrator/Artist: Craig Schommer
Client: Parasole Restaurant Holdings Inc.
Design Firm: Madsen & Kuester Inc.

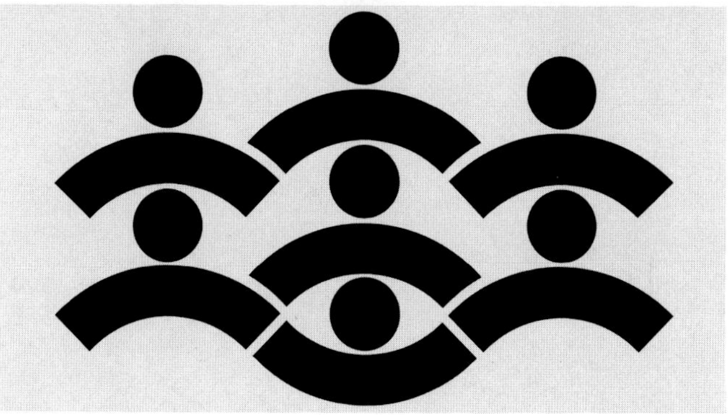

565
Art Director: Timothy T. Trost
Designer: Timothy T. Trost
Client: School for Ophthalmic Technicians, St. Paul-Ramsey
Design Firm: Medical Media Services

566
Art Director: Saul Bass
Designer: Saul Bass, Chuk-Yee Cheng
Client: Kerr Co.
Design Firm: Bass/Yager & Associates

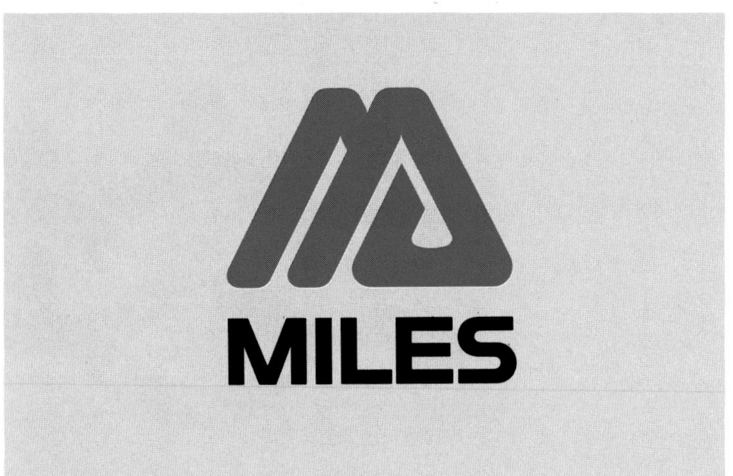

567
Art Director: Saul Bass
Designer: Saul Bass, Chuk-Yee Cheng
Client: Miles Laboratories
Design Firm: Bass/Yager & Associates

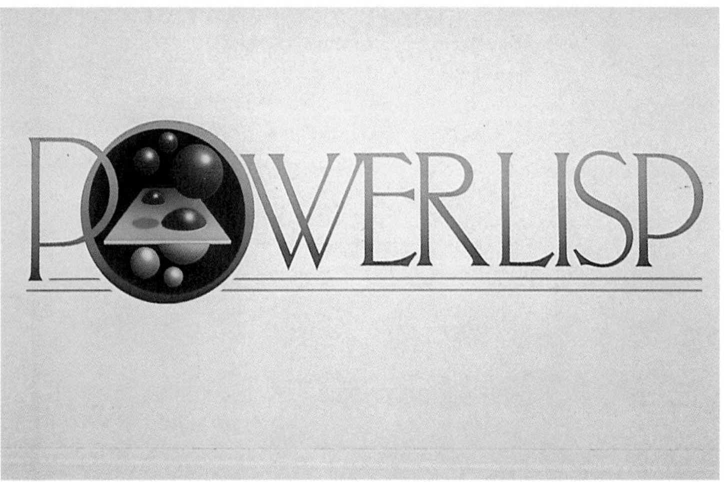

568
Art Director: Robert Cummings
Designer: Michael Stacey
Illustrator/Artist: Dawne Holmes
Creative Director: Robert Cummings
Client: MicroProducts Inc.
Design Firm: Cummings Communications Design Inc.

569
Art Director: Ed Gold
Designer: Mary Perantonakis
Illustrator/Artist: Bert Smith
Writer: John C. Wilson
Client: Publications Des. Prog., Univ. of Balt.

570
Art Director: Robert Cummings
Designer: Michael Stacey
Illustrator/Artist: Michael Stacey
Creative Director: Robert Cummings
Client: MicroProducts Inc.
Design Firm: Cummings Communications Design Inc.

571
Art Director: Michael Toth
Designer: Michael Schwab
Illustrator/Artist: Michael Schwab
Client: Robert Bruce Sweaters

572
Art Director: Patrick SooHoo
Designer: Katherine Lam
Creative Director: Patrick SooHoo
Client: Galardi's Pizza
Design Firm: Patrick SooHoo Designers

573
Art Director: Charles S. Anderson
Designer: Charles S. Anderson
Illustrator/Artist: Charles S. Anderson, Lynn Schulte
Client: Lee Jeans
Design Firm: The Duffy Design Group

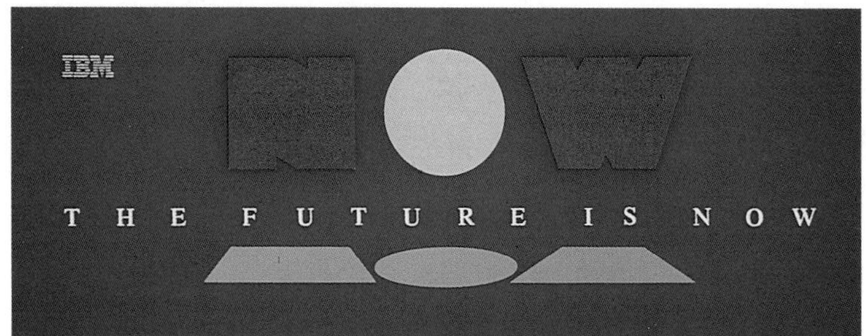

574
Art Director: Linda L. Tom, Michael Orr
Designer: Lorinna Grimmer
Client: IBM Endicott Communications
Agency: IBM Endicott Design Center
Design Firm: Michael Orr & Associates Inc.

575
Art Director: Scott Miller
Designer: Scott Miller
Illustrator/Artist: Robb Wyatt
Creative Director: Lee Hunt
Client: MTV Networks
Design Firm: Scott Miller & Associates

576
Art Director: Ray Sturdivant
Designer: Ray Sturdivant
Illustrator/Artist: Ray Sturdivant
Creative Director: Ray Sturdivant
Client: Lot of Autos
Design Firm: Ray Sturdivant Graphic Design

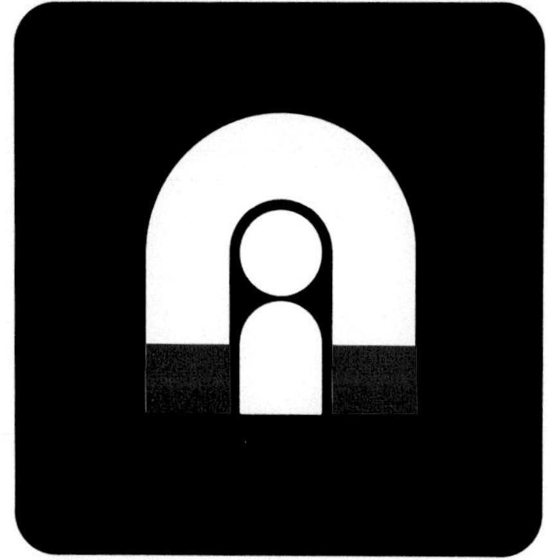

577
Art Director: Scott Mires, John Ball
Designer: John Ball
Illustrator/Artist: Kathy Carpentier-Moore
Client: Magnetic Imaging Center
Design Firm: Mires Design

578
Art Director: David Edelstein, Nancy Edelstein, Lanny French, Carol Davidson
Photographer: Peter Gravelle
Writer: Kathy Cain
Client: Generra Sportswear
Agency: Edelstein Associates Advertising Inc.

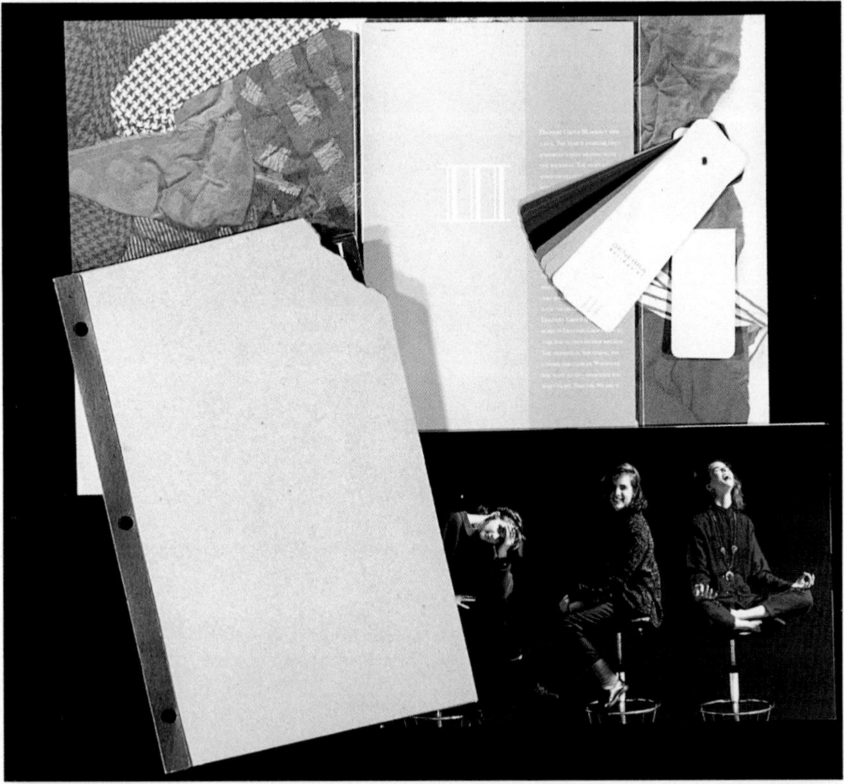

579
Art Director: David Edelstein, Nancy Edelstein, Lanny French
Photographer: Jim Cummins
Writer: Kathy Cain
Client: Generra Sportswear
Agency: Edelstein Associates Advertising Inc.

580
Art Director: Richard Moore, Karen Krieger
Designer: Karen Krieger
Photographer: Bill Farrell
Writer: AT&T Network Systems
Client: AT&T Network Systems
Design Firm: Muir Cornelius Moore Inc.

581

Art Director: Ann Gildea, Frank Rockwell
Designer: Ann Gildea, Margaret Sewell, Kun-Tee Chang
Client: Raytheon Co.
Design Firm: RichardsonSmith Inc.

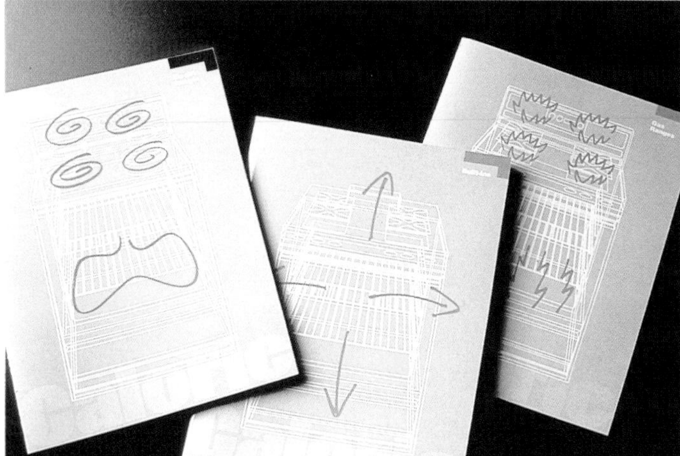

582

Art Director: Thomas Kluepfel
Designer: Katy Delehanty
Photographer: George Hein
Writer: Samuel Swope
Client: Varda Chocolatier
Agency: Drenttel Doyle Partners
Public Relations Director: Fern Berman

583

Art Director: Herbert M. Meyers, Juan Concepcion
Designer: Susan Chalberg, Jerry Dior, Joe Lombardo
Client: Eveready Battery Co., Ralston Purina Co.
Design Firm: Gerstman & Meyers Inc.
Account Manager: Michael Lucas

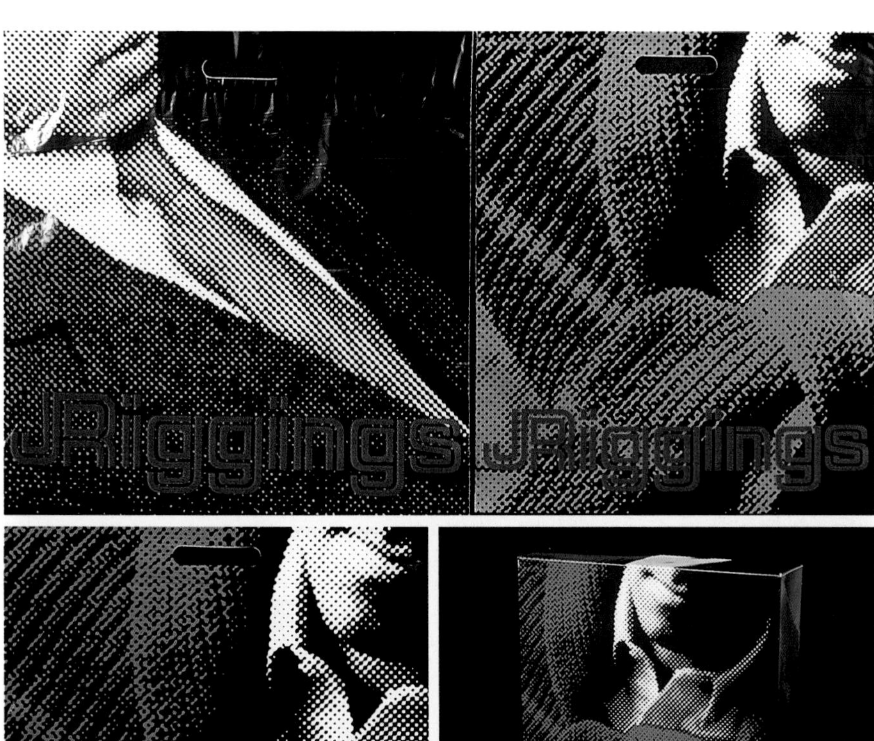

584
Art Director: Robert P. Gersin
Designer: Scott Bolestridge
Client: J. Riggings
Design Firm: Robert P. Gersin Associates Inc.

585
Art Director: Dale Glasser
Designer: Patricia Kovic
Illustrator/Artist: Dale Glasser
Client: Warburton's Inc.
Design Firm: Dale Glasser Graphics

586
Art Director: Mark Handler
Designer: Tom Dolle
Creative Director: Tom Dolle
Client: Citicorp
Design Firm: Handler Group Inc.

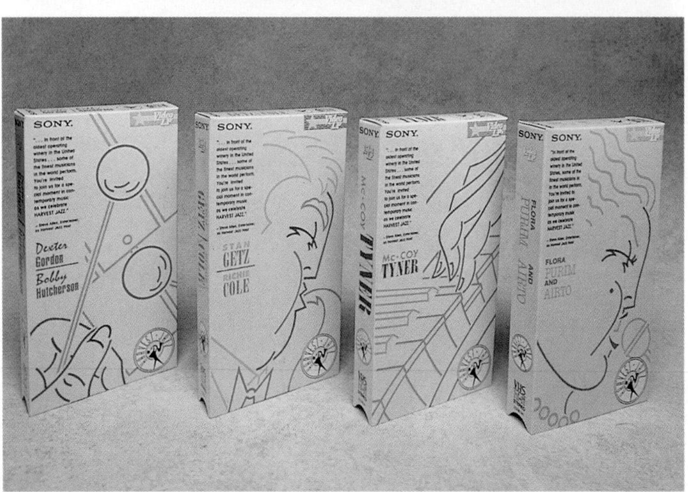

587
Art Director: Pat Davis
Designer: Kathryn Sturges
Photographer: Tom Copi
Brian McMillen
Illustrator/Artist: Kathryn Sturges
Creative Director: Anise Goldman
Client: Sony Video Software Co.
Design Firm: Pat Davis Design
Executive Producer: Paul Kinney Productions

588
Art Director: Dutro Blockson
Designer: Ikuko Lin
Client: Procter & Gamble
Design Firm: Libby Perszyk Kathman

589
Art Director: Nicolas Sidjakov, Jerry Berman
Designer: Dave Curtis
Creative Director: Nicolas Sidjakov, Jerry Berman
Client: Universal Foods
Design Firm: Sidjakov, Berman, Gomez & Partners

590
Art Director: Charles S. Anderson
Designer: Charles S. Anderson
Illustrator/Artist: Charles S. Anderson, Lynn Schulte
Client: Chaps/Ralph Lauren
Design Firm: The Duffy Design Group

591
Art Director: Charles S. Anderson
Designer: Charles S. Anderson
Illustrator/Artist: Charles S. Anderson, Lynn Schulte
Writer: Chuck Carlson
Client: Brooks Shoes
Design Firm: The Duffy Design Group

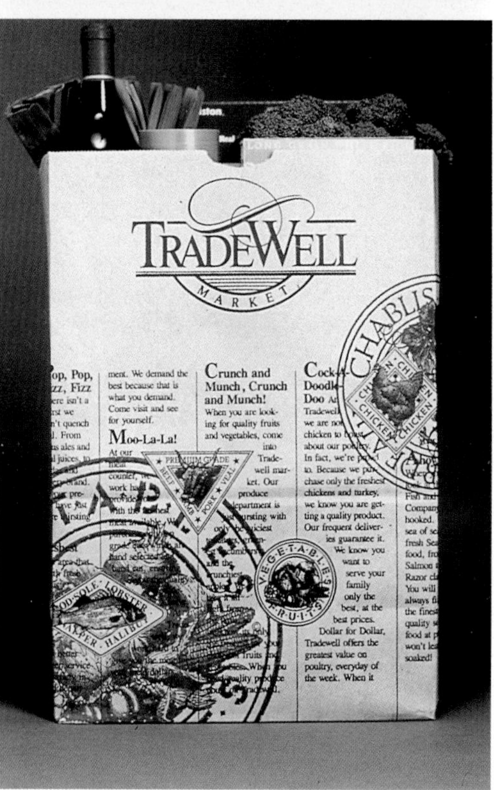

592
Art Director: Jack Anderson
Designer: Jack Anderson, Mary Hermes, Cheri Huber, Julie Tanagi
Writer: Hal Hilts
Client: Tradewell
Design Firm: Hornall Anderson Design Works
Calligraphy: John Fortune

593
Art Director: Paula Yamasaki-Ison
Designer: Katherine Lam, Tricia Rauen
Creative Director: Patrick SooHoo
Client: Los Angeles County Museum of Art
Design Firm: Patrick SooHoo Designers

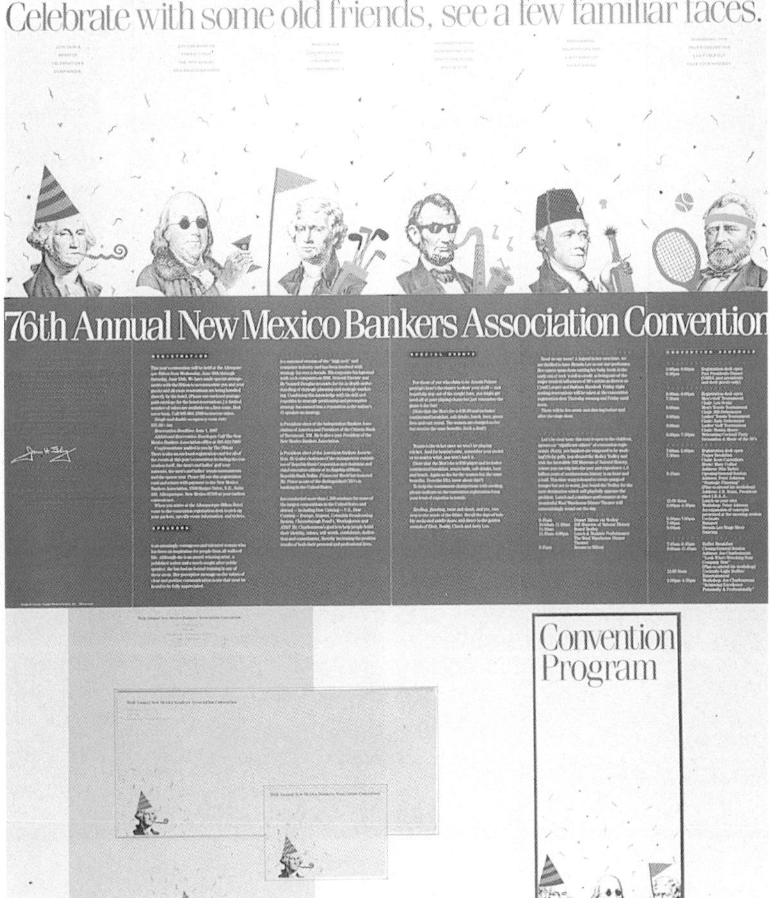

594
Art Director: Steven Wedeen
Designer: Steven Wedeen
Illustrator/Artist: Mark Chamberlain
Writer: Richard Kuhn
Creative Director: Steven Wedeen
Client: New Mexico Bankers Association
Agency: Vaughn/Wedeen Creative Inc.
Design Firm: Vaughn/Wedeen Creative Inc.

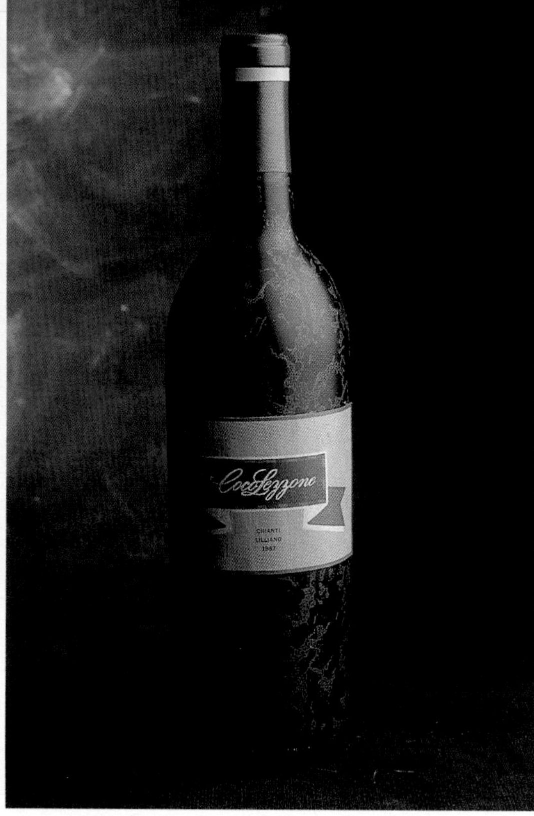

595
Art Director: Haley Johnson
Designer: Haley Johnson
Illustrator/Artist: Haley Johnson
Client: Cocolezzone
Design Firm: The Duffy Design Group

596
Art Director: Robert Cipriani
Designer: Robert Cipriani
Illustrator/Artist: David Hannum
Creative Director: Robert Cipriani
Client: Thinking Machines Corp.
Agency: Cipriani Advertising Inc.
Design Firm: Cipriani Advertising Inc.

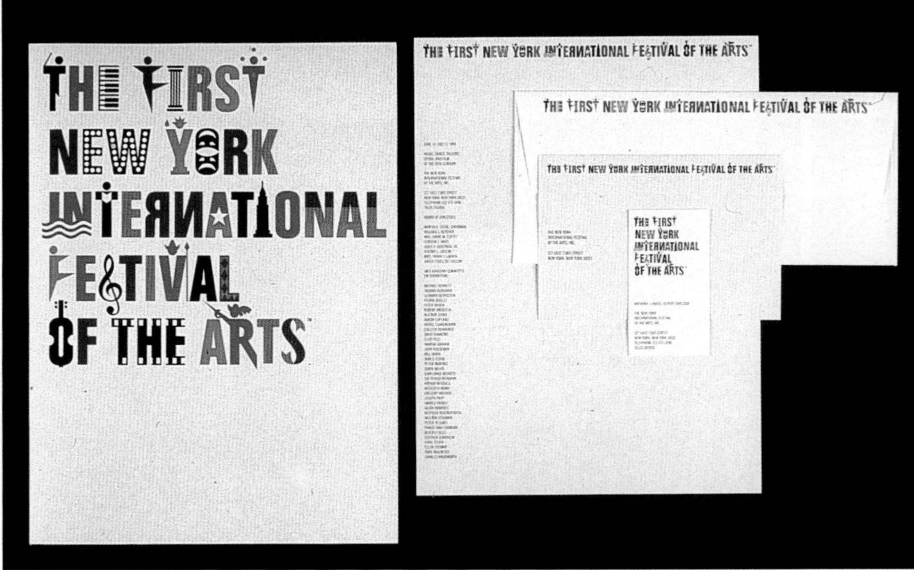

597
Art Director: Ivan Chermayeff
Designer: Bill Anton
Writer: Bill Anton
Client: NY International Festival of the Arts
Design Firm: Chermayeff & Geismar Associates

598
Art Director: Milton Glaser
Designer: Suzanne Zumpano, Milton Glaser
Illustrator/Artist: Milton Glaser
Writer: Julian Koenig
Creative Director: Milton Glaser
Client: Queens College, CUNY
Design Firm: Milton Glaser Inc.
President, Queens College: Shirley Strum Kenny

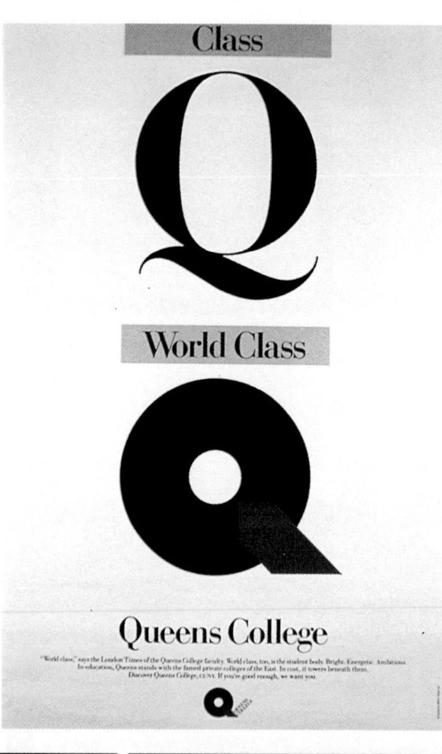

Harvard. Yale. Columbia. Queens.

What's so funny?

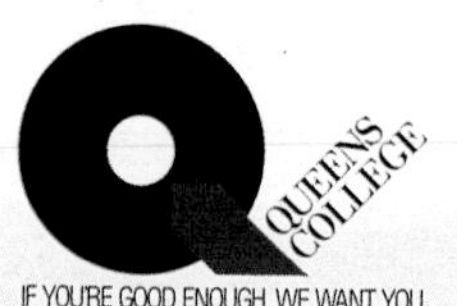

"World class," says the London Times of the Queens College faculty. 4 Stars ★ ★ ★ ★ says the New York Times Guide to Colleges. In facilities, faculty and education, Queens stands with the famed private colleges of the East. In cost, it towers beneath them. And there's nothing funny about that. Discover Queens College, CUNY.

599
Art Director: John T. Grogan
Designer: John T. Grogan, Ken Schwager
Creative Director: John T. Grogan
Design Firm: Rupert/Jensen & Associates

600
Art Director: Peter Harrison, Susan Hochbaum
Designer: Susan Hochbaum
Illustrator/Artist: Paul Davis
Writer: John Berendt
Client: The 21 Club
Design Firm: Pentagram Design

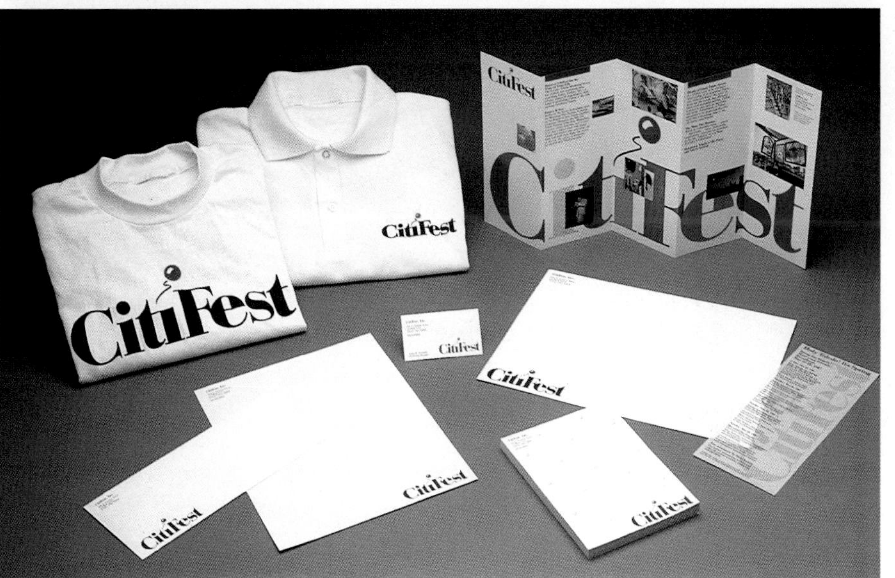

601
Art Director: Terence Langenderfer
Designer: Terence Langenderfer
Photographer: David Lehman
Client: Citifest Inc.
Design Firm: Marketing Communications Group Inc.

603

Art Director: Bruce Willardson
Designer: Margo Zucker, Andy Dreyfus
Client: The Saturn Corp.
Design Firm: Landor Associates, Retail Identity

602

Art Director: Jack Anderson
Designer: Jack Anderson, Luann Bice, Julie Tanagi, Cheri Huber
Creative Director: Jack Anderson
Client: Tradewell
Design Firm: Hornall Anderson Design Works

Humor
COMMITMENT
A
D
FOR THE TRUE BELIEVERS WHO HUNG TOUGH
WHEN THE PHILISTINES WANTED
THE PRODUCT BIGGER AND THE IDEA SMALLER.
IT'S TIME TO ENTER THE 67TH ANNUAL
ART DIRECTORS CLUB SHOW
7
AIGA
DO NOT
DISTURB
NO MOLESTE
PRIERE DE NE
PAS DERANGER
BITTE NICHT
STOREN
ILLUSTRATORS
Anthony
STREET
ROLL
294
A
TEST
KODAK
81 EF
DATE
E1.320
PROD. CO.
Fierberg
DIRECTOR
Morrissey
CAMERAMAN
S.E.Fierberg

PICTURE FRAMING

605
Art Director: Bob Kwait
Designer: Bob Kwait
Illustrator/Artist: Darrel Millsap
Writer: Bob Kwait
Creative Director: Bob Kwait
Client: San Diego Zoo
Agency: Phillips-Ramsey Advertising
Production Artist: Ron Van Buskirk

See you later.
The San Diego Zoo

606
Art Director: Bob Kwait
Designer: Bob Kwait
Illustrator/Artist: Darrel Millsap
Writer: Bob Kwait
Creative Director: Bob Kwait
Client: San Diego Zoo
Agency: Phillips-Ramsey Advertising
Production Artist: Ron Van Buskirk

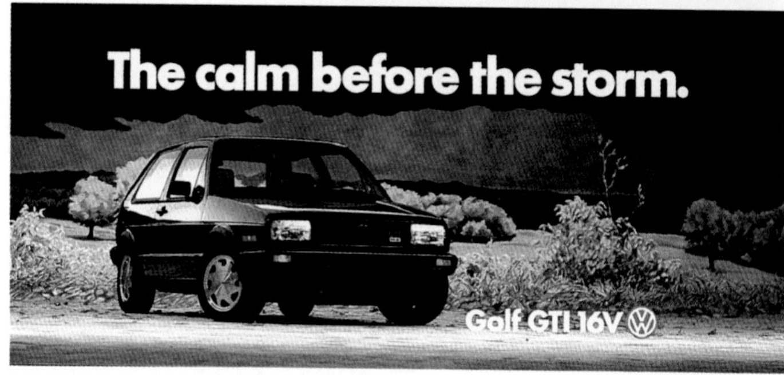

607
Art Director: Steve Thursby
Photographer: Terry Collier
Writer: Terry O'Reilly
Creative Director: Allan Kazmer
Client: Volkswagen Canada Inc.
Agency: DDB Needham Worldwide Advertising

608
Art Director: Marty Weiss
Photographer: Charles Purvis
Writer: Robin Raj
Creative Director: Bill Hamilton
Client: NYNEX Yellow Pages
Agency: Chiat/Day Inc., New York

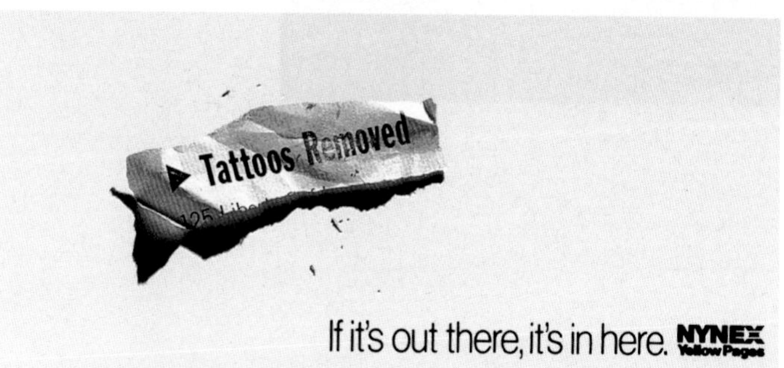

609
Art Director: Marty Weiss
Photographer: Charles Purvis
Writer: Robin Raj
Creative Director: Bill Hamilton
Client: NYNEX Yellow Pages
Agency: Chiat/Day Inc., New York

610
Art Director: Marty Weiss
Photographer: Charles Purvis
Writer: Robin Raj
Creative Director: Bill Hamilton
Client: NYNEX Yellow Pages
Agency: Chiat/Day Inc., New York

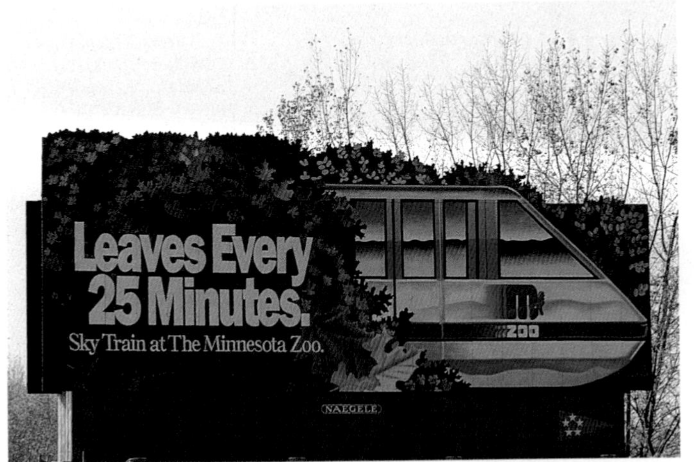

611
Art Director: Steve Sweitzer
Illustrator/Artist: Scott Baker
Writer: Jon Anderson
Creative Director: Jon Anderson
Client: Minnesota Zoo
Agency: Colle & McVoy Advertising

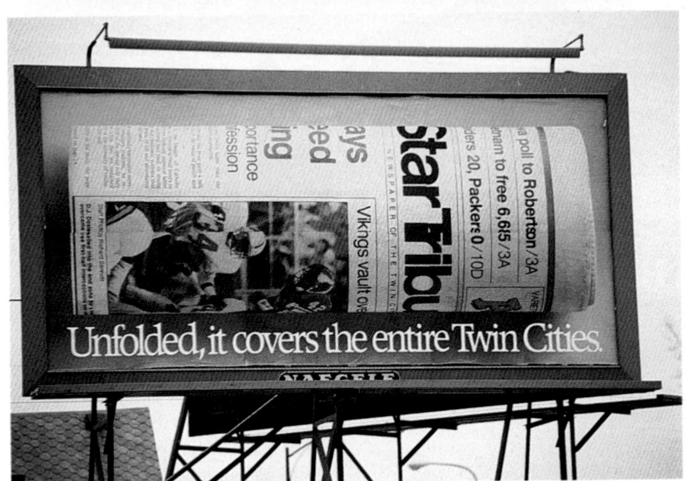

612
Art Director: Kurt Tausche
Writer: Kerry Casey
Creative Director: Bert Gardner
Client: The Minneapolis Star Tribune
Agency: Bozell, Jacobs, Kenyon & Eckhardt

613
Art Director: Sally Oelschlager
Photographer: Steve Umland
Writer: Kerry Casey
Creative Director: Jack Supple
Client: KTCA Channel 2
Agency: Carmichael Lynch
Agency Producer: Barb Knoche

Great Moments In Flight.
7:00 12:15 3:00 6:35
Alaska Airlines To Los Angeles International.

614
Art Director: Clifford Goodenough
Writer: Steve Dolbinski
Creative Director: Ron Sandilands
Client: Alaska Airlines
Agency: Livingston & Co.

Hundreds of chairs.
And occasional tables.
Fleetham
FURNISHINGS & DESIGN
Hennepin Avenue at Lake Street

615
Art Director: Tom Lichtenheld
Designer: Tom Lichtenheld
Writer: Rod Kilpatrick
Creative Director: Tom McElligott
Client: Fleetham
Agency: Fallon McElligott

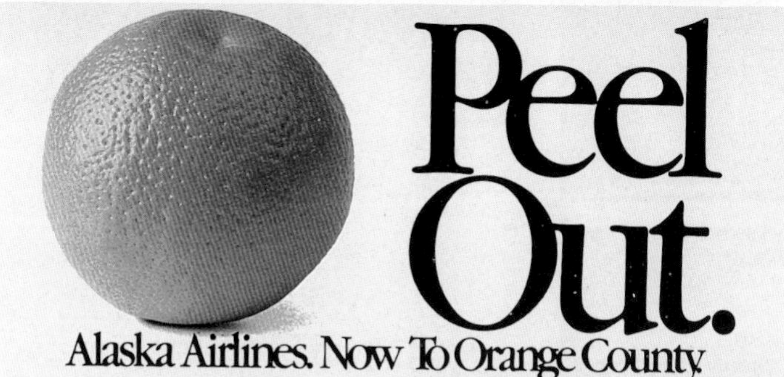

616
Art Director: Clifford Goodenough
Photographer: Larry Gilpin
Writer: Steve Sandoz
Creative Director: Ron Sandilands
Client: Alaska Airlines

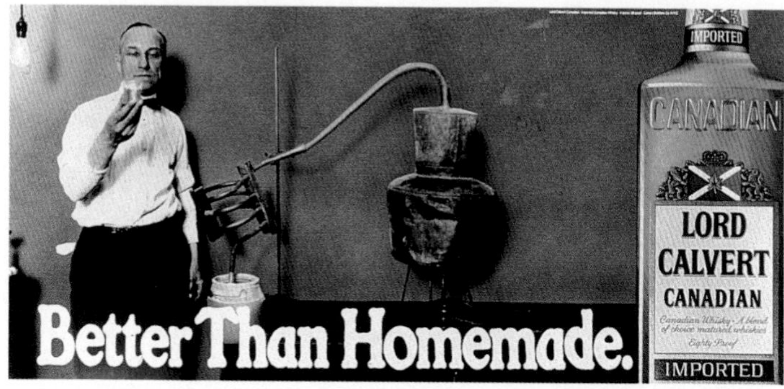

617
Art Director: Irv Klein
Designer: Irv Klein
Illustrator/Artist: Eddie Kunze
Writer: Stephanie Arnold
Client: Seagrams/Lord Calvert
Agency: Levine, Huntley, Schmidt & Beaver

618
Art Director: David Breznau
Photographer: Jeff Nadler
Writer: Ed Gines
Creative Director: Bob Kuperman
Client: Volkswagen of America
Agency: DDB Needham

619
Art Director: Peter Day
Photographer: Shin Sugino
Writer: Viv Tate
Creative Director: Allan Kazmer
Client: Levi Strauss
Agency: DDB Needham Worldwide Advertising

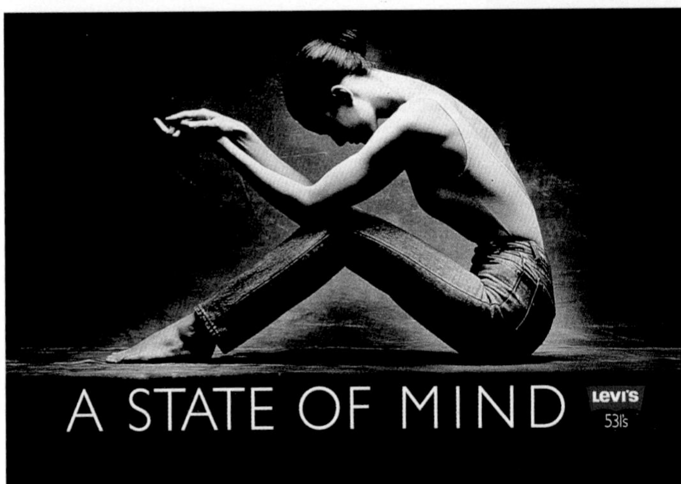

620
Art Director: Judy Penny
Writer: Dan Brown
Creative Director: Richard Pantano
Client: The Boston Museum of Fine Arts
Agency: Hill, Holliday, Connors, Cosmopulos Inc.

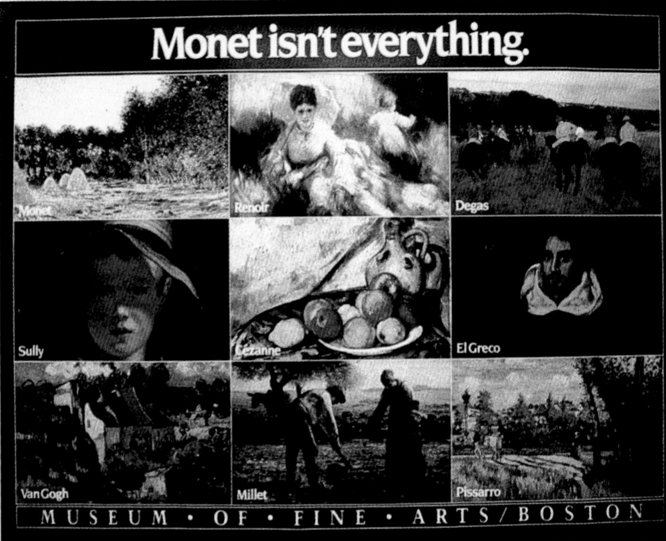

621
Art Director: Judy Penny
Writer: Dan Brown
Creative Director: Richard Pantano
Client: The Boston Museum of Fine Arts
Agency: Hill, Holliday, Connors, Cosmopulos Inc.
Production Manager: Sue McWilliams

622
Art Director: Rocco Campanelli
Photographer: Rocco Campanelli
Writer: Richard Kirshenbaum
Creative Director: Don Deutsch
Client: Emmaus House
Agency: David Deutsch Associates

623
Art Director: Steve Thursby
Photographer: Philip Gallard
Writer: Allan Kazmer
Creative Director: Allan Kazmer
Client: Levi Strauss
Agency: DDB Needham Worldwide Advertising

624
Art Director: Steve Thursby
Photographer: Olga Tracey
Writer: Allan Kazmer
Creative Director: Allan Kazmer
Client: Levi Strauss
Agency: DDB Needham Worldwide Advertising

625
Art Director: Marty Weiss
Photographer: Charles Purvis
Writer: Robin Raj
Creative Director: Bill Hamilton
Client: NYNEX Yellow Pages
Agency: Chiat/Day Inc., New York
Account Management: Amy Saypol, Melissa Bernhardt

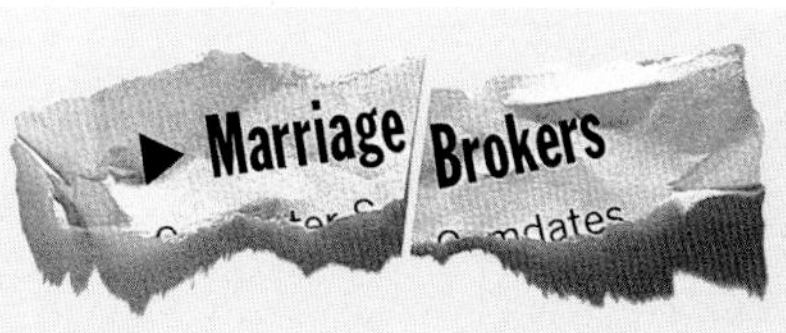

If it's out there, it's in here. NYNEX Yellow Pages

626
Art Director: Marty Weiss
Photographer: Charles Purvis
Writer: Robin Raj
Creative Director: Bill Hamilton
Client: NYNEX Yellow Pages
Agency: Chiat/Day Inc., New York
Account Management: Amy Saypol, Melissa Bernhardt

627
Art Director: Houman Pirdavari
Designer: Houman Pirdavari
Photographer: Robert Giusti
Writer: Sam Avery
Creative Director: Tom McElligott
Client: Federal Express
Agency: Fallon McElligott

628
Art Director: Houman Pirdavari
Designer: Houman Pirdavari
Photographer: Robert Giusti
Writer: Sam Avery
Creative Director: Tom McElligott
Client: Federal Express
Agency: Fallon McElligott

629
Art Director: Houman Pirdavari
Designer: Houman Pirdavari
Photographer: Robert Giusti
Writer: Sam Avery
Creative Director: Tom McElligott
Client: Federal Express
Agency: Fallon McElligott

630
Art Director: Marty Weiss
Photographer: Charles Purvis
Writer: Robin Raj
Creative Director: Bill Hamilton
Client: NYNEX Yellow Pages
Agency: Chiat/Day Inc., New York
Account Management: Amy Saypol,
Melissa Bernhardt

631
Art Director: Marty Weiss
Photographer: Charles Purvis
Writer: Robin Raj
Creative Director: Bill Hamilton
Client: NYNEX Yellow Pages
Agency: Chiat/Day Inc., New York
Account Management: Amy Saypol,
Melissa Bernhardt

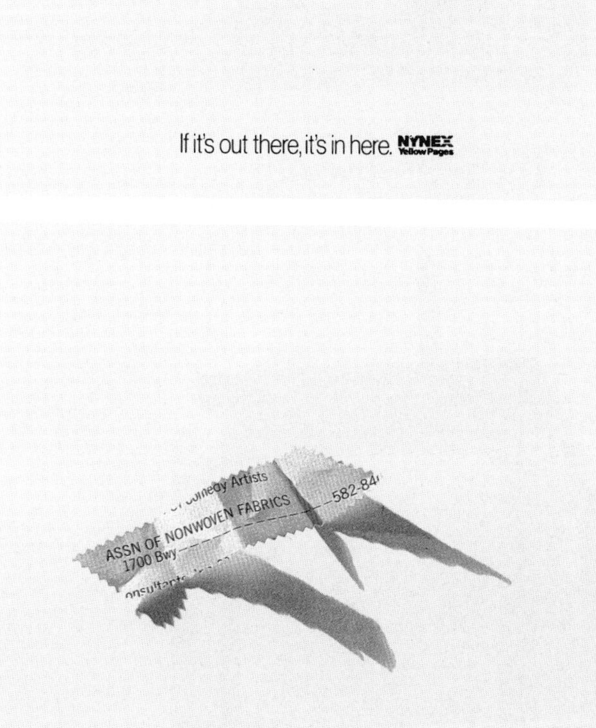

632
Art Director: Marty Weiss
Photographer: Charles Purvis
Writer: Robin Raj
Creative Director: Bill Hamilton
Client: NYNEX Yellow Pages
Agency: Chiat/Day Inc., New York
Account Management: Amy Saypol,
Melissa Bernhardt

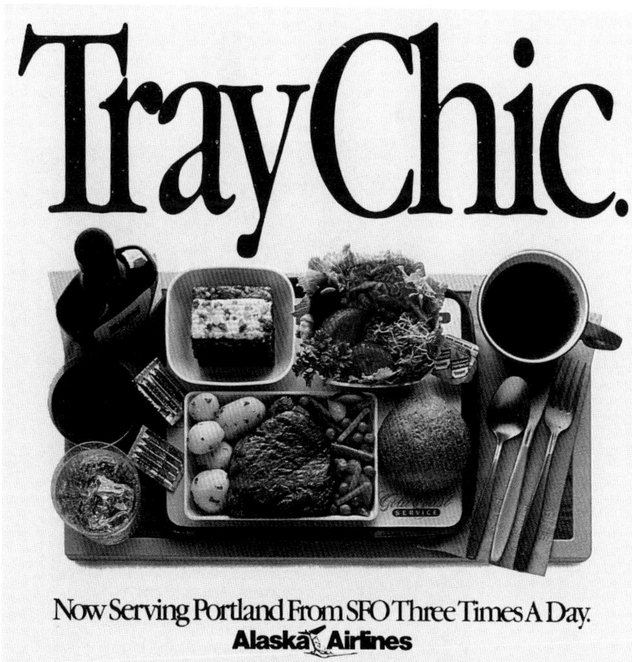

633
Art Director: Clifford Goodenough
Photographer: Stewart Tilger
Writer: Steve Sandoz
Creative Director: Ron Sandilands
Client: Alaska Airlines
Agency: Livingston & Co.

634
Art Director: Steve Thursby
Photographer: Philip Gallard
Writer: Allan Kazmer
Creative Director: Allan Kazmer
Client: Levi Strauss
Agency: DDB Needham Worldwide Advertising

635
Art Director: Robin Smith
Designer: Robin Smith
Photographer: Evan Cohen
Writer: Glen Bentley
Creative Director: Glen Bentley
Client: The Babe Ruth Museum
Agency: VanSant Dugdale

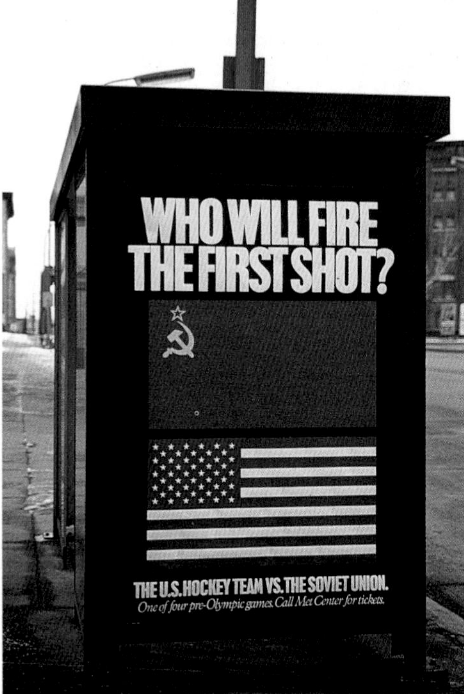

636
Art Director: Bob Brihn
Designer: Bob Brihn
Writer: Jamie Barrett
Creative Director: Tom McElligott
Client: U.S. Olympic Hockey Team
Agency: Fallon McElligott

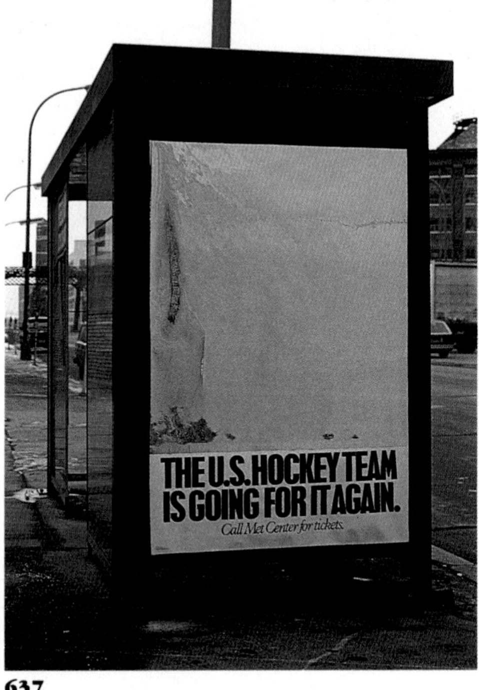

637
Art Director: Bob Brihn
Designer: Bob Brihn
Writer: Jamie Barrett
Creative Director: Tom McElligott
Client: U.S. Olympic Hockey Team
Agency: Fallon McElligott

638
Art Director: Leif Nielsen
Photographer: Ian Campbell
Writer: Steve Conover
Creative Director: Allan Kazmer
Client: Chieftain Products Inc.
Agency: DDB Needham Worldwide Advertising

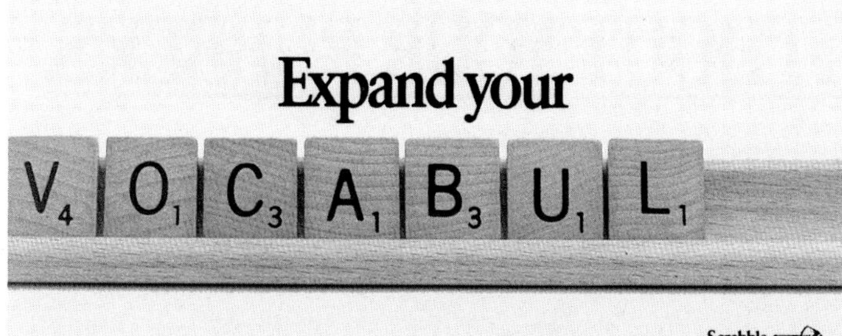

639
Art Director: Leif Nielsen
Photographer: Ian Campbell
Writer: Steve Conover
Creative Director: Allan Kazmer
Client: Chieftain Products Inc.
Agency: DDB Needham Worldwide Advertising

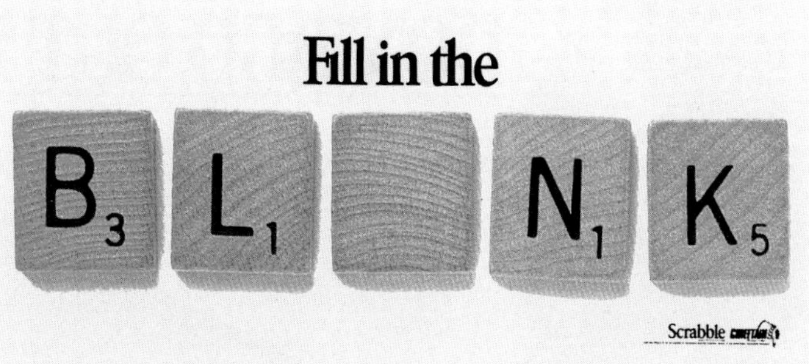

640
Art Director: Leif Nielsen
Photographer: Ian Campbell
Writer: Steve Conover
Creative Director: Allan Kazmer
Client: Chieftain Products Inc.
Agency: DDB Needham Worldwide Advertising

641
Art Director: Tom Lichtenheld
Designer: Tom Lichtenheld
Photographer: Kent Severson
Writer: Rod Kilpatrick
Creative Director: Tom McElligott
Client: The Wall Street Journal
Agency: Fallon McElligott

642
Art Director: Charles Abrams
Photographer: Paccione
Writer: Jennifer Brooke
Creative Director: Charles Abrams
Client: NYC Department of Health
Agency: Saatchi & Saatchi DFS Compton

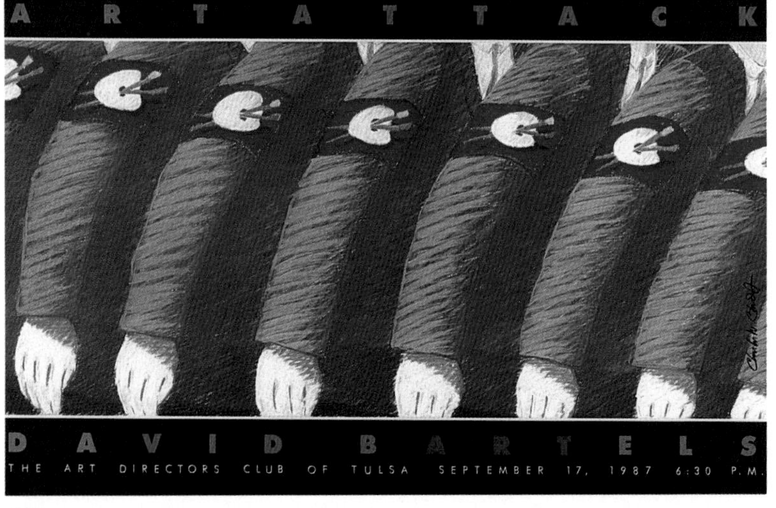

643
Art Director: David Bartels
Designer: Brian Barclay
Illustrator/Artist: Charles Blood
Writer: Cathy Mataloni
Creative Director: David Bartels
Client: The Art Directors Club of Tulsa
Agency: Bartels & Carstens Inc.

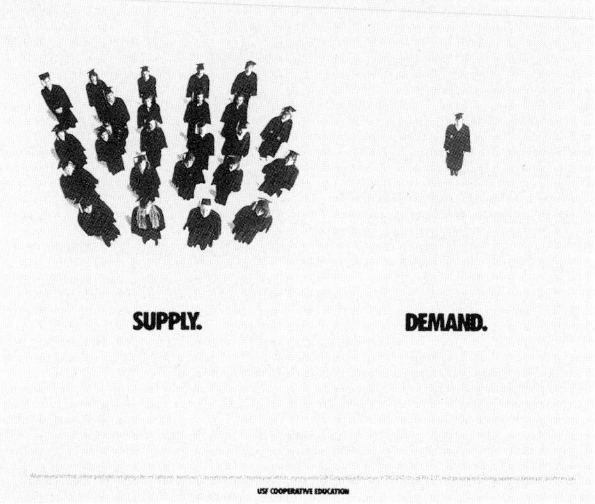

644
Art Director: Michael Wilde, Jim Hill
Photographer: Dick Dickenson
Writer: Michael Wilde, Jim Hill
Creative Director: Ken Bernhardt
Client: Univ. of S. Florida, Coop. Educ. Dept.
Agency: Benito Advertising

645
Art Director: Frederick Murrell
Designer: Karen L. MacGeraughty
Photographer: William Keyser
Writer: Beverly G. Evans
Client: Corning Security Dept.
Design Firm: Corning Corporate Design
Publisher: Upstate Litho

647
Art Director: Craig Tanimoto
Photographer: Joe Lampi
Writer: Dick Thomas
Creative Director: Bert Gardner
Client: SafeRide, Boy Scouts
Agency: Bozell, Jacobs, Kenyon & Eckhardt

646
Art Director: Craig Tanimoto
Photographer: Joe Lampi
Writer: Dick Thomas
Creative Director: Bert Gardner
Client: SafeRide, Boy Scouts
Agency: Bozell, Jacobs, Kenyon & Eckhardt

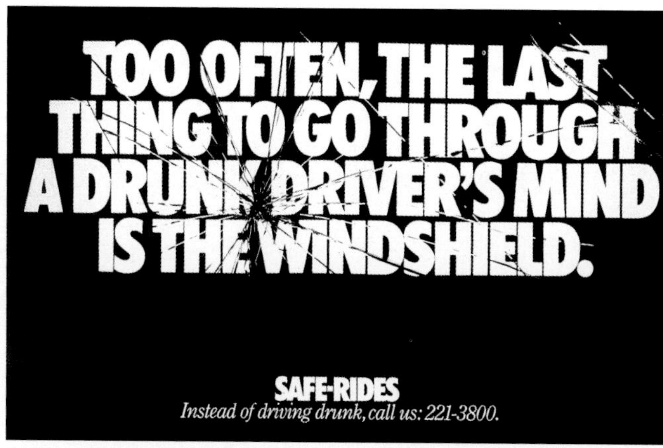

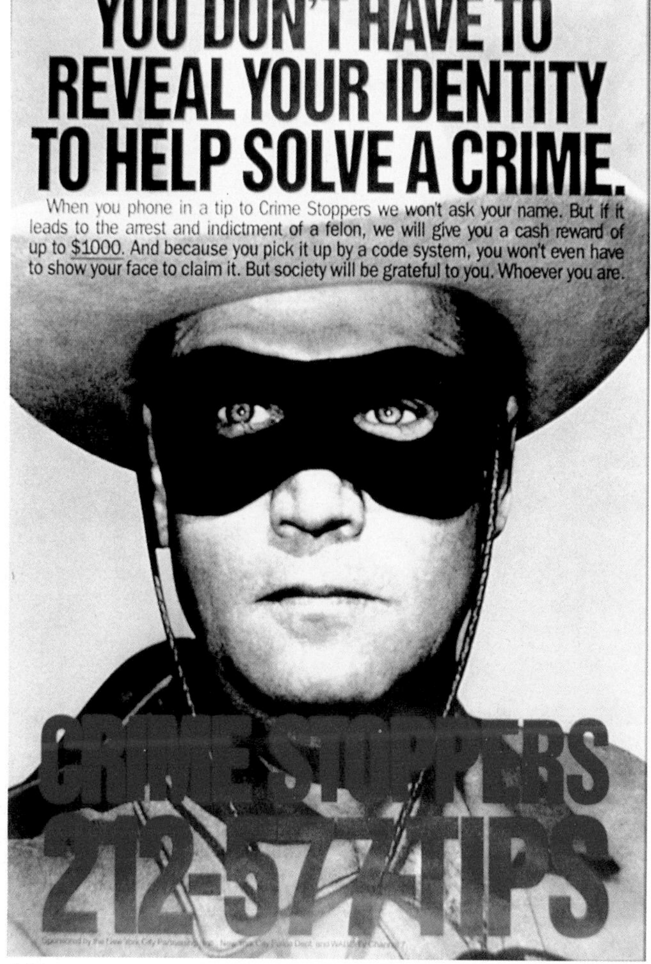

648
Art Director: John Danza
Writer: Frank Fleizach
Client: NYC Partnership, Crimestoppers
Agency: HDM, Dawson, Johns and Black

649

Art Director: Jim Brock
Designer: Jim Brock
Photographer: Bob Jones, Jr.
Writer: John Brockenbrough
Client: Richmond Police Dept.
Agency: Finnegan & Agee

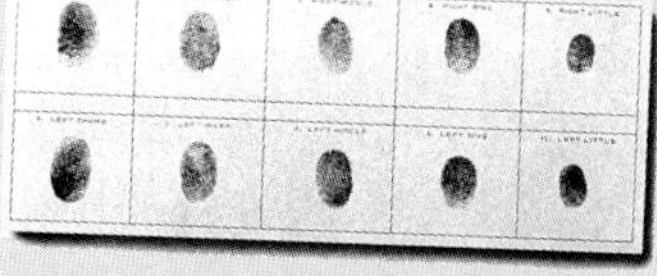

Locating a missing child can be difficult enough without having to worry about accurate identification. And the fact is, there's no more precise method for identifying your child than through fingerprints. Right now fingerprinting is available free. For more information, call the Richmond Bureau of Police, Police Community Services, at 780-1632. We're doing everything we can to ensure the safety of Richmond's children. But we can always use a hand.

THE RICHMOND POLICE

650

Art Director: Jim Mountjoy
Photographer: Jon Silla
Writer: E. L. Jones
Client: Charlotte Symphony
Agency: Loeffler, Ketchum, Mountjoy

Connecticut Special Olympics

Volunteers make the difference

Connecticut Special Olympics
June 19-21, 1987
University of Connecticut, Storrs

A unique program for people with mental retardation, their families and friends

The people of United Technologies are proud to be part of Special Olympics

651

Art Director: Robert Appleton
Designer: Robert Appleton
Client: United Technologies Corp.
Printer: Allied Printing Services
Typographer: Typographic House

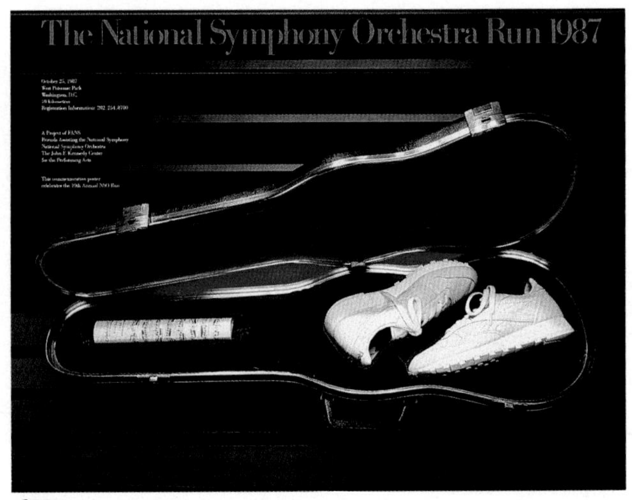

652

Art Director: Kathleen Wilmes Herring
Designer: Kathleen Wilmes Herring
Photographer: Earl Zubkoff
Illustrator/Artist: Cindy Williams DiPalma
Creative Director: Kathleen Wilmes Herring
Client: National Symphony Orchestra, JFK Center
Design Firm: Yankee Doodles
Production Manager: Mark H. Lakefish

653
Art Director: Pamela J. Shanholtzer
Illustrator/Artist: Pamela J. Shanholtzer
Client: Visiting Nurse Association
Design Firm: Robin Shepherd Studios Inc.

654
Art Director: Richard Danne
Designer: Richard Danne, Reid Martin
Photographer: Jim Barber
Writer: Loretta Keane
Creative Director: Richard Danne
Client: Fashion Institute of Technology
Design Firm: Richard Danne & Associates Inc.

655
Art Director: Eric Boelts, Jackson Boelts
Designer: Jackson Boelts, Eric Boelts
Illustrator/Artist: Jackson Boelts
Client: Tucson 20/30 Club
Design Firm: Boelts Bros. Design
Typographer: Arizona Lithographers

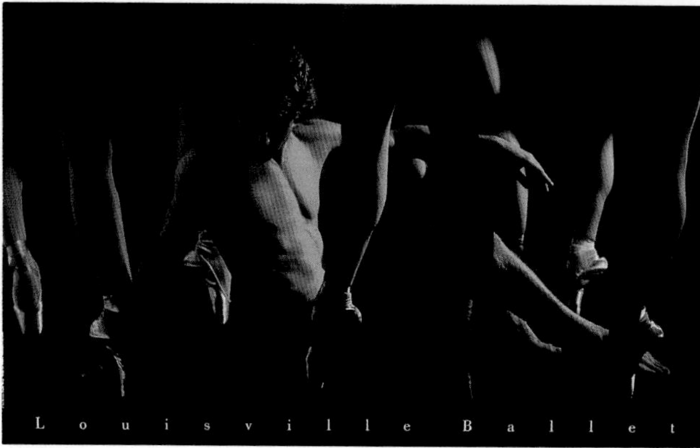

656
Art Director: Ken Herndon
Designer: Ken Herndon
Photographer: Craig Guyon
Client: Louisville Ballet
Design Firm: Ken Herndon Graphic Design

657
Art Director: Burkey Belser
Photographer: Rick McCleary
Illustrator/Artist: Burkey Belser
Client: Filmfest DC

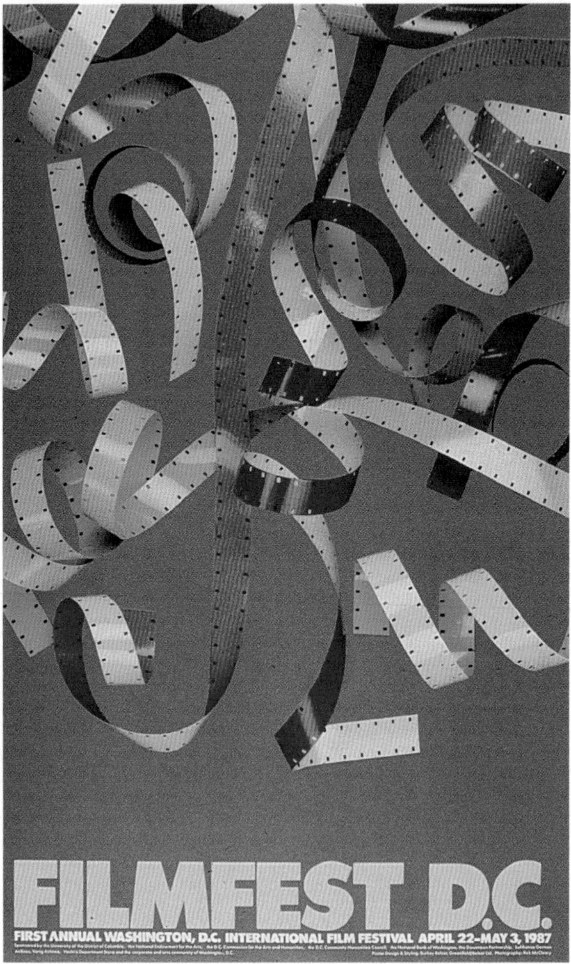

658
Art Director: Beth Ann Knisely
Illustrator/Artist: Joe Krause
Creative Director: Beth Ann Knisely
Client: Detroit New Center Lions Club
Design Firm: Colorpointe Design Inc.
Typography: The Typocraft Co.

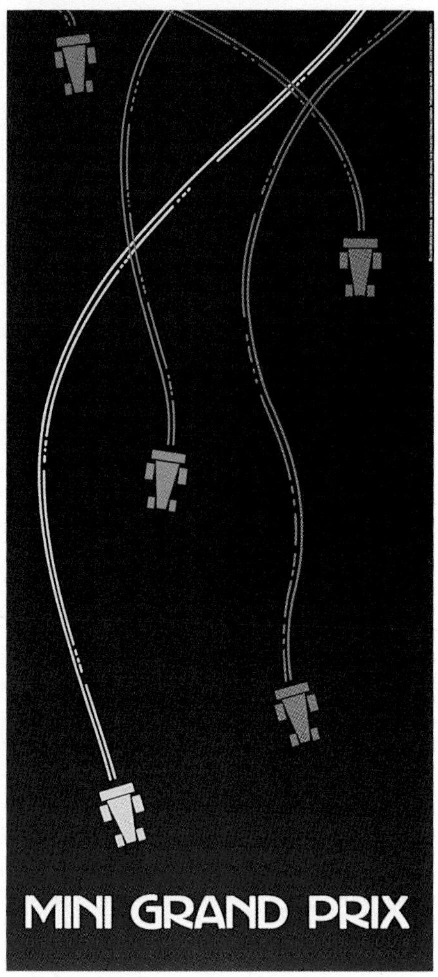

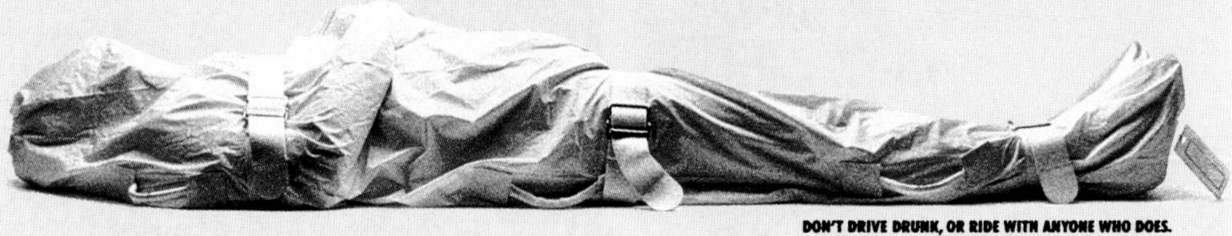

659
Art Director: David Goodnight, Andrew Hirsch
Writer: David Goodnight, Andrew Hirsch
Creative Director: Andrew Langer
Agency: Lowe Marschalk Inc.

660
Art Director: Chuck Anderson
Photographer: Rick Dublin
Writer: Jarl Olsen
Creative Director: Tom McElligott
Client: Harry Singh's
Agency: Fallon McElligott

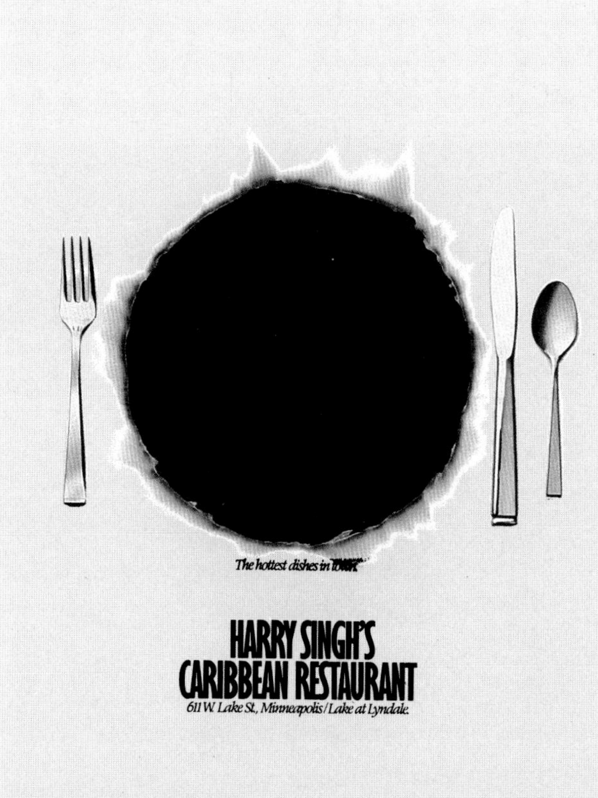

661
Art Director: David Fox
Photographer: Rick Dublin
Writer: Jerry Fury
Creative Director: Jac Coverdale
Client: YMCA
Agency: Clarity, Coverdale, Rueff

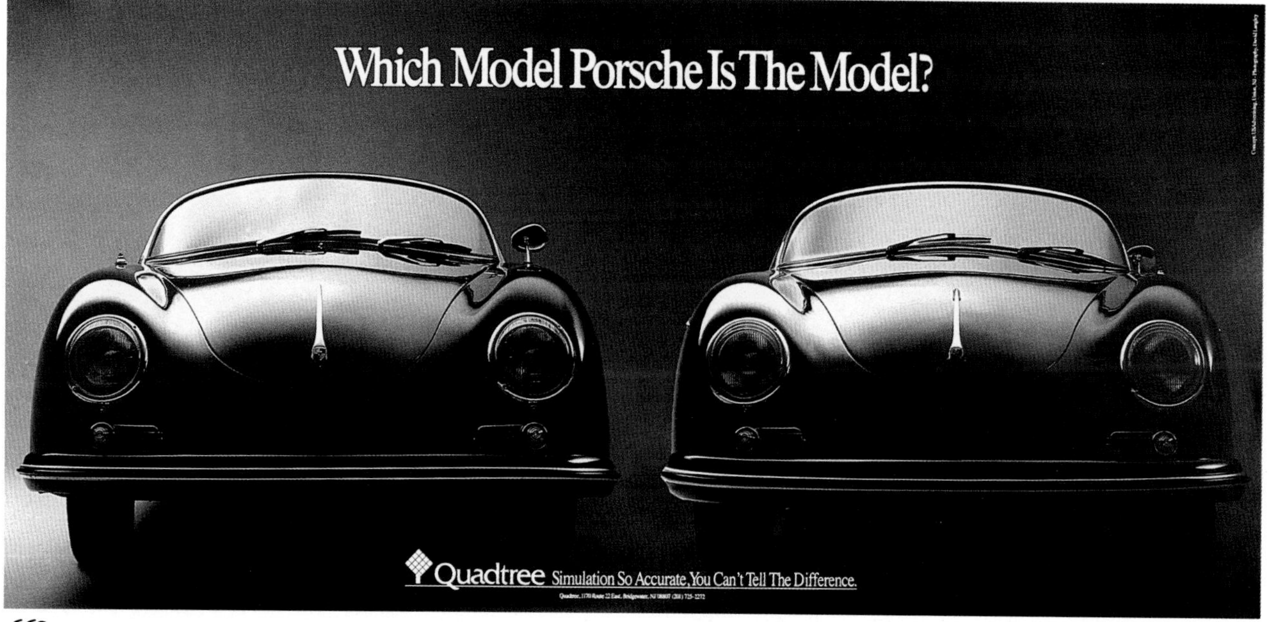

662
Art Director: Rick Paynter
Designer: Rick Paynter
Photographer: David Langley
Writer: Gary Watson
Creative Director: Gary Watson
Client: Quadtree
Agency: Poppe Tyson Inc.

663
Art Director: David Fox
Photographer: Rick Dublin
Writer: Jerry Fury
Creative Director: Jac Coverdale
Client: YMCA
Agency: Clarity, Coverdale, Rueff

664
Art Director: Alan Urban
Designer: Sharon Fisher
Illustrator/Artist: Alan Urban
Design Firm: Urban, Taylor & Associates

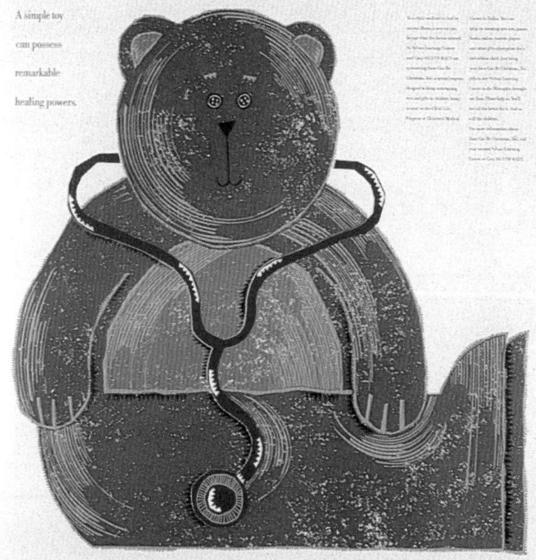

665
Art Director: Ron Sullivan
Designer: Darrel Kolosta, Willie Baronet
Illustrator/Artist: Darrel Kolosta
Writer: Scott Simmons
Creative Director: Ron Sullivan, Mark Perkins
Client: KQZY-105.3 FM, Dallas
Design Firm: Sullivan Perkins

666
Art Director: James Cross
Illustrator/Artist: Rex Peteet
Client: Simpson Paper Co.
Agency: Cross & Associates
Design Firm: Sibley/Peteet Design

667
Art Director: David Bender
Photographer: Gil Cope
Writer: Tom Cunniff
Creative Director: David Bender
Client: Gates
Agency: Janklow Bender

NO OTHER GLOVE COMPANY HAS THE GUTS TO HANG THIS POSTER.

Created from the same plastic used by NASA, our DELRIN® Snap and D Ring is virtually indestructible. Removability eliminates dangerous dangling clips.

DRYLINE™ lining, a new miracle fabric from the makers of Gore-Tex,® actively draws moisture off the skin, transferring it through the Gore-Tex® membrane for quick evaporation.

A GORE-TEX® membrane allows perspiration vapor to escape while preventing the passage of moisture into the glove.

Gates exclusive high density rubberized palm patch of Tuffgrip II™ provides a non-skid no slip surface that works like a vice grip on your ski pole.

A CORDURA® Nylon blend, Ambush® Cloth is the most durable yet flexible shell material available today.

With its millions of microscopic air pockets, THERMOLITE® insulation provides maximum warmth with minimal thickness, and it's virtually crushproof.

Gates

668
Art Director: Bob Corum
Designer: Bob Corum
Illustrator/Artist: Bob Corum
Creative Director: Michael Kelley
Client: Kentucky Derby Festival Inc.
Agency: The Courier-Journal, Promotion Dept.

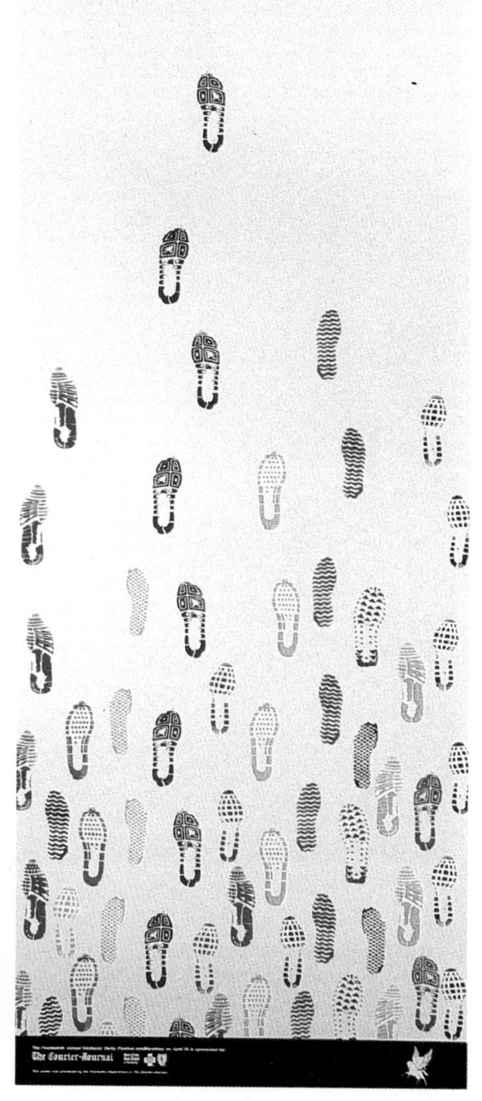

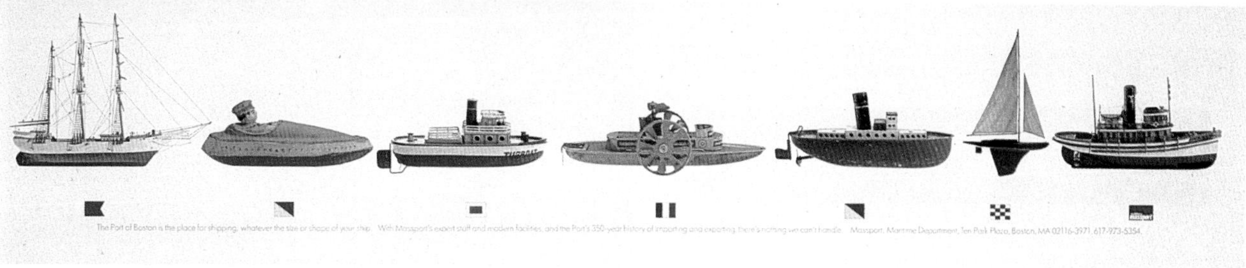

669
Art Director: Gary Greenberg
Designer: Laura Dellovo
Photographer: Bruno Joachim
Illustrator/Artist: Bob Aiello
Writer: Judy Friedman
Creative Director: Gary Greenberg
Client: Massport, Maritime Department
Agency: Rossin, Greenberg, Seronick & Hill

670
Art Director: John Doyle
Designer: John Doyle
Photographer: Myron
Writer: Edward Boches
Client: Advertising Club of Greater Boston
Agency: Mullen

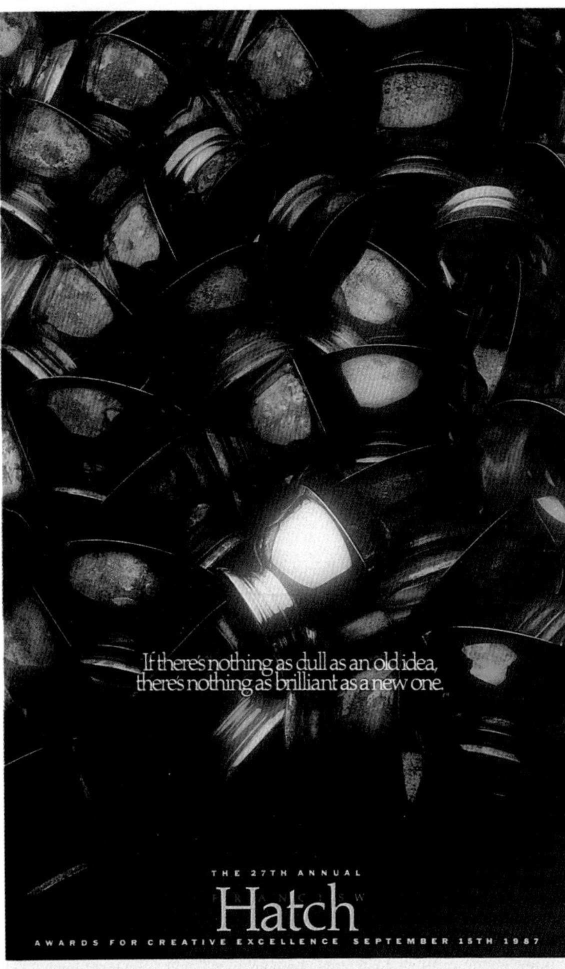

671
Art Director: Seymour Chwast
Designer: Seymour Chwast
Illustrator/Artist: Seymour Chwast
Client: Advertising Women of New York,
Ad Week
Design Firm: The Push Pin Group

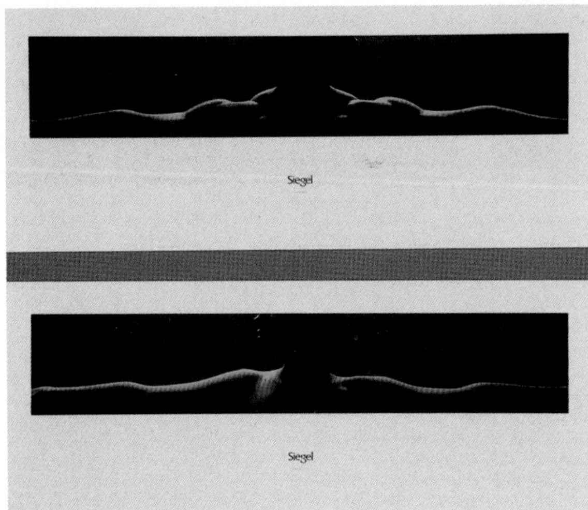

672
Art Director: Dave Page
Designer: Dave Siegel
Photographer: Dave Siegel
Client: Siegel Photographic Inc.
Printer: Woods Lithographics

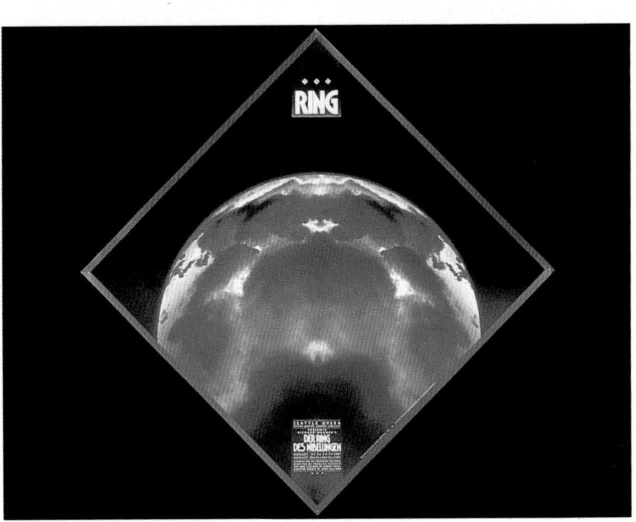

673
Art Director: Paul Matthaeus
Photographer: Dale DeGabriele, DeGabriele Photography
Creative Director: Cynthia Hartwig
Client: The Seattle Opera
Agency: Sharp Hartwig Advertising Inc.
Printing: The Boeing Co.

674
Art Director: Jeanette Carrell
Photographer: Rick Dublin
Writer: Katie Franson
Creative Director: Jack Supple, Frank Haggerty
Client: Cricket Theatre
Agency: Carmichael Lynch
Agency Producer: Barb Knoche

675
Art Director: Cheryl Heller
Designer: Cheryl Heller, Nick Kaldenbaugh
Photographer: Annie Leibovitz
Writer: Joe Lovering
Creative Director: Cheryl Heller
Client: Reebok
Agency: Heller Breene

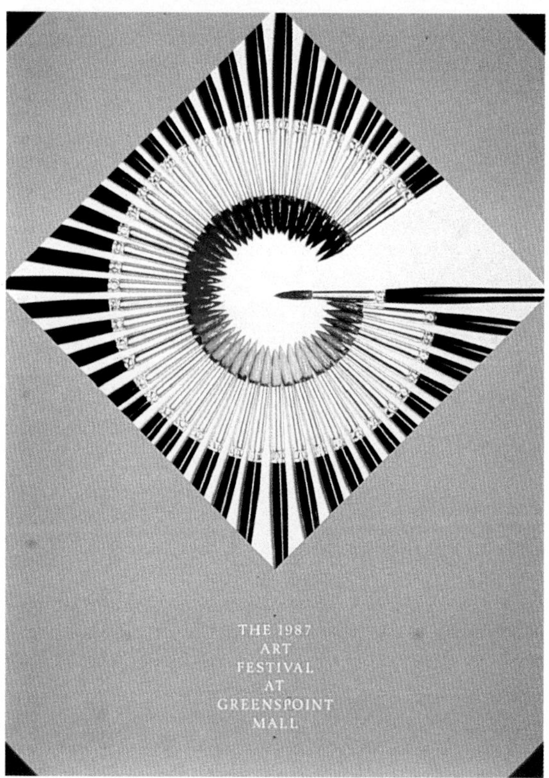

676
Art Director: Chris Hill, David Lerch
Designer: David Lerch
Photographer: Gary Faye
Client: Greenspoint Mall
Agency: Gallagher Advertising
Design Firm: Hill/A Marketing Design Group

677
Art Director: Jeff Jones
Designer: Jeff Jones
Photographer: Mark LaFavor
Writer: John Jarvis
Client: Art Directors/Copywriters Club
Agency: Ruhr/Paragon Inc.

678
Art Director: Sheila McCaffery
Designer: Sheila McCaffery
Creative Director: William McCaffery
Client: Art Directors Club
Agency: McCaffery & Ratner Inc.

679
Art Director: John Vitro
Photographer: David Kramer
Writer: John Robertson
Engraver: Knapp Colour
Lithographer: The Ink Spot

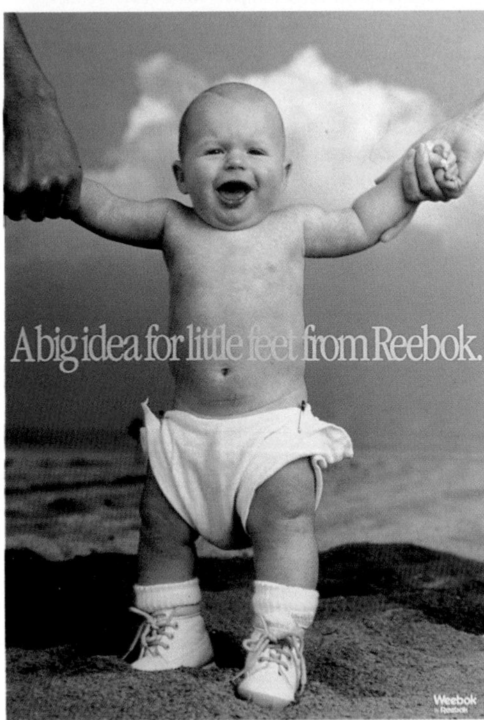

680
Art Director: Cheryl Heller
Designer: Cheryl Heller, Nick Kaldenbaugh
Photographer: Annie Leibovitz
Writer: Joe Lovering
Creative Director: Cheryl Heller
Client: Reebok
Agency: Heller Breene

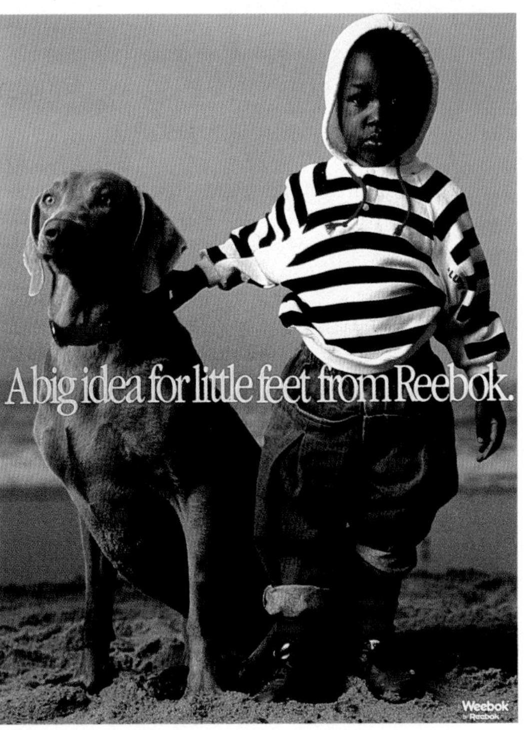

681
Art Director: Cheryl Heller
Designer: Cheryl Heller, Nick Kaldenbaugh
Photographer: Annie Leibovitz
Writer: Joe Lovering
Creative Director: Cheryl Heller
Client: Reebok
Agency: Heller Breene

682
Art Director: Gary Gukeisen
Designer: Gary Gukeisen
Illustrator/Artist: Eric Larson, Art Farm
Creative Director: Roger Yost, Gary Gukeisen
Client: Jantzen Inc.
Agency: Jantzen Ad Dept. Inc.
Design Firm: Art Farm

683
Art Director: Toni Eckmayer
Designer: Bob Buchanan
Illustrator/Artist: John Andrews
Writer: Toni Eckmayer
Creative Director: Toni Eckmayer
Client: EconoPrint
Agency: Zillman Advertising & Marketing Inc.

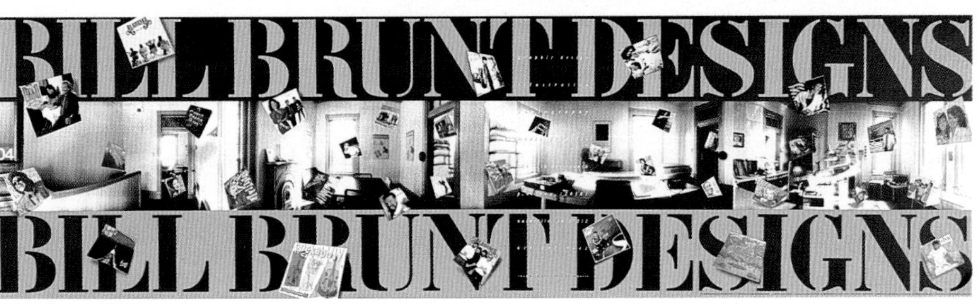

684
Art Director: Bill Brunt
Designer: Bill Brunt
Photographer: Mark Tucker
Illustrator/Artist: Charlie McCallen
Engraver: Harris Graphics

685
Art Director: Scott Ray
Designer: Scott Ray
Writer: Scott Ray
Client: Peterson & Co.
Design Firm: Peterson & Co.

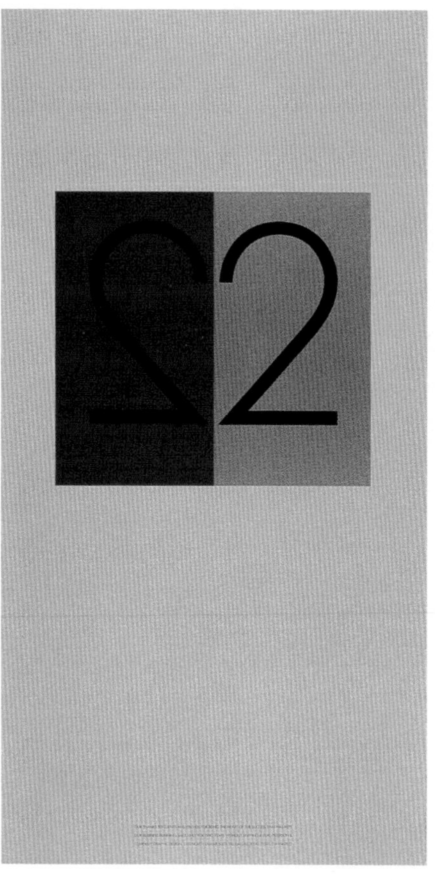

686
Art Director: Martha Lipton, Mark Gerard
Photographer: Simo Neri
Creative Director: Martha Lipton
Client: Avner Eisenberg
Design Firm: M. Lipton Design
Public Relations: Stephen Adler

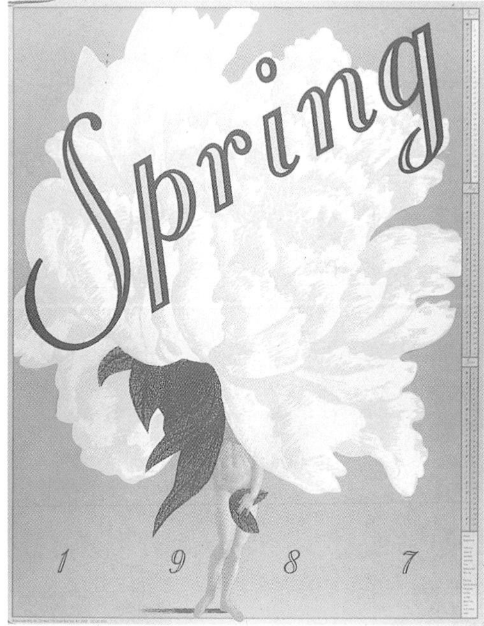

687
Art Director: Paula Scher
Designer: Paula Scher
Illustrator/Artist: Paula Scher
Client: Ambassador Arts
Design Firm: Koppel & Scher

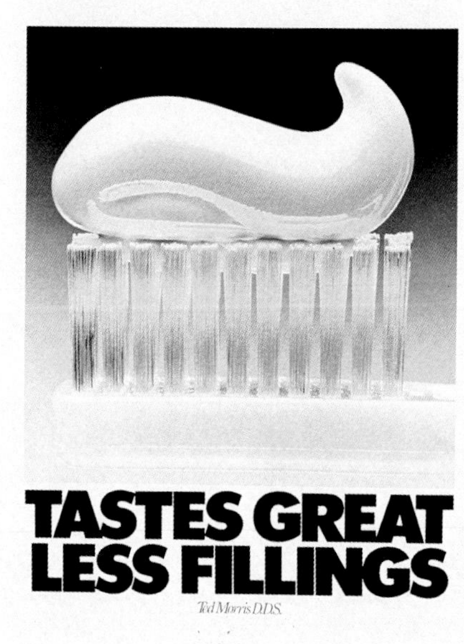

688
Art Director: Jim Mountjoy
Photographer: Jon Silla
Writer: Don Jeffries
Client: Ted Morris, D.D.S.
Agency: Ads-to-Go

689
Art Director: Michael Schwab
Designer: Michael Schwab
Illustrator/Artist: Michael Schwab
Creative Director: Michael Schwab
Client: Perkins Shearer, Denver Symphony
Design Firm: Michael Schwab Design
Printer: Seriphics

690
Art Director: Chris Poisson
Designer: Dino Paul
Photographer: Jeff Noble
Writer: Marianne Curtis
Client: Phoenix Ad Club
Agency: Blood, Sweat & Beers
Printer: Woods Lithographics

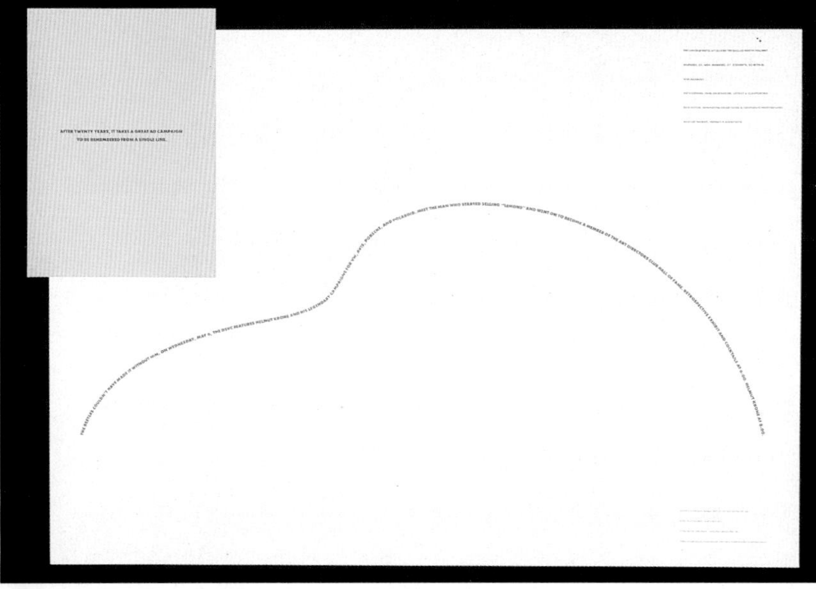

691
Art Director: Ed Zahra, Tommy Lout
Designer: Kent Anderson, Michael Arthur
Illustrator/Artist: Michael Arthur
Writer: Tracy Spinney, Kent Anderson
Client: Dallas Society of Visual Communication
Design Firm: Zahra/Lout Advertising Designers Inc.

692

Art Director: Craig Frazier
Designer: Craig Frazier
Illustrator/Artist: Craig Frazier
Client: Simpson Paper Co.
Design Firm: Frazier Design

693

Art Director: David Carter,
Sanio Waitak Lai
Designer: Sanio Waitak Lai
Illustrator/Artist: Sanio Waitak Lai
Design Firm: David Carter Design
Printer: Spruiell Printing Co.

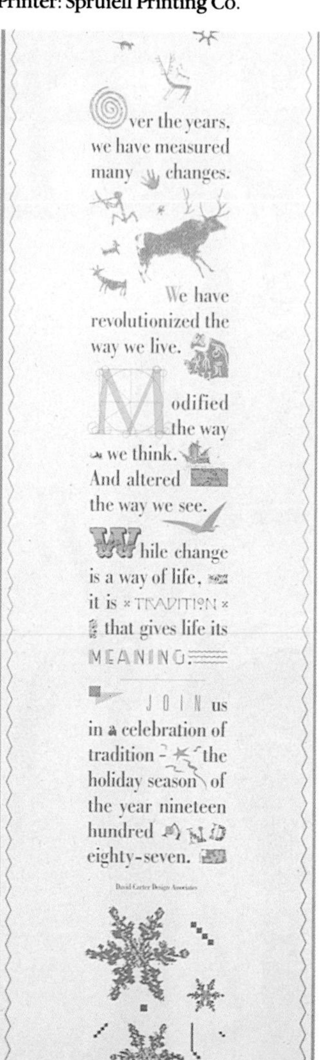

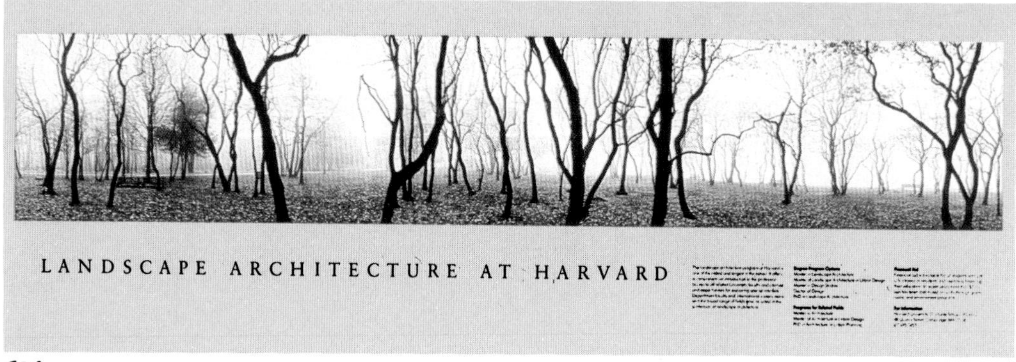

694

Art Director: Clifford Selbert
Designer: Lynn Riddle
Photographer: Jenny Lawton Grassl
Client: Harvard Univ. Graduate School of Design
Design Firm: Clifford Selbert Design Inc.

695

Art Director: Alan Peckolick
Illustrator/Artist: Kinuko Craft
Design Firm: Peckolick & Partners

697

Art Director: Susan Turner
Designer: Susan Turner
Photographer: Jeff Coolidge
Client: Harvard Univ. Department of Music
Design Firm: Clifford Selbert Design Inc.

696

Art Director: Kathy Izard
Illustrator/Artist: Gary Palmer
Writer: E. L. Jones
Creative Director: Jim Mountjoy
Client: North Carolina Zoo
Agency: Loeffler, Ketchum, Mountjoy

698

Art Director: Chris Hill, SWTSU Design Class 1987
Designer: Chris Hill, SWTSU Design Class 1987
Photographer: Gary Faye
Client: Southwest Texas State University
Design Firm: Hill/A Marketing Design Firm

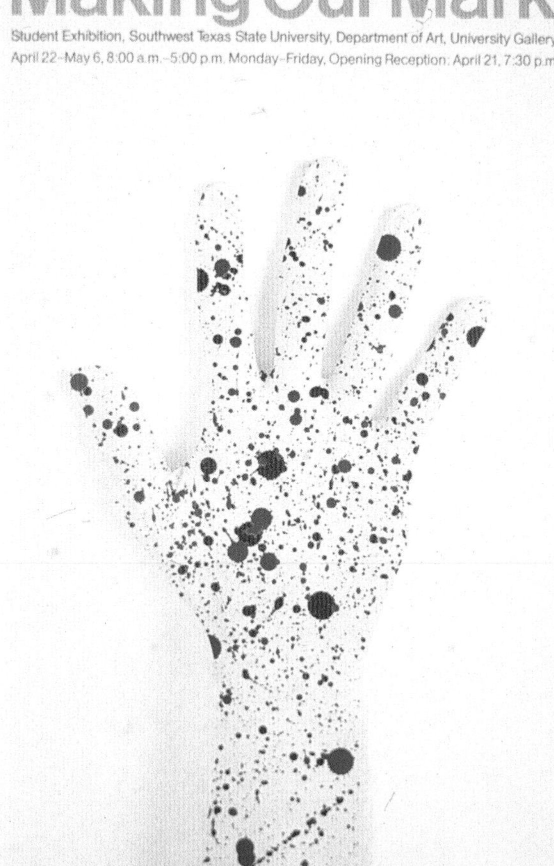

699

Art Director: Haley Johnson
Designer: Haley Johnson
Illustrator/Artist: Haley Johnson
Client: Cocolezzone
Design Firm: The Duffy Design Group

700

Art Director: Stavros Cosmopulos
Designer: Stavros Cosmopulos
Writer: Stavros Cosmopulos
Creative Director: Stavros Cosmopulos
Client: Arrow Composition
Agency: Cosmopulos, Crowley & Daly Inc.
Design Firm: Cosmopulos, Crowley & Daly Inc.
Publication: Direct Mail
Typesetter: Arrow Composition

701

Art Director: McRay Magleby
Designer: McRay Magleby
Illustrator/Artist: McRay Magleby
Client: Brigham Young University
Design Firm: BYU Graphics
Typographer: Jonathan Skousen
Silk Screener: Rory Robinson

702

Art Director: Charles Kreloff
Designer: Charles Kreloff
Illustrator/Artist: Tom Lulevitch
Writer: Michael Cader
Editor: Michael Cader
Client: Peter Workman
Publisher: Workman Publishing
Production Manager: Wayne Kirn

703

Art Director: Charles S. Anderson
Designer: Charles S. Anderson
Illustrator/Artist: Charles S. Anderson, Lynn Schulte
Writer: Chuck Carlson
Client: French Paper
Design Firm: The Duffy Design Group

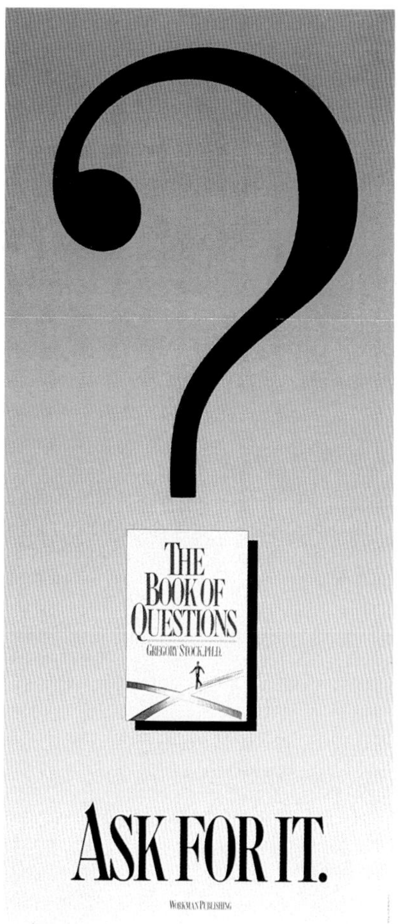

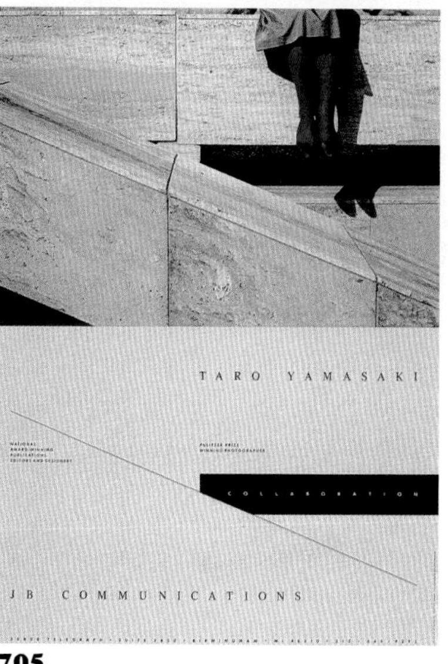

704

Art Director: Sandra Thomson
Designer: Sandra Thomson
Illustrator/Artist: Miles Lewis
Writer: Jack Dillard
Creative Director: Jack Dillard
Client: Charlotte Ad Club
Design Firm: Jeff Gold Design

705

Art Director: Bonnie Detloff Zielinski
Designer: Bonnie Detloff Zielinski
Photographer: Taro Yamasaki
Editor: Janet Burke
Creative Director: Bonnie Detloff Zielinski
Client: JB Communications
Agency: JB Communications
Publisher: JB Communications
Printer: Signet Printing

706
Art Director: Mitchell Boyd
Designer: Mitchell Boyd, Jeff Matz
Photographer: Bettman Archive
Illustrator/Artist: Mitchell Boyd
Writer: Ron McQuien
Client: Howard Johnson, Southeast Region
Agency: Gilpin, Peyton & Pierce

707
Art Director: Charles S. Anderson, Joe Duffy
Designer: Charles S. Anderson, Sara Ledgard
Photographer: Gary McCoy
Illustrator/Artist: Lynn Schulte
Writer: Chuck Carlson
Client: Dorsey & Whitney
Design Firm: The Duffy Design Group

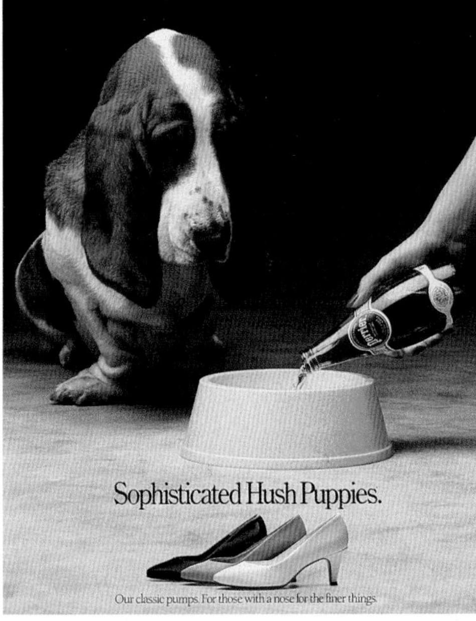

708
Art Director: Bob Barrie
Designer: Bob Barrie
Photographer: Rick Dublin
Writer: Jarl Olsen
Creative Director: Tom McElligott
Client: Hush Puppies
Agency: Fallon McElligott
Model: Jason

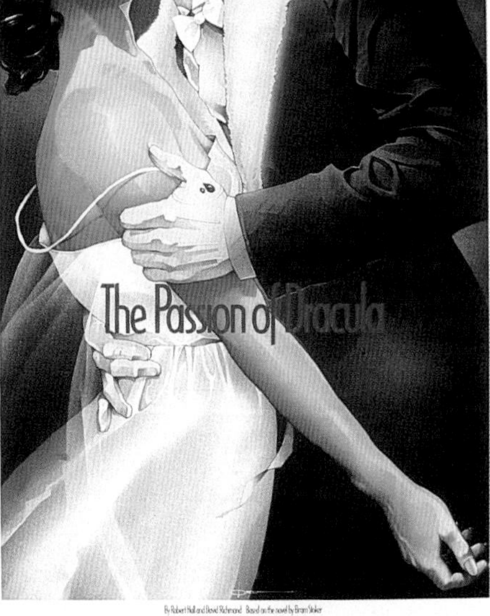

709
Art Director: Elyse Hiller-Shaw, Lee Stewart
Illustrator/Artist: Drew Rose
Creative Director: Virgil Shutze, Ron Fisher
Client: Alliance Theatre
Agency: Hutcheson Shutze

710
Art Director: Tuan Wayne Dao
Photographer: Jonathan Lennard
Client: Kashiyama
Agency: Tuan Dao Design

711
Art Director: Mark Figliulo
Writer: Andy McAfee
Creative Director: John Eding
Client: City of Chicago
Producer: Steve Wagner

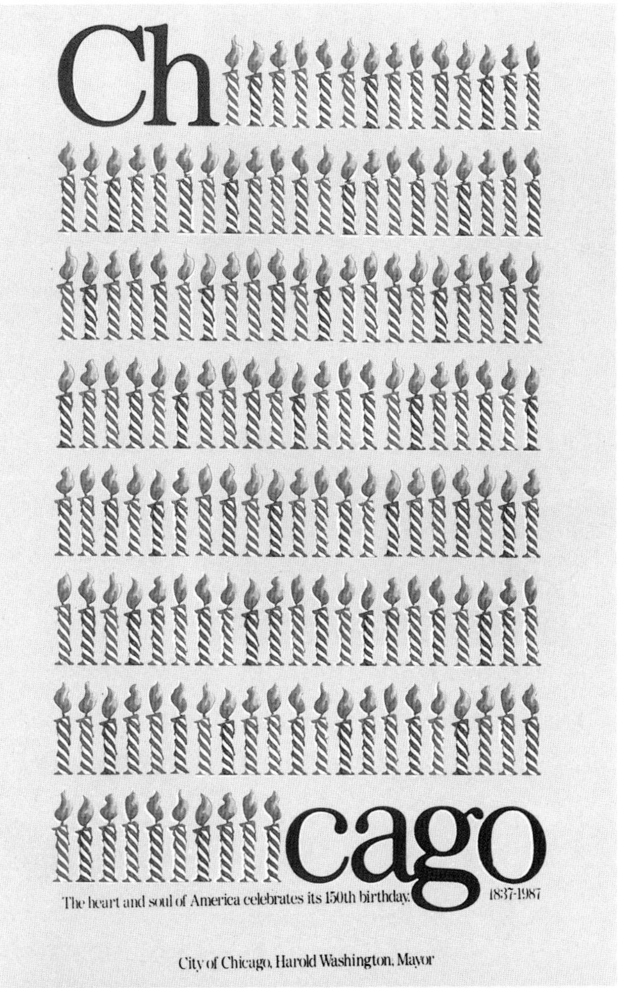

712
Art Director: Jan Rudin
Designer: Jan Rudin
Writer: David M. Bradley
Creative Director: Bob Kwait
Client: San Diego Communicating Arts Group
Agency: Phillips-Ramsey Advertising
Production: Gavin Milner

713
Art Director: Earl Cavanah
Photographer: Jerry Friedman
Writer: Larry Cadman
Creative Director: Sam Scali
Client: Nikon Inc.
Agency: Scali, McCabe, Sloves Inc.
Retoucher: Spano Roccanova

714
Art Director: Saul Bass, Art Goodman
Designer: Saul Bass, Art Goodman
Photographer: George Arakaki
Client: Harper & Row
Design Firm: Bass/Yager & Associates

715
Art Director: Frank Schulwolf
Photographer: Bettman Archive
Writer: Arthur Low
Client: Casinos Pizza Inc.
Agency: Susan Gilbert & Co., Inc.

716
Art Director: Saul Bass
Designer: Saul Bass
Illustrator/Artist: Saul Bass
Client: Napoli 99 Foundation
Design Firm: Bass/Yager & Associates

717
Art Director: Barbara Olejniczak
Designer: Barbara Olejniczak
Photographer: Michael Oldford
Client: Sotheby's

718
Art Director: Ann Rhodes
Photographer: Ann Rhodes
Writer: Dan Balazs
Creative Director: Bill Bruning
Client: HealthPlus, Spokane
Agency: Elgin Syferd

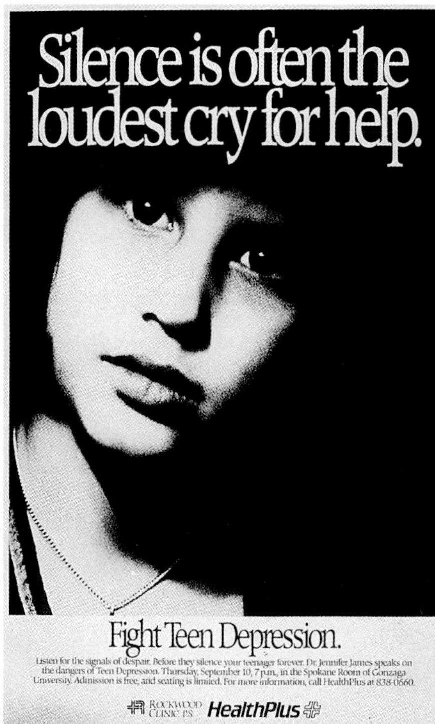

719
Art Director: Angelo Juliano
Designer: Angelo Juliano
Photographer: Ralph Masullo
Writer: Charles Kane
Client: Doug Barasch Productions
Agency: Juliano & Kane
Production: Tim McCabe

720
Art Director: John Muller
Designer: John Muller
Illustrator/Artist: Jay Henning
Creative Director: John Muller
Client: Crown Center Redevelopment Corp.
Agency: Muller & Co.
Design Firm: Muller & Co.

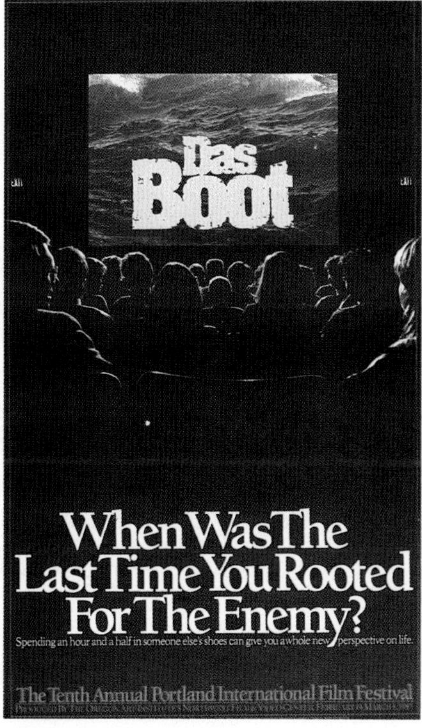

721
Art Director: Warren Eakins
Designer: Warren Eakins
Photographer: Gary Nolton
Writer: Pamela Sullivan
Creative Director: Bill Borders
Client: Oregon Art Institute
Agency: Borders, Perrin & Norrander Inc.

722
Art Director: Kent Hunter
Designer: Kent Hunter
Illustrator/Artist: April Greiman
Creative Director: Aubrey Balkind
Client: National Academy of Cable Programming
Design Firm: GBA Entertainment, The GBA Group

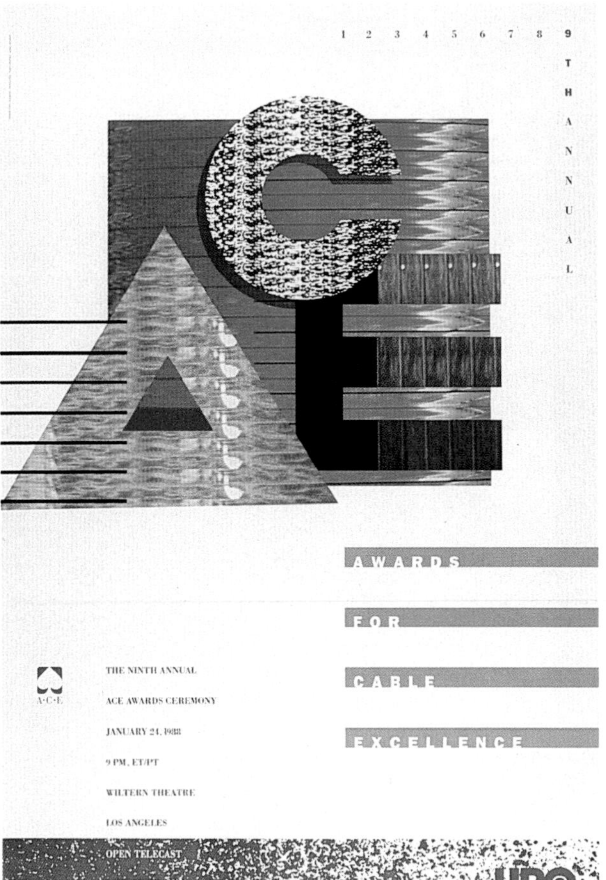

723
Art Director: Monte Dolack
Illustrator/Artist: Monte Dolack

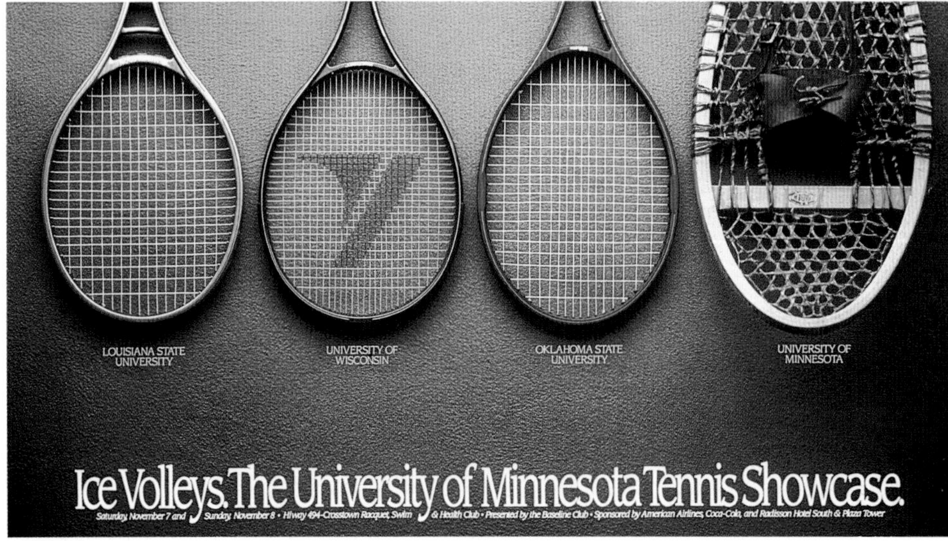

724
Art Director: Pam Conboy
Photographer: Kerry Peterson
Writer: Lyle Wedemeyer
Creative Director: Tom Weyl
Client: Univ. of Minnesota Tennis Showcase
Agency: Martin/Williams Advertising Inc.

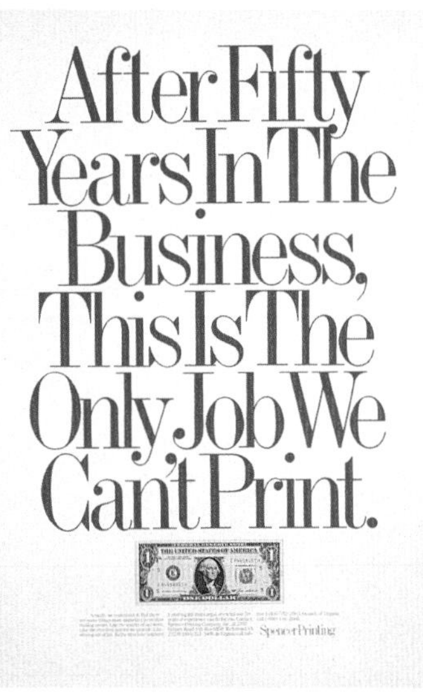

725
Art Director: Cabell Harris
Writer: Joel Jamison
Client: Spencer Printing
Agency: Lawler Ballard Advertising

726
Art Director: Mike Scricco
Illustrator/Artist: Paul Selwyn
Writer: Jack Soos
Creative Director: Mel Maffei, Don Wilson
Client: Strathmore Paper Co.
Agency: Keiler Advertising
Account Manager: Pam Williams
Printer: Allied Printing Services

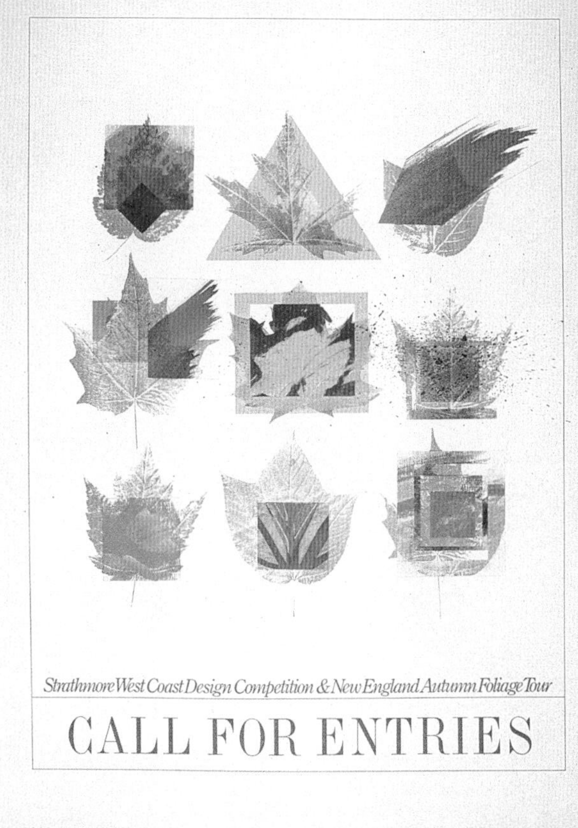

727
Art Director: Pat Gorman
Designer: Cheri Dorr
Creative Director: Pat Gorman
Client: MTV Networks
Design Firm: Manhattan Design

728
Art Director: Olga Arseniev
Designer: Olga Arseniev
Photographer: Dennis Chalkin
Writer: Evert Cilliers
Creative Director: Arnie Arlow, Peter Lubalin
Client: Anheuser Busch
Agency: TBWA Advertising Inc.

729
Art Director: Gad Romann, Barry Tannenholz, Terry Whistler, Denise DeRosiers
Photographer: Horst
Writer: Gad Romann, Barry Tannenholz
Client: Round the Clock Pantyhose
Agency: Romann & Tannenholz

730
Art Director: Mark Johnson
Designer: Mark Johnson
Photographer: Dennis Manarchy
Writer: Phil Hanft
Creative Director: Tom McElligott
Client: Lee Jeans
Agency: Fallon McElligott

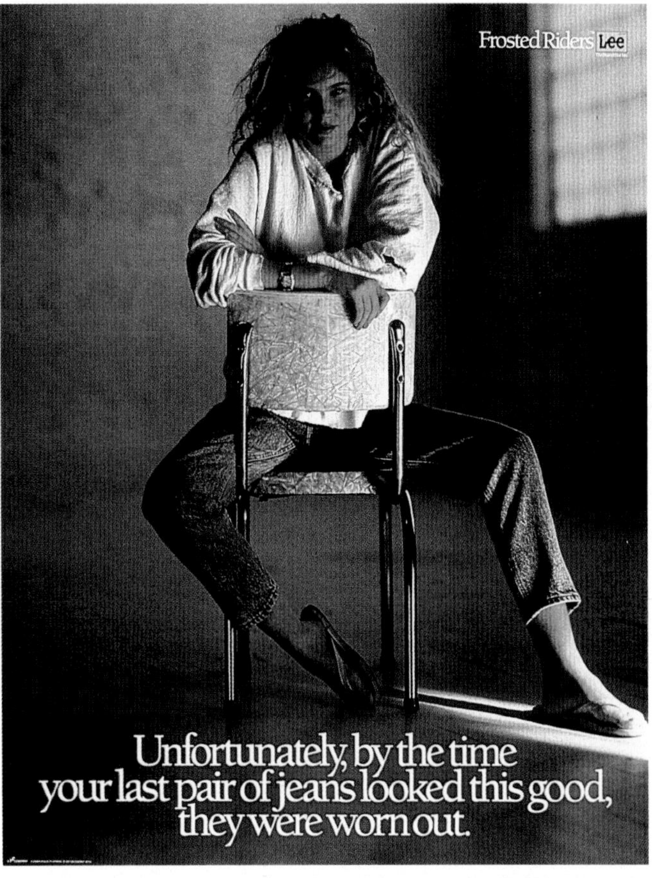

731
Art Director: Mark Johnson
Designer: Mark Johnson
Photographer: Dennis Manarchy
Writer: Phil Hanft
Creative Director: Tom McElligott
Client: Lee Jeans
Agency: Fallon McElligott

732
Art Director: Angela Dunkle
Designer: Angela Dunkle
Photographer: Rick Dublin
Writer: Jamie Barrett
Creative Director: Tom McElligott
Client: Marecek & Cairns
Agency: Fallon McElligott

733
Art Director: Houman Pirdavari
Designer: Houman Pirdavari
Photographer: Steve Umland
Writer: Tom McElligott
Creative Director: Tom McElligott
Client: Brooks
Agency: Fallon McElligott
Model: Daisy

734
Art Director: Tony Mandarino
Designer: Tony Mandarino
Photographer: Tony Mandarino
Client: Tony Mandarino
Engraver: Pioneer Moss

735
Art Director: Stephen Frykholm
Designer: Stephen Frykholm
Client: Herman Miller Inc.
Printer: Continental Iden. Prod.

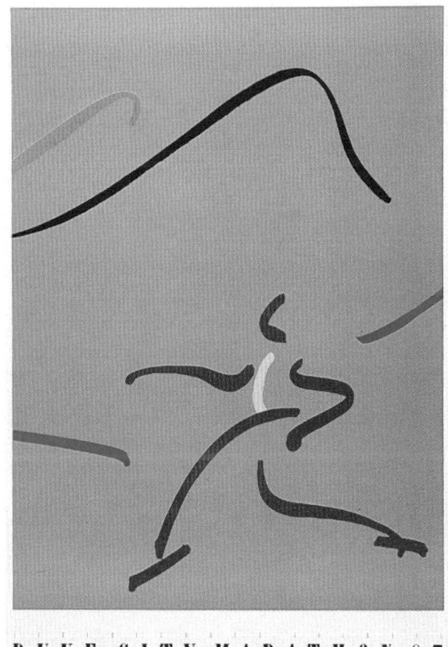

736
Art Director: Rick Vaughn
Designer: Rick Vaughn
Illustrator/Artist: Rick Vaughn
Creative Director: Rick Vaughn
Client: Duke City Marathon
Agency: Vaughn/Wedeen Creative Inc.
Design Firm: Vaughn/Wedeen Creative Inc.

737
Art Director: David Crawford
Illustrator/Artist: Scott Gustafson
Writer: Odette Arnold
Client: Piedmont Airlines
Agency: McKinney & Silver

738
Art Director: Rob Dalton
Designer: Rob Dalton
Writer: George Gier
Creative Director: Tom McElligott
Client: Coleman
Agency: Fallon McElligott

739
Art Director: Bob Brihn
Designer: Bob Brihn
Writer: Jamie Barrett
Creative Director: Tom McElligott
Client: Fallon McElligott
Agency: Fallon McElligott

740
Art Director: Mark Johnson
Designer: Mark Johnson
Photographer: Randy Miller
Writer: Bill Miller
Creative Director: Tom McElligott
Client: Lee Jeans
Agency: Fallon McElligott

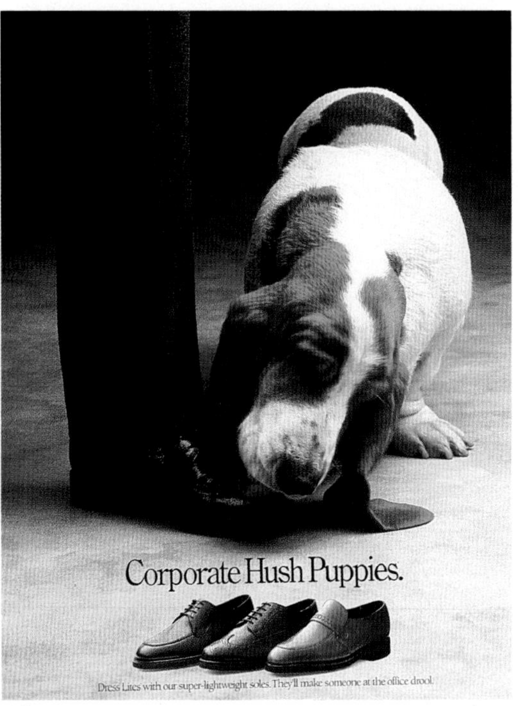

741
Art Director: Bob Barrie
Designer: Bob Barrie
Photographer: Rick Dublin
Writer: Jarl Olsen
Creative Director: Tom McElligott
Client: Hush Puppies
Agency: Fallon McElligott
Model: Jason

742
Art Director: Bob Kwait
Designer: Bob Kwait
Illustrator/Artist: Darrel Millsap
Writer: Bob Kwait
Creative Director: Bob Kwait
Client: San Diego Zoo
Agency: Phillips-Ramsey Advertising
Production Artist: Ron Van Buskirk

743
Art Director: Michael Prieve
Photographer: Richard Noble, Pete Stone
Writer: Jim Riswold
Creative Director: Dan Wieden, David Kennedy
Client: Nike Inc.
Agency: Wieden & Kennedy

Nedene. Jerseymaid's Employee of the Month.

Jerseymaid, Class of '88.

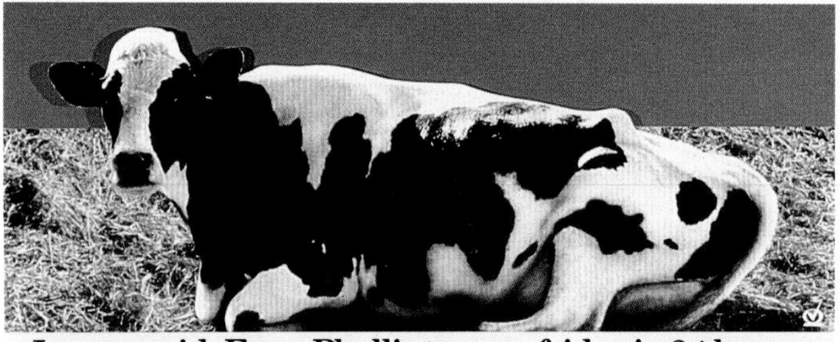

Jerseymaid. From Phyllis to your fridge in 24 hours.

744

Art Director: Betsy Nathane
Photographer: Michael Ruppert
Writer: Robert Chandler
Creative Director: Paul Keye
Client: Jerseymaid Milk Products Co.
Agency: Keye, Donna, Pearlstein

If it's out there, it's in here. NYNEX Yellow Pages

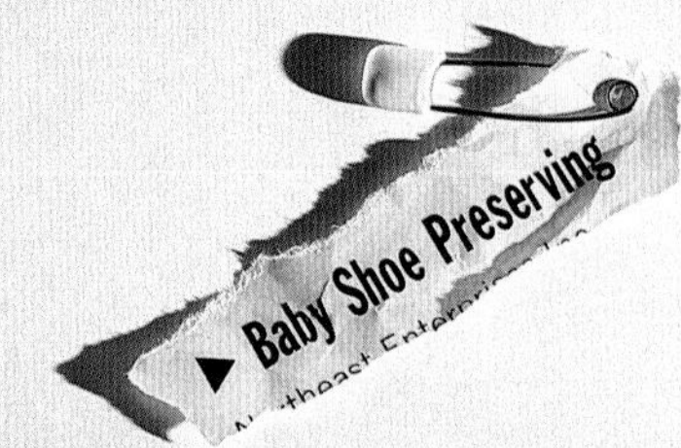

If it's out there, it's in here. NYNEX Yellow Pages

If it's out there, it's in here. NYNEX Yellow Pages

745

Art Director: Marty Weiss
Photographer: Charles Purvis
Writer: Robin Raj
Creative Director: Bill Hamilton
Client: NYNEX Yellow Pages
Agency: Chiat/Day Inc., New York
Account Management: Amy Saypol, Melissa Bernhardt

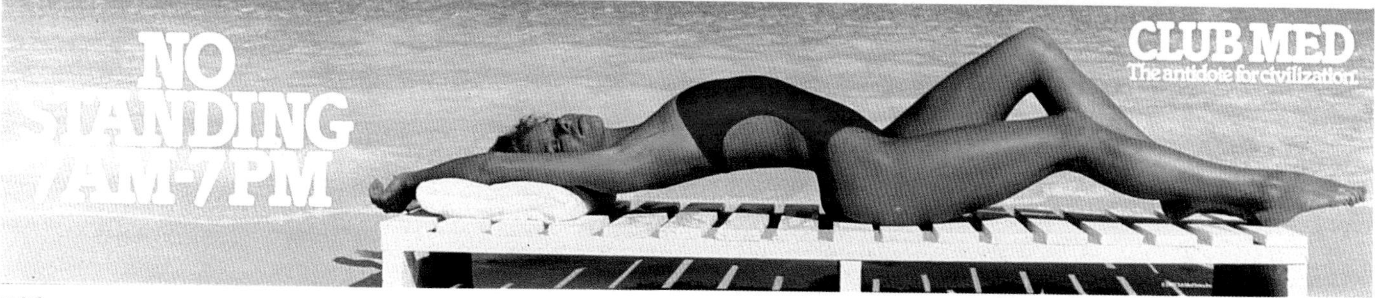

746
Art Director: Ted Shaine, Alain Briere
Photographer: Roy Volkman, Stephen Frink
Writer: Helayne Spivak
Creative Director: Ralph Ammirati
Client: Club Med Sales Inc.
Agency: Ammirati & Puris Inc.

747
Art Director: Leif Nielsen
Photographer: Ian Campbell
Writer: Steve Conover
Creative Director: Allan Kazmer
Client: Chieftain Products Inc.
Agency: DDB Needham Worldwide Advertising

Fill in the
B L N K
Scrabble

Expand your
V O C A B U L
Scrabble

748
Art Director: Steve Sweitzer
Photographer: Ben Saltzman
Writer: Jarl Olsen
Creative Director: Tom McElligott
Client: Ben Saltzman Photography
Agency: Fallon McElligott

749
Art Director: Yvonne Smith
Writer: Yvonne Smith
Agency: Ammirati & Puris Inc.

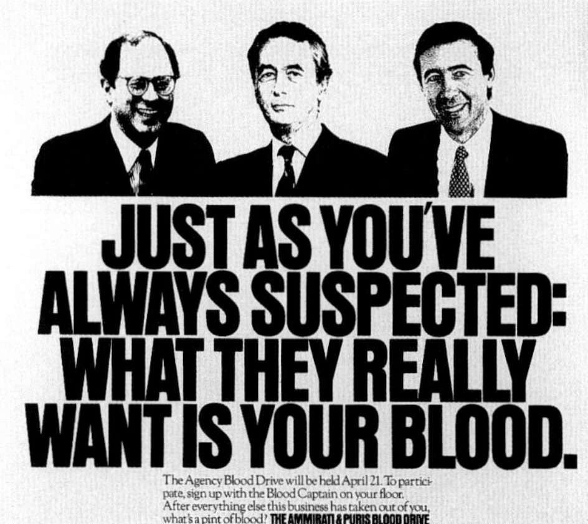

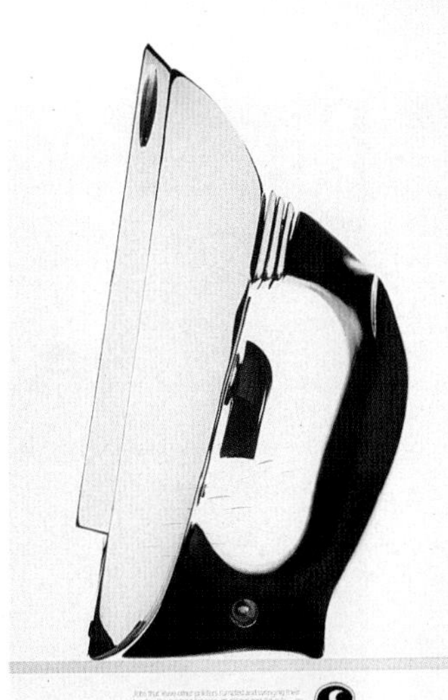

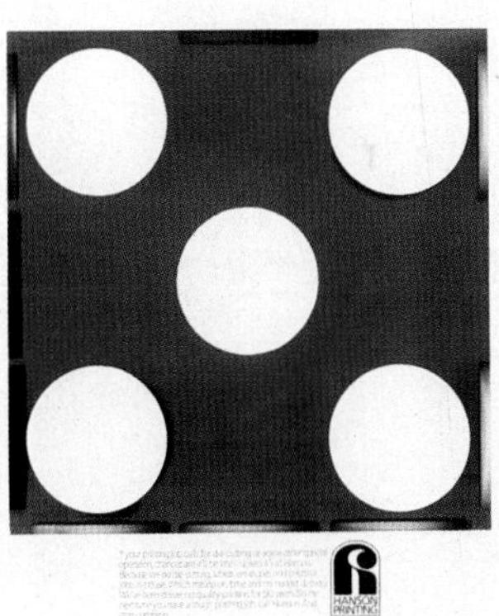

750
Art Director: Joe Vicino
Designer: Joe Vicino
Photographer: Kurt Stier
Writer: Robert L. Cashin
Creative Director: Robert L. Cashin
Client: Hanson Printing Co.
Agency: Robert's & Dana Advertising

751
Art Director: Thom Marchionna
Designer: Joy Modesitt
Photographer: Michael Furman Photography
Writer: Rob Price
Creative Director: Rob Price
Design Firm: Apple Creative Services
Production Manager: Barbara Crow

752
Art Director: Rich Silverstein
Photographer: James Wood
Illustrator/Artist: Jill Sabella
Writer: Peter Wegner
Creative Director: Rich Silverstein
Client: Spoons Restaurants
Agency: Goodby, Berlin & Silverstein

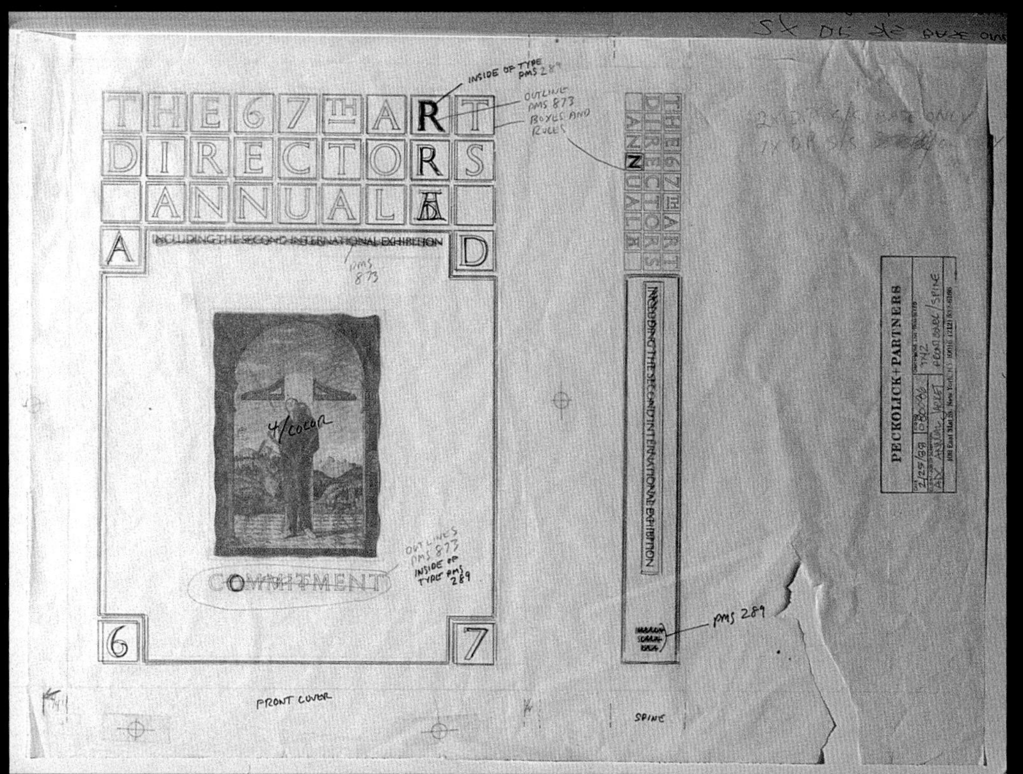
THE 67TH ART
DIRECTORS
ANNUAL
INCLUDING THE SECOND INTERNATIONAL EXHIBITION
A
D
6
7
COMMITMENT
INSIDE OF TYPE PMS 289
OUTLINE PMS 873
BOXES AND RULES
PMS 873
4/COLOR
OUTLINES PMS 873 INSIDE OF TYPE PMS 289
PMS 289
FRONT COVER
SPINE
PECKOLICK+PARTNERS

753 Silver Award

Art Director: Joe Duffy, Charles S. Anderson
Designer: Joe Duffy, Sharon Werner
Illustrator/Artist: Joe Duffy, Sharon Werner
Writer: Chuck Carlson
Client: Dickson's Inc.
Design Firm: The Duffy Design Group

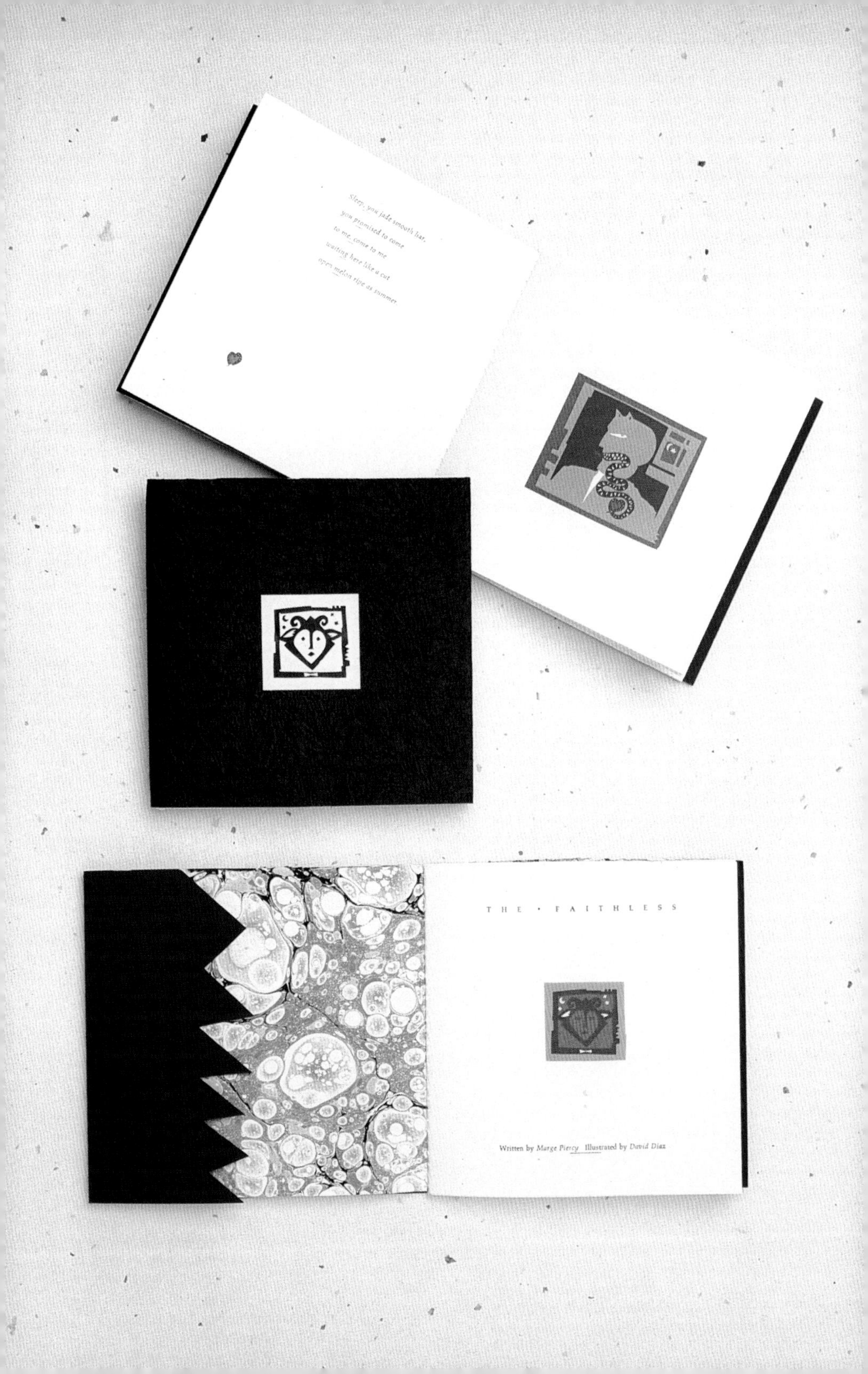

Sleep, you jade smooth bat,
you promised to come
to me, come to me
waiting here like a cut
open melon ripe as summer.

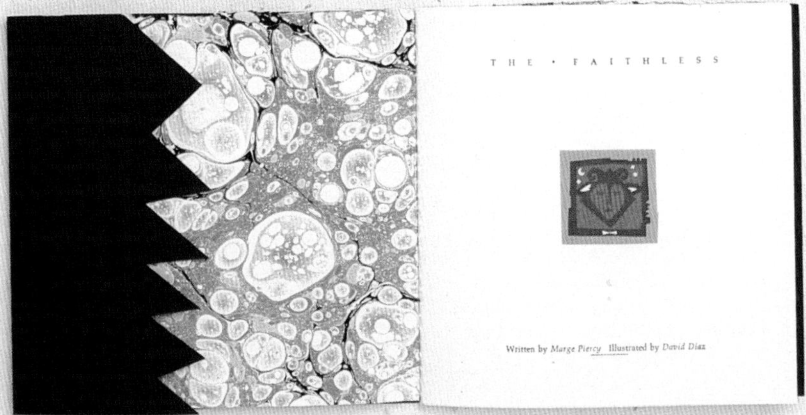

MICHAEL VANDERBYL
San Francisco, California
Gouache on paper

Michael Vanderbyl's Vanderbyl Design serves a wide range of corporate clients, museums, and institutions. Vanderbyl is dean of the School of Design at the California College of Arts and Crafts. His work is included in the permanent collections of the Cooper-Hewitt Museum and the Library of Congress. A frequent recipient of highly respected design awards, Vanderbyl is a member of the Alliance Graphique Internationale and was featured in *Seven Graphic Designers*, edited by Takenobu Igarashi, among other publications.

DUGALD STERMER
San Francisco, California
Pencil and watercolor on paper

Dugald Stermer is a designer, illustrator, and writer. He designed the 1984 Olympic Games medal, has created covers for *Time* magazine, and has produced illustrations for other major publications and for advertising and corporate clients. Stermer is associate editor for Communication Arts magazine. He is the ... *Art of Revolution*, *Vanishing Creatures*, ... upcoming *Vanishing Flora*. ... for his wildlife and botanical ... honored with a one- ... Academy of Sciences.

STARS & STRIPES

By Kit Hinrichs

A Celebration of the American Flag by 96 International Designers and Artists

THE GOLDEN AGE
CLOSE COVER
BEFORE STRIKING
OF MATCHBOOK ART
BY
H. THOMAS STEELE
JIM HEIMANN
ROD DYER
TRAVEL
Trains were said to run faster than speeding bullets. Graceful ocean liners plied vast seas. The open road beckoned travelers by bus and car. Whatever the mode, transportation was a preoccupation of Americans during the first half of the twentieth century, and matchcovers were natural for purveying America's new wonders of the mechanical age. Not only could they sell the practical, such as used cars or coal, but, incorporating images such as streamlined clipper ships of the air, they could be used to suggest faraway destinations—even if the establishment in question was the corner bar or local diner. The matchbook was brought home more often as a keepsake of a location visited than for everyday use.
SANTA CATALINA ISLAND
ISLAND CAFE
AVALON SANTA CATALINA ISLAND
Enjoy Santa CATALINA
"a different world within your reach"
NORTH WESTERN

THE ULTIMATE
ALBUM COVER
ALBUM
ROGER DEAN & DAVID HOWELLS

ADWEEK
PORTFOLIO
PHOTOGRAPHY
INCORPORATING
ART DIRECTORS'
INDEX
PHOTOGRAPH BY SHEILA METZNER

ADWEEK
EAST
PORTFOLIO
CREATIVE SERVICES DIRECTORY
GUEST CHECK
SPEED-O-MATIC
(TYPESETTERS)
INCORPORATING
ART DIRECTORS'
INDEX
THREE-DIMENSIONAL ILLUSTRATION BY ANNA V. WALKER
PHOTOGRAPH BY MATTHEW KLEIN

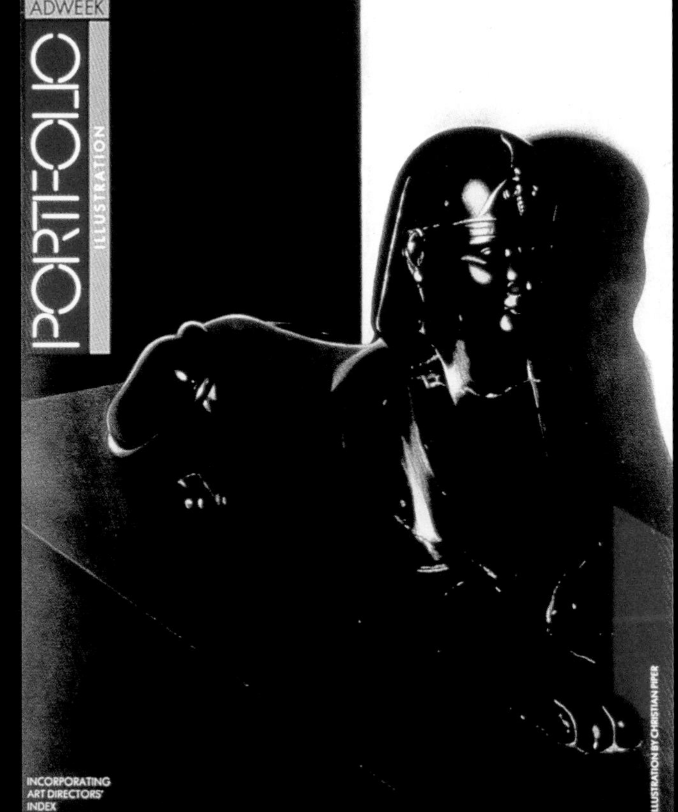
ADWEEK
PORTFOLIO
ILLUSTRATION
INCORPORATING
ART DIRECTORS'
INDEX
ILLUSTRATION BY CHRISTIAN PIPER

759
Art Director: Carol Haralson
Designer: Carol Haralson
Writer: Patty Lou Floyd
Creative Director: Carol Haralson
Client: Council Oak Books
Publisher: Council Oak Books

760
Art Director: Marty Neumeier
Designer: Kathleen Joynes, Marty Neumeier
Illustrator/Artist: Gary Kelley
Writer: Ray Bradbury
Editor: Marty Neumeier
Design Firm: Neumeier Design Team
Publisher: Creative Education

761
Art Director: Marty Neumeier
Designer: Kathleen Joynes, Marty Neumeier
Illustrator/Artist: Gary Kelley
Writer: Ray Bradbury
Editor: Marty Neumeier
Design Firm: Neumeier Design Team
Publisher: Creative Education

763
Art Director: B. Martin Pedersen
Designer: Marino Bianchera, Martin Byland
Writer: Stanley Mason
Editor: B. Martin Pedersen
Creative Director: B. Martin Pedersen
Design Firm: Graphis Press/Graphis U.S.
Publisher: Graphis Press Corp.

762
Art Director: Richard Hess
Designer: Dean Morris, Richard Hess
Writer: Marion Muller
Editor: Richard Hess, Marion Muller
Creative Director: Ira Shapiro
Design Firm: Jonson, Pirtle, Pedersen, Alcorn, Metzdorf & Hess
Publisher: American Showcase Inc.

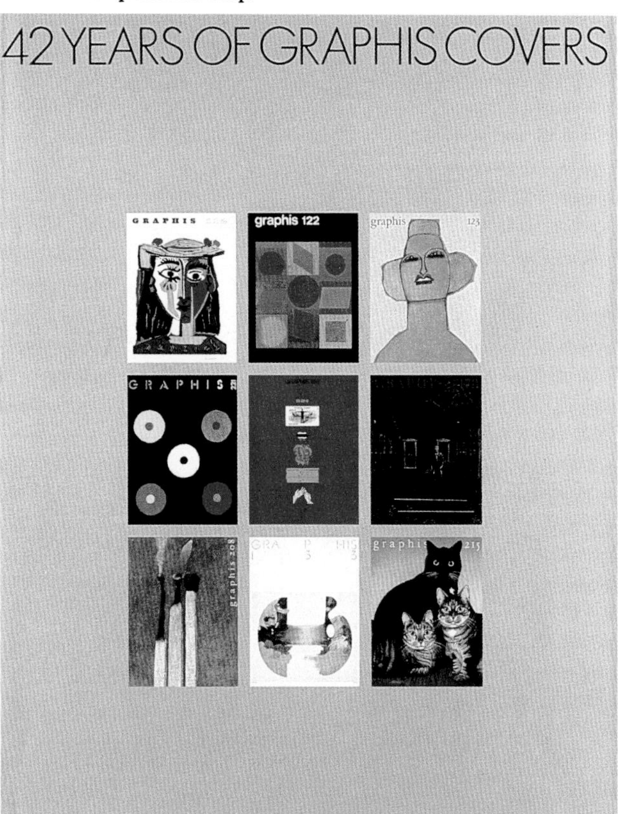

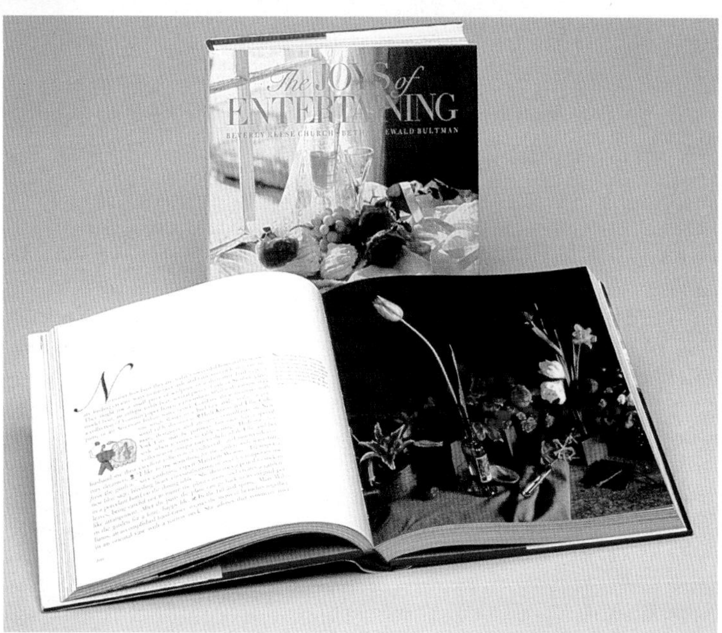

764
Art Director: Sam Antupit
Designer: Joyce Rothschild, Doris Leath
Photographer: O. Winston Link
Editor: Beverly Fazio
Publisher: Harry N. Abrams Inc.

765
Art Director: James Wageman
Designer: James Wageman
Illustrator/Artist: Philippe Weisbecker
Writer: Beverly Reese Church, Bethany Ewald Bultman
Editor: Regina Kahney
Publisher: Robert E. Abrams
Production Manager: Dana Cole

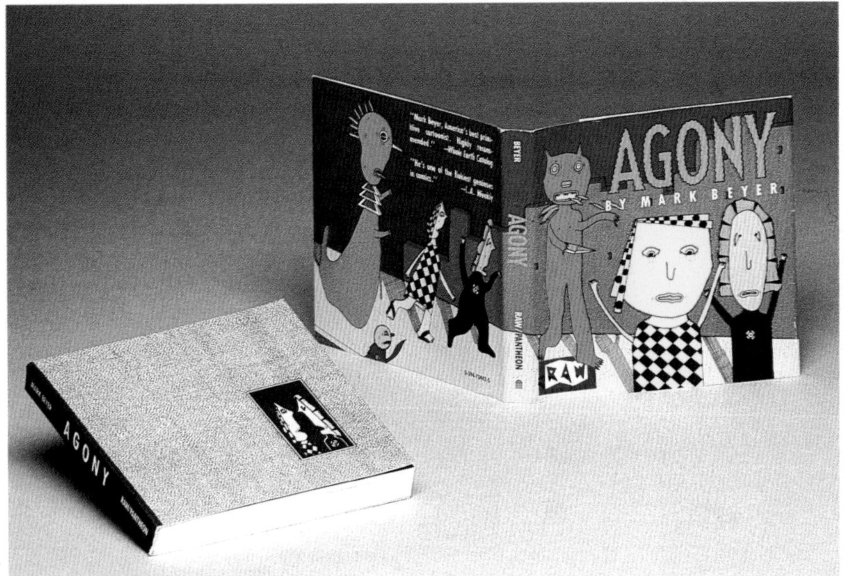

766
Art Director: Louise Fili
Designer: Art Spiegelman
Illustrator/Artist: Mark Beyer
Writer: Mark Beyer
Publisher: Pantheon Books

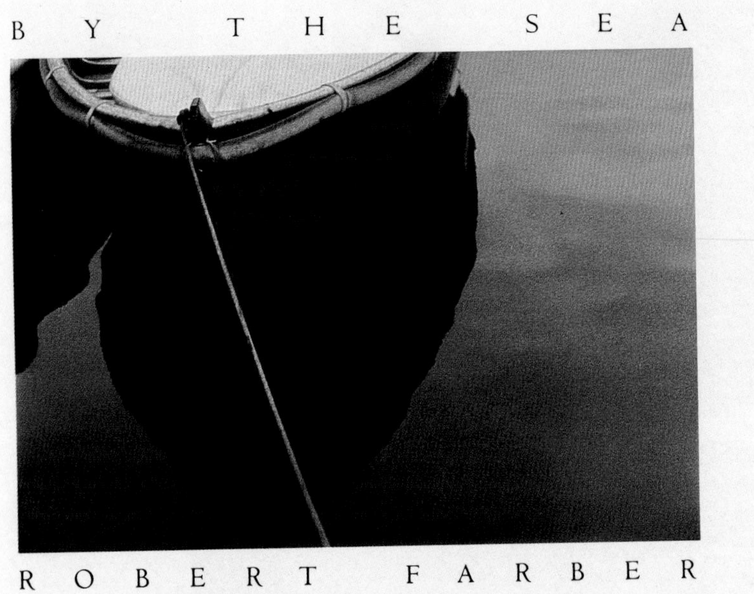

767
Art Director: Larry Vigon
Photographer: Robert Farber
Client: Melrose Publishing Group
Publisher: Jeff Dunas

768
Art Director: Trisha Hanlon
Designer: Trisha Hanlon
Illustrator/Artist: Leo Dillon, Diane Dillon
Writer: Michael Patrick Hearn
Editor: John Keller
Publisher: Little Brown & Co.
Production Manager: Linda Jackson

769
Art Director: Ann Tyler
Designer: Ann Tyler, Renate Gokl
Photographer: William Zehr
Writer: Marcel Franciscono
Editor: Stephen Prokopoff
Client: Krannert Art Museum
Design Firm: Ann Tyler Visual Design
Publisher: Krannert Art Museum, The MIT Press

770
Art Director: René Khatami
Designer: René Khatami
Writer: Baroness Foxhall to C. Phillips
Editor: Alan Axelrod
Publisher: Robert E. Abrams
Production Manager: Dana Cole

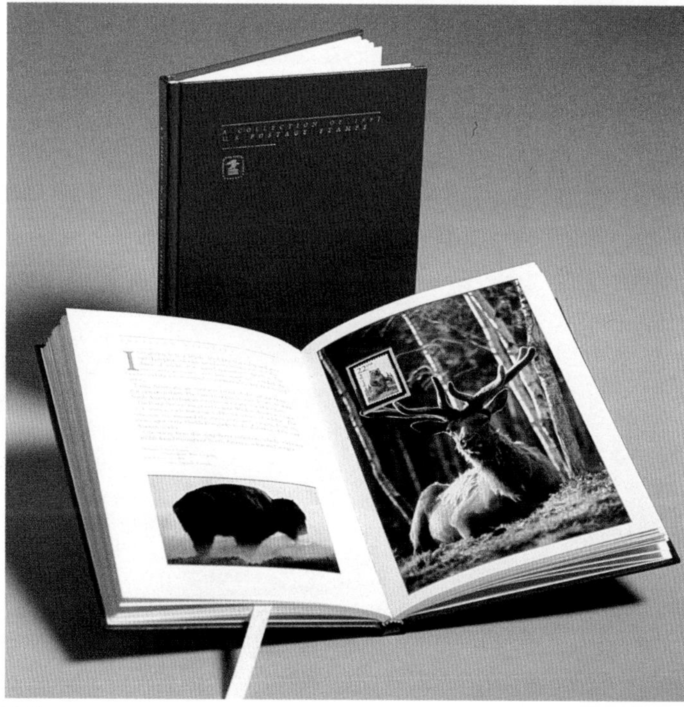

771
Art Director: Thad E. Dilley
Designer: Nancy van Meter
Writer: Valoree Vargo
Editor: Liz Altobell
Creative Director: Terrence W. McCaffrey
Client: United States Postal Service
Agency: United States Postal Service
Publisher: United States Postal Service
Publication: 1987 Collection of Postal Stamps

772
Art Director: Gael Towey
Designer: Rita Marshall
Photographer: Keith Scott Morton
Illustrator/Artist: Etienne Delessert
Writer: Tricia Foley
Editor: Nancy Novogrod
Creative Director: Gael Towey
Client: Having Tea
Publisher: Clarkson N. Potter

773
Art Director: Gael Towey
Designer: Gael Towey
Photographer: Christopher Simon Sykes
Writer: Caroline Seebohm
Editor: Carol Southern
Creative Director: Gael Towey
Client: English Country
Publisher: Clarkson N. Potter

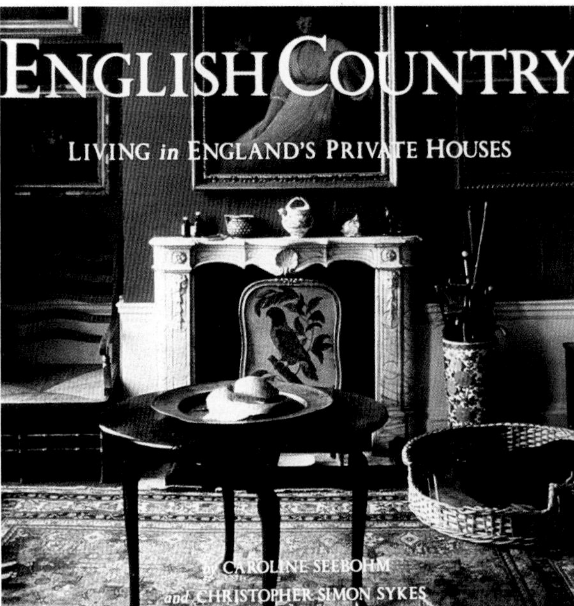

774
Art Director: Wendy Byrne
Designer: Wendy Byrne
Photographer: Ethan Hoffman
Editor: Mark Holborn
Publisher: Aperture

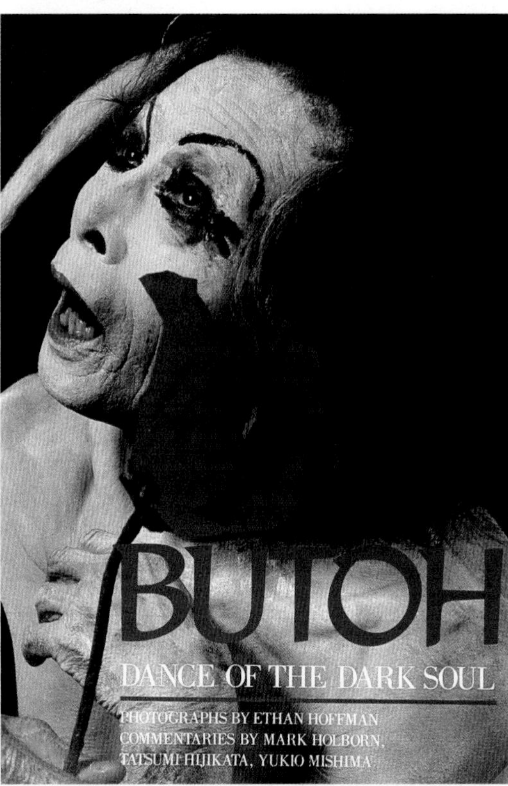

775
Art Director: Pamela Ahern
Designer: Pamela Ahern
Editor: Sharon Gallagher
Publisher: Robert E. Abrams
Consultant: Stephen Neumann
Production Manager: Dana Cole

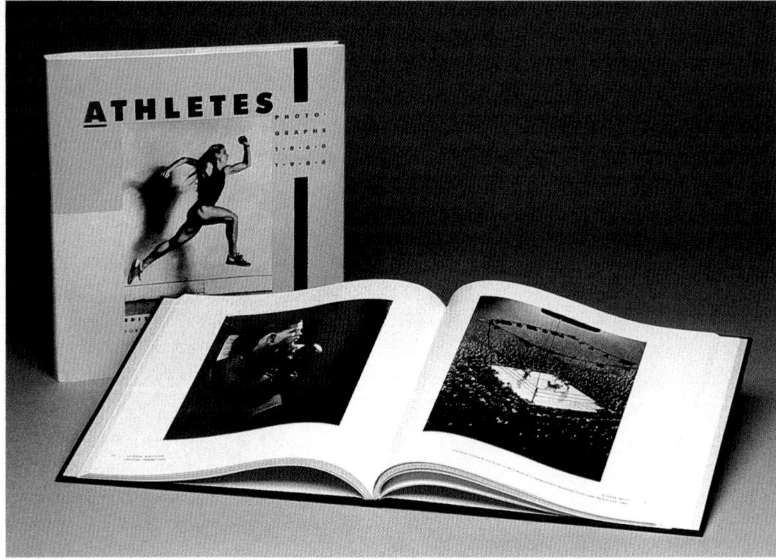

776
Art Director: Virginia Tan
Designer: Peter A. Andersen
Editor: Victoria Wilson
Production Manager: Andrew Hughes

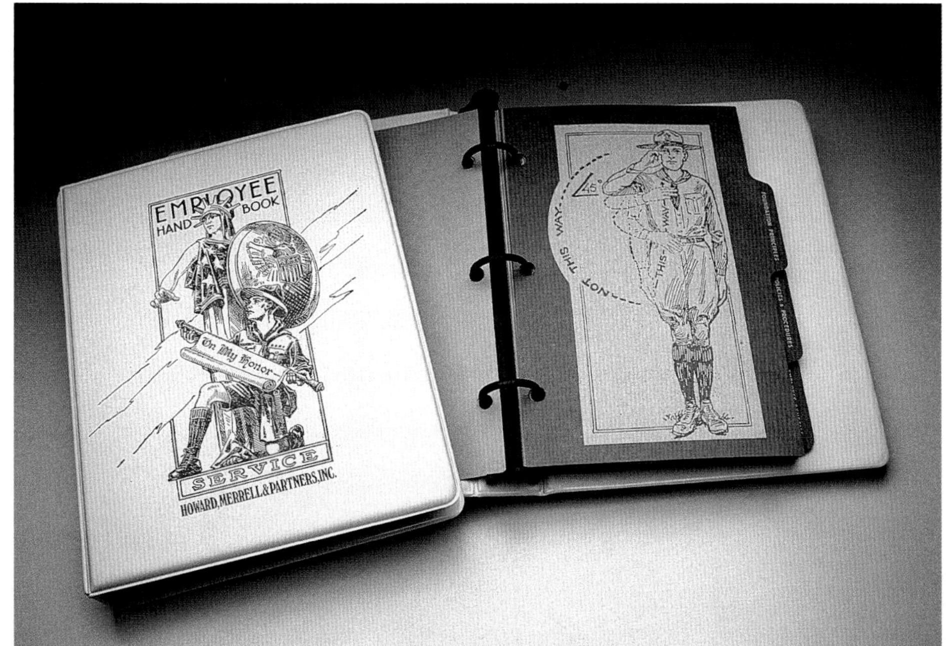

777
Art Director: Joe Ivey
Designer: Joe Ivey
Creative Director: Gary Knutson
Client: Howard, Merrell & Partners
Agency: Howard, Merrell & Partners

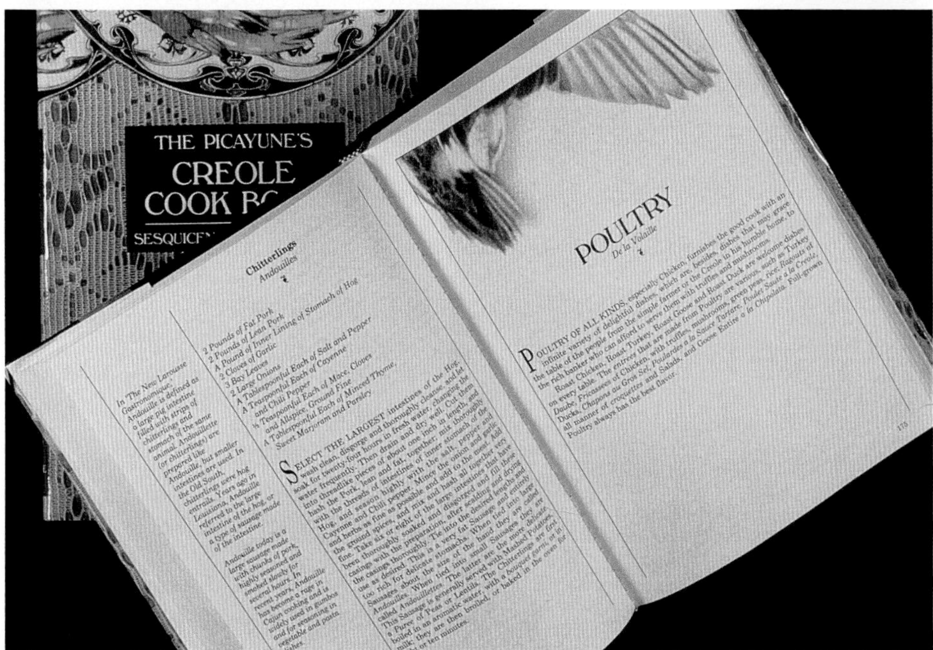

778
Art Director: Wendi Schneider
Designer: Wendi Schneider
Photographer: Wendi Schneider
Writer: Marcelle Bienvenu, Beverly Morris
Editor: Wendi Schneider
Agency: The Times-Picayune Marketing Services Dept.
Publisher: The Times-Picayune
Project Coordinator: Linda Dennery

779
Art Director: Areta Buk
Editòr: Julia Moore, Victoria Craven-Cohn
Client: The Whitney Library of Design
Design Firm: Graphiti Graphics
Editorial Director: Glorya Hale
Production Manager: Hector Campbell
Type: Truffont Typographers

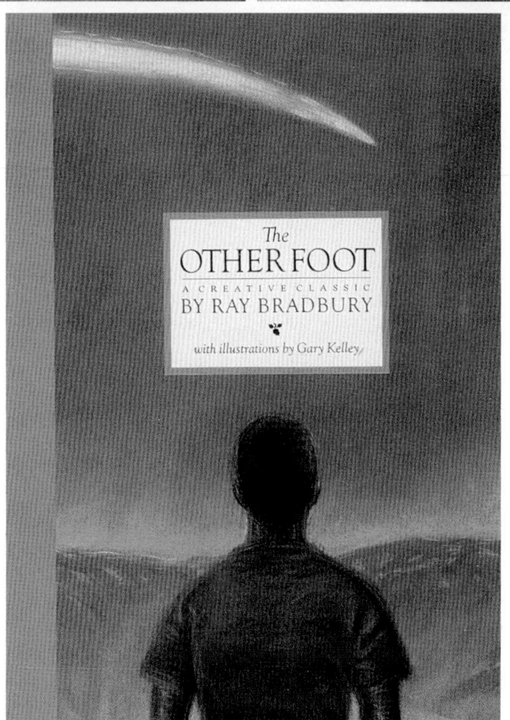

780

Art Director: Marty Neumeier
Designer: Kathleen Joynes, Marty Neumeier
Illustrator/Artist: Gary Kelley
Writer: Ray Bradbury
Editor: Marty Neumeier
Design Firm: Neumeier Design Team
Publisher: Creative Education

781
Art Director: Gerald McConnell
Designer: Robert Anthony
Illustrator/Artist: Elwood P. Smith
Client: Madison Square Press
Design Firm: Robert Anthony Inc.
Publisher: Madison Square Press

782
Art Director: Louise Fili
Designer: Louise Fili
Illustrator/Artist: Robert Goldstrom
Writer: Peter Dickinson
Editor: André Schiffrin
Publisher: Pantheon Books

783
Art Director: Sara Eisenman
Designer: Jose Conde
Illustrator/Artist: Jose Conde
Editor: Ashbel Green
Publisher: Alfred A. Knopf

784
Art Director: Joseph Montebello
Designer: Paul Davis
Illustrator/Artist: Paul Davis
Writer: John Lahr
Editor: Nick Hern, Methuen
Design Firm: Paul Davis Studio
Publisher: Methuen/Harper & Row

785
Art Director: Sam Antupit
Designer: Sam Antupit
Publisher: Harry N. Abrams Inc.

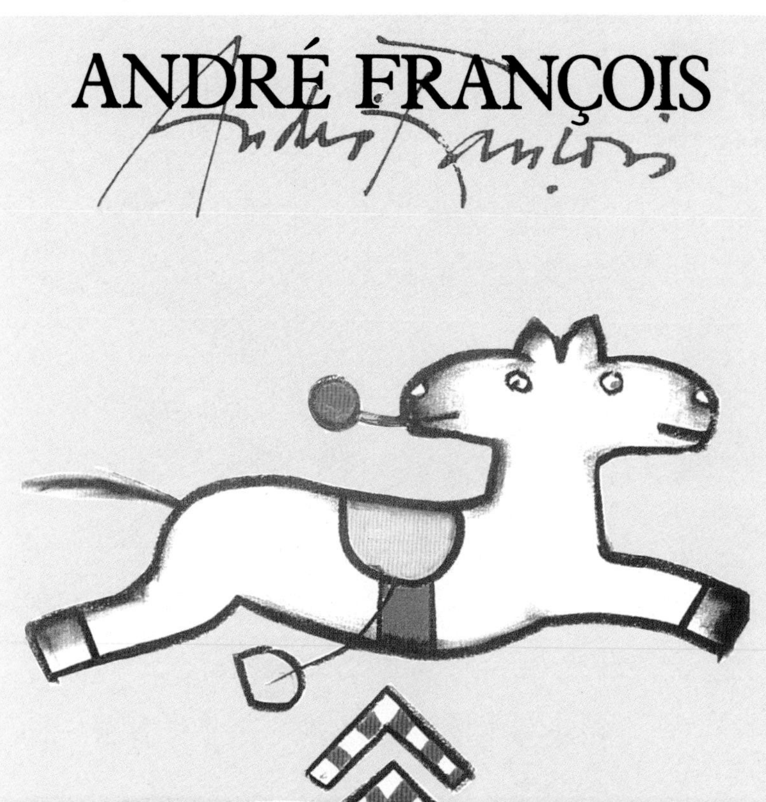

786
Art Director: Louise Fili
Designer: Louise Fili
Illustrator/Artist: John Martinez
Writer: Dan Kavanagh
Editor: André Schiffrin
Publisher: Pantheon Books

787
Art Director: Louise Fili
Designer: Dugald Stermer
Illustrator/Artist: Dugald Stermer
Writer: John Berger
Editor: Tom Engelhardt
Publisher: Pantheon Books

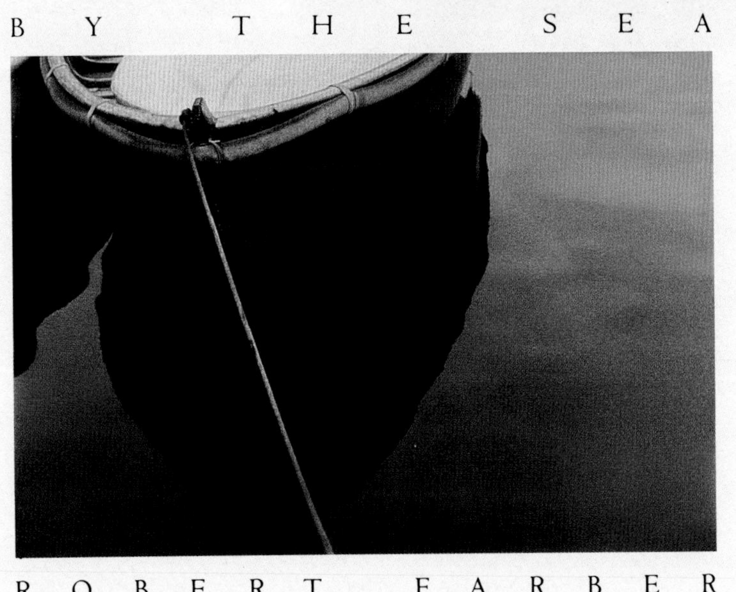

788
Art Director: Larry Vigon
Photographer: Robert Farber
Client: Melrose Publishing Group
Publisher: Melrose Publishing Co.

789
Art Director: R. D. Scudellari
Designer: R. D. Scudellari
Illustrator/Artist: Julian Schnabel
Writer: Julian Schnabel
Editor: David Rosenthal
Publisher: Random House

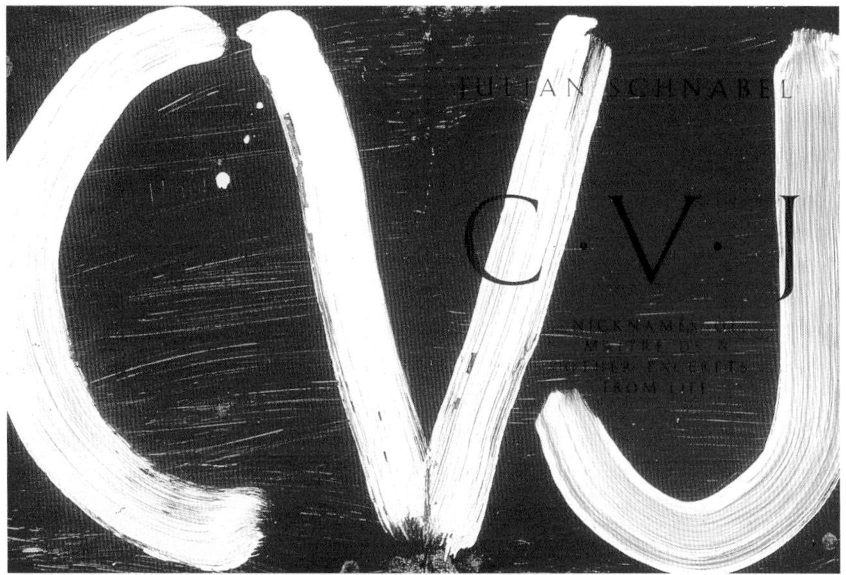

790
Art Director: Louise Fili
Designer: Louise Fili
Illustrator/Artist: Anthony Russo
Writer: Ida Fink
Editor: Sara Bershtel
Publisher: Pantheon Books

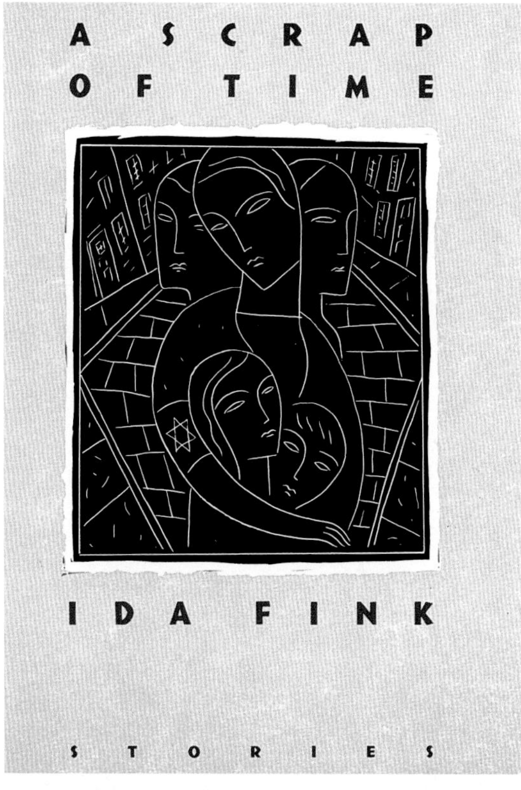

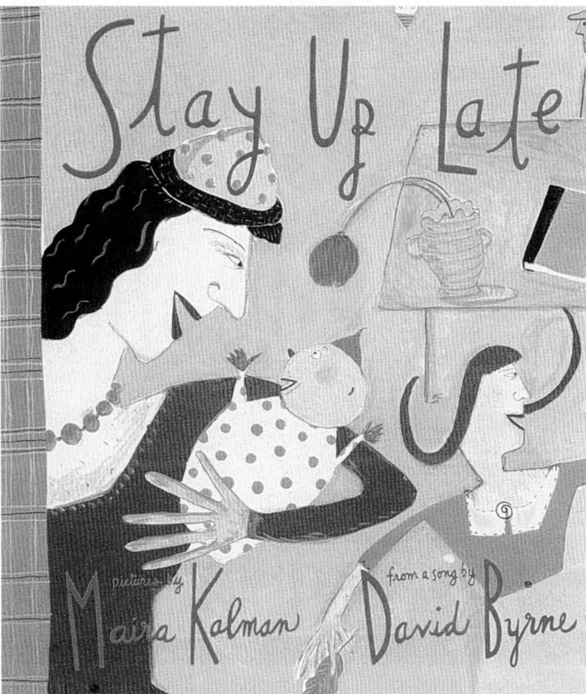

791
Art Director: Tibor Kalman
Designer: Maira Kalman, Timothy Horn
Illustrator/Artist: Maira Kalman
Writer: David Byrne
Editor: Nancy Paulsen
Design Firm: M & Co.
Publisher: Viking-Kestral

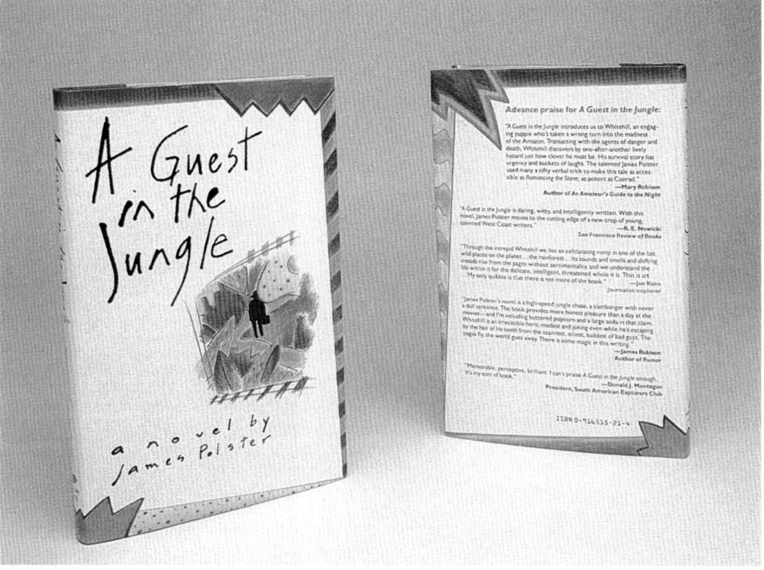

792
Art Director: Sharon Smith
Designer: Sharon Smith
Illustrator/Artist: Dan Hubig, John Hersey
Client: Mercury House
Design Firm: Sharon Smith Design
Publisher: Mercury House
Hand Lettering: Sharon Smith

793
Art Director: Inju Sturgeon, UCLA
Designer: Ken Parkhurst
Illustrator/Artist: Ken Parkhurst
Client: UCLA Extension, Marketing Dept.
Design Firm: Ken Parkhurst & Associates Inc.

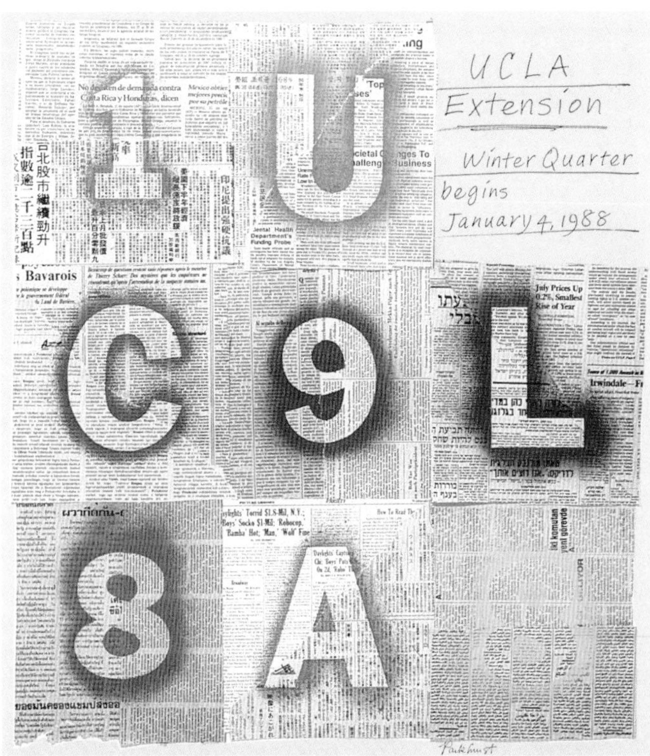

794
Art Director: Marjorie Anderson
Designer: Marjorie Anderson, Joel Meyerowitz
Photographer: Joel Meyerowitz
Editor: Elisabeth Scharlatt
Publisher: Times Books

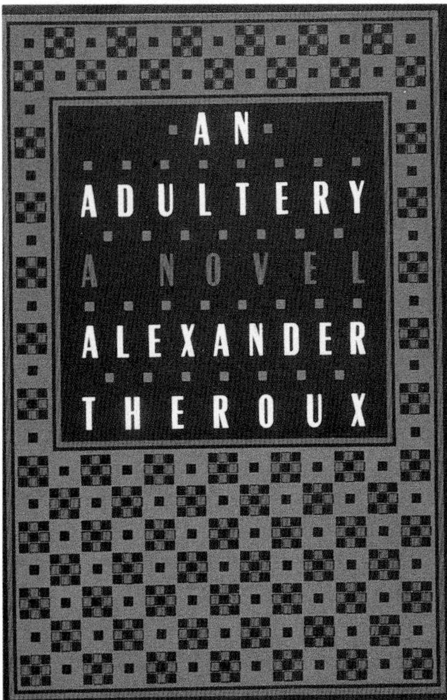

795
Art Director: Frank Metz
Designer: Paula Scher
Design Firm: Koppel & Scher
Publisher: Simon & Schuster Inc.

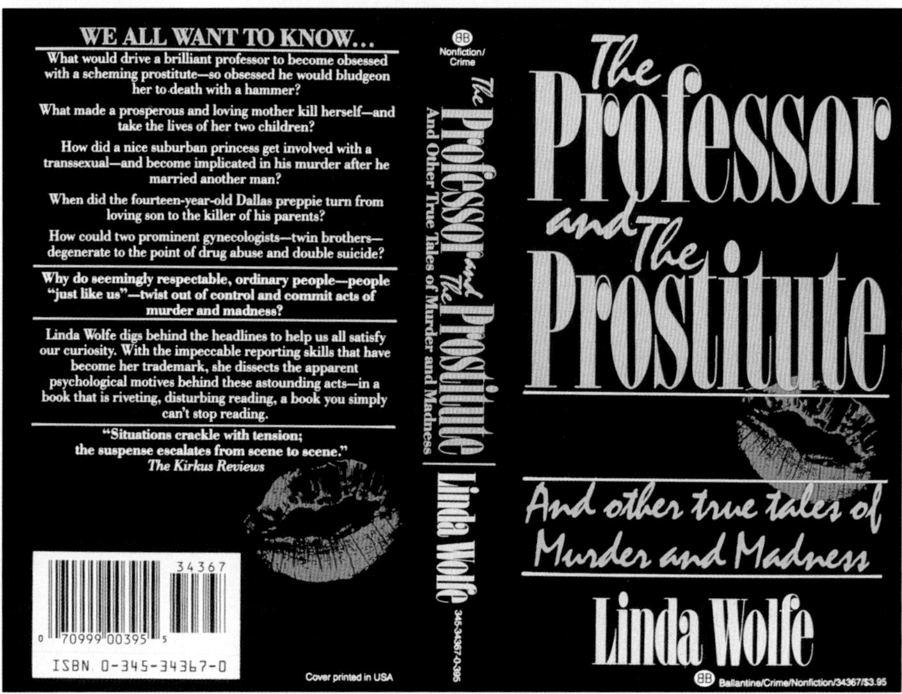

796
Art Director: Donald E. Munson
Designer: Bill Toth
Writer: Jo Sgammato
Editor: Robert Wyatt
Publisher: Ballantine Books

797
Art Director: Frank Metz
Designer: Paula Scher
Design Firm: Koppel & Scher
Publisher: Simon & Schuster Inc.

798
Art Director: Frank Metz
Designer: Robert Anthony
Photographer: Irv Bahrt
Client: Simon & Schuster Inc.
Design Firm: Robert Anthony Inc.
Publisher: Simon & Schuster Inc.

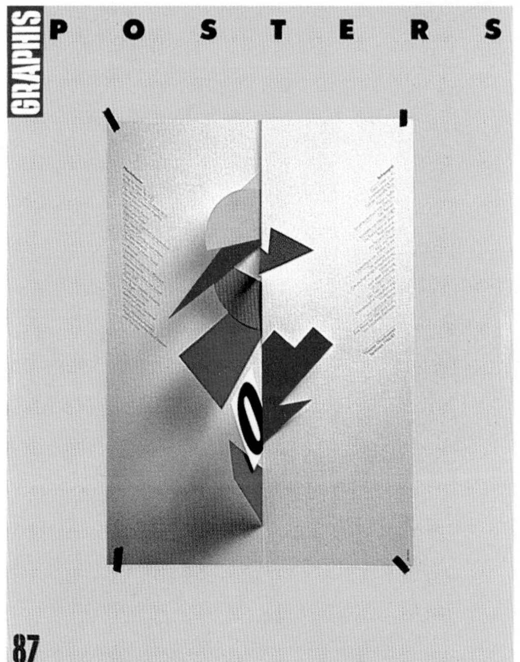

799
Art Director: B. Martin Pedersen
Designer: B. Martin Pedersen
Illustrator/Artist: Holger Matthies, Burkey Belser
Editor: B. Martin Pedersen
Creative Director: B. Martin Pedersen
Design Firm: Graphis U.S. Inc.
Publisher: Graphis Press Corp.

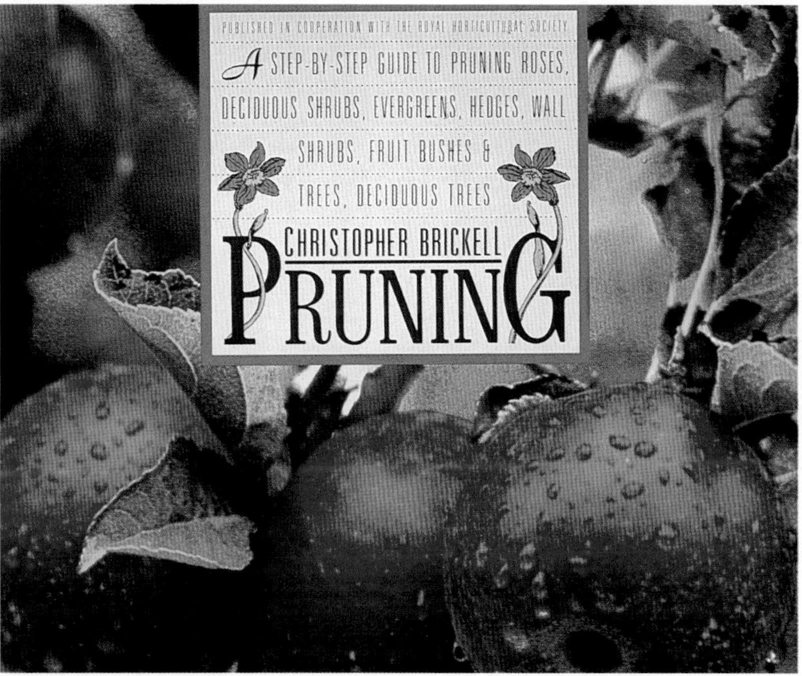

800
Art Director: Jeffrey Morris
Designer: Jeffrey Morris
Photographer: Image Bank
Client: Simon & Schuster

801
Art Director: Stephen Doyle
Editor: David Rieff
Agency: Drenttel Doyle Partners
Publisher: Farrar, Strauss & Giroux

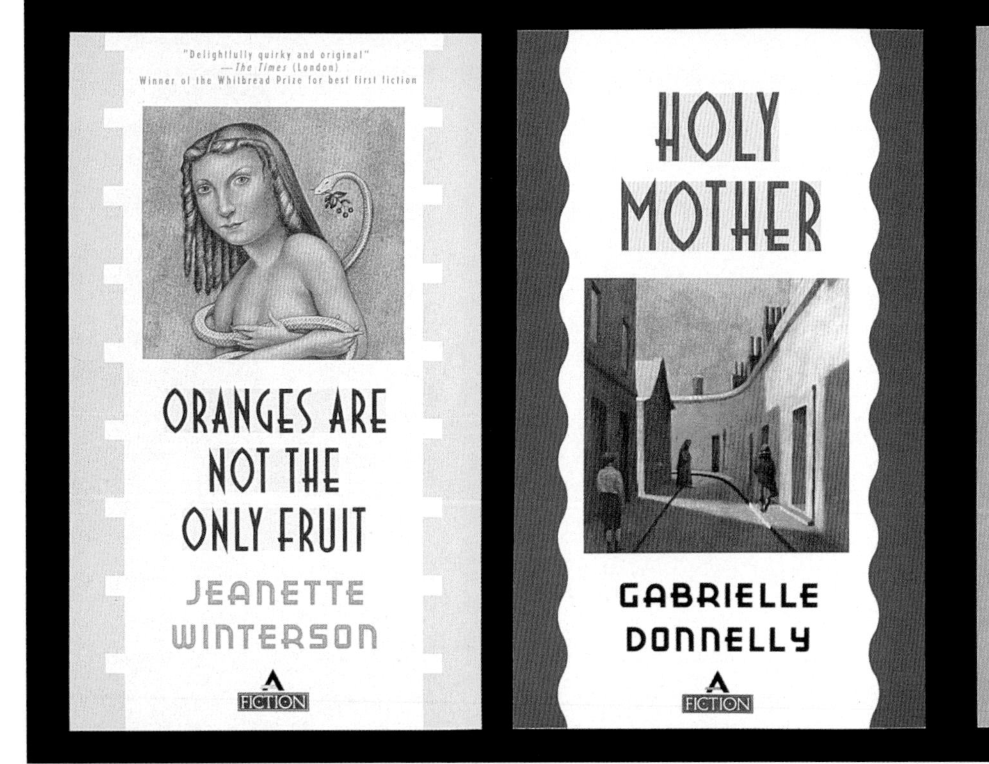

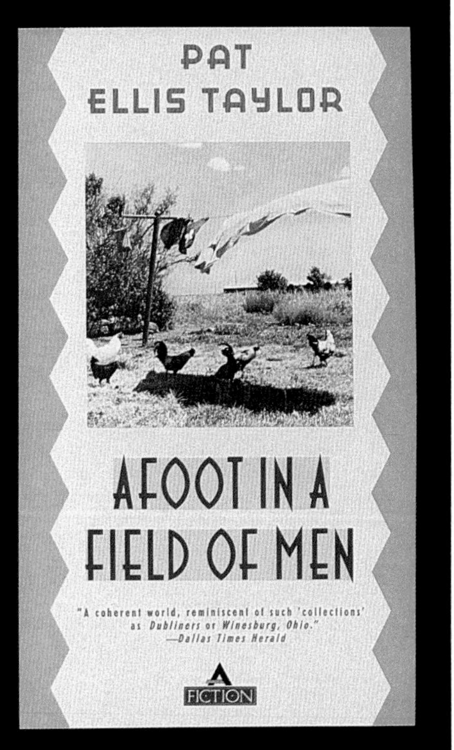

802
Art Director: Robbin Schiff
Designer: Lorraine Louie
Illustrator/Artist: Paola Piglia, Anita Kunz, Steve Carver
Editor: Gary Fisketjohn
Design Firm: Lorraine Louie Design
Publisher: Atlantic Monthly Press

803
Art Director: Louise Noble
Designer: Robert Anthony
Writer: Stephen Birnbaum
Client: Houghton Mifflin Co.
Design Firm: Robert Anthony Inc.
Publisher: Houghton Mifflin Co.

Birnbaum's
Hawaii 1987

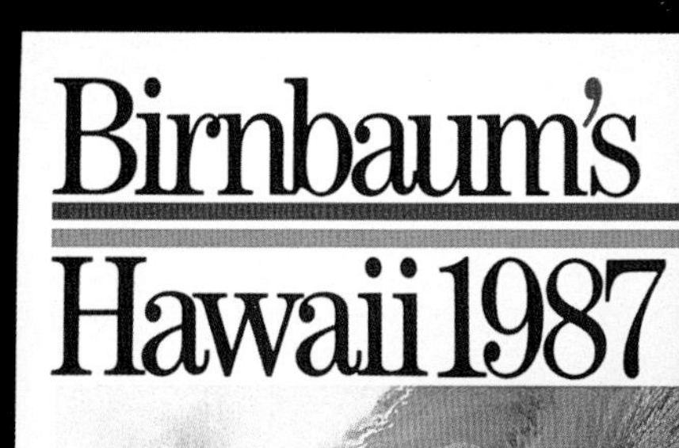

Brown your body on a black sand beach, watch the sunrise from a volcano's rim, surf down waves 30 feet high, ride with cowboys in flowered shirts, go to town on a sugar cane train, nibble the best potato chips on earth, swim with the whales off Maui's coast...

"The information is up-to-date and crisply presented... the judgments knowledgeable..."
—NEW YORK TIMES

Birnbaum's
Mexico 1987

Float in your own flower-filled pool, nap in the bed where Cortés slept, dive from the top of a craggy cliff, test your skill with a charging bull, climb a pyramid the Maya built, taste tequila and turtle soup, visit the villas of the Aztec kings, dance on your hat...

"The information is up-to-date and crisply presented... the judgments knowledgeable..."
—NEW YORK TIMES

Birnbaum's
Great Britain and Ireland 1987

Tread the streets where Shakespeare walked; catch a fish in the Firth of Clyde; shop for tartans, linens, and tweeds; sip a goblet of Celtic mead; ramble through Mumbles, Mousehole, and Mold...

"The information is up-to-date and crisply presented... the judgments knowledgeable..."
—NEW YORK TIMES

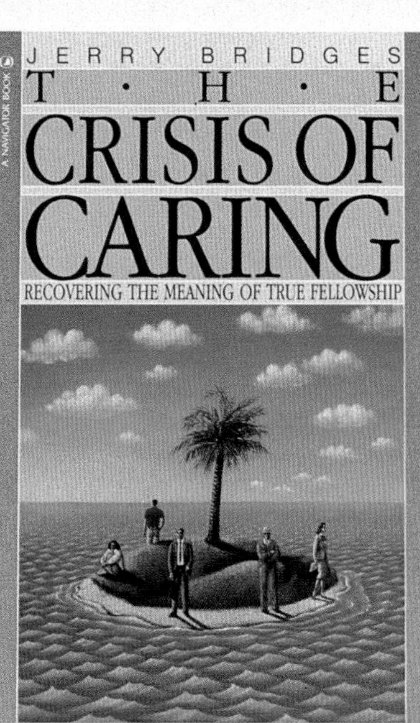

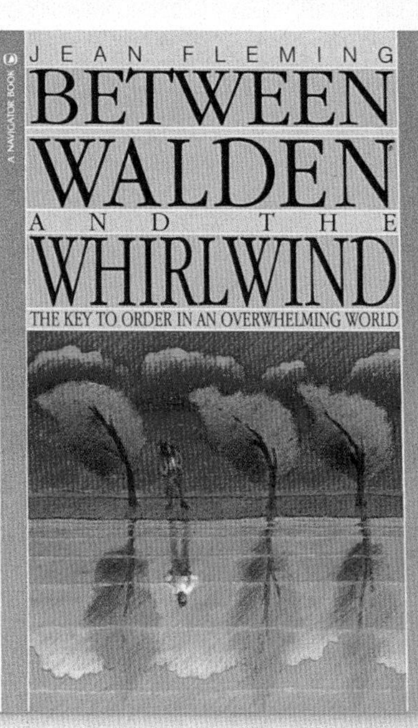

804
Art Director: Stephen T. Eames
Designer: Dan Jamison
Illustrator/Artist: Gary Kelley, Rafal Olbinski, Doug Bowles
Editor: Bruce Nygren
Client: NavPress
Publisher: John Eames
Color Separation: VisiColor

805
Art Director: Susan Mitchell
Designer: Lorraine Louie
Writer: Peter Matthiessen
Design Firm: Lorraine Louie Design
Publisher: Vintage Books

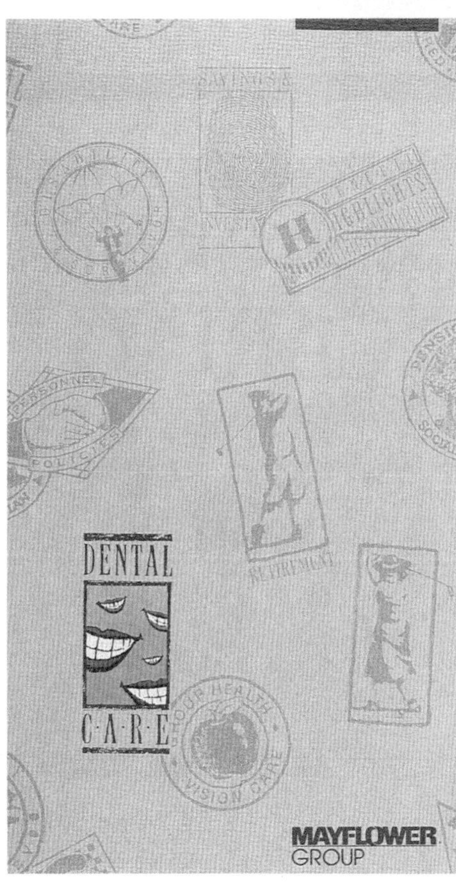

806
Art Director: Jeff Laramore
Designer: Jeff Laramore
Illustrator/Artist: Jeff Laramore, Mike Savitski
Client: Mayflower Group
Agency: Young & Laramore

ILLUSTRATION

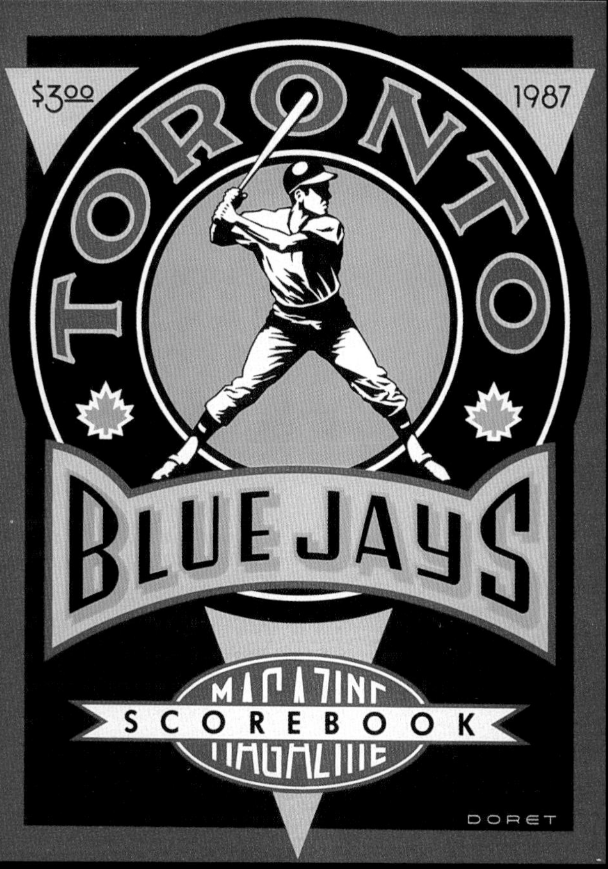
$3.00
1987
TORONTO
BLUE JAYS
SCOREBOOK
DORET

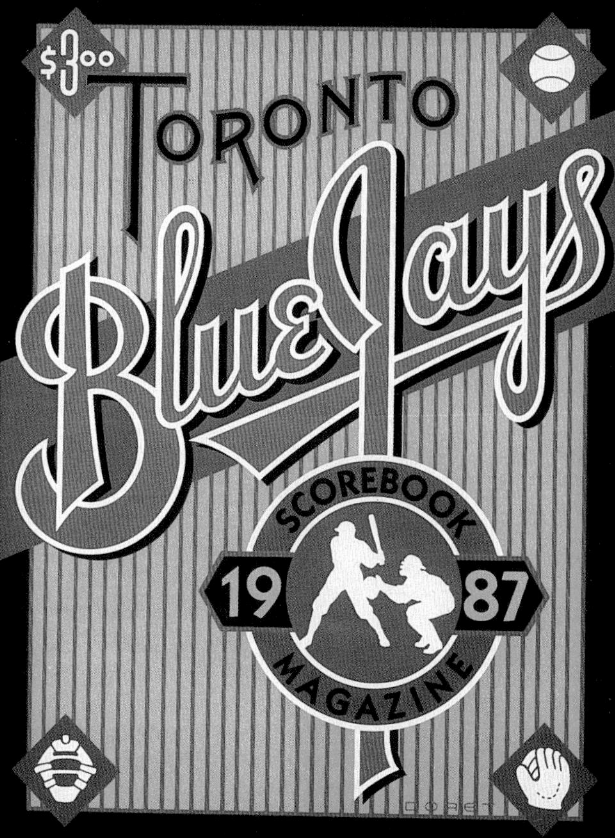
$3.00
TORONTO
BlueJays
SCOREBOOK
19
87
MAGAZINE
DORET

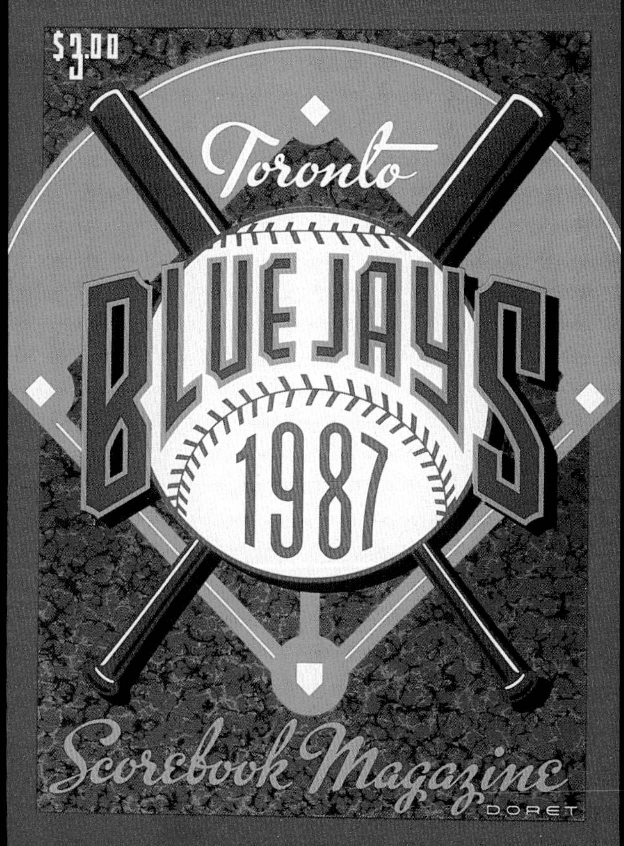
$3.00
Toronto
BLUE JAYS
1987
Scorebook Magazine
DORET

808
Art Director: J. Robert Teringo
Illustrator/Artist: Ned Seidler, Rosalie Seidler
Editor: W. E. Garrett
Client: National Geographic Magazine
Publisher: National Geographic Society
Publication: National Geographic Magazine

809
Art Director: Jeff Hill
Designer: Jeff Hill, John Sposato
Illustrator/Artist: John Sposato
Client: Timex Watches
Agency: Grey Advertising

810
Art Director: Whitney Cookman
Illustrator/Artist: Jim Turgeon
Client: Bantam Books
Representatives: Penny & Stermer Group

811
Art Director: Gary Gretter
Designer: Robert Gray
Illustrator/Artist: Charles Reid
Writer: Jack Kulpa
Editor: Jay Cassell
Publisher: Hearst Corp.
Publication: Sports Afield

Jutting out from a bluff, the rock held the river's finest fishing. Until this year, I considered it all mine.
by Jack Kulpa

The Ledge

Wisconsin's White River is a young man's river. Below the town of Mason, near the northern terminus of U.S. 63, the White drops sharply in its plunge toward Lake Superior, creating a 20-mile stretch of continuous rapids before reaching the dam at Sanborn. Any canoeist who makes that run commits himself to the river, for along that stretch, steep clay cliffs rise like ramparts from the water, difficult to descend and impossible to climb. The tops of the bluffs are battlements of solid timber, and beyond them lies a roadless wilderness of balsam, spruce and pine. A man is on his own if he finds trouble in that chasm, and in early spring trouble can lurk at every bend. Indians say only young fools run rapids—but in spring, the White belongs to reckless young men.

I was thinking about that as I stood on the bridge outside of Mason. The White was high and cloudy with snowmelt, and the bare woods of early spring were filled with its roar. Below me, at the canoe landing, red-winged blackbirds called from dry cattails, the sere stalks submerged in a foot of slush. I watched as a popple log came racing down the river and vanished in the torrent below the first drop.

Each year, for many years now, I had run the White early in the season. The White is one of the finest trout streams in northwestern Wisconsin, but even the most avid anglers avoid the 12-mile stretch of quickwater between Mason and the dam. One reason is the lack of access: No roads or bridges cross the flume, and the old logging trails that once led there have been obliterated by brush. The only practical way to fish it is

"I wanted to see the White just one more time," he told me. Then he spoke of the days when all the brookies went two pounds, when Indians came to spear the suckers and northerns.

812
Art Director: Richard Mantel
Designer: Richard Mantel
Illustrator/Artist: Tom Sciacca
Editor: Susan Breslow
Creative Director: Richard Mantel
Client: New York Magazine
Design Firm: Richard Mantel Studio
Publisher: Edward Kosner
Publication: New York Magazine

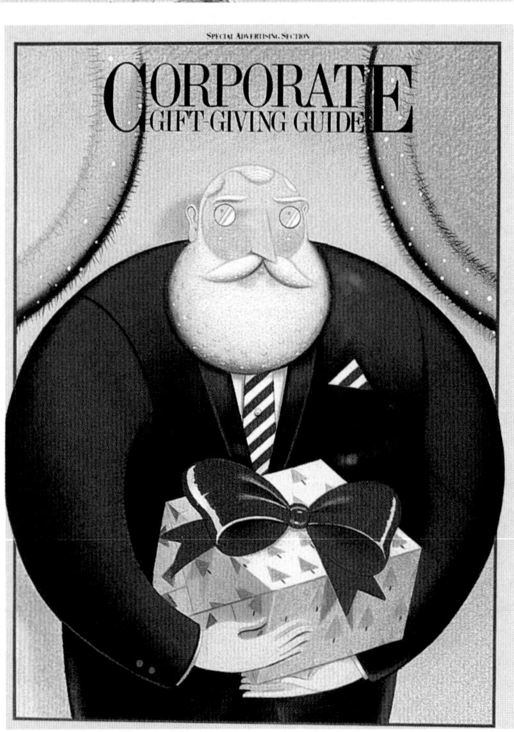

813
Art Director: Richard Mantel
Designer: Richard Mantel
Illustrator/Artist: Dave Calver
Editor: Susan Breslow
Creative Director: Richard Mantel
Client: New York Magazine
Design Firm: Richard Mantel Studio
Publisher: Edward Kosner
Publication: New York Magazine

814
Art Director: Dwayne Flinchum
Illustrator/Artist: Di Macchio
Graphics Director: Frank DeVino
Photo/Art Editor: Hilde Kron

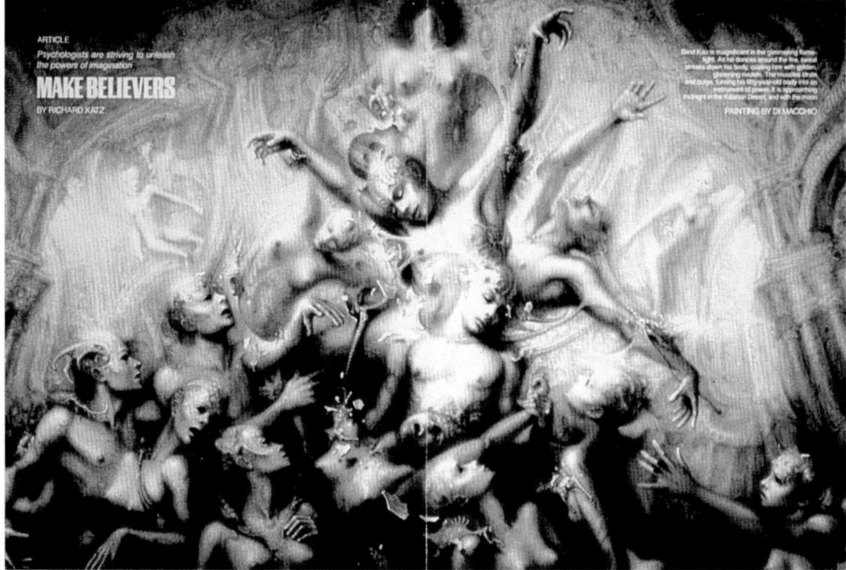

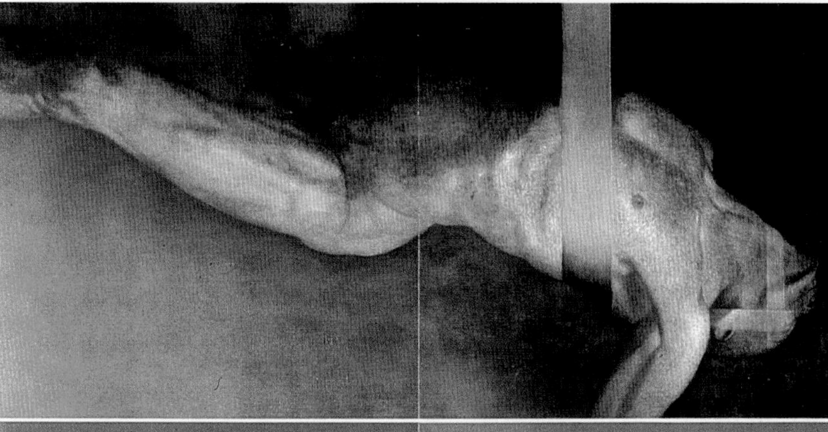

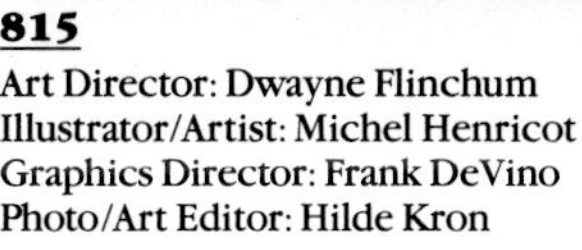

815
Art Director: Dwayne Flinchum
Illustrator/Artist: Michel Henricot
Graphics Director: Frank DeVino
Photo/Art Editor: Hilde Kron

816
Art Director: David Bartels
Designer: David Bartels
Illustrator/Artist: Mark Fredrickson
Creative Director: David Bartels
Client: Piedmont High School
Agency: Bartels & Carstens Inc.
Printer: Pacific Lithograph Co.

817
Art Director: Debbie Kokoruda, Alan E. Cober
Designer: Alan E. Cober, John de Cesare
Illustrator/Artist: Alan E. Cober
Writer: Alan E. Cober
Client: Art Directors Club of Cincinnati

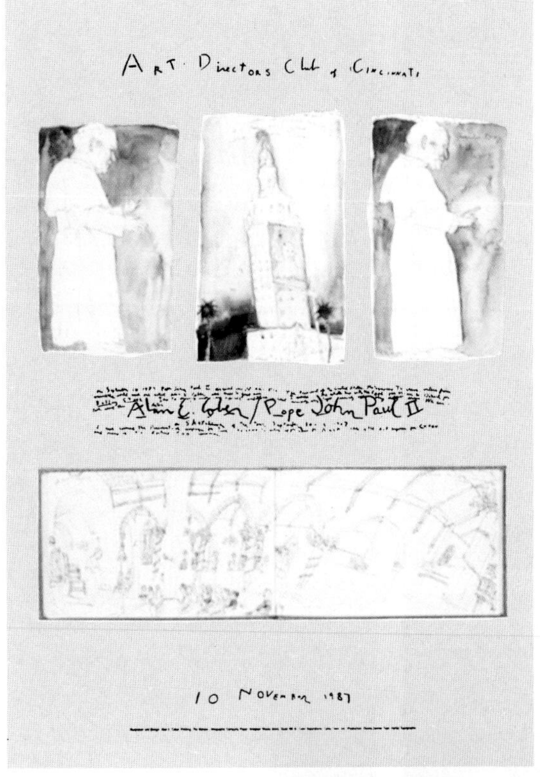

818
Art Director: Bob Conge
Designer: Bob Conge
Illustrator/Artist: Bob Conge
Writer: Steve Roberts
Client: Vietnam Veterans of America, Chapter 20
Agency: Steve Roberts & Co.
Design Firm: Conge Design

819
Art Director: Brian Wilburn
Illustrator/Artist: Bob Depew
Client: LinoTypographers
Agency: Graphic Concepts Group
Typographer: LinoTypographers
Printer: Lewis Label Products

820
Art Director: Rafal Olbinski
Designer: Rafal Olbinski
Illustrator/Artist: Rafal Olbinski
Client: Del Bello Gallery
Design Firm: Rafal Olbinski Studio
Publisher: Paas

821
Art Director: Marilyn R. Murray
Designer: Robert Rodriguez
Illustrator/Artist: Robert Rodriguez
Client: Illustrators Inc.
Publisher: Illustrators Inc.

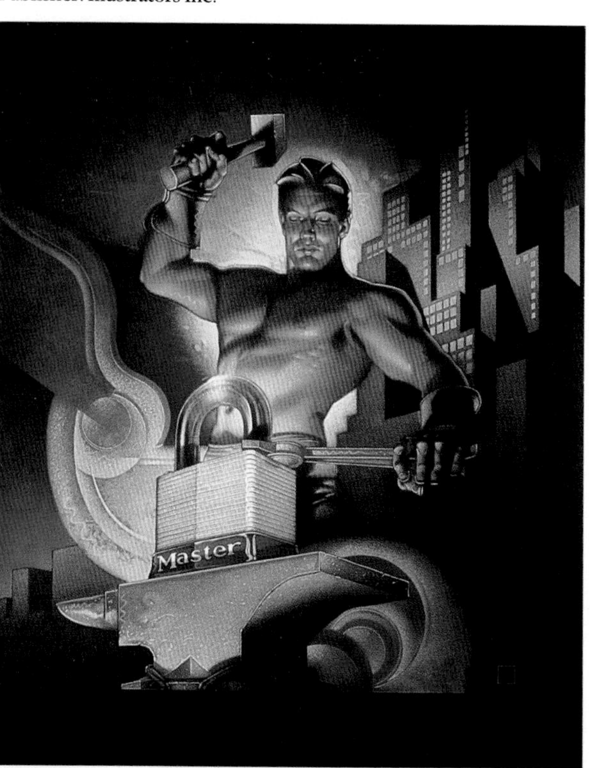

822
Art Director: Chris Hill
Designer: Chris Hill
Illustrator/Artist: Roger Poorman
Client: AIGA, San Francisco
Design Firm: Hill/A Marketing Design Firm

823
Art Director: Alan Peckolick
Illustrator/Artist: Kinuko Craft
Design Firm: Peckolick & Partners

824
Art Director: Gary Teixeira
Designer: Francois Bota
Illustrator/Artist: Francois Bota
Client: WNBC-TV, "Strictly Business"
Producer: Gay Rosenthal

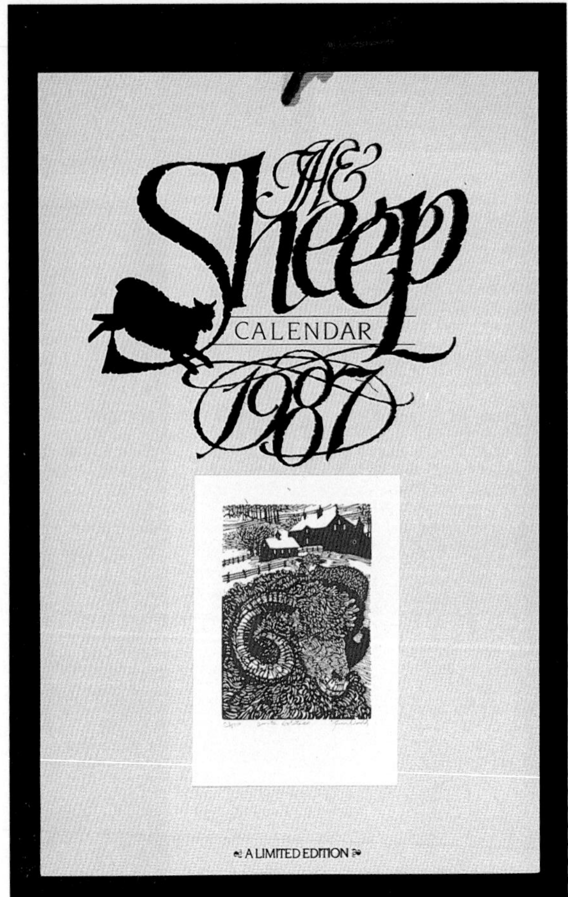

825
Art Director: Jerry Dadds
Illustrator/Artist: Jerry Dadds
Publisher: H. B. Marcoplos
Printer: Collins Litho

826

Art Director: Mike Hicks
Illustrator/Artist: Dugald Stermer
Client: Lantana, Peyton, Collins & Co.,
Security Capital Corp.
Design Firm: Hixo

827

Art Director: Kristen Funkhouser
Designer: Michael Hodgson
Illustrator/Artist: Kristen Funkhouser
Creative Director: Michael Hodgson
Client: L.A. County Museum of Art
Design Firm: Michael Hodgson Design
Publisher: L.A. County Museum of Art
Artist Representative: Richard W. Salzman

PHOTOGRAPHY

AN EPIC STRUGGLE FOR GOLD

It is a staggering scene, seeming to belong in a time in which slaves built monumental works for pharaohs and kings. The ancient, frenzied dream of gold has drawn 400,000 people across the wilderness of Brazil. Digging in the Amazon forests, diving into rivers and gnawing at mountainsides, they move with the rainy season and rumors of new sites. Serra Pelada, in the northern state of Pará, is the largest and richest of these improvised mines. Since a peasant found the first nuggets there in 1980, a mountain has been reduced to a hollow 600 feet deep and half a mile wide. It has yielded 42 tons of gold. Bars, brothels and stores have sprung up nearby; 100,000 people now live alongside the pit. On the following pages, photographer Sebastiao Salgado provides startling images of Serra Pelada, where fortune-seekers have moved a mountain on their backs.

Portfolio by Sebastiao Salgado
Text by Marlise Simons

MOVING A MOUNTAIN *on their backs, Brazilian laborers have gouged out 42 tons of gold at Serra Pelada.*

A CAST OF THOUSANDS *swarms over Serra Pelada (following pages).*

BACK-BREAKING *labor has not deterred 400,000 Brazilians from joining the wilderness gold rush since a peasant found the first nugget in 1980.*

The gold rush is rife with controversy. Prospectors say they like the freedom and camaraderie. But their world, a squalid one built around harsh labor and luck, has spawned an increase in cases of hepatitis, tuberculosis and malaria. And people have been killed in accidents and in violence erupting from rivalries over claims. There are other problems. Ecologists have denounced the contamination of creeks and rivers by the large amounts of mercury used by miners to separate gold from the ore. Independent traders, who roam the gold fields to buy nuggets, reportedly have smuggled large quantities abroad. Politicians and judges are said to have been paid off to overlook wrongdoing. Mining companies, feeling their interests threatened, have urged the government to protect their unworked claims. But the gold seekers have proved heedless of the rights of land owners, invading and exploring wherever they can. "At stake here is the right of every Brazilian to get a share of the riches of the country," said Jairo Rezende, a Serra Pelada prospector. "To see gold, and maybe touch it, maybe not, it drives people mad." ■

LIFE December 1987

A WEEK IN THE LIFE OF A HOMELESS FAMILY

BY ANNE FADIMAN

PHOTOGRAPHS BY MARY ELLEN MARK

According to the U.S. Conference of Mayors, more than one third of the nation's homeless population—and its fastest growing segment—consists of families with children. The reason for this is twofold. At the same time as the number of families living below the poverty line has increased because of unemployment and cuts in welfare benefits, the availability of low-cost housing has dropped because of widespread urban gentrification and a radical decline in the federal budget for subsidized housing. Once a family is homeless, they are likely to encounter discrimination when they seek emergency shelter. In Los Angeles, for example, only 51 of the county's 215 shelters accept families, and of those only 16 accept families with fathers. Though homeless individuals often live outside—on sidewalks, on park benches, beneath freeway overpasses—homeless families are more likely to be hidden from the public eye, living marginally from night to night in shelters, welfare hotels and cars. The Damms, who moved recently to California from Colorado, are such a family. LIFE spent seven days with the Damms during the fifth week in which they had no place to call home.

WEDNESDAY. The Valley Shelter. It is a half hour before dawn, and on the right-hand double bed in Unit 75, the mound under the dirty beige blanket begins to move. There is a similar, larger mound on the other bed, from which a woman's head and a man's arm emerge. The arm explores the space between the beds until it encounters a quart bottle of warm Coca-Cola. The man sits up and takes a swig. He pulls on a pair of jeans, a pair of socks with holes in the toes and a T-shirt that says, "STRESS: The confusion created when the mind overrides the body's desire to choke the living shit out of some asshole who desperately needs it." The woman, who is four months pregnant, walks slowly to the bathroom and takes a cold sponge bath; there has been no hot water in the shelter for five days. The mound on the right-hand bed undulates furiously. The blanket drops to the floor, revealing two small children engaged in a wrestling match. "Chill out, kids," says the man. "This ain't your home."

The Car. An hour and a half later, the Damms leave Crissy, a first-grader, at the Erwin Street School. The car behind them, which drops off a boy about Crissy's age, is a Porsche. The Damms' 1971 Buick Skylark is missing its hood and all the windows on the driver's side. The trunk must be opened with a screwdriver. The radiator leaks. Most of the upholstery on both seats is gone; when the Damms wear shorts, their legs are indented with red impressions from the springs. The car smells. The interior damage is the work of a pit bull terrier named Runtley, who spends most of his time chained to the right front neck rest. Runtley is a status symbol, a potential weapon, a love object and a form of proof that the Damms, as Dean puts it, "are something, even if everyone thinks we're nothing."

When the Damms moved to California a month ago, the car transported, housed and even subsidized them. Before they left their rented trailer outside Colorado Springs, they sold the Skylark's rims, tachometer and gauges. For nearly two years neither Dean nor Linda had found work in Colorado, a state with a high unemployment rate. They knew that even if they did not find jobs in California, the state's welfare allotments for families were the highest in the nation. They left Colorado on September 6 with $80 in cash and everything they owned stuffed into the trunk. The children bounced up and down, excited by the adventure. The peanut butter and jelly sandwiches ran out by the time they crossed the California

The Damm family: Crissy, six; Jesse, four; their mother, Linda, 27, a former nursing-home aide; and their stepfather, Dean, 33, an ex-trucker

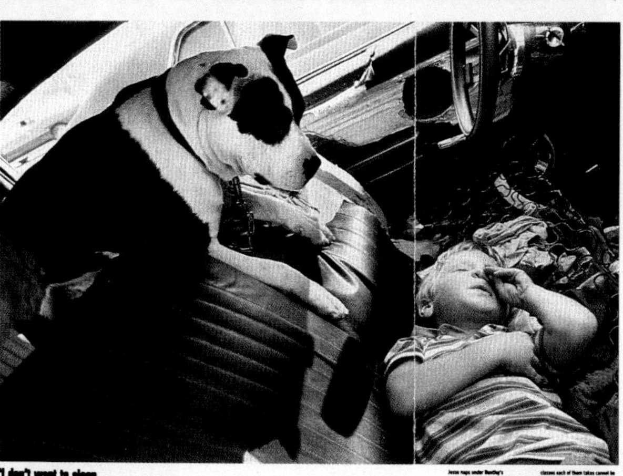

'I don't want to sleep on the street . . .'

Jesse naps under Runtley's guardianship. They both spend most of the day in the car, being carted across the San Fernando Valley on the Damms' chaotic daily itinerary. After one typical 90-mile day, Jesse asked his mother, "Why do we have to travel and travel and travel?" Jesse is too young for school, and there are long waiting lists for subsidized day cares, so either Linda or Dean must constantly be with him. This means that the four hours of daily classes each of them takes cannot be scheduled simultaneously and that neither has time for a part-time job. The instability of their family life has made their children anxious and clinging. These are common symptoms in homeless children, who are also prone to physical ailments caused by malnutrition, poor hygiene and lack of sleep. Only Runtley seems immune to the stresses of homelessness, since he regards the car as his doghouse.

border. The money ran out by the time they got to Victorville. Dean panhandled $5, which bought enough gas to get to Palmdale, where they sold eight rock tapes for $3. They rolled into the San Fernando Valley the night of September 8 with an empty gas tank and less than 10 cents.

Dean had been promised a job with a trucking company, but the offer was rescinded because he had no phone number where he could be contacted. "It's a bitch," says Dean. "You can't get a job unless you have a phone. You can't get a phone unless you have an apartment. You can't get an apartment unless you have a job." Before the Damms were admitted to the Valley Shelter, which they had heard was one of the safest in Los Angeles, they moved seven times in 15 days, staying in their car or in cheap motels patronized by prostitutes and junkies, for which they were given short-term vouchers by social service agencies. These agencies also sometimes gave them bags of food, but much of it was inedible, as it needed to be cooked. They opened the cans with a knife and ate with their hands.

Because the points of their compass—the shelter, the welfare office, Crissy's school, the technical college where Linda studies emergency medical care in the morning and Dean studies telephone installation and repair at night—are so far apart, the Damms are completely dependent on their car, which frequently breaks down. Dean has panhandled five times to pay for gas and repairs. He and Linda have also sold a tent for $10 and their car stereo for $20, and pawned their wedding rings for $15.

The Trimar Blood Center. With the exception of Runtley, whom Dean says he would never sell, the only valuable possession the Damms have left is their blood. Dean has sold whole blood once and plasma six times in the last month. Today he lies on a reclining chair, closes his eyes while 500cc of blood are pumped from his right arm, and waits an hour while the blood is centrifuged and the red blood cells returned to his bloodstream. Dean says he enjoys selling plasma because he is given free Kool-Aid and muffins, and because, with the exception of his school, the blood center is the only clean place he ever goes. When he leaves he gets $10 in cash.

The Valley Shelter. While Dean is at night school, learning the difference between amps, volts and ohms, Linda packs up the family's possessions. In one of the many bureaucratic absurdities they have encountered in their month of homelessness, they are being evicted because they have children. The federal grant that subsidizes shelter fees for families has just expired. If they were childless, the county would pay for an entire month's stay.

The Damms have no luggage. Linda stuffs their clothes into six plastic grocery bags that say, "Congratulations! You're walking out the door with verified savings!" Jesse, who often responds to stress by being especially solicitous of his mother, kneels on the floor and starts folding his T-shirts and pants, many of which came from charitable agencies and fit him only approximately. Crissy, who tends to become hyperactive whenever she sees her parents start to pack, rolls wildly on the bed.

Linda takes Crissy in her arms and rocks her back and forth.

"Where will we sleep tomorrow?" asks Crissy.

Jesse says, "I don't want to sleep on the street. I'll be hit by a car."

"We're not sleeping on the street," says Linda. "We're going camping. We'll hunt for froggies and toast marshmallows. It's going to be *real* fun."

"I'm not sleeping outside," says Crissy. "A snake will eat me."

"Runtley will protect you, honey."

"The snake will eat Runtley."

THURSDAY. County of Los Angeles Social Services. This is Dean's fifth visit to the welfare department, whose official code reads, "Aid shall be so administered . . . as to encourage self-respect, self-reliance, and the desire to be a good citizen, useful to society." Because the office misplaced Dean's birth affidavit, their first welfare check was delayed. Their second check, for their full monthly grant of $753, was accompanied by a mysterious check for $102, the result of a computer error. They were told they immediately had to make the 30-mile round trip to the welfare office to return the $102.

Holding the erroneous check in one hand and Jesse's hand in the other, Dean stands in one line, gets sent to another line and then waits in an office directly under a sign that says, "Courtesy is contagious." Finally a supervisor named Mrs. Finklestein appears, takes the $102 check and tells him she cannot explain why his first check was delayed. On the way out he sits on the security guard's desk. The guard orders him to stand.

"I'm sick of your goddamn system!" yells Dean. "You're jerking my family around! You're treating us like garbage! *We are not garbage!* "

U-Save Auto Parts. As he pays $1.75 for a quart of brake fluid, Dean tells the man behind the cash register about an accident Linda had Monday night. A Datsun driven by a man Dean calls the Iranian slammed into the Skylark and left a large dent. "I'd like to beat that Iranian's brains ➡

She cannot hide her 20 tattoos

Linda waits for Crissy after school. Determined that no one find out her daughter was homeless, Linda would not let her start first grade until she was enrolled in the lunch program, lest her classmates see her lunchbox contained only a lump of moldy cheese. Right: When a charitable agency puts the Damms up in a motel, the children are disoriented by the unaccustomed luxury. Jesse has a crying jag; Crissy, comforted by the warm shower, curls up in a fetal position for an hour.

out," says Dean. "But I'd go to jail, and then where would my family be?"

Big Tujunga Canyon. Fifteen minutes after the Damms arrive in a campground north of the Valley, a sheriff's car pulls up next to them. An officer takes down their license number and asks Dean why his dog is unleashed and how many nights he intends to stay. Since they cannot afford the $5 nightly fee, the Damms drive back dispiritedly to a city park. Dean stands guard while Linda uses the public bathroom, whose doors have been removed so junkies cannot shoot up in private. Then, leaning against the dented fender, Linda toasts marshmallows over a cigarette lighter.

Wino Flats. Violating Municipal Code 85.02, which prohibits using a car as a residence, the Damms spend the night at a nearby roadside breakdown area nicknamed for its customary patrons. Linda spreads clothes on the floor and sleeping bags over the seat springs.

"Do I have to lie on the bump in the floor?" asks Crissy.

"I've made up your bed, and you're gonna sleep in it," snaps Linda.

Linda folds herself onto the backseat. Crissy curls on the floor below her. Dean and Jesse squeeze into a single sleeping bag on the front seat. Runtley sleeps outside, chained to the door handle, and cries all night.

FRIDAY. Jack-in-the-Box. In the rest room, Linda hastily changes into the white uniform she is required to wear to her medical class, pulling a pair of colored shorts on underneath because she does not own any underwear.

Western Technical College. Both Dean and Linda are, according to their teachers, the best students in their classes. There is little in their pasts to suggest that this would be the case. Dean, who was raised on an Illinois farm by his grandparents, dropped out of school after the 10th grade, joined the Army and went AWOL twice. Linda, who was raised in California, Missouri and Michigan by her widowed mother, also dropped out in the 10th grade, married a trailer mechanic, had Crissy and Jesse, left her husband after he started to batter her and took up with an armed robber who beat her as well. Linda and Dean met three years ago when both of them were staying at the same motel. They were married last June. "We'd both been hurt real bad," says Dean, "so we had a lot in common."

Dean heard about Western Tech from a recruiter at the unemployment office, who told them the 26-week courses would help them find $9-an-hour jobs. The Damms have each taken out a $4,500 student loan.

Today Linda takes a three-hour written and practical exam in hematology. "Anyone who does not follow aseptic procedures will fail," announces the professor. "Mrs. Damm, may I inspect your fingernails?"

Linda scrubbed her hands at Jack-in-the-Box, but she cannot hide all 20 of her tattoos, most of which she applied herself when she was a teenager, using a needle dipped in India ink, and tried unsuccessfully to remove a few years later with a red-hot butter knife. The professor frowns.

Linda gets a 94 on the exam.

The Burbank Temporary Aid Center. The Damms drive to a private relief agency—the only one in the Valley where they have not already appealed for help—and are given a $5 gas voucher, $19.41 worth of groceries and a $93.40 voucher for three nights at the Scott Motel. The Scott has become a de facto emergency shelter, since 90 percent of its patrons are homeless people whose fees are paid by charities. The Burbank center sends its clients there because, unlike the proprietors of other local motels, its owners do not complain that their guests are wasting electricity if they leave the lights on all night to keep the cockroaches from crawling on their beds.

Western Technical College. Dean takes an exam on the 25 color-coded wires that hook up a business telephone. He scores 100 percent. ➡

829 Distinctive Merit

Art Director: Tom Bentkowski
Designer: Tom Bentkowski
Photographer: Mary Ellen Mark
Director of Photography: Peter Howe
Publisher: Lisa Valk
Publication: Life
Managing Editor: Patricia Ryan

830

Art Director: Pat Burnham
Designer: Pat Burnham
Photographer: Kurt Markus
Writer: Bill Miller
Creative Director: Tom McElligott
Client: US West
Agency: Fallon McElligott

831

Art Director: Michael Smith
Photographer: Annie Leibovitz
Writer: Jackie End, Bill Hamilton
Creative Director: Bill Hamilton
Client: Arrow
Agency: Chiat/Day Inc.
Account Management: Amy Saypol, Dick O'Connell

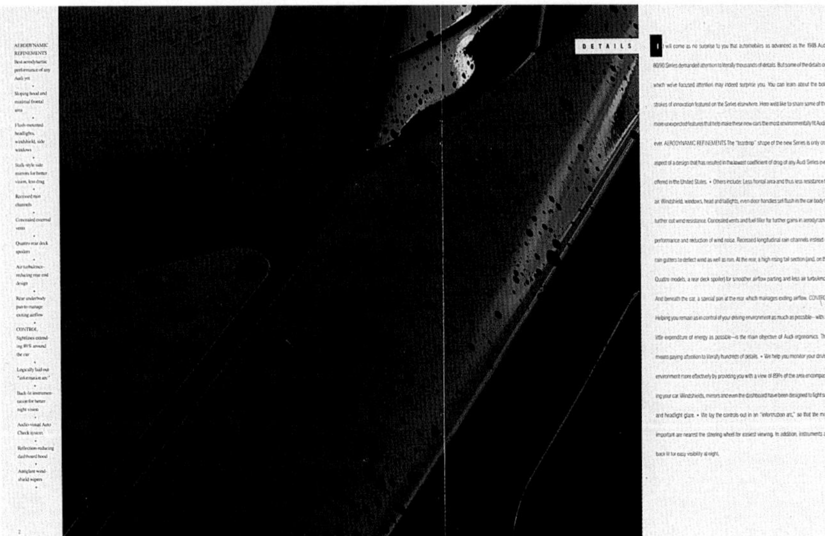

832

Art Director: Barry Shepard
Designer: Barry Shepard
Photographer: Rick Rusing
Client: Audi of America Inc.
Design Firm: SHR Communications Planning & Design

833

Art Director: Barry Shepard
Designer: Barry Shepard
Photographer: Rick Rusing
Client: Audi of America Inc.
Design Firm: SHR Communications Planning & Design

835
Art Director: Bob Barrie
Designer: Bob Barrie
Photographer: Rick Dublin
Writer: Jarl Olsen
Creative Director: Tom McElligott
Client: Hush Puppies
Agency: Fallon McElligott
Model: Jason

834
Art Director: Dan Wilson
Photographer: Mashall Harrington
Writer: Jeff Elkind
Client: San Diego Padres
Agency: Franklin & Associates

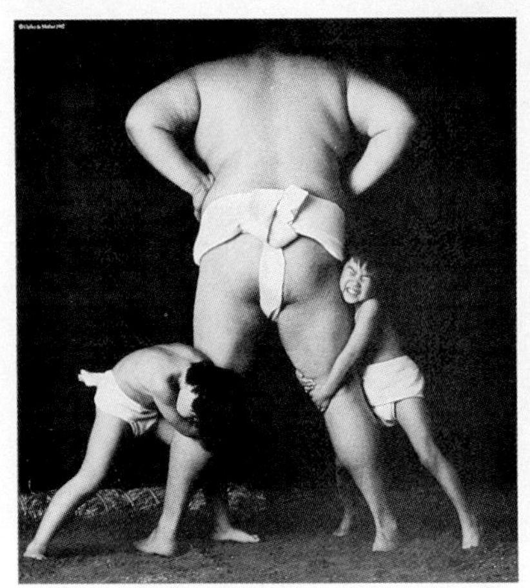

836
Art Director: Tracy Wong, Mike LaMonica
Designer: Tracy Wong, Mike LaMonica
Photographer: David Langley
Client: Ogilvy & Mather
Agency: Shing Unlimited

837
Art Director: Hadas Dembo
Photographer: Laurie Rubin
Publication: The New York Times

838

Art Director: Dean Hanson
Designer: Dean Hanson
Photographer: Richard Olsenius
Writer: Jamie Barrett
Creative Director: Tom McElligott
Client: Fallon McElligott
Agency: Fallon McElligott

Season's Greetings

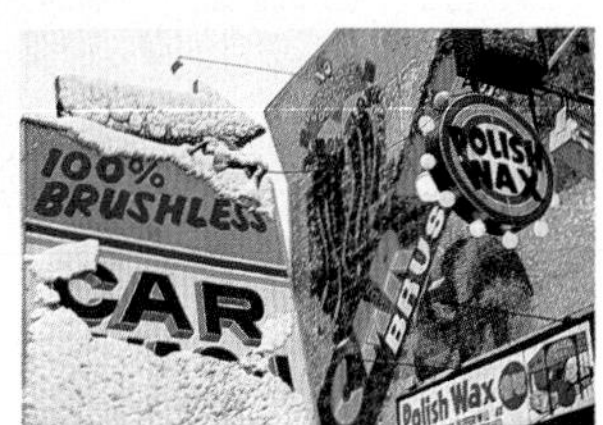

839

Art Director: Don James
Photographer: Don James
Creative Director: Don James
Design Firm: Light Industry
Publisher: Light Industry

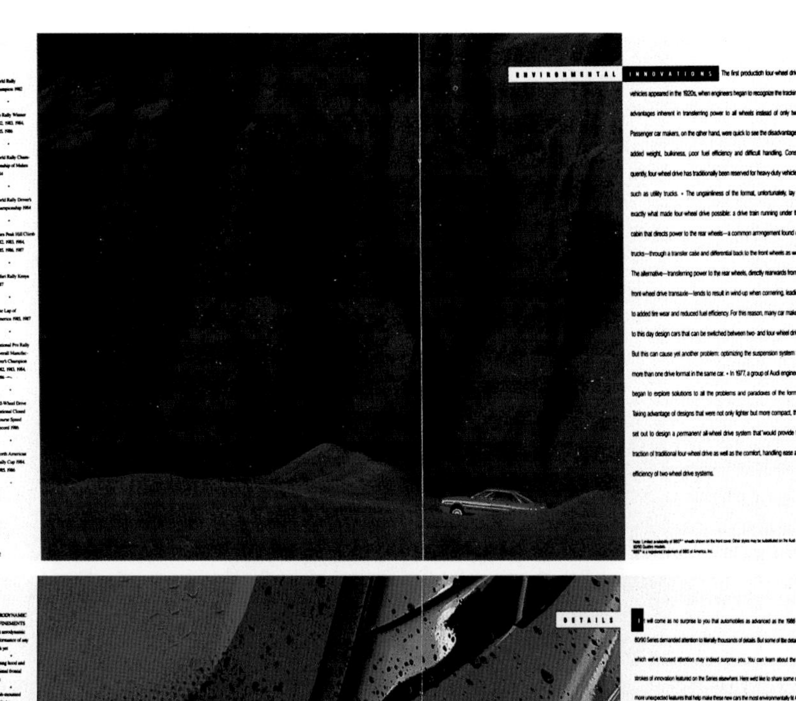

World Rally Champion 1982 • Pro Rally Winner 1982, 1983, 1984, 1985, 1986 • World Rally Championship of Makes 1984 • World Rally Driver's Championship 1984 • Pikes Peak Hill Climb 1982, 1983, 1984, 1985, 1986, 1987 • Safari Rally Kenya 1987 • One Lap of America 1985, 1987 • National Pro Rally Overall Manufacturer's Champion 1982, 1983, 1984, 1986 • All-Wheel Drive National Closed Course Speed Record 1986 • North American Rally Cup 1984, 1985, 1986 •

2

ENVIRONMENTAL INNOVATIONS The first production four-wheel drive vehicles appeared in the 1920s, when engineers began to recognize the tracking advantages inherent in transferring power to all wheels instead of only two. Passenger car makers, on the other hand, were quick to see the disadvantages: added weight, bulkiness, poor fuel efficiency and difficult handling. Consequently, four-wheel drive has traditionally been reserved for heavy-duty vehicles, such as utility trucks. • The ungainliness of the format, unfortunately, lay in exactly what made four-wheel drive possible: a drive train running under the cabin that directs power to the rear wheels—a common arrangement found on trucks—through a transfer case and differential back to the front wheels as well. The alternative—transferring power to the rear wheels, directly rearwards from a front-wheel drive transaxle—tends to result in wind-up when cornering, leading to added tire wear and reduced fuel efficiency. For this reason, many car makers to this day design cars that can be switched between two- and four-wheel drive. But this can cause yet another problem: optimizing the suspension system for more than one drive format in the same car. • In 1977, a group of Audi engineers began to explore solutions to all the problems and paradoxes of the format. Taking advantage of designs that were not only lighter but more compact, they set out to design a *permanent* all-wheel drive system that would provide the traction of traditional four-wheel drive as well as the comfort, handling ease and efficiency of two-wheel drive systems.

AERODYNAMIC REFINEMENTS Best aerodynamic performance of any Audi yet • Sloping hood and minimal frontal area • Flush-mounted headlights, windshield, side windows • Stalk-style side mirrors for better vision, less drag • Recessed rain channels • Concealed external vents • Quattro rear deck spoilers • Air turbulence-reducing rear end design • Rear underbody pan to manage exiting airflow • CONTROL Sightlines measuring 89% around the car • Logically laid out "information arc" • Back-lit instrumentation for better night vision • Audio-visual Auto Check system • Reflection-reducing dashboard hood • Antiglare windshield wipers •

2

DETAILS It will come as no surprise to you that automobiles as advanced as the 1988 Audi 80/90 Series demanded attention to literally thousands of details. But some of the details on which we've focused attention may indeed surprise you. You can learn about the bold strokes of innovation featured on the Series elsewhere. Here we'd like to share some of the more unexpected features that help make these new cars the most environmentally fit Audis ever. AERODYNAMIC REFINEMENTS The "teardrop" shape of the new Series is only one aspect of a design that has resulted in the lowest coefficient of drag of any Audi Series ever offered in the United States. • Others include: Less frontal area and thus less resistance to air. Windshield, windows, head and taillights, even door handles set flush in the car body to further cut wind resistance. Concealed vents and fuel filler for further gains in aerodynamic performance and reduction of wind noise. Recessed longitudinal rain channels instead of rain gutters to deflect wind as well as rain. At the rear, a high rising tail section (and, on the Quattro models, a rear deck spoiler) for smoother airflow parting and less air turbulence. And beneath the car, a special pan at the rear which manages exiting airflow. CONTROL Helping you remain as in control of your driving environment as much as possible—with as little expenditure of energy as possible—is the main objective of Audi ergonomics. That means paying attention to literally hundreds of details. • We help you monitor your driving environment more effectively by providing you with a view of 89% of the area encompassing your car. Windshields, mirrors and even the dashboard have been designed to fight sun and headlight glare. • We lay the controls out in an "information arc," so that the most important are nearest the steering wheel for easiest viewing. In addition, instruments are back lit for easy visibility at night.

Anti-theft sound system coding device • DURABILITY Fully galvanized bodyshell • 27-step paint process • Zinc-rich primer • Hot wax dipping for hidden recesses • Teflon-coated door hinges • Protective rubber pads on underbody lift points • Stainless steel/aluminized steel exhaust system • Gold-plated connectors for fuel injection • Ultrasonically welded wiring connections • REDUCED MAINTENANCE Lifetime lubricants except auto transmission fluid and engine oil • 30,000 mile spark plugs at normal service • ENVIRONMENTAL CONSCIOUSNESS Lead- and cadmium-free paints • Asbestos-free brakes, linings, clutch and gaskets •

DETAILS Front lights that can be switched to deliver flashes powerful enough to function as warning signals even during the daytime. And to protect part of your investment in your car, the sound system actually discourages theft thanks to a feature that renders it inoperative to anyone not knowing a special four digit code. • DURABILITY Full galvanization of the sheet metal used in the bodyshell is only one of the many measures we take to enhance the longevity of the Audi 80/90 Series. • We employ a 27-step paint process that adds protective layers of zinc-rich primer to further increase corrosion resistance. • Hidden recesses throughout the bodyshell are dipped in hot wax, which when cooled remains pliable in order to maintain a protective seal over the finest of crevices. • Under the car, there are special rubber pads at the lift points to prevent rust protection from being scraped off. • Within the engine, gold-plated connectors have been used in the fuel injection system to prevent corrosion. • The exhaust system is constructed almost entirely of stainless steel pipe or aluminized steel. The system actually extracts moisture from the exhaust before it can cause corrosion from the inside out. • REDUCED MAINTENANCE In addition to fighting corrosion, we've also sought to increase durability by replacing parts that in the past required maintenance with new designs that last the life of the car. One example is the synthetic lubricant used for the transaxle and rear differential. Protected by magnetic inserts that pull steel particles out of the oil, this lubricant never needs replacement. ENVIRONMENTAL CONSCIOUSNESS Finally, there are details *absent* from the Audi 80/90 Series that are worth mentioning. Lead- and cadmium-based paints, for example, since these can be environmental hazards. Asbestos, for another example. We have removed it from the brake linings used in the Audi 80/90 Series. These figures are just one of hundreds of details that help keep the 1988 Audi 80/90 Series working *with the environment*.

840

Art Director: Barry Shepard
Designer: Barry Shepard
Photographer: Rick Rusing
Client: Audi of America Inc.
Design Firm: SHR Communications Planning & Design

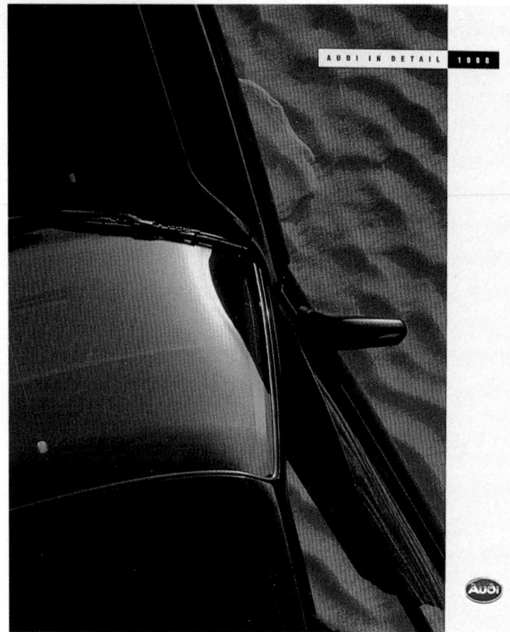

841
Art Director: Barry Shepard
Designer: Barry Shepard
Photographer: Rick Rusing
Client: Audi of America Inc.
Design Firm: SHR Communications Planning & Design

842

Art Director: Michael Smith
Photographer: Dennis Manarchy
Writer: Bryan Buckley
Creative Director: Bill Hamilton
Client: Rockport
Agency: Chiat/Day Inc., New York
Account Management: Steve Friedman

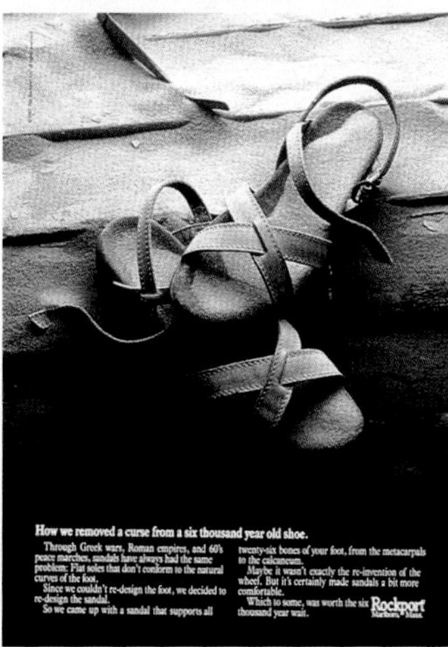

843

Art Director: Michael Smith
Photographer: Dennis Manarchy
Writer: Bryan Buckley
Creative Director: Bill Hamilton
Client: Rockport
Agency: Chiat/Day Inc., New York
Account Management: Bob Jeffrey,
Lori Schrader

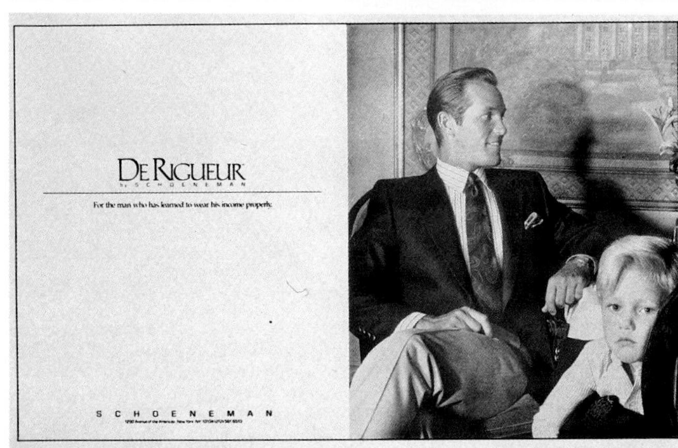

844
Art Director: Gad Romann, Barry Tannenholz, Terry Whistler, Denise DeRosiers
Photographer: Horst
Writer: Gad Romann, Barry Tannenholz
Client: Round the Clock Pantyhose
Agency: Romann & Tannenholz

845
Art Director: Gad Romann, Barry Tannenholz, Suzanne Moss, Denise DeRosiers
Photographer: Thom Gilbert
Writer: Gad Romann, Barry Tannenholz
Client: DeRigueur by Schoeneman
Agency: Romann & Tannenholz

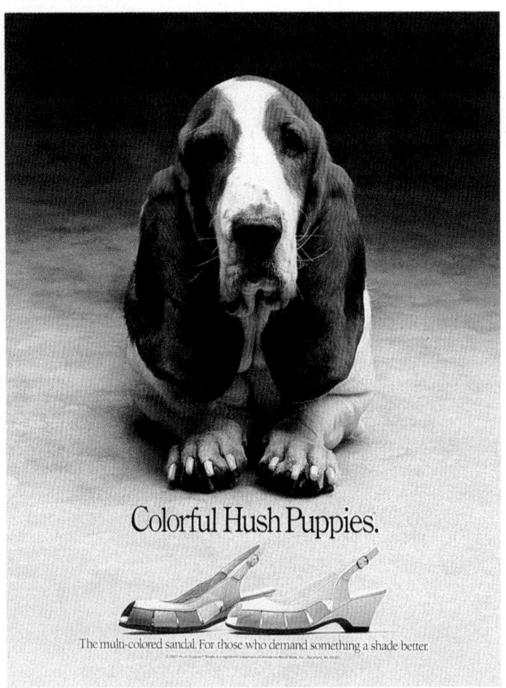

846

Art Director: Bob Barrie
Designer: Bob Barrie
Photographer: Rick Dublin
Writer: Jarl Olsen
Creative Director: Tom McElligott
Client: Hush Puppies
Agency: Fallon McElligott
Model: Jason

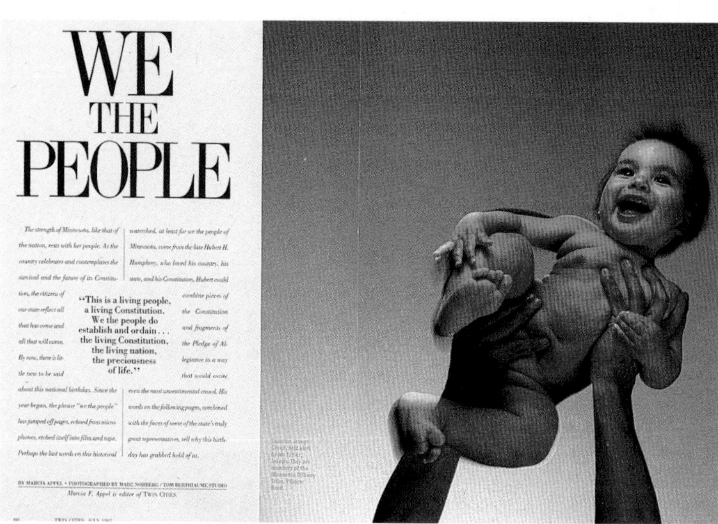

WE THE PEOPLE

The strength of Minnesota, like that of the nation, rests with her people. As the country celebrates and contemplates the survival and the future of its Constitution, the citizens of our state reflect all that has come and all that will come. By now, there is little new to be said about this national birthday. Since the year began, the phrase "we the people" has jumped off pages, echoed from microphones, etched itself into film and tape. Perhaps the last words on this historical watershed, at least for we the people of Minnesota, come from the late Hubert H. Humphrey, who loved his country, his state, and his Constitution. Hubert could combine pieces of the Constitution and fragments of the Pledge of Allegiance in a way that would excite even the most unsentimental crowd. His words on the following pages, combined with the faces of some of the state's truly great representatives, tell why this birthday has grabbed hold of us.

"This is a living people, a living Constitution. We the people do establish and ordain . . . the living Constitution, the living nation, the preciousness of life."

BY MARCIA APPEL • PHOTOGRAPHED BY MARC NORBERG / TOM BERTHIAUME STUDIO

Marcia F. Appel is editor of TWIN CITIES

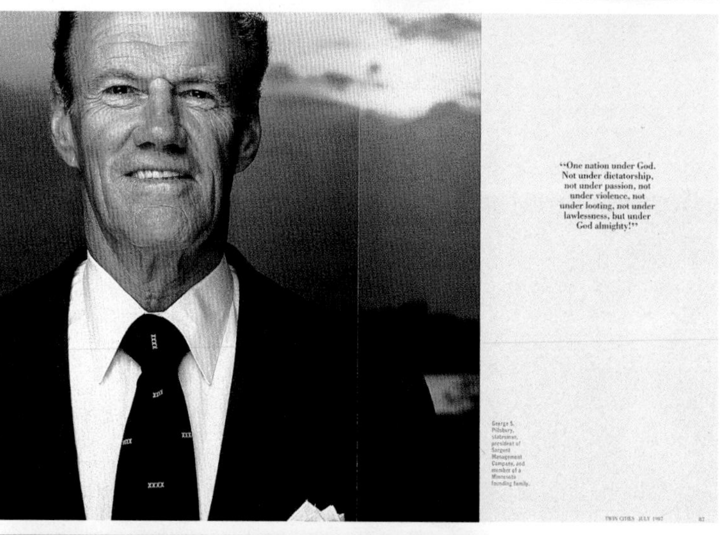

"One nation under God. Not under dictatorship, not under passion, not under violence, not under looting, not under lawlessness, but under God almighty!"

George S. Pillsbury, statesman, president of Sargent Management Company, and member of a Minnesota founding family.

TWIN CITIES JULY 1987 87

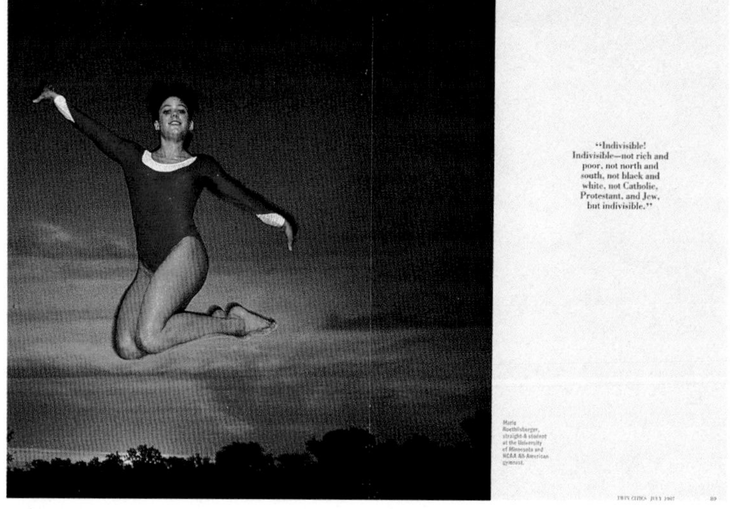

"Indivisible! Indivisible—not rich and poor, not north and south, not black and white, not Catholic, Protestant, and Jew, but indivisible."

Maria Roethlisberger, straight-A student at the University of Minnesota and NCAA All-American gymnast.

TWIN CITIES JULY 1987 89

847

Art Director: Kathleen Timmerman
Designer: Kristi Hedberg
Photographer: Marc Norberg, Berthiaume Studio
Publication: Twin Cities Magazine

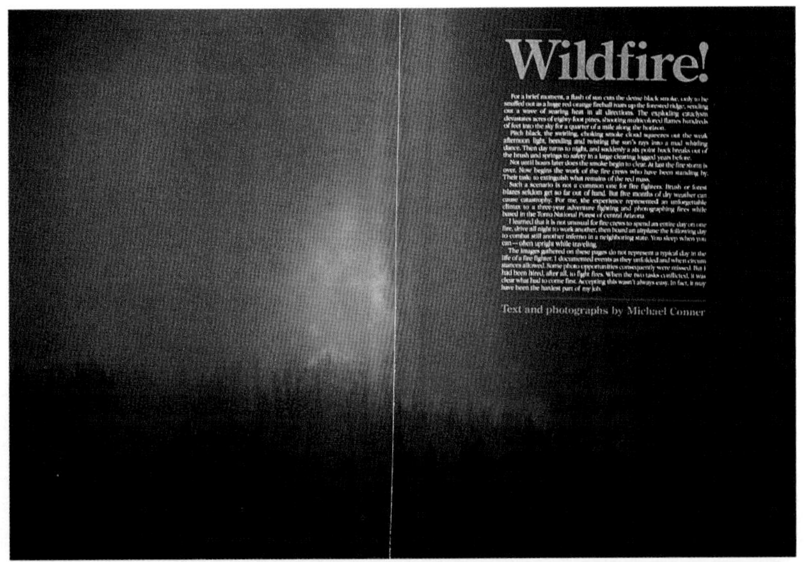

Wildfire!

For a brief moment, a flash of sun cuts the dense black smoke, only to be snuffed out as a huge red orange fireball roars up the forested ridge, sending out a wave of searing heat in all directions. The exploding cataclysm devastates acres of eighty-foot pines, shooting multicolored flames hundreds of feet into the sky for a quarter of a mile along the horizon.

Pitch black, the swirling, choking smoke cloud squeezes out the weak afternoon light, bending and twisting the sun's rays into a mad whirling dance. Then day turns to night, and suddenly a six point buck breaks out of the brush and springs to safety in a large clearing logged years before.

Not until hours later does the smoke begin to clear. At last the fire storm is over. Now begins the work of the fire crews who have been standing by. Their task: to extinguish what remains of the red mass.

Such a scenario is not a common one for fire fighters. Brush or forest blazes seldom get so far out of hand. But five months of dry weather can cause catastrophy. For me, the experience represented an unforgettable climax to a three-year adventure fighting and photographing fires while based in the Tonto National Forest of central Arizona.

I learned that it is not unusual for fire crews to spend an entire day on one fire, drive all night to work another, then board an airplane the following day to combat still another inferno in a neighboring state. You sleep when you can—often upright while traveling.

The images gathered on these pages do not represent a typical day in the life of a fire fighter. I documented events as they unfolded and when circumstances allowed. Some photo opportunities consequently were missed. But I had been hired, after all, to fight fires. When the two tasks conflicted, it was clear what had to come first. Accepting this wasn't always easy. In fact, it may have been the hardest part of my job.

Text and photographs by Michael Conner

Wildfire!

Wildfire!

848

Art Director: Gary Bennett
Designer: Gary Bennett
Photographer: Michael Conner
Writer: Michael Conner
Editor: Merrill Windsor
Client: Arizona Department of Transportation
Publisher: Hugh Harelson
Publication: Arizona Highways
Picture Editor: Peter Ensenberger

ARTS

Echoes

In the early 19th century, our country was young and vast, much of it still wilderness. Culturally, the nation was in its infancy. "[Who] looks at an American picture or statue?" one European journal asked. But by the 1840s there came the stirrings of a response to that scornful declaration: A group of New York artists, fueled by nationalism and in love with nature, had begun traveling the nation to capture its beauty. Known later as the Hudson River School, these painters produced the most lustrous—and illustrious—landscapes in the history of American art. From this month until January 3, in a major exhibition, New York's Metropolitan Museum of Art is presenting American Paradise: The World of the Hudson River School.

LIFE sent landscape photographer Denis Waugh to the locales that inspired some of the most spectacular of these paintings. "I

Kaaterskill Clove, a gorge cut in the Catskill Mountains on the west bank of the Hudson River, inspired a generation of artists. Washington Irving set his 1820 story of Rip Van Winkle there and wrote glowingly of the area's "rocky precipices mantled with primeval forests; deep gorges walled in by beetling cliffs, with torrents tumbling as it were from the sky."

In the 1840s, lured by the rugged scenery, a group of painters formed America's first art colony at the clove's southern end. Asher Brown Durand, an engraver turned painter who was one of the leaders of the Hudson River School, created his *Kaaterskill Clove* (below) in 1866, finishing it in his studio from sketches done on-site.

More than a century later, the view is almost unchanged. About 80 percent of the land visible at right is New York State Forest Preserve. Hidden among trees, Route 23A (the Rip Van Winkle Trail) is no more obtrusive than the stagecoach road it replaced.

American Landscapes of a Century Ago Are Celebrated in a Glorious Exhibit

fell in love with the settings—American scale is so broad," says Waugh, a New Zealander based in Britain. Many of the originals were limned in the Hudson River Valley, but some were done as far away as California and Peru. Wealthy collectors prized them, but after the Civil War the style fell from vogue. The wilderness disappeared too. Some of the painters' sites are now pockets of protected green, flanked by shopping malls and highways. But Waugh has recaptured the wild beauty of the era, making it possible for us to marvel anew at our nation's grandeur.

Henry Hudson explored his great river in 1609. During the Revolutionary War, it was a strategic waterway with a fortress at West Point, 50 miles north of New York City. Ironically, by the time John F. Kensett painted his peaceful *View from Cozzens' Hotel Near West Point* (opposite, bottom) in 1863, graduates of the military academy were fighting one another in the Civil War. Kensett drew and painted all over the countryside, in Massachusetts, Maine, Rhode Island and even Montana, traveling up the Missouri River with a fur trader.

The major painter of the American West at that time was German-born Albert Bierstadt, who grew up in Massachusetts. He visited the Mariposa Grove near Yosemite Valley in 1863, where the sequoias approach 300 feet. He did not paint the setting, perhaps dissuaded by a friend who declared that the giant trees could not be captured on canvas. In the 1870s, however, Bierstadt returned to the area and painted *The Great Trees, Mariposa Grove, California* (top right). The focal point of the picture was the towering "Grizzly Giant."

At his peak, Bierstadt was commanding sums as high as $35,000. But by the 1890s his fortunes and popularity were in deep decline. In 1985 a Bierstadt painting was auctioned for $675,000.

This year what was left of Cozzens' Hotel was torn down. But the Grizzly Giant still stands, as it has since 700 B.C.

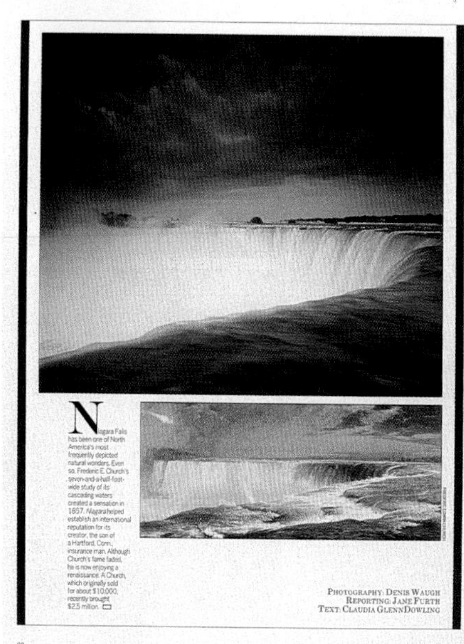

Niagara Falls has been one of North America's most frequently depicted natural wonders. Even so, Frederic E. Church's seven-and-a-half-foot-wide study of its cascading waters created a sensation in 1857. *Niagara* helped establish an international reputation for its creator, the son of a Hartford, Conn., insurance man. Although Church's fame faded, he is now enjoying a renaissance. A Church, which originally sold for about $10,000, recently brought $2.5 million.

PHOTOGRAPHY: DENIS WAUGH
REPORTING: JANE FURTH
TEXT: CLAUDIA GLENN DOWLING

849

Art Director: Tom Bentkowski
Designer: Tom Bentkowski
Photographer: Denis Waugh
Director of Photography: Peter Howe
Publisher: Lisa Valk
Publication: Life
Managing Editor: Patricia Ryan

850

Art Director: Suez Kehl
Designer: Cindy Scudder
Photographer: John Dominis
Writer: Carol McCabe
Editor: Joan Tapper
Client: National Geographic Society
Publisher: National Geographic Society
Publication: National Geographic Traveler
Picture Editor: Winthrop Scudder

851
Art Director: Elizabeth Woodson
Designer: Elizabeth Woodson
Photographer: Diane Padys
Publisher: American Express Publishing Corp.
Publication: Food & Wine

RELIGION

Sisters of the Mists

PHOTOGRAPHY: MARINA YURCHENKO

The Pyukhtitsy Convent near the Estonian city of Kohtla-Järve is one of 15 or so convents and three monasteries still functioning in the U.S.S.R. Between 20 and 50 million Soviets are estimated to be believers in the Russian Orthodox Church, which is tolerated if not embraced by the government. Below: portrait of a novice named Natalya.

Last February at a photography exhibition in Moscow, Westerners were startled and moved by a series of black-and-white pictures documenting life in a convent in northern Estonia. Set on the raw and foggy shores of the Gulf of Finland, the Russian Orthodox monastery seemed to belong more to the Christian world of Tolstoy than to today's U.S.S.R. In fact, the Assumption Convent at Pyukhtitsy was founded by a local nobleman, Count Shakhovskoi, in 1891—long before Estonia fell to the atheistic Soviet state in 1944. It was constructed on the site of a supposed apparition of the Virgin Mary and has operated in remote self-sufficiency ever since. The photographer who penetrated this insular world is a 31-year-old staff member of the Soviet news agency Novosti, Marina Yurchenko. She had first visited the nunnery when she was 15 and attending summer camp nearby. After earning a degree in journalism at Moscow State

University, Yurchenko returned to the convent in 1984 for several days of photography. Her pictures caught the eye of the planners of the book *A Day in the Life of the Soviet Union*. They were preparing to send 50 Soviet and 50 Western photographers to make a one-day pictorial record of the country. Last May 15 the 100 fanned out; Marina Yurchenko, with color film this time, went back to Pyukhtitsy.

"I was concerned that I would merely be repeating my work," says Yurchenko. "But I made an effort to do new things. It is difficult to shoot religious activity because it is private and solemn. When one photographs inside a church, one has crossed a sort of line, a barrier. I decided from the start that I would use no strobe or lights of any kind, and of course that has had an effect on the pictures."

The 144 nuns, comfortable with Yurchenko from her earlier visits, were cooperative subjects. They farm about 60 acres in much the same way as Estonian peasants did a century ago, and except for paying rent to the state, their rites have not been disturbed by the changing regimes in Moscow. The nuns' day begins at six a.m. with mass said by a priest. Breakfast is taken privately in the nuns' cells and is followed by household or farm chores until lunch-

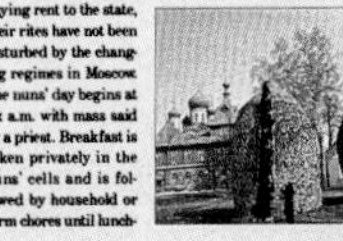

A novice, Dana, retrieves fish from the monastery's ice house. Filled each winter with great blocks cut from a lake, it stores perishable food through the summer. Electric refrigerators in the kitchen keep the day-to-day food. Novices like Dana and those at left, who wear headgear but not habits, are the lowest-ranking. They can serve for up to 25 years before being fully accepted by the order.

The convent relies on horses instead of tractors and automobiles. Bordered by the sea on both north and west, Estonia has a milder climate than the Russian heartland. Yet winter temperatures can fall to below 20°F. The convent buildings have central heating systems, but wood, shown stacked in the nuns' distinctive style, is also burned.

As the wind sweeps in from the sea, Sister Anna meditates in the cemetery that the convent shares with the village of Pyukhtitsy. According to Orthodox doctrine, each departed spirit must undergo a partial judgment during the first 40 days after death, so it is especially important to pray and offer alms for the deceased during this period. Such intercessions can help decide a soul's place on the ladder between damnation and salvation. Thus a nun posthumously forgiven by those on earth for small transgressions she may not even have realized will be judged more kindly. All of which is temporary, for there will be a further accounting, called the Terrible Judgment, when mankind through the ages will know the second coming of Christ.

852

Art Director: Tom Bentkowski
Designer: Tom Bentkowski
Photographer: Marina Yurchenko
Director of Photography: Peter Howe
Publisher: Lisa Valk
Publication: Life
Managing Editor: Patricia Ryan

TOWN & COUNTRY

O Rare Manhattan

's Wonderful! 's Marvelous!

New York. It's red-hot deals, white-hot trading. Or is it? To those who know, it's the show that never closes. Turn a corner and hear a band, meet a dragon or discover a New York beauty. Raised in Tuxedo Park, Susan Rogers Williamson joins the Veteran Corps of Artillery—which first performed when Washington was President—to celebrate in Battery Park's Castle Clinton. Susan, who works at Sotheby's, wears a dress by Manfred Schneider Haute Couture. Cartier pearls. Make-up: Lancôme's Paris en Plaid. Hair and make-up throughout by Garcia.

Photographs by Norman Parkinson/Produced by Alison A. Mazzola and Robert Downs Clark

853

Art Director: Melissa Tardiff
Designer: Maria Bavosa
Photographer: Norman Parkinson
Editor: Frank Zachary
Publisher: Fred Jackson
Publication: Town & Country

854
Art Director: Phyllis Schefer
Photographer: Toscani
Publication: Elle
Publication Director: Régis Pagniez

855
Art Director: Tomas Pantin
Photographer: Tomas Pantin
Creative Director: Kim Iberg
Client: Austin Graphic Arts Society
Agency: Tomas Pantin Inc.
Publisher: Austin Graphic Arts Society

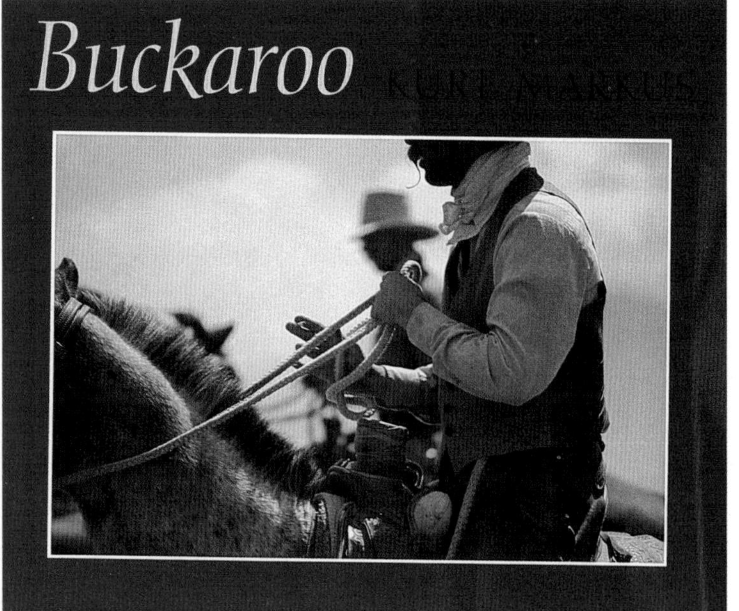

856
Art Director: Kurt Markus, Eleanor Caponigro
Designer: Eleanor Caponigro
Photographer: Kurt Markus
Writer: Kurt Markus
Editor: Russell Martin
Client: U.S. West
Publisher: New York Graphic Society

857

Art Director: Sharon White, Bob Packert
Photographer: Sharon White, Bob Packert
Make-up: Sonny Otero
Hair: Louis Massauro

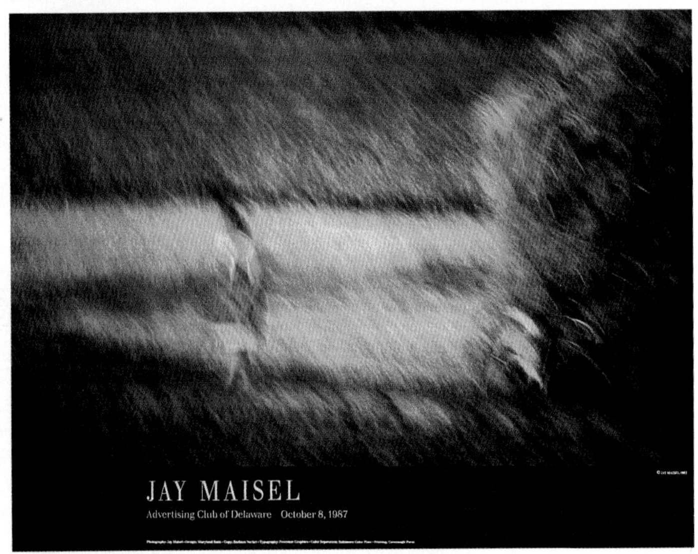

858
Art Director: Cheryl Heller
Photographer: Laurie Rubin
Client: S. D. Warren Paper Co.
Agency: Heller Breene

859
Art Director: Jane Langa, Catherine Sternbergh, Leslie Kedash
Photographer: Jay Maisel
Client: ASMP, St. Louis,
Not Just Another Art Directors Club,
Photographic Resource Center,
Art Directors Club of Delaware

TELEVISION

ROCK DRILLS
60 seconds
OPENING CHIME. SOUND OF MARCHING.
DRILL SERGEANT VO: Attend Hut! Funky Chicken!
SFX: MILITARY SNARE DRUM THROUGHOUT.
SARGE: Duckwalk! ...Moonwalk! ...Disco! ...Windmill! ...Air Guitar! ...James Brown!
SOLDIERS: Huh!
SARGE: Jimi plays Monterey!
VO: If it's out there, it's in here. ...The NYNEX Yellow Pages.
SFX: BOOK SLAMS SHUT.

HIGHER AND HIGHER
60 seconds
CHORUS:
Your love has lifted me higher...
than I've ever been lifted before.
So keep it up.
1ST SOLOIST: So keep it up.
CHORUS: Quench my desire.
2ND SOLOIST: Quench my desire.
CHORUS: And I'll be at your side for ever more.
You know your love keeps on liftin'

Art Director: Marty Weiss
Writer: Robin Raj
Client: NYNEX Information Resources
Director: Kevin Godley, Lol Creme
Producer: Mark Sitley, Steve Amato
Account Manager: Amy Saypol

Art Director: Michael Fazende
Writer: John Stingley
Editor: Jeff Stickles
Client: Emmis Broadcasting
Director: Jeff Gorman
Producer: Judy Brink, Char Loving

Client: NYNEX Information Resources
Director: Kevin Godley, Lol Creme
Producer: Mark Sitley, Steve Amato
Account Manager: Amy Saypol

Editor: Jeff Stickles
Client: Conran's
Director: Henry Sandbank
Producer: Char Loving

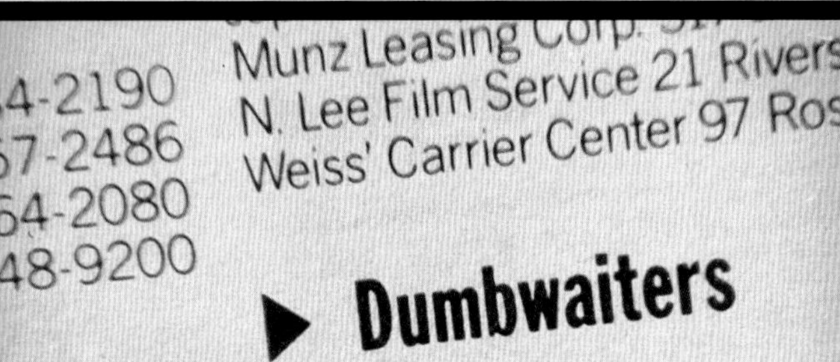

DUMBWAITER
30 seconds
SFX: OPENING CHIME. RESTAURANT SOUNDS.
MAN VO: Excuse me…
WAITER: Sir!
MAN VO: What are your specials today?
WAITER: I don't know.
WOMAN VO: Do your entrees come with salad?
WAITER: I don't know.
MAN VO: Do you have escargots?
WAITER: Escargots? …I don't know.
WOMAN VO: May we see a menu?
WAITER: Yes! No! I don't know.
VO: If it's out there, it's in here….
SFX: PLATES BREAKING.
VO: The NYNEX Yellow Pages.
SFX: BOOK SLAMS SHUT.
VO: Why would anyone need another?

BED
30 seconds
SFX: NATURAL THROUGHOUT.
VO: At Conran's, we don't think beautifully-designed furniture for your dining room…should cost so much…you can't afford furniture for your bedroom. Conran's. Complete home furnishings.

Art Director: Rick Boyko
Writer: Bill Hamilton
Editor: Larry Bridges
Client: Reebok
Director: Mark Coppos
Producer: Mark Sitley, Eric Herrman, Coppos Films
Music: Jonathan Elias; Elias Associates

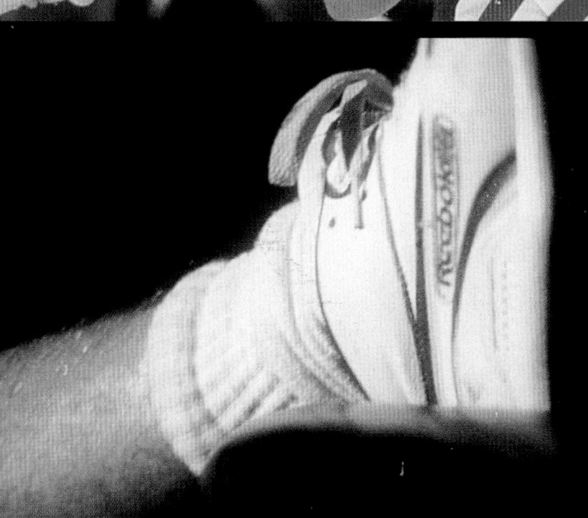

SPORTS CONDITIONING
60 seconds
SFX: BREATHING AND EXAGGERATED SOUND EFFECTS THROUGHOUT.
SILENCE.

Art Director: Keith Lane
Writer: Michael Fortuna, Eric Haggman
Editor: Bill Stuart
Client: WMJX-FM
Producer: Wendy Schwartz
Music: Soundtrack

My husband and I are in the middle of an incredibly stupid argument.

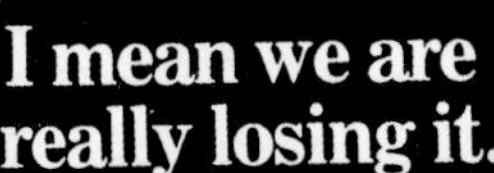

All of a sudden God puts this song on the radio.

ARGUMENT
30 seconds
SFX: "THAT'S WHAT FRIENDS ARE FOR."
GRAPHIC 1: My husband and I are in the middle of an incredibly stupid argument. I mean we are really losing it. All of a sudden God puts this song on the radio. Stopped us right in our tracks. I went out and bought the album.
GRAPHIC 2: We play the great songs.

conran's

870 Distinctive Merit

Art Director: John Morrison
Writer: Robert Chandler
Editor: Dennis Hayes; Dennis Hayes Editorial
Client: Apple/Macintosh
Director: Joe Pytka
Producer: Paul Gold; BBDO, Trish Reeves; BBDO, Pytka

871 Distinctive Merit

Art Director: Bob Ribits, Alex Goslar
Writer: Alex Goslar
Creative Director: Gerry Miller
Client: Procter & Gamble/Cheer
Producer: Angelo Antonucci, Carole Floodstrand, Leroy Koetz; Koetz & Co.

HOME OFFICE
60 seconds
VIC: So they sent you down to check on me?
DICK: Who am I to check up on you? So how's it coming?
VIC: Oh, I don't know. You tell me.
DICK: Where'd you get all this?
VIC: I keep telling you guys, the worst place to get any work done is at work.
DICK: But you're all alone here. I mean no secretary. No production department. No nothin'.
VIC: Oh, I wouldn't exactly say "nothing."

ICE CREAM
45 seconds
MUSIC THROUGHOUT.
ANNCR: Nobody's better in cold than All Temperature Cheer!

872 Distinctive Merit

Art Director: Steve Miller, John Colquhoun, Frank Todaro
Writer: Cliff Freeman, Jane King, Arthur Bijur, Rick LeMoine
Creative Director: Arthur Bijur
Client: North American Philips
Director: Mark Story
Producer: Story, Piccolo, Guliner

Lord Klempston gazed upon Lucretia's loveliness.

and whispered into her ear...

ANNCR (VO): It's time to change your bulb to Philips. Philips Longer Life square bulbs.

LORD KLEMPSTON
30 seconds
1st MAN: Hey, get a load of this. Lord Klempston gazed upon Lucretia's loveliness. Her milky white shoulders were ablaze in the moonlight. Lord Klempston approached her and wrapped his thickly muscled arms around her delicate waist. He then whispered into her ear....
SFX: BULB BLOWS
1st MAN: I can't see.
2nd MAN: Lord Klempston was blind?!
ANNCR: It's time to change your bulb to Philips. Philips Longer Life square bulbs last 33% longer than ordinary round bulbs.

873 Distinctive Merit

Art Director: Mark Shap
Director of Photography: Leslie Dektor
Writer: Veronica Nash
Editor: Jim Edwards
Director: Leslie Dektor
Producer: Tina Raver; Oglivy & Mather, Faith Dektor; Petermann Dektor Productions

STREET DEALER
60 seconds
DEALER 1: Creeps—I don't believe it! Driving in from the suburbs in their daddy's car to score and then trying to beat me down on the price. ...I don't cut my price for nobody. (SCREAMS) Especially for these rich creeps. I got good stuff—you want good stuff—you gonna' pay for it.
DEALER 2: They'll be back.
DEALER 1: Trying to tell me they can take it or leave it. Did you see those little punks, man?
DEALER 2: You're gonna be the first one to take it or leave it.
DEALER 1: Yeah, drivin' their daddy's big car. You know what I'd like to do to them? I'd like to rub their faces.
DEALER 2: You know, they're so stupid, they deserve to be burned.
DEALER 1: They're good for nothing man.
DEALER 2: They're good for something. ...They good for taking money off of.
DEALER 3: Hey man, got some good crack...what do you need?

874
Art Director: David Kennedy
Writer: Dan Wieden
Editor: Bill Abbott
Client: American Honda Motor Scooters
Director: Brent Thomas
Producer: Brent Thomas, Bill Davenport; Wieden & Kennedy

AMERICAN HONDA MOTOR SCOOTERS
30 seconds
VO: What you are about to see is not a car. It's not a motorcycle. What you are about to see is a totally new form of personal transportation. It looks like nothing you've ever seen...and it feels...like nothing you've ever driven.

875
Art Director: Tracy Wong
Animator/Artist: Aardman Animation
Writer: Steve Baer
Client: Duracell Batteries
Director: David Sproxton
Producer: Mootsy Elliot; Ogilvy & Mather

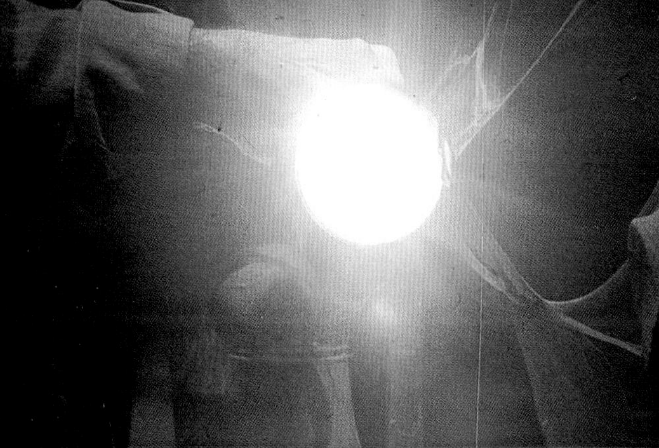

WEB
15 seconds
ANNCR: Even after three years, Duracell Batteries still work.

876
Art Director: Dean Hanson
Writer: Phil Hanft
Editor: Jeff Stickles
Client: Conran's
Director: Henry Sandbank
Producer: Char Loving

EASY CHAIR
10 seconds
VO: At Conran's, we don't believe beautifully designed furniture...should be so expensive...you're afraid to even sit in it.
SFX: BURP.

877
Art Director: Bob Barrie
Writer: Mike Lescarbeau
Editor: Steve Wystrach
Client: Lee Jeans
Director: Mark Coppos
Producer: Char Loving

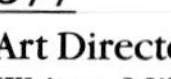

ALIEN
10 seconds
BOY: Is it true Lee jeans fit everybody? Try these on. Well, there you have it. Lee jeans. The brand that fits.

878
Art Director: Bob Brihn
Director of Photography: Tom Krohn
Writer: Jamie Barrett
Editor: Jeff Byers, Tom Krohn
Client: U.S. Olympic Hockey Team
Director: Jeff Byers
Producer: Char Loving

WHEN THE U.S. HOCKEY TEAM PLAYS AT MET CENTER, WE'RE EXPECTING A LOT OF EMPTY SEATS.

SEATS
10 seconds
VO: When the United States hockey team plays at Met Center, we're expecting a lot of empty seats.
SFX: STATIC SOUNDS FROM TV.
VO: Call for tickets today. 853-9300.
SFX: ROAR OF CROWD.

879
Art Director: Paul Boley
Writer: Richard Rand
Creative Director: John Eding
Client: Black & Decker
Producer: Joe Contino, Coast Special Effects

WORKMATE
15 seconds
ANNCR: The Black and Decker Workmate
SFX: MINIMALIST MUSIC TRACK ESTABLISHING BEAT OF ACTION.
NATURAL SOUNDS.
ANNCR: About all it can't help you do is clean up. But at least it gets out of your way. The Black and Decker Workmate.

880
Art Director: Chuck Anderson
Director of Photography: Rick Dublin
Writer: Jarl Olsen
Editor: Dale Cooper
Client: Harry Singh's
Director: Jarl Olsen, Chuck Anderson

BLOWTORCH
10 seconds
ANNCR: What do you think about Harry Singh's?
SFX: WHOOSH.
ANNCR: Hot food lovers can't stop talking about Harry Singh's Caribbean Restaurant. Lake and Lyndale, Minneapolis.

881
Art Director: Steve Miller
Writer: Jane King
Creative Director: Arthur Bijur
Client: North American Philips
Director: Mark Story
Producer: Steve Friedman, Story, Piccolo, Guliner

WOMAN: The magic's gone.

The minute the lights go out, you fall asleep.

ANNCR (VO): It's time to change your bulb to Philips. Philips Longer Life square bulbs.

SOUP COUPLE
15 seconds
WOMAN: Louis, the magic is gone. The minute the lights go out, you fall asleep.
SFX: SPOON DROPPING, MAN'S HEAD FALLING IN SOUP. MAN SNORES INTO SOUP.
ANNCR: It's time to change your bulb to Philips. Philips Longer Life square bulbs last 33% longer than ordinary round bulbs.

882
Art Director: Rich Kimmel
Designer: Rich Kimmel
Director of Photography: Henry Sandbank
Writer: Bill Teitelbaum
Editor: Jerry Hastings
Client: Deere & Co.
Director: Henry Sandbank
Producer: Bob Carney, Greg Carlesimo; Sandbank Films

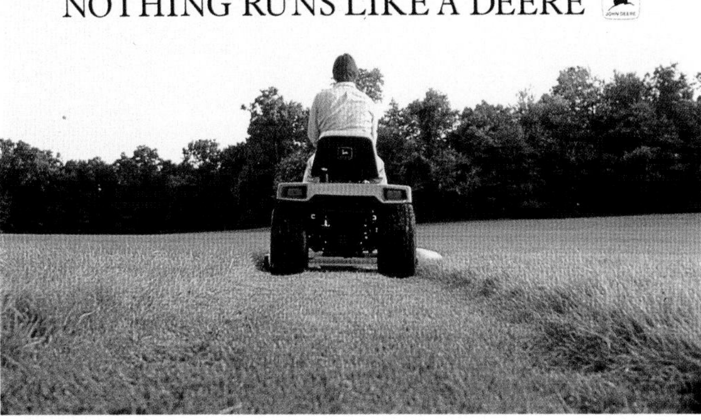

OVERHEAD
15 seconds
MUSIC UP AND UNDER. SYNCH SFX.
VO: Compared to the pieced-together frame of a *typical* lawn and garden tractor, the frame of a John Deere is a single mass of welded steel. And because it isn't *made* of pieces, it doesn't *go* to pieces.

883
Art Director: Morgan Ziller
Director of Photography: Jim Connolly
Writer: Seth Werner
Editor: Richard Ledyard
Client: Wally Winslow
Producer: Sharon Sturgis, Myrna Connolly

A BAD DEAL FOR CHICKENS
10 seconds
ANNCR: It's Church's Family Meal Deal. A great deal for families, a bad deal for chickens.

884
Art Director: Nancy Rice, Nick Rice
Writer: Jim Newcombe
Editor: Tony Fisher
Client: Herman Miller Inc.
Director: Jim Lund
Producer: Deb Tarum, Jim Manson

FLOWER & GARDEN FOOD
15 seconds
SFX: OUTDOOR AMBIANCE, TWEETING BIRDS, ETC.
VO: There may be a better way to fertilize your garden.
SFX: THUNDERING HOOVES, MOOING CATTLE. POUNDING HOOVES UP.
VO: But it's awfully hard on the plants. Greensweep liquid flower and garden plant food.

885
Art Director: Roy Grace
Designer: Roy Grace
Director of Photography: Henry Sandbank
Writer: Diane Rothschild
Editor: Stonecutters
Client: Range Rover of North America
Director: Henry Sandbank
Producer: Lee Weiss, Sandbank Films

RANGE ROVER OF NORTH AMERICA
10 seconds
ANNCR: Introducing Range Rover... a rather exceptional vehicle.

886
Art Director: Tony Hilliard
Director of Photography: John Kraus
Writer: Jim Symon
Editor: Art Dome; ICM Films
Client: GE
Director: Arny Stone
Producer: Geraldine Symon, David Darby; ICM Films

TURKEYS
15 seconds
MUSIC UP, THEN UNDER.
VO: In its lifetime, a Hotpoint refrigerator could hold enough turkeys...to supply your family with Thanksgiving dinners for the next 15,000 years. Hotpoint. For the long run.

887
Art Director: Peter Cohen
Writer: Larry Spector
Editor: Morty Ashkinos
Client: Webster Industries
Director: Mark Story
Producer: Cami Taylor; Story, Piccolo, Guliner, Rachel Novak; Levine, Huntley, Schmidt & Beaver

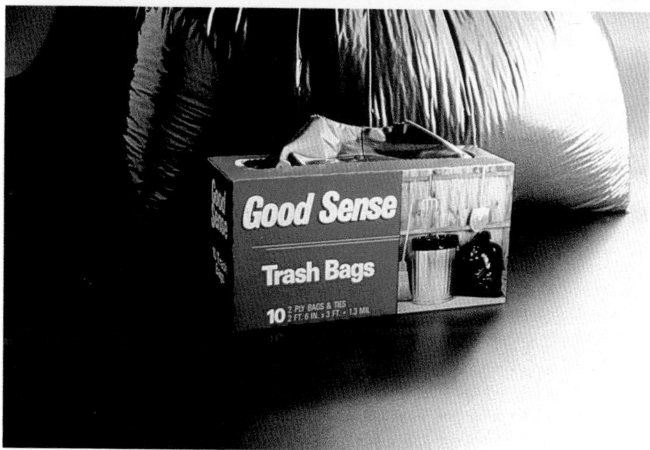

ELEPHANT
15 seconds
MAN: When Good Sense asked me to stand under one of their bags filled with 58 lbs. of elephant fertilizer...I said no. Then they told me it was made of super tough plastic. Obviously that took a load off my mind.
ANNCR: Good Sense. The best things you'll ever throw out.
SFX: BAG DROPPING.

888

Art Director: Leslie Caldwell
Director of Photography: Amir Hamed
Writer: Mike Koelker
Editor: Bob Carr
Client: Levi Strauss & Co.
Director: Leslie Dektor
Producer: Steve Neely, Faith Dektor

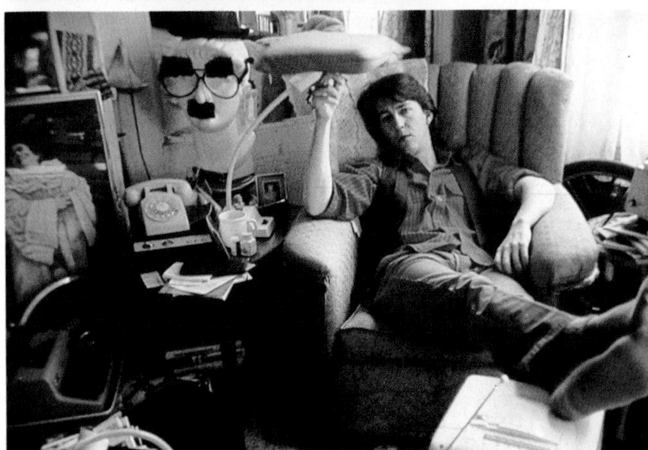

TWO TRICKS
15 seconds
VO: I've got two tricks. This is one of them. The other one isn't as good.
SINGER: Levi's five-oh-one blues.

889

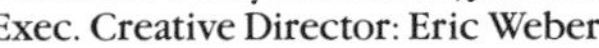

Art Director: Stephen Dolleck
Writer: Terry Gallo
Editor: Allan Eisenberg
Client: Wrangler
Director: Stephen Dolleck, Terry Gallo
Producer: Cheryl Friedland, John Mitchell Ravon
Exec. Creative Director: Eric Weber

COUNTY FAIR
15 seconds
VO: There's a new stone-washed jean made for a man after his work is done.
American Hero Jeans. From Wrangler.

890
Art Director: Peter Cohen
Writer: Larry Spector
Client: Webster Industries
Director: Mark Story
Producer: Cami Taylor; Story, Piccolo, Guliner, Rachel Novak; Levine, Huntley, Schmidt & Beaver

PIE IN FACE
15 seconds
MAN: Unlike paper plates, Good Sense plastic plates will never go limp or leak.
SFX: WHOOSH.
MAN: So you can go back for seconds.
SFX: WHOOSH.
MAN: By the way, we also make plastic cups.
SFX: WHOOSH.
ANNCR: Good Sense. The best things you'll ever throw out.

891
Art Director: Jeff Weiss
Photographer: Moshe Brahka
Creative Director: John Margeotes, John Weiss
Client: Byron Hero
Producer: Therese Jennings

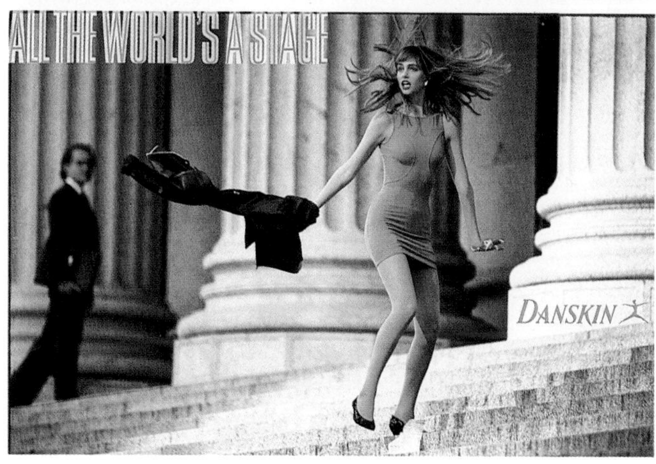

STEPS
10 seconds
MUSIC: TRUMPET FLOURISH.

892
Art Director: Peter Cohen
Writer: Larry Spector
Editor: Morty Ashkinos
Client: Webster Industries
Director: Mark Story
Producer: Cami Taylor; Story, Piccolo, Guliner, Rachel Novak; Levine, Huntley, Schmidt & Beaver

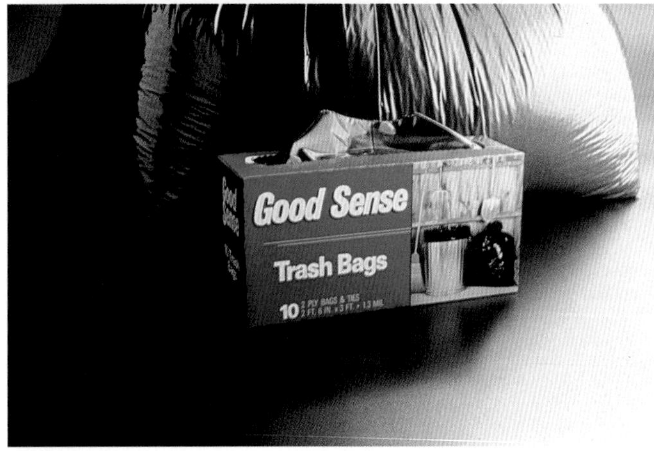

KITTY
15 seconds
MAN: When Good Sense asked me to sit under their bag filled with 58 lbs. of Kitty Litter...I said no. Then they said it was made of super tough plastic. Obviously that took a load off my mind.
ANNCR: Good Sense. The best things you'll ever throw out.
SFX: BAG DROPPING.

893
Art Director: Leslie Caldwell
Director of Photography: Amir Hamed
Writer: Mike Koelker
Editor: Bob Carr
Client: Levi Strauss & Co.
Director: Leslie Dektor
Producer: Steve Neely, Faith Dektor

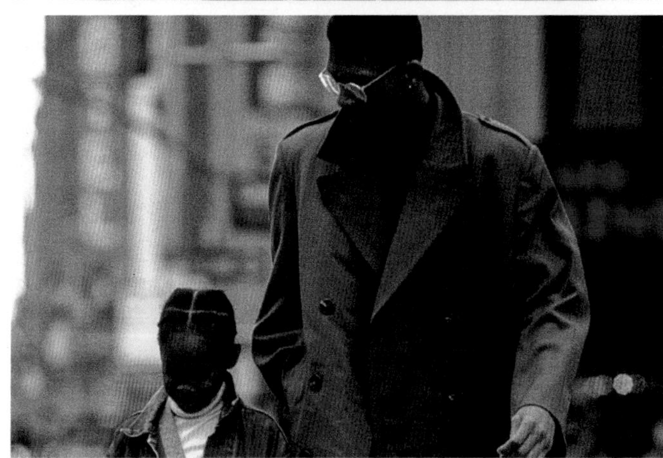

FATHER/DAUGHTER
15 seconds
VO: What can I say? She's my best friend. I'd rather hang out with her than most of the people I know.
SINGERS: Levi's five-oh-one blues.

894
Art Director: Michael Fazende
Writer: John Stingley
Editor: Jeff Stickles
Client: Emmis Broadcasting
Director: Jeff Gorman
Producer: Judy Brink, Char Loving

BIG GLOVE
15 seconds
SFX: BAT CRACK, CARTOONY "ZING" AND "THUMP."
ANNCR: We've made sports easier to catch. WFAN 1050 AM. The world's first 24-hour sports radio station.

895
Art Director: Mike Moser
Writer: Brian O'Neill, Dave O'Hare
Editor: Steve Wystrach
Client: California Cooler
Director: Mark Coppos
Producer: Peter Valentine

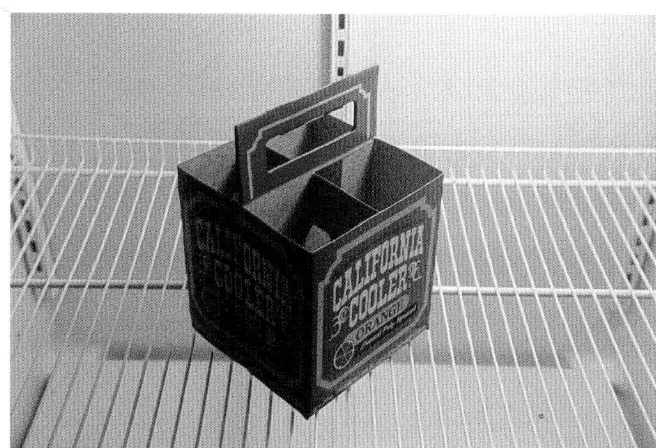

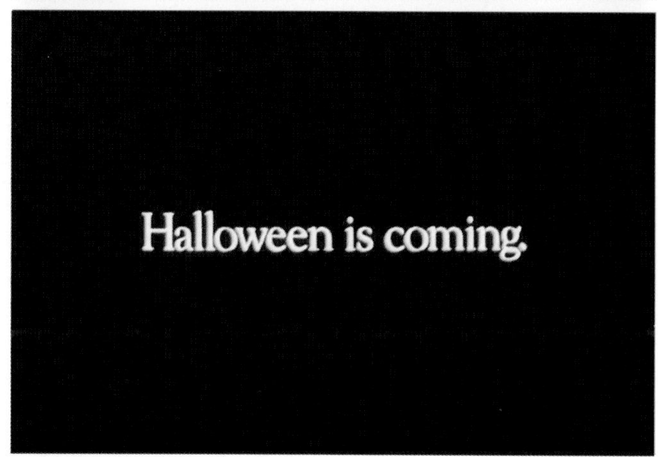

HALLOWEEN
15 seconds
MUSIC: SPOOKY MUSIC UNDER.
VO: Halloween is coming.
SFX: SCREAM
VO: Don't let this happen to you. Stock up for Halloween.

896
Art Director: Dick Grider
Director of Photography: Len Akins
Writer: Nancy Foster
Editor: Don Jacques
Client: BASF Corp.
Director: Joe Conforti
Producer: Nancy Foster; Warner, Bicking & Fenwick, Joe Conforti; JC Productions
Music: Two Pie Are Music

TOUGH WINTER
15 seconds
HARD-DRIVING ELECTRONIC MUSIC MIXED WITH WINTER SFX.
SFX: CRASHHHHH.
SINGERS: Zerexxxxx.
VO: Zerex. The antifreeze that beats winter. Available now.

897
Art Director: Nick Gisonde
Writer: Charlie Breen
Client: Miller Brewing Co.
Producer: Mary McInerney

FOOTBALL STRIKE
15 seconds
VO: At Miller Lite we'd like to say we're sorry if we are in any way responsible for prolonging the football strike. Here's hoping they settle it soon.
VOs: Tastes great! Less filling.

898
Art Director: Bryan McPeak, John Adams
Director of Photography: Mark Story
Writer: Craig Piechura, Neal Spector
Client: Highland
Producer: Kurt Kulas; W. B. Doner & Co., Story, Piccolo & Guliner Production

FREE DELIVERY
15 seconds
SFX: GRUNTING.
VO: The only way to get free delivery at most stores is to deliver it yourself. But Highland offers free delivery on *all* major appliances.
SFX: CRASH.
VO: Just thought you'd like to know.

899
Art Director: Greg Nygard
Photographer: Tony D'Orio
Writer: Steve Silver
Editor: Bob Blanford
Creative Director: Jan Zechman
Client: Dove International
Director: Richard Foster
Producer: Laurie Berger, Deborah McMasters

SWEET DREAMS
15 seconds
MIKE STEFANOS: If my Dad the DoveBar inventor were alive today, he'd probably say, "Son...so what have you come up with?"

900
Art Director: Dick Lemmon
Writer: Mark Fenske
Editor: Bob Blanford
Creative Director: Jan Zechman
Client: Dove International
Producer: Laurie Berger

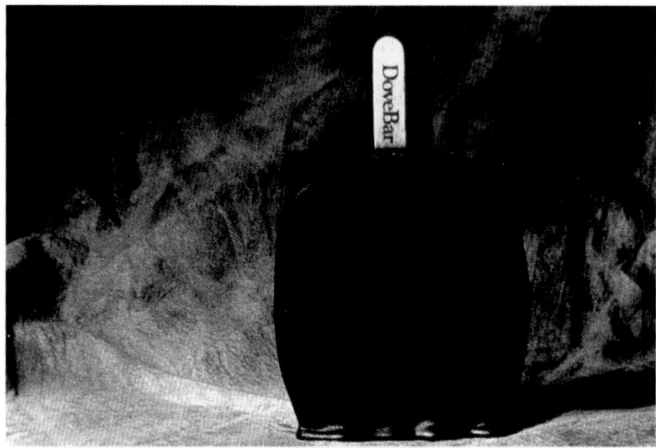

LIFE
15 seconds
MUSIC UNDER.
MICHAEL STEFANOS: I guess most people would think life would be pretty great for a kid whose father invented the DoveBar. Well, you know what? It was.

901
Art Director: Paul Scolaro
Director of Photography: Alex Fernbach
Writer: Tony Gomes
Editor: Don Packer
Client: Conde Nast's Traveler
Director: Alex Fernbach
Producer: Randy Cohen, Kate Eisemann
Sound Effects: Fred Weinberg

GOLF
30 seconds
ANNCR: Brian McCallem brings you on an intriguing journey to the most beautiful golf courses in the Caribbean. Only in the pages of Conde Nast's *Traveler*. The insider's guide to the outside world.

902
Art Director: Earl Cavanah
Writer: Larry Cadman
Editor: Barry Stillwell
Client: Volvo of America Corp.
Director: Henry Sandbank
Producer: Jaki Keuch

HEAVY TRAFFIC
10 seconds
SFX: MUSIC THROUGHOUT.
VO: How well does your car stand up to heavy traffic?
SFX: MUSIC OUT.

903
Art Director: Dick Lemmon
Writer: Mark Fenske
Editor: Bob Blanford
Creative Director: Jan Zechman
Client: Dove International
Producer: Laurie Berger

DAD SAID
15 seconds
SFX: MUSIC UNDER.
MICHAEL STEFANOS: You know, I've based my entire life on something this man said to me 30 years ago. "Son," he said, "I've invented the DoveBar."

904
Art Director: Dean Hanson
Writer: Phil Hanft
Editor: Jeff Stickles
Client: Conran's
Director: Henry Sandbank
Producer: Char Loving

Z-CHAIR
10 seconds
SFX: NO SOUNDS EXCEPT FOR SOUND OF CHAIR MOVING AND MAN'S FOOTSTEPS. SCRAPING SOUND.
VO: At Conran's, we believe furniture should never sacrifice comfort... just to make an impression on your guests.
SFX: FOOTSTEPS.

905
Art Director: Regis Sabol, Paul Brourman
Client: Pittsburgh Brewing Co.
Agency: HBM Creamer Inc.
Director: Richard Kline
Producer: Leslie Lytle

WILD LIFE I
30 seconds
SFX: MUSIC THROUGHOUT.

906
Art Director: Mike Moser
Writer: Brian O'Neill, Dave O'Hare
Editor: Steve Wystrach
Client: California Cooler
Director: Mark Coppos
Producer: Peter Valentine

SMALL PARTY
30 seconds
MUSIC: "WILD THING" VERY LOW.
WOMAN: Well, come over. Okay, I'll see ya in a few minutes.
MUSIC UP.
VO: The original wine cooler has always been the perfect drink to enjoy at a party. California Cooler. Hey, nobody said it had to be a big party.

907
Art Director: Steve Fong
Writer: Dave Woodside
Editor: Steve Wystrach
Client: Worlds of Wonder
Director: Martin Bell
Producer: Karen Carlson

STUFF IT
30 seconds
SFX: BELL RINGS; MUSIC UP.
KID VO: The way I see it, with a Stuff-It binder you will automatically do better at school. You'll be more prepared. You'll keep better notes. You will impress your teachers. Above all, now this is important, you will always take advantage of every opportunity to learn.
MAN VO: Stuff-It. The Binders.
GIRL VO: Nice try, squeak.

908
Art Director: Craig McCord
Writer: David Culp
Editor: Michael Van De Kamer
Client: Best Retail Stores
Director: Gordon Willis, Jr.
Producer: George Kline; George Kline Co.,
Julie Weyand; Tracy-Locke Advertising

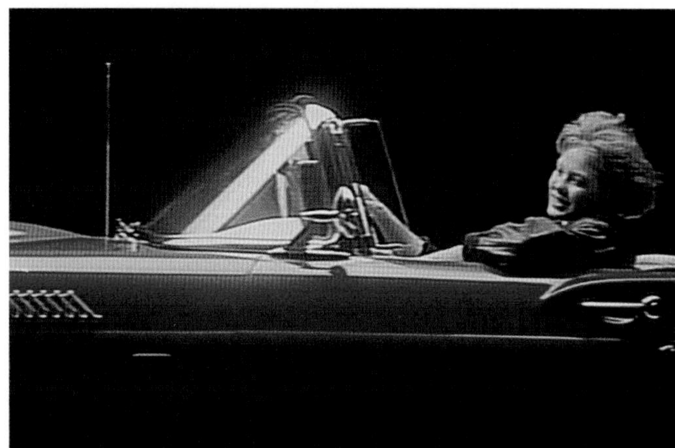

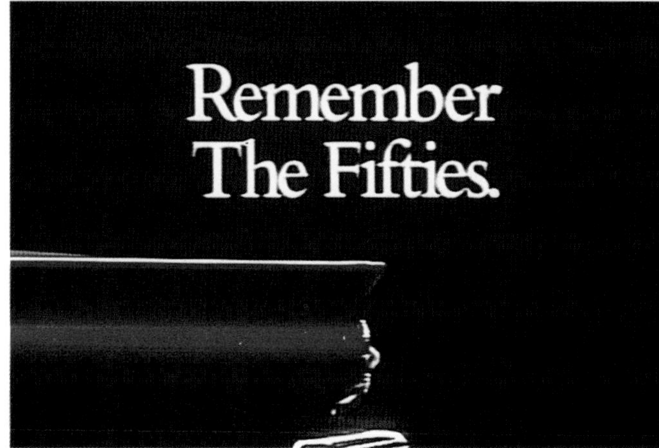

GONE
30 seconds
MUSIC: EARLY ROCK & ROLL SOUND, LOPING TEMPO.
VOCAL: Gone, gone, long gone.
MUSIC UNDER ANNCR.
ANNCR: It's been 30 years coming, but it's going fast. Our 30th-anniversary Remember-the-50s Sale at BEST. Fine jewelry, toys, sporting goods, housewares, electronics. You could even win a vintage '57 T-bird. Register today. Because after this week, BEST's Remember-the-50s Sale will be nothing but a memory.
VOCAL: LONG GONE.

909
Art Director: Cindy Heard, Audrey Devries
Writer: John Dimitri
Editor: Randall Shepard
Creative Director: Neil Scanlan, Bobby Reiser
Client: American Airlines
Director: Jeff Lovinger
Producer: Jerry Chappell

REUNION
30 seconds
MUSIC: UP, THEN UNDER.
SINGER:
The years have passed,
We faced the task,
Those boys I called "my men." I wonder, could the ties we made,
Now join us once again?
VO: Let American Airlines Super Savers take you to the special moments in your life.
SINGER:
The feelings we all share,
We're American Airlines,
Something special in the air.

910
Art Director: John Staffen, Jack Mariucci
Writer: Mike Rogers
Editor: Jacques Dury
Client: Volkswagen
Director: Michael Werk
Producer: Ugo Pergolotti, Joanne Wood

SKID PAD
30 seconds
VO: The engineers of Volkswagen believe our 16-valve engines should deliver a seamless crescendo power. Power from 0 to 60. Passing power from 40 to 60. Autobahn power. Where speeds of 100 mph are considered not the threshold, but the beginning. As you might suspect, the men who delight in developing all this power...insist that it be accompanied by the technology to control it. German engineering. The Volkswagen way.

911
Art Director: James Dalthorp
Photographer: The Image Bank
Writer: Doug Rucker
Editor: Michael Van De Kamer
Client: Mountain Bell Telephone Co.
Agency: Tracy-Locke Advertising
Director: Louis Schwartzberg
Producer: John Seaton; Tracy-Locke Advertising, Energy Productions

AS SURE AS THE SUN
30 seconds
SFX: TELEPHONE AUDIO MONTAGE. MODERN PHONE RING AND PICK-UP.
MALE VO #1: Good morning, Norman–you ready for our conference call?
MALE VO #2: Almost–Karen's just getting the revised estimates.
MALE VO #3: So ol' Bess is a mother, huh?
FEMALE VO #1: I think that's what you call it when you have six adorable puppies.
MALE VO #3: *Six*, Angela–*six*?!
CHILD VO #1: Grandpa, Mommy says you moved away 'cause you're tired!?
MALE VO #4: Not tired, honey, *retired* – you see, that's when grandpa....
VO: With low rates...and quality you can hear...few things in life are as dependable as the value of Long Distance service from Mountain Bell. And there's no question we plan to keep it that way.

912
Art Director: Cathie Campbell, Louise Masano
Designer: John Beard
Director of Photography: Richard Greatrex
Writer: Michael Mark
Client: Revlon
Director: Roger Lyons
Producer: Magi Durham; Hill, Holiday, Connors, Cosmopulos, Mary Ellen Argentieri; Hill, Holiday, Connors, Cosmopulos, Stavros Merjos

INTIMATE PARTY
30 seconds
SFX: ICE TINKLING. MUSIC UNDER THROUGHOUT
VO: Intimate. The uninhibited fragrance from Revlon.

913
Art Director: Susan Picking
Writer: Gary Gusick
Editor: Frankie Ciofridi
Client: Insurance Information Institute
Director: Brent Thomas
Producer: Siegel & Gale, Coppos Films

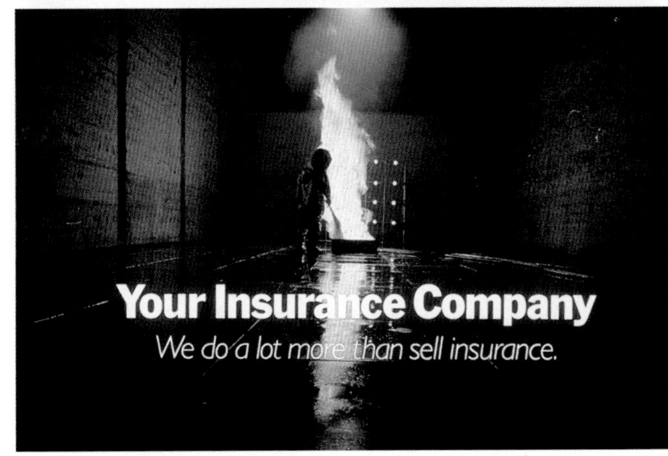

UNDERWRITERS' LABORATORIES
30 seconds
ANNCR: In 1984 a three-man research agency was created to test electrical wiring. In the decades that followed, it tested and set safety standards for products the world over. Its name? Underwriters' Laboratories. Who created Underwriters' Laboratories? You're going to be surprised. Your insurance company. We do a lot more than sell insurance.

914
Art Director: John Staffen, Jack Mariucci
Writer: Mike Rogers
Editor: Jacques Dury
Client: Volkswagen
Director: Michael Werk
Producer: Ugo Pergolotti, Joanne Wood

TWO ENGINEERS
30 seconds
VO: Volkswagen engineers have developed a remarkable fuel injection system. Which gives our Golf and Jetta a 15% increase in horsepower. And top track speeds of over 120. Of course, there are those Volkswagen engineers who believe they've developed something no less remarkable. The brakes. German engineering. The Volkswagen way.

915
Art Director: Janet Ferguson
Writer: Neil Scanlan
Editor: Steve Ho
Client: Territorial House
Director: Peter Moss
Producer: Sam Milgrim, Greg Maya

NEW MEXICO
30 seconds
MUSIC THROUGHOUT
VO: Territorial House Salsa. Thick...with the flavor of New Mexico.

916
Art Director: Bryan Lahr
Writer: Joey Reiman
Client: Temp Force
Director: Candy Clifford
Producer: Thom II
Sound & Music: Leonard Wolf

WORLD WAR III
30 seconds
MUSIC UNDER THROUGHOUT.
MAN VO: Mr. President, Tina's sick today so we've called in a temporary.
MUSIC INCREASES IN INTENSITY.
VO: One mistake can ruin your day. Temp Force. The temporary service that guarantees no mistake.

917
Art Director: Rich Silverstein
Writer: Andy Berlin, Jeff Goodby
Editor: Tom Schachte
Client: Home Express
Director: David Deahl
Producer: Debbie King, Cindy Fluitt, David James
Music Composer/Director: Donal Piestrup

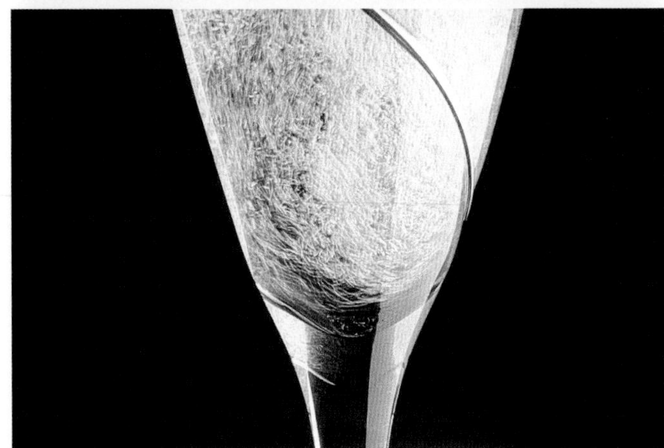

CHAMPAGNE
30 seconds
MUSIC UNDER THROUGHOUT
ANNCR: The great Swiss designer, Le Corbusier, believed that things were not truly beautiful until they were within the reach of many. He would have liked our store.

918
Art Director: Nancy Rorabaugh
Director of Photography: Jerry Cotts
Animator/Artist: Crawford Post Production
Writer: Sarah Bowman
Client: First American Bank
Agency: Pringle Dixon Pringle
Director: Jerry Cotts
Producer: Adam Gross
Sound: Bill Myers

WHAT MONEY CAN'T BUY
30 seconds
VO: The idea is not a new one…that money isn't everything. What is new is that we're a bank and we're saying it. At First American, we recognize the real value of a smile, a kind word, a willingness to listen. And while these things cost us nothing, they can be worth more than all the money in the world. First American. There's more to banking than money.

919
Art Director: John Staffen, Jack Mariucci
Writer: Mike Rogers
Editor: Jacques Dury
Client: Volkswagen
Director: Michael Werk
Producer: Ugo Pergolotti, Joanne Wood

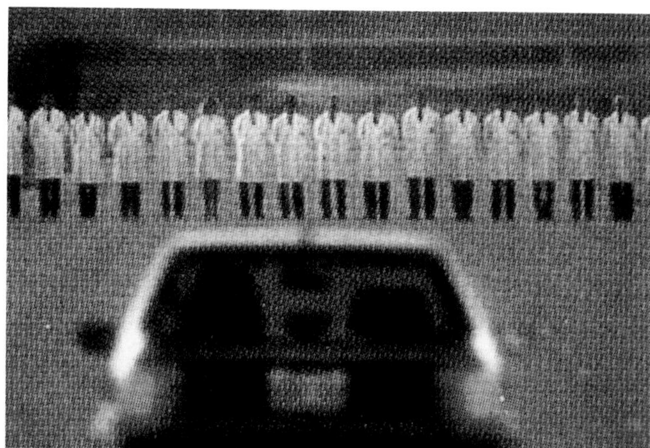

MOVING PARTS
30 seconds
VO: At Volkswagen, our engineers believe car and driver should not merely act…but interact. To them a Volkswagen isn't a vehicle for the driver. But rather an extension…of the driver. Our engineers believe the most important moving part of a Volkswagen…is the one behind the wheel. German engineering. The Volkswagen way.

920
Art Director: John Staffen, Jack Mariucci
Writer: Mike Rogers
Editor: Jacques Dury
Client: Volkswagen
Director: Michael Werk
Producer: Ugo Pergolotti, Joanne Wood

SLALOM
30 seconds
VO: The engineers of Volkswagen have spent years... honing and refining our front-wheel drive, rack and pinion steering, and four-wheel independent suspension. Because the engineers of Volkswagen believe it's not just how fast you go. But rather, how well you go fast. German engineering. The Volkswagen way.

921
Art Director: Janet Ferguson
Writer: Neil Scanlan
Editor: Tim Fulford
Client: American Airlines
Director: Bruce Dowad
Producer: Barry Lisee, John Buxton

EUROPEAN SHADOWS
30 seconds
MUSIC UP.
VO: All over Europe, there's something special in the air–American Airlines. With service to nine European cities.
American Airlines. Something special... to Europe.

922
Art Director: Mark Keller
Director of Photography: Michael Karbelnikoff
Writer: Tim Price
Editor: Larry Bridges
Client: Levi Strauss & Co.
Director: Michael Karbelnikoff
Producer: Florence Babbitt, Cean Chaffin

COAST-TO-COAST
30 seconds
SINGER: I've been from coast to coast searchin' for a clue.
KIDS: I like to wear 'em tight and faded.
I like 'em ripped.... Wear your Levi's however you want.
SINGER: Seems like everybody's got a better point of view.
KIDS: I don't do that. I don't care what's cool. I just wear it the way I want to wear it.

923
Art Director: Dennis D'Amico
Designer: Mel Bourne
Director of Photography: John Crawford
Writer: Robin Raj
Editor: Robert Jubin
Client: NYNEX
Director: Henry Holtzman
Producer: Mark Sitley; Chiat/Day, Stavros Merjos; HSI

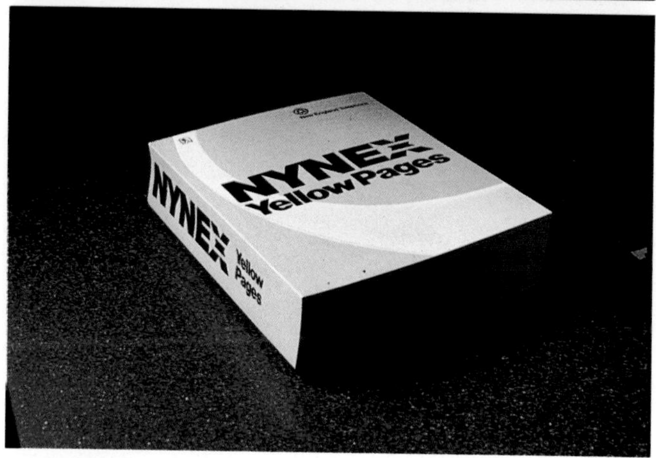

ASK FATHER
30 seconds
SFX: NATURAL SOUNDS.
SALLY: Dad? Why is grass green?
DAD: Because of chlorophyll, honey.
TIMMY: Dad... Is the moon really made of cheese?
SFX: OTHERS SNICKER.
DAD: No, son. The moon is made from molecules.
ALBERTA: Dad?
DAD: Yes?
ALBERTA: The NYNEX Yellow Pages has always had more information than any competing directory. Why would anyone need another?
TIMMY: Dad?
SFX: DIRECTORY FALLS.
VO: NYNEX Yellow Pages.
SFX: HITS TABLE.
VO: It's the one you've always had—it's the only one you need.

924
Art Director: Vance Smith
Writer: Tom Wiecks
Client: Jim Miller
Producer: Craig Henderson Films

SOUNDS LIKE FUN
30 seconds
VO: It was Portland's very first radio station. But then, 62-KGW's always been a bit ahead of its time.
BEACH BOYS: I'm pickin' up good vibrations.
BEATLES: She came in through the bathroom window.
ELTON JOHN: Mars ain't no place to raise your kids.
SLY & THE FAMILY STONE: Different strokes for different folks.
ARETHA FRANKLIN: Sock it to me, sock it to me, sock it to me, sock it to me.

925
Art Director: John Green, Phillip Collier
Director of Photography: Bill Wages
Writer: John Green
Editor: Mike Norman
Client: Kentwood 10-K
Director: Mike Norman
Producer: Kristin Rush; Bauerlein, Gale Goldberg; Emerald Films

ANVIL CHORUS
30 seconds
MUSIC UP: "ANVIL CHORUS."
VO: Until now, the hardest part of working up a thirst was quenching it. Because even though thirst quenchers were good for you, they just didn't taste very good. Introducing 10-K. Finally, a thirst quencher with vitamin C, low sodium, and great taste. So next time you work up a thirst, you'll have something to look forward to. A 10-K.

926
Art Director: Ron Anderson
Writer: Bert Gardner
Editor: Tom Gilman
Client: Check-up Gum/Rydelle Laboratories
Director: Steve Steigman
Producer: Richard Henry

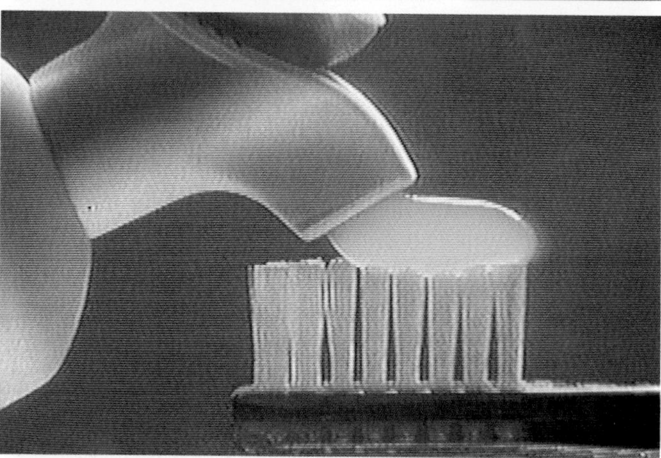

FAMILY PORTRAIT
30 seconds
VO: Something worse than tartar...
SFX: BATTLE SFX UP AND CONT.
VO: is attacking your teeth. It's plaque and dentists agree...plaque is...worse than tartar. Plaque...acids can start...cavities. And plaque...bacteria can lead to...gum disease.
SFX: BOOM.
VO: But there is help.
SFX: MUSIC UP AND CONT. UNDER.
VO: Check-Up toothpaste helps remove plaque...everywhere you brush. Check-Up Gum helps remove plaque between brushings. So switch to Check-up. And fight the plaque that's worse than tartar.

927
Art Director: Robert Reitzfeld
Designer: Robert Reitzfeld
Director of Photography: Henry Sandbank
Writer: David Altschiller
Editor: Randy Ilowite
Client: Ferrero USA Inc.
Director: Henry Sandbank
Producer: Mary Ellen Verrusio; Altschiller Reitzfeld Inc.

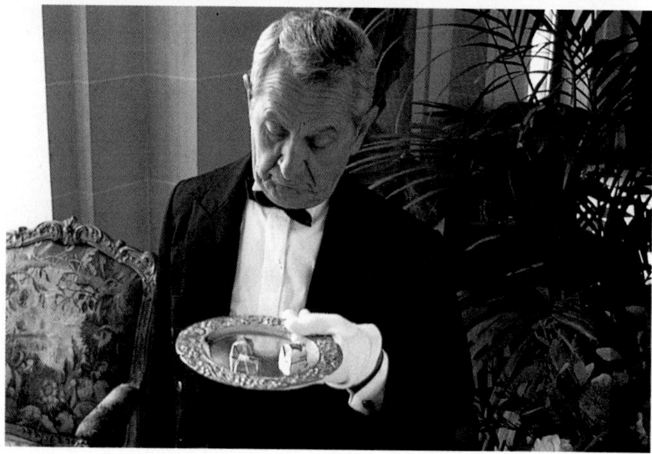

COMPANY'S COMING BRAND CANDYDISH
30 seconds
VO: In Europe...when company is expected...they don't break out the Hershey's Kisses. There are no Goobers or Raisinets in the candy dishes. And Andes are best known as a mountain range. In Europe...they serve a confection a bit more refined. Mon Cheri. The most popular brand of fine milk chocolate in all of Europe. Mon Cheri. The American candydish will never be the same.

928
Art Director: Steve Chase
Writer: Bill Martin
Editor: Kari Skogland
Client: Labatt Brewing Co., Ltd.
Agency: Scali, McCabe, Sloves (Canada) Ltd.
Director: Robert F. Quartly, Nell Frair; Directors Film Co., Patricia Peat; Scali, McCabe, Sloves

BLUE CONDITIONING
30 seconds
SFX: BAR ROOM AMBIENCE THROUGHOUT. CONVERSATION, MUSIC, POOL PLAYING, SOUND OF AIR CONDITIONING. MUSIC UNDER.
VOCAL:
Ready, set, go, man, go!
Are you ready? Are you ready? Are you ready?
Are you ready? Are you really, really ready for a good good time?
Are you really, really ready and that's no lie?
Really, really, ready I'm telling you why.
Are you ready?
Are you ready?
BARMAN: Blue conditioning.
VOCAL: That's why you call for the Blue.

929
Art Director: Michael Vitiello
Writer: Lee Garfinkel
Client: Subaru of America
Director: Steve Horn
Producer: Linda Horn; Steve Horn Inc., Bob Nelson; Levine, Huntley, Schimdt & Beaver

WHEN A MAN LOVES A WOMAN
30 seconds
GIRL: My folks just left.
JAMES: Tonight's the night.
ANNCR: The new Subaru Justy, now with "on demand" 4-wheel drive not only gets you where you want to go—but does it less expensively than any other 4-wheel-drive car in America.
JAMES: Mr. Potts, you're... home?
MR. POTTS: We turned back. The roads are terrible.
SFX: MUSIC UP.
MR. POTTS: So, James, what brings you out on a night like this?

930
Art Director: Richard Crispo
Director of Photography: Bill Bennett
Writer: Bob Ancona
Editor: Luis Landgraf
Creative Director: Martin Macdonald
Client: American Honda Motor Co., Inc.
Director: Brent Thomas
Producer: Joel Squier, Coppos Films

COMFORTABLE
30 seconds
VO: With its 24 valve, 2.7 liter V-6, and advanced anti-lock brakes, this is the performance sedan that's making European automakers uncomfortable. But with such amenities as a leather-trimmed interior and sophisticated stereo system, there's no reason you should feel that way. The Legend Sedan. Precision crafted performance from Acura.

931
Art Director: Peter Cohen
Writer: Larry Spector
Editor: Morty Ashkinos
Client: Webster Industries
Director: Mark Story
Producer: Cami Taylor; Story, Piccolo, Guliner, Rachel Novak; Levine, Huntley, Schmidt & Beaver

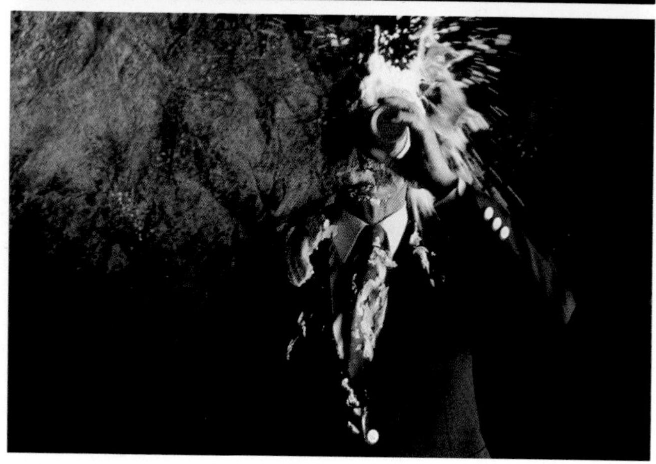

PIE IN FACE-CUPS
30 seconds
MAN: Most paper plates will hold up to maybe one serving of pie.
SFX: WHOOSH.
MAN: After that, they become soggy...and limp. But Good Sense plastic plates stay rigid and don't leak.
SFX: WHOOSH.
MAN: So you can go back for seconds.
SFX: WHOOSH.
MAN: And thirds.
SFX: WHOOSH.
ANNCR: Good Sense plastic plates. The best things you'll ever throw out. By the way, we also make plastic cups.

932
Art Director: Marcia Stone
Writer: Joe Milla
Creative Director: Dan Krumwiede
Client: McDonald's
Agency: Carmichael Lynch
Director: Chris Sanderson
Producer: Cathy Grayson, Nancy Lee

UNDERWATER
30 seconds
MUSIC: "BLUE DANUBE" UNDER THROUGHOUT.
ANNCR: Blub-Blubble-Blubble-Blub-Blub....

933
Art Director: Tom Shortlidge
Writer: Scott Burns
Editor: Michelle Peterson, Jeff Charitz
Client: G. Heileman Brewing Co.
Director: Peter Elliott
Producer: Pat McNaney

CHALKBOARD/PRETZEL
30 seconds
MUSIC: UP AND UNDER.
ANNCR: On the Old Style label you can read exactly what we believe in. We believe a beer should only be brewed with pure artesian spring water. That a beer should be fully kraeusened and naturally carbonated. A beer that is pure and genuine, with nothing artificial. But if you really want to believe, try what's on the inside. Old Style. A beer you can believe in.

934

Art Director: Richard Crispo
Director of Photography: Bill Bennett
Writer: Bob Ancona
Editor: Luis Landgraf
Creative Director: Martin Macdonald
Client: American Honda Motor Co., Inc.
Director: Brent Thomas
Producer: Joel Squier, Coppos Films

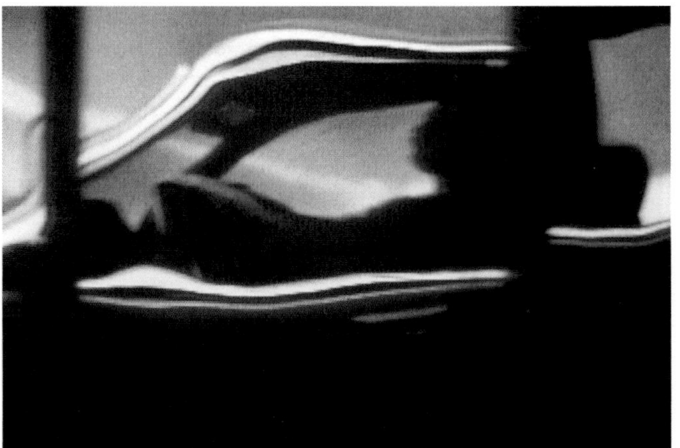

SHATTER
30 seconds
ANNCR: Strange how many automobiles portrayed as state of the art have become mere illusions of innovation. Enter the Acura Legend Coupe. Named "1987 Import Car of the Year" by *Motor Trend*, it is shattering preconceived ideas of what a performance automobile should be. The Legend Coupe. Precision crafted performance. From Acura.

935

Art Director: John Doyle
Writer: Paul Silverman
Editor: Barry Moross
Client: USTrust
Agency: Mullen
Director: Patrick Kelly
Producer: Brenda Smeriglio

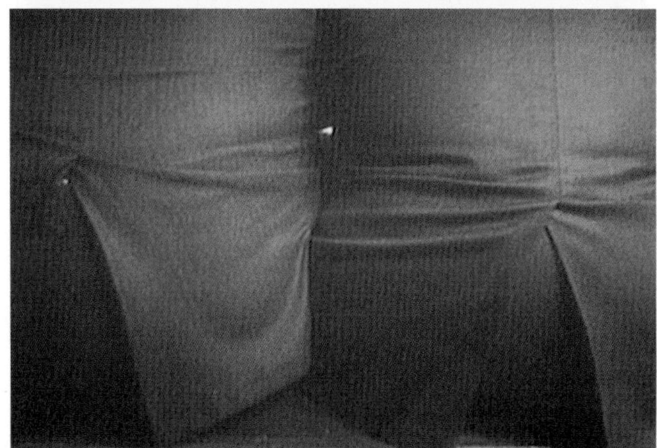

FAT CATS
30 seconds
MUSIC: "SKATER'S WALTZ."
1st BANKER: I don't know, Bill. What do you think?
2nd BANKER: I don't know, Fred. What do you think?
VO: The big banks of Boston have put their heads together. Gone shoulder to shoulder. Merged their vast financial structures. And broadened their customer base. But now that they have twice the assets,...
SFX: BENCH CRACKS.
VO: Will they sit on your loan twice as long? USTrust. We're not your average billion dollar bank.

936
Art Director: Michael Vitiello
Writer: Lee Garfinkel
Editor: Morty Ashkinos
Client: Changing Times
Director: Steve Horn
Producer: Linda Horn; Steve Horn Inc.,
Bob Nelson; Levine, Huntley, Schmidt & Beaver

LIFE CHANGES
30 seconds
1967 HIPPIE: Capitalism stinks, man. Like who needs money, man?
1973 FEMALE COLLEGE STUDENT: Beep Beep must end. Down with the Beep.
ANNCR: Everything changes. To stay informed of changes that affect you personally and financially, read *Changing Times*.
1986 YUPPIE: I'm gonna get rich fast. And retire at 35.
ANNCR: *Changing Times*. Everything you and your money need to know.

937
Art Director: Peter Hirsch
Writer: Ken Majka
Client: Toshiba America Inc.
Agency: Calet, Hirsch, & Spector Inc.
Director: Josh Aronson
Producer: Frank DiSalvo, Gilson & Aronson Films Inc.

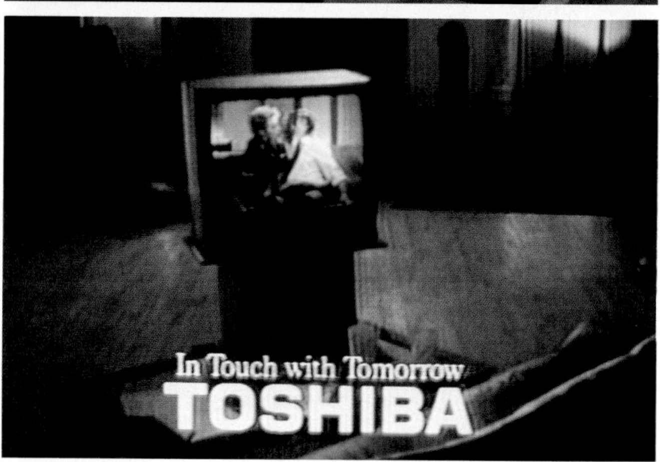

SPECIAL EFFECT
30 seconds
SFX: ROOM AND STREET AMBIANCE.
MUSIC & SONG:
Toshiba. Toshiba.
You got a special effect on me.
You turn me on so effectively.
You put my mind in motion. Such a beautiful notion.
You show me things…
I never thought I would see.
Toshiba. You got a special effect on me.
You got a special effect on me.

938
Art Director: Michael Vitiello
Writer: Lee Garfinkel, Todd Godwin
Editor: Morty Ashkinos
Client: Genesee Brewing Co.
Director: John Bonnano
Producer: Rob Thomas; Levine, Huntley, Schmidt & Beaver

QUESTIONING
30 seconds
COP: I'll make a sound and you tell me what kind of animal it is, okay? Meow.
MAN: Cat. COP: Woof.
MAN: Doggie. COP: Woop.
MAN: Uh. COP: Woop.
MAN: I never heard that one before.
COP: All right, let's start again. Baaach.
MAN: Chicken. COP: Naaa.
MAN: Horsie. COP: Woop.
MAN: I don't know it.
COP: I thought you grew up on a farm.
MAN: I did.
COP: All right then. Woop.
MAN: Boy, could I go for a Genny now.
ANNCR: When you can go for a beer, try the one that's brewed to be the best light beer anywhere. Genny Light.

939
Art Director: Rick Boyko, Miles Turpin
Writer: Elizabeth Hayes
Client: Home Savings of America
Director: Leslie Dektor
Producer: Richard O'Neill, Elaine Hinton, David Prince

THE JONES
30 seconds
MELVYN: It has to be the most thrilling experience for a person to go through. Driving down the street and pulling into our own driveway and, you know, it's like, wow. To go out and water your own grass. These are the things that really hit you. You realize "I'm a homeowner."
ANNCR: Home Savings wanted to give Melvyn and Robin Jones a home loan almost as much as they wanted a home.
MELVYN: All we needed was some institution that would say "We trust you guys."

940
Art Director: Jennifer Owens
Designer: Masami
Director of Photography: Jan Oswald
Animator/Artist: Jeff Jurich
Writer: Jennifer Owens
Editor: Celluloid Studios
Client: Carolina Beverage Corp.
Director: James Wahlberg; Celluloid Studios
Producer: Elizabeth Moore; Celluloid Studios

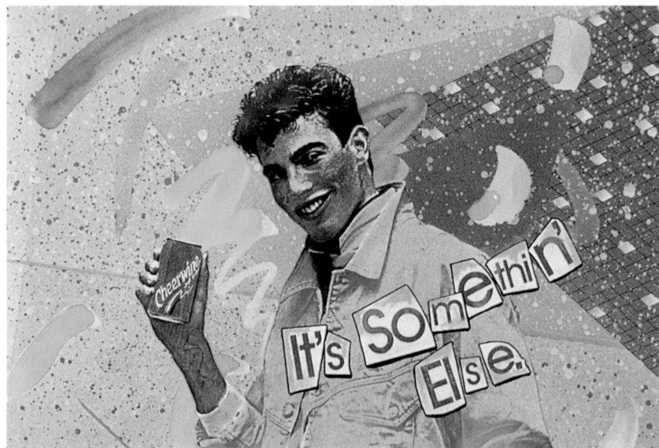

CHEERWINE
30 seconds
Well, your life is kinda boring,
It's the same routine each day.
You need something exciting
Just to take the blahs away.
Yeah, well here's a taste that's different
Even got a different name.
It's Cheerwine
And it doesn't taste the same.
Drink Cheerwine.
Drink Cheerwine.
Well, it's cool to be different
So you better listen up.
Go out and buy this soft drink
And put ice in a cup.
Its taste will satisfy you.
You really gotta try it.
It's Cheerwine, original or diet.
Drink Cheerwine.
Drink Cheerwine.

941
Art Director: Jean Robaire
Writer: John Stein, Chuck Silverman
Client: Nissan Motor Corp.
Director: Norman Seeff
Producer: Richard O'Neill

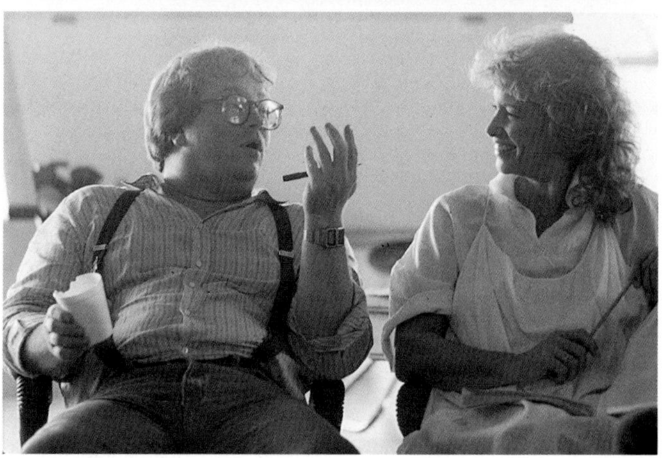

HUMAN ENGINEERING
30 seconds
LOUISE: I think when you start to design a car, you begin with a person…you, you think about the person you're designing for, and you design the car around them.
KAZ: There are other people involved…there are mother-in-laws involved. There are kids involved.
MICHAEL: It's about individuals. It's about how they feel, it's about their egos.
DAVID: What we're doing is humanizing technology by approaching it from a human standpoint.
MICHAEL: I hate to sound like a cliche, but you are what you drive.
DAVID: You sound like a cliche.
SFX: LAUGHTER.
VO: Nissan. Built for the most important race of all. The Human Race.

942
Art Director: John Sullivan
Writer: Doug Pippin, Eric Weber
Client: Martlet Importing Co., Inc.
Director: Michael Butler, Michael Schrom
Producer: Steve Friedman; Saatchi & Saatchi DFS Compton, Peter Sellers; Nadel & Associates
Music: Ry Cooder

MOUNTAIN
30 seconds
VO: In Canada, the wind blows a little colder. The rapids run a little stronger. Some people say you can taste it in the beer. Molson Golden. A little crisper. A little bolder. Molson is Canadian beer.

943
Art Director: Rick Boyko, Miles Turpin
Writer: Elizabeth Hayes, Mary Ann Bixby
Client: Home Savings of America
Director: Leslie Dektor
Producer: Richard O'Neill, Elaine Hinton, David Prince

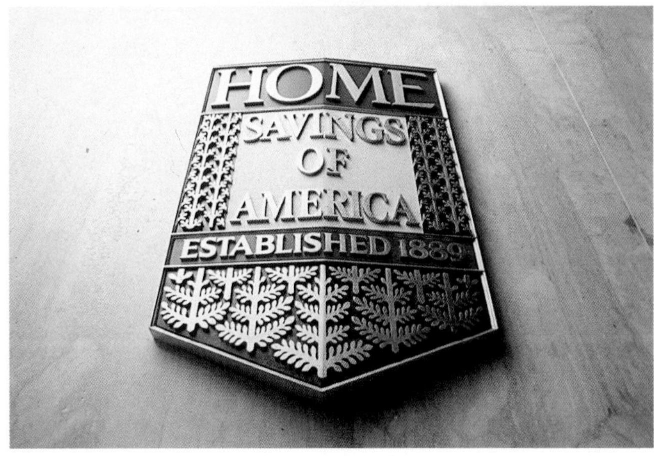

MARY ANN BIXBY
30 seconds
MARY ANN: I'm divorced. I've been divorced for 8 years. This is the first house I have owned on my own. It's not easy. The buck stops with me. But I accept that.
ANNCR: Mary Ann Bixby wasn't alone when she got her home loan. She had Home Savings.
MARY ANN: The day that the wallpaper went up in the hall, my daughter said, "Mom this house sure looks like a female owns it." And I said, "That's fine."

944
Art Director: Mas Yamashita
Writer: David Butler
Client: Porsche Cars North America
Director: Eric Saarinen
Producer: Richard O'Neill

TEST DRIVE
30 seconds
SFX: NATURAL AND MUSIC.
VO: At Porsche, we don't let you buy a car...unless we've test driven it first.

945
Art Director: Jean Robaire
Writer: John Stein, Chuck Silverman
Client: Nissan Motor Corp.
Director: Norman Seeff
Producer: Richard O'Neill

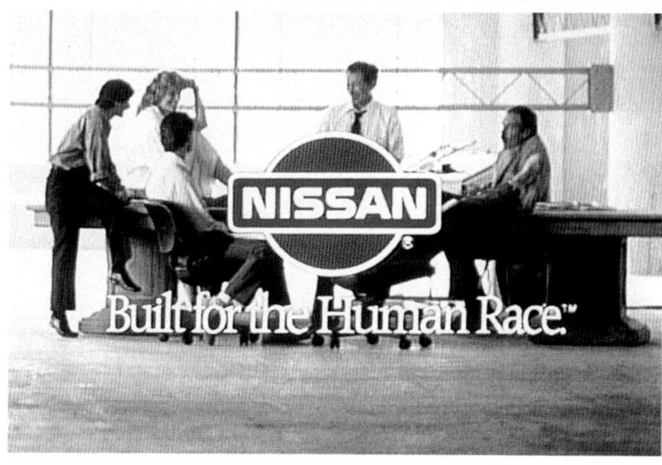

SENTRA
30 seconds
LOUISE: Well, the challenge is to make an inexpensive car that is not cheap.
MICHAEL: We're not talking about an econo-box, we're talking about a real car.
DAVID: When you get in a Sentra, you don't feel like you're in a boxy little car.
CHRIS: People are responding to this, too, because...
LOUISE: There is tremendous consumer satisfaction in this car and that is very satisfying.
MICHAEL: You know what a challenge is? A challenge is...
DAVID: Making my 3-year-old eat meatloaf.
SFX: LAUGHTER.
VO: Nissan. Built for the most important race of all. The Human Race.

946
Art Director: Domingo Perez
Writer: James Jordan
Editor: Steve Bell
Creative Director: Bernie Owett, Richard DiLallo
Director: Bill Marshall
Producer: Sid Horn, Tony Mount

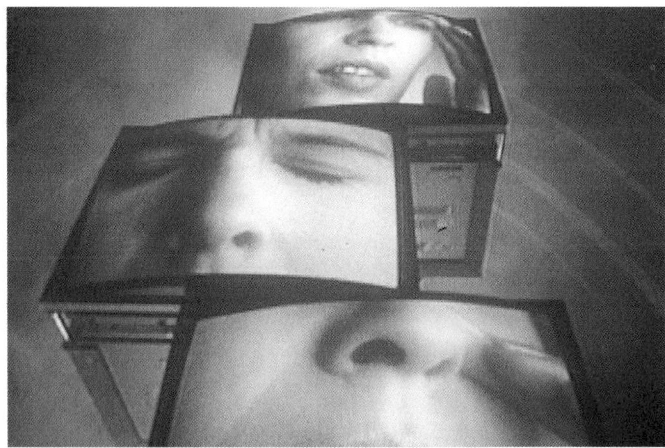

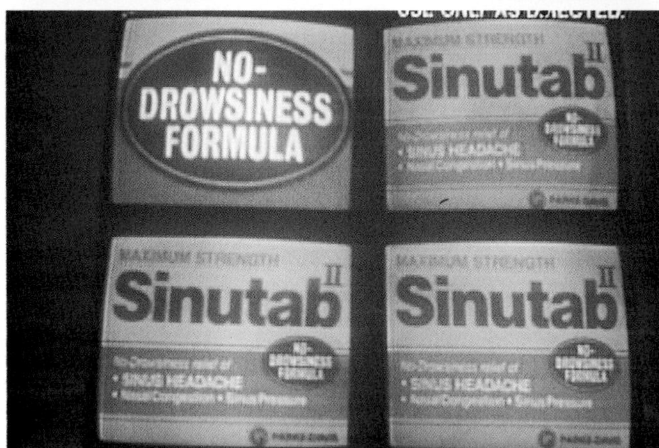

TOWER
30 seconds
ANNCR: Headache, pressure, and congestion. All together. The major symptoms of sinus complex. You need to feel better, but not drowsy. You need Sinutab II no-drowsiness formula. Sinutab II. So you feel altogether better. And awake.

947
Art Director: Rick Boyko, Miles Turpin
Writer: Elizabeth Hayes, Milton Unger, Emma Unger
Client: Home Savings of America
Director: Leslie Dektor
Producer: Richard O'Neill, Elaine Hinton, David Prince

THE UNGERS
30 seconds
MILTON: We've always made it, and I don't worry, because she's a good manager. Whether we have a little or a lot, we make it. One week we were so poor I bought a bushel of carrots and we lived on carrots all week, and now when we go out to dinner and we see carrots, we look at each other and smile. It didn't hurt us. It was fun.
ANNCR: Milton and Emma worked very hard for their retirement. So did Home Savings.
MILTON: We're just ordinary people. We're late bloomers.

948
Art Director: Steve Beaumont
Writer: Steve Rabosky
Client: Nissan Motor Corp.
Director: Norman Seeff
Producer: Richard O'Neill

PATHFINDERS
30 seconds
STEPHEN: There are a lot of people out there who are truck people at heart, but they just want the comfort of a car.
DAVID: What we've done is combined all the aspects of a luxury car and of a tough 4×4.
LLOYD: When you sit inside of a Pathfinder, it's like stepping into a luxurious sedan.
JEFF: You know, it's like a civilized way to go bouncing down a dirt road.
KAZ: It takes you places that aren't even places.
SFX: LAUGHTER.
VO: Nissan. Built for the toughest race of all. The human race.

949
Art Director: Ted Shaine
Writer: Helayne Spivak
Editor: Morty Ashkinos; Morty's Film Service
Client: Club Med Sales Inc.
Director: David Cornell
Producer: Ozzie Spenningsby, Spots Films

WORLD NEWS
30 seconds
VO: The world news Club Med style. Oil spills along the coast.
Foreign relations improving. Gold plunges overseas.
Border dispute settled. Tensions ease in Gulf.
And that's the way it is. At Club Med.

950
Art Director: Jeff Vogt
Writer: Tom Nathan
Editor: Craig Warnick; Jerry Bender Editorial
Client: BMW of North America Inc.
Director: Henry Sandbank
Producer: Colleen O'Connor, Henry Sandbank Films

RETURN TO THE ROAD
30 seconds
VO: Someone once said that the only time a BMW owner willingly removes his car from the road, is to remove the road from his car. The new BMW 325is adds new meaning to that piece of insight. A 39% increase in power, competition tuned suspension, serious aerodynamics. All of which tends to reduce washing the BMW 325is to an act of futility.

951
Art Director: Simon Bowden
Writer: David Metcalf
Editor: Pam Powers, Dennis Hayes
Client: Nikon Inc.
Director: Nick Lewin
Producer: Lewin & Watson,
Jean Muchmore; Scali, McCabe, Sloves Inc.

THE HAND
30 seconds
HORROR MUSIC THROUGHOUT
VINCENT PRICE VO: The new 35mm automatic one-touch from Nikon.
MAID: Ahhhhhhh!!
SFX: CLICK. MUSIC.
PRICE VO: Automatic film load.
BUTLER: Ahhhhhhh!
SFX: CLICK.
PRICE VO: Automatic focusing, automatic smart flash.
BUTLER: Ahhhhhhh!
SFX: CLICK.
PRICE VO: The new Nikon one-touch. It puts great photography at everybody's fingertips.

952
Art Director: Jeff Roll
Writer: Paul Decker
Client: Suzuki of America
Director: Joe Hanright
Producer: Harvey Greenberg, Kira Films

WHAT IT'S LIKE
30 seconds
MICHAEL: Beep, beep, hi!

953
Art Director: Simon Bowden
Director of Photography: Carl Knorr
Writer: David Metcalf
Editor: Dennis Hayes
Client: Volvo of America Corp.
Director: Thom Higgins
Producer: BFCS, Dane Johnson; Scali, McCabe, Sloves, Inc.

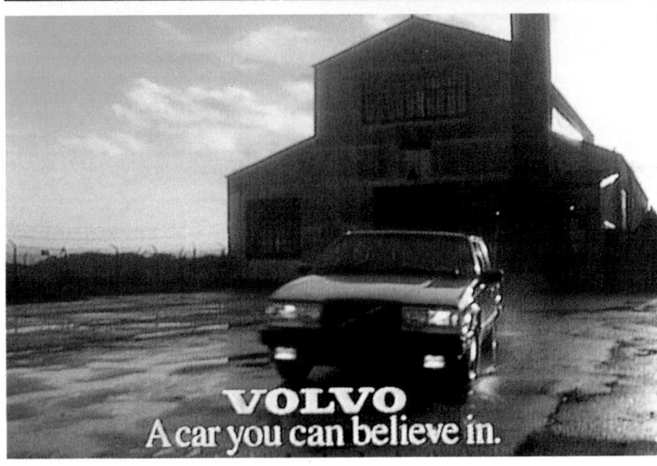

COLLECTOR
30 seconds
MUSIC UNDER: OPERATIC EXCERPT
ANNCR: The 1946 MG.
MUSIC
ANNCR: The 1957 Thunderbird.
MUSIC
ANNCR: The 1988 Volvo 740 Turbo.
MUSIC
ANNCR: A collector's item you can drive every day.

954
Art Director: Bob Phillips
Writer: Rav Friedel
Editor: Morty Ashkinos
Client: BMW of North America Inc.
Director: Steve Horn
Producer: Colleen O'Connor, Steve Horn Productions

LUXURIES RUN DEEP
30 seconds
WOMAN: How much longer 'til we get there?
MAN: About 20 minutes.
VO: Anti-lock brakes, an internationally patented suspension, uncanny control. Conventional luxury sedans are built to survive accidents. The BMW 528e is built to avoid them.
WOMAN: Let's see if they're O.K.

955
Art Director: Ted Shaine, Marcus Kemp
Writer: Rav Friedel
Editor: Craig Warnick; Jerry Bender Editorial
Client: BMW of North America Inc.
Director: Peter Cherry
Producer: Robert Samuel, Cherry Mellon Ibbetson

GUESS WHAT THEY BUY
30 seconds
VO: No one would deny that the Japanese are aficionados of fine machinery. So when they reach that station in life when they can afford really fine machinery, guess what they buy? A car from Germany called the BMW 325i. Making BMW last year's #1 selling luxury import in Japan.

956
Art Director: Marcus Kemp
Writer: Paul Wolfe
Editor: Randy Ilowite; First Edition Editorial
Client: BMW of North America Inc.
Director: Thom Higgins
Producer: Colleen O'Connor, BFCS

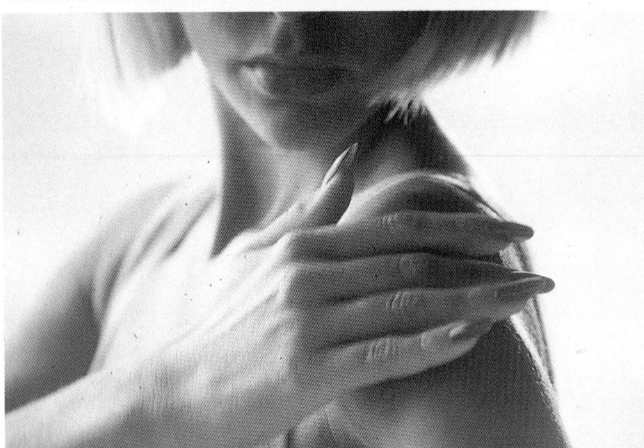

ULTIMATE TANNING MACHINE
30 seconds
VO: The BMW 325i convertible. The ultimate... tanning machine.

957
Art Director: Steve Beaumont
Writer: Steve Rabosky
Client: Nissan Motor Corp.
Director: Norman Seeff
Producer: Richard O'Neill

SWIMMING POOL
30 seconds
JEFFREY: There's two kinds of people. There's car people and truck people... and if you're gonna design trucks, you better know the difference.
DAVID: I was in the desert last week...
SFX: MUSIC BLARING.
DAVID: and there's this guy and he has put a plastic liner...
SFX: SPLASHES.
DAVID: and he's using it for a swimming pool.
SFX: GROUP LAUGHS, CHATTERS.
STEPHEN: People wanna' do that kind of thing with a... truck, they wanna' treat it like it's indestructible.
SFX: TIRES IN THE MUD.
CHRIS: Tough hardbodies can take it.
SFX: TRUCK LEAP AND LAND.
DAVID: This truck is the right tool for the job.
VO: Nissan. Built for the toughest race of all. The Human Race.

958
Art Director: Peter Cohen
Writer: Larry Spector
Editor: Morty Ashkinos
Client: Webster Industries
Director: Mark Story
Producer: Cami Taylor; Story, Piccolo, Guliner, Rachel Novak; Levine, Huntley, Schmidt & Beaver

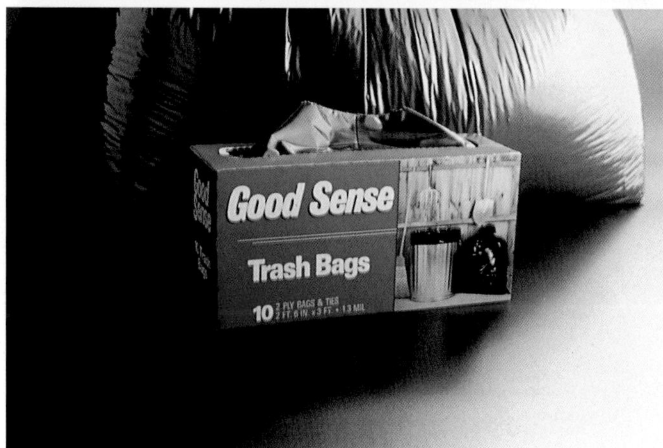

ELEPHANT
30 seconds
MAN: When the people at Good Sense asked me to stand under one of their garbage bags filled with 58 pounds of elephant fertilizer...I said forget it! When they said they'd pay me a fortune, I said...maybe. Then they told me their bags were made of super tough plastic to resist punctures and tears. Which obviously took a big load off my mind.
SFX: ELEPHANT ROARING.
ANNCR: Good Sense.
SFX: BAG DROPPING.
ANNCR: The best things you'll ever throw out.

959
Art Director: Sal DeVito
Writer: Amy Borkowsky
Editor: Howie Lazarus
Client: Genesee Cream Ale
Director: Mark Story
Producer: Cami Taylor; Story, Piccolo, Guliner, Rachel Novak; Levine, Huntley, Schmidt & Beaver

HORSES
15 seconds
VO: This should give you some idea of the difference between beer and Genesee Cream Ale. Smooth Genesee Cream Ale. It's not the same old brewskie.

960
Art Director: Earl Cavanah
Writer: Larry Cadman
Editor: Steve Bodner
Client: Nikon Inc.
Director: Mark Coppos
Producer: Sue Chiafullo

WEDDING
30 seconds
MUSIC: "WEDDING MARCH."
VO: A lot of beautiful moments in life have been messed up by lousy photography.
SFX: CLICK.
ANNCR: But this couldn't happen with the Nikon N4004. It's an autofocus, autoflash 35mm SLR that makes it almost impossible to take a bad picture. The N4004. The only mistake you can make is buying something else.
BRIDE: Uncle Henry, I can't wait to see these pictures.
SFX: CLICK.

961
Art Director: Earl Cavanah
Writer: Larry Cadman
Editor: Barry Stillwell
Client: Volvo of America Corp.
Director: Henry Sandbank
Producer: Jaki Keuch

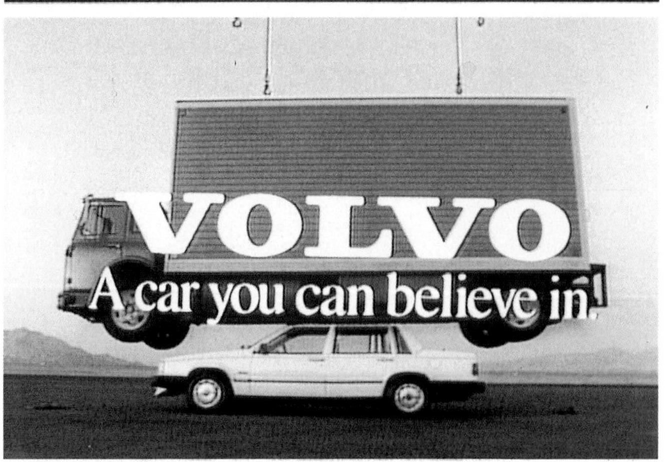

HEAVY TRAFFIC
30 seconds
MUSIC THROUGHOUT.
SFX: CLICK.
VO: How well does your car stand up to heavy traffic?
MUSIC OUT.

962

Art Director: Marty Weiss
Writer: Robin Raj
Client: NYNEX Information Resources
Director: Kevin Godley, Lol Creme
Producer: Mark Sitley, Steve Amato
Account Manager: Amy Saypol

MOTORS-MINIATURE
30 seconds
SFX: OPENING CHIME. SOUND OF CLANGING, MOTOR ON PULLEY.
GUY 1: O.K., bring it forward a little bit...keep it coming.
GUY 2: It ain't gonna fit, Charlie.
SFX: CRANKING SOUND OF MOTOR BEING LOWERED.
GUY 2: Charlie, it ain't gonna fit!
GUY 1: Take it easy...just be gentle with it....
SFX: CRASHING SOUND.
GUY 2: Sorry, Charlie...I knew it wouldn't fit!
GUY 1: Mutters. Wait! Get it up!
GUY 2: I knew it wouldn't fit!...
ANNCR: If it's out there, it's in here....
GUY 2: I knew it wouldn't fit.
ANNCR: The NYNEX Yellow Pages.
SFX: BOOK SLAMS SHUT.
ANNCR: Why would anyone need another?

963

Art Director: Marty Weiss
Writer: Robin Raj
Client: NYNEX Information Resources
Director: Kevin Godley, Lol Creme
Producer: Mark Sitley, Steve Amato
Account Manager: Amy Saypol

PIANO ROLLS
30 seconds
SFX: OPENING CHIME. SOUND OF PIANO ROLLING AS MAN PLAYS COCKTAIL MUSIC. SOUND OF PIANO PLAYING, ROLLING.
VO: If it's out there, it's in here. ...The NYNEX Yellow Pages.
SFX: BOOK SLAMS SHUT.
VO: Why would anyone need another?

964
Art Director: Tim Lachowski
Animator/Artist: Peter Wallach
Writer: Mark Cummins
Client: Michigan State Lottery
Director: Peter Wallach
Producer: Jill Prost; W. B. Doner & Co.,
Sheldon Cohn; W. B. Doner & Co.,
Carole Zeitlin; Peter Wallach Enterprises

MOST WANTED MEN
30 seconds
VO: These are some of Michigan's most wanted men. And if you'd like to apprehend a few more of them for the holidays, play the new instant lottery game Winner Wonderland. Because millions of people could win prizes of up to $1000 instantly. So play Winner Wonderland. And you could have many of Michigan's most wanted men to spend for the holidays. Or you could just throw the book at 'em.

965
Art Director: Ron Arnold
Writer: Bill Hamilton
Editor: Steve Schreiber
Creative Director: Bill Hamilton
Client: Sara Lee
Director: Stan Schofield
Producer: Andrew Chinich, Chiat/Day Inc.,
Richard Cohen; Sandbank Films, Inc.,
Account Management: Ira Matathia
Music: Debby Harry

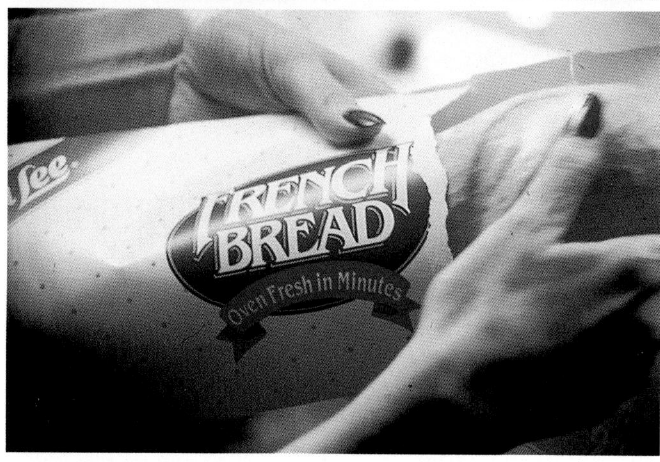

DEBBIE HARRY/FRENCH BREAD
30 seconds
DEBBIE: Hi...here comes my commercial.
MUSIC STARTS.
DEBBIE: First of all, did I tell you this was bread? From Sara Lee. Thirteen minutes in the oven. Smells great.
SFX: TIMER GOES OFF.
DEBBIE: Fresh. Hot. It can't get any hotter than this. I love French bread. Yeah, it's good. Can I cook!

966
Art Director: Marty Weiss
Writer: Robin Raj
Editor: Ciro DeNettis
Client: NYNEX Information Resources
Director: Kevin Godley, Lol Creme
Producer: Mark Sitley, Steve Amato
Account Manager: Amy Saypol

VANITY CASES
30 seconds
SFX: OPENING CHIME. COCKTAIL CHATTER. PIANO.
WOMAN 1: Isn't my hair marvelous? Peter did it, you know.
MAN 1: Didn't we meet in Cannes last year? Or was it Bora Bora?
WOMAN 2: So let's talk about you, darling. What do you think of my dress?
WOMAN 3: Then Rod said, "Let's go to Mick's house."
MAN 2: Both my Ferraris are in the shop...I hate that!
WOMAN 4: I see modeling as a stepping-stone. But what I really want to do is direct!
MAN 3: Uh huh, sure! Oh, you're right. Hi!
VO: If it's out there, it's in here. ...The NYNEX Yellow Pages.
SFX: BOOK SLAMS SHUT.
VO: Why would anyone need another?

967
Art Director: John D'Asto
Writer: Mark Fenske
Editor: Bob Blanford
Creative Director: Jan Zechman
Client: Exchange National Bank
Director: Iain McKenzie
Producer: Laurie Berger

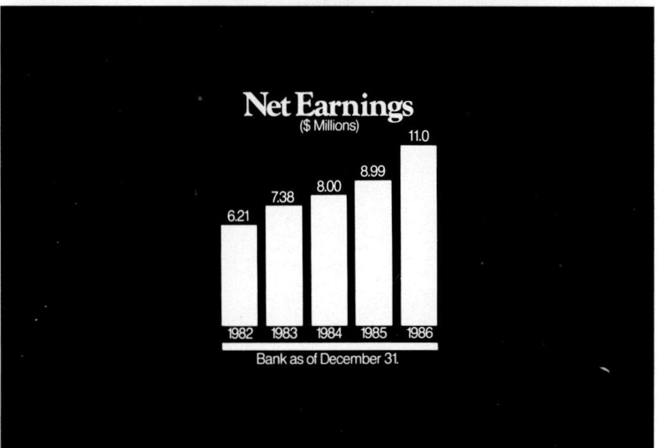

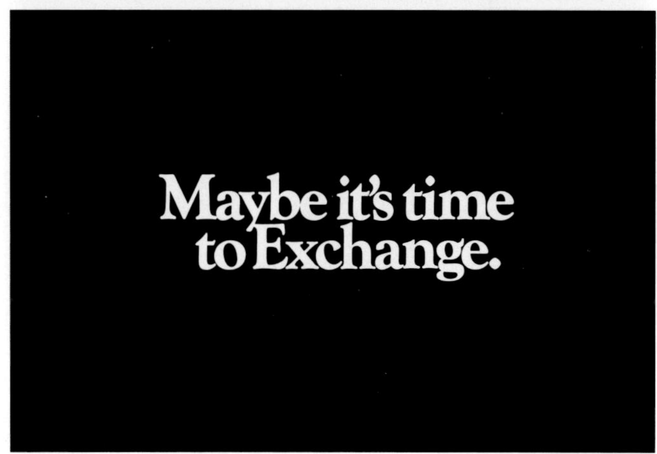

COLUMNS
30 seconds
VO: In Paris you can tell how impressive a bank is by the magnificence of its entranceway. In Amsterdam, by the rank of imposing guards posted by the doors. And in London by the looming grandeur of its facade. So how do you distinguish the best business bank in Chicago? The impressive columns. The Exchange National Bank.

968
Art Director: Simon Nelson
Designer: Chris Dougherty
Director of Photography: Chuck Rosher
Writer: Gwen Nelson
Editor: Charlie Chubak; FilmCore LA
Creative Director: Bryan Birch, BBDO
Client: Sizzler Restaurants
Director: Bob Eggers
Producer: Sterling Ray, Judy Trotter

DRESSING FOR DINNER
30 seconds
DAD: Goggles.
SON: Goggles.
DAD: Hip boots.
SON: Hip boots.
DAD: Slicker.
SON: Slicker.
DAD: Gloves.
SON: Gloves.
DAD: Hat.
SON: Hat.
ANNCR: It's that time again. Sizzler's All-You-Can-Eat Barbequed Beef Ribs. Rib after big juicy rib. For a price you can't beef about.
DAD: Prepare to eat.
SON: Prepare to eat.
DAD: Eat!
SON: Eat!
VO: Sizzler.

969
Art Director: Troy Hayes
Writer: Allen Rubens
Creative Director: David Klehr
Client: Anheuser-Busch/Bud Light
Agency: DDB Needham Worldwide
Director: Bob Eggers
Producer: Grant Hill, Bob Eggers; Eggers Films

PSYCHO
30 seconds
VO: There's a vacancy at the Bates Motel.
SFX: LIGHTNING.
WOMAN: Norman, is that you?
ANNCR: No! It's Spuds McKenzie and it could be you. Look for this display and enter Bud Light's Psycho sweepstakes. To win a Bud Light party with Spuds McKenzie at the Psycho mansion. You can even get a mug like Spuds at participating retailers. Wow!
WOMAN: That Spuds is so cool it's scary.
SFX: SCREAM.

970

Art Director: Peter DeBoer, Arlene Wanetick
Writer: Arlene Wanetick
Creative Director: Peter DeBoer
Client: NEC Home Electronics Inc.
Agency: DDB Needham Worldwide
Producer: Bill Artope, Partner's

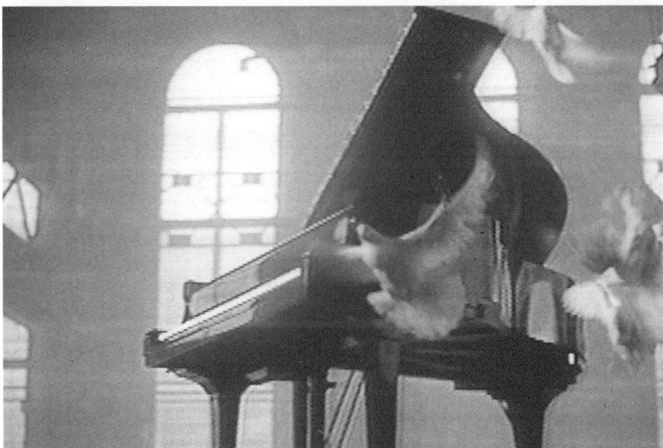

P. J. ROCK
30 seconds
SFX: MUSIC UP.
VO: Discover the NEC Projection TV with surround sound.
SFX: MUSIC AND SINGERS.
VO: N.E.C.

971

Art Director: Cathy Grisham
Director of Photography: Jerry Hartleiben
Writer: Cindy Bokhof
Editor: Tim McGuire
Creative Director: Cathy Grisham, Cindy Bokhof
Client: Maybelline
Agency: DDB Needham Worldwide
Director: Catherine Lefebvre
Producer: Dale French, Catherine Lefebvre

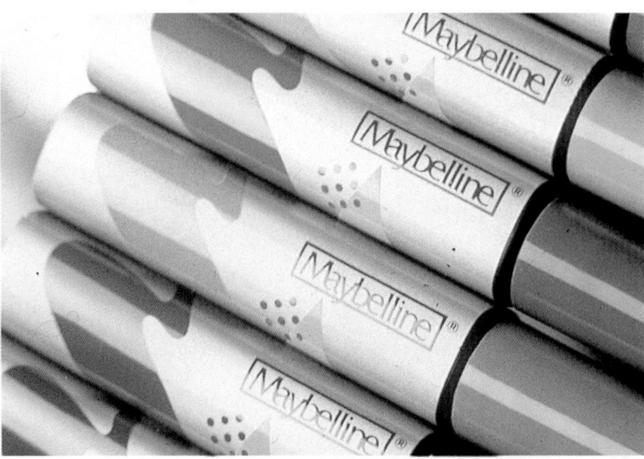

CONTRASTS
30 seconds
SMART: If mascara could satisfy your rational side....
BEAUTIFUL: And your emotional side, it'd be bloomin' brilliant.
SMART: Introducing new Blooming Colors Mascara from Maybelline.
BEAUTIFUL: Colors! Colors! Colors!
SMART: 8 color options.
BEAUTIFUL: Don't fence me in!
SMART: Alternative to black.
BEAUTIFUL: Brilliant. They're mine! All mine!
SMART: Accessorize your eyes.
BEAUTIFUL: New Blooming Colors Mascara!
SUNG: Smart! Beautiful! Maybelline!

972
Art Director: Michael Lawlor
Writer: Charlie Breen
Client: Hyundai Motor America
Producer: Andy Cornelius

GETTING THEM HOME
30 seconds
SFX: TIRES SCREECH, MUSIC UP AND UNDER, HURRIED FOOTSTEPS.
VO: For less than the average price of a new car, you can get two new Hyundai Excels. They're both dependable, have front wheel drive, room for 5, and more standard features than any cars in their class. The only problem is...getting them home. Hyundai. Cars that make sense.

973
Art Director: Nancy Wovers
Director of Photography: Stephen Burum
Animator/Artist: Laine Liska
Writer: Mark Melton
Editor: Don Packer
Client: Keds Corp.
Director: Randy Roberts
Producer: Amy Mizner, Mardi Kleppel; Berkofsky, Smillie, Barrett

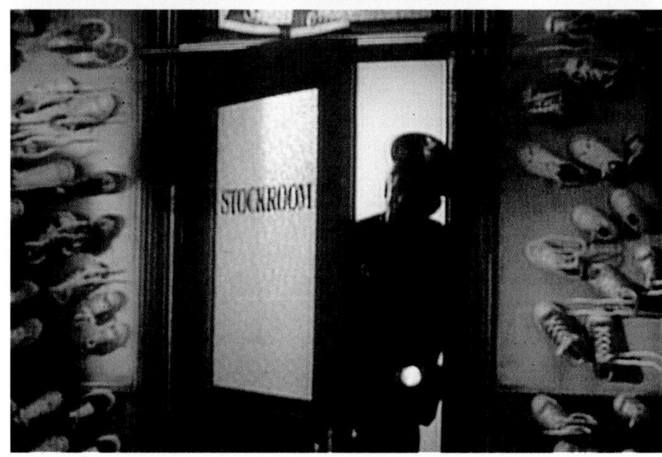

FANCY FOOTWORK
30 seconds
SFX: DOOR CLICKS OPEN; CREAKS AS IT OPENS. LIGHTSWITCH SNAPS OFF. DOOR CLOSES. SYNTHESIZED VOICE. SNEAKER SQUEAKS EXCITEDLY. MORE SNEAKERS SQUEAK AND GIGGLE. FULL MUSIC TRACK KICKS IN: BRIGHT, INSISTENT BEAT. CHORUS OF SMALL SYNTHESIZED VOICES SINGS "KEDS" ON DOWNBEAT. MUSIC CONTINUES. CRASH, BOOM, BANG. MUSIC CUTS OFF ABRUPTLY.
SYNTHESIZED VOICES: Whu-ohhhh!
SFX: HUSHED GIGGLING. GUARD WHISTLES MUSIC ABOVE.
VO: Get a free yoyo when you buy selected Keds right now.

974
Art Director: Geoff Hayes
Writer: Joy Golden
Editor: Morty's
Client: Fromageries Bel
Director: Steve Horn
Producer: Linda Horn, Ed Pollack; TBWA Advertising Inc.

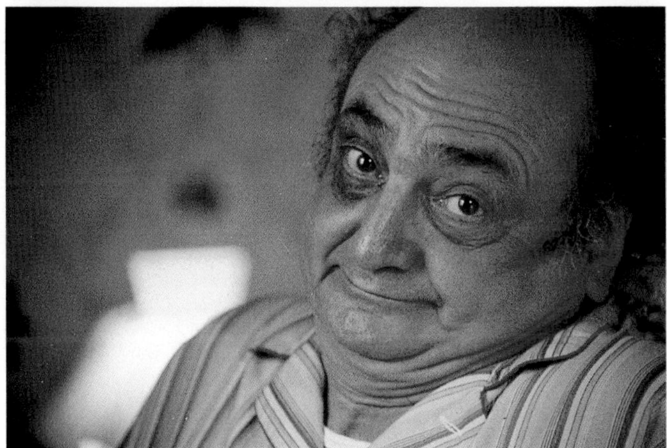

STUART
30 seconds
WOMAN: Last night my husband woke me and said he had a little craving. I said, "I'll give you a little round Laughing Cow in a red net bag." He said, "I don't care if she's in lace with high heels. It's not what I had in mind." I said, "Stuart, Laughing Cow is cheese. Mild Mini Bonbel, Nippy Mini Babybel, and Mini Gouda too. Delicious. Natural bite size." Then he ate 2 little red net bags with 5 mini cheeses in each and said it was the best treat he ever had in bed. So I smacked him.

975
Art Director: Dean Hanson
Writer: Tom McElligott
Client: Lee Jeans
Director: Thom Higgins
Producer: Judy Brink

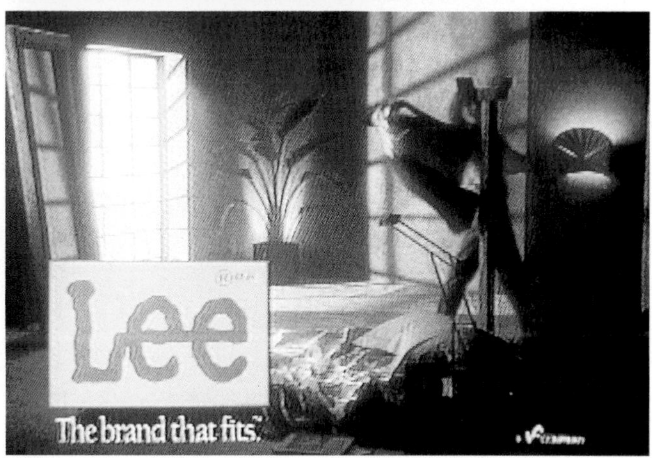

RITUAL
30 seconds
SFX: MUSIC THROUGHOUT.
VO: Every day, millions of American women practice a strange ritual. It's called "getting into jeans." Today there are jeans *designed* to fit a woman's curves... *without* the usual ritual. Lee Relaxed Riders. It's not a better body you need. It's better jeans.

976
Art Director: Bill Yamada
Writer: Marcia Grace
Editor: Jay Gold
Client: Cadbury/Schweppes
Director: Dennis Peil
Producer: Abby Sheridan, Mason Boyd

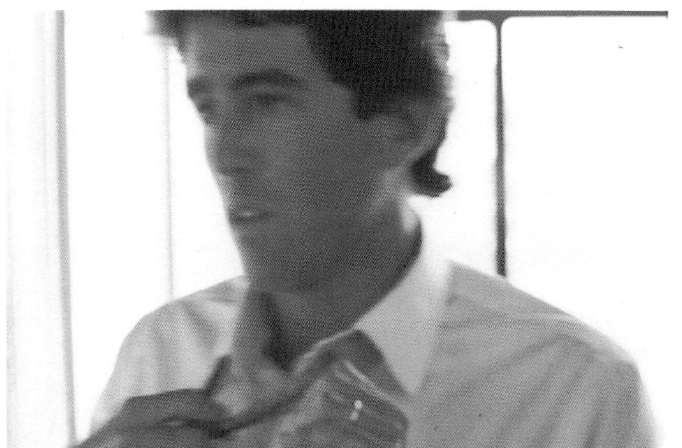

RELAXATION
30 seconds
SFX: MUSIC BEGINS. INCREASES. SINGING BEGINS–"IMAGINATION."
ANNCR: The more refreshing, more distinctive character of Canada Dry Ginger Ale. Regular or Diet. For when your tastes grow up.

977
Art Director: Terry O'Leary
Writer: Doug Feinstein
Editor: Michael Charles
Client: Duracell Batteries
Director: Dick Miller
Producer: Mootsy Elliot, Lisa Miller
Music Director: Karl Westman
Models/Toys: Tony Meininger

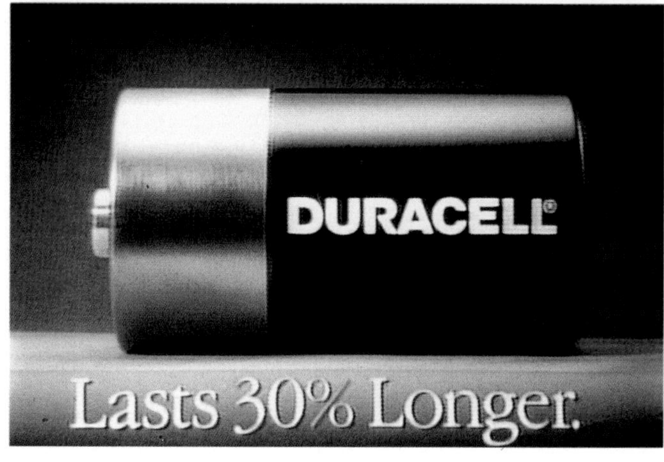

THE CHASE
30 seconds
SFX: MUSIC UP. OLD-FASHIONED SILENT MOVIE STYLE. MUSIC CONTINUES THROUGHOUT.
VO: Today's Duracell.
SFX: SLAM-AROUND.
VO: Lasts 30% longer.

978
Art Director: Dean Hanson
Writer: Phil Hanft
Editor: Jeff Stickles
Client: Conran's
Director: Henry Sandbank
Producer: Char Loving

EASY CHAIR
30 seconds
VO: At Conran's, we don't believe beautifully designed furniture…should be so expensive…you're afraid to even sit in it.
SFX: BURP.

979
Art Director: Pat Burnham
Writer: Bill Miller
Editor: Steve Wystrach
Client: Federal Express
Director: Mark Coppos
Producer: Judy Brink

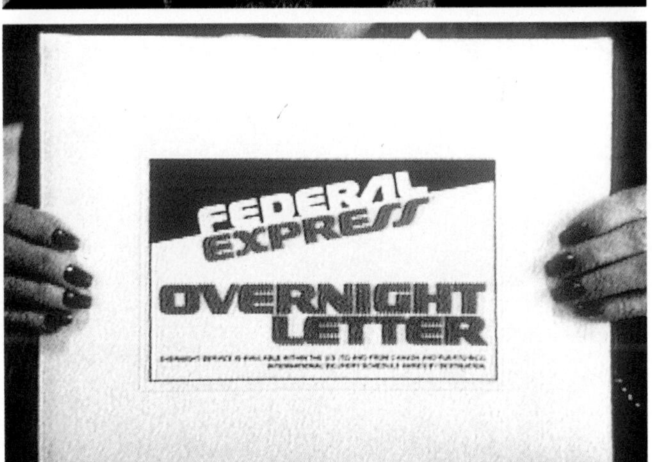

SECRETARY
30 seconds
VO: When it comes to being a secretary, you gotta know how to get things done. You gotta shuffle the paper. You gotta juggle the phones. You gotta know how to handle a rush. You gotta be a pro. You gotta be in charge. You've been this way before. 'Cause when push comes to shove, they know it's you who has to get it out the door. This reminder from Federal Express, that it's not just a package.
SFX: THUMP.
VO: It's your business.

980
Art Director: Fred Massin, Amy Bronstein
Writer: Michele Salmon, Rex Wilder
Creative Director: Stanley Becker
Client: Royal Crown Cola
Director: Henry Sandbank
Producer: Sheldon Levy

RED WAGON
30 seconds
VO: There are some people who like the taste of Coke. And yes, there are some people who like the taste of Pepsi. But there will always be some people who go out of their way for the great taste of RC Cola.

981
Art Director: Dean Hanson
Writer: Tom McElligott
Client: Lee Jeans
Director: Thom Higgins
Producer: Judy Brink

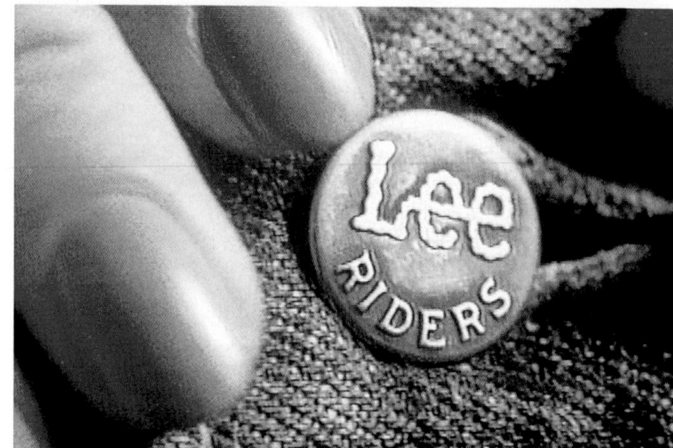

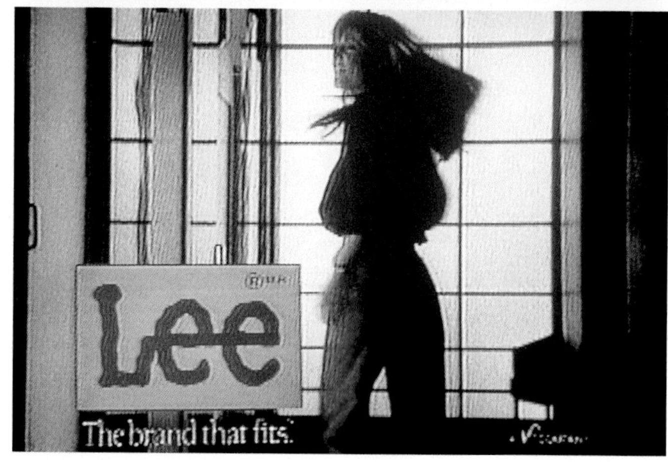

ESTIMATED
30 seconds
SFX: MUSIC THROUGHOUT.
VO: It has been estimated that the average American woman tries on 16.3 pairs of jeans in order to find one pair that fits. An activity that leaves many women blaming their own bodies. But there *are* jeans actually designed to fit the natural curves that make women *look* like women. Lee Relaxed Riders. It's not a better body you need. It's better jeans.

982
Art Director: Philip Halyard
Writer: Kenneth Sandbank
Editor: John Palestrini
Client: Braun Inc.
Director: Patrick Morgan
Producer: Laurie Leokum, RSA Productions

PERFECT COFFEE
30 seconds
SFX: MUSIC THROUGHOUT.
VO: The Braun coffeemaker is designed to brew perfect coffee on those mornings when you just don't have time for instant. Braun. Designed to perform better.

983
Art Director: Pat Burnham
Writer: Bill Miller
Editor: Steve Wystrach
Client: Federal Express
Director: Mark Coppos
Producer: Judy Brink

BIG WHEEL
30 seconds
VO: When it comes to the gear business... you gotta be a big wheel. You gotta know how the world turns. 'Cause you want it to turn your way. You gotta do business in the right circles. You gotta keep your skids greased. You gotta keep your bearings straight. You can't let your customers grind to a halt.
SFX: GEARS MESHING.
VO: This reminder from Federal Express, that it's not just a package.
SFX: THUMP.
VO: It's your business.

984
Art Director: Pat Burnham
Writer: Bill Miller
Editor: Steve Wystrach
Client: Federal Express
Director: Mark Coppos
Producer: Judy Brink

FLYING MAN
30 seconds
VO: When it comes to doing business overseas…you gotta know how to get it over there. You gotta span the globe. You gotta put spin on the ball. You gotta know foreign relations most of all. You gotta know the customs. You can't afford to be stopped at the border. You gotta make things happen…when you get your customer's order. This reminder from Federal Express, that it's not just a package.
SFX: THUMP.
VO: It's your business.

985
Art Director: June Manton
Writer: Sue Read
Client: Thomas J. Lipton
Agency: Lintas USA
Director: Leslie Dektor
Producer: Stan Noble, Leslie Dektor

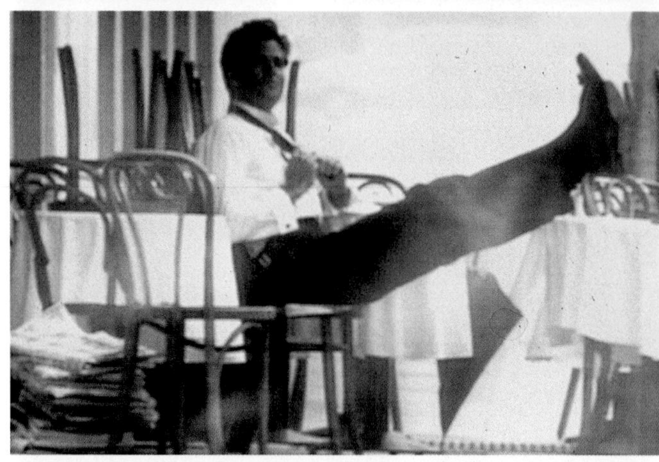

RED DRESS
30 seconds
SINGER:
Look at all those little old ladies drinkin' Lipton Tea.
See them sittin', sippin' Lipton
Proper as can be.
See them rockin'
See them rockin'
Now that's gentility.
Look at all those little old ladies
Drinkin' Lipton Tea.
Look at all those little old ladies
Drinkin' Lipton Tea.

986
Art Director: June Manton
Writer: Sue Read
Client: Thomas J. Lipton
Agency: Lintas USA
Director: Leslie Dektor
Producer: Stan Noble, Leslie Dektor

COOL GUY
30 seconds
SINGER:
Look at all those little old ladies
Drinkin' Lipton Tea.
See them sittin', sippin' Lipton, proper as can be.
See them rockin', see them rockin'.
Now that's gentility.
Lovely.
Look at all those little old ladies
Drinkin' Lipton Tea.
Look at all those little old ladies
Drinkin' Lipton Tea.
Mmmmmm.

987
Art Director: Pat Burnham
Writer: Bill Miller
Editor: Steve Wystrach
Client: Federal Express
Director: Mark Coppos
Producer: Judy Brink

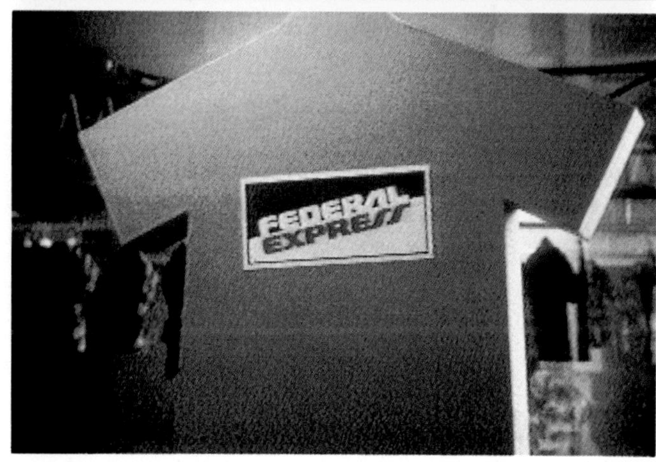

BUTTONED DOWN
30 seconds
VO: When it comes to the clothing business...you gotta cut a big swath. You gotta measure up. You gotta be buttoned down. You gotta dress for success. You gotta know how to sew up a deal. More often than not, you're pressed for time. You can't let your customers fall apart at the seams.
SFX: HANGERS.
VO: This reminder from Federal Express, that it's not just a package.
SFX: THUMP.
VO: It's your business.

988
Art Director: Michael Fazende
Writer: Jarl Olsen
Editor: Tony Fischer
Client: University of Minnesota
Producer: Char Loving

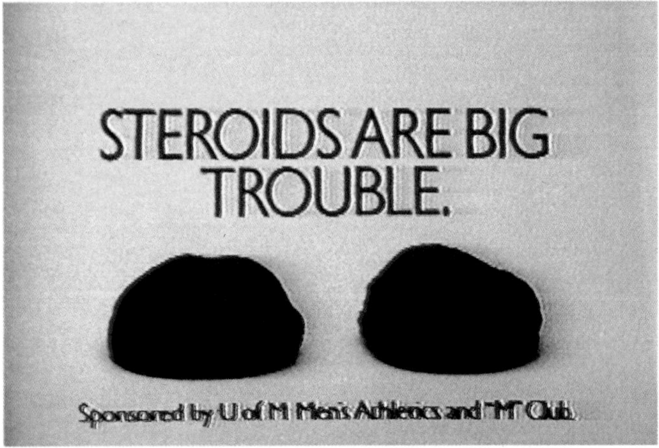

PLUMS
30 seconds
MUSIC: TUBA PLAYING ROUSER SONG.
ANNCR: When a man takes steroids, he introduces a chemical into his body... that acts like a male hormone, so the parts of his body that used to make male hormone shut down. Eventually, they waste away, leaving the man sterile.
MUSIC: LITTLE MORE THAN A HIGH PITCHED WHINE.
ANNCR: A lot of big athletes have taken steroids. But they aren't very big now. Steroids. They're big trouble.

989
Art Director: John Colquhoun
Writer: Arthur Bijur, Cliff Freeman
Creative Director: Arthur Bijur
Director: Mark Story
Producer: Steve Friedman, Story, Piccolo, Guliner

Lord Klempston gazed upon Lucretia's loveliness.

and whispered into her ear...

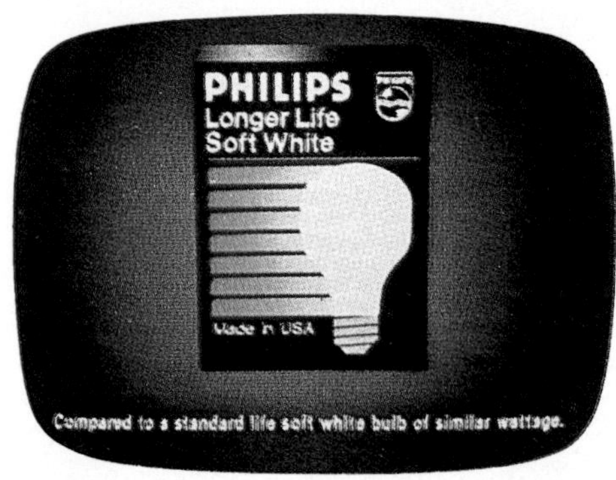

Philips Longer Life square bulbs last 33% longer than ordinary round bulbs.

LORD KLEMPSTON
30 seconds
1st MAN: Hey, get a load of this. Lord Klempston gazed upon Lucretia's loveliness. Her milky white shoulders were ablaze in the moonlight. Lord Klempston approached her and wrapped his thickly muscled arms around her delicate waist. He then whispered into her ear....
SFX: BULB BLOWS.
1st MAN: I can't see.
2nd MAN: Lord Klempston was blind?!
ANNCR: It's time to change your bulb to Philips. Philips Longer Life square bulbs last 33% longer than ordinary round bulbs.

990
Art Director: Pat Burnham
Writer: Bill Miller
Editor: Steve Wystrach
Client: Federal Express
Director: Mark Coppos
Producer: Judy Brink

BIG GLOBE
30 seconds
VO: When it comes to doing business worldwide…you gotta think in global proportions. You gotta know how the world turns…'cause you want it to turn your way.
You gotta speak the language. You gotta travel with a fast crowd. It's a big world out there. You gotta do everything you can to make it smaller.
This reminder from Federal Express, that it's not just a package.
SFX: THUMP.
VO: It's your business.

991
Art Director: Ron Sandilands
Writer: Steve Sandoz
Editor: Peggy Delay
Client: Alaska Airlines
Agency: Livingston & Co.
Director: Joe Sedelmaier
Producer: Cindy Henderson, Sedelmaier Productions
Client Supervisor: John Kelly

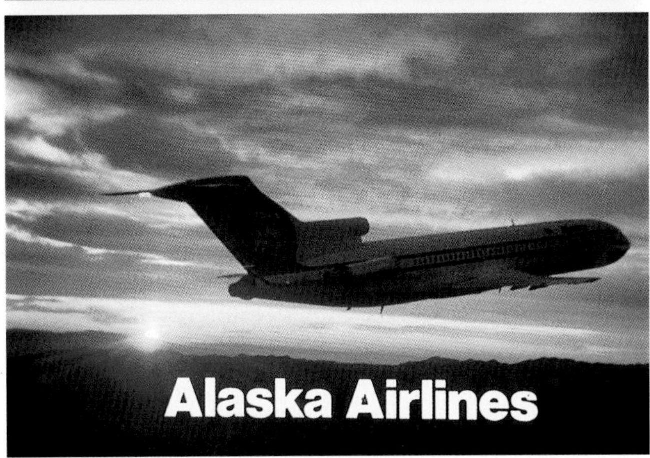

WHAT'S NEXT
30 seconds
VO: Many airlines offer reduced rates. Unfortunately, that's not all they've reduced. It makes you wonder what's next.
MAN: I'd appreciate it, do you have four quarters for a dollar? Anybody have two quarters for a dollar? Yes, miss, do you have two quarters for five dollars, please? Oh boy, I'd really appreciate it.
VO: On Alaska Airlines, we have low fares too. But you'd never know it by the way we treat you.

992
Art Director: Marty Weiss
Writer: Robin Raj
Editor: Ciro DeNettis
Client: NYNEX Information Resources
Director: Kevin Godley, Lol Creme
Producer: Mark Sitley, Steve Amato
Account Manager: Amy Saypol

NOISE CONTROL CONSULTANTS
30 seconds
SFX: OPENING CHIME. SOUND OF RADIO PLAYING LOUD "RAP" MUSIC. LOUD MUSIC CONTINUES. CRASHING SOUND, AS MAN SMASHES RADIO. MUSIC STOPS.
VO: If it's out there, it's in here. ...The NYNEX Yellow Pages.
SFX: BOOK SLAMS SHUT.
VO: Why would anyone need another?

993
Art Director: Marty Weiss
Writer: Robin Raj
Client: NYNEX Information Resources
Director: Kevin Godley, Lol Creme
Producer: Mark Sitley, Steve Amato
Account Manager: Amy Saypol

MANHOLES
30 seconds
SFX: OPENING CHIME. SOUND OF SHOES SQUEAKING. SILENCE. COMICAL SOUND OF SOMETHING FALLING. FALLING SOUND CONTINUES.
VO: If it's out there, it's in here....
SFX: SOUND OF MANHOLE COVER CLANGING, COMING TO REST.
VO: The NYNEX Yellow Pages.
SFX: BOOK SLAMS SHUT.
VO: Why would anyone need another?

994

Art Director: Greg Nygard
Director of Photography: Jules Tomko
Writer: Tom Darbyshire
Editor: Bob Blanford
Creative Director: Jan Zechman
Client: Henri's Food Products
Director: Vivan Mainwaring
Producer: Laurie Berger, Bob Purman

KILLER TOMATOES
30 seconds
VO: And now a word about Henri's. The dressing with the flavor that brings salad to life.
SFX: BOTTLE DROPS. WOMAN SCREAMS BLOODY MURDER. ACTION-PACKED STOCK MUSIC IN. BATTLE SOUNDS. MUSIC CLIMAXES.
VO: Henri's. The dressing with the flavor that brings salad to life. Use at your own risk.

995

Art Director: Dean Stefanides
Writer: Bernie Rosner
Editor: Randy Ilowite
Client: Ralston Purina/O.N.E.
Director: Sarah Moon
Producer: Sue Chiafullo

HUSH PUPPY
30 seconds
VO: One. One dog in a million. When you feel this way, there's one kind of dog food. A dog food with real chicken. That provides optimum nutrition. A dog food as special as your dog. Purina O.N.E. brand dog food. For that one dog. Yours.

996
Art Director: Lorne Craig
Writer: Dian Cross
Editor: Donna Chambers
Creative Director: Alvin Wasserman
Client: McGavin's Bakery
Producer: Dian Cross, Tom Murray; Circle Productions
Cameraman: Philip Linzey

BOWLING BALL
30 seconds
VO: Even though most breads start out fresh...they often sit on the shelf for days. But at McGavin's, we replace our bread every time we visit the store. So reach for McGavin's. ...It's fresh every time.

997
Art Director: Marty Weiss
Writer: Robin Raj
Client: NYNEX Information Resources
Director: Kevin Godley, Lol Creme
Producer: Mark Sitley, Steve Amato
Account Manager: Amy Saypol

HERBS
30 seconds
SFX: OPENING CHIME. SOUND OF PEOPLE TALKING.
MAN 1: Hey! Herbert Fisher! Have you met Herb Grant?
MAN 2: Herb Grant, Tacoma.
MAN 1: Herb's in the plumbing business!
MAN 2: Yeah, I'm all backed up!
SFX: LAUGHTER.
MAN 3: Herb! You know these bums? Herb Riddick, Herb Kaplan.
MAN 4: Hi!
MAN 1: So, the wife and kids are good?
MAN 5: Herb Junior's almost 12.
MAN 1: Woo, next thing you know, there'll be a Herbert Junior Junior!
SFX: LAUGHTER.
VO: If it's out there, it's in here. ...The NYNEX Yellow Pages.
SFX: BOOK SLAMS SHUT.
VO: Why would anyone need another?

998
Art Director: Tom McManus
Writer: David Warren
Editor: Randy Ilowite
Client: Acura
Director: Allen Charles; Charles St. Film
Producer: Georgia Sullivan, Ed Pollack; TBWA Advertising Inc.
Account Supervisor: Russel Schare

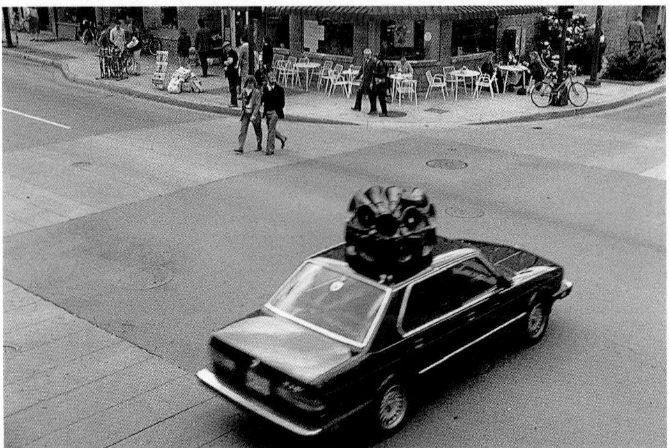

BULLHORN
30 seconds
DRIVER 1: I am a young urban professional....Look at my $42,000 Mercedes....Aren't you impressed?
ANNCR: At Acura, we think the way to impress people is not by showing how much money you spent on your car...but by showing how much car you got for your money.
DRIVER 2: I am a very successful young urban professional....Look at my BMW....Am I not beautiful?
ANNCR: Acura. Cars for people who know better. Priced from $10,000 to $29,000.

999
Art Director: Marty Weiss
Writer: Robin Raj
Client: NYNEX Information Resources
Director: Kevin Godley, Lol Creme
Producer: Mark Sitley, Steve Amato
Account Manager: Amy Saypol

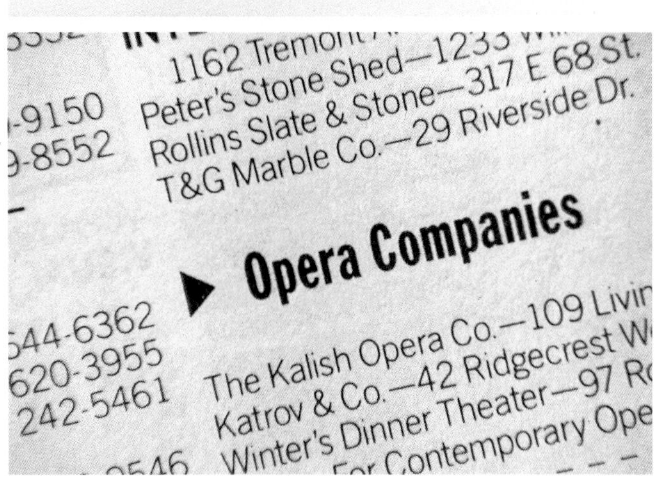

OPERA COMPANIES
30 seconds
SFX: OPENING CHIME. TYPING, PHONE RINGS.
SEC (SINGING THROUGHOUT): Diva Industries, one moment please!
SFX: INTERCOM.
SEC: Yes, Mr. Hummer?
BOSS (SINGS THOUGH INTERCOM): Miss Barnes, you misplaced the Peabody file.
SEC: But Mr. Hummer, I placed it on your desk!
BOSS: No you didn't!
SEC: Yes I did!
BOSS: No you didn't!
SEC: Yes I did!
BOSS: Of all the ridiculous incompetence, Miss Barnes! Find it or I cannot close the deal!
SEC: SINGS A SCALE. Ah ah ah ah ah ah ah ah!
SFX: APPLAUSE.
VO: If it's out there, it's in here....The NYNEX Yellow Pages.
SFX: BOOK SLAMS SHUT.
VO: Why would anyone need another?

1000
Art Director: George Halvorson
Writer: Terry Bremer
Editor: Steve Shepherd; Wilson-Griak
Creative Director: Terry Bremer
Client: The Toro Co.
Agency: John Borchardt; Campbell-Mithun Inc.
Director: Phil Murray
Producer: Mark Carter; Dalton/Fenske & Friends

DRIVEWAY
30 seconds
VO: Until now, plowing through what the snowplow left behind . . .
SFX: BOINK!
VO: was one of the winter's toughest challenges. Now Toro introduces the exclusive Power Shift snowthrower. The Power Shift automatically puts more weight on the front for a more powerful bite on winter's toughest snow. The new Toro Power Shift. The only challenge left... getting out of the driveway to go buy one. Now, haven't you done without a Toro long enough?

1001
Art Director: George Halvorson
Writer: Terry Bremer
Editor: Tom Gilman; City Post
Creative Director: Terry Bremer
Client: The Toro Co.
Director: Dominick Rossetti
Producer: Donald O'Connor; Rossetti Films, Terry Friedlander; Campbell-Mithun Inc.

BOYS
30 seconds
MUSIC & SFX: HEAVY BREATHING AND FOOTSTEPS.
BOYS (SCREAM): Aaaaah!!
DAD: Hi boys.
ANNCR: Only Toro offers the 2-year starting guarantee. This Toro will start on the first or second pull for 2 years, or Toro will fix it free. Guaranteed.
SFX: ENGINE STARTING.
BOYS (SCREAM): Aaaaah!!

1002
Art Director: Maureen White
Writer: Randy Curtis
Editor: Steve Shepherd; Wilson-Griak
Creative Director: Ed Des Lauriers
Client: Sandoz Nutrition Corp.
Director: John Kump
Producer: Chris Wong; Setterholm Productions,
Dan Welter; Setterholm Productions

YOU MAY BE CALLED UPON
30 seconds
ANNCR: It's Captain Midnight! Brought to you by Ovaltine!
CAPTAIN MIDNIGHT: Remember... to do your best, you've got to be at your best. Because someday you may be called upon... to pilot a jet plane across the continent... to take the wheel and bring a great ship safely into port... to drive an ambulance to disaster areas.
That's why I want all Secret Squadron members to drink Ovaltine every day.
ANNCR: And now a late flash from Captain Midnight's Headquarters. Be on the lookout for this new jar of delicious Ovaltine.

1003
Art Director: Mark Haumersen
Animator/Artist: Tom Larson
Writer: John Jarvis
Client: Kemps Ice Cream
Director: John Harvey
Producer: Dain Rodwell; Setterholm Productions,
Lisa Thotland; Martin, Williams Advertising

RHAPSODY IN MOO
30 seconds
LYRICS:
No other cows have our style or grace.
We're the breed that gives Kemps its great taste.
The secret of Kemps, it's the cows.
We hate to start a battle, but those other cows are cattle. The secret of Kemps, it's the cows!
ANNCR: Kemps ice cream. It's the cows.
LYRICS: Moo, moo, moo!

1004
Art Director: Jeff Jones
Writer: Art Novak
Editor: Dale Cooper
Client: Northern States Power
Director: Jim Lund
Producer: Kathy Lally
Production Company: James Productions

DISAPPEARING
30 seconds
SFX: MUSIC.
VO: In many homes, money is disappearing. It's being taken by inefficient heating, drafty windows, and countless other culprits that snatch away dollars. Let NSP check your home's energy use before your money vanishes into thin air. Call NSP for an energy audit.

1005
Art Director: Art Mellor
Writer: H. Robert Greenbaum
Editor: Bob DeRise; A Cut Above
Client: Visa/Visa Card
Director: Fred Petermann
Producer: Tony Frere; BBDO, Petermann-Dektor
Music: Sicurella/Smythe

IMPROV
30 seconds
ANNCR: If you're in Los Angeles and you're looking for a laugh, you don't have to go too far. Just head down Melrose to the Improvisation and you'll get an evening of hoots and howls in a place where a lot of today's top comedians got their start.
But if you go, bring your sense of humor and your Visa card, because at the Improv they don't take anything seriously and they don't take American Express. Visa. It's everywhere you want to be.

1006

Art Director: Randy Papke
Animator/Artist: Bob Kurtz
Writer: Doug Reeves
Client: Lincoln Savings
Agency: Salvati Montgomery Sakoda Inc.
Director: Bob Kurtz
Producer: Lorraine Roberts; Kurtz & Friends

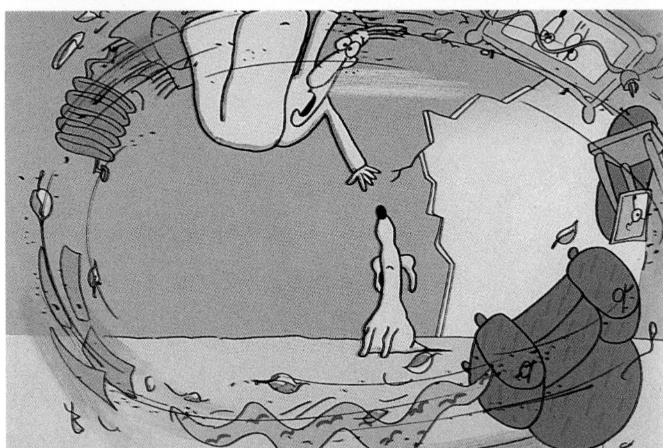

LIFE'S UNEXPECTED OCCURRENCES
30 seconds
VO: Say there's a minor emergency. Say also that you've just socked away all your cash in a long-term CD. Too bad you didn't put it in a Lincoln Savings Access CD. A Lincoln Access CD gives you CD rates, plus access to your money 24 hours a day. The Lincoln Savings Access CD. For life's unexpected little occurrences.

1007

Art Director: John Morrison
Writer: Robert Chandler
Editor: David Dee; Eventime
Client: Apple/Consumer
Director: Bob Giraldi; Giraldi, Suarez Productions
Producer: Barbara Mullins; BBDO, Jennifer Heftler; BBDO, Giraldi, Suarez Productions

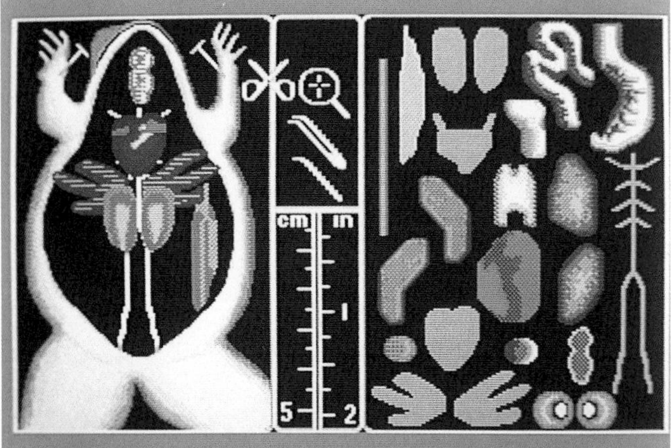

FROG PATHOLOGY
30 seconds
JENIFER: Hi, my name is Jenifer Graham. Last year, in biology class, I refused to dissect a frog. I didn't want to hurt a living thing. I said I would be happy to do it on an Apple Computer. That way—I can learn, and the frog lives.
FROG: Ribbit, ribbit, ribbit.
JENIFER: But that got me into a lot of trouble. And I got a lower grade. So this year, I'm using my Apple II to study something entirely new. Constitutional law.
FROG VO: Ribbit.

1008
Art Director: Sue Kruskopf
Writer: Peggy Poore
Creative Director: Dennis Haley
Client: General Mills Inc.
Director: Ric Machin
Producer: Michael Turoff; Broadcast Arts,
John Borchardt; Campbell-Mithun Inc.

LA BAMBA
30 seconds
ANNCR: What's the secret to Pop Secret Microwave Popcorn?
SFX: MUSIC UP AND UNDER.
ANNCR: Perfect popcorn popped under perfect conditions. Pop Secret's special new corn.
KERNEL: Flip!
KERNEL UNDER: Wheee! (POP! POP! POP!)
ANNCR: Pops lighter and fluffier with fewer unpopped kernels than ever. Pop Secret–from Betty Crocker.
KERNEL: Aieeee!
MUSIC OUT.
ANNCR: It's the only way to pop!!

1009
Art Director: Curt Johnson, Bob Brihn
Writer: Rob Wallace
Client: Target Stores
Director: Jim Lotter
Producer: Mary Schultz
Production Company: Lotter Inc.

VACUUM BAG
30 seconds
VO: This week, you can *really* clean up at Target's Dollar Sale.
SFX: SOUND OF VACCUUM CLEANER, UNDER. MUSIC GRADUALLY INCREASES TEMPO.
VO: Yes, you can pick up all *kinds* of bargains for just a dollar each. During the Dollar Sale. At Target.

1010
Art Director: Olavi Hakkinen
Writer: David Johnson
Editor: Bob DeRise; A Cut Above
Client: Du Pont Stainmaster
Director: Dick Sorenson
Producer: Bob Emerson; BBDO,
Bill Hudson; Hudson Productions
Music: Bob Kirschen, Jerry Alters

COVER UP
30 seconds
VO: Du Pont knows to err... is human. To cover it up... is to be a kid. And to handle it, Du Pont Certified Stainmaster Carpet. Now, even if a stain like this sits for hours... it's a memory in minutes... with Du Pont Stainmaster. The carpet that forgives. Stainmaster. Only from Du Pont.

1011
Art Director: Bill Zabowski
Writer: Pete Smith
Client: 3M Post-it Notes
Director: Garry Sato
Producer: Scott Howard; Coppos Films,
Becky Keller; Martin, Williams Advertising Inc.

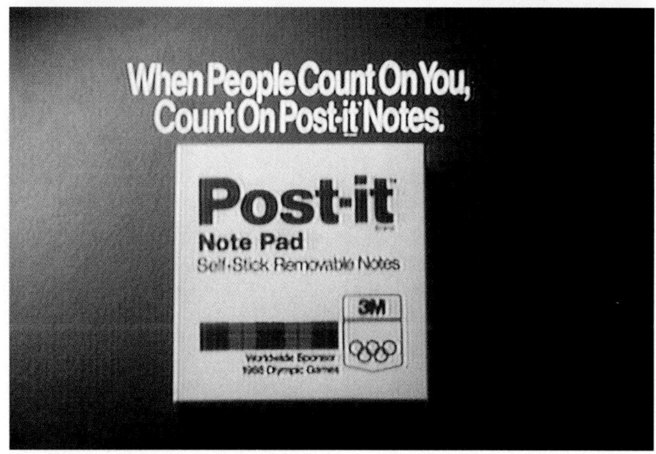

SEE THIS THING/OLYMPICS
30 seconds
SFX: WRITING AND POSTING SOUNDS THROUGHOUT.
VO: When people count on you, count on Post-it Brand Notes.

1012
Art Director: Doug Lew
Writer: Bill Johnson
Editor: Steve Shepherd; Wilson-Griak
Client: TCF Banking & Savings, F.A.
Director: Steve Griak
Producer: Arleen Kulis, Mary Schultz
Production Company: Wilson-Griak

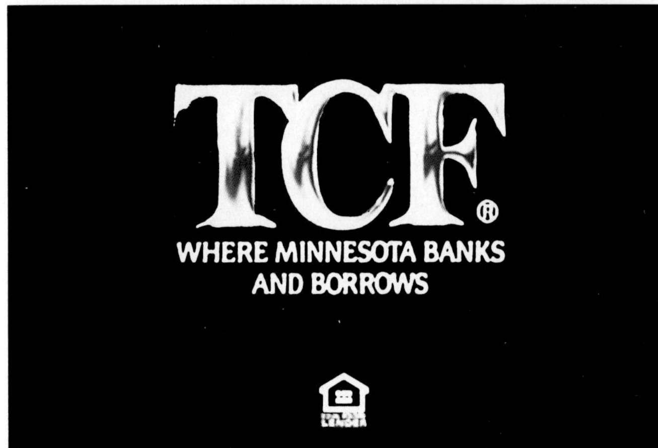

INTERROGATION
30 seconds
BANKER: What can I do for you?
CUSTOMER: Well, my name is John, and I'd like to . . .
SFX: HANDCUFFS CLICK.
ANNCR: When you go to some banks to borrow money, the way you're treated is almost criminal.
BANKER: What do you want the money for?
CUSTOMER: Well, I...I . . .
BANKER: What makes you think we should give you the money?
CUSTOMER: I...I thought you were the ones who had it.
BANKER: Sign this.
CUSTOMER: What's it say?
BANKER: Just sign it.
ANNCR: Escape to TCF. We give you an answer within 8 hours. On all kinds of loans.
CUSTOMER: How long will it take?
BANKER: We'll get back to you.
CUSTOMER: Moan.

1013
Art Director: Ken Sakoda
Writer: Scott Montgomery
Client: Marcy Fitness Products
Agency: Salvati, Montgomery, Sakoda
Director: Oscar Bassinson
Producer: Lorraine Roberts, Bassinson Production
Production Company: Bassinson Production

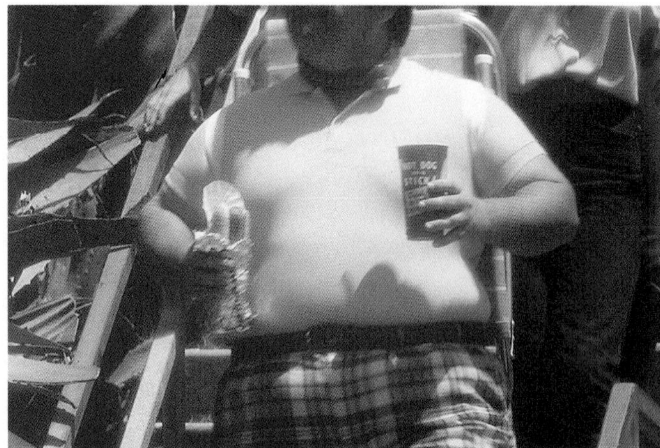

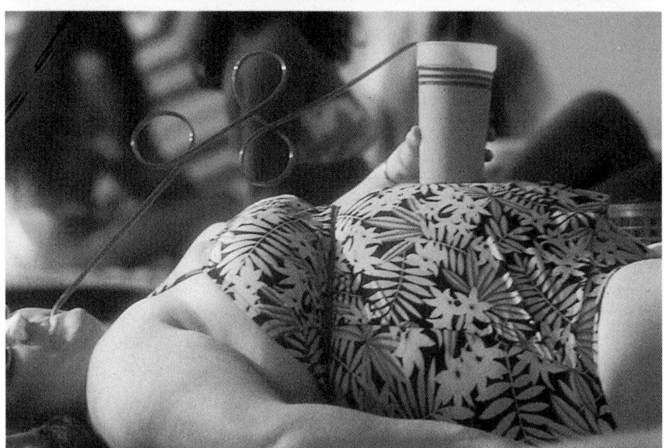

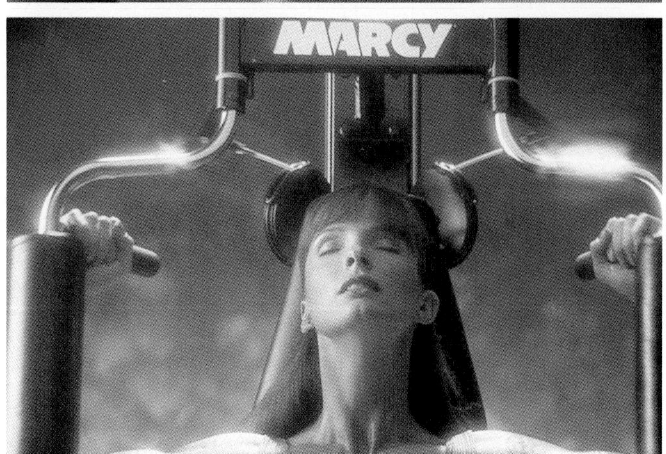

I AIN'T GOT NO BODY
30 seconds
VO: We can turn *any* body...into *some* body. Marcy fitness products. When you finally get serious.

1014
Art Director: Ron Palumbo, Art Mellor
Writer: Doug Kagan, H. Robert Greenbaum
Client: Visa
Producer: Claudio Droguett

PULLING
30 seconds
ANNCR: There are a lot of ways to pull for the U.S. Olympic Team. The easiest is when you pull out your Visa card. Because whenever you use Visa, we'll make a donation to the team. So pull for the team. And, if you go to the '88 Winter Olympics, bring your camera and your Visa card. Because the Olympics don't take place all the time, and this time the Olympics don't take American Express. Visa. It's everywhere you want to be.

1015
Art Director: Curt Johnson
Writer: Rob Wallace
Editor: Tom Lecher
Client: Target Stores
Director: Buck Holzemer
Producer: Kathy Lally
Production Company: Setterholm Productions

DRUMMER
30 seconds
VO: If you don't think you can do much with a dollar these days, just listen to this.
SFX: RHYTHMIC DRUMBEAT, UNDER.
VO: During the Dollar Sale at Target, you can buy everything you see here for just a dollar each. It's a sale that's tough to beat.
SFX: CYMBALS CRASH.
VO: The Dollar Sale at Target.

1016
Art Director: George Halvorson
Writer: Terry Bremer
Editor: Bob Wickland, Wilson-Griak
Creative Director: Terry Bremer
Client: The Toro Co.
Director: Phil Murray
Producer: John Borchardt, Mark Carter; Dalton/Fenske & Friends

NEIGHBORS
30 seconds
VO: The neighbor on the right bought the Toro CCR-2000 last year. Which prompted his neighbor on the left... to get one this year. He soon discovered that it was compact, easy to handle, yet had the power to clear 12 inches of heavy snow. He also discovered that while this Toro, with the unique, curved rotor would throw snow 30 feet to the left... it would also throw it to the right. Now haven't you done without a Toro long enough?

1017
Art Director: Olavi Hakkinen
Writer: David Johnson, Ted Sann
Editor: Bob DeRise; A Cut Above
Client: Du Pont Stainmaster
Director: Mike Moir
Producer: Bob Emerson; BBDO, Mike Moir; Moir Productions
Music: Elias & Assoc.

GREAT SAVES
30 seconds
VO: Recently Du Pont discovered... people with great carpets . . .
SFX: CROWD BEGINS TO CHEER.
VO: had to make great saves. So Du Pont developed... certified Stainmaster carpet.
SFX: CROWD CHEERS WILDLY.
VO: Now, even if a stain like this sits for hours... it's a memory in minutes. With Du Pont Stainmaster. Sooner or later... you're gonna need it.
SFX: CROWD GROANS.
VO: Stainmaster. Only from Du Pont.

1018
Art Director: Tommy Doug Engel, Gary Kaczmarek
Director of Photography: Tom Kramer
Editor: Royce Graham
Client: Chancery Pub & Restaurants
Director: Craig Smith
Producer: Pam Ferderbar; Ferderbar Studios,
Julie Herfel; Lindsay & Stone Advertising Inc.

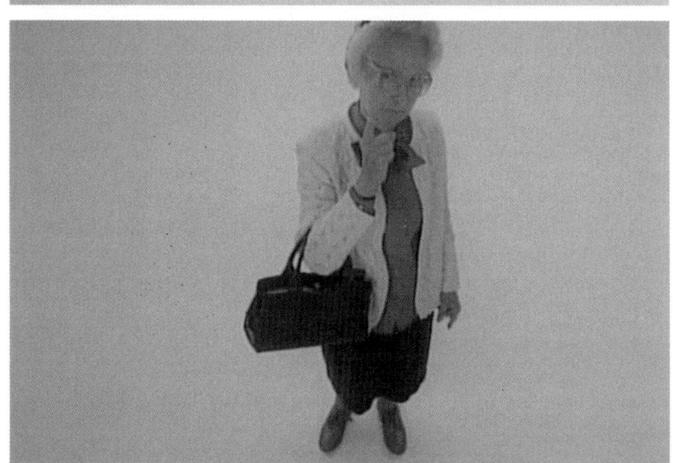

SHAME ON YOU
30 seconds
MUSIC UP AND UNDER.
VO: You mean you're not taking Mother to the Chancery?
MUSIC OUT.

1019
Art Director: Marty Weiss
Writer: Robin Raj
Editor: Ciro DeNettis
Client: NYNEX Information Resources
Director: Kevin Godley, Lol Creme
Producer: Mark Sitley, Steve Amato
Account Manager: Amy Saypol

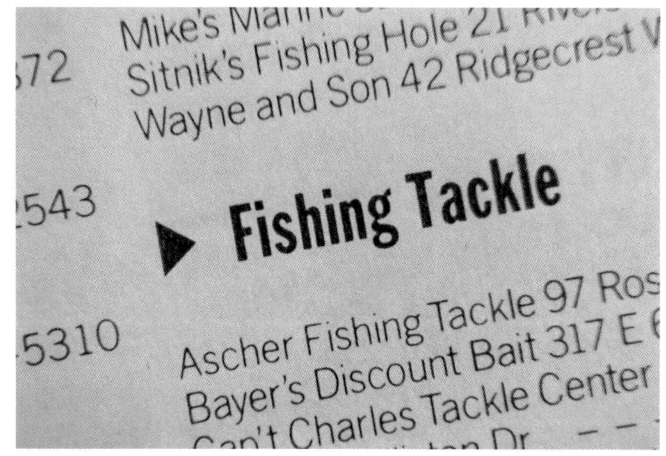

FISHING TACKLE
30 seconds
SFX: OPENING CHIME. SOUND OF FISHING ROD CASTING, BIRDS CHIRPING, WATER SPLASHING, FISHING ROD REELING IN THE LINE, DRAGGING FISH. SOUNDS OF FOOTSTEPS. SOUNDS OF FOOTBALL PLAYER TACKLING AND GRUNTING, CROWD CHEERING.
FOOTBALL PLAYER: Huhh!
VO: If it's out there, it's in here.... The NYNEX Yellow Pages.
SFX: BOOK SLAMS SHUT.
VO: Why would anyone need another?

1020
Art Director: John DeCerchio
Writer: Gary Wolfson
Client: Little Caesars
Director: Jeff Lovinger
Producer: Sheldon Cohn; W. B. Doner & Co.

RUSSIAN
30 seconds
MAN: Uncle Novotny, you were right. This truly is great country. Today I buy first thing.
UNCLE: What?
MAN: This Little Caesars Pizza. I ask man for one, he gives me two. I say, "I sorry, but have money only for one." He tells me, "Here when you buy one, you get second one free."
UNCLE: Free?
MAN: Some country, uh? Tomorrow, I buy car.
VO: Little Caesars. When you make pizza this good, one just isn't enough.

1021
Art Director: Jeff Weiss
Writer: Victor Levin
Creative Director: John Margeotes, John Weiss
Client: Le Clip International
Producer: Therese Jennings

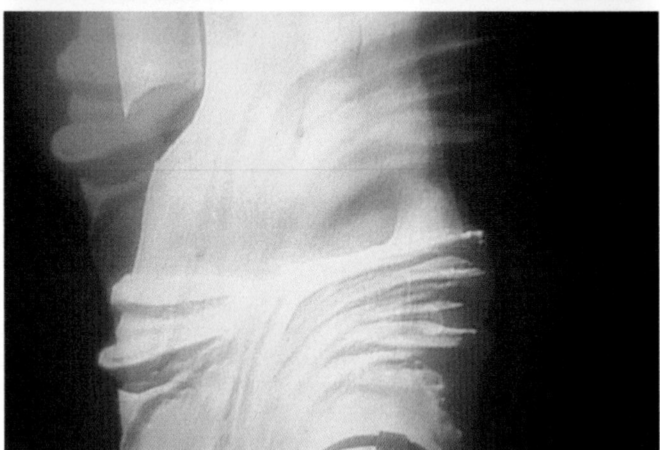

VENUS DE MILO
30 seconds
SFX: CLOCK TICKING UNDER.
VO: For those of us, who, for one reason or another, are not fond of wristwatches, there is, thankfully, Le Clip. Swiss quartz accuracy that takes time off your hands and puts it...anywhere you want. Le Clip. Unhand that watch!

1022
Art Director: Bill Zabowski
Writer: Pete Smith
Client: MedCenters Health Plan

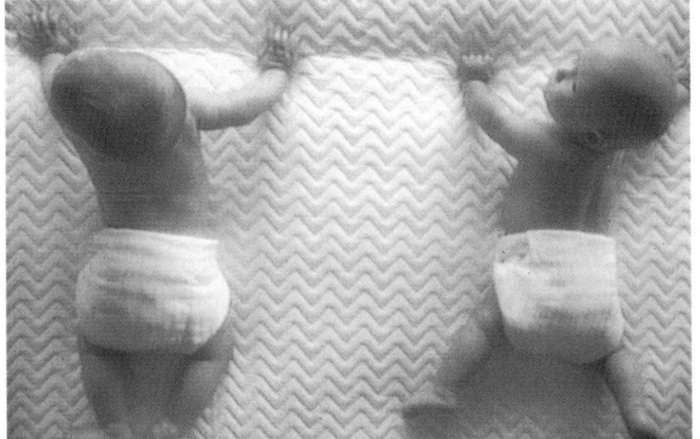

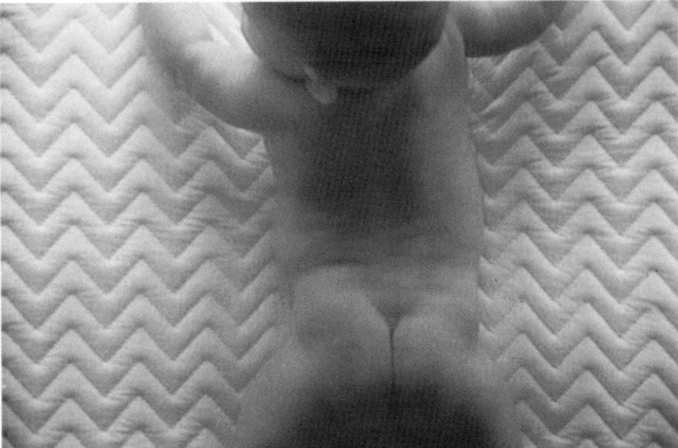

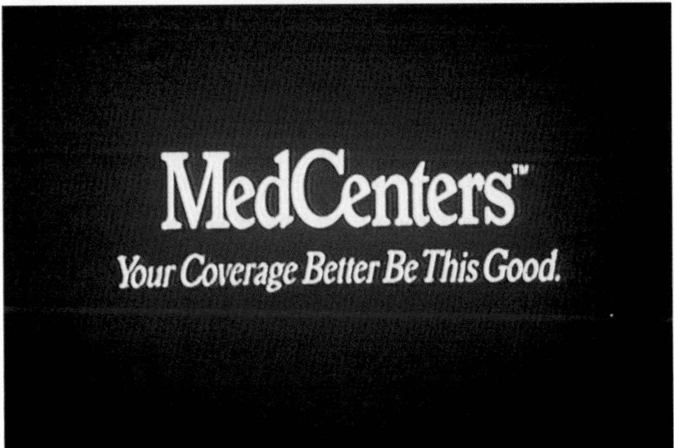

BARE BABIES
30 seconds
VO: At MedCenters Health Plan, we cover you for routine physicals. We cover you for visits to the doctor's office. We cover you for hospital stays and much, much more. While some other plans, maybe even your plan, try to get by with much, much less. MedCenters Health Plan. Your coverage better be this good.

1023
Art Director: Michael Fazende
Writer: John Stingley
Editor: Steve Shepherd; Wilson-Griak
Client: O. M. Scott & Sons
Director: Joe Pytka
Producer: Char Loving

DANDELION
30 seconds
SFX: MUSIC UNDER, CROWD MUMBLING AND TALKING EXCITEDLY.
ANNCR: This spring in Marysville, Ohio, something incredible happened.
KID: Mom, what is it?
ANNCR: Incredible, because Marysville is the home of Scotts lawn products.
SFX: MUSIC CONTINUES.
MAN: Appears to be the Officinale species.
SFX: MUSIC CONTINUES.
WOMAN: We had one in '45. Course, that was before cell-division chemistry.
ANNCR: To Scotts users, lawn problems are just hard to believe. Hey everybody, crabgrass at the Stevens place!
SFX: CROWD GETS VERY EXCITED.
ANNCR: When all there is to do is watch the grass grow, you really get to know grass.

1024
Art Director: Marty Weiss
Writer: Robin Raj
Editor: Ciro DeNettis
Creative Director: Bill Hamilton
Client: NYNEX Information Resources
Director: Kevin Godley, Lol Creme
Producer: Mark Sitley, Steve Amato
Account Manager: Amy Saypol

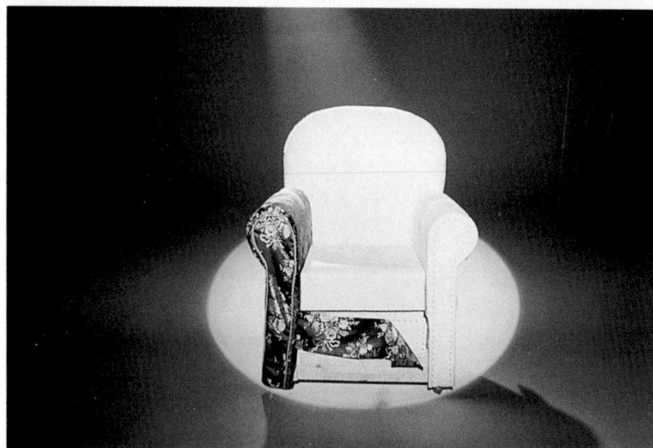

FURNITURE STRIPPING
30 seconds
SFX: OPENING CHIME. STRIPPER MUSIC BEGINS, CLAPPING, WHISTLING. MUSIC AND CROWD NOISE CONTINUE. SOUNDS OF SPRINGS POPPING OFF. MUSIC AND CROWD NOISE CONTINUE.
VO: If it's out there, it's in here. . . .
SFX: CATCALL.
VO: The NYNEX Yellow Pages.
SFX: BOOK SLAMS SHUT.
VO: Why would anyone need another?

1025
Art Director: Bill Boch
Writer: Ron Lawner
Editor: Don Packer
Client: Foot-Joy
Director: Clint Clemens
Producer: Bob Shrieber, White Water Productions

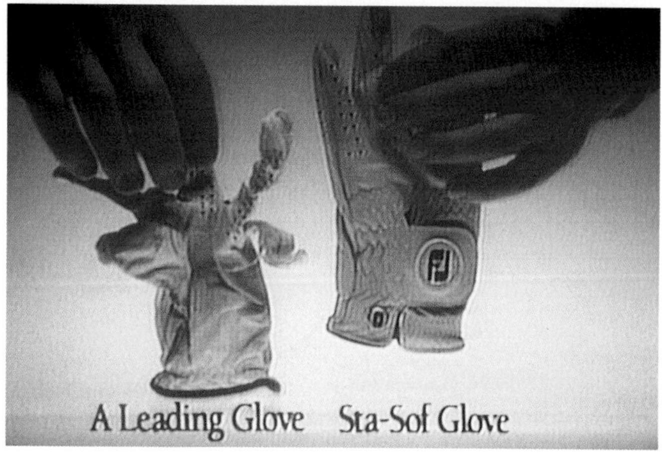

CHOICE ISN'T HARD
30 seconds
VO: You're about to see the difference between a leading golf glove and the Sta-Sof glove by Foot-Joy after 5 rounds of golf. As you can see the competition is stiff. The Sta-Sof glove isn't. With WR200, leather created exclusively for Foot-Joy by Pittard's of England, Sta-Sof gloves dry soft, and stay soft. Sta-Sof. Once you see the difference, the choice isn't hard. Sta-Sof and the new Sta-Sof Cooler. Only from Foot-Joy.

1026
Art Director: Jeff Vogt
Writer: Joe O'Neill
Editor: Craig Warnick; Jerry Bender Editorial
Client: BMW of North America Inc.
Director: Mark Coppos
Producer: Coppos Films, Frank Scherma, Ozzie Spenningsby

400 CARS
30 seconds
VO: Had it survived, it would have sold for nearly $50,000. But in the name of safety... quality... consummate reliability... 400 new BMWs were sacrificed in testing. Extreme?
Not to the person who invests in the 401st. Introducing the new BMW 735i.

1027
Art Director: Mark Moffett
Writer: Mark Silvera
Editor: Hank Corwin; Jerry Bender Editorial
Client: United Parcel Service
Director: Bob Brooks
Producer: Frank Scherma, BFCS

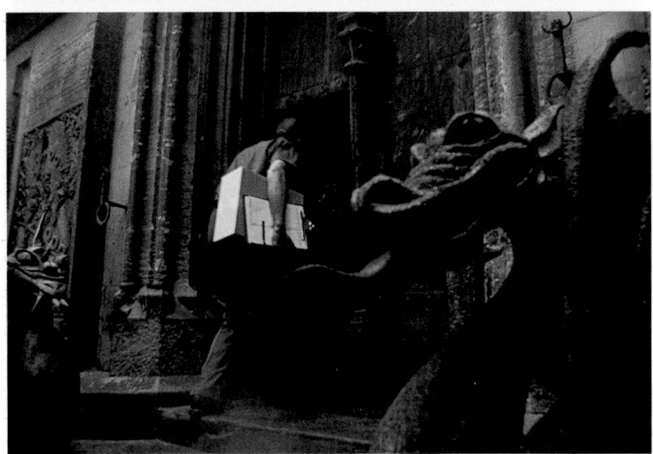

EUROPE
30 seconds
VO: Even today, there are still places in Europe so isolated hardly anyone ever goes there. But, UPS does. With scheduled delivery to every address in every European country it serves. At prices other air delivery companies might find a little scary. UPS. We run the tightest ship in the shipping business.

1028
Art Director: Ralph Ammirati
Writer: Martin Puris
Editor: Craig Warnick; Jerry Bender Editorial
Client: BMW of North America Inc.
Director: Mark Coppos
Producer: Ozzie Spenningsby, Coppos Films

DETAILS
30 seconds
VO: There are those who fervently believe that true perfection is found in the details. At the Bavarian Motor Works we gave that belief a name. We call it... the BMW 735i. Beautiful? To be sure. Yet perhaps the most beautiful thing about it is its spirit.

1029
Art Director: Leslie Caldwell
Director of Photography: Leslie Dektor
Writer: Mike Koelker
Editor: Bob Carr
Director: Leslie Dektor
Producer: Steve Neely; Foote, Cone & Belding, Faith Dektor; Petermann Dektor Productions

QUICK HITS
60 seconds
SFX: MUSIC IN.
SOLO SINGER VO: Use t' see ya when ya had the blues.
Had more trouble than you could use.
Now I see ya on the TV tube.
Everybody loves them five-oh-one blues.
Talkin'....
BACK-UP SINGERS VO: Levi's.
SOLO SINGER VO: Five-oh-one blues. Ooh, yeah!
Ain't it funny how the times have changed?
Even the blues....
TWO SINGERS VO: Been rearranged.
SOLO SINGER VO: Now the crazy part of it,
You don't have to shrink to fit.
Everybody talkin'.
BACK-UP SINGERS VO: Levi's!
SOLO SINGER VO: Five-oh-one blues. Yeah! Talkin'....
BACK-UP SINGERS VO: Levi's!
SINGERS & MUSIC OUT.

1030

Art Director: Renne Richmond
Writer: Doug Feinstein
Editor: Michael Charles
Client: Hardee's
Director: Michael Schrom
Producer: Mootsy Elliot, Susan Bachelder
Special Effects: CHARLEX
Music Director: Karl Westman

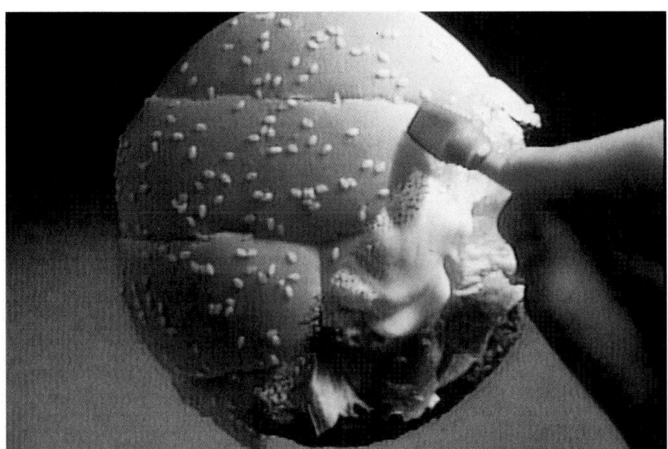

DISGUISE
30 seconds
MUSIC UP. LIGHT, CHEERFUL.
VO: When you take away all the toppings some . . .
SFX: SCRATCH, SCRATCH.
VO: burger places are making. . . such a fuss about these days. . .
SFX: SCRATCH, SCRATCH.
VO: it has to make you wonder . . .
SFX: SCRATCH, SCRATCH.
VO: is there a reason why they aren't making a fuss about . . .
SFX: SCRATCH, SCRATCH.
VO: their burgers? Well, at the heart of every Hardee's quarter-pound burger you'll find nothing but 100% pure American beef that's thick, juicy, and succulent, all by itself. You know unlike all the other places. . . we have nothing to hide. Hardee's. We're out to win you over.

1031

Art Director: Steve Kashtan, Ira Madris
Writer: Patty O'Brien, Bruce Nelson
Editor: Howie Lazarus
Client: Shearson Lehman Brothers
Director: Lester Bookbinder
Producer: Diane Maze
Account Supervisor: Art Richter

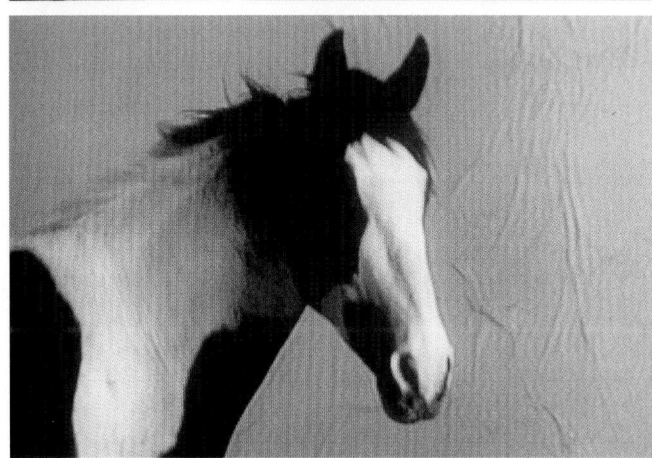

BLACK OR WHITE
30 seconds
ANNCR: Some people see the world as black or white. They limit their world to "yes" or "no," "hot" or "cold." At Shearson Lehman Brothers, however, we believe that choices are only limited by one's imagination. Finding alternatives is capitalism at its best. And why you'll never see the world as simply black and white again. Shearson Lehman Brothers. Minds over money.

1032
Art Director: Frank Todaro
Writer: Rick LeMoine
Creative Director: Arthur Bijur
Client: North American Philips
Director: Mark Story
Producer: Steve Friedman, Story, Piccolo, Guliner

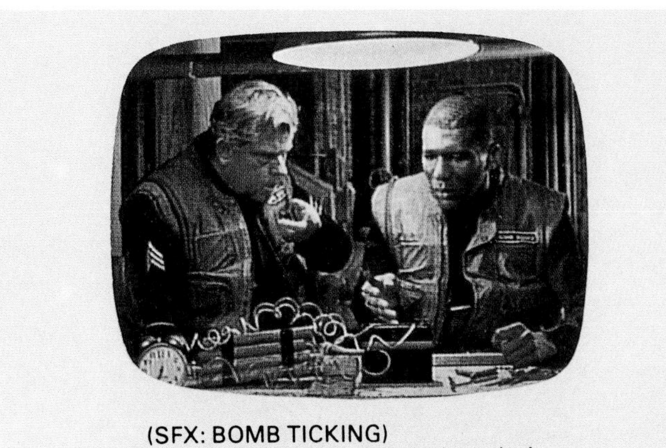
(SFX: BOMB TICKING)
FRANK/CHIEF: Eh, just cut the red wire.

(SFX: BOMB TICKING)

ANNCR (VO): It's time to change your bulb to Philips. Philips Longer Life square bulbs.

BOMB
30 seconds
FRANK: Piece of cake. Cut the red wire.
RICK: What do we do now, Chief?... Chief?
ANNCR: It's time to change your bulb to Philips. Philips Longer Life square bulbs last 33% longer than ordinary round bulbs.

1033
Art Director: Woody Kay
Director of Photography: Amir Ahmed
Writer: Al Lowe
Editor: David Doob
Client: Dexter Shoe Co.
Director: Jeff Gorman
Producer: Sam Shapiro; Johns & Gorman, Beverly Monchun; Pagano, Schenck & Kay

DEXTER SHOE-IN
30 seconds
VO: Comfortable as they are, even Dexter golf shoes can't ease the pain of a less than perfect shot. But at least we are making it easier to get into a pair of Dexters: by taking 10 bucks off our Leather Classics when you trade in your old shoes. Now, if we could only take something off your game. The Great Dexter Shoe-In. Now through June 30th at your pro shop.

1034
Art Director: John Colquhoun
Writer: Cliff Freeman
Creative Director: Donna Weinheim
Client: Royal Crown Cola
Director: Brian Gibson
Producer: Jill Paperno, Brian Gibson & Associates

WHO YOU ARE

IT'S GONNA BE A TOUGH FIGHT.

DIET RITE

ITALIAN DINNER
30 seconds
GUY: Hey, Tony...getting in shape for a hot date?
TONY: No...dinner at my mother's.
MOM: Tony!
SONG:
Everybody's gotta Diet Rite.
It doesn't matter who you are.
It's gonna be a tough fight.
So give yourself the greatest taste.
CHORUS: Diet Rite Cola.
TONY: So you see Ma, I'm drinking Diet Rite–it's salt free.
GIRL: All for you Uncle Tony.
SONG: Everybody's gotta Diet Rite.

1035
Art Director: Donna Tedesco-Hartman
Writer: Yoni Mozeson
Editor: Michael Charles
Client: Hardee's
Director: Michael Schrom
Producer: Mootsy Elliot, Susan Bachelder

CUBE
30 seconds
VO: In this reconstituted, freeze-dried, premixed world of ours, it's hard to find a breakfast that's totally made from scratch. Some syrup on that? Well, at Hardee's our biscuits are made just that way with no shortcuts like some guys use. But then that's probably why they taste so good and why at Hardee's we can truly say Hardee's. We're out to win you over.

1036
Art Director: Dean Hanson
Writer: Tom McElligott
Client: Lee Jeans
Director: Thom Higgins
Producer: Judy Brink

REMEMBER
30 seconds
MUSIC THROUGHOUT.
VO: Remember your first pair of jeans? Because you had a body like a boy, they probably fit you like a boy. The problem was, as your *body* changed, your *jeans* didn't. But there *are* jeans designed to fit you the way you are today. Lee Relaxed Riders. It's not a better body you need. It's better jeans.

1037
Art Director: Carole Deitchman
Animator/Artist: Paul Vester
Writer: Laurie Solomon
Editor: Rick Haber; Synchrofilm
Client: Hershey
Director: Paul Vester
Producer: Kathy DiToro, Keri Batten; Speedy Films
Music: David Dundas

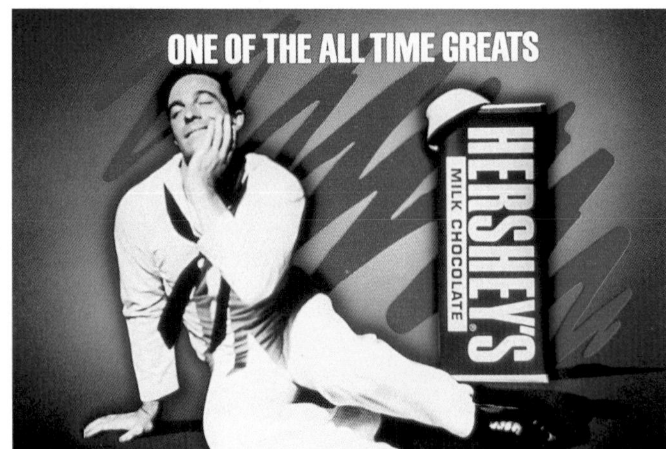

SONG & DANCE
30 seconds
MUSIC:
H-H-H-Hershey's,
One of the All-Time Greats.
Pure milk chocolate,
Almonds.
Nothing but a Hershey's will do.
H-H-H-Hershey's.
One of the All-Time, One of the All-Time Greats,
Hershey, Hershey, Hershey's.
One of the All-Time Greats.
VO: Hershey Bar. One of the All-Time Greats.

1038
Art Director: Michael Fazende
Writer: John Stingley
Editor: Jeff Stickles
Client: Emmis Broadcasting
Director: Jeff Gorman
Producer: Judy Brink, Char Loving

PASSION
30 seconds
SFX: WFAN PLAYING IN BACKGROUND UNDER SOUNDS OF MOANS AND EXCLAMATIONS.
ANNCR: For those with a passion for sports,... now there's WFAN 1050 AM. The world's first 24-hour sports radio station.

1039
Art Director: Bob Barrie
Writer: Mike Lescarbeau
Editor: Jeff Stickles
Client: Continental Illinois
Director: Mark Coppos
Producer: Char Loving

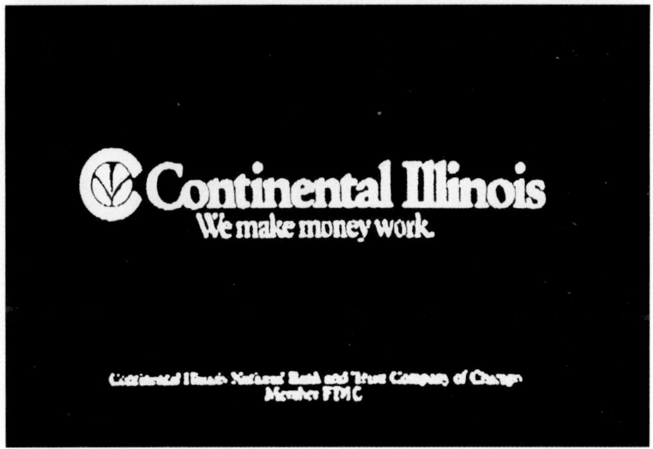

MONITOR
30 seconds
REX: Listen to this woman as a Continental banker would hear her.
WOMAN: My goal is to get steady income from my investments. I want to take my money and make it grow.
SFX: TAPE REWIND UNDER.
REX: Now listen to her as someone else might hear her.
WOMAN: ... take my money. . . .
REX: Wouldn't you rather talk to a Continental banker?
VO: Continental Illinois.... We make money work. Continental Illinois National Bank and Trust Company of Chicago. Member FDIC.

1040

Art Director: Terril Smith
Designer: Propmasters
Writer: Pamela Brooks
Editor: Rick Haber; Synchrofilm
Creative Director: Roy Tuck
Client: Kimberly Clark/Huggies Diapers
Director: Rebecca Karst
Producer: Kathy DiToro, Robin Massin; Filmworks

STAR
30 seconds
VO: Lifestyles of the Young and Famous visits the superstar, Elizabeth. Fresh from the new movie, *Baby Boom*, she reveals the smashing secret of her success. Kleenex Huggies Supertrim Diapers...frankly fabulous with trim-fitting elastic waistbands to help stop leaking. Huggies Supertrim. Diaper to the stars because in this town, you can never be too dry or too happy. Bravo, Elizabeth!

1041

Art Director: Bob Brihn
Writer: George Gier
Editor: Steve Shepherd; Wilson-Griak
Client: Continental Illinois
Director: Mark Story
Producer: Judy Brink

HANDS
30 seconds
REX (DOING HUSBAND AND WIFE VOICES):
WIFE: Honey, don't you think it's about time we redecorated the living room?
HUSBAND: Gee, I'd love to, but we just can't afford it.
WIFE: We could if we got a Home Equity Line of Credit from Continental.
HUSBAND: A Home Equity Line of Credit?
WIFE: Yes, we can use the equity we have in our house to get money for the things we need.
HUSBAND: Sounds great. But how do we apply?
WIFE: Just call 1-800-
REX (BACK TO HIS OWN VOICE): 841-8000 for an application.
VO: Continental Illinois. We make money work.

1042
Art Director: Michael Fazende
Writer: John Stingley
Editor: Jeff Stickles
Client: Emmis Broadcasting
Director: Jeff Gorman
Producer: Judy Brink, Char Loving

BIG GLOVES
30 seconds
ANNCR: Just try catching the sports on most radio stations. Then try WFAN-1050 AM. The world's first 24-hour sports radio station.

1043
Art Director: John Constable
Writer: Dennis Frankenberry
Editor: Scott Wollin
Client: Rocky Rococo
Director: Dennis Gray
Producer: Dennis Frankenberry, Peggy Kelly, Bill Hoare
Production Company: Blue Goose

HONEST
30 seconds
JOHN: When Rocky Rococo asked me to tell you about their delicious pizza by the slice... incredible... they told me I had carte blanche to do whatever I wanted... as long as I didn't resort to cheap tricks just to get your attention. Thank you, Delores. My chiropractor. Honest. You want great pizza without the wait. Rocky Rococo. Pizza by the slice.

1044
Art Director: Joe DelVecchio
Writer: Joe Nunziata, Don Green
Editor: Ciro DeNettis
Creative Director: Joe Nunziata
Client: Dean Witter
Director: Stan Schofield
Producer: Richard Cohen; Sandbank Films, Bob Smith; Lord, Geller, Federico, Einstein

JEANNE EVERT
30 seconds
MUSIC UNDER THROUGHOUT.
JEANNE EVERT: I'm Jeanne Evert. My sister Chris made a fortune with her serve. So investment firms gladly serve her. But I have a firm that helps people like you and me win too. Dean Witter. Right now they're helping me invest...for my future. You see, I've never won the US Open, but Dean Witter still helps me with some very nice returns.
MUSIC: You're somebody at Dean Witter.
VO: A member of the Sears Financial Network.

1045
Art Director: Bryan Lahr
Writer: Carolyn Strickland
Client: Johnson, Lane, Space, Smith & Co., Inc.
Director: Lance Russel, Judy Butin
Producer: 4th Street
Sound & Music: Mark Aramian

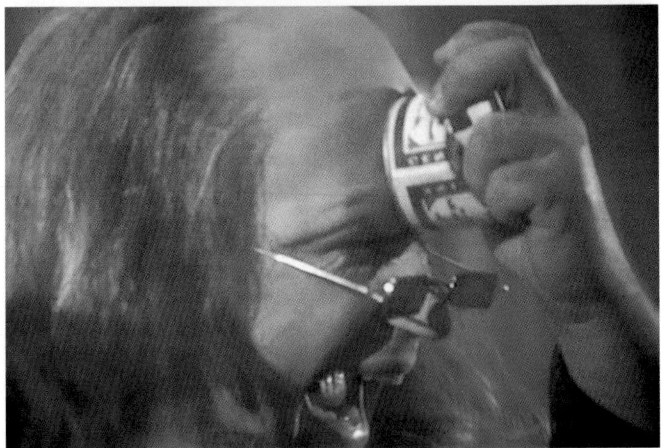

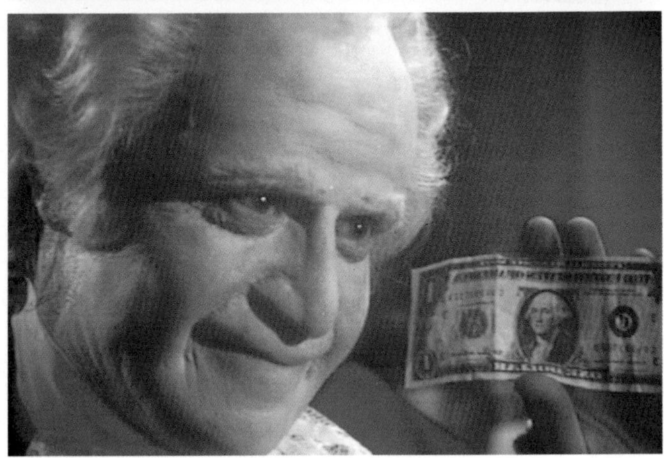

IMMATURE MONEY
30 seconds
ANNCR: It's 1987. Do you know what your money is doing?
CHANTING: Party! Party!
ANNCR: Maybe it's not doing what it should be. Maybe it hasn't grown much since last year. Maybe it's time you called the conservative investment firm of Johnson Lane. Where your money matures.

1046
Art Director: Mike Moser
Writer: Brian O'Neill, Dave O'Hare
Editor: Steve Wystrach
Client: California Cooler
Director: Rick Levine
Producer: Peter Valentine

TRUCKING
30 seconds
MUSIC: "SURFIN' BIRD" BUILDS THROUGHOUT UNTIL GURGLING PART OF "SURFIN' BIRD." MUSIC GROWS FAINT.
VO: Introducing California Cooler Peach. Now available everywhere.

1047
Art Director: Leslie Caldwell
Director of Photography: Amir Hamed
Writer: Mike Koelker
Editor: Yamus
Client: Levi Strauss & Co.
Director: Leslie Dektor
Producer: Steve Neely, Faith Dektor

QUICK HITS
60 seconds
SINGER:
Used to see you when you had the blues.
Had more trouble than you could use.
Now I see you on the TV tube.
Everybody loves them five-oh-one blues.
Talkin' Levi's
Five-oh-one blues.
Oh, yeah!
Ain't it funny how the times have changed?
Even the blues been rearranged.
Now the crazy part of it,
You don't have to shrink to fit.
Everybody talkin' Levi's
Five-oh-one blues.
Talkin' Levi's!

1048
Art Director: Leslie Caldwell
Director of Photography: Amir Hamed
Writer: Mike Koelker
Editor: Bob Carr
Client: Levi Strauss & Co.
Director: Leslie Dektor
Producer: Steve Neely, Faith Dektor

WILDMAN
60 seconds
SINGER:
Feel good and feelin' those five-oh-one blues.
Feel good and feel good, yes it does!
Oh, yeah!
But-button, fly-fly, and yah…
Whow! Oh, yeah!
Have mercy! Help me!
Ow, I can't take this.
Whow!
When I say button-fly go to C.
Button-fly!
I lo…ve it.
Oh, look out!
Levi's five, five, five-oh-one blues.
Oh, yeah!

1049
Art Director: Paul Behnen
Director of Photography: Michael Brown
Writer: Steve Puckett
Editor: Dan Bryant
Client: Health Resources Group
Director: David Cranfill
Producer: Steve Puckett, Dan Bryant
Music: Rhett Parrish

DANCING SHOES
60 seconds
POST SCORED MUSIC IN AND UNDER.
ANNCR: When Russell Johnson was told that his wife had diabetes, he had no idea that it could cause her to go blind. He never dreamed that numbness and poor circulation could make her lose her feet. And he couldn't believe that she could lose control over her own dignity. Russell Johnson had no hint of how devastating diabetes could be to the woman he loved so much. And we intend to make sure he never has to find out.
MUSIC UP AND OUT.

1050
Art Director: Rick Boyko
Writer: Bill Hamilton
Editor: Larry Bridges
Client: Reebok
Director: Mark Coppos
Producer: Mark Sitley, Eric Herrman
Music: Jonathan Elias; Elias Associates

URBAN BASKETBALL
60 seconds
SFX: MUSIC WITH A BEAT, CITY SOUNDS. EXAGGERATED SOUND EFFECTS. SILENCE.

1051
Art Director: Alan Chalfin
Writer: Lee Garfinkel
Client: Subaru of America
Director: Steve Horn
Producer: Linda Horn; Steve Horn Inc.,
Bob Nelson; Levine, Huntley, Schmidt & Beaver

LA BAMBA
45 seconds
ANNCR: The new Subaru XT6 has a powerful 6-cylinder engine. Computerized fulltime 4-wheel drive. And a design which makes it hard to resist. The Subaru XT6. We built our reputation by building a better car.

1052
Art Director: Ivan Horvath
Writer: Ken Segall, Michael Baldwin
Editor: Dennis Hayes
Client: Apple/Macintosh
Director: Joe Pytka
Producer: Paul Gold; BBDO, Trish Reeves; BBDO, Joe Pytka

THE BALANCE SHEET
60 seconds
HELEN: When I fired Walters, he didn't believe it. He kept coming back to work.
DEL: Helen, I just looked at these numbers. Pretty grim. Right…right here.
HELEN: I know, Del. Those are computer costs.
DEL: Didn't we pay for those systems last Quarter?
HELEN: We did. But those are training costs.
DEL: Now let me get this straight. We're spending more on training than we did on the computers?
HELEN: Consultants, instructors, technical support.
DEL: But Helen, Boston doesn't show these costs.
HELEN: They use a different system.
DEL: So?
HELEN: Apparently, with their computers, their people can…train themselves.
DEL: Helen…doesn't that raise a question in your mind?

1053
Art Director: John Lucci
Writer: David Johnson
Editor: Steve Schreiber; Editor's Gas
Client: Pepsi-Cola Co.
Director: Steve Horn
Producer: Barbara Mullins; BBDO,
Steve Horn; Steve Horn Productions
Music: Bob Kirschen; Sunday Productions

JOHNSON/BASEBALL
60 seconds
SFX: CROWD CHEERING.
TV ANNCR: Well this is it fans. It's all come down to this moment. This is where it all gets decided. Johnson steps in…checks the sign.
SFX: ORGAN IN STADIUM.
TV ANNCR: He makes a few adjustments and goes through the motions. Talk about a classic confrontation. The heat is on and boy, you can really feel the tension. Johnson's reaching way down. He's diggin' in. Here's the delivery.
SFX: CAN OPENING…BAT HITTING BALL.
TV ANNCR: Look out. What a shot. He's going back, back, way back. He's headin' for the wall. It is going, going. …It is gone!
ANNCR VO: Pepsi. The choice of a new generation.
TV ANNCR: And that's it folks. The ballgame is over.

1054
Art Director: Michael Vitiello
Writer: Lee Garfinkel
Client: Subaru of America
Director: Steve Horn
Producer: Linda Horn; Steve Horn Inc., Bob Nelson; Levine, Huntley, Schmidt & Beaver

WHEN A MAN LOVES A WOMAN
45 seconds
GIRL: My folks just left.
JAMES: Tonight's the night.
ANNCR: The new Subaru Justy, now with "on demand" 4-wheel drive not only gets you where you want to go–but does it less expensively than any other 4-wheel-drive car in America.
JAMES: Mr. Potts, you're…home?
MR. POTTS: We turned back. The roads are terrible.
SFX: MUSIC UP.
MR. POTTS: So, James, what brings you out on a night like this?

1055
Art Director: Rick Boyko, Miles Turpin
Writer: Elizabeth Hayes
Client: Home Savings of America
Director: Leslie Dektor
Producer: Richard O'Neill, Elaine Hinton, David Prince

THE UNGERS
60 seconds
MILTON: We've always made it, and I don't worry 'cause she's a good manager. Whether we have a little or a lot, we make it.
ANNCR: Milton and Emma Unger, Home Savings customers.
EMMA: We were raised during the depression. It makes a difference. If you have a little money, you start saving it.
MILTON: One week we were so poor I bought a bushel of carrots and we lived on carrots all week. Now when we go out to dinner and we see carrots, we look at each other and smile. It didn't hurt us. It was fun. She was thrifty, she made all her own clothes and she looked like a million bucks. She still does. My hobby is playing the piano at the senior citizens home. It's the only thing I'm good at.
ANNCR: The Ungers worked very hard for their retirement. So did Home Savings.
MILTON: You know, I'm a character, and the little old ladies love that.
EMMA: It really doesn't bother me because I know he really cares for me.
MILTON: Best deal I ever made. I couldn't live without her.

1056
Art Director: Ivan Horvath
Writer: Ken Segall, Michael Baldwin
Editor: Dennis Hayes; Dennis Hayes Editorial
Client: Apple/Macintosh
Director: Joe Pytka
Producer: Paul Gold; BBDO, Trish Reeves; BBDO, Joe Pytka

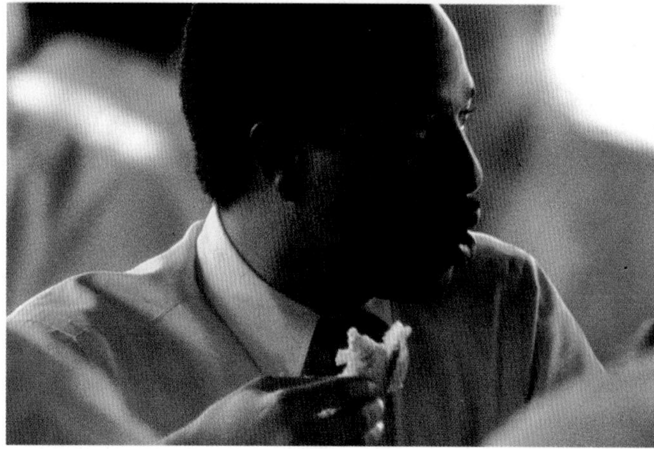

POWER LUNCH
60 seconds
JOEY: Hey Baldwin, how you doin'?
BALDWIN: Pretty good, Joey, how are you?
SAL: Ah, finished already.
WOMAN: Hey, I thought we were supposed to do this in-house.
BALDWIN: That's right. Pass the salt, would you?
New computer.
SAL: Quintile analysis? Gimme a break.
BALDWIN: Well Segall did that.
SAL: I thought he was in the LA office.
BALDWIN: So's Edwards—she did the graphics.
SAL: The market projections?
BALDWIN: Garnett. Chicago.
SAL: How'd you get everybody together in the same place?
BALDWIN: I told you. New computer.
SAL: What kind of system can do that?
BALDWIN (UNINTELLIGIBLY): Mcntsh.
SAL: What?
BALDWIN: Mcntsh. SAL: Pardon me?

1057
Art Director: Lewis Goldstein, Donald Thorin
Director of Photography: Donald Thorin
Editor: John Carol
Client: NBC Entertainment
Producer: Lewis Goldstein; NBC, Bob Bibb; NBC, Jamie Legon; Propaganda Films
Music: Non-Stop Productions

RUNAWAYS
2 minutes, 15 seconds
SFX: MUSIC THROUGHOUT, "RUNAWAY."

1058
Art Director: Linda Kaplan, Peter Farago
Director of Photography: Marvin Kaplan
Writer: Linda Kaplan
Editor: Bill Colucci
Client: Eastman Kodak
Producer: J. Walter Thompson
Music: Fred Thaler, Linda Kaplan

DEAR OLD DAD
60 seconds
Dear ol' dad, how I love you so.
What a time we had.
Does it seem so long ago?
Do you remember
All the thoughts we shared,
All the things we'd say,
All the misty shades of yesterday.
Way back when.
Seeing you now again,
My dear old dad,
Thinking of how it was back then.
And it's so nice to see
You smiling back at me
Year after year with my dear old dad.
So here's to the love and the laughter,
And here's to all the years ever after.
And oh it makes me glad
To look back on all we had.
Let's hear a cheer, for my dear old dad.

1059
Art Director: Nick Striga
Writer: David Cantor
Editor: Steve Schreiber; Editor's Gas
Client: GE/Corporate
Director: Steve Horn
Producer: David Frankel; BBDO, H. Choate; BBDO, Steve Horn; Steve Horn Productions
Music: J. Petersen

PIKE'S PEAK
60 seconds
VO: In 1918, a small team of GE engineers set a new high-altitude record for an aircraft engine. What made it unusual was that they did it without an airplane. Back then no plane could fly high enough to test their new turbo supercharged engine. So…they did the next best thing. They hauled it 14,000 feet up Pike's Peak. After several fits and starts, this remarkable new engine roared to life. And it is the same ingenuity and team spirit that has brought GE from America's first jet engine to the world's most advanced.
AIRLINE CAPTAIN: Ladies and gentlemen, if you look out the left side of the cabin, you'll see Pike's Peak.
VO: Which proves when people work together, there's no telling to what heights they can soar. GE…we bring good things to life.

1060
Art Director: Harvey Hoffenberg
Writer: Ted Sann
Editor: Bob DeRise; A Cut Above
Client: Pepsi-Cola Co.
Director: David Mallet
Producer: David Frankel; BBDO, Trish Reeves; BBDO, M.G.M.M.
Music: David Bowie, Bob Kirschen

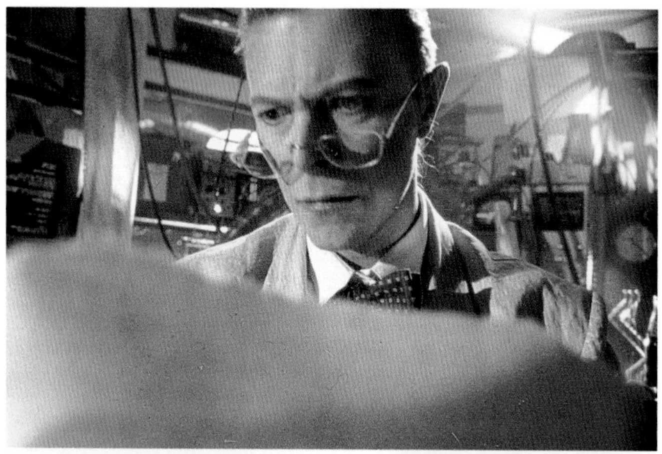

CREATION
60 seconds
ANNCR:
There's no sign of life.
It's just the power to charm.
I'm lying in the rain.
They always wave good-bye.
But I try.
I try.
Now I'm gonna fall for.
Modern love walks beside me,
Modern love at my side.
Modern love now I know.
The choice is mine.
The choice is mine satisfies me.
Choice is mine makes me party.
Choice is mine puts my trust
In my own hand.
Modern love.
Modern love.

1061
Art Director: Roger Mosconi
Writer: Michael Patti
Editor: Dennis Hayes; Dennis Hayes Editorial
Client: Pepsi-Cola Co.
Director: Rick Levine
Producer: Jerry Cammisa; BBDO,
Rick Levine; Rick Levine Productions

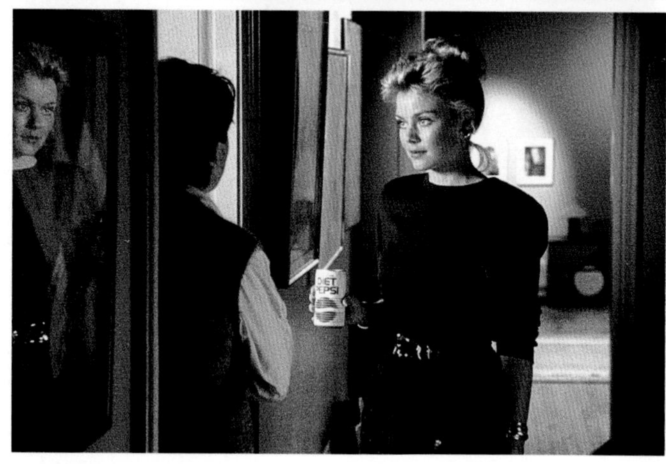

APARTMENT 10G
90 seconds
SFX: KNOCKING ON DOOR.
GIRL: Hi, I just moved in next door. Could I borrow a Diet Pepsi?
MICHAEL J. FOX: Sure, come in. Yes! How about something else?
GIRL: Listen, if you don't have a Diet Pepsi...
FOX: No, no I got it.
SONG:
Headin' up to heaven,
Chasin' down a dream,
Turnin' on my engine, and the tension screams.
I'm on the edge tonight.
GIRL: You okay in there?
SFX: WINDOW BREAKING.
FOX: Here's your Diet Pepsi.
SFX: KNOCKING ON DOOR.
GIRL: That must be my roommate Danny.
FOX: Danny?
GIRL #2: Hi, I'm Danielle. You got another Diet Pepsi?
FOX: Sure.
VO: Diet Pepsi, the choice of a new generation.

1062
Art Director: Melvin Sokolsky
Editor: Jeff Wishengrad
Creative Director: Tony Smith
Client: California Egg Council
Director: Melvin Sokolsky
Producer: Barbara Lewis

THEN AND NOW
60 seconds
LYRIC VO:
In the days of old
An egg meant morning.
But now there's a new day dawning.
'Cause heaven knows
Anything goes
On a bun.
On the run.
In a diet...
For your body's sake.
When it's hot.
When it's not.
Any...thing...goes.
With sauce bernaise
Or chardonnay
In small cafes
Where music plays.
Anything goes with California fresh eggs.

1063
Art Director: Len McCarron
Writer: Rick Meyer, Ted Sann
Editor: Bob DeRise; A Cut Above
Client: Du Pont
Director: Rick Levine
Producer: Regina Ebel; BBDO, Rick Levine; Rick Levine Productions
Music: David Horowitz

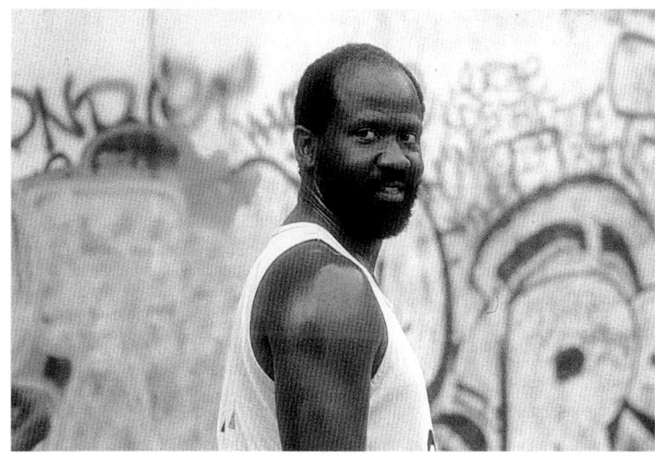

BILL DEMBY
60 seconds
ANNCR: When Bill Demby was in Vietnam, he used to dream of coming home and playing a little basketball with the guys. A dream that all but died when he lost both his legs to a Viet Cong rocket. But then, a group of researchers discovered that a remarkable DuPont plastic could help make artificial limbs that were more resilient, more flexible, more like life itself. Thanks to these efforts, Bill Demby is back. And some say he hasn't lost a step. At DuPont, we make the things that make a difference. Better things for better living.

1064
Art Director: Rick Boyko, Miles Turpin
Writer: Elizabeth Hayes
Client: Home Savings of America
Director: Leslie Dektor
Producer: Richard O'Neill, Elaine Hinton, David Prince

THE JONES
60 seconds
MELVYN: It has to be the most thrilling experience for a person to go through because again you don't really know how it feels until you've been through all the negative things.
ANNCR: Melvyn and Robin Jones, Home Savings customers.
ROBIN: When I saw this house, I said "We'll get a loan."
MELVYN: It was "We were going to get a loan."
ROBIN: And that's when we started going through major anxiety, you know, because we didn't have perfect credit, because, you know, 10 years ago you paid a doctor bill late or something, and then I decided somebody's gonna loan us money to get the house because, you know, we're nice people, stable, we've been on our jobs for a hundred years.
ANNCR: Home Savings didn't give Melvyn and Robin Jones a home loan based on their past. We gave them one based on their future.
ROBIN: I went and picked up the kids.
MELVYN: We opened the door.
ROBIN: And one of them, she said "Are we sleeping here tonight?" And I said "yes," and she ran from room to room with tears in her eyes.

1065
Art Director: John Morrison, Lisa Doan
Writer: Robert Chandler, Robbie Ross
Editor: David Dee; Eventime
Producer: Joe Pytka, Barbara Mullins
Music Director: Bob Kirschen

I'M DIFFERENT
60 seconds
MUSIC IN AND UNDER. RANDY NEWMAN SINGS "I'M DIFFERENT."
I'm different and I don't care who knows it.
Somethin' about me, not the same, yeah.
I'm, different, and that's how it goes.
Ain't gonna play your dumb old game.
I got a different way of walkin',
I got a different kind of smile.
I got a different way of talkin'
Drives the women kind of wild.
CHORUS: He's different.
NEWMAN: Don't care who knows it.
VO: At Apple, we make tools that help ordinary people do extraordinary things. But sometimes, it's more important to help extraordinary people do ordinary things.
NEWMAN SINGS:
I'm different, don't care who knows it.
Ain't gonna play your dumb old game.

1066
Art Director: Bob Ribits, Alex Goslar
Writer: Alex Goslar
Creative Director: Gerry Miller
Client: Procter & Gamble/Cheer
Producer: Angelo Antonucci, Carole Floodstrand, Leroy Koetz; Koetz & Co.

HANKERCHIEF
45 seconds
MUSIC THROUGHOUT.
ANNCR: Nobody's better in cold than All Temperature Cheer!

1067
Art Director: F. Paul Pracilio, Roger Butler, Robert Neuman
Writer: F. Paul Pracilio, Roger Butler, Robert Neuman
Editor: Billy Williams
Client: Smith Barney
Director: Bob Brooks
Producer: Ann C. Marcato, John Cigarini; BFCS

AIRPLANE
60 seconds
LEO MCKERN: "Smith Barney." No, no, a bit strong..."Smith Barney. *They* make money the old-*fashioned* way, *they* earn it." "They make money the old-*fashioned* way, they *earn* it." "Make money the *old*-fashioned way. They *earn* it." Ah, dear, dear...."Smith Barney. They make money. Money. The old-fashioned *way*. They earn *it*." No...."They earn it. They earn it." "They *earrrrn* it." Hmm?
WIFE: Leo, they chose you to be the new spokesman. Do it *your* way.
VO: Introducing Leo McKern for the investment firm of Smith Barney.

1068
Art Director: Kristi Roberts, Susan Hoffman
Writer: Janet Champ
Editor: Larry Bridges
Client: Nike Inc.
Director: Peter Kagen, Paul Greif
Producer: Bill Davenport, Kagen/Greif

REVOLUTION
60 seconds
SFX: MUSIC THROUGHOUT, "REVOLUTION."

1069
Art Director: Mike Oberman
Writer: Christie McMahon
Creative Director: Christie McMahon
Client: Anheuser-Busch/Michelob Light
Agency: DDB Needham Worldwide
Director: Peter Kagan
Producer: Chuck Reese, Stiefel & Co.

DANCE
60 seconds
LYRICS:
Li-li-light up the night.
When the sun goes down,
Gonna light up the night
'Cause one thing soothes me,
One thing moves me.
Gonna light up the night.
Michelob Light.
Golden body, ooh what curves.
Got the taste that I deserve.
Twist it, pour it,
Do it right.
C'mon and light up the night
My-my-my Michelob Light.
Gonna light up the night,
Light up the night,
Michelob Light.
Gonna light up the night.

1070
Art Director: Karen Zateslo Gray
Writer: Margie Gaynor
Creative Director: Cheryl Berman
Client: McDonald's
Producer: John Kaste, Steve Horn; Steve Horn Productions

DADDY'S LITTLE GIRL
45 seconds
DAUGHTER: Hi, Dad.
DAD: How was the dance?
GIRL: All the cute guys are going to McDonald's.
DAUGHTER: Can we go Dad?
DAD: Sure.
DAD VO: When did she start noticing boys?
GIRL: Do you believe Jay O'Brien did that!
DAD VO: There weren't any other men in her life.
GIRLFRIEND: Denny Miller likes you. John Kaste told me.
DAD VO: I was the only one.
GIRLFRIEND: Denny's gonna be at McDonald's.
DAUGHTER (UNDER): I think he's kind of shy.
DAD VO: Seems like just yesterday she climbed on my knee sayin' "Daddy won't you go to McDonald's with me?"
DAUGHTER: Dad, you're not coming in?
DAD VO: Oh... no. I'll just wait here–I'm not hungry.
CREW GIRL: That's one McDLT, one large fries, and one Coca-Cola.
SONG: It's a good time for the great taste of McDonald's.

1071
Art Director: Skip Flanagan
Writer: Herman Parish
Editor: Billy Williams
Creative Director: Jay Jasper
Client: Hallmark Cards
Director: Jeremiah Chechik
Producer: Bernie Wesson; Ogilvy & Mather, Zoe Leader; Ogilvy & Mather

GET WELL
45 seconds
YOUNG MAN: Phone bill. I won a million dollars. Mom? A "Get Well" card! Mom, when I was little you never believed me when I told you I was sick: "Allen, you're not fooling anyone–go to school!" But today, I get a "Get Well" card. Finally I'm grown up. "Allen, you're not fooling anyone–go to work!"
VO: When a loved one is under the weather, you'll find just the right card at Hallmark, the place to go when you care enough to send the very best.

1072
Art Director: David Thall, Alberto Baccari
Writer: Alberto Baccari, David Thall
Editor: Morty's Film Service Ltd.
Client: Citterio USA Corp.
Director: Ron Travisano; Travisano DiGiacomo Films
Producer: Sergio Lentati; Politecne Cinematografica SrL.

THE ITALIAN SLICE OF LIFE
60 seconds
MUSIC UP AND THROUGHOUT.
VO: For over a hundred years... Italians have satisfied their appetite for life ... with Citterio. Prosciutto, Milano Salame, and more. Citterio. The Italian slice of life.

1073
Art Director: Skip Flanagan
Writer: Herman Parish
Editor: Billy Williams, Stuart Waks
Creative Director: Jay Jasper
Client: Hallmark Cards
Director: Jeremiah Chechik
Producer: Bernie Wesson; Ogilvy & Mather,
Zoe Leader; Ogilvy & Mather

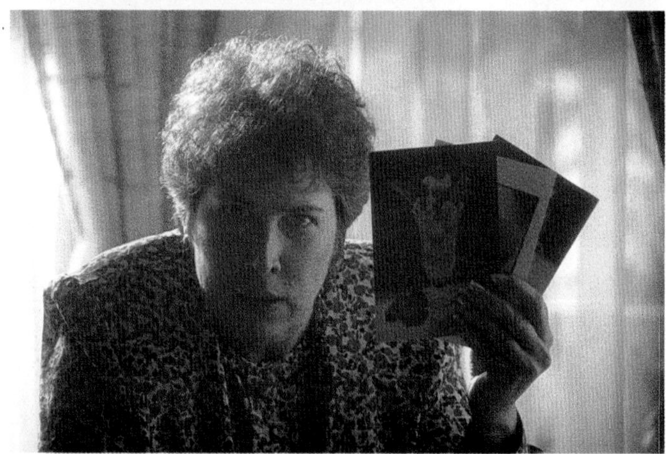

DIET WARS
45 seconds
WOMAN: I predict that this is a card from Janice... all about fattening foods. That's what a true friend does *after* we have made a bet about sticking to our diets. Janice sends me cards with pictures of chocolate on the front: "Wouldn't a box of chocolates taste good right now? Go ahead... no one's looking! Love, Janice." Janice and I have been together through thick–now we're working on thin. The loser buys the winner a *sexy* swimsuit. I just bought these cards for Janice. I predict next week will be a living nightmare for Janice!
VO: Keep up with your best friend. You'll find just the right cards at Hallmark, the place to go when you care enough to send the very best.

1074
Art Director: Barbara Schubeck, Gary Johnston
Writer: Sharon Vanderslice, Kevin O'Neill
Editor: Dennis Hayes
Client: IBM
Director: David Ashwell
Producer: Bob Schenkel; Lord, Geller, Federico, Einstein, Dan Boyle; David Ashwell Films

SOLITAIRE
60 seconds
BURGHOFF: Hello. You want research? Uh, no problem. We work around the clock here. Hold on a second.
SFX: NATURAL.
BURGHOFF: Research here. All trends are up. You're most welcome.
SFX: NATURAL.
BURGHOFF: Hello. Need a shipping date? Hold on a second. Yo! Price change? Yeah, uh, let me switch you.
ANNCR: The new IBM Personal System/2.
BURGHOFF: Shipping. Yeah. It'll be out in 10 days.
ANNCR: The next generation of power, speed, and graphics...
BURGHOFF: Hmmm, the price on that is $89.99, effective Friday. No problem.
ANNCR: to help a company, a department, or a person get their work done.
BURGHOFF: Nice work, everybody.
ANNCR: Introducing the new Personal System/2 from IBM.

1075
Art Director: Dean Hanson
Writer: Tom McElligott
Client: Lee Jeans
Director: Thom Higgins
Producer: Judy Brink

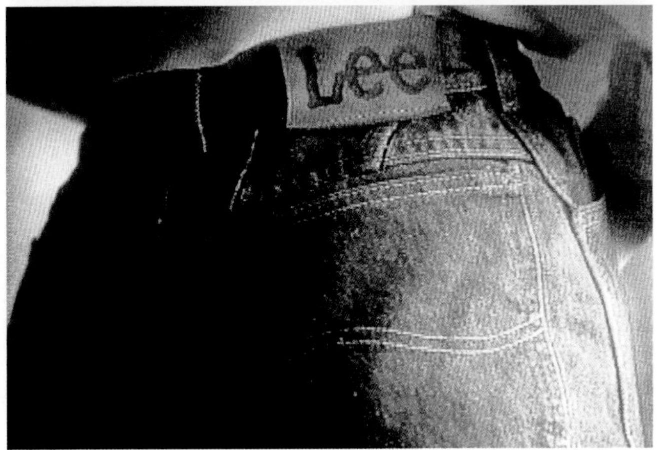

RITUAL
60 seconds
MUSIC THROUGHOUT.
VO: Every day, millions of American women practice a strange ritual. It's called "getting into jeans." Today there are jeans *designed* to fit a woman's curves... *without* the usual ritual. Lee Relaxed Riders. It's not a better body you need. It's better jeans.

1076
Art Director: Bud Watts
Writer: Greg Taubeneck
Creative Director: Greg Taubeneck
Client: United Airlines
Producer: David Beller, Phyllis Koenig; Petermann-Dektor

PEP TALK
60 seconds
NATURAL SOUNDS
COACH: It's fundamentals, fellas. Straight, simple fundamentals. It's the lesson we learn week after week. Now, you think you're gettin' to the top on charm and good looks? Bull! Janotta, you're playing like you got a different agenda. And Koslow, why don't you tell me about missed assignments? And somebody tell me how they're getting to our quarterback.
PLAYER: Coach? Aren't we ahead by 21 points?
COACH: Now, you see that? That's what I'm talking about. As soon as you're satisfied as a football player, we're finished as a football team. Now you think about that. All right, everybody up.
MUSIC: "RHAPSODY IN BLUE."
VO: When you fly over 200 college and pro teams each year, you can't help picking up a few lessons in success.
United. Rededicated to giving you the service you deserve. Come fly the friendly skies.

1077
Art Director: June Manton
Writer: Sue Read
Client: Thomas J. Lipton
Agency: Lintas USA
Director: Leslie Dektor
Producer: Stan Noble, Leslie Dektor

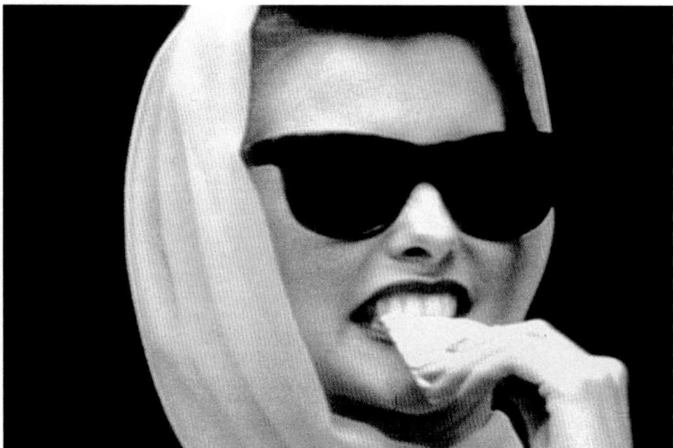

LITTLE OLD LADIES
60 seconds
SONG:
Look at all those little old ladies
Drinkin' Lipton Tea.
See them sittin', sippin' Lipton
Proper as can be.
See them rockin', see them rockin',
Now that's gentility.
Look at all those little old ladies
Drinkin' Lipton tea.
Ooo Look at them ladies,
Ooh they're pretty
Lovely.

1078
Art Director: Bud Watts, Mike Rizzo
Writer: Greg Taubeneck
Creative Director: Greg Taubeneck
Agency: United Airlines
Producer: David Beller, Optimus Inc.

This is a silent commercial

SILENT/CHICAGO
30 seconds
NO AUDIO.

1079
Art Director: Bob Ribits, Alex Goslar
Writer: Alex Goslar
Creative Director: Gerry Miller
Client: Procter & Gamble/Cheer
Producer: Angelo Antonucci, Carole Floodstrand, Leroy Koetz; Koetz & Co.

SOCKS/STEREO
60 seconds
MUSIC THROUGHOUT.
ANNCR: Nobody's better in cold than All Temperature Cheer.

1080
Art Director: Ted Bell, Mike Coffin
Writer: Steffan Postaer
Creative Director: Ron Condon
Client: Heinz Ketchup
Producer: Glant Cohen, Steve Horn; Steve Horn Productions

ROOFTOP
60 seconds
SFX: CITY NOISES. WIND. TRAFFIC. ETC. ...AMBIENT SOUNDS THROUGHOUT.
HERO: Hot dog, please.
VENDOR: Want mustard on that, or what?
HERO: No thanks...I got it covered.
ANNCR: Heinz Ketchup. It's so rich. So thick. Why waste time with anything else? Heinz Ketchup. The best things come to those who wait.

1081
Art Director: Howard Smith
Writer: Seth Fried
Client: Miller Brewing Co./Lite Beer
Producer: Eric Steinhauser

ALIEN
60 seconds
SFX: "HOME ON THE RANGE."
UECKER: Hey guys, great barbeque.
GRESHAM: Yeah, plenty of Miller Lite.
SFX: ALIEN "MUSIC" OVER HARMONICA.
JONES: Mighty fine playing, Jim.
SHOULDERS: Wasn't me....
NITSCHKE: Something tells me we're not alone in the universe.
NUMA (IN JAPANESE): Look! It's terrible! There's a UFO up there!
JONES: Hey, you're right, Numa.
HERRERA: Wonder what they want?
DOBLER: Probably our Miller Lite, 'cause it tastes great.
GROUP: Less filling! Tastes great!
HEINSOHN: Look!
SFX: SPACESHIP-LANDING NOISES.
RODNEY: I tell ya'. We don't get no respect. So this is earth, huh? Where are the girls?
VO: No matter where you're from, there's only one lite beer. Miller Lite.
DANGERFIELD: I tell ya'. It's not easy being us! Oh, what a crowd!

1082
Art Director: Art Mellor
Writer: H. Robert Greenbaum
Editor: David Dee; Eventime
Client: Visa
Director: Joseph Hanwright
Producer: Tony Frere; BBDO, H. Kira Films
Music: Sicurella/Smythe

CALGARY
60 seconds
VO: Just east of the Canadian Rockies is a place where people will go faster and fly further than ever before. The place is Calgary, home of the 1988 Winter Olympics, where a lifetime of work will be measured in seconds. But if you go, bring your camera and your Visa card, because the Olympics don't take place all the time, and this time they don't take American Express. Visa, it's everywhere you want to be.

1083
Art Director: Bobbi John
Writer: Paul Cappelli, Gavin Mulligan, Bernard Bahr
Editor: Dennis Hayes; Dennis Hayes Editorial
Client: Coca-Cola USA
Director: Barry Myers
Producer: Tim White; Spots Films, Mary Ellen Pirozzoli

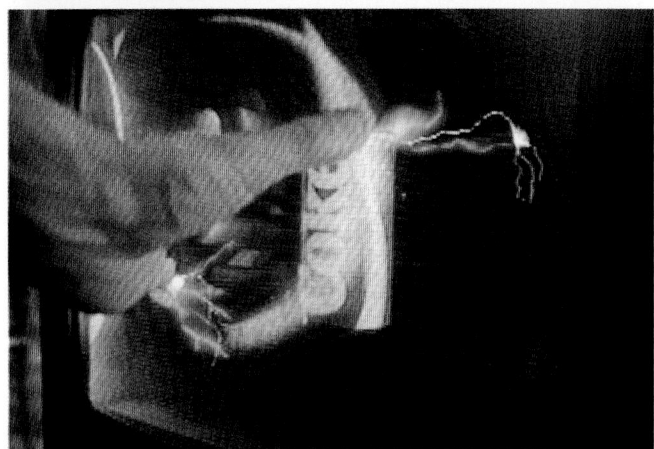

NEW COKE
60 seconds
SFX: BAND SINGING.
NEWSCASTER: The Government has released these...
WOMAN: Hi! I'm Bobby...
VO: Always searching for something better, more modern, refreshing. ...No wonder so many of us are tuning in to the taste of. ...New COKE. Catch the Wave. Coke.

1084
Art Director: Leslie Caldwell
Director of Photography: Amir Hamed
Writer: Mike Koelker
Editor: Jim Edwards
Client: Mervyn's
Director: Leslie Dektor
Producer: Florence Babbitt, Faith Dektor

CINDY BRIGGS
30 seconds
SINGER:
Dear Mervyn's,
The other day my husband said, "I don't know how we could afford to have kids without Mervyn's." He exaggerates a little, we'd manage. But I really don't know what they'd wear, your kids' clothes are the best. Thanks for your help.
Mrs. Cindy Briggs,
Lakewood, Colorado
ANNCR: Sincerely yours, Mervyn's

1085
Art Director: Rich Silverstein
Writer: Andy Berlin, Jeff Goodby
Editor: Tom Schachte
Client: Home Express
Director: David Deahl
Producer: Debbie King, David James
Music Composer/Director: Donal Piestrup

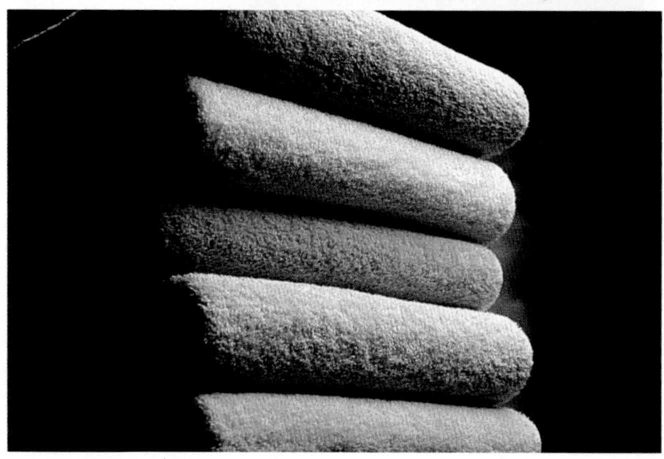

BLUE SATIN
30 seconds
MUSIC UNDER THROUGHOUT.
ANNCR: Fifty years ago, Mies van der Rohe changed the course of modern design with a bold statement: "Less is more." After all those years, we think we've finally hit on exactly what he meant.

1086
Art Director: John Staffen, Jack Mariucci
Writer: Mike Rogers
Editor: Jacques Dury
Client: Volkswagen
Director: Michael Werk
Producer: Ugo Pergolotti, Joanne Wood

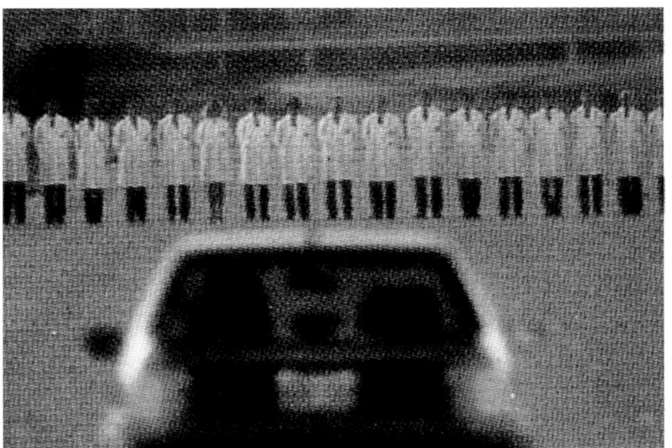

MOVING PARTS
30 seconds
VO: At Volkswagen, our engineers believe car and driver should not merely act...but interact. To them a Volkswagen isn't a vehicle for the driver. But rather an extension...of the driver. Our engineers believe the most important moving part of a Volkswagen...is the one behind the wheel. German engineering. The Volkswagen way.

1087
Art Director: Bob Kwait
Director of Photography: Johnny Dust
Writer: Rich Badami
Editor: Chris Kern; Adventure
Client: San Diego Zoo
Agency: Phillips-Ramsey
Director: Johnny Dust
Producer: Dave Hoogenakker
Music: AdMusic

ORANG
30 seconds
SFX: CLASSICAL MUSIC UNDER THROUGHOUT.

1088
Art Director: Leslie Caldwell
Director of Photography: Amir Hamed
Writer: Mike Koelker
Editor: Bob Carr, Yamus
Client: Levi Strauss & Co.
Director: Leslie Dektor
Producer: Steve Neely, Faith Dektor

COYOTES
30 seconds
SINGERS:
Levi's blue,
Five-oh-one blue.
Shrink-to-fit like the night,
they become one with me.
Button-fly through the night,
they're my indigo Levi's blues.
Five-oh-one blues.
Levi's blue... five-oh-one blues.

1089
Art Director: Rick Carpenter
Director of Photography: Charles Minsky, Jan Dubont
Writer: Dick Sittig
Editor: Larry Bridges, Steve McCoy
Client: American Isuzu Motors
Director: Ron Travisano, Matthew Meshekoff
Producer: Sandra Tuttle, Nancy Koch, Alan Pierce, Robin Benson

BULLET
30 seconds
JOE: How fast is the new Isuzu Impulse Turbo? How does 950 miles per hour sound?
JOE: The Turbo Impulse. Faster than a speeding...
SFX: POP!
JOE: ... well, you know.

1090
Art Director: Sal DeVito
Writer: Amy Borkowsky
Editor: Howie Lazarus
Client: Genesee Brewing Co.
Director: Mark Story
Producer: Cami Taylor; Story, Piccolo, Guliner, Rachel Novak; Levine, Huntley, Schmidt & Beaver

BODY BUILDERS
15 seconds
VO: This should give you some idea of the difference between beer and Genesee Cream Ale. Smooth Genesee Cream Ale. It's not the same old brewskie.

1091
Art Director: Mark Keller
Director of Photography: Michael Karbelnikoff
Writer: Tim Price
Editor: Larry Bridges
Client: Levi Strauss & Co.
Director: Michael Karbelnikoff
Producer: Florence Babbitt, Cean Chaffin

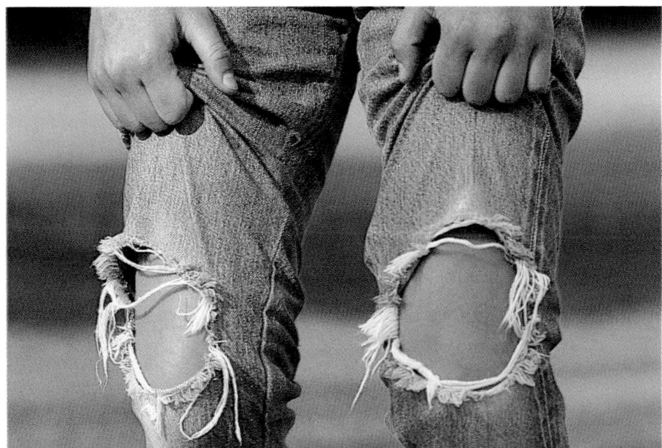

BURNIN' QUESTION
30 seconds
BOY VO: You gotta wear your Levi's baggy. I like 'em tight.
SINGER: It's a burnin' question in the world today.
BOY VO: Yeah, I like my Levi's air conditioned.
SINGER: Watcha wear and watcha do means as much as what you say.
GIRL VO: You know, it's like I don't care how comfortable they are. Just as long as they look cool.
BOY VO: I just wear what I think. What I think is good. I don't care what anyone else says.

1092
Art Director: Sal DeVito
Writer: Amy Borkowsky
Editor: Howie Lazarus
Client: Genesee Brewing Co.
Director: Mark Story
Producer: Cami Taylor; Story, Piccolo, Guliner, Rachel Novak; Levine, Huntley, Schmidt & Beaver

DANCERS
30 seconds
VO: This should give you some idea of the difference between beer and Genesee Cream Ale. Smooth Genesee Cream Ale. It's not the same old brewskie.

1093
Art Director: Rick Boyko
Writer: Bill Hamilton
Editor: Larry Bridges
Client: Reebok
Director: Mark Coppos
Producer: Mark Sitley, Eric Herrman, Coppos Films
Music: Jonathan Elias; Elias Associates

URBAN BASKETBALL
60 seconds
SFX: MUSIC WITH A BEAT, CITY SOUNDS. EXAGGERATED SOUND EFFECTS. SILENCE.

1094
Art Director: Ivan Horvath
Writer: Ken Segall, Michael Baldwin
Editor: Dennis Hayes; Dennis Hayes Editorial
Client: Apple/Macintosh
Director: Joe Pytka
Producer: Paul Gold; BBDO, Trish Reeves; BBDO, Joe Pytka

THE WAR ROOM
60 seconds
LEADER: Five days is no time at all, so let's get moving. First–Ivan, I know your group can make these numbers look presentable. Next. We'll need work from every department. Who's set up for that?
IVAN: Our computers are tied in.
LEADER: Great. Mike–how long for graphics?
MIKE: Two, three days max.
LEADER: Not good enough.
IVAN: Our computers can do it in a day.
LEADER: It's yours. Joni–typesetting and printing?
JONI: About a week, on overtime.
LEADER: Now hold on. Who published this?
IVAN: We did. On the computer.
LEADER: Well do it again. Joe, how long for a production flowchart?
JOE: We're jammed. We'll do it as fast as we can.
LEADER: Ivan, help him out. Last, we need presentation overheads. Any ideas?

1095
Art Director: Jean Robaire, Steve Beaumont
Writer: John Stein, Steve Rabosky, Chuck Silverman
Client: Nissan Motor Corp.
Director: Norman Seeff
Producer: Richard O'Neill

HUMAN ENGINEERING
60 seconds
DAVID: You spend a lot of time in a car. You might as well, if you have the opportunity, make it as livable, as human, as you possibly can.
LOUISE: Yeah, but I think when you start to design a car, you begin with the person, you think about the person who you're designing for and you design the car around it.
KAZ: Also, there are other people involved.
DAVID: But you know, for me, I mean it's where I... I eat breakfast.
LOUISE: And what else?
DAVID & MICHAEL: And lunch and dinner.
LOUISE: A person really needs to feel car it was custom-designed for them.
CHRIS: It's like their little cocoon. They feel... comfortable.
DAVID: It's the Human Engineering thing. It's just not interiors. It has to be the whole car.
LOUISE: That's my point. There's one need we haven't discussed. As long as there's been cars, people have used them to make statements.
MICHAEL: I hate to sound like a cliche, but you are what you drive.
DAVID: You sound like a cliche.
VO: Nissan. Built for the most important race of all. The Human Race.

1096
Art Director: Walt Taylor
Writer: Scott Mackey, Laura Whitacre, Bruce Mansfield, Sue Fay
Client: Northeast Super Stores
Director: Dick Pepperman
Producer: Lawler Ballard Advertising, EUE Screen Gems

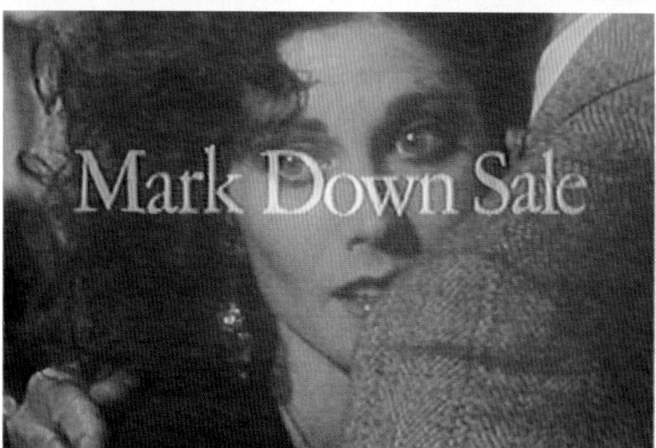

MARK DOWN SALE
30 seconds
SFX: DOORBELL RINGS.
MONICA: Just a minute, darling. Mark, welcome ho…Daddy!
DADDY: Monica…I have some bad news. …It's Mark. …His plane went down.
ANNCR: This is as low as we go. With markdowns of 10 to 50% on selected merchandise. The Mark-Down Sale ends Thursday, at Northeast.

1097
Art Director: Rick Boyko, Miles Turpin
Writer: Elizabeth Hayes
Client: Home Savings of America
Director: Leslie Dektor
Producer: Richard O'Neill, Elaine Hinton, David Prince

THE JONES
60 seconds
MELVYN: It has to be the most thrilling experience for a person to go through, because again you don't really know how it feels until you've been through all the negative things.
ANNCR: Melvyn and Robin Jones, Home Savings customers.
ROBIN: When I saw this house, I said, "We'll get a loan."
MELVYN: It was "We were going to get a loan."
ROBIN: And that's when we started going through major anxiety, you know, because we didn't have perfect credit, because, you know, 10 years ago you paid a doctor bill late or something, and then I decided somebody's gonna loan us money to get the house because, you know, we're nice people, stable, we've been on our jobs for a hundred years.
ANNCR: Home Savings didn't give Melvyn and Robin Jones a home loan based on their past. We gave them one based on their future.
ROBIN: I went and picked up the kids.
MELVYN: We opened the door.
ROBIN: And one of them, she said, "Are we sleeping here tonight?" And I said "yes," and she ran from room to room with tears in her eyes.

1098
Art Director: John Sullivan, Stephen Dolleck
Writer: Doug Pippin, Eric Weber
Client: Martlet Importing Co., Inc.
Director: Michael Butler, Michael Schrom
Producer: Steve Friedman; Saatchi & Saatchi DFS Compton
Music: Ry Cooder

YUKON
30 seconds
VO: In Canada, the cold cuts a little deeper. The winds blow a little wilder. Some people say you can taste it in the beer. Molson Golden. A little crisper. A little bolder. Molson is Canadian beer.

1099
Art Director: Pat Burnham
Writer: Bill Miller
Editor: Steve Wystrach
Client: Federal Express
Director: Mark Coppos
Producer: Judy Brink

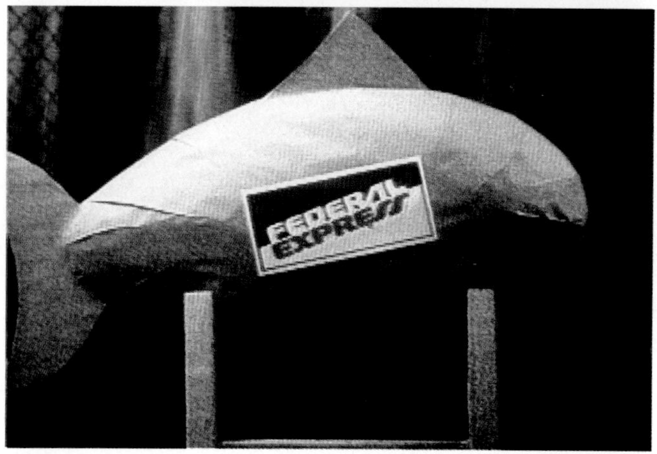

NOSE
30 seconds
VO: When it comes to fresh seafood, you gotta have a nose for the business. You gotta keep things jumping or it's a rotten day. You gotta know what it takes to land the big orders. You can't be content to ride the waves. It's a whale of a job. You gotta take it to the limit. You can't afford to let your customers get away.
SFX: FLIP, THUMP, FLIP.
VO: This reminder from Federal Express, that it's not just a package.
SFX: THUMP.
VO: It's your business.

1100

Art Director: Don Sedei
Director of Photography: Leslie Smith
Writer: Seth Werner, Patrick Scullin
Editor: Richard Gillespie
Client: Dallas Convention & Visitors Bureau
Producer: Sharon Sturgis, Diane Greenwald

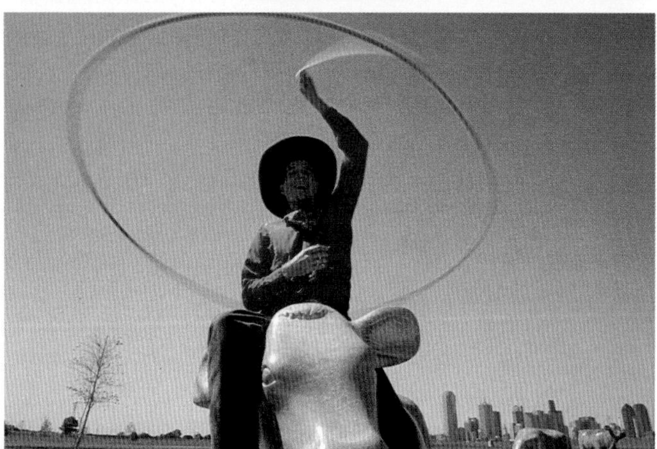

RANDY ERWIN/TRINITY PARK
30 seconds
ANNCR: The city of Dallas isn't really like the one they show you on TV, and frankly, we're kind of happy about that. If you like the show, you'll love the city.

1101

Art Director: Bob Ribits, Alex Goslar
Writer: Alex Goslar
Creative Director: Gerry Miller
Client: Procter & Gamble/Cheer
Producer: Angelo Antonucci, Carole Floodstrand, Leroy Koetz; Koetz & Co.

ICE CREAM
45 seconds
SFX: MUSIC THROUGHOUT.
ANNCR: Nobody's better in cold than All Temperature Cheer!

1102
Art Director: Michael Fazende
Writer: John Stingley
Editor: Jeff Stickles
Client: Emmis Broadcasting
Director: Jeff Gorman
Producer: Judy Brink, Char Loving

BIG GLOVE
30 seconds
ANNCR: Just try catching the sports on most radio stations. Then try WFAN 1050 AM. The world's first 24-hour sports radio station.

1103
Art Director: Matt Fischer
Writer: Chris Howard
Client: Time Inc.
Producer: Roseanne Horn
Agency Music Producer: Craig Hazen

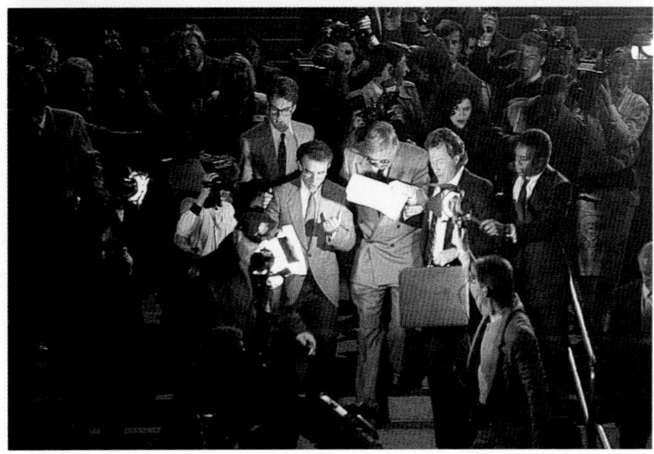

ETHICS
30 seconds
1ST ANNCR: The presidential... did not admit to improper behavior but did...
2ND ANNCR: but disclosures of the TV evangelist's personal misconduct raised questions about possible...
3RD ANNCR: More indictments for insider trading on Wall Street are expected tomorrow. In the meantime...
VO: America, which took such back-thumping pride in its spiritual renewal, finds itself wallowing in a moral morass. Others replayed scandal after scandal. *Time* realized the bigger issue was ethics. *Time*. There's no substitute.

1104
Art Director: Dean Hanson
Writer: Tom McElligott
Client: Lee Jeans
Director: Thom Higgins
Producer: Judy Brink

RITUAL
30 seconds
SFX: MUSIC THROUGHOUT.
VO: Every day, millions of American women practice a strange ritual. It's called "getting into jeans." Today there are jeans *designed* to fit a woman's curves... *without* the usual ritual. Lee Relaxed Riders. It's not a better body you need. It's better jeans.

1105
Art Director: Neil Leinwohl
Writer: Kevin McKeon
Editor: Morty Ashkinos
Creative Director: Lois Korey, Allen Kay
Client: Tri-Honda Auto Dealers Association
Director: Ross Cramer
Producer: Stacey Mokotoff
Executive Producer: Milda Misevicius

HONDATHON
30 seconds
MARCHING BAND MUSIC.
DANNY: Welcome to the Honda Sale of the Century. I'm makin' deals! I'm sellin' cars! The Prelude! The Accord! The CRX! The Civic! I've got hundreds of cars in stock! And I gotta make room! So, I'm makin' deals!
OTHER VOICE: Sir?
DANNY: I'll make a deal for you!
OTHER VOICE: Sir?
SFX: CLASSICAL MUSIC.
CUSTOMER: Sir?
DANNY: What?
CUSTOMER: That blue Accord there?
DANNY: I know. I know. You'll take it.
ANNCR: Honda. The car that sells itself. At your New York, New Jersey, Connecticut Tri-Honda dealer.

1106

Art Director: Jean Robaire
Writer: John Stein
Editor: Larry Bridges
Creative Director: Bob Kuperman
Client: Sea World
Director: Jordan Cronenweth
Producer: Beth Hagen, Riverrun Films

OVERVIEW/UNDERVIEW
30 seconds
SFX: A PIECE OF MUSIC THAT STARTS OUT QUIETLY AND PEACEFULLY.
VO: Sea World. An overview.
SFX: MUSIC CHANGES FAIRLY DRAMATICALLY TO QUICK AND VERY DYNAMIC, THEN PEACEFUL, AS AT BEGINNING.
VO: Sea World. An underview.
SFX: MUSIC BECOMES FAST AND DRAMATIC.
VO: Sea World. No other day makes you feel this way.

1107

Art Director: Michael Lawlor, Howard Smith
Writer: Larry Sokolove, Seth Fried
Client: Miller Brewing Co.
Producer: Eric Steinhauser, Lisa Pailet

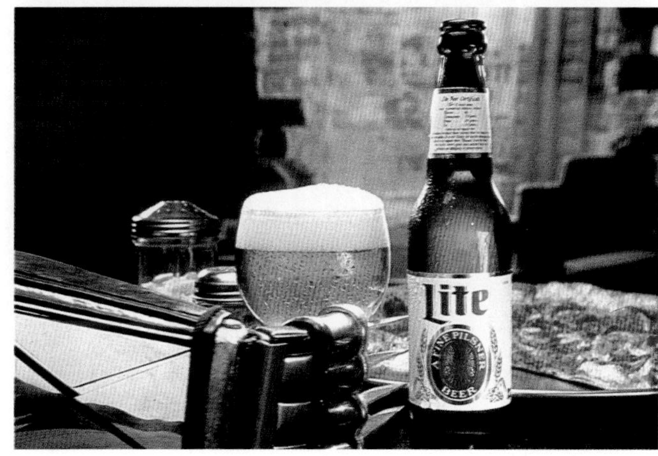

BRUCE PISCOPO
30 seconds
BRUCE: I am master of ancient art of karate, kung fu, and chinese checkers.
SFX: NINJA MOVIE SOUNDS.
BRUCE: But when I'm out socializing, I always reach for a cold Miller Lite.
SFX: NINJA MOVIE SOUNDS.
BRUCE: Lite tastes great. Lite's less filling, too.
SFX: NINJA MOVIE SOUNDS.
BRUCE: Hey, anyone want pepperoni?
SFX: GONG.
VO: Ancient proverb: Only one Lite Beer. Miller Lite.

1108

Art Director: John D'Asto
Writer: Mark Fenske
Editor: Janice Rosenthal
Creative Director: Jan Zechman
Client: Exchange National Bank
Director: Henry Sandbank
Producer: Laurie Berger, Liz Wedlan

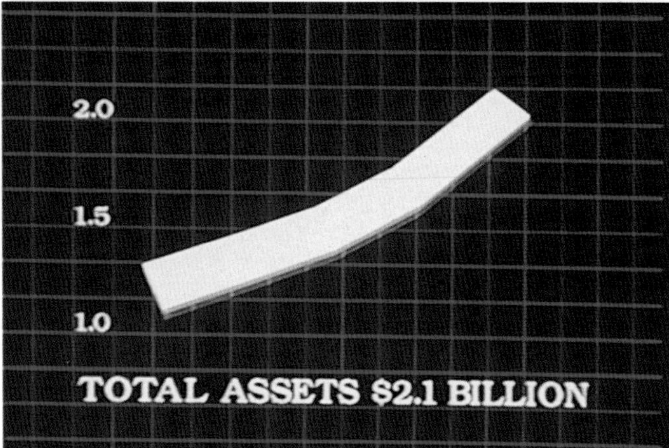

LOBBY
30 seconds
VO: The lobby could have come from the Place Concorde in Paris. The antiques could have come from the Smithsonian in Washington. And the Chagalls could have come from the Guggenheim in New York. But a 5-year performance record that looks like this, could only have come from one business bank in Chicago. The Exchange National Bank. Maybe it's time to Exchange.

1109

Art Director: Alan Chalfin, Mike Vitiello
Writer: Lee Garfinkel
Editor: Morty's
Client: Subaru of America
Director: Steve Horn
Producer: Bob Nelson, Lin Horn

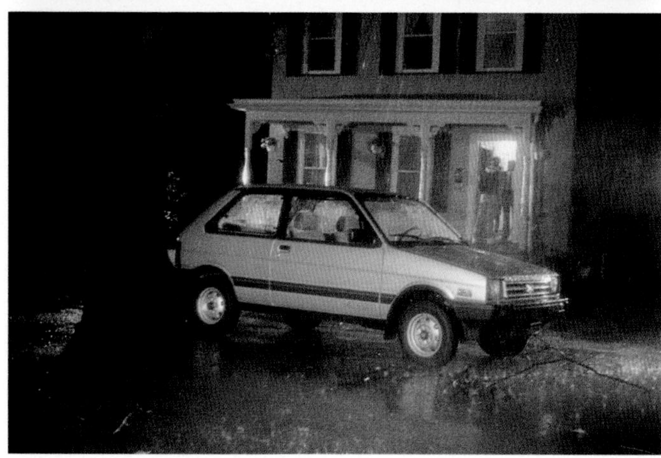

WHEN A MAN LOVES A WOMAN
45 seconds
GIRL: Guess what, my folks just left.
JAMES: Thank you!
ANNCR: The Subaru Justy, with "on demand" 4-wheel drive gets you anywhere you want to go less expensively than any other 4-wheel-drive car.
SFX: DOORBELL.
JAMES: Mr. Potts, you're…home?
MR. POTTS: We turned back. The roads are terrible. So what brings you out on a night like this, James?
SFX: MUSIC UP.

1110
Art Director: Dean Stefanides
Animator/Artist: Etienne Becker
Writer: Bernie Rosner
Editor: Randy Ilowite
Client: Ralston Purina/O.N.E.
Director: Sarah Moon
Producer: Sue Chiafullo

SHIH-TZU
30 seconds
VO: One. One dog in a million. When you feel this way, there's one kind of dog food. A dog food with real chicken, that provides optimum nutrition. A dog food as special as your dog. Purina O.N.E. brand dog food. For that one dog. Yours.

1111
Art Director: Michelle Weibman, Jon Guliner
Writer: Molly Clevenger
Editor: David Friedman
Creative Director: Molly Clevenger
Client: Procter & Gamble/Bounce
Director: Richard Chambers
Producer: Alan Clark, D'Arcy, Masius, Benton & Bowles

FRESH TALK
30 seconds
SFX: MUSIC THROUGHOUT.
1ST WOMAN: Probably the thing that would describe Bounce to me would be outdoors.
2ND WOMAN: It smells like snow. When it's just falling. And you're in it.
3RD WOMAN: Bounce is clean. Fresh.
4TH WOMAN: When you wake up in the morning and there's dew on the ground and you smell that smell, that's what Bounce is.
SONG: For clothes you can't wait to jump into. Jump.
VO: Outdoor fresh Bounce.
SONG: Jump in.
4TH WOMAN: Yeah.
BOY: I think it smells like the blue sky.
4TH WOMAN: Yeah, I...
SONG: Jump in.

1112
Art Director: Brian Aldrich
Writer: Michael Sheehan
Editor: David Doob
Client: McCain Foods
Director: Dan Driscoll
Producer: Jim Fitts, Bill Near

JAY
30 seconds
VO: Superfries from McCain. For the strong, silent type.

1113
Art Director: Joe Gallo
Writer: Bill Klimas
Creative Director: Bill Klimas
Client: Audi of America Inc.
Agency: DDB Needham Worldwide
Director: Dick James
Producer: Chuck Bauer, Dick James

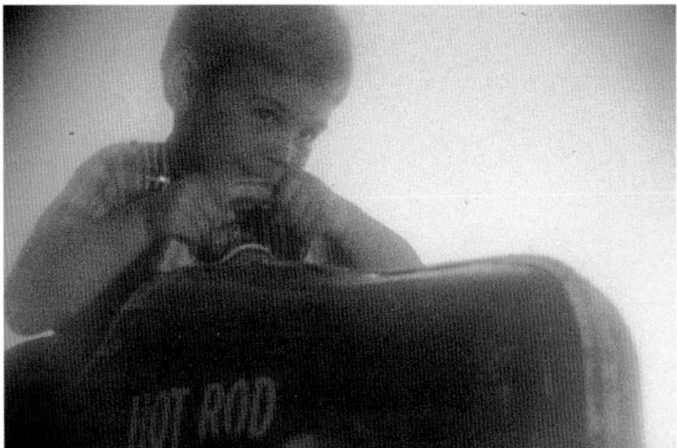

PEDAL CAR
30 seconds
SFX: PEDAL CAR BEING PEDALED. MUSIC UP.
GEOFFREY VO: Remember what it was like to drive a car by the seat of your pants? Your pulse raced. Your heart pounded. You and your car were one.
SFX: MUSICAL TRANSITION.
GEOFFREY VO: If you're ready to feel that way again... you're ready for the new Audi 90 Quattro. Driving is what you hoped it would be. When you were a kid. In a little car. Racing down a hill.

1114
Art Director: Dean Stefanides
Writer: Larry Hampel
Editor: Barry Stillwell
Client: Children's Milk/National Dairy Board
Director: Patrick Russel
Producer: Jaki Keuch

BOTTLE
30 seconds
DAD: What is with those sneakers? Will you please tie the laces.
MOM: Are you ever going to take those sunglasses off? We haven't seen your face in two months.
DAD: Your hair, what's in your hair, motor oil?
MOM: If I've told you once, I've told you a thousand times, don't drink out of the bottle.
VO: This 30 seconds of total coolness has been brought to you by milk.

1115
Art Director: Ted Shaine
Writer: Helayne Spivak
Client: Club Med Sales Inc.
Director: David Cornell
Producer: Ozzie Spenningsby, Spots Films

WORLD NEWS
30 seconds
VO: The world news Club Med style. Oil spills along the coast. Foreign relations improving. Gold plunges overseas. Border dispute settled. Tensions ease in Gulf. And that's the way it is. At Club Med.

1116
Art Director: Mark Oliver
Writer: Mark Oliver
Client: California Fast Food
Director: Mark Oliver, Barry Schwortz
Producer: Mark Oliver Inc., Barry Schwortz; Educational Video

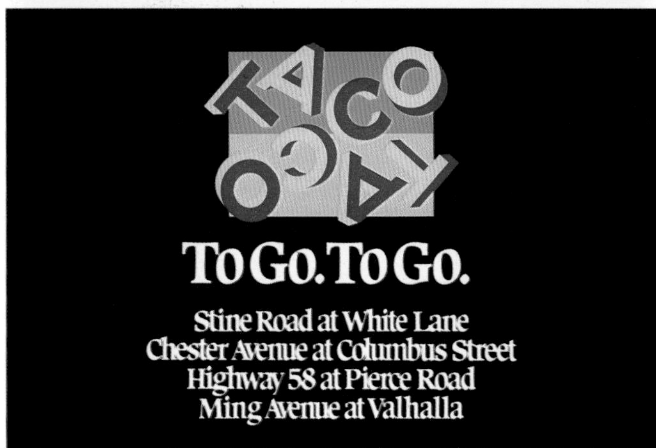

POGO STICK
15 seconds
SFX: DEAD SILENCE. CRRRUUUUNNNNCCCCHHHH! DEAD SILENCE.

1117
Art Director: Mike Oberman
Writer: Christie McMahon
Editor: Tim McGuire
Creative Director: Christie McMahon
Client: Anheuser-Busch/Michelob Light
Agency: DDB Needham Worldwide
Director: Peter Kagan
Producer: Chuck Reese, Stiefel & Co.

DANCE
30 seconds
SINGER:
L-L-Light up the night.
When the sun goes down,
Gonna light up the night.
Silver label, red ribbon.
A taste that's right.
Gonna light up the night.
Michelob Light.
Gonna light up the night.
Gonna light up the night.
Gonna light up the night.
M-m-my Michelob Light.

1118
Art Director: Michael Lawlor
Writer: Charlie Breen
Client: Hyundai Motor America
Producer: Andy Cornelius

GETTING THEM HOME
30 seconds
SFX: TIRES SCREECH, MUSIC UP AND UNDER, HURRIED FOOTSTEPS.
VO: For less than the average price of a new car, you can get two new Hyundai Excels. They're both dependable, have front-wheel drive, room for 5, and more standard features than any cars in their class. The only problem is... getting them home. Hyundai. Cars that make sense.

1119
Art Director: Dean Charlton, Bryan McPeak
Writer: Neal Spector, Dave Michalak, Craig Piechura
Client: Hamady
Producer: David Berne; W. B. Doner & Co.

WINTER
30 seconds
VO: Ah yes, another beautiful Michigan winter. Time to practice speed skating or even try some fancy figure skating moves. Or how about a wild ice fishing party? And even beginners will enjoy Michigan skiing. Need even more excitement? So come to Hamady and celebrate Michigan's sesquicentennial. But remember, no shoes, no shirt, well... you know the rest.

1120

Art Director: Robert Saxon,
Anderson Humphreys, Jay Cooper
Designer: Hannah Hempstead
Writer: Robert Saxon
Client: Megamarket
Director: Hannah Hempstead
Producer: Saxon & Saxon Advertising

BABIES
30 seconds
VO: The dog's master on the left always shops at the supermarket. The dog's master on the right always shops at Megamarket. With the money she saved, the Megamarket shopper had her dog's hair clipped. Bought her a new collar. Sent her to obedience school. Bought her a new house, and something nice to play around with. So while the Megamarket dog is thinking of licking the hand that feeds it, the supermarket dog is thinking of biting it. Megamarket.

1121

Art Director: Joe DelVecchio, Nelsena Burt
Writer: Joe Nunziata, Don Green, Kevin O'Neill
Editor: Ciro DeNettis
Client: Dean Witter
Producer: Bob Smith, Bob Schenkel

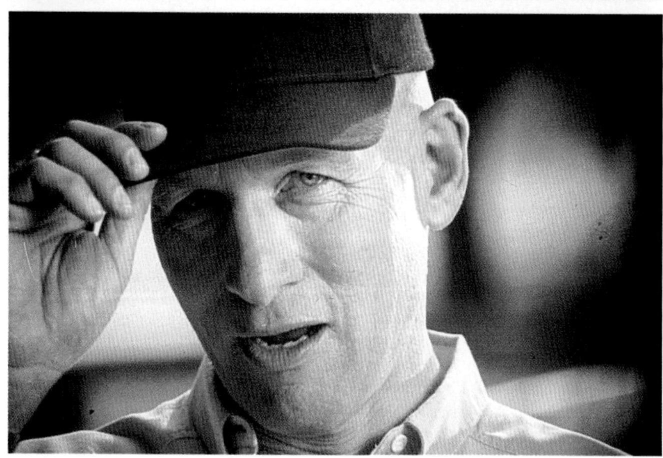

ARTHUR NEWMAN
30 seconds
MUSIC UNDER THROUGHOUT.
ARTHUR NEWMAN: I'm Arthur Newman. Women would love to get their arms around my brother, Paul! And so would investment firms. But, I have a firm that loves to work for people like you and me, too. Dean Witter. You see... I may not be a heart-throb, but Dean Witter still handles my investments with tender loving care.
MUSIC: You're somebody at Dean Witter.
VO: A member of the Sears Financial Network.

1122
Art Director: Dean Hanson
Writer: Phil Hanft
Editor: Jeff Stickles
Client: Lee Jeans
Director: Henry Sandbank
Producer: Char Loving

Z-CHAIR
10 seconds
SFX: NO SOUNDS EXCEPT FOR SOUND OF CHAIR MOVING AND MAN'S FOOTSTEPS. SCRAPING SOUND.
VO: At Conran's, we believe furniture should never sacrifice comfort... just to make an impression on your guests.
SFX: FOOTSTEPS.

1123
Art Director: Michael Vitiello
Writer: Lee Garfinkel, Todd Godwin, Rob Thomas
Editor: Morty Ashkinos
Client: Genesee Brewing Co.
Director: John Bonnano
Producer: Rob Thomas; Levine, Huntley, Schmidt & Beaver

MA, I WON THE LOTTERY
30 seconds
MAN #1: Ma, Ma, I just won the lottery.
MOTHER: Shut up! You know how many people in this neighborhood you owe money to?
MAN #2: Like me.
WOMAN #1: And me.
CHINESE MAN: Me too.
BLACK MAN: How about me?
MAN #3: You owe me.
WOMAN #2: And me.
WOMAN #3: Me too.
MAN #4: Don't forget me.
MAN #5: Pay me.
WOMAN #4: And me.
MAN #6: There he is. Get him!
MAN #1: Boy, could I go for a Genny now.
ANNCR: When you can go for a beer, try the one that's brewed to be the best light beer anywhere. Genny Light.

1124

Art Director: Tom Tieche
Director of Photography: Fred Goodich
Writer: Michael Leonard
Client: United Way
Director: Jon Francis
Producer: Elizabeth O'Toole, Sandra Marshall

ANNE MCLAUREN
60 seconds
ANNE: For a lot of people, this is life. A line of cocaine, a bottle of booze, and whatever it takes to get it. It was my life too. I'd think nothing of driving around all night, looking for a dealer or a liquor store. I'd take my children with me, I didn't care. Drugs were my lover, alcohol my friend. Thank God and thank you for the people who saw that. When you give to the United Way, you support the Concord Family Stress Center. They helped me face the truth that I was killing my family. There are still thousands out there needing that help. But because of you, I'm not one of them. You gave me the courage to change, and you gave my children back their mother. I don't know you but I love you.

1125

Art Director: Walt Taylor
Writer: Rebecca Flora
Client: Virginia Dept. of Alcoholic Bev. Control
Director: Jeff France
Producer: Big City Films, Jeff France; Lawler Ballard Advertising, Bruce Mansfield; Lawler Ballard Advertising

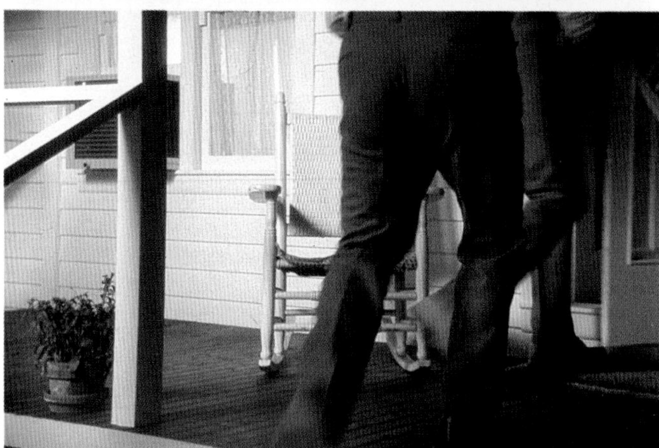

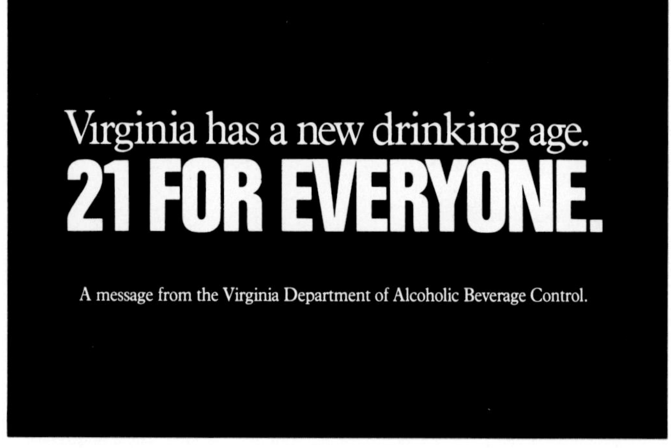

FRANK & ED
10 seconds
VO: In Virginia, if you're under 21, Frank and Ed don't want your support.

1126
Art Director: Pat Le Baron
Writer: Michael Delaney
Editor: Ira Klein
Creative Director: Bernie Owett, Mimi Emilita
Client: Christie Phillips
Director: Gil Cope
Producer: Michael Housman, Mel Gradgio

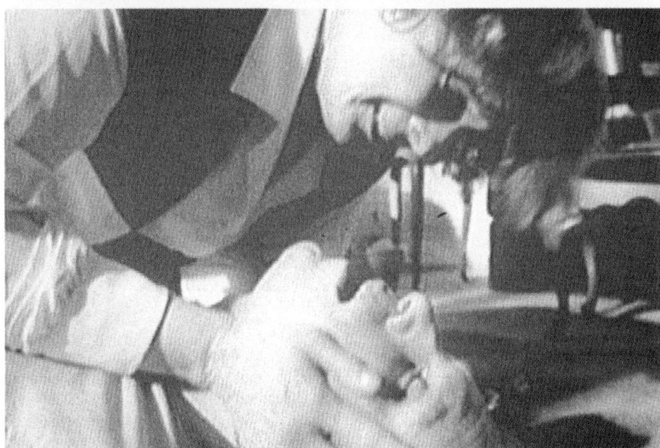

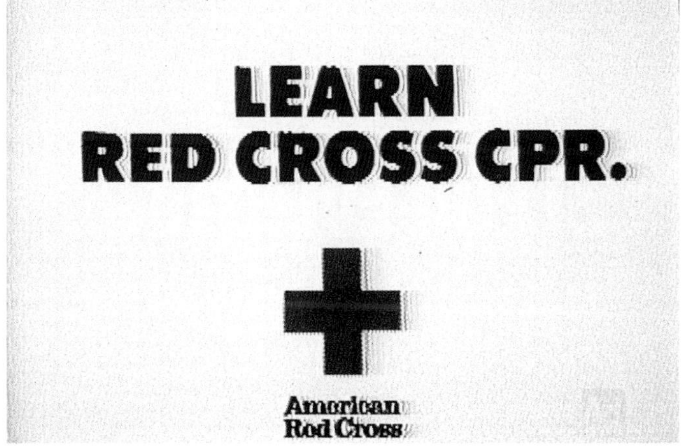

RED CROSS
30 seconds
SFX: CAR TRYING TO TURN OVER.
VO: If your car engine were to stop, you'd probably know what to do to get it started again. The sad fact is, more people know how to jump-start a car than know how to save a life.
SFX: CAR STARTS. HEARTBEAT.
VO: Learn how to jump-start a life. Learn Red Cross CPR.

1127
Art Director: Richard Crispo, Dennis Lim
Writer: Martin Macdonald, Gail Anne Smith
Creative Director: Martin Macdonald
Client: American Lung Association, L.A. Chapter
Director: Jeff Gorman
Producer: Joel Squier, Johns & Gorman

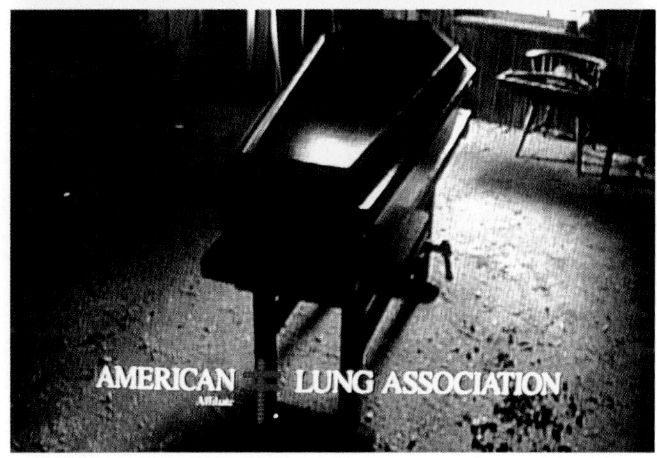

ANOTHER NAIL
30 seconds
VO: Cigarettes. Every one's another nail.

1128
Art Director: Ron Spataro
Writer: John Crawley
Editor: Tom Aberg
Client: United Way
Director: Gordon Willis, Jr.
Producer: John Christian, Diane Greenwald
Music: Tom Faulkner

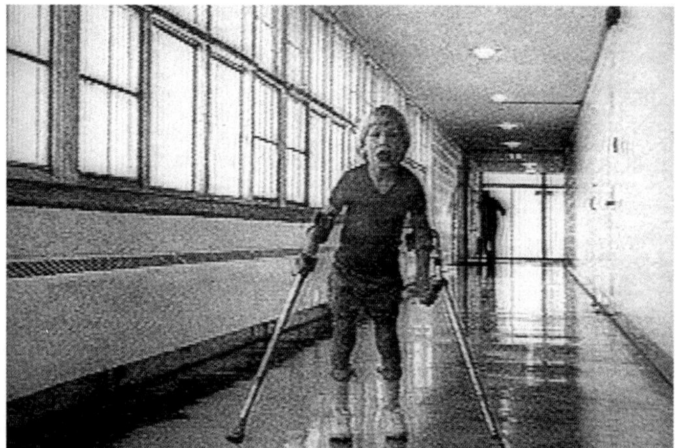
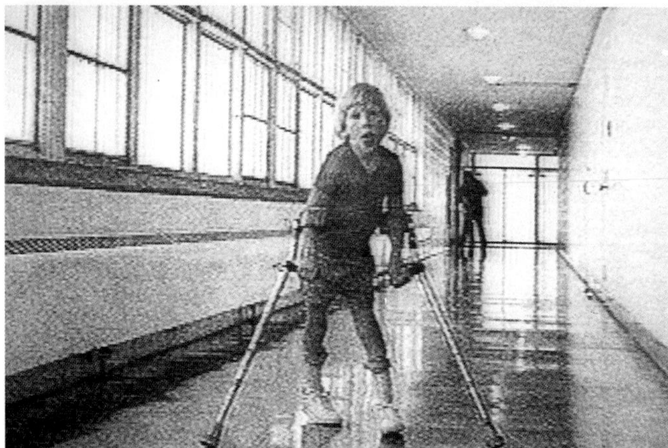

CHILD
30 seconds
VO: It's hard to believe some people still give us excuses–instead of money.

1129
Art Director: Walt Taylor
Writer: Rebecca Flora
Client: Virginia Dept. of Alcoholic Bev. Control
Director: Jeff France
Producer: Big City Films,
Jeff France; Lawler Ballard Advertising,
Bruce Mansfield; Lawler Ballard Advertising

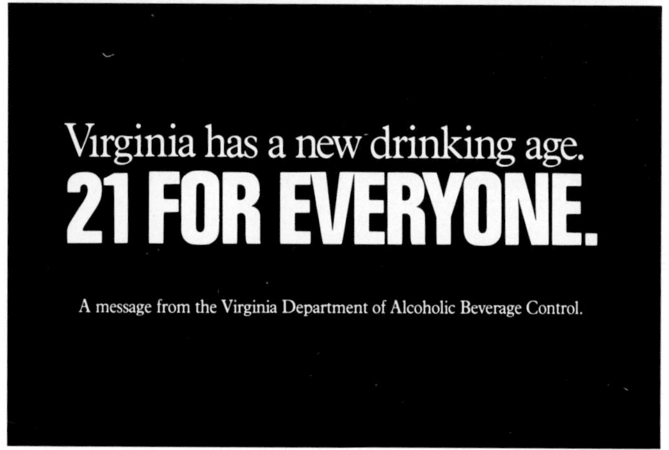

LIGHT
10 seconds
MUSIC UNDER THROUGHOUT.
YOUNG MAN: Gimme a light.
BARTENDER: Gimme some I.D.
VO: Just a reminder, Virginia has a new drinking age.

1130

Art Director: Ron Anderson
Writer: Bert Gardner
Editor: Bob Wickland
Client: First Amendment, Free Speech Committee
Director: Jim Hinton
Producer: Pat Swifka, Patty Petrich, Mike Monten
Music Composer/Director: Tom Lecher

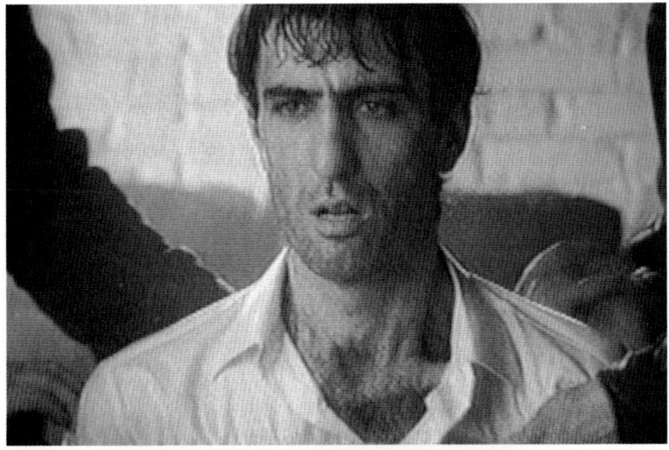

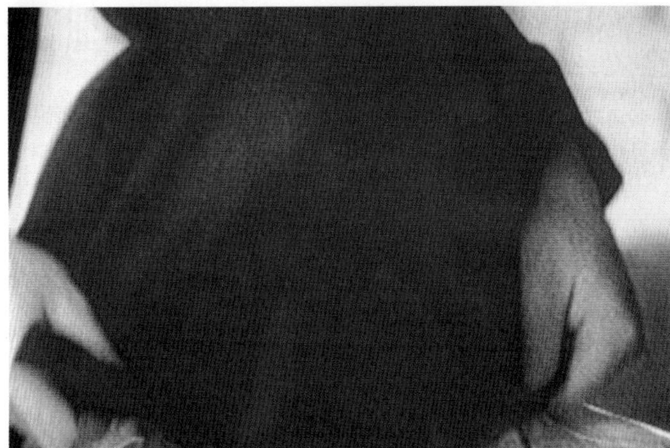

TREASON
30 seconds
VO: In some countries, they have a different word for Freedom of Speech. They call it Treason. Protect the First Amendment.

1131

Art Director: Bruce Hurwit
Writer: Tom Morse
Client: M.S.P.C.A.
Agency: Cosmopulos, Crowley & Daly Inc.
Director: Bob Brown
Producer: Martha Crowley, Tracy Lee Wong; Viz Wiz

Tiger
Kids....30
Grandchildren....73
Great grandchildren....8,192

TIGER
30 seconds
VO: Please, have your housepets spayed or neutered. Call us. We can help.

1132

Art Director: David Olin
Designer: Michael Lerner, David Olin
Writer: Tom Amico, Matt Rechin
Creative Director: Chris N. Perry
Client: Rock n' Roll Hall of Fame
Producer: Michael Lerner, Barry Zeidman; S.O.S. Productions

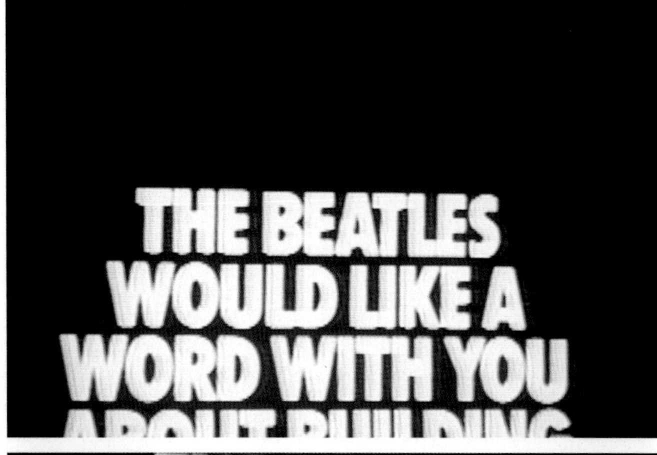

BEATLES
10 seconds
VO: The Beatles would like a word with you. About contributing to the Rock and Roll Hall of Fame.
BEATLES (SUNG): Help!

1133

Art Director: Mark Shap
Director of Photography: Leslie Dektor
Writer: Veronica Nash
Editor: Jim Edwards
Director: Leslie Dektor
Producer: Tina Raver; Ogilvy & Mather, Faith Dektor; Petermann Dektor Productions

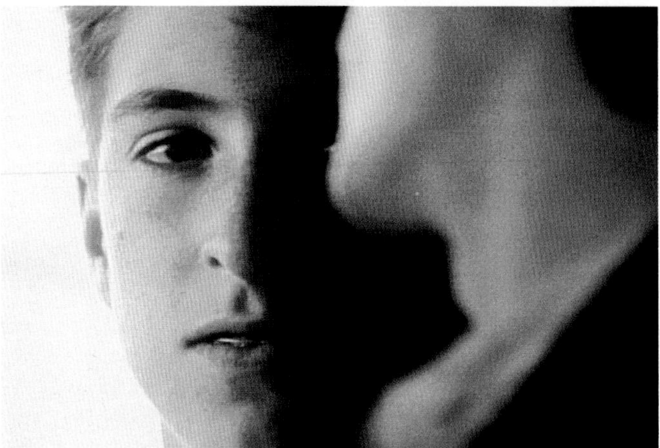

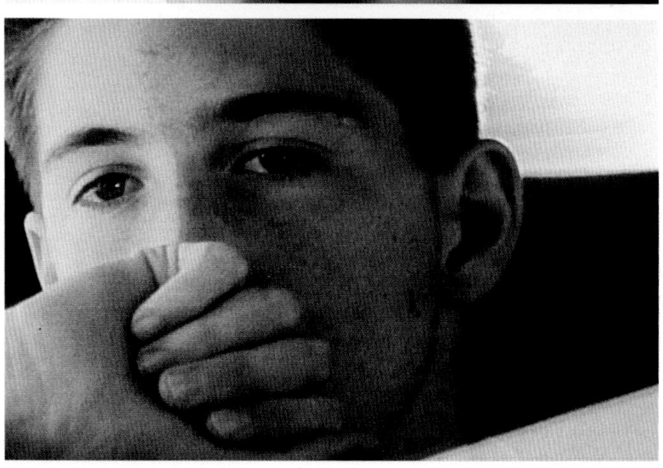

TRICKS OF THE TRADE
60 seconds
SFX: TRAFFIC NOISE.
MAN: You know kid, all you gotta do is be cool. You just give the stuff to your best buddies. You take it to a party. Tell your friends it's a great high. They should just try it. Tell them it can't hurt them.
KID: I can do that.
MAN: Yeah, it's easy. Those kids are going to be a pushover, 'cause they like you. You're a hotshot, right? They'll love you for it.
KID: So how much do I charge?
MAN: Right now, nothing.
KID: Nothing?
MAN: Just give it away. Let 'em have a free taste. Then you watch. You watch and you see who comes back for more.
KID: And then I start charging.
MAN: You're a smart kid. You have a good day at school, Billy boy.
SFX: TRAFFIC NOISE.

1134
Art Director: Randall Saitta, Scott Sorokin
Writer: Charles Borghese, Nancy Librett
Editor: Dick Stone
Client: Amnesty International
Producer: Cynthia Woodward, Bob Ramos Associates,
Nadel & Butler

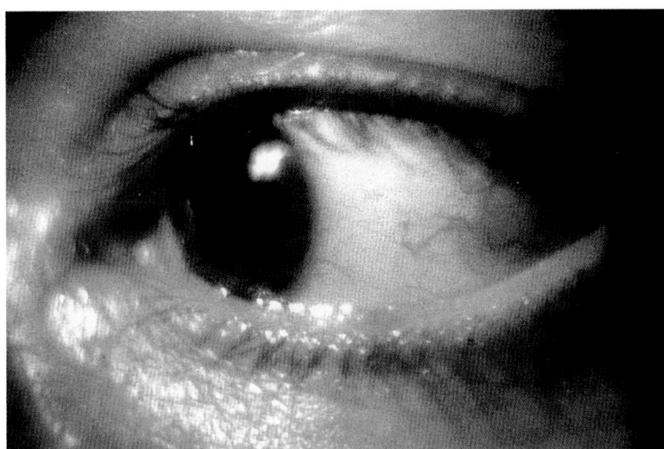

PERFECT COFFEE
30 seconds
MUSIC THROUGHOUT.
VO: The Braun coffeemaker brews perfect coffee, simply. Because life is complicated enough at 7:00 AM. Braun. Designed to perform better.

1135
Art Director: Mark Shap
Director of Photography: Leslie Dektor
Writer: Veronica Nash
Editor: Jim Edwards
Director: Leslie Dektor
Producer: Tina Raver; Ogilvy & Mather,
Faith Dektor; Petermann Dektor Productions

STREET DEALER
60 seconds
DEALER 1: Creeps–I don't believe it! Driving in from the suburbs in their daddy's car to score and then trying to beat me down on the price. . . . I don't cut my price for nobody. (SCREAMS) Especially for these rich creeps. I got good stuff–you want good stuff–you gonna' pay for it.
DEALER 2: They'll be back.
DEALER 1: Trying to tell me they can take it or leave it. Did you see those little punks, man?
DEALER 2: You're gonna be the first one to take it or leave it.
DEALER 1: Yeah, drivin' their daddy's big car. You know what I'd like to do to them? I'd like to rub their faces.
DEALER 2: You know, they're so stupid, they deserve to be burned.
DEALER 1: They're good for nothing man.
DEALER 2: They're good for something. . . . They good for taking money off of.
DEALER 3: Hey man, got some good crack . . . what do you need?

1136
Art Director: Paul Jervis
Writer: Roger Feuerman
Client: Drug-Free America
Producer: Michael Berkman

HOUSEWIFE
30 seconds
SFX: SOAP OPERA VOICES. DOG BARKING OUTSIDE. PHONE RINGING.
VO: One out of every five people who try cocaine get hooked. But that's not your problem. . . .
SFX: SNIFF.
VO: Or is it?
SFX: CHILDREN'S VOICES.

1137
Art Director: Mark Shap
Director of Photography: Leslie Dektor
Writer: Veronica Nash
Editor: Jim Edwards
Director: Leslie Dektor
Producer: Tina Raver; Ogilvy & Mather,
Faith Dektor; Petermann Dektor Productions

GIRL AND DEALER
60 seconds
GIRL: Hi Richie, I really need to talk to you.
DEALER: Yeah, yeah, I got you covered.
GIRL: I only want a little—come on.
DEALER: Sure, I understand.
GIRL: Just a couple of hits. I don't have any money. ... Please.
DEALER: You mean you bring me out here for nothin! That's a no-no, you understand. What are you, stupid? What do I look like?
GIRL: Richie, I just gave you a hundred dollars!
DEALER: That's got nothin' to do with now!
GIRL: Richie, please!
DEALER: Listen to me, no money, no candy, no crack, you understand? Now dissolve. Lose yourself.
GIRL: Richie, come on, don't leave, please!
DEALER: Listen, shh, shh, that girl you're gonna' get—that little red-headed girl—and the both of yous are gonna' come over to my crib.
GIRL: Charlotte?
DEALER: That's right. Go to a nice little party. Understand me? Then I'll take care of ya'.

1138
Art Director: Judy Penny
Writer: Sueanne Peacock
Editor: Century III
Creative Director: Richard Pantano
Client: Emerson College
Producer: Beth Herscott, Century III

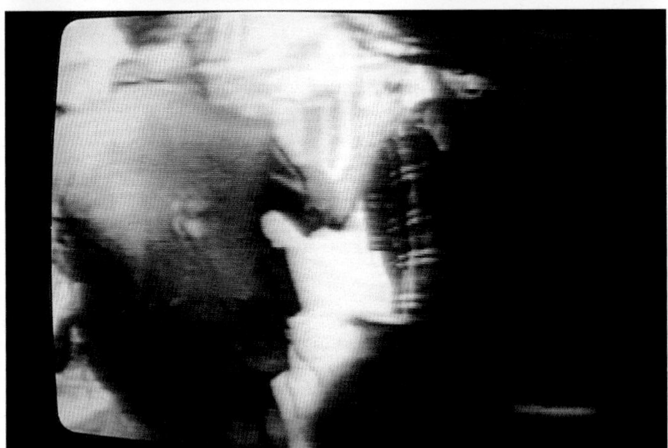

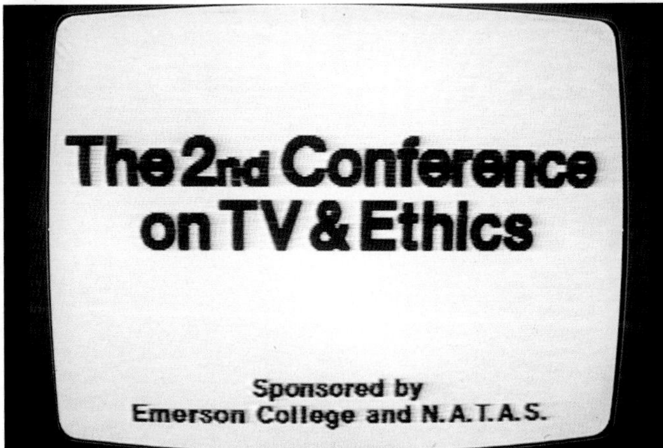

TV & ETHICS
30 SECONDS
VO: When do you turn the cameras off,...and when do you show the truth? When do you protect the viewers,...and when are you keeping them in the dark? When are you influencing history,...and when are you making it? The 2nd Conference on TV & Ethics. You can call now for reservations,...or you can close your eyes.

1139
Art Director: Mark Shap
Writer: Veronica Nash
Editor: Ace & Edie Inc.
Client: 4A's Public Service
Director: Leslie Dektor
Producer: Tina Raver, Faith Dektor

GIRL AND DEALER
60 seconds
GIRL: Hi Richie, I really need to talk to you.
DEALER: Yeah, yeah, I got you covered.
GIRL: I only want a little–come on.
DEALER: Sure, I understand.
GIRL: Just a couple of hits. I don't have any money. ...Please.
DEALER: You mean you bring me out here for nothin' That's a no-no, you understand? What are you, stupid? What do I look like?
GIRL: Richie, I just gave you a hundred dollars!
DEALER: That's got nothin' to do with now!
GIRL: Richie, please!
DEALER: Listen to me, no money, no candy, no crack, you understand? Now dissolve. Lose yourself.
GIRL: Richie, come on, don't leave, please!
DEALER: Listen, shh, shh, that girl you're gonna' get–that little red-headed girl–and the both of yous are gonna' come over to my crib.
GIRL: Charlotte?
DEALER: That's right. Go to a nice little party. Understand me? Then I'll take care of ya'.

1140
Art Director: Jeff Weiss
Director of Photography: Moshe Brahka
Writer: Victor Levin
Creative Director: John Margeotes, John Weiss
Client: City of New York
Producer: Therese Jennings

1141
Art Director: Ron Spataro
Writer: John Crawley
Editor: Tom Aberg
Client: United Way
Director: Gordon Willis, Jr.
Producer: John Christian, Diane Greenwald
Music: Tom Faulkner

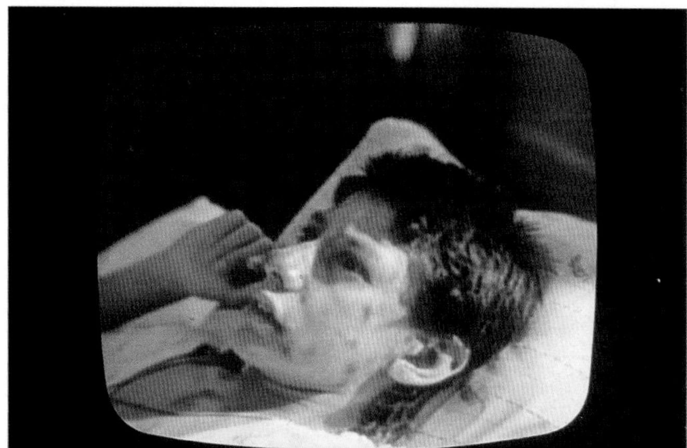

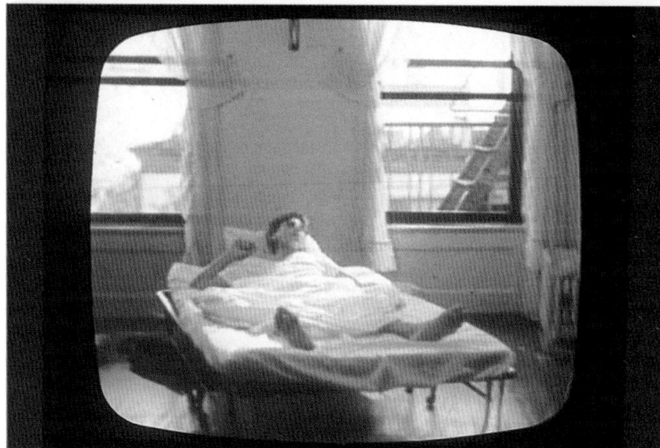

FACE
30 seconds
TEENAGE VO: This is someone who has AIDS. Before AIDS kills him, it can give him a fever that won't go away, and then maybe a brain tumor, or something even worse, that won't go away. Then, finally, he'll go away. PAUSE. You get AIDS by having sex or sharing a needle with someone who has the AIDS virus. So don't. Don't ask for AIDS. Don't get it.

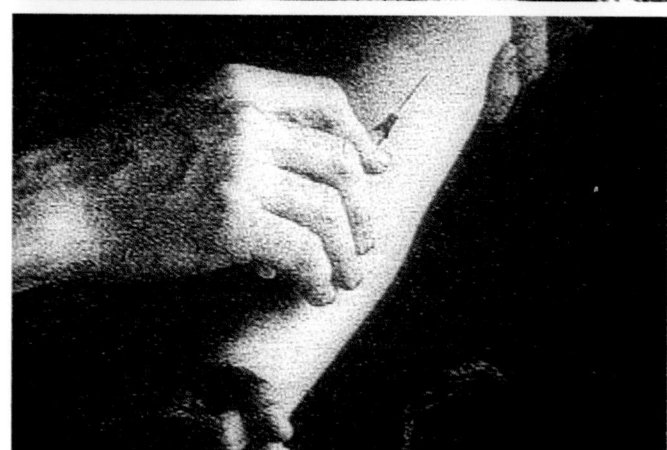

DRUGS
30 seconds
VO: It's hard to believe some people still give us excuses—instead of money.

1142
Art Director: Walt Taylor
Writer: Rebecca Flora
Client: Virginia Dept. of Alcoholic Bev. Control
Director: Jeff France
Producer: Big City Films,
Bruce Mansfield; Lawler Ballard Advertising,
Jeff France; Lawler Ballard Advertising

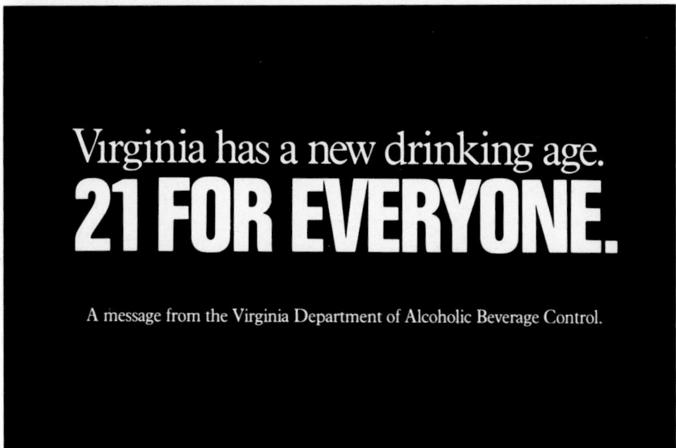

WINE
10 seconds
MUSIC: VANGELIS THEME THROUGHOUT.
VO: Here, in the beautiful Commonwealth of Virginia, we will sell no wine before your time.

1143
Art Director: Paul Jervis
Writer: Roger Feuerman
Client: Drug-Free America
Producer: Michael Berkman

WAKING UP
30 seconds
SFX: RADIO PLAYING. RAINING AND THUNDERING THROUGHOUT.
MAN (WHISPERING): Bye-bye.
VO: One out of every 5 people who try cocaine get hooked. But that's not your problem....
SFX: SNIFF.

1144
Art Director: Paul Fuentes
Director of Photography: Kevin Morrissey
Writer: Chazz Dean, James Siena
Editor: Robert Farringer
Client: Cinemax/Home Box Office
Producer: Karen Sands, Home Box Office
Director of Design: Orest Woronewych

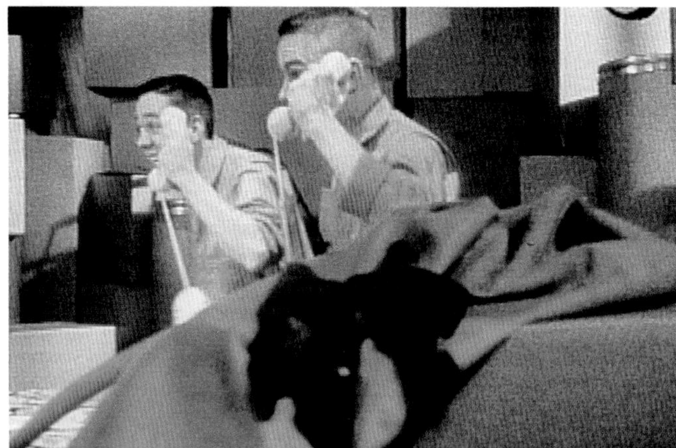

CINEMAX MOVIE CLICHES
50 seconds
CHAZZ DEAN & JAMES SIENA: They're here.
SFX: STABBING MUSIC FROM *PSYCHO*.
JAMES: Stella! Stella!
CHAZZ: Yo, Adrian!
BOTH: Open the pod bay doors please, Hal. Open the pod bay doors please, Hal. Is it safe? Is it safe? Is it safe?
CHAZZ: Here's Johnny!
JAMES: Here's Johnny!
SFX: *JAWS* MUSIC.
BOTH: Elliot, Elliot, Elliot, phone home! Phone home! I am not an animal! Badges? Badges? We don't need no stinking badges. My sister, my daughter, my sister, my daughter, my sister, my daughter. . . .
ANNCR: It's hard work bringing you great movies, but somebody's gotta' do it.

1145
Art Director: Carl Willat
Director of Photography: Don Smith
Writer: Don Smith, Carl Willat
Editor: Carol Brzezinski
Creative Director: Mike Nichols; Disney Channel
Client: The Disney Channel
Producer: Chris Whitney; Colossal Pictures

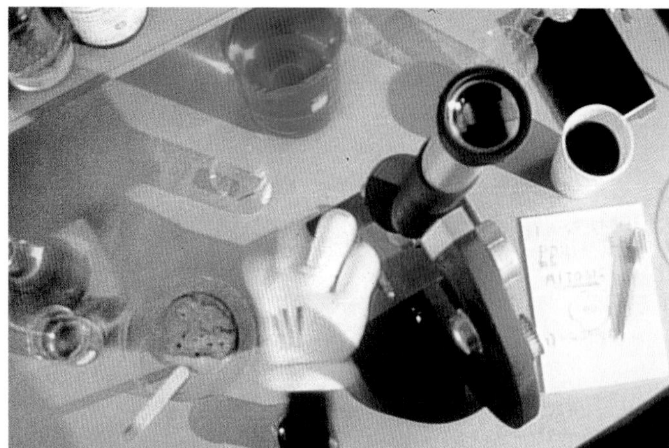

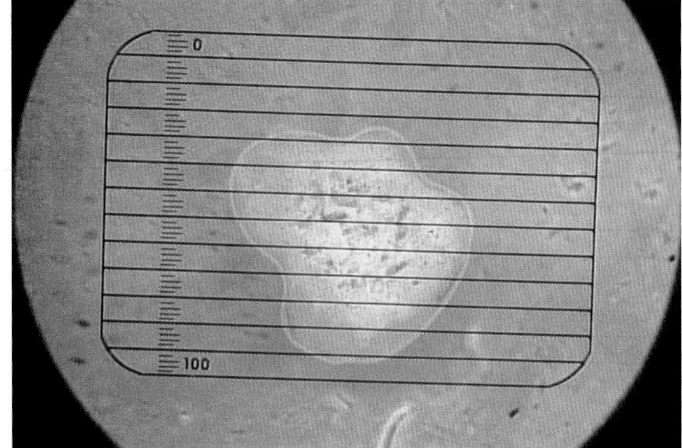

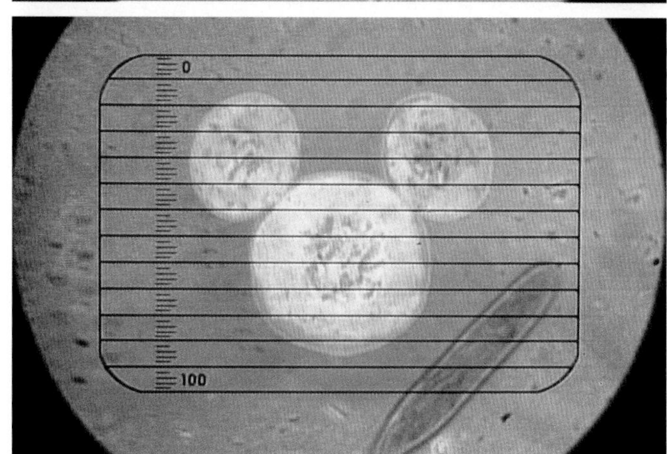

MICKEY MICROSCOPE
20 seconds
NO AUDIO. MUSIC TRACK AND SFX ONLY.

1146
Art Director: George Evelyn, Carl Willat
Writer: George Evelyn, Don Smith, Carl Willat
Creative Director: Mike Nichols; Disney Channel
Client: The Disney Channel
Producer: Chris Whitney; Colossal Pictures

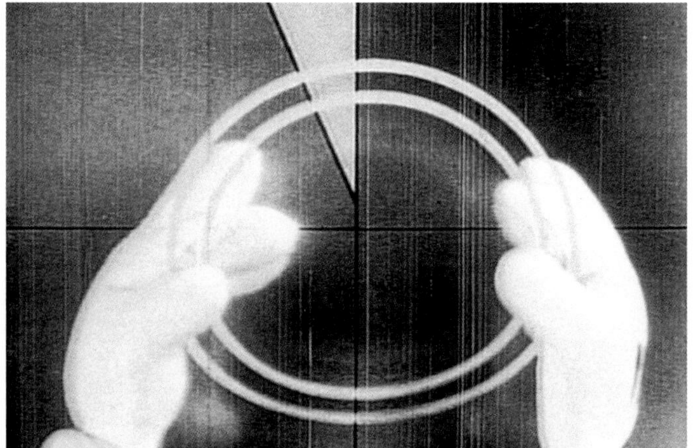

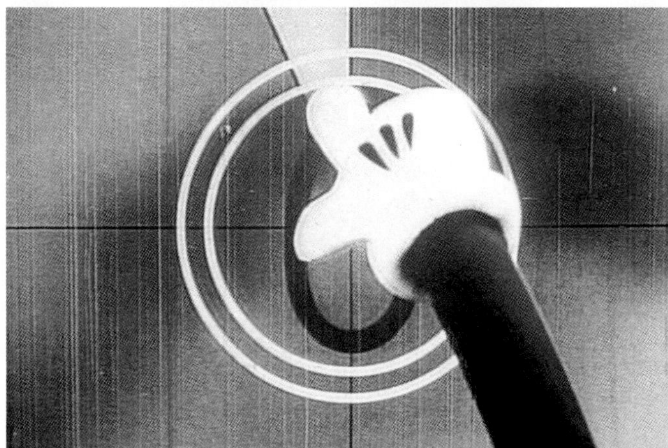

MICKEY COUNTDOWN
15 seconds
NO AUDIO. MUSIC TRACK AND SFX ONLY.

1147
Art Director: George Evelyn
Director of Photography: Don Smith
Animator/Artist: Carl Willat
Editor: Carol Brzezinski
Creative Director: Mike Nichols; Disney Channel
Client: The Disney Channel
Producer: Chris Whitney; Colossal Pictures

MICKEY AND MINNIE FUNHOUSE
34 seconds
NO AUDIO. MUSIC TRACK AND SFX ONLY.

1148
Art Director: Bob Meagher
Writer: Stephanie Gruber
Editor: Bob Meagher
Client: Skil Corp.
Producer: Bob Meagher; Cramer-Krasselt, Stephanie Gruber; Cramer-Krasselt, Archive Film Productions

RAISE YOUR SALES
4 minutes, 20 seconds
SFX: CHRISTMAS MUSIC.
VO: This year your favorite Christmas carol can be the same as last year.
MUSIC: "THE TWIST."
VO: That's right. "The Twist." Remember how customers flocked to your store for the Skil Twist last Christmas?
SFX: DIFFERENT STYLES OF MUSIC THROUGHOUT.
VO: Once again, households all over are depending on you for Christmas presents. That's why the mad, crazy rush for Twists is bound to happen again. And this year we're making it even easier for you. We're making Twists 'round the clock, so you can get as many as you need. We'll also appear on television! We'll be in 88% of the living rooms in America. We're sending [your customers] straight to your store. You'll also get snappy radio scripts for your favorite personality to read on the radio. And ads to run in the the local newspaper. What else? A chance to win, win, win! Yes, win a Caribbean cruise in the Raise-Your-Sales Contest. The consolation prize if you don't win? Sales, sales, sales! Whether you want to raise these kinds of sails or these kinds of sales, a Twist display is sure to bring you luck.

1149
Art Director: Leslie Caldwell
Director of Photography: Amir Hamed
Writer: Mike Koelker
Editor: Dan Brown, Yamus, Bob Carr
Client: Levi Strauss & Co.
Director: Leslie Dektor
Producer: Steve Neely, Faith Dektor

CHAINS
30 seconds
SINGERS:
Used to see you when you had the blues.
Had more trouble than you could use.
Now I see you on the TV tube.
Everybody loves them five-oh-one blues.
Talkin' Levi's
Five-oh-one blues.
Oh, yeah!
Ain't it funny how the times have changed?
Even the blues been rearranged.
Now the crazy part of it,
You don't have to shrink to fit.
Everybody talkin' Levi's
Five-oh-one blues.
Talkin' Levi's!

INTERNATIONAL

DEADLINE: 4 DECEMBER 1987

2

The Art Directors Club, Inc.

SECOND INTERNATIONAL EXHIBITION

CALL FOR ENTRIES

NEW YORK,
NY 10003
U.S.A.

The Art Directors Club of New York is extending its prestigious annual awards program to the international design and advertising community. The 2nd International Exhibition, a juried competition for excellence in print, television and film art direction, will be judged by a distinguished panel of ADC Hall of Fame laureates and designers of international stature.

1150
Art Director: Michael Stockman
Writer: Hajo Depper
Client: Bull AG
Agency: TBWA

1151
Art Director: Koichi Kano
Designer: Koichi Kano
Illustrator/Artist: Arihito Tanno
Writer: Genki Wakabayashi
Client: Toshiba
Agency: Dentsu Inc.
Publication: Nikkan Kogyo Shimbun

1152
Art Director: Jürgen Weber
Photographer: Axel Waldecker
Writer: Heidi Maass
Client: Reinhard Janke
Agency: Wensauer & Partner

1153
Art Director: Jürgen Weber
Photographer: Werner Pawlok, Axel Waldecker
Writer: Heidi Maass
Client: Jelto Hendriok
Agency: Wensauer & Partner

1154
Art Director: Koji Mizuno
Designer: Koji Mizuno
Photographer: Tatsuji Yogi
Writer: Hide Nakano

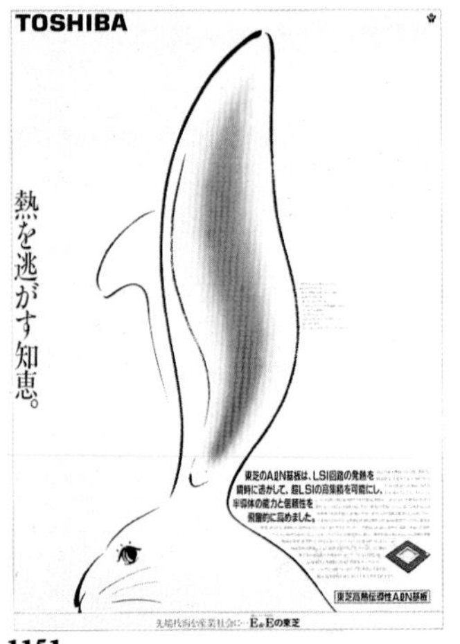

1151

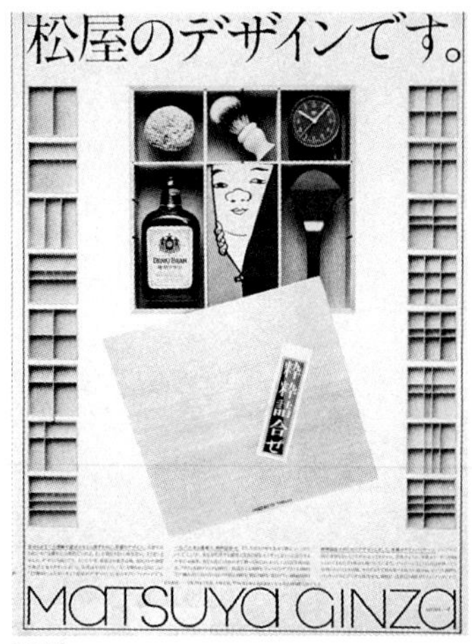

1154

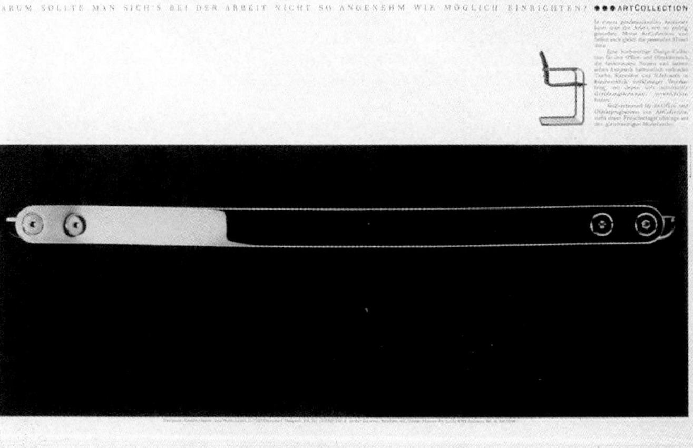

1152

1153

WARUM DER CHEF JETZT LIEBER INS BÜRO GEHT. ●●● ARTCOLLECTION

Ein harmonisches Umfeld ist für den arbeitenden Menschen ebenso wichtig wie für den privaten Menschen zu Hause. Denn nur wer sich wohl fühlt, kann kreativ und leistungsfähig sein.

Deshalb ist ArtCollection zum einen ein Office-Programm mit hohem Design- und Qualitätsanspruch. Und zum anderen die konsequente Verwirklichung eines alten Gedankens: Nämlich arbeiten, um zu leben. Und nicht leben, um zu arbeiten.

Stellvertretend für die Office- und Objektmöbel von ArtCollection bieten wir Ihnen unseren Stuhl »Gamma« aus dem gleichnamigen Programm an.

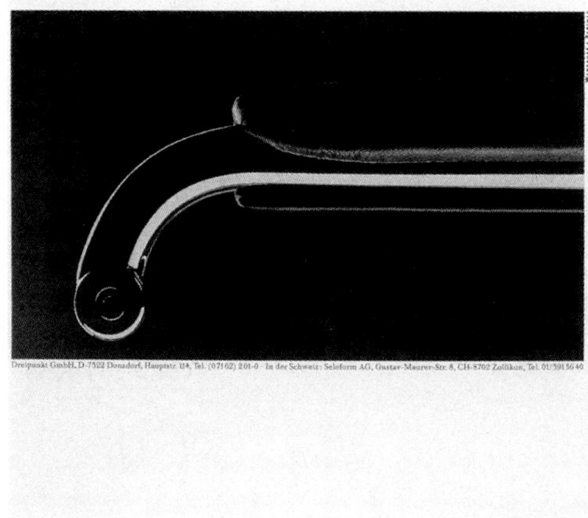

1155

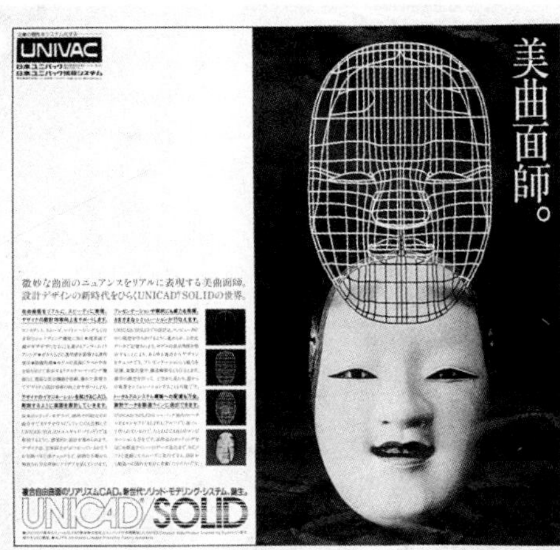

1156

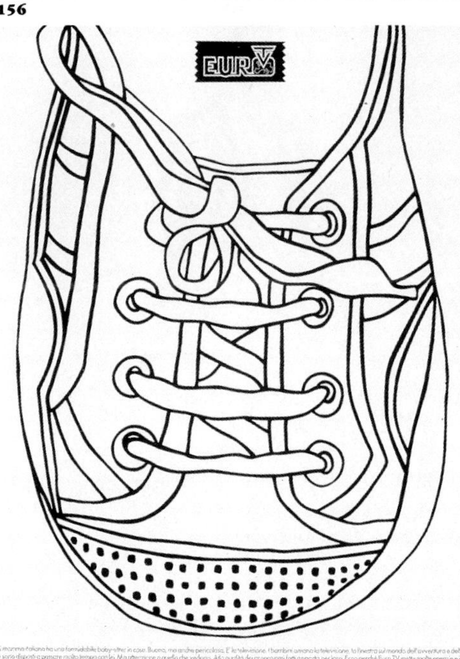

1157

SE VOLETE SAPERE COSA ACCADRÀ IN FUTURO, ACCENDETE QUESTO TV COLOR.

BRIONVEGA

1158

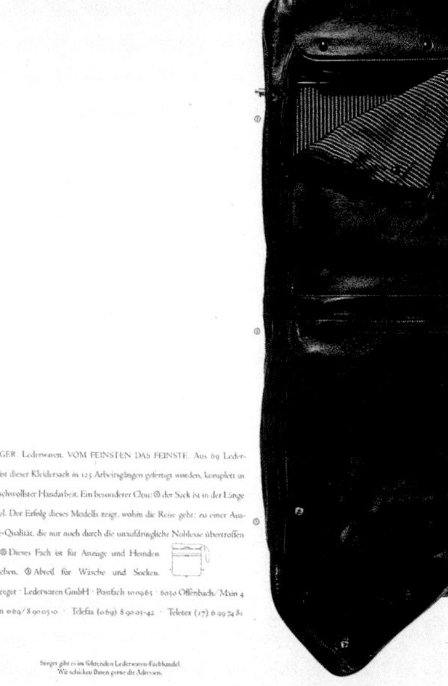

1159

1155
Art Director: Jürgen Weber
Photographer: Axel Waldecker
Writer: Heidi Maass
Client: Reinhard Janke
Agency: Wensauer & Partner

1156
Art Director: Hiroshi Tsurumaki
Designer: Hiroshi Tsurumaki
Writer: Yūsuke Kawamura
Client: Nihon Univac
Agency: Nihon Keizaisha Advertising Ltd.

1157 Silver Award
Art Director: Gavino Sanna
Illustrator/Artist: Gavino Sanna
Writer: Andrea Concato
Creative Director: Gavino Sanna
Client: Euro TV
Agency: Young & Rubicam (Italy) SPA

1158
Art Director: Gavino Sanna
Photographer: Vanni Burkhart
Writer: Nicoletta Cocchi
Creative Director: Gavino Sanna
Client: Brionvega
Agency: Young & Rubicam (Italy) SPA

1159
Art Director: Jürgen Weber
Photographer: Axel Waldecker
Writer: Albert Röhl
Client: Armin Johl
Agency: Wensauer & Partner

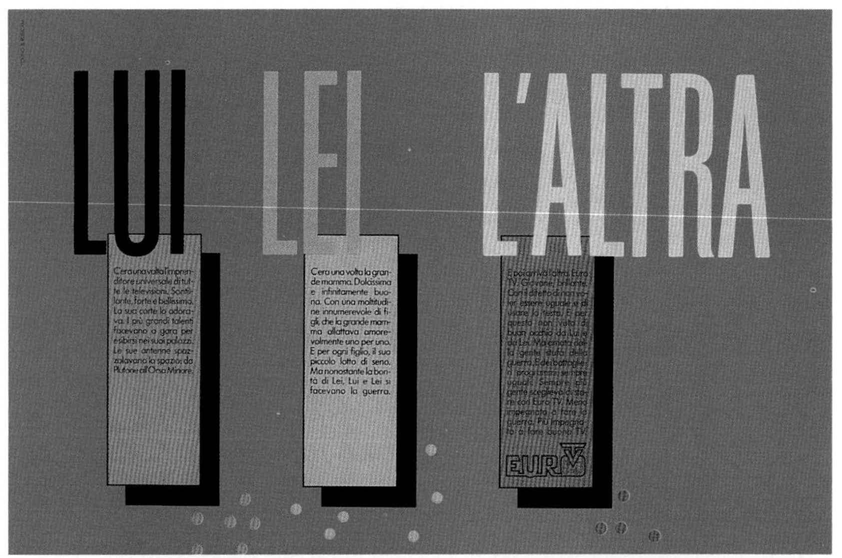

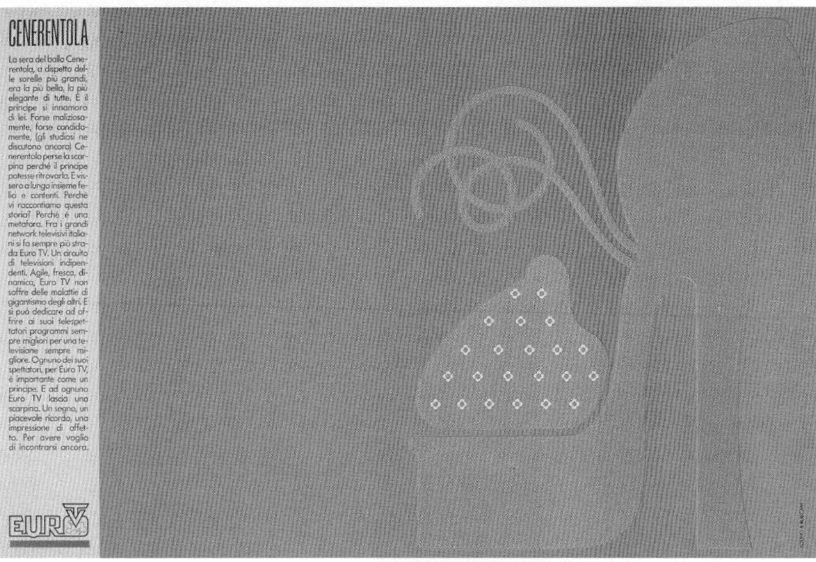

1160
Art Director: Gavino Sanna
Illustrator/Artist: Gavino Sanna
Writer: Andrea Concato
Creative Director: Gavino Sanna
Client: Euro TV
Agency: Young & Rubicam (Italy) SPA

1161
Art Director: Tohru Ikeno
Designer: Shiro Yamaguchi
Illustrator/Artist: Katzu Yoshida
Writer: Masahiro Kiryu
Client: American Express International Inc.
Agency: McCann-Erickson Hakuhodo Inc.
Publisher: Nihon Keizai Shinbun

1162

Art Director: Muneaki Andoh
Designer: Muneaki Andoh
Illustrator/Artist: Takeo Ohno
Writer: Muneaki Andoh, Reiji Yamaguchi
Client: Kirin Beer Co., Ltd.
Agency: Dentsu Inc. (Nagoya)

1163

Art Director: Francesco Rizzi
Photographer: Raffaello Bra'
Illustrator/Artist: Michel Fuzellier
Writer: Nicoletta Cocchi
Creative Director: Gavino Sanna
Client: Sacla'
Strategic Director: Sergio Mambelli

1164 Distinctive Merit

Art Director: Francesco Rizzi
Photographer: Raffaello Bra'
Illustrator/Artist: Michel Fuzellier
Writer: Grazia Usai
Creative Director: Gavino Sanna
Client: Sacla'
Strategic Director: Sergio Mambelli

1165

Art Director: Michael Orr
Photographer: David Body
Writer: David Denton
Client: VAG (UK) Ltd.
Agency: DDB Needham (London)
Publisher: The Observer

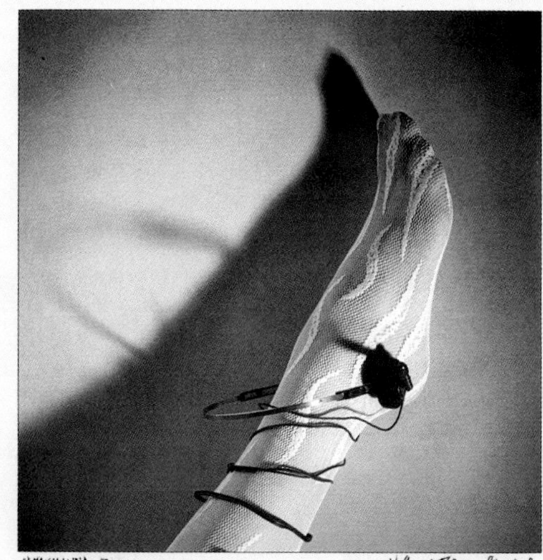

1166
Art Director: Masatoshi Toda
Designer: Mamoru Suzuki
Photographer: Isamu Wakatsuki
Writer: Jun Maki
Client: Isetan

1167
Art Director: Helmut Klein
Photographer: Helmut Klein
Client: Fa. Köck GmbH
Agency: Haupt-Stummer
Producer: Martin Dunkel

1168

Art Director: Ruedi Wyler, Bruno Züttel
Designer: Bruno Züttel
Photographer: Markus Fischer
Writer: Ruedi Maurhofer
Client: Tages-Anzeiger AG (Zurich)
Agency: Ruedi Wyler Werbung

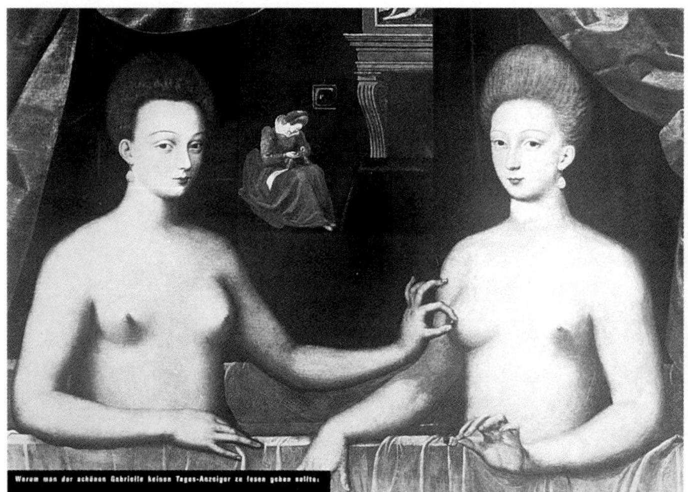

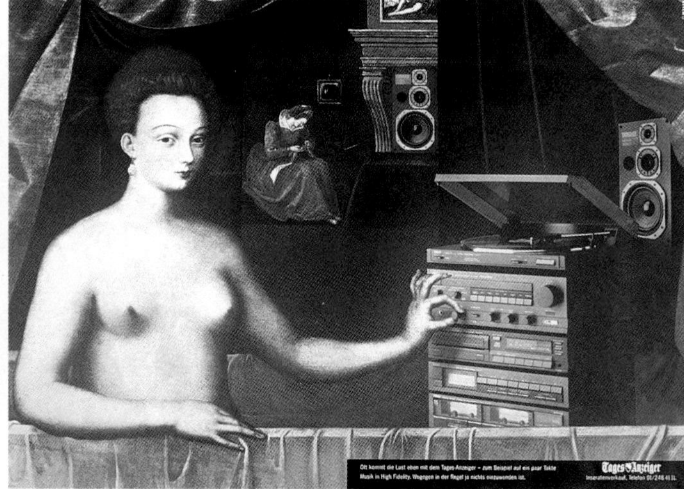

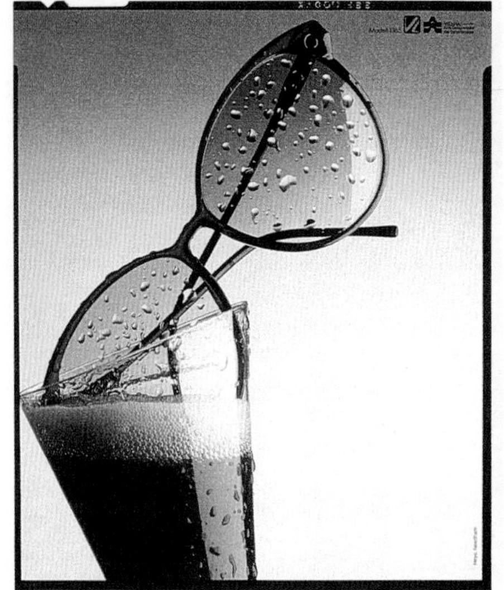

Besonders leicht und perfekt in der Paßform. Nur beim Augenoptiker.

Die Brille. VIENNA Line
PARIS ROMA LONDON WIEN

Besonders leicht und perfekt in der Paßform. Nur beim Augenoptiker.

Die Brille. VIENNA Line
PARIS ROMA LONDON WIEN

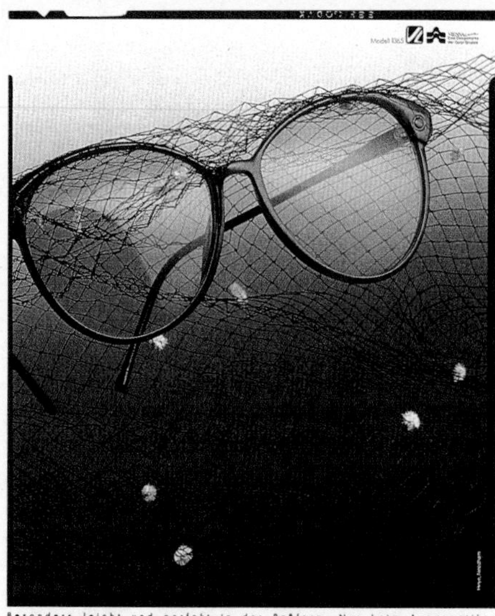

Besonders leicht und perfekt in der Paßform. Nur beim Augenoptiker.

Die Brille. VIENNA Line
PARIS ROMA LONDON WIEN

1169

Art Director: Norbert Herold
Photographer: Jacques Schumacher
Writer: Winnie Bergmann
Client: Optyl Holding Inc.
Agency: Heye & Partner
Producer: Walter Dittrich

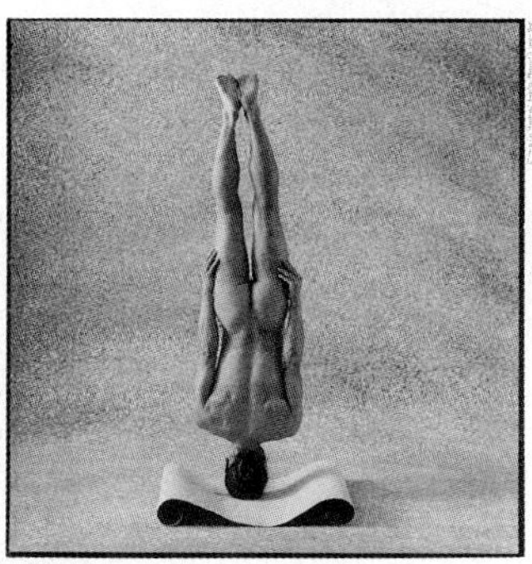

MANY OF THE BEST PICTURES
WERE FIRST SEEN THROUGH A HASSELBLAD 500C/M.

HASSELBLAD

1170

Tini lebt. Hotel, 8. Stock, Zimmer 804. Aus dem Fenster schimmert gedämpftes Licht in die Nacht. Die kleine Tini wartet gemeinsam mit ihrer Puppe Susi auf ihre Eltern. Da dringt Rauch durch die Tür, Feuerzungen lecken in den Raum. Tini kuschelt sich mit ihrer Puppe weinend in eine Ecke. Keiner bemerkt den Brand. Und doch fährt die Feuerwehr vorm Haus bereits die Magirusleiter aus.

Das mikroprozessorgesteuerte Brandmelde-Leitsystem von Schrack hat längst das Feuer entdeckt und die Feuerwehr alarmiert. Über Bildschirm und Drucker wurde der Flächenplan des Hotels mit der Position des Brandherdes übermittelt. Die Feuerwehr kann somit gezielt und ohne Zeitverlust den Brand bekämpfen. Für die Puppe kommt zwar jede Hilfe zu spät. Aber die kleine Tini bleibt unversehrt. Das Brandmelde-Leitsystem von Schrack. Die Spürnase der Feuerwehr.

SCHRACK

„Wer an Utopien nicht glaubt, muß sie realisieren." (E. Harald Schrack)

1171

Many are picked.

Few are chosen.

1172

I don't see the point of getting engaged
I don't see the point of getting
I don't see the point of
I don't see the point
I don't see the
I don't see
I don't
I do

A diamond is forever.

1173

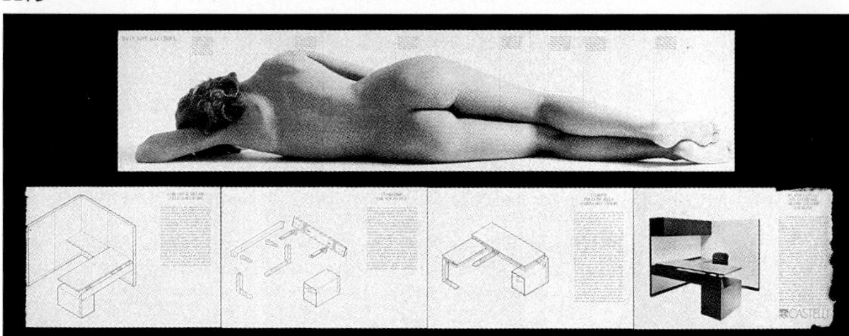

1174

1170 Silver Award
Art Director: Styrbjörn Lyberg
Photographer: Christian Vogt
Writer: Lars Öhjne
Client: Victor Hasselblad A/B
Agency: Öhjne & Co. (Marstrand)

1171
Art Director: Charly Frei
Client: Schrack AG (Vienna)
Agency: Young & Rubicam GmbH

1172 Gold Award
Art Director: Yvonne Sumter
Photographer: Arthur Massey
Writer: Boris Damast
Client: Conga International Foods
Agency: Saatchi & Saatchi Advertising
Publication: Australian Gourmet

1173
Art Director: Paul Austin
Photographer: Charles Settrington
Writer: Paul Austin, John McGrath
Client: Diamond Information Centre
Agency: J. Walter Thompson Co., Ltd.
Typographer: Maggie Lewis

1174
Art Director: Gavino Sanna
Photographer: Vanni Burkhart
Illustrator/Artist: J. P. Maurer
Writer: Maurizia Castellini
Creative Director: Gavino Sanna
Client: Castelli
Agency: Young & Rubicam (Italy) SPA

1175

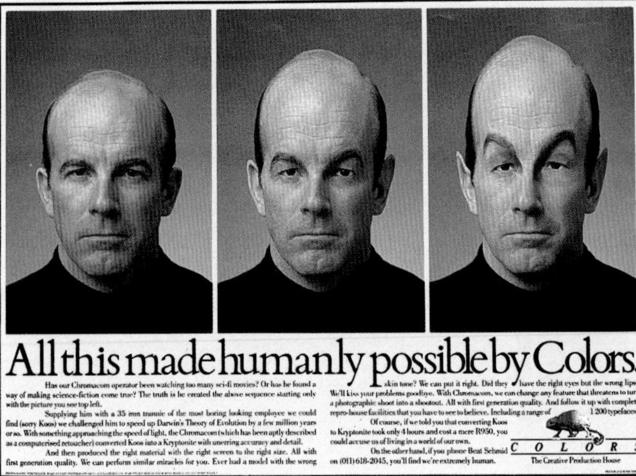

1176

1177

1178

1179

1175
Art Director: Börje Stille
Writer: Ingemar Johannesson
Client: Pappers Gruppen
Agency: Johannesson & Stille

1176
Art Director: Mike Rossi
Photographer: Tom Pollock
Writer: Geoff Coxall
Client: Colors

1177
Art Director: José Zaragoza
Designer: Joca Benavent
Photographer: Fifi Tong
Writer: Claudio Deckes
Client: Wrangler
Agency: DPZ Propaganda
Producer: Anelito De Nóbrega

1178
Art Director: João Simone
Photographer: Fifi Tong
Writer: Claudio Deckes, Stalimir Vieira
Client: Souza Cruz
Agency: DPZ Propaganda
Producer: Anelito De Nóbrega

1179
Art Director: Mike Rossi
Photographer: Tom Pollock
Writer: Geoff Coxall
Client: Colors

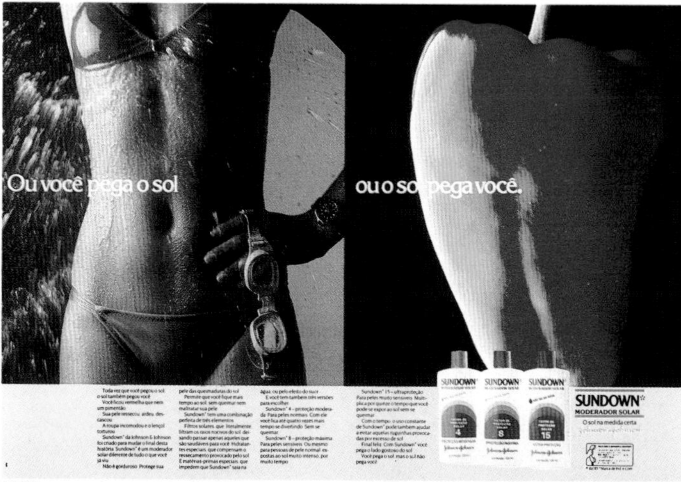

1180

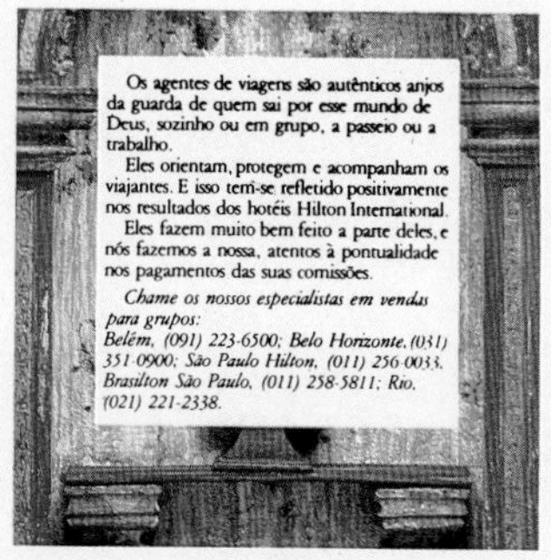

OS ANJOS DA GUARDA DOS NÓSSOS HÓSPEDES.

HILTON INTERNATIONAL BRASIL

Belém (Hilton International Belém) • Belo Horizonte (Brasilton Contagem) • São Paulo (São Paulo Hilton e Brasilton São Paulo).

1183

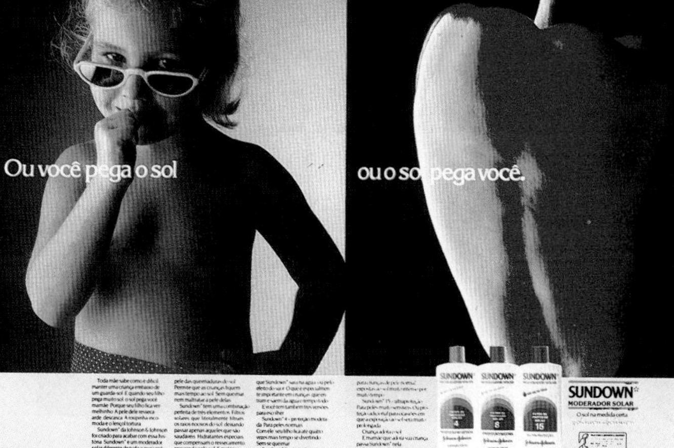

1181

Aproveite a sua viagem para conhecer, ou rever, Belém do Pará (porta de entrada da Amazônia), Belo Horizonte e São Paulo, a maior cidade do País.

Em Belém, Belo Horizonte e São Paulo, existem quatro hotéis Hilton International, para recebê-lo com a mesma eficiência da sua casa e inigualável conforto. Neles, você terá todas as facilidades para o seu trabalho ou lazer e os melhores restaurantes.

Para reservas, chame o seu agente de viagens ou o Hilton Reservation Service: Belém, (091) 223-6500; Belo Horizonte, (031) 351-0900; São Paulo Hilton, (011) 256-0033, Brasilton São Paulo, (011) 258-5811; Rio, (021) 221-2338.

APROVEITE PARA CONHECER OUTROS BRASIS.

HILTON INTERNATIONAL BRASIL

Belém (Hilton International Belém) • Belo Horizonte (Brasilton Contagem)
São Paulo (São Paulo Hilton e Brasilton São Paulo).

1184

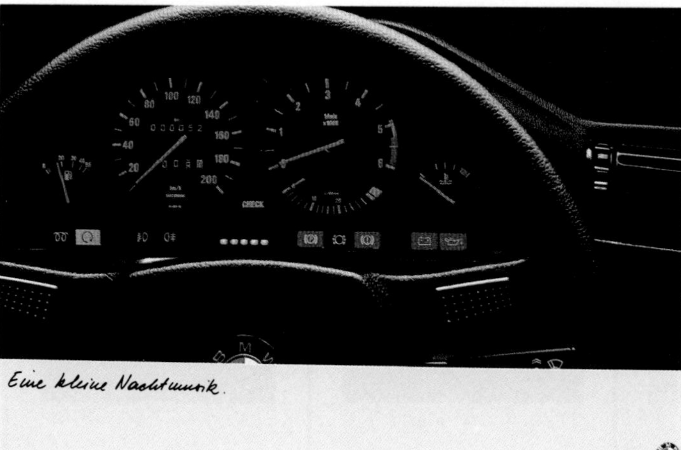

Eine kleine Nachtmusik.

BMW 324td. 6 Zylinder. 2443 ccm. 85 kW/115 PS. 220 Nm/2400 min. Beschleunigung 0–100 km/h: 11,9 sec. Verbrauch nach DIN 70030: 90 km/h 5,2, 120 km/h 6,9, Stadt 8,9 l/100 km. **Freude am Fahren.**

1182

1180
Art Director: Helga Miethke
Photographer: Andreas Heiniger
Writer: Paulo Ghirotti
Client: Johnson & Johnson
Agency: DPZ Propaganda
Producer: Anelito De Nóbrega

1181
Art Director: Helga Miethke
Photographer: Andreas Heiniger
Writer: Paulo Ghirotti
Client: Johnson & Johnson
Agency: DPZ Propaganda
Producer: Anelito De Nóbrega

1182
Art Director: Charly Frei
Writer: Wilfried Vitz
Creative Director: E. Petri
Client: BMW Austria
Agency: Young & Rubicam GmbH
Producer: Herbert Angeli

1183
Art Director: Oswaldo Mendes
Designer: Oswaldo Mendes
Writer: Oswaldo Mendes
Client: Hilton International (Belém)
Agency: Mendes Publicidade Ltda.
Producer: Marcia Martins

1184
Art Director: Oswaldo Mendes
Designer: Oswaldo Mendes
Client: Hilton International (Belém)
Agency: Mendes Publicidade Ltda.
Publisher: Marcia Martins

1185
Art Director: Heinrich Hoffmann, Carlos Ferreira
Photographer: Heinrich Hoffmann
Client: Bernd Berger Mode GmbH
Agency: Michael Conrad & Leo Burnett GmbH

1186 Distinctive Merit
Art Director: Styrbjörn Lyberg
Photographer: Christopher Little
Writer: Lars Öhjne
Client: Victor Hasselblad A/B
Agency: Öhjne & Co. (Marstrand)

1187
Art Director: Styrbjörn Lyberg
Photographer: Greg Gorman
Writer: Lars Öhjne
Client: Victor Hasselblad A/B
Agency: Öhjne & Co. (Marstrand)

1185

1186

1187

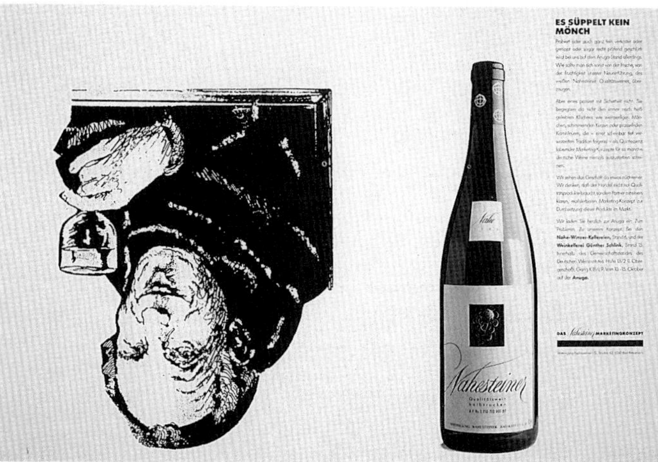

1188
Art Director: Fritz Meyer
Designer: MP-Team
Illustrator/Artist: MP-Team
Writer: MP-Team
Client: Vereinigung Nahesteiner IG
Agency: Meyer
Publication: Lebensmittel-Zeitung
Director: Christoph v. Nell
Director: Günther Schlink

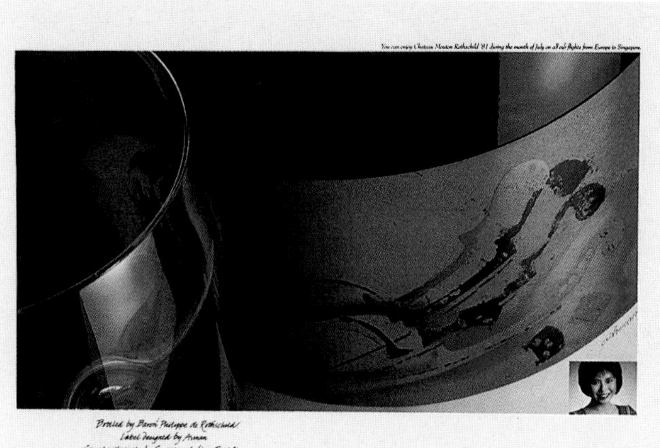

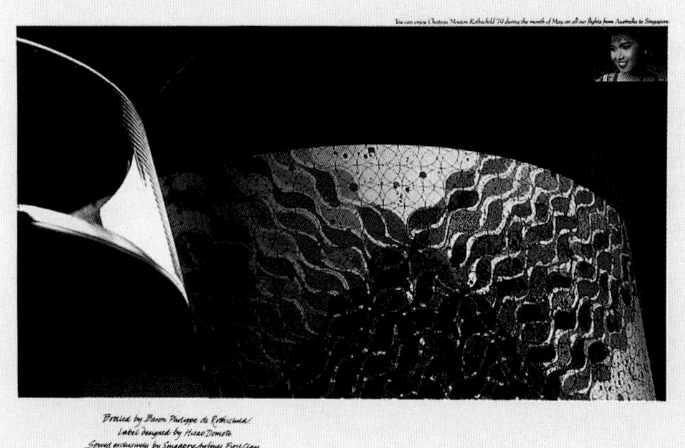

1189 Gold Award
Art Director: Graham Byfield, John Finn
Photographer: Willie Tang
Writer: Adrian Gerson
Client: Singapore Airlines
Agency: Batey Ads Pte., Ltd.

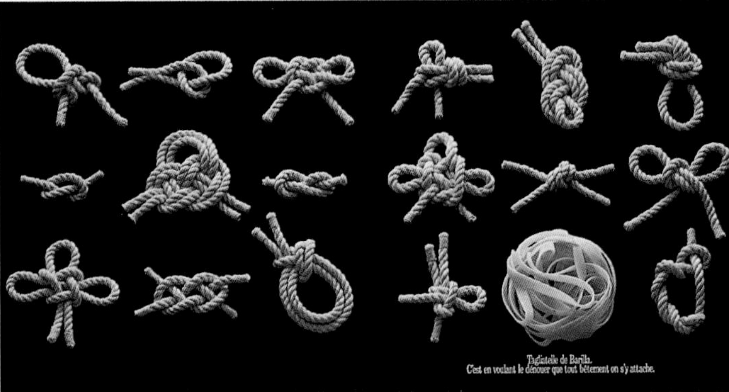

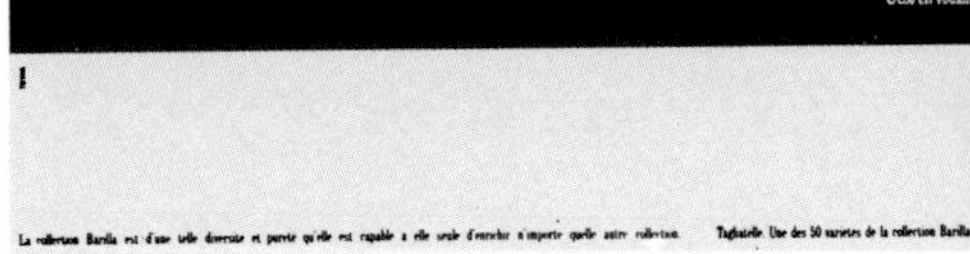

1190 Silver Award
Art Director: Jean-Claude Jouis
Agency: TBWA (Paris)

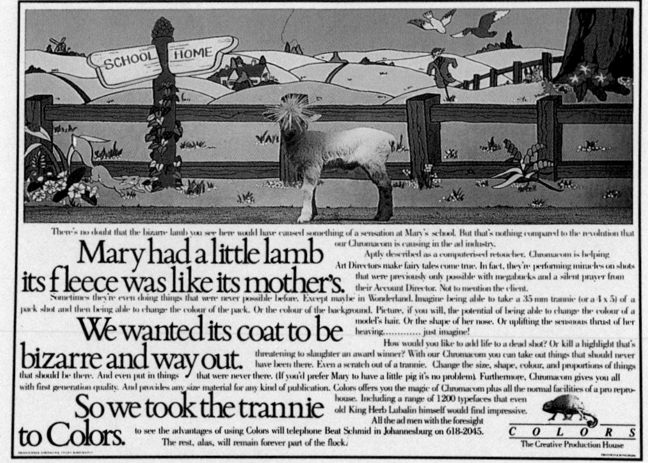

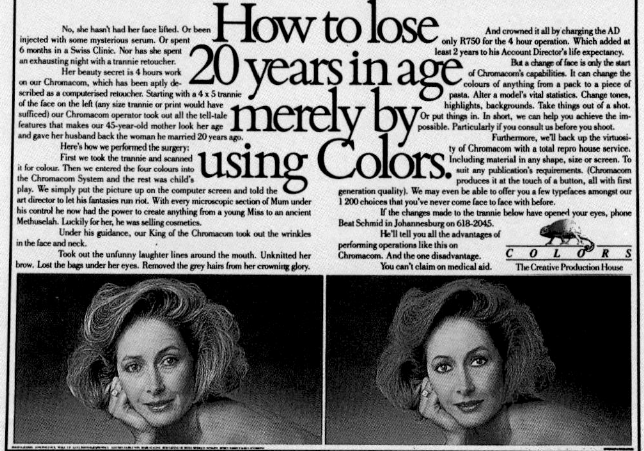

1191 Silver Award
Art Director: Mike Rossi
Designer: Mike Rossi
Photographer: Tom Pollock
Client: Colors

1192
Art Director: Koji Mizutani
Designer: Hirokazu Kurebayashi, Osamu Kitajima
Illustrator/Artist: Ishikura Hiroyuki
Client: Mistui Home Co., Ltd.

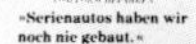

Was wir bauen, sind Einzelstücke in Serie. Wobei sich Individualität nicht darin erschöpft, Ihre Lieblingsfarbe aufzugreifen: Selten verlassen in einem Monat 2 Autos das Werk, die in Technik und Ausstattung gleich sind. Es wäre vielleicht profitabler, Gleichförmigkeit in großen Serien herzustellen. Doch für uns ist etwas anderes entscheidend: die Persönlichkeit des Fahrers. Beratung, Probefahrt sowie Leasing-Angebote: Bitte schicken Sie Ihre Visitenkarte an die Dr. Ing. h. c. F. Porsche AG, Marketingleitung, Postfach 1108, 7140 Ludwigsburg.

PORSCHE

»Erst das Vergnügen, dann die Arbeit,
dann das Vergnügen.«

Morgens im Porsche zur Arbeit, abends im Porsche wieder zurück – ein Wunschtraum, der vielleicht auch Ihrer ist. Es wird niemals der Wunschtraum eines jeden sein. Denn wie die Fahrt in einem Porsche nicht mit der Fahrt in einem Durchschnittsauto zu vergleichen ist, hat auch die Arbeit des Porschefahrers üblicherweise mit einem durchschnittlichen Achtstundentag nicht viel gemein. Woran er allerdings durchaus Vergnügen finden kann. Beratung, Probefahrt und Leasingangebote: Bitte schicken Sie Ihre Visitenkarte an die Verkaufsleitung Inland der Dr. Ing. h. c. F. Porsche AG, Postfach 1108, 7140 Ludwigsburg.

PORSCHE

»Früher oder später kommt man
dahinter, daß Leben auch
etwas mit Erlebnis zu tun hat.«

Porschefahren bedeutet für den einen Freiheit, für andere wiederum Freude an einem faszinierenden Fahrgefühl. Oder ganz einfach Erfüllung eines Wunschtraums. Dieses Erlebnis zu erhalten, ist eines der Ziele von Porsche. Selbst, wenn es sich im Alltag oft nur um eine Form von »Kurzurlaub« zwischen zwei Geschäftsterminen handelt, ist es für so manchen immerhin die Anschaffung eines Porsche wert.

PORSCHE

1193
Art Director: Günther Tibi
Designer: Günther Tibi
Photographer: Dietmar Henneka
Writer: Armin Schmidt, Jürgen Schippers
Client: Porsche
Agency: Wensauer & Partner
Director: Günther Tibi
Advertising Manager: Georg Ledert

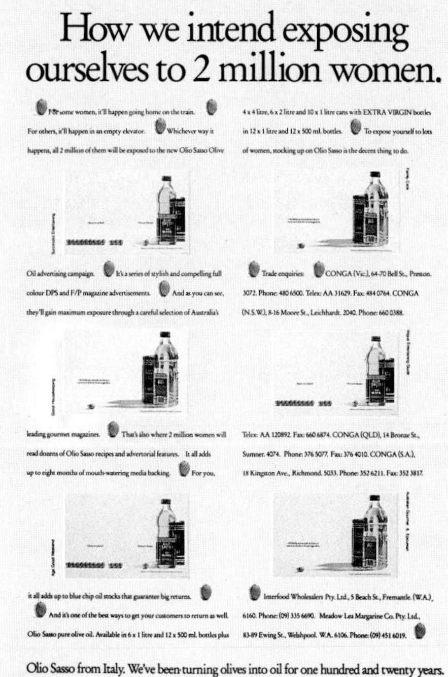

1194

Art Director: Yvonne Sumter, Andrew Hazewinkel
Photographer: Arthur Massey
Writer: Boris Damast, Nicholas Arter
Client: Conga International Foods
Agency: Saatchi & Saatchi Advertising
Publication: Australian Gourmet, Retail World

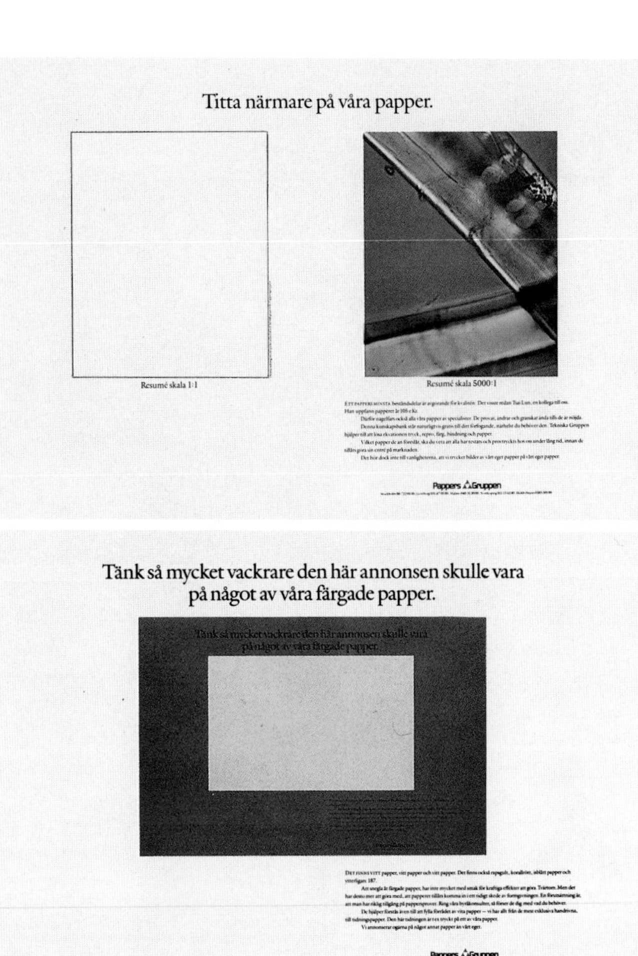

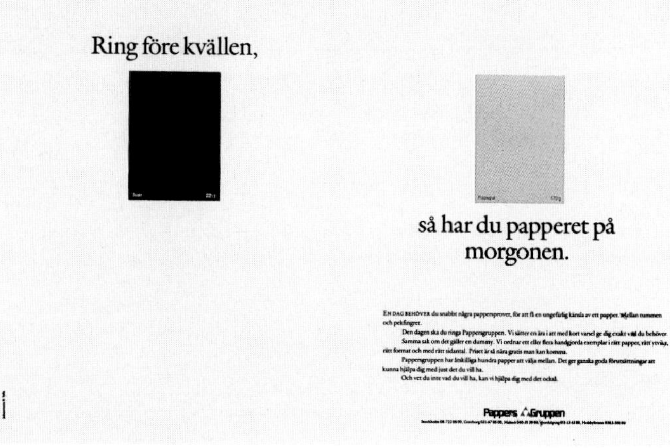

1195

Art Director: Bórje Stille
Writer: Ingemar Johannesson
Client: Pappers Gruppen
Agency: Johannesson & Stille

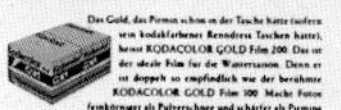
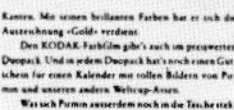
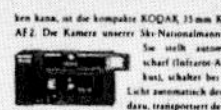
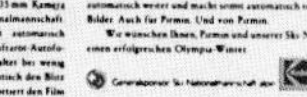

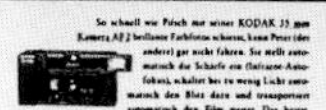

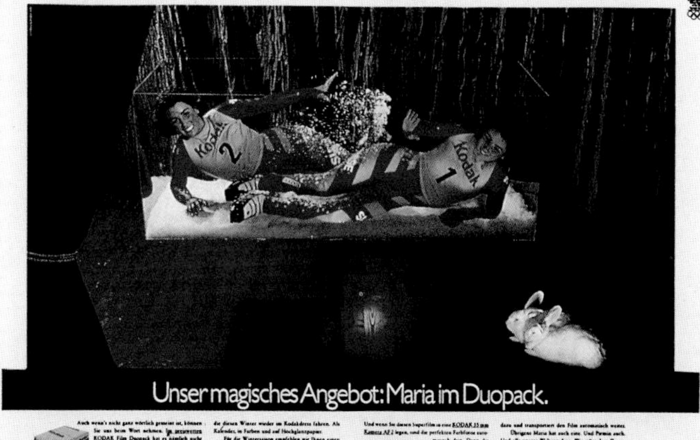

1196

Art Director: Roland Scotoni
Photographer: Michael Joseph
Writer: Hansjörg Zürcher
Client: Kodak S.A.
Agency: Young & Rubicam AG

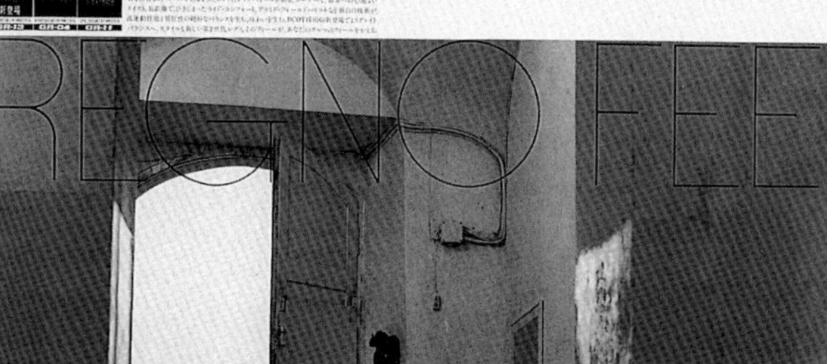

1197

Art Director: Jun-Ichi Morimoto
Designer: Jun-Ichi Morimoto, Hideaki Ozawa
Photographer: Shigeru Bando
Writer: Satoshi Suzuki
Client: Bridgestone Co., Ltd.
Agency: Hakuhodo Inc.
Publisher: Genko Co., Ltd.
Producer: Tomohiro Iizuka

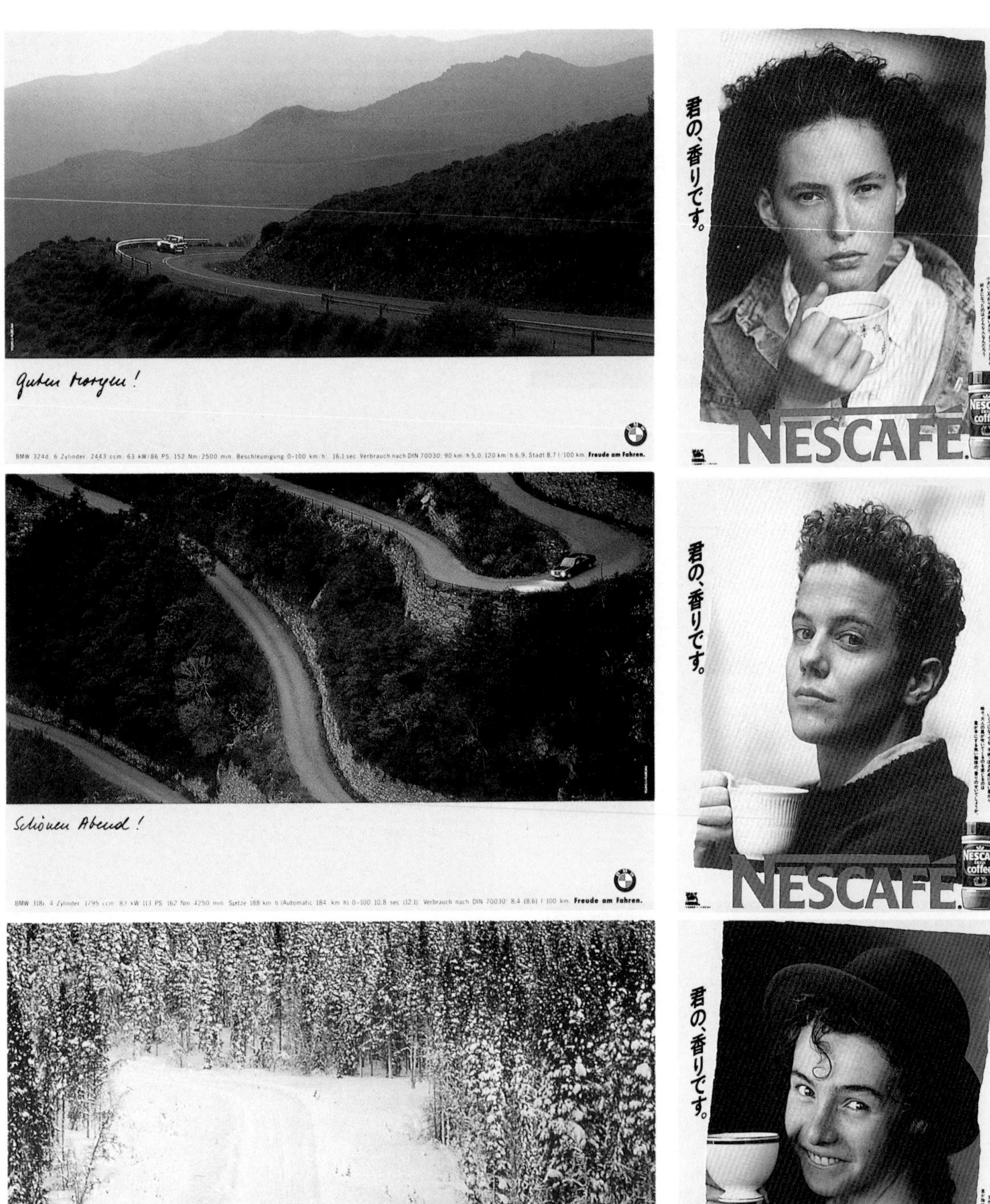

1198 Gold Award

Art Director: Charly Frei
Writer: Wilfried Vitz
Creative Director: Wilfried Vitz
Client: BMW Austria
Agency: Young & Rubicam GmbH
Producer: Herbert Angeli

1199

Art Director: Kazuya Mototani
Designer: Yoshiaki Abe, Shinji Hyuga
Photographer: Minsei Tominaga
Writer: Toshiya Mizoguchi
Client: Nestle Kabushiki Kaisha
Agency: McCann-Erickson Hakuhodo Inc.

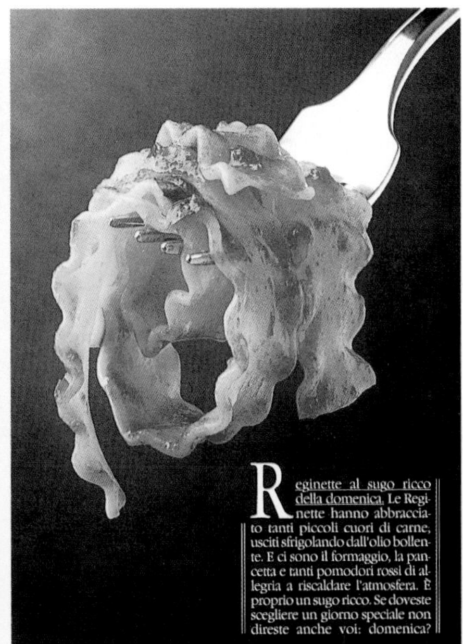

1200

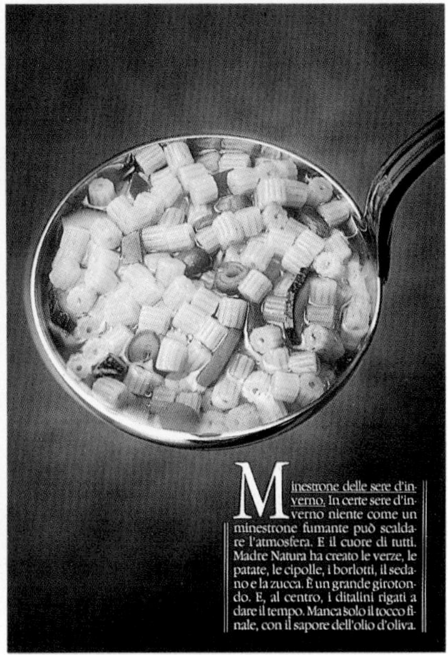

1201

1200
Art Director: Gavino Sanna, R. Fiamenghi
Photographer: Chris Broadbent
Writer: Andrea Concato
Creative Director: Gavino Sanna
Client: Barilla
Agency: Young & Rubicam (Italy) SPA

1201
Art Director: Gavino Sanna, R. Fiamenghi
Photographer: Chris Broadbent
Writer: Andrea Concato
Creative Director: Gavino Sanna
Client: Barilla
Agency: Young & Rubicam (Italy) SPA

1202

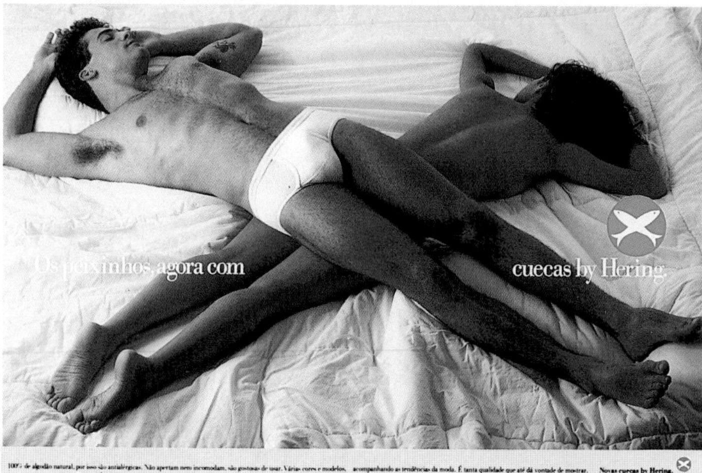

1203

1204

1205

1202

Art Director: Günther Tibi
Designer: Günther Tibi
Photographer: Dietmar Henneka
Writer: Armin Schmidt, Jürgen Schippers
Client: Porsche
Agency: Wensauer & Partner
Director: Günther Tibi
Advertising Manager: Georg Ledert

1203 Distinctive Merit

Art Director: José Zaragoza
Photographer: Moacyr Lugato, Carlos Pazetto, Jorge Monfort
Writer: Neil Ferreira
Client: Hering
Agency: DPZ Propaganda
Producer: Anelito De Nóbrega

1204

Art Director: Daisuke Nakatsuka
Designer: Masato Isobe, Sonomi Sato
Photographer: Shozo Nakamura
Writer: Daisuke Nakatsuka
Client: Shu Uemura Cosmetics Inc.

1205

Art Director: Daisuke Nakatsuka
Designer: Masato Isobe, Sonomi Sato
Photographer: Bishin Jumonji
Writer: Masako Ikumi
Client: Shu Uemura Cosmetics Inc.

1206

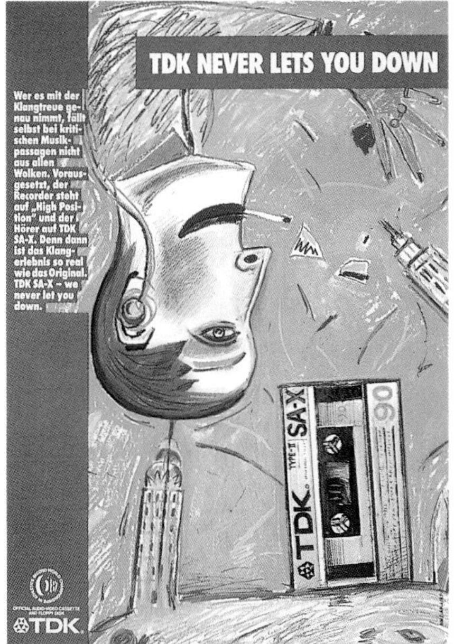

1207

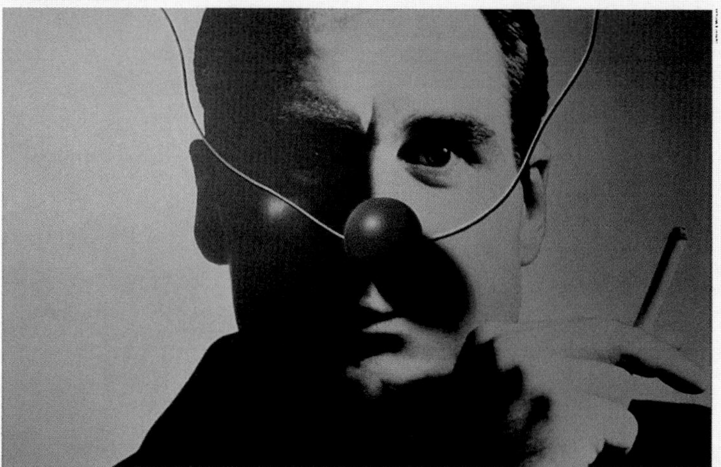

1208

1209

1206
Art Director: João Simone
Photographer: Manolo Moran
Writer: Claudio Deckes
Client: Cristais Hering
Agency: DPZ Propaganda
Producer: Anelito De Nóbrega

1207
Art Director: K. P. Kolberg
Illustrator/Artist: W. Erlbruch
Writer: M. Kellersmann
Client: TDK Electronics Europe
Agency: Baums, Mang & Zimmermann
Publication: Stern

1208
Art Director: Klaus Erwarth
Designer: Jürgen Mick
Photographer: Heinz Schmölzer
Writer: Michael Freund
Client: Trend-Verlag
Agency: Demner & Merlicek

1209
Art Director: Peter Davenport
Designer: Peter Davenport, Russell Bell
Photographer: Brian Griffin
Illustrator/Artist: Ron Sandford
Writer: Les Hutton
Client: London Regeneration Consortium PLC
Publisher: London Regeneration Consortium PLC

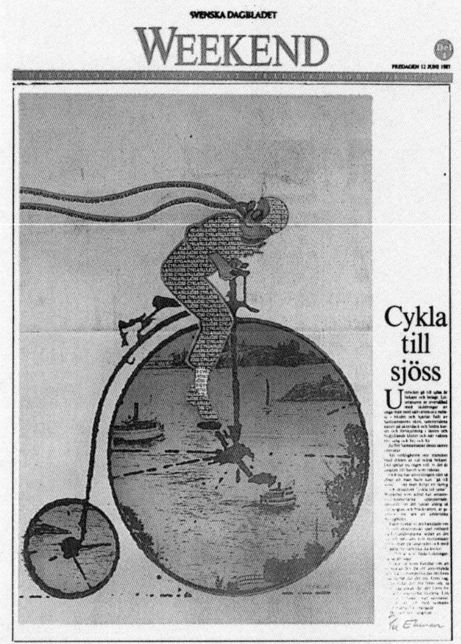

1210

DER

Teuer! Feuer! Blut! Gut! Das Phantom schreit es in die Nacht. Schon bricht ein Brand aus, wachsen Mißgeburten, entstehen Zwietracht und Aufruhr. Zeter und Mordio. Feurio. Holdrio. Owy, owy, klagt Reineke de Vos, als litte er unter Tarzans Jahrhundertgebrüll. Schweigen ist Gold. Welch falscher Schluß. Schrei, wenn Du kannst, Frau, Mann. Zu schreien wie am Spieß, wie der Teufel oder der Zahnbrecher und das zur rechten Zeit, schafft Luft. Explosion ist allemal besser als Implosion. Das dümmste Vieh schreit am lautesten. Und die am lautesten schreien, haben den kleinsten Mut.

SCHREI

1211

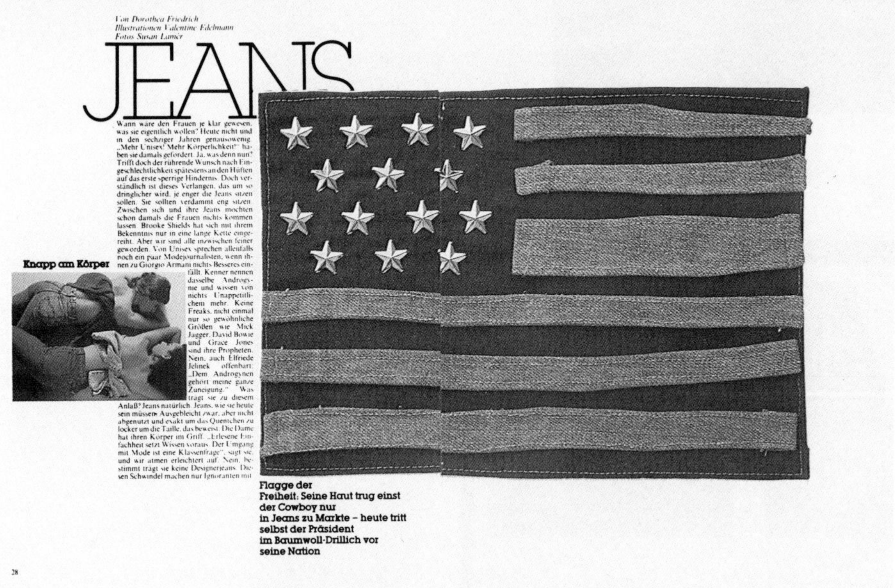

Von Dorothea Friedrich
Illustrationen Valentine Edelmann
Fotos Susan Lamèr

JEANS

Wann wäre den Frauen je klar gewesen, was sie eigentlich wollen? Heute nicht und in den sechziger Jahren genausowenig. „Mehr Unisex! Mehr Körperlichkeit!" haben sie damals gefordert. Ja, was denn nun? Trifft doch der rührende Wunsch nach Eingeschlechtlichkeit spätestens an den Hüften auf das erste sperrige Hindernis. Doch verständlich ist dieses Verlangen, das um so dringlicher wird, je enger die Jeans sitzen sollen. Sie sollten verdammt eng sitzen. Zwischen sich und ihre Jeans mochten schon damals die Frauen nichts kommen lassen. Brooke Shields hat sich mit ihrem Bekenntnis nur in eine lange Kette eingereiht. Aber wir sind alle inzwischen feiner geworden. Von Unisex sprechen allenfalls noch ein paar Modejournalisten, wenn ihnen zu Giorgio Armani nichts Besseres einfällt. Kenner nennen dasselbe Androgynie und wissen von nichts Unappetitlichem mehr. Keine Freaks, nicht einmal nur so gewöhnliche Größen wie Mick Jagger, David Bowie und Grace Jones sind ihre Propheten. Nein, auch Elfriede Jelinek offenbart: „Dem Androgynen gehört meine ganze Zuneigung." Was trägt sie zu diesem Anlaß? Jeans natürlich. Jeans, wie sie heute sein müssen: Ausgebleicht zwar, aber nicht abgenutzt und exakt um das Quentchen zu locker um die Taille, das beweist: Die Dame hat ihren Körper im Griff. „Erlesene Einfachheit setzt Wissen voraus. Der Umgang mit Mode ist eine Klassenfrage", sagt sie, und wir atmen erleichtert auf. Nein, bestimmt trägt sie keine Designerjeans. Diesen Schwindel machen nur Ignoranten mit

Knapp am Körper

Flagge der Freiheit: Seine Haut trug einst der Cowboy nur in Jeans zu Markte – heute tritt selbst der Präsident im Baumwoll-Drillich vor seine Nation

1212

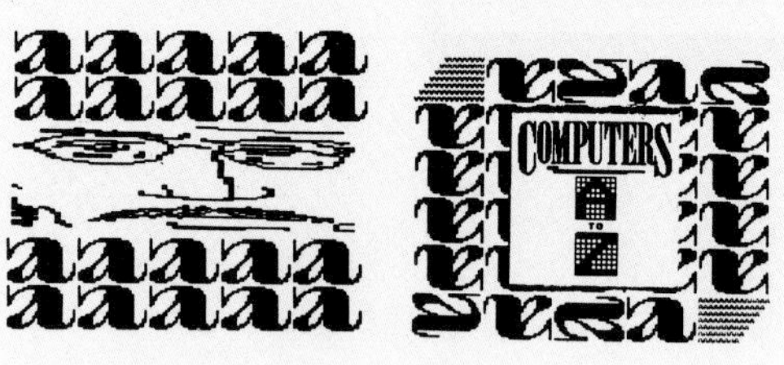

1213

1210
Art Director: Per Ekman
Illustrator/Artist: Katerina Mistal

1211 Gold Award
Art Director: Hans-Georg Pospischil
Designer: Bernadette Gotthardt, Peter Breul
Writer: Ingrid Heinrich-Jost
Publisher: Dr. Bruno Dechamps

1212 Distinctive Merit
Art Director: Hans-Georg Pospischil
Designer: Bernadette Gotthardt, Peter Breul
Photographer: Susan Lamèr
Illustrator/Artist: Valentine Edelmann
Writer: Dorothea Friedrich
Publisher: Dr. Bruno Dechamps

1213
Art Director: Oswaldo Miranda (Miran)
Client: Arte'D
Publisher: Módulo'3
Producer: Copiare Imp.

1214

1215

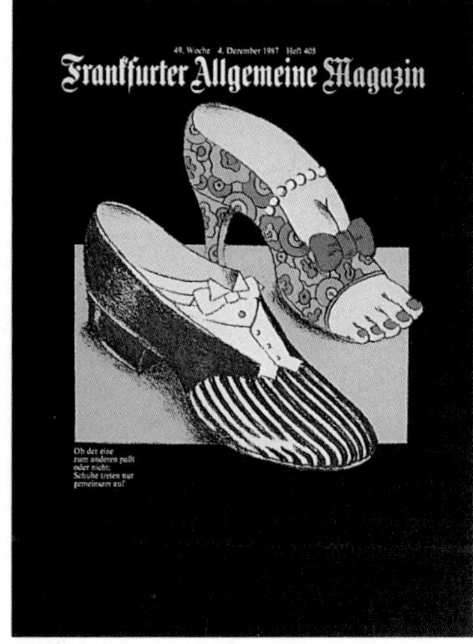

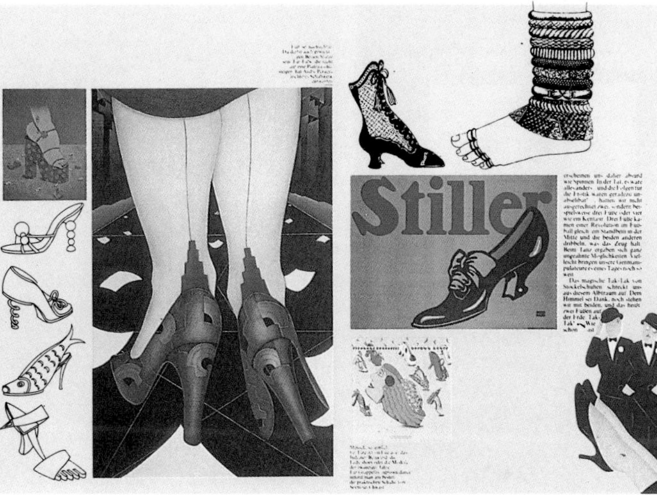

1216

1214
Art Director: Hans-Georg Pospischil
Designer: Bernadette Gotthardt, Peter Breul
Illustrator/Artist: Brad Holland
Writer: Michael Freitag
Publisher: Dr. Bruno Dechamps

1215
Art Director: Hans-Georg Pospischil
Designer: Seymour Chwast
Illustrator/Artist: Seymour Chwast
Agency: The Pushpin Group

1216
Art Director: Hans-Georg Pospischil
Designer: Seymour Chwast
Agency: The Pushpin Group
Publication: Frankfurter Allgemeine

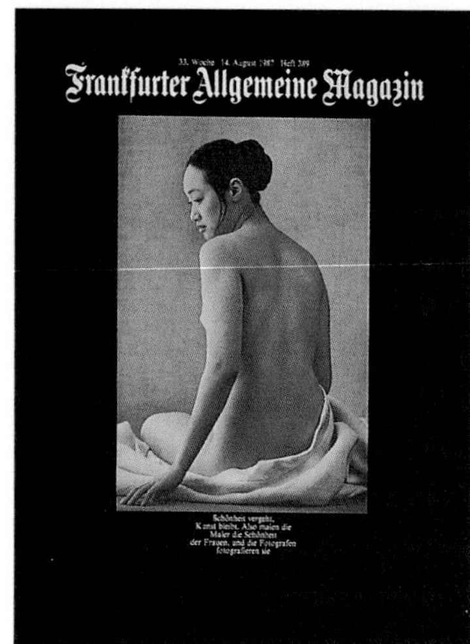

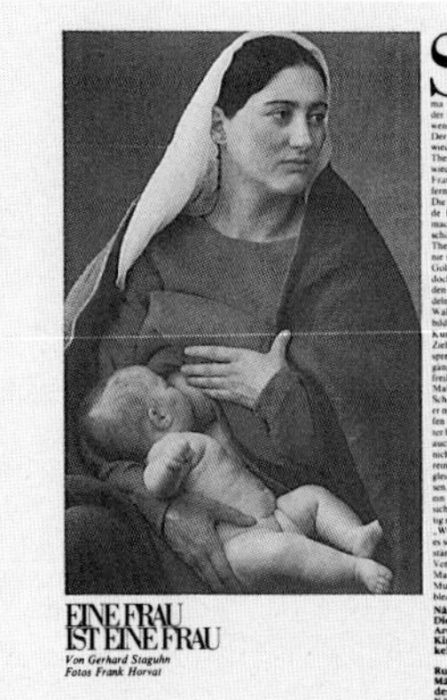

1217

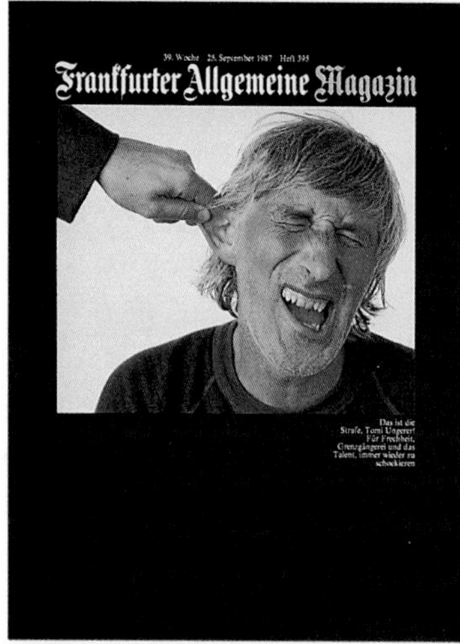

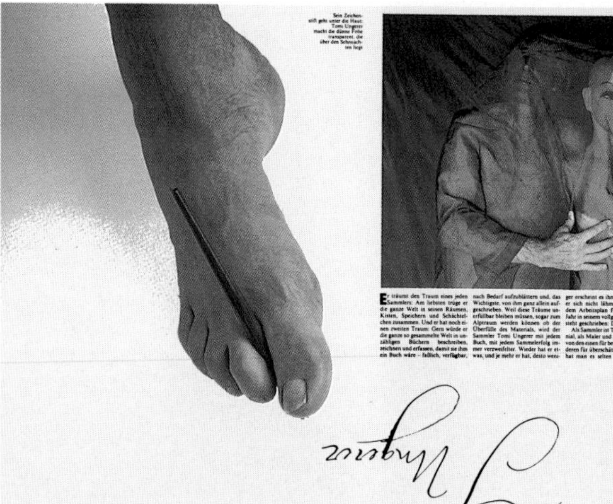

1218

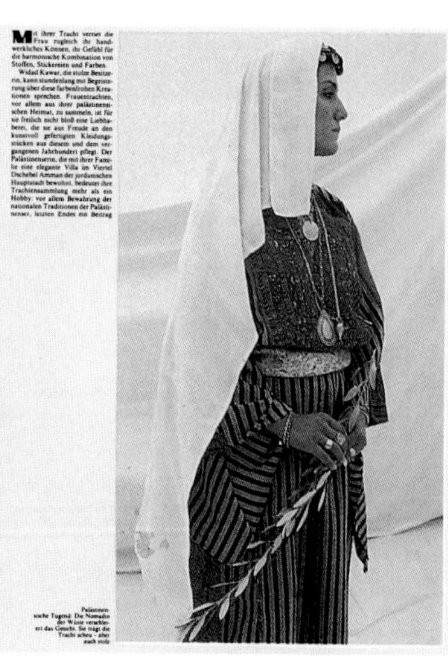

1219

1217
Art Director: Hans-Georg Pospischil
Designer: Bernadette Gotthardt, Peter Breul
Photographer: Frank Horvat
Writer: Gerhard Staguhn
Publisher: Dr. Bruno Dechamps

1218
Art Director: Hans-Georg Pospischil
Designer: Bernadette Gotthardt, Peter Breul
Photographer: Serge Cohen
Writer: Michael Freitag
Publisher: Dr. Bruno Dechamps

1219
Art Director: Hans-Georg Pospischil
Designer: Bernadette Gotthardt, Peter Breul
Photographer: Susan Lamèr
Writer: Wolfgang Köhler
Publisher: Dr. Bruno Dechamps

1220

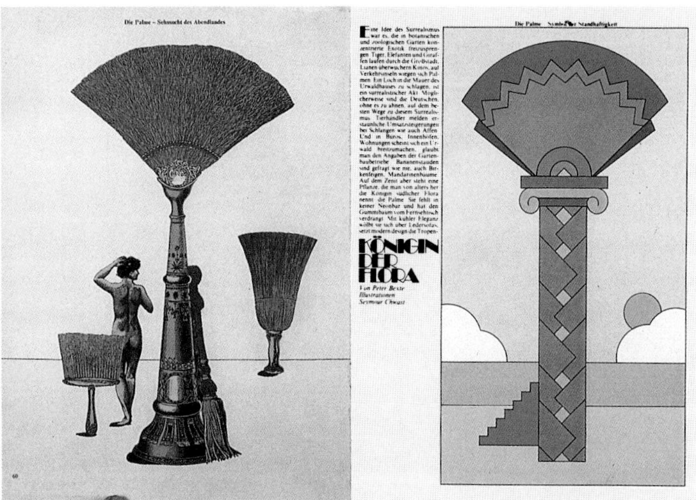

1221

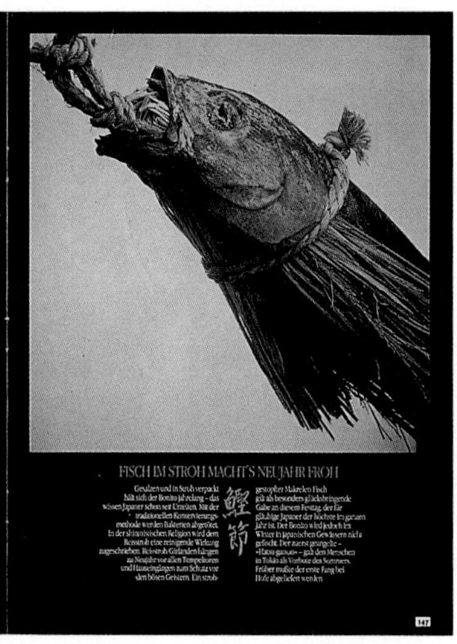

1222

1220

Art Director: Hans-Georg Pospischil
Illustrator/Artist: Seymour Chwast
Writer: Josef Oehrlein
Editor: Thomas Schroder
Client: Frankfurter Allgemeine
Publisher: Dr. Bruno Dechamps
Publication: Frankfurter Allgemeine

1221 Distinctive Merit

Art Director: Hans-Georg Pospischil
Illustrator/Artist: Seymour Chwast
Writer: Peter Bexte
Editor: Thomas Schroder
Client: Frankfurter Allgemeine
Publisher: Dr. Bruno Dechamps
Publication: Frankfurter Allgemeine

1222

Art Director: Thomas Höpker
Designer: Norbert Kleiner
Photographer: Reinhard Wolf
Editor: Gerhard Schnitzer
Creative Director: Gruner & Jahr

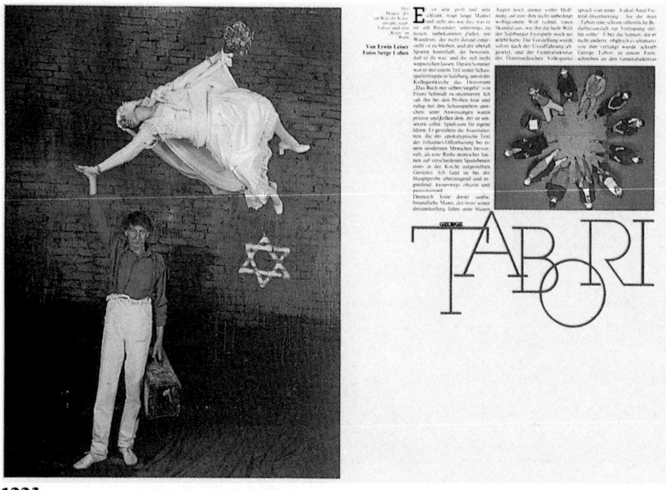

1223

1224

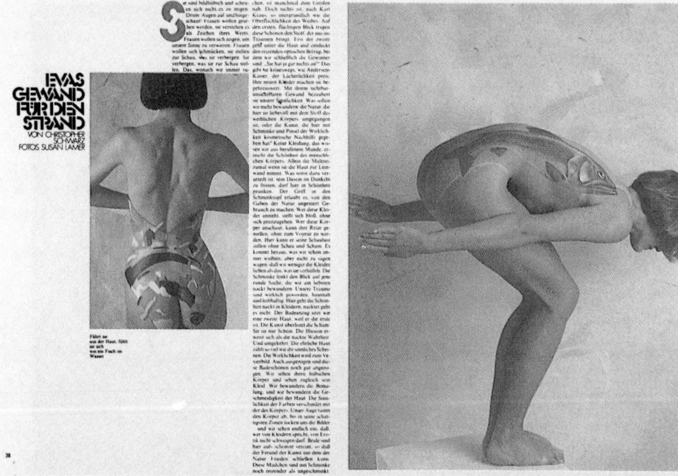

1225

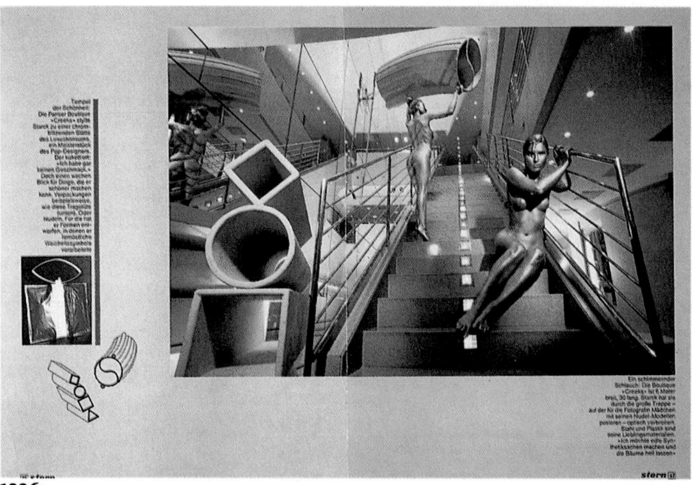

1226

1223
Art Director: Hans-Georg Pospischil
Designer: Bernadette Gotthardt, Peter Breul
Photographer: Serge Cohen
Writer: Erwin Leiser
Publisher: Dr. Bruno Dechamps

1224
Art Director: Hans-Georg Pospischil
Designer: Bernadette Gotthardt, Peter Breul
Illustrator/Artist: Heinz Edelmann
Writer: Jochen Missfeld
Publisher: Dr. Bruno Dechamps

1225 Silver Award
Art Director: Hans-Georg Pospischil
Designer: Bernadette Gotthardt, Peter Breul
Photographer: Susan Lamèr
Writer: Christopher Schwarz
Publisher: Dr. Bruno Dechamps

1226
Art Director: Wolfgang Behnken
Designer: Max Lengwenus
Photographer: Angelika Wald
Editor: Niklas Frank
Creative Director: Gruner & Jahr

LET'S GO

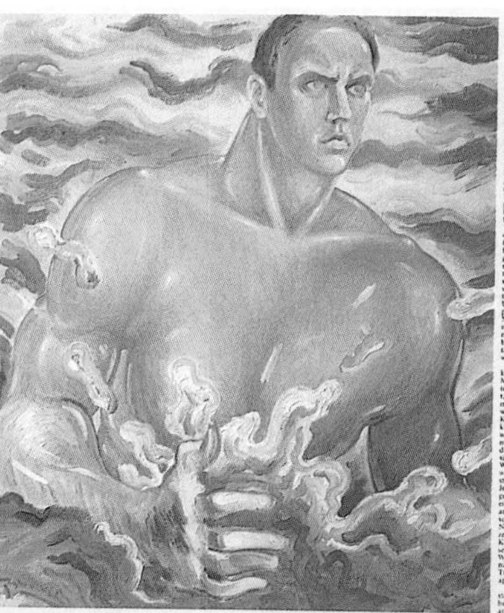

ÜBER DEN DREIFACHEN ATHLETEN

Von Evi Simeoni
Illustrationen Christoph Blumrich

1227

DOMPTEUR DER EITLEN LEUTE

Die Reichen und die Schönen, die Prominenten und die Exzentriker bei Helmut Newton werden sie alle schwach und folgen willig seiner Fotoregie. Für den STERN hat er seine Aufnahmen der Beautiful People kommentiert, die jetzt in einem Bildband erscheinen und gleichzeitig auf einer grossen Fotoschau in Bonn gezeigt werden

stern

1228

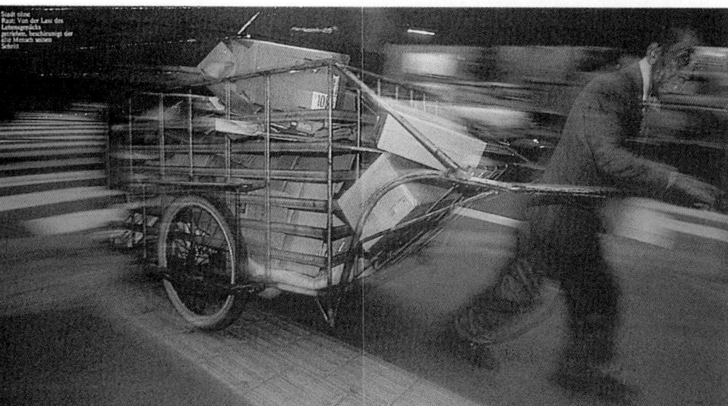

TOKIO

1229

RAUHER ENGEL DER PRÄRIE: DER WESTERNHELD

Von Frank Höselbarth
Illustrationen Heinz Edelmann

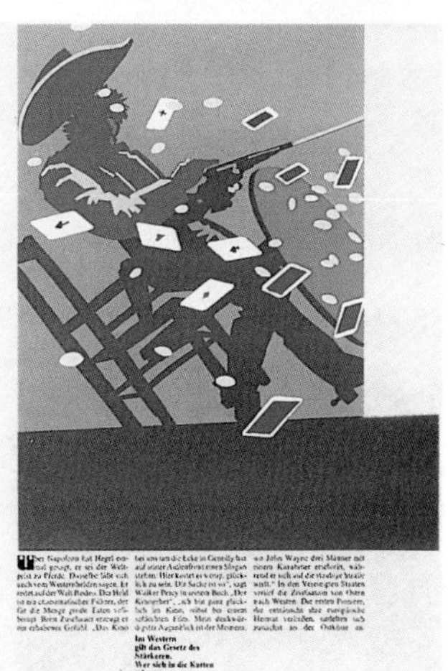

1230

1227

Art Director: Hans-Georg Pospischil
Designer: Bernadette Gotthardt, Peter Breul
Illustrator/Artist: Christoph Blumrich
Writer: Evi Simeoni
Publisher: Dr. Bruno Dechamps

1228

Art Director: Thomas Höpker
Designer: Norbert Kleiner
Photographer: Helmut Newton
Writer: Siegfried Schober
Publisher: Gruner & Jahr

1229

Art Director: Hans-Georg Pospischil
Designer: Bernadette Gotthardt, Peter Breul
Photographer: Wilfried Bauer
Writer: Irmtraud Schaarschmidt-Richter
Publisher: Dr. Bruno Dechamps

1230

Art Director: Hans-Georg Pospischil
Designer: Bernadette Gotthardt, Peter Breul
Illustrator/Artist: Heinz Edelmann
Writer: Frank Höselbarth
Publisher: Dr. Bruno Dechamps

1231

1232

1233

1234

1231
Art Director: Thomas Höpker,
Designer: Norbert Kleiner
Photographer: Christian Von Alvensleben
Publisher: Gruner & Jahr

1232
Art Director: Thomas Höpker
Designer: Peter Hinze
Photographer: Volker Hinz
Writer: Evelyn Holst
Publisher: Gruner & Jahr

1233
Art Director: Rolf Gillhausen, Franz Epping
Designer: Elke Roh Peter
Photographer: VISUM

1234
Art Director: Rolf Gillhausen, Franz Epping
Designer: Andrea Hinrichs
Photographer: Gerd Ludwig

1235

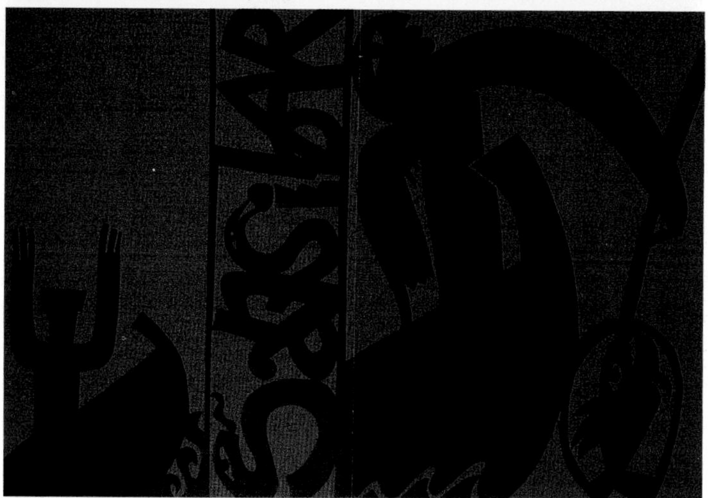
1236

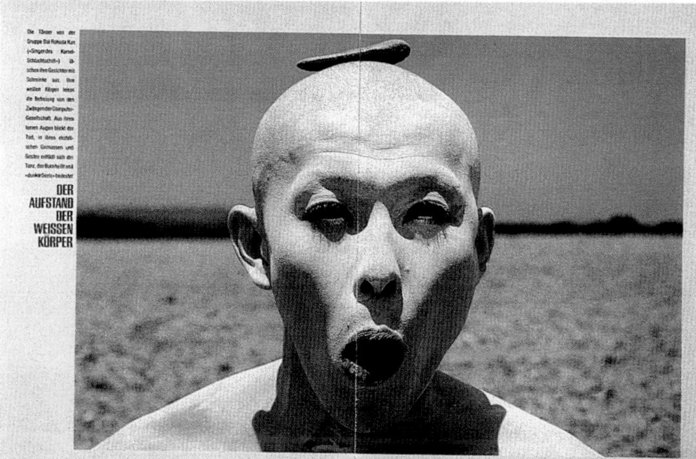

1237

1238

1235
Art Director: Thomas Höpker
Designer: Detlef Schlottmann
Photographer: Dieter Blum
Writer: Dr. Peter Sandmeyer
Client: Stern
Publisher: Gruner & Jahr
Director: Heiner Bremer, Michael Jürgs, Klaus Liedtke

1236
Art Director: Hans-Georg Pospischil
Designer: Bernadette Gotthardt, Peter Breul
Illustrator/Artist: Alfons Holtgreve
Writer: Günter Krabbe
Publisher: Dr. Bruno Dechamps

1237
Art Director: Thomas Höpker
Designer: Norbert Kleiner
Photographer: Tom Jacobi
Writer: Matthias Matussek
Publisher: Gruner & Jahr

1238
Art Director: Thomas Höpker
Designer: Norbert Kleiner
Writer: Mario R. Dederichs
Publisher: Gruner & Jahr

1239
Art Director: Sepp Höss, Bibi Henschel
Photographer: Wolfgang Hohndorf
Writer: Jürgen Werner
Editor: Claus Tiedge
Client: Professional Camera
Publisher: Moderner Verlag (Munich)

1240
Art Director: Michael Barton
Designer: Keiko Hon
Photographer: Patience Arakawa
Editor: Tom Chapman
Client: Japan Air Lines
Publisher: Tohru Moriya

1241
Art Director: Wolfgang Behnken
Designer: Dietmar Schulze
Photographer: Gerhard Vormwald

1242
Art Director: Bulnes & Robaglia
Illustrator/Artist: TATOO, Pierre Hovnanian
Client: S.N.G.

1243
Art Director: Gavino Sanna
Photographer: Chris Broadbent
Writer: Giampaolo Melideo
Creative Director: Gavino Sanna
Client: Barilla
Agency: Young & Rubicam (Italy) SPA

BETTGEFLÜSTER

1239

JOURNAL
Computer
Wenn Maier an den Rechner gehen
Wie die neuen Personal Computer zusammenarbeiten
Die Deutschen haben aufgeholt. Gute Programme stammen längst nicht mehr nur aus den USA
Junge Virtuosen beweisen, wie unsicher Rechenzentren sind
stern

1240

1241

1242

1243

1245

1244

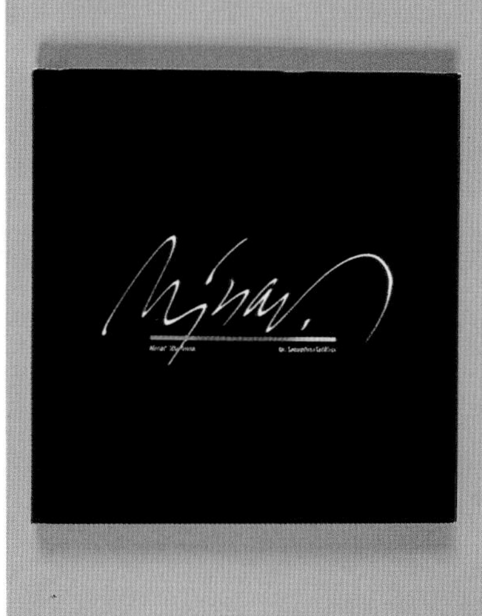

1246

1247

1248

1244
Art Director: David Holmes
Illustrator/Artist: David Holmes
Writer: Duncan Sinclair
Client: Singapore Tourist Promotion Board
Agency: Batey Ads Pte., Ltd.

1245
Art Director: Peter Davenport, Brian Griffin
Designer: Peter Davenport
Photographer: Brian Griffin
Illustrator/Artist: Ron Sandford
Writer: Les Hutton
Client: Rosehaugh Stanhope Developments PLC
Publisher: Rosehaugh Stanhope Developments PLC

1246
Art Director: Oswaldo Miranda (Miran)
Editor: Suzana Munhoz Da Rocha
Publisher: Módulo'3
Producer: Águia Impressora

1247
Art Director: Masatoshi Toda
Designer: Masanori Mizushima
Photographer: Snowdon
Writer: Antonia Williams
Client: Issey Miyake International Inc.
Director: Miyake Design Studio

1248
Art Director: Gavino Sanna
Photographer: Mario Zappalà
Creative Director: Gavino Sanna
Client: Castelli
Agency: Young & Rubicam (Italy) SPA

1249
Art Director: Makoto Saito
Designer: Makoto Saito, Soko Hosonome
Photographer: Tsutomu Wakatsuki
Editor: Fumihiro Nonomura
Client: Michiko (London)
Director: Yasushi Akimoto
Producer: Osami Nakajima, Yasushi Akimoto

1250
Art Director: Randolph Nolte
Designer: Christine Mortag
Client: Nolte European Design Inc.
Agency: Randolph Nolte Creative Consultants

1251
Art Director: Koji Mizutani
Designer: Hirokazu Krebayashi, Kiyokastu Kato, Osamu Kitajima
Illustrator/Artist: Hirokazu Krebayashi, Kiyokastu Kato
Client: African Garden
Agency: African Garden Co.

1252
Art Director: Kijuro Yahagi
Designer: Kijuro Yahagi
Client: Meguro Museum of Art (Tokyo)

1253
Art Director: Jan Lepair
Designer: Jan Lepair
Illustrator/Artist: Norman MacDonald
Writer: Eric Timmer
Client: Drukkerij Slinger
Director: Jan Ulder, M. Ulder

1249

1252

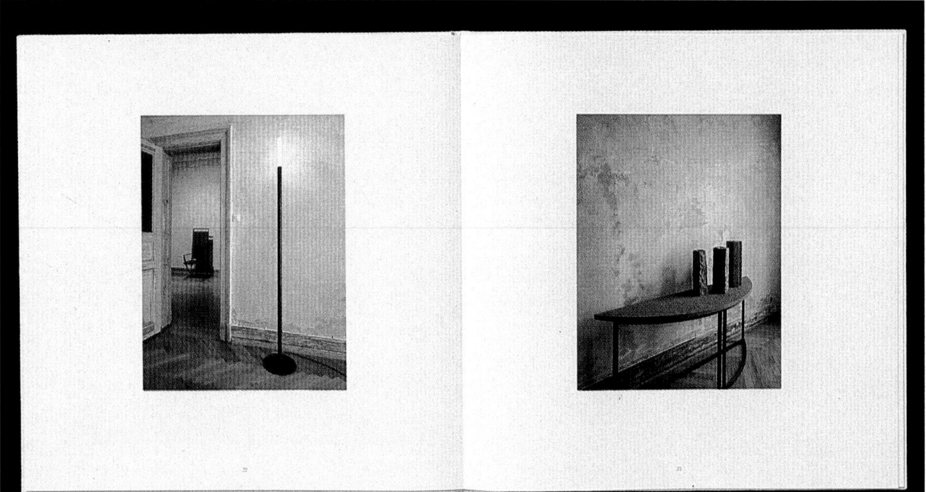
1250

1251

1253

1254

1255

1254
Art Director: Aziz Cami
Designer: Stephen Gibbons
Client: Chris Flood
Agency: Still, Price, Court, Twivy & D'Souza

1255
Art Director: Toshio Yamagata
Designer: Toshio Yamagata
Photographer: Francis Giacobetti, Yukio Shimizu
Writer: Naoko Serikawa
Creative Director: Hiroshi Tanaka
Client: IPSA Co., Ltd.

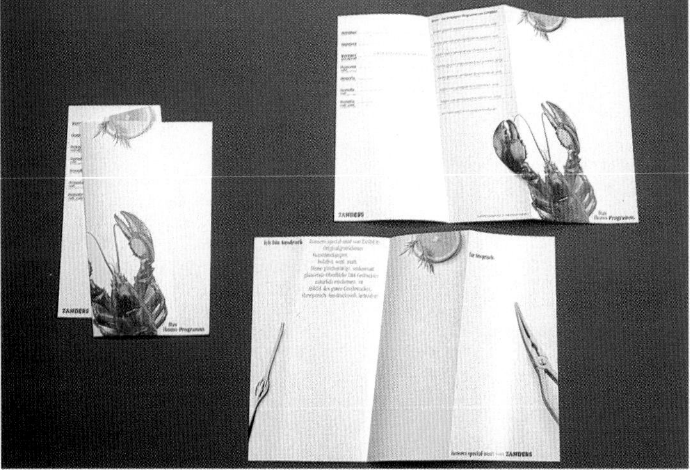

1256

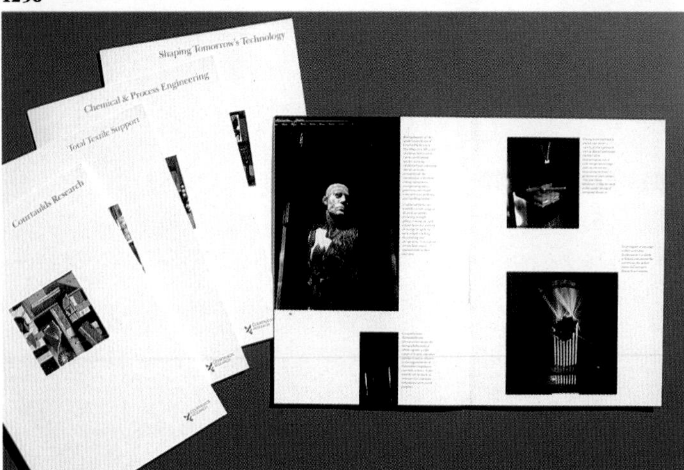

1257

1258

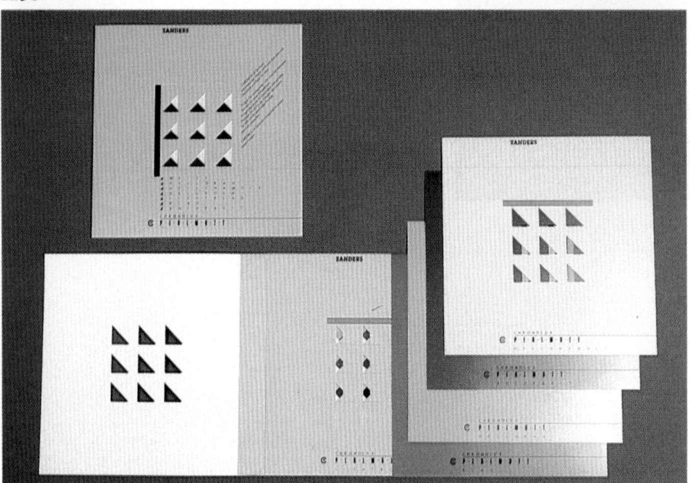

1259

1256
Art Director: Uwe Loesch
Designer: Uwe Loesch
Photographer: Siegbert Kercher
Writer: Uwe Loesch, Friedwald Schüttler
Client: Zanders Feinpapiere AG
Director: Wolfgang Heuwinkel
Producer: Richard Peters
Advertising Manager: F. Schüttler

1257
Art Director: John Lloyd
Designer: David O'Higgins
Photographer: Vic Paris
Illustrator/Artist: David O'Higgins
Client: Courtaulds Research
Agency: Lloyd Northover Ltd.

1258
Art Director: Aziz Cami
Designer: Shaun Dew
Photographer: Brian Griffin
Agency: The Partners

1259
Art Director: Prof. U. Namislow
Designer: Prof. U. Namislow
Client: Zanders Feinpapiere AG
Publisher: Zanders Feinpapiere AG
Director: Wolfgang Heuwinkel
Producer: Wolfgang Witte

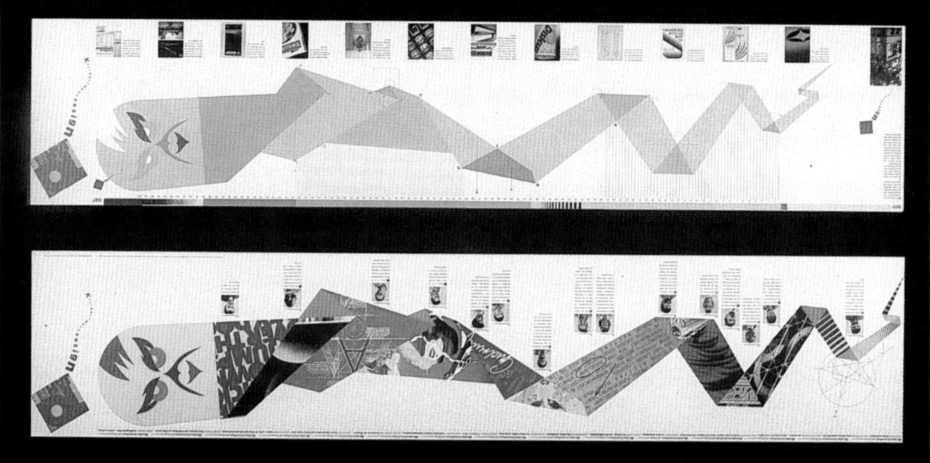

1262

1260

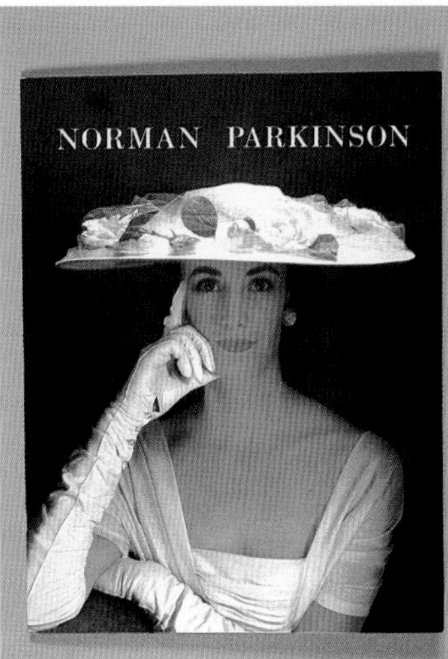

1263

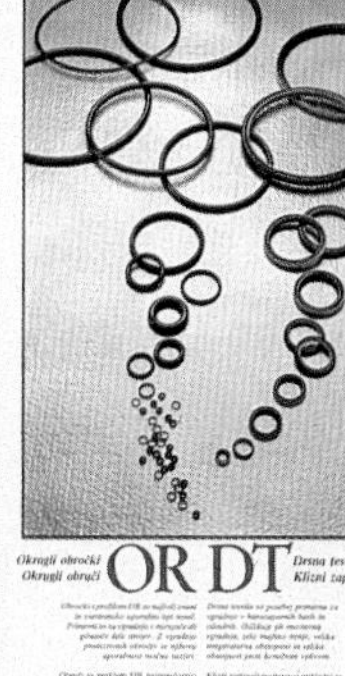

1264

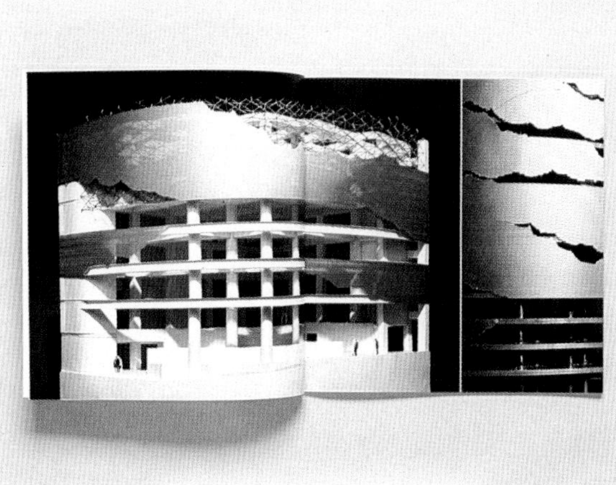

1261

1265

1260

Art Director: Mario Terzic
Designer: Mario Terzic
Illustrator/Artist: Mario Terzic
Writer: Dr. Franz Endler
Client: Österreichische Bundesmuseen
Chief Officer, Austrian Museums: Dr. Johann Marte

1261

Art Director: Osamu Furumura
Designer: Kenichi Yoshida
Photographer: Toshio Arai, Katsuaki Forudate, Tetsu Nakagawa
Writer: Edward Suzuki
Editor: Osamu Furumura
Client: Edward Suzuki Associates Inc.
Agency: Edward Suzuki Associates Inc.

1262

Art Director: Wolfgang Heffe, Roland Mehler
Photographer: Werner Walther
Writer: Knut Hartmann, Roland Mehler
Client: Knut Hartmann Design
Producer: H. & H. Schaufler GmbH, Mainzer Verlagsanstalt und Druckerei, Team 80 GmbH

1263

Art Director: Keith Murgatroyd
Designer: Tracey Radnall
Photographer: Norman Parkinson
Client: Hamilton's Galleries
Agency: RMDA
Producer: Royle Print

1264

Art Director: Edi Berk
Designer: Edi Berk
Photographer: Dragan Arrigler
Writer: Zvone Vreg, Zdenka Lampič
Client: Teng
Agency: Studio Krog
Director: Zvone Vreg
Printer: Učne delavnice

1265

Art Director: Masami Shimizu
Designer: Masami Shimizu
Photographer: Yoshihiko Ueda
Writer: Momoko Takeuchi
Client: Seiyu Co., Ltd.

1266

1268

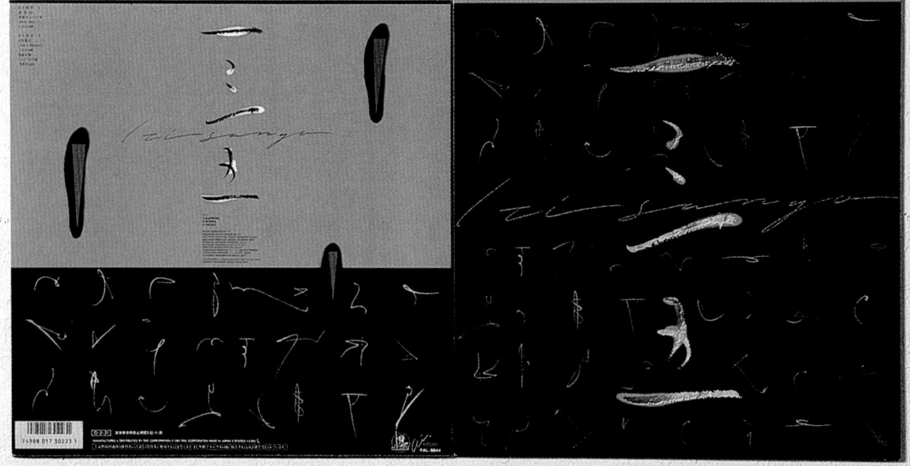
1269

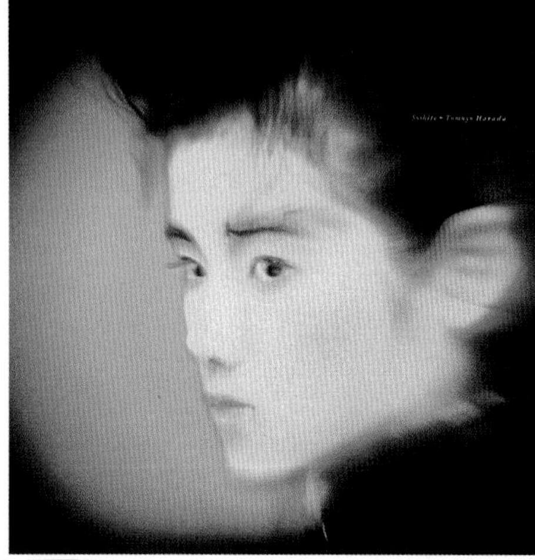
1267

1270

1266
Art Director: Kotaro Hirano
Designer: Kotaro Hirano
Photographer: Tamotsu Fujii
Client: Kitty Music Corp., Inc.

1267
Art Director: Akio Nimbari
Designer: Tomoaki Sakai
Photographer: Sachiko Kuru
Client: CBS/Sony Inc.

1268
Art Director: Yasutaka Kato
Designer: Yasutaka Kato
Photographer: Shigeru Bando
Client: Epic/Sony Inc.

1269
Art Director: Masayuki Yano
Designer: Masayuki Yano
Illustrator/Artist: Koichi Sato

1270
Art Director: Kazutami Nishimoto
Photographer: Harald Sund
Client: Canyon Records

1272

1273

1274

1271

1275

1271 Distinctive Merit
Art Director: Marcello Minale, Brian Tattersfield
Designer: Ian Grindle
Client: San Pellegrino (Italy)
Agency: Bozell, Jacobs, Kenyon & Eckhardt (Italy)

1272 Gold Award
Art Director: Simon Ingleton
Designer: Margaret Nolan
Illustrator/Artist: Andrew Gibb
Client: Asda Stores
Agency: Lloyd Northover Ltd.

1273
Art Director: Keizo Matsui
Designer: Keizo Matsui
Client: Hiroko Koshino International Corp.

1274
Art Director: Hiromi Inayoshi
Designer: Gaku Ohta
Client: Nihon Information Center Co., Ltd.
Agency: Inayoshi Design Inc.
Director: Miha Takagi
Producer: Miha Takagi

1275 Distinctive Merit
Art Director: Ian Grindle
Designer: David Turner, Lucy Walker
Client: Irish Distillers

1276
Art Director: Franz Merlicek
Designer: Franz Merlicek, Stephan Auer
Photographer: Bernhard Angerer
Illustrator/Artist: Bruce Meek
Writer: Dr. Angelo Peer
Client: Evidenzbüro Zuckerfabriken (Vienna)
Agency: Demner & Merlicek

1277
Art Director: Yasuo Tanaka
Designer: Yasuo Tanaka
Writer: Masashi Tatana
Client: Shohgetsu-do Confectionery Co., Ltd.
Agency: Sanuki Printing Co., Ltd.

1278
Art Director: Ken Cato
Designer: Ken Cato, Daryl Turner
Illustrator/Artist: Anita Xhaffer
Client: Cascade Brewery
Agency: Cato Design Inc., Pty., Ltd.

1279
Art Director: Mervyn Kurlansky
Designer: Mervyn Kurlansky, Kenneth Grange, Nancy Koc, Lars Baecklund, Adam White
Client: Shiseido Ltd.

1280
Art Director: Piero Ventura
Designer: Marco J. Ventura
Illustrator/Artist: Marco J. Ventura
Client: Casa Tolomei
Agency: Immagine Design

1276

1279

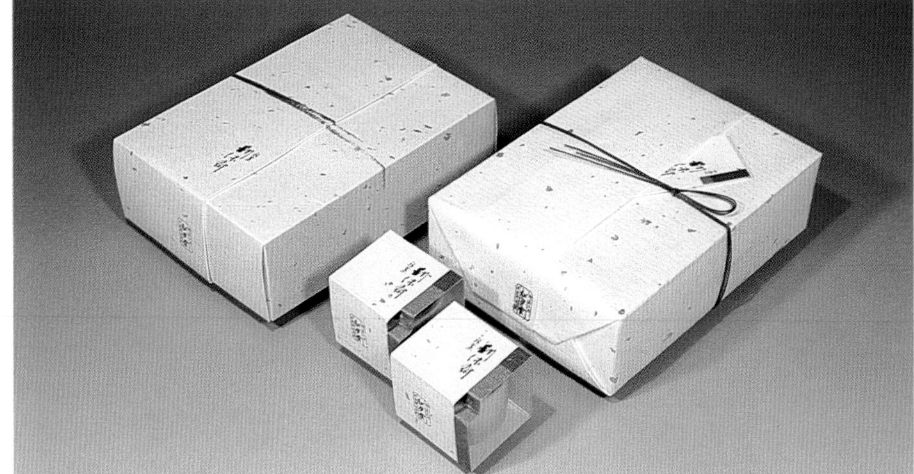

1277

1278

1280

1282

1283

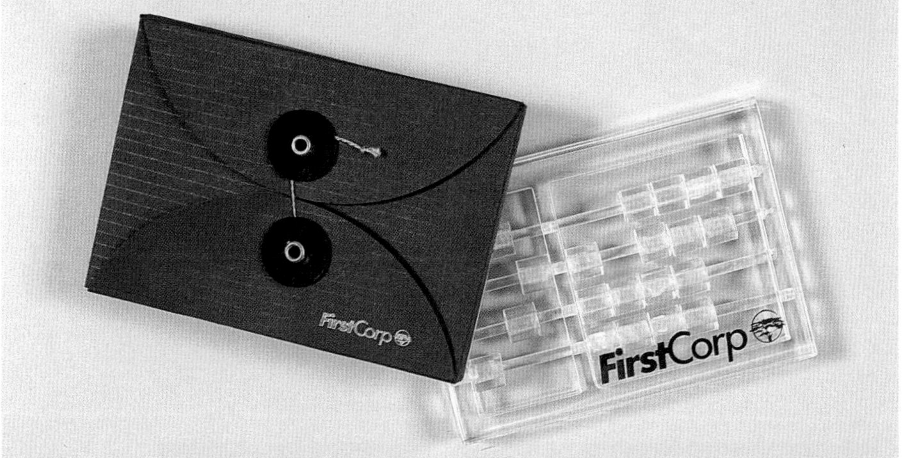

1284

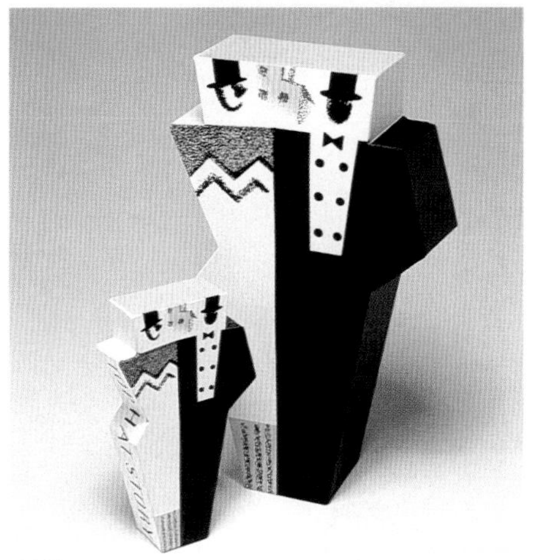

1281

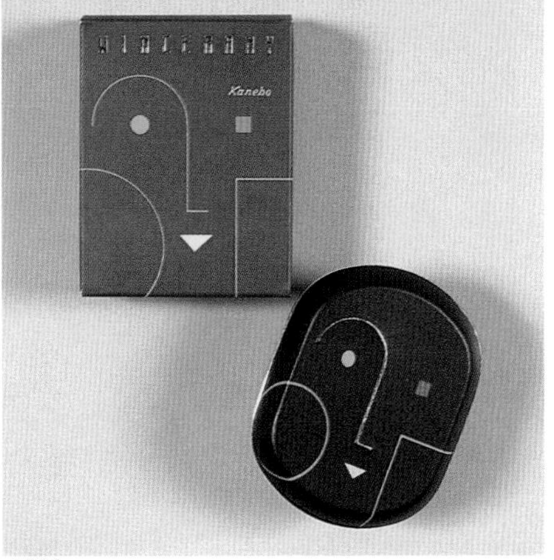

1285

1281
Art Director: Katsu Kimura
Designer: Natsumi Akabane
Illustrator/Artist: Eda Takahashi
Client: Zonart & Co., Ltd.

1282
Art Director: Norico Hirai
Designer: Mitsunori Morita
Illustrator/Artist: Masaya Ito
Client: Uogashi Meicha Ltd.
Agency: Core Produce Ltd.

1283
Art Director: Carsten Jørgensen
Designer: Karin Betschart
Photographer: Carsten Jørgensen
Illustrator/Artist: Carsten Jørgensen
Client: Bodum (Switzerland) AG
Agency: Pi-Design
Director: Jørgen Bodum

1284
Art Director: Kees Schilperoort
Designer: Yvonne Brummer
Client: First Corp. National Merchant Bank
Agency: Pentagraph Pty., Ltd.

1285 Silver Award
Art Director: Shigeru Akizuki
Designer: Shigeru Akizuki, Mayumi Iwakiri
Illustrator/Artist: Shigeru Akizuki
Client: Kanebo Cosmetics Co.

1286
Art Director: Toru Ando
Designer: Toshimi Kunihara
Illustrator/Artist: Sara Midda
Client: Mitsukoshi

1287
Art Director: Toru Ando
Designer: Masanori Kobayashi
Illustrator/Artist: Sara Midda
Client: Mitsukoshi

1288
Art Director: Yasuo Tanaka
Designer: Yasuo Tanaka
Client: Matsushiro Paper Bag Industry Co., Ltd.

1289
Art Director: Norico Hirai
Designer: Mitsunori Morita
Illustrator/Artist: Masaya Ito
Client: Uogashi Meicha Ltd.
Agency: Core Produce Ltd.
Box Construction: Suehito Ando

1290
Art Director: Heinz Mennecken
Illustrator/Artist: Ari Plikart
Client: Grundig AG
Agency: Heye & Partner

1286

1287

1288

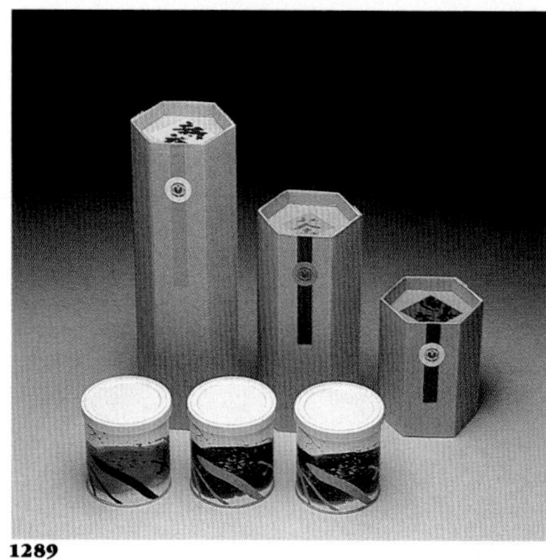
1289

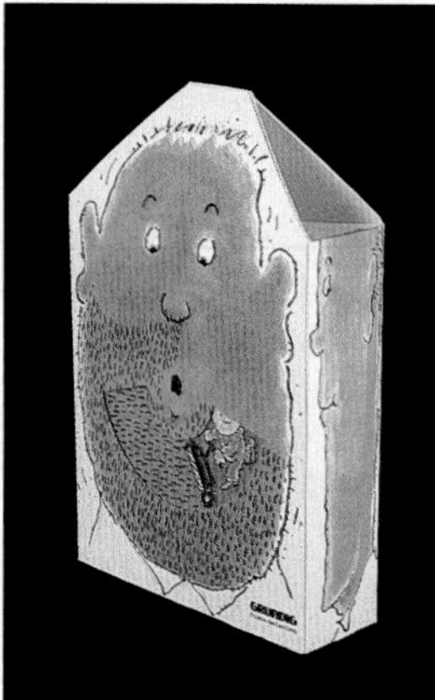
1290

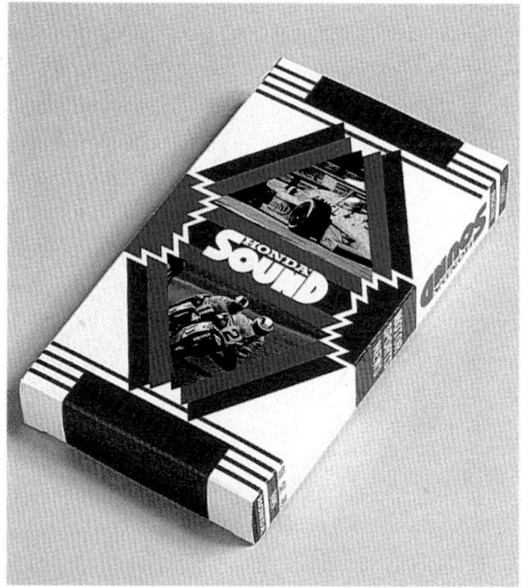

1291

1292

1293

1294

1295

1291
Art Director: Yoshikazu Ogawara
Designer: Yoshikazu Ogawara
Client: Honda Motor Co., Ltd.

1292
Art Director: Hisamoto Naito
Designer: Yoshinari Morimoto
Illustrator/Artist: Seitaro Kuroda
Client: Rokko Oriental Hotel
Agency: Dentsu Inc. (Osaka)

1293
Art Director: Koko Nabatame
Designer: Nabatame Design Office
Client: Nakamuraya Co., Ltd.
Agency: Marui Advertising Co., Ltd.
Calligrapher: Chiyoko Kamura

1294
Art Director: Toru Ando
Designer: Minako Asano
Illustrator/Artist: Sara Midda
Client: Mitsukoshi

1295
Art Director: Kenji Maezawa
Designer: Kenji Maezawa

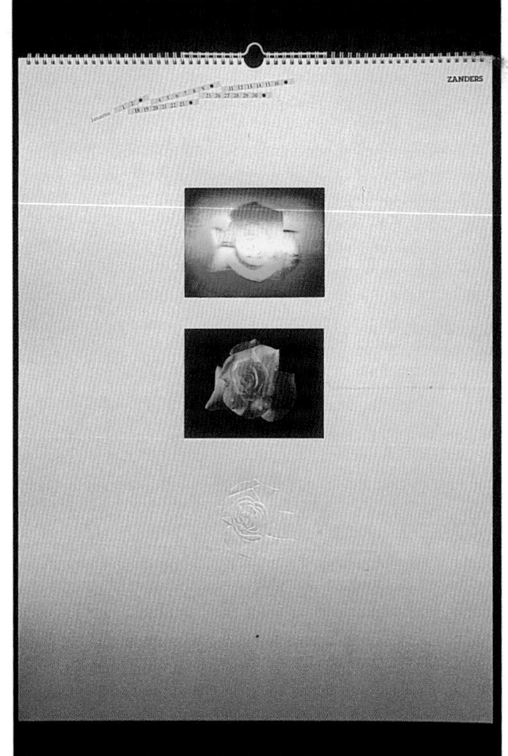

1296

1299

1297

1300

1298

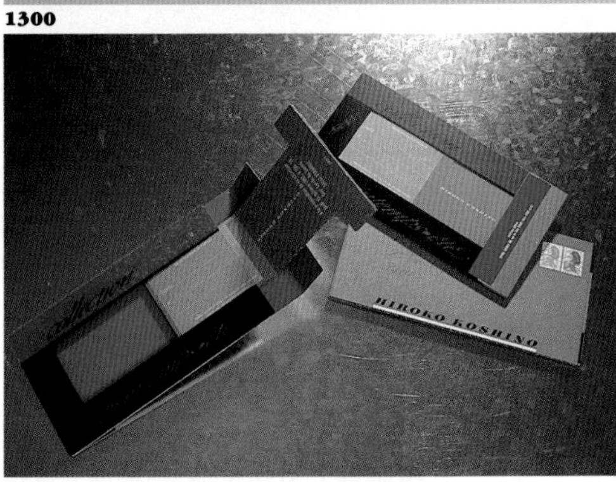

1301

1296 Gold Award
Art Director: Bo Bonfils, Wolfgang Heuwinkel
Designer: Bo Bonfils, Wolfgang Heuwinkel
Illustrator/Artist: Bo Bonfils
Writer: Hermann Pfeiffer
Client: Zanders Feinpapiere AG
Publisher: Zanders Feinpapiere AG
Director: Wolfgang Heuwinkel
Producer: Wolfgang Witte

1297
Art Director: Keizo Matsui
Designer: Keizo Matsui, Eiji Shimizu

1298
Art Director: Masatoshi Toda
Designer: Taku Nakamura
Photographer: Judith Turner
Client: D'Urban

1299 Silver Award
Art Director: John McConnell
Designer: John McConnell, Martin Tilley
Client: Face Photosetting

1300
Art Director: Keizo Matsui
Designer: Keizo Matsui, Eiji Shimizu
Client: Hiroko Koshino International Corp.

1301
Art Director: Keizo Matsui
Designer: Keizo Matsui
Client: Hiroko Koshino International Corp.

1302

1303

1304

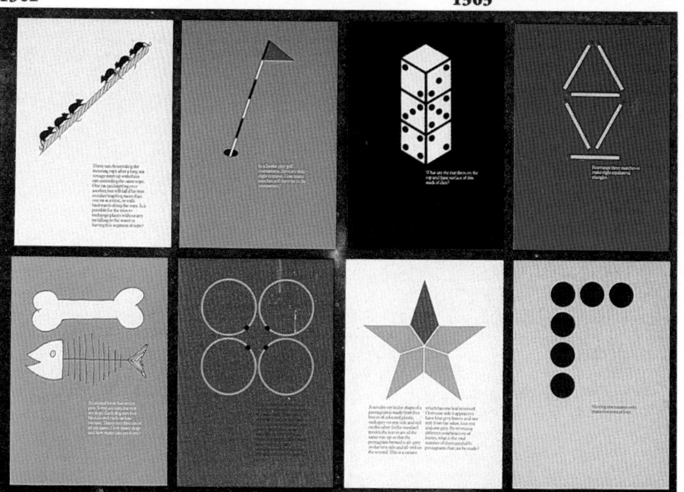

1305

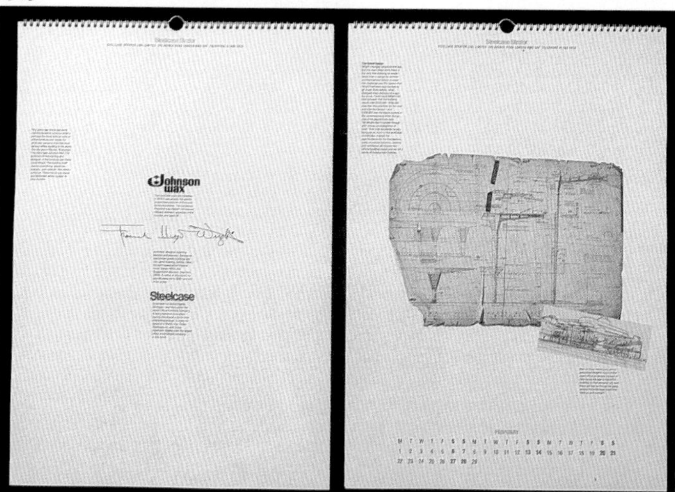

1306

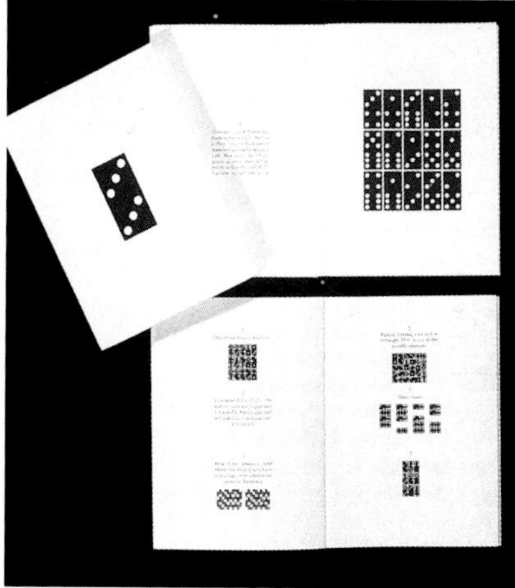

1307

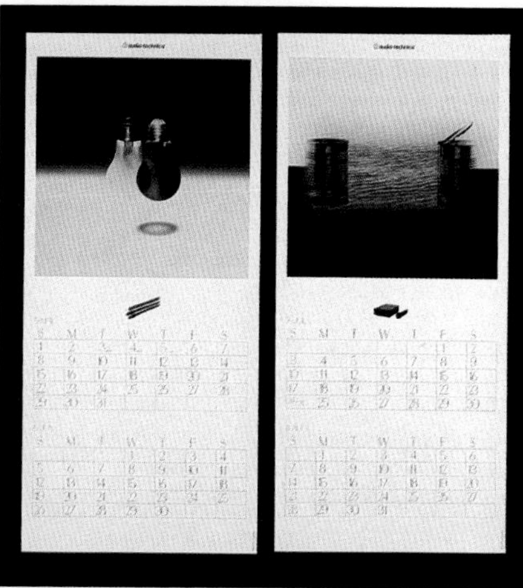

1308

1302
Art Director: Osamu Furuta
Designer: Osamu Furuta
Client: Berkeley Co., Ltd.
Producer: Takako Kudo

1303
Art Director: Daisuke Nakatsuka
Designer: Masato Isobe
Photographer: François Gillet
Writer: Daisuke Nakatsuka, Hiroshi Kuboyama
Client: Dai-Ichi Mutual Life Insurance Co.
Producer: Nobuhiko Koyanagi

1304
Art Director: Hiromi Inayoshi
Designer: Hiromi Inayoshi
Illustrator/Artist: Yasuhiko Taniguchi
Client: Seiwa Corp.
Agency: Inayoshi Design Inc.
Director: Miha Takagi
Producer: Miha Takagi

1305
Art Director: David Hillman
Designer: David Hillman, Amanda Bennett
Client: Oun International

1306
Art Director: Malcolm Swatridge
Designer: James Beveridge
Illustrator/Artist: Maurice Smelt
Client: Honor Thacker

1307
Art Director: David Hillman
Designer: David Hillman, Amanda Bennett
Client: Pentagram Design

1308
Art Director: Susumu Endo
Designer: Susumu Endo
Photographer: Susumu Endo
Client: Audio-Technica Corp.

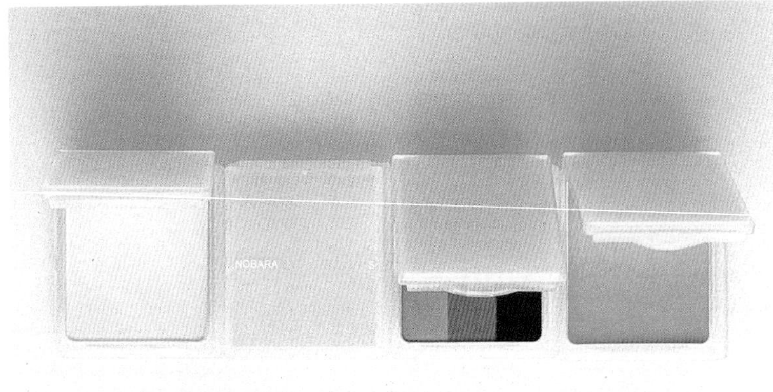

1309

1312

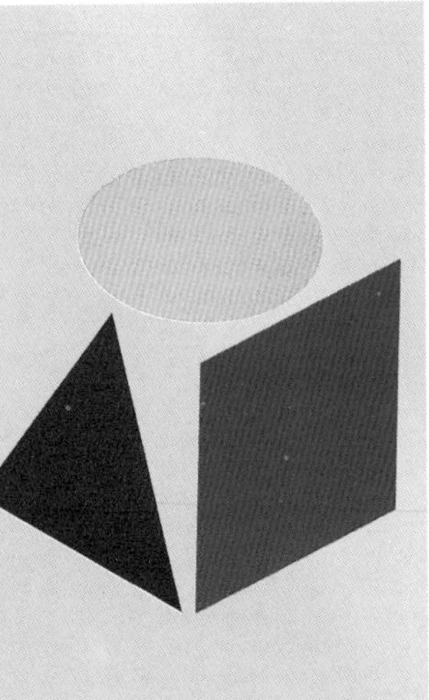

1310

1313

1311

1314

1309
Art Director: Daisuke Nakatsuka
Designer: Sonomi Sato
Creative Director: Shu Uemura
Client: Shu Uemura Cosmetics Inc.

1310
Art Director: Per Arnoldi

1311
Art Director: Hiromi Inayoshi
Designer: Hiromi Inayoshi
Client: Nihon Information Center Co., Ltd.
Agency: Inayoshi Design Inc.
Director: Miha Takagi
Producer: Miha Takagi

1312
Art Director: Minoru Niijima
Designer: Minoru Niijima, Chiaki Aiba
Client: Dan & Aoshima Associates

1313
Art Director: Soko Hosonome
Designer: Soko Hosonome
Photographer: Bin-Shun
Writer: Hideo Kobayashi
Client: Shincho Co., Ltd.

1314
Art Director: Pierre Mendell
Designer: Pierre Mendell
Illustrator/Artist: Heinz Hiltbrunner
Client: International Design Zentrum
Agency: Mendell & Oberer

1315

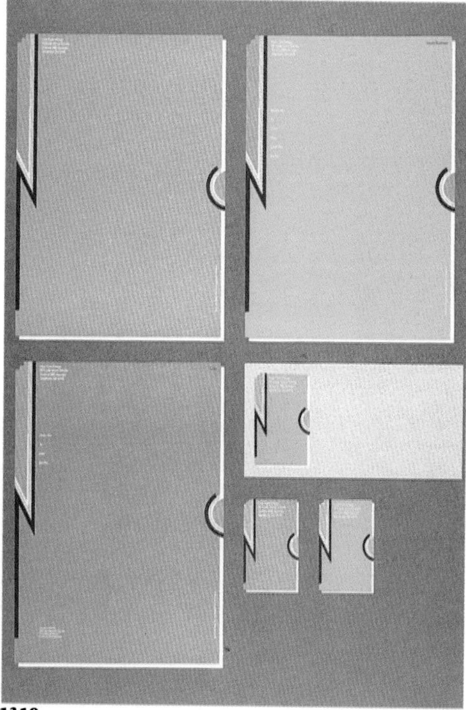

1318

1316

1319

1317

1320

1315
Art Director: Jan Lepair
Designer: Ingrid Van Schoonhoven
Client: Traffic Amsterdam BV
Agency: Jan Lepair Inc.
Director: Jan Ulder
Producer: Ben Van Schoonhoven
Printer: Drukkerij Slinger

1316
Art Director: Douglas Doolittle
Photographer: Mizukoshi Yoshimasa
Client: Mikuni

1317
Art Director: Mervyn Kurlansky
Designer: Mervyn Kurlansky, Robert Dunnet
Client: Museum of Modern Art (Oxford)

1318
Art Director: Ned Culic

1319 Silver Award
Art Director: Mervyn Kurlansky
Designer: Mervyn Kurlansky, Claire Johnson
Client: Eureka! The Children's Museum Ltd.

1320
Art Director: John McConnell
Designer: John McConnell, Leigh Brownsword
Client: London International Festival of Theatre

1321
Art Director: Edi Berk
Designer: Edi Berk
Illustrator/Artist: Zvone Kosovelj
Editor: Studio Krog
Client: Studio Krog
Agency: Studio Krog
Publisher: Studio Krog
Printer: Paralele (Ljubljana)

1322
Art Director: Hiromi Inayoshi
Designer: Hiromi Inayoshi
Illustrator/Artist: Jean-Michel Folon
Client: Inayoshi Design Inc.
Director: Miha Takagi
Producer: Miha Takagi

1323
Art Director: Garth Bell
Designer: Garth Bell
Client: George J. Berg

1324
Art Director: John Harrison, Andrew Zulver, Bill Kirkland

1321

1322

1323

1324

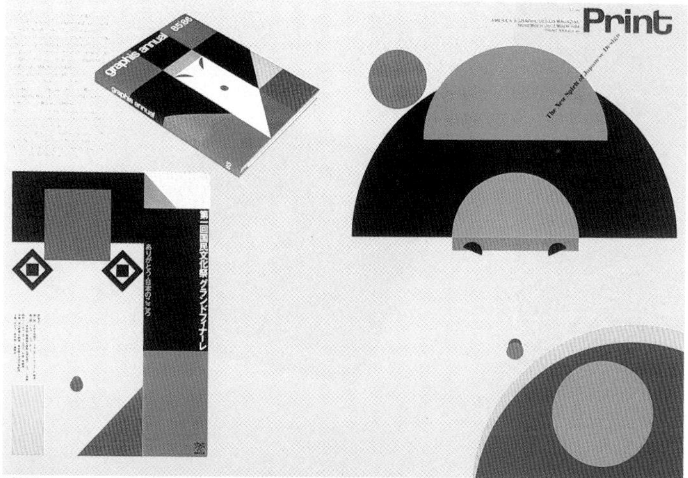

1325

1326

1327

1329

1328

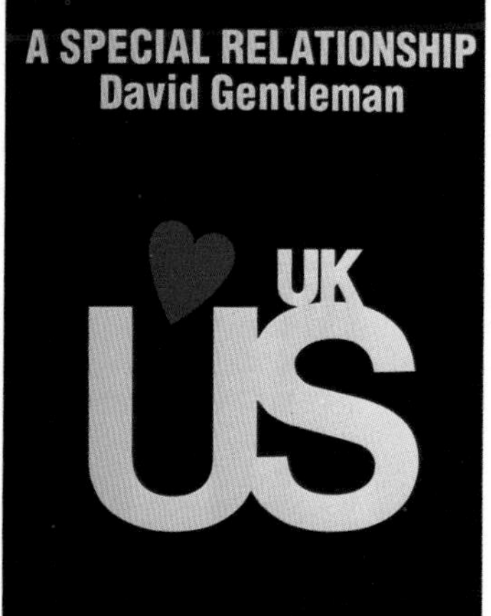

1330

1325 Silver Award
Art Director: Katsuhiro Kinoshita
Designer: Katsuhiro Kinoshita
Writer: Ikko Tanaka
Editor: Katsuhiro Kinoshita
Client: Kodansha Co., Ltd.
Publisher: Kodansha Co., Ltd.
Case & Cover Design: Ikko Tanaka

1326
Art Director: Barbara Baumann, Gerd Baumann
Designer: Barbara Baumann, Gerd Baumann
Illustrator/Artist: Barbara Baumann, Gerd Baumann
Editor: Neugebauer Press (Salzburg)
Agency: Baumann & Baumann
Publisher: Neugebauer Press (Salzburg)

1327 Silver Award
Art Director: Pierre Mendell
Designer: Heinz Hiltbrunner
Editor: Die Neue Sammlung
Agency: Mendell & Oberer
Publisher: Birkhaüser Verlag

1328
Art Director: François G. Baer
Designer: François G. Baer
Photographer: Verena Eggmann, François G. Baer
Client: Diakonissenhaus Bethanien
Publisher: Diakonissenhaus Bethanien

1329
Art Director: Kijuro Yahagi
Designer: Kijuro Yahagi
Client: Meguro Museum of Art (Tokyo)

1330
Art Director: David Gentleman
Designer: David Gentleman
Illustrator/Artist: David Gentleman
Editor: John Bodley
Publisher: Faber & Faber Ltd.

1331

1334

1332

1335

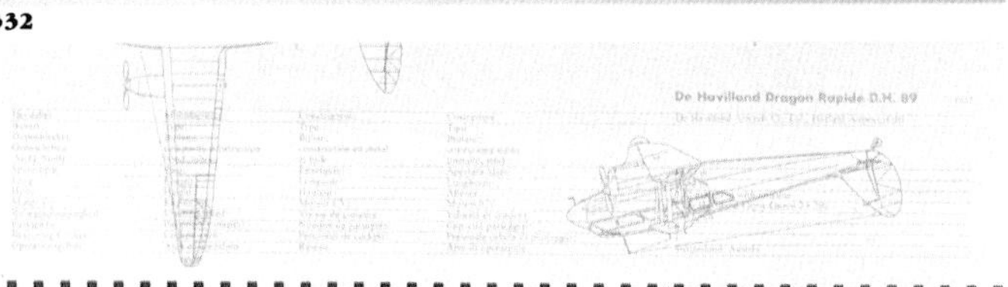

1333

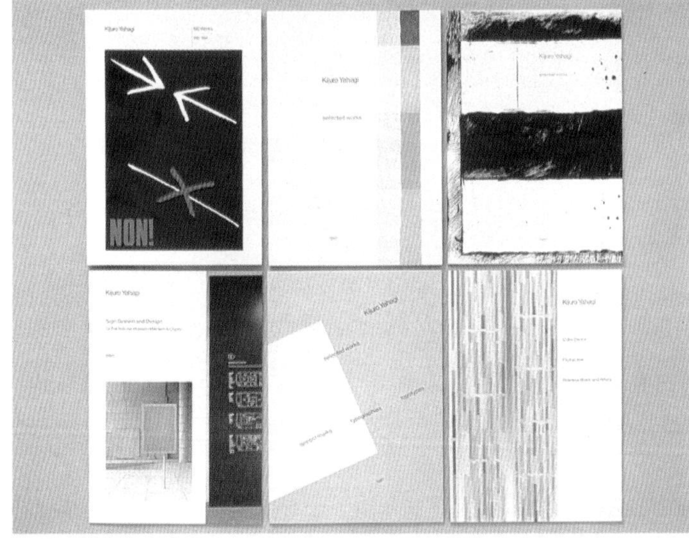

1336

1331
Art Director: Marcello Minale, Brian Tattersfield
Designer: Ian Glazer
Writer: Brian Tattersfield, Rebecca Eliahoo
Editor: Edward Booth-Clibborn
Client: Minale Tattersfield
Publisher: Internos Books

1332
Art Director: Albert Culleré
Designer: Albert Culleré
Photographer: Joan Ribé
Writer: Joan Costa
Publisher: Ediciones CEAC S.A.

1333
Art Director: Stephan Bundi
Illustrator/Artist: Stephan Bundi, Roland Eichenberger, Beat Mäder
Editor: Bert Diener, Fritz Girardin
Client: Swissair AG
Agency: Atelier Bundi
Publisher: Sauerländer AG
Director: Fritz Girardin

1334
Art Director: Hiroyuki Hayashi
Designer: Kiyohisa Nakano
Writer: Takanori Nishijima
Editor: Yuki Kasukawa, NAMCO Ltd.
Agency: Grafix International Inc.
Publisher: Softbank Corp.

1335
Art Director: Tokiyoshi Tsubouchi
Designer: Kazumasa Nagai

1336
Art Director: Kijuro Yahagi
Designer: Kijuro Yahagi
Editor: Kijuro Yahagi
Client: Kijuro Yahagi Co., Ltd.
Publisher: Kijuro Yahagi Co., Ltd.

1337

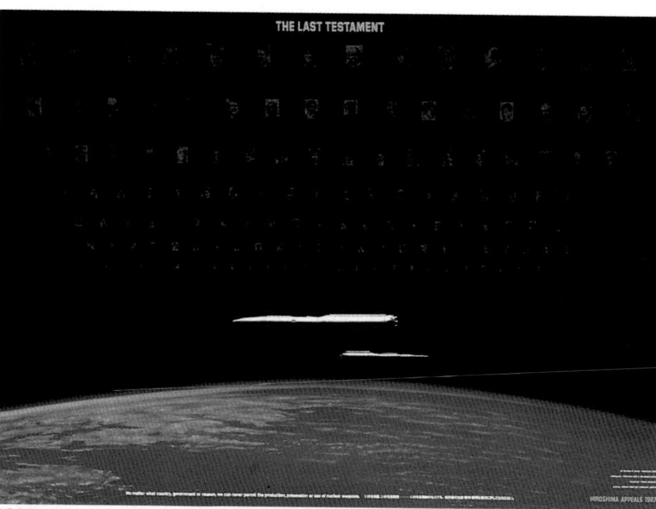

1339

1340

1338

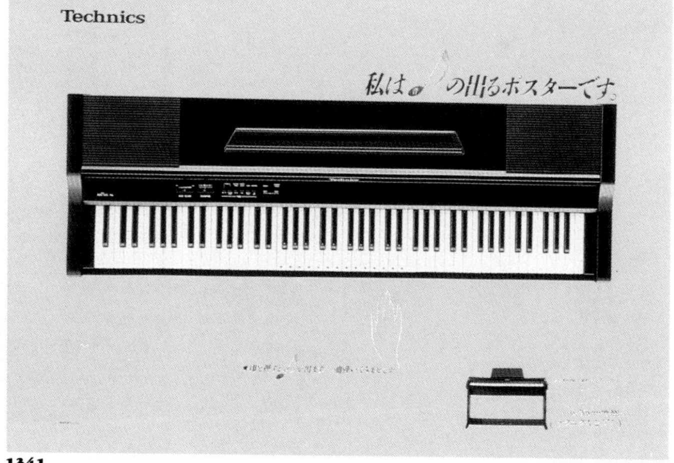

1341

1337
Art Director: Tadanori Itakura
Designer: Tadanori Itakura
Photographer: Seiichi Tanaka
Illustrator/Artist: Mark Kostabi
Writer: Keiko Arai
Client: Ueda College of Fashion
Agency: Dentsu Inc.

1338
Art Director: Günter Rambow
Designer: Günter Rambow
Photographer: Günter Rambow
Client: Hessisches Rundfunk

1339
Art Director: Yasuyuki Uno
Designer: Yasuyuki Uno, Seiichi Satoh
Photographer: Yasuyuki Uno
Illustrator/Artist: Yohji Taguchi
Client: Japan Graphic Designers' Assoc. Inc.

1340
Art Director: Takashi Akiyama
Designer: Takashi Akiyama
Illustrator/Artist: Takashi Akiyama

1341
Art Director: Masaharu Ohtsuka
Designer: Toshiki Saito
Photographer: Koichi Okuwaki
Writer: Noriyuki Fujii
Client: Matsushita Electric Industrial
Agency: Dentsu Inc. (Osaka)

1342

1344

1345

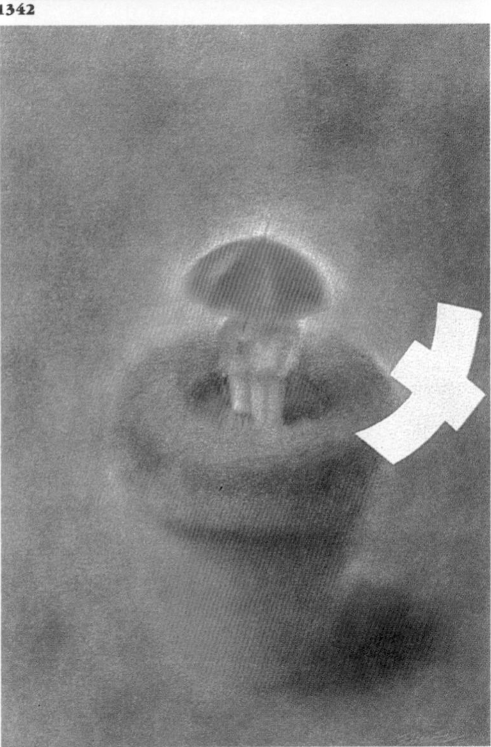
1343

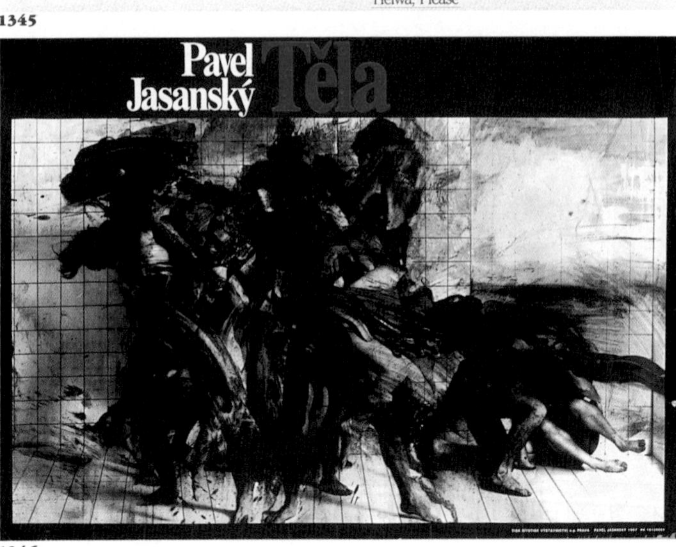

1346

1342
Art Director: Ikko Tanaka
Designer: Ikko Tanaka

1343 Distinctive Merit
Art Director: Masaaki Izumiya
Designer: Hiroshi Kimura, Hiromi Ohmichi, Makoto Endoh
Illustrator/Artist: Hiroshi Watanabe
Writer: Jun Maki
Client: Recruit Co., Ltd.

1344
Art Director: Takaharu Matsumoto
Designer: Takaharu Matsumoto
Photographer: Hiromasa Daimon
Writer: Kōichi Takano
Client: Daihatsu Motor Co., Ltd.

1345
Art Director: Toshiyasu Nanbu
Designer: Toshiyasu Nanbu
Photographer: Tomoharu Mimura
Writer: Toshiyasu Nanbu
Client: Japan Graphic Designers' Assoc. Inc.

1346
Art Director: Pavel Jasansky
Designer: Pavel Jasansky
Editor: Galerie Foma (Prague)
Creative Director: Galerie Foma (Prague)
Client: Galerie Foma (Prague)

1347

1348

1349

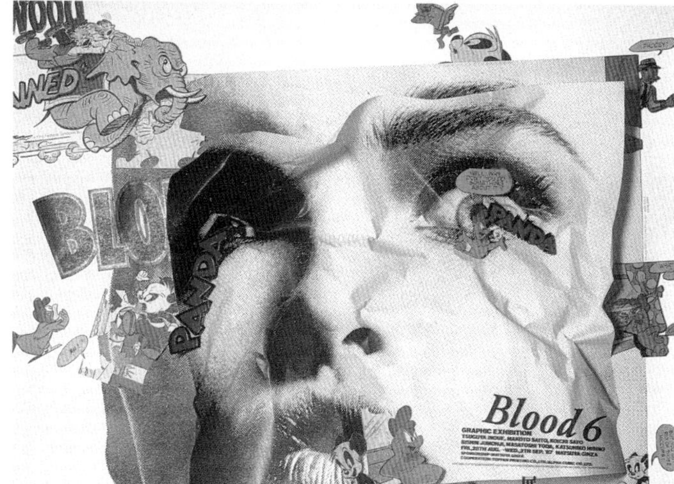

1350

1351

1347
Art Director: Niklaus Troxler
Designer: Niklaus Troxler
Illustrator/Artist: Niklaus Troxler
Client: Reinhold Brown Gallery (New York)

1348
Art Director: Katsuhiro Kinoshita
Designer: Katsuhiro Kinoshita
Illustrator/Artist: Mizumaru Anzai, Yukio Asaga, Pater Sato, Eizin Suzuki, Haruo Takino, Yasuhiro Yomogida
Client: Seibu

1349
Art Director: Masaaki Hiromura
Photographer: Ryuichi Okano
Client: Studio Ebis

1350
Art Director: Makoto Saito
Designer: Makoto Saito
Photographer: Eiichiro Sakata, Hiroshi Sato
Client: Matsuya Co., Ltd.
Printing Direction: Tadashi Kobako

1351
Art Director: Masuteru Aoba
Designer: Masuteru Aoba
Photographer: Masuteru Aoba
Illustrator/Artist: Masuteru Aoba
Client: Recruit Co., Ltd. (G7 Gallery)

1352

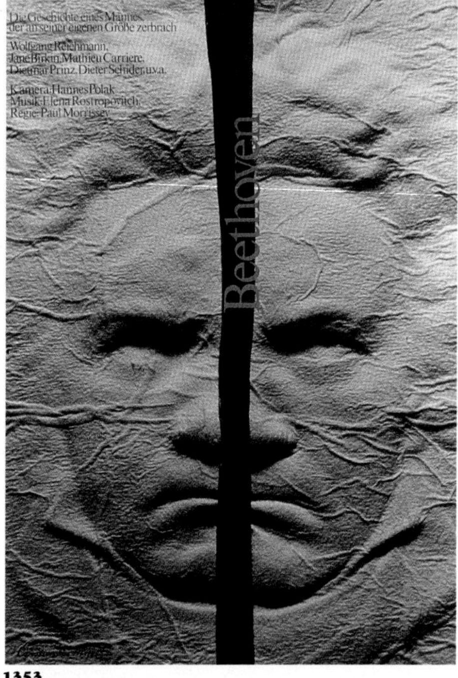

1353

1354

1355

1356

1357

1352
Art Director: Raphie Etgar
Illustrator/Artist: Raphie Etgar
Client: The 40th Anniversary National Committee (Israel)

1353
Art Director: Gerhard Frömel
Designer: Gerhard Umhaller
Photographer: Gerhard Umhaller

1354
Art Director: Makoto Saito
Designer: Makoto Saito, Akihiko Koseki
Photographer: Tsutomu Wakatsuki
Writer: Takeo Nagasawa
Client: Parco Co., Ltd.

1355
Art Director: Péter Pócs
Designer: Péter Pócs
Photographer: Péter Walter
Illustrator/Artist: Péter Pócs
Client: Mücsarnok (Budapest)
Agency: Mücsarnok (Budapest)

1356
Art Director: Harald Draušbaher
Designer: Harald Draušbaher
Photographer: Jože Besnik
Client: Zlatarne Celje

1357
Art Director: Seymour Chwast
Designer: Seymour Chwast
Illustrator/Artist: Seymour Chwast
Writer: Gerd H. Spriesterbach
Client: Zanders Feinpapiere AG
Agency: The Pushpin Group
Publisher: Zanders Feinpapiere AG
Director: Wolfgang Heuwinkel
Producer: Wolfgang Witte

1358

1360

1359

1361

1362

1358
Art Director: Albert Culleré
Designer: Albert Culleré
Photographer: Albert Culleré
Editor: ADG-FAD
Client: ADG-FAD/ICOGRADA

1359
Art Director: Günter Rambow
Designer: Günter Rambow
Photographer: Günter Rambow
Michael van de Sand
Writer: Dr. Bernhard Nordhoff
Client: Kulturamt Kassel

1360
Art Director: Wiliam Kitanov
Designer: Ivan Gazdov
Photographer: Sofi Armenkova
Printer: Vasil Stoyanov

1361
Art Director: Dave Palmer
Photographer: Martin Thompson
Writer: Rick Cook
Client: Kellogg Co. of Great Britain
Agency: J. Walter Thompson Co., Ltd.

1362
Art Director: Kazuhisa Nomura
Designer: Kazuhisa Nomura
Photographer: Hiroto Morioka
Sculptor: Tomokazu Fusaka

1363

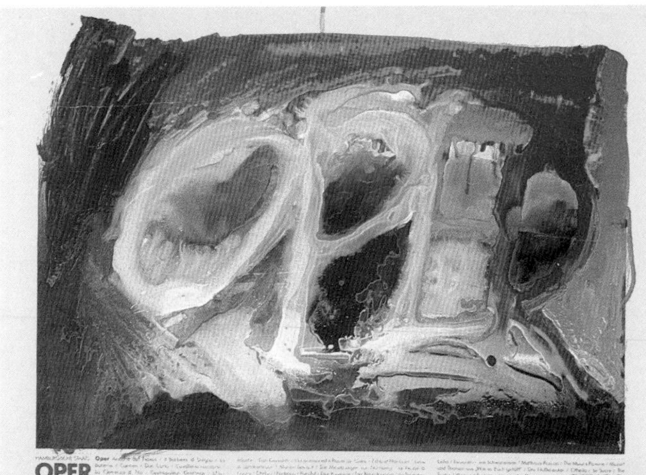

1364

1365

1366

1367

1363
Art Director: Osamu Kawamura
Illustrator/Artist: Osamu Kawamura
Agency: Kawasaki-Si

1364
Art Director: Holger Matthies
Designer: Holger Matthies
Photographer: Holger Matthies
Illustrator/Artist: Holger Matthies
Client: Hamburgische Staatsoper

1365 Silver Award
Art Director: Péter Pócs
Designer: Péter Pócs
Photographer: Péter Walter
Illustrator/Artist: Péter Pócs
Client: József Katona Theather
Agency: József Katona Theather

1366
Art Director: Shunyo Yamauchi
Designer: Shunyo Yamauchi
Photographer: Shunyo Yamauchi
Illustrator/Artist: Shunyo Yamauchi
Client: Japan Graphic Designers' Assoc. Inc.
Publisher: World Design Exposition Association

1367
Art Director: Shunyo Yamauchi
Designer: Shunyo Yamauchi
Photographer: Shunyo Yamauchi
Client: Japan Graphic Designers' Assoc. Inc.
Publisher: Shunyo Yamuchi Design Office

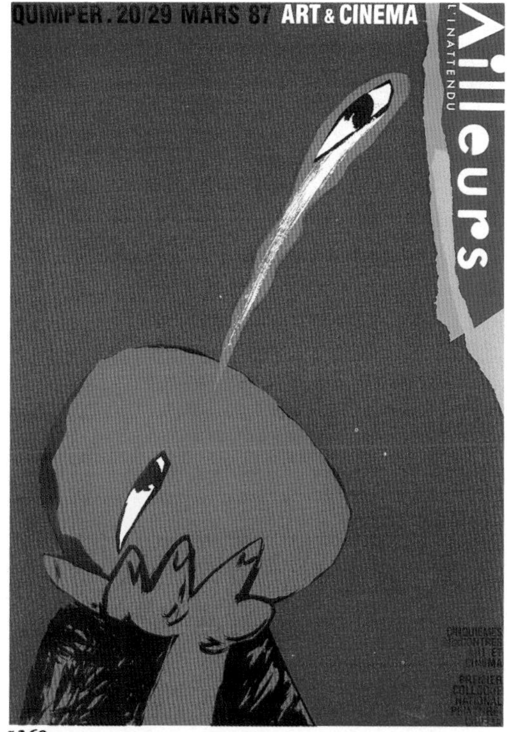

1370

4TH ANNUAL KENT & PENTAGRAM
GRAPHIC DESIGN WORKSHOP 1987
LONDON ENGLAND 4TH ANNUAL
KENT & PENTAGRAM GRAPHIC DESIGN
WORKSHOP 1987 LONDON ENGLAND
4TH ANNUAL KENT & PENTAGRAM
GRAPHIC DESIGN WORKSHOP 1987
LONDON ENGLAND 4TH ANNUAL
KENT & PENTAGRAM GRAPHIC DESIGN
WORKSHOP 1987 LONDON ENGLAND
4TH ANNUAL KENT & PENTAGRAM
GRAPHIC DESIGN WORKSHOP 1987
LONDON ENGLAND 4TH ANNUAL
KENT & PENTAGRAM GRAPHIC DESIGN
WORKSHOP 1987 LONDON ENGLAND
4TH ANNUAL KENT & PENTAGRAM
GRAPHIC DESIGN WORKSHOP 1987
LONDON ENGLAND 4TH ANNUAL
KENT & PENTAGRAM GRAPHIC DESIGN
WORKSHOP 1987 LONDON ENGLAND
4TH ANNUAL KENT & PENTAGRAM
GRAPHIC DESIGN WORKSHOP 1987
LONDON ENGLAND 4TH ANNUAL
KENT & PENTAGRAM GRAPHIC DESIGN
WORKSHOP 1987 LONDON ENGLAND
4TH ANNUAL KENT & PENTAGRAM
GRAPHIC DESIGN WORKSHOP 1987
LONDON ENGLAND 4TH ANNUAL
KENT & PENTAGRAM GRAPHIC DESIGN
WORKSHOP 1987 LONDON ENGLAND

1369

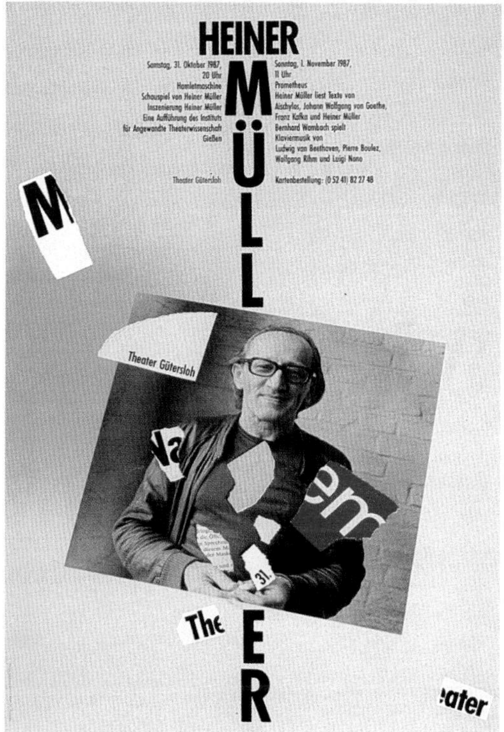

1371

1368
Art Director: Alain Le Quernel
Designer: Alain Le Quernel
Client: Association Gros Plan (Quimper)
Publisher: Association Gros Plan

1369
Art Director: Mervyn Kurlansky
Designer: Mervyn Kurlansky, Herman Lelie
Client: Kent State University

1370
Art Director: Ken Sakaguchi
Designer: Ken Sakaguchi
Photographer: Katsuhiro Ichikawa
Writer: Fuetaro Shinoda

1371
Art Director: Holger Matthies
Designer: Holger Matthies
Photographer: Holger Matthies
Illustrator/Artist: Holger Matthies
Client: Theater Gütersloh

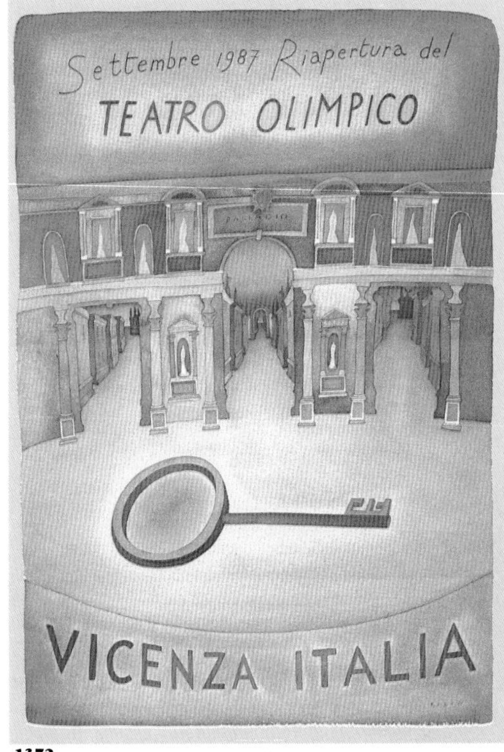

1372

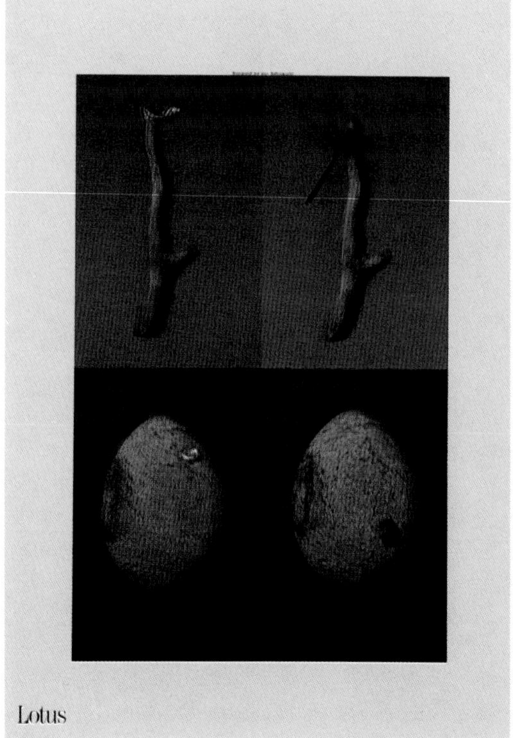

1374

1373

1375

1372
Art Director: Lucia Bandini
Illustrator/Artist: Jean-Michel Folon
Client: Teatro Olimpico di Vicenza
Agency: Errepiudue Veneto (Vicenza)
Publisher: City of Vicenza

1373
Art Director: Tateo Yagi
Designer: Tateo Yagi
Photographer: Hiroshi Shigemura
Client: Omiya Station Building Inc.

1374
Art Director: Ken Sakaguchi
Designer: Ken Sakaguchi
Photographer: Toru Kinoshita

1375
Art Director: Makoto Saito
Designer: Makoto Saito
Photographer: Eiichiro Sakata, Hiroshi Sato
Client: Alpha Cubic Co., Ltd.
Producer: Hiroshi Kaneda

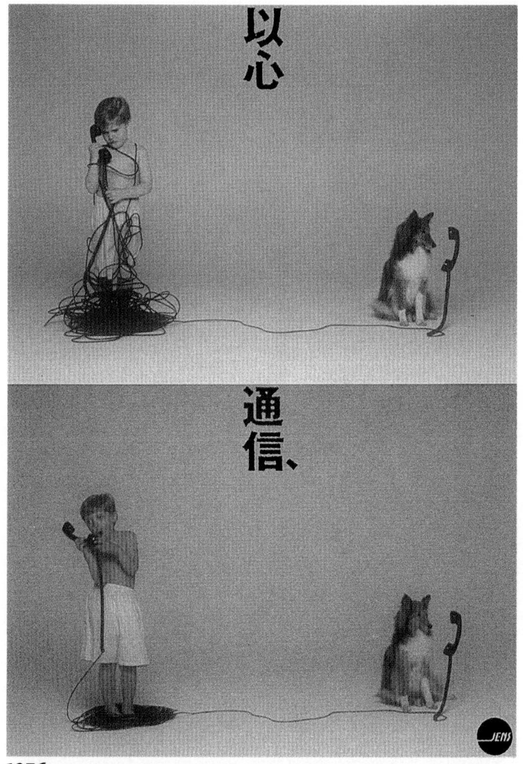

1376

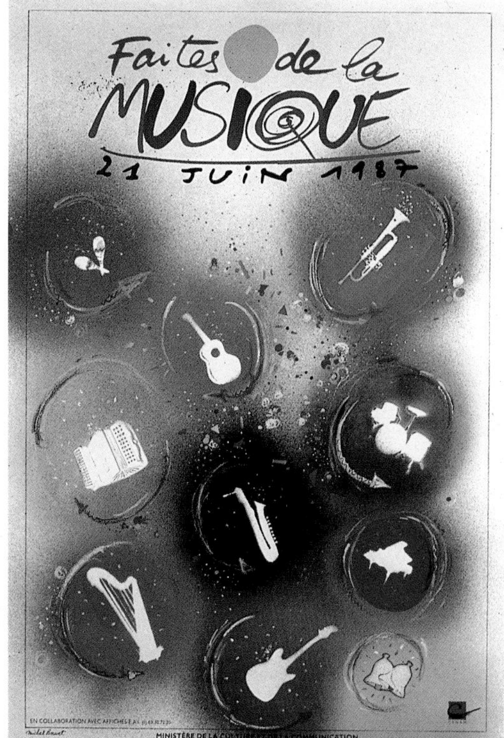

1377

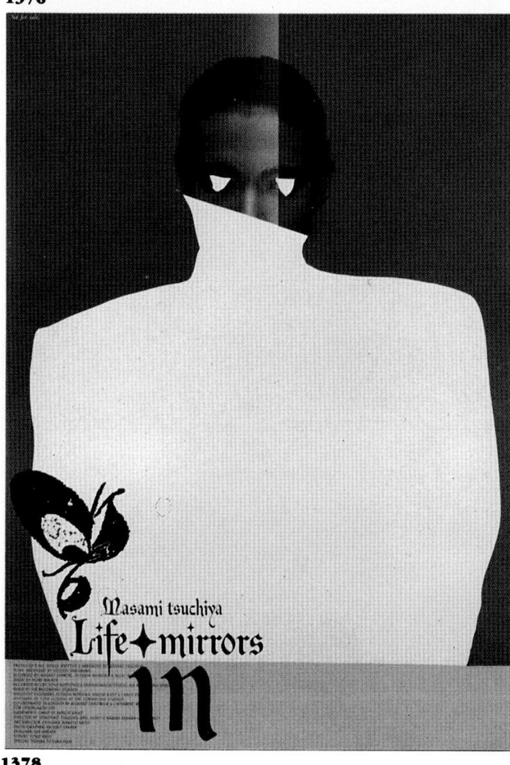

1378

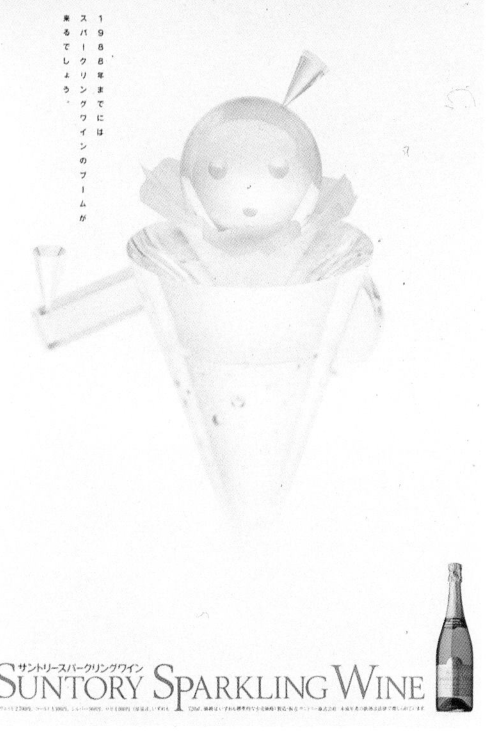

1379

1376
Art Director: Ken Sakaguchi
Designer: Ken Sakaguchi
Photographer: Toru Kinoshita

1377
Art Director: Makoto Saito
Designer: Makoto Saito, Jun Shibata
Photographer: Eiichiro Sakata
Client: Epic/Sony Inc.

1378
Art Director: Michel Bouvet
Designer: Michel Bouvet
Illustrator/Artist: Michel Bouvet
Client: Ministère de la Culture

1379
Art Director: Shigehisa Kitatani, Junko Takahashi
Photographer: Naohiko Hoshino
Illustrator/Artist: Shigehisa Kitatani,
Junko Takahashi
Writer: Hiroshi Ichikura
Agency: Shigehisa Kitatani Design Studio

1380

1381

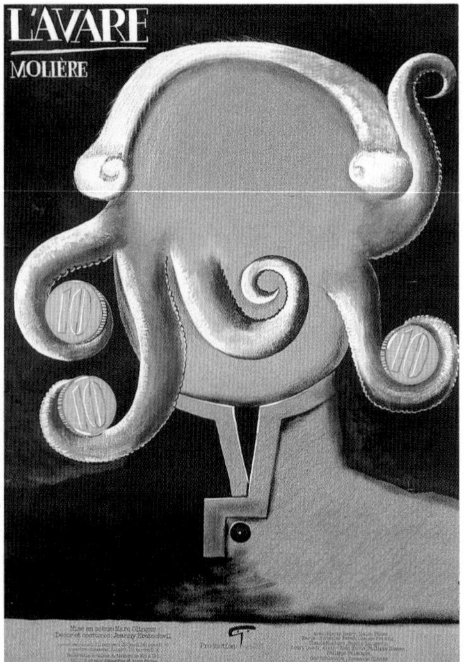

1382

1383

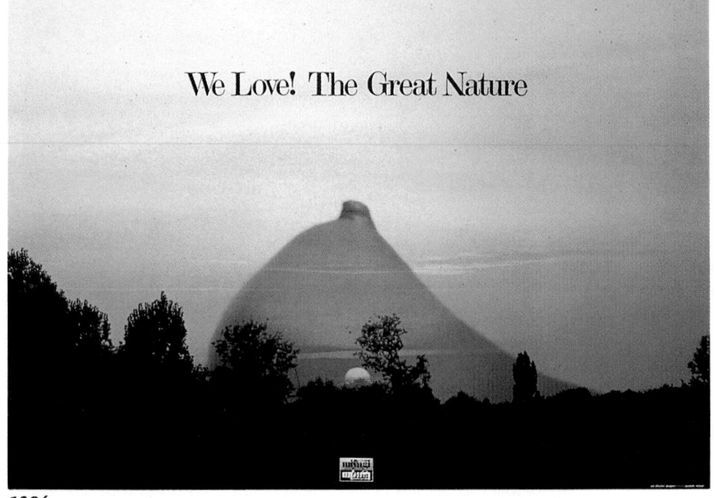

1384

1380
Art Director: Günter Rambow
Designer: Günter Rambow
Photographer: Günter Rambow, Michael van de Sand
Client: Hessisches Literaturbüro

1381
Art Director: Pentti Pilve
Designer: Pentti Pilve
Illustrator/Artist: Pentti Pilve
Writer: Pentti Pilve
Client: A-Lehdet Oy
Agency: Creator Oy

1382
Art Director: Kamen Popov
Designer: Kamen Popov
Illustrator/Artist: Kamen Popov
Client: French Cultural Center, Capucin Theater

1383
Art Director: Haruo Nakamura
Designer: Haruo Nakamura
Photographer: Kohei Onishi
Writer: Koji Yanagishima
Client: Kirin Brewery Co., Ltd.
Agency: Dentsu Inc. (Tokyo)

1384
Art Director: Yasutake Miyagi
Designer: Yasutake Miyagi
Photographer: Yasutake Miyagi
Client: Miyagi Design Studio

1385

1386

1387

1388

1389

1390

1385
Art Director: Per Arnoldi

1386
Art Director: Toyotsugu Itoh
Designer: Toyotsugu Itoh
Illustrator/Artist: Toyotsugu Itoh
Client: Japan Graphic Designers' Assoc. Inc.

1387
Art Director: Stefan Borissov
Illustrator/Artist: Grigor Angelov
Client: Film Distribution (Sofia)
Agency: Film Distribution (Sofia)

1388
Art Director: Per Arnoldi

1389
Art Director: Masuteru Aoba
Designer: Masuteru Aoba
Illustrator/Artist: Masuteru Aoba
Client: A & A

1390
Art Director: Raphie Etgar
Illustrator/Artist: Raphie Etgar
Client: The Train Theater, Mario Kotlier
Director: Yossi Fisher, Jerusalem Foundation

1391

1392

1393

1394

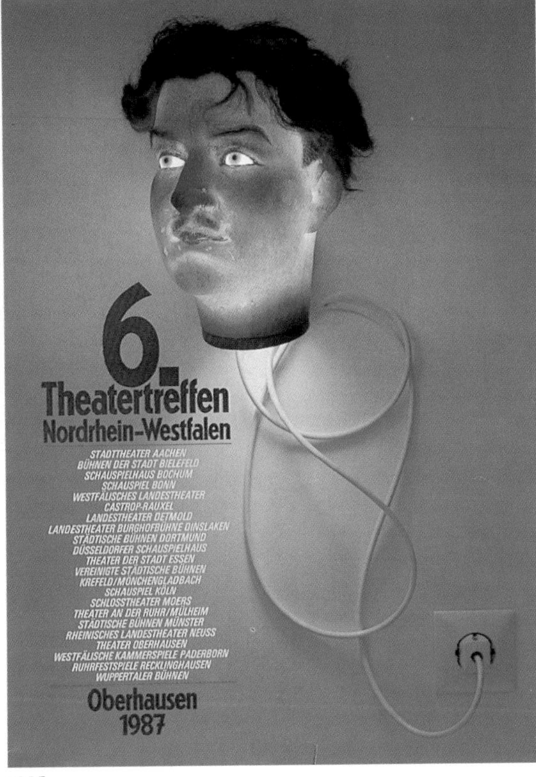

1395

1391
Art Director: Jean-Pol Rouard
Client: Max't Kindt (Brussel's Orchestra)

1392
Art Director: Tadanori Itakura
Designer: Tadanori Itakura, Masakazu Takeda
Photographer: Sakae Takahashi
Writer: Kazuto Naito

1393
Art Director: Michel Bouvet
Designer: Michel Bouvet
Photographer: Jean-Pierre Gapihan
Client: Ris & Danceries

1394
Art Director: Toshio Yamagata
Designer: Yuiro Nakamura
Photographer: Francis Giacobetti
Writer: Naoko Serikawa
Creative Director: Hiroshi Tanaka
Client: IPSA Co., Ltd.

1395
Art Director: Holger Matthies
Designer: Holger Matthies
Photographer: Holger Matthies
Illustrator/Artist: Holger Matthies
Client: Theater Oberhausen

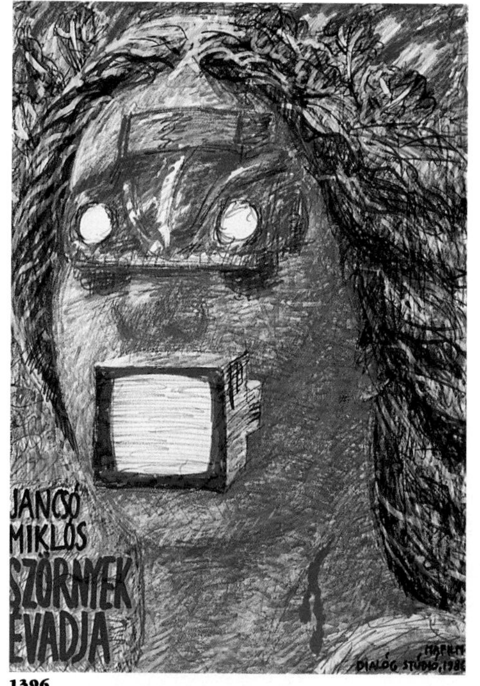

1396

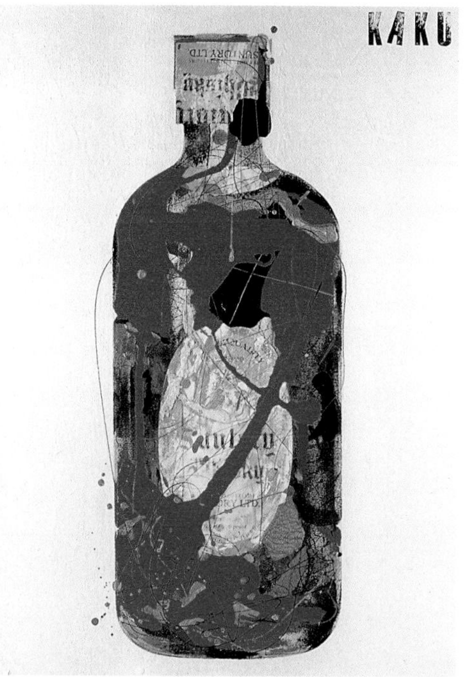

1397

1398

1399

1400

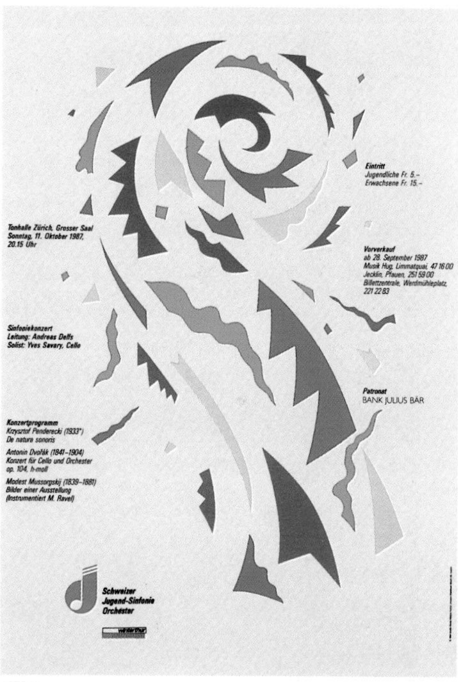

1401

1396
Art Director: Béla Csoma
Designer: György Kemény
Illustrator/Artist: György Kemény
Client: Mokép
Publisher: Mokép
Director: Jozsef Gombár

1397 Silver Award
Art Director: Yasuhiro Sawada
Designer: Yasuhiro Sawada
Illustrator/Artist: Yasuhiro Sawada
Client: Suntory Ltd.
Director: Senji Urushibata

1398
Art Director: Jukka Veistola
Designer: Jukka Veistola
Photographer: Timo Viljakainen
Illustrator/Artist: Jukka Veistola
Writer: Jukka Veistola
Client: The Art Museum of Riga
Agency: Veistola Oy
Typography: Graphic Team

1399
Art Director: Dominique Verrier
Designer: T. A. Lewandowski
Photographer: T. A. Lewandowski
Illustrator/Artist: T. A. Lewandowski
Editor: Theatre de Cinquante (Paris)
Client: Theatre de Cinquante (Paris)
Agency: T. A. Lewandowski
Publisher: Theatre de Cinquante (Paris)
Director: Andreas Voutsinas

1400 Silver Award
Art Director: Uwe Loesch
Designer: Uwe Loesch
Writer: Uwe Loesch, Friedwald Schüttler
Client: Zanders Feinpapiere AG
Publisher: Zanders Feinpapiere AG
Director: Wolfgang Heuwinkel
Producer: Richard Peters
Advertising Manager: F. Schüttler

1401
Art Director: Niklaus Troxler
Designer: Niklaus Troxler
Illustrator/Artist: Niklaus Troxler
Client: Schweizer Jugend-Sinfonie-Orchester
Agency: Niklaus Troxler, Grafik-Studio

1402

1403

1404

1405

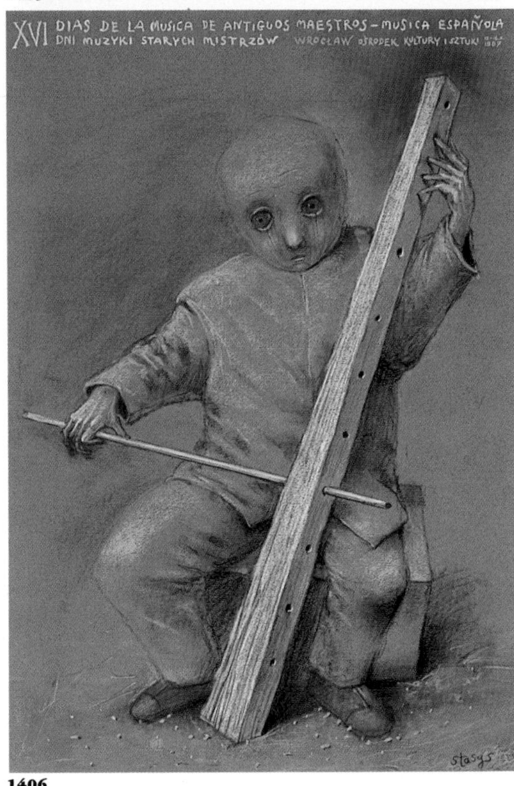

1406

1402
Art Director: Makoto Saito
Designer: Makoto Saito
Photographer: Eiichiro Sakata, Hiroshi Sato
Client: Alpha Cubic Co., Ltd.
Producer: Hiroshi Kaneda

1403
Art Director: Masaki Hirate
Designer: Makiko Takahashi
Photographer: Hiroshi Yoda
Client: Panorama

1404
Art Director: Masaaki Izumiya, Shuji Kasai
Designer: Makoto Endo
Photographer: Masayoshi Sukita
Writer: Isao Kashiwagi, Mitsuhiro Koike
Client: Recruit Co., Ltd.
Agency: Hakuhodo Inc.

1405
Art Director: Péter Pócs
Designer: Péter Pócs
Photographer: László Haris
Illustrator/Artist: Péter Pócs
Client: József Katona Theather
Agency: József Katona Theather

1406 Silver Award
Art Director: Stasys Eidrigevicius
Photographer: Jacek Wolowski
Illustrator/Artist: Stasys Eidrigevicius
Publisher: Cultural Center (Wroclaw)

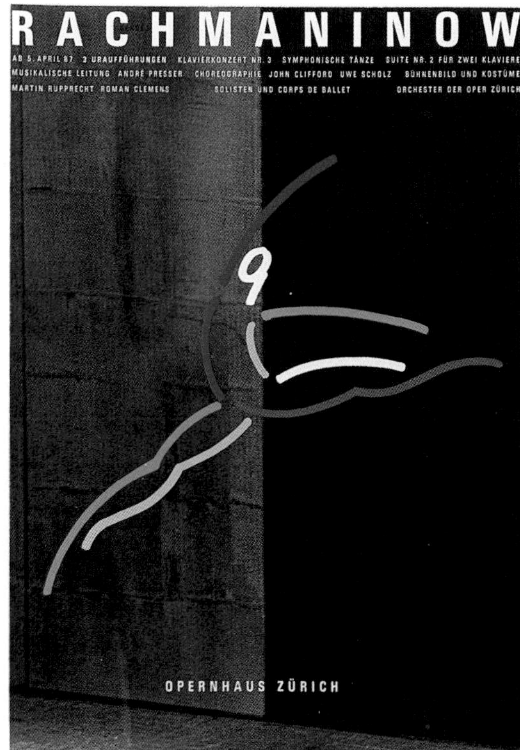

1407

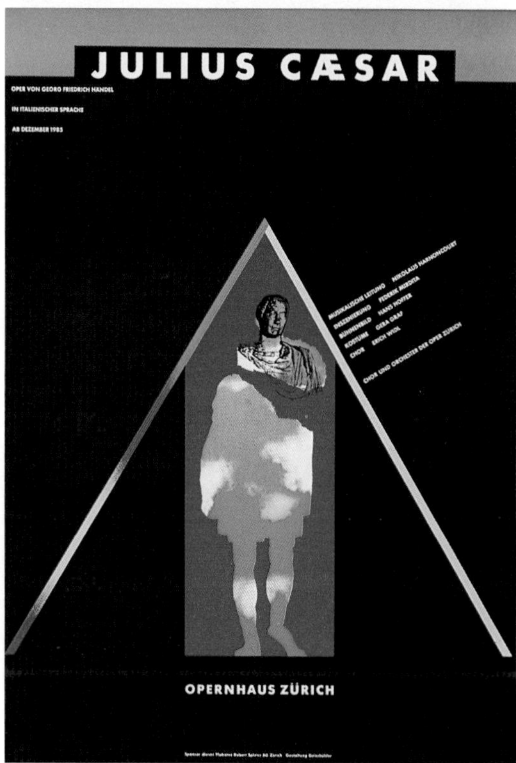

1408

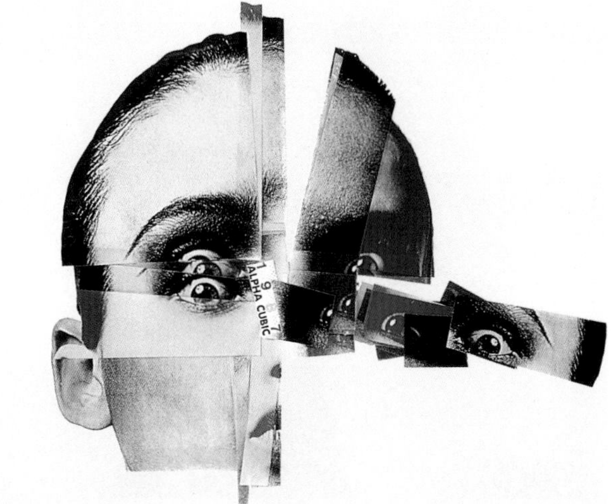

1409

1410

1411

1407 Silver Award
Art Director: K. Domenic Geissbühler
Designer: K. Domenic Geissbühler
Photographer: K. Domenic Geissbühler
Illustrator/Artist: K. Domenic Geissbühler
Editor: Opera House (Zurich)
Client: Opera House (Zurich)
Agency: K. Domenic Geissbühler
Director: Christoph Groszer
Printer: Vontobel Print

1408
Art Director: K. Domenic Geissbühler
Designer: K. Domenic Geissbühler
Illustrator/Artist: K. Domenic Geissbühler
Editor: Opera House (Zurich)
Client: Opera House (Zurich)
Agency: K. Domenic Geissbühler
Director: Christoph Groszer
Printer: Vontobel Print

1409
Art Director: Makoto Saito
Designer: Makoto Saito
Photographer: Eiichiro Sakata
Client: Alpha Cubic Co., Ltd.
Producer: Hiroshi Kaneda

1410
Art Director: Hiromi Inayoshi
Designer: Hiromi Inayoshi
Illustrator/Artist: Yasuhiko Taniguchi
Writer: Aiko Hanai
Client: Seiwa Corp.
Agency: Inayoshi Design Inc.
Director: Miha Takagi
Producer: Miha Takagi

1411
Art Director: Makoto Saito
Designer: Makoto Saito
Photographer: Eiichiro Sakata, Hiroshi Sato
Client: Matsuya Co., Ltd.
Printing Direction: Tadashi Kobako

1412

1413

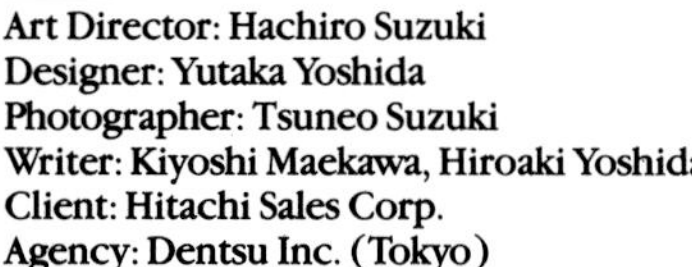

1414

1415

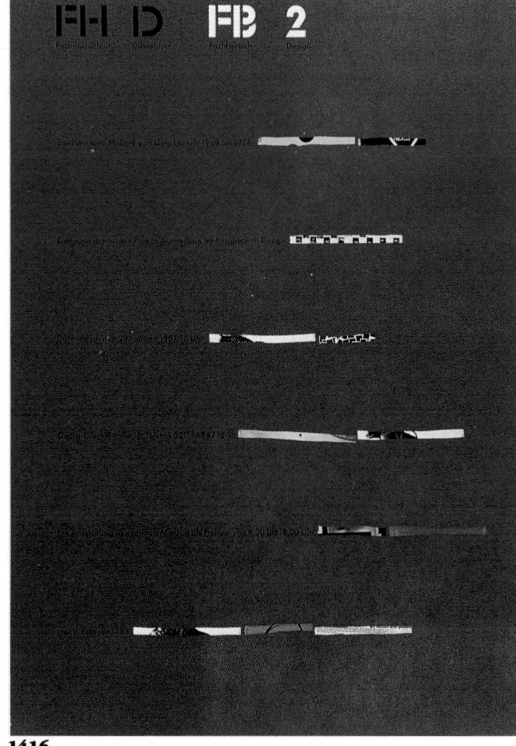

1416

1412
Art Director: Masatoshi Toda
Designer: Masanori Mizushima
Photographer: Mamoru Sugiyama
Illustrator/Artist: Toshio Mori
Writer: Toru Iwakiri
Client: Committee of Nohrino Fuku

1413
Art Director: Yasuhiko Shimura
Designer: Yasuhiko Shimura, Makiko Imanishi
Photographer: Kazunori Tsukuda
Writer: Toshikazu Kido
Client: World Gold Council Ltd.
Agency: McCann-Erickson Hakuhodo Inc.
Director: Keiji Minokura

1414
Art Director: Hachiro Suzuki
Designer: Yutaka Yoshida
Photographer: Tsuneo Suzuki
Writer: Kiyoshi Maekawa, Hiroaki Yoshida
Client: Hitachi Sales Corp.
Agency: Dentsu Inc. (Tokyo)

1415
Art Director: Stasys Eidrigevicius
Photographer: Jacek Wolowski
Illustrator/Artist: Stasys Eidrigevicius
Publisher: Art Gallery (Pulawy)

1416
Art Director: Helfried Hagenberg
Designer: Helfried Hagenberg
Client: Fachhochschule (Düsseldorf)
Publisher: Fachhochschule (Düsseldorf)

1417

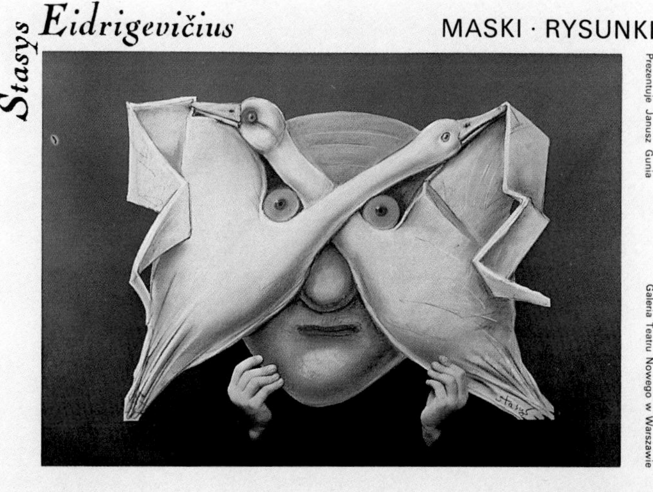

1418

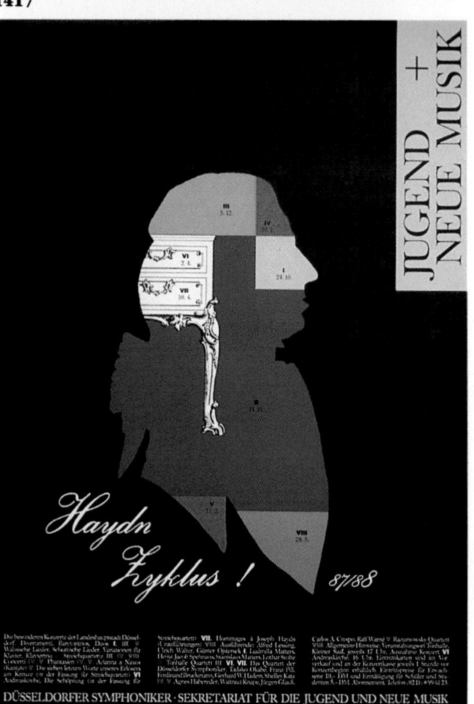

1419

GALERA DE ARTE.

TODA MAGIA DO TRAÇO. TODA EMOÇÃO DA COR. TODA EXPRESSÃO DO GESTO. TODO TALENTO À MOSTRA.

DIA 4 DE JUNHO, CLUBE CAIÇARAS, A PARTIR DAS 20 HORAS.

1420

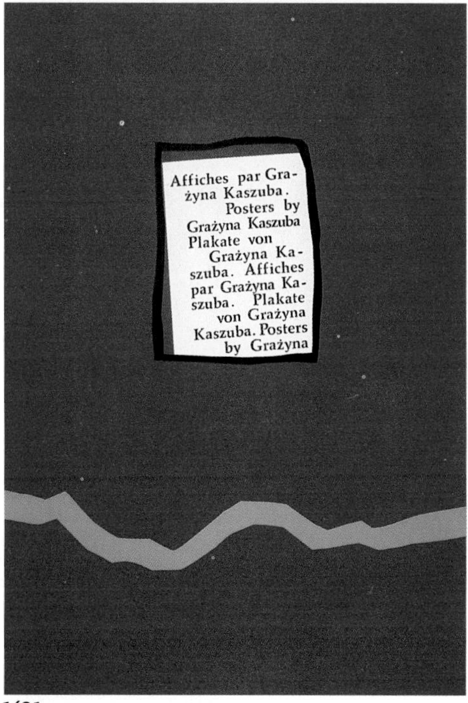

1421

1417
Art Director: Stasys Eidrigevicius
Photographer: Jacek Wolowski
Illustrator/Artist: Stasys Eidrigevicius
Publisher: Teater na Targuwku (Warwaw)

1418
Art Director: Stasys Eidrigevicius
Designer: Krzysztof Jerominek
Photographer: Jacek Wolowski, Krzystof Szeloch
Illustrator/Artist: Stasys Eidrigevicius
Publisher: Teater Nowy (Warsaw)

1419
Art Director: Peter Krüll
Designer: Peter Krüll
Illustrator/Artist: Peter Krüll
Client: Düsseldorfer Symphoniker
Agency: Design Peter Krüll
Director: Dr. Peter Girth
Producer: Offset Company

1420
Art Director: Adeir Rampazzo
Writer: Cibar Ruiz
Agency: Rampazzo Studio

1421
Art Director: Grażyna Kaszuba
Designer: Grażyna Kaszuba

1422

1423

1424

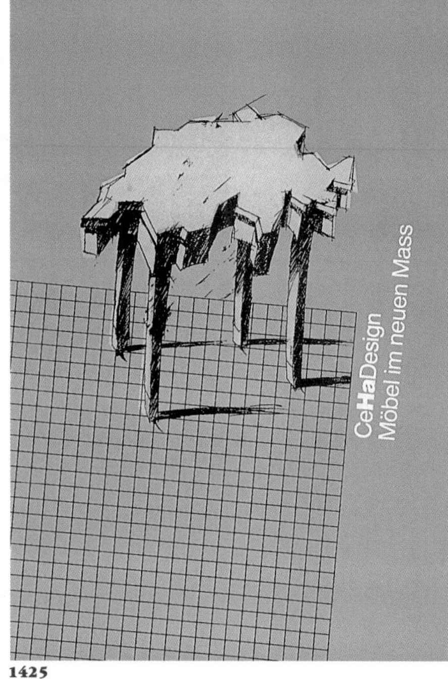

1425

1426

1422
Art Director: Grażyna Kaszuba
Designer: Grażyna Kaszuba
Client: Wilk Graphik Studio

1423
Art Director: Stephan Bundi
Designer: Stephan Bundi
Illustrator/Artist: Stephan Bundi
Client: Cultural Commission (Berne)
Agency: Atelier Bundi

1424
Art Director: Grażyna Kaszuba
Designer: Grażyna Kaszuba
Client: Wilk Graphik Studio

1425
Art Director: Stephan Bundi
Designer: Stephan Bundi
Illustrator/Artist: Stephan Bundi
Client: Ceha Design (Berne)
Agency: Atelier Bundi

1426
Art Director: Stephan Bundi
Designer: Stephan Bundi
Illustrator/Artist: Stephan Bundi
Client: Mühle Hunziken (Rubigen)
Agency: Atelier Bundi

1427

1428

1429

1430

1431

1432

1427
Art Director: Rosemarie Tissi
Designer: Odermatt & Tissi
Publisher: Museum für Gestaltung (Zurich)
Director: Dr. Hansjörg Budliger
Conservator: Martin Heller

1428
Art Director: K. Domenic Geissbühler
Designer: K. Domenic Geissbühler
Illustrator/Artist: K. Domenic Geissbühler, Erich Wonder
Editor: Opera House (Zurich)
Client: Opera House (Zurich)
Agency: K. Domenic Geissbühler
Director: Christoph Groszer
Printer: Vontobel Print

1429
Art Director: K. Domenic Geissbühler
Designer: K. Domenic Geissbühler
Illustrator/Artist: K. Domenic Geissbühler
Editor: Opera House (Zurich)
Client: Opera House (Zurich)
Agency: K. Domenic Geissbühler
Director: Christoph Groszer
Printer: Vontobel Print

1430
Art Director: K. Domenic Geissbühler
Designer: K. Domenic Geissbühler
Illustrator/Artist: K. Domenic Geissbühler
Editor: Opera House (Zurich)
Client: Opera House (Zurich)
Agency: K. Domenic Geissbühler
Director: Christoph Groszer
Printer: Vontobel Print

1431
Art Director: Reinhold Luger
Designer: Reinhold Luger
Client: Bregenz Festival
Producer: Russ-Druck (Lochau)

1432
Art Director: Marc Van de Kerckhove
Illustrator/Artist: Willem Burten
Writer: Guillaume Van der Stighelen
Creative Director: Michel Collart
Client: R. Neirinck
Agency: Young & Rubicam (Brussels)
Publisher: Marcel Vyncke

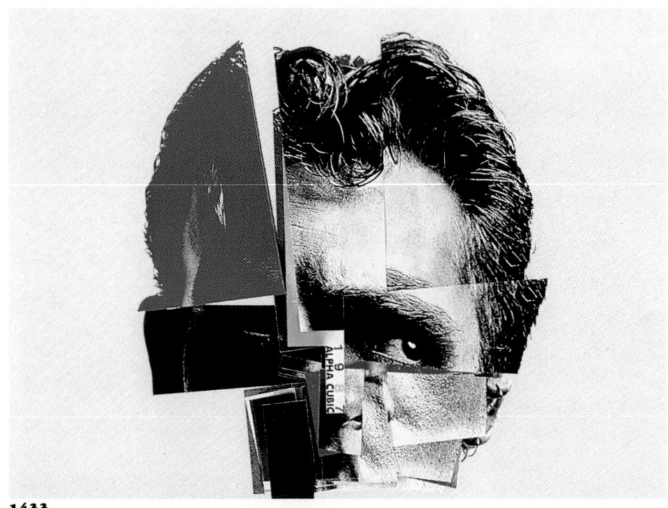

1433

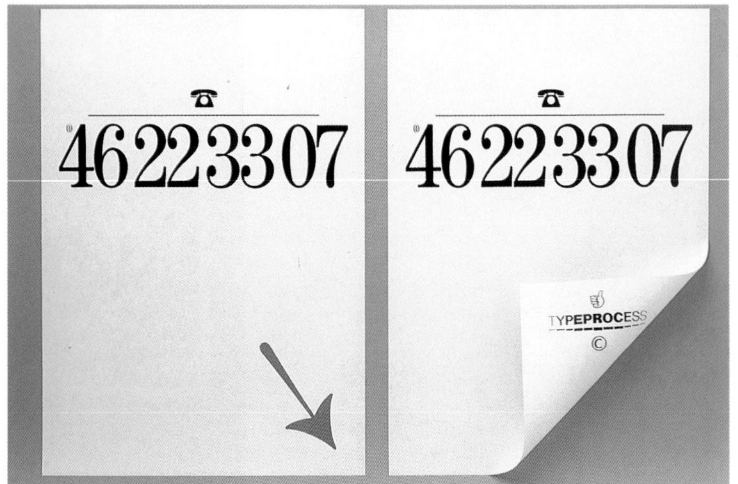

1434

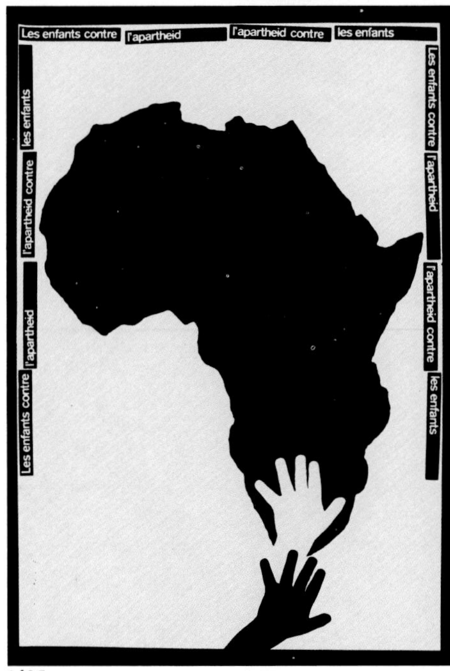

1435

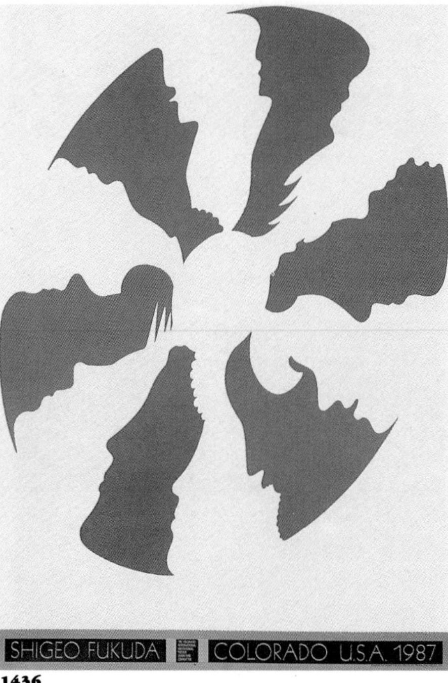

1436

1437

1433 Gold Award
Art Director: Makoto Saito
Designer: Makoto Saito
Photographer: Eiichiro Sakata
Client: Alpha Cubic Co., Ltd.
Producer: Hiroshi Kaneda

1434
Art Director: Garth Bell
Designer: Garth Bell
Client: Typeprocess

1435
Art Director: Thierry Sarfis
Designer: T. A. Lewandowski
Illustrator/Artist: T. A. Lewandowski
Editor: UNESCO (Paris)
Client: UNESCO (Paris)
Agency: T. A. Lewandowski

1436
Art Director: Shigeo Fukuda
Designer: Shigeo Fukuda
Illustrator/Artist: Shigeo Fukuda
Client: Colorado International Invitational Poster Exhibition Committee

1437 Gold Award
Art Director: K. Domenic Geissbühler
Designer: K. Domenic Geissbühler
Illustrator/Artist: K. Domenic Geissbühler
Editor: Opera House (Zurich)
Client: Opera House (Zurich)
Agency: K. Domenic Geissbühler
Director: Christoph Groszer
Printer: Vontobel Print

1438

1439

1438
Art Director: Koji Mazutani
Designer: Hirokazu Kurebayashi, Osamu Kitajima
Illustrator/Artist: Hirokazu Kurebayashi
Client: Swatch
Agency: Cosmo Ad Agency
Producer: Yoshinobu Kitahata

1439
Art Director: Masaaki Izumiya
Designer: Hiroshi Yonemura
Illustrator/Artist: James McMullan
Writer: Jun Maki
Agency: Hakuhodo Inc.

1440

1441

1442

1443

1440
Art Director: Bulnes & Robaglia
Client: Mairie (Paris)
Consultant: François Giannesini

 **1441 Silver Award**
Art Director: Masatoshi Toda
Designer: Mamoru Suzuki
Photographer: Sachiko Kuru
Illustrator/Artist: Masayasu Okabe
Client: Vivre 21

1442
Art Director: Masatoshi Toda
Designer: Taku Nakamura
Photographer: Eiichiro Sakata
Writer: Atuko Iizuka
Client: Vivre 21
Director: Masayasu Okabe

1443
Art Director: Takashi Akiyama
Designer: Takashi Akiyama
Illustrator/Artist: Takashi Akiyama

1444

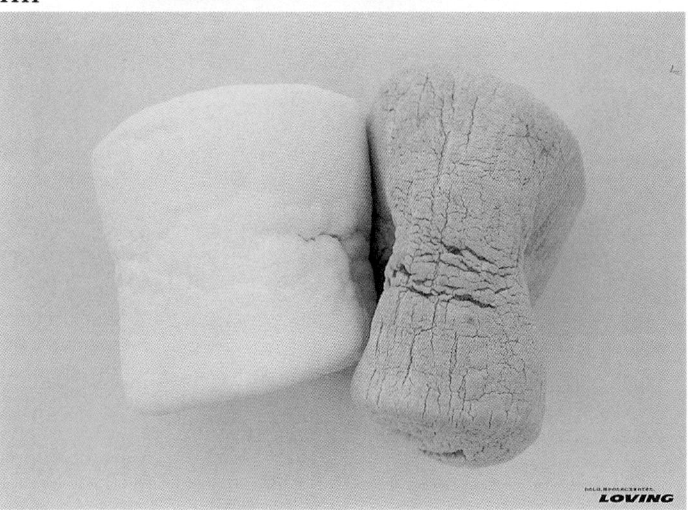

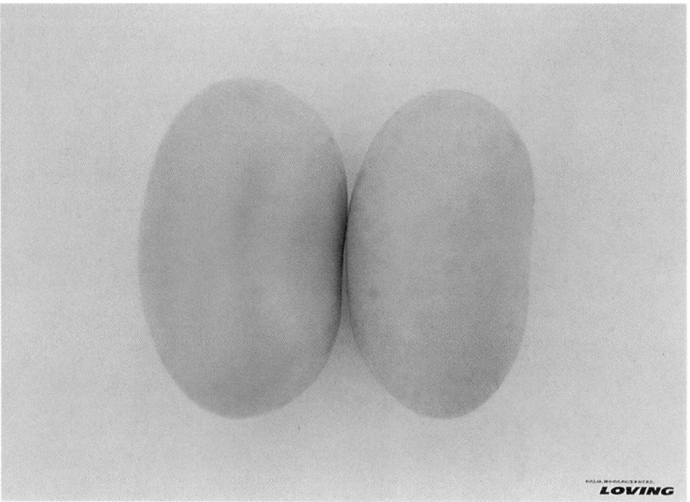

1445

1444
Art Director: Hiromi Inayoshi
Designer: Hiromi Inayoshi
Photographer: Yutaka Sakano
Illustrator/Artist: Katsuhiko Hibino
Writer: Aiko Hanai
Client: Nihon Information Center Co., Ltd.
Agency: Inayoshi Design Inc.
Director: Miha Takagi
Producer: Miha Takagi

1445
Art Director: Hiromi Inayoshi
Designer: Hiromi Inayoshi
Photographer: Atsushi Motoi
Client: Seiwa Corp.
Agency: Inayoshi Design Inc.
Director: Miha Takagi
Producer: Miha Takagi

カラダとアタマの核融合反応。ナイキのフィットネス。

NIKE
FITNESS

カラダとアタマの言文一致運動。ナイキのフィットネス。

NIKE
FITNESS

彼のカラダにふれるな。切れる。

NIKE
FITNESS

1446

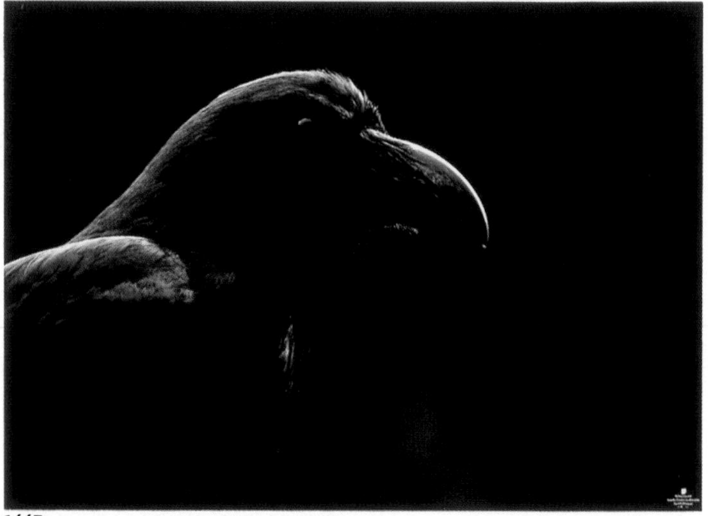

1447

1446

Art Director: Masahiro Sobue
Designer: Yutaka Ohta
Photographer: Shintaro Shiratori
Writer: Shosuke Matuo

1447

Art Director: Toshio Hiragai
Designer: Toshio Hiragai
Photographer: Hironobu Shindo
Illustrator/Artist: Toru Nishi
Client: King Printing Co., Ltd.
Agency: McCann-Erickson Hakuhodo Inc.

1448

1449

1448
Art Director: Takashi Akiyama
Designer: Takashi Akiyama
Illustrator/Artist: Takashi Akiyama

1449 Gold Award
Art Director: Osamu Furumura
Designer: Osamu Furumura
Illustrator/Artist: Osamu Furumura
Client: CBS/Sony
Producer: Akio Ninbari

1450
Art Director: Masato Ohki
Designer: Masato Ohki
Photographer: Masayoshi Sukita
Writer: Rika Enomoto
Creative Director: Kunitaka Okada, Katsumi Asaba
Client: Lacoste/Seibu Department Store
Agency: I & S/Asaba Design Studio
Doll Sculptor: Masato Ohki

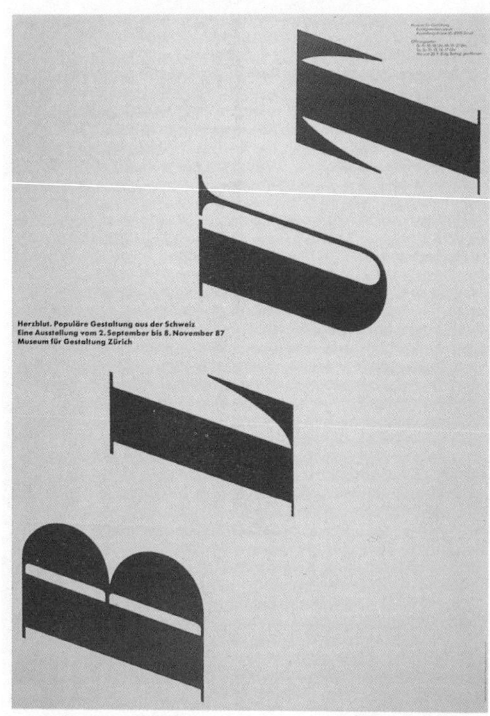

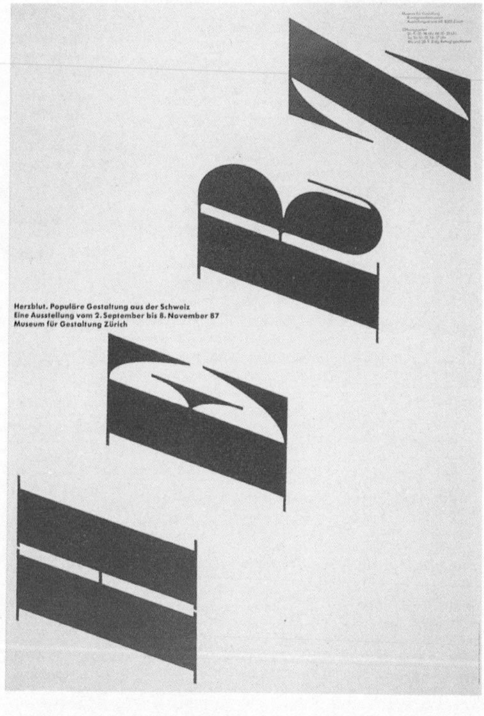

1451
Art Director: Hans-Rudolf Lutz
Designer: Hans-Rudolf Lutz
Publisher: Museum für Gestaltung (Zurich)
Director: Dr. Hansjörg Budliger
Conservator: Martin Heller

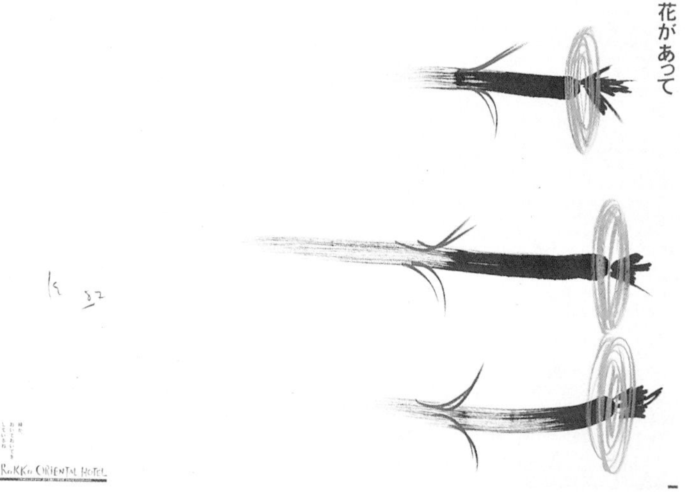

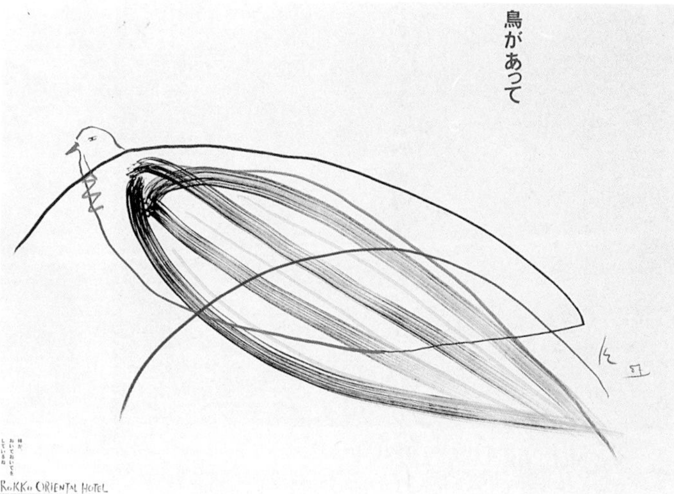

1452
Art Director: Hisamoto Naito
Designer: Yoshinari Morimoto
Illustrator/Artist: Seitaro Kuroda
Writer: Masaki Akama
Client: Rokko Oriental Hotel Co., Ltd.
Agency: Dentsu Inc. (Osaka)

1453
Art Director: Kunihiko Nishiyama
Designer: Akira Ouchi
Illustrator/Artist: Zenji Funabashi
Writer: Kunihiko Nishiyama
Client: Japan Tobacco Inc.
Agency: Dentsu Inc. (Tokyo)

1454
Art Director: Roland Scotoni
Photographer: Hans Feurer
Client: Kodak SA (Lausanne)
Agency: Young & Rubicam AG

1455 Distinctive Merit
Art Director: Klaus Erwarth
Designer: Jürgen Mick
Writer: Michael Freund
Client: Wiener Festwochen
Agency: Demner & Merlicek

1456

1457

1458

1459

1460

1456
Art Director: Ned Culic
Designer: Ned Culic
Illustrator/Artist: Ned Culic
Client: Australian Vintage Travel
Agency: David Lancashire Pty., Ltd.

1457 Silver Award
Art Director: Thomas Lüttge
Designer: Klaus Winterhager
Photographer: Thomas Lüttge
Writer: Andreas K. Heyne
Client: Zanders Feinpapiere AG
Director: Wolfgang Heuwinkel
Concept Director: Wolfgang Heuwinkel

1458
Art Director: Thomas Hönker
Photographer: Tom Jacobi
Publication: Stern
Layout: Norbert Kleiner

1459
Art Director: Hans-Georg Pospischil
Photographer: Stephen Erfurt
Editor: Thomas Schröder
Publisher: Dr. Bruno Dechamps

1460
Art Director: Rols Müeller
Designer: Thomas Schmid
Photographer: Thomas Schmid
Illustrator/Artist: Thomas Schmid
Agency: Bureau for Visual Communications

1461
Art Director: Joël Laroche
Photographer: John Claridge
Editor: Joël Laroche
Publication: Zoom

For the third time in 10 years John Claridge is appearing in ZOOM. A look at the photos published in 1977 proves that even the best can get better. Photography has improved, ZOOM has improved and John Claridge has improved. As a matter of fact, when you look at a 1977 issue of ZOOM, you wonder how something like that could find any readers. Perhaps

John Claridge

the readers have improved as well!
Claridge is 42 years old. Oddly enough, he looks younger. Ten years ago his photo had something rough about it, a kind of graininess which made him look incomplete. A Londoner from the East End, Claridge shares with the American photographer Maisel a childhood of poverty in sordid surroundings. But that is their only point in common because Maisel is a voyeur, the neutral witness of a reality which seems to prepare itself for him.
Claridge is more a director of reality. He organizes his visual world before capturing it. He does not just record it; he makes it beautiful. For that very reason he is above all an advertising photographer. His task is not to witness but to celebrate. Through his lens, even a wrecked car becomes an object of desire. When photographing ordinary objects, Claridge uses the techniques that others save for seductive photographs. And of course, through what one might call the photographer's paradox, which makes a specialist of the Wild West like Allard dream of photographing women, or Larry Dale Gordon talk of photographing something other than models, Claridge professes a passion for black and white which he saves for his «serious photos». That is what occupies three fourths of his time. The rest is reserved for his bread and butter; advertising photography for Fiat, Sony, Air India, BP, Lloyds Bank and, naturally, The Image Bank.

1462
Art Director: Wolfgang Hohndorf
Photographer: Wolfgang Hohndorf
Client: Wolfgang Hohndorf

1463 Gold Award
Art Director: Randolph Nolte
Photographer: Peter Knaup
Client: Schönwald
Agency: Randolph Nolte Creative Consultants

Blue Eyes

1464
Art Director: Philipp Alberto Hohndorf
Photographer: Wolfgang Hohndorf
Client: Wolfgang Hohndorf

1465
Art Director: Philipp Alberto Hohndorf
Photographer: Wolfgang Hohndorf
Client: Wolfgang Hohndorf

1466
Art Director: Philipp Alberto Hohndorf
Photographer: Wolfgang Hohndorf
Client: Wolfgang Hohndorf

1467
Art Director: Masaaki Izumiya
Writer: Koyo Koike
Client: Recruit
Agency: Hakuhodo Inc.

GIANT COMPASS
15 seconds

1468
Art Director: Satoshi Kawarabayashi
Designer: Tatsuya Ishii
Photographer: Yutaka Kobayashi
Writer: Kunihiko Tainaka
Client: Asahi Shimbun Publishing Co.
Agency: Dentsu Inc. (Osaka)
Director: Hirotsuga Horii

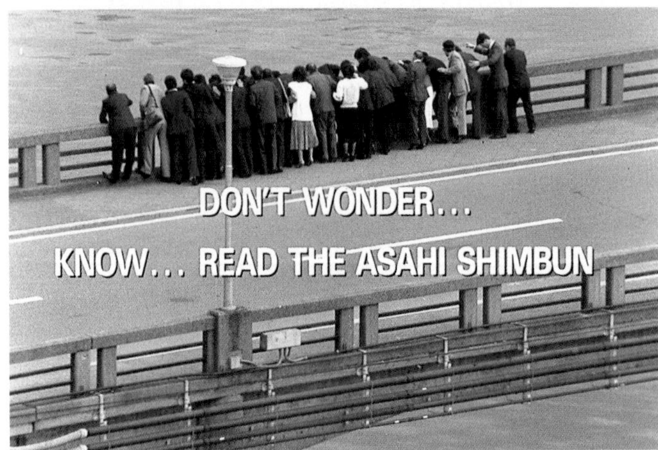

BRIDGE
30 seconds
GROUP: What?...What is what?...What?...What is what?
VO: Don't wonder....Know....Read the Asahi Shimbun.

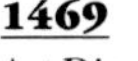
1469
Art Director: Jean-Claude Jouis
Agency: TBWA

AUTUMN LEAVES
30 seconds
MAN: Matresses exist for this!

1470
Art Director: Junichiro Akiyoshi
Photographer: Mitsuhiko Katayama
Writer: Hajime Nishio
Client: Matsushita Electric Industrial Co., Ltd.
Agency: Dentsu Inc. (Osaka)
Director: Masataka Satomi
Producer: Tsuneo Mido

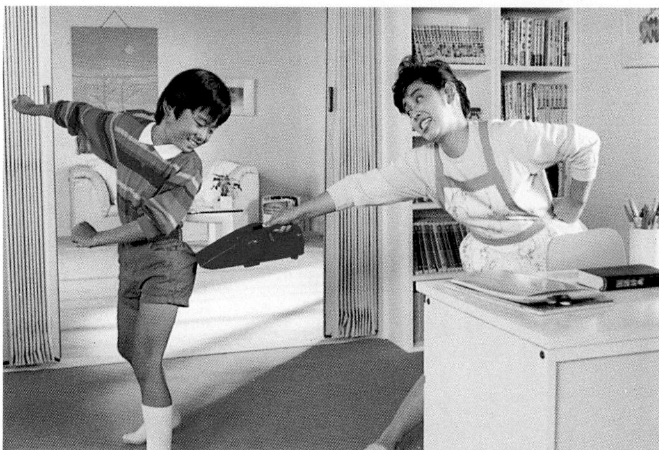

BACK TO YOUR STUDIES
30 seconds
VO: National's Cordless Cleaner, birdie quick and powerful.
MOTHER: Reading comics again?
VO: A powerful 8 volts.
MOTHER: Back to your studies.... Wait.

1471
Art Director: Janet Fox
Writer: Achim Szymanski
Editor: Bruce Leonard
Client: McDonald's Deutschland
Agency: Heye & Partner, Bruce Leonard, Janet Fox, Visiotronic (Munich)

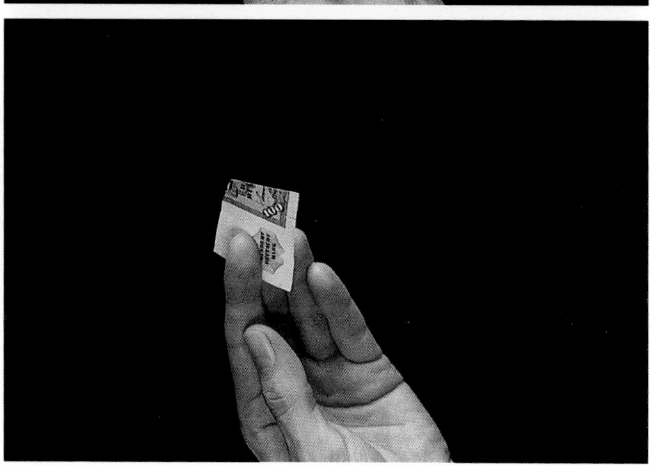

SNIP
15 seconds
SCRIPT UNAVAILABLE.

1472
Art Director: Annette Quinlivan
Writer: Deborah McAdam
Client: 3M Australia Ltd.
Agency: DDB Needham (Sydney) Pty., Ltd.

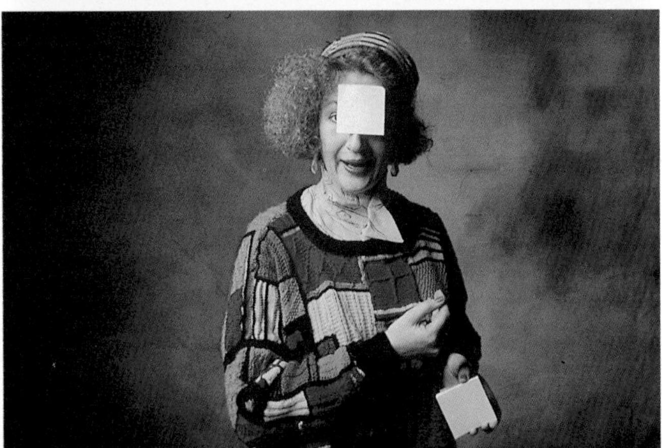

STICKS, DOESN'T IT
30 seconds
ANNIE: You know these little note pad things with the sticky bit on the back that you write messages to each other on? Well, they're called Post-It Notes. Get it stuck in your head. And if you think I'm going to do it again, you're absolutely right. You know these little note pad things with the sticky bit on the back that you write messages to each other on? Well, they're called Post-It Notes. Sticks, doesn't it. That's it. I'm not going to do it again. Get that stuck in your head.

1473
Art Director: Annette Quinlivan
Writer: Deborah McAdam
Client: 3M Australia Ltd.
Agency: DDB Needham (Sydney) Pty., Ltd.

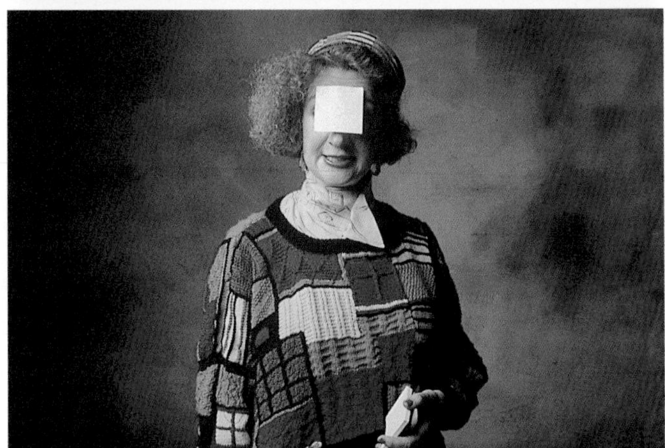
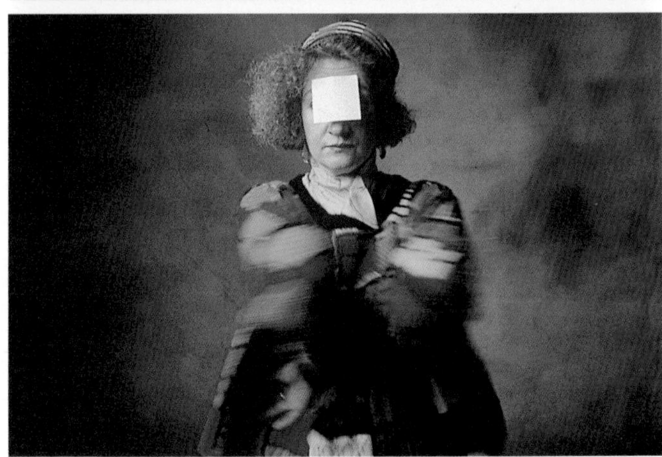

STICKY BIT
15 seconds
ANNIE: You know those little note pad things with the sticky bit on the back that you write messages to each other on? Well, they're called Post-It Notes. Get it stuck in your head.

1474
Art Director: Gary Betts
Writer: Malcolm Green
Editor: BFCS
Client: VAG (UK) Ltd.
Agency: DDB Needham (London)
Director: Mike Seresin
Producer: Howard Spivey

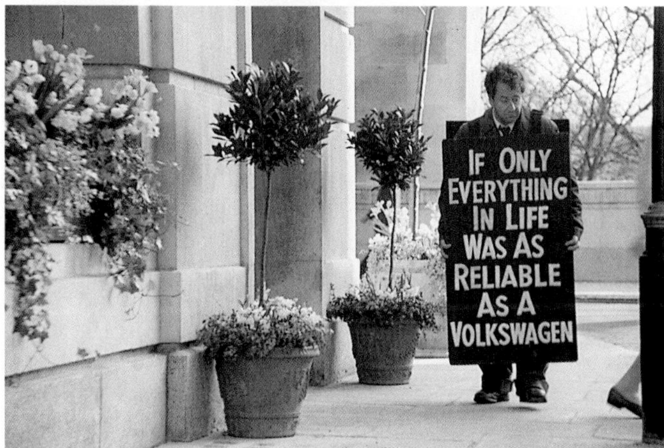

END OF THE WORLD
40 seconds
SFX: MUSIC THROUGHOUT. NO DIALOGUE. STRING QUARTET STARTING SAD, GETTING SADDER, BUT THEN BECOMING HAPPY WHEN THE MAN APPEARS WITH THE VOLKSWAGEN BOARD.

1475
Art Director: Steve Eltringham
Writer: Paul Ridley
Client: Johnson Wax
Agency: DDB Needham (London)
Director: Sid Roberson
Producer: Howard Spivey

RESULTS
30 seconds
MALE VO: In this demonstration, we gave Mrs. Crouch a burnt pan and a nylon scourer....We gave Mrs. Beck an equally burnt pan and a Brillo pad. And so they set to work. The results?... Exactly the same. Mrs. Beck's Brillo pad has given her a perfect shine. Mrs. Crouch's scourer has given her a perfect shine.. and amazing biceps. Brillo. Because cleaning power beats muscle power every time.

1476
Art Director: Garry Walton
Writer: Phil Wiggins
Client: Ti Creda
Agency: DDB Needham (London)
Director: Richard Loncraine
Producer: Angela King

SPIN
30 seconds
ANNCR: I'm here to demonstrate the latest washer/dryer from Creda, Europe's leading tumble-dryer manufacturer. It's not an ordinary washer/dryer . . .it's a drier washer. Its amazing 1150 spin speed forces more water out. So when you tumble-dry, it uses less electricity. . .and its reverse action helps stop your clothes tangling. I don't even need to be ironed.
MALE VO: Incredible? No. . . .Creda.

1477
Art Director: Graham Featherstone
Writer: Barry Greensted
Client: VAG (UK) Ltd.
Agency: DDB Needham (London)
Director: David Bailey
Producer: Howard Spivey

CHANGES
50 seconds
ALAN PRICE SINGING:
Everyone is going through changes
No-one knows what's going on.
And everybody changes places
But the world still carries on.
Love must always change to sorrow
And everyone must play the game.
It's here today and gone tomorrow
But the world goes on the same.

1478 Silver Award
Art Director: Bryan Graves, Michael Elliot
Writer: Susie Henry
Editor: Eddy French
Client: Sandvik
Agency: Waldron, Allen, Henry & Thompson Ltd.
Director: Judy Smith
Producer: Carrie Hart
Animation: Aardman Animation
Model Maker: Chris Lyons

RUNAWAY
30 seconds
SFX: BACKGROUND MUSIC AND NATURAL SOUNDS.
ANNCR: See this old table? I'm going to sand it down. Not with sandpaper...with this.
VO: With new Sandplate you can sand to a perfect finish in a fraction of the time. There's a Sandplate for every sanding job.
ANNCR: Shake hands.
VO: Big or small. And when you're finished, your Sandplate won't be.
ANNCR: Next.
VO: Sandplate from Sandvik.
ANNCR: One at a time, please.

1479 Silver Award
Art Director: Peter Celiz
Writer: Richard Saunders
Client: Rowntree/Kit Kat
Agency: J. Walter Thompson Co., Ltd.
Director: Richard Loncraine
Producer: Hugette De Chassiron

LIMBO
30 seconds
SFX: DING!...HEAVENLY MUZAK....DING!...SCREAMS OF THE DAMNED.
DEVIL: Shuddup!
ANGEL: Morning.
DEVIL: Morning.
SFX: DING! DING!
ANGEL: Well, no rest for the wicked.

1480
Art Director: Takehiko Miura
Photographer: Tetsuji Horino
Writer: Mitsuhiro Wada
Client: Nippon Telegraph & Telephone Corp.
Agency: Dentsu Inc. (Tokyo)
Director: Kikuhide Sekiguchi
Producer: Takeshi Ohnishi, Hideo Wakana

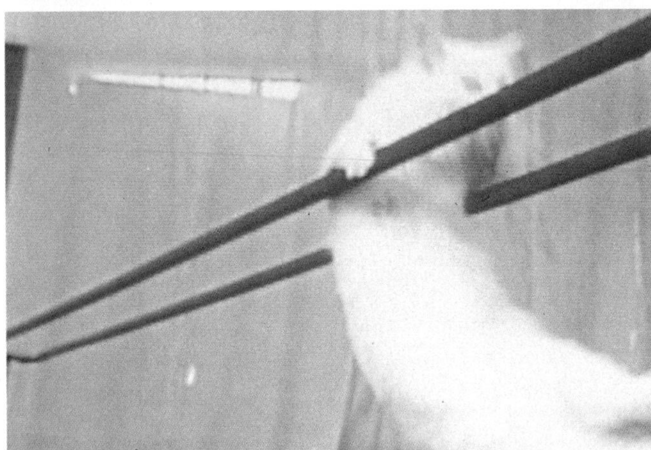

A CAT ON THE HORIZONTAL BAR
15 seconds
VO: If you find a telephone number starting from 0120, it is a toll-free dial. Your call will be automatically charged to the other party. Please remember the toll-free dial when you see a cat on the horizontal bar.

1481
Art Director: Takehiko Miura
Designer: Takehikoiura Miura
Photographer: Tatsuhiko Kobayashi
Writer: Mitsuhiro Wada
Client: Nippon Telegraph & Telephone Corp.
Agency: Dentsu Inc. (Tokyo)
Director: Jun Ichikawa
Producer: Takeshi Ohnishi, Hideo Wakana

LEFT HOME
60 seconds
VO: My telephone doesn't have to stay at home.... What a terrific idea.... New release from NTT.

1482
Art Director: Shuji Kuzugami
Designer: Mamoru Kusakawa
Photographer: Nozumu Sumita
Writer: Yuzo Nishihashi
Client: Matsushita Electric Industrial Co., Ltd.
Agency: Dentsu Inc. (Tokyo)
Director: Toshiaki Nozue
Producer: Itaru Uchijima

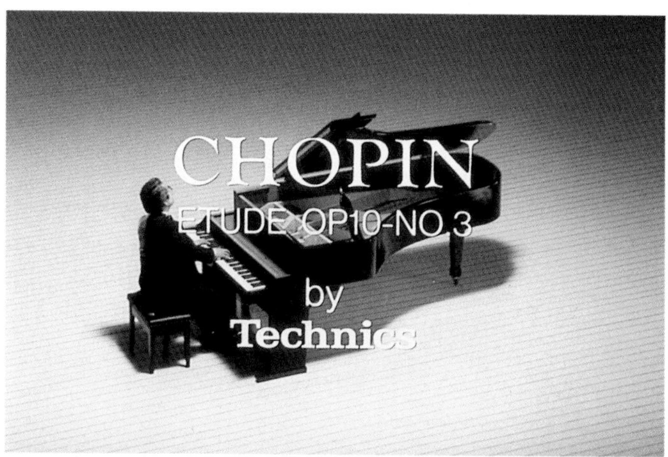

A MINIATURE GRAND PIANO
60 seconds
VO: PCM sound resource gets incredibly close to the fine touch and the acoustic sound of a full concert grand piano in a much smaller size.

1483 Gold Award
Art Director: Joanna Dickerson
Writer: Richard Phillips
Client: British Telecom
Agency: J. Walter Thompson Co., Ltd.
Director: Tony Smith
Producer: Nigel Foster

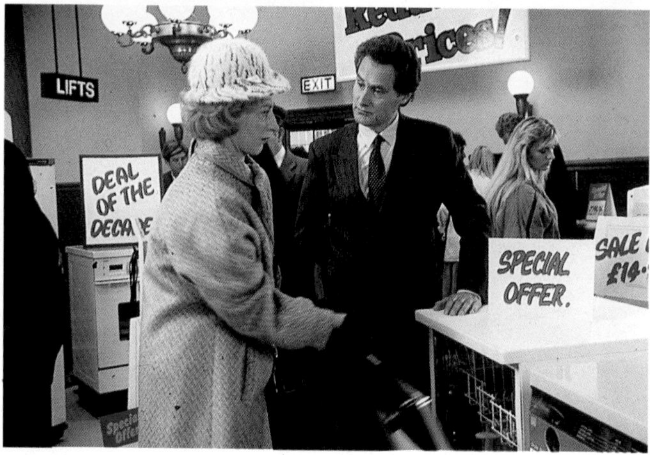

BARGAIN
50 seconds
MAUREEN: Yes. Oh, there you are. I'm interested in this washing machine.
SALES ASSISTANT #1: I'm sorry madam, this one's been reserved.
MAUREEN: Reserved!
SA #1: Yes, by a Mrs. Jones. She telephoned earlier this morning.
MAUREEN: Oh, young man. Could I take this one, please?
SA #2: Certainly.
SA #3: Sorry, George. That's been reserved. Mrs. Jones just phoned.
MAUREEN: Very nice. I've decided I'll take it.
SA #4: Sorry madam, a Mrs. Jones reserved this by phone.
MAUREEN: He's here again with his Mrs. Jones.
MALE VO: If you want the best of the bargains, phone first.
MAUREEN: And this one? Is this also reserved for Mrs. Jones?
SA #4: No madam, would you like it?
MAUREEN: No thank you. If it's not good enough for Mrs. Jones, it's not good enough for me.
MALE VO: British Telecom. It's you we answer to.

1484 Silver Award
Art Director: Rob Morris, Gary Betts, Graham Featherstone
Writer: Tony Brignull, Malcolm Green, Barry Greensted
Editor: BFCS
Client: VAG (UK) Ltd.
Agency: DDB Needham (London)
Director: Mike Seresin, David Bailey
Producer: Howard Spivey

CHANGES
50 seconds
ALAN PRICE SINGING:
Everyone is going through changes
No-one knows what's going on.
And everybody changes places.
But the world still carries on.
Love must always change to sorrow
And everyone must play the game.
It's here today and gone tomorrow
But the world goes on the same.

1485
Art Director: José Zaragoza
Photographer: José Augusto Zanetti
Writer: Neil Ferreira
Editor: Pedro José Garcia
Client: Kaiser Beer
Agency: DPZ Propaganda
Director: Claudio Meyer
Producer: Nova Filmes
Client Contact: Wesley Marine

MEN AT URINALS
30 seconds
SCRIPT UNAVAILABLE.

YEAR-END REVIEW

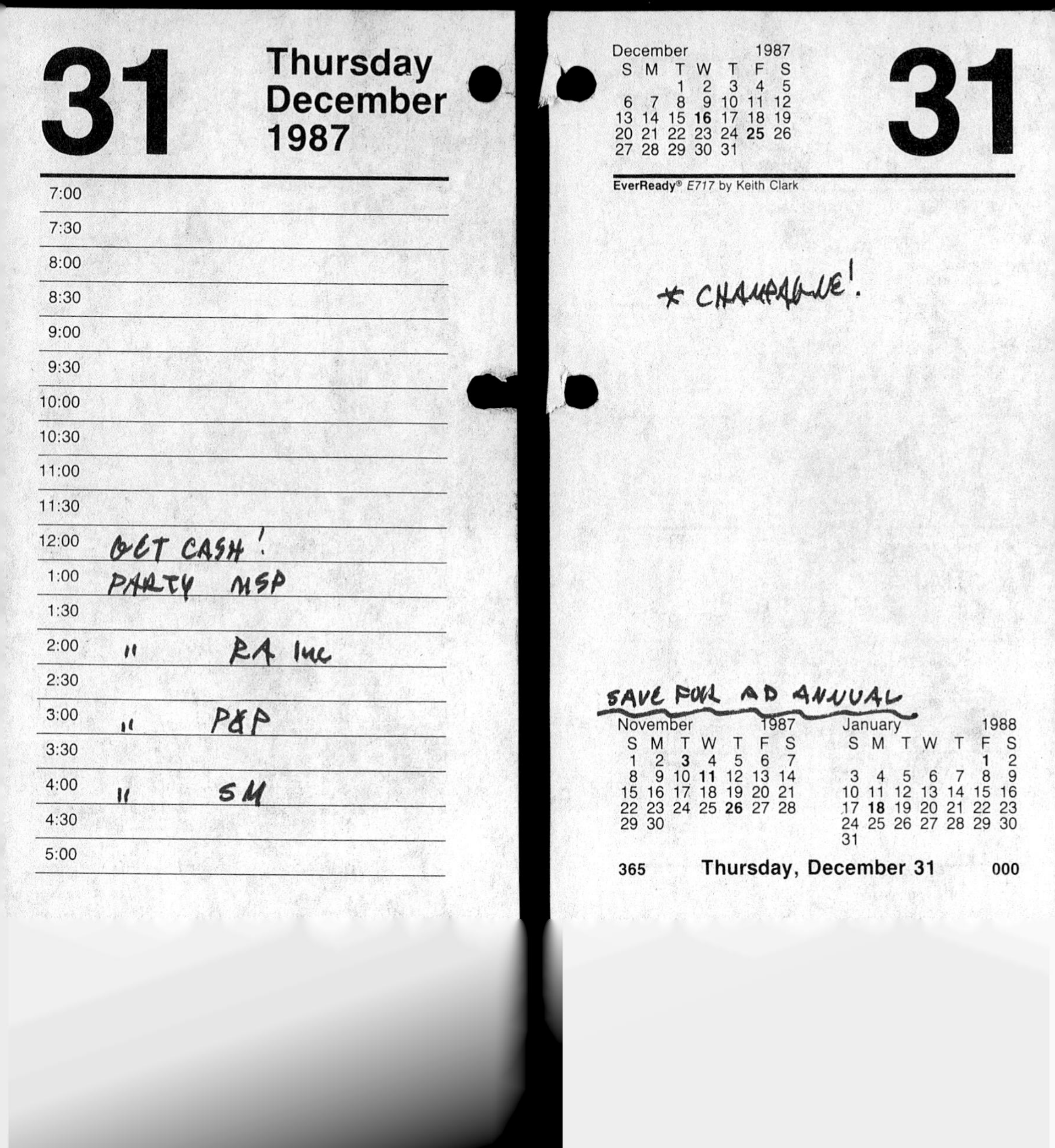

31 Thursday December 1987

7:00
7:30
8:00
8:30
9:00
9:30
10:00
10:30
11:00
11:30
12:00 GET CASH!
1:00 PARTY MSP
1:30
2:00 " RA Inc
2:30
3:00 " P&P
3:30
4:00 " SM
4:30
5:00

December 1987

S	M	T	W	T	F	S
		1	2	3	4	5
6	7	8	9	10	11	12
13	14	15	**16**	17	18	19
20	21	22	23	24	**25**	26
27	28	29	30	31		

31

EverReady® *E717* by Keith Clark

* CHAMPAGNE!

SAVE FOR AD ANNUAL

November 1987

S	M	T	W	T	F	S
1	2	**3**	4	5	6	7
8	9	10	**11**	12	13	14
15	16	17	18	19	20	21
22	23	24	25	**26**	27	28
29	30					

January 1988

S	M	T	W	T	F	S
					1	2
3	4	5	6	7	8	9
10	11	12	13	14	15	16
17	**18**	19	20	21	22	23
24	25	26	27	28	29	30
31						

365 **Thursday, December 31** **000**

PRESIDENT'S REPORT

Commitment. It's the theme Bernie Owett advanced, Alan Peckolick designed, and Kinuko Y. Craft so brilliantly illustrated, and what led to the work that's shown inside this great book.

Commitment. It's the basic fundamental on which the Art Directors Club was founded. A commitment to excellence, to doing the best work, selecting the best, and then showing it at our legendary *Annual Exhibition*. It's what led to the redesign of this annual and publishing it in full color . . . what led to our reaching out and establishing the *International Exhibition*. It led to the creation of the non-profit *Museum of Advertising and Communications Design* that will house the most definitive history of advertising and communications design in the nation. It will eventually include print and television collections from all over the world.

The ADC commitment to excellence includes the continuation of *Evenings with Some of the Greats*, expanded to include panels and presentations about the creation of the great contemporary campaigns, new business successes, and creative breakthroughs. The *Speaker Luncheons* continue to be entertaining and enlightening Wednesday happenings that expose our members and guests to who and what is new and important. The *Members Events Committee* has planned several semi-social, semi-professional gatherings that include issues that affect our profession from "Sex in Advertising" to "Political Advertising," and "The Subject is Wine," with many more topics to come.

The *ADC Gallery* provides the communications/design community with dynamic and informative shows throughout the year, including the Club's *Annual National and International Exhibitions*. We are planning an expanded *World Report on Communications Design* for February 1989 that will be a two-day series of presentations, seminars, and panel discussions of topics including Graphic Design, Advertising, Packaging, and Promotion from the United States and abroad. It will feature leading advertising and design practitioners from around the globe, including the members of our prestigious ADC Hall of Fame.

The newly-designed and computer-produced *ADC Newsletter* will keep you informed – on a regular basis – about what's happening at the Club and with our members. Our *Computer Seminars and Workshops* have been very successful in introducing many people to the mysteries of computer graphics and desk-top publishing. Seminars on computer prepress production techniques will help us stay abreast of the newest developments in design and production. And, there's talk of a mill-supported paper library.

We're committed to serving our expanding membership in every way we can. We believe that it is a primary aspect of the Club's mandate. As with all clubs, we depend on the commitment of the committees and chairpersons to keep things going, and they have been very enthusiastic and creative. We can't live without them and we look forward to having new members swell their ranks. And speaking of commitment, we get a lot of support from our dedicated and – yes – committed staff, led by Diane Moore, Executive Director. Without them this president, or any other, wouldn't last five minutes. My thanks to them as President and as an appreciative member of the Art Directors Club.

Karl H. Steinbrenner

Editorial

Tom Bodkin
Nancy Butkus
Bob Ciano
John Tom Cohoe
Catherine Connors
James Craig
Anna Deus
Bob Eisner
Blanche Fiorenza
Paul Hardy
Anne Jones
Terry Koppel
Sal Lazzarotti
Sue Llewelyn
Alfred Lowry
Tobias Moss
Robert Priest
George Samerjan
David Seager
Eric Seidman
Pandora Spelios
Melissa Tardiff
Shinichiro Tora
Anne Twomey

Television

Cathy Bangel
Jacques Borris
Roger Feuerman
Harvey Gabor
Don Gill
Frank Ginsberg
Lisa Halperin
Michael Hart
Paul Kirner
Irwin Kirz
Pat LeBaron
John Lucci
John Margeotes
Richard Martel
Marce Mayhew
Marty Muller
Marcus Nispel
Jon Parkinson
John Rea
Ronald Rosen
Jill Spacek
Dean Stefanides
Karl H. Steinbrenner
Thomas Vogel
Terry Walker

Bernie Owett

67th National Judging

INTERNATIONAL EXHIBITION COMMITTEE

Before discussing the 2nd Annual International Exhibition, there are two questions all of us connected with this event have been asked. I hope we can answer those questions once and for all. The first question is "Why do we *need* an International Exhibition?" and the second is "What makes the New York Art Directors Club think it is qualified to judge an *International* Exhibition?"

To put the first question "Why do we need an international show?" to rest, we think it is only necessary for you to look around your office, living room, kitchen, and garage. How many of your possessions were manufactured or designed abroad? How many of the products you as an Art Director work on are sold abroad? How many of the stories that fill today's newspapers deal with issues that transcend the boundaries of this country?

Global interdependence is a fact, and we as visual communicators are perhaps in a unique position to learn from, and to benefit from the work being created by our counterparts in the rest of the world.

As to the second question, "What makes the New York Art Directors Club think it is qualified to judge an *International* Exhibition?," we think that a nation and a city made up of immigrants is a logical place for an international anything. And to insure that we would not judge the show in a narrow, nationalistic way, or misjudge a piece through ignorance of the conditions under which it was produced, we invited eight internationally famous art directors from around the globe to help judge the show.

On the weekend of February 6 and 7, they, along with nine members of the ADC Hall of Fame and two Advisory Board members looked at almost 2,000 commercials, ads, posters, magazines, books, and packages to come up with what we honestly feel is one of the most significant collections of work you will see this year.

In addition, the eight international art directors graciously agreed to stay over through Monday February 8 to participate in a panel discussion moderated by Ivan Chermayeff and Massimo Vignelli and held at the Art Directors Club. This was an informal evening without much advance publicity; yet even so, the Club was completely sold out, and there are plans for a more formal conference next year. The International Show has become, after only two years, an integral and important part of the Art Directors Club's activities and perhaps contributes to the global perception that we are the world's premier organization of visual communication.

Andrew Kner, 2nd International Exhibition Co-chairman

Andrew Zwiebel, 2nd International Exhibition Co-chairman

The Judges

William H. Buckley, Advisory Board
Ivan Chermayeff, Hall of Fame
Seymour Chwast, Hall of Fame
Lou Dorfsman, Hall of Fame
Gene Federico, Hall of Fame
Alan Fletcher, England
Roy Grace, Hall of Fame
Gyorgy Haiman, Hungary
Francesco Petit, Brazil
Hans Georg Pospischil, Germany
Eileen Hedy Schultz, Advisory Board
Louis Silverstein, Hall of Fame
Robert Smith, Advisory Board
Henry Steiner, Hong Kong
Ikko Tanaka, Japan
William Taubin, Hall of Fame
Yarom Vardimon, Israel
Massimo Vignelli, Hall of Fame
Maxim Zhukov, Soviet Union

Massimo Vignelli, Francesc Petit, and Ivan Chermayeff at the ADC "World Report on Communication Design" symposium

TRAVELING EXHIBITION COMMITTEE

The Art Directors Club 66th Annual Exhibition traveled extensively throughout the United States during 1987-88. It made stops at:

Utah State Historical Society, Salt Lake City, Utah

Visivo Partnership, Columbus, Ohio

Airport Hilton Inn, Greensboro, North Carolina

Queens Gallery, Charlotte, North Carolina

Koehler Cultural Center, San Antonio, Texas

Art Institute of Atlanta, Georgia

Bixby Gallery, St. Louis, Missouri

Cococino Center for the Arts, Flagstaff, Arizona

Communication Artists of New Mexico, Albuquerque

With the help of ADC nonresident members Masuteru Aoba, Shigeo Okamoto, and Takeo Yao and Japan's *Idea* magazine, the 66th Annual Exhibition and the 1st Annual International Exhibition toured successfully through Japan. The pieces from the 1st Annual International Exhibition were well received and helped establish this event's importance in Japan. There will no doubt be a large Japanese response to the next international call for entries.

Mainichi Broadcasting System again sponsored lectures given in December by ADC Hall of Famer, Len Sirowitz, in Tokyo and Osaka.

From April 20 to May 3, 1988 a joint showing of the 66th Annual Exhibition and the 1st Annual International Exhibition along with selected pieces from the Tokyo Art Directors Club was held in Beijing. This is the first design show of this kind **EVER** presented in the People's Republic of China. It was made possible by the joint efforts of ADC member Shin Tora and officials from the China Exhibition Agency at the National Arts Museum in Beijing. The show was sponsored jointly by the New York and Tokyo Art Directors Clubs. Art directors from Japan and Shin Tora from New York attended the opening of the "First International Art Directors Exhibition" in China.

Minoru Morita,
Traveling Exhibition Chairman

Shinichiro Tora, Board Liaison

The 1st Annual International Show at the Semba Design Center, Osaka; photograph by Shin Tora

GALLERY COMMITTEE

The year 1987 truly expressed the commitment of the ADC gallery to maintain and promote an extremely high standard of professionalism for the entire visual communications community.

We proudly presented shows representing: the Japanese Advertising Association, the Association of Graphic Arts, the Society of Publication Designers Competition, Illustration, and Photography, Advertising Women of New York Fine Arts, the Hall of Fame Patrons, Kodak Photography, the Henry Street Settlement House, Japanese Calendar Auction, Brazilian Graphics, and the School of Visual Arts Student Portfolio and 40th Anniversary.

And, of course, we presented our own Art Directors Club Annual Show. This show exhibited over 2,000 pieces by using partitions on both the main and lower levels and demonstrated the size and flexibility of the gallery.

In short, the gallery is fast becoming the New York City showcase of graphic communication.

Richard Wilde, Gallery Chairman

Steve Heller, Board Liaison

Laura Duggan
Michael Urich

"Hall of Fame Patrons" show, Lower Gallery

Show organizer, Felipe Taborda, at "Brazil Designs"

MEMBERS EVENTS COMMITTEE

Exciting things are happening with the Members Events Committee. We are continuing to plan social/cultural events designed to facilitate interaction among our members. Our committee has been responsible for the panel discussion on sex in advertising, the wine-tasting evening, Christmas and Valentine's Day parties, and much more. We look forward to the continued and increased support of the membership in the upcoming year.

The Members Events Committee would like to thank our new president, Karl H. Steinbrenner and the Board of Directors for their enthusiasm and support of our committee. Special thanks are also due to Diane Moore and her staff for making our events possible.

Diane Depasque,
Members Events Co-Chairwoman

Karl Eric Steinbrenner,
Members Events Co-Chairman

Gladys Barton, Board Liaison
Dennis Arnold
Eva Costabel
Jane Haber
George Gilbert Lott
Shireen Nathoo
Judy Roberts
Herbert M. Rosenthal
Richard Salcer
Paula Thompson
Dorothy Wachtenheim
Keith Waltas

Members Events Committee: back row: Richard Salcer, Dennis Arnold, Keith Waltas, George Lott, Judy Roberts; middle row: Eva Costabel, Jane Haber, Paula Thompson, Dorothy Wachtenheim, Shireen Nathoo; front row: Herb Rosenthal, Diane Depasque, Karl Eric Steinbrenner

MEMBERSHIP COMMITTEE

The membership committee is responsible for reviewing and approving applications for Club membership. We really do check those forms to find out whether that scrawl next to "sponsor" is actually a member's signature and whether that birthdate qualifies an individual for junior membership. We are, however, also concerned with membership in the broader sense–concerned with what the Club can do for its members and vice versa.

It has been our pleasure to welcome 107 new members during the past year and to note the ever-increasing national and international interest in the Club. There are 19 new nonresident members and, of these, 10 are from abroad.

The annual New Members Party was held at the Club on February 25, 1988 and provided an opportunity for old and new members to get acquainted while enjoying the great food and music that are ADC trademarks.

A big "thank you" to Diane Moore, Executive Director, to the ADC staff who help us throughout the year, and to my fellow committee members.

Cissy Bruce, Membership Chairwoman

Lorraine Allen
Adrienne Brooks
Charles Dickenson
Mike Fenga
Blanche Fiorenza
Sal Lazzarotti
Ruth Lubell
Richard MacFarlane
Beverly Schrager
Shinichiro Tora

NEWSLETTER REPORT

This past year has been a busy one for the Club, and consequently, for the Newsletter. ADC members Shinichiro Tora, Dave Stahlberg, and Ralph Casado continued to make significant contributions, while photographers Bob Essel, the Ihara Studio, and staff member Dan Forté helped us include as many smiling faces as possible.

Club president Karl Steinbrenner inaugurated a new column aptly named "President's Corner." His first column was a call to ADC members to communicate with each other via the Newsletter. We echo his words by asking you to keep us informed of all the wonderful things happening in your professional lives.

The Newsletter is currently being reorganized in the hopes of establishing a committee of contributors and columnists. Anyone with great ideas and lots of spare time is invited to contact Dan Forté at the Club. We need your cooperation and suggestions to make this a publication truly reflective of our membership

Ruth Lubell, Newsletter Chairwoman

Karl H. Steinbrenner and new members

Ruth Lubell

WEDNESDAY SPEAKERS LUNCHEON COMMITTEE

We are growing stronger and bolder with each program. The liveliness of our guest speakers on hot topics has spurred multiple discussions and created an environment of stimulating experiences. With such luminaries as Bob Gill, Milton Glaser, Les Goldberg, Art Kane, Duane Michaels, Don Munroe, B. Martin Peterson, and Erik Spielermann, we are creating an awareness of all international areas of our industry.

The expertise of Dee Dee Mancher and ADC staff members Joan Nordlinger, Bonnie Rosenfeld, Glen Kubota, Virginia Petty, Debra Bock Woo, Margaret (Cookie) Busweiler, and S. J. Toy, has made these programs very special and as exciting as ever. We can never adequately thank everyone involved and look forward to a new season of wonderful surprises.

Robin Sweet, Wednesday Speakers Luncheon Chairwoman

Les Goldberg

Robin Sweet, Tony Palladino, and Karl Steinbrenner

PORTFOLIO REVIEW COMMITTEE

This Spring, like so many others, Mondays and Fridays are devoted to the Portfolio Review. Graduating seniors from across the country met one-on-one with Club members from every field of design to discuss their portfolios and their futures.

The schools represented were: C. W. Post Campus of Long Island University; Fashion Institute of Technology, New York City; Kutztown University, Kutztown PA; Moore College of Art, Philadelphia; New York City Technical College; Parsons School of Design, New York City; Pratt Institute, Brooklyn; Pratt Manhattan Center; Syracuse University; Tyler School of Art, Elkins Park PA; University of Delaware, Newark; University of Rochester; Youngstown University, Youngstown OH.

It was a lively and rewarding exchange of ideas that benefited students and art directors alike. For the students, it was a valuable way to have their work critiqued. For the art directors, it was a way to meet and gauge the talent that is about to graduate and begin their careers.

The Portfolio Review Program was successful to a large part because of the cooperation, enthusiasm, and dedication of the art directors who participated. We wish to thank each of them. Special thanks also go to ADC staff members Joan Nordlinger and Virginia Petty who coordinated the entire program.

Ciro Tesoro,
Portfolio Review Co-chairman

Dorothy Wachtenheim,
Portfolio Review Co-chairwoman

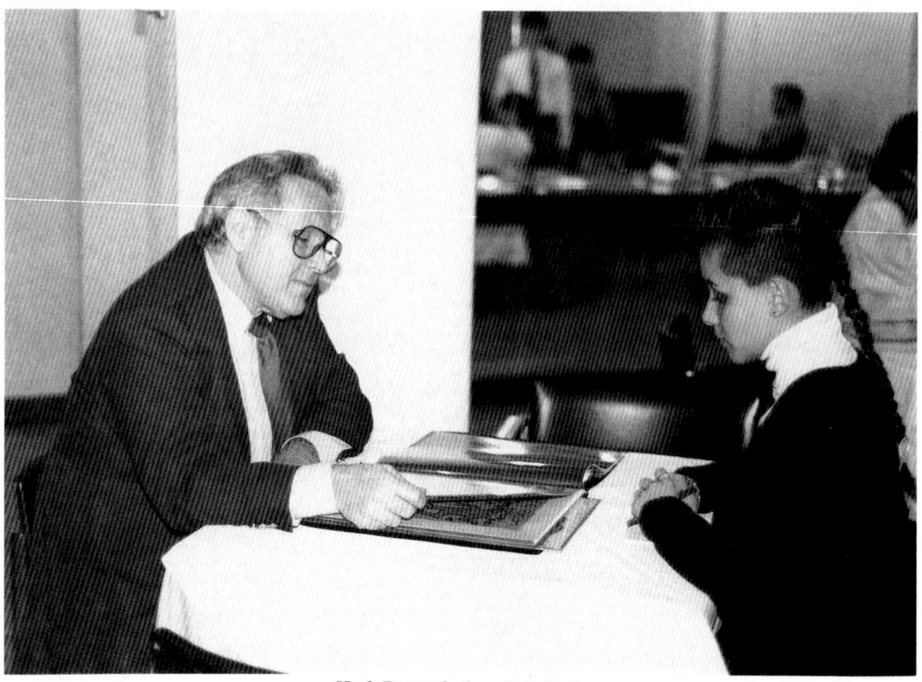

Herb Rosenthal and student

VISUAL COMMUNICATORS EDUCATION FUND INC.

The Visual Communicators Education Fund Inc. is a nonprofit organization within the Art Directors Club. It has one simple mission, to provide tuition scholarships to talented design students attending metropolitan-area art schools. Our endowment fund is modest. Yet, on May 9, 1988, at ceremonies held at the Club, the VCEF gave tuition awards totaling $14,000 to some wonderfully talented students.

The following students received awards of excellence this year.

Cooper Union School of Art

Kathryn Cimis
Kim Elizabeth Powick

Fashion Institute of Technology

Christine Flynn
Julie Herbig
Lisa McGowan
Naomi Taubleb

New York City Technical College

Thanh Du, Roz Goldfarb Award
Elias Jacobs
Richard Wang
Peter Wood
Stephanie Zedlovich

Parsons School of Design

Leslie Greenslet, Richard Taubin Award
Ann Kim
Christine Licata
Manuel Martinez
Edith Stone, Book-of-the-Month Club Award

Pratt Institute

Laura Bonapace
Brian Dempsey

Pratt Manhattan Center

Susan Anson
Andrew Bogucki
Ariel Kotzer
Randy Morrow

School of Visual Arts

Sarika Aggarwal
David Lau
Ed Melnitsky
Sharon Okamoto
Juliana Wright

Bob Blattner, a member of the VCEF Committee since its inception, retired this year. He was responsible for two generous contributions from the Lila Acheson Wallace High Winds Fund, which substantially supports the VCEF. Individual scholarships continue: the Richard Taubin Award, in memory of Mr. & Mrs. Bill Taubin's son; the Book-of-the-Month Club Award, which I obtained for the Fund; and, new this year, a scholarship donated by Roz Goldfarb.

Two years ago, we instituted a new way to raise funds for the scholarships. Entry fees from the Club's Annual Exhibition include a one-dollar contribution to the VCEF. The VCEF is actively seeking your support. We depend solely on individual and corporate contributions to help the endowment fund. Thank you.

Jessica Weber, Visual Communicators Education Fund Inc. President

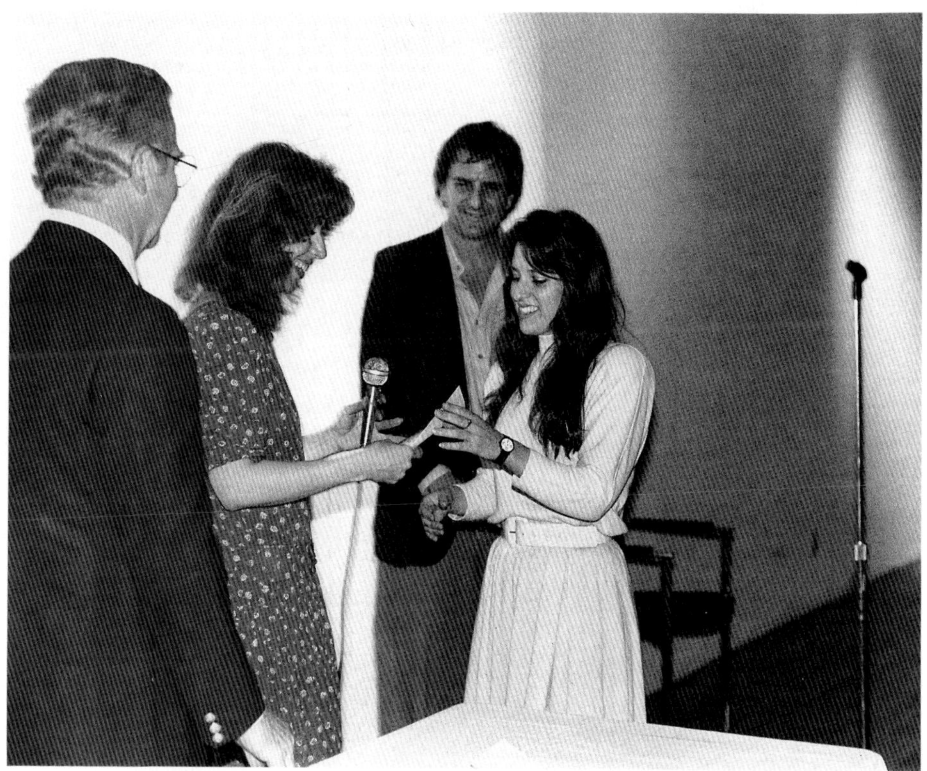

Bill Brockmeier, Jessica Weber, Richard Wilde, and student Award Winner

ADC NATIONAL MEMBERS

A

Donald Adamec
Tina Adamek
Gaylord Adams
Steven Adams
Patricia Addiss
Jane Adler
Peter Adler
Charles Adorney
Ads Magazine
Warren Aldoretta
Charles E. Allen
Lorraine Allen
Carlo Ammirati
Joseph Anderson
Gennaro Andreozzi
Ted Andreseakes
Al Anthony
Robert Anthony
Arnold Arlow
Dennis M. Arnold
Herman Aronson
Rochelle L. Arthur
Tadashi Asano
Marvin Asch
Seymour Augenbraun
Gordon C. Aymar
Joel Azerrad

B

Jeff Babitz
Alberto Baccari
Robert O. Bach
Jeffrey S. Bacon
Ronald Bacsa
Priscilla Baer
Frank Baker
Leslie Baker
Ronald Ballister
Carla Barr
Letitia Barroll
Don Barron
Robert Barthelmes
Gladys Barton
Matthew Baslie
Wendy Bass
Mary K. Baumann
Allen Beaver
Marcia Ben Eli
Ephram E. Benguiat
Edward J. Bennett
Howard Benson
Laurence Key Benson
John Berg
Sy Berkley
Pamme J. Berman
Loren Bernstein
Park Berry
Barbara Bert
Peter J. Bertolami
Frank Bertulis
Robert Best
Roger Black
Janet Blank
Robert H. Blend
Bruce Bloch
David S. Block
Arnold Blumberg
Robert Bode
Ronne Bonder
Geroge Warren Booth
John Boothroyd
Jeroen Bours
Harold A. Bowman
Carolyn Bowyer
Doug Boyd
Douglas C. Boyd
Jean L. Brady
Simeon Braguin
Joan Brandt
Fred J. Braver
Al Braverman
Barry Braverman
Carolyn W. Bray
Denise Breslin
Lynn Dreese Breslin
William P. Brockmeier
Ed Brodsky
Ruth Brody
Adrienne G. Brooks
Joe Brooks
Ilene Renee Brown
Cissy Bruce
Robert Bruce
Bruno E. Brugnatelli
Lee Buchar
William Buckley
Aaron Burns
Herman F. Burns
Laurie Burns
Cipe P. Burtin

C

Bill Cadge
Albert J. Calzetta
Arline Campbell
Jack D. Campbell
Stuart Campbell
Bryan Canniff
Michael R. Capobianco
Tony Cappiello
Thomas Carnase
David E. Carter
Ralph Casado
Angelo Castelli
John R. Centanni
Carol F. Ceramicoli
Edward Cerullo
Jean Chambers
Anthony Chaplinsky Jr.
Vivian Chen
John Cherry
Richard S. Chesler
Roberta Chiarella
Younghee Choi
Shui-Fong Chong
Alan Christie
Stanley Church
Seymour Chwast
Bob Ciano
Jon Cisler
Thomas F. Clemente
Mahlon Cline
Victor Closi
Joann Coates
Joel Cohen
Charles Coiner
Beth Schack Coleman
Michael Coll
Eleanor Colston
Catherine Connors
Daniel Cooper-Bey
Dinah Coops
Lee Corey
Eva Costabel
Sheldon Cotler
Ron Couture
Phyllis Richmond Cox
Robert Cox
Thomas J. Craddock
James Craig
Meg Crane
Brian A. Cranner
Constance Craven
Elaine Crawford
Adam Cricchio
Bob Crozier
Louis F. Cruz
Jerry Cummins
Charles Cutler
Ethel R. Cutler
Gregory F. Cutshaw

D

Royal Dadmun
Derek Dalton
Wendy Damico
David Davidian
Kathryn Davidian
David Davis
Herman Davis
Joseph Davis
Philip Davis
Erick DeMartino
Jan Dechabert
Robert Defrin
Joe Del Soebo
Michael B. Delia
Jerry Demoney
Diane Depasoque
David Deutsch
Frank M. Devino
Francis J. Devito
Peter J. Deweerdt
Gary DiLuca
Joyce C. DiMauro
Charles Dickinson
Arthur Hill Diedrick
Carolyn Diehl
Edward P. Diehl
John Dignam
Al Diorio
Lou Donato
Chel S. Dong
Louis Dorfsman
Marc Dorian
Andra Douglas
Kay Elizabeth Douglas
Nick Driver
Rina Drucker
Faye Eileen Druiz
Ann Dubiel
Donald H. Duffy
William R. Duffy
Laura K. Duggan
Rosalyn C. Dunham
Rudolph Dusek
Michael Dweck

E

Stephen T. Eames
Bernard Eckstein
Peter Edgar
Don Egensteiner
Jack Ehn
Antonie Eichenberg
Zeneth Eidel
Stanley Eisenman
Robert Eisner
Jane Eldershaw
Wallace W. Elton
Malcolm End
David Epstein
Lee Epstein
Lois A. Erlacher
Suren Ermoyan

F

Carolyn Fanelli
Abe Farrell
Gene Federico
Judy Fendelman
Michael Fenga
Roger Ferritter
Michael Fidanzato
Blanche Fiorenza
Gon Firpo
Carl Fischer
Wayne Fitzpatrick
John Flanagan
Morton Fleischer
Gilbert D. Fletcher
Donald P. Flock
Peggy Ford-Fyffe
Jim Forkan
Jan Foster
John Fraioli
Stephen O. Frankfurt
Richard G. Franklin
Gennaro Franzese
Amy Fread
Cheryl Freed
Frederic B. Freyer
Ruby Friedland
Joseph Friedman
Oren Frost
Paul Fuentes
Neil Fujita
Takeshi Fukunaga
Leonard W. Fury

G

Harvey Gabor
Raymond M. Gaeta
Robert Gage
Rosemarie Galioto
Danielle Gallo
Gene Garlanda
David Gatti
Joseph T. Gauss
Alberto P. Gavasci
Howard Geissler
Charles Gennarelli
Gloria Gentile
Joseph Gering
Michael Germarkian
Linda Gersh
John Geryak
Victor Gialleonardo
Edward Gibbs
Carol Bonnie Gildar
Donald Gill
Peter C. Gilleran
Frank C. Ginsberg
Sara Giovanitti
Jon M. Giunta
George Giusti
Milton Glaser
Eric Gluckman
Marc Gobe
Bennet Gold
Bill Gold
Irwin Goldberg
Les Goldberg
Roz Goldfarb
Amy E. Goldman
Eli W. Goldowsky
Jo Ann Goldsmith
Laura J. Goodman
Cyd Gorman
Roy Grace
Diana Graham
Susan Greenbaum
Richard Grider
Jack Griffin
Walter Grotz
Susan Grube
Irving Grunbaum
Nelson Gruppo
Dolores Gudzin
Lurelle Guild
Rollins S. Guild
Jean Emanuel Guyader

H

John B. Haag
Thomas W. Haas
Jane Haber
Hank Hachmann
Robert Hack
Kurt Haiman
Graham Halky
Evertt Halvorsen
Shoichiro Hama
Virginia Murphy Hamill
Edward Hamilton
Frances M. Hamilton
Jerome A. Handman
Paul Hartelius Jr.
George Hartman
Lillian Hartung
Alan Hartwell
Barry Hassell
Carolyn Hawks
Dorothy E. Hayes
Saul Heff
Amy Heit
Shelley L. Heller
Steven Heller
Randall Hensley
Robert S. Herald
Louis F. Hernandez
Susan Herr
Chris Hill
Peter M. Hirsch
Jitsuo Hoashi
Roland Hodes
Marilyn Hoffner
Leslie Hopkins
William Hopkins
Steve Horn
David W. Houser
Jonathan M. Houston
Phillipe-Louis Houze
Joe Hovanec
Elizabeth Howard
Paul Howard
Julie Hubner
Roy Alan Hughes
Thomas M. Hughes
Virginia Hull
Wayne Hulse
Jim Hunt
Jud Hurd
Gary Husk
Melanie Jennings Husk
Morton Hyatt

I

Tom J. Ide
Ana J. Inoa
Henry Isdith
Edward Israel

J

Joseph Jackson
Robert T. Jackson
Harry Jacobs
Holly Jaffe
Lee Ann Jaffee
Jack Jamison
Georgette Jasen
John C. Jay
Bill Jensen
Patricia Jerina
Barbara John
Shaun Johnston
Susan Johnston
Homer Lynn Jolly
Anne M. Jones
Bob Jones
Kristina M. Jones
Roger Joslyn
Len Jossel
Barbara L. Junker

K

Nita J. Kalish
Kiyoshi Kanai
Cheryl Kaplan
Walter Kaprielian
Judy Katz
Rachel Katzen
M. Richard Kaufmann
Ward Kelvin
Ken Kendrick
Alice Kenny
Nancy Kent
Myron W. Kenzer
Michelle Kestin
Ellen Sue Kier
Leslie Kirschenbaum
Gerald Klein
Judith Klein
Mark Kleinfeld
Hilda Stranger Klyde
Andrew Kner
Henry Knoepfler
Ray Komai
Robert F. Kopelman
Nick Koudis
Oscar Krauss
Helmut Krone
Thaddeus B. Kubis
Bill Kuchler
Anna Kurz

L

Howard La Marca
James E. Laird
Abril Lamarque
David R. Lance
Joseph O. Landi
Michael Lanotte
John Larkin
Ann Latrobe
Pearl Lau
Kenneth H. Lavey
Marie Christine Lawrence
Sal Lazzarotti
Jeffery Leder
Daniel Lee
Edwin E. Lee
Robert C. Leung
Richard Levenson
Leslie Leventman
Gus Liapis
Alexander Lieberman
Victor Liebert
Hoi Ling Chu
Barbara Lippert
Beverly Littlewood
Susan Llewllyn
Leo Lobell
George Lois
Henry R. Loomis
Michael Losardo
Rocco Lotito
George Gilbert Lott
Robert Louey
Jackson Lowell
Alfred Lowry
Ruth Lubell
John Lucci
Richard Luden
John H. Luke
Thomas R. Lunde
Larry Lurin
Robert W. Lyon Jr.
Michael J. Lyons

M

Charles MacDonald
Richard MacFarlane
David H. MacInnes
Frank Macri
Sam Magdoff
Louis Magnani
Carol A. Maisto
Anthony Mancino
Jean Marcellino
John Margeotes
David R. Margolis
John S. Marmaras
Andrea Marquez
Bill Marsano
Al Marshall
Daniel Marshall
William R. Martin
Caren J. Martineau
Michael Mastros
Theodore Matyas
Andrea Freund Mauro
Marce Mayhew
Victor J. Mazurkiewicz
William McCaffery
Constance McCaffrey
Kevin McCauley
John McCuen
Mark S. McDowell
Mandi McIntyre
Scott A. Mednick
William Meehan
Nancy A. Meher
Mario G. Messina
Lyle Metzdorf
Jackie Merri Meyer
Emil T. Micha
Eugene Milbauer
Jean Miller
Lawrence Miller
John Milligan
Isaac Millman
William Minko
Michael Miranda
Leonard J. Mizerek
Allan Mogel
Cheryl Mohrman
Joseph Montebello
Burton A. Morgan
Jeffrey Moriber
Minoru Morita
Leonard Morris
William R. Morrison
Thomas Morton
Roger Paul Mosconi
Louie Moses
Roselee Moskowitz
Geoffrey Moss
Tobias Moss
Dale Moyer
Robbi G. Muir
Marty Muller
Ralph J. Mutter

N

Shireen Nathoo
Mattlyn Natoli
Daniel Nelson
John Newcomb
Andrew M. Newman
Stuart Nezin
Deborah Nichols
Mary Ann Nichols
Raymond Nichols
Marcus Nispel
Joseph Nissen
Evelyn C. Noether
David November

C. Alexander Nuckols

O
Frank O'Blak
Bernard O'Connor
John O'Neil
Hugh O'Neill
Jack W. Odette
Noriyuki Okazaki
John Okladek
Susan Alexis Orlie
Garrett P. Orr
Nina Ovryn
Bernard S. Owett

P
Onofrio Paccione
Zlata W. Paces
Maxine Paetro
Robert Paganucci
Robert A. Paige
Brad Pallas
Roxanne Panero
Nicholas Peter Pappas
Jacques Parker
Paul E. Parker Jr.
Grant Parrish
Cynthia Parsons
Joanne Pateman
Charles W. Pates
Arthur Paul
Dianne M. Pavacic
Leonard Pearl
Robert Pearlman
Barbara Pearson
Alan Peckolick
B. Martin Pedersen
Carol Peligian
Paul Pento
Vincent Pepi
Bea Perron
Tony Perrotti
David S. Perry
Harold A. Perry
Roberta Perry
Victoria I. Peslak
John Peter
Peter Scannell Inc.
Christos Peterson
Robert L. Peterson
Robert Petrocelli
Theodore D. Pettus
Allan Philiba
Gerald M. Philips
Alma M. Phipps
Joseph Piatti
George Pierson
Michael Pilla
Ernest Pioppo
Ernest Pioppo
Peter Pioppo
Robert Pliskin
Raymond Podeszwa
George Polk
Richard Portner
Louis Portuesi
Anthony Pozsonyi
Benjamin Pride
Bob Procida
Rory James Pszenitzki
Jay Purvis

Q
Charles W. Queener
Elissa Querze
Anny Queyroy
Mario Quilles
Kathleen Quinn
Mike Quon

R
Judith G. Radice
Paul Rand
Elaine Raphael
Neil Raphan
Samuel Reed
Sheldon Reed
Patrick Reeves
Wendy Reingold
Herbert O. Reinke
Edward E. Ricotta
Arthur Ritter
Valerie Ritter
Michelle M. Roberge
Judy Roberts
Ray Robertson
Bennett Robinson
Harry Rocker
Harlow Rockwell
Andy Romano
Cory L. Rosenberg
Lee Rosenberg
Judy Rosenfeld
Barbara Rosenthal
Ed Rosenthal
Andrew Ross
James Francis Ross
Richard Ross
Warren Rossell
Arnold Roston
Leah Roth
Thomas Roth
Wayne Roth
Iska Rothovius
Mort Rubenstein
Randee Rubin
Thomas P. Ruis
Marta Ruliffson
Robert Miles Runyan
Henry N. Russell
Albert Russo
Don Ruther
Thomas Ruzicka

S
Stewart Sacklow
Moriyoshi Saito
Robert Saks
Richard M. Salcer
Ludvic Saleh
Robert Salpeter
Ina Saltz
George Samerjan
Jim Sant'Andrea Jr.
Carmine Santandrea
Betty B. Saronson
Audrey Satterwhite
Vincent Sauchelli
Hans Sauer
Sam Scali
Ernie Scarfone
Michael Schacht
Peter Schaefer
Paula Scher
Glen Scheuer
Mark Schimmel
Fred Schmidt
Klaus F. Schmidt
Joyce Schnaufer
William H. Schneider
Annette Schonhaut
Beverly Faye Schrager
Sharon Schuermann
Carol Schulter
Eileen Hedy Schultz
Nancy K. Schulz
Victor Scocozza
Ruth Scott
William C. Seabrook III
David M. Seager
Leslie Segal
Sheldon Seidler
Amy Seissler
John L. Sellers
Kaede Seville
Alexander Shear
Mindee H. Shenkman
Orit Shiffman
Minoru Shiokawa
Jerry Siano
Arthur Silver
Joyce Silverman
Louis Silverstein
Milt Simpson
Meera Singh
Leonard Sirowitz
Jack Skolnik
Paul Slutsky
Bernard Brussel Smith
Carol Lynn Smith
Richard Jay Smith
Robert Smith
Edward Sobel
Martin Solomon
Harold Sosnow
Carmen Soubriet
Michelle R. Spellman
Lisa A. Speroni
Victor E. Spindler
Leonard A. St. Louis
Martin St. Martin
David Stahlberg
Mindy Phelps Stanton
Karsten Stapelfeldt
Alexander Stauf
Irena S. Steckiv
Emily Stedman
Douglas Steinbauer
Karl H. Steinbrenner
Karl Eric Steinbrenner Jr.
Vera Steiner
Barrie Stern
Charles M. Stern
Gerald Stewart
Linda Stillman
Stephen Stinehour
Bernard Stone
Otto Storch
William Strosahl
Ira F. Sturevant
Brenda Suler
Ken Sweeny
Robin Sweet

T
Barbara Taff
Robert Talarczyk
Nina Tallarico
Norman Tanen
Jo Ann Tansman
Melissa K. Tardiff
Melco Tashian
Bill Taubin
Jack George Tauss
Mark Tekushan
Trudie Ten Broeke
Ciro Tesoro
Giovanna Testani
Richard Thomas
Bradbury Thompson
Paula Thomson
Marion Thunberg
Robin Ticho
Harold Toledo
Shinichiro Tora
Edward L. Towles
Victor Trasoff
Charles Trovato
Joanne Trovato
Susan B. Trowbridge
Joseph P. Tully
Karen Tureck
Anne Twomey

U
Catherine Ullmann
Claire Ultimo
Frank Urrutia

V
Gerard Vaglio
Michael Valli
A. Barbara Vaughn
Haydee N. Verdia
Elizabeth Thayer Verney
Frank A. Vitale
Constance Von Collande
Thuy Vuong

W
Dorothy Wachtenheim
Allan R. Wahler
Ernest Waivada
Jurek Wajdowicz
Joseph O. Wallace
Keith Walters
Paul Waner
Jill Wasserman
Rose Wasserman
Laurence S. Waxberg
Jessica Weber
Art Weithas
Theo Welti
Ron Wetzel
Ken White
Pamela J. White
Ronald Wickham
Gail Wiggin
Richard Wilde
Rodney Craig Williams
Jack Williamson
Anna Willis
David Wiseltier
Rupert Witalis
Cynthia Wojdyla
David Wojdyla
Henry Wolf
Sam Woo
Elizabeth G. Woodson
Robert S. Woolman
Orest Woronewych
Michael K. Wright
Willliam K. Wurtzel

Y
Ira Yoffe
Zen Yonkovig
Michael Yurick

Z
Bruce Zahor
Carmile S. Zaino
Susan Broman Zambelli
Gary Zamchick
Paul H. Zasada
Sheldon Ziedler
Richard Zoehrer
Alan Zwiebel

ADC INTERNATIONAL MEMBERS

Argentina
Daniel Verdino

Australia
Leighton D. Gage
Ron Kambourian

Austria
M. J. Demner
Franz Merlicek

Bermuda
Paul Smith

Brazil
Oswaldo Miranda
Adeir Rampazzo

Canada
John Brooks
Claude Dumoulin
I. L. Fraiman
Brian C. Hannigan
John Brooke Advertising
Ran Hee Kim
Pierre Pepin

Denmark
Peter Von Schilling

England
John Athorn
Jean Govoni
Keith Murgatroyd
Roland Schenk
Celia Frances Stothard
Len Sugarman

India
Brendan Pereira

Israel
Kalderon Asher
Asher Kalderon
Dan Reisinger

Italy
Titti Fabiani

Japan
Kazuhiko Adachi
Masuteru Aoba
Katsumi Asaba
Yuji Baba
Satoru Fujii
Terunobu Fukushima
Akio Hirai
Mitsutoshi Hosaka
Tadanori Itakura
Yasuyuki Ito
Michio Iwaki
Toshio Iwata
Takahisa Kamijyo
Hideyuki Kaneko
Shiu Kataoka
Naomichi Pete Kobayashi
Ryohei Kojima
Yoshikatsu Kosakai
Kazuki Maeda
Keizo Matsui
Takao Matsumoto
Shin Matsunaga
Hideo Mukai
Keisuke Nagatomo
Michio Nakahara
Yasuharu Nakahara
Makoto Nakamura
Toshiyuki Ohashi
Takkeshi Ohtaka
Shigeo Okamoto
Motoaki Okuizumi
Akio Okumura
Shigeshi Omori
Susumu Sakane
Takayuki Shirasu
Seiji Sugii
Yasuo Suzuli
Itakura Tadanori
Teruaki Takao
Masakazu Tanabe
Ikko Tanaka
Soji George Tanaka
Yusaku Tomoeda
Norio Uejo
Masato Watanabe
Peter Wong
A. Hidehito Yamamato
Joji Yamamoto
Takeo Yao

Mexico
Felix Beltran
Diane Garcia De Tolone
Luis Efren Ramirez Flores

Netherlands
Pieter Branttiga

Norway
Kjell Wollner

Philippines
Emily A. Abrera

Republic of Singapore
Chiet-Hsuen Eng

Sri Lanka
Kosala Rohana Wickramanayake

Switzerland
Bilal Dallenbach
Fernand Hofer
Moritz Jaggi
Hans Looser

West Germany
Uwe Horstmann
Olaf Leu
Hans-Georg Pospischil

ADC AFFILIATE MEMBERS

Avon Products Inc.
Ronald W. Longsdorf
Timothy J. Musios
Perry C. Zompa

Cardinal Type Service Inc.
Mark Darlow
John Froehlich

Constance Kovar & Company
Constance Kovar
Anthony Taibi

NYC Technical College
George Halpern
Seymour Pearlstein

Omnicron Group Inc.
Rayna Brown
Pamela G. Manser

Parsons School of Design
Albert Greenberg
David Levy

Peter Rogers Associates
Henrietta Abrams
Leonard Favara
Peter Rogers

School of Visual Arts
Leslie Brooks

Tisdell/Capescha
Daniel Capescha
Clifford Tisdell

Toppan Printing Company, Ltd.
Takeo Hayano
Ryuichi Minakawa
Teruo Tanabe

Union Camp Corporation
Stewart J. Phelps
Robert S. Todd

INDEX

C

D

E

F

G

L

M

Q

R

S

U

V

W

X

Y

Z

TESSA KIROS

VENEZIA

food & dreams

First published in 2008 by Murdoch Books Pty Ltd
Pier 8/9, 23 Hickson Road, Millers Point NSW 2000

09 10 11 12 13 MUB 10 9 8 7 6 5 4 3 2 1

ISBN-13: 978-0-7407-8516-0
ISBN-10: 0-7407-8516-8

Library of Congress Control Number: 2009923702

www.andrewsmcmeel.com

Photography: Manos Chatzikonstantis
Styling: Michail Touros
Art direction & design: Lisa Greenberg
Editor: Jane Price
Designer: Joanna Byrne
Food editor: Michelle Earl
Production: Alexandra Gonzalez

OVEN VARIATION: You may find cooking times vary depending on the oven you are using. For fan-forced ovens, as a general rule, set the oven temperature to 35°F lower than indicated in the recipe.

TESSA KIROS

VENEZIA

food & dreams

PHOTOGRAPHY BY MANOS CHATZIKONSTANTIS

STYLING BY MICHAIL TOUROS

ART DIRECTION BY LISA GREENBERG

Andrews McMeel Publishing, LLC

Kansas City • Sydney • London

contents

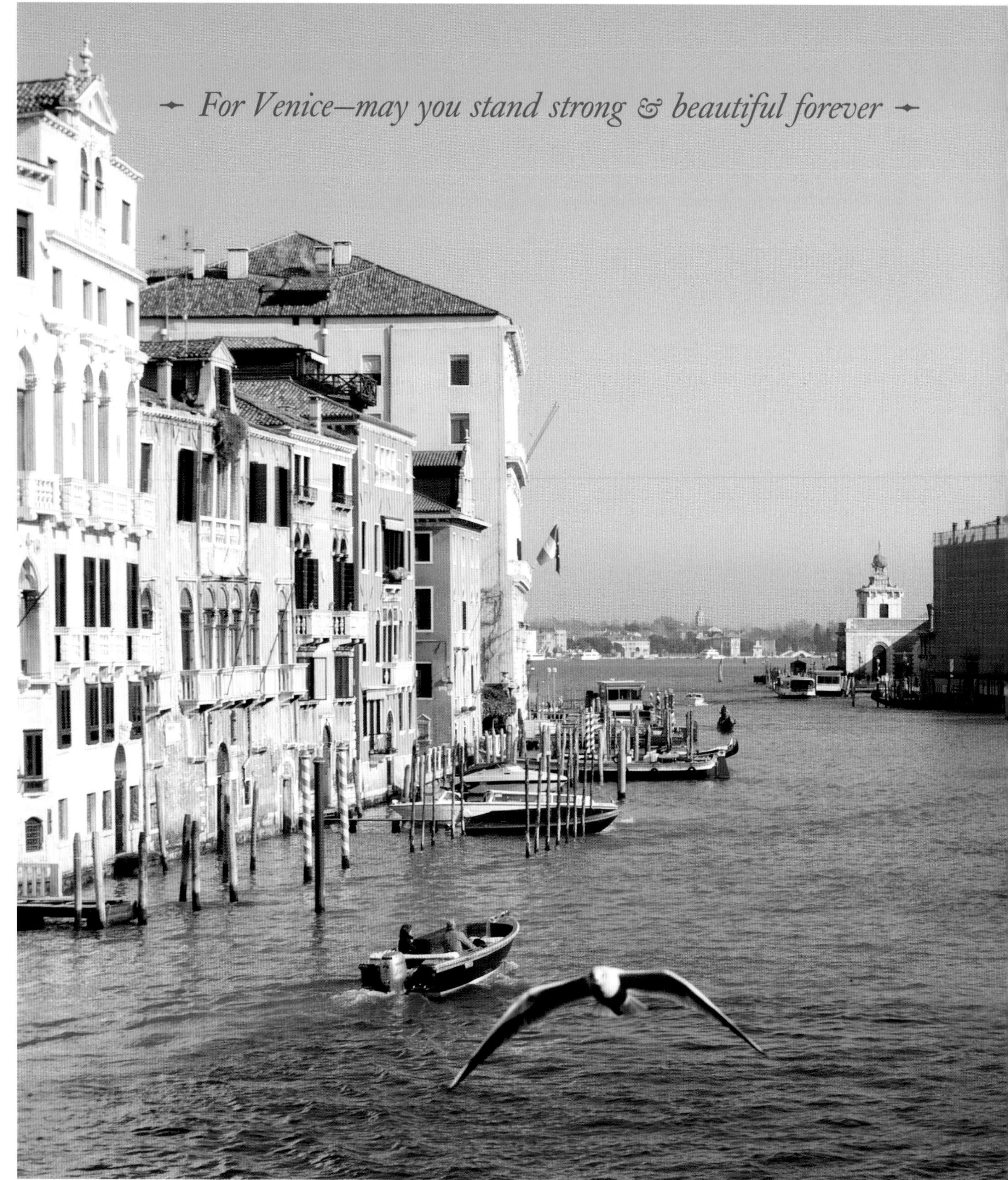

For Venice—may you stand strong & beautiful forever

- PIAZZETTI -

CALLE DEL ACQUA

Dear P,

There is not much I can tell you about Venice...you will have to come and see it for yourself. On the train coming here I could tell from the look in the people's eyes that they were proud, moved and longing...to be in Venice. Whether returning, or going for the first time, longing to be part of the Venetian dream, of the theatre that goes on night and day among Venetian pillars. The unsuspecting car traveller could hardly guess, upon nearing Venice, that below the tangled web of highway could lie such a pearl. The city is like a beautiful mysterious woman who everyone wants to watch and stand as close to as possible; an everchanging powerful lady who flows with the cycle of nature and commands profound respect for her beauty and uniqueness. Like a mermaid sprung unruffled from the deepest waters, she moves and gives with the tides. She is, I find, most beautiful from a distance.

- PIAZZETTI -

CALLE DEL ACQUA

These are the things I ate in Venice. From nearby shores, or inland, further out in the Veneto. Wonderful surprises let me say: things that you would never expect from glancing at the menus of the many tourist-drained locali. Mixed fried and grilled splendors, scallops served in their marvelous shells with simple dressings of olive oil, lemon and parsley. Lovely fresh and small soles, piles and heaps of shiny shells, people eating beautiful cicchetti, glasses of prosecco and other magnificent wines with meatballs, or fried sardines, and a selection of risottos suitable for any of the Doges. Wonderful ink-black spaghetti, or whole-wheat pasta with a sauce of anchovies melted with onions till they die gently. From the fields beyond are faraona, or boiled splendid mixed meats with quince mustard, and liver melted with onions, and gloriously regal-red radicchios. And, I have to say, there is much to confront here: live eels and crabs, snails, raw fish pulled fresh from the waters to be plunged in salt water and served at once, if not raw.

- PIAZZETTI -

CALLE DEL ACQUA

The seafood, in particular, I am told, is best boiled in acqua di mare, so there is no danger of over-salting or under-salting the water; it is always just right!

There are times, you know, when I feel I am a part of the water. Even tucked up in my room with a shawl around me, I can smell the water. I have spray on my boots still from earlier when I was coming home to keep dry. And I can hear the water outside, splashing up out of the canal, joining with the rain and dropping back like a duet, into the canal again. And on this we are all afloat.

Venice is like when you hear a piece of music that scoops down into your soul, or notice a real tear getting ready to drop from the eye of an unlucky child. One of those rare moments when you grasp the magnificence of this world. Yes, Venice is one of those moments.

You will have to come yourself and see,

Love, Tess

Xxx

EATING IN VENICE

__A meal could begin with a glass of Venice's lovely sparkling PROSECCO, *& then continue with one of the very fine wines from the area, such as soave or valpolicella.*
__CICCHETTI *(or chicchetti) are unique to Venice; delicious bites served at any time (although normally appreciated before lunch or dinner). They are often on display as a snack that could end up becoming the whole meal. Sometimes served with a few toothpicks for picking up the bites with. There are special bars that serve only cicchetti.*
__In typical Italian fashion, most meals will begin with the ANTIPASTO, *which might include a platter of the freshest seafood varieties, simply boiled & dressed & splashed with olive oil, lemon, parsley, & some pepper. This bollito misto di mare is very typical & found in simple or rather more complex forms. It relies totally on the freshness & quality of the seafood.*
__Under the PRIMO *category fall soup, gnocchi, pasta, or rice, & these will be made according to the season or occasion.* BIGOLI *is the typically Venetian, slightly rougher, thicker, whole wheat spaghetti, which is wonderful, although various other types of pasta are served, too.*
__RISOTTO *is very much appreciated in Venice & can range from one or more of the many vegetables, fish or even meat. The type of rice used are carnaroli, vialone nano, or arborio. To make a risotto the Venetian way: onda, shake, mantecare. Your risotto will need a broth to take it through its cooking process, usually just made simply with vegetables (brodo di verdure). Here is an example of a quick* VEGETABLE BROTH:

Put 6 cups of water, 1 celery stalk, 1 small, peeled, white onion, 1 large, peeled carrot, 1 thin, clump of parsley, any asparagus off-cuts, 10 or so peppercorns, 2 teaspoons of salt, 1 peeled & squashed garlic clove, & 1 bay leaf into a large saucepan. Bring it all to a boil, then lower the heat, cover, & simmer for 20 to 30 minutes. Strain well, to make about 5 cups.

__For SECONDI *you may find what is most on offer in the many restaurants & homes is the freshest of seafood either fried or simply grilled & drizzled with olive oil & some lemon on the side. This is a dish which relies, once again, on the incredible freshness & quality of the fish. And if you wade through the masses there are also many other Venetian dishes to be tried.*

__Many of the CONTORNI *or sides of seasonal vegetables come from the surrounding lagoon islands such as Sant' Erasmus, which supply many of the vegetables, in particular the wonderful artichokes that make their way to the markets & Venetian tables. The castraure, the typically small & lovely prizes, are the first artichokes to bud on the plant. Artichoke bottoms from the full-grown artichokes are much appreciated, too, & are often sold ready cleaned from buckets of water at the markets.*

__DOLCI *are many & varied to end the meal, or you might just have a few of the cookies typical of the region with a glass of recioto, fragolino, or grappa.*

Caffè. That's it. The Italian way.

Buon appetito

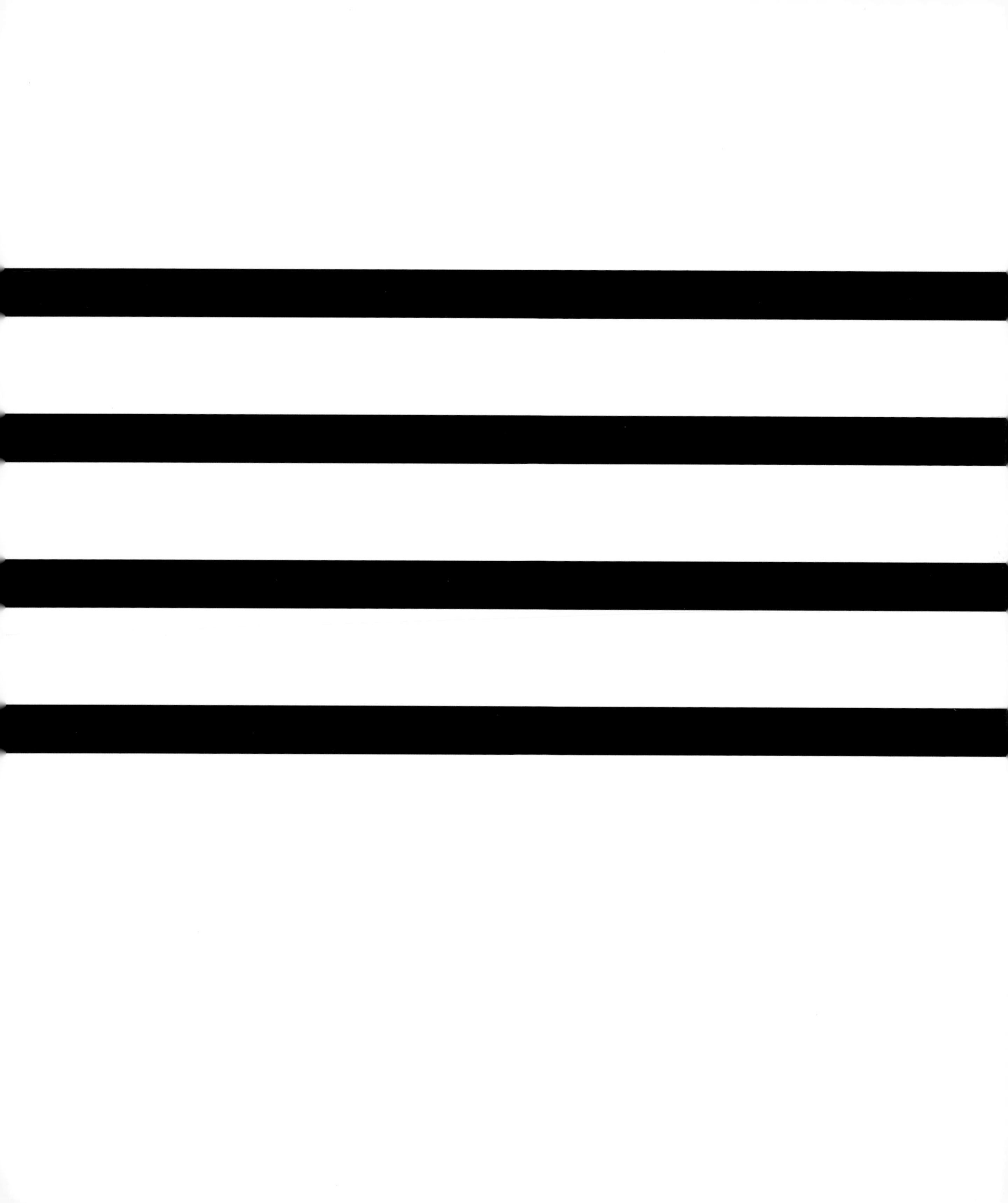

rules & *rossini*

Venice in its labyrinth & enigma; everywhere visible from the windows & mirrors on the top floor at Harry's Bar. Nothing tallies up. Even on Torcello at Locanda Cipriani there was a sudden dip in the grass that didn't seem as if it needed to be there. And the backdrop from the terrace looked like they had been told to recite & play & then the director had forgotten to call stop. Bridges; keyholes peeping into ancient courtyards full of secrets. Alleyways leading directly to steps that would take you right down into the canal if you let them.

I

ESSENTIAL RECIPES

Polenta *(fast & slow)*
Bread bangles Bussolai
Quince mustard Mostarda di frutta
Spritz
Bellini
Rossini
Pomegranate

Polenta

The Venetians are very attached to their polenta—they all know exactly how they like theirs & many people have a specific idea of when it should be served grilled or served soft. They are lucky to be able to buy the lovely white polenta, which is not easy to find elsewhere. This white polenta is cooked slowly until soft & is served under or next to so many dishes. As well as differences in color (you are probably more familiar with yellow polenta than white), it varies in grain size. Coarse-grained polenta, bramata, takes about 40 minutes to cook. Then there is instant polenta (lampo), which has been parboiled & cooks in just a few minutes.

When making soft polenta, the aim is to make it loose rather than stiff. The recipe here is a basic one that is soft enough to spoon well but not so soft that it won't support the accompanying sauce. You may have to test the amount of water you need for the type of polenta you are using, to achieve the result that suits you best (use the package instructions as a guide). But if you are making it to be grilled, then make it a bit less watery than normal. In any case, judge the finished consistency, adding a little more hot water toward the end if necessary.

The recipe opposite is fairly plain & not very salty or buttery. It's suitable for serving with a saucy, flavorsome dish, or for grilling. If you would prefer, you can cook it in broth rather than water, or add a good blob of butter &/or a generous heap of grated Parmesan. Another option is to either stir or tuck a few slices of cheese, such as taleggio or gorgonzola, into the polenta so they melt.

Luisa, my sister-in-law, has a great way to cook polenta without stirring it. You rinse a clean dish cloth, wring it out, then cover the pan with the cloth. Add the lid & make sure the ends of the cloth are away from the flame. Simmer on the lowest possible heat for 40 minutes or so. Check it a couple of times but it should be okay.

If you're not serving the polenta at once, or you have leftovers (half the portion is a good amount for four), there are some lovely things you can make. One option is to pour the polenta into a baking sheet to a depth of about ¾ inch, spreading it with a spatula. When completely cool, cut it into wedges. Heat a small rack on a barbecue grill. When hot, grill the polenta until solid ridges (not too black & burned, though) form on the underside. Polenta cooked this way is often served with food in Venice, or it can be the crostino for a savory topping, or even spread with a little jam for breakfast. To clean your polenta pot, simply leave it to soak in water for a while & then the polenta will peel away.

1 tablespoon olive oil
1 teaspoon salt
1⅔ cups instant polenta

This is the quick way to cook polenta, which in today's rush is probably the way that many make it.

__Fill a pot with about 6 cups of water, then add the oil & salt. Bring the water to a boil. Drizzle the polenta into the water, whisking constantly for a few minutes (or follow the package directions), until it is thick & smooth. It should be a thick pouring consistency. If you think it looks too thick, add a little hot water toward the end. Serve at once.

Makes 8 cups
Serves 4 as an entrée or 8 as an appetizer

1 tablespoon olive oil
1 teaspoon salt
1⅔ cups polenta bramata (or polenta flour) or white polenta (polenta bianca)

The long way:

__Fill a heavy-bottomed pot with about 6 cups of water. When it is boiling, add the oil & salt, then the polenta in a thin stream until it has all been added, whisking in well. When it comes back up to a boil, lower the heat to as low as possible, partly cover with a lid, & simmer for about 40 minutes, whisking often to make sure nothing is sticking & that it is smooth.

Makes 8 cups
Serves 4 as an entrée or 8 as an appetizer

We are approaching San Marco on the Grand Canal & everything looks like paper cut-outs. I prefered the smaller motoscafo that took me to Giudecca. I hate that on some vaporetti there is a hard metal line on the window that cuts everything in half at my exact eye level. I have to dance above & below the line to piece it all together. So typical & theatrical…like all of Venice. -•-

Venice knows about aperitivo. How to do it well & even make a small occasion of it...like everything else. It is the place of the piazza or campo. Nice big squares, rectangles, or any odd shape. For people to use as their gardens. A space to settle into for a while & watch Venetian vitality.

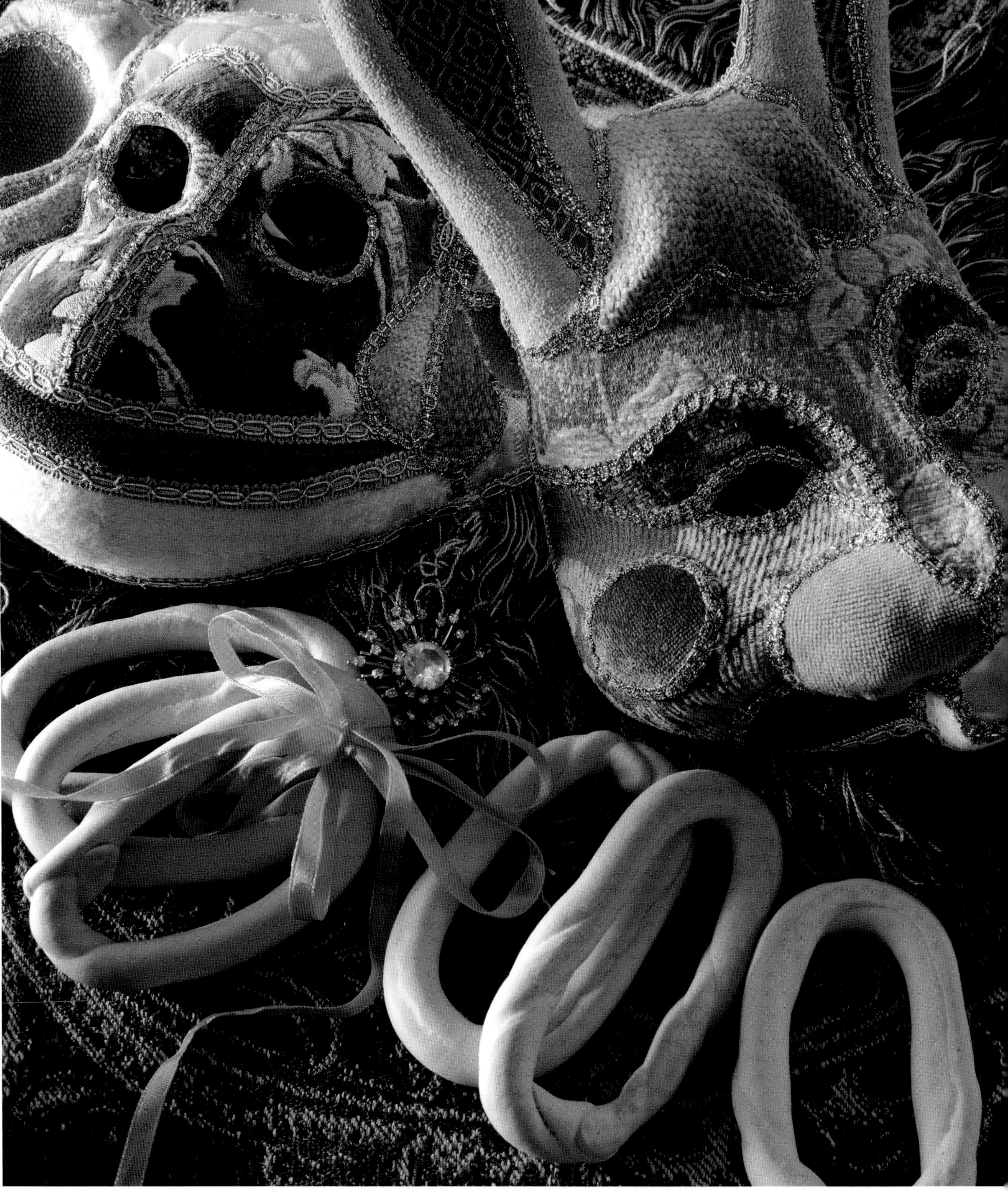

Bussolai

Bread bangles

½ ounce fresh yeast, or
2 teaspoons active dry yeast
1 teaspoon sugar
2 tablespoons butter, melted & cooled
about 4 cups cake flour
1 teaspoon salt

These are bread sticks in the shape of oval bangles–you'll find them served in the bread baskets all over Venice, much like grissini. You have to roll these thin or they will puff up like thin bread rolls in parts, although even if that happens it's no disaster. If you prefer, just roll the dough into rolls & bake–you'll get a wonderful plain, light white bread, much like the soft Venetian bread that, at first, I didn't like but do now. It's great for mopping up all the sauces at the bottom of your plate.

__Crumble the fresh (or sprinkle the dry) yeast into a bowl & add the sugar, butter, ¾ cups of the flour, & 1 cup of lukewarm water & whisk together. Let stand for about 10 minutes, until the yeast starts to activate & bubble up a little. Add the salt & all but ¼ cup of the flour (*you may not need to use it*).

__Mix it all together (*start with a wooden spoon & then use your hands*), adding a little extra flour to the dough & your hands if necessary, to get a nice soft ball. Knead for about 10 minutes, until smooth & elastic. Make a cross on top of the ball of dough, put back into the bowl, then cover the bowl with a dish cloth & let stand in a draft-free, warm place for a couple of hours, until it has puffed up well & doubled in size. Line 2 or 3 baking sheets with parchment paper.

__Preheat the oven to 400°F. Divide the dough into approximately 34 equal pieces or use your scale to measure each piece to ¾ ounce. Using unfloured hands, roll each piece on a smooth surface to a thin rope of 10 to 12 inches long, then press the ends together to make an oval "bracelet." Place the pieces on the baking sheets.

__Bake for about 15 minutes, or until crisp & lightly browned. The bread sticks are best eaten fresh, but you can store them in an airtight container or bag for 1 to 2 weeks.

Makes about 34

Mostarda di frutta

Quince mustard

2 small (about 12 ounces) quinces
4 cups white wine
1 apple
1 pear
2 clementines, or 1 mandarin orange (about 4 ounces in total), peeled, seeded, segmented, & skinned
¼ cup red & green candied cherries, halved
2 tablespoons mixed chopped, candied citrus fruits
1½ cups sugar
1 to 2 tablespoons mustard powder

Luisa says at Christmas they eat Mostarda, mascarpone, & Baicoli. An alternative to having the mustard in the marmalade is to serve a spoonful of mustard alongside.

__Wash the quinces & wipe away their fur. Slice carefully into quarters & tap away any falling seeds. Put them in a saucepan with the wine, bring to a boil, cover, & simmer for 20 minutes, until they are tender & can be peeled easily.
__Meanwhile, peel & core the apple & pear & chop up into rustic pieces.
__Transfer the tender quinces to a bowl using a slotted spoon. Add the apple & pear to the wine, bring back to a boil, then simmer, uncovered, for about 15 minutes, or until tender.
__Thinly peel, core, & cut up the quinces, then return the flesh to the pan of apple & pear. Mix together, then lift out a huge slotted spoonful of the fruit. Purée the rest of the panful with a handheld mixer. Add the unpuréed fruit back to the pan with the clementines (or mandarin), candied fruit, & sugar. Bring to a boil, stirring to dissolve the sugar, then lower the heat & simmer (*strongly at first*) for 1 to 1¼ hours. Mix occasionally, then halfway through turn the heat to very low & mix often so nothing sticks as it thickens & darkens. Once it is lovely & thick, leave to cool.
__Stir in the mustard powder mixed to a loose paste with a little white wine or water (*add it gradually until your prefered mustard flavor is reached*). Spoon into a sterilized jar & keep in the refrigerator for up to a month.

Makes about 3 cups

Spritz

Red & orange

4 to 5 ice cubes
¼ cup aperol or campari
¼ cup white wine or prosecco
¼ cup soda, or seltzer
1 thick chunk of orange with skin
1 olive, shaken out of brine & threaded onto a cocktail stick

This is a much appreciated aperitivo in Venice. To make a Spritz, take a large wineglass & add a good splash of an aperitif, such as campari or its lower-alcohol version, aperol. Next comes a good splash of white wine or prosecco & a few ice cubes. A splash of soda water (club soda, or "seltz" in the bars) is next because it revs everything up from bottom to top, & last, a piece of orange & a green olive on a cocktail stick. The olive is in brine & not rinsed, the lady says. The drink comes halfway to three-quarters up the glass. Very nice.

Everyone has their own version of Spritz. Use aperol or campari or whatever you prefer. Some people say no olive, others no orange, one wants a piece of lemon, one wants prosecco instead of the wine, one no wine at all–it's a bit how you take your coffee–rather personal. So here's a rough guide to how I like my Spritz. Adjust yours to suit your personal preference.

__Put the ice into a large wineglass. Splash in the aperol & then the white wine, next a good whoosh of fizzy water to get everything moving & mixed in. Add the orange & olive on a cocktail stick. That's it.

Serves 1

CONCERT
INTERPRE
VENEZIAN
CHIESA SAN VI

FLORIAN

Bellini

cin cin

1 beautiful sweet ripe white peach (about 5 ounces)
a couple of raspberries
1 cup very cold prosecco, or more if you like

Prosecco has its own kingdom in Venice. Not just any prosecco will do & there is even a separate wine list in some restaurants. Over many lunches I noticed people drinking full rounded plump bottles of chilled prosecco rather than wine, especially with their seafood...beautiful. Never mind stirring it into beautiful puréed white peaches & other fruits. These are the measures I like, but, of course, they're just rough estimates, depending on your glasses & such. They are easy to double or triple for more people, & add more prosecco or fruit, depending on your personal preference. This is nice served with a raspberry, or you could purée a couple of raspberries & add, for a pinkier color.

__Peel your peach with a sharp knife (*or plunge it briefly into boiling water if the skin won't budge*). Halve & stone the peach & purée until smooth. You can sieve your purée or leave it rough–either is good. You can add a little sugar & a drop of lemon if you like once you have tasted your purée (it will depend on your peach).

__Throw in one raspberry per glass. Pour the peach purée into large, beautiful, well-chilled glasses. Stir in the prosecco & wait for it to settle. Serve at once.

Makes 2

cheers

½ cup ripe strawberries, rinsed
1 flat teaspoon sugar (or more depending on your strawberries)
1 teaspoon lemon juice
1 cup very cold prosecco

This is to be made when the strawberries are bursting with their best flavor. I like to make it with small wild strawberries. The amount of sugar will depend on your strawberries, so taste & see.

__Hull the strawberries & cut them into pieces. Sprinkle with sugar & lemon juice. Purée until completely smooth. Pour into 2 glasses. Divide the prosecco between the glasses, mix, let it settle, & then serve immediately.

Serves 2

alla salute

⅓ cup freshly pressed pomegranate juice
1 cup very cold prosecco

This is maybe my favorite for its gentleness of color & taste. Use a citrus presser here (or you could spoon out all the seeds into a wire strainer set over a bowl & press them with a spoon to extract all the juice). A medium pomegranate will give you about ⅓ cup.

__Pour the pomegranate juice into 2 glasses. Pour the prosecco over. Serve.

Serves 2

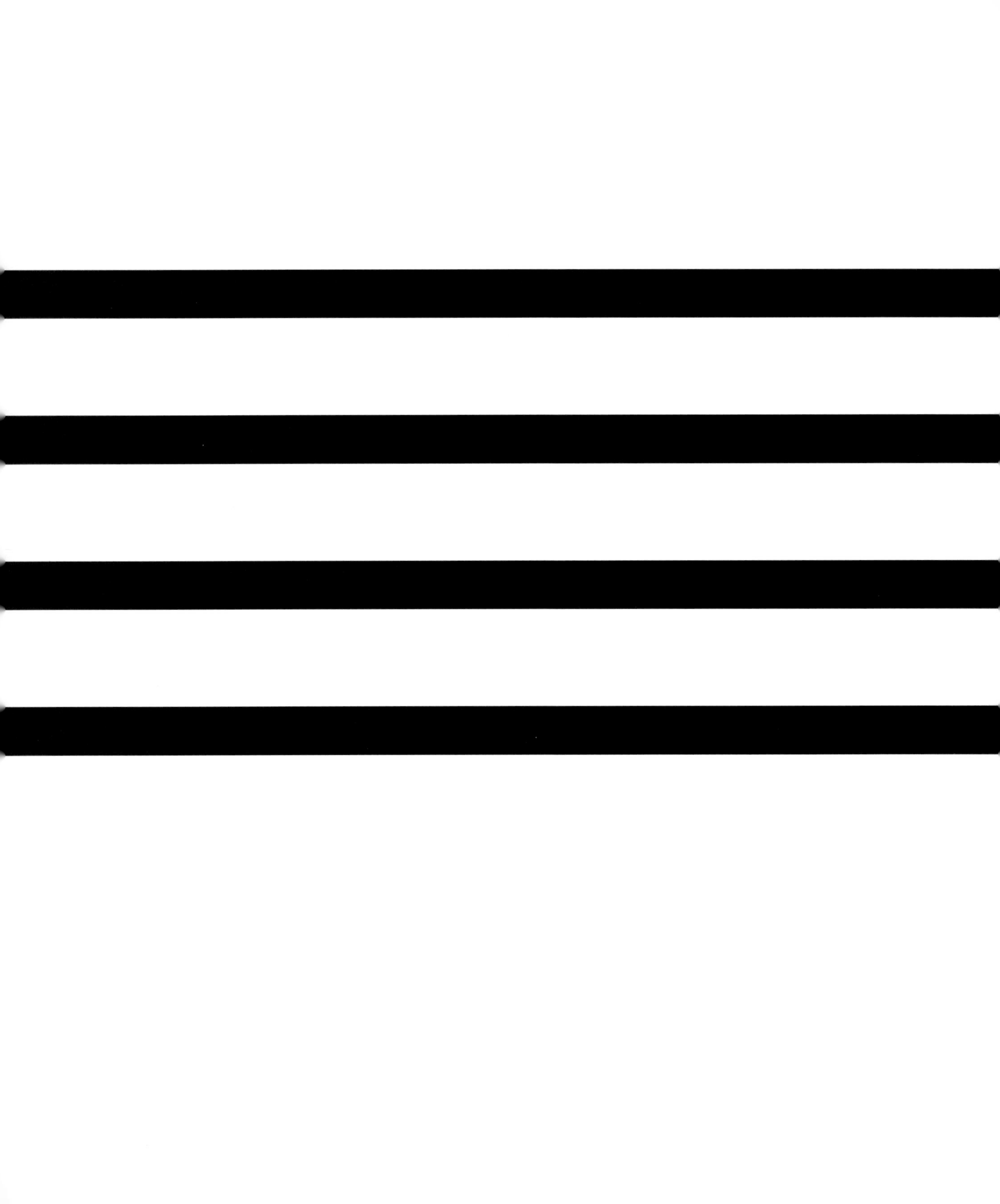

prosecco & *meatballs*

I just went to La Vedova for prosecco. Stunning. He asked me three times to have a polpetta di carne. *So I didn't wait for the fourth (I should have listened to the first). It was a beauty. Big, like a golf ball. Minced beef with boiled potatoes—soft, soft, soft—fried in crumbs until reddish gold & selling like hotcakes. There were other wonderful cicchetti: octopus, fried sardines, scampi, baccala, anchovies, boiled halves of eggs, & delicious-sized glasses & carafes.* ⟜

II

CICCHETTI

AL MARC

AL
CASA DEL PARMIGIANO
in Venezia
dal 1936
CASA DE

Tramezzini

Italian sandwiches

The tramezzini are classic little sandwiches—white bread, stuffed to bursting with mayonnaise & other fillings—that have been updated by the cicchetti bars of modern Venice. They are an important part of Venetian life & are served often with a lovely glass of wine. You need squares of thin white bread with the crusts cut off (about 4 inches), which you then halve into two triangles. The tramezzini are stuffed in the middle & taper down on the corners. Keep them covered if you won't be serving them immediately, so the edges don't curl up. These are what we filled ours with:

__a layer of mayonnaise, then a small slice of ham & 2 artichoke quarters (*the ones bottled in oil*);
__a layer of mayonnaise, a tablespoon or so of crumbled drained tuna, 3 opened-out capers, & a slice of hard-cooked egg in the middle;
__chopped or puréed blanched asparagus mixed with a little mayonnaise (*about 1 tablespoon mayonnaise to 1 tablespoon asparagus purée*), poached scampi, a couple of blanched asparagus tips, & a sprinkling of ground pepper. Add a dab more mayonnaise to keep the top slice of bread in place;
__a layer of tuna salsa (from *Calamari con salsa tonnata* on page 212), some crumbled drained tuna, sliced pickled cucumbers, & a dab more *salsa* on the top piece of bread;
__a layer of mayonnaise, sliced egg, artichoke quarters (*the ones bottled in oil*), & ground pepper;
__or any other filling you like.

Mozzarella in carrozza

Fried mozzarella toasts

Béchamel sauce:
1 scant tablespoon butter
3 teaspoons all-purpose flour
½ cup warm milk
grating of nutmeg

Dipping mixture:
2 eggs
1 tablespoon milk
pinch of salt
all-purpose flour, for coating
dry bread crumbs

For 2 mozzarella & ham sandwiches:
4 slices pan carre or white sandwich bread, crusts removed
4 to 6 slices (not too thick) mozzarella
1 large slice of ham, halved, or 2 small pieces ham
light olive oil, for frying

When in Venice it's great to be able to grab one of these delicious sandwiches for a snack. These are great at Rosticceria in campo San Bartolomeo—there they use tramezzini bread, which is very thin white crustless bread slices often in one long piece. When making these at home, you'll get a similar result with soft, white sandwich bread. Use a small skillet that will fit two sandwiches at a time, so that you don't need too much oil. The sandwiches are dipped in a batter before frying, but I found it simple enough to just dip them in beaten egg & then bread crumbs for the crusty effect. If you like, whisk 3 tablespoons of flour, ½ teaspoon of baking powder, & 2 more tablespoons of milk into your dipping mixture, which is more how the Venetians would make this. Then you need not coat the sandwiches in flour first or in bread crumbs before you fry. These are also good without the béchamel, but then they are less creamy & soft inside. You can make the béchamel ahead of time if you like—it's fine to use cold.

__To make the béchamel sauce, melt the butter in a small heavy-bottomed saucepan. Whisk the flour into the butter & cook for a few minutes, stirring. Reduce the heat to low, then add half the warm milk, whisking well. Add the rest of the milk, a grating of nutmeg, & some salt. Keep whisking until the sauce is smooth & thick, then remove the pan from the heat, cover, & let stand to firm up a bit. Even completely cooled, this is fine to use.

__To make the dipping mixture, beat together the eggs, milk, & salt in a flat bowl.

__For the mozzarella & ham sandwiches, spread 1 scant teaspoon of béchamel sauce over all 4 slices of bread, right to the edge. Lay a piece of ham & 2 or 3 slices of mozzarella onto 2 pieces of the bread so that the topping comes right to the edge. Top with the other pieces of bread to make two sandwiches & press together firmly to seal well. Heat the oil in a skillet—not too hot. Pat the sandwiches in flour, then dip in the dipping mixture to coat well. Shake them out of the mixture & let them drain off a bit, then press in the bread crumbs to coat all over. Fry in the hot oil, turning when

For 2 mozzarella & anchovy sandwiches:
4 slices pan carre or white sandwich bread, crusts removed
top-quality anchovy paste
4 to 6 slices (not too thick) mozzarella cheese
2 large anchovy fillets in olive oil, drained & broken up
light olive oil, for frying

golden & crisp on the bottom to cook the other side, then transfer to a plate lined with kitchen paper. Eat warm, taking care not to burn your mouth on the hot filling.

__For the mozzarella & anchovy sandwiches, spread 1 scant teaspoon of béchamel sauce over all 4 slices of bread. Dab a little anchovy paste onto each piece here & there (*about ¼ teaspoon onto each*). Lay 2 or 3 slices of mozzarella onto 2 pieces of bread to come right to the edge, then top with pieces of anchovy fillet. Top with the other pieces of bread to make 2 sandwiches & press together firmly to seal well. Dip in the flour, egg, & bread crumbs, then fry as above.

Makes 4

Sarde in saor

Sardines sour

about ½ cup olive oil
2 (about 14 ounces) white onions, halved & thinly sliced
a few whole peppercorns, gently squashed
2 bay leaves
½ cup white wine vinegar
15 to 18 whole sardines (about 18 ounces)
all-purpose flour, for dusting
light olive oil, for frying

Every Venetian I have met loves sardines cooked like this—"in saor" means literally "in a sour sauce." My sister-in-law, Luisa, has fond memories of her grandmother often making a big glass bowlful. They make a great snack if you have a crowd to feed—not only because you can easily make many batches, but because they keep so well in the refrigerator. I think they taste best after at least a couple of days to soak up all the delicious flavors. If you are making a large quantity you may have to wash out the pan & start with a fresh batch of oil if the flour starts to burn. If you want to add extra flavor, do as many Venetians do & add a handful of pine nuts & golden raisins to the onions. I use small sardines—you can leave their tails on or off as you prefer.

__Heat the oil in a nonstick skillet that has a lid, add the onions & cook over medium heat. After a few minutes, add the peppercorns, bay leaves, & some salt & pepper, cover, lower the heat, & simmer for 20 to 25 minutes. The onions must not brown but be well softened & nicely cooked, so check occasionally that not all the liquid has been absorbed. If the onions are browning too much, add a few drops of water & continue simmering. Once the onions are soft & cooked down, add the vinegar & simmer without the lid on for another 5 to 10 minutes, until reduced a little, leaving the onions covered in a lovely sauce, but don't let them dry out.

__Meanwhile, to fillet the sardines, cut off the heads, then make a slit down the side of each fish & remove the guts. Open out the sardines flat, making sure they are still hinged together, & place them skin side up on a chopping board. Press each sardine lightly, yet firmly, to open out. Turn each one over & pull out the backbone (*or leave in the bone & just clean them while you are eating them*). Rinse & pat dry with paper towels. Pat well in the flour to coat on both sides.

__Pour enough oil into a large nonstick skillet to cover the bottom abundantly. When the oil is hot add the sardines, turning them only when they are crisp on the bottom. If the flour is falling off the sardines & sticking to the bottom, you may need to lower the heat a little. When both sides are golden & quite crisp, transfer the sardine to a plate lined with paper towels to absorb the excess oil. Sprinkle with fine salt.

__Layer the sardines & onions in a compact bowl, seasoning as you go, creating about three layers. Add the squashed peppercorns & a splash more oil if it looks as if it needs it. Cover & either leave at room temperature if you will be eating within the next few hours or put in the refrigerator, where they will keep for a few days. Each time you eat a sardine, rotate the rest so that they are all covered & not just the ones underneath.

Scampi in saor

Scampi sour

18 to 20 scampi (langoustines, red-claw, or large shrimps)
½ cup olive oil
2 (about 14 ounces) white onions, halved & thinly sliced
a few whole black peppercorns, squashed a little
2 bay leaves
3 tablespoons white wine
½ cup white wine vinegar
all-purpose flour, for coating
light olive oil, for frying

My friend, Sergia, once made me a whole wonderful batch of these to carry home with me on the train & they were delicious. You could add 2 tablespoons of pine nuts & golden raisins to the onion, or even use leek instead of onion. The scampi must be lovely & fresh.

__Peel the scampi. Remove the tail meat by cutting down the center of the underside of the tail with a small, sharp knife & using your fingers to pull out the meat. Devein, wash, pat dry with kitchen paper, & leave in the refrigerator.

__Heat the oil in a nonstick skillet that has a lid & cook the onions for a few minutes before adding the peppercorns, bay leaves, & some salt. Cover, lower the heat, & simmer for 20 to 25 minutes, until well softened but not browned. Check occasionally that not all the liquid has been absorbed. Add the wine, let it bubble up a little, then add the vinegar & simmer, uncovered now, for another 5 to 10 minutes, until it has reduced a bit & its intensity has cooked out, but it is still good & saucy rather than dry.

__Put some flour on a plate & coat the scampi well. Pour enough oil into a large nonstick skillet to cover the bottom abundantly. When the oil is hot, add the scampi, turning them only when they are crisp on the bottom. If the flour is falling off the scampi & sticking to the bottom, you may need to lower the heat a little. When both sides are golden & quite crisp, transfer to a plate lined with paper towels to absorb the oil. Sprinkle with fine salt.

__Put half the onion in a small bowl, top with the scampi & cover with the remaining onion. Scatter some pepper here & there. Add a splash more oil if you think it needs it.

__Cover & either leave at room temperature if you will be eating them within the next few hours, or put in the refrigerator, where they will keep for a few days, soaking up the flavors more & more.

12,50% vol.
Ronchi di Cialla
Controllata
CONTIENE SOLFITI

Moscardini bolliti

Tiny baby octopus

1¼ pounds moscardini or baby octopus
1 small onion, peeled
2 garlic cloves, peeled
2 bay leaves
1 small celery stalk
1 small bunch parsley
about 8 peppercorns
2 tablespoons good-quality, extra-virgin olive oil
juice of half a lemon
1 scant tablespoon chopped parsley
pinch of peperoncino

This is nice as part of a mixed cicchetti plate. Use a great-tasting extra-virgin olive oil for the dressing–it will lift your dish to a different level. Moscardini are tiny red–purple baby octopus, weighing roughly ¾ ounce each. The Venetians also know them as folpeti. They are so small (only a bite or two) that they are often served with toothpicks & are just popped whole into the mouth. If you use the larger baby octopus, they can be halved or cut up into suitable-sized pieces.

__To clean the octopus, cut between the head & tentacles, just below the eyes. Grasp the body & push the beak up & out through the center of the tentacles with your finger. Cut the eyes from the head. To clean the head, carefully slit through one side, avoiding the ink sac, & scrape out any gut. Rinse under running water to remove any grit, then drain.
__Fill a pot with about 6 cups of water & add the onion, a garlic clove, the bay leaves, celery, bunch of parsley, & peppercorns. Season with salt, then bring to a boil. Add the moscardini, then bring back to a boil. Lower the heat, partially cover with a lid, & simmer for about 30 minutes until tender (*you may need to cook the octopus for longer for it to become tender*). Remove from the heat & leave to cool in the liquid for a while.
__Cut the remaining garlic clove in half & rub it around the inside of your serving bowl, then leave the garlic in the bowl.
__Using a slotted spoon, remove the moscardini from the broth & add to the serving bowl.
__Dress with the olive oil, lemon, chopped parsley, peperoncino, & a little salt & black pepper. Season to taste, adding more of anything you think it needs. Serve at room temperature or even cold.

Serves about 6 to 8

Polpo con patate

Octopus & potatoes

1¼ pounds octopus
4 tablespoons olive oil
½ white onion, chopped
2 garlic cloves, chopped
a good pinch of peperoncino
½ cup white wine
1½ cups vegetable broth (page 12)
1¼ pounds (3 medium) potatoes, peeled & cut into chunks
2 tablespoons chopped parsley

This is nice as part of a cicchetti plate or just as an antipasto. It's very easy to double the quantity to serve more people, & you can also completely cook the potatoes separately & then turn them through the cooked octopus.

__To clean the octopus, cut between the head & tentacles, just below the eyes. Grasp the body & push the beak up & out through the center of the tentacles with your finger. Cut the eyes from the head. To clean the head, carefully slit through one side, avoiding the ink sac, & scrape out any gut. Rinse under running water to remove any grit, then drain. Leave the tentacles reasonably long & cut the flesh into bite-size chunks.

__Heat the olive oil in a nice, wide saucepan that has a lid, & sauté the onion until soft & just beginning to turn golden. Add the octopus, mix well, cover, & cook over high heat until almost all of the liquid has evaporated. Add the garlic & peperoncino, folding them in with a wooden spoon. When it smells good, add the wine & cook over steady heat (*uncovered*), until there is very little of it left on the bottom of the pan.

__Pour in the broth & bring to a boil. Lower the heat & simmer for about 30 minutes–covered for the first 10 minutes, then uncovered–until the octopus is very tender.

__Meanwhile, parboil the potato chunks for 10 minutes in a pot of lightly salted boiling water, until just cooked but still firm, then drain.

__Add the potatoes to the octopus at the end of its cooking time when there is just a bit of liquid left, then simmer for 5 minutes together (*the end result is quite dry*). Season to taste.

__Turn off the heat & let stand for 10 to 15 minutes so the potatoes keep absorbing any remaining liquid. Scatter the parsley on top. Serve warm or at room temperature with some salt & a grinding of black pepper.

Serves about 8

Baccala mantecato

Whipped baccala

1 large garlic clove, peeled & well chopped
½ cup olive oil
1¼ pounds baccala (salt cod), soaked
some small bread slices
butter, for frying

I don't know if many Venetian housewives really do make this themselves anymore —I think there are a few commercial places that make it fantastically well & people go there to buy it. I have also seen it made with some warm milk beaten in, which gives it a whiter color, though it may not keep as well. This is normally served on a crostino of polenta. Here it is served with small fried bread crostini, but is even good just with bread.

Baccala mantecato is the plain version; to make Baccala cappuccina, add 2 garlic cloves that have been well chopped to a pulp. Use a handheld blender to mash the fish well, drizzling the oil in very gradually until it has absorbed. Season with ground black pepper & whiz until creamy, then fold in 2 tablespoons of chopped parsley. Serve on polenta crostini. You can even spice it up by adding some crushed peperoncino, lemon juice, or lovely fresh thyme as you mix.

Before you use the salt cod you need to soak it to remove the excess salt. Rinse the cod fillet first, then put it into a large bowl with enough water to completely immerse it. Cover the bowl & refrigerate, changing the water 3 to 4 times a day. Ask your fishmonger how long you need to soak the cod (it's usually 2 to 3 days). If you're unsure, test the cod by breaking off a small fleck, rinsing, & tasting it. The tail part is always a bit more salty. In some places you can buy ready-soaked salt cod, which is very reliable & convenient.

__Put the garlic clove into the oil to flavor it for a while. Drain the baccala, put it into a large saucepan, & cover with water. Bring to a boil, then simmer, skimming, for about 10 minutes. Remove from the heat & let it cool for a while with the lid on. Drain. While the baccala is still warm, remove the skin & bones, & break into flakes in a bowl.

__Remove the garlic clove from the oil, then gradually drizzle the oil into the bowl of baccala, mashing well & stirring with a wooden spoon until all the oil is absorbed. Either use a handheld blender or food processor to pulse the mixture—so some is just bashed from your time with the wooden spoon & some is creamed. It shouldn't need any salt because of the baccala, but add some pepper. That's it—plain & stiff with a consistency a bit like chicken in mayonnaise.

__To serve, sauté some bread slices in butter with a pinch of salt & pepper. Top with a good spoonful of baccala, pepper, & an extra drizzle of olive oil if you like.

Serves many

Polpette di carne

Meatballs

1 pound (about 3 medium) russet potatoes, peeled & cut into chunks
1 garlic clove, peeled
½ pound ground beef
1 tablespoon chopped parsley
2 tablespoons grated Parmesan
1 small egg, lightly beaten
dry bread crumbs
olive oil, for frying

I ate something like these at Alla Vedova, a cicchetteria in front of ca d'Oro vaporetto stop. They were just fantastic. I noticed everyone having them with a beautiful glass of prosecco or vino before dinner. If you then continue, as I did, with all the other cicchetti & more wine, you can call it a day & a night & not need dinner.

These meatballs can be cooked in a skillet or deep fryer. The benefit of the deep fryer is that they will keep their shape better, but it doesn't really matter. If you like, you can make smaller ones. I like them large because they fit in a skillet in one batch & aren't too hard to turn.

You can also make these with part-boiled, mashed or finely chopped beef & some ground pork, so if you have some leftover chopped boiled meats, use them. This recipe makes simple, plain polpette but you could always spice them up a bit with a hint of chile or any other herb.

__Boil the potatoes in lightly salted water until just soft. Drain, then mash until fluffy. Crush the garlic on a board with a sprinkling of salt, until it is mashed to a pulp, removing any green bits if necessary. Add the garlic to the potato & mash together while still warm, then add the beef, & a little salt & mash again, first with a masher, then with a fork until there are no lumps.

__When the potato has cooled a little, add the parsley, Parmesan, & egg, & mix well, adding a little salt or pepper for taste, or whatever else you think would be good. Put in the refrigerator for an hour (*longer, if you prefer*), until they firm up.
__Grab enormous heaped teaspoonfuls of the mixture, rolling them firmly between your palms so you have big balls of about 2-inch diameter. Put the bread crumbs on a plate. Pour enough oil into a large skillet to come about 1 inch up the side of the skillet.
__While the oil is heating, roll the balls in the bread crumbs so they are totally covered. Gently put the balls into the hot oil. Fry them until the undersides form a beautifully golden crust, then turn them gently over with tongs or a spoon, taking care not to pierce them. Fry until golden & crisp, then drain on paper towels. Sprinkle with salt, & serve when they have cooled a little (*they are also good at room temperature*).

Makes 12 to 14

Polpette di tonno

Fish balls

½ pound (2 medium) russet potatoes, unpeeled
1 (6-ounce) can tuna in olive oil
1 garlic clove, very finely crushed
1 small egg, lightly beaten
2 tablespoons chopped parsley
pinch of peperoncino
light olive oil, for frying
dry bread crumbs
lemon, for serving

You can quickly make up even half a portion of these anytime. These also work very well with crab. These are made much smaller than the polpette di carne & are wonderful as a cicchetto with a good glass of wine.

__Boil the potatoes in lightly salted water until just soft. Drain & allow to cool a little. Peel, then mash well.
__Drain the tuna & add to the mashed potato along with the garlic, egg, parsley, peperoncino, some salt, & a little pepper. Mix together well, cover, & refrigerate to firm.
__Heat enough oil in a nonstick skillet to comfortably cover the bottom. Roll the potato mixture into small balls (*I got 25*). Roll them in the bread crumbs & add to the hot oil, gently turning around when crusty so all sides are nicely done. Transfer to a plate lined with paper towels to absorb the excess oil. Sprinkle a little more salt over the top, & squeeze on some lemon juice if you like.

Makes about 25

The children of Venice are the luckiest ones. The most free. No cars. No worried parents. The ideal place for MONOPATTINI. *I pass them walking and hopping to school, passing by the forni to get rolls or focaccia, meeting friends and darting over small bridges, between canals while their parents chatter.*

Sarde fritte

Fried sardines

12 to 15 small sardines (about 9 ounces)
2 very heaped tablespoons chopped parsley
2 large garlic cloves, chopped
1 tablespoon grated Parmesan
1 tablespoon olive oil, plus some for frying
1 egg
dry bread crumbs
lemon juice, for serving

These are lovely any way they come: just fried alone or with a few drops of lemon juice; at room temperature or even cold. Serve these alone or as part of a larger spread of cicchetti.

__To fillet the sardines, cut off the heads, then make a slit down the side of each fish & remove the guts. Open out the sardines flat, making sure they are still hinged together, & place them skin side up on a chopping board. Press each sardine lightly, yet firmly, to open out. Turn each one over & pull out the backbone. Rinse & pat dry with paper towels.

__Mix together the parsley, garlic, Parmesan, olive oil, & some salt & pepper, & stuff gently inside the sardines (*I found I had just enough for my 15 sardines, using about ½ teaspoon for each*).

__Whisk the egg in a small bowl with a pinch of salt. Put the bread crumbs into another small bowl. One at a time, pass the sardines through the egg, holding the fish still & tilting the bowl so that no filling falls out of the sardines. Let the excess drip off & pat the sardines in bread crumbs.

__Heat enough oil to generously cover the bottom of a large nonstick skillet (*where the sardines will hopefully fit in one layer*). Fry until firm, golden, & crusty underneath, then turn gently & cook the other sides. Transfer onto a plate lined with paper towels. Sprinkle with salt, pepper if you like, & some lemon juice.

Serves 4 to 6

Sarde in forno

Roast sardines

15 to 18 whole sardines (about 18 ounces)
5 tablespoons olive oil
1 to 2 bay leaves
4 tablespoons dry bread crumbs, or 5 tablespoons fresh
3 heaped tablespoons chopped parsley
1 teaspoon dried oregano
1 teaspoon finely grated lemon zest
¼ cup white wine

Use small sardines for this recipe. You can add any other herbs or spices you like here. This dish is also lovely at room temperature, which makes it perfect to prepare in advance.

__Preheat the oven to 400°F. To fillet the sardines, cut off the heads, then make a slit down the side of each fish & remove the guts. Open out each sardine flat, making sure it is still hinged together at the tail, & place all of them skin side up on a chopping board. Press each sardine lightly, yet firmly, to open out. Turn each one over & pull out the backbone. Cut off the tail.

__Choose an oven dish that will fit the sardines compactly in a single layer (*but don't put them in the dish yet*). Drizzle 2 tablespoons of the oil into the dish & put the bay leaves on the bottom.

__In a small bowl, mix together the bread crumbs, parsley, oregano, & remaining oil, & season with salt & pepper. Mix well. Pat the sardines in the crumbs on both sides firmly but gently to coat well. Lay the sardines in the oven dish. Scatter the lemon zest over the top, then pour in the wine & roast for about 20 minutes, until the sardines are golden & crusty.

Serves 4 to 6

TROTE
7 50
AL KG.

Acciughe di Luisa

Luisa's anchovies

1 small red onion, finely sliced
3 tablespoons red wine vinegar
about 12 to 15 (7 ounces) fresh anchovies
about 4 tablespoons polenta
olive oil, for frying
1½ tablespoons chopped parsley

Dressing:
juice of half a lemon
3 tablespoons olive oil

The size of anchovies varies greatly & this is also lovely if you can get small sardines (the preparation is the same). These are pressed in polenta, fried, & then dressed with an onion, olive oil & lemon dressing. You can easily make a larger quantity if you like…they keep well in the refrigerator for a day or so & even stay crisp on account of the polenta.

__Put the onion in a bowl. Cover with cold water & the vinegar, let stand for an hour or so, then rinse, drain & pat dry with paper towels.
__To fillet the anchovies, cut off the heads, then make a slit down the side of each fish & remove the guts & bones. Open out each anchovy flat, making sure it is still hinged together with the tail on. Rinse & pat dry very well with paper towels.
__Pat the anchovy fillets in the polenta while your oil is heating in a nonstick skillet. Fry the anchovies in a single layer (*or in two batches, depending on the size of your pan*), until golden & crisp on both sides. Transfer to a plate lined with paper towels.
__In a compact bowl, make a layer of anchovies with some onion & parsley. Make another layer of anchovies, onion, & parsley on top.
__Mix the lemon juice & olive oil to make a dressing & drizzle over the top so that it falls between the fish. Season with salt & pepper. Serve immediately, or cover & let stand to absorb the flavors. This will keep in the refrigerator for a day or so (*after which you could add a bit more dressing if you like*).

Serves 4 to 6

Acciughe di Andrea

Andrea's anchovies

about 12 to 15 (7 ounces) fresh anchovies
½ cup red wine vinegar
1 very small red onion, halved & thinly sliced
1 teaspoon salt
1 teaspoon vinegar
3 tablespoons olive oil
½ teaspoon dried oregano
black pepper
pinch of peperoncino

Andrea is Lidia's son (Lidia's asparagus are on page 252). This has little in common with the salty taste of anchovies as we are used to them—these are marinated to softness & wonderful with bread. For a different version you can leave out the vinegar & add 3 tablespoons of prosecco, the juice of 1½ lemons, some small capers, & a tablespoon of chopped parsley to the finished dish. You could even use small small sardines instead of the anchovies. This is a good dish for leftovers, as the anchovies can stay in their marinade for a day…so you could eat half now, half tomorrow.

__To fillet the anchovies, cut off the heads, then make a slit down the side of each fish & remove the guts. Open out each anchovy flat, making sure it is still hinged together with the tail on. Rinse & pat dry very well with paper towels. Lay flat in a dish in a single layer (*slightly overlapping is fine*).
__Cover with the red wine vinegar (*you may need more, depending on the size of your dish, as all the anchovies need to be just covered*). Cover with plastic wrap & refrigerate for several hours or up to a day.
__Put the onion in a bowl with the salt, vinegar, & enough cold water to cover. Let stand for 1 hour, then drain & pat the onion dry with paper towels.
__Place the anchovies in a colander to drain away all the vinegar. Lay the anchovies flat on a plate with a bit of a lip. Splash with the olive oil & scatter the onions over them. Crush the oregano between your fingers & sprinkle over the anchovies with some black pepper, peperoncino, & salt if you like.
__These can be eaten immediately or kept to marinade longer. They are even good the next day.

Serves 4 to 6

12% vol
Origine Controllata
2005
CONTIENE SOLFITI
12,5% vol
70 cl

Intruglio

Sergia's brew

1 cup drained kalamata olives in oil
⅔ cup drained, pitted taggiasche olives in oil
½ cup drained, large green olives
½ cup drained, sun-dried tomatoes in oil, halved lengthwise
¾ cup caprini (smooth goat's cheese), broken into chunks
1⅓ cups buffalo mozzarella, cut into chunks
½ teaspoon dried oregano
pinch of coarse crushed dried peperoncino
about 1 cup good olive oil

This is delicious as an appetizer, but is also fantastic in summer with tuna, or served over pasta. INTRUGLIO *is actually a Tuscan word that means "brew" or "concoction" Although this is not a Venetian recipe, I feel that it belongs in the book because Sergia, who is the heart & soul of Venice as far as I am concerned, makes it & sells it in her alimentari in the Calle dei Do Mori. Originally, there were 27 alimentari shops in Venice; now there is one: Sergia's. She's like a mix between a great-grandmother owl & a film star. I first met her when I stopped in at her shop & asked where she would send me to eat lunch with locals. So she closed her shop & accompanied me to her friend's, Marinella, & at 4 p.m. we were still drinking Valpolicella & chatting. Now, whenever I stand in Sergia's shop I am amazed by the amount of social goings on: the milk guy who pops in to exchange chatter & news, a quick visit from one of Sergia's seven grandchildren or other relatives, or a conversation with the man who knows about all the foundations of Venice. Sergia keeps introducing everyone & at the same time carries on calmly helping customers in her gentle way. Next comes a guy whom Sergia announces might give me a good recipe for goose, & so time goes on. Sergia knows every bridge & every alley of Venice & loves her city. She shows me her favorite places to sit for an aperitivo & enjoy special views. What a wonderful soul–so incredibly kind & helpful.*

__Mix everything together in a large bowl–don't worry about being gentle. Keep covered in the refrigerator. As the oil chills & solidifies, the mixture will meld into one mass so that you won't be able to work out what it is, but once you remove it from the refrigerator, the oil melts. Store in the fridge, covered with the oil, for up to a week.
__Serve with bread, holding back some of the oil as it may be heavy. This is also lovely with cooked penne.

Serves many

clams & *carpaccio*

Giudecca is a beauty. Calm & serene. Great, big, water views, & no streams & streams of people. It is beautiful to just sit & watch, sipping spritz. This trattoria is the place from which to watch Venice—or the terrace at Cips. To watch Venice, Venetians, tourists, groups, singles, boats, activity…Everything bobbing up & down & carrying on quite naturally on the water. They all have Venice in their veins.

III

ANTIPASTI

Clams & mussels	La saltata di vongole e cozze in bianco
Clams & tomato	La saltata di vongole alla marinara
Scallops	Capesante al forno
Baby octopus in tomato	Moscardini al pomodoro
Mini shrimps	Schie con polenta
Marinated bass	Branzino marinato
Spider crab	Granseola in bella vista
Fish carpaccio with pink peppercorns	Carpaccio di pesce con pepe rosa
Meat carpaccio	Carpaccio di carne

La saltata di vongole e cozze in bianco

Clams & mussels

14 ounces clams in shells
12 ounces black mussels
4 tablespoons olive oil
1 small bunch parsley, plus 2 tablespoons chopped
3 garlic cloves, 1 halved, & 2 roughly sliced
pinch of peperoncino, if you like
bread & lemon wedges, for serving

This is the kind of thing you'll find in many restaurants. It is a lovely generous antipasto that could become a primo if mixed with pasta (you would need about 5½ ounces of cooked spaghetti to serve 2 people). It is also great served with a few handfuls of fries to make a perfect secondo. What I love here is that the garlic is in big pieces that you eat with the clams.

Vongole veraci (carpet shell clams) are good here, but any clams that are not too small will work well. Your clams will probably have been purged of sand already, but check with the fishmonger, otherwise you'll need to soak them for a day in a colander standing in well-salted water, changing the water several times.

__If you've been soaking your clams, give them a good swirl in the water, rinse them, drain, & leave in the colander. To clean the mussels, you need to "debeard" them by pulling away those fiddly bits of algae that stick out. Cut them off with scissors or a knife if you can't detach them, then scrub the shells well with a wire brush to dislodge evidence of the sea. At this stage you need to discard any mussels that are open & don't close when you give them a tap.

__Heat 1 tablespoon of the olive oil in a large skillet that has a lid. Add the bunch of parsley, a grinding of pepper, & the clams & mussels. Put the lid on & steam over medium heat until they all open. There may be a couple of clams that don't open–give them a second chance, but discard any that refuse to open. Transfer the clams & mussels to a bowl. Strain the cooking liquid into a cup, checking that no sand seeps through. If you discover any sand in the cooking liquid, strain it again through a cheesecloth-lined colander. Wipe the skillet clean.

__Add the remaining olive oil, the sliced garlic, & 1 tablespoon of chopped parsley to the skillet. When you can smell the garlic (*taking care not to burn it*), add ½ cup of the cooking water. Increase the heat to high & reduce the sauce, mixing the ingredients together. Once you have a nice sauce that is not too watery & not too thick (*if it reduces too much it may be too salty*), return the clams & mussels to the skillet. Add the rest of the parsley, a grind or two of white pepper, &, if you like, a pinch of peperoncino.

__Meanwhile, toast a couple of pieces of bread, then halve them lengthwise. Rub with the halved garlic & drizzle with a tiny bit of olive oil. Tuck the bread around the edge of the bowl or skillet. Squeeze the lemon over the clams before eating.

Serves 2

As many times as I went out was as many times as I got lost. But I was never lost. I was always somewhere in Venice.

La saltata di vongole alla marinara

Clams & tomato

Tomato sauce:
4 tablespoons olive oil
½ small onion, very finely chopped
1½ cups tomato passata
pinch of peperoncino
2 tablespoons cream

Clams:
3 tablespoons olive oil
2 garlic cloves, chopped
2¼ pounds vongole veraci in shells
½ cup white wine

This is how my lovely sister-in-law, Luisa (half-Venetian, half-Tuscan), likes to make clams. She adds a dash of cream to the tomato sauce, which makes it beautifully sweet & mellow. These can be served with bread or are great tossed into pasta with a little of the pasta cooking water to loosen things up. Try penne, spaghetti, or any pasta you like: you'll need about 10 ounces. You can also add a handful of chopped herbs to the sauce if you like. I have used vongole veraci (carpet shell clams) here, but any vongole are fine. Your clams will probably have been purged of sand already, but check with the fishmonger, otherwise you'll need to soak them for a day in a colander standing in well-salted water, changing the water several times.

__To make the tomato sauce, heat the oil in a skillet & cook the onion over low heat until it almost disappears & is very soft (*it should not be dark but should be very well cooked*). Add the passata, a grinding of salt & pepper, & a good pinch of peperoncino. Simmer, uncovered, for 10 to 15 minutes, until it all thickens into a lovely sauce. Add the cream & allow the sauce to bubble for a few minutes more. Remove the skillet from the heat.
__If you've been soaking your clams, give them a good swirl in the water, rinse them, drain, & leave in the colander. Heat the oil with the garlic in a large skillet that has a lid. Once you start to smell the garlic, add the clams & wine. Increase the heat to maximum & cover the skillet with the lid. Let the clams all steam open. Discard any that refuse to open.
__Take the clams out of the skillet. Check for sand by pressing on the bottom of the skillet with the back of a spoon. If you think there might be sand, then strain the sauce through a colander lined with cheesecloth.
__Add all the clam water to the tomato sauce & simmer for 5 to 10 minutes, until the flavors have merged & the liquid has reduced a little. You want there to be quite a lot of liquid but it shouldn't be too watery. Return the clams to the skillet & heat through for a minute. Serve immediately with bread.

Serves 4

Capesante al forno

Scallops

1 large garlic clove, finely chopped
2 to 3 tablespoons lemon juice
1½ tablespoons finely chopped parsley
2 tablespoons olive oil
6 scallops with coral, on the half shell
dry bread crumbs
2 teaspoons butter

This makes abundant saucy topping for 6 scallops, or even more if the scallops are on the small side. It's easy enough to double the sauce recipe if you want to use more scallops. You can buy scallops already prepared on the half shell.

__Preheat the oven to 425°F. Mix the garlic, lemon, parsley, & olive oil together, & drizzle generously over the scallops. Scatter with bread crumbs (*a three-finger pinch per scallop*), & salt & pepper, & put a small blob of butter on top of each.

__Put the scallops on a baking sheet or in an oven dish lined with aluminum foil (*just to save on cleaning*). Bake for 10 to 15 minutes, until the scallops are tender & the juice is bubbling & crusty golden. Serve with bread.

Serves 2 to 3

Moscardini al pomodoro

Baby octopus in tomato

14 ounces (about 24) small moscardini or baby octopus
4 tablespoons olive oil
1 tablespoon butter
2 garlic cloves, chopped
½ cup red wine
2 cups chopped, canned tomatoes, squashed or briefly pulsed in a blender
1 bay leaf
1 or 2 whole cloves
pinch of peperoncino
1 scant tablespoon chopped parsley
½ quantity soft polenta (page 21)

These exquisite little purple-red octopus are known as "moscardini"...their slightly larger cousins the Venetians call "folpetti." This is also delicious as a sauce for pasta —in that case, you should cut the octopus into pieces.

I ate this in a restaurant along with five other fish bits, followed by a fish lasagne, then a fritto misto, & finally a crema di mascarpone with baicoli. I won't say that I felt fantastic as we waddled to the vaporetto to get home, but it was all delicious & rests now in my mind as a lovely memory. The children played hide & seek through the tiny back canals while the parents were free. In such places, away from the thousands of tourists, the Venetians dine relaxed.

__To clean the octopus, cut between the head & tentacles. Grasp the body & push the beak up & out through the center of the tentacles with your finger. Leave the tentacles whole if they're small, or cut in half if large. The heads can be left whole or halved if large.

__Heat the oil & butter in a wide (*not too big & not too high*) saucepan, then sauté the garlic for 1 minute until it smells good. Add the octopus. When much of the liquid is reduced & the octopus has a good color, add the wine & allow it to bubble until slightly reduced. Add the tomato, bay leaf, cloves, peperoncino, parsley, & salt & pepper, & simmer, covered, for about 30 minutes, checking that nothing is sticking. Pour in ½ cup of water & simmer for 15 minutes before adding another ½ cup of water. Simmer for another 15 minutes, or until the tomatoes have melted down & you have a saucy, soft dish (*if necessary, keep cooking until the octopus is completely tender*). Season to taste. Remove the bay leaf & cloves (*hopefully you can find them*).

__When the octopus is almost ready, cook your polenta (*or, if you're making slow polenta, allow the 40 minutes or so that it needs*). Serve a generous helping of the soft polenta in a bowl with a few pieces of octopus in the middle & some of the sauce over the top.

Serves 4

Schie con polenta

Mini shrimps

9 ounces tiny shrimp
1 bay leaf
3 tablespoons olive oil
2 teaspoons lemon juice, or more to taste
1 garlic clove, peeled & squashed a bit
1 scant tablespoon chopped parsley
¼ quantity soft polenta (page 21)

These shrimp are often served as an antipasto or part of a mixed seafood antipasto in a smaller portion. Schie are miniature shrimp & they are really, really tiny. It will seem crazy as you are peeling them. If you can't get schie, then use the smallest shrimp you can find. Here, they are boiled, peeled, then marinated in garlic & olive oil & served over polenta. Simple & good. You can add any other fresh chopped herbs or seasonings, but this is how I ate them in Venice. Lemon isn't often added to this dish but I enjoy the flavor. If raw garlic doesn't bother you, chop some of that in as well.

__Rinse & drain the shrimp. Bring a small pot of water to a boil, season it with salt, then add the bay leaf & shrimp. Bring back to a boil & boil for 3 minutes or so, until it is all foamy on top.

__Drain the shrimp, let them stand to cool a little, then peel them & put in a bowl with the bay leaf, olive oil, lemon juice, & whole garlic, plus pepper & extra salt if needed. Marinate for a couple of hours at room temperature. Sprinkle with parsley before serving over warm, soft polenta.

Serves 2

The Venetians, I sometimes found, were amazingly generous with giving directions, but not always so amazing at sharing their recipes. They seemed to prefer directing, for the millionth time, a tourist to the fourteenth bridge, rather than be asked if they use white or black pepper with the clams. But I wanted the details of that garlic, hand-slivered by the grandmother…

SOTOPORTEGO
DEL TODESCHINI
1221

Branzino marinato

Marinated bass

3 (10-ounce) whole branzino or other small, whole fish, filleted, skinned, & boned
4-inch piece of tender celery stalk, sliced or chopped
about ¼ small, red bell pepper, cut into small, thin slices
2 garlic cloves, peeled & a bit squashed
juice of 1 lemon
2 tablespoons olive oil
pinch of peperoncino
1 tablespoon chopped parsley

This is lovely as part of a fish antipasto. You can serve this over some rucola, as I ate it in Venice, or just on its own. The fish isn't cooked over heat but the acid of the lemon juice will marinate it right through. It's important to have top-quality fresh, fresh fish. Use white-fleshed boned fillets that are suitable for marinating, such as bass or bream (ask your fishmonger for advice). If you are using fish that has been filleted for you, you will need three 7-ounce fillets.

__First, make sure that all the bones have been removed from the fish, then cut it into thin, rustic chunks & put in a nonreactive bowl. Add the celery, red pepper, garlic, lemon juice, olive oil, a pinch (*as large or small as you like*) of peperoncino, & some salt & pepper. Gently mix everything together. Taste a little of the dressing & check that you are happy with it, adjusting the seasoning if necessary.

__Cover the bowl with plastic wrap & refrigerate for 3 to 4 hours, until the fish is white & no longer translucent (*this indicates that the flesh has been "cooked" by the dressing*). Gently turn the fish, taste a little, & adjust the seasoning if necessary. Remove the whole garlic & sprinkle with parsley to serve.

Serves 4

Granseola in bella vista

Spider crab

1- to 2-pound live crab (spider, mud, sand, or similar)
1 celery stalk, roughly chopped
1 carrot, roughly chopped
1 onion, roughly chopped
a few peppercorns

Dressing:
4 tablespoons extra-virgin olive oil
juice of 1 lemon
1 small garlic clove, squashed
1 tablespoon chopped parsley
pinch of peperoncino

I couldn't get a spider crab at home when I needed it, so I got one in Venice & took it to a restaurant I knew & she gave me the cooking details. It is Marinella from La Buona Forchetta I have to thank. I then got another two crabs from Alvise (from Osteria All' Antica Adelaide), who cooked them for me ready to bring home. Boiled, plucked, dressed plainly with olive oil, garlic, lemon juice—this is everywhere in Venice.

__Put the crab in the freezer for an hour or so to put it to sleep, & make sure you have some ice cubes ready for later on.

__Put the celery, carrot, onion, & peppercorns in a large pot of well-salted water & bring to a boil. Add the crab, bring back to a boil, then cook at a rolling boil according to the crab's weight—less than 10 minutes for a 1-pound crab (sand crabs) or about 15 minutes for 1¾- to 2-pound (mud crabs). Transfer the crab to a container of well-iced water & let stand for 15 minutes to cool completely (*this will make the meat very tender*).

__Lift off the shell with the "lever" on the underside. Clean off the guts & gills, & gently clean off the muck, without immersing the crab or spraying it with water. Lift out the meat. Crack the claws with a sharp tap from the back of a knife to the back of the crab leg (*softer & easier to crack*), & remove the meat. Clean the shell & pile all the meat back into it for serving, putting the roe on top if your crab had any.

__Whisk together the ingredients for the dressing, season with salt & pepper, & drizzle lightly over the crab meat.

Serves 2 to 4, depending on the size of the crab

BOVOLETTI

These are small snails to be boiled & dressed. The Venetian word for spiral is bovolo & these are everywhere, when in season. Bovoletti & polenta is a speciality for Redentore—the Saturday before the third Sunday of July has been a huge celebration since the 1500s, when Venice was saved from the plague. They build a floating bridge from the Zattere to Redentore Church for the weekend. Venetians take their boats with family & friends to Giudecca canal & spend the night, or part of it, eating & drinking wine. The snails are to be found at a fish store or market (even though they are not sea snails at all, but hill snails). Put them in fresh water which is to be changed three times (to purge the snails of their slime) & then heated up very slowly so that the warmth entices the snails to come out of their shells. Then zap them with a strong heat. Eat with garlic, olive oil, parsley, & a squeeze of lemon if you like. Under the fireworks.

Carpaccio di pesce con pepe rosa

Fish carpaccio with pink peppercorns

1 garlic clove, peeled & halved
2 good teaspoons dried pink peppercorns
5 ounces thick tuna fillet, very thinly sliced
5 ounces thick swordfish fillet, very thinly sliced
3 to 4 tablespoons best extra-virgin olive oil
juice of 2 small lemons
pinch of peperoncino
1 scant tablespoon chopped parsley
leaves of 1 fresh thyme sprig

Venetians are used to pulling fish, such as cannolicchi (razor shell clams), out of the water & eating them very plainly there & then, but I have also seen many people enjoying plates of raw seafood, often dressed (as here) with oil & lemon. This is a bit of a variation with pink peppercorns. You can use any type of the freshest seafood such as scampi, cannolicchi, ciacale di mare (mantis shrimp), & the like, or an oyster or two could be added. I have also made this with smoked swordfish, which was really good. There is no real need to marinate the fish at all—once the dressing has been added, it will be very tasty, but I normally marinate for anywhere between 10 minutes to 1 hour. One of the most important requirements is to slice the fish most finely. If you're not confident with your knife skills to do this, ask your fishmonger to slice the fish about ⅛ inch thick.

__You will need two large plates with rims. Rub each plate with the garlic clove, covering as much of the plate as you can. Wrap the peppercorns in a thick piece of paper towels & gently press down with your palms to lightly crush them—it is nice if many remain whole, just lightly pressed to release their flavor.

__Lay the fish slices out flat, with the tuna on one plate & swordfish on the other. If necessary, overlap the pieces. Drizzle half the oil & lemon juice over each plate & scatter half the peppercorns onto each. Season with a pinch of peperoncino, if you like, & some salt & pepper. Let stand at room temperature for 10 minutes or so. Once the fish starts to change color slightly it's ready to serve. (*It could also stay in the refrigerator, covered, for an hour.*)

__Before serving, scatter parsley over one plate & thyme over the other (*I like parsley for the swordfish & thyme for the tuna*). Taste the fish & add a little more salt or other seasoning, if necessary.

Serves 4

Carpaccio di carne

Meat carpaccio

1 beautiful artichoke suitable for eating raw
4 ounces very thinly sliced beef
juice of half a lemon
table & coarse pounded salt
2 tablespoons extra-virgin olive oil
1 tablespoon shaved Parmesan, or asiago stagionato

Harry's Bar made this famous. The carpaccio there is excellent & is served with a creamy mayonnaise sauce drizzled over. Here, I have served it with artichoke & a lemon oil. You could also serve it with arugula, or thin slices of endive, fennel, or celeriac. A couple of blobs of a creamy blue cheese here & there also work well. Serve this as an antipasto for two or a secondo for one. It is lovely as a summer lunch with a green salad on the side & some bread, & then it can take something slightly richer for dessert.

Use well-trimmed & tender, flavorsome lean beef, such as girello or shell steak (use strip loin or porterhouse), tenderloin (mid loin), or beef fillet works well. The diameter of the meat is not important; just add more slices to the plate to cover it, overlapping slightly if necessary. Ask the butcher to trim the meat for you. You may even be able to convince him to slice it, but only if you plan to serve it within an hour or two. If you slice the meat yourself, cut it very cold from the refrigerator to get the thinnest possible slices. It is important that the meat is very thin & very soft. Add some coarse pounded salt in, too, for the texture—table salt with a small amount of bashed coarse salt added.

__Prepare your artichoke first. Trim away the outer leaves & cut a slice off the top. Halve the artichoke & remove the hairy choke if it has one, then cut each half into fine slices 1⁄16 inch thick. (*If you're not serving immediately, keep them covered with cold water & a little lemon juice to prevent them turning black.*)

__If necessary, put the beef slices between two sheets of plastic wrap & pound with a meat mallet until very thin. Arrange them flat on a large plate (*slightly overlapping is fine*). Scatter the artichoke slices over the top. Drizzle with lemon juice, sprinkle with the salt, & drizzle with oil. Now scatter the cheese on top & a good grind of black pepper. Serve with bread, & perhaps the bottle of olive oil, salt, & black pepper on the side, in case you need extra.

Serves 2

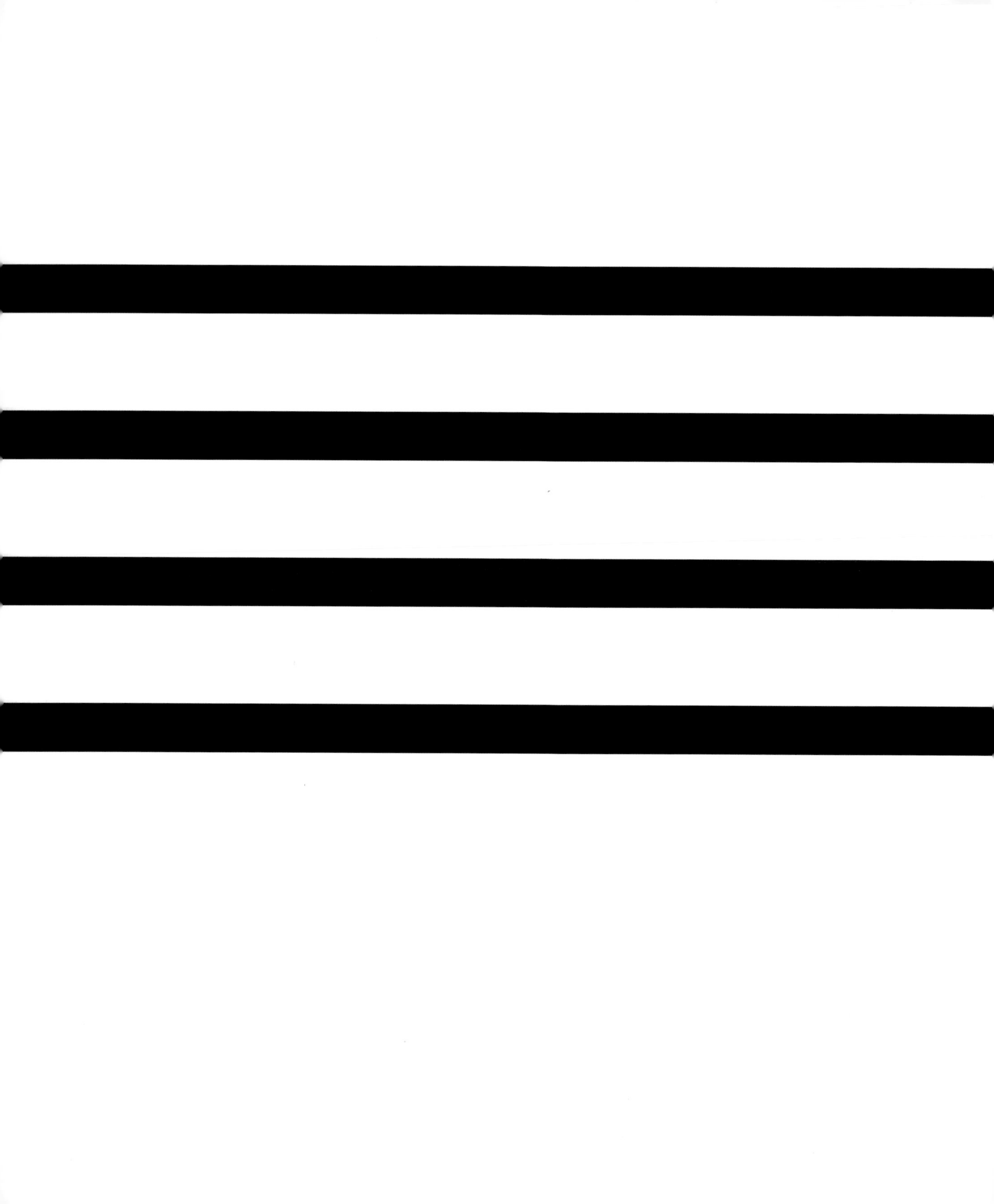

zuppa & *zattere*

The prize goes to who is out at the break of dawn. To watch the sun lighting up some pale colors & just start to brighten up the hyperbole. Follow the low crying of the seagulls. Early morning water & early-bird Venetians chatting, looking out for each other as they do. Witness the backstreet small events…Papà dropping his child off to school by vaporetto. I can see who reads which newspaper. I know the tastes of a gentleman's flowers after a few days & the color of the old ladies' shopping carts as they go to the market. One by one they all slip out of home & onto the stage set. ⟡

IV

ZUPPA/PASTA/ GNOCCHI

Pasta e fagioli

Pasta & beans

1½ cups dried Lamon or borlotti beans
1 carrot, peeled
1 celery stalk
2 garlic cloves, peeled but left whole
2 onions, peeled, 1 left whole & the other finely chopped
4 tablespoons olive oil
1¼ cups chopped pancetta (unsmoked)
pinch of peperoncino
1 tablespoon chopped rosemary
¼ (16-ounce) package dried pasta, such as thin tagliatelle or tagliolini, broken up
thin slices of firm, mature asiago or pecorino, to serve
drizzle of olive oil

This soup is served everywhere in Venice, made with various types of pasta. I particularly like this version that I ate at Marinella's restaurant, La Buona Forchetta, which she served with tagliolini that had been broken up & small triangles of mature asiago. When cooking it at home, you can use any type of short dried pasta (not fresh pasta). I've also seen it with torn & lightly dressed radicchio on top. You can make the soup beforehand & keep it in the refrigerator for a day (you will need to add water when reheating, though).

Lamon beans are the large, creamy, speckled beans found in the Veneto region. They need to be soaked overnight & then cooked for 30 to 45 minutes, until tender. If you can't source Lamon beans, use borlotti beans, which may need longer cooking & perhaps more water.

__Put the beans in a large bowl, cover with cold water, & leave to soak for 8 to 10 hours or overnight. Drain, & put the beans in a large pot with the carrot, celery, garlic, the whole onion, & 8 cups of water. Bring to a boil & skim the surface.

__Lower the heat, partly cover the pot, & simmer from 30 minutes to 1 hour, depending on the type & age of the beans & the heat of the stove. You want the beans to be soft & creamy, but not too mushy. You may need to add 2 cups of hot water midway through cooking, so that you have a good amount of liquid without its being too watery. Season toward the end of the cooking time with salt.

__While the beans are cooking, put the oil & chopped onion into a wide, flat saucepan & sauté until the onion is softened. Add the pancetta & continue sautéing, until the onion & pancetta are golden but not too crisp. Add the peperoncino & some salt & pepper, & stir in the rosemary for a minute or so, then remove the pan from the heat & cover.

__Take the beans off the heat when cooked. Lift out & discard the whole carrot, celery, & onion. Lift out an abundant slotted spoonful of the whole beans & put into the pancetta pan. Take 2 tablespoons of the chopped onion & pancetta mixture & put into the bean pot—a fair swap.

__Purée the bean mixture in a food processor until completely smooth, then return to the pot. Add the pancetta & onion, stir briefly, & bring to a boil. Stir in the pasta pieces & cook for a few minutes until tender. If the soup is too thick for your liking, add more hot water.

__Season with more salt & pepper if necessary. Ladle the soup into bowls & top each bowl with a couple of thin triangles of cheese so they melt a bit. Add a drizzle of olive oil & a grinding of pepper.

Serves 4 to 5

Zuppa di piselli spezzati

Split pea soup

2⅓ cups dried split peas
2 tablespoons olive oil, plus some for the croutons
¼ cup chopped unsmoked pancetta
1 tablespoon well-chopped rosemary
1 white onion, peeled
1 celery stalk (not too big)
1 carrot, peeled but left whole
4 slices country bread with crusts, roughly cut into 2-inch pieces
grated Parmesan

The split peas in Venice are green, but you can use yellow if you like. If you aren't going to serve the soup immediately, you'll need to add water when reheating it, then stir well, because you'll find that the soup has almost set into a thick block.

__Soak the peas in a big bowl of cold water for an hour or two. Drain well.

__Heat the oil in a large saucepan & sauté the pancetta lightly until softened & pale golden, being careful not to let it become crispy. Add the rosemary to the pan & sauté for another minute. Add the drained peas, stir well, & then add the whole onion, celery stalk, carrot, & about 6 cups of water. Bring to a boil, skimming occasionally, then lower the heat & simmer well for about 30 minutes, until many of the peas have dissolved. Stir occasionally to help the peas break up, then keep simmering for another 10 to 15 minutes, stirring regularly so that it doesn't stick, until the liquid has reduced to make a thick soup. If it's still too thin, keep cooking until it thickens. Season with salt & pepper (*or save the pepper for serving*).

__When the soup is almost cooked, remove the carrot, celery, & onion with a slotted spoon (*these won't be served, but you can eat them anyway if you like*).

__Meanwhile, to make the croutons, scatter the bread on a baking sheet, drizzle lightly with olive oil, & bake in the oven for about 8 minutes at 350°F until crisp. Sprinkle with salt.

__Ladle the soup into bowls, then add a grinding of black pepper, a good scattering of Parmesan, & a small bowl of croutons on the side for each (*& a pinch of peperoncino if anyone likes*).

Serves 4 to 6

Zuppa di pesce

Fish soup

Brodo di pesce:

4 to 6 large shrimp
3 cicale, cleaned & left whole
3 to 4 whole small fish (about 1¾ pounds in total weight)
1 large carrot, peeled & halved
1 celery stalk with leaves, halved
1 white onion, peeled
1 large garlic clove, peeled
1 dried bay leaf
about 8 peppercorns
1 teaspoon salt
1 bunch parsley

Soup base:

4 tablespoons olive oil, plus 2 tablespoons extra
1 small white onion, finely chopped
1 small carrot, very thinly sliced slightly on the diagonal
2 garlic cloves, chopped
1 tablespoon chopped parsley, plus a little extra
½ cup white wine

When making the broth for this soup, it's worth seeking out cicale—a mantis shrimp popular in Venice that is known to make a lovely broth. However, if you can't get cicale then use an extra couple of large shrimp, leaving these ones whole to add their flavor to the broth. You can also freeze any leftover brodo & use later as the base for a lovely plain risotto.

Use small whole fish for the broth...I like to use different types for their flavor—scorfani (scorpion fish), gallinella (gurnard), pescatrice (anglerfish), or bream, mullet, or whiting, depending on what is available from your fishmonger. I haven't used their flesh here for the soup, but you can if you like—or you could use it to make fish croquettes (Polpette di tonno, page 57).

__Begin by peeling & deveining the shrimp. Keep the shells & heads for the brodo & put the meat in the refrigerator to use for the soup.

__Put all the brodo ingredients in a pot with the shrimp shells & heads, add 6 cups of water, & bring to a gentle boil. Lower the heat, then cover & simmer for about 30 minutes. Remove from the heat. Let stand, covered, until it cools a little. Strain through a fine sieve so you end up with a clear broth.

__To make the soup base, heat 4 tablespoons of the olive oil in a wide, heavy-bottomed pan & sauté the onion, until it is pale golden & well cooked. Add the carrot, garlic, & parsley, & stir well until you can smell the garlic, then add the wine. Let the wine bubble away until it has evaporated, then add the tomato & season lightly with salt & pepper & peperoncino. Simmer, uncovered, for 10 minutes or so, crushing the tomato with a wooden spoon so that there are no lumps.

__Strain 4 cups of the fish brodo into the pot with the tomato, & slowly increase the heat, stirring to blend in all the ingredients. Once it has come to a simmer, cook for another 5 minutes or so to allow all the flavors to mix through.

1 cup roughly puréed, canned, or peeled fresh tomatoes
pinch of dried peperoncino

4 slices country bread with crusts, roughly cut into 1-inch pieces
olive oil, for drizzling
2 (5½-ounce) firm, white fish fillets
a little all-purpose flour
1 garlic clove, peeled
2 tablespoons cognac or brandy

__Meanwhile, to make the croutons, scatter the bread on a baking sheet, drizzle lightly with a little olive oil, & bake in the oven for about 8 minutes at 350°F until crisp. Sprinkle lightly with salt.

__While the croutons are baking, remove any skin or bones from the fish fillets, pat dry with paper towels, & cut into 1½ inch pieces. Coat them very lightly in flour, flapping them against your free palm to get rid of any excess. Take the shrimp from the refrigerator & cut each one into 3 or 4 pieces. Coat them lightly with flour.

__Heat the remaining 2 tablespoons of olive oil in a large nonstick skillet (*it should just cover the bottom*) with the whole garlic clove. Panfry the fish fillets quickly over high heat, until crusty golden on the base, then turn over & add the shrimp, cooking until they just brighten & turn opaque. Lightly season with salt, add the cognac, & ignite the pan, standing well back. Sprinkle lightly with a bit more parsley & a grind of pepper.

__Dish the fish into four hot deep bowls & cover with boiling hot broth. Serve immediately with croutons on the side.

Serves 4

Bigoli in salsa

Healthy pasta with anchovies & onion

9 salt-packed anchovy fillets
8 tablespoons olive oil
2 large white onions, thinly sliced
¼ cup white wine
black peppercorns, coarsely cracked with a hammer or rolling pin
1 scant tablespoon chopped parsley
8½ ounces bigoli or thick whole-wheat spaghetti

This is everywhere & no wonder, since it is made from such simple but beautiful ingredients—the typical lovely thick wholewheat spaghetti, plump anchovies in salt, onions, & freshly cracked black pepper. Traditionally this dish was served at room temperature. Ceramic dishes of this would be laid out on the tables of osterie ready for the customers.

You could try this using red onion, or adding a sprig or two of fresh thyme to the onions while they cook. Or throw in a few small olives...Parmesan may not normally be served, but I love it here. Use thick spaghetti if you don't have bigoli. Black pepper is a must here.

__Rinse the anchovy fillets in cold water, then debone & pat dry with paper towels. Heat the oil in a large nonstick skillet that has a lid, add the onions, & cover. Sauté over low heat for 20 to 30 minutes (*as Sergia says, they must die slowly in the oil*). When you see the onions start to color, add the wine & let it simmer briefly, then add 3 tablespoons of water, cover again, & cook until the onions are soft & most of the liquid has evaporated.

__Add the anchovies to the skillet, breaking them up over the heat so that they melt into the onion a little. Add the coarsely cracked pepper & parsley, & remove the pan from the heat.

__Meanwhile, cook the pasta in boiling salted water, following the instructions on the package. Drain, reserving a little of the cooking water. Add the pasta to the skillet & toss, adding a little of the cooking water if necessary to blend it all together. Serve with more black pepper.

Serves 3

Gnocchi con scampi

Scampi & gnocchi

9 to 10 scampi (langoustines, red-claw, or large shrimps) —you need about 5½ ounces scampi meat
1 tablespoon butter
1 tablespoon cognac, or brandy
1 tablespoon cream
1 tablespoon chopped parsley

Tomato sauce:
½ (14-ounce) can peeled tomatoes
3 tablespoons olive oil
½ white onion, finely chopped
2 garlic cloves, chopped
¼ cup white wine
pinch of peperoncino

Gnocchi:
1½ pounds (4 medium) russet potatoes, washed but unpeeled
1 cup all-purpose flour, less if possible

This will serve 4 to 6 people, depending on what else you're serving at the table. I am making the assumption that you would prefer a small serving of something rich & that you'll probably be following with a Fritto misto (page 182) or mixed grill, you may have already had a crab salad as an antipasto & you'll want space for some mascarpone cream afterwards, or perhaps you'll just manage a Sgroppino (page 268). Maybe you'll be lunching outside on a terrace looking at miles & miles of water or lagoon. Who can tell?

In Italy, we get potatoes that say on the bag they are perfect for gnocchi. If that doesn't happen where you live, try to choose russet potatoes of a uniform size so that they will all cook to more or less the same softness at the same time.

__First, clean the scampi. Peel, remove the heads, & devein. Cut up the flesh into 3 or 4 pieces. Rinse, pat dry with paper towels, & set aside.

__To make the tomato sauce, put the tomatoes in a food processor & pulse until quite smooth. Heat the oil in a large skillet, & sauté the onion until it melts & is pale golden but well cooked. Add the garlic &, when you can smell it, add the wine & let it bubble up until it has evaporated & the onion is frying again. Then add the pulsed tomatoes, some salt & pepper, & peperoncino, & simmer over low heat for about 15 minutes, or until you have a nice loose sauce, not too thick. Add the cream and bubble up for a moment. Keep warm while you make the gnocchi.

__To make the gnocchi, cook the potatoes in their skins in boiling salted water until soft. Remove & drain. Cool a little, then peel. Pass the warm potato through a potato ricer. Mix in as much of your flour as necessary to make a very soft dough—the less flour you have to use, the better & softer your gnocchi will be. Cut off chunks of the mixture & gently roll out logs about ¾ inch thick, without pressing down too hard. Cut into pieces about 1 inch long.

__Meanwhile, melt the butter in a small saucepan over the highest heat until it starts fizzing. Add the scampi pieces & cook until they are golden on the bottom, all the liquid has evaporated, & the scampi are once again frying in the butter & there are some crusty bits here & there. Add a little salt, & when the scampi are golden in places & the flesh is bright white & soft, add the cognac & ignite the pan, standing back so that you don't burn yourself. Add the scampi to the tomato sauce.

__ Bring a large pot of salted water to a boil. Add half the gnocchi to the boiling water & cook until they bob up to the surface, then lift out with a slotted spoon. Add to the hot tomato sauce while you cook the second batch. Once the gnocchi have all been added to the tomato sauce, increase the heat to high & add about 4 tablespoons of the gnocchi cooking water to loosen things up a little. Fold everything together.

__ Allow the sauce to bubble away & toss the pan by flicking your wrist to coat everything rather than stabbing at the gnocchi with a spoon to mix together. Serve immediately into flat bowls or plates, with chopped parsley & a grinding of black pepper.

Serves 4 (abundantly) or 6 (scantily)

Gnocchi di zucca

Winter squash gnocchi

2½ pounds winter squash
1 egg, lightly beaten
about ½ teaspoon salt
about 1⅓ cups all-purpose flour
oil, for dipping
1 stick butter
2 or 3 sage sprigs
a good grating of nutmeg, to serve
lots of grated Parmesan, to serve

I learnt to make these from my friend Julia. This gnocchi dish is made without potato & is wonderfully soft & sweet. You will not be able to roll out the puréed vegetable as you would with potato gnocchi; instead use two spoons to form quenelles. The amount of flour is very approximate here and will depend entirely on how much liquid your winter squash contains. The quality of the squash is really important so choose a sweet, bright orange one. When cooking, you need to cook & dry out your winter squash well at the beginning without crisping it too much.

__Preheat the oven to 350°F. Line a baking sheet with foil. Peel the winter squash & remove the seeds. Cut the flesh into large slices. Roast the squash on the sheet for about 30 minutes until tender, but not too browned (*or they will be difficult to purée*). Transfer to a plate & allow to cool a little.
__Purée all the slightly warm squash as smoothly as possible, so it is evenly colored & there are no chunks in the finished gnocchi. Scrape into a bowl, add the egg & salt, & mix well. Add the flour, mixing it in well (*try to put in as little as possible*), until you have a mixture that holds its shape on a spoon.
__Bring a saucepan of salted water to a boil. Pour some olive oil into a cup. If you are not going to be serving your gnocchi at once, have a slightly oiled or buttered sheet ready so that they won't all stick together while they wait.
__Put the butter & sage in a small skillet & heat until the butter turns golden & the sage becomes crisp, but be careful not to let it burn.
__When the water is boiling, lightly dip 2 teaspoons in the oil, then form quenelles by passing the squash back & forth between the spoons. Gently lower the gnocchi into the water, then lift out with a slotted spoon when they bob up to the top. Put them in the heated butter or on your oiled sheet.
__Sauté the gnocchi in the hot butter for a minute or so. Spoon onto plates, drizzling the butter over & around. Serve immediately with nutmeg, Parmesan, & black pepper.

Serves 4

Spaghetti con castraure e gamberi

Spaghetti with tiny artichokes & shrimps

6 large, sweet shrimp (about 9 ounces), peeled & deveined
6 castraure artichokes
juice of half a lemon
⅓ (16-ounce) package spaghetti
3 tablespoons olive oil
2 garlic cloves, chopped
2 tablespoons chopped parsley
2½ tablespoons butter
pinch of peperoncino
¼ cup prosecco, or white wine

Castraure are small artichokes—the tiny bitter beauties that come from the Venetian vegetable garden island of Sant' Erasmus. If you can't find castraure use a couple of ordinary, larger artichokes instead. This is my kind of primo & definitely what I would order if I saw it on a restaurant menu. I adore artichokes cooked in all possible ways. Use large, fresh, sweet, succulent shrimp: I used three per serving as they were large, but you might decide to add more. You can leave them unpeeled for effect, but cut a slit to devein & make them easier to eat with hands at the table…

__Rinse the shrimp & pat dry with paper towels. Prepare your artichokes: if you're using tiny castraure just cut them in half; for larger artichokes, trim away the outer leaves & cut a slice off the top. Halve the artichoke & remove the hairy choke if it has one, then cut each half into fine slices ⅛ inch thick. (*If you're not serving immediately, keep them covered with cold water & a little lemon juice to prevent their turning black.*)
__Meanwhile, bring a large pan of salted water to a boil & add the pasta.
__Heat the oil in a large skillet & add half the garlic. When you start to smell the garlic, add the artichokes (*drained if they have been in lemon water*). Season, add half the parsley, & sauté for a few minutes. Cook over steady heat for about 5 minutes, until just tender but still with a bit of crunch, then lift out to a side plate, scraping out all the sauce so the pan is dry.
__Add the butter to the skillet. When it's fizzling, add the shrimp & turn up to the highest heat possible. Cook until they have a gold crust on the bottom, then turn & sprinkle with salt, peperoncino, the rest of the parsley, & some black pepper. When the shrimp are opaque with a deep gold crust here & there, add the prosecco, & bubble up fast to give some good sauce in the pan.
__Drain the pasta (*saving a little of the water*), & add to the shrimp pan along with the artichokes. Add a little pasta water if necessary to bring it together. Toss through quickly & serve with a shrimp or two on top & black pepper.

Serves 2

Linguine al granchio

Crab linguini

5½ ounces linguini
4 tablespoons olive oil
2 garlic cloves, crushed
8 ripe cherry tomatoes, cut into thirds
2 tablespoons chopped parsley
about 5 ounces fresh crab meat

This is how Giorgia from the Rialto fish market would make her pasta—it is the simplest of simple. If you're buying a fresh crab, you'll need one that weighs about 1¼ pounds to give you this amount of meat. This is very often served with tagliolini in Venice, & you could add a dash of peperoncino. If you want to buy a live crab & cook it yourself, follow the method for Granseola in bella vista (page 93).

__Bring a large saucepan of water to a boil, add salt, & cook the pasta according to the instructions on the package. When the pasta is nearly ready, heat 3 tablespoons of the olive oil & the garlic in a large skillet (*it will hold your pasta, too, later*). Add the tomato & half the parsley. Cook for a minute or so, then add the crab meat, & cook for another minute or so with a pinch of salt.

__Drain the pasta, saving a little of the cooking water. Add the pasta to the skillet, & heat for a minute, adding a little of the cooking water if necessary to bring it all together.

__Turn off the heat & add the rest of parsley & olive oil. Serve immediately with a grinding of black pepper.

Serves 2

Spaghetti con vongole e calamari

Spaghetti with clams & calamari

¾ pound clams in shells
2 calamari
⅓ (16-ounce) package spaghetti
4 tablespoons olive oil
2 garlic cloves, chopped
3 tablespoons chopped parsley
½ cup white wine
pinch of peperoncino

The important thing here is timing: the calamari has to be tender & you need the seafood cooking while you par-cook the spaghetti. Then they can be tossed together at the right moment & the spaghetti can finish off its cooking in the lovely thick seafood sauce. I like to use vongole veraci (carpet shell clams). Your clams will probably have been purged of sand already, but check with the fishmonger, otherwise you'll need to soak them for a day in well-salted water, changing the water several times.

__If you've been soaking your clams, give them a swirl in the water, rinse them, drain, & leave in the colander. To prepare the calamari, firmly pull the head & innards from the body & wash the body well. Cut off the head just below the eyes, leaving the tentacles in one piece if they're small. Discard the head, pull the transparent quill out of the body, & rinse out the tube. Peel off the outer membrane & slice the tube into slices about ⅛ inch thick. Pat dry with paper towels (*you should have about 6 ounces of cleaned calamari*).

__Meanwhile, heat 2 tablespoons olive oil in a skillet that has a lid. Add half the garlic &, when it smells good, add the clams, 1 tablespoon of parsley, & 3 tablespoons of white wine. Cover & cook over high heat until the clams open. Discard any that refuse to open. Transfer the clams to a large bowl, removing the shells from half of them. Add all the clam water to the bowl (*if you have any suspicions there may be sand in the cooking water you can strain it through a cheesecloth-lined colander*). Wipe out the pan with paper towels.

__Heat the remaining oil in the skillet with the rest of garlic. Add the calamari, 1 tablespoon parsley, peperoncino, & a pinch of salt. Cook over high heat, until the calamari changes color. Add the rest of the wine & let it reduce a little. Remove from the heat & add the clams & juices to the calamari.

__Meanwhile, cook the spaghetti in boiling salted water until almost ready. Drain, add to the seafood, & toss over high heat to thicken the clam sauce until it coats the spaghetti. Serve with olive oil, black pepper, & parsley.

Serves 2

For all the water surrounding me in Venice, for all the time spent on it and watching it, there is relatively little swimming potential. I kept wishing I could dive in and I couldn't. There are so many places with much less water…and a lot more possibility for swimming.

Pasticcio di pesce

Monkfish & bavette lasagne

about 3 pounds whole monkfish, scaled & gutted, or 1 monkfish head, eyes & tongue removed
4 tablespoons olive oil
1 large onion, chopped
2 garlic cloves, chopped
½ cup white wine
a good grating of nutmeg
2 sprigs of thyme
1 small peperoncino, crumbled
1 tablespoon chopped parsley
1 cup tomato passata
½ (16-ounce) package bavette pasta (or other dried pasta)
3 tablespoons grated Parmesan

Béchamel sauce:
7 tablespoons butter
⅔ cup all-purpose flour
3 cups warm milk
a good grating of nutmeg

This is Lidia from Lido's wonderful recipe for coda di rospo (monkfish). You must try it—it's a beauty & well worth the effort. You buy a whole fish & use the head to make this flavorful pasta "pie" & the rest of it for a second course of mixed grilled fish (page 186) with salad, or have the monkfish with tomato (page 187) the next day. The recipe is designed for monkfish but you could use snapper, though I can't promise the flavor will be the same. If you prefer, use the tail instead of the head for this recipe: just cook the fish in the same way, then remove all the bones & mash the flesh into the ragù—you will get more meat, but it will also be less gelatinous than the head. If some of the steps sound too challenging, ask your fishmonger to prepare the fish for you, then you just have to take out all the bones with your fingers, using gloves if necessary, squashing the meat between your fingers as though playing with sand. All this removing of eyes & teeth might seem like a nightmare—but once you've tasted it you'll forget the details. The thyme is great here, & oregano or marjoram would be just as good.

This meal is lovely the next day, too: just cover with foil & reheat in the oven.

__If you are using the whole fish, skin it completely. Cut the head away from the body. Cut away the fins to make a neat tail with central bone. Set the tail end aside to use for stock or another dish.

__Heat 3 tablespoons of the oil in a wide saucepan that has a lid & sauté the onion until very soft, then add the garlic, cooking briefly before adding the fish head. Sauté the fish until well colored on both sides, then pour in the wine. Allow the wine to bubble away until it has evaporated a little, then season with nutmeg, thyme, peperoncino, parsley, salt, & pepper. Add the tomato passata & bring to a boil. Once it is boiling, add 2 cups of hot water, then cover & simmer for an hour until everything is soft.

__Allow the mixture to cool. When the fish is cool enough to touch, lift out the head, & then carefully remove all the meaty bits, squashing down the pulp patiently with your hands to ensure only flesh remains & all the bones & teeth have been removed.

__Return the fish flesh to the pan. Remove & discard the thyme sprigs. Return to the heat for another 15 minutes or so, until the mixture thickens, stirring so that nothing sticks to the bottom of the pan.
__Preheat the oven to 400°F. Cook the pasta in boiling salted water & drain 2 to 3 minutes before it is completely cooked. Transfer the pasta to a large bowl & mix in the remaining tablespoon of oil. Allow to cool.
__Meanwhile, make the béchamel sauce. Melt the butter in a heavy-bottomed saucepan. Whisk the flour into the butter, then add a little salt & pepper, & cook for a few minutes, stirring. Reduce the heat to low, then begin adding the warm milk. It will be immediately absorbed, so work quickly, whisking with one hand while slowly pouring the milk with the other. When the sauce is smooth & thick, add the nutmeg, remove the pan from the heat, & let it cool (*it should thicken even more*). Adjust the seasoning.
__Once the fish ragù has cooled down a bit, stir the cooked pasta into it along with one-third of the béchamel. Stir through gently so that it's all mixed in. You'll need an oven dish that's about 9 inches by 14 inches & is 2 inches high (*I like my oval dish here*). Dollop one-third of the béchamel over the bottom of the oven dish. Pour the pasta & fish over gently (*not flattening it, but just shaking so it settles*). Dollop the rest of the béchamel sauce over the top to more or less cover the mixture, then scatter the Parmesan evenly over the top. Bake for about 20 minutes, until a lovely golden crust has formed here & there. Serve warm to hot. This is close to stunning…

Serves 8

Lasagne di pesce

Seafood lasagne

2¼ pounds small clams
1¼ pounds mussels
4 tablespoons olive oil
24 lasagna noodles (uncooked), about 10 by 2¼ inches
2 or 3 garlic cloves, peeled, but left whole
about ½ cup white wine
about 2 tablespoons chopped parsley, plus a small bunch
a blob of butter
½ pound fillet of san pietro (John Dory), cernia (dusky grouper), or snapper, cut into strips
5 to 6 peeled scampi (langoustines, red-claw, or large shrimps), cut into thirds
3 tablespoons grated Parmesan

Béchamel sauce:
7 tablespoons butter
⅔ cup all-purpose flour
2½ cups warm milk
a good grating of nutmeg

For this I use a rectangular dish of 13 by 10 inches where the pasta fits exactly. If you prefer something smaller or an oval dish, which is fine, you will either need less pasta or you'll have to cut it up & turn it to fit in the dish. Use any seafood you like here. Your clams will probably have been purged of sand already, but check with the fishmonger, otherwise you'll need to soak them for several hours in a colander standing in well-salted water, changing the water several times.

__Have your lasagne dish ready. If you've been soaking your clams, give them a good swirl in the water, rinse them, drain, & leave in the colander. To clean the mussels, you need to "debeard" them by pulling away fiddly bits of algae that stick out. Cut them off with scissors or a sharp knife if you can't detach them, then scrub the shells well with a wire brush to dislodge evidence of the sea. At this stage, you need to discard any mussels that are open & don't close when you give them a tap.

__Bring a pot of water to a boil, salt it, & add 1 tablespoon of the oil. Cook the pasta according to the time given on the package, or until almost cooked (*it will all go in the oven & continue cooking*). Remove, refresh in cold water, & lay out the noodles on a baking sheet lined with clean dishcloths, making a couple of layers as necessary to accommodate all the pasta.

__Heat 2 tablespoons of the olive oil in a wide, heavy-bottomed saucepan or deep skillet that has a lid. Add a clove of garlic &, when the garlic smells good, add the mussels & clams with half the white wine, a grinding of black pepper, & the thin bunch of parsley. Cover with the lid & cook over high heat until all the mussels & clams open. There may be a couple that don't open–give them a second chance, but discard any that refuse to open. Transfer the clams & mussels into a bowl. Strain the cooking liquid into a cup, checking that no sand seeps through. If you discover any sand in the cooking liquid, strain it through a cheesecloth-lined colander. Reserve 1 cup of the cooking broth. When cool enough to touch, remove the mussels & clams from the shells. Chop the mussels, but leave the clams whole unless very large.

__Heat the remaining tablespoon of olive oil & a blob of butter in a nonstick skillet. Add the fish pieces, scampi, & a clove or two of garlic. Sauté very briefly over high heat until crusty here & there & just cooked. Season with salt & pepper, then add the rest of the wine & reduce a little so that it is still saucy. Remove from the heat & remove the garlic. Add the mussels, clams, & chopped parsley, tossing together.
__Make the béchamel sauce. Melt the butter in a heavy-bottomed saucepan. Whisk the flour into the butter, then add a little salt & pepper, & cook for a few minutes, stirring. Reduce the heat to low, then begin adding the warm milk. It will be immediately absorbed, so work quickly, whisking with one hand while slowly pouring the milk with the other. Once the milk is finished, add the nutmeg & switch to using the reserved cooking broth. When the sauce is smooth & thick, remove from the heat & adjust the seasoning.
__Preheat the oven to 350°F. Assemble the lasagne. Dollop 2 large serving spoonfuls of béchamel sauce into the bottom of the dish, spreading it to cover. Lay 6 sheets of pasta across over the béchamel sauce, overlapping slightly if necessary. The next 3 layers will be repeated 3 times: a good dollop or two of béchamel, one-third of the fish mixture, & 6 sheets of pasta. Once the final layer of pasta has been added, spread 2 final dollops of béchamel abundantly over the top. Lightly tap the dish to let the lasagne settle. Sprinkle Parmesan over the top, then bake for 20 to 30 minutes until partly golden. Allow to cool slightly before cutting. Serve with a light drizzle of good olive oil on the plate.

Serves 6 to 8

Lasagne di radicchio

Radicchio lasagne

1¾ pounds radicchio di Treviso (or red chicory)
6 tablespoons olive oil
1 onion, thinly sliced
¼ cup white wine
24 lasagna noodles (uncooked), about 10 by 2¼ inches
6 tablespoons grated Parmesan
a blob of butter

Béchamel sauce:
7 tablespoons butter
⅔ cup all-purpose flour
3 cups warm milk
a good grating of nutmeg

This is as lovely & bitter as radicchio itself, so you have to like the beautiful leaf to appreciate this lasagne. The radicchio you will use here is the raddicho di Treviso, which is long rather than round. They vary in size, so you'll need between two & four for this weight. You'll need a rectangular oven dish that's about 13 by 9½ inches, so that the lasagna noodles will fit perfectly–once they are boiled they swell up to larger than their uncooked size. You will need 18 lasagna noodles, but cook a couple extra just in case.

__Cut away & discard the tough white stalk from the bottom of the radicchio. Roughly cut up the rest into chunky strips along the length, wash, & drain.

__Heat 5 tablespoons of the oil in a large skillet & sauté the onion until soft & pale golden. Add the wine & cook until evaporated. Add the radicchio, cover, & simmer over low heat until it surrenders its hardness. Add salt & pepper & cook, stirring now & then with a wooden spoon, until it is soft & there is hardly any liquid left in the skillet. Remove the lid for the last 5 minutes or so.

__Bring a pot of water to a boil, salt it, & add the last tablespoon of olive oil. Cook the pasta according to the time given on the package, or until almost cooked (*it will all go in the oven & continue cooking*). Remove, refresh in cold water, & lay out the noodles on a baking sheet lined with clean dishcloths, making a couple of layers as necessary to accommodate all the pasta.

__Make the béchamel sauce. Melt the butter in a heavy-bottomed saucepan. Whisk the flour into the butter, then add a little salt & pepper, & cook for a few minutes, stirring. Reduce the heat to low, then begin adding the warm milk. It will be immediately absorbed, so work quickly, whisking with one hand while slowly pouring the milk with the other. When the sauce is smooth & thick, add the nutmeg, remove the pan from the heat, & let it cool (*it should thicken even more*). Adjust the seasoning.

__Preheat the oven to 350°F. Assemble the lasagne. Dollop 2 large serving spoonfuls of béchamel sauce into the bottom of the oven dish, spreading it to cover. Lay 6 sheets of pasta over the béchamel, overlapping them if necessary. Splatter half the radicchio (*not in a neat perfect layer*) over the pasta. Dollop some more béchamel over the radicchio & spread gently here & there. Scatter with about 2 tablespoons of the Parmesan. Now add another layer of pasta, the rest of the radicchio, some more béchamel (*not all of it—save ½ cup for the top*), & another couple of tablespoons of Parmesan. Add the final layer of pasta & cover roughly with the rest of the béchamel. Sprinkle with the rest of the Parmesan & add a few blobs of butter. Bake for 20 to 30 minutes, until lovely & crusty here & there. Allow to cool a little before serving.

Serves 6 to 8

Around the ghetto is something to see on a Friday night. It makes me sad not to be part of something so big. But they did invite me in for Kiddush & kittkah.

Spaghetti alla busara

Spaghetti with tomato & scampi

8 small scampi (langoustines, red-claw, or large shrimps) with heads (about 2½ inches)
3 tablespoons olive oil
½ small white onion, finely chopped
1 cup peeled, canned, or chopped fresh tomatoes
pinch of peperoncino
1 tablespoon butter
1 bay leaf
2 garlic cloves, chopped
1 heaped tablespoon chopped parsley
¼ cup prosecco
⅓ (16-ounce) package thick spaghetti

In the restaurants of Venice, the scampi are sometimes served whole with the shells & heads intact. It certainly looks impressive, but can be difficult to eat, so you decide whether you want to peel them. I recommend seeking out small scampi & keeping the heads on for flavor, but peel the bodies for easier eating. Some small scampi are quite easy to peel once they have been cooked, so they would be fine to serve with the shells intact.

__First, clean the scampi. Remove the shells from the bodies & devein (*& remove the heads if you prefer*), rinse, & set aside.

__Heat 2 tablespoons olive oil in a skillet, & sauté the onion until completely softened, stirring often. Add the tomatoes, a pinch of peperoncino, & some salt. Simmer, uncovered, for 10 to 15 minutes, squashing the tomatoes down with a wooden spoon occasionally, until the tomatoes melt & are free of lumps & you have a nice sauce. Keep warm.

__Heat the butter & the last tablespoon of olive oil in a large nonstick skillet. When hot, add the scampi & bay leaf, & sauté over very high heat until the bottom of the scampi becomes golden & forms a bit of a crust. Turn the scampi over, add a pinch of salt, a pinch of peperoncino, & then the garlic. Now add the parsley. Finish cooking the scampi, until you can smell the garlic & both sides of the scampi are just cooked, then pour in the prosecco (*or white wine if you don't have prosecco*), & simmer rapidly until it has evaporated. The scampi meat must be soft but not overcooked.

__Meanwhile, cook the pasta in boiling salted water until tender. Drain, reserving a dash of the cooking water in case it may be needed to loosen the sauce. Add the spaghetti to the scampi & scrape the tomato into the skillet as well. Toss everything together as gently as possible, preferably by flicking the skillet to coat all & not mash things up. Add some of the reserved pasta cooking water if it seems too dry. Serve immediately with black pepper.

Serves 2

Spaghetti al ragù di pesce

Spaghetti with fish

¼ pound large shrimp (about 6 to 7)
½ pound clams in shells
½ pound mussels
4 tablespoons olive oil
1 onion, finely chopped
2 garlic cloves, chopped
1¼ cups canned chopped tomatoes (or fresh, very ripe equivalent, peeled & chopped)
¼ pound (3 to 4) moscardini or baby octopus, cleaned & chopped
pinch of peperoncino
2-inch piece cinnamon stick
2 whole cloves
½ cup white wine
2 (4-ounce) boneless fish fillets, such as san pietro (John Dory) or cernia (or snapper), chopped
2 tablespoons chopped parsley
⅔ (16-ounce) package spaghetti or bigoli

A "ragù" like this might have been made by a fisherman's wife to use up the fish that was not sold that day. The fish would have been put into a terra-cotta pot with many spices & left to simmer slowly on the side of the stove. You can use 2 fillets of the same fish, or choose different ones. You could swap the lovely cinnamon & cloves here for some fresh thyme or other herb & a more everyday flavor. Use bigoli or a thicker spaghetti for this rather than a thinner one.

Your clams will probably have been purged of sand already, but check with the fishmonger, otherwise you'll need to soak them for a day in a colander standing in well-salted water, changing the water several times.

__Peel & devein the shrimp. Roughly chop the shrimp meat & set aside. If you've been soaking the clams, give them a good swirl in the water, rinse them, drain, & leave in the colander. To clean the mussels, you need to "debeard" them by pulling away fiddly bits of algae that stick out. Cut them off with scissors or a sharp knife if you can't detach them, then scrub the shells well with a wire brush to dislodge evidence of the sea. At this stage, you need to discard any mussels that are open & don't close when tapped.

__Heat the oil in a wide pot. Sauté the onion until almost melted & pale golden. Add the garlic &, once you start to smell the garlic, add the tomatoes, mashing them in with a potato masher. Bring the sauce to a boil. Add the moscardini, peperoncino, cinnamon, & cloves, & simmer, covered, for 40 minutes or so, until the moscardini are tender. Check a couple of times that they are not drying out or sticking to the pot–if so, add more water. If necessary, cook for a further 10 minutes, until they are very tender.

__Meanwhile, put the clams, mussels, & wine into a saucepan, cover with a lid, & cook over high heat. Let the clams & mussels all steam open. There may be a couple that don't open–give them a second chance, but discard any that refuse to open. Remove from the pan, reserving the cooking broth (*if you have any suspicions there may be sand in your broth, strain it through a cheesecloth-lined colander*).

__Remove all of the meat from the shells, discarding the shells. Chop the mussel & clam meat, & add it to the pan with the octopus. Add the shrimp, fish pieces, 1 tablespoon of the parsley, & ¾ cup of the clam & mussel broth. Simmer, uncovered, for about 10 minutes, until it looks like a good ragù (*rich & quite thick*). Pick out the cinammon & cloves if you can find them.
__Meanwhile, cook the pasta in boiling salted water until tender. Drain well, reserving about ½ cup of cooking water. Add the spaghetti to the ragù with as much of the water as you need to loosen the sauce, tossing through quickly & gently over the heat for a moment.
__Divide the ragù evenly among warm serving plates. Serve imediately with a scattering of parsley & a grind of black pepper, plus a little extra ground peperoncino if you feel it needs it.

Serves 4

Spaghetti al nero di seppie

Spaghetti with squid ink

⅔ pound squid, with ink sac
3 tablespoons olive oil
2 garlic cloves, chopped
pinch of ground peperoncino
1 tablespoon chopped parsley, plus some for serving
½ cup white wine
⅓ (16-ounce) package spaghetti

This is an aesthetically dramatic dish—jet black—which is how I like it, but if you prefer a softer look, add less squid ink. If your squid doesn't come with an ink sac or if it doesn't yield much ink, you can use a package of squid ink. Abroad, these are sold by some fishmongers & delicatessens, often in a package containing 2 portions, ⅛ ounce each. You should only need to use ⅛ ounce (about 0.15 ounce) here, but you can add another if you want the result to be darker. Alternatively, you can make the sauce without any squid ink at all & mix it with black, ready-made squid ink spaghetti.

__To prepare the squid, pull the head & innards from the body. Separate the ink sac from the rest of the innards without puncturing, then rinse gently & put in a bowl. Wash the body. Cut off the head just below the eyes, leaving the tentacles in one piece, & discard the head. Pull out the transparent quill, rinse the tube, & peel off the outer membrane. Cut the squid body into ¼-inch strips & the tentacles into pieces. Pat dry with paper towels.

__Heat the oil in a nonstick skillet that has a lid & add the squid. Cook over high heat until the liquid begins to evaporate, then add the garlic, peperoncino, & parsley, & season with salt & pepper. When you can smell the garlic, add the wine & bring it to a simmer. Once it is bubbling up, cover with the lid, lower the heat, & simmer for 10 to 15 minutes, until most of the liquid has been absorbed.

__Cut the ink sac into a cup & mix with ¾ cup of water. Pour into the skillet. Add a little more water to rinse out the inky cup, pouring it into the skillet. Cover & simmer for 15 minutes or until the squid is tender (*check that it does not dry out & add water if necessary*). Season with salt.

__Meanwhile, cook the pasta in boiling salted water until tender. Drain, reserving ½ cup of the cooking water. Add the pasta & cooking water to the skillet with the squid & toss well to coat with sauce. Serve with a little extra parsley & a good grinding of black pepper.

Serves 2

Fig. 14
Fig. 12
Fig. 11
Fig. 10
Fig. 13
Fig. 15
Fig. 16
Fig. 17
Fig. 18
97.
Perruquier Barbier, Perruques

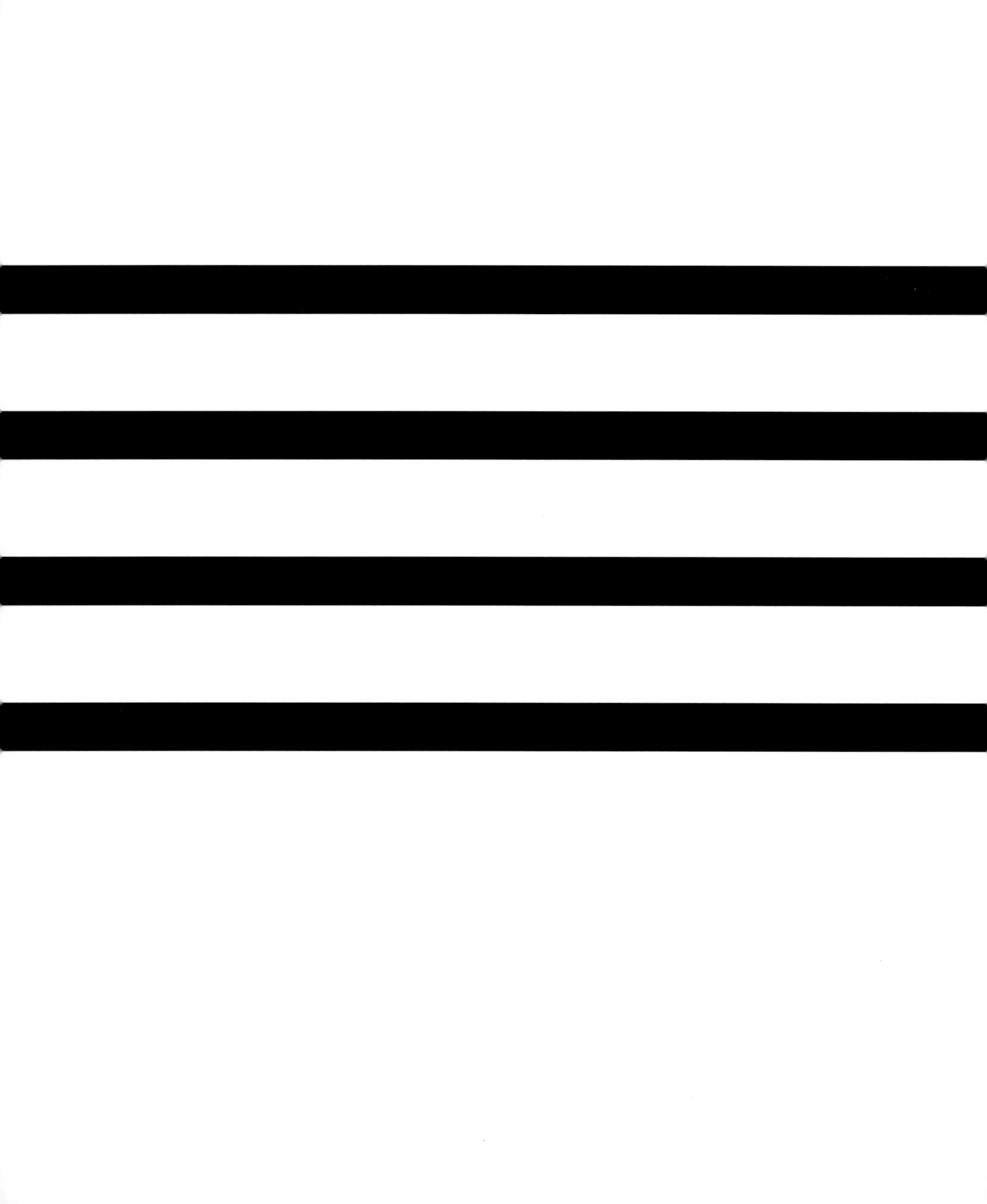

patience & *risotto*

There is a vaporetto etiquette to be followed. Move in quick. Don't loiter. Go straight inside or right to the other end to allow all the others to squash in too. (Unless you only have a couple of stops, then get on, sharp left or right near the opening—or proceed immediately to the other side if your stop will be on the other side of the zigzag.) Ideally, a sort of cross is left clear in the middle for passing through. Almost at your stop, you start pressing through the masses. Gently. Quietly. Without necessarily letting on that that is what you are actually doing. So that you happen to be on the side where you will be disembarking just before the vaporetto comes to a clanging kidney-jolting halt. If this hasn't worked, then you should say "permesso" in a fairly firm kind of way to let people know that you urgently need to get past. ⊸

V

RISOTTO

Clam risotto	Risotto di vongole
Radicchio risotto	Risotto di radicchio
Seafood risotto	Risotto di pesce
Asparagus & scampi risotto	Risotto di asparagi e scampi
Vegetable risotto	Risotto di verdure
Rice & peas	Risi e bisi
Rice & potatoes	Riso e patate
Risotto with meat	Risotto con le seccole
Winter squash risotto	Risotto di zucca
Milk risotto	Risotto al latte
Risotto with cabbage	Risotto con la verza

Risotto di vongole

Clam risotto

2¼ pounds small clams in shells
2 tablespoons olive oil
1 large garlic clove, chopped
1 tablespoon chopped parsley
½ cup prosecco

Risotto:
2 tablespoons olive oil
1 tablespoon butter
1 small white onion, chopped
2 garlic cloves, chopped
4 tablespoons chopped parsley
1¼ cups Arborio rice
pinch of peperoncino
¼ cup prosecco
4 cups hot vegetable broth (page 12)

I ate this in a restaurant where they used mussels & scampi as well as the clams, & their risotto had a ton of green parsley flecks that made me feel glad. The vegetable broth should have a delicate flavor–maybe add a spinach or chard leaf to the pot when you're making it. I loved using the prosecco, but you can easily replace it with white wine. If you like, add a few drops of lemon juice to serve. Rice is often estimated at 4 tablespoons per person as an appetizer portion in Italy.

I used lupini gandi clams, which are very good, but use whatever you can get. Your clams will probably have been purged of sand already, but check with the fishmonger, otherwise you'll need to soak them for a few hours in a colander standing in well-salted water, changing the water several times.

__If you've been soaking your clams, give them a good swirl in the water, rinse them, drain, & leave in the colander. Heat the olive oil with the garlic in a large skillet that has a lid. Once you start to smell the garlic, add the parsley, then the clams, prosecco, & some white or black pepper. Increase the heat to maximum & put the lid on the skillet. Let the clams all steam open–if there are a couple of clams that don't open, give them a second chance, but discard any that refuse to open. Remove from the heat and allow to cool a little.

__When the clams are cool enough to handle, take them out of the skillet, reserving the cooking liquid (*there should be about ¾ cup*). Remove the clam meat from the shells–you can keep a few in their shells to garnish the risotto. Roughly chop the clam meat if they're large, otherwise leave them. If you think there might be sand in the cooking liquid, strain it through a cheesecloth-lined colander.

__Heat the oil & butter in a wide, heavy-bottomed saucepan or a skillet with high sides. Sauté the onion until golden. Add the garlic & 1 tablespoon of the parsley. Add the rice & peperoncino & stir well, until the rice is coated with the buttery oil. You should not need to add salt because the clams are quite salty. Pour in the prosecco, lower the heat to a simmer, & cook, stirring regularly, until almost all the liquid has evaporated. Add the clam broth &

about 2 cups of the vegetable broth & continue cooking, stirring regularly & adding another cup of broth whenever it is absorbed, for about 20 minutes until the rice is tender.

__About 5 minutes before the risotto is ready, stir in the clams & remaining parsley, & the rest of the broth if you think it needs it. Season to taste. The risotto should still have some liquid & the rice grains should be slightly firm yet creamy. Serve with ground white or black pepper, & a drizzle of great olive oil.

Serves 4

We stand up in the gondolas to cut straight across the canal. Just like Venetians. Legs apart so we don't lose our balance. We dare not sit down & seem like tourists–but learn to stand & balance.

Once I get past the arriving and pushing through the crowds, I sink into a glorious, soft, and very much present vitality. Past the muchness I find simplicity. A marine serenity. Another reality. A magical, aqua-colored one.

Risotto di radicchio

Radicchio risotto

about 1¼ pounds radicchio di Treviso (or red chicory)
4 tablespoons olive oil
½ white onion, chopped
about ½ teaspoon salt
1 cup red wine
1¼ cups Arborio rice
5 cups hot vegetable broth (page 12)
1 tablespoon butter
2 tablespoons grated Parmesan

This is a lovely risotto with a beautiful rounded bitterness, not at all sharp. It's perfect for lunch on a winter's day, or as a primo before a dish such as the Faraona (page 216). The radicchio you will use here is radicchio di Treviso, which is long rather than round. They vary in size, but about 2 large ones should give you this weight. For a different flavor, you could stir in ⅔ cup of grated taleggio or another cheese when you add the butter & Parmesan at the end. Use a rice such as arnaroli or Arborio. The Venetians like vialone nano for risotto because it absorbs large amounts of liquid & produces the wet, soupy style of dish they prefer.

_Cut away & discard the tough white stalk from the bottom of the radicchio. Wash well & drain. Cut into quarters lengthwise, then chop along the length into rustic pieces.
_Heat the olive oil in a wide, heavy-bottomed saucepan or a skillet with high sides. Sauté the onion until golden & well-cooked through. Add the radicchio & salt, & cook for 10 to 15 minutes, until the radicchio collapses. Add the wine, let it bubble up, & then add the rice. Allow it to bubble up for a few minutes to reduce the wine & blend into the flavors.
_Add 2 cups of hot broth & continue cooking, stirring regularly, then adding another 2 cups of broth as it is absorbed, for about 20 minutes, or until the rice is tender. Just before the rice is cooked, add the rest of the broth (*you might only need half of it*) & mix to make sure nothing is sticking. The risotto should still have some liquid & the rice grains should be firm, yet soft & creamy.
_Turn off the heat, season to taste, & gently stir in the butter & Parmesan with a wooden spoon. Serve immediately with a good grinding of black pepper & lots of grated Parmesan if you like.

Serves 4

Risotto di pesce

Seafood risotto

Brodo:
1 onion, peeled & cut in half
1 carrot, peeled
1 celery stalk
thin bunch of parsley
4 or 5 whole peppercorns
1 teaspoon salt

½ pound (about 4) scampi (langoustines, red-claw, or large shrimps), unpeeled
⅓ pound (about 4) shrimp
⅔ pound small clams in shells
1 pound mussels
7-ounce piece of firm, white fish (such as snapper, mackerel, halibut, or monkfish)
6 tablespoons olive oil
3 garlic cloves, 2 chopped & 1 left whole
3 tablespoons chopped parsley
1 cup white wine
2 tablespoons cognac
1 cup Arborio rice
1 tablespoon butter
1 tablespoon grated Parmesan

The Venetians have a wonderful selection of wines to drink & splash into their cooking. The sparkling white, prosecco, is much of a habit & will be often ordered throughout the meal.

I ate a fantastic version of this at the Trattoria alla Madonna, which is something of an institution—a huge space with 40 men in soft, white jackets serving. Licio strode up to me like Papa Bear & made wise suggestions of what I should order (he should know: he's been there for more years than you'd guess). He took me right into the kitchen, threading me through the 40 waiters to see the "onda" (wave), the shake, rock, & roll that the chef does to "mantecare" (mix & meld) the risotto at the end of its cooking process. Quite impressive.

Your clams will probably have been purged of sand already, but check with the fishmonger, otherwise you'll need to soak them for a few hours in a colander standing in well-salted water, changing the water several times.

_Peel & devein the scampi & shrimp, keeping all the heads & shells. Cut the tails into 3 or 4 pieces & set aside.

_To make the broth, rinse the shells & heads & put them in a pot with half the onion, the carrot, celery, parsley, peppercorns, salt, & 5 cups of water. Bring to a boil, lower the heat, & simmer, covered, for about 20 minutes. Strain, discarding the solids, & set aside.

_Meanwhile, if you've been soaking the clams, give them a good swirl in the water, rinse them, drain, & leave in the colander. To clean the mussels, you need to "debeard" them by pulling away fiddly bits of algae that stick out. Cut them off with scissors or a sharp knife if you can't detach them, then scrub the shells well with a wire brush to dislodge evidence of the sea. At this stage, you need to discard any mussels that are open & don't close when you give them a tap. Cut up the fish into pieces.

_Heat 1 tablespoon of the oil in a skillet with a lid, add the chopped garlic, & sauté for a minute before adding the clams, mussels, 1 tablespoon chopped of parsley, & ½ cup of white wine. Cover with the lid & cook over high heat until all the mussels & clams open. There may be a couple of clams & mussels that don't open—give them a second chance, but discard any that refuse to open.

__Remove the skillet from the heat &, when cool, transfer all the clams & mussels to a large bowl, reserving the cooking liquid. Remove the clams & mussels from their shells. If you have any suspicions there may be sand in the cooking water you can strain it through a cheesecloth-lined colander.

__Heat 2 tablespoons of the olive oil in a small nonstick skillet with the whole clove of garlic. Add the fish pieces, sauté over medium–high heat to just cook them, then add the scampi & sauté for another minute before adding 1 tablespoon of parsley, a small sprinkling of salt & pepper, & the cognac. Ignite the skillet, standing well back as it lights up, & then turn off the heat & let it finish burning. Keep aside for the moment, discarding the garlic clove.

__Now for the final risotto step. If necessary, warm the strained broth. Heat the remaining olive oil in a wide, heavy-bottomed saucepan or high-sided skillet. Chop the remaining onion half & sauté until well-softened. Add the rice & stir well for a minute or so, until it is well mixed with the onion & coated with oil. Add the other ½ cup of wine & cook until almost evaporated. Then add the mussel/clam broth (*you should have a generous cupful*) & let it bubble away on a good simmer.

__When you see the rice puffing up & that there is not much liquid left, add about 1 cup of the broth & cook, stirring, until almost all the liquid has evaporated. Continue in this way, adding more broth (*you'll need about 3 cups in total*) & stirring for about 20 minutes, until the rice is cooked. Season to taste. Once the risotto is creamy & cooked with some thick liquid, lower the heat, then add the fish & seafood, butter, Parmesan, & remaining parsley. Now for the *onda*...This is the gentle shaking & rocking of the pan that melds the risotto together so that everything comes together like a sweet opera. Serve immediately.

Serves 4

Risotto di asparagi e scampi

Asparagus & scampi risotto

12 to 16 scampi (red-claw, langoustines, or large shrimps)

Brodo:
1 large carrot
½ onion
1 bay leaf
a few peppercorns

13 ounces (about 19) asparagus spears
½ onion, finely chopped
4 tablespoons olive oil
1 cup Arborio rice
½ cup white wine
1 tablespoon cognac
1 tablespoon butter
2 tablespoons grated Parmesan

This is also good & delicate with just scampi or just asparagus. Some people don't serve Parmesan with seafood, but I put a bit in here.

__To make the brodo, peel & clean the scampi, & cut each one in half down the middle. Set the meat aside for the moment, but rinse the heads & shells, & put them in a pot with 6 cups of water, the carrot, onion, bay leaf, peppercorns, & some salt. Bring to a boil, then simmer for 30 minutes. Strain, & keep the broth hot.

__Discard the woody ends from the asparagus & cut off the tips. Put the tips aside & chop the stems. Heat 3 tablespoons of the olive oil in a large saucepan & sauté the onion until well softened. Add the chopped asparagus & sauté briefly.

__Add the rice, turning it through so that it is well coated with oil. Add the white wine & let it bubble up until much of it has evaporated. Add 2 cups of broth, stir well, & simmer for 10 to 15 minutes, or until almost of it has been absorbed. Add another 2 cups of broth, stir, & cook for another 5 to 10 minutes. (*Add another ½ cup of broth if you want a creamier risotto.*)

__When the risotto is almost ready, heat the remaining oil in a small skillet, add the scampi & asparagus tips, & cook over high heat for 2 minutes, turning the scampi over when they have a pale golden crust underneath. Add the cognac, stand back & ignite the skillet. Add a little salt & toss it all together, then take off the heat.

__Stir the butter & Parmesan into the risotto, then tip the scampi & asparagus tips into the risotto. Add salt if needed, quickly toss it all through & serve immediately with ground black pepper.

Serves 4

Risotto di verdure

Vegetable risotto

8 ounces (about 12) asparagus spears
5 cups hot vegetable broth (page 12)
2 fresh artichokes
juice of half a lemon
4 tablespoons olive oil
1 small white onion, chopped
2 zucchinis, sliced
1 cup fresh, or frozen, peas
1 cup Arborio rice
½ cup white wine
2 tablespoons butter
3 to 4 tablespoons grated Parmesan
2 tablespoons chopped parsley
all-purpose flour, for coating
light olive oil
handful of mint sprigs

The winning stroke here is the fried artichokes on top, as suggested by my friend Sergia. The combination of the artichokes & fresh mint to pull through the risotto as you are eating is truly great. When you are making your vegetable broth, be sure to add the trimmings from the asparagus to give a depth of flavor.

__Trim the asparagus & slice on the diagonal, leaving the tips whole. Add the trimmings to your vegetable broth as it simmers.
__To prepare your artichokes, trim away the outer leaves & cut a slice off the top. Halve the artichoke & remove the hairy choke if it has one, then cut each half into fine slices ⅛ inch thick. (*Keep them covered with cold water & a little lemon juice to prevent their turning black.*)
__Heat the olive oil in a wide pot & sauté the onion until well softened. Add the asparagus, zucchini, & peas, & sauté on high heat for a minute to just take in the flavors. Add the rice, turning it through so that it is well coated with oil. Season with salt & pepper, then add the wine, & allow it let to bubble away. Add 2 cups of hot broth, lower the heat, & simmer for about 10 minutes, until much of the broth has been absorbed. Add another cup of hot broth, stirring gently & adding another cup of broth when necessary as it is absorbed, for about 20 minutes, or until the rice is tender & creamy. Don't let the risotto get so dry that you have to keep stirring.
__Remove from the heat, then *mantecare* by adding the butter, Parmesan, & parsley, & stirring gently. Add salt to taste if needed.
__Just before your risotto is ready, drain the artichokes, pat dry with paper towels, & pat lightly in flour on both sides. Use a nonstick skillet that will fit the artichokes in one layer if possible. Just cover the bottom with oil & heat up. Add the artichokes & fry until golden & crisp on both sides. Transfer onto a plate lined with paper towels to drain. Serve the risotto with a heap of hot, fried artichokes on top, plus fresh mint, extra Parmesan, & black pepper.

Serves 4

Risi e bisi

Rice & peas

2 pounds (about 6 cups) fresh peas, shelled, or 1 pound (about 3 cups) frozen peas
7 cups hot vegetable broth (page 12)
12 thin slices cured, unsmoked pancetta/rigatino (the peppery, salty variety)
3 tablespoons olive oil
1 small white onion, chopped
2 tablespoons chopped parsley
1 cup Arborio rice
½ cup white wine
1 tablespoon butter
2 tablespoons grated Parmesan, plus extra for serving

This dish was traditionally good enough for the doges. It becomes an altogether different plate if you use shelled home-grown peas, & add the jackets to your broth as it simmers. If you are serving for 6 people, you will want to have 4 more slices of pancetta to crisp up for the top. You could also add a fresh herb in here last minute.

__If you are using fresh peas, shell them & add the pods to your vegetable broth as it cooks.
__Chop 4 slices pancetta, reserving the rest for later. Heat the oil in a wide, heavy-bottomed saucepan or deep skillet. Sauté the onion until golden & cooked through well. Add the chopped pancetta & cook briefly until softened. Add the peas & 1 tablespoon of the parsley & simmer for a minute. Add the rice & stir until it is well coated with the oil. Pour in the wine & allow it to bubble up for a few minutes to reduce the wine & mix into the flavors.
__When much of the wine has been absorbed, add 2 cups of hot broth & continue cooking, stirring regularly & adding another 2 cups of broth as it is absorbed, for about 20 minutes, or until the rice is tender. Season to taste. Just before the rice is cooked, add another 1 or 2 cups of the broth & mix to make sure nothing is sticking. Taste for seasoning, but remember that you will be adding Parmesan. Add the butter, the second tablespoon of chopped parsley, & 2 tablespoons of Parmesan, & stir. (*This should be a loose risotto, with some thick liquid running around the side, like a lovely soupy rice.*)
__Meanwhile, heat up a nonstick skillet (*you shouldn't need any oil*) & fry the thin slices of pancetta until crisp & golden.
__Serve the risotto with black pepper & a good scattering of Parmesan. Top with a couple of slices of crisp pancetta for each serving, & sprinkle with more parsley & grated Parmesan or pecorino, if you like.

Serves 4 to 6

Riso e patate

Rice & potatoes

Chicken broth:
2 (¾-pound) chicken leg quarters
1 small onion, cut in half
1 carrot, cut in half
1 celery stalk with leaves, cut in half
1 garlic clove, peeled, but left whole
1 bay leaf
1½ teaspoons salt

1 small leek, trimmed
3 tablespoons olive oil
1¼ cups Arborio rice
¼ cup white wine
1 pound (about 3 medium) russet potatoes, peeled & cut into chunks
1 scant tablespoon finely chopped rosemary
1 tablespoon butter
grated Parmesan, for serving

Normally I don't go for double carbohydrate, but I really liked this & so did the rest of the family. I made it with a chicken broth, which I loved, but you could use a vegetable broth for a lighter flavor. (If you prefer to use a pressure cooker, you will only need to cook the broth for 20 minutes.)

You can cut up the potatoes small if you like, but I prefer just holding the potato in my hand & chipping this way & that to get irregular chips that can still fit on a fork, or spoon, or in the mouth. If you're preparing the potatoes in advance, put the pieces in a bowl & cover with cold water.

_Put all the broth ingredients in a large saucepan & pour in 7 cups of water. Bring to a boil, then lower the heat, partly cover, & simmer for an hour or so. Remove the chicken pieces & vegetables from the broth, then strain into a bowl & skim off any fat from the surface. Keep warm. (*Make sandwiches with the chicken if you like.*)

_Slice the leek lengthwise a few times & wash under running water. Pat dry with paper towels & chop. Heat the olive oil in a wide, heavy-bottomed pan & sauté the leek until softened & lightly golden. Stir in the rice until well coated in the oil. Add the wine & stir until evaporated. Add the potato pieces & rosemary & stir well.

_Add 3 cups of the warm chicken broth, & simmer for about 10 minutes until most of the broth has been absorbed, then add another 2 cups of broth & simmer for a further 10 minutes.

_Add the final cup of broth, stir, & cook for a few more minutes until the risotto is quite soupy. Season to taste & stir in the butter just before serving. Serve with Parmesan & ground black pepper.

Serves 4 to 5

Risotto con le seccole

Risotto with meat

2 tablespoons olive oil
2 tablespoons butter
1 white onion, chopped
⅔ pound seccole (good-quality meat trimmings), finely chopped
1 cup valpolicella or other red wine
about 5 cups meat broth
1¼ cups Arborio rice
grated Parmesan, for serving

I was surprised at how much I liked this. It is a wonderfully masculine dish. It's especially wonderful with the broth from Bollito di carne (page 227), but you can make it with a lighter meat or chicken broth, or even vegetable broth. Traditionally, this was probably a very simple dish; by using good-quality red wine & broth from the bollito, this version becomes something quite noble. Seccole are the scraps of meat left attached to vertebra & bones—the trimmings. Here I have used the trimmings from top-quality cuts, like rump or sirloin steak.

__Heat the oil & butter in a wide, heavy-bottomed pan or a deep skillet that has a lid. Sauté the onion until golden & well cooked through. Add the seccole & cook until all the liquid from the meat has evaporated & it starts browning & frying in the oil. Season with salt & pepper. Add the wine, allow it to bubble up & almost evaporate, then add 1 cup of the broth. Cover with a lid & simmer on low for about an hour, until the meat is tender & tasty & there is some thick sauce in the bottom of the pan (*check occasionally that nothing is sticking & add a little more broth or water if it seems necessary*).
__Add the rice & stir well. Add 2 cups of hot broth & continue cooking, stirring regularly. Cook for about 20 minutes, or until the rice is tender, adding another 2 cups of broth when it has been absorbed. (*There should be enough salt in the broth, but taste & see if you need to add extra.*) Stir in the remaining cup of broth if it looks as if it's needed. The risotto should still have some liquid & the rice grains should be firm yet creamy.
__Remove from the heat. Serve immediately with a good grating of Parmesan & a grinding of black pepper.

Serves 4

Risotto di zucca

Winter squash risotto

1¾ pounds winter squash
2 tablespoons olive oil
2 tablespoons butter
1 white onion, finely chopped
2½ ounces thick-sliced sweet pancetta without rind, chopped
1 sage sprig
pinch of peperoncino
1 cup Arborio rice
½ cup white wine
5 cups hot vegetable broth (page 12)
2 tablespoons grated Parmesan, plus extra for serving
1 heaped tablespoon chopped parsley

You need to have a lovely sweet-tasting winter squash here—the flavor of your squash is what will make this so special. Winter squash simmered with white onion is also often served as a contorno.

__Peel the squash, remove the seeds, & chop the flesh into 1¼-inch pieces. You should have about 1⅓ pounds of pieces of winter squash.

__Heat the olive oil & half the butter in a wide, heavy-bottomed saucepan or a deep skillet that has a lid. Sauté the onion until golden. Add the pancetta & sage, & cook briefly until softened—don't let the pancetta become crisp. Add the pieces of squash & season with a little salt & pepper & a good pinch of peperoncino. Cover with the lid & simmer, stirring once or twice, for 15 minutes or so, until the squash is tender & some of the pieces have collapsed & some have kept their shape.

__Add the rice & stir well. Add the wine, lower the heat to a simmer, & cook, stirring often, until almost all of the liquid has evaporated. Add about 2 cups of the broth & continue cooking, stirring regularly & adding more broth as it is absorbed, for about 20 minutes, or until the rice is tender. You may not need the final cup of broth. The risotto should still have some liquid & the rice grains should be firm, yet soft & creamy.

__Add the remaining tablespoon of butter & the Parmesan & parsley to the risotto. Remove the pan from the heat, stir with a wooden spoon, or do the "onda" & shake the pot to combine it well. Remove the sage sprig. Serve immediately with a good twist of black pepper & scattering of Parmesan.

Serves 4

Risotto al latte

Milk risotto

6 cups milk
3 tablespoons olive oil
1 small onion, or French shallot, peeled but left whole
1⅓ cups Arborio rice
a good grating of nutmeg
1 tablespoon unsalted butter
4 tablespoons grated Parmesan

It's very important to serve this risotto as soon as it comes off the stove. Also, make sure you use a block of good Parmesan that you grate yourself, not a ready-grated one from a package—as you can see, there are so few ingredients in this simple risotto that you can't disguise any flavors. What you see is what you get. If you like, you could add a few blobs of a stronger cheese like Gorgonzola at the end, but that is another thing altogether.

__Warm the milk in a large saucepan.
__Heat the olive oil in a wide, heavy-bottomed saucepan or a deep skillet. Sauté the whole onion to flavor the oil. Add the rice & stir well until it is coated in oil. Season with salt. Add half the warm milk, lower the heat to a simmer, & cook, stirring often, until almost all the liquid has evaporated. Add another 2 cups of the milk & continue cooking, stirring regularly, for 20 minutes or so, or until the rice is tender, adding the last of the milk toward the end to make a sloppy risotto. Taste that there is enough salt (*even though you will be adding Parmesan, you will need enough salt here*). Remove the onion.
__Add a nice grating of nutmeg, the butter, & Parmesan, & remove from the heat. Stir together. Serve immediately with an extra heap of Parmesan & a grinding of black pepper.

Serves 4 to 6

Risotto con la verza

Risotto with cabbage

4 tablespoons olive oil
1 white onion, chopped
1 or 2 sausages (7 ounces in total), skinned & crumbled
1⅔ pounds cabbage, trimmed, cored, & outer leaves removed, thinly sliced
1 cup Arborio rice
6 cups hot vegetable broth (page 12)
½ cup white wine
2 tablespoons butter
3 tablespoons grated Parmesan

The sausages here need to be pork ones like the Italian salsiccia that you can remove the casings from & then crumble the sausage meat. Make sure your broth is salted, or then check the risotto well for seasoning, as there is a lot of cabbage added. I used savoy here–the cabbage can also be made as a side dish.

__Heat the olive oil in a wide, heavy-bottomed saucepan or deep skillet that has a lid. Sauté the onion until softened, then add the sausage meat & cook until pale golden. Add the cabbage & some salt, then stir everything together, put the lid on & let it cook down, making sure nothing is sticking. Add 1 cup of the hot broth, cover, & simmer for another 20 minutes or so, stirring from time to time until tender. Season to taste.

__Add the rice, stir well, & then add the wine & cook until almost all the liquid has evaporated. Add about 2 cups of the vegetable broth & continue cooking, stirring regularly, & adding another 2 cups of broth when it is absorbed, for about 20 minutes, or until the rice is tender. About 5 minutes before the risotto is ready, stir in the remaining broth. The risotto should still have some liquid & the rice grains should be firm, yet soft & creamy.

__Once the risotto is creamy & cooked with some thick liquid, lower the heat & stir in the butter & Parmesan. Serve immediately with extra Parmesan & a grinding of black pepper over the top.

Serves 4 to 6

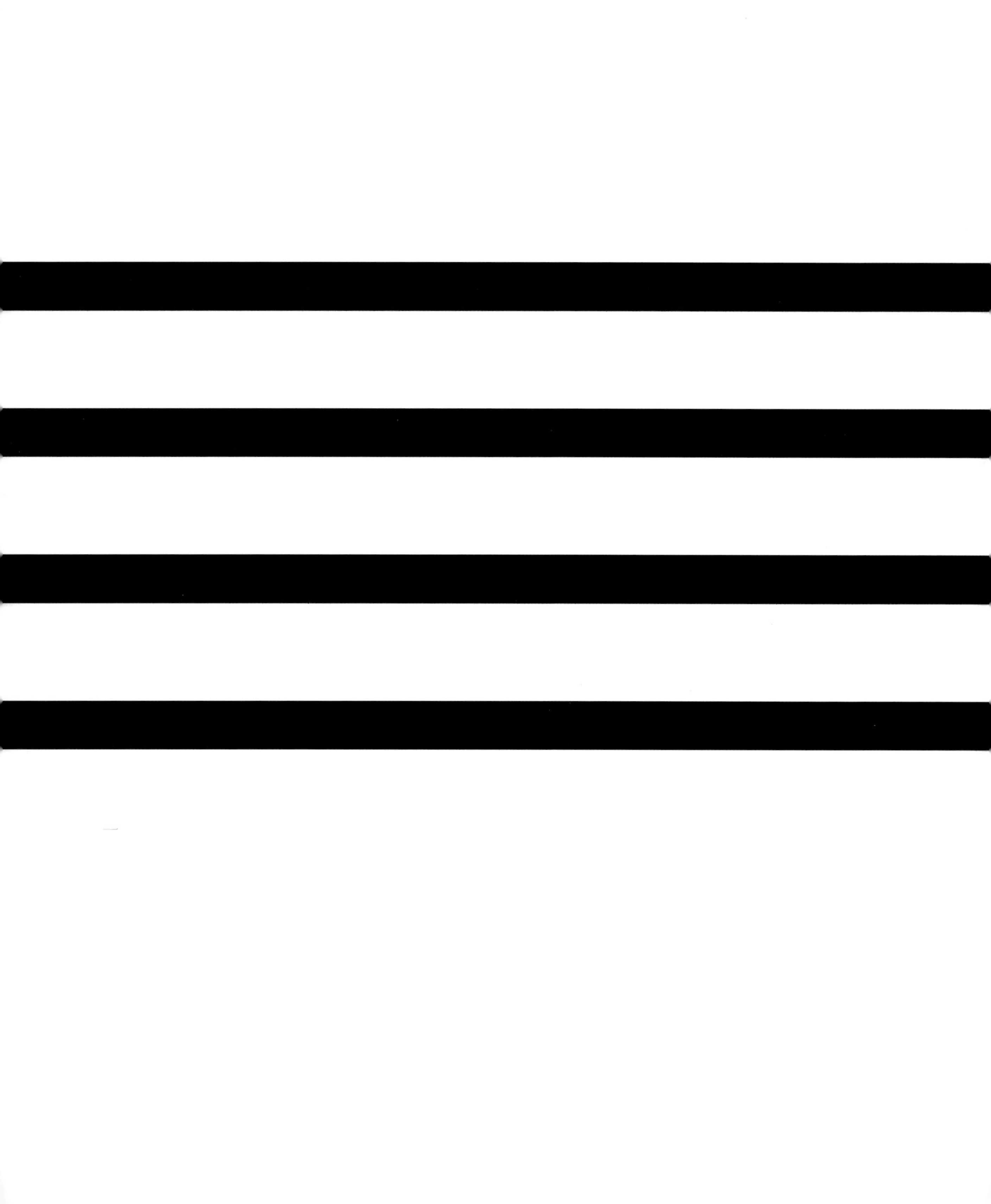

galoshes & *high-heels*

Today is cold, gray, & raining. Flooding, actually. Men in hats & raincoats. Umbrellas everywhere & acqua alta. Galoshes & high heels. Mist. The canals are completely alive. We pass by the golden facade on the right. You would think you'd need to buy a ticket to look at that building, sparkling even on this watercolored day. ⟜

VI

SECONDI

Mixed fried fish	Fritto misto di pesce
Mixed grilled fish	Grigliata mista di pesce
Monkfish with tomato	Coda di rospo al pomodoro
Liver & onions	Fegato alla veneziana
Baccala baked in milk	Baccala alla vincentina
Osso buco with rice & peas	Osso buco con riso e piselli
Braised beef with amarone	Brasato con amarone di valpolicella
Squid stewed with ink	Seppie in nero con polenta
Fish with potatoes & mushrooms	Rombo con patate e funghi al forno
Fish fillets with artichokes	San pietro in padella con carciofi
Roast eel	Anguilla al forno
Eel with tomato	Anguilla in umido
Calamari with tuna mayonnaise	Calamari con salsa tonnata
Sausages & polenta	Luganega e polenta
Roasted guinea fowl with peverada	Faraona arrosto con la salsa peverada
Chicken in tomato	Pollo con pomodoro in tecia
Birds with polenta	Uccelli con polenta
Duck with anchovies & capers	Anatra in padella con acciughe e capperi
Pork in milk	Maiale al latte
Venetian sausage with beans	Musetto con fagioli piccanti
Pasta in broth	Pasta in brodo
Mixed boiled meats	Bollito di carne
Red bell pepper & anchovy sauce	Salsa piccante di peperone e acciughe
Eggplant in oil & vinegar	Melanzane sotto olio e aceto

Fritto misto di pesce

Mixed fried fish

8 calamari
light olive oil, for frying
8 scampi tails (red-claw, langoustines), or large shrimps, peeled & deveined
2 small, whole sole (2½ ounces each) or other small fish, cleaned & gutted
all-purpose flour, for dusting
lemon, for serving

This is everywhere in Venice, featuring many different seafoods...sometimes with the tiny whole baby squid much appreciated by the Venetians. Eel is also appreciated, or you could use any fresh fish you like; sometimes vegetable sticks are on the platter, too. This is a combination I liked. Generally, the amounts for a fritto in Venice tend to be rather generous, but you can judge for yourself. I prefer to eat this for lunch rather than dinner & just have a salad on the table as well. Many Venetians say you don't need lemon here–they prefer to taste just the freshness of fish. You decide.

_To prepare the calmari, firmly pull the head & innards from the body & wash the body well. Cut off the head just below the eyes, leaving the tentacles in one piece if they're small. Discard the head, pull the transparent quill out of the body, & rinse out the tube. Peel off the outer membrane & cut the tube into chunky rings, about 1½ inches thick.

_Heat enough olive oil in a large deep saucepan or wok to comfortably fry the fish. Pat all the seafood dry with paper towels, pat in flour & shake off the excess. Your oil must be *very hot* before you add anything. Start with the sole (*they will take the longest to cook*) & a few calamari if they fit. Once the sole are crisp & golden on both sides (*& cooked on the inside*), lift out with a slotted spoon onto a plate lined with paper towels.

_Add all the calamari to the pan, & the scampi, too, if they fit. When golden, lift out to drain on more paper towels. Transfer to a dish (*lined with paper for serving, if necessary*).

_Serve immediately with salt & black pepper...lemon for squeezing...cold white wine or prosecco.

Serves 2

Grigliata mista di pesce

Mixed grilled fish

2 sole (about ½ pound each), cleaned & gutted
1 monkfish tail (about ⅓ pound)
1 bream (about ¾ pound), cleaned & gutted
4 scampi (red-claw, langoustines, or large shrimps), deveined but not peeled
4 large shrimps, deveined but not peeled
4 small squid or calamari, cleaned
1 garlic clove, peeled & halved
chopped parsley, olive oil, & lemon, for serving

Here you can use any variety of small fish, perhaps snapper or bream. In Venice, fish is often served on its own as a second course with very little done to it–just a sprinkling of parsley, lemon, olive oil, salt & pepper. This mixed fish grill is a rather grander situation. Add scallops, or different fillets, such as John Dory, as you like. Eel, too, is also very much appreciated on the grill as it loses some of its fat–many people prefer it cooked this way to any other. You can be very flexible here, adding or doubling, leaving out, as you will…Here is what I used:

__Heat up your barbecue or electric grill. Clean the seafood if you are doing it yourself. Rub your serving platters with the cut garlic clove & sprinkle with a little parsley. Grill the seafood until cooked through & settle onto the plates with an immediate drizzling of olive oil & a sprinkling of salt & parsley (*these will contribute to some juice on plate*). Everyone can decide if they want more oil or lemon & ground pepper. Serve immediately with a lovely salad & some bread.

Serves 4

Coda di rospo al pomodoro

Monkfish with tomato

1 monkfish tail (about 1¾ pounds), or 6 fish steaks
4 tablespoons olive oil
1 large onion, chopped
2 garlic cloves, chopped
1½ cups tomato passata
1 small peperoncino, crushed
½ cup white wine
1 tablespoon chopped parsley
soft polenta (page 21), for serving

This is a lovely, simple secondo that is easy to make in advance & then reheat just before the polenta is ready. If you have cooked the Pasticcio di pesce (page 128), this is perfect for using up the rest of the fish. But if you're just cooking this on its own, buy firm white fish steaks, such as snapper, or any chunky cutlets.

__If you are using a whole monkfish tail, cut it into 6 or 7 steaks along the central bone, each steak to be about 1¼ inches thick.

__Heat the olive oil in a large skillet that has a lid & sauté the onion until well softened. Add the garlic &, when you can smell it, add the passata along with some salt, pepper, & the peperoncino. Simmer, covered, for 10 minutes or so.

__Add the fish to the skillet & sauté in the tomato, then turn over & briefly cook the other side. Sprinkle a little salt over the fish & add the wine. Once the wine has mostly bubbled away, lower the heat slightly, cover, & simmer for about 15 minutes, until cooked through. If the sauce is looking too dry, add a few tablespoons of water as necessary. Sprinkle with the parsley & serve with soft polenta.

Serves 4 to 6

Fegato alla Veneziana

Liver & onions

½ pound calf liver
1 tablespoon butter
2 tablespoons olive oil
½ pound (about 3 small) white onion, halved & thinly sliced
a few sage sprigs
⅓ cup white wine
1 heaped tablespoon chopped parsley
soft or broiled polenta (page 21), for serving

This is on every menu in Venice. You can easily double the recipe if you're serving more than two people. Some people use two pans & cook the onions & liver separately, then combine them into one pan shortly before serving. The most important thing here is that the liver is top quality, so when it's cooked it should be very soft. Sergia adds a couple of unpeeled apple slices, too, to make the onions more "digestible." While it may not be very traditional, I like the sage in here.

__Wash the liver in cold water, pat dry with paper towels, & cut away any sinew. Slice into 1/16- to ⅛-inch pieces. Then cut more or less into triangles about 2¾ by ¾ inches.

__Melt the butter in a large nonstick skillet that has a lid, then add the oil. When hot, add the onion & cook, stirring, for a couple of minutes to get them going before adding the sage & a little salt. Cover & simmer over low heat for 15 to 20 minutes, until soft & very pale golden. Add the wine if anything looks like it could be starting to catch or in the last 10 minutes or so. Stir often so that nothing sticks.

__Remove the lid, transfer the onions to a plate, increase the heat right up, & add the liver. Cook for a few minutes, until cooked through & just starting to change color, turning halfway so both sides are browned. Once cooked, add salt & pepper, & return the onions to the skillet & stir well. Remove from the heat & add the parsley. Serve immediately with polenta.

Serves 2

Baccala alla vicentina

Baccala baked in milk

1⅔ pounds baccala (salt cod), soaked
all-purpose flour, for dusting
5 tablespoons olive oil
1 large white onion, halved & thinly sliced
2 garlic cloves, chopped
about 6 large anchovy fillets in olive oil, drained & broken into pieces
2 tablespoons chopped parsley
3 cups milk
small handful halved, pitted black or green olives

Lidia says that this is mainly served as a second course with broiled polenta & broiled radicchio, so that they have dolce (sweet), amaro (bitter), & polenta on the one plate, which is a perfect combination. You need a baking dish that can also go onto the stovetop (mine measures 12 by 8½ inches).

Before you use the salt cod, you need to soak it to remove the excess salt. Rinse the cod fillet first, then put it into a large bowl with enough water to completely immerse it. Cover the bowl & refrigerate, changing the water 3 to 4 times a day. Ask your fishmonger how long you need to soak the cod (it's usually 2 to 3 days). If you're unsure, test the cod by breaking off a small fleck, rinsing, & tasting it. The tail part is always a bit more salty. In some places you can buy ready-soaked salt cod, which is very reliable & convenient.

__Preheat the oven to 350°F. Drain the baccala & break it into pieces about 2 by 1½ inches, discarding the skin & bones. Lay on a baking sheet, sift flour over both sides, then beat on your palm to get rid of the excess.

__Heat the oil in your heatproof baking dish & sauté the onion until softened & pale gold. Add the garlic &, when you can smell it, add 3 of the anchovies, squashing them into the onion so that they almost "melt." Stir well, add the parsley & arrange the baccala pieces on top, mixing through so that all the flavors are combined. Add 2 or 3 grindings of black pepper.

__Pour the milk into the dish, moving the baccala pieces so the milk seeps down. Add the rest of the anchovies. Cover the dish with foil & put in the oven. Bake for about 1 hour, then uncover & cook for 30 minutes, or until the baccala & onion have soaked up almost all of the milk & there is a golden crust on top. If you are using olives, scatter them over the top 10 minutes before the end. Turn off the oven & remove the dish. Let stand to allow the fish to finish absorbing the rest of the liquid. If it seems too liquidy, return to the oven (*the residual heat will help the fish absorb the milk more quickly*).

Serves 4

Osso buco con riso e piselli

Osso buco with rice & peas

6 veal osso buchi
all-purpose flour, for dusting
2 tablespoons olive oil, plus 4 tablespoons extra
2 celery stalks, roughly chopped
1 medium carrot, roughly chopped
1½ white onions, roughly chopped
2 garlic cloves, peeled but left whole
1 tablespoon finely chopped rosemary
1 cup white wine
grated Parmesan, for serving

Risotto:
1 tablespoon olive oil
1 tablespoon butter
½ white onion, finely chopped
1⅓ cups Arborio rice
½ cup white wine
5 cups vegetable broth (page 12)

This is a lovely piatto unico. The key to this recipe is to time the cooking, so that the risotto & peas are both ready as you take the osso buco out of the oven...so start on the risotto about 30 minutes before the osso buco is ready, & start the peas 10 minutes after you've begun cooking the risotto. Alternatively, cook the osso buco at your leisure & then just heat through, adding a little water, when you want. I like to use vegetable broth for the risotto because it adds an extra dimension of flavor & takes little effort to make.

For the veal, you'll need a piece of shank that weighs about 2¼ pounds, cut into 6 pieces. Each piece should be about ¾ inch thick & 4 inches in diameter, though it will depend on the size of the shank.

_Preheat the oven to 350°F. Snip the osso buchi in a few places around the edge to prevent curling. Pat dry the meat with paper towels. Put onto a chopping board & sprinkle with salt & pepper, then dust flour on each side. Shake off the excess flour.

_Heat the 2 tablespoons olive oil in a nonstick skillet &, when the oil is hot, add the osso buchi & fry for a few minutes on each side until golden & sealed.

_Meanwhile, pulse the celery, carrot, & onion, along with the garlic, in a food processor until evenly chopped. Heat the extra 4 tablespoons of olive oil in a heatproof casserole dish about 12 by 10 inches. Add the chopped vegetable mixture & cook in the oven until the vegetables are softened, adding the rosemary to flavor for a few minutes longer.

_Put the osso buchi in a single layer on top of the vegetables in the dish. Sprinkle with a little salt, add the wine, & ½ cup of water. Cover with foil & bake for 30 minutes. Turn the osso buchi over gently so that the meat holds its shape & doesn't lose any marrow. Cover & return to the oven for another 20 to 30 minutes, or until tender. Remove the foil & return to the oven for about 30 minutes, until the meat is lovely & tender, & the sauce syrupy & not watery.

Peas:
1 tablespoon olive oil
½ white onion, peeled
¾-ounce slice of pancetta
1 garlic clove, peeled &
squashed a bit
1 pound frozen peas
2 scant tablespoons
chopped parsley

__Meanwhile, make the risotto. Heat the olive oil & butter in a wide, heavy-bottomed saucepan or skillet with high sides. Sauté the piece of onion until golden. Add the rice & stir until it is coated with the buttery oil. Season with salt & pepper. Add the wine, lower the heat to a simmer, & cook, stirring often, until almost all the liquid has evaporated. Add about 1 cup of the broth & continue cooking, stirring regularly & adding more broth as it is absorbed, for about 20 minutes, until the rice is tender. The risotto should still have some liquid & the rice grains should be firm, yet soft & creamy.

__While the risotto is cooking, cook the peas. Heat the oil in a saucepan & sauté the half onion (*still in one piece*), pancetta, & garlic until it smells good. Add the peas, stir well, then add 1 tablespoon of parsley, ½ cup of water, & some salt & pepper, & simmer for about 15 minutes, until the peas are tender but still a nice green. Remove the onion, pancetta, & garlic clove. Drain the peas & scatter with the rest of the parsley.

__When everything is ready, serve the risotto, squashing the rice down a little, with the peas to one side & an osso buco on top. Spoon on some of the lovely sauce & give a good scattering of grated Parmesan & black pepper.

Serves 6

I keep feeling as if everyone is staring at me on the vaporetto. But—it is not me I realize. It is Venice. And the masterpieces everywhere, this show, this muchness of everything, everywhere.

Brasato con amarone di valpolicella

Braised beef with amarone

2¾ pounds chuck, blade, or shin steak in one piece, trimmed of fat
4 tablespoons olive oil
2 carrots, halved
1 celery stalk, halved
1 white onion, halved
1 tablespoon butter
3 cups amarone di valpolicella, or other red wine
soft polenta (page 21), for serving

Usually, the wine used in cooking would be the one to drink, but you may decide here to drink a great amarone & choose a less expensive bottle for cooking. Or a beautiful deep red wine instead. The cut of meat here is important as it has to become very soft. Ask your butcher to recommend a great piece of meat. I used La sfaldatura di bistecca dissosata, which is deboned steak & particularly good for a brasato. It is often made with shin of beef. A brasato (stew or braise) is usually cooked on the stovetop. Here I have started off the cooking on the stovetop & then finished it in the oven where you don't need to give it a glance for a couple of hours. Because the pot will be going from stovetop to oven, it needs to be heatproof. I use my large, cast-iron one with lid that is 12 inches across & almost as deep. Serve with a nice dollop of soft polenta.

__Preheat the oven to 350°F. Roughly tie the meat with kitchen string to hold its shape while cooking. Heat the oil in a heatproof casserole, add the meat, & seal well on all sides until golden here & there. Season well with salt & pepper (*this is important so that you don't get flavorless meat later*). When the meat is almost browned all over, add the vegetables & butter, & then sauté so that the vegetables get a bit of a color.

__Add the wine &, once it starts bubbling, cover with the lid & put in the oven. Cook for 1 hour, then lower the oven temperature to 325°F & cook for a further 1½ hours, or until tender, turning the meat once or twice.

__Lift the meat from the dish, remove the string, & rest on a board while you finish the sauce. Use a handheld blender to purée the vegetables until smooth. You may need to cut the vegetables up a little first, or add a little liquid from the pot to get a smooth purée.

__Cut the meat into 12 or so thick slices. Serve two or three slices of meat per person with a dollop of the sauce over the top & polenta on the side.

Serves 4 to 6

Seppie in nero con polenta

Squid stewed with ink

3 large squids (about 1¾ pounds in total weight) with ink sacs
3 tablespoons olive oil
2 garlic cloves, chopped
½ cup white wine
1 (14-ounce) can crushed tomatoes
1 heaped tablespoon chopped parsley
pinch of peperoncino
polenta (preferably white) (page 21), for serving

Squid stewed with ink is often made without the tomato; if you decide you'd like to make it that way, you may need to add an extra ½ cup of wine & water so that the sauce doesn't dry out. It can also be made as a primo, mixed into spaghetti. The deep jet black color of this dish is very dramatic & can deter timid diners, but the taste is wonderful. When I was cooking I couldn't see anything but black—I kept hoping that none of my rings would fall into the pot.

If you're making slow-cooked polenta, you'll need to start on it about the same time as you start cooking the squid. If your squid doesn't come with ink sacs or if they don't yield much ink, you can supplement with a package of squid ink. Abroad, these are sold by some fishmongers & delicatessens, often in a package containing 2 portions, ⅛ ounce each. Use 1 portion & see how black the squid becomes before adding the other. Alternatively, you can make this without any squid ink at all—just don't tell people they are eating seppie in nero.

__To prepare the squid, pull the head & innards from the body. Separate the ink sac from the rest of the innards without puncturing it, & then rinse gently & put in a bowl. Wash the body well. Cut off the head just below the eyes, leaving the tentacles in one piece, & discard the head. Pull out the transparent quill, rinse the tube, & peel off the outer membrane. Cut the squid body & tentacles into chunks. Pat dry with paper towels.

__Heat the oil in a wide saucepan & add the squid. Cook over high heat until the liquid begins to evaporate & the squid turns golden on the bottom. Add the garlic, turning with a wooden spoon. When you can smell the garlic, add the wine & let it evaporate a little.

__Cut the ink sacs into a cup & mix with 3 tablespoons of water, then add this to the pot. Add the chopped tomatoes, parsley, peperoncino, & some salt & pepper. Cook for 5 minutes until it all starts bubbling up, then cover, lower the heat, & simmer gently for about 40 minutes until the squid is tender & there is a good amount of sauce (*cook for longer, adding more liquid if necessary, until your squid is tender*).

__Check occassionally that nothing is sticking to the bottom of the pan. Add a little more water if it starts to thicken too much. Season to taste.

__Put a generous mound of polenta on each plate, then top with a good dollop of squid. Scatter with extra parsley, if you like–or just leave it all stark black.

Serves 4

The vast open water highway makes me happy. To get on a quiet vaporetto & take a long ride away from the circus. Let my thoughts float out over the ripples of the water before they come back & settle into me again.

Rombo con patate e funghi al forno

Fish with potatoes & mushrooms

about 1¾ pounds whole, flat fish, such as turbot or flounder
2 garlic cloves, peeled but left whole
1 thin bunch of parsley
coarse salt
4 tablespoons olive oil
1¼ pounds (3 medim) russet potatoes, peeled
¼ cup white wine
⅔ pound fresh mushrooms, porcini, field, or swiss browns, sliced

I love this method of cooking whole fish, because it's so easy to do all your preparation well ahead. You clean & prepare the fish, & lay it in an oven dish with the oil & salt, then put it in the refrigerator for a few hours until you're ready to cook it. During this time the salt penetrates the fish. When you're ready, take it out, add the potatoes, & pop it straight into the oven. If you're short of time, of course you don't have to put it in the refrigerator, you can just cook it right away. Don't overcook the fish or it will lose its delicate softness &, once it's cooked, serve it immediately.

This dish is lovely with or without the mushrooms, which are added 10 to 15 minutes before the end of the cooking time. I use porcini here, for the flavor they add.

__Gut, clean, & scale the fish but leave the head on (*your fishmonger can do this for you*). Wash the whole fish & pat dry with paper towels. Stuff the fish cavity with the garlic & parsley. Sprinkle in some coarse salt & pepper, & scatter some on the outside, too. Put the fish in a large baking dish. If you don't think there will be room for the whole fish & the potatoes in your dish, cut away the fins with a pair of kitchen shears. Drizzle the olive oil into the bottom of the dish. Cover with plastic wrap & put in the refrigerator for a few hours to allow the salt to penetrate.

__Meanwhile, slice the potatoes into very thin rounds (1/16 inch) & keep them covered in a bowl of water so that they don't darken.

__Preheat the oven to 400°F & take the fish out of the refrigerator. Drain the potatoes & pat dry with paper towels. Scatter around the fish in as flat a layer as possible. Bake in the oven for about 15 minutes until lightly golden. Drizzle the wine over the fish & return to the oven for another 15 minutes (*by this stage the potatoes should be quite golden*). Sprinkle a little fine salt over the potatoes, add the mushroom slices, & season them with a little extra salt & pepper. Cook in the oven for a final 10 minutes or so until everything is cooked. When serving, carefully remove the fish skin & bones.

Serves 4

San pietro in padella con carciofi

Fish fillets with artichokes

2 fresh artichokes
juice of half a lemon
4 tablespoons olive oil
2 garlic cloves, peeled, & squashed a bit
1 tablespoon chopped parsley
2 san pietro (John Dory) fillets (about ½ pound each)
¼ cup white wine

San pietro (John Dory) is a very delicate fish & cooking for too long will cause it to break up. If you buy it whole & fillet it yourself, then use the head & trimmings to make a fish broth for risotto (page 159). Of course, you could use other firm white fish fillets here. If it's helpful to prepare the artichokes in advance; keep them in a bowl of cold water with a little lemon juice to prevent them discoloring.

__To prepare the artichokes, trim away the outer leaves & cut a slice off the top. Halve each artichoke & remove the hairy choke if it has one, then cut each half into fine slices ⅛ inch thick. (*Keep them covered with cold water & a little lemon juice to prevent their turning black.*)
__Heat half the olive oil in a skillet. Add the artichokes & one of the garlic cloves, & season with salt. Sauté gently for 5 to 10 minutes until softened & flavored, then remove the garlic & add the parsley. Scrape out the artichokes onto a plate & wipe the skillet clean.
__Meanwhile, pat the fish dry with paper towels. Heat the remaining oil & garlic clove in the skillet & add the fish. Cook until just pale golden underneath, then turn over & add the wine. Lower the heat, shake the skillet to loosen the fish, & add salt & pepper. When the wine has bubbled up, add the artichokes to the side. Remove from the heat & serve with a grinding of pepper.

Serves 2

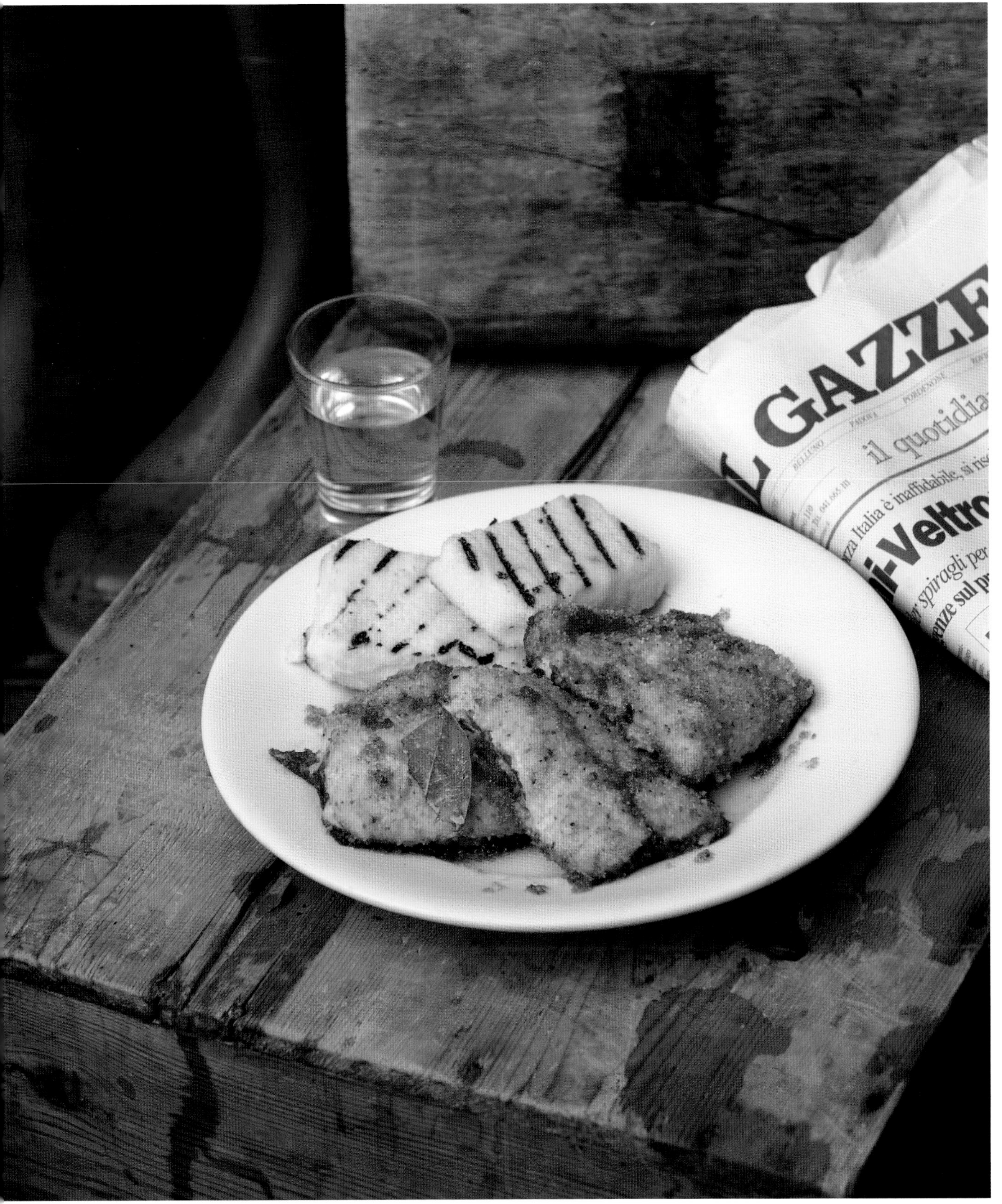
GAZZE
BELLUNO PADOVA PORDENONE
il quotidia
Italia è inaffidabile, si ris
i-Veltro
spiragli per

Anguilla al forno

Roast eel

8 eel fillets (about 2 pounds)
5 tablespoons olive oil
dry bread crumbs
3 bay leaves
2 garlic cloves, peeled but left whole
¼ cup white wine
lemon wedges & broiled polenta (page 21), for seving

They say no one cooks eel like the Venetians do. You can make this with any oily fish fillets, such as hake, mackerel, or mullet. I used mullet fillets & they worked beautifully. My father-in-law, Mario, loves eel—this is his recipe. If you're using eel, you can remove the skin if you prefer.

_Preheat the oven to 400°F. Cut the eel into pieces of about 3 inches & pat dry on paper towels. Drizzle 3 tablespoons of olive oil into a good-sized roasting pan. Pat the eel in bread crumbs, salt, & pepper, & arrange in the pan with the bay leaves & garlic. Drizzle with the remaining oil.

_Roast for about 20 minutes or until golden, then add the wine & cook for another 5 minutes or so, until it bubbles up & is saucy & roasty looking. Serve with lemon wedges & broiled polenta.

Serves 4

Anguilla in umido

Eel with tomato

about 3 tablespoons olive oil
1 onion, finely chopped
1 garlic clove, peeled, but left whole
1 (14-ounce) can crushed tomatoes
8 eel fillets (about 2 pounds)
all-purpose flour, for dusting
¼ cup white wine
2 tablespoons chopped parsley
soft polenta (page 21), for serving

You can make this with any oily fish fillets, such as hake, mackerel, or mullet. Eel has a very distinctive flavor & there are people who love it & people who don't. Much eel is eaten in the Veneto, where it is known as bisato, & there are many different ways to prepare it. It has a delicate, slightly sweet taste & is also enjoyed fried & broiled. You can also sauté eel in a skillet with butter, white wine, & garlic, & scatter with chopped parsley & serve with polenta.

__Heat 3 tablespoons of olive oil in a large skillet, add the onion, & sauté to soften. Add the garlic &, when you can smell it, add the tomatoes & some salt & pepper, & simmer for 10 minutes or so.

__Meanwhile, cut the eel into pieces of about 3 inches. Pat dry the eel on paper towels & lightly coat with flour. Heat a little oil in another skillet & fry the eel on both sides until lightly browned. Add salt & pepper, then pour away any oil from the skillet before adding the wine. Let it bubble up & reduce.

__Scrape all of the eel into the skillet of tomatoes, add ½ cup of water, & simmer for 10 to 15 minutes, until nicely cooked. Add a little more water if it needs it. Sprinkle with parsley & serve hot with polenta.

Serves 4

Calamari con salsa tonnata

Calamari with tuna mayonnaise

4 calamari (about 1 pound)
½ (7-ounce) canned tuna in oil, drained
1 large tablespoon capers in vinegar, drained
3 tablespoons mayonnaise (below)
freshly chopped parsley, to serve
lemon wedges, for serving

Mayonnaise:
2 egg yolks
1 teaspoon lemon juice, plus 1 to 2 extra teaspoons
scant 1 cup light olive oil

This recipe is a variation of Italy's famous Vitello tonnato. Someone told me about it on the island of Lido, but using boiled squid or calamari, & I couldn't wait to try it. Here, I've grilled the calamari, but you might like to try it boiled sometime.

This is great. I've made it as a main, but it also works well for more people as an antipasto. You don't have to make your own mayonnaise–use a top-quality bought one. A lightly dressed salad is good with this.

__First, make the mayonnaise. Whisk the yolks in a small bowl with a teaspoon of lemon juice & a pinch of salt. Drizzle in the olive oil, whisking all the while, until the mayonnaise is thick & creamy. Add more lemon juice to taste. This makes about ¾ cup & will keep for a week in the refrigerator in a sterilized jar. You'll need 3 tablespoons of the mayonnaise for this recipe.

__To prepare the calamari, firmly pull the head & innards from the body & wash the body well. Cut off the head just below the eyes, leaving the tentacles in one piece if small. Discard the head, pull the transparent quill out of the body, & rinse out the tube. Peel off the outer membrane & cut the tube down the length of one side, then open it out into a steak. Snip the edges & score the top with a sharp knife in slashes or a crisscross pattern.

__Pulse the tuna & capers in a food processor until roughly smooth. Scrape out into a bowl & mix in 3 tablespoons of mayonnaise. Season to taste.

__Preheat the electric grill to hot. Put the calamari steaks flat on the grill, with the tentacles, in a single layer (*or cook in batches*). Cook until deep golden so that they take the taste of the grill rack, then turn over & cook the other side until soft, tender, opaque white, & with a few grill marks. The steaks probably won't stay completely flat (*I held with tongs the parts that were threatening to curl*). Put them flat onto plates, allow them to cool a bit (*if too hot, will melt the mayonnaise too much*), & cover with 1 tablespoon of the salsa tonnata. Scatter with parsley & black pepper & serve immediately with lemon wedges.

Serves 2

NEZIA

Luganega e polenta

Sausages & polenta

4 thin slices (about 2¼ ounces) pancetta, chopped
3 thin slices (about 2¼ ounces) lardo, chopped
6 good pork sausages (luganege) (about 1½ pounds), pricked all over
1 small onion, sliced
1 cup white wine
polenta (page 21) & grated Parmesan, for serving

This is a simple & rich dish; the kind you won't see on restaurant menus but that Venetians would make at home to eat in front of a wintery fire. Use good pork sausages, & I like to use a mixture of lardo & pancetta here. Lardo is rather a precious thing—"lardo di colonnato" is a traditional Tuscan delicacy of cured pork fat & it is prized all over Italy. When sliced very thinly, the majority of the slice is pork fat with just a tiny piece of prosciutto-type meat. Pancetta is very well-cured pork, much drier & with much more meat than lardo. Together they are a great combination. I use white wine here, but red is also good. Serve this rich dish with polenta & perhaps a nice plate of radicchio or Verza soffogata (page 253).

__Sauté the pancetta & lardo in a dry, nonstick skillet over medium heat until some of the oil seeps out, then add the sausages. Cook the sausages until they are slightly golden in places. Transfer the pancetta & lardo to a plate, so that they won't become too crisp, & add the onion to the skillet. Cook until the onion is golden & soft (*your sausages might not look lovely & brown yet, but they will have more time in the skillet later*).

__Return the pancetta & lardo to the skillet & fry for a few minutes, until everything is nicely melded together. Add the wine & simmer for 30 minutes, turning the sausages over once until they are golden on the bottom, the wine has evaporated, & everything once again looks as if it is frying in the oil. (*If you don't intend to be serving immediately, cover with a lid.*) Serve a sausage & some of the sauce & rich oil over a serving of polenta. Scatter with Parmesan.

Serves 6

Faraona arrosto con la salsa peverada

Roasted guinea fowl with peverada

1 guinea fowl (about 2½ pounds)
1 tablespoon butter
2 teaspoons finely chopped rosemary
2 teaspoons finely chopped sage
1 large garlic clove, chopped
¼ cup finely chopped pancetta
5 long thin slices cured pancetta
4 tablespoons olive oil
1 cup white wine

Salsa peverada:
¼ pound chicken livers
¾ ounce guinea fowl liver
1 thick slice (about 3 ounces) soft salami, skin removed, chopped
2 tablespoons olive oil
1 teaspoon finely grated lemon zest
juice of 1 small lemon
2 garlic cloves, chopped
1 tablespoon chopped parsley

This is quite lovely, noble-looking &, most of all, easy to make. It's rather like doing a roast chicken with a bit of a stuffing sauce on the side. Prepare as for a chicken, keeping the liver if your guinea fowl comes with one. This is particularly lovely with cabbage or the roast pumpkin & mushrooms (page 248). I have seen many different versions of this sauce; some elaborate with vinegar, crumbed bread, anchovies, onions, or various spices, & it works very well next to any roast poultry. If your bird doesn't come with the liver, just increase the chicken liver accordingly.

__Preheat the oven to 425°F. Rinse the guinea fowl inside & out & pat dry with paper towels. Season lightly inside & out. Mix together the butter, rosemary, sage, garlic, & chopped pancetta, & stuff inside the bird.

__Lay the sliced pancetta over the bird widthwise, so that the top & sides are covered, & then tie up with string. Put half the olive oil in a roasting pan, put the bird in the pan & drizzle with the rest of the oil. Roast for 15 minutes or so, until golden & sizzling on the bottom, then pour in half the wine. Turn down the oven temperature to 350°F, & roast for another 40 to 45 minutes, adding the rest of the wine about 30 minutes, once it is bubbling nicely. Once or twice baste the bird with the pan juices. Poke a fork into the thickest part of the thigh & check the juices are clear (*cook for 10 to 15 minutes more if needed, but it's important not to overcook it & dry it out*). Remove from the oven and let stand for 10 minutes before untying the bird & cutting up into portions.

__Meanwile, make the peverada: clean the livers of any sinew & then chop them well. Put all the ingredients in a small saucepan with salt & simmer for 10 minutes or so, until the livers are cooked. Add a good couple of grindings of pepper. Serve a spoonful of this warm, along with a portion of roast guinea fowl with its lovely pan juices.

Serves 4

Pollo con pomodoro in tecia

Chicken in tomato

1 (2¾-pound) chicken, cut into 8 pieces
1 white onion, quartered
1 carrot
1 small celery stalk
1 garlic clove, peeled but left whole
4 tablespoons olive oil
1 tablespoon chopped parsley
1 tablespoon finely chopped rosemary
pinch of ground peperoncino
¾ cup red wine
2 (14-ounce) cans crushed tomatoes
polenta (page 21), for serving

I usually make this in my cast-iron pot. If possible, use an attractive pot that you can take straight to the table from the stove. The whole chicken, cooked until meltingly soft, has a wonderful flavor, but if you prefer absolutely no bones, then just use large chicken breasts.

There is a lot of tomato sauce here, which is lovely with polenta to soak it up. You can make your polenta the quick method or the 40-minute way–just make sure you allow enough time for it to be ready with the chicken. Or, make the chicken in advance & warm it up to serve just before your polenta is ready. Boiled or mashed potatoes or rice work well here, too.

_To prepare the chicken, remove the skin, fat, & any stray bones. Put the onion, carrot, celery, & garlic into a food processor & pulse until roughly chopped but not too small.

_Heat the olive oil in a large pot & sauté the chopped vegetables & parsley until they start to smell good. Add the chicken & sauté until it changes color & has browned here & there, turning so that it cooks evenly.

_Add a generous amount of salt & pepper, then add the rosemary & peperoncino. Sauté to flavor well, then add the wine, & cook to reduce a little. Add the tomatoes & let it all bubble up, then simmer, partly covered, for about 1 hour, adding 1 cup of water after about 40 minutes as it is absorbed & looks like it needs it. Taste the sauce & add salt & pepper if necessary.

_Meanwhile, start making the polenta (*either the short or long way*), but keep in mind that it must be eaten as soon as it's ready. Leave the chicken covered (*lid completely on*) until you serve it…with a scattering of parsley if you like. Check carefully when you serve, for any small bones that may have come loose during the long cooking time.

Serves 4

Uccelli con polenta

Birds with polenta

12 small birds, cleaned, or 6 small quail, halved & cleaned
12 long, thin slices pancetta
2 tablespoons butter
2 tablespoons olive oil
2 ounces sweet pancetta, chopped
2 sage sprigs
¾ cup white wine
polenta (page 21), for serving

In Venice small birds are used for this—tordi, merli, or fringuelli. We used fringuelli, which Mariella happened to have in her freezer. Ten small birds weighed about ½ pound each. You will probably find quail are more readily available, depending on where you live, but if you do use the small birds you'll only need to roast them for 30 minutes. I use slices of peppery pancetta for wrapping them.

__Preheat the oven to 350°F. Lightly salt & pepper the inside of the birds, wrap each one with a slice of pancetta, & secure with a toothpick.

__Heat the butter & olive oil in a small heatproof casserole, & sauté the chopped pancetta & sage until the pancetta has melted. Add the birds in a single layer, sauté for a moment on both sides, & then add the wine. Transfer the dish to the hot oven & roast for 30 minutes, or 50 minutes if you're using quail, until cooked & tender. Serve with soft polenta.

Serves 4

Anatra in padella con acciughe e capperi

Duck with anchovies & capers

1 (3-pound) duck, cut into 8 pieces
1 white onion, chopped
1 ounce sweet pancetta, chopped
6 large anchovy fillets in olive oil, drained
2 tablespoons capers in vinegar, drained
2 garlic cloves, chopped
2 teaspoons finely chopped rosemary
2 teaspoons chopped sage leaves
1½ cups white wine

Cutting up a duck is not as easy as cutting up a chicken…so you might want to ask your butcher to do it for you. Cut it in half first, & then cut each half into four pieces. If your duck looks terribly fatty, then cut some of that away. You may need to singe away any bits of feather, too—scrape away the remnants with a sharp knife. You will need a large nonstick skillet with high sides & a lid that fits well—& even better if you can take it straight to the table for serving. This is lovely with radicchio in padella & roast potatoes…

__Dry-fry the duck pieces in a large nonstick skillet until brown on all sides, then season with salt & pepper (*not too much salt as you'll have anchovies in the sauce*).
__Transfer the duck pieces onto a plate, & add the onion to the duck fat in the skillet. Cook until pale golden, then add the pancetta & anchovies, mashing them into the oil with a wooden spoon. When they have melted & the pancetta is softened, add the capers, garlic, rosemary, & sage.
__When you can smell the garlic, return the duck to the skillet & add the wine. Cover with the lid & simmer for almost an hour, then add about ½ cup of water. Cook for another 20 minutes, then remove the lid & turn the duck pieces. Simmer for a further 10 to 15 minutes to get a glossy, sticky sauce in the skillet. The duck should be golden brown & very tender—check with a fork.

Serves 4

Maiale al latte

Pork in milk

2 quite small fennels, trimmed & halved lengthwise
about 1¾ pounds pork loin, with only a little fat on top
1 sage sprig
1 rosemary sprig
3 tablespoons olive oil
1 tablespoon butter
2 garlic cloves, peeled but left whole
½ cup white wine
about 2½ cups milk

The sauce may look as though it is curdled, but it tastes wonderful. If you really don't like the look of it, you can purée to render it smooth, but it is traditionally served as it is cooked. This is one of those dishes that does not reheat particularly well, so time it to be finished when you're ready to serve. You'll need a good big pot: large enough to fit the meat but not too wide, & leaving enough room for the fennel to be added later.

__Bring a small saucepan of salted water to a boil. Add the fennel & boil for about 5 minutes until quite tender (*it will have more time in the pot later*). Transfer the fennel with a slotted spoon onto a plate. Cut the fennel halves in half again, leaving them attached at the bottom. Set aside for the moment.

__Tie up the loin piece with kitchen string, fastening the sage on one side & the rosemary on the other. Heat the olive oil & butter in your pot &, when it is fizzling, add the pork & cook until it is lovely & golden on all sides, adding the garlic toward the end of cooking so that it doesn't burn. Once the pork is browned all over, season generously with salt & pepper (*this is important for the final flavor*).

__Pour in the wine & let it bubble up until there is a great-smelling syrupy juice in the bottom of the pot. Add 2 cups of the milk. Bring to a boil, then lower the heat & simmer, covered, for about 1¼ hours, checking toward the end that the sauce is not evaporating too much. Carefully, add the fennel around the meat; warm the rest of the milk & pour that in, too. Sprinkle with a little salt if you think it needs it. Cook, uncovered, for another 15 minutes, or until the pork & fennel are tender.

__Remove the pot from the heat & let it stand for about 10 minutes, then lift the meat out of the sauce. Remove the string & cut the pork into fairly thick slices. Serve the pork & fennel with a generous helping of sauce & add a good grinding of black pepper.

Serves 4

Musetto con fagioli piccanti

Venetian sausage with beans

2½ cups dried Lamon or borlotti beans
1 musetto (cotechino) sausage (about 1⅓ pounds)
2 garlic cloves, peeled but left whole
1 sage sprig
4 tablespoons olive oil
1 white onion, chopped
1¾ ounces cured pancetta or rigatino, chopped
1 scant tablespoon finely chopped rosemary
2 pinches ground peperoncino
1½ (14-ounce) cans crushed tomatoes

Musetto is a wintery Venetian dish—lovely in slices with a good dollop of mustard (Dijon is great), bread, & a heap of the Veneto's beautiful taupy-red, speckled Lamon beans. These beans are also a beauty with broiled salsiccia, or other sausages that you like—& if you can't find Lamon, just use borlotti beans.

Musetto is a Venetian sausage (also popular served with mashed potato or polenta), that I saw being kept in a separate warm broth to keep it soft & moist, then taken out with a long fork to slice as someone ordered a portion. I bought my musetto from my friend Sergia, who has the alimentari there, & she gave me the full cooking instructions. Cotechino sausage is similar enough to use here, just larger across its diameter. If you can only find the precooked cotechino, follow the preparation instructions on the package.

__Soak the beans overnight in a bowl with plenty of water to cover.

__Stick about 8 toothpicks into the musetto & leave them in (*to let the fat come out during the cooking*), then put in a pot of water & bring to a boil. Partly cover the saucepan & boil gently for about 1½—even 2—hours, adding more water if necessary (*or follow the instructions on the package if your cotechino is precooked*). Test with a fork to check that it is lovely & tender, then remove from the heat.

__Meanwhile, drain the beans, put in a big pot of fresh water with the garlic & sage, & bring to a boil. Partly cover the pot & cook for anything from 30 to 50 minutes (*depending on your beans*) until tender, but not too overcooked (*they get another few minutes of cooking later*). Add some salt toward the end of their cooking time. Drain, keeping about a cup of the cooking liquid, & remove the garlic & sage.

__Meanwhile, heat the olive oil in a high, wide saucepan, & sauté the onion until it is soft & pale golden. Add the pancetta & sauté for a minute more, then add the rosemary & peperoncino. Add the tomatoes & a little salt, & simmer for 10 to 15 minutes, punching the tomatoes down with a wooden spoon so the pieces dissolve.

__Add the beans to the pan & toss through gently without mashing them. Add about ½ cup of the reserved bean water (*or more if it looks necessary*), & simmer for a few minutes to mix with all the flavors. Season to taste & simmer for 5 minutes or so, until it is all just right.

__Now…lift the musetto out of its cooking liquid &, if you are not serving it immediately, you could keep it in a pot of warm vegetable broth so it stays tender, just as they do at Do Mori ciccheteria in Venice. Cut into slices about ½ inch thick, removing the skin, & serve with a heap of warm beans & your favorite mustard & bread.

Serves 6 to 8

Pasta in brodo

Pasta in broth

This is a primo, but fits here because it is lovely made with the complex meat broth from the bollito misto (opposite). Serve it before the bollito.

__If you are making pasta "in brodo" for 4 people, put about 6 cups of broth into a saucepan & bring to a boil. Check that your broth is well seasoned. Snap up ¼ pound of spaghetti (*break the strands into about 6 pieces*) & cook in boiling, salted water until ready (*or you could use tortellini or tagliatelle instead*). Spoon into bowls, pour in the broth, & serve with a generous scattering of Parmesan.

Serves 4

Bollito di carne

Mixed boiled meats

15-ounce piece veal or beef tongue
½ boiling chicken (about 2 pounds), rinsed
1⅔ pound piece chuck steak, or blade steak
1 pound oxtail (about 3 thick slices)
1-pound piece veal shoulder
14 ounces beef shin
1 large carrot, peeled
1 large onion, peeled
1 celery stalk
1 bunch of parsley
1 bay leaf
10 peppercorns
3 teaspoons salt

This is rather celebrational & Christmassy. Luisa says they serve this, then follow with a dessert of mascarpone, some more mostarda, & baicoli biscuits. Serve the meats with the Salsa piccante di peperone e acciughe (overleaf) & some other accompaniments, such as fresh horseradish sauce & Mostarda (page 28).

The idea with this recipe is to cook the meats, then use the delicious broth that remains to make Pasta in brodo (opposite), or a lovely meat risotto, such as Risotto con le seccole (page 172), & serve that as your primo or the next day. The mixed boiled meats are then served as the main course, & you can vary the cuts of meats to suit your tastes & needs. You'll need a large pot to make this–I have a 2-gallon stockpot, but if you don't have such a large one, make a smaller batch.

__Put the tongue in a small pot & cover with salted water. Bring to a boil, then simmer, covered, for about 1½ hours until tender (*it will cook for another hour later on, but needs to be cooked enough now to strip off the skin*). Drain, leave until cool enough to handle, then pull off the skin.

__Wash all the meat & pat dry with paper towels. Put the carrot, onion, celery, parsley, bay leaf, peppercorns, & salt in your huge pot with 16 cups of water. Bring to a boil, then add the various meats. Return to a boil & simmer, covered, over a good heat, so it's rolling gently but not bursting everywhere, for about 1 hour. Add the tongue & cook for another hour. If necessary, top up with a bit more water. To check that the meat is ready, stick a fork into each cut & remove when tender (*the chicken may need to be removed before the other meats*). Remove from the heat & season with salt if you think it needs it.

__Serve immediately, or leave to cool a little. Carefully transfer the meat to a warm serving dish, cut up & cover so that it doesn't dry out. Strain the broth into a large bowl, then cover & refrigerate if you're not using it immediately. (*Once the broth sets you could remove the layer of fat on top.*)

Serves 6

Salsa piccante di peperone e acciughe

Red bell pepper & anchovy sauce

- *½ cup olive oil*
- *4 very large anchovy fillets in oil, drained*
- *1 tablespoon all-purpose flour*
- *1 garlic clove, peeled & halved*
- *2 small red bell peppers, seeded & cut into pieces*
- *1 tablespoon capers in vinegar, drained*
- *¾ cup vegetable broth, not too salty (page 12)*
- *2 teaspoons white wine vinegar*

Luisa's grandmother always made this to serve with a bollito misto. You can also serve it with a simple plate of boiled chicken, fish, or grilled meat. It's also great drizzled onto grilled bread.

__Heat the olive oil & anchovies in a small saucepan, whisking so the anchovies dissolve. Add the flour, whisking until smooth.

__Add the garlic, pepper, & capers. Bring to a slow boil, then add the vegetable broth. Lower the heat & simmer for about 15 minutes, whisking now & then so that nothing sticks. Allow to cool a little, then purée thoroughly using a handheld blender. When completely cool, stir in the vinegar.

Makes 1½ cups

Melanzane sotto olio e aceto

Eggplant in oil & vinegar

15 ounces (about 2 or 3) long, thin eggplants
1 tablespoon coarse salt
1½ cups white wine vinegar
2 garlic cloves, peeled but left whole
2 bay leaves
a few peppercorns & whole peperoncini
about 1 cup good olive oil

These eggplant pickles are lovely to eat with the bollito (page 227), or even as part of an antipasto. You need to use the long, slender eggplants here, so you'll get strips with the skin & not have too many pieces that are just flesh. You might like to add a couple of dried peperoncini or peppercorns to the container when packing the eggplant pieces in oil. The eggplant will keep for a month or longer, as long as it's covered with oil. The container (glass or ceramic) must be cleaned & then sterilized with boiling water before use. Leave it to dry in a warm oven.

__Cut the eggplants into ¾-inch-thick slices along their length. Then cut across those slices into ½-inch pieces. Put in a colander, scatter with the salt, & let stand over a large bowl for an hour or so.

__Put the vinegar & 1 cup of water in a pot & bring to a boil. Rinse the eggplants, shake well, then add to the pot. When the liquid comes back to a boil, lower the heat slightly, & cook for 4 to 5 minutes–no more. Remove from the heat, transfer the eggplant with a slotted spoon into the colander, & allow to cool. (*You can keep the lovely vinegar if you think you might make more eggplant pickles over the next few days.*)

__When cool, pack the eggplant into a sterilized container with the garlic & bay leaves. Add a few peppercorns & peperoncini, if you like. Cover with the oil (*the amount you need will depend on your container*). Press down on the eggplant to make sure there are no air bubbles. Seal. Leave for a couple of days before eating. Serve with some of the oil in a bowl on the side.

Serves 6 to 8

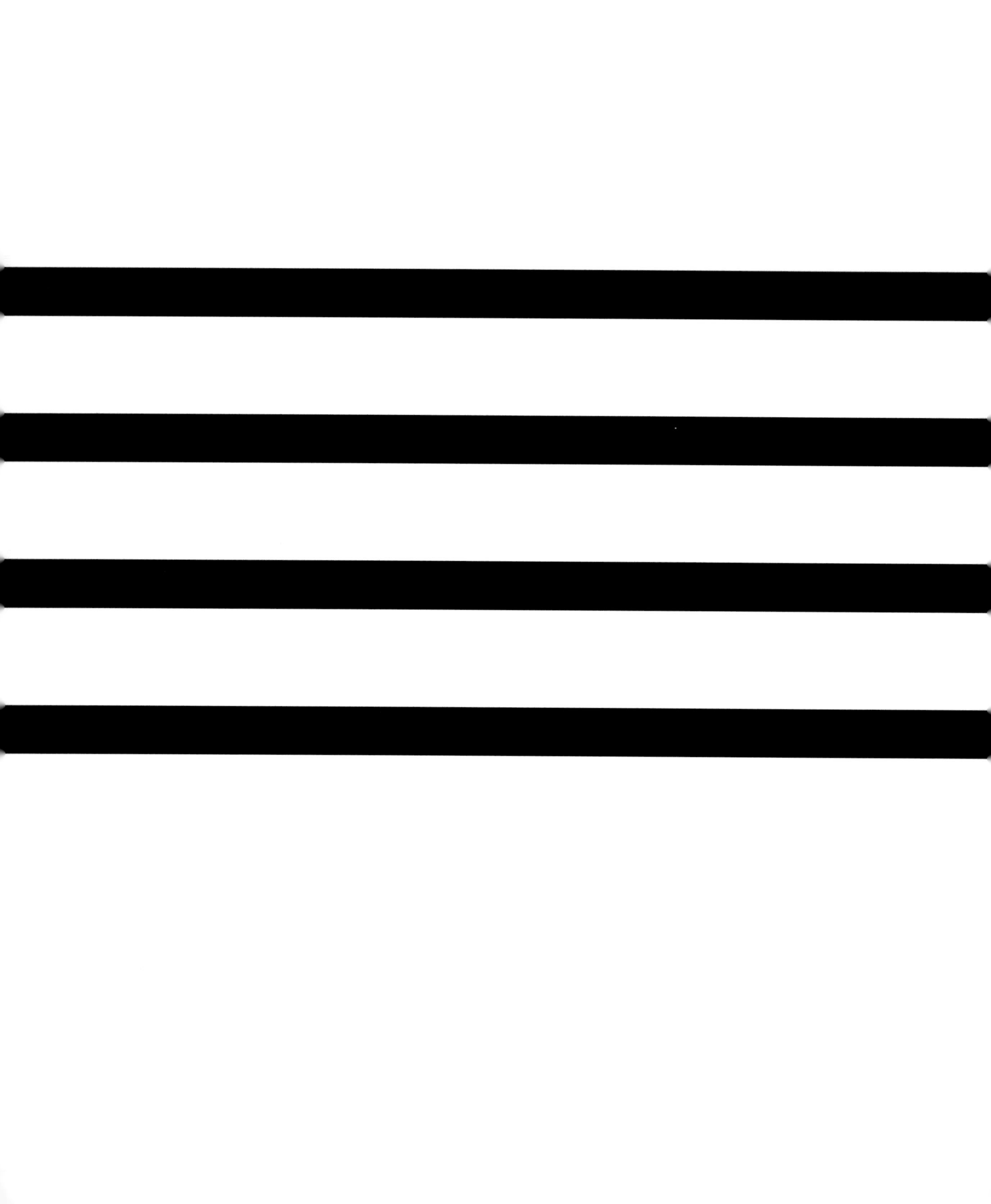

radicchio & *roses*

I love Pellestrina & its slow sadness. After sgroppinos & tiramisu, at that same round table at the entrance where the ladies had been peeling miniature shrimps & were now cracking cooked crabs, I ask if they'll give me the recipe. They say, PER UN CURIOSO CI VUOLE UN BUGIARDO–FOR A CURIOUS PERSON ONE NEEDS A LIAR! *Our friend, whom we have just met over lunch, takes us back on his jeanneau. His son Sebastian, age seven, knows a lot. He tells me there is fresh thyme in the pasticcio. They told him so once.*

VII

CONTORNI

Tiny whole artichokes	Castraure in padella
Artichoke bottoms	Fondi di carciofo
Radicchio with anchovies	Radicchio con acciughe
Radicchio in lemon	Radicchio al limone
Roast winter squash & mushrooms	Zucca e funghi al forno
Bell peppers	La peperonata
Lidia's wild asparagus	Asparagi selvatici di Lidia
Suffocated cabbage	La verza soffogata

Rialto
Rialto

Castraure in padella

Tiny whole artichokes

about 25 castraure
or baby artichokes
juice of half a lemon
2 garlic cloves, chopped
4 tablespoons olive oil
2 tablespoons chopped parsley

Castraure are beauties—the small, bitter, first artichokes that bud on the island of Sant' Erasmus (a nice vaporetto ride from the fondamenta Nuova). They are considered a prize & are much appreciated—so small & perfect that it is not necessary to take out a choke. Make as many as will fit in a large nonstick skillet (I have said about 25 here, but yours may be of a different size). If you don't have castraure, use ordinary artichokes, quartered. Or baby artichokes. If you have some vegetable broth, then definitely use that instead of the water here.

__Remove the outer leaves of the castraure & cut off all but ¾ inch of the stems. Cut off the outer, bitter, dark green bit. Cut off the tops, about a third of the way down. As you prepare them, drop the castraure into a bowl of water with the lemon juice added to prevent their discoloring.

__Heat the garlic & olive oil in nonstick skillet & add the drained castraure in a single layer. Cook until you can smell the garlic. Add the parsley, mix well, & season with salt & a grind of black pepper. Add about ½ cup of water, cover the pan, & simmer over low heat for about 10 minutes.

__Remove the lid, turn up the heat a touch, & simmer for another few minutes until the water has all gone & just the oil is left in a bit of sauce at the bottom. Serve warm or at room temperature, with the remaining oil poured over, & a squeeze of lemon & black pepper if you like.

Serves 5 to 6

Fondi di carciofo

Artichoke bottoms

8 artichokes
juice of half a lemon
1 garlic clove, chopped
1 tablespoon chopped parsley
3 tablespoons olive oil

These are everywhere. I believe many Venetians buy the Frisbee-size artichoke bottoms ready prepared that I have seen in abundance in the Rialto market. The first outer tough leaves can be thrown away. The next layer of leaves can be saved in a bowl with water & lemon juice. Drain them later & dip the tips in a ramekin of olive oil, lemon, salt, & pepper, & scrape off with your teeth. The softer inner leaves & all trimmings can go into a vegetable soup or salad.

Use the bigger, wider variety of artichokes if possible. You can make many more of these in your pan—as many as will fill it, depending on their size.

__Cut away the stalk of the artichoke, leaving only an inch. The cut that piece off & trim away the outer bitter parts to get to the inner core. (*These can go into a soup.*) The bottoms of the artichokes here need to be flat but the first inner stem bit is good, so save that. Cut away an inch off the top so that it is flat. Now pull away the first tough leaves & discard.

__Next, layer the leaves to be saved in a bowl of water with the lemon juice added. The leaves, which are still a bit hard, can be eaten in pinzimonio (*raw, dipped in lemon & olive oil*). Then get to the inner bits & trimmings & pop them into the soup pot. If the choke is hairy, cut it away with a small knife or pointed spoon & just have the bottom. If you are not ready to cook the artichokes, keep them in lemon water for now.

__Have a pot of broth or water boiling, add the artichoke bottoms and boil gently for 5 to 10 minutes, or until tender, then lift out with a slotted spoon.

__Heat the oil in a nonstick skillet. Add the artichokes & sauté for 2 minutes over high heat to give a nice color to both sides. Add the garlic, & sauté, stirring until you can smell it, season, & add the parsley. Cover with a lid & cook for a few minutes, until the artichokes are tender. Leave the lid on until you serve, with some of the parsleyed garlic oil drizzled over.

Serves 4 to 8

Radicchio con acciughe

Radicchio with anchovies

1 large radicchio di Treviso (about 9 ounces), halved lengthwise
2 tablespoons olive oil
1 large garlic clove, peeled & squashed a bit
4 large anchovy fillets in oil, drained
1 heaped tablespoon capers, drained
1 brimming tablespoon red wine vinegar

This is quite definite in flavor—yet with a delicate dressing. Mix through well & season to taste before adding anything more to your plate.

_Slice the radicchio into ¾-inch-thick, easy-to-eat slices, discarding the tough white stalk. Wash well, drain, & arrange on a platter.
_Heat the olive oil, garlic clove, & the anchovies in a small pan over very gentle heat, mashing the anchovies with a fork until dissolved. Remove the pan from the heat & stir in the capers. Allow to cool a little, stirring with a wooden spoon. Remove the garlic clove.
_Drizzle the flavored oil over the radicchio. Add the vinegar to the saucepan, swirling it around to gather all the pan flavors, then drizzle it over the radicchio. Take the platter to the table, or dish up onto individual plates. Serve immediately with a good twist of black pepper & some bread. Beautiful simplicity.

Serves 2 to 3

Radicchio al limone

Radicchio in lemon

3 to 4 small or 2 large radicchio di Treviso
5 tablespoons olive oil
juice of 1 large lemon

Nice. Bitter. Easy. This is great when radicchio is in season, & is a lovely side dish with the liver & onions (page 190), or any secondo you think would go well. Apart from being such a gorgeous color, radicchio is also very good for us. You need the longer Treviso radicchio for this—the round puffy ones are from nearby bustling Chioggia. With any luck all your radicchio will be similar inside—but the ones with a lot of "anima" (the white stem) will need to be left over the heat a while longer. It's important that they are soft, but not collapsing, & are nice & crusty from the cooking. When you cut them, leave the leaves attached at the stem—some leaves may fall away, but you will serve them intact. For a spicy kick, add some crumbled peperoncino to the pan. You can make radicchio al vino rosso by using 1/3 cup of red wine instead of the lemon juice.

__You will need a large, good-quality nonstick skillet that has a lid. Halve or quarter the radicchio, depending on the size, so that they fit in your skillet in a single layer. Trim away any hard outer leaves if necessary, but leave the leaves attached to the stem. Wash the bottom. Pat dry with paper towels.

__Heat the olive oil in the skillet, add the radicchio pieces, cut side down, & sauté over high heat until the bottoms are cooked & golden. Gently turn over & cook for a few minutes to get the underside going, then sprinkle with some salt & pepper & pour over the lemon juice.

__Put the lid on, lower the heat to medium, & simmer for about 10 minutes, until the radicchio is soft but still attached at the stems, & there is some pink syrupy sauce in the pan. The bottom of the radicchio should be crusty here & the leaves should be soft & delicious. Cook for longer & add a little more liquid if necessary. Sprinkle a little more salt (*& some pepper, if you like*) over the top. Best served warm, but also good at room temperature.

Serves 4 to 6

Zucca e funghi al forno

Roast winter squash & mushrooms

1¾ pounds winter squash
5 tablespoons olive oil
about 14 ounces fresh porcini, or field, or swiss brown mushrooms, cut into chunks
2 garlic cloves, chopped
1 tablespoon finely chopped rosemary
about 3 tablespoons grated Parmesan

This is Luisa's dish. It's a beauty—simple & lovely. You can make it ahead of time & pop it into a hot oven to reheat for a moment just before serving. I tend to use my round 12-inch baking dish to make this, but you could use a rectangular one of about 10½ by 9 inches, & about 2 inches deep. You can easily add more winter squash & mushrooms here—just fill up your dish.

_Preheat the oven to 350°F. Peel the winter squash, remove the seeds, & cut the flesh into ¼-inch slices. You should have about 1⅓ pounds of sliced winter squash.

_Drizzle some of the olive oil into your baking dish. Add the slices of squash, mushrooms, garlic, & rosemary, & season with salt & pepper, then drizzle with the rest of the olive oil. Turn well, using your hands or a wooden spoon, then spread everything out more or less rustically.

_Bake for 30 to 40 minutes, until the squash is tender & golden in places & the mushrooms are crisp & golden here & there. Scatter with Parmesan & bake for another 5 or 10 minutes. Serve warm or even at room temperature.

Serves 4 to 6

LINUM

La peperonata

Bell peppers

2 red & 1 yellow large pepper (about 2¼ pounds in total)
about 5 tablespoons olive oil
1 white onion, chopped
2 garlic cloves, chopped
about 3 tablespoons white wine vinegar
3 to 4 anchovy fillets in oil, drained
small handful of small capers in vinegar, drained
2 tablespoons chopped parsley

This is a classic dish using bell peppers. There are several variations on the recipe: some cooks add tomato or eggplant, some use no anchovies & capers, some just red peppers. I love it with the capers & anchovies. It's lovely warm, or even cold from the refrigerator (as Giovanni likes it), & it is great on toasted bread. This is one of those beautiful dishes where you can taste every ingredient.

__Rinse & dry the peppers, then remove the seeds & stem, & cut the flesh into nice rustic chunks.

__Heat the olive oil in a large skillet that has a lid. Sauté the onion until soft & turning golden here & there. Add the peppers & cook on a strong simmer until they get going well. Add a tiny amount of salt (*you will be adding anchovies later*). Stir in the garlic, cover with the lid, & simmer for about 15 minutes, until the peppers have surrendered their firmness–a bit gold in places is good. Stir with a wooden spoon occasionally to check that nothing is sticking, but there should be enough liquid created from the peppers.

__Splash in the vinegar & simmer, uncovered, for another 10 minutes, or until it has all joined in a syrupy way in the bottom of the skillet & looks good.

__Add the anchovies to a bare space in the sauce in the bottom of the skillet, mashing them to dissolve, then mix well & simmer for a few minutes more. Add the capers, parsley, & some black pepper, & mix well before removing from the heat.

Serves 6

Asparagi selvatici di Lidia

Lidia's wild asparagus

about $2\frac{1}{4}$ pounds thin, wild asparagus (or the thinnest asparagus you can buy)
3 cups white vinegar
1 cup red wine
2 teaspoons salt
plenty of olive oil
2 garlic cloves, peeled & halved
about 12 whole peppercorns

Lidia used to collect the long, thin, wild asparagus on an island of the lagoon called Caroman. She would pick it by hand at the edge of the small wood, where it grew in the sand—long, long, & thin, thin.

We cooked the asparagus in 2 batches in a skillet large enough to fit them lying flat. But if you don't have a large (or very tall) skillet, you can do it in a smaller one & in several batches, as long as they are all cooked in the vinegar equally. If your asparagus is of normal thickness, you can still make this but cook it in the vinegar for a minute or two longer. You'll need a tall container to store the asparagus; it must be first cleaned, then sterilized with boiling water & left to dry in a warm oven.

It may seem a lot of oil, but the flavor is wonderful—it is great drizzled over salads, boiled potatoes, & rice salads.

__Snap off the tough ends of the asparagus, then wash the stalks. Heat the vinegar, red wine, & salt in a large skillet or a tall pot. Bring to a boil. Add the asparagus, in batches if necessary, so that they are immersed in the vinegar. Bring back to a boil & boil for 2 to 3 minutes, depending on the thickness of the asparagus.

__You won't need the lovely pink vinegar here, but you can save it for cooking another batch, so drain the asparagus, then lay it out onto a clean cloth to cool, & dry thoroughly. When cold, take a tall sterilized jar that will fit all the stalks (*or a rectangular dish*), & pour in a cup of olive oil. Pack in the garlic, peppercorns, & asparagus, & add another cup of oil, or enough to cover the asparagus completely. Sprinkle the tops with a little more salt.

__Leave for a few days before eating, as is, or with salads, rice salads, or cold pasta. These get better with time & will keep well for a month if the asparagus is immersed in the oil.

Serves many

La verza soffogata

Suffocated cabbage

about 1⅔ pounds whole savoy cabbage
3 tablespoons olive oil
1 white onion, thinly sliced
½ cup white wine
about 3 tablespoons tomato passata
pinch of peperoncino

This is a great accompaniment for the Luganega e polenta (page 215) or just some sausages & lovely bread. Savoy is great here but you can use any type of cabbage. Remove a few of the darker, tougher outer leaves to use in a soup—it helps if most of your leaves are similarly tender so the cooking times don't differ too much, although it is also nice to have some variation in texture. I have also tasted this with a little splash of vinegar, which must have been added with the wine.

__Rinse the cabbage & divide into quarters lengthwise. Cut away the hard bottom stalk in a triangle shape. Cut the cabbage into ⅜-inch-thick slices.

__Heat the olive oil in a large nonstick saucepan that has a lid, & gently sauté the onion until pale golden & softened. Add the cabbage and some salt, & cook, covered, until the volume reduces & the bottom is pale gold. Add the wine & allow it to bubble for a minute or so without the lid on. Add the tomato passata, peperoncino, & 2 cups of water. Bring back to a boil, cover, lower the heat, & simmer gently for about 30 minutes, stirring occasionally with a wooden spoon to check that nothing is sticking.

__Remove the lid & cook for another 10 minutes or so on a higher heat, so that the liquid almost completely evaporates. If the cabbage is still hard, continue cooking for a little longer—adding a little more water if it needs it—until the cabbage is meltingly soft & tastes quite sweet. Remove from the heat. Season to taste. This is best served warm, but is also good at room temperature.

Serves 6

sweets & *secrets*

Waiting in the line of cars to get onto the ferry to leave, I ask the taxi driver in front what's going on. Unless they bring a second boat we won't get on—there are too many, he says quite casually. I glance at my watch. So, if we don't make this one we will get on the 11:40, he says rather calmly, as I panic & ask him how this is possible. "Eh, eh," he says, "we Venetians are used to it." If you didn't book for the fast line, then that's how it is. When you live with the sea you have to be calm. The water is slow but inexorable. Is that a Venetian saying? I ask him. Not exactly, he says, but there are many similar. The Venetians are pensive & elusive at once, accepting, like the tides of their waters. ⟞

VIII

DOLCI

Tiramisù

Tiramisu

3 fresh eggs, preferably organic, separated
3 heaping tablespoons sugar
1¼ cups mascarpone
about ½ cup strong coffee
about 3 tablespoons rum, cognac, or kirsch
about 30 pavesini or small ladyfingers
unsweetened cocoa powder, for dusting

This can be varied as much as you like: make it less sweet, more sweet; serve it with gratings of semisweet chocolate on top; use whatever alcohol you like, such as Grand Marnier, whiskey, or marsala. It's also very easy to make double the amount.

My friend Claudia makes this for the children with no alcohol. She mixes milk in with the coffee for a lighter version.

You can either make this in individual dishes or one large one. Small dishes need to be 2 inches high & long enough across the bottom to fit the ladyfingers, so at least 2¾ inches. I prefer individual ones, but if you'd like to make this in one large dish, it should be about 10 by 7 inches & 2 inches deep. Mine is lightly wider at the top, so I usually have to add more ladyfingers to the top layer than I did to the bottom.

__Whip the egg whites until very fluffy & white. Next (*you don't need to wash the beaters*), whip the egg yolks & sugar in a bowl until it is very creamy. Mix in the mascarpone & give a quick whisk, then fold in the egg whites until lovely, full, & *voluminoso.*

__Make your coffee (*if you're using a moka, listen for the beautiful "ready" sound*). Pour the coffee into a bowl (*if you like, stir in 1 teaspoon of sugar to sweeten it*). Allow to cool a little, then splash in your alcohol.

__Have your 6 dishes ready & dollop 1 tablespoon of marscarpone into each bowl. Dip a couple of ladyfingers at a time into the coffee until they have soaked it up, then shake them out well so any excess coffee drips back into the bowl & you don't end up with soggy cake. Lay the ladyfingers over the mascarpone in the bowl. Top with another couple of dollops of mascarpone, then more cake, then a final couple of dollops of mascarpone–don't go all the way to the top of your dishes. Chill them baking sheet in the refrigerator for at least a few hours & dust with cocoa before serving.

__If you are making the tiramisù in 1 large dish, dollop about 3 tablespoons of the mascarpone mix into the dish & smudge it to just cover the bottom, so that the ladyfingers will stick. Arrange a layer of dipped fingers like 2 rows of soldiers facing each other (about 8 per row). Dollop about half of the mascarpone cream over this layer, then another layer of cake, & the rest of mascarpone. Cover with plastic wrap & chill for at least a couple of hours. Dust with cocoa before serving.

Serves 6

Tiramisù di Sergia

Sergia's tiramisu

15 small amaretti cookies, plus 3 extra, if you like
3 tablespoons Martini Rosso (sweet vermouth)
1 egg, separated
1 heaping tablespoon sugar
1 cup mascarpone
unsweetened cocoa powder, for dusting

Sergia taught me this recipe—a lovely bittersweet variation on a classic—which is so very quick to make. It has less cookies & doesn't involve the layering of a traditional tiramisu. Make sure you have elegant glasses on a stem for serving. This recipe only makes a small amount, perfect for filling 3 of my lovely stemmed glasses, but you can easily double the quantities if necessary.

__Into each of 3 glasses put 5 amaretti, laying them as flat as you can. Splash the amaretti with a tablespoon of vermouth, & then let stand so that the liquid is absorbed by the cookies.

__Meanwhile, whip the egg white until very fluffy & white. Next (*you don't need to wash the beaters*), whip the egg yolk & the sugar very well in a small bowl until it is pale and very creamy. Mix in the mascarpone & give a quick whisk, then fold in the egg white until lovely, full, & *voluminoso.*

__Dollop the cream into the glasses (*you are just having one layer here*). Cover with plastic wrap & chill in the refrigerator for a couple of hours. When you are ready to serve, add another cookie to the top of each glass if you like (*it is good for scooping up the mascarpone*), & add a generous sifting of cocoa powder.

Serves 3

Crema di mascarpone

Mascarpone cream

2 egg yolks
1½ tablespoons sugar
4 drops vanilla extract
1 cup mascarpone
a couple of good pinches of ground cinnamon
1 tablespoon brandy
baicoli (page 264) or biscotti, for serving

Serve this in a small bowl or ramekin with a pile of baicoli (page 264) stacked up like dominoes—this is how I ate it in Venice. Or serve with biscotti that you can use as the spoon. You can use another liqueur, such as rum, or grappa, or a mixture, if you like.

_Beat the yolks, sugar, & vanilla with electric beaters until creamy & firm as possible (*very important*).

_Quickly whisk in the mascarpone & cinnamon until well combined. Then add the brandy to loosen it slightly to a lovely cream. Dollop into 4 small ramekins. Cover with plastic wrap & chill in the refrigerator for at least 1 hour before serving, so that the cream isn't droopy. Serve with baicoli or biscotti.

Makes 4 gracious servings

There is still time to admire the water in front before the boat arrives & listen to the fisherman. A boatman clanking on a nail with a hammer. A couple of ladies swapping remedies while the wind is lifting. Just another day in beautiful Venice.

Zaletti

Polenta cookies

⅔ cup golden raisins
2 tablespoons grappa or brandy
1 stick & 1 tablespoon unsalted butter
½ cup sugar
1 teaspoon vanilla extract
1 egg, plus 1 egg yolk
1 cup cake flour
1 cup fine yellow polenta
1 teaspoon baking powder
¼ cup pine nuts

These are lovely tasting & lovely textured, with a good crispness even among their softness, on account of the polenta. I have seen many versions & many various sizes.

__Soak the raisins in the grappa or brandy. Meanwhile, cream the butter, sugar, & vanilla using electric beaters, until creamy. Beat in the eggs with a pinch of salt. Add the combined flour, polenta, & baking powder, & mix together with a wooden spoon to get a not-too-solid paste. Pour in the raisins & grappa, & the pine nuts, & work them well into the mixture.

__Cover & refrigerate the dough for about 30 minutes until it is firm.

__Preheat the oven to 325°F. Line 2 baking sheets with parchment paper. Remove the dough & put it on a floured work surface. Divide the dough into two salami shapes about 1½ inches in diameter. Cut into ½-inch-thick disks, then shape these into lozenges about 2¾ inches long.

__Put the cookie dough onto the baking sheet, allowing enough room for them to spread as they bake. Bake for about 15 minutes, until firm & lightly colored. Cool on a wire rack, then store in an airtight container.

Makes about 40

Baicoli

Crisp cookies

½ ounce fresh yeast, or
2 teaspoons active dry yeast
¾ cup warm milk
1 stick & 6 tablespoons
unsalted butter, softened
⅓ cup sugar
about 4 cups cake flour,
plus a little extra
1 egg white

I fiddled with a couple of recipes & ended up liking this one, even though it is quite different to actual baicoli. But everyone I asked in Venice said they had never & would never make their own, but of course they can just pop down to any shop to buy them, so why would they? Anyway, yours will not be the same as the manufactured types, so expect a few broken ones. This is a nice cookie to have on the side—like a not-too-sweet version of melba toast—that you can stack up like dominoes as Venetians do alongside a dessert such as Crema di mascarpone (page 262), or to eat with Mostarda (page 28).

__Sprinkle the dried (*or crumble up the fresh*) yeast into a bowl, add the lukewarm milk, & whisk together. Let stand until the yeast starts to activate & bubble up a little. Cream the butter & sugar with an electric mixer.

__Add the activating yeast to the creamed butter & then sift in the flour, egg white, & a pinch of salt. Mix well with a wooden spoon, then with your hands, adding a little extra flour to the dough & your hands, to get a nice soft ball. Make a cross on top, cover the bowl with a dishcloth, & leave in a draft-free warm place for a couple of hours until the dough has puffed up. Line a very large baking sheet (*or 2 sheets*) with parchment paper.

__Punch the dough down & divide it into 4 salami shapes about 12 inches long & 1½ inches across, using a little extra flour if necessary. Put them on the baking sheet. Cover loosely with a dish cloth, then let stand for 1½ to 2 hours, until they have well risen. Preheat the oven to 350°F.

__Bake for 15 to 20 minutes, or until light golden & cooked. Turn off the oven & leave the loaves inside to cool completely for 24 hours—they will harden in this time. Slice each loaf into 1/16-inch-thick slices.

__Preheat the oven to 325°F. Lay the cookie pieces on a baking sheet & bake for 10 minutes, turning once, until crisp but not brown. Allow to cool on a wire rack & then store in an airtight container.

Makes many

Torta di amaretti

Amaretti tart

Pastry:
⅓ cup cold unsalted butter, chopped
2 cups cake flour
1 teaspoon baking powder
⅓ cup sugar
2 eggs

Crema:
2 eggs
⅔ cup superfine sugar
⅔ cup blanched or coarsely ground almonds

about 2¾ ounces amaretti cookies
about 4 tablespoons rum, or cognac
2 heaped tablespoons orange marmalade

My sister-in-law, Luisa, taught me this recipe. She has been making it for a while & doesn't remember where she got it from. It's essentially a tart made up of layers: pastry, marmalade, amaretti &, finally, a creamy egg custard with ground almonds. The number of amaretti you need to cover the bottom of your pastry will depend on their size—if they're small you'll need a few more. If you have homemade orange marmalade, it's great in this tart.

__To make the pastry, mix the butter in a bowl with the flour, baking powder, & sugar until it resembles bread crumbs. Add the eggs & mix until combined. (*Alternatively, pulse together in a food processor.*) Press the dough into a ball, flatten a little, & cover with plastic wrap. Chill for at least 1 hour in the refrigerator (*you can make this a day in advance, or even freeze it at this stage*).

__To make the crema, beat the eggs with the sugar for about 5 minutes, until thick & pale. If you are using blanched almonds, pulse them in a food processor until coarsely ground. Whisk the ground almonds into the egg mixture with a fork.

__Put the amaretti on a plate. Splash bit by bit with the alcohol until they have absorbed most of it. Preheat the oven to 325°F.

__Wet a sheet of parchment paper (about 13 inches by 19 inches), scrunching it up completely. Then unscrunch it & shake off the water. Flatten it onto your work surface, drying it with a clean cloth. Roll out your dough onto the paper with another sheet of parchment paper on top to help roll it without sticking to the rolling pin. Roll the pastry out to line the bottom & side of a 9½-inch springform cake pan. If the weather is hot, you may have to refrigerate the pastry again. Peel away the top layer of parchment paper, & lift the pastry & bottom layer of paper into the pan, pressing the pastry down well (*you will find this easier to do using floured fingers*). The pastry rim should be about ¾ inch lower than the top of the pan, & the parchment paper underneath the pastry will help you lift it out for serving.

__Prick the bottom of the pastry a few times with a fork. Spread the marmalade over the bottom of the pastry. Layer the soaked amaretti biscuits over the marmalade in a single layer, completely covering the bottom.
__Gently pour the crema into the cake pan–it should come almost to the top of the pastry. Cook the tart for 30 to 40 minutes, until the filling is well set & a bit cracked here & there & the pastry is cooked through & pale golden. If you like, you can dust the tart with confectioners' sugar to serve, but I think it is sweet enough as it is.

Serves 8 to 10

Gelato al limone

Lemon ice cream

zest of 1 lemon, cut into big strips
1 cup sugar
½ cup & 2 tablespoons lemon juice
1 cup chilled cream

__Put the lemon zest & sugar in a small saucepan with ½ cup of water. Bring to a boil, stirring to dissolve the sugar. Lower the heat & simmer gently, without stirring, for 5 to 10 minutes, until the mixture becomes syrupy & tastes of lemon. Take out the pieces of lemon zest. Allow the mixture to cool, then pour in the lemon juice.
__Whisk the cream until it's fairly stiff & then whisk in the cooled lemon syrup. Allow to cool, then transfer to an airtight container & put in the freezer. After 1 hour give the mixture an energetic whisk with a hand whisk or electric mixer. Return to the freezer & then whisk again after another couple of hours. When the ice cream is nearly firm, give one last whisk.
__Alternatively, pour the mixture into an ice-cream machine (*if you have one*) & churn, following the manufacturer's instructions.

Serves 6

Sgroppino

Lemon chill

½ pound lemon ice cream (page 267)
about 4 tablespoons chilled prosecco
about 2 tablespoons chilled vodka

You can make your own or buy lemon ice cream for this recipe. If you are making the ice cream, make it the day before so that it has time to become firm & then all you have to do on the day is briefly whizz the ice cream with the alcohol. You can add as much prosecco & vodka as you like here, depending how soft your ice cream is & how strong you want this to be. Since I like to serve this after lunch, I've made it fairly mild, bearing in mind that you may have started the meal with prosecco, then moved onto wine & are not looking at passing out for the afternoon. It's much more summery with less alcohol anyway. Many people serve this as a palate cleanser instead of as a dessert. If it's very hot then put your glasses in the freezer for a few minutes before serving.

_Scoop the ice cream into a blender. Splash in the prosecco & vodka, & whizz (*the more alcohol you add the more liquidy the mixture will end up*). Pour into glasses & serve immediately before it melts.

Serves 2

Sbriciolona

Crumbler cake

1⅓ cups unpeeled almonds
1 egg
⅔ cup sugar
1 teaspoon vanilla extract
2 sticks & 2 tablespoons unsalted butter, softened
2 cups all-purpose flour
thick cream or ice cream, for serving

Be prepared to tread on crumbs around the table after eating sbriciolona. Sbriciolare is Italian for "crumble," & that's exactly what the name implies: crumbly. This is beautiful with sweetened whipped or thick cream that the crumbs can cling to, or just with a glass of something moscato-ish. In Venice, fragolino, a red or white sweet wine, is what they like to drink.

__Preheat the oven to 350°F. Use a blob from the butter to grease an 11-inch springform cake pan & lightly dust it with flour. Put the almonds in a food processor & pulse until quite fine but with some chunks left (*alternatively, bash them with your rolling pin*).

__Whip the egg with the sugar & vanilla until nice & creamy. Put the softened butter on a plate & mash until smooth, but not melted. Gradually, whisk the flour, butter, & a pinch of salt into the egg mixture. Add the ground almonds & work them in with your hands to make a rough pastry.

__Pat the mixture into the cake pan, dollops at a time, flattening it to roughly cover the bottom. It won't look perfect, but it will spread while baking. Bake for about 40 minutes, or until golden brown.

__Allow to cool, then cut into wedges if you can (*it's crumbly*). To serve, either whip some cream with a little vanilla extract & sugar, or simply serve with ice cream, which holds the crumbs in its cloud of thickness.

Serves 8 to 10

Mele cotte con amaretti

Cooked apples with amaretti

4 lovely apples
10 small amaretti cookies
¼ cup golden raisins
3 tablespoons sugar
2 tablespoons grappa or brandy
2 tablespoons unsalted butter
1½ cups white wine
2 strips orange peel

This is a very simple, homestyle dessert. I like to make it with 2 green & 2 red apples —not because I can see any difference at the end, but it looks great before it goes into the oven! If you're serving more than 4 people, you can easily add a couple more apples & just increase the other ingredients accordingly. It's best to use a baking dish that fits the apples fairly snugly.

__Preheat the oven to 350°F. Core the apples, leaving the apples in one piece. Prick the peel a few times with the point of a sharp knife.

__Using a mortar & pestle (*or rolling pin or heavy bottle*), crush the amaretti with the raisins & 1 tablespoon of the sugar, until roughly smashed. Add the grappa, mix well, & stuff into the center of each apple.

__Put the apples in a baking dish & sprinkle 1 tablespoon of sugar evenly over the tops. Divide the butter into four & put a blob on top of each apple. Pour the wine around the apples, then add the final tablespoon of sugar & the orange peel to the wine. Cover loosely with foil & bake for about 20 minutes, or until tender. Uncover & cook for another 20 minutes, basting the apples with the pan juices a couple of times, until they are well cooked but not split.

__Remove the cooked apples from the dish, turn the oven temperature right up, & return the dish to the oven to reduce the sauce until golden (*or do this on the stovetop*). Serve the apples warm, or at room temperature, with the juice spooned over & around.

Serves 4

Gelato di amaretto

Amaretto ice cream

2½ ounces amaretti cookies
1 cup milk
3 egg yolks
½ cup sugar
½ teaspoon vanilla extract
1 cup heavy whipping cream

This is not as amaro as you may think. It has a gentle Italian elegance about it, I find, & goes well after any meal, but especially autumn & winter dishes like Bigoli in salsa or duck.

__Crush the amaretti very well with a mortar & pestle or rolling pin. Put the milk in a heavy-bottomed, small saucepan & heat gently. Meanwhile, whip the yolks very well with the sugar & vanilla until pale & thick. Before the milk comes to a boil, whisk a little into the creamy eggs, whipping so that the eggs don't scramble. When it's well mixed, pour it all back into the saucepan over very low heat & whisk well for a couple of minutes–just to slightly cook the eggs, but please don't scramble them into lumps.
__Remove from the heat & allow to cool slightly. Whisk in the cold cream & then the amaretti cookies. Leave to cool completely, then transfer to an airtight container lid & put in the freezer. After 1 hour, give the mixture an energetic whisk with a hand whisk or electric mixer. Return to the freezer & then whisk again after another couple of hours. When the ice cream is nearly firm, give one last whisk & freeze again overnight to firm up.
__Alternatively, pour the mixture in an ice-cream machine & churn, following the manufacturer's instructions. Transfer to an airtight container, then leave overnight in the freezer to firm up.

Serves 4 to 6

Zabaione

Eggs & marsala

4 egg yolks
⅓ cup superfine sugar
⅓ cup & 2 tablespoons marsala

Here, zabaione is served the classic way, sweet & warm. But you may like to add some whipped cream to make it a softer pudding...If so, whip ¾ cup of cream until lovely & billowy, then fold it gently, but thoroughly, into the zabaione. You could also add a pinch of ground cinnamon, or grated lemon zest, or a dash of vanilla extract, although I love the simplicity of marsala here. Another variation is to replace the marsala with the same amount of espresso—use your empty eggshells to measure the marsala...6 half-shells will give you the right amount. In Italy, zabaione was traditionally served to the newlywed man so he had energy to get through the wedding night!

__Quarter-fill a saucepan with water. Bring the water to a boil, then turn down the heat to a low simmer.

__Put the egg yolks, sugar, & a few drops of the marsala in a wide, stainless-steel bowl, & beat with an electric mixer until thick & creamy. Lift the bowl onto the pot of simmering water, making sure the bowl doesn't touch the water. Turn the heat to the lowest possible level. Beat the mixture over the hot water for about 20 minutes until it is *voluminoso*, adding the rest of the marsala bit by bit; when the mixture is very thick & creamy add the rest. Occasionally, gently scrape down the side of the bowl but try to avoid any cooked bits getting into the pudding. After about 20 minutes of beating, the mixture should be thick & creamy, so remove it from the heat & keep whisking a bit while it cools.

__Spoon into lovely glass cups & serve while still slightly warm. Or keep covered in the refrigerator. Serve with baicoli (*page 265*), amaretti, or other hard cookies such as biscotti that you can use as a spoon.

Serves 4 to 6

Gelato di zabaione

Zabaglione ice cream

6 egg yolks
1 cup sugar
1½ cups milk
½ cup marsala
1½ cups heavy whipping cream

I love this gelato. Serve on its own or with a plain cookie like a baicolo (page 265). I hope you have a big ice-cream machine for this, but if not, just make half a portion. Use your empty eggshells to measure the marsala…about 5 half-shells full here.

__Whip the egg yolks & sugar until pale & thick. While you are beating, slowly heat the milk in a small, heavy-bottomed saucepan. Before the milk comes to a boil, whisk a little of it into the creamy eggs, whipping so that the eggs don't scramble. When it is all mixed together, scrape the whole lot back into the saucepan & return to very low heat, whisking well for a couple of minutes–just to slightly cook the eggs, but don't let the eggs scramble into lumps.

__Remove the saucepan from the heat & allow to cool. Whisk in the marsala & stir in the cold cream, then leave to cool completely. Transfer to an airtight container & put in the freezer. After 1 hour, give the mixture an energetic whisk with a hand whisk or electric mixer. Return to the freezer & then whisk again after another couple of hours. When the ice cream is nearly firm, give one last whisk and freeze overnight to firm up.

__Alternatively, pour the mixture into an ice-cream machine & churn, following the manufacturer's instructions. Transfer to an airtight container, then leave overnight in the freezer to firm up.

Serves 6 to 8

Bussola

"S" or round cookies

1 stick & 1 tablespoon cold, unsalted butter, chopped
2 cups cake flour
½ cup sugar
2 egg yolks
1½ teaspoons vanilla extract
1½ teaspoons finely grated lemon zest
2 tablespoons milk

These are the famous S-shaped or plain round firm cookies that are great to serve with something like fragolino, & come in many variations. They are also great with a small dish of wild strawberries & another of vanilla ice cream. These must be the ones that the boatman said come from Burano, with its lovely colored houses…they are kept in underwear drawers because of their beautiful smell & last forever because of the citrus. Only in Venice could I believe such a tale.

__Mix the butter with the flour & sugar until it resembles bread crumbs. Combine the egg yolks, vanilla extract, lemon zest, & milk in a bowl. Pour the crumb mixture into the bowl & mix until it comes together. (*Alternatively, pulse together in a food processor.*) Turn out onto a board & bring it together to make a fat 8-inch-long log. Wrap in plastic wrap & chill in the refrigerator for about 1 hour or more.
__Preheat the oven to 325°F. Line two baking sheets with parchment paper. You will need a lightly floured surface & flour for your hands.
__Keep half the dough in the refrigerator to keep it cool while you work with the other half. Cut slices about ¼ inch thick along the log & roll each slice out to 3 inches by ½ inch thick. Form each one into an S shape. (*Alternatively, roll them into 4-inch ropes & join the ends to make circles instead.*)
__Put each "S," or circle, onto the baking sheet. Bake for 10 to 15 minutes, or until pale but golden here & there–they shouldn't be too hard as they will harden once out of the oven.

Makes about 50

Focaccia Veneziana

Venetian focaccia

¾ ounce fresh yeast, or
3 teaspoons active dry yeast
1 cup warm milk
½ cup sugar
7 tablespoons unsalted butter, melted & cooled
3 egg yolks
2¾ cups cake flour
finely grated zest of 1 small lemon

Topping:
⅓ cup sugar
2 good tablespoons large-granule sugar

This has little in common with the bread called focaccia, but is more a brioche-pandoro thing. I tasted one from the pasticceria Puppa in Cannareggio & was completely sold on it, so I found a recipe in my sister-in-law's old book A TOLA CO I NOSTRI VECI *by Mariu Salvatori de Zuliani (thank goodness, I had Luisa to translate the Venetian dialect instructions to me).*

__Dissolve the yeast in the milk & whip with a whisk. Add the sugar, butter, egg yolks, flour, & a pinch of salt, mixing at the end with your hands or a strong whisk, to form a soft dough. Cover with plastic wrap, then a dishcloth & leave for 12 hours in warm place until well risen. Uncover & mix it all again with your hands (*even though it is very soft*), kneading in the lemon zest. Lightly butter a 9-cup cake pan (*or line with a paper mold*).

__Plop the dough into the cake pan as evenly as possible–it will seem as if there is a lot of room left, but it will rise, so cover the top again with plastic wrap & then a dishcloth, & leave in a warm place again for a couple of hours. Preheat the oven to 350°F.

__Remove the plastic wrap & bake the dough for about 40 minutes, until golden on top, covering with foil for the last 15 minutes if you think it is browning too much. A skewer poked into the center should come out clean.

__Meanwhile, make the sugar syrup. Put the sugar in a small saucepan with 3 tablespoons of water, stir to dissolve the sugar, then let it simmer without stirring for 5 to 8 minutes, until thickened a bit. Cool for a minute & then brush over the cooled focaccia. Sprinkle the sugar granules over the top so they stick.

Makes 1 big cake…

INDEX

INDEX

INDEX

INDEX

GRAZIE

__To all who helped in the making of this book—I am truly grateful.

__Thank you Artemis & Kyriakos for showing me the good life in Venice. Thank you Luisa (for being my half-Venetian sister-in-law!), & for making the collecting & cooking so much smoother & grazioso. Thank you to your sister, Lidia, your nephew, Andrea, & your mom, Dina.

__I had the fortuna of meeting amazing Venetians who made my journeys wonderful. Thank you all for your spontaneous help: Sergia Regolino, Alimentari in Calle dei do Mori; Marinella Jop from La Buona Forchetta ristorante; Giorgia from Rialto fish market (Pescheria Giorgia & Gianni Fabbris); Alvise Ceccato from ristorante Antica Adelaide; Licio Sfriso from trattoria alla Madonna; Stefano Nicolao from Nicolao Atelier costume hire for allowing us into your beautiful costume kingdom; Valerio Pagnacco & Mariagrazia Dammico, Flavia Cordioli Mognetti for your gracious help; Houshang Rachtian from Casa d'Aste Antiques for gallantly allowing us to photograph your red monkey; to the artist Gianni Roberti for your painting on the wall of the Antica Mola trattoria. Thank you also to Franco, Sebastian, & Stefano.

__To all away from Venice—thank you Mario, Wilma, Angela-Maria, Lisa, Richard, Sue, Andrea, Barbara, Mariella, Claudia, Marzia, Scilla & Roberto, Luciano, & Stefania, Antonella, Paolo, Julia, Jem, Anabelle, Peta, Anna, Jan, Rebecca, Nicci, & Marisa for all your very much appreciated help & encouragement.

__Thank you Anna Rosa Migone from Saena Vetus Antiques in Siena for allowing us to use some of your valued pieces.

__Thank you Popsi for your solidity & for adapting so well to all situations, & to my beautiful wonders, Yasmine & Cassia—thank you for making everything so much more fun always.

__Thank you Mom, Dad, Ludi, & Nin for your support always.

__Thank you to all at Murdoch Books, to Jane & Jo, & the many involved in production. Thanks Michelle, for going further than you had to. Thank you Kay for dealing the card of opportunity.

__To my team. A grande thank you: Michail, I acknowledge your ability to style mountains out of molehills. Manos, your beautiful sensitivity with your camera, & Lisa—the best art director friend one could hope for.

Tess x

INSPIRATION COOKBOOKS:

La cucina del Veneto, Emilia Valli
A tola co i nostri veci, Mariù Salvatori de Zuliani
A Tavola con I Dogi, Pino Agostini, Alvise Zorzi
Venice & Food, Sally Spector

INSPIRATION READING:

The Passion, Jeanette Winterson
Across the River & into the Trees, Ernest Hemingway
The City of Falling Angels, John Berendt
Acqua Alta, Donna Leon
Venetian Stories, Jane Turner Rylands
Venice for Pleasure, J. G. Links
The Stones of Venice, John Ruskin